LEARNING CRIMINAL PROCEDURE

by

Ric Simmons
Chief Justice Thomas J. Moyer Professor for the Administration of Justice and Rule of Law
Moritz College of Law, The Ohio State University

Renée McDonald Hutchins
Professor of Law and Co-Director, Clinical Law Program
The University of Maryland Francis King Carey School of Law

LEARNING SERIES

Mat #41382786

The publisher is not engaged in rendering legal or other professional advice, and this publication is not a substitute for the advice of an attorney. If you require legal or other expert advice, you should seek the services of a competent attorney or other professional.

444 Cedar Street, Suite 700
St. Paul, MN 55101
1-877-888-1330

Printed in the United States of America

ISBN: 978-0-314-28670-3

To Cyrus, Aquila, and Zeke

RS

To the Jays and Julian

RMH

PREFACE

This book is the latest installment in the Learning Series of law school textbooks. LEARNING CRIMINAL PROCEDURE offers a new, and hopefully more effective, method of teaching students the legal principles that define the field of criminal procedure. Most legal textbooks focus on appellate decisions and ask readers to deduce the legal rules from the cases. In contrast, this book presents the legal rules at the beginning of each chapter in the clearest language possible, and then explores the scope and exceptions to the rules using examples drawn from the case law. This format of presenting the material, which was first conceived by Professor Debby Merritt, has proven to be very successful in teaching law students. It is also remarkably easy for professors to use in the classroom. If you have used any books from the Learning series before, you will find the style and formatting to be very familiar.

Unlike some other books in the Learning series, LEARNING CRIMINAL PROCEDURE does provide students with excerpts of actual opinions at the end of many of the chapters. However, their purpose is not to teach the law, but rather to let readers understand the logic and policy considerations behind the legal principles that they have already learned earlier in the chapter.

Many law students have helped with this effort by providing substantive suggestions, research assistance, and proofreading. We would like to thank (in alphabetical order) Maria Bruno, Keith Edwards, Elizabeth Gorman, Russell Gray, Zach Horton, Brenda Kathurima, Ashley Loyke, Scott McCormick, Stephanie Noronha, Kristen Poetzel, Maryam Rezayat, Liane Rousseau, Akeel St. Jean, Christina Taylor, and Amond Uwadineke. Also, Allyson Hennelly and Susan Edwards at Ohio State and Jenny Rensler at Maryland Carey provided support services that were essential for getting this book published.

We would also like to thank Professor Michael Mannheimer for providing suggestions for the text and for the teacher's manual. And of course, we cannot close without thanking our families for providing us with immense amounts of support during the entire book-writing process.

Ric Simmons
Renée McDonald Hutchins

September 2014

TABLE OF CONTENTS

DETAILED TABLE OF CONTENTS

STUDY GUIDE: HOW TO USE THIS BOOK

This book approaches legal study differently than the typical casebook. Most obviously, it does not expect you to deduce legal rules from the case law. Instead, it explicitly sets out the rules of law for the various aspects of criminal procedure and then gives concrete examples of how the law works in practice. In addition to telling you plainly what the rules are, most chapters also include review questions so that you can apply what you have learned. Also, many chapters reproduce significant portions of some of the seminal cases so that you can appreciate more fully the source of the legal rules.

The book also contains several other special features designed to aid your learning. Here are some tips on how to get the most out of this book:

1. Learning the Basics. The materials in this book teach the rules of criminal procedure through textual discussion, analysis of the relevant cases, and concrete examples. The text does not require you to extract principles from cases. By the end of each chapter, you should understand the basic features of the law discussed in that chapter.

a. Key Concepts. Most chapters begin with a text box labeled "Key Concepts" and marked with the key icon. These boxes serve two purposes. **First,** they will alert you to the most important concepts that you should focus on when reading the chapter. **Second,** when you review the materials, you should be able to glance at the Key Concept box for each chapter and readily recall the meaning of those concepts. In addition to appearing at the beginning of each chapter, the Key Concepts appear in the **Detailed Table of Contents**. You can use that table as a very quick overview of the course.

b. Quick Summary. Each chapter ends with a "Quick Summary" of the contents, designated by the "summary folder" icon. These boxes do not contain all of the information you need to know from the chapter. You need to master details from the chapter, not just the summary principles. But, these summaries will give you a mental framework for organizing the material in the chapter. After reading each chapter, look at the Quick Summary and see how many details you can recall to accompany each principle.

2. Black Letter Law. Understanding criminal procedure requires much more than simply learning the specific legal rules set out by the courts and legislatures. But learning these specific legal rules is a necessary first step in the process. The federal law of criminal procedure comes from many sources: the text of the United

States Constitution, court cases interpreting the Constitution, federal legislation, and the Federal Rules of Criminal Procedure. Much of this law also applies to the states as well, but states have also created their own law in many different areas.

To aid your understanding, we have summarized the relevant black letter law for each topic we cover. The law will be set out early in each chapter, after a brief introduction, and highlighted and blocked off in a grey box for easy reference. Key words or terms are underlined and are discussed immediately following the legal rule. Here is an example from early in the book:

> Government surveillance will constitute a "search" and thereby implicate the Fourth Amendment if:
>
> (1) the defendant exhibited a subjective expectation of privacy in the area or item that was the object of the surveillance, and this expectation was one that society is prepared to recognize as reasonable and legitimate;
>
> OR if
>
> (2) law enforcement officers intruded onto a "constitutionally protected area" in order to conduct the surveillance.

In addition to understanding the black letter law, you will also need to know the source of the particular legal rule—for example, whether it is from the United States Supreme Court, or a federal statute, or some other authority. Although this is not a traditional casebook, most of the law of criminal procedure derives from Supreme Court cases, and so it is important for you to know the names of the major cases in the field. Unlike many other criminal procedure books, this book does not discuss cases that have merely "historic" value—that is, cases that were once significant but have since been overruled. All of the cases that are referenced in the book are necessary to understanding the current state of the law as well as potential future developments.

A word of caution: unlike a subject such as evidence or civil procedure, many of the rules for criminal procedure have to be derived from case law. Frequently the rule is well-settled law, but occasionally the case law will be open to interpretation and there may be disagreement among the lower courts as to what the rule actually is. On these occasions the book will present the general consensus as to what the rule is, but will then note the disagreement and discuss the other possible interpretations.

3. Applying the Law. After each section explaining the specific rule under discussion, we provide one or more examples of how the rule applies in practice.

These examples are intended to help you understand the scope of the rule, as well as to understand how courts apply the rule in different situations. Some of these examples are pure hypotheticals, while others are based on actual cases. In most instances, the name of the case will be provided so that you know the source of that particular aspect of the rule.

4. Open Questions. As noted above, some legal principles of criminal procedure are still open to dispute. Even when a principle is clear, its application may vary depending on the facts of the case. These materials note when legal issues are unresolved, as well as when application of a principle depends on the facts of the case. In addition to textual explanations, icons mark these points so they are easy to recognize:

The walking-flying fish indicates points of law that are still evolving. Evolving issues include (1) legal principles that most parties assume are settled, but that a thoughtful attorney might challenge; (2) issues on which a conflict exists among the federal circuits or between states; (3) unsettled questions raised by recent Supreme Court decisions; and (4) issues that courts have not yet addressed. The evolving fish identifies these issues, which are discussed further in the text.

The balancing scales indicate issues on which the legal principle is clear, but the court's decision will depend on the facts of the case. Legal counsel's ability to apply the governing principle to the facts is particularly important in these situations. When you study these issues, the legal principle may seem straightforward. Think, however, about how you would apply the principle to a variety of factual situations. Applying the principle, rather than simply knowing it, is critical to these issues.

5. Organization. Each chapter in this book addresses a particular principle of Criminal Procedure. The chapters are self-contained, although later chapters build on earlier ones. True mastery of criminal procedure, however, requires an ability to understand how different parts of the law interact with each other. To help you build that understanding, the book uses **Overview Chapters** and **Overview Paragraphs** to offer specific information about how rules relate to one another or to trials in general. When you see the overview icon at the beginning of a chapter, it means that the entire chapter is an organizational one, helping you relate rules to one another. When the icon appears beside a particular paragraph, it means that the paragraph positions the material within the broader scope of criminal procedure jurisprudence.

6. Policy Debates. Although this book focuses on explaining what the law is and how it operates, it is impossible to fully understand criminal procedure without occasionally delving into the underlying policy issues that the rules raise and the ethical problems that attorneys face when applying these rules. Therefore, at various points in the text, indicated by the debate icon, the book will examine a policy debate in depth usually by quoting some portions of a Supreme Court decision.

7. Practice Questions. One of the best ways of learning criminal procedure is to apply the knowledge to specific fact patterns. Many of the chapters include a number of review questions at the end that allow you to apply the law you have just learned. Some of these questions will have certain right or wrong answers; others will require you to consider both sides of the issue and then exercise your judgment as to the correct decision. The question icon will indicate a series of practice questions.

8. From the Courtroom. Although the book does not require you to learn the legal rules by looking only at cases, it is occasionally necessary for you to become familiar with the most significant cases in the field. This is because it is important to understand the source of the rules that you are learning, and because you need to know the policy arguments that are made by the Justices that are deciding these cases. Thus, you will not only be given the rule and a discussion of the scope of the rule, but also a chance to read the primary source of these rules, so you can see how the law is explained by the courts. The gavel icon will introduce these significant cases.

9. How to Prepare for Class. You should read the assigned materials before class! All professors say that, but there is a particular reason to read these materials before class. With the case method, some students (especially in upper level courses) find that it is efficient to read the cases very lightly—or not at all—and wait for class to illuminate the principles contained in the cases. The materials in this book, however, teach the basics directly; there's no quicker way to learn them.

Your professor, moreover, may not review the basics in class. Instead, the professor may focus class on review questions, advanced problems, policy discussions, and simulations. If you don't know the basics, you will not benefit much from these classes.

10. How to Prepare for Exams. You should find these materials helpful, both in preparing for the exam in this course and when reviewing for the bar exam. The techniques outlined below will help you prepare well for both exams:

a. Be sure that you understand the Key Concepts in each chapter. These appear both at the beginning of the chapter and in the Detailed Table of Contents.

b. Read over the Quick Summary for each chapter. In addition to understanding the summary, you should be able to recall details relating to each of the points in the summary.

c. Review the black letter law in each chapter to ensure you understand the basic legal provisions for each topic.

d. Review Overview chapters and paragraphs to be sure that you understand how the different provisions of criminal procedure interact with one another. Reviewing the Table of Contents will also reveal important relationships.

e. Take special note of evolving issues and know how you would argue both sides of those issues. You may argue these issues some day in court and you almost certainly will have to argue some of them on an exam.

f. Pay special attention to "balancing scale" or fact-based principles. These principles often seem easy, but the essence of these rules lies in their application. You need to know how to apply these rules carefully to the facts of a problem, seeing arguments that both sides might raise.

Criminal procedure is a fascinating topic to study, involving fundamental issues of justice, fairness, and the proper extent of government power. So let's get started…

1

Introduction to Criminal Procedure

Key Concepts

- "Investigation" v. "Adjudication"
- Stages of a Criminal Case
- Overview of Police

A. Introduction. *Criminal Procedure* is defined as the rules governing "the procedural steps through which a criminal case passes, commencing with the initial investigation of a crime and concluding with the unconditional release of the offender."[1] Traditionally the topic is divided into two broad categories:

1. The "investigation" process covers the period from the beginning of the criminal investigation up until the point where a suspect has been identified and arrested. The study of this half of criminal procedure examines the rules governing and limiting how police can conduct their investigation, specifically the rules on searches and seizures, interrogations, and identification procedures. For the most part, the investigatory stage of the criminal process is governed by the Supreme Court's interpretation of the Fourth, Fifth, and Sixth Amendments to the Constitution. However, there are also federal laws, state constitutions, and state laws that apply.

2. The "adjudication" process covers the period from the point of the arrest through the end of sentencing. This involves the rules governing bail, discovery and pre-trial motions, and jury trials. This half of the subject is roughly analogous to the study of Civil Procedure, and it is governed primarily by the Rules of Criminal Procedure, though there are certain constitutional limitations that apply as well.

There are two important aspects of the criminal justice system that Criminal Procedure does **not** cover. First, it does not cover **substantive criminal law**—that is, the elements of crimes such as murder, rape, and burglary, nor the related concepts such as *mens rea*, defenses, acting in concert, and so on. Substantive criminal law is typically covered in the first-year Criminal Law class.

---

[1] Black's Law Dictionary, 337 (5th ed. 1979).

Second, Criminal Procedure does not include a study of **trial evidence**—that is, what information a jury is or is not allowed to hear during trial, and how that information is presented to a jury. This topic is typically covered in a separate class on evidence. It is true that if the police violate the law during their investigation, one potential remedy is the exclusionary rule, which means that the court may preclude the state from using the illegally-acquired evidence at trial. But the policy and governing law behind the exclusionary rule are separate and distinct from the rules that govern the admissibility of evidence at trial.

B. The Process of Criminal Justice: Investigation. What follows is a very broad overview of how a typical criminal case moves through the criminal justice system. One important caveat: almost no criminal case will follow this "typical" path exactly. Every jurisdiction has its own rules for different stages of the process, and every case will have its own individual differences. Nonetheless, it is still important to understand the overall arc of a criminal case.

In most people's minds, the criminal justice process begins when an individual commits a crime. However, this definition is both too broad and too narrow.

It is too broad because the majority of crimes go unnoticed by law enforcement, either because there are no victims or witnesses or because the witnesses and victims decide not to report the offense. Thus, the occurrence of a crime in most cases does not trigger the beginning of a criminal case. Over half of all violent crimes and two-thirds of all property crimes are unreported.[2] In terms of raw numbers, this means that roughly fourteen million crimes a year are never reported to the police.[3] And these numbers only include crimes with identifiable victims, such as assault or theft, not "victimless" crimes such as narcotic sales, prostitution, or possession of narcotics or illegal firearms.[4] Thus, most crimes in this country not only go unpunished but literally go unnoticed by the criminal justice system.

On the other hand, the definition is also too narrow because sometimes a criminal investigation will occur even though no crime has actually occurred. The report of a crime may have been false, or what appeared to be criminal activity may turn out to be innocent. As long as the police become aware that a crime may have been committed, they have the option of starting a criminal investigation, if only a very brief one. For example, police officers may see a suspect conduct a furtive exchange on a street corner known for drug activity, and then stop and frisk the suspect. Or the police may pull someone over for speeding, notice that she is act-

[2] U.S. Dep't of Just., Bureau of Justice Statistics, Criminal Victimization 2004 (Dec. 2008, NCJ 224390) (hereinafter "DOJ Crime Victimization 2004") (showing a 46% reporting rate for violent crimes, and a 37% reporting rate for property crimes).

[3] Id.

[4] DOJ Crime Victimization 2004, supra note 2.

ing nervous, and ask for permission to search the car. In many of these cases, the police officer may have mistaken innocent conduct for potential criminal activity.

Therefore, it is most accurate to say that a criminal investigation begins when the police become aware that a crime may have been committed. Police officers become aware of potential crimes in a number of different ways:

1. A report by a citizen, either a victim or a witness;

2. Personal observation of suspicious or illegal behavior; or

3. A referral from some other government agency.

Although most criminal cases begin in one of these three places, there are dozens of different spots where they can end. Their ultimate endpoint will depend on the subsequent investigation and trial. Frequently the police will investigate briefly and determine that there is no criminal conduct occurring, such as when they stop and frisk a suspect but find nothing. Sometimes the police will decide not to investigate potential criminal behavior because the criminal activity is not worth the resources necessary to pursue it. In these cases, the police exercise their discretion to prioritize which crimes even enter the criminal justice system. This discretion can be exercised by individual officers, who may see individuals engaged in relatively minor criminal activity such as disorderly conduct, public drunkenness, defacement of property, or engaging in a bar fight and try to resolve the situation without making an arrest. Or, the discretion may come from higher up. For example, the police chief or even the mayor may respond to community pressure and set a policy that police resources should be devoted to certain types of crimes—domestic violence, gun possession, drunk driving—which means that fewer resources will be devoted to enforcing other crimes.

If the police do decide to pursue an investigation, they can undertake a number of different steps. In some cases the first step the police take will be to engage in **surveillance**. This can take many different forms: police can follow the suspect, watch video from public or private security cameras, enter the suspect's house and look for evidence, wiretap his telephone, subpoena his bank records, or intercept and read his e-mails.

All of these different types of surveillance are regulated to different degrees by the Fourth Amendment and various statutes. Generally, the more intrusive the method of surveillance, the higher the standard the police must meet before being allowed to conduct the surveillance. If the police merely want to observe the suspect in a public place or engage the suspect in a consensual conversation, they are free to do so without showing any justification for their actions. If they want to briefly detain the suspect and conduct a quick pat-down for weapons, known as a "**stop and frisk**," they must possess "**reasonable suspicion**" that the suspect is guilty and that he may be armed. If they want to look through his home, they are conducting a **search** and will be required to show **probable cause** and probably get a **search warrant** from a judge before they conduct the search. (However, there are various exceptions to the warrant requirement that allow the police to conduct searches without a warrant under certain circumstances.) Finally, if the police want to conduct a wiretap on the suspect's telephone or intercept the suspect's emails, they will need to get a "**Title III order**" from a court ahead of time, which will require them to show probable cause and meet a number of other requirements.

In addition to conducting surveillance on the suspect himself, the police might also engage in other, less intrusive investigative techniques: they may interview witnesses, gather evidence from the crime scene, or conduct forensic analysis of items that they recover.

Eventually the police may want to conduct an **interrogation** of the suspect, or they may want to conduct an **identification procedure** (such as a line-up) to see if witnesses can confirm that the suspect is in fact the perpetrator of the crime. These actions can take place either before or after an arrest, and each is strictly regulated by the Fifth Amendment, the Sixth Amendment, and the Due Process Clause of the Fourteenth Amendment to Constitution.

Finally, once the police have some evidence to substantiate their belief that the suspect is indeed the individual who committed the crime, they oftentimes decide that formal charges should be brought against the defendant. At this point, the suspect will be arrested and usually held in jail until his first court appearance. The police will process the suspect—take his fingerprints, take his photograph, and conduct a thorough search of his person, seizing and storing most of his personal possessions. For minor offenses, the suspect may be given the chance to post "stationhouse bail," which allows him to remain free until his court appearance. For very minor offenses, the suspect often is not be arrested at all—he is merely given a summons and told to report to court on a certain date. It should be noted that the interrogation and identification procedure may happen before or after the suspect is arrested—although once the suspect is arrested, she receives a number of significant rights, such as the right to remain silent and the right to have an attorney present during questioning.

For the most part, this completes the "investigation" portion of the case, although the police may continue to gather evidence after the defendant's arrest.

C. The Police. As we study the rules governing criminal investigations, you should keep in mind that these rules are essentially rules which regulate police behavior. In other words, these are rules describing what police are and are not allowed to do when they are investigating a crime. Thus, in understanding how these rules operate in practice—and in order to critically evaluate whether the rules make sense—it is useful to have at least a brief understanding of who the police are.

When we talk about "the police," we are using shorthand which could refer to any of the approximately eighteen thousand different law enforcement agencies throughout the country. These can be broken up into two broad categories: "state and local" and "federal."

Most of the interactions that individuals have with law enforcement are interactions with state and local police—officers, sheriffs, deputies and troopers who work for the city, county, or state. Across the country there are over 1.1 million uniformed state and local law enforcement officers. Some of these police agencies are quite large—the largest, the New York City Police Department, has over 35,000 uniformed officers and is larger than the army of some European countries. However, over half of the existing police agencies employ fewer than ten officers.[5]

Among the local police, one in eight is a woman, and one in four is a member of an ethnic minority. These proportions mean that most police departments are whiter and more male than the general population. Improvement though has been seen over the past few decades.[6] The technology that the police use has been changing as well: over the past decade, there have been dramatic increases in the number of local police who have the opportunity to use computers in the field (currently 90%), who have video cameras mounted on their dashboard (66%), and who are armed with Tasers (75%). Also, 75% of police officers work for a department that uses a predictive "crime mapping" system such as COMPSTAT to identify the locations where criminal activity is statistically more likely to occur. Departments then target resources in these areas to proactively prevent crime from occurring.[7] Concerns have been voiced that this "predictive" concentration of police resources in fact creates a feedback loop that bears little relationship to actual patterns of crime occurrence. Privacy advocates have also questioned whether the increased police use of technology is moving us too far in the direction of a surveillance state.

---

[5] U.S. Dep't of Just., Bureau of Justice Statistics, Census of State law Enforcement Agencies, 2008, at http://www.bjs.gov/index.cfm?ty=pbdetail&iid=2216.

[6] U.S. Dep't of Just., Bureau of Justice Statistics, Local Police Departments, 2007, at http://www.bjs.gov/content/pub/pdf/lpd07.pdf.

[7] Id.

Federal law enforcement is only about one tenth the size of the state and local police—there are over 120,000 federal law enforcement officials, spread among ninety different bureaus and agencies. Over one-third of these officers—more then 40,000—work for one agency: Customs and Border Protection. A significant portion of the remaining officials are employed by three other agencies (Federal Bureau of Prisons, Federal Bureau of Investigation, and Immigration and Custom Enforcement) with over 10,000 officers each.[8] One in six federal officers is a woman, and one in three is a member of an ethnic minority. Federal law enforcement officers generally are better educated, better trained, and better paid than their state and local counterparts. Many small towns have no minimum educational requirement for their law enforcement officers. Large cities typically require at least a high school education, or even some college education. In contrast, most federal law enforcement agencies require a college degree as a condition of employment.

Though our use of the term "police" is intended to be capacious, there is one group of people we are **not** talking about when we use the term. That group is private security forces—private detectives or guards who work for companies or are hired by neighborhood associations. These "private police" are at least as numerous as the public police,[9] and their actions have a significant impact on the criminal justice system. However, they differ from public police in two significant ways.

First, the private police (like the public police) exercise discretion as to which crimes get priority, and (as with the public police) this leads to lax enforcement of some criminal laws and strict enforcement of other criminal laws. However, the goal of private police is not to protect society in general or to further justice. Rather, the primary focus of private police forces is to serve the interests of their private employer. Thus, when private security officers exercise discretion, they are not responding to public pressure or prioritizing more serious crimes in order to ensure the safety of the population. Instead, they are dealing with criminal activity in whatever way best meets the needs of their employer. This means that many of the criminals apprehended by private security will frequently be dealt with outside of the criminal justice system—a trespasser may be asked to leave the property; a dishonest employee may be fired; a violent patron in a bar may be thrown out onto the street. Reporting a crime and then cooperating with the police and prosecutor takes time, which is expensive for the employer, and thus pursuing a criminal case may literally not be worth it.

[8] U.S. Dep't of Just., Bureau of Justice Statistics, Federal Law Enforcement Officers, 2008, available at http://www.bjs.gov/index.cfm?ty=pbdetail&iid=4372.

[9] U.S. Dep't of Labor, Bureau of Labor Statistics, May 2006 National Occupational Employment and Wage Estimates 28, available at http://www.bls.gov/oes/current/oes_nat.htm#b33-0000.

Second, private security officers are not bound by the same rules and laws that limit public police. As we will see in **Chapter 4**, the constitutional limits on investigations only apply to state actors—those who are employed by the government or who are acting on the government's behalf. Thus, if a private security officer enters a home to search for evidence without a warrant, or if she interrogates a suspect without informing him of his *Miranda* rights, the defendant has no recourse in the criminal justice system. On the other hand, the private security officer is not protected by any kind of government immunity, so the defendant can bring a private cause of action against her (and her employer) for any abuses that occur.

The wide variety of police organizations—and of police officers—makes it hard to speak generally about "the police." However, as we examine the rules of criminal investigation, keep in mind that although all police officers receive some training about the legal rules that govern their behavior, almost none of the police officers are lawyers.

Having completed this short detour into the nature of the police, let us return to tracking the "typical" criminal case as it makes its way through the criminal justice system.

D. The Process of Criminal Justice: Adjudication. In most cases, once the defendant has been arrested and processed, the role of the police officer becomes secondary, and the case is turned over to a prosecuting attorney. (In the parlance of television dramas, this is the end of the "Order" part of the case and the beginning of the "Law" part of the case.) The prosecutor is usually the one who writes the formal criminal **complaint** against the suspect and submits it to the court after the police have completed their investigation. However, many cases follow a different path. Sometimes (particularly in federal cases), the prosecutor becomes involved much earlier: the prosecutor and law enforcement officers work together from the very beginning of the investigation. Sometimes the law enforcement officers consult with the prosecutor at various stages during the investigation to determine whether a certain surveillance method is legal. They might also work together to gauge the type of evidence needed to make the case stronger. In other cases, the prosecutor may become involved much later in the process: in many smaller jurisdictions, and for minor crimes, the police officers draw up the criminal complaint and submit it to the judge, and the prosecutor only becomes involved at the first court hearing.

At whatever point the prosecutor is brought into the case, she will begin by conducting her own evaluation. First, she will decide whether there are sufficient allegations to charge the suspect. Second, she will decide whether it is worth the required state resources to pursue those charges. The decision whether to pursue charges is the first of many opportunities for a prosecutor to exercise **prosecutorial discretion**. Prosecutorial discretion refers to the essentially unreviewable power a prosecutor has in managing a criminal case—it includes the decision of what charge should be brought or even whether any charges are appropriate at all, whether to make an offer during plea bargaining, and what sentence to recommend if there is a conviction. Ideally, prosecutors are meant to exercise their discretion in ways that represent the interests of the public and result in the most just outcome of the case. In reality, prosecutors may be responding to a variety of different motivations when they exercise their discretion, and sometimes their discretion is exercised in ways that are unrelated to these goals.

Once the criminal complaint is drafted and submitted to the court, the suspect—now known as the defendant—will be brought in front of a judge for the first court appearance of his criminal case. This first appearance is known as the "**initial appearance**" or "**arraignment**." Before the arraignment, he will probably meet his defense attorney for the first time—but again, the timing of this first meeting will vary depending on the case. Some suspects will consult with an attorney before they come into any contact with law enforcement. Others will contact an attorney after a search or before an interrogation. On the other hand, if the defendant does not have or cannot afford his own attorney, he may not get an attorney until after the arraignment. The Supreme Court has held that every individual charged with a crime has the right to an attorney. If such an individual cannot afford their own attorney, the government must provide one for them at no charge.

At the arraignment, the prosecutor will formally present the charges to the defendant. If the complaint does not properly set out a crime, the defendant may make a **motion to dismiss**, and the judge will dismiss the case. Beyond a request for dismissal, there are other, far more common forms of relief a defendant might seek at this first hearing.

For example, at arraignment, a defendant might ask to be released on **bail**. Bail is a form of pre-trial release. To resolve the question of bail, a magistrate or other judicial officer considers a number of factors, including the seriousness of the alleged offense, the defendant's record, the likelihood the defendant will reappear for trial if released, and public safety. Both the prosecutor and the defense are afforded an opportunity to make arguments regarding the appropriate pre-trial release determination.

Pre-trial release can take a number of forms. For example, the defendant may be released on his own recognizance, which means he is free to go but promises (by signing a formal assurance) to return to court for his next court appearance. In many jurisdictions, if the defendant fails to appear on the next court date, a separate criminal charge can be brought for the failure to appear. If a judge determines that he needs greater assurances that the defendant will reappear, the judge might set bail, which is an amount of money that the defendant (or a friend or family member) must pay to the court to allow the defendant to be released. Oftentimes, the defendant will have to "post" or pay to the court only a small percentage of the full bail amount that is set. If the defendant does return, the defendant gets the money back.

The arraignment is also the first time that the defendant has a chance to answer the charges brought against him. A defendant is required to enter a plea at the time of arraignment. This plea can either admit responsibility (*e.g.*, guilty) or not (*e.g.*, not guilty). Though most defendants plead "not guilty" at the time of arraignment, approximately 94% of state cases and 96% of federal cases are ultimately resolved by a defendant pleading guilty. Such guilty pleas are often entered in return for a reduced charge and/or a reduced sentence. This is a process known as **plea bargaining**, and it is yet another stage at which the prosecutor exercises tremendous discretion.

In deciding what offer to make the defendant, the prosecutor generally receives very little oversight. A number of factors might influence a prosecutor's decision to make a particular defendant an offer. For example, a prosecutor might be guided by the chances of winning the case at trial. A prosecutor also might consider the most just outcome for the case. The negotiation might also be guided by political agendas. At times a political leader or chief prosecutor may establish crime control priorities that dictate whether particular cases can be resolved through the plea negotiation process. Sometimes referred to as "no drop" policies, such prosecutorial priorities might demand that certain types of cases (*e.g.*, domestic violence cases or drug cases over a certain threshold) must be taken to trial unless the defendant is willing to plead to the full panoply of charges. At times there are less legitimate motives that influence prosecutors as well: a defendant's race, financial status, and political stature have all been documented as influencing prosecutorial decision-making about who is "deserving" of the best deals.

There are two reasons why the system tends to give prosecutors a substantial amount of leverage in plea bargaining. First, the proliferation of criminal statutes over the past few decades means that prosecutors are frequently able to bring multiple charges, even in cases involving just a single instance of criminal conduct. Prosecutors act well within their legal authority when they charge cases in this manner, but many commentators have questioned the justness of such charging practices. Often some of the charges filed will carry significant mandatory minimums. In negotiating a plea bargain, the prosecutor can offer to dismiss many of the charges and still have enough crimes left to reach their desired outcome. Second, the maximum sentence for many crimes is so high that the defendant has a strong incentive to make a deal in order to avoid a lengthy prison sentence.

This means that the prosecutor, rather than the judge, often has the real power in deciding what sentence the defendant will receive.

If the criminal case is a felony, the prosecutor must meet one more procedural requirement before moving forward: she must obtain an **indictment** or an **information** against the defendant. Indictments and informations serve the same purpose—they are formal charging documents that allow a felony to go to trial. The difference is an indictment is handed down by a **grand jury**, while an information is issued by a judge after a **preliminary hearing**. In indictment jurisdictions, the prosecutor presents the case to a grand jury, which must confirm that there is probable cause to believe that the defendant committed the crimes charged. The presentation typically involves the prosecutor bringing witnesses to testify to the grand jury. Inside the grand jury, there is no judge, no defendant, and no defense attorney. In addition, the rules of evidence usually do not apply. Given the lack of adversarial process, grand juries almost always return an indictment after a presentation.

Many jurisdictions have abandoned the grand jury requirement and allow a judge to issue an information after a preliminary hearing. The legal standard is the same—the prosecutor must demonstrate that there is probable cause to believe that the defendant committed the crime—but the process is very different. The hearing is conducted in front of the judge, with the defendant and the defense attorney present, and the defendant has the right to cross-examine witnesses, call his own witnesses, and testify himself if he wants.

After the arraignment and/or indictment, both sides begin to prepare for trial. This generally involves further investigation by both the prosecutor and the defense attorney. There may also be continued plea negotiations as both sides learn more about the strengths and weaknesses of the case.

One essential piece of trial preparation is known as **discovery**. To avoid trial by ambush, this is a process by which the parties disclose some of the evidence in their possession. For certain materials, like witness statements and expert reports, the parties both shoulder a legal obligation to turn over evidence. However, in practice, because the prosecutor bears the burden and usually controls the bulk of the evidence, the prosecution often turns over far more information than the defendant. As experienced attorneys will confirm, the information provided in discovery is the beginning, not the end, of trial preparation. It should be a springboard for each side's own exhaustive investigation and thorough legal analysis. However, this is a somewhat idealized version of the system. As many legal commentators have noted, the criminal justice system is underfunded and sometimes overwhelmed with cases, particularly on the state level. A lack of resources, time, experience, or skill too often mean that defense attorneys representing indigent clients proceed to trial without having undertaken the necessary degree of investigation and analysis needed to mount a credible response to the prosecution's charges. The sheer number of cases in large jurisdictions means that many prosecutors are also forced to prepare for trial without adequate investigation and preparation.

In addition to statutory discovery obligations, the prosecution alone bears an additional constitutional duty to disclose exculpatory evidence that is material to the defense. This information is known as ***Brady*** **material**, based on the Supreme Court case that created the obligation.

The transfer of information does not end with discovery. In advance of most trials the parties file a series of motions in an effort to more clearly define the precise contours of the trial proceedings. This flurry of pre-trial paperwork is often referred to as "**motions practice**."

In the criminal arena, there are a series of motions (beyond the standard discovery motions) that are fairly commonplace. For example, the defendant has the opportunity to challenge the legality of the police conduct during the investigation. Such challenges are raised in what is known as a **motion to suppress**. In such a motion, the defendant presents arguments to support any claim he may have that the police violated his rights during their investigation of the case. These motions are usually argued in a **suppression hearing**. If the defendant wins the suppression hearing, the typical remedy is exclusion. This means that the evidence gained through the use of illegal police tactics may not be used as direct evidence against the defendant at trial. Sometimes, this will mean the case against the defendant must be dismissed, because the suppressed evidence—the drugs recovered from the defendant's pocket, the confession the defendant made at the precinct, or the identification by the eyewitness—was a critical part of the prosecutor's case. If there is inadequate proof of guilt absent the illegally obtained evidence, the prosecutor has no choice but to dismiss the case.

In addition to suppression motions, a variety of other pre-trial matters might be decided during motions practice. Most practitioners will tell you that trial judges do not like surprises. Consequently, a well-prepared lawyer will do what she can to resolve any foreseeable disputes in advance. A **motion in limine** (sometimes referred to as a motion to exclude) might be used to set the appropriate boundaries of admissible evidence and argument. In such a motion, the moving party would argue that particular evidence or arguments should be excluded from the trial for stated reasons. A party might also file what is known as a 404(b) motion to obtain an advance ruling on the particular "bad acts" of the defendant that can be introduced.

Following motions practice, if no plea agreement can be reached, the case moves to trial. Some cases are tried as "bench trials," meaning a judge will receive the prosecution's evidence and decide the defendant's guilt. However, many other cases are tried to a jury. Since the right to a jury trial belongs to the defendant in most cases, the determination of whether a case is tried as a bench trial or as a jury trial is usually up to the defendant. If the defendant elects a bench trial (or is for some other reason not eligible for a jury trial), the trial will simply begin with the prosecution calling its first witness. If, however, the defendant is entitled to and elects a jury trial the first step in the trial will be picking a jury.

To pick the jury, a panel of potential jurors, known as the venire, is called into the courtroom. The venire consists of many more jurors than are actually needed in the case. To winnow the venire down to the actual trial (or petit) jury, the jurors in the venire are subjected to **voir dire** (pronounced "vwah deer," although some jurisdictions pronounce the term "vwah die-er"). Voir dire is the Latin term used to describe the process of examining jurors. Depending upon where you practice, voir dire may be controlled entirely by the lawyers or it may be controlled entirely by the trial judge (though the lawyers are always allowed some input regarding the questions asked). If this questioning reveals that a juror is not objectively suited to hear the case (for example, they personally know one of the witnesses or they were the recent victim of a crime similar to the one charged and are still traumatized by it), that juror will be removed from the panel for what is known as "cause." Once all "cause" challenges have been resolved, a group of potentially fair jurors remains. However, the process is not over.

The lawyers next have a chance to remove jurors who, though presumptively fair—*i.e.*, not subject to removal for cause—are still not suited for the case in the lawyer's view. Using what is known as peremptory strikes, the lawyers will remove the jurors that they do not want from the trial jury. For example, in a child abduction and murder case, the defense may not want parents of young children on the jury; or in a case involving a lot of police testimony, the prosecutor may want to strike a juror who has indicated some animosity towards the police. As a matter of statutory law, each side is assigned a precise number of peremptory challenges that they can use at their discretion.

The use of peremptory challenges is the subject of considerable debate (and the subject of specific constitutional constraints). Because reasons typically are not needed before a peremptory is exercised, the process is rife with the potential for discrimination. If one party believes that the other is using their peremptory challenges in a discriminatory manner (for example, if the prosecutor is striking all of the black jurors in a case where the defendant is black), the party can bring a "***Batson* challenge**" and force her opponent to provide a race-neutral justification for his actions.

Putting aside the question of discrimination, experienced lawyers are also fairly divided in their views of the actual usefulness of peremptories. Many lawyers report that the gut intuitions underlying peremptory strikes are misguided assumptions that are too often inaccurate. "After cause challenges are worked out, just give me the first twelve jurors in the box," is an oft repeated phrase.

When the process of selecting the jury is finally complete, the prosecutor will present her case. This is done with opening arguments, which advise the fact finder what the prosecution expects the evidence to show, and the presentation of witness testimony and other evidence to prove the defendant is guilty of the crimes charged.

The prosecutor bears the burden of proof. In light of the significant consequences that flow from a criminal conviction, this burden is substantial. The prosecution must prove that the defendant is guilty beyond a reasonable doubt. For his part, the defendant is presumed innocent—a presumption that does not lift unless and until the prosecution overcomes its burden. The defendant theoretically bears no burden, and thus does not need to present any argument or evidence to prevail—the jury must only be convinced by the end of trial that the prosecutor has not proven her case beyond a reasonable doubt. As a practical matter, though, most lawyers will tell you it is incumbent upon the defense to, at a minimum, present a coherent counter-narrative to rebut the prosecution's case—either through argument or the actual presentation of evidence.

At the end of the prosecutor's case, the defendant will make another motion to dismiss. At this stage, the motion is called a motion for judgment of acquittal (or an MJOA) in many jurisdictions. In this motion, the defense argues that even if the prosecutor's witnesses are telling the truth, there is still not sufficient evidence to convict the defendant. If the motion is granted, the case is dismissed, and the defendant is released. If, as is more typically the case, the motion is denied, the defendant has the right to put on his own case and to testify on his own behalf. After the defense case, the prosecutor then has a chance for rebuttal. At the end of the defense case (or the rebuttal case if one is presented), the defense has one more opportunity to seek dismissal of the charges.

If the renewed motion for judgment of acquittal is denied, the lawyers are given an opportunity to make closing arguments. During such arguments, the lawyers explain why the evidence presented either did (or did not) establish the defendant's guilt. The case is then submitted to the jury. To aid the jury in its deliberations, the judge instructs the jury on the law. These instructions typically include 1) a discussion of the elements of the specific charges, 2) the principles that guide all criminal trials—like the presumption of innocence and the burden of proof—and 3) any issues specific to the case, like affirmative defenses. In most jurisdictions, the judge will not "marshal" or summarize the evidence; instead that task is left to the lawyers. The jury then retires to deliberate.

In most jurisdictions, a unanimous verdict is required, but some jurisdictions allow for non-unanimous verdicts. If the defendant is convicted, the case proceeds to sentencing. If the defendant is acquitted, his liberty is restored. By the rules of **double jeopardy**, the prosecutor cannot again bring charges against him for the same crime.

Once the verdict has been reached, the jury is usually dismissed, and the judge decides the sentence. The only major exception to this rule is capital cases, in which the jury remains for the sentencing hearing to decide whether the defendant receives the death penalty. Sometimes the judge sets sentencing for immediately following the trial. However, more often sentencing is delayed for a matter of weeks or months to allow the parties to gather evidence. This evidence is then presented at a sentencing hearing in which both sides present arguments along with any evidence they may have as to what sentence the defendant should receive.

After sentencing, the defendant may appeal the conviction. Though a convicted defendant has an absolute right to appeal in most cases, this right must be affirmatively invoked. This is done by filing what is known as a **notice of appeal**. The notice is a short, one-page boilerplate document that, in most jurisdictions, must be filed within thirty days of sentencing in the trial court. It announces the defendant's intention to challenge his conviction. The filing of the notice triggers the appellate process, including the preparation of the trial transcript, the compiling of the record, and the transfer of the necessary materials to the appellate court. If the defendant purposely fails to file a timely notice, the right to appeal is waived.

Once the case moves to the appellate stage, the parties' labels change. Assuming the defendant appealed the case, the "defendant" becomes the "appellant," and the "prosecution" becomes the "appellee." The appeal of a criminal conviction can challenge either the process that resulted in the guilty verdict or the actual substantive finding of guilt. For example, the defendant might argue that his request to suppress evidence was incorrectly decided and evidence that should have been precluded was consequently presented to the jury. Or, he might argue that the judge gave the jury improper instructions regarding the elements of the crime with which he was charged. Both of these are examples of procedural attacks. Alternatively, the defendant might argue that the evidence presented was legally insufficient to establish his guilt. This would constitute a substantive challenge.

As a result of the constitutional constraint on double jeopardy, the State is not only precluded from retrying the defendant, but also generally cannot file an appeal. In only the narrowest band of circumstances is the State allowed to challenge an adverse trial result. For example, the State is allowed to challenge an adverse suppression ruling. The State is not, in contrast, allowed to challenge a jury's "not guilty" verdict.

Following a direct appeal, most states provide the opportunity for further review in what is known as the post-conviction phase of the case. (In decades past, this stage was often referred to as "state habeas," but with the adoption of post-conviction procedures in most jurisdictions, the terminology has been modified.) In the post-conviction phase once again labels change. The "appellant" becomes the "petitioner," and the "appellee" becomes the "respondent." Post-conviction challenges are available in most states pursuant to a statutory scheme that carefully constrains both the types of claims that can be brought and the number of times relief of that specific form may be sought (or reviewed). In post-conviction, the defendant may not raise challenges that have already been litigated on direct appeal. There is typically a prohibition on claims that have been previously "waived" as well. Assuming a claim is neither waived nor finally litigated, post-conviction presents the defense with an opportunity to present new attacks on the process. Ineffective assistance of trial or appellate counsel, a prosecutor's misconduct, and newly discovered bias on the part of the judge or jury are common post-conviction claims. Significantly, newly discovered evidence of actual innocence is not, in most jurisdictions, a source of post-conviction relief. Rather, claims of actual innocence are often brought pursuant to separate state statutory schemes that authorize writs of actual innocence (or other post-trial relief).

If relief is granted in post-conviction, the most common remedy is a remand for new trial. This is because the challenge in post-conviction is to the process that resulted in the finding of guilt. Thus, the fitting remedy in most cases is to afford a new process. Upon remand, the prosecution has the discretion to retry the defendant on all, some, or none of the original charges.

Beyond the state post-conviction process, the final stage of review available in most criminal cases is federal habeas. As in state post-conviction, a claim of actual innocence is generally not thought to be a viable habeas claim. The Supreme Court has indicated that actual innocence is a "gateway" that may excuse other procedural hurdles. However, the Court has yet to squarely resolve whether actual innocence constitutes a substantive federal habeas claim in its own right.

Federal habeas claims are governed by the Anti-Terrorism Effective Death Penalty Act ("AEDPA") and 28 U.S.C. § 2254 (state prisoners) and § 2255 (federal prisoners). These statutes impose significant substantive and procedural limits on habeas claimants. For example, a federal habeas court will consider only clearly established violations of the Constitution. Violations of state laws or state constitutions are irrelevant. Similarly, a firm time bar of one year is imposed on habeas petitions. Though there are some opportunities for "tolling" of this limitation, as a general rule, any federal claim must be brought within 365 days of the litigant's conviction becoming final in state court. In practice, the one-year filing deadline has proven virtually impossible for most state prisoners to meet. Consequently, though theoretically available, the vast majority of state prisoners are afforded no federal review of their convictions.

For those state prisoners who can meet the filing deadline, the relief sought in a federal habeas claim is a **writ of habeas corpus**. Generally the odds of success on habeas petitions are quite low. In seeking a balance between finality and fairness, the criminal justice system has front-loaded most resources into the trial process itself.

The flow chart on the next page provides a brief visual summary of the possible paths of a criminal case that you have just read about.

Now that we have traced the procedural path that a case generally takes through the criminal justice system, the next chapter considers the various policy questions which arise when we create or amend the rules which govern this process.

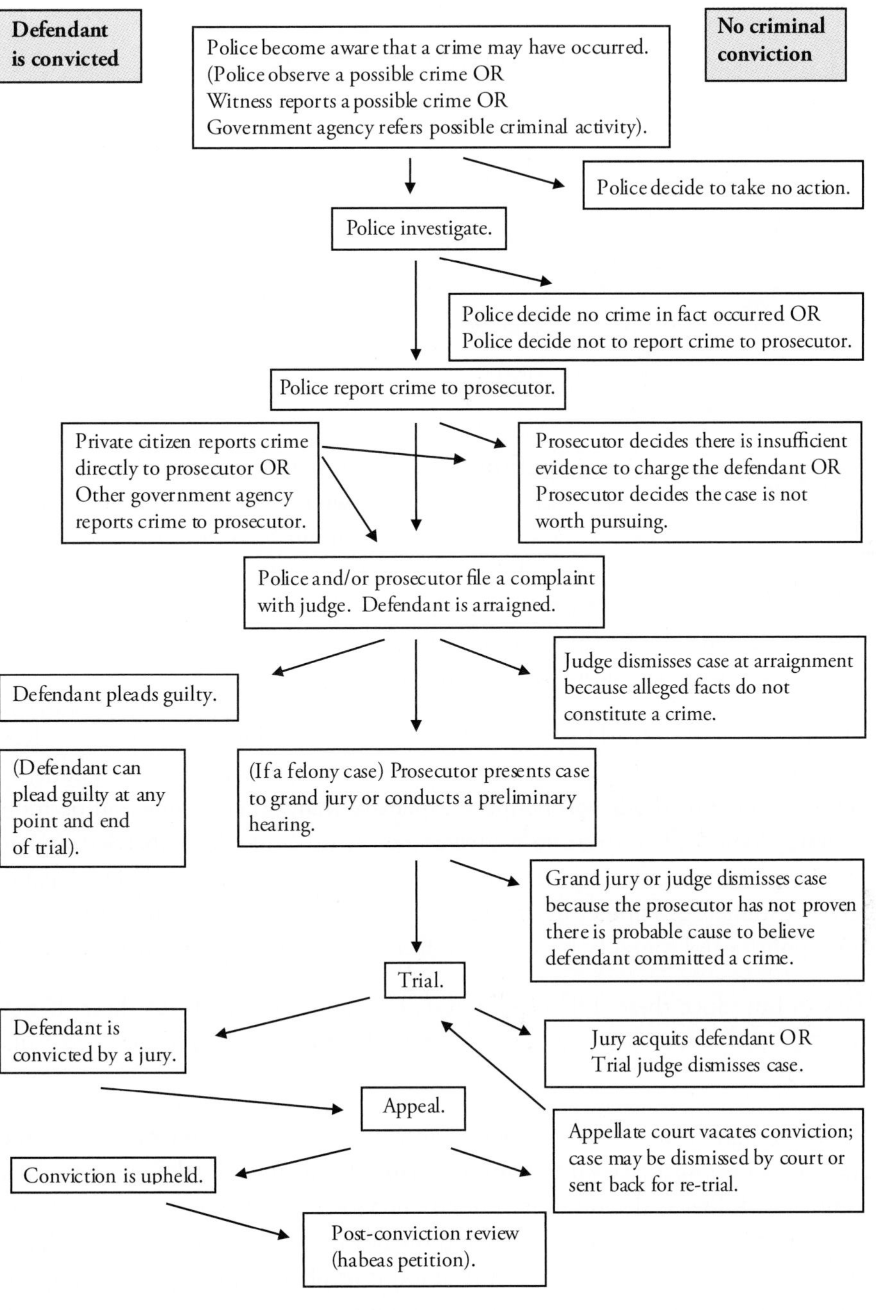
Defendant is convicted
No criminal conviction
Police become aware that a crime may have occurred. (Police observe a possible crime OR Witness reports a possible crime OR Government agency refers possible criminal activity).
Police decide to take no action.
Police investigate.
Police decide no crime in fact occurred OR Police decide not to report crime to prosecutor.
Police report crime to prosecutor.
Private citizen reports crime directly to prosecutor OR Other government agency reports crime to prosecutor.
Prosecutor decides there is insufficient evidence to charge the defendant OR Prosecutor decides the case is not worth pursuing.
Police and/or prosecutor file a complaint with judge. Defendant is arraigned.
Defendant pleads guilty.
Judge dismisses case at arraignment because alleged facts do not constitute a crime.
(Defendant can plead guilty at any point and end of trial).
(If a felony case) Prosecutor presents case to grand jury or conducts a preliminary hearing.
Grand jury or judge dismisses case because the prosecutor has not proven there is probable cause to believe defendant committed a crime.
Trial.
Defendant is convicted by a jury.
Jury acquits defendant OR Trial judge dismisses case.
Appeal.
Appellate court vacates conviction; case may be dismissed by court or sent back for re-trial.
Conviction is upheld.
Post-conviction review (habeas petition).

2

Common Themes

Key Concepts

- Various Conflicting Interests in Criminal Procedure
- Liberty v. Security
- Rules v. Discretion
- Cost v. Accuracy

A. Introduction. Unlike substantive criminal law, which struggles with the question of **what** should be criminalized and **how severe** the punishment should be, Criminal Procedure is concerned with how we determine who is guilty of a crime. In a perfect world, every person who is guilty of a crime would be apprehended and punished according to the substantive criminal law, while the innocent would be left alone to go about their business.

Of course, this ideal world is impossible to attain, and therefore important decisions must be made about what methods are used to determine who is guilty of a crime. Some methods will be more expensive than others; some will be more accurate; some will infringe to a greater extent on individual liberties; and so on. Thus, the rules for criminal procedure can be seen as representing a balance between numerous competing interests. It is in setting this balance that questions, politics and morality become significant in the field of criminal procedure.

We will introduce these different interests here and then return to these themes throughout the book as we discuss specific rules and laws that attempt to strike this balance.

The most significant set of competing interests is the question of **liberty and privacy** against **security and crime control**. By definition, the existence of a criminal code lowers the amount of liberty in a society. Likewise, giving power to the police to investigate these crimes and the power to a prosecutor and a judge to adjudicate these crimes also limits the amount of liberty enjoyed by the population. A completely anarchic society with no police and no courts would give its citizens complete freedom from the government, while a totalitarian surveillance state allowing law enforcement to search, arrest, and interrogate anyone at any time would theoretically result in a very low crime rate.

A second set of competing interests involves the balance between setting up **strict, well-defined rules** and giving the various actors in the system **discretion to make their own decisions**. Rules give the system predictability and consistency, and help to prevent arbitrary or discriminatory enforcement of the laws. Discretion, however, gives each individual actor the opportunity to evaluate the unique facts and circumstances of each case in order to ensure that each individual is treated fairly.

A third set of competing interests is the tension between **cost and accuracy**. Put another way, this tension might be seen as between **finality and fairness**. Certain steps in the criminal justice system can be streamlined to make them quicker, less expensive, and less subject to review. But frequently a process focused on speed and finality results in more overall mistakes being made in determining accurately who is guilty and who is not.

B. Liberty v. Security. This is perhaps the most well-known debate in the field of criminal procedure. Over two hundred years ago, Benjamin Franklin famously declared, "[t]hey who can give up essential liberty to obtain a little temporary safety, deserve neither liberty nor safety."[1] But everyone agrees that it is necessary to give up some liberty in order to achieve a necessary level of safety. The question is, "what kind of liberty and how much?"

In many ways, our criminal justice system can be seen as a system of rules necessary to protect liberty against the ever-encroaching populist desire for more security. The Bill of Rights was originally adopted in order to protect individual rights against the power of the government, and it includes numerous protections against government overreach, such as the warrant requirement, the protection against self-incrimination, and the grand jury requirement. As Justice Stewart once wrote, "in times of unrest, whether caused by crime or racial conflict or fear of internal subversion, this basic law and the values that it represents may appear unrealistic or 'extravagant' to some. But the values were those of the authors of our fundamental constitutional concepts."[2] As we proceed through the course, you will see how these various protections have been interpreted by the courts—sometimes in ways that strengthen the protections and sometimes in ways that weaken them.

Also, when determining the guilt of a defendant, our system is theoretically weighted in the early stages towards ensuring that the innocent are not convicted, rather than ensuring that every guilty person is punished. Prior to trial, the prosecutor must disclose to the defense not only all information that may prove the

---

1 Benjamin Franklin, Memoirs of the Life and the Writings of Benjamin Franklin 270 (London, Henry Colburn 1818).

2 Coolidge v. New Hampshire, 403 U.S. 443, 455 (1971).

defendant's guilt, but also all information that tends to exculpate him. During trial, the prosecutor has the burden of proof, and must demonstrate guilt beyond a reasonable doubt. Evidentiary rules limit the type of information that may be admitted in an effort to prevent undue prejudice. However, after a conviction the pendulum begins to swing away from fairness and toward finality. An appellant may only present issues on appeal that are within the scope of the appellate court's review and that have been preserved in the lower court. Future challenges to the conviction become increasingly circumscribed by both substantive and procedural hurdles.

Although the criminal trial system is formally weighted towards reducing the risk that an innocent will be punished, it should be noted that there are many informal factors that influence the system in other ways. For example, the amount of money a suspect has will make it more or less likely that she will go unpunished, without regard for innocence or guilt. A suspect with money can hire an attorney who may be able to intervene in the case long before the arrest and initial court appearance. In contrast, a suspect with less money must wait until the initial court appearance to meet with an appointed attorney, after the police have had an opportunity to question her. (The appointed attorney, though not necessarily of a poorer quality, will almost certainly be overworked, under-resourced and consequently less able to focus as much attention on the indigent client). An indigent defendant is also less likely to be able to make bail. This will mean the individual will likely remain in prison while awaiting trial—making it harder to prepare her own defense and also increasing the pressure on her to plead guilty.

Finally, you should keep in mind that the interests of liberty and security are not always in conflict. Many investigatory techniques increase security without diminishing our liberty—or at least, without diminishing the liberty of innocent people. For example, alarms and surveillance cameras on private property allow for criminal activity to be detected and proven more easily, but do not curtail the freedom of individuals who do not trespass on private property.

C. Rules v. Discretion. In any legal or political system, important choices must be made regarding the amount of power that is given to individual actors in the system. On the one hand, we should live under a system of laws and not be subject to the unfettered whims of the authorities. In a democratic society, the legislature should set the rules and the police, prosecutors, and courts who apply these rules need to follow the will of the elected representatives. However, there are a number of reasons why it is not only desirable but also necessary to give discretion to the various actors in the system:

1. The rules and laws set out by courts and legislatures are by necessity **too broad** to fit every possible fact pattern. This is true for both the substantive criminal law and for rules of criminal procedure.

For substantive criminal law, consider a basic crime like battery. Most battery laws are written quite simply, for example:

An individual who recklessly or knowingly causes physical injury or substantial physical pain to another is guilty of battery. Battery is a first-degree misdemeanor, punishable by up to one year in jail.

This law leaves a fair amount of discretion for police officers deciding when to make an arrest, and prosecutors deciding whether to bring charges. What is "physical injury" and when is pain "substantial?" When does negligent behavior rise to the level of recklessness? Similarly, judges are given significant discretion in setting punishment—an individual who is found guilty could be given a sentence anywhere between probation and one year in jail.

The law could, of course, be written more specifically in order to curtail the discretion of the police, prosecutors, and judges. For example, it could give examples of what rises to the level of "physical injury," such as a cut or abrasion over a half an inch in length, or a bruise which is over an inch in diameter. And it could link various injuries to specific punishments—for example, one month in jail for an injury to the leg which causes the victim to noticeably limp for up to one day, or three months in jail if the victim went to the hospital for his injuries. But such specificity would quickly become cumbersome and would still be unable to cover every possible configuration of injuries that might occur. Thus, there has to be room for the individual decision-makers to exercise independent judgment as to what each defendant deserves.

The same considerations exist for the procedural rules. For example, the Supreme Court has held that a police officer may briefly detain a suspect if the officer has "reasonable suspicion" that the suspect is involved in criminal activity.[3] Again, the courts could try to describe every possible scenario which gives rise to reasonable suspicion, but that would be impossible. Instead, the Court has provided a broad standard to police officers and allows them the flexibility to work within that standard. Cases are then reviewed individually to determine whether the officer's conduct complies with the broad standards that have been structured.

2. Even the most carefully crafted rule will need to have exceptions for **unusual cases** which could not be foreseen by the rule's drafters. Take the battery example discussed earlier. The law probably sets out narrow exceptions for self-defense or necessity. But are there any other circumstances in which a case should not be brought? What if the victim struck

[3] Terry v. Ohio, 392 U.S. 1 (1968).

the defendant first and then taunted him to hit back? What if the defendant just learned that the victim had sexually assaulted his wife? What if the defendant and the victim were both intoxicated and got into a fight in a bar? A mechanical application of the rules would lead to punishment—identical punishment—for each of these circumstances. Giving discretion to the police officers and prosecutors who handle these cases allows them to consider whether a specific defendant deserves significant punishment, nominal punishment, or perhaps no punishment at all.

3. Most rules are created by **centralized authority**—federal or state legislatures, or federal or state supreme courts. But most crime is enforced on the local level by city or county police, and is adjudicated in city or state courts. A law which may have the support of a majority of state or federal legislatures may not have support in certain jurisdictions.

   For example, assume the New York state legislature criminalizes both marijuana possession and unlicensed firearm possession. The citizens—and thus the police—in New York City may be utterly unconcerned with whether an individual smokes pot in his apartment, but they may wish to devote substantial resources to arresting and imprisoning people with illegal guns. In contrast, the police officers who patrol a wealthy suburb of Albany may have no problems with gun violence, but may be aware that drug abuse is commonplace among local high school students. Thus, the suburban police may set up special task forces to track down users of marijuana, and make no special effort to arrests those who illegally possess guns.

4. There are **so many criminal laws** on the books that it would literally be impossible to enforce them all. Thus, various authorities throughout the process need to prioritize and decide which crimes under which circumstances deserve more attention than others. They may do so based on one of the three reasons above—the law is written so broadly that it is over-inclusive; there are extraordinary circumstances involved for this specific defendant; or the law passed by the centralized authority is not important to the local authority. Or they may simply not have the resources to enforce every single criminal law, so they make political or moral judgments about which laws are important enough to enforce.

To understand the amount of discretion that exists in the criminal justice system, consider how many different individuals and institutions have the ability to exempt a suspect from facing the criminal process or a guilty defendant from receiving the punishment that she deserves under the law:

- The police officer may decide not to make an arrest, even though she has sufficient evidence of criminal activity.

- The prosecutor may decide not to move forward with the charges, even though he believes he could prove the case beyond a reasonable doubt.

- The grand jury (if the case is a felony) may refuse to indict the case, even though the prosecutor has set out sufficient evidence for an indictment.

- The trial jury may refuse to convict the defendant, even though the case has been proven beyond a reasonable doubt.

- The governor or President may pardon the defendant or commute the defendant's sentence after conviction.

None of these decisions is reviewable by an independent authority. That is, no institution can force the police officer to make an arrest, nor the prosecutor to bring charges, nor the grand jury to indict, nor the trial jury to convict.

In practice, a decision not to move forward by any of these individuals or institutions is relatively rare, particularly for serious crimes. Furthermore, political pressure often influences actors in the system against exempting the guilty defendant from punishment. However, the ability to completely exempt the guilty from punishment is only the most extreme example of discretion. For example, police can issue summons instead of making an arrest; prosecutors can make generous plea offers instead of asking for the maximum sentence; and judges can sentence a convicted defendant to probation instead of prison time.

Having just set out all these reasons why discretion is necessary and frequently desirable, it is important to also note the dangers of allowing different authorities and institutions to exercise discretion. In addition to the idea that discretionary exercise of authority is contrary to democratic principles, there is the concern that individual actors or institutions may exercise their discretion in arbitrary or discriminatory ways. Our country has a long and ugly history of racial discrimination in the criminal justice system, involving mostly white law enforcement officials and prosecutors selectively enforcing the law against racial minorities. This concern still persists today, from issues of racial profiling in traffic stops and stop-and-frisks to the disproportionate application of the death penalty against people of color.

And sometimes the exercise of discretion reflects other values or perspectives held by the decision-maker that are not widely shared. For example, for decades many police would not make an arrest for domestic violence because such conduct was considered to be a "family matter" which should not involve the police. Similarly, for many years prosecutors would frequently refuse to go forward with sexual assault charges if the victim was not sexually chaste, out of a belief (or a concern that a jury would believe) that the victim would not be credible.

Finally, allowing individual actors to exercise discretion necessarily means that there will be less consistency across the system. Individual defendants who commit the same crime under the same circumstances will receive different punishments—perhaps dramatically so—depending on which police officer, prosecutor, or judge handles their case. This lack of consistency leads to unfairness in the system—though perhaps less unfairness than would exist from a mechanical application of the rules to every defendant equally.

As we proceed through the course, you should ask yourself whether the system gives the appropriate amount of discretion at each stage of the criminal justice system. You should also consider which individuals or institutions should be given discretion—are some more trustworthy than others? And finally, think about whether there are ways to monitor or review the exercise of discretion—and if so, who or what should be trusted with that watchdog role.

D. Cost v. Accuracy. Since 1992, the Innocence Project has been working to exonerate and free prisoners who have been wrongfully convicted of serious felonies. In twenty years they have found over three hundred demonstrably innocent people who were imprisoned for crimes they did not commit. And these three hundred represent just a small fraction of the total number of innocent people who are currently languishing in the criminal justice system. Although there is no way to calculate the actual error rate with precision, the most reliable studies have predicted a systemic error rate of between 3% and 5%.[4] This would represent at least 30,000 innocent people who are found guilty of felonies and at least 300,000 innocent people who are found guilty of misdemeanors each year.

Mistakes occur in the other direction as well, of course. In fact, every time an innocent person is falsely convicted of a crime, by definition there is a guilty person who was **not** convicted. And in countless other cases, guilty criminals are wrongfully acquitted because the jury makes a mistake, or because the prosecutor fails to present an effective case, or because a witness fails to appear or comes across as not credible.

If you were to ask a hundred people what error rate they were willing to accept in the criminal justice system, some might say that any amount of error is unacceptable: we should never convict an innocent person of a crime, nor should we allow a guilty person to go unpunished. In reality though, most Americans seem willing to accept some amount of error in the criminal justice system. Since 1999,

[4] D. Michael Risinger, Innocents Convicted: An Empirically Justified Factual Wrongful Conviction Rate, 97 J. Crim. L. & Criminology 761, 769–780 (suggesting that previous studies have over- and under-estimated the error rate, and predicting a "corrected" estimation of between 3.3% and 5%).

a consistent and overwhelming majority of Harris poll participants (95%) has expressed the belief that the system sometimes convicts innocent people.[5] When asked to estimate the system's likely error rate, the average prediction among those polled was twelve mistakes in every 100 convictions (or 12%). Although this estimate is probably too high, the acknowledgement of the existence of error is rather rational. Precision is impossible[6]—if only because it would not be feasible to devote the amount of resources required to ensure that every single case is correctly decided. The real questions are: how much money are we willing to spend and how much inaccuracy are we willing to tolerate? As with all questions regarding state resources, the money we spend on the criminal justice system must come from somewhere: higher taxes or fees, or less money for schools, roads, or social services.

Thus, the criminal justice system faces another challenging trade-off: cost v. accuracy (or as described above finality v. fairness). Partly this is merely a question of allocation of resources: if a city is able to hire more police, more public defenders, more prosecutors, and more judges, the city would almost certainly be able to determine the guilt or innocence of suspects more accurately. But partly this is also a question of the rules that are created.

For example, consider a defendant who has just been convicted of a crime at trial. What are his rights to challenge the conviction in another proceeding? A state could create a rule which allows not only for an immediate appeal, but also for the defendant to automatically re-open his case every year, with a new lawyer to look for irregularities in the trial, new investigators to search for evidence of innocence, and a new appellate court to review the conviction. This rule would probably uncover some number of defendants who were wrongly convicted, but it would be so costly that no state has chosen to adopt it. Conversely, the rule could be changed so that no defendant could ever appeal his conviction at trial. This would save a substantial amount of money, but it would mean that a far lower number of wrongfully convicted defendants would be able to establish their right to relief—thus, no state has adopted this rule either.

Instead, most states have adopted a rule in which the defendant has the right to one direct appeal to the intermediate appellate court. If the defendant loses that appeal, he is almost certainly out of luck—he has the right to a discretionary appeal to the highest court of the state, but that court is very unlikely to take the case. In most states, he also has the ability to launch a "collateral attack"—for example, a hearing in state court to evidence that trial counsel was ineffective; or a hearing in federal court to prove that his constitutional rights were violated—but

[5] Regina Corso, Over Three in Five Americans Believe in Death Penalty, The Harris Poll 1, 1 (Mar. 18, 2008), available at www.harrisinteractive.com/vault/harris-interactive-poll-research-over-three-in-five-americans-believe-in-death-penalty-2008-03.pdf (March 18, 2008).

[6] Kansas v. Marsh, 548 U.S. 163, 199 (2006) (Scalia, J., concurring).

he must meet a very high standard to even get the case heard. Some states do not even create an automatic right to the initial appeal, and only review some of the convictions at trial—a rule which saves money but results in more wrongful convictions going uncorrected.

As you progress through this course, you will notice that the criminal justice system tends to focus its resources at certain points in the process. For example, the decision to begin a prosecution generally requires three separate institutions to agree that a prosecution is warranted: the police officer who makes the initial arrest, the prosecutor who decides to go forward with the case, and an independent judge who reviews the charges to ensure there is probable cause to believe the defendant is guilty of the crimes charged. Such redundancy requires more resources, but because a formal criminal charge is a serious infringement of liberty, the expenditure of resources is deemed worthwhile. But this focus on certainty at the charging stage means that there are fewer resources to ensure certainty at earlier stages—for example, police officers can conduct many different kinds of surveillance, some of which are quite intrusive, without needing the approval of prosecutors or judges.

In the adjudication phase, the criminal justice system also focuses its resources at a specific point: the criminal trial. The defendant is given many rights at trial—the right to an attorney, the right to a jury, the right to subpoena his own witnesses and cross-examine witnesses against him, and so on. Trials are a very formal process, involving attorneys, judges, court reporters, bailiffs, court officers, clerks, and jurors and witnesses who are called away from their jobs to testify. They may take days or even weeks to complete. Even the standard of proof—beyond a reasonable doubt—is meant to increase the level of accuracy. However, there is no question that these protections also increase the cost, since the prosecutor must expend a large amount of resources on the trial in order to ensure that she can prove her case. But as we have seen, once the trial is over, we give the defendant very limited means to challenge the conviction—he essentially gets one appeal in which the higher court reviews the trial record for legal errors

Unsurprisingly, the criminal justice system has adapted to find more efficient ways of getting the job done by avoiding the points at which the cost is the highest. Realizing that an arrest and a formal charge are expensive, police will seek to carry out surveillance and even interrogations on a broad number of individuals before making an arrest of an individual suspect. And the inexpensive practice of plea bargaining has effectively replaced the expensive trial as the primary means of determining guilt in the system. These adaptations certainly decrease the cost of running the system—that was why they were developed. But perhaps they result in a loss of accuracy, or of one of the other competing values in the system.

In critically evaluating the rules and laws of criminal procedure, you should think about how each rule balances each of these sets of competing interests and how you might strike a different balance. You should also think about whether there is a way to improve the rule without engaging in a trade-off; that is, whether there may be a way to advance one of these interests without incurring a cost to another interest.

Quick Summary

In creating rules of Criminal Procedure, there are many different competing interests to take into account.

The criminal justice system exists in order to reduce crime, usually by apprehending and punishing those who commit crime. But investigating crime and adjudicating guilt necessarily infringes on valuable individual liberties to at least some extent. As a general rule, the courts must apply the rights found in the Constitution to protect individual rights against a more populist desire to increase the power of police and prosecutors.

As in any complex system, a balance must be struck between setting out strict rules that must be followed without exception in order to maintain consistency, and allowing for flexibility and discretion on the part of individual actors. This balance is especially critical in the criminal justice system. On the one hand we need the laws to apply to everyone equally. On the other hand we need the system to result in justice for each individual case.

Finally, it is critical that the criminal justice system accurately identify those who are guilty of criminal activity, both to ensure that the guilty are punished, but also to ensure that the innocent are not falsely accused and convicted. Unfortunately, some amount of error is unavoidable in the system. Presumably though the more resources we spend on the system, the lower the error rate becomes. Since we do not have unlimited resources, we must decide how much we are willing to spend and how much inaccuracy we are willing to tolerate.

3

Sources of the Law

Key Concepts

- Fourth, Fifth, Sixth, Eighth Amendments
- Increased Significance of Statutes
- Influence of Politics on the Law of Criminal Procedure

A. The Federal Constitution. The Bill of Rights was ratified in 1791, two years after the United States Constitution, and it was designed to limit the powers of the federal government. In particular, the Fourth, Fifth, Sixth, and Eighth Amendments provided protections for those suspected or accused of a crime:

- The **Fourth Amendment** contains restrictions on when and how law enforcement can conduct searches and seizures of individuals and property.
- The **Fifth Amendment** requires a grand jury indictment for all felony cases; precludes the prosecution from re-trying a defendant if he is acquitted; forbids the government from forcing a defendant to give testimony against himself; and requires "due process" in every criminal case.[1]
- The **Sixth Amendment** requires the government to give the defendant a "speedy and public trial"; gives the defendant the right to a jury trial in the jurisdiction where the crime was committed; requires the government to inform the defendant of the charges against him; gives the defendant the right to cross-examine the witnesses brought against him and the right to subpoena witnesses in his own behalf; and gives the defendant the right to the effective assistance of an attorney.
- The **Eighth Amendment** prohibits "excessive bail" and "cruel and unusual punishment."

[1] In the realm of civil law, the Fifth Amendment also requires the government to give just compensation to private property owners when it takes their property for public use.

Originally, the Bill of Rights only provided protection against the **federal** government. Consequently, it did not restrict the ability of states to pass laws which violated its protections. (Many states had similar protections in their own state constitutions, as noted below). Thus, a course in criminal procedure in the 19th century would be very state-specific, since every state had its own rules and standards. However, in 1868, in the aftermath of the Civil War, the States adopted the Fourteenth Amendment, which states in its first section:

> . . . No State shall make or enforce any law which shall abridge the privileges or immunities of citizens of the United States; nor shall any State deprive any person of life, liberty, or property, without due process of law; nor deny to any person within its jurisdiction the equal protection of the laws.

The general intent of this section of the Fourteenth Amendment was to place some limitations on the power of individual state governments, much the same way that the Bill of Rights placed limitations on the power of the federal government. For many decades after the passage of the Fourteenth Amendment, there was an ongoing judicial debate about exactly what those limitations were. Specifically, the Supreme Court struggled to define the exact relationship of the Amendment to the Bill of Rights.

Some Supreme Court Justices argued that the Due Process clause of the Amendment should be interpreted to mean that the entire Bill of Rights applied to state governments to the same extent as it did to the federal government. This was known as the "full incorporation" doctrine.[2] Others argued that the Due Process clause only incorporated some of the Amendments contained in the Bill of Rights. This was known as the "selective incorporation" doctrine.[3] Still others argued that the Due Process clause did not incorporate any of the Amendments contained in the Bill of Rights, but was intended instead to create a separate set of "fundamental rights" that could be enforced against the state. This was known as the "fundamental rights" doctrine.[4]

In the end, the Supreme Court settled on the "selective incorporation" doctrine, and one by one the Court has decided which of the rights that are guaranteed in the Bill of Rights should be applied as against the states. Over time, the Court held that the overwhelming majority of the Bill of Rights is to be applied against the states, which means that the provisions of these "incorporated" amendments now limit the states as well as the federal government. With regard to the "criminal procedure amendments," the Fourth, Fifth, Sixth and Eighth Amendments, there is one notable exception. The exception is the provision of the Fifth Amendment which requires a grand jury indictment for all felony cases. This provision is

---

[2] See, e.g., Adamson v. California, 332 U.S. 46, 71-72 (1947) (Black, J. dissenting).

[3] See, e.g., Williams v. Florida, 399 U.S. 78, 130-31 (Harlan, J., concurring).

[4] See, e.g., Adamson, 332 U.S. at 66 (Frankfurter, J., concurring).

binding on the federal government only[5] (though it turns out that some states have a similar requirement in their own constitutions).

Furthermore, the Court has also almost always held that when a provision of the Bill of Rights is applied to the states, the scope and contours of that right with regard to the state government are identical to the scope and contours of that right with regard to the federal government. In other words, when a right (such as the right against self-incrimination) is "incorporated" and thereby applied to the states, the Court will import all of the case law and jurisprudence that interprets, describes, and limits that right (such as the *Miranda* rule requiring police officers to notify a suspect after arrest of his right against self-incrimination). Here too, there is one exception to the rule: the right to a jury trial has been incorporated, but the common law rule requiring **unanimous** jury verdicts applies only to federal trials, not to state trials.[6]

What this means for students and young lawyers studying criminal procedure is that the law in this area has to a large extent been federalized—many of the same laws and rules that are enforced in federal court are also enforced in every state court. However, as we will see below, there are still some differences between the federal government and the states, as well as between different states. Moreover, as more recent Supreme Court decisions have reduced the constitutional footprint and are becoming increasingly willing to defer to the states, legislatures are becoming an increasing source of criminal procedural guidance.

B. The (Preliminary) Shift Away from Case Law. In many ways, the contemporary field of Criminal Procedure began in the 1950's and 1960's. This was the time of the Warren Court, when Chief Justice Earl Warren led a relatively liberal Supreme Court that issued dozens of high-profile decisions that in many respects broadened and strengthened individual rights. Many of these cases became well-known outside of legal circles, such as *Gideon v. Wainwright*,[7] which guaranteed counsel for indigent defendants during a criminal trial; *Brady v. Maryland*,[8] which required the prosecutor to turn over any material exculpatory evidence to the defense attorney; and *Miranda v. Arizona*,[9] which held that the police must give an arrested suspect a series of warnings before beginning an interrogation.

It was during this era that many of the original casebooks of criminal procedure were first published, and they (justifiably) placed a heavy focus on the Supreme Court's role in creating and defining the rules on criminal procedure by interpreting the United States Constitution. Today, the Constitution and the Supreme

[5] Hurtado v. California, 110 U.S. 516 (1884).

[6] Williams v. Florida, 399 U.S. 78 (1970).

[7] 372 U.S. 335 (1963).

[8] 373 U.S. 83 (1963).

[9] 384 U.S. 436 (1966).

Court's decisions are still significant, but these decisions are not the only source of law governing criminal procedure. There are two reasons for this shift:

1. Over the past couple of decades, the Supreme Court has repudiated many of the constitutional protections previously afforded individual rights. This has, in many cases, relegated the Constitution to the sidelines of criminal procedure. Republican legislatures have taken advantage of the Court's more conservative approach and passed laws that give greater power to law enforcement. Liberal legislatures, on the other hand, have sought to fill the gap in individual liberties by passing laws that protect suspects. State supreme courts, too, have taken a more active role in defining the contours of individual liberty under their state constitutions.

2. New technologies in law enforcement and surveillance are being developed at an unusually brisk pace. It takes a good deal of time for the Supreme Court to make a new rule or define the precise application of an existing rule to a new scenario. The issue in question needs to be challenged in court by a defendant, then usually be the subject of numerous circuit court decisions, perhaps creating a circuit split, before the Supreme Court eventually decides the problem is important enough to warrant attention. For questions involving traditional methods of criminal investigation, such as the rules surrounding interrogations, or the standards police must meet before obtaining a search warrant, the Court has this luxury of time. But often for rapidly changing surveillance technologies, in the time it takes the Court to take up a particular method of technologically enhanced surveillance tools being used on the ground are years beyond the question being considered. Thus, rules governing intercepting e-mails, searching computer data, or monitoring internet searches are more likely to be set by federal and state legislatures than the courts.

To be sure, the United States Constitution and the Supreme Court's interpretations of the Constitution are still the primary framework for the law of criminal procedure. The Constitution plays an important role in defining the minimum levels of required protection. However, modern students and modern practitioners need to be familiar not only with Supreme Court case law, but also various federal and state statutes. As a practical matter, the relative nimbleness of legislatures has become an important tool in defining the appropriate use of cutting-edge technologies.

In the adjudication aspect of the course, federal and state statutes are even more significant. Specifically, the federal government and every state has promulgated the Rules of Criminal Procedure, which—like the Rules of Evidence or the Rules of Civil Procedure—are a codified set of laws which lawyers and judges must follow as they prepare for and engage in litigation.

C. Federal Statutes. As noted in the first section, the federal constitution is not the only source of law in criminal procedure. Federal statutes, state constitutions, state statutes, and even administrative regulations also regulate how the government investigates and adjudicates crime. In particular, certain federal laws have gained significance as criminal activity and law enforcement surveillance have evolved:

Title III of The Omnibus Crime Control and Safe Streets Act Wiretap Act of 1968 ("Title III"), which set out standards and rules for wiretapping telephones after the Supreme Court ruled that the police could not conduct wiretapping without prior judicial authorization.

The Electronic Communication and Privacy Act ("ECPA"), which extends Title III to electronic communications.

The Pen Register Act, which creates rules for tracing phone numbers and address information on digital communication.

The Stored Communications Act ("SCA"), which regulates the government's ability to obtain digitally-stored data.

The Foreign Intelligence Services Act ("FISA"), which restricts how the federal government can gather and use information. Though initially conceived as a regulation on foreign intelligence gathering, modern administrations have increasingly used the provisions of the Act in connection with domestic surveillance as well.

The Federal Rules of Criminal Procedure ("F.R.C.P."), which, like its civil law counterpart, codifies the law for every stage of the criminal adjudication process.

D. State Laws. Although the *de facto* federalization of the Bill of Rights means that no state can offer less protection than the United States Constitution provides, there is nothing stopping a state from creating rules that create more protection than the Constitution offers. For example, the Supreme Court has held that, absent extraordinary circumstances, the Fourth Amendment requires the government to bring a defendant before a judge for a probable cause hearing within forty-eight hours of the arrest.[10] Many states, however, have a stricter requirement; for example, New York requires the government to bring a defendant before a judge within twenty-four hours of the arrest. Even if a state does not seek to expand the individual rights of suspects, there are a number of areas—particularly in the adjudication phase—where the Bill of Rights is silent, and so state laws have been passed to fill in the gaps. For example, most rules regarding discovery are governed by statute, not by the Constitution.

---

[10] County of Riverside v. McLaughlin, 500 U.S. 44 (1991).

In addition, every state has its own rules of criminal procedure, which are similar, but not identical, to the Federal Rules of Criminal Procedure.

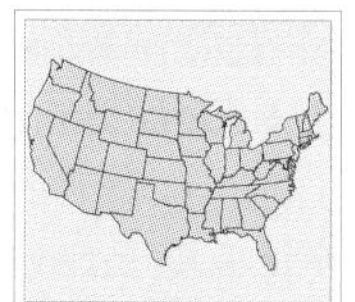

This book will focus primarily on federal law, and on the majority rule of the states in cases where federal law does not control. However, the book will point out the areas where state laws differ in significant ways, and will use the icon to the left to notify you of the differences. Throughout your study and practice of criminal procedure, you always need to keep in mind that every jurisdiction will have its own unique set of rules depending on the state laws.

E. Law and Politics. The laws and rules of Criminal Procedure are, by and large, the result of the political views of the individuals who drafted them. Of course, this is true for any field you will study in law school, but the influence of politics on Criminal Procedure is both more transparent and more subtle than in many of your other classes.

It is more transparent because unlike most classes—Property, Civil Procedure, Evidence—the laws and rules of the criminal justice system have immediate and obvious political significance. Whether the police should be required to obtain a warrant before they can collect the cell phone records of a suspected terrorist is very much a political question. How much do we value our right to privacy? How aggressive do we want to be in the war against terror? How much do we trust the police to use the power we give them judiciously and in a non-discriminatory manner? These are questions which are (and should be) debated in legislatures and written about in the opinion papers of newspapers. They are also questions about which you may already have strong beliefs, depending on your own political preferences.

On the other hand, the political aspect of Criminal Procedure is more subtle because so many of the laws come from the Supreme Court's interpretation of the Constitution. The Constitution itself is a document that is beyond politics—nearly every American agrees with the principles of the Constitution, and every office-holder takes an oath to support it. But the text of the Constitution is very brief and very vague. So when we say that the Constitution establishes a certain rule, we are really saying that a majority of the Supreme Court at the time of a certain decision ruled that the Constitution established a certain rule. Thousands of other rules have been established by circuit courts as they apply the Supreme Court's decisions, and hundreds of thousands of individual rulings are made by trial judges and magistrates when they apply these rules to individual defendants.

Although judges are supposed to be above the law, and most judges would not admit that their political preferences influence decisions, there is no doubt that judges' political beliefs affect their decisions to some degree. Every time a Supreme Court Justice retires, the political nature of the job becomes apparent, as the President is expected to appoint a "liberal" or "conservative" judge, depending on the President's own ideology. The nominee's confirmation hearing often becomes a political circus with spirited attacks launched by senators of the opposite political persuasion and focused adoration offered by senators of the President's party. Once on the bench, a Justice is usually labeled as liberal or conservative, and reliable voting blocs develop for each area of law. In fact, political scientists have measured and ranked the ideological tendencies of every recent Supreme Court Justice based on their decisions, thus quantifying the phenomenon. When one voting bloc becomes dominant—as the liberal bloc did in the Warren Court in the 1960's, or the conservative bloc did in the Rehnquist Court in the 1990's—the effect on the nation's policies can be dramatic.

The influence of a judge's political leanings is significant on every level of the judiciary. On the Supreme Court level, justices define terms such as "cruel and unusual punishment" and "probable cause," or set out the scope of the right to counsel or the right against self-incrimination. These decisions are bound by the text of the Constitution and by prior precedent, but the justice's own political preferences guide her within those limits. Meanwhile, at the trial court level, judges will quickly gain a reputation for being liberal or conservative based on their pattern of conduct in questions of bail determination, plea bargaining decisions, and sentencing.

As you consider the cases that we discuss in this book, think about the judges or courts making their decisions in two stages. First, what range of choices did the judges or justices have when faced with their decision? And second, what choice did each judge or justice make from within that range? The first question is the legal question: the text of the law and earlier interpretations of the law will restrict the range of possible outcomes for the judge. The second is the political question: given the restrictions created by the law, the judge was able to exercise some independent political judgment and make a decision. As we read through the text of the Constitution, the binding precedents, and the applicable statutes, think about how much discretion the laws actually give to the judges who are interpreting them.

Quick Summary

The primary source of Criminal Procedure law remains the Supreme Court's interpretations of the Bill of Rights, specifically the Fourth, Fifth, Sixth, and Eighth Amendments. This reality, however, is slowly changing as federal and state legislatures pass statutes to fill in the gaps in the Supreme Court jurisprudence, and as states pass their own laws which may create stronger individual rights than those guaranteed under the United States Constitution. Also, in the adjudication stage, the Federal Rules of Criminal Procedure have codified most of the steps taken in preparation for and during litigation of criminal cases. Finally, be aware of the influence that a judge or justice's political preferences may have on the decisions that they issue.

4

When Does the Fourth Amendment Apply?

Key Concepts

- Limitations on the Fourth Amendment
- Which "People" Are Protected
- State Action

A. Introduction and Policy. We begin our discussion of surveillance regulation with an introduction to the Fourth Amendment. Although there are many different sources of law for surveillance regulation, the Fourth Amendment is still the foundation around which the rest of the law is built.

First, let us examine the text of the Fourth Amendment:

> The right of the people to be secure in their persons, houses, papers, and effects, against unreasonable searches and seizures, shall not be violated, and no Warrants shall issue, but upon probable cause, supported by Oath or affirmation, and particularly describing the place to be searched, and the persons or things to be seized.[1]

As you might imagine, these fifty-four words have been the subject of countless pages of interpretation and analysis by judges, professors, and other experts. By now, over two hundred years after the Fourth Amendment was ratified, many of the words have become terms of art with their own special meaning, and sometimes those meanings are quite counter-intuitive.

The Framers intended some of the terms to be broad and vague. "Unreasonable" and "probable cause" were meant to require judicial interpretation and thus their meaning has evolved with time as the Court has considered the operation of the Amendment upon different fact patterns. Other terms might seem straightforward but, in fact, have been interpreted to require sophisticated legal definitions. For example, the terms "search" and "seizure" have specific meanings that have undergone dramatic changes over the past fifty years. In addition, the term "seizure" has been defined in two different ways, depending on whether an item or a person is being "seized." (We will discuss the definition of "search" in **Chapter 6** and the definitions of "seizure" in **Chapter 9**.)

[1] U.S. Const. amend. IV.

Still other terms have required new interpretations as technology has advanced. For example, the Amendment declares a right to be secure in your "person[], houses, papers, and effects." Accordingly, on its face, the Amendment might appear not to apply to the wiretapping of a telephone call or the interception of an e-mail. But the Supreme Court has broadly interpreted the Amendment to encompass both tangible and intangible items. Thus, it applies to computer data and private conversations to the same extent that it applies to paper diaries and suitcases.

We begin our discussion of the Fourth Amendment with an important preliminary question: under what circumstances does the Amendment apply?

There are three important limitations to the protection provided by the language of the Fourth Amendment:

1. The Fourth Amendment does not protect the rights of people who are citizens of and reside in another country, nor does it apply to everyone who is currently residing in this country.

2. The Fourth Amendment only applies when government agents (or those who are working on their behalf) violate a person's privacy rights or liberty interests. This is known as the **state action** requirement.

3. The Fourth Amendment only applies when **the person whose rights have been violated** challenges the violation.

These limitations are not obvious from the text of the Amendment. In fact, the plain meaning of the Amendment's language would lead some readers to conclude that these limitations do not exist.

1. The term "the people" in the first line could be interpreted as meaning all people residing in this country; in fact, it only refers to residents of this country who are legally present or have developed sufficient community ties here.

2. The passive verb "shall not be violated" in the second line implies that the Amendment protects privacy rights from **any** kind of infringement, whether the infringer is a public or private actor. Instead, the Amendment is interpreted as though it were written in the active tense, with a subject, as: "The state shall not violate. . . ."

3. The Amendment is silent as to who can challenge a violation, which could lead the reader to believe that **anyone** could sue or otherwise challenge government action. Instead, only the person whose rights were violated can challenge the government action.

Thus, the first clause of the Amendment can be re-written more accurately (though no doubt less eloquently) as follows:

> If **a government agent** violates the right **of a resident of the United States** to be secure in his or her person, houses, papers, and effects against unreasonable searches and seizures, **the individual whose rights have been violated can seek a remedy against the government**.

In this chapter, we discuss the "people" who are protected by the Fourth Amendment and examine how the state action doctrine applies. The question of whose rights are violated by an illegal search—analogous to a standing requirement in civil law—is a bit more complicated. Therefore we will delay that explanation until **Chapter 22.** However, you should keep it in mind as we move through our discussion of the Fourth Amendment.

B. Who is Protected?

The Supreme Court has never precisely defined which "people" are covered by the Fourth Amendment. However, it has said the following:

> To be protected by the Fourth Amendment, the subject of the surveillance must be "part of our national community" or have "otherwise developed sufficient connection with this country to be considered part of that community."[2]
>
> The Fourth Amendment does not apply to any surveillance conducted by a foreign government and then turned over to domestic law enforcement to be used in domestic courts.

Unfortunately we have very little guidance as to how to interpret the phrases "part of our national community" and "significant connection with this country." There has only been one Supreme Court case to directly address this issue, and it had a relatively unusual fact pattern:

> **Example—*United States v. Verdugo-Urquidez*, 494 U.S. 259 (1990):** René Martín Verdugo-Urquidez, a citizen and resident of Mexico, was charged in the United States with drug trafficking. Verdugo-Urquidez was arrested by Mexican police and extradited to the United States, where he was held in a San Diego prison while awaiting trial.

[2] United States v. Verdugo-Urquidez, 494 U.S. 259, 265 (1990).

In order to gain evidence against Verdugo-Urquidez, U.S. Drug Enforcement ("DEA") agents, working with Mexican police, searched Verdugo-Urquidez's residences in Mexicali and San Felipe, Mexico. The searches turned up incriminating documents, which the government sought to introduce against Verdugo-Urquidez at trial. Verdugo-Urquidez moved to suppress the documents, arguing that the DEA searches in Mexico violated his Fourth Amendment rights.

Analysis: The Supreme Court held that Verdugo-Urquidez was not protected by the Fourth Amendment. He was not a citizen of this country, and he did not have sufficient connection to the country to be part of the national community. Although he was present in the country at the time of the searches, his presence was involuntary and short-term, "not of the sort to indicate any substantial connection with our country."

The Verdugo-Urquidez case left a number of questions unanswered. On the one hand, the Court noted that Verdugo-Urquidez might deserve protection if his involuntary presence in the country had been for a longer period of time (for example, if he had served a number of years in prison). On the other hand, the Court implied that not every undocumented resident who is voluntarily in the United States deserves the protections of the Fourth Amendment. At minimum, the Court's language suggested that only an undocumented resident who is voluntarily in the country and who has "accepted some societal obligations" of being in the country will be protected.

Although *Verdugo-Urquidez* does not provide as much guidance as we would like, we can still draw some conclusions about which categories of people are protected by the Fourth Amendment:

	Surveillance Inside the United States	**Surveillance Outside the United States Conducted by United States Agents**	**Surveillance Outside the United States Conducted by Foreign Agents**
Citizen	Protected	Protected	Not protected
Legal Resident	Protected	May be protected; depends on legal resident's "connection to the national community."	Not protected
Undocumented resident	Probably protected; depends on undocumented resident's "connection to the national community."	Not protected	Not protected

As the United States government continues to aggressively pursue foreign nationals both inside and outside the United States, we can expect to see more litigation on this issue in the near future.

C. State Action Requirement. Although the text of the Fourth Amendment makes no mention of a state action requirement, the Supreme Court has held that the "origin and history clearly show that it was intended as a restraint upon the activities of sovereign authority, and was not intended to be a limitation upon other than governmental agencies."[3] Thus, there is no Fourth Amendment violation if a private party is conducting the surveillance. However, the government cannot get around the state action requirement merely by directing a private actor to carry out the actual search or seizure. If the government orders or requests a private party to conduct the search or seizure, that private party will be considered a "state actor."

> The limitations of the Fourth Amendment only apply to a search that is carried out by a government agent, or a private party who is
>
> - acting under orders or after a request by a government agent; or
>
> - acting pursuant to a law that requires or strongly encourages the private party to conduct the search

This rule leaves two issues in need of clarification. First, when are state employees **not** considered "state actors?" And second, under what conditions are private individuals considered "state actors?"

1. What Is a "Government Agent"? Obviously any government official with law enforcement duties counts as a government agent. But the Supreme Court has given a broad interpretation to the "state action" requirement, so that it includes (nearly) every individual who works for the government:

> **Example—*New Jersey v. T.L.O.*, 469 U.S. 325 (1985):** A teacher in a public high school in New Jersey caught a fourteen-year-old freshman smoking in the bathroom. The teacher brought the girl, whose initials were T.L.O., to the assistant vice principal. When the girl denied smoking, he searched her purse. Inside he found not only a pack of cigarettes but also cigarette rolling paper, marijuana, letters implicating T.L.O. in marijuana dealing, a list of students who owed her money, and a substantial amount of cash, all in one-dollar bills. The assistant vice princi-

[3] Burdeau v. McDowell, 256 U.S. 465, 475 (1921).

pal turned all the evidence over to the police. The police arrested T.L.O. and charged her with dealing marijuana. She challenged the search of her purse, arguing that it was an illegal search and therefore the evidence found inside should be excluded from her trial. The prosecutor responded that the assistant vice principal was not a state actor, and so the Fourth Amendment did not apply to his actions.

Analysis: The Supreme Court held that the assistant vice principal was a state actor. It noted that past cases held "the Fourth Amendment applicable to the activities of civil as well as criminal authorities: building inspectors, Occupational Safety and Health Act inspectors, and even firemen entering privately owned premises to battle a fire." The Court went on to note that "[the] basic purpose of this Amendment, as recognized in countless decisions of this Court, is to safeguard the privacy and security of individuals against arbitrary invasions by governmental officials."[4]

A later Supreme Court opinion found "state action" where the executive director of a public hospital ordered a search of a doctor's office to find evidence of misuse of state property and sexual harassment.[5]

However, it is not accurate to say that **every** action by a government employee satisfies the "state action" component of the Fourth Amendment. If a government employee is off-duty and finds evidence of criminal activity while engaging in purely private affairs, there is no state action.[6] And although it is settled that a government employee is a state actor if she is conducting a search (like the school administrator in *T.L.O.* or the building inspectors or safety inspectors referenced in *T.L.O.*), some lower courts have held that a government employee should not be viewed as a "state actor" if she is performing tasks that would also be performed by a private actor. For example, doctors and other medical personnel at public hospitals who examine patients, or conduct blood or urine tests for purely medical purposes will not be deemed to be state actors merely because their employer is a public institution.[7] However, the exact contours of when government employees will be considered to be state actors have not yet been fully defined by the Supreme Court.

---

[4] New Jersey v. T.L.O., 469 U.S. 325, 335 (1985) (internal citations and quotations omitted). Although the Court held that there was state action, it went on to rule that the search was permissible because of the "special needs" doctrine, which we cover in **Chapter 18**.

[5] O'Connor v. Ortega, 480 U.S. 709 (1987).

[6] See, e.g., United States v. Ginglen, 467 F.3d 1071 (7th Cir. 2006).

[7] See, e.g., United States v. Chukwubike, 956 F.2d 209 (9th Cir. 1992).

2. When Does a Private Individual Become a State Actor? Generally, information gathered by private detectives, private delivery services, credit card companies, internet service providers, or any other private entity is not covered by the Fourth Amendment. Thus, law enforcement agents are free to subpoena information from private entities about anyone they are investigating. Information about the purchases, movements, cell phone activity, internet searches, and hundreds of other details about every individual are routinely collected by private companies, and even packaged and sold to other companies for marketing purposes. As this privately-collected information becomes more comprehensive and detailed, it is becoming a valuable resource for law enforcement.

There is a difference, however, between the government gathering information that has already been collected by private parties and government-initiated searches. If a government agent **initiates** the search for information, the private actor conducting the actual search is transformed into a state actor.

Law enforcement officials routinely rely on private third parties to do the actual work of collecting information. When FBI agents want to tap the phone or monitor the e-mail traffic of a suspect, they contact the telephone company or the internet service provider to set up the monitoring system. Police officers also frequently rely on informants—private individuals who enter into conversations with suspects while wearing a recording device, or who seek out physical evidence to bring to the police. Law enforcement officers also occasionally work with private parties to set up sting operations to catch individuals embezzling from a company or committing other types of financial crimes.

> **Example**—Steve Wilson rented out the top floor of his duplex to a man named Jamie Dawson. After having Dawson as a tenant for a few months, Wilson began to suspect that Dawson may be engaged in illegal activity. He noticed people coming and going from the unit at odd hours of the night, and smelled strange odors coming from the apartment. Wilson went to the police and told them of his suspicions. But the police told him that he did not have enough information for them to obtain a warrant. The police then suggested that Wilson enter Dawson's home the next time Dawson was away, look for anything incriminating, and return to them if he found something.
>
> The next day Wilson waited until Dawson left the apartment. He then let himself in with his spare key and looked around. He found over ten thousand dollars in cash, twenty small baggies of crack cocaine, and a small amount of powder cocaine. He quickly left the apartment and headed straight for the police precinct, where he reported what he found. The police immediately

got a warrant based on the information, searched the apartment, recovered the contraband, and arrested Dawson. Dawson moved to suppress the evidence, arguing that the original search by Wilson violated his rights under the Fourth Amendment.

Analysis: The court should find that Wilson was a state actor when he entered Dawson's apartment to search for contraband. Wilson was acting under specific instructions from the police. If Wilson had searched through Dawson's apartment and found the contraband **before** he spoke to the police, the Fourth Amendment would not apply to his actions and the evidence would be admissible. (Note: depending on the terms of the lease, Wilson potentially committed a trespass against his neighbor and could face criminal or civil liability for entering Dawson's home without permission. However, this does not affect the Fourth Amendment analysis.)

Because Wilson was a state actor in this case (and because his conduct clearly constituted a search), the court would move to the next step of the analysis to determine whether the search was legal under the Fourth Amendment. As we will see in **Chapter 11**, law enforcement agents (or in this case private parties who are state actors) may not search a home without a search warrant. Therefore, the search was illegal and the evidence would be excluded.

However, if a government agent merely **encourages** a private party to engage in searches generally, that is not enough to turn the private party into a state actor. For example, if the police have a long-standing agreement with an informant that they will pay money for incriminating information, and the informant conducts a search to find the information, the informant is not a state actor with regard to that search. And general warnings by the police to be on the lookout for suspicious behavior or posting rewards for information leading to an arrest do not transform private parties into state actors.

A private party will, however, be considered a state actor if a law or regulation requires or strongly encourages the private party to conduct a certain kind of search:

Example—*Skinner v. Railway Labor Executives' Ass'n*, 489 U.S. 602 (1989): In order to detect and prevent alcohol abuse by railway workers, the Federal Railroad Administration ("FRA") passed a series of rules regulating all private railroad companies. One set of rules, known as "Subpart C," required railroad companies to conduct blood and urine tests on all employees who were involved in a train accident. Another set of rules, known as "Subpart D," authorized (but did not require) railroad companies to conduct blood and urine tests any time a manager had reasonable suspicion that an employee was under the influence of drugs or alcohol.

The railroad employees union sued the FRA, arguing that the blood and urine tests under Subparts C and D were unconstitutional searches. The FRA argued as one of its defenses that the railroad companies, not the FRA itself, was conducting the tests, so there was no state action involved.

Analysis: The Supreme Court held that the mandatory drug tests required by Subpart C were covered by the Fourth Amendment because "[a] railroad that complies with [these] regulations does so by compulsion of sovereign authority" and therefore is an agent of the government.

The Court held that the discretionary drug tests authorized by Subpart D also constituted state action, given the totality of the circumstances. The Court looked to the "degree of the Government's participation in the private party's activities"[8] and concluded that the discretionary testing procedures were not "primarily the result of private initiative."[9] The regulations pre-empted all pre-existing state or local regulations, and they stated that the company's right to conduct these tests could not be bargained away in labor negotiations. The regulations also said that the results of certain tests had to be shared with the FRA. Thus, Subpart D did not passively authorize these tests but instead showed a strong government "preference" that the tests take place.

However, just because the government **authorizes** a private party to carry out a certain type of surveillance does not necessarily mean that state action exists. In *Skinner,* the Court held that the discretionary drug and urine tests represented state action because of the FRA's encouragement, endorsement, and participation of such tests.[10]

---

[8] Skinner v. Railway Labor Executives' Ass'n, 489 U.S. 602, 614 (1989).

[9] Id. at 615.

[10] Id. at 615-16.

Quick Summary

Notwithstanding the plain language of the Fourth Amendment, its application is limited in numerous ways. First, it only protects individuals with a sufficient connection to the United States, such as United States citizens, legal permanent residents, and probably undocumented residents who have become part of the national community. Second, it only applies to surveillance conducted by "state actors," which includes government agents and private parties who undertake surveillance which is ordered, specifically requested, or legally required by the government. Finally, surveillance which violates the Fourth Amendment can only be challenged by individuals who are the victims of the illegal surveillance. We will discuss this requirement, which is similar to a standing requirement, in **Chapter 22**.

Review Questions

1. The Pakistani-Canadian Drug Dealer. Sakhwat Umah, a Pakistani-born Canadian citizen, illegally crossed the United States/Canadian border in the forests of upstate New York. After two days of sleeping in the wilderness, he made his way to Niagara Falls, New York, where he met some of his cousins who lived in an apartment there. He stayed in the apartment for seven days, helping them cut and package cocaine, which they sold on the streets of the town.

After nine days in the country, Umah was outside the apartment building smoking a cigarette when two federal drug enforcement officers spotted him. Knowing that drug dealers frequented the neighborhood and knowing that ethnic Pakistanis were involved in the drug trade in Niagara, the officers approached Umah, threw him against the wall, and searched him. They found five small bags of cocaine and arrested him. Umah is now challenging the detention and the search in a suppression hearing. The government argues that the Fourth Amendment does not apply to him. Should Umah receive the protection of the Fourth Amendment?

2. The Forced Urine Test. Virginia Platt was a secretary at the University of Michigan, a public university. One afternoon Platt's supervisor smelled what she believed to be alcohol on Platt's breath. Since any consumption of alcohol during work hours was strictly prohibited by Platt's employment contract, the supervisor escorted Platt to the university hospital and demanded that she take a urine test to see whether she was intoxicated. The urine test showed no evidence of intoxication but did show that Platt had smoked marijuana within the last twenty-four hours. Upon learning this, the supervisor fired Platt.

Platt is now suing the university for violating her civil rights, arguing that the supervisor was a state actor who forced her to undergo a urine test. The university argues that the supervisor, though technically a public employee, was not a state actor at the time she ordered the urine test. Was the supervisor a state actor?

3. FedEx Delivers Cocaine. Jerry Zimmerman was a security specialist working for Federal Express when he smelled the odor of laundry soap coming from one of the packages. Zimmerman knew that drug dealers frequently use overnight couriers to deliver drugs. He also knew that they sometimes disguise the smell of the drugs with laundry soap. He proceeded to open the package and found two bags of white powder wrapped in laundry detergent. He immediately called the Drug Enforcement Agency pursuant to a company policy and notified them of the suspicious substance.

A DEA agent arrived and field tested the substance, confirming that it was cocaine. The DEA agent then requested that Federal Express perform a controlled delivery of the package. The cocaine was replaced with bags of corn starch, and the package was delivered by a Federal Express employee to its destination in Tampa, Florida. When the deliveryman rang the doorbell, Lacey Kraig answered the door and accepted the package. The Federal Express employee stepped inside the house while Kraig was signing for the package, and he looked into the kitchen, where he saw dozens of small plastic bags filled with white powder. After Kraig signed for the package, the DEA obtained a search warrant based on (1) the original contents of the package, as observed by Zimmerman and tested by the DEA agent, (2) Kraig's acceptance of the package and (3) the deliveryman's observations of the kitchen of her house. DEA agents executed the warrant and found cocaine inside Kraig's house.

Kraig moved to suppress the cocaine, arguing that the warrant was based on evidence that had been gathered in violation of her Fourth Amendment rights. At the suppression hearing, the trial judge made the following findings of fact:

During the course of his employment at Federal Express, Zimmerman contacted the DEA at least eight times and has testified as a government witness in two cases. He has never worked as an informant for the DEA and has never been rewarded by the DEA for his aid. However, Zimmerman routinely attended an annual meeting of Federal Express security personnel, and every year at that meeting, representatives from the DEA gave a lecture and provided booklets describing the various methods used by drug dealers who were shipping narcotics and how to spot them. The DEA officers at those meetings did not request that common carriers broaden the scope of their search to include drugs or related contraband, but noted that they would quickly respond to calls to assist when suspected contraband is found.

Which actions in this investigation are state actions for the purposes of the Fourth Amendment, and which are merely the actions of a private party?

4. Foiled Theft of Kay Jewelers. Timothy Smith entered a Kay Jeweler's at a shopping mall and asked to see a diamond ring. The salesman gave him the ring and watched as Smith examined the ring. The salesman suspected that during this brief examination Smith substituted a ring with cubic zirconium for the real diamond ring and planned on giving the fake ring back to the salesman while keeping the diamond ring. The salesman signaled for a colleague to call mall security, which is a private security firm that patrols the mall. A mall security officer soon entered the store. Smith saw the officer, quickly returned the real ring, and left the store. The manager of Kay Jeweler's called the security officer over and said she suspected Smith of having stolen rings from the store in the past and asked the officer to "grab him and hold him until the police arrive."

The mall officer called the sheriff's office and asked for them to send a deputy to the mall. The mall officer then followed Smith into the parking lot, where he stopped Smith and searched him. He did not find any fake ring, but he did find ammunition and an illegal handgun. Smith was detained at the mall security office until the sheriff's deputy arrived. The mall officer described what happened and handed the gun and ammunition over to the deputy. Smith was charged with illegal possession of a firearm. He is now moving to suppress the gun, arguing that it was the result of an illegal search. Was the mall officer a state actor at the time of the search?

5

Overview of Limitations on Searches

Key Concepts

- The "Reasonableness" Clause and the "Warrant" Clause
- The Warrant Presumption
- Different Legal Standards for Different Types of Surveillance
- More Intrusive Surveillance Usually Requires a Higher Legal Standard

A. The Fourth Amendment and the Warrant Presumption. As noted in the last chapter, the first step in any Fourth Amendment analysis is to determine whether the Fourth Amendment even applies to the investigative conduct. We have already discussed the first three pre-requisites to applicability:

1. Is the person challenging the surveillance one of "the people" who the Fourth Amendment protects?

2. Has government action taken place?

3. Is the person challenging the violation the one whose rights were allegedly violated?

In this chapter we introduce the last requirement that must be met before the Fourth Amendment applies: Is the government conduct intrusive enough to constitute a "search" under the Fourth Amendment?

This terminology sometimes causes confusion among students, since the word "search" has an everyday meaning and a specialized legal meaning. Its everyday meaning is "to look through in order to find something."[1] This meaning is broadly used to refer to all investigative conduct that is intended to gather information. The Supreme Court, however, has used the word "search" as a term of art to refer to the subset of investigative conduct that implicates the Fourth Amendment. Thus, if the investigative conduct is classified as a "search," the protections of the Fourth Amendment apply. If the investigative conduct is not classified as a "search," the protections of the Fourth Amendment are irrelevant.

---

[1] Webster's New World Dictionary 559 (Simon & Schuster, 1st ed. 1996).

In order to avoid confusion, in this book we will use the terms "Fourth Amendment Search" or "search under the Fourth Amendment" when referring to the word "search" as a term of art.

So when is a search considered to be a Fourth Amendment Search? We will examine this question in depth in the next chapter. For the immediate purposes of this overview, you should note that investigatory conduct is classified as a Fourth Amendment Search if it infringes on the suspect's reasonable expectation of privacy or if the officer physically intruded into a constitutionally protected area to gather information.

Once we have determined that the Fourth Amendment applies, the next step is to **categorize** the search in order to determine whether the requirements of the Fourth Amendment are satisfied. In other words, you must figure out what legal standards are imposed by the Fourth Amendment and then determine whether those standards have been met.

To begin this discussion, let us turn back to the Fourth Amendment and consider the principal and most troubling ambiguity in its text:

> The right of the people to be secure in their persons, houses, papers, and effects, against unreasonable searches and seizures, shall not be violated, and no Warrants shall issue, but upon probable cause, supported by Oath or affirmation, and particularly describing the place to be searched, and the persons or things to be seized.[2]

Note that the Amendment is composed of two parts. The first part (known as the "reasonableness clause") sets out a rule prohibiting "unreasonable" searches. The second part (known as the "warrant clause") sets out the rules for issuing warrants. But what is the relationship between the two clauses? There are a number of possibilities. In theory, the plain language of the amendment could be interpreted to mean any of the following:

1. All searches are categorically unreasonable unless authorized by a valid warrant; or

2. Most searches are presumptively unreasonable unless authorized by a valid warrant, though from time to time, there may be the need to permit exceptions to the general rule; or

3. The existence of a warrant is just a factor that should be considered when deciding whether searches are reasonable; or

[2] U.S. Const. amend. IV.

4. The reasonableness and warrant clauses should be considered in isolation—the first sets out the rule for searches, and the second sets out the rule for issuing warrants.

Judges and commentators have debated this ambiguity for centuries without coming to a completely satisfying resolution. Currently, the official state of the law is option #2; the Supreme Court has repeatedly held that a search is presumptively unreasonable and thus unconstitutional if a warrant has not been issued, but the government can overcome that presumption if the search falls into one of the "carefully delineated" categories of warrant exceptions that the Court has created. On the other hand, if a warrant has been issued, the search is presumptively reasonable and thus constitutional, though the defendant can challenge the validity of the warrant itself in court.

This rule used to be known as the "warrant requirement," meaning that any search **without** a warrant was unreasonable and thus unconstitutional, unless one of a few, narrow exceptions applied. However, as the "few, narrow" exceptions grew in number and breadth, the term "warrant requirement" was replaced with the term "warrant presumption," to better reflect the reality that warrantless searches are now only **presumed** to be unreasonable.

In practice, however, many scholars have noted that the Court's shift in terminology is not adequately descriptive of what is happening on the ground. In their view, the *de facto* state of affairs operates in a manner closer to option #3— i.e., a warrant is an important factor in determining whether a challenged search was reasonable and therefore constitutional, but there are many ways (other than a warrant) that the government can demonstrate the legality of its conduct. These scholars observe that, as a practical matter, law enforcement can legally carry out so many searches without a warrant that the term "presumption" may not even be accurate.

Students exploring this subject for the first time, however, should be clear that notwithstanding the scholarly debate just described (and explored in greater detail below), the Supreme Court, to date, continues to adhere to the notion of a "warrant presumption." It is, thus, a useful starting point when learning the rules for searches and thinking about whether the Fourth Amendment has been satisfied.

B. Beyond the Warrant Presumption: Matching the Type of Surveillance with the Correct Legal Standard. The analysis described in Section A. reflects the Court's explicit framework for thinking about the regulation of searches. However, evaluating whether the warrant presumption applies is not the only way to think about the protections provided by the Fourth Amendment. Alternatively, one might consider the Court's Fourth Amendment jurisprudence as creating different categories of surveillance, each with a different set of legal requirements. This section will help you to understand how you might organize the Court's Fourth Amendment cases around these categories instead of around the warrant presumption.

First, it is necessary to classify the **type of surveillance** that has occurred. This, in turn, will establish the **legal requirements** the government must meet in order to conduct the surveillance.

The legal requirements usually consist of two factors:

1. The **level of suspicion** the government agent must demonstrate before being allowed to conduct the surveillance, and

2. Whether **judicial pre-approval** is required; that is, whether the government agent must demonstrate the necessary level of suspicion to a court before the surveillance takes place (by obtaining a warrant or perhaps a different order mandated by statute), or whether she is allowed to conduct the surveillance first and then justify it afterwards in a suppression hearing.

So how many different types of surveillance and corresponding legal standards has the Court recognized? Quite a few, as it turns out:

1. Suveillance in **public places** that does not require any physical intrusion into a private area, such as following a suspect over a public road or using a surveillance camera to watch a suspect in a park, is completely **unregulated** by the Fourth Amendment.

2. Surveillance which occurs for a reason **other than traditional law enforcement purposes**, such as building code inspections or immigration checkpoints, need only be **reasonable**.

3. **Stopping and frisking a suspect for weapons** requires the law enforcement officer to have reasonable suspicion that criminal activity is afoot and reasonable suspicion that the suspect is armed.

4. Surveillance which intrudes on the suspect's **reasonable expectation of privacy** is classified as a "search":

    a. Some searches fit into one of the **warrant exception** categories, such as searches of cars or searches of individuals right after they are arrested. These searches usually require the law enforcement officer to have probable cause that a crime occurred and that the search will turn up evidence of that crime.

b. Searches which do **not** fit into one of the many warrant exceptions require a warrant which specifies what will be searched and what items can be seized. The warrant will be issued by a judge or a magistrate only if the law enforcement officer can demonstrate that there is **probable cause** that a crime occurred and that evidence of that crime can be found by conducting this search.

5. Surveillance which is **extraordinarily intrusive**, such as conducting surgery on the suspect or forcing her to give blood, requires a warrant, but the warrant must both show probable cause and establish that the extraordinarily intrusive procedure is reasonable given the circumstances.

Finally, you should remember that the Fourth Amendment is not the only source of limitation on government surveillance. As we saw in **Chapter 3**, Congress has passed a number of laws which set out their own legal requirements for different types of surveillance. Laws restricting surveillance are most often applicable if the government is using technology that was not contemplated by the drafters of the Fourth Amendment, such as telephone wiretapping, monitoring of e-mails, and searching through data stored in remote internet service providers. We will discuss these statutes in **Chapters 20 and 21**; for now, as we focus on the Fourth Amendment, simply keep in mind that Congress has also created its own limitations on surveillance.

Quick Summary

The Supreme Court has interpreted the two clauses of the Fourth Amendment to mean that if the state actor conducts a "search," then the warrant presumption applies. If so, the government must either obtain a warrant before conducting the surveillance, or it must demonstrate that an exception to the warrant presumption existed at the time of the search. Over the next few chapters, we will discuss the definition of "search": the requirements for a warrant and the numerous exceptions to the warrant requirement.

Sometimes, however, considering whether the warrant presumption applies is not the only way to conduct the analysis. There are many categories of surveillance that do not fit neatly within the warrant presumption analysis—frisks for weapons, special needs searches, and extraordinarily intrusive searches—each of which require the government to meet a different legal standard to establish their legality. We will consider each of these types of surveillance as well. Finally, there are a number of federal statutes that restrict government surveillance. We will conclude our discussion of surveillance regulation by discussing those laws.

6

When Is a Search a "Fourth Amendment Search"?

Key Concepts

- *Katz* test
- "Reasonable Expectation of Privacy"
- No Protection in What Is Held Out to the Public
- "Open Fields" v. "Curtilage"

A. Introduction and Policy. Law enforcement officers gather information in hundreds of different ways. Some ways do not appear to infringe on privacy interests: for example, a police officer might observe individuals walking on a public sidewalk, might access driving records from a public database, or might pick up forensic evidence left behind at a crime scene. Other types of surveillance are much more intrusive: for example, an officer might enter a suspect's home and look around, wiretap his telephone, or hack into his email account. Still others are somewhere in between, such as when an officer sorts through a suspect's garbage, uses a specially-trained dog to detect narcotics in an automobile, or looks through the window of a house at night with infrared goggles.

Some of these methods of gathering information are regulated by the Fourth Amendment, and some are not. As we discussed in the last chapter, the Fourth Amendment only regulates investigatory conduct which rises to the level of a "search" under the Fourth Amendment.

Until 1967, the test for determining whether government conduct constituted a "Fourth Amendment search" was relatively simple, if a bit formalistic. The Supreme Court held in a series of cases that government conduct implicated an individual's Fourth Amendment rights only if the government agents trespassed on the suspect's property rights. For example, when the government wanted to wiretap a telephone, its conduct did not constitute a Fourth Amendment search if it merely placed a device on the telephone lines outside the suspect's property.[1] This was because the suspect had no property rights which extended beyond the four walls of his home, and thus the use of the wiretap did not infringe upon any protected rights.

[1] Olmstead v. United States, 277 U.S. 438 (1928).

A pair of cases from the middle of the twentieth century demonstrates the extreme formalism of the property-rights doctrine. In *Goldman v. United States*, law enforcement officers used an electronic listening device to eavesdrop on the defendant's conversations in his office. In order to hear the conversations, they gained entry to the office next door and placed a "slap-mike" on the wall that adjoined his office. The Supreme Court held that there was no trespass onto the defendant's property, and so the government conduct did not constitute a search.[2] Just six years later, in *Silverman v. United States*, government agents again eavesdropped on a defendant's conversations inside his office. However, this time the agents accomplished their eavesdropping by using a "spike-mike," which they inserted through a hole in the adjoining office's wall and rested against a heating duct owned by the defendant on his side of the wall. In *Silverman*, the Court held that a trespass occurred (the contact of the spike-mike with the heating duct), however minor. This finding of a technical trespass led the *Silverman* Court to conclude that, unlike in *Goldman*, the government's conduct amounted to a Fourth Amendment search.[3]

This trespass-based analysis was finally set aside by the Court in 1967 in the seminal case of *Katz v. United States*.[4] In *Katz*, federal agents placed an electronic listening device on the outside of a public telephone booth and recorded the defendant's conversations about illegal wagering. The government did not have a warrant authorizing this surveillance and argued that they did not need one: under the *Goldman/Silverman* trespass doctrine, their surveillance was not a Fourth Amendment search because it did not infringe on the defendant's property rights. The Court rejected that argument, holding that "the Fourth Amendment protects people, not places,"[5] and therefore "the reach of that Amendment cannot turn upon the presence or absence of a physical intrusion onto any given enclosure."[6]

What, then, does the reach of the Amendment turn upon? The answer is found in Justice Harlan's concurrence in *Katz*, where he stated that government surveillance is a Fourth Amendment search if it violates an individual's "reasonable expectation of privacy."[7] This phrase is now known as the *Katz* test, and it remains the primary standard by which courts determine whether a specific type of investigatory conduct is regulated by the Fourth Amendment.

[2] 316 U.S. 129 (1942).

[3] 365 U.S. 505 (1961).

[4] 389 U.S. 347 (1967).

[5] Id. at 351.

[6] Id. at 353.

[7] Although the majority opinion in *Katz* decided the case, it did not provide an easy test for determining when a search occurred. Justice Harlan's concurrence coined the "reasonable expectation of privacy" language, and it is this language that has been applied in subsequent Supreme Court cases as the official test for whether a search has occurred.

B. The Law. The *Katz* test, as originally set out, reads as follows:

> [T]here is a twofold requirement, first that a person have exhibited an actual (subjective) expectation of privacy and second, that the expectation be one that society is prepared to recognize as "reasonable."[8]

Later cases have clarified this rule in two critical ways. First, the defendant's subjective expectation of privacy must not only be **reasonable**, but it must also be **legitimate**; that is, it must protect something that the defendant has a legal right to possess. Thus, because an individual has no legitimate expectation of privacy in possessing contraband, a surveillance technique which only detects the presence or absence of contraband (such as using a drug-sniffing dog) does not constitute a "search". We will discuss these types of searches in **Chapter 7** below.

Second, the recent Supreme Court case of *United States v. Jones*[9] held that the *Goldman/Silverman* "trespass doctrine" still has force. As the *Jones* Court explained, the *Katz* test **supplements** rather than **replaces** the trespass doctrine. Thus, if the government intrudes on a constitutionally protected area in order to gather information—even if the information they end up gathering is information otherwise available to the public—a Fourth Amendment search has occurred and the Fourth Amendment is implicated. We will discuss the *Jones* case in Section C.6, below.

Therefore, the *Katz* test, as it is currently understood, would be more accurately stated like this:

> Government surveillance will constitute a "search" and thereby implicate the Fourth Amendment if:
>
> (1) the defendant exhibited a subjective expectation of privacy in the area or item that was the object of the surveillance, and this expectation was one that society is prepared to recognize as <u>reasonable</u> and <u>legitimate</u>;
>
> OR if
>
> (2) law enforcement officers intruded onto a "<u>constitutionally protected area</u>" in order to conduct the surveillance.

C. Applying the Law. Even with all of these clarifications, the core of the test remains the same: A court will ask whether the defendant had a subjective expec-

[8] Id. at 361 (Harlan, J., concurring).

[9] United States v. Jones, 132 S. Ct. 94 (2012).

tation of privacy in the area or item being searched, and whether the defendant's expectation was reasonable. As we will see when we examine the case law, the Supreme Court's view of what is "reasonable" may not always coincide with your own view of what is reasonable, or even with the view of a majority of Americans.

For example, the Court has determined that we have no reasonable expectation of privacy in our activities in public areas, in open lands that are not next to our house, in areas that can be viewed from the air, and in the garbage that we throw away. As a general rule, we have no reasonable expectation of privacy for anything that we have "knowingly exposed to the public."

1. Public Areas. With one possible caveat discussed below, police surveillance of public areas is never a Fourth Amendment search. If an individual has knowingly exposed information to the public, she does not have a reasonable expectation of privacy in that information. For example, any activity which is carried out on roads, sidewalks, parking lots, commercial establishments open to the public, shopping malls, or parks has been knowingly exposed to the public, and therefore government surveillance of that activity will not implicate the Fourth Amendment.

The manner of surveillance does not matter, as long as the police only gather information which is exposed to the public; for example, the police can install video cameras in public spaces and watch and record everyone's movements, but they cannot place electronic listening devices to record private conversations that occur in public. Similarly, law enforcement officers can search through public databases such as handgun registration records, incorporation records from the secretary of state, or court filings. Thus, there is quite a lot of surveillance and investigation that can be done without implicating the Fourth Amendment:

> **Example:** Detective Lee is investigating an armed bank robbery that took place at First National Bank. She begins by viewing the videotape from the security cameras in the bank, which shows three men in ski masks and sweatshirts stealing money at gunpoint from one of the tellers at 4:30 PM and driving away in a red car. A police surveillance camera at a nearby intersection records a similar red car driving rapidly away from the bank at 4:33 PM, with a license plate that reads "KM-2451." She searches the records of the department of motor vehicles and learns that the license plate belongs to Matt Anselm, who lives on the outskirts of town. She logs onto Facebook and reads through all the publically available information about Anselm—his friends, where he works, and where he went to high school. Detective Lee notes the name of several known criminals among

the friends. She then drives out to Anselm's house in an unmarked car. She sees Anselm's car parked on the street next to the house and walks over to it, shining her flashlight inside and observing a ski mask in the back seat. She goes back to her own car and waits. Over the next few hours, Detective Lee sees a number of people drive up to Anselm's house, enter the house, and leave a few minutes later. Detective Lee records all of their license plate numbers and takes pictures of all of them.

Finally Anselm gets into his car and drives away. Detective Lee secretly follows him. Anselm first stops at a jewelry store and goes in. Detective Lee follows him into the store and observes him buying an expensive watch with cash. Anselm then drives to a nearby motel, parks his car, and enters the lobby. Detective Lee follows him through the lobby and down one of the corridors until Anselm reaches Room 255 and enters. She notes all this information down and returns to her car.

Analysis: None of Detective Lee's conduct constitutes a Fourth Amendment search under the *Katz* test (even as modified by *Jones*), and thus none of her conduct is regulated by the Fourth Amendment.

At some point in her investigation, the detective may develop probable cause to believe that a more intrusive investigation will reveal contraband or evidence of a crime. She can then apply for a warrant using the information that she has learned and ask to search Anselm's home, his car, or Room 255 of the hotel room—all of which are private areas in which Anselm can claim a reasonable expectation of privacy.

As mentioned above, there is one possible caveat to this rule: Using modern technology such as a GPS device or even a surveillance drone, government agents now have the ability to track an individual's movements in public places twenty-four hours a day for weeks or months at a time. The *Jones* case questioned the constitutionality of such a prolonged surveillance, saying that even though the government is only gathering information which is exposed to the public, the amount of information they receive may violate the suspect's reasonable expectation of privacy. We will discuss this case further in the next chapter.

2. "Open Fields" v. "Curtilage". The Supreme Court has ruled that an individual has no reasonable expectation of privacy in open fields that she owns near her home—even if those fields are enclosed by a fence and posted with "No Trespassing" signs. Large tracts of farmland or empty property will be called "open fields" by the Court, even if they are enclosed by a fence.

Example—*Oliver v. United States,* 466 U.S. 170 (1984): Two narcotics agents had suspicions that Oliver was growing marijuana on his farm. They drove to Oliver's farm, parked their car next to a locked gate with a sign that read "No Trespassing," and walked along a footpath that led around the gate. They walked into the property for a few hundred yards, past a barn and a parked camper. At one point a man emerged from the camper and yelled at them to stop walking because hunting was not allowed on the property. The agents identified themselves as police officers, and the man disappeared. After a few more minutes of searching, the officers found a field of marijuana plants. Oliver later moved to suppress the marijuana, claiming that the officers violated his reasonable expectation of privacy when they trespassed onto his private land to conduct their surveillance.

Analysis: The Court held that neither the plain language of the Fourth Amendment, nor the history of the common law, nor the *Katz* test supported the defendant's position. The language of the Fourth Amendment protects only "persons, houses, papers, and effects," not open fields. In fact, the original draft of the Fourth Amendment protected persons, houses, papers, and property, but the language was amended to replace the broader term "property" with "effects." At the time of the founding, the law specifically excluded open fields from the term "effects." Thus, in the Court's view this was clear evidence that the Framers did not intend the Amendment to protect open fields. Moreover, historically, common law courts have always made a distinction between the "curtilage," which is the land immediately surrounding the home, and the open fields beyond the home.

Most importantly, individuals do not have a "reasonable expectation of privacy" in land which is not immediately adjacent to their home and which is not being used for personal or private activities. "[O]pen fields do not provide the setting for those intimate activities that the Amendment is intended to shelter from government interference or surveillance . . . . Moreover, as a practical matter these lands usually are accessible to the public in ways that a home, an office, or commercial structure would not be. It is not generally true that fences or 'No Trespassing' signs effectively bar the public from viewing open fields in rural areas."[10]

However, an individual **does** have a reasonable expectation of privacy in the land immediately adjacent to her house, such as a front porch or a back yard, since that land is used for more personal, domestic activities. The case law describes this adjacent land as the "curtilage" of the home.

Therefore, the critical question when police officers are conducting surveillance on a suspect's property is whether the officers merely enter "open fields" or whether

[10] Oliver v. United States, 466 U.S. 170, 179 (1984).

they intrude on the suspect's "curtilage." In *United States v. Dunn*, the Court provided a four-factor test to determine whether an area was an open field or a curtilage:

- The proximity of the area claimed to be curtilage to the home;
- Whether the area is included within an enclosure surrounding the home;
- The nature of the uses to which the area is put; and
- The steps taken by the resident to protect the area from observation by people passing by.[11]

None of these factors is dispositive; instead, they should be examined together by a court to decide whether "the area in question is so intimately tied to the home itself that it should be placed under the home's umbrella of Fourth Amendment protection."[12]

> **Example—*United States v. Dunn*, 480 U.S. 294 (1987)**: An agent of the Drug Enforcement Agency (DEA) and a member of the Houston Police Department tracked a container of phenylacetic acid to a barn on Ronald Dunn's property. Based on this evidence, they suspected that Dunn was manufacturing amphetamine on his property. To investigate their suspicions, the two entered Dunn's property without a warrant to search for evidence.
>
> Dunn owned a 198-acre ranch, which was completely encircled by a perimeter fence. Inside of this perimeter fence were a number of other fenced-in areas on the property, including an innermost fence, which encircled just Dunn's house and a nearby small greenhouse. Two barns were located on the property, inside the perimeter fence and approximately fifty yards away from the fenced-in area that surrounded the house. The front portion of the larger barn was enclosed by yet another wooden fence.
>
> The investigating agents crossed over the outer fence and one other interior fence and approached the house until they were midway between the residence and the barns. At that point they smelled a "very strong odor" of phenylacetic acid coming from the barns. The agents then approached the smaller barn, looked inside, and saw empty boxes. The agents crossed over the wooden

11 United States v. Dunn, 480 U.S. 294, 301 (1987).

12 Id.

fence enclosing the larger barn and shined a flashlight through the gates of the barn to look inside. They saw what they believed to be a laboratory used to manufacture illegal drugs. They then left the property and used this information in an affidavit for a search warrant. When executing the search warrant, the officers found illegal drugs as well as ample evidence that drugs were being manufactured on the premises.

Dunn challenged the validity of the warrant, claiming that the officers violated his Fourth Amendment rights when they entered his property and looked inside the barn without a warrant.

Analysis: The Court held that the barn was in the "open field" of the defendant's property and not its curtilage, and therefore the initial viewing of the interior of the large barn was not a search. The Court applied its four-factor test to the situation:

1. The barn was fifty yards from the fence surrounding the house and sixty yards from the house itself; according to the Court, this was a "substantial distance."
2. The barn was not located within the area surrounding the house that was enclosed by a fence. "The fence surrounding the residence serves to demark a specific area of land immediately adjacent to the house that is readily identifiable as part and parcel of the house," and the barn was located on a distinctly different part of the property.
3. The agents had good reason to believe that the barn was not being used for intimate activities of the home. Aerial photographs had shown that the truck transporting the container of phenylacetic acid was backed up to the barn, and the agents detected "a very strong odor" of phenylacetic acid coming from the barn. This indicated that the barn was being used to manufacture illegal drugs, and not to engage in actions "associated with the activities and privacies of domestic life."
4. Dunn had not done very much to protect the barn area from observation by those standing in the open fields. Although there were numerous fences between the public road and the barn, "the fences were designed and constructed to corral livestock, not to prevent persons from observing what lay inside the enclosed areas."[13]

3. "Flyover" Surveillance. The Court has held that surveillance from airplanes and helicopters is not a Fourth Amendment search, even if the law enforcement officers are viewing a constitutionally protected area, so long as the agents are flying in navigable airspace. In these "flyover" cases, the Court once again looked to the *Katz* test and reasoned that because air travel is so ubiquitous, individuals

[13] Id. at 302–3.

do not have a reasonable expectation of privacy in anything that can be seen from a passing airplane:

> **Example—*California v. Ciraolo*, 476 U.S. 207 (1986)**: Police officers received an anonymous tip that Ciraolo was growing marijuana in his backyard. However, when the officers went to the home to investigate, they found they could not observe the backyard from the public street because of a ten-foot fence that completely surrounded the property. The officers then rented a private plane and flew over Ciraolo's property at 1,000 feet. From that vantage point they identified and photographed marijuana plants growing in Ciraolo's backyard. Ciraolo moved to suppress this evidence, arguing that the police conducted a warrantless search of his fenced backyard—clearly part of his home's curtilage.

Analysis: The Supreme Court agreed that the police conducted a surveillance of Ciraolo's curtilage, but ruled that the surveillance was not a "search" within the meaning of the Fourth Amendment because the marijuana had been "knowingly exposed to the public." "[T]he mere fact that an individual has taken measures to restrict some views of his activities [does not] preclude an officer's observations from a public vantage point where he has a right to be and which renders the activities clearly visible." Because members of the public routinely travel by air, and any of them could have glanced down and seen the marijuana plants, the plants had been knowing exposed to the public, and the police surveillance was not a Fourth Amendment search.[14]

The Court in *Ciraolo* did not expressly apply the four *Dunn* factors to determine whether the defendant's backyard was curtilage instead of "open field," and some students find it difficult to reconcile the Court's decision not to protect the fenced-in backyard in *Ciraolo*. It is true that the area observed by the police in *Ciraolo* clearly satisfied two of the factors for curtilage: The backyard was close to Ciraolo's home, and it was completely surrounded by not one but two fences, the first eight feet high, the second ten feet high. However, as explained above, no one *Dunn* factor is determinative, and the other two factors weigh in favor of the backyard as an "open field". Ciraolo was using the area to grow marijuana, not to engage in intimate activities, and although Ciraolo protected the area from one type of viewing—those walking past on the street—he did nothing to protect the area from aerial passersby.

This last factor—that fact that the backyard was visible to the public from the air—seemed to be the most critical in *Ciraolo.* The Court confirmed this "flyover doctrine" in a later case, in which the police officers flew a helicopter four-hun-

---

[14] California v. Ciraolo, 476 U.S. 207, 213 (1986).

dred feet above the ground to view marijuana plants growing inside a greenhouse with a partially open roof. Because "any member of the public could legally have been flying over [the defendant's] property in a helicopter at the altitude of four-hundred feet and could have observed [the] greenhouse," the contents of the greenhouse had been "knowingly exposed to the public."[15]

4. Containers in Public. Just because the outside of a container is exposed to the public does not mean that law enforcement officers can open it and search through it. Instead, law enforcement officers are only allowed to look at what has been "knowingly exposed to the public." For example, law enforcement officers can look through the windows of a parked car without implicating the Fourth Amendment, but they cannot open the door and start looking through the glove compartment. Likewise, they can freely observe that a person is carrying a purse or a briefcase or a box, but they are limited as to when they are allowed to look inside those containers. This rule is frequently applied to the luggage that people carry with them while travelling.

> **Example—*Bond v. United States*, 529 U.S. 334 (2000)**: Steven Bond was travelling on a Greyhound bus from California to Arkansas. He had packed a soft-sided green canvas bag as luggage, and along with the rest of the passengers he stored the bag up above his seat on the overhead rack. As the bus passed through Texas, it stopped at a border patrol checkpoint, and Special Agent Cantu boarded the bus to confirm that all the passengers were legally in the United States.
>
> After Agent Cantu had completed that task, he walked up from the back of the bus towards the front, squeezing each of the bags in the overhead compartment as he passed by them. When he passed by Bond's green canvas bag, he squeezed it and felt a suspicious hard brick-like object inside. He asked Bond for permission to search the bag and Bond consented. When Agent Cantu opened the bag, he found a brick of methamphetamine wrapped in duct tape.
>
> Bond was arrested, and he later sought to have the methamphetamine suppressed, arguing that when Agent Cantu squeezed his bag, he was conducting a "search" without a warrant or probable cause. The government argued that the bag was exposed to the public and that Bond could reasonably expect other people would handle it and be able to feel its contents from the outside.

[15] Florida v. Riley, 488 U.S. 445, 446 (1989).

Analysis: The Court acknowledged that by placing his bag in the overhead compartment, Bond could "expect that it would be exposed to certain kinds of touching and handling,"[16] but agreed with Bond that "Agent Cantu's physical manipulation of his luggage far exceeded the casual contact [Bond] could have expected from other passengers."[17] Society reasonably expects that luggage will not be felt "in an exploratory manner" by members of the public or law enforcement.[18]

In dissent, Justice Breyer mocked the majority for creating a "jurisprudence of squeezes"[19] and argued that the "squeezing" done by the border patrol agent did not differ in any material way from "the treatment that overhead luggage is likely to receive from strangers in a world of travel that is somewhat less gentle than it used to be."[20]

It should be noted that Bond was challenging the initial squeezing of the luggage, not the actual search of the luggage. Because the initial squeeze was an illegal search, everything that the squeeze led to was precluded. This is because of the "fruit of the poisonous tree" doctrine, which we will discuss in **Chapter 23.**

5. Garbage. Although generally we have a reasonable expectation of privacy in the contents of containers, this rule does not apply to garbage. The Court has held that garbage is a special case because the contents of garbage have been abandoned by its owner, and there is arguably some understanding that others may rummage through garbage. Therefore, individuals do not have a reasonable expectation of privacy in the garbage they leave on the sidewalk to be picked up by trash collectors. Although a person may have a subjective belief that the contents of the garbage are private, this is not a belief that society is willing to accept as reasonable:

> **Example—*California v. Greenwood*, 486 U.S. 35 (1988):** The Long Beach police had suspicions that Billy Greenwood was selling narcotics from his home. To confirm these suspicions, Detective Stracner asked the neighborhood's regular trash collector to keep Greenwood's garbage separate from the rest of the garbage he picked up and deliver the trash to her instead of taking it to the local dump. The trash collector did as instructed. Detective Stracner then sifted through the trash and found evidence of narcotics use in the home. Stracner used this information in an affidavit to get a warrant to search Greenwood's home, where she found sufficient evidence of Greenwood's narcotics trafficking to arrest him. Greenwood later challenged the warrant, arguing that

---

16 Bond v. United States, 529 U.S. 334, 338 (2000) (citations and internal quotations omitted).

17 Id. at 338.

18 Id. at 338–39.

19 Id. at 342 (Breyer, J., dissenting).

20 Id. at 340 (Breyer, J., dissenting).

Stracner's examination of his garbage was a "search" under the Fourth Amendment.

Analysis: The Supreme Court held that examining Greenwood's garbage was not a "search" under the Fourth Amendment. The Court understood why Greenwood may have subjectively believed the contents of his trash were private: "The trash, which was placed on the street for collection at a fixed time, was contained in opaque plastic bags, which the garbage collector was expected to pick up, mingle with the trash of others, and deposit at the garbage dump." Also, "the trash was only temporarily on the street, and there was little likelihood that it would be inspected by anyone." However, the Court decided that "[i]t is common knowledge that plastic garbage bags left on or at the side of a public street are readily accessible to animals, children, scavengers, snoops, and other members of the public." Because Greenwood placed the garbage "in an area particularly suited for public inspection and, in a manner of speaking, public consumption, for the express purpose of having strangers take it, he could have had no reasonable expectation of privacy in the inculpatory items that he discarded."[21]

6. The Rebirth of the Trespass Doctrine as "Physical Intrusion." As mentioned in Part B., above, the recent Supreme Court case of *United States v. Jones* has revised (or "clarified") the *Katz* test by holding that the old *Goldman/Silverman* "trespass doctrine" is also still in effect. There had been hints that the Court was still clinging to aspects of the trespass doctrine after *Katz*. For example, in *Ciraolo*, the original flyover case, the Court noted that the police officers made their observation in a "physically nonintrusive manner"; while in *Riley*, the helicopter flyover case, the plurality noted that the helicopter had flown in a legally navigable airspace and had not created "undue noise, and no wind, dust, or threat of injury." But lawyers and scholars were nevertheless surprised by the robust re-affirmation of the trespass doctrine in *Jones*.

Example—*United States v. Jones*, 132 S.Ct. 945 (2012): The police suspected that Antoine Jones was involved in narcotics trafficking, so they attached a GPS tracking device to the undercarriage of his wife's car while it was parked in a public parking lot. For the next twenty-eight days, the GPS device reported every movement of the defendant's Jeep across public roads and parking lots, generating 2,000 pages of data. The government used this evidence at Jones' eventual trial for narcotics trafficking, and Jones objected to the government's conduct on Fourth Amendment grounds. The government argued (1) the initial placement of the GPS device on Jones' car was not a "search,"

[21] California v. Greenwood, 486 U.S. 35, 39–41 (1988) (citations and internal quotations omitted).

because the undercarriage of the car was "knowingly exposed to the public," and (2) tracking Jones' movements for thirty days was not a "search," because the government only tracked his car's movements over public highways, which was also "knowingly exposed to the public."

Analysis: The majority opinion of the Court did not reach the second issue, because it held that held that the government agents conducted a "search" when they placed the GPS device onto the defendant's car for the purpose of gathering information.[22] Justice Scalia, writing for the majority, reasoned that when the Fourth Amendment was adopted, it was meant to protect individuals from physical intrusion onto their property. Justice Scalia also reasoned that the *Katz* case was not meant to reduce the level of protection the Fourth Amendment provided.[23] Therefore, a search occurs if the government "obtains information by physically intruding on a constitutionally protected area."[24] The majority opinion emphasized that a trespass alone is not sufficient to establish a search; law enforcement must trespass with the purpose of obtaining information.[25]

Four justices in a concurrence argued that the "trespass" doctrine had been replaced, not supplemented, by the *Katz* decision. Thus, they reached the second issue in the case, and held that tracking the defendant's movements over public highways for thirty days did in fact constitute a search. We will consider the concurring opinions in *Jones* in the next chapter.

In *Jones*, the Court stayed away from the term "trespass," instead preferring the term "physical intrusion." This is because the Court wanted to make clear that although intruding onto the physical property of the suspect can violate the Fourth Amendment, the extent of this protection is not identical to the suspect's right to exclude others under property law.

The"physical intrusion" doctrine was applied again one year later in *Florida v. Jardines.*[26] In *Jardines*, police officers took a trained drug detection dog to the front door of the defendant's house and allowed the dog to sniff for drugs. After the dog alerted, the police obtained a search warrant and found drugs in the defendant's house. The defendant argued that the police had conducted an illegal search when they brought the drug dog to his front door.

As we will see in **Chapter 7,** the use of a drug-detection dog in itself is not a search because it can only detect evidence of illegal activity, and nobody has a reasonable and legitimate expectation of privacy in illegal activity. But the *Jardines* Court

[22] United States v. Jones, 132 S. Ct. 945, 948 (2012).

[23] Id.

[24] Id. at 950, n.3.

[25] Id. at 951, n.5.

[26] 133 S.Ct. 1409 (2013).

was not concerned with whether the drug dog violated the defendant's reasonable expectation of privacy; instead, the majority ruled that a search occurred because the police physically intruded on the defendant's property for the purpose of obtaining information. The front porch and area in front of the front door are clearly the "curtilage" of the home. And although a homeowner gives an implied invitation to individuals who want to come up to the front door and deliver packages or knock to see if someone is home, the homeowner does **not** give an implied invitation to a police officer who brings a drug detection dog to sniff around the front of the house. Thus, the case could be decided on property-rights grounds alone. As the Court explained:

> Thus, we need not decide whether the officers' investigation of Jardines' home violated his expectation of privacy under *Katz*. One virtue of the Fourth Amendment's property-rights baseline is that it keeps easy cases easy. That the officers learned what they learned only by physically intruding on Jardines' property to gather evidence is enough to establish that a search occurred.[27]

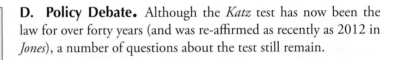

D. Policy Debate. Although the *Katz* test has now been the law for over forty years (and was re-affirmed as recently as 2012 in *Jones*), a number of questions about the test still remain.

First, the test is vague enough that it arguably allows judges to exercise too much discretion as to which expectations of privacy are "reasonable" and which are not. Justice Hugo Black first raised this objection when he dissented in the *Katz* opinion, warning that granting courts such "omnipotent lawmaking authority" can be unwise. Justice Black continued: "I do not believe that it is the proper role of this Court to rewrite the [Fourth] Amendment in order 'to bring it into harmony with the times' and thus reach a result that many people believe to be desirable."[28] Not only might it be improper for the Court to strive for a result that most citizens believe to be desirable, it may be impossible. As you have seen, many of the decisions the Supreme Court has made about what is "reasonable" may not exactly correspond to what the majority of Americans might think is "reasonable"—as a number of commentators have noted, most Americans do not expect the police to dig through their garbage or observe their backyard with a helicopter hovering four-hundred feet above their home. Justice Scalia has criticized the amount of discretion that the *Katz* test gives to judges:

[27] Id. at 1414.

[28] Katz, 389 U.S. at 364 (Black, J., dissenting).

> In my view, the only thing the past three decades have established about the *Katz* test . . . is that, unsurprisingly, those "actual (subjective) expectations of privacy" "that society is prepared to recognize as 'reasonable,'" bear an uncanny resemblance to those expectations of privacy that this Court considers reasonable. When that self-indulgent test is employed . . . to determine whether a "search or seizure" within the meaning of the Constitution has occurred (as opposed to whether that "search or seizure" is an "unreasonable" one), it has no plausible foundation in the text of the Fourth Amendment. That provision did not guarantee some generalized "right of privacy" and leave it to this Court to determine which particular manifestations of the value of privacy "society is prepared to recognize as 'reasonable.'"
>
> When that self-indulgent test is employed . . . to determine whether a "search or seizure" within the meaning of the Constitution has occurred (as opposed to whether that "search or seizure" is an "unreasonable" one), it has no plausible foundation in the text of the Fourth Amendment. That provision did not guarantee some generalized "right of privacy" and leave it to this Court to determine which particular manifestations of the value of privacy "society is prepared to recognize as 'reasonable.'" Rather, it enumerated ("persons, houses, papers, and effects") the objects of privacy protection to which the Constitution would extend, leaving further expansion to the good judgment, not of this Court, but of the people through their representatives in the legislature.[29]

Of course, other Supreme Court Justices disagree. Justice Harlan, who created the test in his concurrence in *Katz*, conceded that Supreme Court Justices would look to their own values in determining what expectations of privacy are reasonable. But whereas Justice Scalia regards this possibility as an example of inappropriate judicial activism, Justice Harlan embraced this role for the judiciary:

> Since it is the task of the law to form and project, as well as mirror and reflect, we should not, as judges, merely recite the expectations and risks without examining the desirability of saddling them upon society. The critical question, therefore, is whether under our system of government, as reflected in the Constitution, we should impose on our citizens the risks of [a given surveillance method] without at least the protection of a warrant requirement.

[29] Minnesota v. Carter, 525 U.S. 83, 97–98 (1998).

> This question must, in my view, be answered by assessing the nature of a particular practice and the likely extent of its impact on the individual's sense of security balanced against the utility of the conduct as a technique of law enforcement. For those more extensive intrusions that significantly jeopardize the sense of security which is the paramount concern of Fourth Amendment liberties, I am of the view that more than self-restraint by law enforcement officials is required and at the least warrants should be necessary.[30]

Justice Thurgood Marshall agreed with Justice Harlan on this point, arguing that "by its terms, the constitutional prohibition of unreasonable searches and seizures assigns to the judiciary some prescriptive responsibility."[31]

At its base, this dispute is an excellent example of the ongoing debate between those who advocate judicial restraint, such as Justice Scalia, and those who argue in favor of a living constitution, such as Justice Harlan. Is it truly the task of the law—or more specifically, the judiciary—to "form and project, as well as mirror and reflect?" If so, what values should the judiciary be projecting? If not, how should the courts decide what meaning attaches to the vague terms in the Fourth Amendment?

Another question is how the *Katz* test can be applied to new technologies. As surveillance technologies become more sophisticated—and more widespread—our reasonable expectation of privacy is evolving. The flyover cases are a good example of this—150 years ago, an individual who placed a twelve-foot fence around his backyard would surely have a reasonable expectation of privacy in his activities inside the fence, because nobody could fly over the backyard to observe it, and so the area was not exposed to the public. Today, however, airplane travel is so common that any area without a roof is at least theoretically exposed to the public and therefore, in the Court's view, not deserving of Fourth Amendment protection. But newer technologies are being developed every day, and these technologies will allow police—and members of the public—access to quite a bit of information that today we consider private. At what point do these new technologies change our reasonable expectation of privacy? We will explore this issue in the following chapter.

---

30 United States v. White, 401 U.S. 745, 786–87 (1971) (Harlan, J., dissenting) (citations omitted).

31 Smith v. Maryland, 442 U.S. 735, 750 (1979) (Marshall, J., dissenting).

Quick Summary

Under the *Katz* test, surveillance by law enforcement is considered a "search" if the defendant exhibited a subjective expectation of privacy in the area or item that was the object of the surveillance, and this expectation was one that society recognizes as reasonable and legitimate.

Through its case law, the Supreme Court has provided extensive guidance as to what types of expectation of privacy society may recognize as "reasonable." An individual has no reasonable expectation of privacy in anything she knowingly exposes to the public, nor in anything situated in the "open fields" of her property, nor in anything that is visible from the air, nor in the garbage she leaves out on the sidewalk. On the other hand, an individual does have a reasonable expectation of privacy in the "curtilage" of a home, and, generally, in the contents of containers in public, even to the extent that law enforcement officers cannot squeeze or manipulate those containers without implicating the Fourth Amendment.

Also, the *Katz* test is not the only way that government surveillance could constitute a search. Under the *Jones* test, a surveillance is a "search" if law enforcement officers trespassed onto a "constitutionally protected area" in order to conduct the surveillance.

Review Questions

1. Breaking Into a Building. The Essex County Fugitive Task Force, a police unit specializing in tracking down fugitives, was searching for James Rogers, an indicted felon who failed to appear in court. The Task Force received information that Rogers was living in a ground-floor apartment in a large apartment building. The Task Force approached the apartment building, but found that the door to the building was locked, and a sign was posted in the door reading: "No visitors are permitted in this building unless accompanied by a resident. Anyone not accompanied by a resident will be prosecuted as a trespasser." A member of the Task Force went around to the back of the building and found a partially open window which gave him access to a common stairwell inside the building. An officer from the Task Force crawled through the window and came to the front to let in the rest of his team. The officers then listened outside the apartment where Rogers was allegedly staying and heard Rogers's voice, which one of the officers recognized. The officers waited outside the apartment and when Rogers emerged, they arrested him and searched him, finding an unlicensed gun in his pocket.

Rogers now challenges his arrest and the subsequent search. Did the police conduct a Fourth Amendment search when they entered the lobby of his building and listened outside his door?

2. Raiding the Homeless Shelter. At five o'clock in the morning, twenty agents of the United States Marshall Service conducted an operation to try to locate and apprehend a number of individuals with outstanding arrest warrants. Believing that many of these individuals were homeless, the agents raided a local homeless shelter which was at the time housing nearly five hundred individuals. The door to the homeless shelter was locked, but when one of the agents knocked on the door, a staff member unlocked the door and opened it and the agents all forced their way in over the staff member's protests. The agents proceeded to awaken every individual sleeping in the shelter and demand identification or names and birthdates from each of them.

As the agents roused Nathan Park, they noticed a small object that was visible beneath his pillow. One of the agents grabbed the object and found that it was a crack pipe with a rock of crack cocaine in it. The agent seized the object and charged Park with possession of a controlled substance. Park now challenges the entrance into the shelter and the seizure of his property as a violation of his Fourth Amendment rights.

Did the agents conduct a Fourth Amendment search of Park's property?

3. Civil Commitment. The California Civil Commitment Unit for Sex Offenders ("CCCUSO") housed patients who had been civilly and involuntarily committed after having been classified as violent sexual predators. All of the common areas of the CCCUSO are monitored by video cameras. Individual patients sleep in private quarters with doors that can be closed but not locked. The patients share single-use restrooms and showers that are attached to the common area, and the doors to these rooms can be locked, though administrators can unlock and enter the doors if necessary. Initially, there were no video cameras in the private quarters nor in the restrooms.

The administrators of the facility received a report that one of the patients allegedly sexually assaulted another in a single-use restroom attached to a common area. In order to deter further such assaults, the administration decided to install cameras in every restroom in the facility. The inmates of the CCCUSO sued the administration, arguing that the cameras in the restroom violated their reasonable expectation of privacy.

Does the use of the video cameras constitute a Fourth Amendment search of the patients at the facility?

4. Blockading a Forest Road. Larry Qualls, a United States Forest Service investigator in South Dakota, received a report that two of the forestry roads had been illegally blockaded with boulders. He investigated the area and noticed tractor tire tracks on the road. The tracks led towards the driveway of Larry Ventling. There were two "No Trespassing" signs posted next to the driveway. Qualls drove up Ventling's driveway and then went to Ventling's front door. While he was there, he saw tire tracks on Ventling's property that matched the tracks on the forestry road, and he also saw a tractor equipped with a front-end loader parked on the property. He knocked on the door and spoke briefly to Larry Ventling's wife, who ordered him to leave the property. As Qualls left, he took pictures of the tire tracks on the property.

Qualls went to a magistrate and obtained a warrant based on the information he gathered. He then searched Ventling's property and confirmed that the tires on Ventling's tractor were the ones that made the tracks near the blockades. Ventling was arrested, and he moved to suppress the evidence, arguing that Qualls conducted an illegal warrantless search of his property before obtaining the warrant. The government argued that Qualls did not conduct a "search," because he did not enter the house or the curtilage of Ventling's home.

Did Qualls conduct a Fourth Amendment search of Ventling's property prior to getting a warrant?

FROM THE COURTROOM

KATZ v. UNITED STATES

United States Supreme Court
389 U.S. 347 (1967)

[Justice STEWART delivered the opinion of the Court.]

[Justice DOUGLAS filed a concurring opinion, which was joined by Justice BRENNAN.]

[Justice HARLAN filed a concurring opinion.]

[Justice WHITE filed a concurring opinion.]

[Justice BLACK filed a dissenting opinion.]

[Justice MARSHALL took no part in the consideration or decision of this case.]

The petitioner was convicted in the District Court for the Southern District of California under an eight-count indictment charging him with transmitting wagering information by telephone from Los Angeles to Miami and Boston in violation of a federal statute. At trial the Government was permitted, over the petitioner's objection, to introduce evidence of the petitioner's end of telephone coversations, overheard by FBI agents who had attached an electronic listening and recording device to the outside of the public telephone booth from which he had placed his calls. In affirming his conviction, the Court of Appeals rejected the contention that the recordings had been obtained in violation of the Fourth Amendment, because '(t)here was no physical entrance into the area occupied by, (the petitioner).' We granted certiorari in order to consider the constitutional questions thus presented.

The petitioner had phrased those questions as follows:

'A. Whether a public telephone booth is a constitutionally protected area so that evidence obtained by attaching an electronic listening recording device to the top of such a booth is obtained in violation of the right to privacy of the user of the booth.

'B. Whether physical penetration of a constitutionally protected area is necessary before a search and seizure can be said to be violative of the Fourth Amendment to the United States Constitution.'

We decline to adopt this formulation of the issues. In the first place the correct solution of Fourth Amendment problems is not necessarily promoted by incantation of the phrase 'constitutionally protected area.' Secondly, the Fourth Amendment cannot be translated into a general constitutional 'right to privacy.' That Amendment protects individual privacy against certain kinds of governmental intrusion, but its protections go further, and often have nothing to do with privacy at all.[4] Other provisions of the Constitution protect personal privacy from other forms of governmental invasion. But the protection of a person's general right to privacy-his right to be let alone by other people-is, like the protection of his property and of his very life, left largely to the law of the individual States.

Because of the misleading way the issues have been formulated, the parties have attached great significance to the characterization of the telephone booth from which the petitioner placed his calls. The petitioner has strenuously argued that the booth was a 'constitutionally protected area.' The Government has maintained with equal vigor that it was not. But this effort to decide whether or not a given 'area,' viewed in the abstract, is 'constitutionally protected' deflects attention from the problem presented by this case. For the Fourth Amendment protects people, not places. What a person knowingly exposes to the public, even in his own home or office, is not a subject of Fourth Amendment protection. But what he seeks to preserve as private, even in an area accessible to the public, may be constitutionally protected.

The Government stresses the fact that the telephone booth from which the petitioner made his calls was constructed partly of glass, so that he was as visible after he entered it as he would have been if he had remained outside. But what he sought to exclude when he entered the booth was not the intruding eye-it was the uninvited ear. He did not shed his right to do so simply because he made his calls from a place where he might be seen. No less than an individual in a business office, in a friend's apartment, or in a taxicab, a person in a telephone booth may rely upon the protection of the Fourth Amendment. One who occupies it, shuts the door behind him, and pays the toll that permits him to place a call is surely entitled to assume that the words he utters into the mouthpiece will not be broadcast to the world. To read the Constitution more narrowly is to ignore the vital role that the public telephone has come to play in private communication.

The Government contends, however, that the activities of its agents in this case should not be tested by Fourth Amendment requirements, for the surveillance technique they employed involved no physical penetration of the telephone booth from which the petitioner placed his calls. It is true that the absence of such penetration was at one time thought to foreclose further Fourth Amendment inquiry, for that Amendment was thought to limit only searches and seizures of tangible property. But '(t)he premise that property interests control the right of the Government to search and seize has been discredited.' Thus, although a closely divided Court supposed in *Olmstead* that surveillance without any trespass and without the seizure of any material object fell outside the ambit of the Constitution, we have since departed from the narrow view on which that decision rested. Indeed, we have expressly held that the Fourth

---

[4] 'The average man would very likely not have his feelings soothed any more by having his property seized openly than by having it seized privately and by stealth. * * * And a person can be just as much, if not more, irritated, annoyed and injured by an unceremonious public arrest by a policeman as he is by a seizure in the privacy of his office or home.'

Amendment governs not only the seizure of tangible items, but extends as well to the recording of oral statements overheard without any 'technical trespass under * * * local property law.' Once this much is acknowledged, and once it is recognized that the Fourth Amendment protects people-and not simply 'areas'-against unreasonable searches and seizures it becomes clear that the reach of that Amendment cannot turn upon the presence or absence of a physical intrusion into any given enclosure.

We conclude that the . . . 'trespass' doctrine . . . can no longer be regarded as controlling. The Government's activities in electronically listening to and recording the petitioner's words violated the privacy upon which he justifiably relied while using the telephone booth and thus constituted a 'search and seizure' within the meaning of the Fourth Amendment. The fact that the electronic device employed to achieve that end did not happen to penetrate the wall of the booth can have no constitutional significance.

The question remaining for decision, then, is whether the search and seizure conducted in this case complied with constitutional standards. In that regard, the Government's position is that its agents acted in an entirely defensible manner: They did not begin their electronic surveillance until investigation of the petitioner's activities had established a strong probability that he was using the telephone in question to transmit gambling information to persons in other States, in violation of federal law. Moreover, the surveillance was limited, both in scope and in duration, to the specific purpose of establishing the contents of the petitioner's unlawful telephonic communications. The agents confined their surveillance to the brief periods during which he used the telephone booth, and they took great care to overhear only the conversations of the petitioner himself.

Accepting this account of the Government's actions as acccurate, it is clear that this surveillance was so narrowly circumscribed that a duly authorized magistrate, properly notified of the need for such investigation, specifically informed of the basis on which it was to proceed, and clearly apprised of the precise intrusion it would entail, could constitutionally have authorized, with appropriate safeguards, the very limited search and seizure that the Government asserts in fact took place. Only last Term we sustained the validity of such an authorization, holding that, under sufficiently 'precise and discriminate circumstances,' a federal court may empower government agents to employ a concealed electronic device 'for the narrow and particularized purpose of ascertaining the truth of the * * * allegations' of a 'detailed factual affidavit alleging the commission of a specific criminal offense.' Discussing that holding, the Court in *Berger v. State of New York*, 388 U.S. 41, said that 'the order authorizing the use of the electronic device' in *Osborn* 'afforded similar protections to those * * * of conventional warrants authorizing the seizure of tangible evidence.' Through those protections, 'no greater invasion of privacy was permitted than was necessary under the circumstances.' Here, too, a similar judicial order could have accommodated 'the legitimate needs of law enforcement' by authorizing the carefully limited use of electronic surveillance.

. . .

[B]y bypassing a neutral predetermination of the scope of a search leaves individuals secure from Fourth Amendment violations 'only in the discretion of the police.'

These considerations do not vanish when the search in question is transferred from the setting of a home, an office, or a hotel room to that of a telephone booth. Wherever a man may be, he is entitled to know that he will remain free from unreasonable searches and seizures. The government agents here ignored 'the procedure of antecedent justification * * * that is central to the Fourth Amendment,' a procedure that we hold to be a constitutional precondition of the kind of electronic surveillance involved in this case. Because the surveillance here failed to meet that condition, and because it led to the petitioner's conviction, the judgment must be reversed.

It is so ordered.

Judgment reversed.

Mr. Justice MARSHALL took no part in the consideration or decision of this case.

[The concurring opinion of Justice DOUGLAS, which was joined by Justice BRENNAN, is omitted.]

Mr. Justice HARLAN, concurring.

I join the opinion of the Court, which I read to hold only (a) that an enclosed telephone booth is an area where, like a home, and unlike a field, a person has a constitutionally protected reasonable expectation of privacy; (b) that electronic as well as physical intrusion into a place that is in this sense private may constitute a violation of the Fourth Amendment; and (c) that the invasion of a constitutionally protected area by federal authorities is, as the Court has long held, presumptively unreasonable in the absence of a search warrant.

As the Court's opinion states, 'the Fourth Amendment protects people, not places.' The question, however, is what protection it affords to those people. Generally, as here, the answer to that question requires reference to a 'place.' My understanding of the rule that has emerged from prior decisions is that there is a twofold requirement, first that a person have exhibited an actual (subjective) expectation of privacy and, second, that the expectation be one that society is prepared to recognize as 'reasonable.' Thus a man's home is, for most purposes, a place where he expects privacy, but objects, activities, or statements that he exposes to the 'plain view' of outsiders are not 'protected' because no intention to keep them to himself has been exhibited. On the other hand, conversations in the open would not be protected against being overheard, for the expectation of privacy under the circumstances would be unreasonable.

The critical fact in this case is that '(o)ne who occupies it, (a telephone booth) shuts the door behind him, and pays the toll that permits him to place a call is surely entitled to assume' that his conversation is not being intercepted. The point is not that the booth is 'accessible to the public' at other times, but that it is a temporarily private place whose momentary occupants' expectations of freedom from intrusion are recognized as reasonable.

In *Silverman v. United States*, 365 U.S. 505, we held that eavesdropping accomplished by means of an electronic device that penetrated the premises occupied by petitioner was a violation of the Fourth Amendment. That case established that interception of conversations reasonably intended to be private could constitute a 'search and seizure,' and that the examination or taking of physical property was not required. . . . In *Silverman* we found it unnecessary to re-examine *Goldman v. United States*, 316 U.S. 129, which had held that electronic surveillance accomplished without the physical penetration of petitioner's premises by a tangible object did not violate the Fourth Amendment. This case requires us to reconsider *Goldman*, and I agree that it should now be overruled. Its limitation on Fourth Amendment protection is, in the present day, bad physics as well as bad law, for reasonable expectations of privacy may be defeated by electronic as well as physical invasion.

Finally, I do not read the Court's opinion to declare that no interception of a conversation one-half of which occurs in a public telephone booth can be reasonable in the absence of a warrant.

As elsewhere under the Fourth Amendment, warrants are the general rule, to which the legitimate needs of law enforcement may demand specific exceptios. It will be time enough to consider any such exceptions when an appropriate occasion presents itself, and I agree with the Court that this is not one.

[The concurring opinion of Justice WHITE is omitted.]

[The dissenting opinion of Justice BLACK is omitted.]

FROM THE COURTROOM

UNITED STATES v. JONES

United States Supreme Court, 2012
132 S.Ct. 945

[Justice SCALIA delivered the opinion.]

[Justice SOTOMAYOR joined the opinion and filed a concurring opinion.]

[Justice ALITO, GINSBURG, BREYER, and KAGAN filed a concurring opinion.]

We decide whether the attachment of a Global-Positioning-System (GPS) tracking device to an individual's vehicle, and subsequent use of that device to monitor the vehicle's movements on public streets, constitutes a search or seizure within the meaning of the Fourth Amendment.

I

In 2004 respondent Antoine Jones, owner and operator of a nightclub in the District of Columbia, came under suspicion of trafficking in narcotics and was made the target of an investigation by a joint FBI and Metropolitan Police Department task force. Officers employed various investigative techniques, including visual surveillance of the nightclub, installation of a camera focused on the front door of the club, and a pen register and wiretap covering Jones's cellular phone.

Based in part on information gathered from these sources, in 2005 the Government applied to the United States District Court for the District of Columbia for a warrant authorizing the use of an electronic tracking device on the Jeep Grand Cherokee registered to Jones's wife. A warrant issued, authorizing installation of the device in the District of Columbia and within [ten] days.

On the 11th day, and not in the District of Columbia but in Maryland, agents installed a GPS tracking device on the undercarriage of the Jeep while it was parked in a public parking lot. Over the next [twenty-eight] days, the Government used the device to track the vehicle's movements, and once had to replace the device's battery when the vehicle was parked in a different public lot in Maryland. By means of signals from multiple satellites, the device established the vehicle's location within [fifty] to [one-hundred] feet, and communicated that location by cellular phone to a Government computer. It relayed more than 2,000 pages of data over the [four]-week period.

The Government ultimately obtained a multiple-count indictment charging Jones and several alleged co-conspirators with, as relevant here, conspiracy to distribute and possession with intent to distribute five kilograms or more of cocaine and fifty grams or more of cocaine base, in violation of 21 U.S.C. §§ 841 and 846. Before trial, Jones filed a motion to suppress evidence obtained through the GPS device. The District Court granted the motion only in part, suppressing the data obtained while the vehicle was parked in the garage adjoining Jones's residence. It held the remaining data admissible, because " '[a] person traveling in an automobile on public thoroughfares has no reasonable expectation of privacy in his movements from one place to another.'" (quoting *United States v. Knotts*, 460 U.S. 276, 281 (1983)). Jones' trial in October 2006 produced a hung jury on the conspiracy count.

In March 2007, a grand jury returned another indictment, charging Jones and others with the same conspiracy. The Government introduced at trial the same GPS-derived locational data admitted in the first trial, which connected Jones to the alleged conspirators' stash house that contained $850,000 in cash, [ninety-seven] kilograms of cocaine, and 1 kilogram of cocaine base. The jury returned a guilty verdict, and the District Court sentenced Jones to life imprisonment.

The United States Court of Appeals for the District of Columbia Circuit reversed the conviction because of admission of the evidence obtained by warrantless use of the GPS device which, it said, violated the Fourth Amendment. The D.C. Circuit denied the Government's petition for rehearing en banc, with four judges dissenting. We granted certiorari.

II

A

The Fourth Amendment provides in relevant part that "[t]he right of the people to be secure in their persons, houses, papers, and effects, against unreasonable searches and seizures, shall not be violated." It is beyond dispute that a vehicle is an "effect" as that term is used in the Amendment. We hold that the Government's installation of a GPS device on a target's vehicle, and its use of that device to monitor the vehicle's movements, constitutes a "search."

It is important to be clear about what occurred in this case: The Government physically occupied private property for the purpose of obtaining information. We have no doubt that such a physical intrusion would have been considered a "search" within the meaning of the Fourth Amendment when it was adopted. *Entick v. Carrington*, 95 Eng. Rep. 807 (C.P. 1765), is a "case we have described as a 'monument of English freedom' 'undoubtedly familiar' to 'every American statesman' at the time the Constitution was adopted, and considered to be 'the true and ultimate expression of constitutional law'" with regard to search and seizure. In that case, Lord Camden expressed in plain terms the significance of property rights in search-and-seizure analysis:

> "[O]ur law holds the property of every man so sacred, that no man can set his foot upon his neighbour's close without his leave; if he does he is a trespasser, though he does no damage at all; if he will tread upon his neighbour's ground, he must justify it by law."

The text of the Fourth Amendment reflects its close connection to property, since otherwise it would have referred simply to "the right of the people to be secure against unreasonable searches and seizures"; the phrase "in their persons, houses, papers, and effects" would have been superfluous.

Consistent with this understanding, our Fourth Amendment jurisprudence was tied to common-law trespass, at least until the latter half of the 20th century. Thus, in *Olmstead v. United States*, 277 U.S. 438 (1928), we held that wiretaps attached to telephone wires on the public streets did not constitute a Fourth Amendment search because "[t]here was no entry of the houses or offices of the defendants."

Our later cases, of course, have deviated from that exclusively property-based approach. In *Katz v. United States*, 389 U.S. 347, 351 (1967), we said that "the Fourth Amendment protects people, not places," and found a violation in attachment of an eavesdropping device to a public telephone booth. Our later cases have applied the analysis of Justice Harlan's concurrence in that case, which said that a violation occurs when government officers violate a person's "reasonable expectation of privacy".

The Government contends that the Harlan standard shows that no search occurred here, since Jones had no "reasonable expectation of privacy" in the area of the Jeep accessed by Government agents (its underbody) and in the locations of the Jeep on the public roads, which were visible to all. But we need not address the Government's contentions, because Jones's Fourth Amendment rights do not rise or fall with the *Katz* formulation. At bottom, we must "assur[e] preservation of that degree of privacy against government that existed when the Fourth Amendment was adopted." As explained, for most of our history the Fourth Amendment was understood to embody a particular concern for government trespass upon the areas ("persons, houses, papers, and effects") it enumerates.[3] *Katz* did not repudiate that understanding.

Less than two years later the Court upheld defendants' contention that the Government could not introduce against them conversations between *other* people obtained by warrantless placement of electronic surveillance devices in their homes. The opinion rejected the dissent's contention that there was no Fourth Amendment violation "unless the conversational privacy of the homeowner himself is invaded "[W]e [do not] believe that *Katz*, by holding that the Fourth Amendment protects persons and their private conversations, was intended to withdraw any of the protection which the Amendment extends to the home. . . ."

---

[3] Justice ALITO's concurrence (hereinafter concurrence) doubts the wisdom of our approach because "it is almost impossible to think of late-18th-century situations that are analogous to what took place in this case." But in fact it posits a situation that is not far afield—a constable's concealing himself in the target's coach in order to track its movements. There is no doubt that the information gained by that trespassory activity would be the product of an unlawful search—whether that information consisted of the conversations occurring in the coach, or of the destinations to which the coach traveled.

In any case, it is quite irrelevant whether there was an 18th-century analog. Whatever new methods of investigation may be devised, our task, *at a minimum*, is to decide whether the action in question would have constituted a "search" within the original meaning of the Fourth Amendment. Where, as here, the Government obtains information by physically intruding on a constitutionally protected area, such a search has undoubtedly occurred.

More recently, in *Soldal v. Cook County*, 506 U.S. 56 (1992), the Court unanimously rejected the argument that although a "seizure" had occurred "in a 'technical' sense" when a trailer home was forcibly removed, no Fourth Amendment violation occurred because law enforcement had not "invade[d] the [individuals'] privacy," the Court explained, established that "property rights are not the sole measure of Fourth Amendment violations," but did not "snuf[f] out the previously recognized protection for property." As Justice Brennan explained in his concurrence in *Knotts*, *Katz* did not erode the principle "that, when the Government *does* engage in physical intrusion of a constitutionally protected area in order to obtain information, that intrusion may constitute a violation of the Fourth Amendment." We have embodied that preservation of past rights in our very definition of "reasonable expectation of privacy" which we have said to be an expectation "that has a source outside of the Fourth Amendment, either by reference to concepts of real or personal property law or to understandings that are recognized and permitted by society."*Katz* did not narrow the Fourth Amendment's scope.

. . .

The Government . . . points to our exposition in *New York v. Class*, 475 U.S. 106 (1986), that "[t]he exterior of a car . . . is thrust into the public eye, and thus to examine it does not constitute a 'search.' " That statement is of marginal relevance here since, as the Government acknowledges, "the officers in this case did *more* than conduct a visual inspection of respondent's vehicle." By attaching the device to the Jeep, officers encroached on a protected area. In *Class* itself we suggested that this would make a difference, for we concluded that an officer's momentary reaching into the interior of a vehicle did constitute a search.

Finally, the Government's position gains little support from our conclusion in *Oliver v. United States*, 466 U.S. 170 (1984), that officers' information-gathering intrusion on an "open field" did not constitute a Fourth Amendment search even though it was a trespass at common law. Quite simply, an open field, unlike the curtilage of a home, see *United States v. Dunn*, 480 U.S. 294 (1987), is not one of those protected areas enumerated in the Fourth Amendment. The Government's physical intrusion on such an area—unlike its intrusion on the "effect" at issue here—is of no Fourth Amendment significance.[8]

B

The concurrence begins by accusing us of applying "18th-century tort law." That is a distortion. What we apply is an 18th-century guarantee against unreasonable searches, which we believe must provide *at a minimum* the degree of protection it afforded when it was adopted. The concurrence does not share that belief. It would apply

[8] Thus, our theory is not that the Fourth Amendment is concerned with "any technical trespass that led to the gathering of evidence." The Fourth Amendment protects against trespassory searches only with regard to those items ("persons, houses, papers, and effects") that it enumerates. The trespass that occurred in *Oliver* may properly be understood as a "search," but not one "in the constitutional sense."

exclusively Katz's reasonable-expectation-of-privacy test, even when that eliminates rights that previously existed.

The concurrence faults our approach for "present[ing] particularly vexing problems" in cases that do not involve physical contact, such as those that involve the transmission of electronic signals. We entirely fail to understand that point. For unlike the concurrence, which would make *Katz* the *exclusive* test, we do not make trespass the exclusive test. Situations involving merely the transmission of electronic signals without trespass would *remain* subject to *Katz* analysis.

In fact, it is the concurrence's insistence on the exclusivity of the *Katz* test that needlessly leads us into "particularly vexing problems" in the present case. This Court has to date not deviated from the understanding that mere visual observation does not constitute a search. We accordingly held in *Knotts* that "[a] person traveling in an automobile on public thoroughfares has no reasonable expectation of privacy in his movements from one place to another." Thus, even assuming that the concurrence is correct to say that "[t]raditional surveillance" of Jones for a 4-week period "would have required a large team of agents, multiple vehicles, and perhaps aerial assistance," our cases suggest that such visual observation is constitutionally permissible. It may be that achieving the same result through electronic means, without an accompanying trespass, is an unconstitutional invasion of privacy, but the present case does not require us to answer that question.

And answering it affirmatively leads us needlessly into additional thorny problems. The concurrence posits that "relatively short-term monitoring of a person's movements on public streets" is okay, but that "the use of longer term GPS monitoring in investigations *of most offenses* " is no good. That introduces yet another novelty into our jurisprudence. There is no precedent for the proposition that whether a search has occurred depends on the nature of the crime being investigated. And even accepting that novelty, it remains unexplained why a [four]–week investigation is "surely" too long and why a drug-trafficking conspiracy involving substantial amounts of cash and narcotics is not an "extraordinary offens[e]" which may permit longer observation. What of a [two]–day monitoring of a suspected purveyor of stolen electronics? Or of a [six]–month monitoring of a suspected terrorist? We may have to grapple with these "vexing problems" in some future case where a classic trespassory search is not involved and resort must be had to *Katz* analysis; but there is no reason for rushing forward to resolve them here.

. . .

The judgment of the Court of Appeals for the D.C. Circuit is affirmed.

It is so ordered.

[The concurring opinion of Justice SOTOMAYOR is omitted.]

Justice ALITO, with whom Justice GINSBURG, Justice BREYER, and Justice KAGAN join, concurring in the judgment.

This case requires us to apply the Fourth Amendment's prohibition of unreasonable searches and seizures to a 21st-century surveillance technique, the use of a Global Positioning System (GPS) device to monitor a vehicle's movements for an extended period of time.

Ironically, the Court has chosen to decide this case based on 18th-century tort law. By attaching a small GPS device to the underside of the vehicle that respondent drove, the law enforcement officers in this case engaged in conduct that might have provided grounds in 1791 for a suit for trespass to chattels. And for this reason, the Court concludes, the installation and use of the GPS device constituted a search.

This holding, in my judgment, is unwise. It strains the language of the Fourth Amendment; it has little if any support in current Fourth Amendment case law; and it is highly artificial.

I would analyze the question presented in this case by asking whether respondent's reasonable expectations of privacy were violated by the long-term monitoring of the movements of the vehicle he drove.

I

A

The Fourth Amendment prohibits "unreasonable searches and seizures," and the Court makes very little effort to explain how the attachment or use of the GPS device fits within these terms. The Court does not contend that there was a seizure. A seizure of property occurs when there is "some meaningful interference with an individual's possessory interests in that property," and here there was none. Indeed, the success of the surveillance technique that the officers employed was dependent on the fact that the GPS did not interfere in any way with the operation of the vehicle, for if any such interference had been detected, the device might have been discovered.

The Court does claim that the installation and use of the GPS constituted a search, but this conclusion is dependent on the questionable proposition that these two procedures cannot be separated for purposes of Fourth Amendment analysis. If these two procedures are analyzed separately, it is not at all clear from the Court's opinion why either should be regarded as a search. It is clear that the attachment of the GPS device was not itself a search; if the device had not functioned or if the officers had not used it, no information would have been obtained. And the Court does not contend that the use of the device constituted a search either. On the contrary, the Court accepts the holding in *United States v. Knotts*, 460 U.S. 276 (1983), that the use of a surreptitiously planted electronic device to monitor a vehicle's movements on public roads did not amount to a search.

The Court argues—and I agree—that "we must 'assur[e] preservation of that degree of privacy against government that existed when the Fourth Amendment was adopted.'" But it is almost impossible to think of late-18th-century situations that are analogous to what took place in this case. (Is it possible to imagine a case in which a constable secreted himself somewhere in a coach and remained there for a period of time in order to monitor the movements of the coach's owner?)[3] The Court's theory seems to be that the concept of a search, as originally understood, comprehended any technical trespass that led to the gathering of evidence, but we know that this is incorrect. At common law, any unauthorized intrusion on private property was actionable, but a trespass on open fields, as opposed to the "curtilage" of a home, does not fall within the scope of the Fourth Amendment because private property outside the curtilage is not part of a "hous[e]" within the meaning of the Fourth Amendment.

B

The Court's reasoning in this case is very similar to that in the Court's early decisions involving wiretapping and electronic eavesdropping, namely, that a technical trespass followed by the gathering of evidence constitutes a search. In the early electronic surveillance cases, the Court concluded that a Fourth Amendment search occurred when private conversations were monitored as a result of an "unauthorized physical penetration into the premises occupied" by the defendant. *Silverman v. United States*, 365 U.S. 505, 509 (1961). In *Silverman*, police officers listened to conversations in an attached home by inserting a "spike mike" through the wall that this house shared with the vacant house next door. This procedure was held to be a search because the mike made contact with a heating duct on the other side of the wall and thus "usurp[ed] . . . an integral part of the premises."

By contrast, in cases in which there was no trespass, it was held that there was no search. Thus, in *Olmstead v. United States*, 277 U.S. 438 (1928), the Court found that the Fourth Amendment did not apply because "[t]he taps from house lines were made in the streets near the houses." Similarly, the Court concluded that no search occurred in *Goldman v. United States*, 316 U.S. 129 (1942), where a "detectaphone" was placed on the outer wall of defendant's office for the purpose of overhearing conversations held within the room.

This trespass-based rule was repeatedly criticized. In *Olmstead*, Justice Brandeis wrote that it was "immaterial where the physical connection with the telephone wires was made." Although a private conversation transmitted by wire did not fall within the literal words of the Fourth Amendment, he argued, the Amendment should be understood as prohibiting "every unjustifiable intrusion by the government upon the privacy of the individual." See also, *e.g.*, *Silverman*, *supra*, at 513 (Douglas, J., concurring) ("The concept of 'an unauthorized physical penetration into the premises,' on which the present decision rests seems to me beside the point. Was not the wrong . . .

[3] The Court suggests that something like this might have occurred in 1791, but this would have required either a gigantic coach, a very tiny constable, or both—not to mention a constable with incredible fortitude and patience.

done when the intimacies of the home were tapped, recorded, or revealed? The depth of the penetration of the electronic device—even the degree of its remoteness from the inside of the house—is not the measure of the injury"); *Goldman, supra*, at 139 (Murphy, J., dissenting) ("[T]he search of one's home or office no longer requires physical entry, for science has brought forth far more effective devices for the invasion of a person's privacy than the direct and obvious methods of oppression which were detested by our forebears and which inspired the Fourth Amendment.").

Katz v. United States, 389 U.S. 347 (1967), finally did away with the old approach, holding that a trespass was not required for a Fourth Amendment violation. *Katz* involved the use of a listening device that was attached to the outside of a public telephone booth and that allowed police officers to eavesdrop on one end of the target's phone conversation. This procedure did not physically intrude on the area occupied by the target, but the *Katz* Court "repudiate[ed]" the old doctrine, and held that "[t]he fact that the electronic device employed . . . did not happen to penetrate the wall of the booth can have no constitutional significance," ("[T]he reach of th[e] [Fourth] Amendment cannot turn upon the presence or absence of a physical intrusion into any given enclosure"); see *Rakas* (describing *Katz* as holding that the "capacity to claim the protection for the Fourth Amendment depends not upon a property right in the invaded place but upon whether the person who claims the protection of the Amendment has a legitimate expectation of privacy in the invaded place"); *Kyllo, supra*, at 32 ("We have since decoupled violation of a person's Fourth Amendment rights from trespassory violation of his property."). What mattered, the Court now held, was whether the conduct at issue "violated the privacy upon which [the defendant] justifiably relied while using the telephone booth."

Under this approach, as the Court later put it when addressing the relevance of a technical trespass, "an actual trespass is neither necessary *nor sufficient* to establish a constitutional violation." In *Oliver*, the Court wrote:

> "The existence of a property right is but one element in determining whether expectations of privacy are legitimate. 'The premise that property interests control the right of the Government to search and seize has been discredited.'"

. . .

III

Disharmony with a substantial body of existing case law is only one of the problems with the Court's approach in this case.

I will briefly note four others. First, the Court's reasoning largely disregards what is really important (the *use* of a GPS for the purpose of long-term tracking) and instead attaches great significance to something that most would view as relatively minor (attaching to the bottom of a car a small, light object that does not interfere in any way with the car's operation). Attaching such an object is generally regarded as so trivial that it does not provide a basis for recovery under modern tort law. But under the Court's reasoning, this conduct may violate the Fourth Amendment. By contrast, if long-term monitoring can be accomplished without committing a technical trespass—suppose, for example, that the Federal Government required or persuaded auto manufacturers to include a GPS tracking device in every car—the Court's theory would provide no protection.

Second, the Court's approach leads to incongruous results. If the police attach a GPS device to a car and use the device to follow the car for even a brief time, under the Court's theory, the Fourth Amendment applies. But if the police follow the same car for a much longer period using unmarked cars and aerial assistance, this tracking is not subject to any Fourth Amendment constraints.

In the present case, the Fourth Amendment applies, the Court concludes, because the officers installed the GPS device after respondent's wife, to whom the car was registered, turned it over to respondent for his exclusive use. But if the GPS had been attached prior to that time, the Court's theory would lead to a different result. The Court proceeds on the assumption that respondent "had at least the property rights of a bailee," but a bailee may sue for a trespass to chattel only if the injury occurs during the term of the bailment. So if the GPS device had been installed before respondent's wife gave him the keys, respondent would have no claim for trespass—and, presumably, no Fourth Amendment claim either.

Third, under the Court's theory, the coverage of the Fourth Amendment may vary from State to State. If the events at issue here had occurred in a community property State or a State that has adopted the Uniform Marital Property Act, respondent would likely be an owner of the vehicle, and it would not matter whether the GPS was installed before or after his wife turned over the keys. In non-community-property States, on the other hand, the registration of the vehicle in the name of respondent's wife would generally be regarded as presumptive evidence that she was the sole owner.

Fourth, the Court's reliance on the law of trespass will present particularly vexing problems in cases involving surveillance that is carried out by making electronic, as opposed to physical, contact with the item to be tracked. For example, suppose that the officers in the present case had followed respondent by surreptitiously activating a stolen vehicle detection system that came with the car when it was purchased. Would the sending of a radio signal to activate this system constitute a trespass to chattels? Trespass to chattels has traditionally required a physical touching of the property. In recent years, courts have wrestled with the application of this old tort in cases involving unwanted electronic contact with computer systems, and some have held that even the transmission of electrons that occurs when a communication is sent from one computer to another is enough. But may such decisions be followed in applying the Court's trespass theory? Assuming that what matters under the Court's theory is the law of trespass as it existed at the time of the adoption of the Fourth Amendment, do these recent decisions represent a change in the law or simply the application of the old tort to new situations?

. . .

[The concurrence goes on to analyze the government surveillance using the traditional *Katz* test and ultimately agrees with the judgment that the government violated the Fourth Amendment.]

7

The Fourth Amendment and New Technologies

Key Concepts

- New Surveillance Technology Constitutes a Search if it Reveals Information about a Constitutionally Protected Area
- Defendant's "Reasonable Expectation of Privacy" Must Be Legitimate

A. Introduction and Policy. According to *Katz*, government surveillance will be deemed a Fourth Amendment search if the surveillance infringes on the suspect's "reasonable expectation of privacy."[1] If the police enter your home and rifle through your dresser drawers, they are obviously conducting a search: you have a subjective belief that the contents of your dresser drawer should remain private, and that is a belief that society as a whole recognizes as reasonable. However, if a police officer watches you meet a friend in a public park, she is not conducting a search: you probably did not expect the fact that you were meeting your friend to remain private, and even if you did, most members of society would not think that your expectation was reasonable. But what if you were meeting your friend in a deserted area of a public park where nobody else was around? Would you have a reasonable expectation of privacy that your meeting should stay secret? Perhaps not: a police officer could be watching you with binoculars from hundreds of yards away. What if it was nighttime and pitch dark—but a police officer was using binoculars with infrared scanners? What if you knew for certain that there was nobody else for miles around—but the police officer downloaded an image of the meeting from a passing satellite orbiting overhead?

These questions can be re-stated as follows: does the question of whether you have a reasonable expectation of privacy depend on the type of technology that the police are using to conduct their surveillance? The answer is no—if you have a reasonable expectation of privacy in a certain activity, that activity will be protected by the Fourth Amendment no matter how the police conduct their surveillance.

However, whether you have a reasonable expectation of privacy **does** depend on the type of technology that you reasonably expect the police to be using. This is a subtle but critical distinction. As a general rule, if law enforcement agents make

[1] Katz v. United States, 389 U.S. 347, 358 (1967) (Harlan, J., concurring).

observations from a lawful vantage point using common technologies that most people in society use on a regular basis—such as binoculars or a flashlight (or, as we saw in the last chapter, an airplane flying overhead)—you cannot reasonably expect that any activities which may be subject to those types of surveillance are private. But, if they are only able to observe or hear you by using specialized technology that is not in everyday use—such as a directional microphone or infrared technology—then your expectation of privacy is reasonable.

The Court faced this issue directly in the 2001 case of *Kyllo v. United States.*[2] Government agents wanted to determine whether the defendant was using high-intensity heat lamps to grow marijuana inside his house. Without a warrant, they used a thermal imager to detect the heat that was emitting from the house. The thermal imager revealed suspicious patterns of heat radiation in certain areas of the home that were consistent with heat lamps. Armed with this information, the government agents acquired a warrant and searched the defendant's house, where they did indeed find marijuana. The defendant argued that the initial use of the thermal imager was a search of his house, and it was therefore unconstitutional without a warrant.

Kyllo presented the Supreme Court with a good first case with which to tackle the question of new technologies. On the one hand, the police were learning details about the inside of someone's home—traditionally the most private type of information there is. On the other hand, the police were doing nothing more than recording the heat leaving the home—they were not looking **inside** the house at all, merely using a tool to measure heat that was **outside** the house. Thus, the Court had to decide which factor was more important: the type of information that was being gathered, or the method that was being used to gather the information.

In a 5-4 decision, the Court chose to focus on the type of information that was being gathered. Justice Scalia wrote the majority opinion, ruling that the use of the thermal imager was a Fourth Amendment search because the defendant could reasonably expect that the details of the inside of his house should be private. As Justice Scalia famously explained, using the thermal imager could reveal "at what hour each night the lady of the house takes her daily sauna and bath"—a fact that most of us would consider to be "intimate."[3] Whether the government was using an X-ray machine to look through the walls or a thermal imager to sense heat that had already left the walls was irrelevant to the decision.

B. The Law. The *Kyllo* case set out the Supreme Court's most recent rule on using surveillance technology:

---

[2] 533 U.S. 27 (2001).

[3] Id. at 38.

> Using technology during a surveillance will be deemed a "search" if law enforcement obtains information "that could not otherwise have been obtained without physical intrusion into a constitutionally protected area, at least where . . . the technology in question is not in general public use."[4]

This test has two separate prongs. First, the court looks to see whether law enforcement obtained any information **"that could not otherwise have been obtained without physical intrusion into a constitutionally protected area."** For example, if police use satellite technology to take pictures of a suspect meeting a friend in a public park, the surveillance is not a search because the police could have conceivably acquired the same information through simple visual observation. The method that the law enforcement officers used is immaterial. What is relevant is the fact that they did not have to intrude into a constitutionally protected area to gather the information they sought. On the other hand, if the police use a parabolic microphone to hear conversations inside a home that would otherwise be inaudible to anyone outside the home, they are conducting a search, because without the use of the technology, there would be no way for them to hear the conversation.

But what if the police use a technology that is a common part of our everyday lives? This is the second prong of the test. If "**the technology . . . is in general public use,**" the Court's language in *Kyllo* suggests that police can use it to detect information that they otherwise could not detect. We have already seen that the police can lawfully fly over a home and look into the home's curtilage;[5] they can also use flashlights and binoculars.[6] This is because these technologies are so commonly used that a suspect cannot assume his activities are private if those activities can be detected by such everyday devices.

Of course, whether or not a specific technology is in "general public use" may not be obvious, and at any rate may change as certain technologies become more widespread. We will explore this question further in Part C.4, below.

C. Applying the Law.

1. Monitoring Public Areas with Surveillance Technology, Part I. Though subject to certain exceptions, as a general rule, it does not matter what **method** the police use when monitoring a suspect's movements in a public place—they can use

[4] Kyllo v. United States, 533 U.S. 27, 27 (2001).
[5] California v. Ciraolo, 476 U.S. 207 (1986).
[6] United States v. Lee, 274 U.S. 559 (1981).

video surveillance or tracking technology, as long as the information they gather only involves activities that the suspect has knowingly exposed to the public.

> **Example—*United States v. Knotts*, 460 U.S. 276 (1983):** Federal agents suspected that Knotts was manufacturing illegal drugs. With the permission of the chemical company, they were able to install a small radio transmitter into a five-gallon container of chloroform that was purchased by one of Knotts' confederates. They then used the radio transmitter to track the container of chloroform to a cabin over a hundred miles away. The agents observed the cabin for three days and developed probable cause to search the cabin. They acquired a warrant, searched the cabin, and found machines used to manufacture amphetamine, as well as fourteen pounds of amphetamine. Knotts and his co-defendants challenged the warrant, arguing that tracking the car using a radio transmitter was a Fourth Amendment search, and therefore required a warrant.

Analysis: The Court held that, where the surveillance did not amount to round-the-clock, long-term surveillance, the defendants had no reasonable expectation of privacy in their movements along public roads. The police could have followed Knotts and his co-defendants along the roads in an unmarked car to visually observe their movements. Consequently, the fact that they used a tracking device to gather the same information did not alter the analysis under the Fourth Amendment. "Insofar as the respondent's complaint appears to be simply that scientific devices such as the beeper enabled the police to be more effective in detecting crime, it simply has no constitutional foundation. We have never equated police efficiency with unconstitutionality, and we decline to do so now."[7]

The *Knotts* case above is invariably contrasted with *United States v. Karo*, which the Court decided one year later. In *Karo,* federal agents installed a similar radio transmitter into a can of ether and tracked the defendant's movements over public roads. However, in *Karo*, the officers continued to monitor the movements of the can of ether after it was transferred into a private house. The Supreme Court held that a "search" occurred from the moment the police began monitoring movements inside the private houses:

> The monitoring of an electronic device such as a beeper is, of course, less intrusive than a full-scale search, but it does reveal a critical fact about the interior of the premises that the Government is extremely interested in knowing and that it could not have otherwise obtained without a warrant. The case is thus not like *Knotts*, for there the beeper told the authorities nothing about the interior of Knotts' cabin. The information

[7] United States v. Knotts, 460 U.S. 276, 284 (1983).

> obtained in *Knotts* was "voluntarily conveyed to anyone who wanted to look . . . here, as we have said, the monitoring indicated that the beeper was inside the house, a fact that could not have been visually verified."[8]

Thus, *Knotts* and *Karo* established a clear dividing line between public and private surveillance. *Knotts* also suggested another line that the Court might need to draw when it hinted that surveillance technology may someday become so sophisticated that "twenty-four hour surveillance of any citizen of this country will be possible, without judicial knowledge or supervision."[9] The Court explained that if such advances ever occur, "there will be time enough then to determine whether different constitutional principles may be applicable."[10]

This language proved to be prophetic. Twenty-nine years after the *Knotts* decision, police surveillance technology had improved from radio transmitters to GPS devices.

2. Monitoring Public Areas with Surveillance Technology, Part II. In 2012, the Supreme Court in *United States v. Jones* was asked to decide whether it was possible that continuous monitoring of a suspect's public movements could ever be a search. As we saw in the last chapter, the majority opinion of the Court ducked this question by reviving the pre-*Katz* "physical trespass" theory and ruling that the government surveillance was a search because the government infringed on the defendant's property rights when they placed the GPS device on the bottom of her car. But the *Jones* case was also significant for its concurring opinions:

> **Example—*United States v. Jones*, 132 S. Ct. 945 (2012):** The police suspected that Jones was involved in narcotics trafficking, so they attached a GPS tracking device to the undercarriage of his wife's car while it was parked in a public parking lot. For the next twenty-eight days, the GPS device reported every movement of the vehicle across public roads and parking lots, generating 2,000 pages of data. The government used this evidence at Jones' eventual trial for narcotics trafficking, and Jones objected on Fourth Amendment grounds.

Analysis: The majority of the Court held that use of the GPS was a Fourth Amendment search because of the physical trespass required to install the GPS-enabled tracking device onto the defendant's vehicle (see **Chapter 8**). But in two separate concurrences, five of the Justices also reached the question of whether the government violated the defendant's reasonable expectation of privacy. The concurrences argued that the continuous monitoring of the defendant's public

[8] Knotts, 460 U.S. at 283.

[9] United States v. Karo, 468 U.S. 705, 708-10, 715-16 (1984).

[10] Id. at 283-84.

movements over a four-week period did in fact infringe on the defendant's reasonable expectation of privacy. The concurrences re-affirmed *Knotts*' holding that it is not a Fourth Amendment search to use an electronic device to track one trip on a public road, but argued that it is reasonable for the defendant to assume that the police would not track her for such an extended period of time.[11]

However, the concurrences refrained from creating a bright-line rule to determine when this type of monitoring shifted from a *Knotts* non-search to a comprehensive *Jones*-type Fourth Amendment search. Instead, the Justices merely noted that "the line was surely crossed before the four-week mark."[12]

Courts and scholars have used the term "mosaic" to describe the doctrine articulated in the *Jones* concurrences.[13] The theory is that although one piece of data regarding an individual's movement in public does not infringe on the individual's privacy to any significant extent, hundreds or thousands of pieces of information describing where an individual has travelled in public over a one-month period can be pieced together to reveal quite a bit of private information. As one lower court noted:

> Disclosed in [GPS] data . . . will be trips the indisputably private nature of which takes little imagination to conjure: trips to the psychiatrist, the plastic surgeon, the abortion clinic, the AIDS treatment center, the strip club, the criminal defense attorney, the by-the-hour motel, the union meeting, the mosque, synagogue or church, the gay bar and on and on.[14]

Justice Sotomayor quoted this language in her concurrence in *Jones,* noting that "[t]he Government can store such records and efficiently mine them for information years into the future."[15] As of now, the *Jones* concurrences are merely dicta. But this is surely an area that the Court will return to in order to clarify its position. Although the Court decided the *Jones* case based on the physical trespass of the GPS device on the defendant's car, future cases will likely not involve any physical trespass at all. For example, most individuals carry cell phones whose locations are monitored and recorded by the private cell phone carrier. The government can subpeona an individual's location data from the private company and receive essentially the same information it acquired from the GPS in the *Jones* case, although this time with no physical trespass. Whether this activity will be termed a Fourth Amendment search through application of the mosaic theory is still an open question.

---

[11] United States v. Knotts, 460 U.S. 276, 277-78, 284 (1983).

[12] United States v. Jones, 132 S. Ct. 945, 964 (2012) (Alito, J., concurring).

[13] See. e.g., United States v. Maynard, 615 F.3d 544, 562 (U.S. App. D.C. 2010).

[14] People v. Weaver, 12 N.Y.3d 433, 441–42 (N.Y. 2009).

[15] United States v. Jones, 132 S. Ct. 945, 956 (2012) (Sotomayor, J., concurring).

3. Encryption. For hundreds of years, many criminals, spies, and privacy advocates have encoded their communications in an attempt to keep their messages private. Of course, any amount of encryption will *de facto* give the communication some amount of privacy from the government because the encoding ensures that the message will be difficult for anyone other than the intended recipient to read. The stronger the encryption, the more privacy the message will have. In fact, most modern encryption programs are so powerful that they are literally impossible to decode without the proper key. But this analysis sidesteps an important legal question: does encryption create a reasonable expectation of privacy in the contents of the message? In other words, if the police do find a way to decode an encrypted message or computer file (perhaps by learning the key from a third party), are they conducting a search when they decode the document?

The answer is probably not—encryption on its own probably does not create a reasonable expectation of privacy. Imagine the following scenario, based on a hypothetical from Professor Orin Kerr:[16]

> **Example:** Lex Luthor attempts to blackmail the city of Metropolis. He takes out a full-page advertisement in the city newspaper that reads: "I will destroy Times Square at noon tomorrow unless you wire me $100 million dollars. Here is my secret plan, encrypted so that you will never be able to read it:
>
> J XJMM MFBXF B CPNC VOEFS B QBSLFE DIFWSPMFU UBYJDBC XJUI NPOUBOB MJDFOTF QMBUFT.
>
> The police work all morning on the code and at 11:50 AM they realize that it is a simple substitution cypher: A has been replaced with B, B with C, and so on. They decode the message to read:
>
> I WILL LEAVE A BOMB UNDER A PARKED CHEVROLET TAXICAB
>
> WITH MONTANA LICENSE PLATES.
>
> The police quickly rush to Times Square, find the car, and defuse the bomb just in time. They then arrest Luthor, and during Luthor's trial they seek to admit the decoded message. Luthor moves to preclude this evidence, since the police did not acquire a warrant before decoding the message.

[16] Orin S. Kerr, The Fourth Amendment in Cyberspace: Can Encryption Create a "Reasonable Expectation of Privacy?", 33 Conn. L. Rev. 503, 519-20 (2001).

Analysis: Although Luthor may claim to have a subjective expectation of privacy in his message, his expectation is not reasonable. Instead, courts have analogized encrypted documents to speaking in a foreign language—the speakers may hope that nobody around is able to understand what they are saying, and if the language is an obscure one, they probably will be able to keep the conversation private, but they always assume the risk that what they are saying can be understood by someone. Likewise, a person who encrypts a document assumes the risk that the government will be able to crack the code.

Of course, most encrypted documents are not published in newspapers. If the incriminating encrypted file was on Luthor's personal computer, then the government agents would be conducting a Fourth Amendment search when they read the file—but only because it was kept in a location in which Luthor had a reasonable expectation of privacy, not because of the encryption.

This is far from settled law, however. All of the arguments against encryption creating a reasonable expectation of privacy are based on analogies: encrypted documents are analogous to foreign languages that the police are able to translate, or to shredded documents that police piece back together. Some commentators come to the opposite conclusion by using a different analogy: encryption is like a "lock" that individuals use to hide documents they wish to keep secret, and using this lock is the equivalent of closing an open front door or sealing an opaque container, either of which would create a reasonable expectation of privacy. Since the courts have not yet passed judgment on this issue, good advocacy on either side could convince a judge that a specific encrypted document does or does not deserve Fourth Amendment protection.

4. "Sense-Enhancing" Devices. *Kyllo* tells us that the key question to ask in determining whether a Fourth Amendment search has occurred is whether the technology used in the surveillance is in general public use. This is consistent with the Court's general principle that law enforcement officers are allowed to use relatively unsophisticated devices to aid in their surveillance. It would be unreasonable for an individual to assume that any information or activity which can be detected by such devices should remain private. For example, it is generally permissible for police to use binoculars to look through a suspect's window, or to use a flashlight to scan the backseat of her car, because these are common, unsophisticated technologies that the suspect would reasonably expect others (including the police) to use. But when police used an 800 millimeter telescope from a quarter-mile away to look through the defendant's apartment window, a lower court ruled that using such "powerful" and "sophisticated visual aids" constituted a Fourth Amendment search.[17]

---

[17] United States v. Kim, 415 F. Supp. 1252 (D. Haw. 1976).

This does not mean that a Fourth Amendment search occurs every time the police use sophisticated technology that is not in public use. If the police officers are using advanced technology merely to learn about an activity or gain information which has been knowingly exposed to the public, they are not committing a Fourth Amendment search. The key is to focus on the type of information being recovered, not the technology used to recover it:

> **Example—*Dow Chemical Co. v. United States*, 476 U.S. 227 (1986):** The Environmental Protection Agency conducted an on-site inspection of Dow Chemical's plant with the company's consent. After the company denied a second on-site inspection, the EPA flew a plane over the facility and took pictures with a "precision aerial mapping camera." This was a camera that cost in excess of $22,000 and was able to take several photos in rapid succession, which allowed the EPA to conduct a "stereoscopic examination" that could simulate depth perception.
>
> Dow learned about the high-resolution photographs and sued the EPA in civil court. Dow sought an injunction against further such surveillance, arguing that the EPA was using the sophisticated camera to conduct an unlawful warrantless Fourth Amendment search of its property.

Analysis: The Supreme Court held that the high-quality photographs of Dow's facilities did not constitute a Fourth Amendment search, because "the photographs here are not so revealing of intimate details as to raise constitutional concerns."[18] The majority decision conceded that the precision camera used by the EPA was a very sophisticated device, but noted that the resulting photographs "remain limited to an outline of the facility's buildings and equipment."[19]

The *Dow* case was a close call, however: the decision was 5-4, and even the majority noted in dicta that "surveillance of private property by using highly sophisticated surveillance equipment not generally available to the public, such as satellite technology, might be constitutionally proscribed absent a warrant."[20] The Court also found it significant that the EPA was conducting surveillance on an "industrial complex [that] is more comparable to an open field"[21] than the curtilage of a private home. Given these considerations, it is probably accurate to treat the precision camera in *Dow* as the limit to what the government is allowed to do without a warrant.

---

18 Id. at 238.

19 Dow Chemical Co. v. United States, 476 U.S. 227 (1986).

20 Id.

21 Id. at 239.

The question of whether a surveillance tool is in general public use may also depend on how the device being used. In this regard, courts sometimes draw a distinction between "sense-enhancing" and "sense-replacing" devices. A "sense-replacing" device does not merely magnify an image or sound, but it allows law enforcement officers to detect information they could otherwise never detect. A device that can "see through" clothing or walls would count as a sense-replacing device—for example, a metal detector or an X-ray machine. Because most sense-replacing devices are not in general public use, this type of surveillance is almost always considered to be a search (the metal detectors that we routinely pass through at airports or courthouses are considered Fourth Amendment searches, but they fall under the "special needs" exception to the warrant requirement, as described in **Chapter 18**). Indeed, the dispute in *Kyllo* largely revolved around the different Justices' categorizations of the thermal imager: the majority portrayed the device as a "sense-replacing" device that allowed the police to see through the walls of the house, while the dissent portrayed the thermal imager as merely a "sense-enhancing" device that enhanced the ability of officers to detect heat on the outside of the house.

5. "Legitimate" Expectation of Privacy and Binary Surveillance. The *Katz* test tells us that surveillance implicates the Fourth Amendment if it infringes on the suspect's reasonable expectation of privacy. Later, the Court refined the definition of "reasonable" to emphasize that the suspect's expectation must not only be "justified" but also "legitimate." Assume, for example, that a burglar breaks into a family's isolated vacation home, knowing that the family will not come visit the home for weeks. After he steals all the jewelry in the home, he sits down in the living room and begins to smoke a marijuana cigarette. At that point the police, alerted by a neighbor, burst into the room and see the burglar holding a marijuana cigarette in one hand and a bag of stolen jewelry in the other. The burglar later argues that his Fourth Amendment rights have been violated: he reasonably believed that he would not be disturbed in the living room of an empty, private home. Have the police in fact violated his rights?[22]

The obvious answer is no—the burglar had no right to be inside the home in the first place, and so he cannot argue that he had a reasonable expectation of privacy. This is because his expectation of privacy, though perhaps **justified**, is not **legitimate**, because his presence on the property is unlawful. Thus, the Supreme Court has made it clear that a reasonable expectation of privacy must also involve a **legitimate** interest in the place or property being searched.

This may seem to be a minor point, but it has taken on greater significance with the advent of a new type of surveillance: binary surveillance. In this context, the term "binary" means there are only two possible outcomes—contraband is pres-

[22] This is based on a hypothetical in Rakas v. Illinois, 439 U.S. 128, 143 n.12 (1978).

ent, or contraband is not present—and no other information. The best example of this form of surveillance is a drug-sniffing dog—a dog who will alert only if she detects the presence of narcotics. Theoretically, when the police use a drug dog to sniff someone's car or suitcase, there are only two possible outcomes of the sniff: the police will know that drugs are present, or they will know that drugs are not present. The Supreme Court has held that binary surveillance of this sort is **not** a search. This is because the only information provided to law enforcement is that contraband is present, and the suspect has no legitimate expectation of privacy in possessing contraband:

> **Example—*Illinois v. Caballes*, 543 U.S. 405 (2005):** Roy Caballes was driving from Chicago to Las Vegas when he was pulled over for speeding at 5:04 PM. State trooper Daniel Gillette called the stop into headquarters to check the validity of Caballes' license. He then began writing a warning ticket. Trooper Craig Graham heard the transmission and decided to take his drug detection dog out to the location.
>
> Ten minutes later, while Trooper Gillette was still writing the ticket, Trooper Graham arrived and led his dog around Caballes' car. In less than a minute, the dog alerted to the trunk. The state troopers opened the trunk of the car and found over $250,000 worth of marijuana. Caballes was sentenced to twelve years in prison after a bench trial, but he appealed the verdict, claiming that the dog sniff of his car was a "search" that was conducted without a warrant or probable cause.

Analysis: The Supreme Court upheld Caballes' conviction, ruling that the use of a drug dog was not a search, because it did not "compromise any legitimate interest in privacy." Any surveillance which discloses only the absence or presence of contraband is not a Fourth Amendment search.

The Court distinguished the drug dog from the thermal imager that was used in *Kyllo*. The thermal imager was capable of detecting lawful activity—intimate details of the home—in addition to unlawful activity. "The legitimate expectation that information about perfectly lawful activity will remain private is categorically distinguishable from [Caballes'] hopes or expectations concerning the non-detection of contraband in the car trunk. A dog sniff . . . that reveals no information other than the location of a substance that no individual has any right to possess does not violate the Fourth Amendment."[23]

The *Caballes* case involves a number of important issues, some of which we have not yet discussed. First, there was the ten to twelve minute delay between the

[23] Illinois v. Caballes, 543 U.S. 405, 409-10 (2005).

time Caballes was pulled over and the time the drug dog actually alerted to the trunk. This is known as a seizure. We will discuss the seizure rules in **Chapter 9.** For now, suffice it to say there are rules governing how long officers can detain individuals under different circumstances. Under these rules, the seizure of Caballes was not sufficiently lengthy so as to make his stop unlawful.

Another issue involves the search that occurred when police officers opened Caballes' trunk. Unlike the drug sniff, this was indeed a search under the Fourth Amendment, and so it required a warrant or some exception to the warrant requirement. As we will see in **Chapter 15,** there is an "automobile exception" to the warrant requirement which allows police officers to search a car without a warrant if they have probable cause. The trial court in *Caballes* concluded that the drug dog's alert, plus other suspicious facts about the defendant,[24] generated probable cause. While the length of the detention and the opening of the trunk were relevant issues, the key holding of *Caballes* was that a binary surveillance does not constitute a Fourth Amendment search.

Another example of binary surveillance is the use of a field test to determine whether a substance contains narcotics. In a field test, police apply a set of chemicals to a suspicious substance. If the chemicals react, the substance has tested positive for some type of illegal controlled substance. If there is no reaction, the police have not learned anything else about the substance.[25] Consequently, the use of such tests does not violate the Fourth Amendment.

To date, the most common application of the binary search doctrine has been in the area of drug dogs. This is likely to change in the near future, however. New technologies are being developed which will enable machines or software to transform an illegal search into a legal binary surveillance. For example, in locations where guns are illegal (such as on school grounds or in many bars), law enforcement officers will be able to use gun detectors which use X-rays to see through clothing or closed containers. Such detectors are equipped with image recognition software that analyzes the images it "sees" internally to determine if any of the images resemble a gun. If the software does not recognize the image of a gun, the detector will do nothing. However, if the image is consistent with the outline of a gun, the detector will beep or flash a light, which is the only possible output that it would give to the user. Significantly, if the detector projected all of what it "saw" on a screen, using the device would constitute a Fourth Amendment search. But since the technology only reveals the presence or the absence of an illegal item, it is a type of binary surveillance and is not a Fourth Amendment search.

---

[24] The lower courts noted that the defendant appeared nervous when being questioned and that he claimed to have never been arrested before, when the license check confirmed that he had in fact been arrested twice for drug crimes. People v. Caballes, 802 N.E.2d 202, 202–04 (Ill. 2003).

[25] See United States v. Jacobsen, 466 U.S. 109 (1984).

Law enforcement officers could also employ internet sniffer software that intercepts data travelling through the internet. The software examines all pictures being transmitted and compares those images to known images of child pornography. If images consistent with child pornography are detected, a copy of the image is sent to law enforcement along with the identifying information of the individual who sent it.

As of now, the Fourth Amendment does not regulate binary surveillance, which means that—absent any statutory restrictions—police officers could use gun detectors, internet sniffers, and other technological binary surveillance methods with impunity, as long as their only output was to tell law enforcement whether something illegal was going on. Because these searches only reveal the presence of illegal conduct, they do not infringe on an individual's "legitimate expectation of privacy."

6. Wiretapping, Computer Surveillance, and Statutory Restrictions on Technological Surveillance. With the advent of the telephone, criminals received an enormous boost in their ability to communicate and make plans in secret. This boost was further enhanced in the twentieth century by the widespread availability of computers, the internet, and cell phones. Of course, law enforcement was quick to counter with new surveillance technologies: wiretapping telephones, monitoring computer transmissions, copying hard drives, and using cell phone records to track a suspect's movements.

With regard to data storage, lower courts have consistently applied the *Katz* test to searches of electronic storage media, such as computer hard drives. Judges have analogized electronic data storage with closed containers, such as a briefcase or a purse, in which individuals have a reasonable expectation of privacy. Thus, law enforcement agents are engaging in a Fourth Amendment search when they access the data on a computer or smart phone, and the search is illegal without a warrant or an applicable exception to the warrant requirement.

Courts have struggled to determine how the Fourth Amendment applies to new methods of communication. However, a few principles are relatively clear by applying the *Katz* test to these types of surveillance. First, individuals have a reasonable expectation of privacy in the content of their telephone conversations. Thus, the Fourth Amendment requires a warrant before the government can wiretap a telephone. In theory, this same reasonable expectation of privacy should also extend to electronic communications, such as e-mail and texting. However, as we will see in the next chapter, the "third party doctrine" might provide the government a loophole which will allow it to evade the warrant requirement for electronic communication. In short, it is not clear how much protection the Fourth Amendment provides for electronic communication.

In practice, however, the Fourth Amendment is not the primary focus for evaluating telephonic or electronic communication. As noted earlier, the Fourth Amendment is not the only restriction on how law enforcement conducts its surveillance. Congress and state legislatures have passed a number of laws to regulate police investigations. Nowhere is this more true than in the context of new technologies, specifically surveillance of electronic communication and storage. We will consider these statutes in detail in **Chapters 20 and 21,** but for now you should realize that in order to conduct any real-time surveillance of communications, law enforcement must comply with statutory requirements which are far more onerous than the Fourth Amendment's warrant requirement.

Quick Summary

According to the *Kyllo* test, a new surveillance technology will be deemed a Fourth Amendment search if it allows the police to obtain information "that could not otherwise have been obtained without physical intrusion into a constitutionally protected area." Thus, the thermal imager in *Kyllo* constituted a search because it could have provided police with information about the intimate activities inside the suspect's home. If the police use technology that is in "general public use," such as a flashlight or binoculars, however, they are allowed to look into constitutionally protected areas because it is unreasonable for the suspect to expect privacy in such situations.

Encryption probably does not create a reasonable expectation of privacy, and thus the decoding of encryption alone would not typically be seen as raising questions under the Fourth Amendment. However, that is not to say such surveillance raises no Fourth Amendment concerns. Individuals have a reasonable expectation of privacy in their electronic communications and the contents of their computers. Thus, the police usually must conduct a Fourth Amendment search to access the file or communication that is being decoded, thereby implicating constitutional concerns.

A person's reasonable expectation of privacy must be legitimate, so if the surveillance only detects the presence or absence of illegal activity (a "binary" surveillance), then the surveillance does not constitute a Fourth Amendment search.

Review Questions

1. Tracking a Stolen Phone. A few minutes after midnight, Carolyn Frey was robbed at gunpoint in downtown San Francisco. The perpetrator took her purse, which contained her wallet and a cell phone. When the police learned that the cell phone had a GPS feature, they contacted Sprint, which was Frey's cell phone provider. Sprint told them if Frey signed a release, the company could "ping" the phone and Sprint could then tell the police the location of the phone within ten meters. Frey signed the release, Sprint pinged the phone, and Sprint then informed the police that the telephone was at the intersection of 16th and Mission Street.

Some police officers proceeded to that location and saw Charles Bane, who matched the description of the perpetrator, getting into a car at 16th and Mission Streets. The car began driving north on Mission Street toward 15th Street, and after a second ping Sprint confirmed that the phone was now heading north, passing Mission and 15th Streets. The police officers stopped the car and saw Frey's purse in the backseat. They arrested Bane and charged him with the theft. Bane challenged the use of the GPS, arguing that it infringed on his reasonable expectation of privacy. Did the police use of the GPS violate Bane's Fourth Amendment rights?

2. Credit Card Data. Police received an anonymous tip that a woman named Frieda Davis was committing credit card fraud. The informant told police that Davis would apply for numerous credit cards in her own name, and then doctor the magnetic strip on the back of the card so that when it was swiped it charged someone else's account.

In order to confirm the tip, the police conducted a sting operation at the local Wal-Mart where Davis regularly made purchases. When Davis came to the cash register to purchase some items, she handed her credit card to the cashier, who handed it to an undercover police officer standing nearby. The undercover officer used a device which scanned the magnetic strip on the card and then displayed the number of the account linked to the strip. The officer compared that number to the account number on the front of the card and found that the two were different. He then arrested Davis and searched her pocketbook, finding six different credit cards, all with her name and account number on the front, but all with magnetic strips linked to different account numbers on the back.

Davis was charged with credit card fraud. She challenged the use of the credit card scanner, arguing that the initial scanning of the first credit card was an illegal search of her property. Did the police violate Davis' Fourth Amendment rights?

3. Drones and Soil Samples. Narcotics officers in southern California flew small, unmanned drones over hundreds of acres of farmland. The drones flew at approximately 200 feet of altitude and took thousands of pictures of both the fields and the backyards of farmers. The officers then reviewed the photos, and saw what appeared to be marijuana plants in three different locations:

(a) In a cornfield owned by a man named Gerald Kounter, the photos unambiguously revealed the presence of marijuana plants growing about a half-mile from Kounter's house. The police submitted these photos to a magistrate and obtained a search warrant for Kounter's property and an arrest warrant for Kounter.

(b) In the backyard of a house owned by Theresa Gilmore, the photos also unambiguously revealed the presence of marijuana plants. The plants were inside a fenced backyard only a few feet from Gilmore's house. The police submitted these photos to a magistrate and obtained a search warrant for Gimore's property and an arrest warrant for Gilmore.

(c) In an empty field owned by Andrew Young, the photos revealed what appeared to be opium plants, but the fidelity of the photos was not clear enough to establish probable cause. The area was in a large field over a quarter of a mile from Young's house, not enclosed by any fence and apparently not used for anything other than growing crops. The FBI investigated further by sending two agents onto Young's land without Young's knowledge or consent. When they reached the spot where the potential opium had been growing, they saw that whatever plant had been there had recently been harvested. They then took a small soil sample from the ground and brought it back to their laboratory. Using a new method of chemical analysis, the technicians in the lab were able to determine that opium had recently been grown in the soil. The FBI took this information to a magistrate and obtained a search warrant for Young's house, where they found opium being processed into heroin.

Kounter, Gilmore, and Young were all charged with drug offenses and they all claimed the surveillance of their property by the drone was an unconstitutional search. Young also argued that the analysis of the soil from his property was also an unconstitutional search. How should the court rule in each of these cases?

FROM THE COURTROOM

KYLLO v. UNITED STATES

United States Supreme Court, 2001
533 U.S. 27

[Justice SCALIA delivered the opinion of the Court.]

[Justice STEVENS filed a dissenting opinion, which was joined by Chief Justice REHNQUIST and Justices O'CONNOR and KENNEDY.]

This case presents the question whether the use of a thermal-imaging device aimed at a private home from a public street to detect relative amounts of heat within the home constitutes a "search" within the meaning of the Fourth Amendment.

I

In 1991 Agent William Elliott of the United States Department of the Interior came to suspect that marijuana was being grown in the home belonging to petitioner Danny Kyllo, part of a triplex on Rhododendron Drive in Florence, Oregon. Indoor marijuana growth typically requires high-intensity lamps. In order to determine whether an amount of heat was emanating from petitioner's home consistent with the use of such lamps, at 3:20 a.m. on January 16, 1992, Agent Elliott and Dan Haas used an Agema Thermovision 210 thermal imager to scan the triplex. Thermal imagers detect infrared radiation, which virtually all objects emit but which is not visible to the naked eye. The imager converts radiation into images based on relative warmth—black is cool, white is hot, shades of gray connote relative differences; in that respect, it operates somewhat like a video camera showing heat images. The scan of Kyllo's home took only a few minutes and was performed from the passenger seat of Agent Elliott's vehicle across the street from the front of the house and also from the street in back of the house. The scan showed that the roof over the garage and a side wall of petitioner's home were relatively hot compared to the rest of the home and substantially warmer than neighboring homes in the triplex.

Agent Elliott concluded that petitioner was using halide lights to grow marijuana in his house, which indeed he was. Based on tips from informants, utility bills, and the thermal imaging, a Federal Magistrate Judge issued a warrant authorizing a search of petitioner's home, and the agents found an indoor growing operation involving more than 100 plants. Petitioner was indicted on one count of manufacturing marijuana, in violation of 21 U.S.C. § 841(a)(1). He unsuccessfully moved to suppress the evidence seized from his home and then entered a conditional guilty plea.

The Court of Appeals for the Ninth Circuit remanded the case for an evidentiary hearing regarding the intrusiveness of thermal imaging. On remand the District Court found that the Agema 210 "is a non-intrusive device which emits no rays or beams and shows a crude visual image of the heat being radiated from the outside of the house"; it "did not show any people or activity within the walls of the structure"; "[t]he device used cannot penetrate walls or windows to reveal conversations or human activities"; and "[n]o intimate details of the home were observed." Based on these findings, the District Court upheld the validity of the warrant that relied in part upon the thermal imaging, and reaffirmed its denial of the motion to suppress. A divided Court of Appeals initially reversed, but that opinion was withdrawn and the panel (after a change in composition) affirmed, with Judge Noonan dissenting. The court held that petitioner had shown no subjective expectation of privacy because he had made no attempt to conceal the heat escaping from his home, and even if he had, there was no objectively reasonable expectation of privacy because the imager "did not expose any intimate details of Kyllo's life," only "amorphous 'hot spots' on the roof and exterior wall." We granted certiorari.

II

The Fourth Amendment provides that "[t]he right of the people to be secure in their persons, houses, papers, and effects, against unreasonable searches and seizures, shall not be violated." "At the very core" of the Fourth Amendment "stands the right of a man to retreat into his own home and there be free from unreasonable governmental intrusion." With few exceptions, the question whether a warrantless search of a home is reasonable and hence constitutional must be answered no..

On the other hand, the antecedent question whether or not a Fourth Amendment "search" has occurred is not so simple under our precedent. The permissibility of ordinary visual surveillance of a home used to be clear because, well into the 20th century, our Fourth Amendment jurisprudence was tied to common-law trespass. Visual surveillance was unquestionably lawful because "'the eye cannot by the laws of England be guilty of a trespass.'" . . . As we observed in *California v. Ciraolo,* 476 U.S. 207, 213 (1986), "[t]he Fourth Amendment protection of the home has never been extended to require law enforcement officers to shield their eyes when passing by a home on public thoroughfares."

One might think that the new validating rationale would be that examining the portion of a house that is in plain public view, while it is a "search" despite the absence of trespass, is not an "unreasonable" one under the Fourth Amendment. But in fact we have held that visual observation is no "search" at all—perhaps in order to preserve somewhat more intact our doctrine that warrantless searches are presumptively unconstitutional. In assessing when a search is not a search, we have applied somewhat in reverse the principle first enunciated in *Katz v. United States,* 389 U.S. 347 (1967). *Katz* involved eavesdropping by means of an electronic listening device placed on the outside of a telephone booth—a location not within the catalog ("persons, houses, papers, and effects") that the Fourth Amendment protects against unreasonable searches. We held that the Fourth Amendment nonetheless protected Katz from the warrantless eavesdropping because he "justifiably relied" upon the privacy of the telephone booth.

As Justice Harlan's oft-quoted concurrence described it, a Fourth Amendment search occurs when the government violates a subjective expectation of privacy that society recognizes as reasonable. We have subsequently applied this principle to hold that a Fourth Amendment search does *not* occur—even when the explicitly protected location of a *house* is concerned—unless "the individual manifested a subjective expectation of privacy in the object of the challenged search," and "society [is] willing to recognize that expectation as reasonable." . . .

The present case involves officers on a public street engaged in more than naked-eye surveillance of a home. We have previously reserved judgment as to how much technological enhancement of ordinary perception from such a vantage point, if any, is too much. While we upheld enhanced aerial photography of an industrial complex in *Dow Chemical,* we noted that we found "it important that this is *not* an area immediately adjacent to a private home, where privacy expectations are most heightened."

III

It would be foolish to contend that the degree of privacy secured to citizens by the Fourth Amendment has been entirely unaffected by the advance of technology. For example, as the cases discussed above make clear, the technology enabling human flight has exposed to public view (and hence, we have said, to official observation) uncovered portions of the house and its curtilage that once were private. The question we confront today is what limits there are upon this power of technology to shrink the realm of guaranteed privacy.

The *Katz* test—whether the individual has an expectation of privacy that society is prepared to recognize as reasonable—has often been criticized as circular, and hence subjective and unpredictable. While it may be difficult to refine *Katz* when the search of areas such as telephone booths, automobiles, or even the curtilage and uncovered portions of residences is at issue, in the case of the search of the interior of homes—the prototypical and hence most commonly litigated area of protected privacy—there is a ready criterion, with roots deep in the common law, of the minimal expectation of privacy that *exists,* and that is acknowledged to be *reasonable.* To withdraw protection of this minimum expectation would be to permit police technology to erode the privacy guaranteed by the Fourth Amendment. We think that obtaining by sense-enhancing technology any information regarding the interior of the home that could not otherwise have been obtained without physical "intrusion into a constitutionally protected area," constitutes a search—at least where (as here) the technology in question is not in general public use. This assures preservation of that degree of privacy against government that existed when the Fourth Amendment was adopted. On the basis of this criterion, the information obtained by the thermal imager in this case was the product of a search.[2]

---

[2] The dissent's repeated assertion that the thermal imaging did not obtain information regarding the interior of the home is simply inaccurate. A thermal imager reveals the relative heat of various rooms in the home. The dissent may not find that information particularly private or important, but there is no basis for saying it is not information regarding the interior of the home. The dissent's comparison of the thermal imaging to various circumstances in which outside observers might be able to perceive,

The Government maintains, however, that the thermal imaging must be upheld because it detected "only heat radiating from the external surface of the house." The dissent makes this its leading point, contending that there is a fundamental difference between what it calls "off-the-wall" observations and "through-the-wall surveillance." But just as a thermal imager captures only heat emanating from a house, so also a powerful directional microphone picks up only sound emanating from a house-and a satellite capable of scanning from many miles away would pick up only visible light emanating from a house. We rejected such a mechanical interpretation of the Fourth Amendment in *Katz,* where the eavesdropping device picked up only sound waves that reached the exterior of the phone booth. Reversing that approach would leave the homeowner at the mercy of advancing technology—including imaging technology that could discern all human activity in the home. While the technology used in the present case was relatively crude, the rule we adopt must take account of more sophisticated systems that are already in use or in development. The dissent's reliance on the distinction between "off-the-wall" and "through-the-wall" observation is entirely incompatible with the dissent's belief, which we discuss below, that thermal-imaging observations of the intimate details of a home are impermissible. The most sophisticated thermal-imaging devices continue to measure heat "off-the-wall" rather than "through-the-wall"; the dissent's disapproval of those more sophisticated thermal-imaging devices is an acknowledgement that there is no substance to this distinction. As for the dissent's extraordinary assertion that anything learned through "an inference" cannot be a search that would validate even the "through-the-wall" technologies that the dissent purports to disapprove. Surely the dissent does not believe that the through-the-wall radar or ultrasound technology produces an 8–by–10 Kodak glossy that needs no analysis (*i.e.,* the making of inferences). And, of course, the novel proposition that inference insulates a search is blatantly contrary to *United States v. Karo,* 468 U.S. 705 (1984), where the police "inferred" from the activation of a beeper that a certain can of ether was in the home. The police activity was held to be a search, and the search was held unlawful.

The Government also contends that the thermal imaging was constitutional because it did not "detect private activities occurring in private areas." It points out that in *Dow Chemical* we observed that the enhanced aerial photography did not reveal any "intimate details." *Dow Chemical,* however, involved enhanced aerial photography of an industrial complex, which does not share the Fourth Amendment sanctity of the home. The Fourth Amendment's protection of the home has never been tied to measurement of the quality or quantity of information obtained. In *Silverman,* for example, we made clear that any physical invasion of the structure of the home, "by even a fraction of an inch," was too much, and there is certainly no exception to the warrant requirement for the officer who barely cracks open the front door and sees

---

without technology, the heat of the home—for example, by observing snowmelt on the roof—is quite irrelevant. The fact that equivalent information could sometimes be obtained by other means does not make lawful the use of means that violate the Fourth Amendment. The police might, for example, learn how many people are in a particular house by setting up year-round surveillance; but that does not make breaking and entering to find out the same information lawful. In any event, on the night of January 16, 1992, no outside observer could have discerned the relative heat of Kyllo's home without thermal imaging.

nothing but the nonintimate rug on the vestibule floor. In the home, our cases show, *all* details are intimate details, because the entire area is held safe from prying government eyes. Thus, in *Karo,* the only thing detected was a can of ether in the home; and in *Arizona v. Hicks,* 480 U.S. 321 (1987), the only thing detected by a physical search that went beyond what officers lawfully present could observe in "plain view" was the registration number of a phonograph turntable. These were intimate details because they were details of the home, just as was the detail of how warm—or even how relatively warm—Kyllo was heating his residence.

Limiting the prohibition of thermal imaging to "intimate details" would not only be wrong in principle; it would be impractical in application, failing to provide "a workable accommodation between the needs of law enforcement and the interests protected by the Fourth Amendment," To begin with, there is no necessary connection between the sophistication of the surveillance equipment and the "intimacy" of the details that it observes—which means that one cannot say (and the police cannot be assured) that use of the relatively crude equipment at issue here will always be lawful. The Agema Thermovision 210 might disclose, for example, at what hour each night the lady of the house takes her daily sauna and bath—a detail that many would consider "intimate"; and a much more sophisticated system might detect nothing more intimate than the fact that someone left a closet light on. We could not, in other words, develop a rule approving only that through-the-wall surveillance which identifies objects no smaller than [thirty-six] by [thirty-six] inches, but would have to develop a jurisprudence specifying which home activities are "intimate" and which are not. And even when (if ever) that jurisprudence were fully developed, no police officer would be able to know *in advance* whether his through-the-wall surveillance picks up "intimate" details—and thus would be unable to know in advance whether it is constitutional.

The dissent's proposed standard—whether the technology offers the "functional equivalent of actual presence in the area being searched,"—would seem quite similar to our own at first blush. The dissent concludes that *Katz* was such a case, but then inexplicably asserts that if the same listening device only revealed the volume of the conversation, the surveillance would be permissible. Yet if, without technology, the police could not discern volume without being actually present in the phone booth, Justice STEVENS should conclude a search has occurred. Cf. *Karo,* 468 U.S., at 735. (STEVENS, J., concurring in part and dissenting in part) ("I find little comfort in the Court's notion that no invasion of privacy occurs until a listener obtains some significant information by use of the device . . . . A bathtub is a less private area when the plumber is present even if his back is turned"). The same should hold for the interior heat of the home if only a person present in the home could discern the heat. Thus the driving force of the dissent, despite its recitation of the above standard, appears to be a distinction among different types of information—whether the "homeowner would even care if anybody noticed." The dissent offers no practical guidance for the application of this standard, and for reasons already discussed, we believe there can be none. The people in their houses, as well as the police, deserve more precision.

We have said that the Fourth Amendment draws "a firm line at the entrance to the house." That line, we think, must be not only firm but also bright—which requires clear specification of those methods of surveillance that require a warrant. While it is certainly possible to conclude from the videotape of the thermal imaging that occurred in this case that no "significant" compromise of the homeowner's privacy has occurred, we must take the long view, from the original meaning of the Fourth Amendment forward.

> "The Fourth Amendment is to be construed in the light of what was deemed an unreasonable search and seizure when it was adopted, and in a manner which will conserve public interests as well as the interests and rights of individual citizens." *Carroll v. United States,* 267 U.S. 132 (1925).

Where, as here, the Government uses a device that is not in general public use, to explore details of the home that would previously have been unknowable without physical intrusion, the surveillance is a "search" and is presumptively unreasonable without a warrant.

Since we hold the Thermovision imaging to have been an unlawful search, it will remain for the District Court to determine whether, without the evidence it provided, the search warrant issued in this case was supported by probable cause—and if not, whether there is any other basis for supporting admission of the evidence that the search pursuant to the warrant produced.

The judgment of the Court of Appeals is reversed; the case is remanded for further proceedings consistent with this opinion.

It is so ordered.

Justice STEVENS dissented, joined by Chief Justice REHNQUIST and Justices O'CONNOR and KENNEDY.

. . .

II

Instead of trying to answer the question whether the use of the thermal imager in this case was even arguably unreasonable, the Court has fashioned a rule that is intended to provide essential guidance for the day when "more sophisticated systems" gain the "ability to 'see' through walls and other opaque barriers." The newly minted rule encompasses "obtaining [1] by sense-enhancing technology [2] any information regarding the interior of the home [3] that could not otherwise have been obtained without physical intrusion into a constitutionally protected area . . . [4] at least where (as here) the technology in question is not in general public use." In my judgment, the Court's new rule is at once too broad and too narrow, and is not justified by the Court's explanation for its adoption. As I have suggested, I would not erect a constitutional impediment to the use of sense-enhancing technology unless it provides its user with the functional equivalent of actual presence in the area being searched.

Despite the Court's attempt to draw a line that is "not only firm but also bright," the contours of its new rule are uncertain because its protection apparently dissipates as soon as the relevant technology is "in general public use." Yet how much use is general public use is not even hinted at by the Court's opinion, which makes the somewhat doubtful assumption that the thermal imager used in this case does not satisfy that criterion.[5] In any event, putting aside its lack of clarity, this criterion is somewhat perverse because it seems likely that the threat to privacy will grow, rather than recede, as the use of intrusive equipment becomes more readily available.

It is clear, however, that the category of "sense-enhancing technology" covered by the new rule is far too broad. It would, for example, embrace potential mechanical substitutes for dogs trained to react when they sniff narcotics. But in *United States v. Place,* 462 U.S. 696 (1983), we held that a dog sniff that "discloses only the presence or absence of narcotics" does "not constitute a 'search' within the meaning of the Fourth Amendment," and it must follow that sense-enhancing equipment that identifies nothing but illegal activity is not a search either. Nevertheless, the use of such a device would be unconstitutional under the Court's rule, as would the use of other new devices that might detect the odor of deadly bacteria or chemicals for making a new type of high explosive, even if the devices (like the dog sniffs) are "so limited both in the manner in which" they obtain information and "in the content of the information" they reveal. If nothing more than that sort of information could be obtained by using the devices in a public place to monitor emissions from a house, then their use would be no more objectionable than the use of the thermal imager in this case.

The application of the Court's new rule to "any information regarding the interior of the home," is also unnecessarily broad. If it takes sensitive equipment to detect an odor that identifies criminal conduct and nothing else, the fact that the odor emanates from the interior of a home should not provide it with constitutional protection. The criterion, moreover, is too sweeping in that information "regarding" the interior of a home apparently is not just information obtained through its walls, but also information concerning the outside of the building that could lead to (however many) inferences "regarding" what might be inside. Under that expansive view, I suppose, an officer using an infrared camera to observe a man silently entering the side door of a house at night carrying a pizza might conclude that its interior is now occupied by someone who likes pizza, and by doing so the officer would be guilty of conducting an unconstitutional "search" of the home.

Because the new rule applies to information regarding the "interior" of the home, it is too narrow as well as too broad. Clearly, a rule that is designed to protect individuals from the overly intrusive use of sense-enhancing equipment should not be limited to a home. If such equipment did provide its user with the functional equivalent of access to a private place—such as, for example, the telephone booth involved in *Katz,* or an office building—then the rule should apply to such an area as well as to a home.

[5] The record describes a device that numbers close to a thousand manufactured units; that has a predecessor numbering in the neighborhood of 4,000 to 5,000 units; that competes with a similar product numbering from 5,000 to 6,000 units; and that is "readily available to the public" for commercial, personal, or law enforcement purposes, and is just an 800–number away from being rented from "half a dozen national companies" by anyone who wants one. Since, by virtue of the Court's new rule, the issue is one of first impression, perhaps it should order an evidentiary hearing to determine whether these facts suffice to establish "general public use."

The final requirement of the Court's new rule, that the information "could not otherwise have been obtained without physical intrusion into a constitutionally protected area," also extends too far as the Court applies it. As noted, the Court effectively treats the mental process of analyzing data obtained from external sources as the equivalent of a physical intrusion into the home. . . . [T]he process of drawing inferences from data in the public domain should not be characterized as a search.

. . .

III

Although the Court is properly and commendably concerned about the threats to privacy that may flow from advances in the technology available to the law enforcement profession, it has unfortunately failed to heed the tried and true counsel of judicial restraint. Instead of concentrating on the rather mundane issue that is actually presented by the case before it, the Court has endeavored to craft an all-encompassing rule for the future. It would be far wiser to give legislators an unimpeded opportunity to grapple with these emerging issues rather than to shackle them with prematurely devised constitutional constraints.

I respectfully dissent.

FROM THE COURTROOM

ILLINOIS v. CABALLES

United States Supreme Court, 2005
543 U.S. 405

[Justice STEVENS delivered the opinion of the Court.]

[Justice SOUTER filed a dissenting opinon.]

Justice GINSBURG filed a dissenting opinion, which was joined by Justice SOUTER.]

[Chief Justice REHNQUIST took no part in deciding the case.]

Illinois State Trooper Daniel Gillette stopped respondent for speeding on an interstate highway. When Gillette radioed the police dispatcher to report the stop, a second trooper, Craig Graham, a member of the Illinois State Police Drug Interdiction Team, overheard the transmission and immediately headed for the scene with his narcotics-detection dog. When they arrived, respondent's car was on the shoulder of the road and respondent was in Gillette's vehicle. While Gillette was in the process of writing a warning ticket, Graham walked his dog around respondent's car. The dog alerted at the trunk. Based on that alert, the officers searched the trunk, found marijuana, and arrested respondent. The entire incident lasted less than [ten] minutes.

Respondent was convicted of a narcotics offense and sentenced to [twelve] years' imprisonment and a $256,136 fine. The trial judge denied his motion to suppress the seized evidence and to quash his arrest. He held that the officers had not unnecessarily prolonged the stop and that the dog alert was sufficiently reliable to provide probable cause to conduct the search. Although the Appellate Court affirmed, the Illinois Supreme Court reversed, concluding that because the canine sniff was performed without any "'specific and articulable facts'" to suggest drug activity, the use of the dog "unjustifiably enlarg[ed] the scope of a routine traffic stop into a drug investigation."

The question on which we granted certiorari is narrow: "Whether the Fourth Amendment requires reasonable, articulable suspicion to justify using a drug-detection dog to sniff a vehicle during a legitimate traffic stop." Thus, we proceed on the assumption that the officer conducting the dog sniff had no information about respondent except that he had been stopped for speeding; accordingly, we have omitted any reference to facts about respondent that might have triggered a modicum of suspicion.

Here, the initial seizure of respondent when he was stopped on the highway was based on probable cause and was concededly lawful. It is nevertheless clear that a seizure that is lawful at its inception can violate the Fourth Amendment if its manner of execution unreasonably infringes interests protected by the Constitution. A seizure that is justified solely by the interest in issuing a warning ticket to the driver can become unlawful if it is prolonged beyond the time reasonably required to complete that mission. In an earlier case involving a dog sniff that occurred during an unreasonably prolonged traffic stop, the Illinois Supreme Court held that use of the dog and the subsequent discovery of contraband were the product of an unconstitutional seizure. We may assume that a similar result would be warranted in this case if the dog sniff had been conducted while respondent was being unlawfully detained.

In the state-court proceedings, however, the judges carefully reviewed the details of Officer Gillette's conversations with respondent and the precise timing of his radio transmissions to the dispatcher to determine whether he had improperly extended the duration of the stop to enable the dog sniff to occur. We have not recounted those details because we accept the state court's conclusion that the duration of the stop in this case was entirely justified by the traffic offense and the ordinary inquiries incident to such a stop.

Despite this conclusion, the Illinois Supreme Court held that the initially lawful traffic stop became an unlawful seizure solely as a result of the canine sniff that occurred outside respondent's stopped car. That is, the court characterized the dog sniff as the cause rather than the consequence of a constitutional violation. In its view, the use of the dog converted the citizen-police encounter from a lawful traffic stop into a drug investigation, and because the shift in purpose was not supported by any reasonable suspicion that respondent possessed narcotics, it was unlawful.

In our view, conducting a dog sniff would not change the character of a traffic stop that is lawful at its inception and otherwise executed in a reasonable manner, unless the dog sniff itself infringed respondent's constitutionally protected interest in privacy. Our cases hold that it did not.

Official conduct that does not "compromise any legitimate interest in privacy" is not a search subject to the Fourth Amendment. We have held that any interest in possessing contraband cannot be deemed "legitimate," and thus, governmental conduct that *only* reveals the possession of contraband "compromises no legitimate privacy interest." This is because the expectation "that certain facts will not come to the attention of the authorities" is not the same as an interest in "privacy that society is prepared to consider reasonable." In *United States v. Place*, 462 U.S. 696 (1983), we treated a canine sniff by a well-trained narcotics-detection dog as "*sui generis* " because it "discloses only the presence or absence of narcotics, a contraband item." Respondent likewise concedes that "drug sniffs are designed, and if properly conducted are generally likely, to reveal only the presence of contraband." Although respondent argues that the error rates, particularly the existence of false positives, call into question the premise that drug-detection dogs alert only to contraband, the record contains no evidence or findings that support his argument. Moreover, respondent does not suggest that an erroneous alert, in and of itself, reveals any legitimate private information, and, in this case, the trial judge found that the dog sniff was sufficiently reliable to establish probable cause to conduct a full-blown search of the trunk.

Accordingly, the use of a well-trained narcotics-detection dog—one that "does not expose noncontraband items that otherwise would remain hidden from public view,"—during a lawful traffic stop, generally does not implicate legitimate privacy interests. In this case, the dog sniff was performed on the exterior of respondent's car while he was lawfully seized for a traffic violation. Any intrusion on respondent's privacy expectations does not rise to the level of a constitutionally cognizable infringement.

This conclusion is entirely consistent with our recent decision that the use of a thermal-imaging device to detect the growth of marijuana in a home constituted an unlawful search. *Kyllo v. United States*, 533 U.S. 27 (2001). Critical to that decision was the fact that the device was capable of detecting lawful activity—in that case, intimate details in a home, such as "at what hour each night the lady of the house takes her daily sauna and bath." The legitimate expectation that information about perfectly lawful activity will remain private is categorically distinguishable from respondent's hopes or expectations concerning the nondetection of contraband in the trunk of his car. A dog sniff conducted during a concededly lawful traffic stop that reveals no information other than the location of a substance that no individual has any right to possess does not violate the Fourth Amendment.

The judgment of the Illinois Supreme Court is vacated, and the case is remanded for further proceedings not inconsistent with this opinion.

It is so ordered.

Justice SOUTER, dissenting.

I would hold that using the dog for the purposes of determining the presence of marijuana in the car's trunk was a search unauthorized as an incident of the speeding stop and unjustified on any other ground. I would accordingly affirm the judgment of the Supreme Court of Illinois, and I respectfully dissent.

In *United States v. Place*, 462 U.S. 696 (1983), we categorized the sniff of the narcotics-seeking dog as "*sui generis*" under the Fourth Amendment and held it was not a search. The classification rests not only upon the limited nature of the intrusion, but on a further premise that experience has shown to be untenable, the assumption that trained sniffing dogs do not err. What we have learned about the fallibility of dogs in the years since *Place* was decided would itself be reason to call for reconsidering *Place*'s decision against treating the intentional use of a trained dog as a search. The portent of this very case, however, adds insistence to the call, for an uncritical adherence to *Place* would render the Fourth Amendment indifferent to suspicionless and indiscriminate sweeps of cars in parking garages and pedestrians on sidewalks; if a sniff is not preceded by a seizure subject to Fourth Amendment notice, it escapes Fourth Amendment review entirely unless it is treated as a search. We should not wait for these developments to occur before rethinking *Place*'s analysis, which invites such untoward consequences.

At the heart both of *Place* and the Court's opinion today is the proposition that sniffs by a trained dog are *sui generis* because a reaction by the dog in going alert is a response to nothing but the presence of contraband. Hence, the argument goes, because the sniff can only reveal the presence of items devoid of any legal use, the sniff "does not implicate legitimate privacy interests" and is not to be treated as a search.

The infallible dog, however, is a creature of legal fiction. Although the Supreme Court of Illinois did not get into the sniffing averages of drug dogs, their supposed infallibility is belied by judicial opinions describing well-trained animals sniffing and alerting with less than perfect accuracy, whether owing to errors by their handlers, the limitations of the dogs themselves, or even the pervasive contamination of currency by cocaine. Indeed, a study cited by Illinois in this case for the proposition that dog sniffs are "generally reliable" shows that dogs in artificial testing situations return false positives anywhere from 12.5% to 60% of the time, depending on the length of the search. In practical terms, the evidence is clear that the dog that alerts hundreds of times will be wrong dozens of times.

Once the dog's fallibility is recognized, however, that ends the justification claimed in *Place* for treating the sniff as *sui generis* under the Fourth Amendment: the sniff alert does not necessarily signal hidden contraband, and opening the container or enclosed space whose emanations the dog has sensed will not necessarily reveal contraband or any other evidence of crime. This is not, of course, to deny that a dog's reaction may provide reasonable suspicion, or probable cause, to search the container or enclosure; the Fourth Amendment does not demand certainty of success to justify a search for evidence or contraband. The point is simply that the sniff and alert cannot claim the certainty that *Place* assumed, both in treating the deliberate use of sniffing dogs as *sui generis* and then taking that characterization as a reason to say they are not searches subject to Fourth Amendment scrutiny. And when that aura of uniqueness disappears, there is no basis in *Place*'s reasoning, and no good reason otherwise, to ignore the actual function that dog sniffs perform. They are conducted to obtain information about the contents of private spaces beyond anything that human senses could perceive, even when conventionally enhanced. The information is not provided by independent third parties beyond the reach of constitutional limitations, but gathered by the government's own officers in order to justify searches of the traditional sort, which may or may not reveal evidence of crime but will disclose anything meant to be kept private in the area searched. Thus in practice the government's use of a trained narcotics dog functions as a limited search to reveal undisclosed facts about private enclosures, to be used to justify a further and complete search of the enclosed area. And given the fallibility of the dog, the sniff is the first step in a process that may disclose "intimate details" without revealing contraband, just as a thermal-imaging device might do, as described in *Kyllo v. United States*, 533 U.S. 27 (2001).

It makes sense, then, to treat a sniff as the search that it amounts to in practice, and to rely on the body of our Fourth Amendment cases, including *Kyllo*, in deciding whether such a search is reasonable. As a general proposition, using a dog to sniff for drugs is subject to the rule that the object of enforcing criminal laws does not, without more, justify suspicionless Fourth Amendment intrusions.

. . .

The Court today does not go so far as to say explicitly that sniff searches by dogs trained to sense contraband always get a free pass under the Fourth Amendment, since it reserves judgment on the constitutional significance of sniffs assumed to be more intrusive than a dog's walk around a stopped car. For this reason, I do not take the Court's reliance on *Jacobsen* as actually signaling recognition of a broad authority to conduct suspicionless sniffs for drugs in any parked car . . . or on the person of any pedestrian minding his own business on a sidewalk. But the Court's stated reasoning provides no apparent stopping point short of such excesses. For the sake of providing a workable framework to analyze cases on facts like these, which are certain to come along, I would treat the dog sniff as the familiar search it is in fact, subject to scrutiny under the Fourth Amendment.

[The dissenting opinion of Justice GINSBURG, with whom Justice SOUTER joins, is omitted.]

8

The Fourth Amendment and Third Parties

Key Concepts

- Information Shared with Third Parties Is Generally Not Protected By the Fourth Amendment
- Address Information Is Always Unprotected; Content Information May Be Protected

A. Introduction and Policy. *Katz* tells us that a surveillance implicates the Fourth Amendment if it infringes on the suspect's reasonable expectation of privacy. But what if the suspect has shared the private information with a third party? This can happen in a number of different contexts: the suspect could tell confidential information to a friend; she could hand over private documents to a company like a bank or an accountant for processing or safekeeping; or she could entrust a private communication to a telephone company or an internet server, expecting the company to deliver the message to its recipient. Alternatively, information might be revealed to a third party if the suspect allows a friend to stay in her home or drive her car, thereby allowing the friend to observe all kinds of information. Later on, that friend might report what he heard to the police, or the company might turn over the documents or communication to the government. Does the suspect forfeit her reasonable expectation of privacy in certain information just because she has shared that information with one other person or a company?

For the most part, the answer is yes. When an individual shares information with a third party, the Court has found that he or she assumes the risk that the third party will turn the information over to the police. According to the majority opinion in *Katz*, a suspect does not receive Fourth Amendment protection for any information that she "knowingly exposes to the public."[1] The Supreme Court has interpreted "knowing exposure to the public" to mean "knowing exposure to any single individual or company"—at least if the individual or company with whom the suspect shared the secret becomes willing to (or is later required to) turn the information over to law enforcement.

This rule was controversial when it was created back in the 1960s. Justice Marshall, who dissented in the case which originally set out this rule, noted that "[i]mplicit in the concept of assumption of risk is some notion of choice."[2] He pointed out

[1] United States v. Katz, 389 U.S. 347, 351 (1967).

[2] Smith v. Maryland, 422 U.S. 735, 749 (1979) (Marshall, J., dissenting).

that in many cases, individuals were not really "choosing" to share information; they were effectively forced to share in order to function in the complex economy of the 1960s. For example, every telephone number that a person dials is by necessity shared with the telephone company, and the only way to avoid that information from becoming public would be to forgo the use of the telephone entirely, which was not a realistic alternative.

Today, the concerns voiced some fifty years ago are increasingly salient. Modern life requires the knowing disclosure of staggering amounts of information to third parties. For example, credit card companies, banks, and other financial institutions have exhaustive records of most financial transactions that we conduct. Internet and cellular service providers maintain detailed information about phone calls, texts, and e-mails. And much of the information that we store on our computers is transferred to and sometimes stored on distant servers, such as cloud computing, which involves storing data at a remote location. We are already seeing some lower courts challenging the third-party rule in certain contexts, and, as noted in **Chapter** 7, at least one Supreme Court Justice has hinted at the need to change the doctrine.

B. The Law. The general rule of law regarding third parties as they relate to the Fourth Amendment is as follows:

> If an individual <u>knowingly</u> <u>shares</u> information with a third party, the government can retrieve that information <u>from the third party</u> without implicating the Fourth Amendment.

The rule is referred to somewhat interchangeably as the "third-party disclosure" or "assumption of risk" doctrine. This is because, as noted above, the Court has found when you share information with a third party you assume the risk that they will disclose that information to law enforcement.

There are a few important points to note about this rule. First, the government must receive the information **from the third party**. In other words, the third-party doctrine only allows the government access to the information if the third party turns the information over to the government; the suspect still maintains a reasonable expectation of privacy in the information in every other way. For example, assume Jim sends a letter to his friend Sally detailing his involvement in a recent kidnapping. Jim types the letter on his laptop, prints out a copy, and sends it to Sally. The letter now exists both in digital form on his computer's disk drive and as a hard copy that Sally receives. If Sally decides to take the letter and give it to the police, the police can read the letter without implicating Jim's Fourth Amendment rights—that is, they are not conducting a search within the meaning of the Fourth Amendment when they read the letter. In other words, Jim has assumed the risk that Sally will give the letter to the government. Note that this risk includes both the risk that Sally will **voluntarily** turn the information over to the government and the risk that the government will force Sally to turn over the information by subpoenaing the letter.

However, Jim still has a reasonable expectation of privacy in the letter which is stored on his hard drive. If the police open up his laptop, access the document on his hard drive, and read the letter, they have conducted a Fourth Amendment search. In other words, the third-party doctrine does **not** state that an individual gives up all privacy rights when he or she shares information with a third party; he only assumes the risk that the third party will turn the information over to the government. Significantly, the third-party doctrine does not apply to the contents of letters given to the post office, since postal employees are legally forbidden from opening the letter and reading its contents.

Second, information that an individual shares with a third party can end up in the government's hands in one of two ways. If the third party believes the information is incriminating and wants the government to know about it, she can voluntarily contact the government and hand over the information. But even if the third party does not want to share the information, the government can force disclosure if it knows that the third party has the information. The requirements for a subpoena are relatively minimal: the request must be specific, it may not create an undue burden, and the information being sought must be relevant to a criminal investigation. Therefore, a third party who does not wish to turn over information pursuant to a subpoena can try to challenge or quash the subpoena, but is unlikely to succeed. For example, the Department of Justice can reach out to a search engine such as Google and ask for the search terms used by visitors to the site. Google can challenge the subpoena, but only by arguing that the subpoena is overbroad or creates an undue burden on Google—not by arguing that the information is protected by the Fourth Amendment.

Third, the third-party doctrine only applies if the suspect "**knowingly**" shares information with a third party. If the government directs a third party to eavesdrop on the suspect or to secretly copy the suspect's private records without the suspect's knowledge, the third party (as a government agent) has conducted a Fourth Amendment search.

Finally, the law is currently in flux regarding what it means to "**share**" information. The third-party disclosure rule originally established in the 1960s and 1970s was fairly capacious. A suspect was deemed to have "shared" information (and thus assumed the risk of disclosure) anytime she gave a third party legal access to the information. This was true even if the suspect provided access to the information for limited reasons. It was also true without regard for how the third party typically used the information. But this broad understanding of "sharing" has fallen under attack given the advent of modern digital communication. Internet service providers (ISPs) have access to the contents of all of the information that they transmit: address information, search engine requests, web pages that are visited, and the contents of texts and e-mails. A formalist interpretation of the third-party doctrine would mean that the government could request (or force) the ISP to turn over all of this information to law enforcement without implicating the Fourth Amendment. In light of these (and other) concerns, numerous circuit courts are now attempting to redefine what type of "sharing" will trigger application of the third-party disclosure doctrine.

C. Applying the Law. This rule applies in many different contexts, from the use of police informants to the entrusting of documents to companies. We will start with the easiest (and least controversial) aspects of this rule, and move to the more complicated (and most controversial) applications.

1. Police Informants. The Supreme Court has held that the Fourth Amendment does not apply when a suspect tells information to a "friend" who then gives the information to the police:

> **Example—*Hoffa v. United States*, 385 U.S. 293 (1966):** In 1962, labor leader Jimmy Hoffa was tried for numerous violations of federal law. Federal prosecutors suspected that Hoffa might be bribing some of the jurors in order to avoid conviction. Thus, during the trial the prosecutors worked with Edward Partin, a local labor leader, to try to determine the truth of their suspicions. Partin was under indictment for his own crimes, so he was willing to help the government in its case against Hoffa. Partin visited Hoffa in his hotel suite several times during the trial. During these visits, Partin heard Hoffa make a number of incriminating statements, both to Partin and to others in the room while Partin was present. For example, at one point Hoffa told Partin he would "pay fifteen or twenty thousand dollars, whatever—whatever it cost to get to the jury;" and at other points Partin heard Hoffa ordering others to deliver bribes to various jurors. Partin duly reported all of these statements to federal prosecutors.
>
> Hoffa's trial ended in a hung jury, and prosecutors then brought bribery charges against Hoffa. At Hoffa's bribery trial, Partin testified as to the statements he heard Hoffa make. Hoffa objected to this testimony, arguing that using Partin in this way violated his Fourth Amendment rights. Hoffa was ultimately convicted of the bribery, and he appealed the issue to the Supreme Court.

Analysis: The Supreme Court rejected Hoffa's arguments, noting that "[n]either this Court nor any member of it has ever expressed the view that the Fourth Amendment protects a wrongdoer's misplaced belief that a person to whom he voluntarily confides his wrongdoing will not reveal it."[3]

The *Hoffa* case was decided before *Katz*, and so the Court based its decision in part on the argument that the informer Partin had not physically trespassed into Hoffa's suite. But, the Supreme Court affirmed the *Hoffa* ruling in numerous cases after *Katz*, noting that ". . . however strongly a defendant may trust an apparent colleague, his expectations in this respect are not protected by the Fourth Amendment when it turns out that the colleague is a government agent regularly communicating with the authorities."[4] In terms of the *Katz* test, a defendant does not have a "justifiable and constitutionally protected expectation that a person with whom he is conversing will not then or later reveal the conversation to the police."[5] In other words, it is not "reasonable" to assume that the person to whom you are speaking will not report those words to law enforcement, because "inescapably, one contemplating illegal activities must realize and risk that his companions may be reporting to the police."[6]

The Fourth Amendment is also not implicated if the informant is wearing electronic equipment to record the defendant's words,[7] nor if the informant is wearing a wire which transmits the words immediately to the police.[8] Police are also permitted to go undercover themselves and masquerade as a colleague or fellow criminal in order to hear and observe evidence of criminal behavior.[9]

The critical factor in all of these scenarios is that the defendant must know that the third party is present (though of course the defendant will not know that the third party is an informant or an undercover officer). If the police attempt to eavesdrop with an undercover officer who is hiding in the room, or if they place an electronic listening device without the knowledge of any party to the conversation, they have conducted a search under *Katz*—indeed, that was the precise government conduct at issue in *Katz*.

2. Hotel Maids, Landlords, and House Guests—Third Party Access to Protected Areas. Suppose that Carl is planning to rob a bank. In order to better prepare for his crime, he rents a hotel room near the bank for a few nights before the robbery will occur. He scouts the location numerous times. After each trip, he comes back to his hotel room to take notes on what he has seen and draw maps

[3] Hoffa v. United States, 385 U.S. 293, 302 (1966).
[4] United States v. White, 401 U.S. 745, 749 (1971).
[5] Id.
[6] Id. at 752.
[7] Lopez v. United States, 373 U.S. 427 (1963).
[8] White, 401 U.S. 745.
[9] Lewis v. United States, 385 U.S. 206 (1966).

of the location. While he is out one day, the maid enters the room and becomes suspicious after seeing the maps of the bank and the notes Carl has taken. She reports her observations to the police. Have Carl's Fourth Amendment rights been violated?

The answer is no, for two reasons. For the purposes of the *Katz* test, she has not violated Carl's reasonable expectation of privacy. Carl could not reasonably expect that a maid would not see the information he left in plain view in the room. Carl does have a reasonable expectation of privacy in the hotel room generally, just as Katz had when he closed the door of his telephone booth. And as we saw in **Chapter 6**, Carl has standing to object to a search of his hotel room, even though he is only renting it. However, he has implicitly given the maid access to the room, and so he cannot reasonably assume she will keep what she sees confidential.

The second reason, as discussed in **Chapter 4**, is that the maid is not a state actor, and so none of her actions are covered by the Fourth Amendment. If the police asked her to go into the room and look for incriminating information, she would be acting as an agent of law enforcement, and the conduct might indeed be a search. However, if she is simply entering the room to clean it as part of her daily duties at the hotel, the state action element would be missing.

Just as the maid's discovery and disclosure of Carl's information was not a Fourth Amendment search, neither is a landlord entering a renter's house to make regular repairs and finding child pornography on the kitchen counter, or an overnight house guest finding an illegal firearm in the closet. The real question is: what are the police allowed to do next? They are not allowed to simply enter the hotel room, apartment, or home; the defendant still maintains a reasonable expectation of privacy in those areas. Nor can the maid, landlord, or house guest give the police permission to search these areas. As we will see in **Chapter 16**, third parties can only give police consent to search an area under very limited conditions. Thus, the only thing the police can do is to use the information provided by the maid (or landlord or house guest) to establish probable cause in a warrant application. Once armed with the warrant, the police will be able to enter the premises and conduct a legal search.

3. Companies as Third Parties. In the course of our everyday life, we share information not just with other individuals but also with private companies. Sometimes we purposefully share this information, such as when we send financial documents to banks or accountants. At other times we do so out of necessity, such as when we let the post office know the addresses of the letters that we send or let the credit card company know the names of all of the stores where we make purchases. Still at other times we may not even realize the company is tracking the information we provide: for example, that our grocery store keeps a database of all the different types of food that we buy. In today's society, we share more information than ever before. We purposefully place information on social media websites like Facebook or store documents in the "cloud" on remote servers. And all of our e-mails and texts are transmitted and stored by private companies.

The legal restrictions that police face in trying to access this information come from both the Fourth Amendment and statutory law. In this section we will deal only with the Fourth Amendment issues. In **Chapters 20** and **21**, we will consider the statutory regime.

Under the Fourth Amendment, the general rule is the same as it is for when we share information with individuals: every time we share information with a private company, we assume the risk that the private company will turn the information over to the police. This rule is evolving, and is subject to a couple of caveats, but it is a good place to start when learning this doctrine.

The first Supreme Court case to address this issue under the *Katz* test was *United States v. Miller*.[10] In *Miller*, agents of the Federal Bureau of Tobacco, Alcohol, and Firearms suspected the defendant was illegally producing alcohol without the proper permits and without paying taxes. In order to confirm these suspicions, the agents subpoenaed the defendant's financial records from two of his banks. The records confirmed certain illegal purchases and were part of the evidence presented to the grand jury against the defendant. The Supreme Court held that the subpoena of the bank records was not a search, because the financial documents were not "personal records" but rather "negotiable instruments" that would routinely be reviewed by the government for "criminal, tax, and regulatory investigations and proceedings."[11] Furthermore, Miller "knowingly expose[d]" the information to the public when he placed the checks or deposit slips into the stream of commerce and therefore could not claim he had a reasonable expectation of privacy in the documents.

Miller was a logical step from the third-party doctrine that the Court had already adopted in the informant cases such as *Hoffa*. And the fact that it dealt with purely commercial records made it a relatively easy step to take. Then four years later came the *Smith* case:

> **Example—*Smith v. Maryland*, 442 U.S. 735 (1979):** After Patricia McDonough was robbed, she began receiving obscene and threatening phone calls from an unidentified man, whom she presumed was the robber. She also saw a 1975 Monte Carlo automobile driving slowly by her house shortly after one of the calls, and she recognized the car as being one that was parked

[10] 425 U.S. 435 (1975).

[11] Id. at 444.

nearby when she was robbed. She wrote down the license plate and called the police, and the police traced the car to Michael Smith.

The police immediately contacted the telephone company and requested that the phone company place a "pen register" on Smith's telephone line. This device records every telephone number that the phone subscriber dials, although it does not record the content of the calls. The next day, the police saw that Smith placed a call to McDonough's home. They used this information to obtain a search warrant to search Smith's home. The police searched Smith's home, found incriminating evidence, and arrested him. McDonough later identified Smith in a line-up as the man who robbed her. Before trial, Smith moved to preclude the evidence from the pen register (and all the evidence that it subsequently led to), arguing that the pen register was a search that was conducted without a warrant. The motion was denied. Smith was thereafter convicted and sentenced to six years in prison. The search issue was appealed all the way to the United States Supreme Court.

Analysis: The Court held the use of the pen register was not a search and affirmed Smith's conviction. The Court applied the *Katz* test and concluded that Smith did not have a legitimate, reasonable expectation of privacy in the numbers that he dialed from his telephone. First, he probably did not have a subjective expectation of privacy because he knew that he was conveying the dialing information to the telephone company. Second, even if he did have a subjective expectation of privacy, this was not an expectation that society was bound to recognize as reasonable because Smith "voluntarily conveyed numerical information to the telephone company and 'exposed' that information to its equipment."[12] Thus, he "assumed the risk that the company would reveal to police the numbers he dialed."[13]

Smith conceded that all of this would be true if the telephone company still employed human operators to place calls—then he would have dictated the number to another human being and would thereby have been aware that someone else knew the number. However, Smith argued that most modern (that is, 1979) telephone companies use electronic switching to place calls, so no individual person ever actually knows the numbers that are dialed. Smith also noted that most telephone companies do not choose to make any record of local telephone numbers dialed, since that is not required for billing purposes. In a ruling which was to become critically important in the ensuing decades, the Court rejected the distinctions Smith urged them to draw:

[12] Smith v. Maryland, 442 U.S. 735, 744.

[13] Id.

> The fortuity of whether or not the phone company in fact elects to make a quasi-permanent record of a particular number dialed does not, in our view, make any constitutional difference. Regardless of the phone company's election, petitioner voluntarily conveyed to it information that it had facilities for recording and that it was free to record.[14]

Smith was a 5-3 decision, with Justices Stewart, Brennan, and Marshall dissenting. Justice Stewart explained why in the dissent's view the phone numbers dialed should be protected by *Katz*:

> The numbers dialed from a private telephone—although certainly more prosaic than the conversation itself—are not without "content." Most private telephone subscribers may have their own numbers listed in a publicly distributed directory, but I doubt there are any who would be happy to have broadcast to the world a list of the local or long distance numbers they have called. This is not because such a list might in some sense be incriminating, but because it easily could reveal the identities of the persons and the places called, and thus reveal the most intimate details of a person's life.[15]

In his own dissent Justice Marshall attacked the majority's use of the "assumption of risk" doctrine:

> Implicit in the concept of assumption of risk is some notion of choice. At least in the third-party consensual surveillance cases, which first incorporated risk analysis into Fourth Amendment doctrine, the defendant presumably had exercised some discretion in deciding who should enjoy his confidential communications. [Citations to *Hoffa* and similar cases]. By contrast here, unless a person is prepared to forgo use of what for many has become a personal or professional necessity, he cannot help but accept the risk of surveillance. It is idle to speak of "assuming" risks in contexts where, as a practical matter, individuals have no realistic alternative.[16]

These two arguments—that the Court should distinguish between "content" information and "non-content" information and that "assumption of risk" becomes meaningless in the context of modern commercial realities—are two critical flaws in the *Smith* doctrine. As we will see, later cases have begun to attack *Smith* on precisely these grounds. Before we do, however, it is worth emphasizing that *Smith* and *Miller* are still good law: according to current Supreme Court prec-

---

[14] Id. at 745.

[15] Id. at 748 (Stewart, J., dissenting).

[16] Id. at 750 (Marshall, J., dissenting).

edent, individuals have no Fourth Amendment rights in any information they voluntarily turn over to third party corporations.

4. Content v. Address Distinction in Electronic Communication. There are two legally important distinctions between *Smith* and *Katz.* The first, and the one which the Court relied on in *Smith*, is based on our "reasonable expectation of privacy" in the information the police are trying to intercept—an outgoing telephone number in *Smith* and the content of a telephone conversation in *Katz.* Telephone companies record and perhaps store telephone numbers during their everyday course of business, and everyone who uses a telephone should reasonably expect that their telephone numbers that they dial are not a secret. Under Fourth Amendment jurisprudence, once the information is knowingly shared with any third party, the dialer assumes the risk that the third party will share the information with the government. The same is not true for the content of telephone conversations: we **can** reasonably expect that the telephone company is neither recording nor storing that information. However, the person with whom we are conversing is also a third party, of course, so we still assume the risk that she may be recording the conversation or may report its contents to the police.

The second distinction is in the type of information the government is acquiring. In *Smith,* the government was merely seeking the identity of the person the defendant was calling—what we call the "address" information. In *Katz*, the government was seeking the contents of the conversation itself. Given the private nature of most phone conversations, we have a reasonable expectation of privacy in the content of our communication but not in the address information.

Thus, in the context of telephone communications, the "address" information is not protected because it is (1) shared with a third party; and (2) not considered to be as private as the contents of the communication. This is also true with traditional mail: the address of a letter is shared with the post office, and it is considered to be less private than the contents of the letter. Thus, the address on the outside of a letter is not protected by the Fourth Amendment, but the contents of the letter are protected.[17]

"Address" information is defined as **non-content information used to facilitate communication**. Address information must necessarily be shared with a third party in order for the communication to take place. Likewise, address information is seen as far less private than content information (Justice Stewart's *Smith* dissent notwithstanding). Thus, this information has never been protected by the Fourth Amendment. Viewed from a historical standpoint, this makes sense. At the time of the nation's founding, the only way to communicate with someone outside your own household was to travel to them in person (in which case you

[17] Ex parte Jackson, 96 U.S. 727 (1877).

could be followed) or write them a letter (in which case the address of the letter was open to the public). Law enforcement officials routinely institute "mail covers" on a suspect, in which they order the post office to copy the addresses of every outgoing and incoming piece of mail that a suspect sends or receives. As long as the delivery of the mail is not significantly delayed, which would constitute a seizure (see **Chapter 9**), the Fourth Amendment is not implicated.

But in the context of electronic communication, one of the distinctions between address information and content information disappears. Third party companies (such as internet service providers) record and store content information the same way that they record or store address information. Because *Smith v. Maryland* was based only on this first distinction—the fact that address information is recorded by the telephone company—a literal application of *Smith* would mean that the content information in electronic communication is not protected. Therefore, as we have evolved into the age of digital communications, courts have begun to test the *Smith* precedent to see if it still applies when the information being recorded is content information.

Courts have consistently applied this doctrine to address information with regard to electronic communications as well:

> **Example—*United States v. Forrester*, 512 F.3d 500 (9th Cir. 2008):** Police suspected that Mark Forrester and Dennis Alba were running a laboratory manufacturing the drug Ecstasy. To investigate these suspicions, the government contacted PacBell Internet, Alba's internet service provider and asked them to install a "mirror port" on Alba's account. The mirror port recorded the to/from addresses of Alba's e-mail messages, the total volume of information sent to or from his account, and the Internet Protocol ("IP") addresses of the websites that Alba visited. An IP address is a number which uniquely identifies a location on the internet—a website will typically have only one IP address even if it has thousands of different pages on the site.
>
> At trial, the defendants argued that the use of the mirror port was a search. The trial court denied the defense motion, and the defendants appealed to the Ninth Circuit.

Analysis: The Ninth Circuit held that the mirror port should receive the same constitutional treatment as the pen register in *Smith*, for two reasons. First, the information acquired by the government was information that Alba and Forrester voluntarily turned over to a third party. Consequently, they "should know that this information is provided to and used by internet service providers for the specific purpose of directing the routing of information."[18] Second, the e-mail addresses and IP addresses do not provide any significant content information—they do not tell the government any more information than the government learns from outgoing phone numbers. That is, the information tells the government "where" the communication is going but not "what" is being communicated.

The court acknowledged that IP addresses have some "content-like" information: "the government may make educated guesses about what was said in the messages or viewed on the websites based on its knowledge of the e-mail to/from addresses and IP addresses."[19] But it concluded that this was no different from the educated guesses that the government could make from looking at outgoing phone numbers: "like IP addresses, certain phone numbers may strongly indicate the underlying contents of the communication; for example, the government would know that a person who dialed the phone number of a chemicals company or a gun shop was likely seeking information about chemicals or firearms."[20]

So "address" information is not protected by the Fourth Amendment, whether in written, telephonic, or electronic form. But what protections are afforded the "content" information in the electronic context? Internet service providers such as PacBell Internet record and store both address and content information for every text and e-mail that they process.

Indeed, from a physical standpoint, there is no real difference between the two types of information. An e-mail or text is broken up into small "packets" of binary data, some of which contain address information, and some of which contain content information. The data is processed by computers and stored in servers, and it is only when recipients receive the text or open the e-mail that the software then breaks the packets apart to display address information in one part of the screen and content information in another.

From a privacy standpoint, there is a significant distinction between content information and address information—one is much more personal and intimate than the other. Unfortunately, the holding of *Smith v. Maryland* did not rely on that distinction: according to the language of the Court, all that matters is whether the information is shared with the third-party company or not.

The Ninth Circuit in *Forrester*, aware of this potential problem, made a comment in dicta which suggested that *Smith* should be interpreted narrowly in the context of electronic communications. It noted that the address information at issue in *Forrester* was completely analogous to *Smith*'s phone numbers because "like telephone numbers, which provide instructions to the switching equipment that processed those numbers, e-mail to/from addresses and IP addresses

[18] United States v. Forrester, 512 F.3d 500, 510 (9th. Cir. 2008).

[19] Id. at 509–510.

[20] Id.

are not merely passively conveyed through third party equipment, but rather are voluntarily turned over in order to direct the third party's servers."[21] Thus, the Ninth Circuit in *Forrester* implied that there was a difference between information "passively conveyed through third party equipment" (such as the content of the e-mails) and information "voluntarily turned over in order to direct the third party's servers" (such as the address information).[22]

The Ninth Circuit later relied on this argument in *Quon v. Arch Wireless Operating Company* when it held that the texts that were sent and received from a pager were protected by the Fourth Amendment, because they were "content" information rather than "address" information. The court held that the fact that the third party servicer was able to access the content of the texts was "irrelevant."[23]

Two years later, the Sixth Circuit agreed with this principle:

> **Example—*United States v. Warshak*, 631 F.3d 266 (2010):** Steven Warshak ran a company that sold herbal supplements, including a wildly popular pill called "Enzyte," which allegedly increased the size of a man's erection. Advertisements for Enzyte claimed that it increased a man's penis size from between 12% and 31%; that the pill had been developed by doctors at Stanford University; and that customers experienced a 96% satisfaction rate. In reality, none of these claims were true.
>
> The government began investigating Warshak's fraudulent business practices. Government agents obtained a court order compelling NuVox Communications, Warshak's ISP, to copy the content of every e-mail sent to and received by Warshak's account and turn the copies over to the government. NuVox complied with the order and ultimately delivered approximately twenty-seven thousand e-mails to the government over a fifteen-month period. During this time, Warshak was never informed about the monitoring program. After Warshak was indicted, he challenged the government's actions, claiming they violated his rights under the Fourth Amendment.

Analysis: The Sixth Circuit held that the government's actions violated the Fourth Amendment. The court stated that the intercepted e-mails were analogous not to the phone numbers in *Smith*, but instead to the content of the phone call in *Katz* or the content of a letter sent through the post office.

---

[21] Id. at 510.

[22] Id. (internal quotation marks omitted).

[23] Quon v. Arch Wireless Operating Co., 529 F.3d 892 (9th Cir. 2008).

The court followed the Ninth Circuit's arguments in distinguishing the case from *Miller* and *Smith*. In *Miller*, the banks were the intended recipients of the financial documents; in *Smith*, the telephone company had to use the telephone numbers to direct the calls. In contrast, Warshak's ISP was merely the intermediary who was meant to "passively convey" the contents of the e-mails.[24]

The *Warshak* case was a repudiation of *Smith* and a victory of legal realism over legal formalism. The Sixth Circuit bypassed the specific rules and language in *Smith* and instead focused more broadly on underlying principles:

> Since the advent of email, the telephone call and the letter have waned in importance, and an explosion of internet-based communication has taken place. People are now able to send sensitive and intimate information, instantaneously, to friends, family, and colleagues half a world away. Lovers exchange sweet nothings, and businessmen swap ambitious plans, all with the click of a mouse button. Commerce has also taken hold in email. Online purchases are often documented in email accounts, and email is frequently used to remind patients and clients of imminent appointments. In short, "account" is an apt word for the conglomeration of stored messages that comprises an email account, as it provides an account of its owner's life. By obtaining access to someone's email, government agents gain the ability to peer deeply into his activities.[25]

Although a few circuit courts have limited *Smith* by focusing on the address/content distinction rather than the third-party doctrine, this issue is far from settled. Other circuit courts have held that an individual has no reasonable expectation of privacy in e-mails, because the e-mails are sent through a third-party ISP.[26]

Even the distinction between address information and content information is now becoming blurry. The *Forrester* case held that the IP addresses of websites that an individual visits on her computer counts as "address" information, because it only indicates the website that the individual has accessed. What about the precise URL,[27] which indicates the exact page of the website the individual is examining? For example, a record of the IP address that I accessed ("170.149.100.10") will only tell you that I went to the New

[24] United States v. Warshak, 631 F.3d 266 (6th Cir. 2010). The Sixth Circuit ultimately allowed the use of the emails at trial because it found that the government relied in good faith on a statute known as the Stored Communications Act ("SCA"). We will talk about the SCA in **Chapter 21**, and about the good faith reliance doctrine in **Chapter 23**.

[25] Id. at 284.

[26] Rehburg v. Paulk, 598 F.3d 1268 (11th Cir. 2010).

[27] "URL" stands for "Unifom Resource Locator," and refers to the string of characters that we see in our web browsers when we navigate to a certain web site, such as "http://www.nytimes.com/".

York Times website. A record of the URL that I accessed ("http://www.nytimes.com/2013/01/17/opinion/gun-reform-for-a-generation.html?ref=todayspaper") will tell you that I looked at that day's editorial regarding gun control legislation. Is that still merely "address" information? What about the search terms that a person types into Google? All of these are questions that courts are still struggling to answer, and frequently they try to answer these questions by comparing the cases to their analog equivalent: is a URL more like the address on an envelope or the contents of a letter? In cases like this, good advocacy—and knowledge of how modern communication technology actually works—can sway a judge to one side or the other.

5. The End of the *Smith v. Maryland* Doctrine? We have already seen that the lower courts are beginning to challenge *Smith* in cases like *Warshak* and *Forrester*. For its part, the Supreme Court has refused to explain how *Smith* might apply to electronic communications. Recently, the Court had a chance to rule on the issue of how *Katz* applied to the employer-issued pagers in *Quon*, but it explicitly refused to answer the question, saying that the technology (and society's expectations of the technology) was still evolving:

> The judiciary risks error by elaborating too fully on the Fourth Amendment implications of emerging technology before its role in society has become clear. In *Katz*, the Court relied on its own knowledge and experience to conclude that there is a reasonable expectation of privacy in a telephone booth. It is not so clear that courts at present are on so sure a ground. Prudence counsels caution before the facts in the instant case are used to establish far-reaching premises that define the existence, and extent, of privacy expectations enjoyed by employees when using employer-provided communication devices. Rapid changes in the dynamics of communication and information transmission are evident not just in the technology itself but in what society accepts as proper behavior.[28]

More recently, Justice Sotomayor addressed this issue in her concurrence in the recent *Jones* case:

> [I]t may be necessary to reconsider the premise that an individual has no reasonable expectation of privacy in information voluntarily disclosed to third parties [Citation to *Smith*]. This approach is ill suited to the digital age, in which people reveal a great deal of information about themselves to third parties in the course of carrying out mundane tasks. People disclose the phone numbers that they dial or text to their cellular providers; the URLs that they visit and the e-mail addresses with which they

[28] City of Ontario v. Quon, 130 S. Ct. 2619, 2629 (2010) (citations omitted).

correspond to their Internet service providers; and the books, groceries, and medications they purchase to online retailers. . . .

I for one doubt that people would accept without complaint the warrantless disclosure to the Government of a list of every Web site they had visited in the last week, or month, or year. But whatever the societal expectations, they can attain constitutionally protected status only if our Fourth Amendment jurisprudence ceases to treat secrecy as a prerequisite for privacy. I would not assume that all information voluntarily disclosed to some member of the public for a limited purpose is, for that reason alone, disentitled to Fourth Amendment protection.[29]

As of now, Justice Sotomayor is a lone voice on the Court asking to review this question, but that will not be the case for very long. As we will see in **Chapter 21**, the federal government's position is that the Patriot Act allows law enforcement to collect lists of websites that people visit: the very information that Justice Sotomayor believed people would not accept being disclosed. This position—and the conflicting circuit court interpretations of *Smith*—seem almost certain to force the Supreme Court to deal with these questions head-on.

D. Policy Debate. The third-party doctrine once again brings up the issue of how courts should determine whether a "reasonable expectation of privacy" exists. The majority in *Smith* essentially found that when you share otherwise confidential information with another person or company, it is not "reasonable" to assume they will not go to the police. This "assumption of risk" theory has a couple of potential flaws. First, is assumption of risk even an appropriate measure of what is reasonable? In his dissent in *Smith*, Justice Marshall argued that "whether privacy expectations are legitimate within the meaning of *Katz* depends not on the risks an individual can be presumed to accept when imparting information to third parties, but on the risks he should be forced to assume in a free and open society."[30]

Another problem with using the assumption of risk rationale is that the suspect's awareness of risks can be manipulated by the government. Justice Marshall noted that "law enforcement officials, simply by announcing their intent to monitor the content of random samples of first-class mail or private phone conversations, could put the public on notice of the risks they would thereafter assume in such

[29] United States v. Jones, 132 S. Ct. 945, 957 (Sotomayor, J., concurring).
[30] Smith, 442 U.S., at 750 (Marshall, J., dissenting).

communications."[31] In this sense, the government could limit or eliminate Fourth Amendment protection simply by explaining to citizens that a certain type of surveillance would become commonplace.

The *Smith* majority rejected this concern as overly alarmist, arguing that at some point the Court would intervene to protect this type of manipulation by the government. In other words, in interpreting the term "reasonable and legitimate expectation of privacy," it is **usually** sufficient to look to what society does in fact legitimately expect will be kept private. But if this expectation has been "conditioned" by "influences alien to well-recognized Fourth Amendment freedoms," it would be appropriate for the Court to substitute its own normative beliefs about what should be kept private.[32]

The third-party doctrine has also come under attack for creating an "all or nothing" theory of privacy. The most expansive reading of the doctrine would mean that an individual who chooses to share information with only one person has effectively given that one person the right to expose the information to the entire world. As Justice Marshall noted:

> Privacy is not a discrete commodity, possessed absolutely or not at all. Those who disclose certain facts to a bank or phone company for a limited business purpose need not assume that this information will be released to other persons for other purposes.[33]

One response to this argument is that the third-party doctrine does not in fact mean that a suspect gives up all rights to privacy when she shares information with one person; the suspect still has the right to prevent everyone else (including the government) from acquiring the information from the suspect. All the third-party doctrine means is that the suspect has assumed the risk that the third party will choose to share the information. This response is not very compelling, however, because the government has the right to force the third party to disclose the information through subpoena power; thus, the suspect is not really assuming the risk that the third party will betray them, but rather assuming the risk that the government will not learn about the possibility of this investigatory tactic.

---

[31] Id. (Marshall, J., dissenting (citing Anthony Amsterdam, Perspectives on the Fourth Amendment, 58 Minn. L. Rev. 349, 384, 407 (1974))).

[32] Id. at 740 n.5.

[33] Id. at 749 (Marshall, J., dissenting).

Quick Summary

When a suspect shares information with a third party, the information is generally not protected by the Fourth Amendment if that third party decides to take that information to the police. This doctrine originally was developed in the context of informants. In that context, if a suspect has a confidential conversation with a colleague, the suspect assumes the risk that the colleague will go to the police, even if the suspect subjectively believed the information would be kept secret. The doctrine evolved to cover other sorts of information such as records turned over to third-party companies, including financial records given to banks and phone numbers given to the phone company in order to place calls.

In the modern era of digital communications, the notion that one "assumes the risk" when they turn information over to a third party has become somewhat problematic. Modern life requires that we share quite a bit of personal, intimate information with third parties. To begin to address this concern, some courts have focused on the distinction between "address information," which is transmitted to the third party in order to allow the third party to deliver a communication, and "content information," which is passively conveyed by the third party. And as in other areas where we are using new technologies to store and send information, there is a complex and growing statutory regime which also applies to this area, which will be discussed in **Chapters 20 and 21.**

Review Questions

1. Consequences of an Unwanted Pregnancy. Donald Robeson had recently gotten his under-aged girlfriend Carla pregnant, and he was fearful that her parents would have him arrested for unlawful sexual conduct with a minor. Robeson solved this problem by hiring someone to kill Carla. When investigating Carla's death, the police identified Robeson as Carla's boyfriend, and he became a suspect.

Robeson worked as an accountant for a small firm downtown. The police contacted his employer and asked to see Robeson's computer files and any record of his internet activity. Robeson's firm owned the computer that he used at work, and the IT department had the ability to access Robeson's computer at any time. Furthermore, when Robeson started work at the firm seven years ago, he signed a contract which acknowledged that the firm had the right to monitor his computer files and his internet activity. On Robeson's hard drive they found a copy of a letter written to Carla urging her to get an abortion. In reviewing his internet searches they found that he had searched for "how to have a miscarriage" and "how to kill a baby."

The police then contacted AT&T, Robeson's internet service provider, and asked for a record of all of the internet searches that Robeson conducted over the past month from his home computer. AT&T keeps such records for all of its consumers and then sells the information to advertising and marketing agencies. The police learned that Robeson had searched for "hit man" and "contract killing."

The police used this information to obtain a search warrant, and the search of Robeson's house turned up incriminating evidence. Robeson was arrested and charged with the murder. He is now challenging the search of his office computer, his office internet activity, and his home internet searches. How should the court rule on his motion?

2. False Facebook Friends. The police suspected that a known gang member named Melvin Coolidge had participated in a number of violent assaults. As part of their investigation, they logged onto his Facebook page, but Coolidge's main page revealed nothing incriminating. The police then contacted one of Coolidge's Facebook friends, who gave police her Facebook password and allowed them to login as her. By reading the material that Coolidge has posted exclusively for his friends, the police saw that Coolidge had posted messages in which he bragged about his past acts of violence. The police sought to use this information against Coolidge at his later trial. Coolidge argued that the police's examination of his "friends only" information on Facebook was an unconstitutional search.

3. The Nosy Roommate. Sarah Poole, Wendy Reynolds, and Glenda Ashton were freshmen in college sharing a suite. The door to the suite was always kept locked, but there were no locks on the individual bedrooms inside the suite. After a few weeks, Poole suspected that Reynolds and Ashton were using cocaine in the room when Poole was not around. One day when Reynolds was in class, Poole went into Reynolds's room and searched through Reynolds's dresser. In one of the drawers behind some sweatshirts Poole found a Ziploc bag containing a white powder.

Poole immediately took the powder to the police, who tested it and confirmed that it was cocaine. She explained where the cocaine came from and the police asked her to go back and search through Ashton's room as well. She returned to the suite and searched Ashton's bedroom, and under the bed she found a paper bag containing marijuana. She brought this to the police as well. That night the police arrested Reynolds for possession of cocaine and Ashton for possession of marijuana. Both women moved to suppress the evidence, arguing that Poole's search of their rooms was unconstitutional. How should the court rule?

4. NSA and Phone Records. In the wake of a terrorist bombing at the Boston Marathon, the National Security Administration ("NSA") made hundreds of requests of cell phone providers such as Verizon and Sprint in order to try to determine who made calls from the location of the bombing. The NSA did not request the content of any conversation (which at any rate was not recorded by the cell phone providers); instead, for each individual they wanted to know how many phone calls the person made over the week leading up to the bombing, who they called, how long each conversation lasted, and where the call was made from. The ACLU brought a class-action lawsuit on behalf of all of the customers of these providers, arguing that the NSA should not be given this information unless it had a warrant for a specific person's records. Did the NSA violate the Fourth Amendment?

FROM THE COURTROOM

SMITH v. MARYLAND

United States Supreme Court, 1979
442 U.S. 735

[Justice BLACKMUN delivered the opinion of the Court.]

[Justice POWELL took no part in the consideration or decision of this case.]

[Justice STEWART filed a dissenting opinion, which Justice BRENNAN joined.]

Justice MARSHALL filed a dissenting opinion, which Justice BRENNAN joined.]

This case presents the question whether the installation and use of a pen register[1] constitutes a "search" within the meaning of the Fourth Amendment, made applicable to the States through the Fourteenth Amendment.

I

On March 5, 1976, in Baltimore, Md., Patricia McDonough was robbed. She gave the police a description of the robber and of a 1975 Monte Carlo automobile she had observed near the scene of the crime. After the robbery, McDonough began receiving threatening and obscene phone calls from a man identifying himself as the robber. On one occasion, the caller asked that she step out on her front porch; she did so, and saw the 1975 Monte Carlo she had earlier described to police moving slowly past her home. On March 16, police spotted a man who met McDonough's description driving a 1975 Monte Carlo in her neighborhood. By tracing the license plate number, police learned that the car was registered in the name of petitioner, Michael Lee Smith.

The next day, the telephone company, at police request, installed a pen register at its central offices to record the numbers dialed from the telephone at petitioner's home. The police did not get a warrant or court order before having the pen register installed. The register revealed that on March 17 a call was placed from petitioner's home to McDonough's phone. On the basis of this and other evidence, the police obtained a warrant to search petitioner's residence. The search revealed that a page in petitioner's

[1] "A pen register is a mechanical device that records the numbers dialed on a telephone by monitoring the electrical impulses caused when the dial on the telephone is released. It does not overhear oral communications and does not indicate whether calls are actually completed." A pen register is "usually installed at a central telephone facility [and] records on a paper tape all numbers dialed from [the] line" to which it is attached.

phone book was turned down to the name and number of Patricia McDonough; the phone book was seized. Petitioner was arrested, and a six-man lineup was held on March 19. McDonough identified petitioner as the man who had robbed her.

Petitioner was indicted in the Criminal Court of Baltimore for robbery. By pretrial motion, he sought to suppress "all fruits derived from the pen register" on the ground that the police had failed to secure a warrant prior to its installation. The trial court denied the suppression motion, holding that the warrantless installation of the pen register did not violate the Fourth Amendment. Petitioner then waived a jury, and the case was submitted to the court on an agreed statement of facts. The pen register tape (evidencing the fact that a phone call had been made from petitioner's phone to McDonough's phone) and the phone book seized in the search of petitioner's residence were admitted into evidence against him. Petitioner was convicted, and was sentenced to six years. He appealed to the Maryland Court of Special Appeals, but the Court of Appeals of Maryland issued a writ of certiorari to the intermediate court in advance of its decision in order to consider whether the pen register evidence had been properly admitted at petitioner's trial.

The Court of Appeals affirmed the judgment of conviction, holding that "there is no constitutionally protected reasonable expectation of privacy in the numbers dialed into a telephone system and hence no search within the fourth amendment is implicated by the use of a pen register installed at the central offices of the telephone company." Because there was no "search," the court concluded, no warrant was needed. Three judges dissented, expressing the view that individuals do have a legitimate expectation of privacy regarding the phone numbers they dial from their homes; that the installation of a pen register thus constitutes a "search"; and that, in the absence of exigent circumstances, the failure of police to secure a warrant mandated that the pen register evidence here be excluded. Certiorari was granted in order to resolve indications of conflict in the decided cases as to the restrictions imposed by the Fourth Amendment on the use of pen registers.

II

A

The Fourth Amendment guarantees "[t]he right of the people to be secure in their persons, houses, papers, and effects, against unreasonable searches and seizures." In determining whether a particular form of government-initiated electronic surveillance is a "search" within the meaning of the Fourth Amendment,[4] our lodestar is *Katz v. United States,* 389 U.S. 347 (1967). In *Katz,* Government agents had intercepted the contents of a telephone conversation by attaching an electronic listening device to the outside of a public phone booth. The Court rejected the argument that a "search" can occur only when there has been a "physical intrusion" into a "constitutionally

[4] In this case, the pen register was installed, and the numbers dialed were The telephone company, however, acted at police request. In view of this, respondent appears to concede that the company is to be deemed an "agent" of the police for purposes of this case, so as to render the installation and use of the pen register "state action" under the Fourth and Fourteenth Amendments. We may assume that "state action" was present here.

protected area," noting that the Fourth Amendment "protects people, not places." Because the Government's monitoring of Katz' conversation "violated the privacy upon which he justifiably relied while using the telephone booth," the Court held that it "constituted a 'search and seizure' within the meaning of the Fourth Amendment."

Consistently with *Katz,* this Court uniformly has held that the application of the Fourth Amendment depends on whether the person invoking its protection can claim a "justifiable," a "reasonable," or a "legitimate expectation of privacy" that has been invaded by government action.[5] *E.g., Rakas v. Illinois,* 439 U.S. 128, 143 (1978).

B.

In applying the *Katz* analysis to this case, it is important to begin by specifying precisely the nature of the state activity that is challenged. The activity here took the form of installing and using a pen register. Since the pen register was installed on telephone company property at the telephone company's central offices, petitioner obviously cannot claim that his "property" was invaded or that police intruded into a "constitutionally protected area." Petitioner's claim, rather, is that, notwithstanding the absence of a trespass, the State, as did the Government in *Katz,* infringed a "legitimate expectation of privacy" that petitioner held. Yet a pen register differs significantly from the listening device employed in *Katz,* for pen registers do not acquire the *contents* of communications. This Court recently noted:

"Indeed, a law enforcement official could not even determine from the use of a pen register whether a communication existed. These devices do not hear sound. They disclose only the telephone numbers that have been dialed—a means of establishing communication. Neither the purport of any communication between the caller and the recipient of the call, their identities, nor whether the call was even completed is disclosed by pen registers."

Given a pen register's limited capabilities, therefore, petitioner's argument that its installation and use constituted a "search" necessarily rests upon a claim that he had a "legitimate expectation of privacy" regarding the numbers he dialed on his phone.

This claim must be rejected. First, we doubt that people in general entertain any actual expectation of privacy in the numbers they dial. All telephone users realize that they must "convey" phone numbers to the telephone company, since it is through telephone company switching equipment that their calls are completed. All subscrib-

---

[5] Situations can be imagined, of course, in which *Katz'* two-pronged inquiry would provide an inadequate index of Fourth Amendment protection. For example, if the Government were suddenly to announce on nationwide television that all homes henceforth would be subject to warrantless entry, individuals thereafter might not in fact entertain any actual expectation or privacy regarding their homes, papers, and effects. Similarly, if a refugee from a totalitarian country, unaware of this Nation's traditions, erroneously assumed that police were continuously monitoring his telephone conversations, a subjective expectation of privacy regarding the contents of his calls might be lacking as well. In such circumstances, where an individual's subjective expectations had been "conditioned" by influences alien to well-recognized Fourth Amendment freedoms, those subjective expectations obviously could play no meaningful role in ascertaining what the scope of Fourth Amendment protection was. In determining whether a "legitimate expectation of privacy" existed in such cases, a normative inquiry would be proper.

ers realize, moreover, that the phone company has facilities for making permanent records of the numbers they dial, for they see a list of their long-distance (toll) calls on their monthly bills. In fact, pen registers and similar devices are routinely used by telephone companies "for the purposes of checking billing operations, detecting fraud and preventing violations of law." Electronic equipment is used not only to keep billing records of toll calls, but also "to keep a record of all calls dialed from a telephone which is subject to a special rate structure." Pen registers are regularly employed "to determine whether a home phone is being used to conduct a business, to check for a defective dial, or to check for overbilling." Although most people may be oblivious to a pen register's esoteric functions, they presumably have some awareness of one common use: to aid in the identification of persons making annoying or obscene calls. Most phone books tell subscribers, on a page entitled "Consumer Information," that the company "can frequently help in identifying to the authorities the origin of unwelcome and troublesome calls." Telephone users, in sum, typically know that they must convey numerical information to the phone company; that the phone company has facilities for recording this information; and that the phone company does in fact record this information for a variety of legitimate business purposes. Although subjective expectations cannot be scientifically gauged, it is too much to believe that telephone subscribers, under these circumstances, harbor any general expectation that the numbers they dial will remain secret.

Petitioner argues, however, that, whatever the expectations of telephone users in general, he demonstrated an expectation of privacy by his own conduct here, since he "us[ed] the telephone *in his house* to the exclusion of all others." But the site of the call is immaterial for purposes of analysis in this case. Although petitioner's conduct may have been calculated to keep the *contents* of his conversation private, his conduct was not and could not have been calculated to preserve the privacy of the number he dialed. Regardless of his location, petitioner had to convey that number to the telephone company in precisely the same way if he wished to complete his call. The fact that he dialed the number on his home phone rather than on some other phone could make no conceivable difference, nor could any subscriber rationally think that it would.

Second, even if petitioner did harbor some subjective expectation that the phone numbers he dialed would remain private, this expectation is not "one that society is prepared to recognize as 'reasonable.' " This Court consistently has held that a person has no legitimate expectation of privacy in information he voluntarily turns over to third parties. *E. g., United States v. Miller,* 425 U.S. 435, 442–444 (1976). In *Miller,* for example, the Court held that a bank depositor has no "legitimate 'expectation of privacy'" in financial information "voluntarily conveyed to . . . banks and exposed to their employees in the ordinary course of business." The Court explained:

"The depositor takes the risk, in revealing his affairs to another, that the information will be conveyed by that person to the Government. . . . This Court has held repeatedly that the Fourth Amendment does not prohibit the obtaining of information revealed to a third party and conveyed by him to Government authorities, even if the information is revealed on the assumption that it will be used only for a limited purpose and the confidence placed in the third party will not be betrayed."

Because the depositor "assumed the risk" of disclosure, the Court held that it would be unreasonable for him to expect his financial records to remain private.

This analysis dictates that petitioner can claim no legitimate expectation of privacy here. When he used his phone, petitioner voluntarily conveyed numerical information to the telephone company and "exposed" that information to its equipment in the ordinary course of business. In so doing, petitioner assumed the risk that the company would reveal to police the numbers he dialed. The switching equipment that processed those numbers is merely the modern counterpart of the operator who, in an earlier day, personally completed calls for the subscriber. Petitioner concedes that if he had placed his calls through an operator, he could claim no legitimate expectation of privacy. We are not inclined to hold that a different constitutional result is required because the telephone company has decided to automate.

Petitioner argues, however, that automatic switching equipment differs from a live operator in one pertinent respect. An operator, in theory at least, is capable of remembering every number that is conveyed to him by callers. Electronic equipment, by contrast can "remember" only those numbers it is programmed to record, and telephone companies, in view of their present billing practices, usually do not record local calls. Since petitioner, in calling McDonough, was making a local call, his expectation of privacy as to her number, on this theory, would be "legitimate."

This argument does not withstand scrutiny. The fortuity of whether or not the phone company in fact elects to make a quasi-permanent record of a particular number dialed does not in our view, make any constitutional difference. Regardless of the phone company's election, petitioner voluntarily conveyed to it information that it had facilities for recording and that it was free to record. In these circumstances, petitioner assumed the risk that the information would be divulged to police. Under petitioner's theory, Fourth Amendment protection would exist, or not, depending on how the telephone company chose to define local-dialing zones, and depending on how it chose to bill its customers for local calls. Calls placed across town, or dialed directly, would be protected; calls placed across the river, or dialed with operator assistance, might not be. We are not inclined to make a crazy quilt of the Fourth Amendment, especially in circumstances where (as here) the pattern of protection would be dictated by billing practices of a private corporation.

We therefore conclude that petitioner in all probability entertained no actual expectation of privacy in the phone numbers he dialed, and that, even if he did, his expectation was not "legitimate." The installation and use of a pen register, consequently, was not a "search," and no warrant was required. The judgment of the Maryland Court of Appeals is affirmed.

It is so ordered.

Mr. Justice STEWART, with whom Mr. Justice BRENNAN joins, dissenting.

I am not persuaded that the numbers dialed from a private telephone fall outside the constitutional protection of the Fourth and Fourteenth Amendments.

In *Katz,* the Court acknowledged the "vital role that the public telephone has come to play in private communication[s]." The role played by a private telephone is even more vital, and since *Katz* it has been abundantly clear that telephone conversations carried on by people in their homes or offices are fully protected by the Fourth and Fourteenth Amendments. As the Court [has] said,"the broad and unsuspected governmental incursions into conversational privacy which electronic surveillance entails necessitate the application of Fourth Amendment safeguards."

Nevertheless, the Court today says that those safeguards do not extend to the numbers dialed from a private telephone, apparently because when a caller dials a number the digits may be recorded by the telephone company for billing purposes. But that observation no more than describes the basic nature of telephone calls. A telephone call simply cannot be made without the use of telephone company property and without payment to the company for the service. The telephone conversation itself must be electronically transmitted by telephone company equipment, and may be recorded or overheard by the use of other company equipment. Yet we have squarely held that the user of even a public telephone is entitled "to assume that the words he utters into the mouthpiece will not be broadcast to the world."

The central question in this case is whether a person who makes telephone calls from his home is entitled to make a similar assumption about the numbers he dials. What the telephone company does or might do with those numbers is no more relevant to this inquiry than it would be in a case involving the conversation itself. It is simply not enough to say, after *Katz,* that there is no legitimate expectation of privacy in the numbers dialed because the caller assumes the risk that the telephone company will disclose them to the police.

I think that the numbers dialed from a private telephone—like the conversations that occur during a call—are within the constitutional protection recognized in *Katz.* It seems clear to me that information obtained by pen register surveillance of a private telephone is information in which the telephone subscriber has a legitimate expectation of privacy. The information captured by such surveillance emanates from private conduct within a person's home or office—locations that without question are entitled to Fourth and Fourteenth Amendment protection. Further, that information is an integral part of the telephonic communication that under *Katz* is entitled to constitutional protection, whether or not it is captured by a trespass into such an area.

The numbers dialed from a private telephone—although certainly more prosaic than the conversation itself—are not without "content." Most private telephone subscribers may have their own numbers listed in a publicly distributed directory, but I doubt there are any who would be happy to have broadcast to the world a list of the local or long distance numbers they have called. This is not because such a list might in some sense be incriminating, but because it easily could reveal the identities of the persons and the places called, and thus reveal the most intimate details of a person's life.

I respectfully dissent.

Mr. Justice MARSHALL, with whom Mr. Justice BRENNAN joins, dissenting.

The Court concludes that because individuals have no actual or legitimate expectation of privacy in information they voluntarily relinquish to telephone companies, the use of pen registers by government agents is immune from Fourth Amendment scrutiny. Since I remain convinced that constitutional protections are not abrogated whenever a person apprises another of facts valuable in criminal investigations, I respectfully dissent.

Applying the standards set forth in *Katz,* the Court first determines that telephone subscribers have no subjective expectations of privacy concerning the numbers they dial. To reach this conclusion, the Court posits that individuals somehow infer from the long-distance listings on their phone bills, and from the cryptic assurances of "help" in tracing obscene calls included in "most" phone books, that pen registers are regularly used for recording local calls. But even assuming, as I do not, that individuals "typically know" that a phone company monitors calls for internal reasons[1] it does not follow that they expect this information to be made available to the public in general or the government in particular. Privacy is not a discrete commodity, possessed absolutely or not at all. Those who disclose certain facts to a bank or phone company for a limited business purpose need not assume that this information will be released to other persons for other purposes.

The crux of the Court's holding, however, is that whatever expectation of privacy petitioner may in fact have entertained regarding his calls, it is not one "society is prepared to recognize as 'reasonable'." In so ruling, the Court determines that individuals who convey information to third parties have "assumed the risk" of disclosure to the government. This analysis is misconceived in two critical respects.

Implicit in the concept of assumption of risk is some notion of choice. At least in the third-party consensual surveillance cases, which first incorporated risk analysis into Fourth Amendment doctrine, the defendant presumably had exercised some discretion in deciding who should enjoy his confidential communications. By contrast here, unless a person is prepared to forgo use of what for many has become a personal or professional necessity, he cannot help but accept the risk of surveillance. It is idle to speak of "assuming" risks in contexts where, as a practical matter, individuals have no realistic alternative.

More fundamentally, to make risk analysis dispositive in assessing the reasonableness of privacy expectations would allow the government to define the scope of Fourth Amendment protections. For example, law enforcement officials, simply by announcing their intent to monitor the content of random samples of first-class mail or private phone conversations, could put the public on notice of the risks they would thereafter

[1] Lacking the Court's apparently exhaustive knowledge of this Nation's telephone books and the reading habits of telephone subscribers, I decline to assume general public awareness of how obscene phone calls are traced. Nor am I persuaded that the scope of Fourth Amendment protection should turn on the concededly "esoteric functions" of pen registers in corporate billing, functions with which subscribers are unlikely to have intimate familiarity.

assume in such communications. Yet, although acknowledging this implication of its analysis, the Court is willing to concede only that, in some circumstances, a further "normative inquiry would be proper." No meaningful effort is made to explain what those circumstances might be, or why this case is not among them.

In my view, whether privacy expectations are legitimate within the meaning of *Katz* depends not on the risks an individual can be presumed to accept when imparting information to third parties, but on the risks he should be forced to assume in a free and open society. By its terms, the constitutional prohibition of unreasonable searches and seizures assigns to the judiciary some prescriptive responsibility. As Mr. Justice Harlan, who formulated the standard the Court applies today, himself recognized: "[s]ince it is the task of the law to form and project, as well as mirror and reflect, we should not . . . merely recite . . . risks without examining the desirability of saddling them upon society." *United States v. White,* 401 U.S. 745, 786 (1971). In making this assessment, courts must evaluate the "intrinsic character" of investigative practices with reference to the basic values underlying the Fourth Amendment. And for those "extensive intrusions that significantly jeopardize [individuals'] sense of security . . . . more than self-restraint by law enforcement officials is required."

The use of pen registers, I believe, constitutes such an extensive intrusion. To hold otherwise ignores the vital role telephonic communication plays in our personal and professional relationships, as well as the First and Fourth Amendment interests implicated by unfettered official surveillance. Privacy in placing calls is of value not only to those engaged in criminal activity. The prospect of unregulated governmental monitoring will undoubtedly prove disturbing even to those with nothing illicit to hide. Many individuals, including members of unpopular political organizations or journalists with confidential sources, may legitimately wish to avoid disclosure of their personal contacts. Permitting governmental access to telephone records on less than probable cause may thus impede certain forms of political affiliation and journalistic endeavor that are the hallmark of a truly free society. Particularly given the Government's previous reliance on warrantless telephonic surveillance to trace reporters' sources and monitor protected political activity, I am unwilling to insulate use of pen registers from independent judicial review.

Just as one who enters a public telephone booth is "entitled to assume that the words he utters into the mouthpiece will not be broadcast to the world so too, he should be entitled to assume that the numbers he dials in the privacy of his home will be recorded, if at all, solely for the phone company's business purposes. Accordingly, I would require law enforcement officials to obtain a warrant before they enlist telephone companies to secure information otherwise beyond the government's reach.

FROM THE COURTROOM

UNITED STATES v. WARSHAK

Sixth Circuit Court of Appeals, 2010
631 F.3d 266

[Judge BOGGS delivered the opinion].

[Judge KEITH filed a concurring opinion].

. . .

I. STATEMENT OF THE FACTS

A. Factual Background

In 2001, Steven Warshak ("Warshak") owned and operated a number of small businesses in the Cincinnati area. One of his businesses was TCI Media, Inc. ("TCI"), which sold advertisements in sporting venues. Warshak also owned a handful of companies that offered a modest line of so-called "nutraceuticals," or herbal supplements. While the companies bore different names and sold different products, they appear to have been run as a single business, and they were later aggregated to form Berkeley Premium Nutraceuticals, Inc. ("Berkeley"). In Berkeley's early days, the company's workforce was relatively minute; the company employed approximately [twelve] to [fifteen] people, nearly all of whom were Warshak's friends and family. Among them was his mother, Harriet Warshak ("Harriet"), who processed credit-card payments.

As the company grew, Warshak brought on additional employees to facilitate expansion, but he remained extremely "hands-on" with respect to the company's operations. In 2001, he hired James Teegarden, who eventually became Berkeley's Chief Operating Officer. Warshak also hired Shelley Kinmon to oversee the company's sales, later elevating her to the role of Vice–President. In 2002, Sue and Greg Cossman, Warshak's sister and brother-in-law, joined the company. Sue worked in Customer Care, where she dealt with customer complaints. Greg came in as the President of the company and thereafter functioned in various other capacities. That year also saw the hiring of Sam Grote, who was brought on board to work in the marketing department.

To sell its products, Berkeley took orders over the phone, but it also made sales through the mail and over the Internet. Customers purchased products with their credit cards, and their credit-card numbers were entered into a database along with other information. During sales calls, representatives would read from sales scripts, which listed the major points to cover during the transaction. Shelley Kinmon testified that Warshak had the final word on the content of the scripts. Often, the scripts would include a description of the desired product, as well as language intended to persuade more pliant customers to make additional purchases.

In the latter half of 2001, Berkeley launched Enzyte, its flagship product. At the time of its launch, Enzyte was purported to increase the size of a man's erection. The product proved tremendously popular, and business rose sharply. By 2004, demand for Berkeley's products had grown so dramatically that the company employed 1500 people, and the call center remained open throughout the night, taking orders at breakneck speed. Berkeley's line of supplements also expanded, ballooning from approximately four products to around thirteen. By year's end, Berkeley's annual sales topped out at around $250 million, largely on the strength of Enzyte.

1. *Advertising*

The popularity of Enzyte appears to have been due in large part to Berkeley's aggressive advertising campaigns. The vast majority of the advertising—approximately 98%—was conducted through television spots. Around 2004, network television was saturated with Enzyte advertisements featuring a character called "Smilin' Bob," whose trademark exaggerated smile was presumably the result of Enzyte's efficacy. The "Smilin' Bob" commercials were rife with innuendo and implied that users of Enzyte would become the envy of the neighborhood.

In addition to the television commercials, however, there were also advertisements in other media, such as print and radio. In 2001, just after Enzyte's premiere, advertisements appeared in a number of men's interest magazines. At Warshak's direction, those advertisements cited a 2001 independent customer study, which purported to show that, over a three-month period, 100 English-speaking men who took Enzyte experienced a 12 to 31% increase in the size of their penises. The 2001 study was also referenced in radio advertisements and appeared on the company's website, as well as in brochures and sales calls. James Teegarden later testified that the survey was bogus. He stated that, prior to the appearance of the advertisements, Warshak instructed him to create a spreadsheet and to fill it with fabricated data. Teegarden testified that he plucked the numbers out of the air and generated the spreadsheet over a twenty-four hour period.

A number of advertisements also indicated that Enzyte boasted a 96% customer satisfaction rating. Teegarden testified that that statistic, too, was totally spurious. Before the claim began showing up in Berkeley's literature, Warshak had asked him to harvest 500 names from the customer database and to "mark an 'X' by either satisfied or very satisfied on say 475 of those." As for the remaining [twenty-five], Teegarden "was to put not satisfied." Thereafter, the customer-satisfaction statistic cropped up in Berkeley's print advertisements and in the "sales pitches, brochures, [and on the] Internet."

Finally, numerous print and radio advertisements boasted that Enzyte was the brainchild of reputable doctors with impressive educational pedigrees. According to the ads, "Enzyte was developed by Dr. Fredrick Thomkins, a physician with a biology degree from Stanford and Dr. Michael Moore, a leading urologist from Harvard." The ads also stated that the doctors had collaborated for thirteen years in developing a supplement designed to "stretch and elongate." In reality, the doctors were just as fictitious as "Smilin' Bob." Investigators who contacted Stanford and Harvard learned that neither man existed.

2. *The Auto–Ship Program*

The "life blood" of the business was its auto-ship program, which was instituted in 2001, shortly before Enzyte hit the market. The auto-ship program was a continuity or negative-option program, in which a customer would order a free trial of a product and then continue to receive additional shipments of that product until he opted out. Before each new continuity shipment arrived on the customer's doorstep, a corresponding charge would appear on his credit-card statement. The shipments and charges would continue until the customer decided to withdraw from the program, which required the customer to notify the company.

In the early days of the auto-ship program, customers who ordered products over the phone were not told that they were being enrolled. From August 2001 to at least the end of December 2002, customers were simply added to the program at the time of the initial sale without any indication that they would be on the hook for additional charges. Apparently, products were shipped with literature explaining the program, but no authorization was sought in advance of the shipment. According to Teegarden, Warshak explained that the auto-ship program was never mentioned because "nobody would sign up." If nobody signed up, "you couldn't make revenue."

. . .

B. Procedural History

In September 2006, a grand jury sitting in the Southern District of Ohio returned a 112–count indictment charging Warshak, Harriet, TCI, and several others with various crimes related to Berkeley's business.

Before trial, numerous motions were filed. First, Warshak moved to exclude thousands of emails that the government obtained from his Internet Service Providers. That motion was denied.

. . .

Over fifteen months later, in January 2008, the case proceeded to trial. Approximately six weeks later, the trial ended and the defendants were convicted of the majority of the charges. Warshak was acquitted of Counts 14–22, 24–26, and 28, which charged him with making false statements to banks, and he was also acquitted of Counts 109–110, which charged him with misbranding offenses. Harriet was acquitted of Count 28, which alleged that she made false statements to a bank. She was convicted on Counts 27, 30–31, 99–101, and 107.

On August 27, 2008, the defendants were sentenced. Warshak received a sentence of [twenty-five] years of imprisonment. He was also ordered to pay a fine of $93,000 and a special assessment of $9,300. In addition, he was ordered to surrender $459,540,000 in proceeds-money-judgment forfeiture and $44,876,781.68 in money-laundering-judgment forfeiture. Harriet was sentenced to [twenty-four] months of imprisonment, ordered to pay a special assessment of $800, and held jointly and severally liable for the forfeiture judgments. TCI was sentenced to five years of probation and ordered to pay a fine of $160,000 and a special assessment of $6,400.

Following a series of unsuccessful post-trial motions, the defendants timely appealed.

II. ANALYSIS

A. The Search & Seizure of Warshak's Emails

Warshak argues that the government's warrantless, *ex parte* seizure of approximately [twenty-seven thousand] of his private emails constituted a violation of the Fourth Amendment's prohibition on unreasonable searches and seizures. . . . We find that the government *did* violate Warshak's Fourth Amendment rights by compelling his Internet Service Provider ("ISP") to turn over the contents of his emails.

. . .

2. *Factual Background*

Email was a critical form of communication among Berkeley personnel. As a consequence, Warshak had a number of email accounts with various ISPs, including an account with NuVox Communications. In October 2004, the government formally requested that NuVox prospectively preserve the contents of any emails to or from Warshak's email account. The request was made pursuant to 18 U.S.C. § 2703(f) and it instructed NuVox to preserve all future messages.[14] NuVox acceded to the government's request and began preserving copies of Warshak's incoming and outgoing emails—copies that would not have existed absent the prospective preservation request. Per the government's instructions, Warshak was not informed that his messages were being archived.

In January 2005, the government obtained a subpoena under § 2703(b) and compelled NuVox to turn over the emails that it had begun preserving the previous year. In May 2005, the government served NuVox with an *ex parte* court order under § 2703(d) that required NuVox to surrender any additional email messages in Warshak's account. In all, the government compelled NuVox to reveal the contents of approximately 27,000 emails. Warshak did not receive notice of either the subpoena or the order until May 2006.

[14] Warshak appears to have accessed emails from his NuVox account via POP, or "Post Office Protocol." When POP is utilized, emails are downloaded to the user's personal computer and generally deleted from the ISP's server.

3. *The Fourth Amendment*

The Fourth Amendment provides that "[t]he right of the people to be secure in their persons, houses, papers, and effects, against unreasonable searches and seizures, shall not be violated, and no Warrants shall issue, but upon probable cause. . . ." U.S. CONST. amend. IV. The fundamental purpose of the Fourth Amendment "is to safeguard the privacy and security of individuals against arbitrary invasions by government officials."

Not all government actions are invasive enough to implicate the Fourth Amendment. "The Fourth Amendment's protections hinge on the occurrence of a 'search,' a legal term of art whose history is riddled with complexity." A "search" occurs when the government infringes upon "an expectation of privacy that society is prepared to consider reasonable." This standard breaks down into two discrete inquiries: "first, has the [target of the investigation] manifested a subjective expectation of privacy in the object of the challenged search? Second, is society willing to recognize that expectation as reasonable?"

Turning first to the subjective component of the test, we find that Warshak plainly manifested an expectation that his emails would be shielded from outside scrutiny. As he notes in his brief, his "entire business and personal life was contained within the . . . emails seized." Given the often sensitive and sometimes damning substance of his emails, we think it highly unlikely that Warshak expected them to be made public, for people seldom unfurl their dirty laundry in plain view. Therefore, we conclude that Warshak had a subjective expectation of privacy in the contents of his emails.

The next question is whether society is prepared to recognize that expectation as reasonable. This question is one of grave import and enduring consequence, given the prominent role that email has assumed in modern communication. Cf. *Katz*, 389 U.S. at 352 (suggesting that the Constitution must be read to account for "the vital role that the public telephone has come to play in private communication"). Since the advent of email, the telephone call and the letter have waned in importance, and an explosion of Internet-based communication has taken place. People are now able to send sensitive and intimate information, instantaneously, to friends, family, and colleagues half a world away. Lovers exchange sweet nothings, and businessmen swap ambitious plans, all with the click of a mouse button. Commerce has also taken hold in email. Online purchases are often documented in email accounts, and email is frequently used to remind patients and clients of imminent appointments. In short, "account" is an apt word for the conglomeration of stored messages that comprises an email account, as it provides an account of its owner's life. By obtaining access to someone's email, government agents gain the ability to peer deeply into his activities. Much hinges, therefore, on whether the government is permitted to request that a commercial ISP turn over the contents of a subscriber's emails without triggering the machinery of the Fourth Amendment.

In confronting this question, we take note of two bedrock principles. First, the very fact that information is being passed through a communications network is a paramount Fourth Amendment consideration. *See United States v. U.S. Dist. Court*,

407 U.S. 297 (1972) ("[T]he broad and unsuspected governmental incursions into conversational privacy which electronic surveillance entails necessitate the application of Fourth Amendment safeguards."). Second, the Fourth Amendment must keep pace with the inexorable march of technological progress, or its guarantees will wither and perish. *See Kyllo v. United States*, 533 U.S. 27, 34 (2001) (noting that evolving technology must not be permitted to "erode the privacy guaranteed by the Fourth Amendment"); *see also* Orin S. Kerr, *Applying the Fourth Amendment to the Internet: A General Approach*, 62 Stan. L.Rev. 1005, 1007 (2010) (arguing that "the differences between the facts of physical space and the facts of the Internet require courts to identify new Fourth Amendment distinctions to maintain the function of Fourth Amendment rules in an online environment").

With those principles in mind, we begin our analysis by considering the manner in which the Fourth Amendment protects traditional forms of communication. In *Katz*, the Supreme Court was asked to determine how the Fourth Amendment applied in the context of the telephone. There, government agents had affixed an electronic listening device to the exterior of a public phone booth, and had used the device to intercept and record several phone conversations. The Supreme Court held that this constituted a search under the Fourth Amendment, notwithstanding the fact that the telephone company had the capacity to monitor and record the calls. In the eyes of the Court, the caller was "surely entitled to assume that the words he utter[ed] into the mouthpiece w[ould] not be broadcast to the world." The Court's holding in *Katz* has since come to stand for the broad proposition that, in many contexts, the government infringes a reasonable expectation of privacy when it surreptitiously intercepts a telephone call through electronic means. *Smith*, 442 U.S. at 746. (Stewart, J., dissenting) ("[S]ince *Katz*, it has been abundantly clear that telephone conversations are fully protected by the Fourth and Fourteenth Amendments.").

Letters receive similar protection. While a letter is in the mail, the police may not intercept it and examine its contents unless they first obtain a warrant based on probable cause. This is true despite the fact that sealed letters are handed over to perhaps dozens of mail carriers, any one of whom could tear open the thin paper envelopes that separate the private words from the world outside. Put another way, trusting a letter to an intermediary does not necessarily defeat a reasonable expectation that the letter will remain private. *See Katz*, 389 U.S. at 351 ("[W]hat [a person] seeks to preserve as private, even in an area accessible to the public, may be constitutionally protected.").

Given the fundamental similarities between email and traditional forms of communication, it would defy common sense to afford emails lesser Fourth Amendment protection. Email is the technological scion of tangible mail, and it plays an indispensable part in the Information Age. Over the last decade, email has become "so pervasive that some persons may consider [it] to be [an] essential means or necessary instrument[ ] for self-expression, even self-identification." It follows that email requires strong protection under the Fourth Amendment; otherwise, the Fourth Amendment would prove an ineffective guardian of private communication, an essential purpose it has long been recognized to serve. As some forms of communication begin to diminish, the Fourth Amendment must recognize and protect nascent ones that arise. *See War-*

shak I, 490 F.3d at 473 ("It goes without saying that like the telephone earlier in our history, e-mail is an ever-increasing mode of private communication, and protecting shared communications through this medium is as important to Fourth Amendment principles today as protecting telephone conversations has been in the past.").

If we accept that an email is analogous to a letter or a phone call, it is manifest that agents of the government cannot compel a commercial ISP to turn over the contents of an email without triggering the Fourth Amendment. An ISP is the intermediary that makes email communication possible. Emails must pass through an ISP's servers to reach their intended recipient. Thus, the ISP is the functional equivalent of a post office or a telephone company. As we have discussed above, the police may not storm the post office and intercept a letter, and they are likewise forbidden from using the phone system to make a clandestine recording of a telephone call—unless they get a warrant, that is. It only stands to reason that, if government agents compel an ISP to surrender the contents of a subscriber's emails, those agents have thereby conducted a Fourth Amendment search, which necessitates compliance with the warrant requirement absent some exception.

In *Warshak I,* the government argued that this conclusion was improper, pointing to the fact that NuVox contractually reserved the right to access Warshak's emails for certain purposes. While we acknowledge that a subscriber agreement might, in some cases, be sweeping enough to defeat a reasonable expectation of privacy in the contents of an email account, we doubt that will be the case in most situations, and it is certainly not the case here.

As an initial matter, it must be observed that the mere *ability* of a third-party intermediary to access the contents of a communication cannot be sufficient to extinguish a reasonable expectation of privacy. In *Katz,* the Supreme Court found it reasonable to expect privacy during a telephone call despite the ability of an operator to listen in. Similarly, the ability of a rogue mail handler to rip open a letter does not make it unreasonable to assume that sealed mail will remain private on its journey across the country. Therefore, the threat or possibility of access is not decisive when it comes to the reasonableness of an expectation of privacy.

Nor is the *right* of access. As the Electronic Frontier Foundation points out in its *amicus* brief, at the time *Katz* was decided, telephone companies had a right to monitor calls in certain situations. Specifically, telephone companies could listen in when reasonably necessary to "protect themselves and their properties against the improper and illegal use of their facilities." In this case, the NuVox subscriber agreement tracks that language, indicating that "NuVox *may* access and use individual Subscriber information in the operation of the Service and as necessary to protect the Service." Thus, under *Katz,* the degree of access granted to NuVox does not diminish the reasonableness of Warshak's trust in the privacy of his emails.

Our conclusion finds additional support in the application of Fourth Amendment doctrine to rented space. Hotel guests, for example, have a reasonable expectation of privacy in their rooms. This is so even though maids routinely enter hotel rooms to replace the towels and tidy the furniture. Similarly, tenants have a legitimate expectation of privacy in their apartments. That expectation persists, regardless of the incursions of handymen to fix leaky faucets. Consequently, we are convinced that some degree of routine access is hardly dispositive with respect to the privacy question.

Again, however, we are unwilling to hold that a subscriber agreement will *never* be broad enough to snuff out a reasonable expectation of privacy. As the panel noted in *Warshak I,* if the ISP expresses an intention to "audit, inspect, and monitor" its subscriber's emails, that might be enough to render an expectation of privacy unreasonable. But where, as here, there is no such statement, the ISP's "control over the [emails] and ability to access them under certain limited circumstances will not be enough to overcome an expectation of privacy."

We recognize that our conclusion may be attacked in light of the Supreme Court's decision in *United States v. Miller*, 425 U.S. 435 (1976). In *Miller,* the Supreme Court held that a bank depositor does not have a reasonable expectation of privacy in the contents of bank records, checks, and deposit slips. The Court's holding in *Miller* was based on the fact that bank documents, "including financial statements and deposit slips, contain only information voluntarily conveyed to the banks and exposed to their employees in the ordinary course of business." The Court noted,

"The depositor takes the risk, in revealing his affairs to another, that the information will be conveyed by that person to the Government. . . . [T]he Fourth Amendment does not prohibit the obtaining of information revealed to a third party and conveyed by him to Government authorities, even if the information is revealed on the assumption that it will be used only for a limited purpose and the confidence placed in the third party will not be betrayed."

But *Miller* is distinguishable. First, *Miller* involved simple business records, as opposed to the potentially unlimited variety of "confidential communications" at issue here. Second, the bank depositor in *Miller* conveyed information to the bank so that the bank could put the information to use "in the ordinary course of business." By contrast, Warshak received his emails through NuVox. NuVox was an *intermediary,* not the intended recipient of the emails. Thus, *Miller* is not controlling.

Accordingly, we hold that a subscriber enjoys a reasonable expectation of privacy in the contents of emails "that are stored with, or sent or received through, a commercial ISP." The government may not compel a commercial ISP to turn over the contents of a subscriber's emails without first obtaining a warrant based on probable cause. Therefore, because they did not obtain a warrant, the government agents violated the Fourth Amendment when they obtained the contents of Warshak's emails. Moreover, to the extent that the [Stored Communications Act ("SCA")] purports to permit the government to obtain such emails warrantlessly, the SCA is unconstitutional.

[The court went on to conclude that although the government violated the defendants' Fourth Amendment rights when they accessed his e-mails, they acted in good faith reliance on the Stored Communications Act, and therefore the e-mails did not have to be precluded from trial].

9

What is a "Seizure"?

Key Concepts

- Seizure of Objects: "Meaningful Interference"
- Seizure of Individuals: "Reasonably Believe Not Free to Leave"
- Seizure Must be "Reasonable" in Scope and Duration

A. Introduction and Policy. In the past three chapters, we have discussed when government surveillance is classified as a "search," which triggers full constitutional protection. We now turn briefly to the other aspect of Fourth Amendment law: seizures. Whereas surveillance involves the government gathering information from a suspect, seizures involve the government exercising some kind of control over an item or an individual pursuant to a criminal investigation. When the police take a gun out of a dresser drawer in someone's home or pull a package of white powder out of a suspect's pocket, they are seizing those objects. Likewise, when they pull over a car or order someone on the street to stop, they are seizing a person.

Frequently the two actions—searches and seizures—go together. For example, a typical search warrant will give police officers the authority to search for and seize certain items specified in the warrant. And under the "plain view" exception to the warrant requirement, police officers are allowed to look around any space where they are lawfully present, and are allowed to seize any item whose illegal nature is "immediately apparent," such as fruits of a crime, instruments of a crime, or contraband.[1] But, just as there occasionally can be a search without a seizure (as with the thermal imager in *Kyllo*), there can also be a seizure without a search. For example, if the police take a suitcase from a suspect at the airport and hold it for five days before returning it without looking inside, the suitcase has been seized but not searched.

In the context of searches, we have seen that generally the police must provide a stronger justification for more intrusive searches. Similarly, there is a continuum of seizures. If the police are seizing an object or detaining a person, the scope and duration of that seizure must be reasonable under the circumstances, so more intrusive seizures must be supported by greater justifications.

---

[1] Coolidge v. New Hampshire, 403 U.S. 443, 466 (1971). See **Chapter 14**.

B. The Law. There are different rules for seizures of property and seizures of people. In this chapter we will primarily discuss seizures of property. We will consider what sort of police conduct constitutes a seizure, and we will discuss the legal showing required before police can seize property. We will then discuss briefly what constitutes seizure of a person. However, the legal showing required to seize a person—and at what point that seizure becomes an arrest—is a bit more complicated and deserves its own chapter, so we will wait and discuss those issues in **Chapter 19.** By way of overview and introduction, here are the rules:

For seizures of property:

> An item is seized when a government agent exercises "some meaningful interference with an individual's possessory interest in that property."[2]
>
> In order to seize an item without a warrant, it must be "immediately apparent" to the officer that the item is contraband, fruits of a crime, instrumentalities of a crime, or evidence of a crime.[3] The extent and duration of the seizure must be reasonable under the circumstances.

An item is seized when the government agent "**exercises meaningful interference with an individual's possessory interest.**" Note the rule does not cover **all** interference with a possessory interest—only a **meaningful** interference. In property law, a possessory interest in an object or land means that the owner can exclude everyone else from using it or taking it. Fourth Amendment law is somewhat more forgiving: a trivial interference with this right does not constitute a seizure; instead, the government's action must involve a **meaningful** interference with that possessory interest. For example, if a government agent takes a soil sample from a field, he has interfered with the property interest of the field's owner, but the interference is so trivial that he has not "seized" the owner's property.

Police are allowed to seize any item which appears to be contraband (such as narcotics), the fruits or consequence of a crime (such as stolen property), the instrumentality of a crime (such as a gun which they suspect was used in a recent crime), or evidence of a crime (such as distinctive clothing which was described by an eyewitness). Before the item may be seized, however, the fact that it is contraband, a consequence, an instrumentality, or evidence must be "**immediately apparent**" to the police officer. We will examine examples of the "immediately apparent" doctrine below.

---

2 Coolidge, 403 U.S. at 466 (1971).

3 United States v. Karo, 468 U.S. 705, 712 (1984).

The last part of the rule recognizes that not all seizures are the same. A police officer may handle an item for only a few minutes, or she may deprive the owner of the item permanently. The courts have said that the duration of the seizure must be reasonable—thus, the greater the level of suspicion that the item is contraband or the fruit, instrumentality, or evidence of a crime, the longer and more intrusive the seizure can be. This is a fact-based judgment that courts must make given the totality of the circumstances.

The rule for seizures of people is a bit more complicated:

> An individual is seized when a reasonable person in the suspect's position would believe he or she is not free to leave or otherwise terminate the encounter.[4]
>
> In order to briefly seize an individual (otherwise known as a "stop"), the law enforcement officer must have reasonable suspicion based on specific and articulable facts that criminal activity is afoot.[5]
>
> Any seizure of a person which consists of more than "a brief investigatory detention" is considered an arrest.[6]
>
> A law enforcement officer may arrest an individual without a warrant if she has probable cause to believe the individual committed a felony. If the officer has probable cause to believe the individual committed a misdemeanor, her authority to arrest will depend on the laws of that jurisdiction.
>
> In order to arrest an individual inside his or her home, the law enforcement officer must obtain an arrest warrant. (This is done by demonstrating probable cause to a neutral magistrate).

A person is seized if "**a reasonable person in his or her position would believe he or she is not free to leave**." Obviously, if a police officer physically grabs and restrains a person, she has been seized. But a seizure can also occur if the police officer exercises a show of authority over the person and the person submits to that authority. Thus, for example, if a police officer yells: "Freeze!" and the person stops, she has been seized. On the other hand, if a police officer yells: "Freeze!" and the person continues to run away, she has not been seized.

---

[4] United States v. Mendenhall, 446 U.S. 544, 553 (1980); Florida v. Royer, 460 U.S. 491, 503 (1983).

[5] Terry v. Ohio, 392 U.S. 1, 27 (1968).

[6] Id. at 500.

Finally, all of the above tests only apply to **warrantless** seizures of items and individuals. If a police officer has probable cause to seize an item or arrest an individual, the officer can always obtain a warrant to seize the item or make the arrest. (The item can then be held for the duration of the investigation, while the individual can be held for up to forty-eight hours under federal law before he must be brought before a judge, who will review the detention in a court proceeding known as an arraignment). We will discuss warrants in more depth in **Chapter 11.**

In analyzing the seizure of an item or a person, the first question of the analysis is whether a seizure occurred at all. If so, the court will then determine whether the initial seizure was proper, and then weigh the duration and scope of the seizure against the justification for the seizure. In the next section we will discuss each of these steps—and how they differ depending on whether an item or a person is being seized.

C. Applying the Law.

1. Has an Item Been Seized? The first question you must consider is whether a seizure has happened at all. As discussed above, a law enforcement officer "seizes" an item when she "meaningfully interferes with an individual's possessory interest." Usually if a government agent physically takes the item from the suspect, even temporarily, she is seizing the item. The same is true if the government agent interferes with an item while it is in transit. But sometimes the interference with the suspect's control is minimal. For example, an officer who takes a few cups of water from a suspect's lake or a few tablespoons of soil from a suspect's land is not conducting a seizure.

The interference with a possessory interest is sometimes very trivial (for example, briefly picking up an item and then putting it down again, or moving an object so that other objects can be seen more clearly). In such cases, courts will determine there is no seizure.

> **Example—*Arizona v. Hicks*, 480 U.S. 321 (1987):** While investigating a nearby shooting, police officers lawfully entered Hicks' apartment to look for a gun. One of the officers noticed an expensive stereo which seemed out of place in the otherwise "squalid" apartment. The officer pulled the stereo components out from the wall in order to read the serial numbers on the back, copied the numbers onto a piece of paper, and then called in the numbers to see if the stereo had been reported as stolen. After he learned that the stereo was in fact stolen property, he arrested Hicks for the theft. Hicks then challenged the officer's

actions, claiming that he illegally seized the stereo and illegally searched it.

Analysis: The Supreme Court held that the officer did not "seize" the stereo because moving the equipment a few inches did not constitute a meaningful interference with the defendant's possessory interest. And the Court held that copying information from the back of the stereo onto a piece of paper was also not a seizure, because "the mere recording" of those numbers did not meaningfully interfere with the defendant's possessory interest.

The Court did find that moving the stereo in order to read the numbers on the back constituted a search, since it "exposed to view concealed portions" of the apartment's contents and therefore intruded upon the defendant's reasonable expectation of privacy. (The court went on to find that the search was illegal because it did not fit within the plain view doctrine, which will be discussed in **Chapter 14**.)[7]

As we will see below, the *Hicks* holding that the mere copying of information does not constitute a seizure has serious and perhaps unforeseen ramifications for the digital age.

What the above example also shows is that the search and seizure analyses are independent. As in *Hicks*, a search can exist even if a seizure does not. In other cases, the reverse is true: the surveillance does not rise to the level of a search, but the interference with the suspect's possessory interest is significant enough that a seizure occurs.

Example—*United States v. Jacobsen*, 466 U.S. 109 (1984): Employees at a Federal Express office noticed that a package had been damaged in transit. Pursuant to company policy regarding damaged packages, the employees opened the package and inspected its contents. Inside they found a tube containing three baggies of a white powder. They immediately called the Drug Enforcement Agency.

When the DEA agents arrived, they took the white powder out of the bags and performed a field test on the substance to see whether it contained cocaine. The test came back positive. Based on this information the agents obtained a search warrant against the addressee, a man named Jacobsen. Jacobsen was subsequently arrested and charged with possession of cocaine with intent to distribute. He moved to suppress the drugs, arguing that the agents illegally

[7] Arizona v. Hicks, 480 U.S. 321 (1987).

searched his package and illegally seized the substance within to conduct the field test.

Analysis: The Supreme Court rejected Jacobsen's arguments. First, the Court found that no "search" occurred. Next the Court determined that although a "seizure" occurred, it was reasonable under the circumstances.

Regarding the search analysis, the Court first noted that the initial opening of the package by the Federal Express employees could not be a search because it was conducted by a private party, so there was no government action. The later field test by the DEA agents was also not a search, because it was a binary surveillance—it could not reveal anything about the substance other than the fact that it was or was not an illegal substance, and therefore did not infringe on a legitimate expectation of privacy.

Regarding the seizure analysis, the Court held that the DEA agents first exercised dominion and control over the package when they made the decision to conduct the field test. The defendant had entrusted the package to Federal Express and did not expect the government to be able to have any control over it. The seizure became more intrusive when the actual field test was conducted, since a portion of the cocaine was destroyed, which converted the temporary seizure of the package into a permanent seizure of some of the substance inside the package.

Thus, the Court concluded that there were two "seizures" in the case. The Court then turned to the question of whether the seizure was permissible. We will discuss that question in Sections 2 and 3, below.

Admittedly, there is not much distinction between facts of *Hicks* and the facts of *Jacobsen*. In *Hicks,* there was no seizure when the government moved stereo components a few inches and copied down some serial numbers from the back of the components. In *Jacobsen*, there were two seizures when the government "took control" over a package that had been entrusted to a third party and then destroyed a minimal amount of the substance during a chemical test. Thus, we can see that there is a very low threshold for whether a "seizure" of property takes place.

Recently, courts have been forced to deal with a new question regarding seizures: when is the data in a computer "seized"? Consider the following hypothetical:

Example: FBI Special Agent Frieda Downing suspected Josiah Harris of possessing child pornography. One day she followed Harris into a public park, and saw Harris sit down at a picnic table and open up his laptop and start working on it. After a few minutes Harris left the table to purchase a soft drink from a concession stand, leaving his computer unattended. Agent Downing quickly walked over to the computer, pulled out the jump drive, and plugged it into her own computer. She then created a folder called "Harrisflash" and copied the entire contents of the flash drive into the folder without seeing any of the data being copied. Before Harris returned, she replaced the flash drive into Harris' computer. The entire process took less than thirty seconds, and there was no way that Harris could have known that the flash drive had been copied.

Back at the FBI's office, Agent Downing ran a search on the "Harrisflash" folder, running a program that looked for .jpg files which were known to contain child pornography. The program returned fifty-two "hits." Downing took this information to a magistrate, obtained a warrant to search the folder, and then opened up the folder, confirming that there were fifty-two photographs containing child pornography. Harris was arrested and charged with possession of child pornography. He now challenges the seizure and subsequent search of the data on his computer.

Analysis: Most courts would conclude that Agent Dowling did not commit a seizure, because she did not meaningfully interfere with the Harris' possessory interest in the flash drive. She also arguably did not interfere with Harris' possessory interest in the data any more than the police interfered with the defendant's possessory interest in his stereo serial numbers in *Hicks*. In *Hicks*, the Court held that moving the stereo equipment a few inches was not a seizure, and that copying down the serial numbers onto a piece of paper was also not a seizure. This might be considered analogous to what Agent Dowling did here—she moved the flash drive a few feet, and then returned it to its original position, and she copied information without disturbing the original version of that information. Thus, under *Hicks*, there was no seizure here.

Although we are discussing seizures in this chapter, remember that you must always conduct a search analysis as well. When conducting a search analysis, the Harris fact pattern is much more like *Jacobsen* than *Hicks*. The surveillance in this case (running a computer program which can only detect the absence or presence of child pornography) is almost certainly not a search, since it is merely a binary surveillance—just like the field test in *Jacobsen*, which could only detect the absence or presence of a controlled substance.

However, neither *Hicks* nor *Jacobsen* seem to get at the real issue in the fact pattern. Under both analyses the court is focusing on the government's control over the physical object containing the data, not its exercise of control over the data itself. A court will focus on the potential "seizure" of the tangible object—in this case, the flash drive—and not on the seizure of the information. Thus, the legal rules miss the significant part of the government's action.

For example, what if we changed the fact pattern slightly to state that Agent Dowling used her own flash drive, plugged it into Harris' computer while he was away, and copied all of his document files onto her flash drive? Under *Hicks*, nothing at all has been "seized," because Agent Dowling has not physically moved any of Harris' belongings. She exercised some control over his computer for a few seconds, but not long enough to rise to the level of a seizure, especially because he was not using the computer at the time and was not even aware of her actions. The mere copying of information—by making a photocopy or copying a computer file—is not considered a seizure. (It may, of course, still be considered a search, as it was in the *Hicks* case).

One problem may be that the current laws on seizure were developed in an era of physical items and paper documents, and these rules need to be updated to reflect modern perceptions of intellectual property and modern methods of storing information. Courts faced a similar challenge before *Katz* with regard to searches; according to pre-*Katz* law, a surveillance was not a "search" unless it interfered with a property interest. But in *Katz* the Court was willing to hold that something as intangible as a telephone conversation could be the subject of a "search," and that the true test was whether the surveillance interfered with the suspect's reasonable expectation of privacy.

The current state of seizure law is analogous to the pre-*Katz* state of search law. Information has always been valuable, but now information can be stored and instantly copied without any transfer of physical property. In the old days, the government obtained records and information by seizing a journal or a book or a file cabinet, which clearly constituted a seizure. Today, information can be copied from a hard drive or copied while in transit without its owner even knowing about it. Is this a "meaningful interference with the owner's possessory interest"?

Imagine, for example, the scenario described in **Chapter 7**, where government agents use "internet sniffers" which intercept all of the digital communication coming and going from a suspect's account to search for child pornography. If the sniffer software only reveals the absence or presence of illegal images, it will not be considered a search, since it is not interfering with the any legitimate expectation of privacy. Under current seizure laws, this is not a seizure either, since it does not meaningfully interfere with the suspect's possessory interest. But as courts see more and more of these "information only" searches, they may be more willing to broaden the definition of a seizure.

2. Seizing Items: When Is It Permissible? After a court determines that a seizure has occurred, it turns to the next question: whether the seizure was reasonable.

This can be split into two distinct questions: first, was the initial seizure justified? And second, was the extent and duration of the seizure reasonable under the circumstances? We will consider these questions in order.

If the police officer has probable cause to seize an item, she can always go to a judge or magistrate and obtain warrant, which will state with particularity the items to be seized. In the absence of a warrant, however, the Supreme Court has stated that an item may be seized if it is "immediately apparent" that the item is (1) contraband, (2) the instrumentality of a crime, (3) the fruits of a crime, or (4) evidence of a crime. This rule applies to officers who are acting without a warrant and to officers who seek to seize an item that is not specified in their warrant.

The term "immediately apparent" is a bit misleading. The incriminating nature of the item must be immediately ascertainable. However, the incriminating nature need not be "apparent" in the sense of obvious or certain. Instead, as discussed in **Chapter 14,** the officer need only have probable cause that the item falls into one of the four categories in order to justify the seizure. But the officer must have probable cause immediately upon detecting the object; she is not allowed to engage in a thorough examination before determining that she has probable cause.

> **Example:** Dan Michaels, a high school student, was driving through town when his car broke down. He began to push his car towards a local service station, when a police officer approached and asked if he needed help. As the two pushed the car together, the police officer looked inside the car and saw a bottle of prescription pills on the passenger side of the car. The bottle had no label. The officer had seen a report that a number of high school students in town were illegally taking pharmaceutical drugs, and suspected that Michaels did not have a prescription for the pills.
>
> After they finished pushing the car to the service station, the police officer reached into the car and grabbed the pill bottle. Michaels immediately protested, claiming that he had a prescription for the pills, but that the label had fallen off of the bottle. The police officer did not believe Michaels and said he was going to hold onto the pill bottle until Michaels could provide documentation that he did indeed have a prescription for the pills. Two hours later, Michaels appeared at the police station with a copy of his prescription, and the officer returned the bottle. Michaels is now suing the police department, arguing that the officer conducted an unlawful seizure.

Analysis: A court would probably hold that this was an unlawful seizure by the police. The first step would be to determine whether a seizure occurred at all—that is, whether taking possession of the pill bottle for two hours represented a "meaningful interference" with Michaels' possessory interest. This almost certainly is the case, given the nature of the item taken and the amount of time that the officer held it. If the officer had merely picked up the pill bottle, inspected it, and then replaced it, there would not have been a seizure (though there might have been a search).

The court would then determine whether the contraband nature of the bottle was "immediately apparent" at the time of the seizure. This would be a judgment call by the court: if a police officer knows that prescription drugs are being abused by local high school students and then sees a high school student in possession of a prescription pill bottle without a label, is the contraband nature of the bottle "immediately apparent"? Most judges would probably say no, meaning the officer had no right to seize the bottle. On the other hand, if an experienced narcotics officer saw a bag of white powder that she believed to be cocaine, a judge would almost certainly conclude that the contraband nature of the item was immediately apparent to police officer.

If the court did conclude that it was "immediately apparent" that the pill bottle was contraband, it would then need to decide whether the seizure was reasonable—that is, whether the level of suspicion the officer had at the time of the seizure justified the scope and duration of the seizure that occurred. We turn to this question in the next section.

3. Seizing Items: How Intrusive Can the Seizure Be? Even if an object has been properly seized, the extent and duration of the seizure must be reasonable. Courts consider two factors to determine whether a seizure is reasonable:

1. The extent of the interference in the suspect's possessory interest—that is, the scope and duration of the seizure; and
2. The level of suspicion the police had at the time of the seizure. If the police were acting only on reasonable suspicion, only a brief seizure is permitted. If the police were acting on probable cause, a more extensive seizure is permitted.

In the end, the reasonableness analysis is a fact-based inquiry. In the *Jacobsen* case discussed in Section C.1, above, the Court held that a field test conducted on the defendant's Federal Express package was reasonable because (1) the seizure was minimally intrusive, since the package's delivery was delayed by at most a few hours, and the amount of drugs destroyed in the test was negligible, and (2) the police were fairly certain at the time of the seizure that the package did in fact contain cocaine.

Many factors can contribute to a court's analysis of the scope and duration of the seizure. Consider the following:

Example—*United States v. Place*, 462 U.S. 696 (1983): As Raymond Place purchased a ticket to fly from Miami to New York, his actions raised the suspicions of federal agents. They stopped him to ask some questions. During this questioning, Place consented to a search of his checked bags. However, the agents let him board his plane without conducting the search because his flight was about to take off. At the request of the agents in Miami, two federal agents were waiting for Place when he landed at La Guardia airport in New York. They watched him as he moved through the airport, and his actions again seemed suspicious. After Place retrieved his luggage, the agents approached him and asked for permission to search his suitcases. This time Place refused. The agents then explained that they were going to take his suitcases to a federal magistrate and get a search warrant. Place was invited to come with them, but he refused, instead getting a telephone number from one of the agents which he could call to retrieve his bags later.

The agents took Place's bags to Kennedy airport, where they had a drug-sniffing dog on duty. The dog sniffed Place's bags and reacted positively to one of them. This was ninety minutes after the officers had taken the bags from Place. Because it was Friday afternoon, the police held the luggage until Monday morning, when they obtained a search warrant, opened the bag, and found over one kilo of cocaine. Place moved to suppress the seizure and search of his bags.

Analysis: The Supreme Court held there was no pre-warrant "search" of Place's bag, because the sniff from the drug dog was only a binary search. However, the Court held that taking possession of Place's luggage was a meaningful interference with his possessory interest, and therefore a seizure occurred.

The Court found that the initial seizure was permissible. "When an officer's observations lead him reasonably to believe that a traveler is carrying luggage that contains narcotics," he can "detain the luggage briefly to investigate the circumstances that aroused his suspicion, provided that the investigative detention is properly limited in scope."

The Court then turned to the question of whether the scope of the seizure was "reasonable" under the circumstances and determined that it was not. At the time of the seizure, the police only had reasonable suspicion that Place's bags contained narcotics. This low level of suspicion would justify a brief investigation but not a ninety minute seizure. The federal agents also exacerbated the intrusion of the seizure—making it even more unreasonable—in four ways: (1) such a lengthy seizure could have been avoided if the agents in New York had arranged to have a drug-sniffing dog at the proper airport when Place arrived; (2) the agents failed to accurately inform Place about where they were taking his luggage; (3) the agents failed to tell Place the length of time they would keep the luggage; and (4) the agents did not tell Place specifically how to get the luggage back if no contraband was found.

Once the dog alerted to one of Place's bags, the police had probable cause to believe that the bag contained narcotics. Probable cause is a higher level of suspicion which can justify a longer and more intrusive seizure. Therefore, keeping the bag from that point until the warrant was issued three days later was reasonable. But because the duration of the seizure before the dog sniff was unreasonable, the drugs found in the bags had to be suppressed.[8]

4. Seizing a Person. Police also have the authority to seize individuals. This is often referred to as "detaining" the suspect. As with seizures of objects, the Fourth Amendment creates a sliding scale that runs from no-seizure-at-all to a full blown arrest. The longer or more intrusive the detention, the greater the justification needed to authorize it. At the lowest end of the register is a consensual encounter between a police officer and a suspect. Such an encounter does not constitute a "seizure" and thus does not implicate the Fourth Amendment. Police officers engaged in such consensual encounters do not need to offer any justification for the approach and a suspect engaged in such an encounter is free to walk away at any time.

The next level up is a brief encounter in which the suspect is forced to stop by the police for a few moments. This sort of temporary seizure is known as a "stop", and it requires "reasonable suspicion" that the suspect is involved in a crime.

The most substantial type of seizure recognized by the Court is an arrest. An arrest occurs when the suspect is detained for a significant period of time and (usually) results in the suspect being criminally charged. Police must have probable cause before they can conduct an arrest. Finally, if the arrest takes place inside the suspect's home, the police must, under ordinary circumstances, first obtain a warrant from a judge (supported by probable cause). There is an exception for hot pursuit—that is, if the police are chasing a fleeing suspect who then runs into her home—which we will discuss in detail in **Chapter 17.**

[8] United States v. Place, 462 U.S. 696 (1983).

Overview – Seizure of a person

	Consensual encounter	Stop	Arrest	Arrest within home
How Long?	Until suspect decides to leave	"Reasonable time"* to resolve suspicion	48 hours before D must see judge	48 hours before D must see judge
Justification Required?	None	Reasonable suspicion	Probable cause or arrest warrant	Arrest warrant (or hot pursuit)

A "reasonable time" depends on the facts and circumstances of the case, but generally anything up to twenty minutes has been deemed reasonable, while *Place* tells us that ninety minutes is certainly unreasonable.

The preliminary question, then, is whether (and when) a seizure actually occurs—that is, the difference between a consensual encounter and a "stop." In answering this question, courts will apply a purely objective test: would a reasonable person in the suspect's position believe she is free to leave?

Obviously if the suspect attempts to leave and is ordered to stay or is physically prevented from leaving, a seizure has occurred: the Supreme Court has held that a seizure occurs "when the officer, by means of physical force or show of authority, has in some way restrained the liberty of a citizen."[9] However, the question of a seizure is not always so clear-cut. In the absence of this direct evidence of physical force or a show of authority, the Supreme Court has listed the following factors as relevant to the question of whether the objective circumstances establish a seizure:

- The "threatening presence of several officers."
- The display of a weapon by an officer.
- The physical touching of the suspect.
- Use of language or tone of voice indicating that compliance with the officer's request is required.
- The youth of the suspect.

The Court applied this test to a police-suspect encounter on a Greyhound bus:

[9] Terry, 392 U.S. at 19 n.16.

Example—*United States v. Drayton*, 536 U.S. 194 (2002): Christopher Drayton and his friend Clifton Brown were traveling from Florida to Michigan on a Greyhond bus. The bus made a scheduled stop in Tallahassee, Florida, so that the bus could get refueled and cleaned. All the passengers were required to get off the bus. When the passengers returned to the bus, the driver left the bus to complete paperwork, and three Tallahassee Police Department officers boarded the bus. The officers were dressed in plain clothes and carried concealed weapons, but their badges were visible.

The officers were conducting a routine drug and weapons interdiction program. One of the officers knelt on the driver's seat and faced the rear of the bus. Another officer walked to the back of the bus and stood there. The third officer started at the back of the bus and worked his way forward, speaking with each passenger as he came forward and asking them to identify their luggage in the overhead rack. The officer later testified that any passengers who refused to speak with him or who wanted to leave the bus would have been allowed to do so, though he did not tell this to any of the passengers. During each of these encounters, the officer was about twelve to eighteen inches away from each passenger, and he stood a little in front or behind them so that he did not block their access to the aisle.

The officer reached Drayton and Brown, held up his badge, identified himself as a police officer, explained he was looking for drugs and illegal weapons, and asked if they had any bags on the bus. After the two individuals identified their bag, the officer asked for permission to search it, which Brown gave. No drugs were found in the bag. The officer then asked Brown: "Do you mind if I check your person?" and Brown answered "Sure." The officer searched Brown and found hard objects taped to his thighs that felt like drug packages. The officer arrested Brown and found nearly half a kilo of cocaine taped to Brown's thighs.

The officer then asked Drayton, "Mind if I check you?" and Drayton responded by lifting his hands about eight inches from his legs. Lang conducted a patdown of Drayton's thighs and detected hard objects similar to those found on Brown. Drayton was also searched and the officer found 295 grams of cocaine taped to his thighs.

Drayton challenged the search, arguing that he had been seized while on the bus and so therefore the ensuing consent, search, and arrest were invalid.

Analysis: The Supreme Court held that the police conduct did not constitute a seizure. Because the police officer did not block the aisle and spoke in conversational tone of voice, no reasonable person would believe that he or she was unable to leave the bus or terminate the encounter. The Court noted: "There was no application of force, no intimidating movement, no overwhelming show of force, no brandishing of weapons, no blocking of exits, no threat, no command, not even an authoritative tone of voice. It is beyond question that had this encounter occurred on the street, it would be constitutional."[10] The fact that it took place on a bus made it even less like a seizure, according to the Court, because it took place in front of so many other people, making the police presence less intimidating.

Three Justices filed a sharp dissent. In their mind, this type of encounter could easily have been a seizure had it occurred on the street: "[C]onsider three officers, one of whom stands behind [a] pedestrian, another at his side toward the open sidewalk, with the third addressing questions to the pedestrian a foot or two from his face."[11] Especially if this happened in a narrow alleyway, the presence of the officers may indeed seem threatening to the extent that they "overbear a normal person's ability to act freely, even in the absence of explicit commands or the formalities of detention."[12] The situation was even more coercive on a bus, when the driver left the bus and turned it over to the three police officers. In such a situation, the dissent argued, the fact that the officer used a quiet tone of voice is irrelevant: "A police officer who is certain to get his way has no need to shout."[13]

Thus, judges may disagree whether a "reasonable person" in the suspect's position would feel free to leave or otherwise terminate the encounter.

Although judges may disagree about how a reasonable person may react in any given situation, there is no question that the reasonable person standard is the appropriate test. In other words, the seizure test is purely objective. Thus, it does not matter whether the police officer intended to seize the suspect. If a police officer approaches a suspect and engages in casual conversation without any show of force or authority, the interaction will not be considered a seizure even if the police officer later admits that she would not have let the suspect leave if he tried to do so. Likewise, if the officer grabs the suspect by the arm and holds him, but the officer honestly believes that the suspect was allowed to leave at any time, the court will determine that the suspect was seized despite the officer's honest belief to the contrary.

---

[10] United States v. Drayton, 536 U.S. 194 (2002).

[11] Id. at 210 (Souter, J., dissenting).

[12] Id. (Souter, J., dissenting).

[13] Id. at 21. (Souter, J., dissenting).

The subjective belief of the suspect himself is also not determinative of whether he has been seized. Of course, his own statements or actions will be factors the court considers in determining whether a reasonable person would believe himself free to leave or end the encounter.

> **Example:** Police officers suspected that Wendell was involved in a series of burglaries. They called Wendell at his home and asked if he would come down to the police station to answer some questions. Wendell said he was willing to come down, but he couldn't make it until noon the next day.
>
> The next day at noon, Wendell drove to the police station and was met by three uniformed police officers. They took him into a room and had him sit at a table. They closed the door to the room but left it unlocked. Two officers sat at the table across from him, while the third stood by the door. Wendell looked up at the door and said: "Am I under arrest all of a sudden?" One of the officers at the table shook his head and said: "No, of course not, we just want to ask you a few questions." Has Wendell been seized by the police at this point?

Analysis: A court will probably determine that Wendell has not been seized, but there are good arguments on each side. On the one hand, when Wendell arrived at the station, he was met by three officers in uniform, making the interaction seem less like a consensual conversation. In addition, one of the officers stood by the door during the meeting, which a reasonable person might interpret as a signal that he was not allowed to simply walk out the door whenever he felt like it.

On the other hand, the original contact from the police came in the form of a request, and Wendell was allowed to choose his own time to meet with the police and drove his own car to the station without any police escort. Furthermore, before the conversation even began, he was told he was not under arrest. These are all objective factors which would lead a reasonable person to believe that they were in fact free to leave.

What if the police officer physically grabs the suspect and the suspect escapes and runs away? Or what if the police officer makes a "show of authority" but the suspect ignores the show of authority and flees? The Supreme Court faced that question in a case called *Hodari D.* and found that a suspect's failure to submit means there has been no seizure:

> **Example—*California v. Hodari D.*, 499 U.S. 621 (1991):** Officer Pertuso and his partner were on patrol when they saw a group of youths huddled around a parked car. When the youths saw the police officers' car, they immediately fled in different

directions. Officer Pertuso got out of the car and pursued the youth on foot, cutting through streets until he was able to jump in front of Hodari D., one of the fleeing suspects. Seeing the police officer blocking his path, Hodari D. threw a small rock to the ground and was then tackled by Pertuso. The police officer handcuffed Hodari D. and then went to inspect the rock he had thrown on the ground. The rock turned out to be crack cocaine. Hodari D. was arrested for drug possession, and moved to suppress the crack from evidence.

Analysis: The Court held that Hodari D. was not seized until he had been physically restrained by the officer. The Court's analysis turned on when Hodari D. was "seized" by the police officer. If the seizure occurred at the time Hodari D. first fled , then he dropped the drugs after having been "seized," and therefore the police would have to prove that the seizure was justified under the Fourth Amendment. If, on the other hand, he was not seized until he was tackled and handcuffed, he abandoned his property before the seizure, and the police were free to recover the abandoned property without implicating the Fourth Amendment.

"The word 'seizure' . . . does not remotely apply, however, to the prospect of a policeman yelling 'Stop, in the name of the law!' at a fleeing form that continues to flee. . . . An arrest requires either physical force . . . or, where that is absent, submission to the assertion of authority."[14]

As *Hodari D.* makes clear, a police encounter will not move on the sliding scale from "entirely consensual" to "subject to the strictures of the Fourth Amendment" until the police have applied physical force or a suspect has submitted to a show of authority.

Once we know that a person has been seized, there are still questions the court must consider. For example, the court must decide whether the seizure was a brief detention requiring only reasonable suspicion to justify it; or if the seizure was an arrest requiring probable cause. The line between stops and arrests is examined in **Chapter 19**, which examines the *Terry* case and its progeny in greater detail. For now, note only that there are two distinct types of seizures—stops and arrests—each permitting various degrees of intrusion by law enforcement and each requiring very different levels of justification.

You should also know that the consequences of an illegal stop or an illegal arrest are different from the consequences of an illegal search. If the police conduct an illegal search, the defendant can move to suppress the fruits of that search. Similarly, if an item is illegally seized, that item may be suppressed. But a suspect who is illegally detained or arrested has no direct remedy. She cannot move to

[14] California v. Hodari D, 499 U.S. 621, 626 (1991).

"suppress the arrest" or argue that the charges against her should be dropped because the stop was illegal. Instead, an improper seizure has legal relevance only because it may indirectly affect whether a subsequent search was legal, or because a statement made by the suspect while in custody may be inadmissible.

For example, when a police officer conducts a legal stop, she may be permitted to frisk the suspect for weapons. Likewise, when a police officer makes a lawful arrest, she is generally allowed to search the suspect without a warrant. If in these cases the defendant can prove that the stop or the arrest was illegal, then any search which based on that stop becomes an illegal search, and the fruits of that search will most likely be suppressed from trial.

5. Police Discretion in Seizing a Person. One of the important themes in criminal procedure is the tension between creating strict rules which ensure uniform application of the law and giving discretion to decision-makers to allow for flexibility. At this very early stage of the investigatory process, police officers are given wide discretion as to whether to conduct a seizure—or even whether to charge an individual with a crime. The following two case shows the extent to which the Supreme Court has deferred to police discretion in deciding whether to make a seizure:

> **Example—*Atwater v. City of Lago Vista*, 532 U.S. 218 (2001):** Texas law required every passenger in the front seat of a vehicle to wear a seat belt. A violation of this law resulted in a fine of between $25 and $50. The law also expressly allowed a police officer to make an arrest for any violation, though officers were also allowed to give a citation instead of an arrest.
>
> Gail Atwater was driving her truck with her three-year-old and five-year-old children as passengers, and none of them were wearing seat belts. Officer Turek of the Lago Vista police department pulled her over for the violation and immediately began yelling at her, saying "We've met before," and "You're going to jail." He called for backup and asked for Atwater's license and proof of insurance. Atwater told him she could not provide them because her purse had been stolen. Atwater's children began to cry, and Atwater asked if she could take them to a friend's house, but the officer refused. One of Atwater's friends showed up at the scene to take possession of the children. Atwater was arrested, handcuffed, taken to the police precinct, booked, and placed in a holding cell for an hour. She then was taken in front of a magistrate and released on $310 bond.

Atwater ultimately pled guilty to the charge of driving without a seat belt. She then sued Officer Turek and the City of Lago Vista, arguing that her arrest violated her Fourth Amendment right against unreasonable seizures. Atwater asked the courts to create a rule which prohibited an arrest for minor crimes that carried no possibility of jail time if there was no compelling need for immediate detention.

Analysis: In a 5-4 decision, the Supreme Court held that Atwater's arrest was not an unreasonable seizure and refused to create any rule limiting the police power to arrest.

The Court first reviewed the common law history of warrantless misdemeanor arrests and concluded that at the time that the Fourth Amendment was drafted, there was no unanimity as to whether state officials were given the power to execute a warrantless arrest for a misdemeanor. The Court did note, however, that in modern times all fifty states permitted such arrests.

The Court then explained that a rule that restricted the arrest power beyond the probable cause requirement would be too difficult to apply in practice. A police officer on the scene, for example, might have no way of knowing whether the offense carries the possibility of jail time—for example, whether a crime carries jail time may depend on whether the defendant has a prior record, or whether the amount of marijuana recovered is less than or greater than one ounce.

Although the Court held that the officer's conduct in Atwater's case was "foolish" and "at best" showed extremely poor judgment, the Court did not believe that there was widespread abuse of the arrest power among police officers. This was because legislatures and police department rarely permitted arrests for minor offenses, given the expense and time involved in making an arrest. And in the event that good sense did not prevail within legislatures and police departments, both institutions were politically accountable for their actions, which would serve as an ultimate check on potential abuses of the arrest power.[15]

Thus, as long as police officers have probable cause to believe that a crime has occurred, and as long as the statute authorizes an arrest for that crime, there is no constitutional limitation on the officer's arrest power. No matter how trivial the crime, the officer has the power to arrest if he or she believes it is appropriate.

The same rule applies to seizures that fall short of an arrest. A police officer who has reasonable suspicion that an individual is involved in criminal activity has the right to forcibly detain that person for questioning and observation, if the officer believes it is the best course of action. As we will see when we discuss *Terry*, if the officer chooses to forcibly stop the suspect, she may also have the right to frisk

[15] Atwater v. City of Lago Vista, 532 U.S. 218 (2001).

the suspect for weapons. Of course the officer is not **required** to make an arrest or seizure. Instead, she could attempt to resolve the suspicion with a consensual encounter. Both the stop and the frisk are valuable investigative tools for the police officer, but they both also involve a significant loss of liberty on the part of the suspect.

On the one hand, it would be nonsensical to require the police to forcibly detain **everyone** for whom they have a reasonable suspicion of criminal activity—there needs to be some room for police to focus their investigations more efficiently. On the other hand, there is a real concern that police officers at times exercise this discretion in a discriminatory manner.

Police officers are given considerable discretion in their encounters with civilians. For example, consider a police officer on foot patrol walking through a crowded park. She observes two individuals nearby standing next to a park bench, passing a cigarette back and forth. She approaches them, and one of the individuals sees her approach, stubs out the cigarette, and puts it in his pocket. Assuming we are in a jurisdiction where marijuana is illegal, the officer now probably has reasonable suspicion to detain the person with the cigarette. Thus, she could order him to stand still, grab him, and perhaps even frisk him to look for weapons. Then she could ask him questions about the cigarette in his pocket until she either develops probable cause to arrest him or the reasonable suspicion is dispelled.

But she could also simply walk up to the individual, greet him politely, and then ask what he was doing and what was in his pocket, leaving the individual free to ignore her and leave if he wanted to. This investigative technique may seem less useful, but in fact a suspect may be more willing to admit to a small infraction of the law under friendly, unthreatening questioning than under forcible interrogation. And the officer may be more likely to get further cooperation from the suspect with a softer approach—perhaps he will be more willing to give her information about the drug trade in the area that would be useful for a longer term investigation.

The officer must consider one other important factor in making her decision. There are a lot of members of the community standing around watching—what message does she want to convey to them? That she—and by extension other police officers in the neighborhood—are tough, no-nonsense law enforcement agents who will not hesitate to assert their authority when a person is suspected of breaking the law? Or that she—and by extension other police officers in the neighborhood—are reasonable individuals who respect the rights of their fellow citizens? Either message may be useful, depending on the reputation that the officer wants to cultivate with members of the community.

Finally, assume the police officer is able to develop probable cause that the suspect does in fact possess marijuana. She now has a number of options:

1. She can formally arrest him—that is, handcuff him, book him, and place him in jail, where he will likely stay until his arraignment, which may be twelve or more hours away.

2. She could give him a citation—she gives the suspect a ticket and tells him to appear at a specific court at a given time a few days or weeks in the future. At that time the defendant may plead guilty to a fine and never spend a minute in jail.

3. She could decide not to pursue any criminal charges against the suspect—she would simply confiscate the marijuana cigarette, give the suspect a warning, and let him go about his business.

How the police officer exercises this discretion can obviously have an enormous impact on the suspect himself, not to mention the state of police/community relations in the neighborhood.

6. Pretextual Seizures. Allowing the police so much discretion raises the problem of pretextual seizures—that is, seizures in which it is apparent the police are in fact seizing a person for an illegitimate reason, but claim they are seizing the individual for a legitimate reason. The Supreme Court has consistently refused to examine the subjective intent of the individual officers in evaluating the constitutionality of a seizure, and merely looks to whether the officer had the right to conduct the seizure. For example, in the context of vehicle stops, the Court has held that as long as the police officer had a **legal** reason for making the seizure, it is irrelevant what her **actual** reason was for making the seizure:

> **Example—*Whren v. United States,* 517 U.S. 806 (1996):** Plainclothes vice-squad officers of the District of Columbia police were in an umarked car in a "high drug area" of the city when they saw a car with "youthful occupants" stopped at a stop sign. The car stayed at the stop sign for more than twenty seconds, during which time the driver looked down into the lap of his passenger. When the police executed a U-turn to head back towards the car, the car turned to its right without signaling and sped off at an "unreasonable" speed.
>
> At this point the police believed the occupants of the car possessed illegal drugs, but legally they did not even have reasonable

suspicion that this was true. However, they did have probable cause to pull the car over for traffic violations, so they pulled alongside the car and ordered the driver to put the car in park. One of the officers approached the car to give the driver a traffic warning and he saw two large plastic bags of crack cocaine in the hands of one of the occupants. The police ordered all of the occupants out of the car and searched the car, finding various other illegal drugs. All of the occupants were arrested.

One of the occupants of the car, Michael Whren, challenged the stop and temporary seizure of the car. Whren argued that even though the police had the right to stop the car for the minor traffic violation, the traffic violation was a mere pretext for the officers' actual motivations.

Analysis: The Court unanimously upheld the seizure, stating that the actual motivations of individual officers who conduct a seizure were irrelevant in evaluating the constitutionality of the seizure. There is nothing to "prevent the police from doing under the guise of enforcing the traffic code what they would like to do for different reasons."[16]

The defendant also asked the Court to adopt an "objective" rule which would require a judge to determine "whether the officer's conduct deviated materially from usual police practices;" in other words, whether a reasonable officer in the same circumstances would not have made the stop for the reasons given." The Court refused to adopt this standard as well, holding that it was unworkable, since it would be very difficult to determine what the "usual police practices" would be for a certain jurisdiction and for the given facts of a case. More significantly, the Court rejected (as it would later do in *Atwater*) any application of a "reasonableness" test to the police officer's decision to make a seizure or an arrest. As long as the police officer possesses probable cause, she is permitted to execute the stop or the arrest, respectively, regardless of her own internal motivations.

We will see this principle applied in many different contexts throughout the class: as long as the police officer has the right to do something, courts will not inquire as to the subjective motivation of the police officer when she does it. The Fourth Amendment is arguably not meant to regulate the reasons behind police conduct, only the objective conduct itself.

7. Use of Deadly Force While Seizing an Individual. Frequently police officers seize an individual merely by ordering them to stop. Sometimes, however, police use force to conduct a seizure—and occasionally they use deadly force. Just as

[16] Whren v. United States, 517 U.S. 806, 814 (1996).

with other aspects of seizures, the level of force used by the police when conducting a seizure must be reasonable. The police can respond with deadly force if it is necessary to prevent a suspect from the imminent use of deadly force against themselves or others. But what if the police are simply trying to stop a suspect from escaping?

> **Example—*Tennessee v. Garner*, 47 U.S. 1 (1985):** Two Memphis police officers responded to a report of a burglary at a home. When they arrived, Officer Wright radioed their status while Officer Hymon went to the back of the home. Officer Hymon heard the backdoor slam and saw an individual—later known to be Edward Garner—run across the backyard and crouch next to a six-foot chain fence. With his flashlight, the officer saw Garner's hands and face, and was "reasonably sure" that the suspect was not armed. Officer Hymon yelled out "Police! Halt!" Garner began to climb the fence and Officer Hymon shot him in the back of the head. Garner was taken to the hospital and died on the operating table. At the time of the shooting, he had been carrying items that had been stolen from the house.
>
> Garner's family sued the state of Tennessee, arguing that Officer Hymon violated Garner's Fourth Amendment rights by conducting an unreasonable seizure. Tennessee argued that if Officer Hymon had not shot Garner, Garner would have jumped over the fence and disappeared into the darkness. Thus, Tennessee argued that Officer Hymon acted reasonably because he had employed the only possible method to prevent the escape of a fleeing felon.

Analysis: The Supreme Court held that Officer Hymon's method of seizure was unreasonable because the use of deadly force is not justified to apprehend nonviolent suspects. The Court noted that although Officer Hymon clearly had probable cause to seize Garner, the **method** of the seizure must be reasonable. Reasonableness is measured by balancing the extent of the intrusion against the need for it.

Tennessee argued that the use of deadly force to apprehend a fleeing, nonviolent felon is necessary because it deters others felons from attempting to flee from the police and therefore increases the number of perpetrators who peacefully surrender to police. The Court rejected this argument, noting that a majority of the police departments in the country prohibited the use of deadly force and thus had apparently concluded that allowing such force would not have a significant impact on the conduct of future criminals in similar situations. This questionable interest needed to be balanced against the state's fundamental interest in protecting human life.[17]

After *Garner* was decided, many lawyers and courts attempted to create simple, bright-line rules for when the use of deadly force was appropriate. Two decades later, however, the Supreme Court heard another case on this issue and clarified the flexible nature of the "reasonableness" standard:

> **Example—*Scott v. Harris*, 550 U.S. 372 (2007):** A county deputy in Georgia recorded Victor Harris' car driving at 73 miles per hour in a 55 miles-per-hour zone. The deputy put on his light and siren and began to follow Harris, but Harris did not pull over. Instead, Harris increased his speed to 85 miles per hour and fled from the deputy. More deputies were called in to assist in the chase, including Deputy Timothy Scott. During the ensuing chase, Harris' car swerved around more than a dozen other cars, crossed over the double yellow line, ran multiple red lights, frequently drove in the center left-turn-only lane, and collided with Deputy Scott's car at one point to escape being trapped in a shopping center parking lot. The Supreme Court described the episode as "a Hollywood-style car chase of the most frightening sort, placing police officers and innocent bystanders alike at great risk of serious injury."[18]
>
> Six minutes and ten miles after the chase began, Deputy Scott received permission to "take out" Harris' car. Using a controlled maneuver, Deputy Scott accelerated and hit the rear bumper of Harris' car. Harris lost control of the car, which ran off the roadway, down an embankment, flipped over, and crashed. Harris was severely injured and ended up a quadriplegic as a result of the crash. Harris sued the sheriff's office, arguing that based on *Garner*, the method of seizure was unreasonable under the circumstances.

Analysis: The Supreme Court ruled that Deputy Scott's actions were reasonable. The Court acknowledged that Deputy Scott applied deadly force to Harris, but the Court rejected the argument that *Garner* was controlling. Harris argued that, under *Garner*, deadly force was only justified if (1) the suspect posed an immediate threat of harm to others; (2) deadly force was necessary to prevent escape; and (3) some warning was given to the suspect. But the Court rejected such a

[17] Tennessee v. Garner, 471 U.S. 1, 9 (1985).

[18] Scott v. Harris, 550 U.S. 372, 379-380 (2007).

mechanical application of *Garner*, explaining that the reasonableness test was a flexible standard in which the judge should balance the justification for the use of deadly force against the level of intrusion it involves.

In this case (unlike in *Garner*), there was a strong justification for the use of deadly force because the suspect's actions posed "an actual and imminent threat to the lives of any pedestrians who might have been present, to other civilian motorists, and to the officers involved in the chase."[19] The level of intrusion was high (as it is in all deadly force cases), since Deputy Scott's actions "posed a high likelihood of serious injury or death to respondent." But it still was not as high as in *Garner*, which involved "the near certainty of death posed by . . . shooting a fleeing felon in the back of the head."[20] The use of deadly force was also justified because Harris, who was the more culpable party, was knowingly putting many others at risk with his conduct, whereas Deputy Scott was only attempting to prevent Harris from harming others.

Thus, "[a] police officer's attempt to terminate a dangerous high-speed car chase that threatens the lives of innocent bystanders does not violate the Fourth Amendment, even when it places the fleeing motorist at risk of serious injury or death."[21]

Harris did not overrule *Garner*; it simply clarified that the applicable test was a flexible one. However, after *Garner* and *Harris*, we know that any method of seizure which will likely result in serious physical injury or death—such as shooting at the suspect or running his car off the road—only has a chance of being permissible if it is used against a suspect who presents an actual and imminent threat to the lives or safety of others.

However, once the police have determined that the suspect does present such an imminent threat, they are allowed to use whatever type of deadly force is reasonably necessary to neutralize that threat. In the 2014 decision *Plumhoff v. Rickard*, the driver led police on a *Harris*-like chase through traffic for over five minutes at speeds that at time exceeded 100 miles per hour. After the driver consistently refused to stop, two officers fired fifteen shots into the passenger compartment of a car, killing the driver and his passenger. The Supreme Court held that the officers' conduct was reasonable, and that the amount of force used was not excessive. "[I]f police officers are justified in firing at a suspect in order to end a severe threat to public safety, the officers need not stop shooting until the threat has ended."[22]

However, once the police have determined that the suspect does present such an imminent threat, they are allowed to use whatever type of deadly force that is reasonably necessary to neutralize that threat. In the 2014 decision *Plumhoff v.*

[19] Id. at 384.
[20] Id.
[21] Id. at 386.
[22] Plumhoff v. Rickard, 134 S.Ct. 2012 (2014).

Rickard, the driver led police on a *Harris*-like chase through traffic for over five minutes at speeds that at time exceeded 100 miles per hour. After the driver consistently refused to stop, two officers fired fifteen shots into the passenger compartment of a car, killing the driver and his passenger. The Supreme Court held that the officers' conduct was reasonable, and that the amount of force used was not excessive. "[I]f police officers are justified in firing at a suspect in order to end a severe threat to public safety, the officers need not stop shooting until the threat has ended."[23]

While the method of **seizure** must be calibrated based on the severity of the suspected offense, the Court has not imposed a similar limitation on the method of **search** following arrest. Once an arrestee is lawfully arrested and is being booked into detention to be housed at a correctional facility, the Court has found that any type of search—even a strip search—is permitted even if the arrestee is being booked for a fairly minor offense.[24]

There was one other significant aspect of the *Harris* case: the majority opinion placed the police officer's dashboard video record of the chase as part of the official Supreme Court record. This is symbolic of the way new technologies have transformed the way courts review police/citizen interaction. Less than a generation ago, the way that police treated suspects on the street was largely hidden from view. When the suspect challenged the police conduct at a later hearing—either in a suppression hearing in his own criminal case or as part of a civil trial when the suspect sued the police—the court's only versions of the facts was the sworn testimony of the suspect and the police officer. As you might expect, courts tended to resolve any factual dispute in favor of the police officer instead of the suspected criminal.

Now, however, dashboard cameras are standard equipment for many police cars. And even if there is no dashboard camera, a police officer would be foolish to assume that the interaction was not recorded by a surveillance camera or someone nearby with a cell phone camera. In the *Harris* case, the evidence provided by the video favored the government because it convinced the Supreme Court that the defendant's driving was dangerously reckless. But in many other cases, the video provides nearly incontrovertible evidence that the police themselves behaved unreasonably.

[23] Plumhoff v. Rickard, 134 S.Ct. 2012 (2014).

[24] Florence v. Chosen Board of Freeholders, 132 S.Ct. 1510 (2012).

Quick Summary

Like searches, seizures must be "reasonable" under the Fourth Amendment. The Court has interpreted reasonableness on a sliding scale—as seizures become more intrusive, they require a greater justification.

An object is seized when the police meaningfully interfere with the owner's possessory interest. Generally police officers are required to obtain a warrant which lists with specificity the items which are to be seized. However, in the absence of a warrant, police are allowed to seize an object if it is contraband, fruits of a crime, instrumentalities of a crime, or evidence of a crime. A brief seizure is permitted if the police have reasonable suspicion, and a longer seizure is permitted if the police have probable cause, but in either case the illicit nature of the object must be immediately apparent to the officer.

An individual is seized when a reasonable person in the suspect's position would believe she is not free to leave. The test is a wholly objective one, independent of whether the police officer or the suspect actually believed the suspect was free to go. Individuals may be briefly seized (known as a "stop") upon a mere showing of reasonable suspicion. However, a longer and more intrusive seizure (known as an arrest) will require a greater justification. Before the police can arrest someone in her own home, they must obtain an arrest warrant supported by probable cause. Finally, the *manner* of seizure must be reasonable; the police may not use deadly force against a fleeing suspect unless the suspect poses an imminent and serious threat to the safety of others.

Review Questions

1. Shooting a Lion. Charles Newberry called the police and reported that his pet lioness Nila had escaped his enclosure and was loose in the town. Newberry explained that the lioness was a harmless pet with no claws. The police found the lioness and shot her once with a tranquilizer gun. The chief of police then called the officers on the scene and said that the lioness had to be killed. The officers on the scene waited for Nila to collapse from the effects of the tranquilizer and then approached her and shot her in the back of the head. Newbery is now suing for unlawful seizure of his pet lioness.

Did the police officers "seize" Nila? If so, was the seizure reasonable?

2. Scrap Metal on the Driveway. One afternoon the police received a report from Abigail Howe, who claimed that David Nasser, her neighbor, had dumped a pile of scrap metal onto her driveway so that she could not leave her garage. Officer James Gavin responded to the call. Officer Gavin was Howe's brother-in-law, and he had known Howe for many years. When he arrived on the scene he saw that Nasser had indeed dumped a small pile of scrap metal in his front yard, and that a few pieces of metal were lying partially on Howe's driveway, but they was not nearly enough to prevent access to Howe's garage. Nevertheless, Howe told Gavin that she wanted the metal to be moved, because it was unsightly and she was having a number of people over for a party that night. Officer Gavin asked Nasser to move the metal to his backyard, and he refused. After more requests from Howe, Gavin agreed to move the metal himself. He spent five minutes moving the metal from Nasser's front yard to the side yard, where it would be out of view. As he was moving the metal, he uncovered a large copper pipe with a serial number on it. He copied the serial number down and later ran it through a police database, which informed him that the pipe had been stolen from a junkyard a few days earlier. Based on this information, he returned to Nasser's home and arrested him for possession of stolen property.

Nasser is now moving to suppress the evidence of the copper pipe, arguing that Officer Gavin learned its serial number only because he was conducting an unlawful seizure of his metal. Did Officer Gavin "seize" the metal? If so, was it reasonable?

3. A Late-Night Encounter. Officer David West saw a car parked outside of a Sprint telephone store at 1:30 in the morning. The location was part of Officer West's usual patrol area, so he knew that the Sprint store had been burglarized twice over the past three weeks. He pulled up behind the car, shined a spotlight inside of it, and ran the license plate. The license check revealed that the owner of the car had been arrested for drug possession last year. Officer West then approached the car on foot with his flashlight and noticed a person, later identified as Samuel O'Neil, in the driver's seat. Officer West asked O'Neil to roll down his window and O'Neil complied. As Officer West shined his flashlight into the car, he asked what O'Neil was doing there. O'Neil said his car wouldn't start and he was waiting for a fried to come by with jumper cables. Officer West then asked O'Neil to try to start the car and O'Neil tried and could not. Officer West then asked O'Neil to hand over his license and registration, and O'Neil gave him a license with a different name on it. Officer West then ordered O'Neil out of the car and frisked him. The frisk turned up an illegal gun and O'Neil was arrested.

O'Neil is now challenging his search and seizure at a suppression hearing. At what point (if any) during this encounter was O'Neil seized?

4. Confrontation at the Bus Depot. Darla Matthews, a sixteen year old girl, was traveling by herself on a Greyhound bus from Denver to visit her aunt in St. Louis. Halfway through the trip, the bus stopped at the bus depot in Kansas City for fifteen minutes. Two uniformed police officers in the Kansas City bus depot saw Darla get off the bus, go immediately into the women's restroom and stay there for over ten minutes. When she emerged from the restroom, her walk was unsteady and she seemed disoriented. The police officers believed that she had used illegal drugs in the restroom, and they approached her. She stopped when she saw them and put her bag on the ground next to her. The officers stood between her and the bus she needed to board and asked her for her identification. She pulled out her driver's license and gave it to them. While one of them looked at the driver's license, the other one picked up her bag and asked if he could look through it. Darla said he could not, and told them that the bus was about to leave and she didn't want to miss it. The first officer looked at her for a moment and said: "You can go if you want to; we're not stopping you." However, he made no movement to return the driver's license, and his partner still held onto her bag. After five seconds of silence, Darla sighed and said "OK, fine, go ahead and search my bag." The second officer opened her bag and looked inside, finding two packets of heroin and a syringe with heroin residue inside.

Darla was arrested for illegal possession of narcotics, and she now moves to suppress the heroin, claiming that her consent only came after an illegal seizure. The prosecution argues that she was never seized, because she was always free to leave. Was Darla seized?

FROM THE COURTROOM

UNITED STATES v. PLACE

United States Supreme Court, 1983
462 U.S. 696

[Justice O'CONNOR delivered the opinion of the Court.]

[Justices BRENNAN filed a concurring opinion, which Justice MARSHALL joined.]

[Justices BLACKMUN filed a concurring opinion, which Justice MARSHALL joined.]

This case presents the issue whether the Fourth Amendment prohibits law enforcement authorities from temporarily detaining personal luggage for exposure to a trained narcotics detection dog on the basis of reasonable suspicion that the luggage contains narcotics. Given the enforcement problems associated with the detection of narcotics trafficking and the minimal intrusion that a properly limited detention would entail, we conclude that the Fourth Amendment does not prohibit such a detention. On the facts of this case, however, we hold that the police conduct exceeded the bounds of a permissible investigative detention of the luggage.

I

Respondent Raymond J. Place's behavior aroused the suspicions of law enforcement officers as he waited in line at the Miami International Airport to purchase a ticket to New York's LaGuardia Airport. As Place proceeded to the gate for his flight, the agents approached him and requested his airline ticket and some identification. Place complied with the request and consented to a search of the two suitcases he had checked. Because his flight was about to depart, however, the agents decided not to search the luggage.

Prompted by Place's parting remark that he had recognized that they were police, the agents inspected the address tags on the checked luggage and noted discrepancies in the two street addresses. Further investigation revealed that neither address existed and that the telephone number Place had given the airline belonged to a third address on the same street. On the basis of their encounter with Place and this information, the Miami agents called Drug Enforcement Administration (DEA) authorities in New York to relay their information about Place.

Two DEA agents waited for Place at the arrival gate at LaGuardia Airport in New York. There again, his behavior aroused the suspicion of the agents. After he had claimed his two bags and called a limousine, the agents decided to approach him.

They identified themselves as federal narcotics agents, to which Place responded that he knew they were "cops" and had spotted them as soon as he had deplaned. One of the agents informed Place that, based on their own observations and information obtained from the Miami authorities, they believed that he might be carrying narcotics. After identifying the bags as belonging to him, Place stated that a number of police at the Miami Airport had surrounded him and searched his baggage. The agents responded that their information was to the contrary. The agents requested and received identification from Place—a New Jersey driver's license, on which the agents later ran a computer check that disclosed no offenses, and his airline ticket receipt. When Place refused to consent to a search of his luggage, one of the agents told him that they were going to take the luggage to a federal judge to try to obtain a search warrant and that Place was free to accompany them. Place declined, but obtained from one of the agents telephone numbers at which the agents could be reached.

The agents then took the bags to Kennedy Airport, where they subjected the bags to a "sniff test" by a trained narcotics detection dog. The dog reacted positively to the smaller of the two bags but ambiguously to the larger bag. Approximately 90 minutes had elapsed since the seizure of respondent's luggage. Because it was late on a Friday afternoon, the agents retained the luggage until Monday morning, when they secured a search warrant from a magistrate for the smaller bag. Upon opening that bag, the agents discovered 1,125 grams of cocaine.

Place was indicted for possession of cocaine with intent to distribute in violation of 21 U.S.C. § 841(a)(1). In the District Court, Place moved to suppress the contents of the luggage seized from him at LaGuardia Airport, claiming that the warrantless seizure of the luggage violated his Fourth Amendment rights. The District Court denied the motion. Applying the standard of *Terry v. Ohio,* 392 U.S. 1 (1968), to the detention of personal property, it concluded that detention of the bags could be justified if based on reasonable suspicion to believe that the bags contained narcotics. Finding reasonable suspicion, the District Court held that Place's Fourth Amendment rights were not violated by seizure of the bags by the DEA agents. Place pleaded guilty to the possession charge, reserving the right to appeal the denial of his motion to suppress.

On appeal of the conviction, the United States Court of Appeals for the Second Circuit reversed. The majority assumed both that *Terry* principles could be applied to justify a warrantless seizure of baggage on less than probable cause and that reasonable suspicion existed to justify the investigatory stop of Place. The majority concluded, however, that the prolonged seizure of Place's baggage exceeded the permissible limits of a *Terry*-type investigative stop and consequently amounted to a seizure without probable cause in violation of the Fourth Amendment.

We granted certiorari, and now affirm.

II

The Fourth Amendment protects the "right of the people to be secure in their persons, houses, papers, *and effects,* against unreasonable searches and seizures." (Emphasis added.) Although in the context of personal property, and particularly containers, the

Fourth Amendment challenge is typically to the subsequent search of the container rather than to its initial seizure by the authorities, our cases reveal some general principles regarding seizures. In the ordinary case, the Court has viewed a seizure of personal property as *per se* unreasonable within the meaning of the Fourth Amendment unless it is accomplished pursuant to a judicial warrant issued upon probable cause and particularly describing the items to be seized. Where law enforcement authorities have probable cause to believe that a container holds contraband or evidence of a crime, but have not secured a warrant, the Court has interpreted the Amendment to permit seizure of the property, pending issuance of a warrant to examine its contents, if the exigencies of the circumstances demand it or some other recognized exception to the warrant requirement is present.[25] For example, "objects such as weapons or contraband found in a public place may be seized by the police without a warrant," because, under these circumstances, the risk of the item's disappearance or use for its intended purpose before a warrant may be obtained outweighs the interest in possession.

In this case, the Government asks us to recognize the reasonableness under the Fourth Amendment of warrantless seizures of personal luggage from the custody of the owner on the basis of less than probable cause, for the purpose of pursuing a limited course of investigation, short of opening the luggage, that would quickly confirm or dispel the authorities' suspicion. Specifically, we are asked to apply the principles of *Terry v. Ohio, supra,* to permit such seizures on the basis of reasonable, articulable suspicion, premised on objective facts, that the luggage contains contraband or evidence of a crime. In our view, such application is appropriate.

In *Terry* the Court first recognized "the narrow authority of police officers who suspect criminal activity to make limited intrusions on an individual's personal security based on less than probable cause." In approving the limited search for weapons, or "frisk," of an individual the police reasonably believed to be armed and dangerous, the Court implicitly acknowledged the authority of the police to make a *forcible stop* of a person when the officer has reasonable, articulable suspicion that the person has been, is, or is about to be engaged in criminal activity. That implicit proposition was embraced openly in *Adams v. Williams,* 407 U.S. 143 (1972), where the Court relied on *Terry* to hold that the police officer lawfully made a forcible stop of the suspect to investigate an informant's tip that the suspect was carrying narcotics and a concealed weapon. See also *Michigan v. Summers*, 452 U.S. 692 (1981) limited detention of occupants while authorities search premises pursuant to valid search warrant); *United States v. Cortez,* 449 U.S. 411 (1981) (stop near border of vehicle suspected of transporting illegal aliens); *United States v. Brignoni-Ponce*, 422 U.S. 873 (1975) (brief investigative stop near border for questioning about citizenship and immigration status).

[25] In *Sanders,* the Court explained: "The police acted properly-indeed commendably-in apprehending respondent and his luggage. They had ample probable cause to believe that respondent's green suitcase contained marihuana. . . . Having probable cause to believe that contraband was being driven away in the taxi, the police were justified in stopping the vehicle . . . and seizing the suitcase they suspected contained contraband."
The Court went on to hold that the police violated the Fourth Amendment in immediately searching the luggage rather than first obtaining a warrant authorizing the search. . . .

The exception to the probable-cause requirement for limited seizures of the person recognized in *Terry* and its progeny rests on a balancing of the competing interests to determine the reasonableness of the type of seizure involved within the meaning of "the Fourth Amendment's general proscription against unreasonable searches and seizures." We must balance the nature and quality of the intrusion on the individual's Fourth Amendment interests against the importance of the governmental interests alleged to justify the intrusion. When the nature and extent of the detention are minimally intrusive of the individual's Fourth Amendment interests, the opposing law enforcement interests can support a seizure based on less than probable cause.

We examine first the governmental interest offered as a justification for a brief seizure of luggage from the suspect's custody for the purpose of pursuing a limited course of investigation. The Government contends that, where the authorities possess specific and articulable facts warranting a reasonable belief that a traveler's luggage contains narcotics, the governmental interest in seizing the luggage briefly to pursue further investigation is substantial. We agree. As observed in *United States v. Mendenhall,* "[t]he public has a compelling interest in detecting those who would traffic in deadly drugs for personal profit."

Respondent suggests that, absent some special law enforcement interest such as officer safety, a generalized interest in law enforcement cannot justify an intrusion on an individual's Fourth Amendment interests in the absence of probable cause. Our prior cases, however, do not support this proposition. In *Terry,* we described the governmental interests supporting the initial seizure of the person as "effective crime prevention and detection; it is this interest which underlies the recognition that a police officer may in appropriate circumstances and in an appropriate manner approach a person for purposes of investigating possibly criminal behavior even though there is no probable cause to make an arrest." Similarly, in *Michigan v. Summers* we identified three law enforcement interests that justified limited detention of the occupants of the premises during execution of a valid search warrant: "preventing flight in the event that incriminating evidence is found," "minimizing the risk of harm" both to the officers and the occupants, and "orderly completion of the search." The test is whether those interests are sufficiently "substantial," not whether they are independent of the interest in investigating crimes effectively and apprehending suspects. The context of a particular law enforcement practice, of course, may affect the determination whether a brief intrusion on Fourth Amendment interests on less than probable cause is essential to effective criminal investigation. Because of the inherently transient nature of drug courier activity at airports, allowing police to make brief investigative stops of persons at airports on reasonable suspicion of drug-trafficking substantially enhances the likelihood that police will be able to prevent the flow of narcotics into distribution channels.

Against this strong governmental interest, we must weigh the nature and extent of the intrusion upon the individual's Fourth Amendment rights when the police briefly detain luggage for limited investigative purposes. On this point, respondent Place urges that the rationale for a *Terry* stop of the person is wholly inapplicable to investigative detentions of personalty. Specifically, the *Terry* exception to the probable-cause requirement is premised on the notion that a *Terry* -type stop of the person is substantially less intrusive of a person's liberty interests than a formal arrest. In the property context, however, Place urges, there are no degrees of intrusion. Once the owner's property is seized, the dispossession is absolute.

We disagree. The intrusion on possessory interests occasioned by a seizure of one's personal effects can vary both in its nature and extent. The seizure may be made after the owner has relinquished control of the property to a third party or, as here, from the immediate custody and control of the owner.[26] Moreover, the police may confine their investigation to an on-the-spot inquiry—for example, immediate exposure of the luggage to a trained narcotics detection dog—or transport the property to another location. Given the fact that seizures of property can vary in intrusiveness, some brief detentions of personal effects may be so minimally intrusive of Fourth Amendment interests that strong countervailing governmental interests will justify a seizure based only on specific articulable facts that the property contains contraband or evidence of a crime.

In sum, we conclude that when an officer's observations lead him reasonably to believe that a traveler is carrying luggage that contains narcotics, the principles of *Terry* and its progeny would permit the officer to detain the luggage briefly to investigate the circumstances that aroused his suspicion, provided that the investigative detention is properly limited in scope.

. . .

III

There is no doubt that the agents made a "seizure" of Place's luggage for purposes of the Fourth Amendment when, following his refusal to consent to a search, the agent told Place that he was going to take the luggage to a federal judge to secure issuance of a warrant. As we observed in *Terry*, "[t]he manner in which the seizure . . . [was] conducted is, of course, as vital a part of the inquiry as whether [it was] warranted at all." We therefore examine whether the agents' conduct in this case was such as to place the seizure within the general rule requiring probable cause for a seizure or within *Terry*'s exception to that rule.

---

[26] One need only compare the facts of this case with those in *United States v. Van Leeuwen,* 397 U.S. 249 (1970). There the defendant had voluntarily relinquished two packages of coins to the postal authorities. Several facts aroused the suspicion of the postal officials, who detained the packages, without searching them, for about [twenty-nine] hours while certain lines of inquiry were pursued. The information obtained during this time was sufficient to give the authorities probable cause to believe that the packages contained counterfeit coins. After obtaining a warrant, the authorities opened the packages, found counterfeit coins therein, resealed the packages and sent them on their way. Expressly limiting its holding to the facts of the case, the Court concluded that the [twenty-nine]-hour detention of the packages on reasonable suspicion that they contained contraband did not violate the Fourth Amendment.

As one commentator has noted, "*Van Leeuwen* was an easy case for the Court because the defendant was unable to show that the invasion intruded upon either a privacy interest in the contents of the packages or a possessory interest in the packages themselves."

At the outset, we must reject the Government's suggestion that the point at which probable cause for seizure of luggage from the person's presence becomes necessary is more distant than in the case of a *Terry* stop of the person himself. The premise of the Government's argument is that seizures of property are generally less intrusive than seizures of the person. While true in some circumstances, that premise is faulty on the facts we address in this case. The precise type of detention we confront here is seizure of personal luggage from the immediate possession of the suspect for the purpose of arranging exposure to a narcotics detection dog. Particularly in the case of detention of luggage within the traveler's immediate possession, the police conduct intrudes on both the suspect's possessory interest in his luggage as well as his liberty interest in proceeding with his itinerary. The person whose luggage is detained is technically still free to continue his travels or carry out other personal activities pending release of the luggage. Moreover, he is not subjected to the coercive atmosphere of a custodial confinement or to the public indignity of being personally detained. Nevertheless, such a seizure can effectively restrain the person since he is subjected to the possible disruption of his travel plans in order to remain with his luggage or to arrange for its return.[27] Therefore, when the police seize luggage from the suspect's custody, we think the limitations applicable to investigative detentions of the person should define the permissible scope of an investigative detention of the person's luggage on less than probable cause. Under this standard, it is clear that the police conduct here exceeded the permissible limits of a *Terry*-type investigative stop.

The length of the detention of respondent's luggage alone precludes the conclusion that the seizure was reasonable in the absence of probable cause. Although we have recognized the reasonableness of seizures longer than the momentary ones involved in *Terry, Adams,* and *Brignoni-Ponce,* the brevity of the invasion of the individual's Fourth Amendment interests is an important factor in determining whether the seizure is so minimally intrusive as to be justifiable on reasonable suspicion. Moreover, in assessing the effect of the length of the detention, we take into account whether the police diligently pursue their investigation. We note that here the New York agents knew the time of Place's scheduled arrival at LaGuardia, had ample time to arrange for their additional investigation at that location, and thereby could have minimized the intrusion on respondent's Fourth Amendment interests. Thus, although we decline to adopt any outside time limitation for a permissible *Terry* stop,[28] we have never approved a seizure of the person for the prolonged [ninety]-minute period involved here and cannot do so on the facts presented by this case.

---

[27] "At least when the authorities do not make it absolutely clear how they plan to reunite the suspect and his possessions at some future time and place, seizure of the object is tantamount to seizure of the person. This is because that person must either remain on the scene or else seemingly surrender his effects permanently to the police." 3 W. LaFave, Search and Seizure § 9.6, p. 61 (1982 Supp.).

[28] Cf. ALI, Model Code of Pre-Arraignment Procedure § 110.2(1) (1975) (recommending a maximum of 20 minutes for a *Terry* stop). We understand the desirability of providing law enforcement authorities with a clear rule to guide their conduct. Nevertheless, we question the wisdom of a rigid time limitation. Such a limit would undermine the equally important need to allow authorities to graduate their responses to the demands of any particular situation.

Although the [ninety]-minute detention of respondent's luggage is sufficient to render the seizure unreasonable, the violation was exacerbated by the failure of the agents to accurately inform respondent of the place to which they were transporting his luggage, of the length of time he might be dispossessed, and of what arrangements would be made for return of the luggage if the investigation dispelled the suspicion. In short, we hold that the detention of respondent's luggage in this case went beyond the narrow authority possessed by police to detain briefly luggage reasonably suspected to contain narcotics.

IV

We conclude that, under all of the circumstances of this case, the seizure of respondent's luggage was unreasonable under the Fourth Amendment. Consequently, the evidence obtained from the subsequent search of his luggage was inadmissible, and Place's conviction must be reversed. The judgment of the Court of Appeals, accordingly, is affirmed.

It is so ordered.

[The concurring opinion of Justice BRENNAN, which was joined by Justice MARSHALL, is omitted].

[The concurring opinion of Justices BLACKMUN, which was joined by Justice MARSHALL, is omitted].

FROM THE COURTROOM

SCOTT v. HARRIS

United States Supreme Court, 2007
550 U.S. 372

[Justice SCALIA delivered the opinion of the Court.]

[Justices GINSBURG and BREYER joined in the majority and filed concurring opinions.]

[Justice STEVENS filed a dissenting opinion.]

We consider whether a law enforcement official can, consistent with the Fourth Amendment, attempt to stop a fleeing motorist from continuing his public-endangering flight by ramming the motorist's car from behind. Put another way: Can an officer take actions that place a fleeing motorist at risk of serious injury or death in order to stop the motorist's flight from endangering the lives of innocent bystanders?

I

In March 2001, a Georgia county deputy clocked respondent's vehicle traveling at [seventy-three] miles per hour on a road with a [fifty-five]–mile–per–hour speed limit. The deputy activated his blue flashing lights indicating that respondent should pull over. Instead, respondent sped away, initiating a chase down what is in most portions a two-lane road, at speeds exceeding 85 miles per hour. The deputy radioed his dispatch to report that he was pursuing a fleeing vehicle, and broadcast its license plate number. Petitioner, Deputy Timothy Scott, heard the radio communication and joined the pursuit along with other officers. In the midst of the chase, respondent pulled into the parking lot of a shopping center and was nearly boxed in by the various police vehicles. Respondent evaded the trap by making a sharp turn, colliding with Scott's police car, exiting the parking lot, and speeding off once again down a two-lane highway.

Following respondent's shopping center maneuvering, which resulted in slight damage to Scott's police car, Scott took over as the lead pursuit vehicle. Six minutes and nearly 10 miles after the chase had begun, Scott decided to attempt to terminate the episode by employing a "Precision Intervention Technique ('PIT') maneuver, which causes the fleeing vehicle to spin to a stop." Having radioed his supervisor for permission, Scott was told to "'[g]o ahead and take him out.'" Instead, Scott applied his push bumper to the rear of respondent's vehicle. As a result, respondent lost control of his vehicle, which left the roadway, ran down an embankment, overturned, and crashed. Respondent was badly injured and was rendered a quadriplegic.

Respondent filed suit against Deputy Scott and others under Rev. Stat. § 1979, 42 U.S.C. § 1983, alleging, *inter alia,* a violation of his federal constitutional rights, viz. use of excessive force resulting in an unreasonable seizure under the Fourth Amendment. In response, Scott filed a motion for summary judgment based on an assertion of qualified immunity. The District Court denied the motion, finding that "there are material issues of fact on which the issue of qualified immunity turns which present sufficient disagreement to require submission to a jury." On interlocutory appeal, the United States Court of Appeals for the Eleventh Circuit affirmed the District Court's decision to allow respondent's Fourth Amendment claim against Scott to proceed to trial. Taking respondent's view of the facts as given, the Court of Appeals concluded that Scott's actions could constitute "deadly force" under *Tennessee v. Garner,* 471 U.S. 1 (1985), and that the use of such force in this context "would violate [respondent's] constitutional right to be free from excessive force during a seizure. Accordingly, a reasonable jury could find that Scott violated [respondent's] Fourth Amendment rights." The Court of Appeals further concluded that "the law as it existed [at the time of the incident], was sufficiently clear to give reasonable law enforcement officers 'fair notice' that ramming a vehicle under these circumstances was unlawful." The Court of Appeals thus concluded that Scott was not entitled to qualified immunity. We granted certiorari, and now reverse.

II

In resolving questions of qualified immunity, courts are required to resolve a "threshold question: Taken in the light most favorable to the party asserting the injury, do the facts alleged show the officer's conduct violated a constitutional right? This must be the initial inquiry." If, and only if, the court finds a violation of a constitutional right, "the next, sequential step is to ask whether the right was clearly established . . . in light of the specific context of the case." Although this ordering contradicts "[o]ur policy of avoiding unnecessary adjudication of constitutional issues," we have said that such a departure from practice is "necessary to set forth principles which will become the basis for a [future] holding that a right is clearly established," We therefore turn to the threshold inquiry: whether Deputy Scott's actions violated the Fourth Amendment.

III

A

The first step in assessing the constitutionality of Scott's actions is to determine the relevant facts. As this case was decided on summary judgment, there have not yet been factual findings by a judge or jury, and respondent's version of events (unsurprisingly) differs substantially from Scott's version. When things are in such a posture, courts are required to view the facts and draw reasonable inferences "in the light most favorable to the party opposing the [summary judgment] motion." In qualified immunity cases, this usually means adopting (as the Court of Appeals did here) the plaintiff's version of the facts.

There is, however, an added wrinkle in this case: existence in the record of a videotape capturing the events in question. There are no allegations or indications that this videotape was doctored or altered in any way, nor any contention that what it depicts differs from what actually happened. The videotape quite clearly contradicts the version of the story told by respondent and adopted by the Court of Appeals. For example, the Court of Appeals adopted respondent's assertions that, during the chase, "there was little, if any, actual threat to pedestrians or other motorists, as the roads were mostly empty and [respondent] remained in control of his vehicle." Indeed, reading the lower court's opinion, one gets the impression that respondent, rather than fleeing from police, was attempting to pass his driving test:

> "[T]aking the facts from the non-movant's viewpoint, [respondent] remained in control of his vehicle, slowed for turns and intersections, and typically used his indicators for turns. He did not run any motorists off the road. Nor was he a threat to pedestrians in the shopping center parking lot, which was free from pedestrian and vehicular traffic as the center was closed. Significantly, by the time the parties were back on the highway and Scott rammed [respondent], the motorway had been cleared of motorists and pedestrians allegedly because of police blockades of the nearby intersections."

The videotape tells quite a different story. There we see respondent's vehicle racing down narrow, two-lane roads in the dead of night at speeds that are shockingly fast. We see it swerve around more than a dozen other cars, cross the double-yellow line, and force cars traveling in both directions to their respective shoulders to avoid being hit.[6] We see it run multiple red lights and travel for considerable periods of time in the occasional center left-turn-only lane, chased by numerous police cars forced to engage in the same hazardous maneuvers just to keep up. Far from being the cautious and controlled driver the lower court depicts, what we see on the video more closely resembles a Hollywood-style car chase of the most frightening sort, placing police officers and innocent bystanders alike at great risk of serious injury.

At the summary judgment stage, facts must be viewed in the light most favorable to the nonmoving party only if there is a "genuine" dispute as to those facts. Fed. Rule Civ. Proc. 56(c). As we have emphasized, "[w]hen the moving party has carried its burden under Rule 56(c), its opponent must do more than simply show that there is some metaphysical doubt as to the material facts . . . . Where the record taken as a whole could not lead a rational trier of fact to find for the nonmoving party, there is no 'genuine issue for trial.'" "[T]he mere existence of *some* alleged factual dispute between the parties will not defeat an otherwise properly supported motion for summary

[6] Justice STEVENS hypothesizes that these cars "had already pulled to the side of the road or were driving along the shoulder because they heard the police sirens or saw the flashing lights," so that "[a] jury could certainly conclude that those motorists were exposed to no greater risk than persons who take the same action in response to a speeding ambulance." It is not our experience that ambulances and fire engines careen down two-lane roads at 85–plus miles per hour, with an unmarked scout car out in front of them. The risk they pose to the public is vastly less than what respondent created here. But even if that were not so, it would in no way lead to the conclusion that it was unreasonable to eliminate the threat to life that respondent posed. Society accepts the risk of speeding ambulances and fire engines in order to save life and property; it need not (and assuredly does not) accept a similar risk posed by a reckless motorist fleeing the police.

judgment; the requirement is that there be no *genuine* issue of *material* fact." When opposing parties tell two different stories, one of which is blatantly contradicted by the record, so that no reasonable jury could believe it, a court should not adopt that version of the facts for purposes of ruling on a motion for summary judgment.

That was the case here with regard to the factual issue whether respondent was driving in such fashion as to endanger human life. Respondent's version of events is so utterly discredited by the record that no reasonable jury could have believed him. The Court of Appeals should not have relied on such visible fiction; it should have viewed the facts in the light depicted by the videotape.

B

Judging the matter on that basis, we think it is quite clear that Deputy Scott did not violate the Fourth Amendment. Scott does not contest that his decision to terminate the car chase by ramming his bumper into respondent's vehicle constituted a "seizure." "[A] Fourth Amendment seizure [occurs] . . . when there is a governmental termination of freedom of movement through means intentionally applied." ("If . . . the police cruiser had pulled alongside the fleeing car and sideswiped it, producing the crash, then the termination of the suspect's freedom of movement would have been a seizure"). It is also conceded, by both sides, that a claim of "excessive force in the course of making [a] . . . 'seizure' of [the] person . . . [is] properly analyzed under the Fourth Amendment's 'objective reasonableness' standard." The question we need to answer is whether Scott's actions were objectively reasonable.

1

Respondent urges us to analyze this case as we analyzed *Garner,* 471 U.S. 1. We must first decide, he says, whether the actions Scott took constituted "deadly force." (He defines "deadly force" as "any use of force which creates a substantial likelihood of causing death or serious bodily injury," If so, respondent claims that *Garner* prescribes certain preconditions that must be met before Scott's actions can survive Fourth Amendment scrutiny: (1) The suspect must have posed an immediate threat of serious physical harm to the officer or others; (2) deadly force must have been necessary to prevent escape; and (3) where feasible, the officer must have given the suspect some warning. Since these *Garner* preconditions for using deadly force were not met in this case, Scott's actions were *per se* unreasonable.

Respondent's argument falters at its first step; *Garner* did not establish a magical on/off switch that triggers rigid preconditions whenever an officer's actions constitute "deadly force." *Garner* was simply an application of the Fourth Amendment's "reasonableness" test, to the use of a particular type of force in a particular situation. *Garner* held that it was unreasonable to kill a "young, slight, and unarmed" burglary suspect, by shooting him "in the back of the head" while he was running away on foot, and when the officer "could not reasonablyhave believed that [the suspect] . . . posed any threat," and "never attempted to justify his actions on any basis other than the need to prevent an escape." Whatever *Garner* said about the factors that *might have* justified shooting the suspect in that case, such "preconditions" have scant applicability to this case, which has vastly different facts. " *Garner* had nothing to do with one car striking another or even with car chases in general . . . . A police car's bumping a fleeing car is, in fact, not much like a policeman's shooting a gun so as to hit a person. Nor is the threat posed by the flight on foot of an unarmed suspect even remotely comparable to the extreme danger to human life posed by respondent in this case. Although respondent's attempt to craft an easy-to-apply legal test in the Fourth Amendment context is admirable, in the end we must still slosh our way through the factbound morass of "reasonableness." Whether or not Scott's actions constituted application of "deadly force," all that matters is whether Scott's actions were reasonable.

2

In determining the reasonableness of the manner in which a seizure is effected, "[w]e must balance the nature and quality of the intrusion on the individual's Fourth Amendment interests against the importance of the governmental interests alleged to justify the intrusion." Scott defends his actions by pointing to the paramount governmental interest in ensuring public safety, and respondent nowhere suggests this was not the purpose motivating Scott's behavior. Thus, in judging whether Scott's actions were reasonable, we must consider the risk of bodily harm that Scott's actions posed to respondent in light of the threat to the public that Scott was trying to eliminate. Although there is no obvious way to quantify the risks on either side, it is clear from the videotape that respondent posed an actual and imminent threat to the lives of any pedestrians who might have been present, to other civilian motorists, and to the officers involved in the chase. It is equally clear that Scott's actions posed a high likelihood of serious injury or death to respondent—though not the near *certainty* of death posed by, say, shooting a fleeing felon in the back of the head, or pulling alongside a fleeing motorist's car and shooting the motorist. So how does a court go about weighing the perhaps lesser probability of injuring or killing numerous bystanders against the perhaps larger probability of injuring or killing a single person? We think it appropriate in this process to take into account not only the number of lives at risk, but also their relative culpability. It was respondent, after all, who intentionally placed himself and the public in danger by unlawfully engaging in the reckless, high-speed flight that ultimately produced the choice between two evils that Scott confronted. Multiple police cars, with blue lights flashing and sirens blaring, had been chasing respondent for nearly [ten] miles, but he ignored their warning to stop. By contrast, those who might have been harmed had Scott not taken the action he did were entirely innocent. We have little difficulty in concluding it was reasonable for Scott to take the action that he did.

But wait, says respondent: Couldn't the innocent public equally have been protected, and the tragic accident entirely avoided, if the police had simply ceased their pursuit? We think the police need not have taken that chance and hoped for the best. Whereas Scott's action—ramming respondent off the road—was *certain* to eliminate the risk that respondent posed to the public, ceasing pursuit was not. First of all, there would have been no way to convey convincingly to respondent that the chase was off, and that he was free to go. Had respondent looked in his rearview mirror and seen the police cars deactivate their flashing lights and turn around, he would have had no idea whether they were truly letting him get away, or simply devising a new strategy for capture. Perhaps the police knew a shortcut he didn't know, and would reappear down the road to intercept him; or perhaps they were setting up a roadblock in his path. Given such uncertainty, respondent might have been just as likely to respond by continuing to drive recklessly as by slowing down and wiping his brow.

Second, we are loath to lay down a rule requiring the police to allow fleeing suspects to get away whenever they drive *so recklessly* that they put other people's lives in danger. It is obvious the perverse incentives such a rule would create: Every fleeing motorist would know that escape is within his grasp, if only he accelerates to 90 miles per hour, crosses the double-yellow line a few times, and runs a few red lights. The Constitution assuredly does not impose this invitation to impunity-earned-by-recklessness. Instead, we lay down a more sensible rule: A police officer's attempt to terminate a dangerous high-speed car chase that threatens the lives of innocent bystanders does not violate the Fourth Amendment, even when it places the fleeing motorist at risk of serious injury or death.

* * *

The car chase that respondent initiated in this case posed a substantial and immediate risk of serious physical injury to others; no reasonable jury could conclude otherwise. Scott's attempt to terminate the chase by forcing respondent off the road was reasonable, and Scott is entitled to summary judgment. The Court of Appeals' judgment to the contrary is reversed.

It is so ordered.

[Justice GINSBURG's concurring opinion and Justice BREYER's concurring opinion are omitted.]

Justice STEVENS, dissenting.

Today, the Court asks whether an officer may "take actions that place a fleeing motorist at risk of serious injury or death in order to stop the motorist's flight from endangering the lives of innocent bystanders." Depending on the circumstances, the answer may be an obvious "yes," an obvious "no," or sufficiently doubtful that the question of the reasonableness of the officer's actions should be decided by a jury, after a review of the degree of danger and the alternatives available to the officer. A high-speed chase in a desert in Nevada is, after all, quite different from one that travels through the heart of Las Vegas.

. . .

[T]he factual statements by the Court of Appeals quoted by the Court, were entirely accurate. That court did not describe respondent as a "cautious" driver as my colleagues imply, but it did correctly conclude that there is no evidence that he ever lost control of his vehicle. That court also correctly pointed out that the incident in the shopping center parking lot did not create any risk to pedestrians or other vehicles because the chase occurred just before 11 p.m. on a weekday night and the center was closed. It is apparent from the record (including the videotape) that local police had blocked off intersections to keep respondent from entering residential neighborhoods and possibly endangering other motorists. I would add that the videos also show that no pedestrians, parked cars, sidewalks, or residences were visible at any time during the chase. The only "innocent bystanders" who were placed "at great risk of serious injury," were the drivers who either pulled off the road in response to the sirens or passed respondent in the opposite direction when he was driving on his side of the road.

I recognize, of course, that even though respondent's original speeding violation on a four-lane highway was rather ordinary, his refusal to stop and subsequent flight was a serious offense that merited severe punishment. It was not, however, a capital offense, or even an offense that justified the use of deadly force rather than an abandonment of the chase. The Court's concern about the "imminent threat to the lives of any pedestrians who might have been present," while surely valid in an appropriate case, should be discounted in a case involving a nighttime chase in an area where no pedestrians were present.

What would have happened if the police had decided to abandon the chase? We now know that they could have apprehended respondent later because they had his license plate number. Even if that were not true, and even if he would have escaped any punishment at all, the use of deadly force in this case was no more appropriate than the use of a deadly weapon against a fleeing felon in *Tennessee v. Garner,* 471 U.S. 1 (1985). In any event, any uncertainty about the result of abandoning the pursuit has not prevented the Court from basing its conclusions on its own factual assumptions. The Court attempts to avoid the conclusion that deadly force was unnecessary by speculating that if the officers had let him go, respondent might have been "just as likely" to continue to drive recklessly as to slow down and wipe his brow. That speculation is unconvincing as a matter of common sense and improper as a matter of law. Our duty to view the evidence in the light most favorable to the nonmoving party would foreclose such speculation if the Court had not used its observation of the video as an excuse for replacing the rule of law with its ad hoc judgment. There is no evidentiary basis for an assumption that dangers caused by flight from a police pursuit will continue after the pursuit ends. Indeed, rules adopted by countless police departments throughout the country are based on a judgment that differs from the Court's.

Although *Garner* may not, as the Court suggests, "establish a magical on/off switch that triggers rigid preconditions" for the use of deadly force, it did set a threshold under which the use of deadly force would be considered constitutionally unreasonable:

> "Where the officer has probable cause to believe that the suspect poses a threat of serious physical harm, either to the officer or to others, it is not constitutionally unreasonable to prevent escape by using deadly force. Thus, if the suspect threatens the officer with a weapon or there is probable cause to believe that he has committed a crime involving the infliction or threatened

> infliction of serious physical harm, deadly force may be used if necessary to prevent escape, and if, where feasible, some warning has been given."

Whether a person's actions have risen to a level warranting deadly force is a question of fact best reserved for a jury. Here, the Court has usurped the jury's factfinding function and, in doing so, implicitly labeled the four other judges to review the case unreasonable. . . .

The Court today sets forth a *per se* rule that presumes its own version of the facts: "A police officer's attempt to terminate a dangerous high-speed car chase *that threatens the lives of innocent bystanders* does not violate the Fourth Amendment, even when it places the fleeing motorist at risk of serious injury or death." Not only does that rule fly in the face of the flexible and case-by-case "reasonableness" approach applied in *Garner* and *Graham v. Connor*, 490 U.S. 386 (1989), but it is also arguably inapplicable to the case at hand, given that it is not clear that this chase threatened the life of any "innocent bystande[r]." In my view, the risks inherent in justifying unwarranted police conduct on the basis of unfounded assumptions are unacceptable, particularly when less drastic measures—in this case, the use of stop sticks or a simple warning issued from a loud-speaker—could have avoided such a tragic result. In my judgment, jurors in Georgia should be allowed to evaluate the reasonableness of the decision to ram respondent's speeding vehicle in a manner that created an obvious risk of death and has in fact made him a quadriplegic at the age of [nineteen].

I respectfully dissent.

10

Probable Cause

Key Concepts

- Basis of Knowledge
- Reliability of Informant
- Totality of the Circumstances
- Practical Considerations of Everyday Life
- Reasonable Ground for Belief in Guilt

A. Introduction and Policy. Probable cause is perhaps one of the most well-known standards in criminal procedure. It is used very often in practice: it is the standard that law enforcement officials must meet before making any warrantless arrest, as well as the standard they must meet before conducting most warrantless searches. It is also the standard that guides judicial officers when issuing search warrants or arrest warrants. In short, if the law enforcement officer has probable cause (usually abbreviated to "PC") they can almost always conduct the search or make the arrest. If the law enforcement officer does not have probable cause, they cannot make an arrest and will have a much more difficult time justifying a search. Thus, many police investigations are initially focused on "developing probable cause" against an individual so that the investigation can be taken to the next level.

The probable cause standard exists to create a barrier between citizens and rash or unjustified police action. However, the Court has explained that the standard should not be understood as so demanding that it will unduly interfere with law enforcement. "The rule of probable cause is a practical, nontechnical conception affording the best compromise that has been found for accommodating these often opposing interests. Requiring more would unduly hamper law enforcement. To allow less would be to leave law-abiding citizens at the mercy of the officers' whim or caprice."[1] Indeed, though acknowledging the standard is not perfect, the Court has nonetheless found it to "embod[y] 'the best compromise that has been found for accommodating the often opposing interests' in 'safeguarding citizens from rash and unreasonable interferences with privacy' and in 'seeking to give fair leeway for enforcing the law in the community's protection.'"[2]

---

[1] Gerstein v. Pugh, 420 U.S. 103, 112 (1975).

[2] Dunaway v. New York, 442 U.S. 200, 208 (1979); see also Gerstein v. Pugh, 420 U.S. 103, 112 (1975).

In describing this constitutional balance between the needs of law enforcement and the needs of the citizenry, the Court has commented that "the requisite 'balancing' has been performed in centuries of precedent and is embodied in the principle that seizures are 'reasonable' only if supported by probable cause."[3] However, for all its common use, nailing down a precise definition of probable cause presents a challenge. As the Court itself has said, "[a]rticulating precisely what . . . 'probable cause' mean[s] is not possible"[4] because "probable cause is a fluid concept—turning on the assessment of probabilities in particular factual contexts—not readily, or even usefully, reduced to a neat set of legal rules."[5]

The best way to understand the concept of probable cause is to review the body of probable cause precedents that have developed over time. Probable cause is a fact-specific determination. Consequently, there is rarely a guarantee that a finding of probable cause in one case will demand a similar conclusion in another.[6] However, by seeing courts apply the concept in a number of different contexts, you will be able to get a sense of when the evidence that is being gathered rises to the level of probable cause.

Probable cause is most often defined by describing what it is not. Thus, we know that probable cause is evidence amounting to significantly less than what is required to establish guilt beyond a reasonable doubt or by a preponderance of the evidence.[7] In this same vein, probable cause does not require as much as "prima facie evidence, or, in other words, such evidence as, in the absence of exculpatory proof, would justify condemnation."[8] In this sense, the term "probable cause" is something of a misnomer—it does not actually mean that a fact is "probable" in the sense that it is more likely than not.

On the other hand, we know that probable cause requires more than rumor, report, or strong suspicion. It is also more demanding than reasonable suspicion. However, the Court has been reluctant to say exactly how much more. Probable cause should be understood not as a precise quantification of evidence, but rather as a non-technical function of probabilities. There is a common-sense element to the concept: factors relevant to probable cause "are the factual and practical considerations of everyday life on which reasonable and prudent men, not legal technicians, act."[9]

---

[3] Dunaway v. New York, 442 U.S. 200, 214 (1979).

[4] Ornelas v. United States, 517 U.S. 690, 695 (1996).

[5] Illinois v. Gates, 462 U.S. 213, 231 (1983).

[6] Id. at 698.

[7] Id. at 121.

[8] Locke v. United States, 7 Cranch 339, 348 (1813).

[9] Brinegar v. United States, 338 U.S. 160, 175 (1949).

B. The Law. One way to conceptualize the analysis of probable cause is as a series of three questions—when, what and how. First, you must determine *when* the probable cause standard applies. Next, you must decide *what* precisely the standard requires. And, finally, you must consider *how* to determine whether it exists. The first inquiry is a matter of circumstance; the second, a matter of substance; and the final, a matter of process.

The answer to each of these questions can be summarized as follows:

When:

1. Law enforcement officers may not make an arrest without demonstrating probable cause that a crime has occurred and that the arrestee is the one who committed the crime.

   If the officers are seeking an arrest warrant, they must demonstrate probable cause to a judge before the warrant is issued.

   If the officers make a warrantless arrest, they must demonstrate to a judge within a reasonable time after the arrest that probable cause existed at the time of the arrest.

2. In order to obtain a search warrant, law enforcement officers must have probable cause that a crime occurred and that evidence of that crime is present at the location of the proposed search. The officers must demonstrate this probable cause to a judge before the warrant is issued.

3. In order to conduct a warrantless search using the automobile exceptions to the warrant requirement, law enforcement officers must have probable cause before the search begins that a crime occurred and that evidence of that crime is present inside the car. They must demonstrate this to a judge at a suppression hearing after the search.

4. In order to bring a case to trial, the prosecutor must demonstrate to a judge or a grand jury probable cause that a crime occurred and that the defendant was the one who committed the crime.

What:

"Probable cause" means:

Evidence that would "warrant a man of prudence and caution in believing that the offense has been committed";[10] or

a "reasonable ground to believe that the accused [is] guilty";[11] or

"facts and circumstances within the arresting officers' knowledge and of which they had reasonably trustworthy information [that] are sufficient in themselves to warrant a man of reasonable caution in the belief that an offense has been or is being committed."[12]

How:

Probable cause will be determined by examining the totality of the circumstances. Two of the primary relevant factors to this assessment are:

(a) the <u>quality of the source</u> of the information (veracity or reliability of the source); and

(b) the <u>quantity of the information</u> provided (the "basis of knowledge" provided by the source).

We will now examine each of these questions in more detail.

1. When Is Probable Cause Required? As you have read in earlier chapters, the Fourth Amendment provides, "The right of the people to be secure in their persons, houses, papers, and effects, against unreasonable searches and seizures, shall not be violated, and no Warrants shall issue, but upon **probable cause**, supported by Oath or affirmation, and particularly describing the place to be searched, and the persons or things to be seized." As the text suggests, the probable cause standard is used when warrants are issued—"no Warrants shall issue but upon probable cause." But as we can see from the above statement of the law, probable cause is also used in a variety of other circumstances—when the police make a warrantless arrest; when the government seeks civil forfeiture of criminal assets; when evaluating the constitutionality of a warrantless search using the automobile

---

[10] See Carroll v. United States, 267 U.S. 132, 161 (1925) (citing Locke v. United States, 7 Cranch (11 U.S.) 339 (1813)).

[11] Id.

[12] Draper v. United States, 358 U.S. 307, 313 (1959).

exception; and when determining whether prosecutors have sufficient evidence to take a defendant to trial.

The probable cause standard is a critical component of the warrant requirement, which essentially is the process by which police officers get pre-clearance before conducting a search or making an arrest. The Supreme Court has repeatedly held that the probable cause determination should, where possible, be made in the first instance by a neutral and detached magistrate.[13] These sorts of probable cause assessments are forward-looking processes, with a judicial officer determining in advance whether the evidence that the police have against a suspect justifies the requested search or arrest.

However, pre-authorization by a judge is not always required. As the Court commented forty years ago, "[m]aximum protection of individual rights could be assured by requiring a magistrate's review of the factual justification prior to any arrest [or search], but such a requirement would constitute an intolerable handicap for legitimate law enforcement."[14] Consequently, a significant number of probable cause determinations are made in the first instance by the police officer on the street.

Of course, even when the police officer makes the initial determination of probable cause, judicial review of the officer's decision is required, although in such cases the judicial review occurs after the police conduct. For the most part, the probable cause standard is the same in both the pre-clearance context and the post-conduct review context. However, the Supreme Court has occasionally suggested that greater deference is appropriate when reviewing a judicial official's determination of probable cause:[15]

> [W]hen a search is based upon a magistrate's, rather than a police officer's, determination of probable cause, the reviewing courts will accept evidence of a less "judicially competent or persuasive character than would have justified an officer in acting on his own without a warrant," and [a reviewing court] will sustain the judicial determination so long as "there was substantial basis for the magistrate to conclude that [evidence was] probably present."

In theory, this deference would encourage law enforcement to obtain a warrant instead of conducting a warrantless search or arrest. However, the true extent to which courts apply a lower standard to a magistrate's finding of probable cause is

[13] See, e.g., Gerstein v. Pugh, 420 U.S. 103, 113 (1975).

[14] Id. at 114.

[15] Aguilar v. Texas, 378 U.S. 108, 111 (1964); see also Illinois v. Gates, 462 U.S. 213, 236 (1983) ("[W]e have repeatedly said that after the fact scrutiny by courts of the sufficiency of an affidavit should not take the form of *de novo* review.").

unclear. In fact, in one recent case, the Supreme Court suggested that deference is not appropriate no matter the source of the probable cause determination. In *Ornelas v. United States*, the Court found that *de novo* review of a lower court's probable cause determination is appropriate. "We have never, when reviewing a probable-cause or reasonable suspicion determination ourselves, expressly deferred to the trial court's determination."[16] In a puzzling display of mental gymnastics, the *Ornelas* Court first endorsed its earlier decision that "the scrutiny applied to a magistrate's probable-cause determination to issue a warrant is less than that for warrantless searches"; and then held that "as a general matter, determinations of reasonable suspicion and probable cause should be reviewed *de novo* on appeal."[17] As a practical matter, this means lawyers litigating probable cause assessments should be careful to identify the precise binding local precedent governing the standard of review for such determinations.

It is clear that, even in the case of judicial determinations of probable cause, a reviewing court must conduct a meaningful review and not become a rubber stamp for the lower court decision.[18]

In addition to identifying when probable cause applies, you should also be familiar with the numerous instances when it does not. There are two higher standards that are of particular relevance to the criminal law:

a. To convict a defendant of a criminal offense, more than probable cause is needed. A criminal conviction may only stand if the prosecution has established guilt by proof beyond a reasonable doubt.

b. When the government seeks civil forfeiture of criminal assets, it must prove its case by a preponderance of the evidence. Preponderance of the evidence is evidence that "though insufficient to free the mind wholly from all reasonable doubt, is still sufficient to incline a fair and impartial mind to one side of the issue rather than the other."

On the opposite end of the spectrum, there is a collection of three scenarios in which the Court has held that something less than probable cause is acceptable:

a. When police officers behave in a way that does not amount to Fourth Amendment activity (i.e., search or seizure), the police do not have to overcome any particular evidentiary burden. For example, a police officer is free to stand on a street corner and watch whoever may happen to pass, even if she has absolutely no reason to suspect those she observes.

---

[16] 517 U.S. 690, 697 (1996).

[17] Id. at 699.

[18] Id.

b. When the police are engaged in pre-arrest investigatory activity, they need only possess *reasonable suspicion* that criminal activity is afoot and the suspect is armed and dangerous in order to briefly detain a suspect and conduct a protective frisk for weapons. (We will discuss these "*Terry* stops" in **Chapter 19**.)

c. When conducting a search that was conducted for a purpose different from the traditional law enforcement purpose of criminal investigation, law enforcement officers only need to act "reasonably." (We will discuss these "special needs searches" in **Chapter 18**.)

2. What is Probable Cause? What exactly must a police officer know before "probable cause" will be found? Though the Court has consistently resisted a singular understanding of probable cause, it has given considerable guidance with regard to the substance of the standard. Essentially, probable cause is sufficient evidence to cause a man of reasonable caution to believe that an offense has been or is being committed.

Probable cause is less than what is needed for proof beyond a reasonable doubt. It is also less than prima facie evidence of guilt.[19] At their core, the various descriptions of probable cause convey the clear view that "probable cause is a reasonable ground for belief of guilt, and that the belief of guilt must be particularized with respect to the person to be searched or seized."[20]

Determining the existence of probable cause is necessarily a heavily fact-dependent assessment that requires case-by-case evaluation. Nonetheless, the Court has offered some general guidance concerning the practical operation of the above standards.

First, the Court has instructed that mere presence in the area of criminal activity will not justify an inference of probable cause.[21] This is not to suggest that there is nothing suspicious about being present at the scene of a crime. Presence when coupled with other facts may be adequate to overcome the probable cause hurdle. But, suspicion based on presence alone will not suffice. Moreover, to the extent that presence establishes any quantum of suspicion at all, such suspicion is completely destroyed when a single guilty party (other than the accused) is identified.[22]

Probable cause also is not established by a failure to protest or otherwise resist arrest. Nor will an arrestee's prior criminal history, without more, be adequate

---

[19] Gates, 462 U.S. at 235.

[20] Maryland v. Pringle, 540 U.S. 366, 371 (2003).

[21] United States v. Di Re, 332 U.S. 581, 592 (1948).

[22] Id. at 594.

to establish probable cause.[23] Finally, probable cause cannot be generated retroactively. Accordingly, a search cannot be justified by what it turns up—the law enforcement officer must demonstrate that he possessed probable cause at the point **before** the search began.[24]

The "**what**" of probable cause has a temporal component as well as a factual component. As we have seen, the factual element demands that police offer adequate factual grounds for their belief that the accused is engaged in criminal activity (or that a particular location will contain evidence of that activity). The **temporal** component demands that these factual allegations exist close in time to the challenged police conduct. As the Supreme Court pointed out, "the proof must be of facts so closely related to the time of the issue of the warrant as to justify a finding of probable cause at that time."[25]

For example, the day after a bank robbery, the police may use witness statements, surveillance footage, and employee work records to determine that a particular suspect robbed the bank and has stashed the proceeds of the robbery inside the ice cream stand where he works. However, even if this factual record is adequate to justify a warrant, the police may not sit on the information for a month before seeking judicial authorization to search the stand. Though the information might be factually sufficient to create probable cause, it must go one step further. The facts must establish probable cause to believe the money will actually be at the stand **at the time of the proposed search**. By waiting a month, the likelihood that the money is still located in the stand is substantially diminished.

Delayed assertion of information to support probable cause renders the information "stale." Stale facts are insufficient, standing on their own, to support a finding of probable cause. The Court has never issued a precise limit by which to assess when information becomes stale, and thus inadequate, to justify a probable cause finding, although in one case the Court has rejected information that was delayed by twenty-one days.[26]

The concept of staleness has been incorporated into the actual language of many warrants. As a statutory matter, most warrants expire on their own terms ten days after they are issued. Indeed, in one of the Court's most recent explorations into warrantless search procedures, the need for evaluation under the warrant exceptions was necessary because law enforcement officers obtained a warrant but then waited until the eleventh day after issuance to execute its terms.[27] By the eleventh

[23] Beck v. Ohio, 379 U.S. 89 (1964); but see Brinegar v. United States, 338 U.S. 160 (finding that the arresting officer's knowledge of Brinegar's criminal history coupled with other objective facts was adequate).

[24] Sibron v. New York, 392 U.S. 40, 62–63 (1968).

[25] Sgro v. United States, 287 U.S. 206, 210 (1932).

[26] Id. at 212.

[27] United States v. Jones 132 S.Ct. 945, 948 (2012).

day, the warrant had expired, and thus the police conduct had to be evaluated as a warrantless search.

Staleness contemplates searches occurring too late. Anticipatory search warrants present an opposite issue of timing. Anticipatory search warrants, as you will learn in **Chapter 11**, are warrants that are issued with a triggering condition. Once the triggering condition occurs, probable cause exists to believe evidence of criminal activity will be found on the target premises. Thus, the question of probable cause in the context of anticipatory search warrants is one of the searches happening too soon, not too late. To combat this concern, anticipatory search warrants require both probable cause to believe the evidence will be found once the triggering condition occurs, and probable cause to believe the triggering condition will happen.[28]

3. How to Prove Probable Cause. Once you know that a probable cause assessment is required, and you understand the meaning of the probable cause standard, the next issue is how that assessment should be made. In most cases, the existence of probable cause is a fairly straightforward inquiry. A reviewing court will consider "the events leading up to the arrest, and then decide 'whether these historical facts, viewed from the standpoint of an objectively reasonable police officer, amount to' probable cause."[29] These historical facts are generally provided by the investigating officer who is requesting the warrant or who is justifying his search or seizure, but they may be provided by another person or people and then simply reported to the judge by the investigating officer. Whenever the police officer is relying on information relied by another person, that person is known as the "informant."

When the police officer herself has firsthand knowledge of the information, the officer swears to the truth of the facts in the warrant application, or (in the context of an after-the-fact hearing), the officer testifies under oath that the facts are true. Then the court simply determines whether the information rises to the level of probable cause. But, when the information in support of probable cause is provided (in whole or in part) by an informant, the court's job is more difficult; the judge must consider both whether the amount of information is sufficient **and** whether the informant who provided the information is trustworthy.

Courts used to deal with these two inquires as two separate prongs of a test, called the *Aguilar-Spinelli* test based on the two cases that gave rise to it.[30] Under *Aguilar-Spinelli*, when making a probable cause assessment involving an informant, courts were required to separately consider 1) the informant's "**basis of**

---

[28] United States v. Grubbs, 547 U.S. 90, 96–97 (2006).

[29] Maryland v. Pringle, 540 U.S. 366, 371 (2003) (citing Ornelas v. United States, 517 U.S. 690, 696 (1996)).

[30] Aguilar v. Texas, 378 U.S. 108 (1964); Spinelli v. United States, 393 U.S. 410 (1969).

knowledge" and then 2) his "**veracity**" (referred to at times as the informant's "reliability"). Each of the two prongs came to be understood as imposing an independent and compulsory hurdle. If the informant failed to satisfy either prong, the information was excluded from the probable cause assessment.[31]

The government could satisfy the "basis of knowledge" prong by providing "some of the underlying circumstances from which the informant concluded that the" evidence was where the informant claimed it was.[32] Put more directly, under *Aguilar-Spinelli*, the government had to apprise the court not only what the informant believed (*e.g.*, "there are drugs in the defendant's vacation home") but also those facts that led the informant to her conclusion—that is, the informant's "basis of knowledge" for knowing these facts (e.g., "I attended a party last night at the defendant's home in the Hamptons. At the party, I went upstairs to use the second guest bathroom and saw a massive pile of heroin on top of a filing cabinet in the study. I have used heroin for years and know it when I see it. After I used the restroom, I snuck into the study and helped myself to some of the drugs. That was the best hit I've had in a long time.").

While the "basis of knowledge" prong focused on the informant's claims, the "veracity" prong focused on the informant herself. The "veracity" prong required the government to offer "some of the underlying circumstances from which the officer concluded that the informant . . . was 'credible' or his information 'reliable.'"[33] For example, an officer might disclose that she had worked with an informant for many years and information supplied by the informant resulted in successful arrests on several occasions. In *Spinelli*, the officer swore that his informant was reliable, but did not offer any additional information to support this conclusion. Accordingly, the *Spinelli* Court found the information provided by the police informant there could not be considered in the probable cause balance.

In the years after the creation of the *Aguilar-Spinelli* test, lower courts applied it strictly. This strict application led to routine rejection of police investigations based substantially on information provided by anonymous informants. "Ordinary citizens, like ordinary witnesses, generally do not provide extensive recitations of the basis of their everyday observations."[34] Likewise, if an officer had no prior involvement with an informant or did not know the informant, it was impossible to provide evidence in support of the "reliability" prong of the *Aguilar-Spinelli* test.

These two observations led the Court to conclude that "anonymous tips seldom could survive a rigorous application of either of the *Spinelli* prongs" and that

---

[31] Illinois v. Gates, 462 U.S. 213, 228 (1983).

[32] Aguilar, 378 U.S. at 114.

[33] Id.

[34] Gates, 462 U.S. at 237.

the two-prong *Aguilar-Spinelli* test required "an excessively technical dissection of informants' tips."[35] Accordingly, in *Illinois v. Gates*, the Court rejected the formal application of the two-pronged *Aguilar-Spinelli* case and turned to a **totality-of-the-circumstances** test to assess the existence of probable cause.[36]

The *Gates* totality-of-the-circumstances test, which is now generally applied to all probable cause assessments, requires a comprehensive evaluation of the information known to police. While the *Aguilar-Spinelli* inquiries into an informant's basis of knowledge and veracity are still relevant, they are not as rigidly applied. "[A] deficiency in one may be compensated for, in determining the overall reliability of a tip, by a strong showing as to the other, or by some other indicia of reliability."[37] Moreover, independent police corroboration of details provided by the informant may be used to support probable cause, even if the tip alone is insufficient. However, corroboration of any minor detail, no matter how trivial, will not do. "[T]he additional information acquired by the arresting officers must in some sense be corroborative of the informer's tip that the arrestees committed the felony or . . . were in the process of committing the felony."[38] Corroboration of predictions about the suspect's future behavior also weighs heavily in favor of probable cause.

Courts are relatively lenient regarding the **type** of information that can be used to establish probable cause. Thus, although hearsay evidence is typically excluded from the trial stage of a criminal case, it is freely admitted in connection with probable cause determinations. As to such evidence, the Court has said there must be only a "substantial basis for crediting the hearsay."[39]

Whether hearsay or non-hearsay, the evidence must also be sufficient to allow the reviewing magistrate or court to make an independent determination about the existence of probable cause. Therefore, the government's burden of production requires more than conclusory assertions that probable cause exists. The Court has held that "[s]ufficient information must be presented to the magistrate to allow that official to determine probable cause; his action cannot be a mere ratification of the bare conclusions of others."[40] Hence, a statement that "the undersigned plaintiff has probable cause to believe the accused violated the narcotics laws," would be insufficient. Instead, the underlying circumstances and details that form the basis for that opinion must also be offered.

---

[35] Id.

[36] 462 U.S. 213, 234–35.

[37] Id. at 233.

[38] Whiteley v. Warden, 401 U.S. 560, 567 (1971).

[39] United States v. Ventresca, 380 U.S. 102, 108 (1965).

[40] Gates, 462 U.S. at 239.

C. Applying the Law. To understand how courts determine whether probable cause exists, we will first examine the two best known factors in the test ("basis of knowledge" and "veracity"). Then we will see how these two factors are applied in the broader context of the totality-of-the-circumstances test. Then we will look at a few specific categories of probable cause determinations.

1. Basis of Knowledge. In any determination of probable cause, there is some conclusion that the police officer is trying to establish. It could be the fact that the defendant committed a crime and therefore should be arrested (or the arrest which already took place was proper). It could be that evidence of a crime will be found at a particular location and therefore the police should be allowed to search in that location to find the evidence. In order to establish probable cause, the police officer needs to convince a judge that a person of reasonable caution would believe that there is a fair probability that the conclusion is correct.

The "basis of knowledge" factor essentially involves evaluating the facts the informant sets forth that lead him to his conclusion. For example, assume the police officer is trying to establish that the defendant stole a tablet computer from an electronics store. Here are three versions of facts that a officer might present to a court to try to establish probable cause:

A. An informant told me: "I saw the defendant running down the street holding something hidden under his coat."

B. An informant told me: "I saw the defendant running down the street. I looked behind him, and I saw the front window of the electronics store had been broken."

C. An informant told me: "I saw the defendant running down the street holding something hidden under his coat. I looked behind him, and I saw the front window of the electronics store had been broken."

Although both (A) and (B) describe suspicious behavior, neither set of facts on its own is likely to establish probable cause. (C) will likely be enough to establish probable cause, although it is a close call.

Another issue that arises in evaluating the basis of knowledge factor is ensuring that the informant explains exactly how she acquired the information. For example, an informant who merely says: "Terrance Williams hacked into a number of Chase bank accounts and stole money" does very little to satisfy the basis of knowledge factor because it does not explain **how** the informant knows this information. In contrast, an informant who says: "I was with Terrance Williams on July 22nd in his home, and I personally saw him hack into a number of Chase bank accounts and steal money" shows a significant basis of knowledge because the informant states that she personally witnessed the crime. Of course, the informant may be lying, but that has nothing to do with the basis of knowledge factor; that has to do with the reliability factor.

Another way of satisfying the basis of knowledge prong is if the information has a high degree of detail. The fact that the informant knows specific details about the criminal activity implies that she has a strong basis of knowledge. For example, assume the informant states: "On July 22nd, beginning at 10:35 P.M., Terrance Williams hacked into three different bank accounts kept at Chase bank. The first belonged to Ronald Dawson, account number 5557887. The second belonged to Debra Glowski, account number 7342113. The third belonged to Francine Harding, account number 9335493. Williams hacked into the bank accounts by using a computer program and a high-speed processor to guess every possible username and password combination until it hit upon a successful combination." Although this informant does not say directly how she knows this information, the high degree of detail is evidence that she has a strong basis of knowledge about the activity. Again, the informant may be lying about these details, but that is a question of reliability, not basis of knowledge.

Example—*Draper v. United States*, 358 U.S. 307 (1959): Agent Marsh was a federal narcotics officer stationed in Denver, Colorado. He worked with an informant named Hereford who periodically provided him with useful information about drug trafficking in the city. One day Hereford called Agent Marsh and told him that a man named James Draper was going to deliver heroin into the city. Hereford said that Draper "had gone to Chicago the day before by train [and] that he was going to bring back three ounces of heroin [and] that he would return to Denver either on the morning of the 8th of September or the morning of the 9th of September also by train." Hereford explained that Draper was a black man with a light brown complexion, twenty-seven years of age, five feet eight inches tall, and weighing about 160 pounds. Hereford indicated that Draper would be wearing a light colored raincoat, brown slacks and black shoes. He also said that Draper would be carrying "a tan zipper bag," and that he habitually "walked real fast."

Agent Marsh waited at the train station, and on September 9th he saw a person precisely fitting Hereford's description disembark from the train from Chicago and walk quickly through the station. Agent Marsh arrested the individual (who turned out to be James Draper) and then searched him incident to the arrest. Agent Marsh found two envelopes containing heroin in Draper's hand.

Draper was charged with transporting narcotic drugs. He challenged his arrest and subsequent search at a suppression hearing after his arrest. Draper argued that Agent Marsh did not possess probable cause to arrest him, and therefore the arrest and subsequent search were unconstitutional. The case eventually reached the Supreme Court.

Analysis: The Court held that Agent Marsh did possess probable cause to arrest Draper. Regarding the basis of knowledge factor, the Court noted that the level of detail provided by the informant led to a reasonable inference that the informant had gained his information in a reliable way. As we will see in the next section, the Court also found that the informant was reliable, and therefore the information ranked high on the second factor as well.

In contrast, when the informant only provides conclusory statements about the defendant's illegal activity, or provides very few details without explaining how he came to know them, a court should find the basis of knowledge factor to be lacking:

Example—*Spinelli v. United States*, 393 U.S. 410 (1969): The FBI suspected William Spinelli of running an illegal gambling operation in St. Louis. They applied for and received a warrant to search his office, and the search turned up substantial evidence of Spinelli's criminal activity. Spinelli was convicted of gambling, but he appealed the conviction, arguing that the magistrate had improperly issued the warrant because the police had not demonstrated probable cause.

The FBI's warrant application contained the following relevant information:

1. "[A] confidential reliable informant [states] that William Spinelli is operating a handbook and accepting wagers and disseminating wagering information by means of the telephones which have been assigned the numbers WUdown 4-0029 and WYdown 4-0136."

2. The FBI followed Spinelli and saw him enter into a certain apartment in St. Louis. A check with the phone company showed that the apartment contained two telephones, that had been assigned the numbers WYdown 4-0029 and WYdown 4-0136.

3. Spinelli was "known" to federal law enforcement as a gambler and an associate of gamblers.

The case was appealed to the United States Supreme Court.

Analysis: The Court held that the magistrate erred when it issued the warrant, because the application did not show a sufficient basis of knowledge.

> We are not told how the FBI's source received his information—it is not alleged that the informant personally observed Spinelli at work or that he had ever placed a bet with him . . . . In the absence of a statement detailing the manner in which the information was gathered, it is especially important that the tip describe the accused criminal activity in sufficient detail that the magistrate may know that he is relying on something more substantial than a casual rumor circulating in the underworld or an accusation based merely on an individual's general reputation.[41]

The Court contrasted the paltry level of detail in Spinelli's case to the large amount of detail in *Draper*—a description in "minute particularity" of the clothing the suspect would be wearing and an accurate prediction of when he would be arriving. In contrast, the only detail that the informant gave about Spinelli's activity was the fact that he used two telephones, and "this meager report could easily have been obtained from an offhand remark heard at a neighborhood bar."[42]

2. Veracity. In the above examples, we only considered the **amount** of information provided by the informant. For the veracity prong, courts consider the **reliability** of that information—in other words, how likely is it that the informant is telling the truth?

In many cases, the police officer seeking to establish probable cause can testify directly to what she has seen—in other words, there is no "informant." In such cases, the veracity factor is not a significant consideration because the police officer is testifying under oath (or in the case of a warrant application, swearing in an affidavit) that the information is correct:

Example: An undercover police officer standing in a park watches a suspect sitting on a park bench. Over the course of fifteen minutes, he sees three different people approach the suspect and give him money. After receiving the money, the suspect then reaches into a paper bag underneath the park bench and hands each person a small plastic baggie. The police officer then moves in and arrests the suspect. He searches the paper bag incident to

41 Spinelli v. United States, 393 U.S. 410, 416 (1969).

42 Id. at 417.

the arrest and sees ten small baggies each containing a rock of crack cocaine.

The suspect then challenges the arrest and subsequent search, claiming that the officer did not have probable cause to make the arrest.

Analysis: The police officer had probable cause to make the arrest. His basis for knowledge was strong—he witnessed the suspect engage in suspicious behavior on three separate occasions, and the behavior was suspicious enough to cause a person of reasonable caution to believe that there was a fair probability that drug sales were occurring. In addition, the police officer himself will testify at the suppression hearing, under oath and subject to cross-examination. To the extent that reliability issues are present, the hearing judge will be able to immediately assess them based upon personal observation of the witness, so there is no issue of informant reliability external to the proceedings.

In other cases, however, the police officer is reporting facts that were told to her by an informant. In these cases, the reviewing court must evaluate the reliability of the informant. An anonymous tip from an informant with no known track record has almost no reliability on its own. An anonymous tip from an informant who has provided correct information in the past has a much higher level of reliability. A tip from an individual who is willing to provide her name and address also has a much higher level of reliability, even if she has never provided information to the police before.

If the police are concerned that their informant's level of reliability is so low that his information cannot establish probable cause, they can increase the level of reliability by confirming some of the details provided by the informant. Confirmation of even seemingly innocent details may help to increase the level of reliability, and thereby make the informant's statements about the defendant's illicit behavior more likely to be believed:

Example—*Draper v. United States*, 358 U.S. 307 (1959): In the previous section, we saw that the high level of detail provided by the informant in *Draper* demonstrated the informant's significant basis of knowledge. In order to determine whether there was probable cause, however, the Court also needed to determine the reliability of the informant.

Analysis: Because so many details from the informant's report had been corroborated by the police before the arrest, the Court found that the informant was reliable. As the Court explained in a later case:

> Independent police work in [*Draper*] case corroborated much more than one small detail that had been provided by the informant . . . . [T]he police, upon meeting the inbound Denver train on the second morning specified by informer Hereford, saw a man whose dress corresponded precisely to Hereford's detailed description. It was then apparent that the informant had not been fabricating his report out of whole cloth . . . . [43]

Of course, in the *Draper* case the informant also had a proven track record with the federal agents. However, the Court has implied that even if this had been the informant's first contact with law enforcement, the number of corroborated details in *Draper* would give the informant a high level of reliability.

Significantly, the Court found that the informant in *Draper* was reliable even though the only details the police had confirmed were predictions of totally innocent behavior: arriving on a certain train, dressing a certain way, and walking quickly. But the fact that these predictions were correct made it more likely that the informant was honest about the final prediction—that the suspect would be carrying heroin.

3. Totality of the Circumstances: As noted above, when determining probable cause, a court will need to look at both the informant's reliability and her basis of knowledge. However, the totality-of-the-circumstances test means that the court can be flexible in evaluating these two factors: even if one of these factors is very weak, the court can still find there is probable cause if the other factor is particularly strong. The *Gates* case itself provides an excellent example:

> **Example—*Illinois v. Gates*, 462 U.S. 213 (1983):** A detective in the Chicago suburbs received a handwritten letter from an unknown informant. The note reported that a couple named Lance and Susan Gates, who lived on a named road in the town, were selling drugs. The letter reported that the couple picked up their drugs in Florida and then resold them in Illinois. According to the source, the wife usually drove to Florida and immediately flew back to Illinois. She would leave the car to be loaded with drugs. The husband would then fly to Florida from Illinois and drive the loaded car back. The letter reported that the couple had an upcoming trip of this nature planned in the next day or two. The letter closed with information that the couple presently had more than $100,000 worth of drugs in the basement of their home.

---

[43] Id.

Acting on the information contained in the letter, the detective confirmed that a "Lance Gates" had a driver's license issued to an address on the street identified in the letter. The detective also learned that an "L. Gates" was scheduled to fly on Eastern Airlines from Chicago to West Palm Beach, Florida in two days. Federal agents in Florida observed Mr. Gates get off the flight and take a taxi to a nearby hotel. At the hotel, they watched him enter a room registered to a Susan Gates. The next morning Gates and an unidentified woman got into a car bearing Illinois license plates and drove north on a highway heading in the direction of the Chicago area.

The letter coupled with the information the detective gleaned during his investigation was submitted to a magistrate and a warrant was issued to search the Gates' home and car. When the Gateses returned to their home in the Chicago-area twenty-two hours later, the police arrested them and searched their home and car. The police found 350 pounds of marijuana in the car. Additional drugs, money and weapons were found in the house.

The Gateses challenged the lawfulness of the searches. They argued that the information provided by in the anonymous letter was inadequate to establish probable cause. Specifically, the Gateses argued that the basis of the informant's knowledge was poor, and the informant's veracity (or reliability) could not be established.

Analysis: The Supreme Court held that the magistrate was correct to find probable cause, and thus the warrant was properly issued.

The Court agreed that the informant's basis of knowledge and veracity were important factors in determining whether probable cause existed. The Court also implied that one of these factors—basis of knowledge—was not satisfied in this case. The informant did not explain how the information provided was known. Moreover, the level of detail provided was not enough to demonstrate first-hand knowledge.

However, the Court explained that it was incorrect to treat the two factors as independent prongs that must each be proven in order to establish probable cause. In the Court's view, the totality-of-the-circumstances test was "far more consistent with [the Court's] prior treatment of probable cause."[44]

[44] Illinois v. Gates, 462 U.S. 213, 230 (1983).

Thus, the relevant question for the *Gates* Court was whether, on balance, the information known to the officer established probable cause to believe the Gateses were engaged in criminal activity. The relevant pool of information included not just the information and predictions supplied by the informant, but also the information the officer gathered independently to corroborate the informant's claims. Since the detective in *Gates* independently corroborated a substantial amount of the information including details concerning the future actions of the Gateses, the Court found adequate support for the probable cause finding. "It is enough that there was a fair probability that the writer of the anonymous letter had obtained his entire story either from the Gates[es] or someone they trusted. And corroboration of major portions of the letter's predictions provides just this probability."[45]

In short, judges making probable cause determinations should still evaluate the basis of knowledge and the reliability of the informant. However, the *Gates* totality-of-the-circumstances test is flexible and lets courts find probable cause even if one of these factors is particularly weak, as long as the overall amount of information that is provided meets the probable cause standard.

4. The "Mere Presence" Factor. As you have read, mere presence at the scene of criminal activity is not adequate to establish probable cause. But, how does this oft-repeated maxim play out when police come upon a group of people all of whom are in close proximity to obvious criminal activity? Over the course of approximately sixty years, the Court decided a trio of cases that resolved this question:

> **Example—*United States v. Di Re*, 332 U.S. 581(1948):** A government investigator in Buffalo, New York was working to combat the trade in counterfeit gasoline rations. The investigator learned from an informant, Reed, that Reed was scheduled to purchase counterfeit rations later that day from a man named Buttitta. The informant also provided the name of the place where the sale would transpire.
>
> The investigator and a Buffalo police officer trailed Buttitta's car to the named location. When they arrived, Buttitta had already parked. The two officers approached Buttitta's car, and found the informant Reed sitting alone in the back seat. In his hand, Reed was holding two gasoline rations. When asked by the officers where he got them, Reed indicated Buttitta. Buttitta was sitting in the front of the car in the driver's seat. A man named Michael De Re was sitting in the passenger's seat.

[45] Id. at 246.

The officers arrested Buttitta and Di Re. During a search at the stationhouse, the police found counterfeit gasoline and fuel oil rations in Di Re's pocket. They also found one hundred counterfeit gasoline rations stashed between Di Re's shirt and his underwear. Di Re challenged his arrest as unlawful. Di Re maintained that his presence in the front seat of the car and his failure to protest his innocence were insufficient to establish probable cause.

Analysis: Di Re's arrest was unlawful and the rations should have been excluded from evidence. The police had no information about Di Re before coming upon him in the car. When they arrived at the car, Di Re did not do or say anything to suggest he was involved with the exchange of counterfeit gas rations. There was also no evidence that Di Re was in the car when the rations were exchanged or that he heard or took part in any conversation about the exchange. Indeed, when asked the source of the counterfeit rations, Reed identified only Buttitta. Reed made no mention of Di Re. "Any inference that everyone on the scene of a crime is party to it must disappear if the Government informer singles out the guilty person."[46]

In finding that probable cause did not exist to arrest Di Re, the Court took special note of the fact that the crime had taken place "in broad daylight, in plain sight of passersby, in a public street of a large city, and where the alleged substantive crime is one which does not necessarily involved any act visibly criminal."[47] On those facts, the Court found it not at all "probable" that Di Re was a part of the illegal conduct taking place in his presence.

However, in a second "passenger in a car" case, involving a crime more "visibly criminal," the Court came to an opposite conclusion:

Example—*Maryland v. Pringle*, 540 U.S. 366 (2003): Joseph Pringle was the front seat passenger in a Nissan Maxima that was stopped for speeding just after 3:00 a.m. outside of Baltimore, Maryland. Also in the car were the driver, Donte Partlow, and a back seat passenger, Otis Smith. In response to a request for documents from the police officer who made the stop, the driver Partlow reached in front of Pringle and opened the glove compartment. As Partlow did this, the officer observed a large roll of cash inside the compartment. Partlow retrieve his registration and handed it over along with his license. A document check revealed nothing out of order. Nonetheless, the officer returned

[46] Di Re, 332 U.S. at 594.

[47] Id.

to the car and ordered Partlow to step out. When a second police car arrived on the scene, the officer asked permission to search the car. Partlow agreed. The search uncovered $763 dollars in rolled up bills in the glove box and five baggies of cocaine. The cocaine was tucked behind the back seat armrest, which was raised so that it was flush with the back seat.

When the officer inquired about the money and the drugs none of the three men claimed ownership. The officer then advised the men if no one confessed, they would all be arrested. When no one spoke up, all three men were arrested. At the station, following *Miranda* warnings, Pringle confessed to owning the cocaine. When he confirmed that the others in the car were not aware of the presence of the drugs, they were released.

Pringle challenged his arrest, arguing that under *Di Re*, his mere presence in the car did create probable cause to believe he was involved in criminal activity. Accordingly, he maintained that his confession, which was a product of that arrest, should have been suppressed.

Analysis: The Supreme Court upheld the arrest. There is no question that once the officer located the drugs in the rear seat of the car, he had probable cause to believe criminal activity was afoot. The only question was whether there was sufficient evidence from which the officer might reasonably believe that Pringle was the one who committed the crime. The Court found there was.

Nearly $800 in cash was found rolled up in the glove compartment that was directly in front of Pringle. In addition, the five baggies of cocaine, though not visible, were easily accessible to any of the men in the car. In the Court's view, car passengers are often engaged in common pursuits with the driver and other occupants. The Court also found it implausible that those engaged in the enterprise of drug dealing, which the quantity of drugs and cash suggested, would allow innocent people into their midst. "We think it an entirely reasonable inference from these facts that any or all three of the occupants had knowledge of, and exercised dominion and control over, the cocaine."[48]

Many find the Court's unanimous decision in *Pringle* troubling. Though drug dealing is a "visibly criminal" enterprise, there was no evidence in *Pringle* that either the cash or the drugs were visible to the two passengers in the car. Indeed, the evidence indisputably indicated that 1) the cash could not be seen until the glove compartment was opened by the driver, 2) the drugs, which were tucked

[48] Maryland v. Pringle, 540 U.S. 366, 372 (2003).

between the rear seat and the arm rest, were not visible at all, 3) there was another person sitting in the back seat, and 4) Pringle neither owned nor operated the car. Under these circumstances, many commentators have challenged the *Pringle* Court's conclusion that it was "probable" Pringle had knowledge of the cocaine's presence. These commentators suggest that by finding probable cause, the Court in reality allowed sufficient suspicion to be generated by mere presence (at least with regard to suspected narcotics distribution).

Though this critique has logical appeal, the *Pringle* decision should not be understood as creating a blanket "drug conspiracy" exception to the broader "mere presence" rule. Critical to the *Pringle* Court's decision was the fact that the criminal activity occurred in a confined physical space. The Court also found decisive the fact that nothing about the circumstances made any one of the three men **less** likely to have been involved in the offense. Where such "singling out" evidence is available, probable cause as to those who are not singled out will be undermined.

The *Pringle* decision has also been critiqued as reducing the quantum of suspicion needed to establish probable cause. In *Pringle*, as a purely mathematical proposition, if only one of the men was guilty of a crime, then there was only a 33⅓% chance that Pringle was the one committing a narcotics offense. Nonetheless, the Court found that the officer had probable cause to arrest Pringle. Critics of this conclusion argue that the Court's decision signals that "probable cause" can now be quantified as a 33⅓% chance that the suspect committed a crime. This is well below what courts and practitioners have understood the term "probable" to mean.

However, the Court, both in *Pringle* and since, has made clear it has not adopted a precise quantitative definition of the term: "[t]he probable cause standard is incapable of precise definition or quantification into percentages because it deals with probabilities and depends on the totality of the circumstances."[49]

What if drug dealing is suspected in a physical space larger than a car? For example, assume the police suspect a particular commercial establishment as being the location of drug sales. Does the *Pringle* Court's "common criminal enterprise" inference apply to anyone found on the premises?

> **Example—*Ybarra v. Illinois*, 444 U.S. 85 (1979):** After receiving information from a confidential informant, Aurora, Illinois police officers secured a warrant to search the Aurora Tap Tavern. As the warrant revealed, the officers reasonably suspected that the bartender at the Tavern was selling heroin and was keeping his stash in a drawer at the bar.

[49] Id. at 373 (emphasis added); see also Florida v. Harris, 133 S.Ct. 1050, 1055 (2013) (noting that the "test for probable cause is not reducible to 'precise definition or quantification'").

Seven or eight officers executed the warrant. Upon entering the bar, the officers announced why they were there, and then proceeded to pat down each of the dozen or so customers inside. Ventura Ybarra was one such customer. The first time Ybarra was frisked, the frisking officer indicated he felt a cigarette package with objects in it in Ybarra's pants pocket. After completing frisks of the other patrons, the officer then returned to Ybarra. This time the officer relocated the item in Ybarra's pants pocket and pulled it out. He found a cigarette box with six tinfoil packets inside. Each of the packets contained a substance that was later determined to be heroin.

Ybarra challenged the constitutionality of his search, arguing that probable cause did not exist to justify the intrusion.

Analysis: The search of Ybarra was improper. The search warrant that justified the search of the Tavern established probable cause to believe drugs might be found in the Tavern and on just one person in it—the bartender. Nothing that the police learned upon their arrival at the bar shifted the focus of these suspicions to Ybarra. Ybarra did not say or do anything to suggest he might be suspicious to the officers. "In short, the agents knew nothing in particular about Ybarra, except that he was present, along with several other customers, in a public tavern at a time when the police had reason to believe that the bartender would have heroin for sale."

Unlike in *Pringle*, the suspicion that the officers possessed in *Ybarra* attached to the bar and the bartender in isolation. "[A] person's mere propinquity to others independently suspected of criminal activity does not, without more, give rise to probable cause to search that person."[50]

As the decisions in *Di Re*, *Ybarra*, and *Pringle* make clear, probable cause is a highly fact sensitive inquiry that turns on all of the specific circumstances in a particular case. Being in close proximity to drug dealing might generate suspicion if you are in an automobile, but not if you are in a bar. On the other hand, being in the close confines of a car may justify no suspicion at all if the criminal activity taking place is not readily apparent. In case after case, courts have waded through the facts before them to determine whether a reasonable probability exists for particularized suspicion. As you move out into practice, deciding whether probable cause exists in your case will necessarily require reference to prior court decisions. But, you should also always step back and make a commonsense assessment of your particular facts. More often than prior decisions, it is this practical assessment of facts that guides courts' probable cause cases.

[50] Ybarra v. Illinois, 444 U.S. 85, 91 (1979).

5. Building Inspections. One specific factual circumstance is worth mentioning before we finish our probable cause overview. Although the Court has been fairly consistent in its estimation of the quantum of evidence necessary to establish probable cause, building inspections represent a significant outlier.

In *Camara v. San Francisco*,[51] the Court determined that, with regard to building inspections, probable cause means something less than what we understand it to mean in the context of criminal investigations. You will read more about *Camara* in **Chapter 18** and its discussion of the special needs exception to the Warrant Requirement. For now, you should note only that within the singular confines of building inspections, probable cause to inspect a particular dwelling can be established by simply pointing to "reasonable legislative or administrative standards for conducting an area inspection."[52] As a practical matter, this means that where a regulatory scheme for periodic building inspections is in place, probable cause to search any single building in the covered area can be established based on little more than the passage of time since the last inspection. Clearly, this quantum of proof would not be adequate in a standard criminal case.

[51] 387 U.S. 523 (1967).

[52] Id. at 538.

Quick Summary

Probable cause is the standard that governs a wide swath of official police conduct. Probable cause is required as a constitutional matter for all conduct that is subject to the Warrant Clause of the Fourth Amendment. In addition, the Court has determined that a significant amount of police action that is not pre-authorized by a warrant requires the justification of probable cause.

Probable cause is not a rigid concept and takes on meaning only in application. The Court has also indicated that probable cause, though not perfect, is the best compromise yet identified to balance the citizenry's right to be free from unreasonable police action with the competing needs of law enforcement.

Probable cause must support both a reasonable belief that criminal activity is afoot and a reasonable belief that the target of police action is involved with that criminal activity. The existence of probable cause is evaluated using a totality-of-the-circumstances test. This test considers all of the information known to the police. Information provided by others is fairly weighed in the balance. If information provided by others is insufficient standing alone to establish probable cause, the police may bolster their suspicion by corroborating the information that has been provided.

Review Questions

1. **Searching a Crack House.** The police are applying for a search warrant for a house at 55 W. Neil Avenue. Consider the following possible facts which might support a warrant application:

A. An anonymous tip from an informant that crack cocaine is being sold out of the house.

B. Police observations over the course of a four-hour period one night revealing that eleven different individuals entered the home, stayed for less than a minute, and then left.

C. A background check of the resident of the house reveals that he has two prior convictions for narcotics trafficking over the past seven years.

D. A uniformed police officer approached the door of the home and asked to search the home, and the resident refused.

E. Police observation that there is a "high concentration" of small Ziploc baggies on the sidewalks and in the gutters within a one-block radius of the house; when tested, a number of the Ziplocs show crack cocaine residue.

You are the issuing magistrate and will only issue a warrant if you determine there is probable cause. Which combination of factors (if any) would lead you to conclude there was probable cause to believe that drugs are being sold out of the house?

i. A. alone?

ii. B. alone?

iii. A. and B.?

iv. A. and C.?

v. A. and D.?

vi. A. and E.?

2. **Tipped Off by a Family Member.** The police respond to a 911 call and find a person identifying himself as Gary Carson. Gary tells the police that his brother

David carries an illegal firearm and Gary is afraid that David will use it "and hurt someone or get himself hurt." Gary tells the police that David works as a mechanic in a car garage, and he urges the police to arrest him right away. The police proceed to the car garage, and arrest Gary. They search him subsequent to his arrest and find a gun in an ankle holster. He is charged with illegal possession of a firearm.

Gary is now moving to suppress the gun, arguing that the police did not have probable cause to arrest him, and therefore the subsequent search was illegal.

a. Did the police have probable cause to make the arrest? If not, what further information could they have acquired to ensure they had probable cause?

b. Suppose that when the police arrested Gary, they searched him but found no gun. Gary is now suing the police for unlawful arrest, and the police argue that they had probable cause. Does the fact that no gun was found make the analysis different than it is in (a)?

3. Stolen Electronics. At 2:00 AM on the morning of September 23rd, a Best Buy store was burgled. The perpetrators approached the lone security guard on foot, knocked him unconscious, and stole dozens of laptop computers, over twenty iPads, and a Panasonic sixty-inch Plasma TV. The security guard revived at about 2:15 and called the police. He told them that there were three men that attacked him and that they were wearing all black and that they "looked Hispanic." Police immediately fanned out through the neighborhood to look for the perpetrators.

a. At 2:30 approximately five blocks from the store, Officer Martin saw David Rodriguez, who is Hispanic, carrying three laptop computers in his arms. The man was walking at a normal pace in a direction away from the store. When Officer Martin asked him to stop, Rodriguez did so. Officer Martin asked to see the laptops and Rodriguez said: "I'm sorry, officer, I know my rights and I don't want to be searched by the police." Officer Martin then arrested Rodriguez and confiscated the laptops.

   It turned out the laptops were not stolen—Rodriguez was a college student and he was carrying his laptop and his friends' laptops back from a study session. However, in a search incident to the arrest, Officer Martin found a marijuana cigarette in Rodriguez's pocket. Rodriguez was charged with possession of marijuana, and he is now challenging the arrest, arguing that Martin did not have probable cause. How should the court rule?

b. At 2:35 approximately one-half mile from the store, Officers Harrison was in his patrol car and saw a beat-up red pickup truck parked on the road. Inside the bed of the pickup truck was a Panasonic sixty-inch Plasma TV, still in its original box. Officer Harrison can testify that he is familiar with the neighborhood and knows that it is "an extremely poor neighborhood—almost everyone there lives on government assistance." Thus, he believed that it was very unlikely that anyone living there could afford such an expensive television set. As the officer got out of the truck to examine the TV, Cynthia Gomez, who is Hispanic, emerged from a nearby home and walked over to the truck. Officer Harrison asked if she owned the truck and the TV. Gomez said she owned both. Officer Harrison asked to see a receipt for the TV, and Gomez said she didn't have one. She then got in her truck to drive away, and Officer Harrison arrested her. He took her and the television back to the Best Buy, and the store manager confirmed the TV was the same one that had been stolen. Gomez than confessed that she knew the TV was stolen and that her boyfriend showed up five minutes before Officer Harrison arrived, told her he stole a television, loaded it into her truck, and asked her to drive it to his mother's house.

   Based in part on this confession, Gomez was charged with possession of stolen property and obstruction of an official police investigation. Gomez is now challenging the arrest and thus the subsequent confession, arguing that Officer Harrison did not have probable cause at the time of the arrest. How should the court rule?

c. At 2:37 approximately six blocks from the store, Officer Cho saw Stanley Underhill, who was not Hispanic and was wearing a dark blue shirt and blue jeans. Underhill was walking at a brisk pace away from the store and he was carrying an iPad. Officer Cho approached Underhill and said: "Sir! I'd like to ask you a few questions!" Underhill turned and saw Officer Cho and immediately started running. Officer Cho chased Underhill, tackled him, and placed him under arrest. He then seized the iPad and searched Underhill. Underhill had an unlicensed gun in his waistband. The iPad had not been stolen from Best Buy.

   Underhill was charged with illegal possession of a weapon, and he challenged his arrest and subsequent search. How should the court rule?

FROM THE COURTROOM

ILLINOIS v. GATES

United States Supreme Court, 1983
462 U.S. 213

Justice REHNQUIST delivered the opinion of the Court.

Justice WHITE concurred in the judgment.

Justices BRENNAN, MARSHALL, and STEVENS dissented.

Respondents Lance and Susan Gates were indicted for violation of state drug laws after police officers, executing a search warrant, discovered marijuana and other contraband in their automobile and home. Prior to trial the Gates' moved to suppress evidence seized during this search. The Illinois Supreme Court affirmed the decisions of lower state courts granting the motion. It held that the affidavit submitted in support of the State's application for a warrant to search the Gates' property was inadequate under this Court's decisions in *Aguilar v. Texas*, 378 U.S. 108 (1964) and *Spinelli v. United States*, 393 U.S. 410 (1969).

We granted certiorari to consider the application of the Fourth Amendment to a magistrate's issuance of a search warrant on the basis of a partially corroborated anonymous informant's tip. . . .

We . . . conclude that the Illinois Supreme Court read the requirements of our Fourth Amendment decisions too restrictively. . . .

II

We now turn to the question presented in the State's original petition for certiorari, which requires us to decide whether respondents' rights under the Fourth and Fourteenth Amendments were violated by the search of their car and house. A chronological statement of events usefully introduces the issues at stake. Bloomingdale, Ill., is a suburb of Chicago located in DuPage County. On May 3, 1978, the Bloomingdale Police Department received by mail an anonymous handwritten letter which read as follows:

> "This letter is to inform you that you have a couple in your town who strictly make their living on selling drugs. They are Sue and Lance Gates, they live on Greenway, off Bloomingdale Rd. in the condominiums. Most of their buys are done in Florida. Sue his wife drives their car to Florida, where she leaves it to be loaded up with drugs, then Lance flys down and drives it back.

Sue flys back after she drops the car off in Florida. May 3 she is driving down there again and Lance will be flying down in a few days to drive it back. At the time Lance drives the car back he has the trunk loaded with over $100,000.00 in drugs. Presently they have over $100,000.00 worth of drugs in their basement.

They brag about the fact they never have to work, and make their entire living on pushers.

I guarantee if you watch them carefully you will make a big catch. They are friends with some big drugs dealers, who visit their house often.

Lance & Susan Gates

Greenway
in Condominiums"

The letter was referred by the Chief of Police of the Bloomingdale Police Department to Detective Mader, who decided to pursue the tip. Mader learned, from the office of the Illinois Secretary of State, that an Illinois driver's license had been issued to one Lance Gates, residing at a stated address in Bloomingdale. He contacted a confidential informant, whose examination of certain financial records revealed a more recent address for the Gates, and he also learned from a police officer assigned to O'Hare Airport that "L. Gates" had made a reservation on Eastern Airlines flight 245 to West Palm Beach, Fla., scheduled to depart from Chicago on May 5 at 4:15 p.m.

Mader then made arrangements with an agent of the Drug Enforcement Administration for surveillance of the May 5 Eastern Airlines flight. The agent later reported to Mader that Gates had boarded the flight, and that federal agents in Florida had observed him arrive in West Palm Beach and take a taxi to the nearby Holiday Inn. They also reported that Gates went to a room registered to one Susan Gates and that, at 7:00 a.m. the next morning, Gates and an unidentified woman left the motel in a Mercury bearing Illinois license plates and drove northbound on an interstate frequently used by travelers to the Chicago area. In addition, the DEA agent informed Mader that the license plate number on the Mercury registered to a Hornet station wagon owned by Gates. The agent also advised Mader that the driving time between West Palm Beach and Bloomingdale was approximately [twenty-two] to [twenty-four] hours.

Mader signed an affidavit setting forth the foregoing facts, and submitted it to a judge of the Circuit Court of DuPage County, together with a copy of the anonymous letter. The judge of that court thereupon issued a search warrant for the Gates' residence and for their automobile. The judge, in deciding to issue the warrant, could have determined that the *modus operandi* of the Gates had been substantially corroborated. As the anonymous letter predicted, Lance Gates had flown from Chicago to West Palm Beach late in the afternoon of May 5th, had checked into a hotel room registered in the name of his wife, and, at 7:00 a.m. the following morning, had headed north, accompanied by an unidentified woman, out of West Palm Beach on an interstate highway used by travelers from South Florida to Chicago in an automobile bearing a license plate issued to him.

At 5:15 a.m. on March 7th, only [thirty-six] hours after he had flown out of Chicago, Lance Gates, and his wife, returned to their home in Bloomingdale, driving the car in which they had left West Palm Beach some [twenty-two] hours earlier. The Bloomingdale police were awaiting them, searched the trunk of the Mercury, and uncovered approximately 350 pounds of marijuana. A search of the Gates' home revealed marijuana, weapons, and other contraband. The Illinois Circuit Court ordered suppression of all these items, on the ground that the affidavit submitted to the Circuit Judge failed to support the necessary determination of probable cause to believe that the Gates' automobile and home contained the contraband in question. This decision was affirmed in turn by the Illinois Appellate Court and by a divided vote of the Supreme Court of Illinois.

The Illinois Supreme Court concluded—and we are inclined to agree—that, standing alone, the anonymous letter sent to the Bloomingdale Police Department would not provide the basis for a magistrate's determination that there was probable cause to believe contraband would be found in the Gates' car and home. The letter provides virtually nothing from which one might conclude that its author is either honest or his information reliable; likewise, the letter gives absolutely no indication of the basis for the writer's predictions regarding the Gates' criminal activities. Something more was required, then, before a magistrate could conclude that there was probable cause to believe that contraband would be found in the Gates' home and car.

The Illinois Supreme Court also properly recognized that Detective Mader's affidavit might be capable of supplementing the anonymous letter with information sufficient to permit a determination of probable cause. In holding that the affidavit in fact did not contain sufficient additional information to sustain a determination of probable cause, the Illinois court applied a "two-pronged test," derived from our decision in *Spinelli*.[3] The Illinois Supreme Court, like some others, apparently understood *Spi-*

[3] In *Spinelli*, police officers observed Mr. Spinelli going to and from a particular apartment, which the telephone company said contained two telephones with stated numbers. The officers also were "informed by a confidential reliable informant that William Spinelli [was engaging in illegal gambling activities]" at the apartment, and that he used two phones, with numbers corresponding to those possessed by the police. The officers submitted an affidavit with this information to a magistrate and obtained a warrant to search Spinelli's apartment. We held that the magistrate could have made his determination of probable cause only by "abdicating his constitutional function." The Government's affidavit contained absolutely no information regarding the informant's reliability. Thus, it did not satisfy *Aguilar*'s requirement that such affidavits contain "some of the underlying circumstances" indicating that "the informant . . . was 'credible' " or that "his information [was] 'reliable.'" In addition, the tip failed to satisfy *Aguilar*'s requirement that it detail "some of the underlying circumstances from which the informant concluded that . . . narcotics were where he claimed they were. We also held that if the tip concerning Spinelli had contained "sufficient detail" to permit the magistrate to conclude "that he [was] relying on something more substantial than a casual rumor circulating in the underworld or an accusation based merely on an individual's general reputation," 393 U.S. at 416, then he properly could have relied on it; we thought, however, that the tip lacked the requisite detail to permit this "self-verifying detail" analysis.

nelli as requiring that the anonymous letter satisfy each of two independent requirements before it could be relied on. According to this view, the letter, as supplemented by Mader's affidavit, first had to adequately reveal the "basis of knowledge" of the letter writer—the particular means by which he came by the information given in his report. Second, it had to provide facts sufficiently establishing either the "veracity" of the affiant's informant, or, alternatively, the "reliability" of the informant's report in this particular case.

The Illinois court, alluding to an elaborate set of legal rules that have developed among various lower courts to enforce the "two-pronged test,"[4] found that the test had not been satisfied. First, the "veracity" prong was not satisfied because, "there was simply no basis [for] . . . conclud[ing] that the anonymous person [who wrote the letter to the Bloomingdale Police Department] was credible." The court indicated that corroboration by police of details contained in the letter might never satisfy the "veracity" prong, and in any event, could not do so if, as in the present case, only "innocent" details are corroborated. In addition, the letter gave no indication of the basis of its writer's knowledge of the Gates' activities. The Illinois court understood *Spinelli* as permitting the detail contained in a tip to be used to infer that the informant had a reliable basis for his statements, but it thought that the anonymous letter failed to provide sufficient detail to permit such an inference. Thus, it concluded that no showing of probable cause had been made.

We agree with the Illinois Supreme Court that an informant's "veracity," "reliability," and "basis of knowledge" are all highly relevant in determining the value of his report. We do not agree, however, that these elements should be understood as entirely separate and independent requirements to be rigidly exacted in every case,[5] which the opinion of the Supreme Court of Illinois would imply. Rather, as detailed below, they should be understood simply as closely intertwined issues that may usefully illuminate the commonsense, practical question whether there is "probable cause" to believe that contraband or evidence is located in a particular place.

---

[4] In summary, these rules posit that the "veracity" prong of the *Spinelli* test has two "spurs"—the informant's "credibility" and the "reliability" of his information. Various interpretations are advanced for the meaning of the "reliability" spur of the "veracity" prong. Both the "basis of knowledge" prong and the "veracity" prong are treated as entirely separate requirements, which must be independently satisfied in every case in order to sustain a determination of probable cause. Some ancillary doctrines are relied on to satisfy certain of the foregoing requirements. For example, the "self-verifying detail" of a tip may satisfy the "basis of knowledge" requirement, although not the "credibility" spur of the "veracity" prong. Conversely, corroboration would seem not capable of supporting the "basis of knowledge" prong, but only the "veracity" prong . . . .

[5] The entirely independent character that the *Spinelli* prongs have assumed is indicated both by the opinion of the Illinois Supreme Court in this case, and by decisions of other courts. One frequently cited decision, *Stanley v. State*, 19 Md.App. 507 (Md.App.1974), remarks that "the dual requirements represented by the 'two-pronged test' are 'analytically severable' and an 'overkill' on one prong will not carry over to make up for a deficit on the other prong."

III

This totality-of-the-circumstances approach is far more consistent with our prior treatment of probable cause[6] than is any rigid demand that specific "tests" be satisfied by every informant's tip. Perhaps the central teaching of our decisions bearing on the probable cause standard is that it is a "practical, nontechnical conception." "In dealing with probable cause, . . . as the very name implies, we deal with probabilities. These are not technical; they are the factual and practical considerations of everyday life on which reasonable and prudent men, not legal technicians, act." Our observation in *United States v. Cortez*, 449 U.S. 411, 418 (1981), regarding "particularized suspicion," is also applicable to the probable cause standard:

> The process does not deal with hard certainties, but with probabilities. Long before the law of probabilities was articulated as such, practical people formulated certain common-sense conclusions about human behavior; jurors as factfinders are permitted to do the same-and so are law enforcement officers. Finally, the evidence thus collected must be seen and weighed not in terms of library analysis by scholars, but as understood by those versed in the field of law enforcement.

As these comments illustrate, probable cause is a fluid concept—turning on the assessment of probabilities in particular factual contexts-not readily, or even usefully, reduced to a neat set of legal rules. Informants' tips doubtless come in many shapes and sizes from many different types of persons. As we said in *Adams v. Williams*, 407 U.S. 143 (1972), "[i]nformants' tips, like all other clues and evidence coming to a policeman on the scene may vary greatly in their value and reliability." Rigid legal

---

6 Our original phrasing of the so-called "two-pronged test" in *Aguilar* suggests that the two prongs were intended simply as guides to a magistrate's determination of probable cause, not as inflexible, independent requirements applicable in every case. In *Aguilar*, we required only that:

> the magistrate must be informed of *some of the underlying circumstances* from which the informant concluded that . . . narcotics were where he claimed they were, and *some of the underlying circumstances* from which the officer concluded that the informant . . . was 'credible' or his information 'reliable.'" (emphasis added).

As our language indicates, we intended neither a rigid compartmentalization of the inquiries into an informant's "veracity," "reliability" and "basis of knowledge," nor that these inquiries be elaborate exegeses of an informant's tip. Rather, we required only that *some* facts bearing on two particular issues be provided to the magistrate. Our decision in *Jaben v. United States,* 381 U.S. 214 (1965), demonstrated this latter point. We held there that a criminal complaint showed probable cause to believe the defendant had attempted to evade the payment of income taxes. We commented that:

> Obviously any reliance upon factual allegations necessarily entails some degree of reliability upon the credibility of the source. . . . Nor does it indicate that each factual allegation which the affiant puts forth must be independently documented, or that each and every fact which contributed to his conclusions be spelled out in the complaint. . . . *It simply requires that enough information be presented to the Commissioner to enable him to make the judgment that the charges are not capricious and are sufficiently supported to justify bringing into play the further steps of the criminal process.*" *Id.*, at 224–225 (emphasis added).

rules are ill-suited to an area of such diversity. "One simple rule will not cover every situation."[7]

Moreover, the "two-pronged test" directs analysis into two largely independent channels—the informant's "veracity" or "reliability" and his "basis of knowledge." There are persuasive arguments against according these two elements such independent status. Instead, they are better understood as relevant considerations in the totality-of-the-circumstances analysis that traditionally has guided probable cause determinations: a deficiency in one may be compensated for, in determining the overall reliability of a tip, by a strong showing as to the other, or by some other indicia of reliability.

If, for example, a particular informant is known for the unusual reliability of his predictions of certain types of criminal activities in a locality, his failure, in a particular case, to thoroughly set forth the basis of his knowledge surely should not serve as an absolute bar to a finding of probable cause based on his tip. Likewise, if an unquestionably honest citizen comes forward with a report of criminal activity—which if fabricated would subject him to criminal liability—we have found rigorous scrutiny of the basis of his knowledge unnecessary. Conversely, even if we entertain some doubt as to an informant's motives, his explicit and detailed description of alleged wrongdoing, along with a statement that the event was observed first-hand, entitles his tip to greater weight than might otherwise be the case. Unlike a totality-of-the-

[7] The diversity of informants' tips, as well as the usefulness of the totality-of-the-circumstances approach to probable cause, is reflected in our prior decisions on the subject. In *Jones v. United States*, 362 U.S. 257, 271 (1960), we held that probable cause to search petitioners' apartment was established by an affidavit based principally on an informant's tip. The unnamed informant claimed to have purchased narcotics from petitioners at their apartment; the affiant stated that he had been given correct information from the informant on a prior occasion. This, and the fact that petitioners had admitted to police officers on another occasion that they were narcotics users, sufficed to support the magistrate's determination of probable cause.

Likewise, in *Rugendorf v. United States*, 376 U.S. 528 (1964), the Court upheld a magistrate's determination that there was probable cause to believe that certain stolen property would be found in petitioner's apartment. The affidavit submitted to the magistrate stated that certain furs had been stolen, and that a confidential informant, who previously had furnished confidential information, said that he saw the furs in petitioner's home. Moreover, another confidential informant, also claimed to be reliable, stated that one Schweihs had stolen the furs. Police reports indicated that petitioner had been seen in Schweihs' company, and a third informant stated that petitioner was a fence for Schweihs.

Finally, in *Ker v. California*, 374 U.S. 23 (1963), we held that information within the knowledge of officers who searched the Ker's apartment provided them with probable cause to believe drugs would be found there. The officers were aware that one Murphy had previously sold marijuana to a police officer; the transaction had occurred in an isolated area, to which Murphy had led the police. The night after this transaction, police observed Ker and Murphy meet in the same location. Murphy approached Ker's car, and, although police could see nothing change hands, Murphy's *modus operandi* was identical to what it had been the night before. Moreover, when police followed Ker from the scene of the meeting with Murphy he managed to lose them after performing an abrupt U-turn. Finally, the police had a statement from an informant who had provided reliable information previously, that Ker was engaged in selling marijuana, and that his source was Murphy. We concluded that "[t]o say that this coincidence of information was sufficient to support a reasonable belief of the officers that Ker was illegally in possession of marijuana is to indulge in understatement." *Id.* at 36.

circumstances analysis, which permits a balanced assessment of the relative weights of all the various indicia of reliability (and unreliability) attending an informant's tip, the "two-pronged test" has encouraged an excessively technical dissection of informants' tips,[9] with undue attention being focused on isolated issues that cannot sensibly be divorced from the other facts presented to the magistrate.

As early as *Locke v. United States*, 7 Cranch. 339, (1813), Chief Justice Marshall observed, in a closely related context, that "the term 'probable cause,' according to its usual acceptation, means less than evidence which would justify condemnation. . . . It imports a seizure made under circumstances which warrant suspicion." More recently, we said that "the *quanta* . . . of proof" appropriate in ordinary judicial proceedings are inapplicable to the decision to issue a warrant. Finely-tuned standards such as proof beyond a reasonable doubt or by a preponderance of the evidence, useful in formal trials, have no place in the magistrate's decision. While an effort to fix some general, numerically precise degree of certainty corresponding to "probable cause" may not be helpful, it is clear that "only the probability, and not a prima facie showing, of criminal activity is the standard of probable cause."

We also have recognized that affidavits "are normally drafted by nonlawyers in the midst and haste of a criminal investigation. Technical requirements of elaborate specificity once exacted under common law pleading have no proper place in this area." Likewise, search and arrest warrants long have been issued by persons who are neither lawyers nor judges, and who certainly do not remain abreast of each judicial refinement of the nature of "probable cause." The rigorous inquiry into the *Spinelli* prongs and the complex superstructure of evidentiary and analytical rules that some have seen implicit in our *Spinelli* decision, cannot be reconciled with the fact that many warrants are quite properly, issued on the basis of nontechnical, common-sense

---

[9] Some lower court decisions, brought to our attention by the State, reflect a rigid application of such rules. In *Bridger v. State*, 503 S.W.2d 801 (Tex. Ct. App. 1974), the affiant had received a confession of armed robbery from one of two suspects in the robbery; in addition, the suspect had given the officer $800 in cash stolen during the robbery. The suspect also told the officer that the gun used in the robbery was hidden in the other suspect's apartment. A warrant issued on the basis of this was invalidated on the ground that the affidavit did not satisfactorily describe how the accomplice had obtained his information regarding the gun.

Likewise, in *People v. Palanza*, 55 Ill.App.3d 1028 (Ill. App. 1978), the affidavit submitted in support of an application for a search warrant stated that an informant of proven and uncontested reliability had seen, in specifically described premises, "a quantity of a white crystalline substance which was represented to the informant by a white male occupant of the premises to be cocaine. Informant has observed cocaine on numerous occasions in the past and is thoroughly familiar with its appearance. The informant states that the white crystalline powder he observed in the above described premises appeared to him to be cocaine." The warrant issued on the basis of the affidavit was invalidated because "There is no indication as to how the informant or for that matter any other person could tell whether a white substance was cocaine and not some other substance such as sugar or salt."

Finally, in *People v. Brethauer*, 174 Colo. 29 (Colo. 1971), an informant, stated to have supplied reliable information in the past, claimed that L.S.D. and marijuana were located on certain premises. The affiant supplied police with drugs, which were tested by police and confirmed to be illegal substances. The affidavit setting forth these, and other, facts was found defective under both prongs of *Spinelli*.

judgments of laymen applying a standard less demanding than those used in more formal legal proceedings. Likewise, given the informal, often hurried context in which it must be applied, the "built-in subtleties," of the "two-pronged test" are particularly unlikely to assist magistrates in determining probable cause.

Similarly, we have repeatedly said that after-the-fact scrutiny by courts of the sufficiency of an affidavit should not take the form of *de novo* review. A magistrate's "determination of probable cause should be paid great deference by reviewing courts." "A grudging or negative attitude by reviewing courts toward warrants" is inconsistent with the Fourth Amendment's strong preference for searches conducted pursuant to a warrant "courts should not invalidate . . . warrant[s] by interpreting affidavit[s] in a hypertechnical, rather than a commonsense, manner."

If the affidavits submitted by police officers are subjected to the type of scrutiny some courts have deemed appropriate, police might well resort to warrantless searches, with the hope of relying on consent or some other exception to the warrant clause that might develop at the time of the search. In addition, the possession of a warrant by officers conducting an arrest or search greatly reduces the perception of unlawful or intrusive police conduct, by assuring "the individual whose property is searched or seized of the lawful authority of the executing officer, his need to search, and the limits of his power to search." Reflecting this preference for the warrant process, the traditional standard for review of an issuing magistrate's probable cause determination has been that so long as the magistrate had a "substantial basis for . . . conclud[ing]" that a search would uncover evidence of wrongdoing, the Fourth Amendment requires no more.[10] We think reaffirmation of this standard better serves the purpose of encouraging recourse to the warrant procedure and is more consistent with our traditional deference to the probable cause determinations of magistrates than is the "two-pronged test."

Finally, the direction taken by decisions following *Spinelli* poorly serves "the most basic function of any government": "to provide for the security of the individual and of his property." The strictures that inevitably accompany the "two-pronged test" cannot avoid seriously impeding the task of law enforcement. If, as the Illinois Supreme Court apparently thought, that test must be rigorously applied in every case, anonymous tips seldom would be of greatly diminished value in police work. Ordinary citizens, like ordinary witnesses . . . generally do not provide extensive recitations of the basis of their everyday observations. Likewise, as the Illinois Supreme Court observed in this case,

[10] We also have said that "Although in a particular case it may not be easy to determine when an affidavit demonstrates the existence of probable cause, the resolution of doubtful or marginal cases in this area should be largely determined by the preference to be accorded to warrants." This reflects both a desire to encourage use of the warrant process by police officers and a recognition that once a warrant has been obtained, intrusion upon interests protected by the Fourth Amendment is less severe than otherwise may be the case. Even if we were to accept the premise that the accurate assessment of probable cause would be furthered by the "two-pronged test," which we do not, these Fourth Amendment policies would require a less rigorous standard than that which appears to have been read into *Aguilar* and *Spinelli.*

the veracity of persons supplying anonymous tips is by hypothesis largely unknown and unknowable. As a result, anonymous tips seldom could survive a rigorous application of either of the *Spinelli* prongs. Yet, such tips, particularly when supplemented by independent police investigation, frequently contribute to the solution of otherwise "perfect crimes." While a conscientious assessment of the basis for crediting such tips is required by the Fourth Amendment, a standard that leaves virtually no place for anonymous citizen informants is not.

For all these reasons, we conclude that it is wiser to abandon the "two-pronged test" established by our decisions in *Aguilar* and *Spinelli.* In its place we reaffirm the totality-of-the-circumstances analysis that traditionally has informed probable cause determinations. The task of the issuing magistrate is simply to make a practical, common-sense decision whether, given all the circumstances set forth in the affidavit before him, including the "veracity" and "basis of knowledge" of persons supplying hearsay information, there is a fair probability that contraband or evidence of a crime will be found in a particular place. And the duty of a reviewing court is simply to ensure that the magistrate had a "substantial basis for . . . conclud[ing]" that probable cause existed. We are convinced that this flexible, easily applied standard will better achieve the accommodation of public and private interests that the Fourth Amendment requires than does the approach that has developed from *Aguilar* and *Spinelli.*

Our earlier cases illustrate the limits beyond which a magistrate may not venture in issuing a warrant. A sworn statement of an affiant that "he has cause to suspect and does believe that" liquor illegally brought into the United States is located on certain premises will not do. *Nathanson v. United States*, 290 U.S. 41 (1933). An affidavit must provide the magistrate with a substantial basis for determining the existence of probable cause, and the wholly conclusory statement at issue in *Nathanson* failed to meet this requirement. An officer's statement that "affiants have received reliable information from a credible person and believe" that heroin is stored in a home, is likewise inadequate. As in *Nathanson*, this is a mere conclusory statement that gives the magistrate virtually no basis at all for making a judgment regarding probable cause. Sufficient information must be presented to the magistrate to allow that official to determine probable cause; his action cannot be a mere ratification of the bare conclusions of others. In order to ensure that such an abdication of the magistrate's duty does not occur, courts must continue to conscientiously review the sufficiency of affidavits on which warrants are issued. But when we move beyond the "bare bones" affidavits present in cases such as *Nathanson* and *Aguilar*, this area simply does not lend itself to a prescribed set of rules, like that which had developed from *Spinelli.* Instead, the flexible, common-sense standard articulated in *Jones*, *Ventresca*, and *Brinegar* better serves the purposes of the Fourth Amendment's probable cause requirement.

Justice BRENNAN's dissent suggests in several places that the approach we take today somehow downgrades the role of the neutral magistrate, because *Aguilar* and *Spinelli* "preserve the role of magistrates as independent arbiters of probable cause. . . ." Quite the contrary, we believe, is the case. The essential protection of the warrant requirement of the Fourth Amendment, as stated in *Johnson v. United States*, 333 U.S. 10 (1948), is in "requiring that [the usual inferences which reasonable men draw from evidence] be drawn by a neutral and detached magistrate instead of being judged by the officer engaged in the often competitive enterprise of ferreting out crime." Nothing in our opinion in any way lessens the authority of the magistrate to draw such reasonable inferences as he will from the material supplied to him by applicants for a warrant; indeed, he is freer than under the regime of *Aguilar* and *Spinelli* to draw such inferences, or to refuse to draw them if he is so minded.

The real gist of Justice BRENNAN's criticism seems to be a second argument, somewhat at odds with the first, that magistrates should be restricted in their authority to make probable cause determinations by the standards laid down in *Aguilar* and *Spinelli*, and that such findings "should not be authorized unless there is some assurance that the information on which they are based has been obtained in a reliable way by an honest or credible person." However, under our opinion magistrates remain perfectly free to exact such assurances as they deem necessary, as well as those required by this opinion, in making probable cause determinations. Justice BRENNAN would apparently prefer that magistrates be restricted in their findings of probable cause by the development of an elaborate body of case law dealing with the "veracity" prong of the *Spinelli* test, which in turn is broken down into two "spurs"—the informant's "credibility" and the "reliability" of his information, together with the "basis of knowledge" prong of the *Spinelli* test. That such a labyrinthine body of judicial refinement bears any relationship to familiar definitions of probable cause is hard to imagine. Probable cause deals "with probabilities. These are not technical; they are the factual and practical considerations of everyday life on which reasonable and prudent men, not legal technicians, act."

Justice BRENNAN's dissent also suggests that "words such as 'practical,' 'nontechnical,' and 'common sense,' as used in the Court's opinion, are but code words for an overly-permissive attitude towards police practices in derogation of the rights secured by the Fourth Amendment." An easy, but not a complete, answer to this rather florid statement would be that nothing we know about Justice Rutledge suggests that he would have used the words he chose in *Brinegar* in such a manner. More fundamentally, no one doubts that "under our Constitution only measures consistent with the Fourth Amendment may be employed by government to cure [the horrors of drug trafficking]," but this agreement does not advance the inquiry as to which measures are, and which measures are not, consistent with the Fourth Amendment. "Fidelity" to the commands of the Constitution suggests balanced judgment rather than exhortation. The highest "fidelity" is achieved neither by the judge who instinctively goes furthest in upholding even the most bizarre claim of individual constitutional rights, any more than it is achieved by a judge who instinctively goes furthest in accepting the most restrictive claims of governmental authorities. The task of this Court, as of other courts, is to "hold the balance true," and we think we have done that in this case.

IV

Our decisions applying the totality-of-the-circumstances analysis outlined above have consistently recognized the value of corroboration of details of an informant's tip by independent police work. In *Jones v. United States*, we held that an affidavit relying on hearsay "is not to be deemed insufficient on that score, so long as a substantial basis for crediting the hearsay is presented." We went on to say that even in making a warrantless arrest an officer "may rely upon information received through an informant, rather than upon his direct observations, so long as the informant's statement is reasonably corroborated by other matters within the officer's knowledge." Likewise, we recognized the probative value of corroborative efforts of police officials in *Aguilar*—the source of the "two-pronged test"—by observing that if the police had made some effort to corroborate the informant's report at issue, "an entirely different case" would have been presented.

Our decision in *Draper v. United States*, 358 U.S. 307 (1959), however, is the classic case on the value of corroborative efforts of police officials. There, an informant named Hereford reported that Draper would arrive in Denver on a train from Chicago on one of two days, and that he would be carrying a quantity of heroin. The informant also supplied a fairly detailed physical description of Draper, and predicted that he would be wearing a light colored raincoat, brown slacks and black shoes, and would be walking "real fast." Hereford gave no indication of the basis for his information.[12]

On one of the stated dates police officers observed a man matching this description exit a train arriving from Chicago; his attire and luggage matched Hereford's report and he was walking rapidly. We explained in *Draper* that, by this point in his investigation, the arresting officer "had personally verified every facet of the information given him by Hereford except whether petitioner had accomplished his mission and had the three ounces of heroin on his person or in his bag. And surely, with every other bit of Hereford's information being thus personally verified, [the officer] had 'reasonable grounds' to believe that the remaining unverified bit of Hereford's information—that Draper would have the heroin with him—was likewise true."

The showing of probable cause in the present case was fully as compelling as that in *Draper*. Even standing alone, the facts obtained through the independent investigation of Mader and the DEA at least suggested that the Gates were involved in drug trafficking. In addition to being a popular vacation site, Florida is well-known as a source of narcotics and other illegal drugs. Lance Gates' flight to Palm Beach, his brief, overnight stay in a motel, and apparent immediate return north to Chicago in the family car,

---

[12] The tip in *Draper* might well not have survived the rigid application of the "two-pronged test" that developed following *Spinelli*. The only reference to Hereford's reliability was that he had "been engaged as a 'special employee' of the Bureau of Narcotics at Denver for about six months, and from time to time gave information to [the police] for small sums of money, and that [the officer] had always found the information given by Hereford to be accurate and reliable." Likewise, the tip gave no indication of how Hereford came by his information. At most, the detailed and accurate predictions in the tip indicated that, however Hereford obtained his information, it was reliable.

conveniently awaiting him in West Palm Beach, is as suggestive of a pre-arranged drug run as it is of an ordinary vacation trip.

In addition, the magistrate could rely on the anonymous letter, which had been corroborated in major part by Mader's efforts—just as had occurred in *Draper.*[13] The Supreme Court of Illinois reasoned that *Draper* involved an informant who had given reliable information on previous occasions, while the honesty and reliability of the anonymous informant in this case were unknown to the Bloomingdale police. While this distinction might be an apt one at the time the police department received the anonymous letter, it became far less significant after Mader's independent investigative work occurred. The corroboration of the letter's predictions that the Gates' car would be in Florida, that Lance Gates would fly to Florida in the next day or so, and that he would drive the car north toward Bloomingdale all indicated, albeit not with certainty, that the informant's other assertions also were true. "Because an informant is right about some things, he is more probably right about other facts,"—including the claim regarding the Gates' illegal activity. This may well not be the type of "reliability" or "veracity" necessary to satisfy some views of the "veracity prong" of *Spinelli,* but we think it suffices for the practical, common-sense judgment called for in making a probable cause determination. It is enough, for purposes of assessing probable cause, that "corroboration through other sources of information reduced the chances of a reckless or prevaricating tale," thus providing "a substantial basis for crediting the hearsay."

Finally, the anonymous letter contained a range of details relating not just to easily obtained facts and conditions existing at the time of the tip, but to future actions of third parties ordinarily not easily predicted. The letter writer's accurate information as to the travel plans of each of the Gates was of a character likely obtained only from the Gates themselves, or from someone familiar with their not entirely ordinary travel plans. If the informant had access to accurate information of this type a magistrate could properly conclude that it was not unlikely that he also had access to reliable information of the Gates' alleged illegal activities.[14] Of course, the Gates' travel plans

---

[13] The Illinois Supreme Court thought that the verification of details contained in the anonymous letter in this case amounted only to "the corroboration of innocent activity," and that this was insufficient to support a finding of probable cause. We are inclined to agree, however, with the observation of Justice Moran in his dissenting opinion that "[i]n this case, just as in *Draper*, seemingly innocent activity became suspicious in the light of the initial tip." And it bears noting that *all* of the corroborating detail established in *Draper*, was of entirely innocent activity. . . .

This is perfectly reasonable. As discussed previously, probable cause requires only a probability or substantial chance of criminal activity, not an actual showing of such activity. By hypothesis, therefore, innocent behavior frequently will provide the basis for a showing of probable cause; to require otherwise would be to *sub silentio* impose a drastically more rigorous definition of probable cause than the security of our citizens demands. We think the Illinois court attempted a too rigid classification of the types of conduct that may be relied upon in seeking to demonstrate probable cause. In making a determination of probable cause the relevant inquiry is not whether particular conduct is "innocent" or "guilty," but the degree of suspicion that attaches to particular types of non-criminal acts.

[14] The dissent seizes on one inaccuracy in the anonymous informant's letter-its statement that Sue Gates would fly from Florida to Illinois, when in fact she drove—and argues that the probative value of the entire tip was undermined by this allegedly "material mistake." We have never required that

might have been learned from a talkative neighbor or travel agent; under the "two-pronged test" developed from *Spinelli*, the character of the details in the anonymous letter might well not permit a sufficiently clear inference regarding the letter writer's "basis of knowledge." But, as discussed previously, probable cause does not demand the certainty we associate with formal trials. It is enough that there was a fair probability that the writer of the anonymous letter had obtained his entire story either from the Gates or someone they trusted. And corroboration of major portions of the letter's predictions provides just this probability. It is apparent, therefore, that the judge issuing the warrant had a "substantial basis for . . . conclud[ing]" that probable cause to search the Gates' home and car existed. The judgment of the Supreme Court of Illinois therefore must be

Reversed.

[Justice WHITE'S concurrence is omitted]

Justice BRENNAN, with whom Justice MARSHALL joins, dissenting.

. . .

III

The Court's complete failure to provide any persuasive reason for rejecting *Aguilar* and *Spinelli* doubtlessly reflects impatience with what it perceives to be "overly technical" rules governing searches and seizures under the Fourth Amendment. Words such as "practical," "nontechnical," and "commonsense," as used in the Court's opinion, are but code words for an overly permissive attitude towards police practices in derogation of the rights secured by the Fourth Amendment. Everyone shares the Court's concern over the horrors of drug trafficking, but under our Constitution only measures consistent with the Fourth Amendment may be employed by government to cure this

---

informants used by the police be infallible, and can see no reason to impose such a requirement in this case. Probable cause, particularly when police have obtained a warrant, simply does not require the perfection the dissent finds necessary.

Likewise, there is no force to the dissent's argument that the Gates' action in leaving their home unguarded undercut the informant's claim that drugs were hidden there. Indeed, the line-by-line scrutiny that the dissent applies to the anonymous letter is akin to that we find inappropriate in reviewing magistrate's decisions. The dissent apparently attributes to the magistrate who issued the warrant in this case the rather implausible notion that persons dealing in drugs always stay at home, apparently out of fear that to leave might risk intrusion by criminals. If accurate, one could not help sympathizing with the self-imposed isolation of people so situated. In reality, however, it is scarcely likely that the magistrate ever thought that the anonymous tip "kept one spouse" at home, much less that he relied on the theory advanced by the dissent. The letter simply says that Sue would fly from Florida to Illinois, without indicating whether the Gates' made the bitter choice of leaving the drugs in their house, or those in their car, unguarded. The magistrate's determination that there might be drugs or evidence of criminal activity in the Gates' home was well-supported by the less speculative theory, noted in text, that if the informant could predict with considerable accuracy the somewhat unusual travel plans of the Gates, he probably also had a reliable basis for his statements that the Gates' kept a large quantity of drugs in their home and frequently were visited by other drug traffickers there.

evil. We must be ever mindful of Justice Stewart's admonition in *Coolidge v. New Hampshire*, 403 U.S. 443 (1971), that "[i]n times of unrest, whether caused by crime or racial conflict or fear of internal subversion, this basic law and the values that it represents may appear unrealistic or 'extravagant' to some. But the values were those of the authors of our fundamental constitutional concepts." In the same vein, *Glasser v. United States*, 315 U.S. 60 (1942), warned that "[s]teps innocently taken may, one by one, lead to the irretrievable impairment of substantial liberties."

Rights secured by the Fourth Amendment are particularly difficult to protect because their "advocates are usually criminals." But the rules "we fashion [are] for the innocent and guilty alike." By replacing *Aguilar* and *Spinelli* with a test that provides no assurance that magistrates, rather than the police, or informants, will make determinations of probable cause; imposes no structure on magistrates' probable cause inquiries; and invites the possibility that intrusions may be justified on less than reliable information from an honest or credible person, today's decision threatens to "obliterate one of the most fundamental distinctions between our form of government, where officers are under the law, and the police-state where they are the law."

Justice STEVENS, with whom Justice BRENNAN joins, dissenting.

The fact that Lance and Sue Gates made a [twenty-two]-hour nonstop drive from West Palm Beach, Florida, to Bloomingdale, Illinois, only a few hours after Lance had flown to Florida provided persuasive evidence that they were engaged in illicit activity. That fact, however, was not known to the magistrate when he issued the warrant to search their home.

What the magistrate did know at that time was that the anonymous informant had not been completely accurate in his or her predictions. The informant had indicated that "Sue drives their car to Florida *where she leaves it to be loaded up with drugs. . . . Sue flies back after she drops the car off in Florida.*" Yet Detective Mader's affidavit reported that she "left the West Palm Beach area driving the Mercury northbound."

The discrepancy between the informant's predictions and the facts known to Detective Mader is significant for three reasons. First, it cast doubt on the informant's hypothesis that the Gates already had "over $100,000 worth of drugs in their basement." The informant had predicted an itinerary that always kept one spouse in Bloomingdale, suggesting that the Gates did not want to leave their home unguarded because something valuable was hidden within. That inference obviously could not be drawn when it was known that the pair was actually together over a thousand miles from home.

Second, the discrepancy made the Gates' conduct seem substantially less unusual than the informant had predicted it would be. It would have been odd if, as predicted, Sue had driven down to Florida on Wednesday, left the car, and flown right back to Illinois. But the mere facts that Sue was in West Palm Beach with the car,[1] that she was

---

[1] The anonymous note suggested that she was going down on Wednesday, but for all the officers knew she had been in Florida for a month.

joined by her husband at the Holiday Inn on Friday,[2] and that the couple drove north together the next morning[3] are neither unusual nor probative of criminal activity.

Third, the fact that the anonymous letter contained a material mistake undermines the reasonableness of relying on it as a basis for making a forcible entry into a private home.[4]

Of course, the activities in this case did not stop when the magistrate issued the warrant. The Gates drove all night to Bloomingdale, the officers searched the car and found 400 pounds of marijuana, and then they searched the house. However, none of these subsequent events may be considered in evaluating the warrant, and the search of the house was legal only if the warrant was valid. I cannot accept the Court's casual conclusion that, *before the Gates arrived in Bloomingdale*, there was probable cause to justify a valid entry and search of a private home. No one knows who the informant in this case was, or what motivated him or her to write the note. Given that the note's predictions were faulty in one significant respect, and were corroborated by nothing except ordinary innocent activity, I must surmise that the Court's evaluation of the warrant's validity has been colored by subsequent events.[7]

. . .

When the Court discusses the merits [of this case] it attaches no weight to the conclusions of the Circuit Judge of DuPage County, Illinois, of the three judges of the Second District of the Illinois Appellate Court, or of the five justices of the Illinois Supreme Court, all of whom concluded that the warrant was not based on probable cause. In

---

[2] Lance does not appear to have behaved suspiciously in flying down to Florida. He made a reservation in his own name and gave an accurate home phone number to the airlines. And Detective Mader's affidavit does not report that he did any of the other things drug couriers are notorious for doing, such as paying for the ticket in cash, dressing casually, looking pale and nervous, improperly filling out baggage tags, carrying American Tourister luggage, not carrying any luggage, or changing airlines en route.

[3] Detective Mader's affidavit hinted darkly that the couple had set out upon "that interstate highway commonly used by travelers to the Chicago area." But the same highway is also commonly used by travelers to Disney World, Sea World, and Ringling Brothers and Barnum and Bailey Circus World. It is also the road to Cocoa Beach, Cape Canaveral, and Washington, D.C. I would venture that each year dozens of perfectly innocent people fly to Florida, meet a waiting spouse, and drive off together in the family car.

[4] The Court purports to rely on the proposition that "if the [anonymous] informant could predict with *considerable accuracy* the *somewhat unusual travel plans* of the Gates, he probably also had a reliable basis for his statements that the Gates kept a large quantity of drugs in their home." (emphasis added). Even if this syllogism were sound, its premises are not met in this case.

[7] *Draper v. United States,* 358 U.S. 307 (1959), affords no support for today's holding. That case did not involve an anonymous informant. On the contrary, as the Court twice noted, Mr. Hereford was "employed for that purpose and [his] information had always been found accurate and reliable." In this case, the police had no prior experience with the informant, and some of his or her information in this case was unreliable and inaccurate.

a fact-bound inquiry of this sort, the judgment of three levels of state courts, all of whom are better able to evaluate the probable reliability of anonymous informants in Bloomingdale, Illinois, than we are, should be entitled to at least a presumption of accuracy. . . .[8]

[8] The Court holds that what were heretofore considered two independent "prongs"—"veracity" and "basis of knowledge"—are now to be considered together as circumstances whose totality must be appraised. "A deficiency in one may be compensated for, in determining the overall reliability of a tip, by a strong showing as to the other, or by some other indicia of reliability." Yet in this case, the lower courts found *neither* factor present. And the supposed "other indicia" in the affidavit take the form of activity that is not particularly remarkable. I do not understand how the Court can find that the "totality" so far exceeds the sum of its "circumstances."

11

Issuing and Executing a Warrant

Key Concepts

- Warrant "Preference"
- Oath or Affirmation
- Probable Cause
- Particularity
- Neutral and Detached Magistrate
- Arresting Inside the Home

A. Introduction and Policy. As we have already seen, police officers are given a large amount of discretion in their jobs. They have the ability to decide whether to make an arrest, whether to search an individual or a car that they have stopped, and whether to stop and frisk a suspect or engage him in a friendly conversation. In fact, it could be argued that the police exercise more discretion—in ways affecting more people—than any other actor in the criminal justice system.

But although the police are given a lot of discretion, many of their decisions are reviewed later by a magistrate or judge. If the reviewing court determines that the police officer did not have the proper justification for her actions, the fruits of the search will likely be inadmissible under the exclusionary rule. In other words, when the police officers act without prior judicial authority there is always a chance that their decisions will be second-guessed by a reviewing court and the evidence they recover will be thrown out.

Furthermore, there are certain things that a police officer is almost never allowed to do without prior judicial approval, such as searching or making an arrest inside of a home. In order to take these actions, a police officer, in most cases, must first obtain a warrant from the court.

A warrant is a legal document which gives the police officer judicial authority to undertake a search and/or make an arrest. If a police officer obtains a warrant before acting, she can be far more confident that her actions will withstand later challenge by the defendant. As we will see, defendants can challenge a warrant just as they can challenge an officer's warrantless action, but such challenges rarely succeed. In this chapter, we will examine how to get a warrant and how warrants are used. In the next chapter, we will begin to examine the many ways in which a police officer can conduct a search without a warrant.

B. The Law. Warrants are described in the second clause of the Fourth Amendment, the aptly named "warrant clause," which provides:

> . . . no Warrants shall issue, but upon probable cause, supported by Oath or affirmation, and particularly describing the place to be searched, and the persons or things to be seized.[1]

As we discussed in **Chapters 4 and 5,** the Fourth Amendment contains a fair amount of ambiguity. There are questions both about how the reasonableness clause should be interpreted and about the precise relationship between the reasonableness clause and the warrant clause. But the warrant clause itself is relatively straightforward. There are four requirements for obtaining a warrant, including one which is not specifically mentioned in the text but which is implied from the term "warrant" itself:

1. A warrant must be supported by an oath or affirmation.
2. A warrant must be supported by probable cause that a crime has occurred and (in the case of a search warrant) that fruits, instrumentalities, or evidence of that crime are located at the particular location described.
3. A warrant must describe the place to be searched and/or the person or things to be seized with particularity.
4. A warrant must be issued by a neutral and detached magistrate.

The first of these requirements is integral to the next two. In order to obtain a warrant, a law enforcement officer submits a sworn affidavit or gives sworn testimony (both of which contain an **oath or affirmation**, meaning that the statement is made under penalty of perjury). In this affidavit or testimony, the officer sets out the facts that demonstrate probable cause and describes in some detail the place to be searched and the items to be seized (or in the case of an arrest warrant, the person to be seized).

We have already discussed the second requirement in **Chapter 10**: the warrant must be supported by **probable cause**. To encourage the use of warrants, the Supreme Court has noted that probable cause is a slightly easier standard to meet in the context of a warrant application than it would be when a judge reviews a warrantless search or arrest after the fact. "In a doubtful or marginal case, a search under a warrant may be sustainable where without one it would fail."[2] Indeed, there are cases in which the Supreme Court has rejected a warrantless search be-

[1] U.S. Const. amend. IV.

[2] United States v. Ventresca, 380 U.S. 102, 106 (1965).

cause of a lack of probable cause, but stated that it would have found probable cause if the officers had used the same information to obtain a search warrant.[3]

Also note that if the government is applying for a search warrant, it must submit evidence not only to establish probable cause to believe a crime occurred, but also must submit evidence from which a court might find probable cause to believe that evidence of that crime will be found at the location named in the warrant.

Third, the Fourth Amendment requires "**particularity**"—which means that the warrant must specify exactly what the officers are looking for and where they are allowed to look. This requirement was a reaction to the British practice of issuing "writs of assistance" during colonial times. These writs, which were issued by British courts to customs officials in an attempt to combat smuggling, permitted the officials to search anyone's property at any time without any need to show cause. The colonial resentment of these general warrants led the Founders to insert the particularity requirement into the Fourth Amendment in order to prevent such abuses in the future.

Finally, the warrant must be issued by a "**neutral and detached magistrate**." In a very real sense, this final requirement is the whole purpose of the warrant preference—to limit the discretion of police officers by having a judicial officer review the search or arrest before it occurs. As the Supreme Court noted:

> The point of the Fourth Amendment, which often is not grasped by zealous officers, is not that it denies law enforcement the support of the usual inferences which reasonable men draw from evidence. Its protection consists in requiring that those inferences be drawn by a neutral and detached magistrate instead of being judged by the officer engaged in the often competitive enterprise of ferreting out crime. Any assumption that evidence sufficient to support a magistrate's disinterested determination to issue a search warrant will justify the officers in making a search without a warrant would reduce the Amendment to a nullity and leave the people's homes secure only in the discretion of police officers.[4]

In other words, the warrant presumption—and specifically its neutral and detached magistrate requirement—ensures that the judiciary acts as a check on the executive power to conduct searches.

---

[3] See, e.g., Johnson v. United States, 333 U.S. 10 (1948); Chapman v. United States, 365 U.S. 610 (1961).

[4] Johnson, 333 U.S. at 13–14.

C. Applying the Law.

1. How to Obtain a Warrant: Statements Made Under "Oath or Affirmation." The warrant process is initiated by a law enforcement officer submitting an affidavit or sworn oral testimony to a magistrate or judge. If the warrant request is part of a complex or long-term investigation, the officer may be working with a prosecutor, but frequently he creates the affidavit on his own. The affidavit or testimony sets out the facts that are personally known to the officer (known as the "affiant"), or the facts that the officer has been told by others, which lead the officer to believe that probable cause exists. The affiant also describes with specificity the location to be searched and the items to be seized. Usually the affiant will also include a proposed search warrant, already written and ready for the judge's or magistrate's signature. The proposed warrant will borrow language heavily from the affidavit in describing the places to be searched and the things to be seized.

The affiant submits the application and proposed warrant to the magistrate or judge. Usually this is done in person, in the judge's chambers. However, many jurisdictions also permit warrant applications by phone or by e-mail so that the police officer need not travel to the courthouse. These remote methods for securing warrants mean that more and more frequently, police officers can apply for—and receive—warrants while they are waiting outside the scene of the crime.

After the application is submitted, the magistrate or judge reviews the application and makes her own determination as to (1) whether probable cause exists and (2) whether there is sufficient specificity in the request of what is to be searched and what can be seized. The review is done *ex parte*—the target of the warrant is not notified and there is no opposing counsel to cross-examine the affiant or to argue against the warrant being issued. In response to an application, the magistrate or judge can do one of three things:

1. If she believes that both of these requirements are met, she will sign the proposed warrant and give it back to the officer, who will proceed to execute the warrant.

2. If she believes that probable cause exists but that the proposed warrant lacks sufficient particularity, she can edit or re-write the proposed warrant with her own language with the proper degree of particularity.

3. If she believes that probable cause is not established, or she believes there is insufficient particularity, she can refuse to sign the warrant and instead return it to the officer. If the officer has further information which can save the warrant, some jurisdictions will allow an officer to supplement the warrant affidavit with oral testimony which will cure the problem.

Otherwise, the officer must conduct further investigation and return with more information.

In theory, the magistrate or judge conducts a careful, thorough review of the affidavit or testimony to ensure that probable cause exists. However, many critics complain that in practice the process is more perfunctory than precise. These critics observe that the majority of applications contain mostly boilerplate language, and many warrants are issued after less than five minutes of review.[5] Also, in larger jurisdictions, police officers will forum-shop. That is, they learn which judicial officers are most likely to issue a warrant and strategically submit their applications to those magistrates.[6]

If the magistrate or judge issues the warrant, the law enforcement officer executes the warrant. The warrant will be time-limited; that is, the officer must execute the warrant within a certain amount of time after it has been issued. A copy of the warrant (which includes the particularized list of places to be searched and items to be seized) is left at the premises being searched. Following execution, the officer then returns the warrant to the issuing magistrate or judge with an inventory describing what (if anything) was seized as a result of the search. Also known as a "warrant return," this step is intended to insure that judicial oversight was provided from the beginning to the end of the process.

Recently many jurisdictions have permitted the electronic submission of affidavits and issuance of warrants. This allows police officers to obtain a warrant far more quickly and efficiently—perhaps in a matter of only a few minutes, while waiting in a squad car outside the targeted premises. In this procedure, the police officer can type up the affidavit on a computer and then e-mail it to the magistrate with an electronic signature. The magistrate will usually orally administer the oath over the telephone, review the affidavit, and then e-mail the warrant back to the police officer waiting at the scene.[7]

2. The Subpoena Power. Search warrants are not the only way for the government to gather information from suspects. Prosecutors can also subpoena testimony, documents, and items from private citizens. In some jurisdictions, the prosecutor must use the authority of an investigative grand jury to issue a subpoena. (A grand jury is a body of lay people that is convened in many jurisdictions to investigate cases and formally charge defendants. As we will see in **Chapter 35**, most grand juries are under the *de facto* control of the prosecutor). In other jurisdictions, the prosecutor is given the subpoena power directly. This means they are allowed to issue subpoenas independently, without resorting to

[5] David E. Steinberg, Zealous Officers and Neutral Magistrates: The Rhetoric of the Fourth Amendment, 43 Creighton L. Rev. 1019, 1046 (2010).

[6] Id.

[7] See, e.g., Mich. Comp. Laws § 780.651 (1966).

any supervisory authority. Either way, subpoenas require the suspect to turn over incriminating information or items to the government.

From the government's point of view, a subpoena has a number of advantages over a search warrant. In most jurisdictions, the prosecutor need not show probable cause or even reasonable suspicion that the items or documents sought will reveal evidence of criminal activity. Instead, to obtain a subpoena, the prosecutor need only demonstrate a "reasonable possibility" that the material will "produce information relevant to the general subject of the . . . investigation."[8] Moreover, a search warrant forces the government to utilize more resources because police officers must go out and execute the warrant. In contrast, a subpoena requires the suspect to do all the work, for it is the suspect who must gather the documents and other items requested and deliver them to the prosecutor. Moreover, prosecutors can be fairly confident in the authenticity and completeness of the material produced because hiding or altering anything that is requested by a subpoena is considered a separate crime.

Although the subpoena method does present a number of advantages to the prosecutor, it does require some amount of cooperation from the suspect. Subpoenas may be effective in certain cases, such as white collar crime cases or long-term investigations in which the suspects tend to have retained counsel who are more likely to convince their clients to respond to the subpoena. However, subpoenas are not used as often in "street crime" cases. A murder suspect is unlikely to respond to a subpoena for the murder weapon, and a drug dealer is unlikely to turn in the narcotics he has been selling. Attempting to use a subpoena in these contexts would be counter-productive, since it would alert the suspect and allow him to hide or destroy the evidence. The search warrant is invaluable in situations where law enforcement does not want the suspect to have prior notice or otherwise cannot trust that the suspect will comply with a subpoena.

3. "Neutral and Detached Magistrate." The magistrate who issues the warrant need not actually be a judge or even an attorney. Different states authorize different types of people to issue search warrants, such as justices of the peace or even court clerks. The only competency requirement is that the person issuing the warrant must be "capable of determining whether probable cause exists for the requested arrest or search."[9]

In addition to this requirement, the magistrate must also be neutral and detached, which means (at a minimum) that she must be a member of the judicial branch of government:

---

8 United States v. R. Enters, Inc., 498 U.S. 292 (1991).

9 Shadwick v. City of Tampa, 407 U.S. 345 (1972).

Example—*Coolidge v. New Hampshire,* 403 U.S. 443 (1971): Police suspected Edward Coolidge of murdering a fourteen-year-old girl. After investigating Coolidge for over two weeks, the police presented the evidence to the state attorney general, who under New Hampshire law was also a justice of the peace and thereby authorized to issue search and arrest warrants. The attorney general had taken an active role in the investigation, and later he was to be the lead prosecutor in the case. After hearing the evidence put forward by the police, he issued an arrest warrant for Coolidge, and a search warrant for his two cars. The police then arrested Coolidge and impounded and searched his car. Coolidge later challenged the warrant on the grounds that the Attorney General was not a "neutral and detached magistrate."

Analysis: The Supreme Court agreed that the state attorney general could not be a neutral and detached magistrate. Thus, the warrant was invalid. Although state law permitted the attorney general to issue warrants, such a procedure was unconstitutional, because prosecutors and police officers cannot be considered neutral.[10]

The neutrality requirement also means that if the reviewing magistrate is given any financial incentive to favor law enforcement, she will not be considered "neutral and detached." For example, the Court struck down a "fee system," in which a volunteer justice of the peace was paid five dollars for every warrant she issued, but paid nothing for warrant applications that she denied.

Even members of the judiciary who receive no direct compensation can fail the neutrality requirement if they participate in the execution of the warrant:

Example—*Lo-Ji Sales v. New York,* 442 U.S. 319 (1979): A New York State police officer purchased a movie from an adult bookstore. He showed the movie to a Town Justice, who determined that the movie violated New York's obscenity laws. The officer then applied for a search warrant to search the adult bookstore and seize all other "obscene" material found there. The Town Justice approved the warrant which contained language authorizing the seizure of "[the] following items that the Court independently [on examination] has determined to be possessed in violation of [the obscenity law]." However, no items were listed after this sentence. Instead, the Town Justice agreed to accompany police officers during the search to examine items that were found and tell the officers which should be considered "obscene."

[10] Coolidge v. New Hampshire, 403 U.S. 443 (1971).

As planned, the Town Justice joined seven police officers and three prosecutors and raided the adult bookstore. The Town Justice viewed excerpts of over two dozen movies and hundreds of magazines, indicating to the law enforcement officials which ones they were permitted to seize. The entire search lasted nearly six hours. As the search progressed, the police officers filled in the warrant with the names and descriptions of the movies, magazines, and other items that the Town Justice told them to seize.

The owner of the bookstore challenged the search warrant in court, and the case was appealed to the Supreme Court.

Analysis: The Court held that the warrant lacked particularity. At the time the warrant was issued, it did not specify which items were to be seized, and the Constitution does not permit "open-ended" warrants, to be filled out after the search is completed.[11]

The Court also held that the Town Justice did not act as a neutral and detached magistrate. "He allowed himself to become a member, if not the leader, of the search party which was essentially a police operation. Once in the store, he conducted a generalized search under authority of an invalid warrant; he was not acting as a judicial officer but as an adjunct law enforcement officer."

The Supreme Court contrasted the *Lo-Ji* case with an earlier case, *Heller v. New York*,[12] in which police officers asked the judge to go to an adult movie theater as a regular paying patron. After viewing the movie and deciding that it was obscene, the judge signed a search warrant for the theater and arrest warrants for the theater manager, the projectionist, and the ticket taker. The Court found that in *Heller*, the judge's trip to the scene was merely a way for the police to present evidence establishing probable cause. In contrast, in *Lo-Ji*, the magistrate "undertook not merely to issue a warrant, but to participate with the police and prosecutors in its execution."[13]

4. Sufficient "Particularity." A search warrant must state with particularity the place to be searched and the items to be seized. This requirement exists not only to prevent the issuing of "general warrants," which could be abused by law enforcement, but also to ensure that the police officers do not make a mistake when they execute the warrant. Thus, particularity in describing a location is sufficient if it unambiguously describes one premises (such as a home or an office). Generally the street address is used, but a distinctive description of the location is also sufficient.

---

[11] Lo-Ji Sales v. New York, 442 U.S. 319 (1979).

[12] Heller v. New York, 413 U.S. 483 (1973).

[13] Lo-Ji Sales, 442 U.S. at 328 n.6.

One problem that arises because of the particularity requirement is that occasionally the warrant will appear to have sufficient particularity, but will in fact contain an ambiguity or an error which only comes to light during the execution of the warrant:

> **Example:** A police officer receives information from a confidential informant who claims that he has first-hand knowledge that heroin is being sold out of Apartment D in the downtown apartment complex located at 4250 Broad Street. The informant also tells the police officer that some of the drugs are stored in a car which is parked outside the apartment complex. The car is described as a blue Honda Accord with the license plate ERG-4521.
>
> The police officer writes all of this information in her warrant application, including the informant's past history of providing accurate information and the informant's basis of knowledge for knowing about these drugs. After reviewing the application, the magistrate issues a search warrant authorizing the search of "Apartment D at 4250 Broad Street" and "A blue Honda Accord automobile parked in the parking lot of 4250 Broad Street with the license plate ERG-4521."
>
> The affiant takes a team of police officers to the location to execute the warrant. But when the team enters the apartment complex, the affiant realizes that the building has five floors, and there is an apartment "D" on each floor. She also looks through the parking lot, and sees no car that exactly fits the description given in the warrant. However, she does see a blue Honda Accord with the license plate ERB-4521.
>
> The police raid all five Apartments "D" in the complex, and seize and search the Honda Accord. The police find thirty packets of heroin in apartment D on the fourth floor of the building, and another twenty ounces of heroin in the car. The other four apartment D's reveal no contraband or evidence of criminal activity. The two occupants of the apartment where the heroin was found are arrested. One of them is the owner of the car. They challenge the warrant in court.

Analysis: The warrant lacked particularity with regard to the apartment, but is probably valid with regard to the automobile.

The magistrate was correct to issue the warrant given the information available to him. The confidential informant's information would be sufficient to establish probable cause under the totality of the circumstances because the informant has demonstrated past reliability and has first-hand knowledge of the location of the heroin. Furthermore, the warrant as issued appeared to describe with sufficient the place being searched.

However, when the police went to execute the warrant, it became clear that the warrant's description of the apartment was not adequate. The search of all five apartments would therefore be unconstitutional. On the other hand, the search of the car would probably be upheld. Although the description of the automobile contained a minor error, the accurate information—the color and type of car, the location where it was parked, and five of the six digits of the license plate—were sufficient to meet the particularity requirement. If there were more errors, or more significant errors, a court would probably invalidate that part of the warrant as well.

In addition to requiring a specific description of the area to be searched, the particularity requirement also applies to the list of items to be seized. Sufficient particularity exists as long as enough information is given to preclude the possibility of the police seizing the wrong property. Frequently courts will approve relatively vague descriptions of items if there is no way for the police to know anything more. For example, if police officers are investigating a murder in which the victim was killed with a rifle, they may apply for a search warrant for the suspect's home that seeks to seize any rifle of the particular caliber involved in the crime. However, if the police are searching for a specific rifle that was stolen in a burglary, they would probably need to include the serial number of the rifle being sought, since that is information that is available to them at the time they applied for the warrant.

Finally, if the items in question are contraband, such as narcotics or illegal firearms, a general description of the type of contraband being sought will be deemed sufficient. For example, "all cocaine and marijuana" would be sufficient; there would be no need to describe how the cocaine is packaged or the particular type of marijuana that might be found.

5. Executing a Warrant. When police officers execute a warrant, the particularity requirement will also serve to limit the specific areas where they can search. This is because officers are only allowed to look inside containers that might conceivably contain the items listed in the warrant. For example, if they are investigating a shooting and looking for a gun, they cannot search through the defendant's computer files.

Savvy police officers may draft their affidavit in a way that maximizes the types of places that can be searched. For example, if they are investigating a location where narcotics are suspected to be sold, they will ask for permission to search not only for narcotics and for cash, but also for "any records of inventory, purchases, or sales of narcotics, whether in paper or digital form." If this language is approved, it will allow the officers to search not only rooms and closets and under beds, but also any computers that they may find in the home. Similarly, if the police officers are investigating a burglary of an appliance store, they will ask for permission to look not only for the appliances that were stolen, but also "cell phones which may have been used in the planning or execution of the crime." If this language is ultimately included in the warrant, it would allow police officers to search inside small containers, such as desk drawers and coat pockets, where they would otherwise not be allowed to search if they were only looking for appliances.

Of course, judges and magistrates need to ensure that there is a sufficient nexus between the items that are listed in the search warrant and the probable cause that has been demonstrated. Remember that "probable cause" in the context of a search warrant means that the government must present evidence sufficient to warrant a man of reasonable caution that relevant evidence of the crime exists at the particular locations named in the warrant. Thus, not every allegation of narcotics sales will support the government's contention that evidence of the criminal activity will be found on computers at the location. Similarly, not every allegation of burglary will support a government claim that cell phones were used to plan the crime. The magistrate will reject a bare assertion by the government that computer files, cell phones, or other items are relevant to the crime being investigated. There must be sufficient facts alleged to support any such link.

For the most part, the police may only seize items that are specifically listed in the warrant. However, as explained in **Chapter 9**, police officers may also seize any other item in plain view if it is "immediately apparent" to the officer that the item is contraband, fruits of a crime, instrumentalities of a crime, or evidence of a crime.

Although a search warrant is issued without notice to the target, police traditionally are required to "knock and announce" their presence before entering a home. As we will see in **Chapter 20**, police officers are exempted from the knock and announce rule if they can demonstrate in their application that there is reasonable suspicion that knocking and announcing would be dangerous, futile, or would allow for the destruction of evidence. In addition, even officers who were subject to the knock-and-announce rule at the time the warrant was issued might be exempted from the rule at the time of the execution if they can demonstrate that a new exigency arose during the warrant's execution.

Once the police are at the location exercising the search warrant, what can they do to the individuals who are present at the location? As we saw in the *Ybarra* case in **Chapter 10,** the police cannot automatically search every individual who happens to be present at the location during the search. Instead, the police may only search individuals if the police have probable cause to believe those individuals have evidence that is specified in the search warrant that might be concealed or destroyed. Thus, they cannot search any individuals who are merely present at the location with no apparent connection to the illegal activity or individuals who arrive at the scene during the execution of the warrant. Likewise, the police cannot search anyone present at the scene if the search warrant only specifies items which are too large to be hidden on someone's person.

However, the Supreme Court has given police much broader powers when it comes to **seizing** individuals who are present:

> **Example—*Michigan v. Summers*, 452 U.S. 692 (1981):** Detroit police officers were preparing to execute a search warrant on a house, when they encountered George Summers walking down the front steps of the house. They asked him to help them into the house, and afterwards they detained him while they searched the house. After finding narcotics in the basement of the house, the police arrested Summers, searched him incident to a lawful arrest, and found eight and a half grams of heroin. Summers was ultimately charged with possession of narcotics based on the heroin that was found on his person.
>
> Summers then challenged his arrest and subsequent search, arguing that the police had no right to detain him initially as he was leaving the house. At that point, Summers argued, there was no probable cause or even reasonable suspicion to justify the detention.

Analysis: The Court upheld the seizure of Summers, holding that the temporary seizure of an individual present at the location of the search warrant is permissible for three reasons:

First, the law enforcement officers have a strong interest in preventing the occupants from fleeing in the likely case that contraband is in fact found during the search.

Second, allowing occupants to move around freely during the search could pose a serious risk to the police officers, while allowing them to leave and perhaps alert others could also endanger the police. Thus, "[t]he risk of harm to both the police and the occupants is minimized if the officers routinely exercise unquestioned command of the situation."[14]

[14] Michigan v. Summers, 452 U.S. 692, 703 (1981).

Third, the occupants of the location are frequently able to assist the police officers in conducting the search. They may be able to open locked doors or locked containers, thereby preventing unnecessary damage to their property during the search.

The Court allowed the police to detain Summers even though he was in the process of leaving just as the police officers arrived on the scene to execute the warrant. In a later case, the Court clarified that the *Summers* rule does not apply to individuals who leave the location **just before** the warrant is executed. Police may not seize individuals who have already left, because those individuals pose no danger to the police, they are unlikely to be helpful in the search, and the possibility that they may flee after a successful search is too tenuous to support a violation of their liberty interests.[15]

6. Challenging a Warrant. When a magistrate or judge issues a search warrant, she has determined that the affiant has presented facts which establish probable cause. Nonetheless, even after a warrant has been executed, the defendant has the right to challenge the warrant in a suppression hearing. Essentially, the defendant can challenge the warrant in one of three ways: a facial challenge to the warrant's sufficiency; a claim that information establishing probable cause was illegally secured; or an assertion that the affiant provided false information.

1. A challenge to the facial sufficiency of the warrant. With such a challenge, the defendant would argue that the magistrate or judge who issued the warrant incorrectly determined that probable cause existed. As described in **Chapter 10**, this requires the reviewing judge to examine the statements made by the affiant and evaluate both (a) the reliability of the informant who provided the information to the affiant; and (b) whether that information establishes a true likelihood that a crime occurred and that evidence of that crime can be found at the target location.

   In order to encourage the police to obtain warrants, most jurisdictions shift the burden of proof onto the defendant when challenging the sufficiency of a warrant. In other words, if the defendant is seeking to preclude evidence that was found during a **warrantless** search, the prosecutor bears the burden at the suppression hearing of proving that probable cause existed. However, if the defendant is seeking to preclude evidence that was found during a search conducted pursuant to a warrant, the defendant bears the burden of proving that probable cause did not exist.

2. A claim that the information used to generate probable cause was illegally obtained. For example, the defendant could argue that the a police officer illegally entered his house, saw drugs and guns on the table, and then applied for a warrant based on the fact that she saw drugs and guns inside the house.

[15] Bailey v. United States, 133 S.Ct. 1031 (2013).

Such a challenge must be combined with the facial sufficiency challenge to be effective. In other words, the defendant must argue first that certain facts presented in the affidavit were illegally obtained, and should therefore be disregarded. Next the defendant must argue that without the illegally obtained facts the warrant is facially insufficient because it fails to establish probable cause.

3. A claim that the affiant gave false information to the magistrate. Unlike the facial challenge, this challenge does not claim that the affidavit fails to establish probable cause. Instead, the defendant would argue that the affiant either lied in the application or was reckless with regard to the truth of what he said.

   For many years, this type of challenge was not permitted by the courts. Courts held that there was no need to review the credibility of the affiant, because the magistrate who issued the warrant was in the best position to make that assessment. In *Franks v. Delaware*, the Supreme Court changed this rule and allowed this type of challenge. *Franks* was a case in which the defendant used all three types of challenges at the suppression hearing:

   Example—*Franks v. Delaware,* 438 U.S. 154 (1978): Police suspected Jerome Franks of raping Cynthia Bailey while threatening her with a knife, and they sought a search warrant for his apartment. In the application for the warrant, Detective Brooks included the following information in the "probable cause" section of the affidavit:

   1. After being arrested for an unrelated crime, the defendant asked if he was being arrested for raping Bailey.

   2. The victim gave a statement to the police in which she described the perpetrator's age, race, height, and build. The victim also stated that the perpetrator was wearing "a white thermal undershirt, black pants with a silver or gold buckle, a brown leather three-quarter-length coat, and a dark knit cap."

   3. Detective Brooks interviewed the defendant's employers, James Williams and Wesley Lucas. Williams "revealed to your affiant that the normal dress of Jerome Franks does consist of a white knit thermal undershirt and a brown leather jacket" while "Lucas revealed to your affiant that in addition to the thermal undershirt and jacket, Jerome Franks often wears a dark green knit hat."

The magistrate issued the search warrant, and the police searched Franks' apartment, where they recovered a thermal undershirt, a knit hat, dark pants, a leather jacket, and a single-blade knife.

The defendant challenged the warrant on three grounds.

First, he argued that the warrant was not facially sufficient because it did not establish probable cause that Franks was the perpetrator. That is, assuming that the affiant honestly reported everything that the defendant, victim, and defendant's employers said, those statements were not sufficient to establish probable cause.

Second, he argued that his statement (wherein he asked if he was being arrested for raping Bailey) was obtained in violation of his Miranda rights and, therefore, could not be used to help establish probable cause. Franks further maintained that once his statement was disregarded, the remainder of the affidavit was not sufficient to establish probable cause. Finally, he argued that Detective Brooks was dishonest when he reported the statements made by the defendant's employers. Franks claimed that Brooks did not in fact interview his employers—that in fact his employers spoke to other police officers and said things that were quite different from what Brooks reported.

The trial court ruled against the defendant with regard to the first two challenges. In addition, the court precluded the third challenge, holding that Franks was not allowed to challenge the veracity of the affiant when attacking the warrant. Franks appealed all the way to the Supreme Court.

Analysis: The Supreme Court held that Franks should have been allowed to challenge the affiant's credibility in the suppression hearing, holding that a "flat ban on impeachment of veracity [of the affiant] could denude the probable-cause requirement of all real meaning."

The requirement that a warrant not issue "but upon probable cause, supported by Oath or affirmation," would be reduced to a nullity if a police officer was able to use deliberately falsified allegations to demonstrate probable cause, and, having misled the magistrate, then was able to remain confident that the ploy was worthwhile.

The Court also determined that other possible sanctions against a dishonest affiant, such as a perjury prosecution, administrative discipline, a contempt of court proceeding, or a civil suit were all inadequate to effectively deter this kind of conduct. But the Court also emphasized that affiants should be presumed credible, and the defendant must overcome this presumption with specific facts that challenge specific statements in the affidavit. Conclusory statements or unsubstantiated allegations will not be sufficient to satisfy the defense burden.

The Court also stated that a *Franks* challenge was only permissible if it alleged intentional, knowing, or reckless misstatements on the part of the affiant. The defendant cannot attack the warrant if the affiant made an innocent mistake or was merely negligent as to the truth.

The Court remanded the case to the trial court for another suppression hearing in which the judge would consider the defendant's challenge to the affiant's credibility.

Note that *Franks* only allows a challenge if the defendant alleges that the **affiant** lied to the issuing magistrate. There is no challenge allowed if the defendant alleges that the **informant** lied to the affiant. This is because the credibility (or lack thereof) of the informant was part of the original test for probable cause—the issuing magistrate already considered the reliability of the informant (along with the informant's basis of knowledge) when deciding whether to issue the warrant. The validity of the warrant is based on the information known to the officer (and thus the magistrate) at the time of the warrant application—thus, proof at a later date that the informant was lying is not relevant to the validity of the warrant.

7. **Arrest Warrants.** Like search warrants, arrest warrants are subject to the requirements of an oath or affirmation, probable cause, and particularity. "Probable cause" in this context means evidence sufficient to warrant a man of reasonable caution to believe a crime occurred and that the individual named in the arrest warrant committed that crime. Usually this burden is met using the same process that exists for search warrants: sworn testimony or an affidavit submitted to a magistrate. Probable cause for an arrest warrant can also be established if a grand jury returns an indictment against an individual. Therefore, after an indictment has been issued, a magistrate should issue an arrest warrant against the individuals named in the indictment without any need to inquire about the facts of the case. We will discuss grand juries and indictments in **Chapter 35**.

In the context of arrest warrants, the particularity requirement means that the warrant must uniquely identify the individual to be arrested, either by name, by occupation, by home address, or by personal appearance. "Where a name that would reasonably identify the subject to be arrested cannot be provided, then some other means reasonable to the circumstances must be used to assist in the identification of the subject of the warrant."[16] For example, a warrant may be issued for "the owner of the house located at 55 W. 5th Avenue" or for "the individual known as 'Slick' who works as a bartender at Lucky's Pub at 1525 W. Main Street."

Finally, unlike search warrants, which expire after a limited amount of time, arrest warrants remain valid indefinitely.

8. When and Why Do Police Use Arrest Warrants? As we saw in **Chapter 9,** police have the authority to make an arrest in a public place without a warrant as long as they have probable cause to believe the suspect is guilty of a crime. As with any warrantless action, this arrest will be reviewed by a judge, and if the judge concludes that probable cause did not exist, the arrest and any search made pursuant to that arrest are illegal. Thus, police officers often seek to obtain an arrest warrant in order to protect themselves from an after-the-fact finding by the judge that the arrest was improper.

However, there is one situation in which an arrest warrant is almost always mandatory—when the police seek to arrest an individual inside his own home:

> **Example—*Payton v. New York,* 445 U.S. 573 (1980):** After two days of investigating the murder of a gas station attendant, New York police detectives developed probable cause that Theodore Payton was the perpetrator. A team of police officers went to Payton's apartment in the Bronx without a warrant to arrest him. At the time, New York State law permitted police officers to enter an individual's home to make a felony arrest without a warrant. The officers saw lights on inside the apartment and heard music playing, but nobody responded to their knocking. After half an hour, the police broke down the metal door and entered the apartment. Payton was not present, but in plain view the police saw and recovered a .30 caliber shell casing.
>
> Payton later surrendered to the police, and the shell casing was used in the trial against him. He moved to suppress the casing, arguing that the warrantless entry into his home violated the Fourth Amendment.

[16] United States v. Swanner, 237 F.Supp. 69, 71 (E.D. Tenn. 1964).

Analysis: The Supreme Court agreed with Payton and ruled that police may not enter a home to make an arrest without an arrest warrant. The Supreme Court noted that the home has always received special protection under the Fourth Amendment. Consequently, police officers entering a home and forcibly seizing its occupant must be considered an extremely severe intrusion.

The Fourth Amendment protects the individual's privacy in a variety of settings. "In none is the zone of privacy more clearly defined than when bounded by the unambiguous physical dimensions of an individual's home. . . . [At] the very core [of the Fourth Amendment] stands the right of a man to retreat into his own home and there be free from unreasonable governmental intrusion."[17]

Also, the Court noted that it would be inconsistent to allow warrantless arrests inside the home given the fact that police are not permitted to enter a home to conduct a warrantless search. Indeed, the very facts of *Payton* demonstrate why this is true. The police entered the home without a warrant, and while searching for the suspect, they found evidence in plain view that they later used against him in court. In other words, allowing a warrantless arrest inside a home would give the police the ability to conduct a (limited) warrantless search inside a home. Forcing the police to obtain an arrest warrant "interpose[s] the magistrate's determination of probable cause between the zealous officer and the citizen."

Although the Supreme Court vehemently defended the sanctity of the home in *Payton*, it later acknowledged that there was an exception to this rule: if the police are in "hot pursuit" of a suspect, and the suspect retreats into his home, the police are allowed to pursue the criminal into the home. We will consider the "hot pursuit" exception, as well as other emergency or "exigent circumstances" exceptions to the warrant requirement, in **Chapter 17.**

There are two other important issues to consider with regard to the issue of arrests within the home. First, what constitutes a "home" for the purposes of the Fourth Amendment? We will see in **Chapter 22** that a defendant must have standing to challenge a search. In other words, a defendant must demonstrate that the police officers violated **his** Fourth Amendment rights and not the rights of a third party. Similarly, to receive the protection of the *Payton* rule, the defendant must demonstrate that the police officers entered **his** home (or a space that is the equivalent of such) without a warrant. As the Supreme Court's decision in *Minnesota v. Olson* makes clear, the Court has liberally interpreted the definition of a "home" in this context:

Example—*Minnesota v. Olson*, 495 U.S. 91 (1990): After developing probable cause to believe that Robert Olson participated in the robbery of a gas station, the police entered the house where he was temporarily staying and arrested him without a

[17] Payton v. New York, 445 U.S. 573, 589 (1980).

warrant. Olson was taken to the police station and made incriminating statements during a subsequent interrogation

Although Olson had spent the previous night in the house, the government argued that the house was not Olson's "home" and no warrant was required to arrest him there. The government proposed a twelve-factor test for courts to use in determining whether the location qualified as a defendant's home. These factors included whether the defendant stored clothes at the location, whether he received mail there, whether he was given a key to the location, and whether he was ever left alone there by the owner.

Analysis: The Court found Olson's arrest was illegal. Rejecting the state's "needlessly complicated" test, the Court held that a defendant can claim the protection of a "home" as long as he is an overnight guest in the location. In supporting this rule, the Court explained why a "home" is given such broad protections under the Fourth Amendment:

To hold that an overnight guest has a legitimate expectation of privacy in his host's home merely recognizes the everyday expectations of privacy that we all share. Staying overnight in another's home is a longstanding social custom that serves functions recognized as valuable by society. . . . [W]e think that society recognizes that a houseguest has a legitimate expectation of privacy in his host's home.

From the overnight guest's perspective, he seeks shelter in another's home precisely because it provides him with privacy, a place where he and his possessions will not be disturbed by anyone but his host and those his host allows inside. We are at our most vulnerable when we are asleep because we cannot monitor our own safety or the security of our belongings. It is for this reason that, although we may spend all day in public places, when we cannot sleep in our own home we seek out another private place to sleep, whether it be a hotel room, or the home of a friend. Society expects at least as much privacy in these places as in a telephone Booth—"a temporarily private place whose momentary occupants' expectations of freedom from intrusion are recognized as reasonable. . . ."

The second issue raised by the arrest of someone inside a home is whether an arrest warrant authorizes the police to enter a third party's home to find and arrest the suspect named in the warrant:

Example—*Steagald v. United States*, 451 U.S. 204 (1981): Federal agents obtained an arrest warrant for Ricky Lyons, a fugitive who was wanted for drug crimes. After securing the arrest warrant, the agents received a tip that Lyons was staying at a certain address in Atlanta. When the agents arrived at the house, they saw two people standing outside. They frisked both men, checked their identification, and determined that neither was Lyons. They then entered the house and searched it for Lyons. Lyons was not present, but the officers did observe a substance they believed to be cocaine.

The officers secured the house, obtained a search warrant based on the suspected cocaine they had seen, and returned to do a more thorough search of the house. During this subsequent search, the officers recovered forty-three pounds of cocaine. Thereafter, they arrested the owner of the house, Gary Steagald, and charged him with drug crimes. Steagald challenged the search warrant, arguing that it was based on probable cause that was the result of the police officer's unlawful presence in his home.

Analysis: The Supreme Court invalidated the warrant, holding that the police had no authority to enter Steagald's house. The Court emphasized the difference between an arrest warrant and a search warrant. The arrest warrant requirement protects an individual from the unauthorized seizure of his **person** inside his home; the search warrant protects an individual's interest in the privacy of his home and possessions. Thus, when a neutral and detached magistrate authorizes the arrest of a person, she does not implicitly allow the police to enter into anyone's private home to search for that person.

The Court was also worried that a contrary decision would essentially eviscerate the search warrant requirement, because the police could use an arrest warrant as a pretext to conduct warrantless searches of homes. "Armed solely with an arrest warrant for a single person, the police could search all the homes of that individual's friends and acquaintances." The Court cited a recent case in which the police searched three hundred homes while looking for two fugitives as evidence of the potential for this abuse.

Given this rule, how should the police officers have proceeded in this case? If the informant's tip was sufficient to provide probable cause that Lyons was in Steagald's house, the police could have used that probable cause to obtain a search warrant to enter Lyons' house to look for Steagald. Once legally there pursuant to the search warrant, they would be permitted to observe and seize any contraband that they saw in plain view as they looked for Lyons.

If the informant's tip was not sufficient to create probable cause that Lyons was present in the home, the police could have tried to get consent from someone inside the house to enter and look for him. If they could not get consent, they would have to conduct surveillance on the house until Lyons either left the house, in which case he could be arrested in a public place, or until they saw him inside the house, in which case they would have the probable cause necessary to obtain a warrant.

One final reminder: there is no direct remedy for an unconstitutional **arrest**. If a defendant successfully establishes that an arrest in unconstitutional, there is no remedy unless police conducted a search or interrogation as a result of the illegal arrest. If so, the items seized by the police or the statements made by the defendant would be inadmissible. For example, in *Payton*, the illegal entry led to an illegal observation and seizure of the shotgun shell; in *Olson*, the defendant was interrogated shortly after his illegal arrest and made inculpatory statements. If such evidence is not obtained, however, there is no remedy within the confines of the criminal justice process for the illegal arrest. (As we will discuss in **Chapter 23**, the defendant could sue the government in a civil case to seek damages, but such claims are difficult to win.)

Quick Summary

Before police conduct a search, they must either obtain a warrant or ensure that the search falls into one of the many exceptions to the warrant requirement. In order to obtain a search warrant, the police must submit an affidavit or sworn testimony (1) under oath or affirmation which sets out (2) probable cause to believe that a crime has occurred and that instrumentalities, evidence, or fruits of that crime will be present at the location, and (3) that describes with particularity the areas to be searched and the items to be seized. This application must be submitted to a (4) neutral and detached magistrate.

Probable cause is a somewhat lower standard to meet when applying for a warrant before the search than when trying to defend a warrantless search after the search has been completed. The **particularity** requirement is meant to prevent the issuance of "general warrants," and it is typically met when the warrant describes the location and items to a level of specificity that removes all ambiguity as to where to look and what to seize. A magistrate is **neutral and detached** as long as she is a member of the judicial branch and does not receive any incentive, financial or otherwise, for issuing a warrant.

The requirements for an arrest warrant are identical to those for a search warrant. Warrantless arrests are allowed in any public place based on probable cause, but the police must have an arrest warrant in order to arrest someone inside his own home. If the police arrest a suspect inside of a third party's home, a search warrant for the home is also needed before the arrest can be effected.

Sample affidavit for a warrant (From *Franks* case):

IN THE MATTER OF: Jerome Franks, B/M, DOB: 10/9/54 and 222 S. Governors Ave., Apt. #3, Dover, Delaware. A two room apartment located on the South side, second floor, of a white block building on the west side of S. Governors Avenue, Between Loockerman Street and North Street, in the City of Dover. The ground floor of this building houses Wayman's Barber Shop.

STATE OF DELAWARE

COUNTY OF KENT ss:

Be it remembered that on this 9th day of March A. D. 1976 before me John Green, personally appeared Det. Ronald R. Brooks and Det. Larry Gray of the Dover Police Department who being by me duly sworn depose and say:

That they have reason to believe and do believe that in the 222 S. Governors Avenue, Apartment #3, Dover, Delaware. A two room apartment located on the south side second floor of a white block building on the west side of S. Governors Avenue between Loockerman Street and North Street in the City of Dover. The ground floor of this building houses Wayman's Barber Shop the occupant of which is Jerome Franks there has been and/or there is now located and/or concealed certain property in said house, place, conveyance and/or on the person or persons of the occupants thereof, consisting of property, papers, articles, or things which are the instruments of criminal offense, and/or obtained in the commission of a crime, and/or designated to be used in the commission of a crime, and not reasonably calculated to be used for any other purpose and/or the possession of which is unlawful, papers, articles, or things which are of an evidentiary nature pertaining to the commission of a crime or crimes specified therein and in particular, a white knit thermal undershirt; a brown 3/4 length leather jacket with a tie-belt; a pair of black mens pants; a dark colored knit hat; a long thin bladed knife or other instruments or items relating to the crime.

Articles, or things were, are, or will be possessed and/or used in violation of Title 11, Sub-Chapter D, Section 763, Delaware Code in that [see attached probable-cause page].

Wherefore, affiants pray that a search warrant may be issued authorizing a search of the aforesaid 222 S. Governors Avenue, Apartment #3, Dover, Delaware. A two room apartment located on the south side second floor of a white block building on the west side of S. Governors Avenue between Loockerman St. and North Street, in the City of Dover in the manner provided by law.

/s/ Det. Ronald R. Brooks

Affiant

/s/ Det. Larry D. Gray

Affiant

SWORN to (or affirmed) and subscribed before me this 9th day of March A. D. 1976.

/s/ John Green

Judge Ct 7

The facts tending to establish probable cause for the issuance of this search warrant are:

1. On Saturday, 2/28/76, Brenda L. B. , W/F/15, reported to the Dover Police Department that she had been kidnapped and raped.

2. An investigation of this complaint was conducted by Det. Boyce Failing of the Dover Police Department.

3. Investigation of the aforementioned complaint revealed that Brenda B. -- -- -- , while under the influence of drugs, was taken to 222 S. Governors Avenue, Apartment 3, Dover, Delaware.

4. Investigation of the aforementioned complaint revealed that 222 S. Governors Avenue, Apartment #3, Dover, Delaware, is the residence of Jerome Franks, B/M DOB: 10/9/54.

5. Investigation of the aforementioned complaint revealed that on Saturday, 2/28/76, Jerome Franks did have sexual contact with Brenda B. -- -- -- without her consent.

6. On Thursday, 3/4/76 at the Dover Police Department, Brenda B. -- -- -- revealed to Det. Boyce Failing that Jerome Franks was the person who committed the Sexual Assault against her.

7. On Friday, 3/5/76, Jerome Franks was placed under arrest by Cpl. Robert McClements of the Dover Police Department, and charged with Sexual Misconduct.

8. On 3/5/76 at Family Court in Dover, Delaware, Jerome Franks did, after being arrested on the charge of Sexual Misconduct, [make] a statement to Cpl. Robert McClements, that he thought the charge was concerning Cynthia Bailey not Brenda B.

9. On Friday, 3/5/76, Cynthia C. Bailey, W/F/21 of 132 North Street, Dover, Delaware, did report to Dover Police Department that she had been raped at her residence during the night.

10. Investigation conducted by your affiant on Friday, 3/5/76, revealed the perpetrator of the crime to be an unknown black male, approximately 5'7', 150 lbs., dark complexion, wearing white thermal undershirt, black pants with a belt having a silver or gold buckle, a brown leather 3/4 length coat with a tie belt in the front, and a dark knit cap pulled around the eyes.

11. Your affiant can state, that during the commission of this crime, Cynthia Bailey was forced at knife point and with the threat of death to engage in sexual intercourse with the perpetrator of the crime.

12. Your affiant can state that entry was gained to the residence of Cynthia Bailey through a window located on the east side of the residence.

13. Your affiant can state that the residence of Jerome Franks is within a very short distance and direct sight of the residence of Cynthia Bailey.

14. Your affiant can state that the description given by Cynthia Bailey of the unknown black male does coincide with the description of Jerome Franks.

15. On Tuesday, 3/9/76, your affiant contacted Mr. James Williams and Mr. Wesley Lucas of the Delaware Youth Center where Jerome Franks is employed and did have personal conversation with both these people.

16. On Tuesday, 3/9/76, Mr. James Williams revealed to your affiant that the normal dress of Jerome Franks does consist of a white knit thermal undershirt and a brown leather jacket.

17. On Tuesday, 3/9/76, Mr. Wesley Lucas revealed to your affiant that in addition to the thermal undershirt and jacket, Jerome Franks often wears a dark green knit hat.

18. Your affiant can state that a check of official records reveals that in 1971 Jerome Franks was arrested for the crime of rape and subsequently convicted with Assault with intent to Rape.

Review Questions

1. Searching for Stolen Property. Tyrone Brown was arrested by Lansing police for a string of break-ins. He told police he stashed the stolen property at his girlfriend Stella Wheeler's house. After he pointed out the house to police, the police obtained a warrant to search the house.

The warrant listed the property to be "searched and seized" as "including but not limited to personal property (shotguns, long guns, computer and stereo equipment, cameras, DVD players, video game systems, big screen televisions, necklaces, rings, other jewelry, coin collections, music equipment, car stereo equipment) taken in approximately nineteen burglaries."

The police executed the warrant and seized three cameras, three gold bracelets, a gold chain, gold earrings, a gold ring, two watches, a radio, a laptop computer, a nineteen-inch television, a PlayStation, a Gameboy, a video camera, and a car stereo. Some of these items had been stolen, but many of them (two of the cameras, all of the jewelry, and the Playstation) belonged to Wheeler.

Wheeler was subsequently arrested and charged with possession of stolen property. She challenged the constitutionality of the warrant, arguing that it did not state the items to be seized with sufficient particularity.

2. Searching a Hard Drive. David Evers, Jr. ("Junior") learned from his niece Marlene that his father, David Evers, Sr. ("Evers"), had sexually assaulted Marlene twice, taken pictures of her body, and saved the pictures on his computer. Junior searched the computer and found a sexually suggestive video of Marlene. He then called the police.

Based on Junior's information, the police obtained a search warrant for the Evers' home. The warrant instructed the police to search and seize "any digital cameras, photos, or personal computers that may contain evidence of the crimes."

When the police executed the warrant, they took two computers from Evers' bedroom. A quick search showed that images had been deleted before the police search. The officers turned the computers over to a forensic agent, who scanned the hard drive and recovered forty photos which had been deleted, all depicting sexually explicit images of Marlene in her underwear. Evers filed a motion to suppress the photos, arguing the sophisticated technological search of his hard drive exceeded the scope of the warrant, which failed to describe the computers with particularity.

3. Jailer as Magistrate. In a small rural county in Ohio, Police County Commissioner Michelle Madison routinely signed search warrants. Madison was hired and could be fired by the County Jailer, who was a law enforcement official. Madison's duties consisted of the following: handling the purchase orders for all jail bills; assisting the jailer with the yearly budget; maintaining the records of the jail's commissary account; handling the Jailer's correspondence; processing handled inmates' work release requests; assisting inmates with their child support obligations; and facilitating inmates' drug rehabilitation placements.

Madison did not carry a weapon; nor did she wear a badge or uniform. She never arrested anyone, did not participate in the ongoing training required of deputy jailers, and was not on the regular rotation of duties for monitoring prisoners.

Paul Uviller was arrested after the police executed a search warrant against him and recovered stolen property. Uviller challenged the constitutionality of the warrant, arguing that Madison was not a neutral and detached magistrate but rather a law enforcement official. The state argued that Madison was an administrative assistant who did not participate in day-to-day law enforcement activities, and therefore was eligible to issue warrants.

4. Arrests at a Crack House. The police suspected that two brothers, Jared and Nick Gordon, were selling crack cocaine out of an abandoned building in the city. The building was an old apartment building that had been taken over by the city as part of a tax foreclosure six years ago; it had been abandoned ever since then. The brothers sold the cocaine out of Apartment 2D in the building. They usually sold from 10 PM until 3 AM; then one of them would sleep on a cot in the apartment to guard the stash while the other went to their legitimate apartment for the rest of the night. In addition to the cot, the brothers each kept a change of clothes in the apartment and a few personal items. The building had no running water and no electricity.

One night an undercover police officer knocked on the door of Apartment 2D and when Jared answered the door, the officer asked for two bags of crack cocaine. Jared took the officers money and handed him two small plastic bags. In an attempt to lure him out of the apartment, the officer said: "By the way, you had better do something about the problem in the lobby." Jared said: "What problem?" and stepped out into the hallway. The officer then grabbed him and placed him under arrest. Jared yelled: "Nicky! The cops!" and Nick closed the door. Two other policemen then broke down the door and arrested Nick inside the apartment. Jared and Nick were both searched incident to arrest, and the police found five bags of crack cocaine on Jared. The police also saw twenty bags of crack cocaine sitting on the table when they were in the apartment making the arrest.

Jared and Nick both challenged their arrest. They concede that the drug sale provided the police with probable cause, but they argue that the police should have had an arrest warrant since Nick was in his home when he was arrested, and Jared was lured out of his home by the police under false pretenses.

FROM THE COURTROOM

LO-JI SALES v. NEW YORK

United States Supreme Court, 1979
442 U.S. 319

Mr. Chief Justice BURGER delivered the unanimous opinion of the Court.

We granted certiorari on claims that the seizure of magazines, films, and other objects from petitioner's bookstore violated guarantees of the First, Fourth, and Fourteenth Amendments.

I

On June 20, 1976, an investigator for the New York State Police purchased two reels of film from petitioner's so-called "adult" bookstore. Upon viewing them, he concluded the films violated New York's obscenity laws. On June 25, he took them to a Town Justice for a determination whether there was reasonable cause to believe the films violated the state obscenity laws so as to justify a warrant to search the seller's store. The Town Justice viewed both films in their entirety, and he apparently concluded they were obscene. Based upon an affidavit of the investigator subscribed before the Town Justice after this viewing, a warrant issued authorizing the search of petitioner's store and the seizure of other copies of the two films exhibited to the Town Justice.

The investigator's affidavit also contained an assertion that "similar" films and printed matter portraying similar activities could be found on the premises, and a statement of the affiant's belief that the items were possessed in violation of the obscenity laws. The warrant application requested that the Town Justice accompany the investigator to petitioner's store for the execution of the search warrant. The stated purpose was to allow the Town Justice to determine independently if any other items at the store were possessed in violation of law and subject to seizure. The Town Justice agreed. Accordingly, the warrant also contained a recital that authorized the seizure of "[t]he following items that the Court independently [on examination] has determined to be possessed in violation of Article 235 of the Penal Law . . . ." However, at the time the Town Justice signed the warrant there were no items listed or described following this statement. As noted earlier, the only "things to be seized" that were described in the warrant were copies of the two films the state investigator had purchased. Before going to the store, the Town Justice also signed a warrant for the arrest of the clerk who operated the store for having sold the two films to the investigator.

The Town Justice and the investigator enlisted three other State Police investigators, three uniformed State Police officers, and three members of the local prosecutor's office—a total of eleven—and the search party converged on the bookstore. The store clerk was immediately placed under arrest and advised of the search warrant. He was the only employee present; he was free to continue working in the store to the extent the search permitted, and the store remained open to the public while the party conducted its search mission which was to last nearly six hours.

The search began in an area of the store which contained booths in which silent films were shown by coin-operated projectors. The clerk adjusted the machines so that the films could be viewed by the Town Justice without coins; it is disputed whether he volunteered or did so under compulsion of the arrest or the warrant. The Town Justice viewed twenty-three films for two to three minutes each and, satisfied there was probable cause to believe they were obscene, then ordered the films and the projectors seized.

The Town Justice next focused on another area containing four coin-operated projectors showing both soundless and sound films. After viewing each film for two to five minutes again without paying, he ordered them seized along with their projectors.

The search party then moved to an area in which books and magazines were on display. The magazines were encased in clear plastic or cellophane wrappers which the Town Justice had two police officers remove prior to his examination of the books. Choosing only magazines that did not contain significant amounts of written material, he spent not less than ten seconds nor more than a minute looking through each one. When he was satisfied that probable cause existed, he immediately ordered the copy which he had reviewed, along with other copies of the same or "similar" magazines, seized. An investigator wrote down the titles of the items seized. All told, 397 magazines were taken.

The final area searched was one in which petitioner displayed films and other items for sale behind a glass enclosed case. When it was announced that each box of film would be opened, the clerk advised that a picture on the outside of the box was representative of what the film showed. Therefore, if satisfied from the picture that there was probable cause to believe the film in the box was obscene, the Town Justice ordered the seizure of all copies of that film. As with the magazines, an investigator wrote down the titles of the films seized, a total of 431 reels. Miscellaneous other items, including business records, were also seized, but no issue concerning them is raised here.

Throughout the day, two or three marked police cars were parked in front of the store and persons who entered the store were asked to show identification and their names were taken by the police. Not surprisingly, no sales were made during the period the search party was at the store, and no customers or potential customers remained in the store for any appreciable time after becoming aware of the police presence.

After the search and seizure was completed, the seized items were taken to a State Police barracks where they were inventoried. Each item was then listed on the search warrant, and late the same night the completed warrant was given to the Town Justice. The warrant, which had consisted of two pages when he signed it before the search, by late in the day contained sixteen pages. It is clear, therefore, that the particular description of"things to be seized" was entered in the document after the seizure and impoundment of the books and other articles.

The items seized formed the basis for a three-count information charging petitioner with obscenity in the second degree under New York law. The counts were based upon the three main groups of items seized: the magazines, Count I; the films for sale to the public, Count II; and the films and coin-operated projectors, Count III. Before trial, petitioner moved to suppress all the evidence upon which the three counts were based because it had been searched for and seized in violation of the First, Fourth, and Fourteenth Amendments. The motion was denied. Petitioner then entered a guilty plea to all three counts and was fined $1,000 on each. Accordingly, the obscenity of the magazines and films having been the subject of a judicial confession, there is no issue of obscenity in the case. Only the validity of the warrant and the search and seizure of the property are before us.

New York permits appeal of a denial of a motion to suppress even after a plea of guilty to the charge. Pursuant to this procedure, petitioner appealed and the intermediate appellate court for that judicial district affirmed the convictions. A timely application for leave to appeal to the New York Court of Appeals was denied.

II

This search warrant and what followed the entry on petitioner's premises are reminiscent of the general warrant or writ of assistance of the 18th century against which the Fourth Amendment was intended to protect. Except for the specification of copies of the two films previously purchased, the warrant did not purport to "PARTICULARLY DESCRIB[E] . . . THE . . . THINGS to be seized." Based on the conclusory statement of the police investigator that other similarly obscene materials would be found at the store, the warrant left it entirely to the discretion of the officials conducting the search to decide what items were likely obscene and to accomplish their seizure. The Fourth Amendment does not permit such action. Nor does the Fourth Amendment countenance open-ended warrants, to be completed while a search is being conducted and items seized or after the seizure has been carried out.

This search began when the local justice and his party entered the premises. But at that time there was not sufficient probable cause to pursue a search beyond looking for additional copies of the two specified films, assuming the validity of searching even for those. And the record is clear that the search began and progressed pursuant to the sweeping open-ended authorization in the warrant. It was not limited at the outset as a search for other copies of the two "sample" films; it expanded into a more extensive search because other items were found that the local justice deemed illegal.

. . .

III

We have repeatedly said that a warrant authorized by a neutral and detached judicial officer is "a more reliable safeguard against improper searches than the hurried judgment of a law enforcement officer 'engaged in the often competitive enterprise of ferreting out crime.'" The State contends that the presence and participation of the Town Justice in the search ensured that no items would be seized absent probable cause to believe they were obscene, and that his presence enabled petitioner to enjoy an immediate adversary hearing on the issue.

The Town Justice did not manifest that neutrality and detachment demanded of a judicial officer when presented with a warrant application for a search and seizure. We need not question the subjective belief of the Town Justice in the propriety of his actions, but the objective facts of record manifest an erosion of whatever neutral and detached posture existed at the outset. He allowed himself to become a member, if not the leader, of the search party which was essentially a police operation. Once in the store, he conducted a generalized search under authority of an invalid warrant; he was not acting as a judicial officer but as an adjunct law enforcement officer. When he ordered an item seized because he believed it was obscene, he instructed the police officers to seize all "similar" items as well, leaving determination of what was "similar" to the officer's discretion. Indeed, he yielded to the State Police even the completion of the general provision of the warrant. Though it would not have validated the warrant in any event, the Town Justice admitted at the hearing to suppress evidence that he could not verify that the inventory prepared by the police and presented to him late that evening accurately reflected what he had ordered seized.

We also cannot accept the State's contention that it acted in compliance with *Heller v. New York,* 413 U.S. 483 (1973). There, based on police reports of probable violation of state law, a judge viewed a film in a theater as an ordinary paying patron; on the basis of his observation of the entire performance, he then issued a warrant for the seizure of the particular viewed film as evidence. There was no claim that seizure of the single copy impeded the exhibitor's continued business pending decision on the issue of obscenity. Heller's claim was that not even one of his films could be lawfully seized without a prior adversary hearing. We rejected that claim and held that seizure on the warrant so issued by a neutral judicial officer on probable cause after viewing one film was constitutionally permissible so long as, on request, a prompt adversary hearing was available on the issue of obscenity. "With such safeguards, we do not perceive that an adversary hearing *prior* to a seizure [of a single sample film] by lawful warrant would materially increase First Amendment protection."

. . .

In contrast, the local justice here undertook to telescope the processes of the application for a warrant, the issuance of the warrant, and its execution. It is difficult to discern when he was acting as a "neutral and detached" judicial officer and when he was one with the police and prosecutors in the executive seizure, and indeed even whether he thought he was conducting, *ex parte,* the "prompt" postseizure hearings on obscenity called for by *Heller. Heller* does not permit the kind of activities revealed by this record.[6]

[6] We do not suggest, of course, that a "neutral and detached magistrate" loses his character as such merely because he leaves his regular office in order to make himself readily available to law enforcement officers who may wish to seek the issuance of warrants by him. For example, in *Heller,* the judge signed the search warrant for the seizure of the film in the theater itself. But as we have just pointed out, *Heller* cannot control this case where the local Town Justice undertook not merely to issue a warrant, but to participate with the police and prosecutors in its execution.

IV

Perhaps anticipating our disposition of the case, the State raises a different theory from the one advanced in its opposition to the petition for certiorari and on which it had relied in the state courts. The suggestion is that by virtue of its display of the items at issue to the general public in areas of its store open to them, petitioner had no legitimate expectation of privacy against governmental intrusion, and that accordingly no warrant was needed. But there is no basis for the notion that because a retail store invites the public to enter, it consents to wholesale searches and seizures that do not conform to Fourth Amendment guarantees. The Town Justice viewed the films, not as a customer, but without the payment a member of the public would be required to make. Similarly, in examining the books and in the manner of viewing the containers in which the films were packaged for sale, he was not seeing them as a customer would ordinarily see them.

Any suggestion that petitioner through its clerk consented to the sweeping search also comes too late. After Lo-Ji's agent was placed under arrest and was aware of the presumed authority of the search warrant, his conduct complying with official requests cannot, on this record, be considered free and voluntary. Any "consent" given in the face of "colorably lawful coercion" cannot validate the illegal acts shown here. Our society is better able to tolerate the admittedly pornographic business of petitioner than a return to the general warrant era; violations of law must be dealt with within the framework of constitutional guarantees.

The judgment of the Appellate Term of the Supreme Court of the State of New York for the Ninth and Tenth Judicial Districts is reversed, and the case is remanded for further proceedings not inconsistent with this opinion.

FROM THE COURTROOM

MINNESOTA v. OLSON

United States Supreme Court, 1990
495 U.S. 91

Justice WHITE delivered the opinion of the Court.

Chief Justice REHNQUIST and Justice BLACKMUN dissented.

The police in this case made a warrantless, nonconsensual entry into a house where respondent Robert Olson was an overnight guest and arrested him. The issue is whether the arrest violated Olson's Fourth Amendment rights. We hold that it did.

I

Shortly before 6 a.m. on Saturday, July 18, 1987, a lone gunman robbed an Amoco gasoline station in Minneapolis, Minnesota, and fatally shot the station manager. A police officer heard the police dispatcher report and suspected Joseph Ecker. The officer and his partner drove immediately to Ecker's home, arriving at about the same time that an Oldsmobile arrived. The driver of the Oldsmobile took evasive action, and the car spun out of control and came to a stop. Two men fled the car on foot. Ecker, who was later identified as the gunman, was captured shortly thereafter inside his home. The second man escaped.

Inside the abandoned Oldsmobile, police found a sack of money and the murder weapon. They also found a title certificate with the name Rob Olson crossed out as a secured party, a letter addressed to a Roger R. Olson of 3151 Johnson Street, and a videotape rental receipt made out to Rob Olson and dated two days earlier. The police verified that a Robert Olson lived at 3151 Johnson Street.

The next morning, Sunday, July 19, a woman identifying herself as Dianna Murphy called the police and said that a man by the name of Rob drove the car in which the gas station killer left the scene and that Rob was planning to leave town by bus. About noon, the same woman called again, gave her address and phone number, and said that a man named Rob had told a Maria and two other women, Louanne and Julie, that he was the driver in the Amoco robbery. The caller stated that Louanne was Julie's mother and that the two women lived at 2406 Fillmore Northeast. The detective-in-charge who took the second phone call sent police officers to 2406 Fillmore to check out Louanne and Julie. When police arrived they determined that the dwelling was a duplex and that Louanne Bergstrom and her daughter Julie lived in the upper unit but were not home. Police spoke to Louanne's mother, Helen Niederhoffer, who lived in the lower unit. She confirmed that a Rob Olson had been staying upstairs but was not then in the unit. She promised to call the police when Olson returned. At 2 p.m., a pickup order, or "probable cause arrest bulletin," was issued for Olson's arrest. The police were instructed to stay away from the duplex.

At approximately 2:45 p.m., Niederhoffer called police and said Olson had returned. The detective-in-charge instructed police officers to go to the house and surround it. He then telephoned Julie from headquarters and told her Rob should come out of the house. The detective heard a male voice say, "tell them I left." Julie stated that Rob had left, whereupon at 3 p.m. the detective ordered the police to enter the house. Without seeking permission and with weapons drawn, the police entered the upper unit and found respondent hiding in a closet. Less than an hour after his arrest, respondent made an inculpatory statement at police headquarters.

The Hennepin County trial court held a hearing and denied respondent's motion to suppress his statement. The statement was admitted into evidence at Olson's trial, and he was convicted on one count of first-degree murder, three counts of armed robbery, and three counts of second-degree assault. On appeal, the Minnesota Supreme Court reversed. The court ruled that respondent had a sufficient interest in the Bergstrom home to challenge the legality of his warrantless arrest there, that the arrest was illegal because there were no exigent circumstances to justify a warrantless entry,[1] and that respondent's statement was tainted by that illegality and should have been suppressed. Because the admission of the statement was not harmless beyond reasonable doubt, the court reversed Olson's conviction and remanded for a new trial.

We granted the State's petition for certiorari, and now affirm.

II

It was held in *Payton v. New York,* 445 U.S. 573 (1980), that a suspect should not be arrested in his house without an arrest warrant, even though there is probable cause to arrest him. The purpose of the decision was not to protect the person of the suspect but to protect his home from entry in the absence of a magistrate's finding of probable cause. In this case, the court below held that Olson's warrantless arrest was illegal because he had a sufficient connection with the premises to be treated like a householder. The State challenges that conclusion.

Since the decision in *Katz v. United States,* 389 U.S. 347 (1967), it has been the law that "capacity to claim the protection of the Fourth Amendment depends . . . upon whether the person who claims the protection of the Amendment has a legitimate expectation of privacy in the invaded place." *Rakas v. Illinois,* 439 U.S. 128 (1978). A subjective expectation of privacy is legitimate if it is "'one that society is prepared to recognize as "reasonable."'"

[1] Because the absence of a warrant made respondent's arrest illegal, the court did not review the trial court's determination that the police had probable cause for the arrest. Hence, we judge the case on the assumption that there was probable cause.

The State argues that Olson's relationship to the premises does not satisfy the twelve factors which in its view determine whether a dwelling is a "home."[4] Aside from the fact that it is based on the mistaken premise that a place must be one's "home" in order for one to have a legitimate expectation of privacy there,[5] the State's proposed test is needlessly complex. We need go no further than to conclude, as we do, that Olson's status as an overnight guest is alone enough to show that he had an expectation of privacy in the home that society is prepared to recognize as reasonable.

As recognized by the Minnesota Supreme Court, the facts of this case are similar to those in *Jones v. United States,* 362 U.S. 257 (1960). In *Jones,* the defendant was arrested in a friend's apartment during the execution of a search warrant and sought to challenge the warrant as not supported by probable cause.

> "[Jones] testified that the apartment belonged to a friend, Evans, who had given him the use of it, and a key, with which [Jones] had admitted himself on the day of the arrest. On cross-examination [Jones] testified that he had a suit and shirt at the apartment, that his home was elsewhere, that he paid nothing for the use of the apartment, that Evans had let him use it 'as a friend,' that he had slept there 'maybe a night,' and that at the time of the search Evans had been away in Philadelphia for about five days."[6]

The Court ruled that Jones could challenge the search of the apartment because he was "legitimately on [the] premises." Although the "legitimately on [the] premises"

---

[4] The [twelve] factors are:
(1) the visitor has some property rights in the dwelling;
(2) the visitor is related by blood or marriage to the owner or lessor of the dwelling;
(3) the visitor receives mail at the dwelling or has his name on the door;
(4) the visitor has a key to the dwelling;
(5) the visitor maintains a regular or continuous presence in the dwelling, especially sleeping there regularly;
(6) the visitor contributes to the upkeep of the dwelling, either monetarily or otherwise;
(7) the visitor has been present at the dwelling for a substantial length of time prior to the arrest;
(8) the visitor stores his clothes or other possessions in the dwelling;
(9) the visitor has been granted by the owner exclusive use of a particular area of the dwelling;
(10) the visitor has the right to exclude other persons from the dwelling;
(11) the visitor is allowed to remain in the dwelling when the owner is absent; and
(12) the visitor has taken precautions to develop and maintain his privacy in the dwelling.

[5] Of course, 2406 Fillmore need not be respondent's "home," temporary or otherwise, in order for him to enjoy a reasonable expectation of privacy there. "[T]he Fourth Amendment protects people, not places," and provides sanctuary for citizens wherever they have a legitimate expectation of privacy. Mr. Katz could complain because he had such an expectation in a telephone booth, not because it was his "home" for Fourth Amendment purposes. Similarly, if Olson had a reasonable expectation of privacy as a one-night guest, his warrantless seizure was unreasonable whether or not the upper unit at 2406 Fillmore was his home.

[6] Olson, who had been staying at Ecker's home for several days before the robbery, spent the night of the robbery on the floor of the Bergstroms' home, with their permission. He had a change of clothes with him at the duplex.

standard was rejected in *Rakas* as too broad, the *Rakas* Court explicitly reaffirmed the factual holding in *Jones:*

> "We do not question the conclusion in *Jones* that the defendant in that case suffered a violation of his personal Fourth Amendment rights if the search in question was unlawful. . . .
>
> "We think that *Jones* on its facts merely stands for the unremarkable proposition that a person can have a legally sufficient interest in a place other than his own home so that the Fourth Amendment protects him from unreasonable governmental intrusion into that place." 439 U.S. at 141–142.

Rakas thus recognized that, as an overnight guest, Jones was much more than just legitimately on the premises.

The distinctions relied on by the State between this case and *Jones* are not legally determinative. The State emphasizes that in this case Olson was never left alone in the duplex or given a key, whereas in *Jones* the owner of the apartment was away and Jones had a key with which he could come and go and admit and exclude others. These differences are crucial, it is argued, because in not disturbing the holding in *Jones,* the Court pointed out that while his host was away, Jones had complete dominion and control over the apartment and could exclude others from it. We do not understand *Rakas,* however, to hold that an overnight guest can never have a legitimate expectation of privacy except when his host is away and he has a key, or that only when those facts are present may an overnight guest assert the "unremarkable proposition," that a person may have a sufficient interest in a place other than his home to enable him to be free in that place from unreasonable searches and seizures.

To hold that an overnight guest has a legitimate expectation of privacy in his host's home merely recognizes the everyday expectations of privacy that we all share. Staying overnight in another's home is a longstanding social custom that serves functions recognized as valuable by society. We stay in others' homes when we travel to a strange city for business or pleasure, when we visit our parents, children, or more distant relatives out of town, when we are in between jobs or homes, or when we house-sit for a friend. We will all be hosts and we will all be guests many times in our lives. From either perspective, we think that society recognizes that a houseguest has a legitimate expectation of privacy in his host's home.

From the overnight guest's perspective, he seeks shelter in another's home precisely because it provides him with privacy, a place where he and his possessions will not be disturbed by anyone but his host and those his host allows inside. We are at our most vulnerable when we are asleep because we cannot monitor our own safety or the security of our belongings. It is for this reason that, although we may spend all day in public places, when we cannot sleep in our own home we seek out another private place to sleep, whether it be a hotel room, or the home of a friend. Society expects at least as much privacy in these places as in a telephone booth—"a temporarily private place whose momentary occupants' expectations of freedom from intrusion are recognized as reasonable."

That the guest has a host who has ultimate control of the house is not inconsistent with the guest having a legitimate expectation of privacy. The houseguest is there with the permission of his host, who is willing to share his house and his privacy with his guest. It is unlikely that the guest will be confined to a restricted area of the house; and when the host is away or asleep, the guest will have a measure of control over the premises. The host may admit or exclude from the house as he prefers, but it is unlikely that he will admit someone who wants to see or meet with the guest over the objection of the guest. On the other hand, few houseguests will invite others to visit them while they are guests without consulting their hosts; but the latter, who have the authority to exclude despite the wishes of the guest, will often be accommodating. The point is that hosts will more likely than not respect the privacy interests of their guests, who are entitled to a legitimate expectation of privacy despite the fact that they have no legal interest in the premises and do not have the legal authority to determine who may or may not enter the household. If the untrammeled power to admit and exclude were essential to Fourth Amendment protection, an adult daughter temporarily living in the home of her parents would have no legitimate expectation of privacy because her right to admit or exclude would be subject to her parents' veto.

Because respondent's expectation of privacy in the Bergstrom home was rooted in "understandings that are recognized and permitted by society," it was legitimate, and respondent can claim the protection of the Fourth Amendment.

. . .

IV

We therefore affirm the judgment of the Minnesota Supreme Court.

It is so ordered.

Chief Justice REHNQUIST and Justice BLACKMUN dissent.

12

Introduction to the Exceptions to the Warrant Requirement

Key Concepts

- "Specifically Established" and "Well-Delineated"
- S-P-A-C-E-S

As you read in **Chapter 5**, the Court has long determined that the relationship between the two clauses of the Fourth Amendment mean that, as a general matter, searches and seizures conducted in the absence of a warrant are *per se* unreasonable. Almost from the beginning, though, the Court has simultaneously acknowledged the need for exceptions to this general rule. In recognizing these exceptions, the Court has often repeated that reasonableness, not a warrant, is the ultimate touchstone of the Fourth Amendment. Consequently, the Court has found it reasonable for the police to proceed without a warrant under certain circumstances. For example, the Court has crafted exceptions where there is a special law enforcement need, where the target of the search or seizure enjoys diminished expectations of privacy, and where the law enforcement intrusion is seen as only minimal.[1]

The warrant requirement might be thought of as a blanket of Fourth Amendment protection that covers each person. The exceptions to the warrant requirement might then be described as holes that have been cut in that protection—areas where individuals are left more exposed. Drawing the analogy out just a bit further, how we view any particular exception depends on how we feel about the quality of the original blanket and how the holes cumulatively affect its integrity. How we might feel about any particular exception also depends on what part of the metaphorical body the original blanket covered and how big a hole the exception cuts. Figuratively speaking, if the area where the hole now lies originally covered only a small part of your heel, the withdrawal of protection might not matter much. If however, the blanket originally covered a large part of your torso and the hole now leaves you significantly exposed to the elements, the withdrawal of protection might matter quite a bit more.

---

[1] Illinois v. McArthur, 531 U.S. 326 (2001).

Generally, in crafting and refining each new exception, the Court has tended to describe the area of protection being withdrawn as a heel—not a torso. Thus, for each exception recognized, the Court has not deemed the individual interests left exposed as particularly weighty and has characterized the hole cut as relatively unimportant to the blanket's ongoing durability. In contrast, critics champion the importance of a warrant requirement, and suggest that the holes being cut by exceptions are individually significant, and cumulatively devastating—leaving the requirement more a threadbare, moth-eaten scrap than a warm and robust covering.

The Court has consistently indicated that there are "only a few specifically established and well-delineated exceptions."[2] But at least one Supreme Court justice (and many commentators) have suggested that the exceptions to the warrant requirement are "legion." The two views can be reconciled by understanding the **categories** of exceptions, rather than considering the **particular facts** of each case in which an exception has been applied: it is true that there are only six specific categories, but many of them are broadly applicable to vast amounts of police conduct.

To aid in your memorization of the categories, we have adopted the mnemonic S-P-A-C-E-S. S-P-A-C-E-S stands for the six exceptions to the warrant requirement that the Court has recognized and named. They are 1) Search Incident to a Lawful Arrest; 2) Plain View; 3) Automobiles; 4) Consent; 5) Exigent Circumstances; and 6) Special Needs. Over the course of the next six chapters, we will analyze the policy underlying each of these exceptions and the specific rules that define them. First, let's examine a brief description of each exception and the scope of warrantless police conduct that it permits:

Named Exception	Brief Description	Scope
Search Incident to a Lawful Arrest	Once the police have lawfully arrested a suspect, they may search to find weapons or to prevent the destruction of evidence. If an arrestee was the recent occupant of a car, the search is also justified by a desire to find evidence of the crime of arrest.	The search may encompass the arrestee, any containers on her person, any items under her control, and any area into which the arrestee might reach to secure a weapon or destroy evidence ("wingspan"); in cars, area of search includes entire passenger compartment.
Plain View	If the police observe immediately apparent contraband from a lawful vantage point, and they have lawful access to the item, they may search or seize it.	Once lawfulness of the search is establish, the police may engage in a thorough exploration of the item in plain view.

[2] Katz v. United States, 389 U.S. 347, 357 (1967).

Automobile	When the police have probable cause to believe an automobile contains contraband, they may search it.	The entire car may be searched, including any containers contained therein that might conceal the object of the search. If probable cause attaches only to a single container in the car, only that container may be searched.
Consent	If an individual with actual or apparent authority to consent grants permission, the police may conduct a warrantless search.	If express limitations to the consent are provided, those limitations govern. If no express constraints were provided, the search is limited to a reasonably objective understanding of what the speaker authorized.
Exigent Circumstances	Where the police have especially pressing or urgent needs that rise to the level of "exigency," they may search or seize without a warrant.	The search may not exceed the bounds of the exigency. Items in "plain view," however, may be seized.
Special Needs	When the police act with a primary purpose other than general law enforcement, the warrant requirement will not apply.	The scope of special needs searches varies depending upon the special need being advanced.

In thinking through the validity of government action, you should first ask yourself whether the challenged conduct is even governed by the Fourth Amendment—was there government action, and did the complaining party have a reasonable expectation of privacy in the area or item searched or seized. If the answer to this inquiry is yes, you should next consider whether the police conduct was "reasonable" within the meaning of the Fourth Amendment.

The easiest way for police conduct to be deemed reasonable is if it was authorized by a validly executed warrant. However, the six exceptions to the warrant requirement that you will explore over the next several chapters provide an alternate route to legitimacy. If warrantless conduct is permitted by one of the six exceptions, the Fourth Amendment's command of reasonableness will be satisfied, so long as officers limit their conduct to the scope authorized by the relevant exception.

Though the exceptions to the warrant requirement were all borne out of divergent factual scenarios, what they have in common is the Court's sense that imposing a warrant requirement in these six instances would unduly hamper law enforcement without significantly advancing the rights protected by the Fourth Amendment. For example, requiring a warrant for the search or seizure of items of contraband in plain view would not substantially advance privacy interests, but would significantly undercut law enforcement's ability to prevent crime. To evoke our earlier analogy, the warrant requirement in this context offers only minimal protection—covering a heel, not a torso—and so allowing plain view items to be searched or seized without a warrant is not a terribly significant hole in the blanket of constitutional protection previously afforded.

Another feature shared by many of the exceptions is some sense of a need for prompt action. Thus, for example, automobile searches, searches incident to a lawful arrest, and exigent circumstances searches all share the notion that delayed police action will be less productive police action.

Many commentators have suggested that the exceptions to the warrant requirement have been interpreted too broadly. Thus, the automobile exception, which was first recognized in connection with a car in transit, has been expanded to include cars which are held in police custody. Similarly, the search incident to a lawful arrest, which was originally recognized in the dynamic arrest situation to avoid harm to officers and evidence, has been expanded to include searches even after an arrestee is completely subdued. The Court's expansive reading of warrant exceptions has caused some to question whether the Court is fully committed to a warrant requirement at all. However, while the policy debates rage about the advisability and the future viability of the warrant requirement, for the time being the Court has indicated that it is an integral part of Fourth Amendment protection. As you study the coming chapters, you should therefore understand the exceptions to the warrant requirement as just that: exceptions to a broader rule that acknowledges the importance of interposing a neutral and detached magistrate between the citizenry and the police.

13

Exceptions to the Warrant Requirement: Search Incident to a Lawful Arrest

Key Concepts

- Officer Safety and Preservation of Evidence
- "Wingspan" Rule
- Special Rules for Arrests of Car Occupants

A. Introduction and Policy. Recall that the exceptions to the warrant requirement can be remembered with the mnemonic S-P-A-C-E-S. The first exception—the "S" in "SPACES"—represents an exception known as a search incident to a lawful arrest.

This exception has long been recognized in both English and American law. Such a search encompasses the person of the arrestee, any containers that she is carrying, and her immediate surroundings. However, it must be "incident to" the arrest—that is, it must be, contemporaneous with the arrest and conducted in a location that is not too far removed from the location of the arrest.

Why do we make an exception to the warrant requirement in this context? The courts have offered a number of different rationales. First, an officer making a lawful arrest already has probable cause to believe that the suspect has committed a crime, and so there is a good chance that evidence of that crime may be found on or near the person at the time of the arrest. Of course, in theory the arresting officer could detain the arrestee at the place of arrest immediately after the arrest and send another officer to obtain a warrant. But in reality that would be a very impractical (and potentially dangerous) procedure. Second, the arrestee may have a weapon or some other item which he could use to injure the officer and/or facilitate his escape from custody. And finally, an individual who has just been arrested has a lessened privacy interest. Thus, the intrusion is considered not as great as if the warrantless search were being conducted on an average citizen.

This search incident to a lawful arrest doctrine (sometimes referred to as the "SILA" doctrine) has a lengthy and well-established pedigree. As early as 1914 in *Weeks v. United States*, the Supreme Court unhesitatingly acknowledged "the right on the part of the Government, always recognized under English and American law, to search **the person** of the accused when legally arrested to discover and seize the fruits or evidences of crime."[1] The exception thus permits a full and thorough in-the-field search of the arrestee's person, including any containers found on the arrestee.[2]

Given the rationale behind the rule, it makes sense for the rule to encompass not just the items that are carried by the arrestee, but also any items that she may be able to access. Thus, eleven years after *Weeks*, the Court in *Carroll v. United States* broadened the doctrine's reach to include not just the arrestee and containers found on her, but also any items within the arrestee's control.[3]

B. The Law. A search incident to a lawful arrest is an exception to the Warrant Requirement. As you have read, this means that though warrantless searches are generally disfavored by the Constitution, they are allowed if the circumstances of the warrantless search indicate that it was associated with a legitimate arrest:

> When a law enforcement officer performs a lawful arrest of an individual, the officer may conduct a contemporaneous search of:
>
> 1. The arrestee's person;
> 2. Containers found on the arrestee;
> 3. Items within the arrestee's control; and
> 4. The physical space around the arrestee.

The first three of these areas are fairly self-explanatory and have, consequently, been little examined by the Court following their initial sanction. However, the same has not been true for the fourth—the physical space around the arrestee. As you will read in Section C below, the Court has given considerable thought to just how big the searchable area around the arrestee should be. Under current law, the police are allowed to search the area within the arrestee's reach or "wingspan."

The search incident to a lawful arrest exception has two other critical elements. The first requires, as the name suggests, that the search must be an "incident of" or "incidental to" an arrest. This means that the search must flow from and be reasonably associated with the arrest itself. The first constraint this element imposes is temporal. For example, the warrantless search of an arrestee occurring seven days after arrest would not be "incident to" the arrest. Consequently, though some other exception may justify a warrantless search delayed by a week,

---

1 Weeks v. United States, 232 U.S. 383, 392 (1914).
2 United States v. Robinson, 414 U.S. 218 (1973).
3 Carroll v. United States, 267 U.S. 132, 158 (1925).

such a search would not be permissible under the search incident to a lawful arrest exception. In addition to placing temporal limits on the search, the "incident to" requirement also places spatial constraints on the search. As the Court has said, "[o]nce an accused is under arrest and in custody, then a search made at another place, without a warrant, is simply not incident to the arrest."[4] We will explore in the next section just how far removed the search may be.

The second element suggested by the exception's label—search incident to a **lawful arrest**—is that the exception only applies if there is a "lawful arrest."[5] Thus, if a person is briefly detained for reasonable suspicion (see **Chapters 9 and 19**), but not arrested, a full warrantless search of that person cannot be justified as a search incident to a lawful arrest. Similarly, if the arrest is invalid (for example, because the police did not have probable cause) the subsequent search of the arrestee cannot be excused as a search incident to a lawful arrest.

A related proposition is also true. Not only is a lawful arrest necessary for application of the exception, in large measure it is also sufficient. The authority to search pursuant to the exception flows directly and completely from the fact of the arrest itself.[6] Consequently, though you read above about the original justifications for the exception—officer safety, hindrance of escape, and preservation of evidence—it has long been recognized that the prosecution is not required to prove the existence of any one of these justifications before application of the exception will be adopted in any particular case. Instead, the prosecution need only demonstrate the lawfulness of the arrest. "Since it is the fact of custodial arrest which gives rise to the authority to search, it is of no moment that [an officer] did not indicate any subjective fear of the [arrestee] or that he did not himself suspect [the arrestee] was armed."[7] In fact, the Court has found that a formal arrest based on probable cause will insulate a warrantless search conducted incident to that arrest even if that search violates state law.[8]

A search incident to a lawful arrest may also include the passenger compartment of a car if the arrestee is a recent occupant of the vehicle. Known as the *Belton* doctrine, this rule was originally understood to provide officers with virtually limitless authority to search cars whenever they arrested a recent occupant. However, the Court recently created a significant limitation to the *Belton* doctrine: If the arrestee has been secured (*i.e.*, handcuffed or otherwise brought under police control), officers do not have automatic authority to search the interior of the

---

[4] Preston v. United States, 376 U.S. 364, 367 (1964).

[5] Knowles v. Iowa, 525 U.S. 113 (1998); but see Cupp v. Murphy, 412 U.S. 291 (1973) (finding that the search incident to a lawful arrest rationale allowed the police to conduct a "limited" search consisting of scraping under the suspect's fingernails where the suspect was temporarily detained at the stationhouse upon probable cause to believe he had committed a murder).

[6] Gustafson v. Florida, 414 U.S. 260 (1973).

[7] United States v. Robinson, 414 U.S. 218, 236 (1973).

[8] Virginia v. Moore, 553 U.S. 164 (2008).

car. Instead, the police officers must be able to demonstrate either an actual and continuing threat to their safety, or a reasonable belief that evidence related to the crime of arrest is present in the vehicle.

This recent modification of the search incident to a lawful arrest exception has raised interesting questions regarding the prosecutor's burden to establish justification for such searches. These questions are explored in greater detail in Section D below.

C. Applying the Law. The search incident to a lawful arrest exception has received repeated scrutiny from the Supreme Court. Notwithstanding the Court's continued examination, current doctrine is largely consistent with its beginnings. For example, the exception remains applicable only to contemporaneous searches that are not too distant in time or location from the arrest. Similarly, the spatial limits on the search, though somewhat tumultuous in their development and currently broader than originally articulated by the Court, have now found an equilibrium that is logically related to the exception's origins.

Like many other aspects of the Fourth Amendment, the search incident to a lawful arrest exception certainly faced the pressure to answer the needs of law enforcement. This pressure caused some significant expansion of the doctrine in the 1980s and 1990s, a period in which the doctrine was interpreted expansively when applied to searches incident to the arrest of a recent occupant of a vehicle. However, early in the 21st century the Court curtailed this expansion, imposing limits that largely advance the exception's original justifications. As you will read in Part C.6, below, we are at the beginning of another period of reevaluation as the Court considers the reach of the exception in the face of portable technology.

1. Right to Search Incident to Lawful Arrest is Automatic. Although the SILA doctrine's original justifications were to protect officers, prevent escape, and prevent destruction of evidence, the Supreme Court has broadened the power over the years to the point where the right to search incident to an arrest is automatic, even if it does not fulfill any of the doctrine's original purposes:

> **Example—*United States v. Robinson,* 414 U.S. 218 (1973):** Officer Richard Jenks saw Willie Robinson driving late one evening near 8th and C Streets in northeast Washington, D.C. Based on prior contacts with Robinson, the officer had probable cause to believe that he was driving on a revoked driver's license, which was an arrestable offense. Accordingly, he pulled Robinson over and placed him under arrest. Following the arrest, Officer Jenks searched Robinson. During a pat-down of the front of Robinson's body, Jenks felt something in the left breast

pocket of Robinson's coat. Jenks reached into the pocket and retrieved a crumpled cigarette pack. He manipulated the pack and felt objects inside. He did not know what they were, so he opened the pack and found fourteen gel capsules of heroin. Robinson was ultimately convicted of possessing the heroin and he appealed his case to the Supreme Court.

Analysis: The Supreme Court approved the warrantless search of Robinson as a search incident to a lawful arrest. Robinson had argued that the search could not be justified as a search incident to an arrest because (1) the officer had no reason to believe that the crumpled cigarette pack contained a weapon or an item to help Robinson escape; and (2) Robinson had been arrested for driving with a suspended license, and there was no reason for the officer to believe that he would find further evidence of that crime inside the cigarette pack. The Supreme Court held that "the fact of the lawful arrest [alone] establishes the authority to search,"[9] and that no further showing is necessary to justify the search.

This "automatic" right to conduct a search incident to a lawful arrest has been weakened ever so slightly in the context of searches of automobiles incident to an arrest (see Section 3, below), but otherwise it is still good law.

2. Limits on Geographic Range of Search: Generally. As you have read, the Court in *Weeks* and *Carroll* expanded the scope of the search incident exception beyond the arrestee's person to include items within the arrestee's "control." A few years later, in *United States v. Agnello,* the Court stated in dictum that the search incident exception also allowed the police to search the "place" of arrest.[10] In the years after *Agnello*, the Court struggled to identify the appropriate boundaries of *Agnello*'s "place" expansion. At first the Court suggested that the exception authorized search of an area that included the entire house or office space in which the arrest occurred.[11] However, through a whip-sawing development of the doctrine, this wide-ranging interpretation was ultimately rejected.[12] The search incident to a lawful arrest doctrine as currently interpreted applies to the area immediately surrounding the arrestee "from within which he might gain possession of a weapon or destructible evidence."[13] Put somewhat differently, this area might be understood to include any area the arrestee can readily access.

---

[9] United States v. Robinson, 414 U.S. 218, 235 (1978).

[10] Agnello v. United States, 269 U.S. 20 (1925).

[11] See, e.g., Marron v. United States, 275 U.S. 192 (1927). Consider also Harris v. United States, 331 U.S. 145 (1947) and United States v. Rabinowitz, 339 U.S. 56 (1950), which were both overturned by Chimel v. California, 395 U.S. 752 (1969).

[12] See, e.g., United States v. Lefkowitz, 285 U.S. 452; Trupiano v. United States, 334 U.S. 699 (1948).

[13] Chimel v. California, 395 U.S. 752, 763 (1969).

As a matter of common sense, this rule of "ready access" when applied to someone arrested on the street would not permit the warrantless search of a suitcase in the playground three doors down or a duffel bag stashed under a mailbox on the corner across the street (though there may be other justifications for such searches). When a person is arrested inside of a home, however, the lines of demarcation become a bit fuzzier. Does the area from which she might gain possession of a gun include the entire home? Does it include only the room in which the arrestee is standing? Should different rules apply depending upon whether the arrest occurs in a one-bedroom apartment or a twenty-room mansion? The Court answered these questions in its review of the search of Ted Chimel's three-bedroom home:

Example—*Chimel v. United States*, 395 U.S. 752 (1968): Police officers in Santa Ana, California obtained an arrest warrant for Ted Chimel in connection with the burglary of a local coin shop. When the officers arrived at Chimel's house, his wife let them in. Chimel returned home from work approximately fifteen minutes later. The officers immediately placed him under arrest. They then asked Chimel if they could search the residence. He told them they could not.

The officers ignored Chimel's refusal, advising him that a search of the home was permitted incident to his arrest. Thereafter, the officers had Mrs. Chimel walk them around the three-bedroom home. For approximately the next forty-five minutes, the officers searched the entire house including the attic, a small workshop, and the garage. In the master bedroom and the sewing room, the officers ordered Mrs. Chimel to open drawers and move things around. During the search, the officers found a number of items that were later introduced as evidence in the burglary prosecution.

At trial, Chimel objected to the admission of the evidence. He argued that the search of his home infringed the Fourth Amendment's ban on unreasonable searches. However, the California courts reviewing the case found that the search of the home fell squarely within the search incident to a lawful arrest exception to the warrant requirement. Four years after Chimel's conviction, the Supreme Court took up the dispute.

Analysis: The search of Chimel's home was not justified as an incident of his arrest. The search incident to a lawful arrest exception to the warrant requirement is validated by just three aims—preventing harm to the arresting officer; preventing escape; and preventing the destruction of evidence. These justifications make it entirely reasonable to permit the search of areas from which the arrestee might actually gain possession of a weapon or evidence. However, these rationales do not justify roving searches that include "any room other than that in which an arrest occurs—or, for that matter, for searching through all the desk drawers or other closed or concealed areas in that room itself."[14]

These identified contours of the search incident exception are unaffected by the size of the dwelling in which the arrest occurs. Whether the arrest occurs in a one-room hovel or a palatial manor, the permissible zone of police exploration is confined to the area within the arrestee's reach. The search of Chimel's house extended far beyond this permissible zone and was thereby unconstitutional.

Following *Chimel*, the searchable zone incident to an arrest was understood to include the area surrounding the arrestee and any containers in the area that the arrestee might access at the time of the arrest. The *Chimel* doctrine is sometimes referred to as the "wingspan" doctrine because it authorizes a search of the area within the arrestee's grasp or "wingspan." Consistent with its defined contours, the area does not extend outside the home when the arrest occurs inside;[15] and does not extend inside the home when the arrest occurs outside.[16]

3. Limits on Geographic Range of Search: Cars. In addition to homes and other buildings, the Court has also considered the spatial limits of a search incident to a lawful arrest when the exception is applied to the arrest of a car's recent occupant. Theoretically, such a search could be limited any number of ways. For example, consistent with *Chimel*, the searchable area might be thought to "float" around the arrestee, and thus, to turn on whether the arrestee is still inside the car at the time of the search. Also consistent with *Chimel*, one could envision the limits as being confined to just that area of the car from which the arrestee was seized. Alternatively, consistent with *Agnello*, the permissible area of search might be thought to include the car's entire interior. Recognizing that a clear rule had been established by *Robinson* in connection with the search of a person incident to a lawful arrest, the Court in *Belton* set out to create similar clarity for the search of cars pursuant to the exception:

> **Example—*New York v. Belton*, 453 U.S. 454 (1981):** A state trooper was driving an unmarked car on the New York Thruway when a car sped past him. The officer chased the car down and pulled it over. There were four men in the car. After asking for the driver's license and registration, the officer noticed an odor of burnt marijuana coming from the car. He also saw an envelope on the floor of the car marked "Supergold," a packaging he

[14] Chimel v. California, 395 U.S. 752 (1969).

[15] Coolidge v. New Hampshire, 403 U.S. 443, 456–57 (1971).

[16] Vale v. Louisiana, 399 U.S. 30, 35 (1970).

associated with marijuana. The officer ordered all four men out of the car and placed them under arrest. None of the men were handcuffed, but he separated them along the side of the roadway. He then searched the backseat of the car.

On the backseat of the car, the officer found Belton's black leather jacket. The officer unzipped a pocket on the jacket and retrieved cocaine. Belton was charged and convicted of drug offenses. He challenged the search of his jacket, arguing that it did not fall within the scope of a search incident to his lawful arrest because he had no access to it.

Analysis: The search of Belton's jacket was entirely lawful.

The Court's decision in *Chimel* recognized the space that is searchable incident to a lawful arrest includes any areas within the immediate control of the arrestee. The passenger compartment of a car is a fairly confined area. Even if it is not a foregone conclusion the area will be accessed by an arrestee, it is possible. Consequently, it is appropriate to assume "that articles inside the relatively narrow compass of the passenger compartment of an automobile are in fact generally, even if not inevitably, within 'the area into which an arrestee might reach in order to grab a weapon or evidentiary item.'"[17] Under the authority of *Chimel*, the entire passenger compartment of the car may therefore be searched incident to the arrest of one of the car's occupants.

Furthermore, the permissible search area includes all containers. Consequently, the search may include the glove compartment and consoles, and any luggage, boxes, bags, or clothing. The permissible search area does not, however, include the trunk.

Though the majority in *Belton* described its rule as squarely within the *Chimel* doctrine, the dissenters complained that the holding in fact constituted a vast broadening of *Chimel*'s authority. In the dissenters' view, *Belton* approved a new "area search" incident to lawful arrest even though, on the facts before it (and presumably on the facts of many cases yet to come) there was no chance the arrestee could have accessed the area: "In its attempt to formulate a 'single, familiar standard' to guide police officers . . . the Court today disregards [*Chimel*'s] principles, and instead adopts a fiction—that the interior of a car is **always** within the immediate control of an arrestee who has recently been in the car."[18] The dissenters warned that the *Belton* rule was a "dangerous precedent" that was unconstrained by the justifications underlying creation of the search incident to a lawful arrest exception.[19]

---

[17] New York v. Belton, 453 U.S. 454, 460 (1981).

[18] Id. at 466 (Brennan, J., dissenting) (emphasis in original).

[19] Id. at 468.

In the years following the *Belton* decision, the dissenters' concerns were realized. *Belton* could have been interpreted narrowly, allowing a car search incident to an arrest when (and only when) a recent occupant has been arrested and was still within reaching distance of the car. The rule, however, came to be understood much more comprehensively: It effectively created a prerogative of the police, unrelated to conditions at the time of the search, to search a car whenever someone who had been in the car was arrested. Searches of an arrestee's vehicles were approved in cases involving only the most strained concern for officer safety or evidence destruction. For example, the *Belton* doctrine was cited to support a car search even though the police did not make contact with the arrestee until he was walking away from the vehicle.[20] It was also cited to support the search of a car parked outside of an auto repair shop even though the driver of the car was arrested inside the establishment.[21] The case was cited to support a car search after the arrestee was transported from the scene.[22] And, in Justice Scalia's words, the number of cases involving car searches after the arrestee was handcuffed and sitting in the back of a police car "are legion."[23]

Describing the post-*Belton* state of affairs, Justice O'Connor wrote, "lower court decisions seem now to treat the ability to search a vehicle incident to the arrest of a recent occupant as a police entitlement rather than as an exception justified by the twin rationales of *Chimel*."[24] In 2009, responding to calls from "courts, scholars, and Members of this Court who have questioned [*Belton*'s] clarity and its fidelity to Fourth Amendment principles," the Court set out to restore balance to the SILA exception as applied to cars[25]:

> **Example—*Arizona v. Gant*, 556 U.S. 332 (2009):** Police received an anonymous tip that drugs were being sold out of a residence in Tucson, Arizona. Officers visited the residence and asked to speak with the owner. Rodney Gant, who answered the door, told the officers the owner would be back shortly. The officers left. They also conducted a records check and determined that Rodney Gant had a suspended license and an outstanding arrest warrant for driving on a suspended license.
>
> The officers returned to the house later in the evening. They arrested a man in the back of the house (for providing a false name), and a woman parked in front of the house (for possession of drug paraphernalia). Gant then pulled into the driveway.

[20] Thornton v. United States, 541 U.S. 615 (2004).

[21] Black v. State, 810 N.E.2d 713, 716 (Ind. 2004).

[22] United States v. McLaughlin, 170 F.3d 889 (9th Cir. 1999).

[23] Thornton, 541 U.S. at 628 (Scalia, J., concurring in judgment).

[24] Id. at 614 (O'Connor, J., concurring in part).

[25] Arizona v. Gant, 556 U.S. 332, 338 (2009).

Gant got out of his car, shut the door and had walked ten to twelve feet away from the vehicle when he was arrested. The police handcuffed Gant and locked him in the back of a patrol car. After Gant was secured, the officers searched his car and recovered a gun and a bag of cocaine. When asked why they had searched Gant's car, one of the officers testified, "Because the law says we can do it."

Following conviction, and a somewhat meandering course through the state courts, Gant's case arrived in the Supreme Court. The state argued that *Belton* clearly authorized the search. Gant argued that the evidence was unlawfully obtained.

Analysis: The search of Gant's car was unconstitutional.

The search incident to a lawful arrest exception is defined by *Chimel* when applied to searches of places. In *Chimel*, the Court explained that permissible area of search was defined by the arrestee's "reaching distance." This boundary appropriately recognized and was driven by concerns for officer safety and evidence destruction. *Belton* simply applied *Chimel* to the context of car searches. Consequently, the decision in *Belton* is circumscribed by *Chimel*'s twin rationales: "If there is no possibility that an arrestee could reach into the area that law enforcement officers seek to search, both justifications for the search incident to arrest exception are absent and the rule does not apply."[26]

As a practical matter, this limitation means that searches of vehicles incident to an occupant's arrest are authorized under *Chimel* and *Belton* only if the arrestee is "unsecured and within reaching distance of the passenger compartment at the time of the search." Understanding *Belton* any more broadly "would serve no purpose except to provide a police entitlement, and it is anathema to the Fourth Amendment to permit a warrantless search on that basis."[27]

The justifications for the search incident exception that were recognized in *Chimel* were not, however, the only justifications for the doctrine. The twin rationales of officer safety and evidence preservation justify the search incident exception in all arrest contexts. But, a third rationale for the exception exists in the specific context of vehicles: "[W]hen it is reasonable to believe evidence relevant to the crime of arrest might be found in the vehicle,"[28] a third justification for a search incident to the arrest of a recent occupant exists.

In Gant's case, he was secured in the back of a police car at the time his own car was searched. The twin rationales of *Chimel*, therefore, could not justify the search. Furthermore, he was arrested for a traffic violation: "Gant was arrested for driving

[26] Id. at 339.

[27] Id. at 347.

[28] Id. at 343.

with a suspended license—an offense for which police could not expect to find evidence in the passenger compartment of Gant's car."[29] The alternative rationale for a search incident in the vehicle context—the likelihood of discovering offense-related evidence—therefore also provided no justification for the search.

As commentators have recognized, the modified framework advanced in *Gant* provided both substantial limitation, and significant expansion of the search incident doctrine. The limitation, as noted, reigned in the broad reach of *Belton* by restoring the twin justifications of *Chimel* in the context of searches of cars incident to arrest—evidence preservation and officer safety. A search of an arrestee who had been subdued by police was not supported by either of these rationales. However, the *Gant* Court did not stop there. It also found that the search incident doctrine (at least in the context of a car search) could also be justified by a desire to locate evidence of the crime of arrest. Previously, such warrantless evidentiary explorations had been recognized only under the automobile exception to the warrant requirement, which required probable cause. The *Gant* Court's "reasonable belief" language did not appear to require probable cause—indeed, the Court noted that the warrantless search it was recognizing was something other than the search already authorized by the automobile exception. In this regard then, *Gant* broadened the search incident exception by applying it in an entirely new context.

Application of the search incident to a lawful arrest exception in this context can cause great confusion for students. This is because the warrantless search of cars is authorized not only by the search incident exception, but also by its own discrete exception to the warrant requirement. This second exception—the "A" in SPACES—is the automobile exception. As you will read in **Chapter 15**, the automobile exception allows the police to search a car whenever officers have probable cause to believe the vehicle contains evidence of criminal activity. Students must be careful to note the significant differences between the automobile exception on the one hand, and the search of a car conducted pursuant to the search incident to a lawful arrest exception, on the other.

First, when a car is searched pursuant to the search incident to a lawful arrest exception, the suspicion justifying the search attaches primarily to the **person** not to the **car**. Under this exception, the car is permissibly searched because the person arrested was a recent occupant. Absent probable cause to arrest (and the actual arrest of) a recent occupant, the search of the car is not permitted pursuant to the search incident exception.

In contrast, with the automobile exception, the suspicion justifying the search attaches to the **car**. The car is permissibly searched under that exception because the police have probable cause to believe the **car** contains evidence of criminal activity. In applying the automobile exception, it consequently matters little whether the police actually arrest any of the car's occupants.

---

[29] Id. at 344.

As the Court explained in *Gant*, a second difference is that whenever a car search is justified by the "reasonable belief" justification for a search incident, the reasonable belief must be as to the existence of evidence of **the crime of arrest**. As the Court noted, "[i]n many cases, as when a recent occupant is arrested for a traffic violation, there will be no reasonable basis to believe the vehicle contains relevant evidence."[30] (Note that the search of the **person** incident to a lawful arrest need not be tied to the crime of the arrest, as noted in the *Robinson* case; only the search of a **car** incident to a lawful arrest).

No similar constraint binds the automobile exception. Assuming the existence of probable cause, that exception permits a search of the car for evidence relevant to any offense.

A third difference between the two types of searches regards the permissible area of exploration. As we have seen, the search incident to lawful arrest exception only allows the search of the passenger compartment of the car. Under the automobile exception, the entire car is the approved target (including the trunk).

4. Limits on Timing of Search. In addition to enjoying a limited geography, the search incident to a lawful arrest exception also is cabined by temporal constraints:

> **Example—*United States v. Chadwick*, 433 U.S. 1 (1977):** Gregory Machado and Bridget Leary boarded a train from San Diego to Boston. The two brought with them a large footlocker. Train personnel in San Diego noted that the trunk appeared heavy for its size. They also noted that the trunk was leaking talcum powder, a substance often used to mask the scent of marijuana. Train officials notified law enforcement in San Diego, who in turn notified their counterparts in Boston.
>
> When the train arrived in Boston, drug enforcement agents were waiting with a drug detection dog. They did not, however, have a warrant. After Machado and Leary unloaded the trunk they placed it on the floor of the station and sat down on it. The agents released the dog. Unnoticed by Machado and Leary, the dog signaled for the presence of marijuana.
>
> When Chadwick arrived, the three loaded the footlocker in to the trunk of Chadwick's waiting car. While the trunk was still open, and before the car was started, the agents arrested all three and seized the footlocker. The suspects and the evidence were transported to the Federal Building in Boston. Approximately

[30] Gant, 556 U.S. at 343.

an hour and a half after the arrests, the agents finally opened the footlocker. Marijuana was found inside.

At trial, Chadwick and the others objected to the admission of the evidence. They objected to the search, which was removed both in time and in distance from the scene of the original arrests. The State argued that the search of the footlocker was constitutional because the footlocker was seized at the time of the arrests, and was searched as soon after the arrests as was practicable.

Analysis: The search of the footlocker could not be justified as a proper search incident to a lawful arrest. Searches incident to a lawful arrest are motivated by the desire to protect evidence and advance officer safety. In keeping with these justifications, the arrestee and any area within the arrestee's immediate reach may be searched incident to the arrest. However, the search of luggage that can no longer be accessed by the arrestee is not permissibly included within the scope of such a search:

"Once law enforcement officers have reduced luggage and other personal property not immediately associated with the person of the arrestee to their exclusive control, and there is no longer any danger that the arrestee might gain access to the property to seize a weapon or destroy evidence, a search of that property is no longer an incident of the arrest."[31]

Where the search was conducted more than an hour after the footlocker had been reduced to the exclusive control of the agents, the Court found the warrantless search of Chadwick's footlocker was unconstitutional.

The amount of time that the police are allowed to delay the search after the arrest depends on the circumstances, though usually the search must be contemporaneous. In *Chadwick*, there was no reason for the one-hour delay after the agents gained control of the footlocker. However, if there is a legitimate reason to delay the search, the court may allow a one hour delay or even a longer delay. In a case which probably represents the outer limits of this rule, the Supreme Court held that a delay of ten hours did not invalidate a search incident to an arrest. The police were investigating a break-in at the local post office, and the perpetrator's forced entry had left paint chips on the window sill and on the window's mesh cover. Ten hours after the police arrested a suspect, they seized his clothing and found paint chips matching the evidence at the scene. The Court held that this seizure was lawful because the delay was occasioned in part by the fact that substitute clothing was not available until the next morning. Under these circumstances, the Court agreed that "[w]hile the legal arrest of a person should

[31] United States v. Chadwick, 433 U.S. 1, 15 (1977).

not destroy the privacy of his premises, it does—for at least a reasonable time and to a reasonable extent—take his own privacy out of the realm of protection from police interest in weapons, means of escape and evidence."[32]

5. Must Be a "Lawful Arrest." As the name of the exception implies, the police cannot conduct a search incident to an arrest unless they actually make an arrest. This is true even if they had the legal right to make an arrest but chose not to do so:

> **Example—*Knowles v. Iowa*, 525 U.S. 113 (1998):** Patrick Knowles was stopped for driving 43 miles-per-hour in a 25 miles-per-hour zone. Under Iowa law, the officer who stopped Knowles could either arrest Knowles or issue a citation. The officer chose the latter. Nonetheless, the officer also conducted a full search of Knowles' car under an Iowa statute that permitted such in-the-field searches whenever the authority to arrest existed. The officer found marijuana and a pipe. Knowles was convicted of the drug offense, and he challenged the search.

Analysis: The Supreme Court found the search of Knowles' car could not be justified under the search incident doctrine because Knowles was only issued a citation: "[W]hile the concern for officer safety in this context may justify the 'minimal' additional intrusion of ordering a driver and passengers out of the car, it does not by itself justify the often considerably greater intrusion attending a full field-type search."[33]

Students should note that the Court has provided somewhat conflicting guidance with regard to the formal arrest requirement. In at least one case, the Court found that the formal detention of a person at the stationhouse upon probable cause (even though not resulting in an actual arrest) was sufficient to justify a limited warrantless search under the search incident to a lawful arrest exception. However, the specifics of that case were unique, and the Court has yet to apply the holding beyond its facts:

> **Example—*Cupp v. Murphy*, 412 U.S. 291 (1973):** In *Murphy*, the Court allowed the limited search of a suspect even though he had not been formally arrested. Daniel Murphy was suspected of his estranged wife's murder. When notified of the killing by police, Murphy agreed to come to the station to give a statement. An officer at the police station noticed Murphy had a dark stain under his thumbnail that the officer suspected was blood. When the stain was drawn to Murphy's attention, he first placed his hands

[32] United States v. Edwards, 415 U.S. 800, 809 (1974).

[33] Knowles v. Iowa, 525 U.S. 113, 117 (1998).

behind his back, and then placed his hand in his pocket, where officers heard the sound of his keys rattling. Police forcibly took fingernail scrapings from Murphy in an effort to obtain evidence of the crime. The scrapings revealed trace amounts of Mrs. Murphy's skin and blood, as well as fabric from her nightgown. Murphy challenged the warrantless search, arguing that it was not justified by an exception to the warrant requirement.

Analysis: The Supreme Court found that the warrantless seizure of the fingernail scrapings was justified by the search incident exception, even though Murphy had not been officially arrested. The police had probable cause to arrest Murphy when he arrived at the station. There was also no question that Murphy was detained against his will at the station for the period necessary to collect the scrapings. The Court found that under these circumstances, the search incident exception applied: "On the fact of this case, considering the existence of probable cause, the very limited intrusion undertaken incident to the stationhouse detention, and the ready destructibility of the evidence, we cannot say that this search violated the Fourth and Fourteenth Amendments."[34]

Beyond the unique circumstances found in *Murphy*, however, students should apply the general rule that a formal arrest is a necessary prerequisite to proper application of the search incident exception.

6. Searching Cell Phones and Other Digital Evidence. As we have seen, the search incident to a lawful arrest doctrine was originally motivated by dual concerns for officer safety and evidence preservation. Early on the Court found that these dual concerns justified the expansion of SILA searches to encompass physical containers on the arrestee's person, such as the cigarette package at issue in *Robinson*. In more recent years, lower courts relied on *Robinson* to allow searches of address books,[35] wallets,[36] purses,[37] and many other types of "containers," provided those searches were incident to a lawful arrest.

New questions arose, however, with the growing popularity of cell phones in the early 21st century. Individuals began carrying around digital "containers" that held vastly more information than would have been physically possible before. When a suspect carrying a cell phone was arrested, the arresting officer would frequently conduct an on-the-spot, warrantless search through the suspect's phone, examining her call log, contact list, address book, date book, browsing history, texts, photos, videos, and anything else that the officer thought might provide

[34] Cupp v. Murphy, 412 U.S. 291, 296 (1973).

[35] United States v. Carrion, 809 F.2d 1120 (5th Cir. 1987).

[36] United States v. Watson, 669 F.2d 1374 (11th Cir. 1982).

[37] United States v. Lee, 501 F.2d 890 (D.C. Cir. 1974).

useful information about criminal activity. The lower courts were split on the constitutionality of such searches. Some courts treated cellphones and other such devices like the cigarette package in *Robinson* and allowed the searches. Other courts, however, found that cellphones and other digital devices constituted a *sui generis* category that justified an altogether different legal rule. The case ultimately reached the United States Supreme Court:

> **Example—*Riley v. California*, 134 S.Ct. 2473 (2014):** Police officers pulled over David Riley for driving with expired registration tags, and ultimately arrested him for driving with a suspended license. During the search incident to the arrest, an officer found a cell phone in Riley's pocket. The officer looked through the text messages and contact lists and saw incriminating information linking Riley to the Bloods street gang. Later at the precinct, another officer searched through the entire phone and found videos connecting Riley to the Bloods gang as well as photos that connected him to a shooting. Riley was ultimately charged with the shooting, and the prosecutor offered some of the evidence from his cell phone against him at trial. Riley moved to suppress the evidence, but the court ruled that the evidence was properly obtained as part of a search incident to an arrest. Riley was convicted, and he appealed the issue all the way to the Supreme Court.
>
> In the companion case, a police officer saw Brima Wurie engage in what he believed to be a drug sale. The officer arrested Wurie and transported him to the station. At the station, officers seized Wurie's cellphone. As Wurie was being processed, the officers noticed that his phone kept receiving incoming calls from a caller identified as "my house." Searching through the phone's internal directory, the officers identified the phone number associated with the "my house" label. They then tracked the number to a physical address. They ultimately searched the property and found drugs, drug paraphernalia and weapons. Wurie moved to suppress this evidence as the fruit of the illegal search of his telephone. The district court denied the motion, and Wurie was convicted. Wurie appealed the issue, and it arrived in the Supreme Court along with Riley's case.

Analysis: The Supreme Court unanimously ruled that the searches of Riley and Wurie's phones were unconstitutional. The Court conceded that *Robinson* gave police the automatic right during an arrest to search inside any container for evidence or weapons, even if there was no reason to believe there were any evidence or weapons inside. However, the Court held that cell phones—and digital evidence more broadly—are fundamentally different from physical evidence that a suspect may be carrying on his person.

First, the Court noted that the reasons underlying the search incident to lawful arrest doctrine did not apply with the same force to digital evidence. There is no real way the information inside a cell phone could present a danger to the officer. Accordingly, there can be no justification for a search of such devices based on officer safety. The government had argued that the danger of destruction of evidence was greater with cell phones than with physical evidence, since an accomplice could erase the data on the phone with a remote signal using a technique known as "remote wiping." The Court dismissed this concern as merely theoretical, since the government had only provided "a couple of anecdotal examples of remote wiping triggered by an arrest."[38] The Court also noted that the police could prevent destruction of evidence by turning the phone off, removing its battery, or placing the phone inside a specialized aluminum foil bag that blocks remote signals.

On the other side of the balancing test, the Court noted that the intrusion of privacy was far greater with respect to the digital evidence on cell phones than it would be for any type of physical search. Cell phones can carry an immense amount of data, and the data they carry cuts broadly across all aspects of a person's life. Thus, "[m]odern cell phones, as a category, implicate privacy concerns far beyond those implicated by the search of a cigarette pack, a wallet, or a purse."[39]

The government had proposed a compromise solution: that police officers be allowed to search a cell phone if they had "reason to believe" evidence of the crime could be found inside. This compromise position was grounded in the Court's earlier language in *Gant*, which authorized searches of cars incident to a recent occupant's arrest if the police had reason to believe evidence of the offense of arrest might be found inside the vehicle. However, the Court rejected the proposed compromise as well, stating that cell phones have so much potential information, "[i]t would be a particularly inexperienced or unimaginative law enforcement officer who could not come up with several reasons to suppose evidence of just about any crime could be found on a cell phone."[40]

Interestingly, the rule that Court adopted in *Riley* did not draw a distinction between the smartphone at issue in *Riley*, and the less sophisticated cell phone that was subject to search in *Wurie*. Even though the phone in *Wurie* did not contain the massive amounts of information present on Riley's phone, and even though the police search in *Wurie* was far more limited than the search in *Riley*, the Supreme Court held that the same analysis applied in both cases.

---

[38] Riley v. California, 573 U.S. __, slip opinion at 13 (2014).

[39] Id. at 17.

[40] Id. at 23.

The Court was also careful to note that though no other exception had been articulated in the instant cases, other exceptions to the warrant requirement might justify a search of a cellphone in a future case. For example, if the police needed to check the cell phone immediately to locate a bomb that was about to detonate or find a child who had been abducted, the police would be permitted to search the cell phone under the exigent circumstances exception. This exception to the warrant requirement is discussed in greater detail in **Chapter 17.**

Finally, it is important to note that the *Riley* decision echoed many of the arguments that were raised in the concurring opinions in the *Jones* case regarding GPS tracking, which had been decided one year earlier. Four of the justices in *Jones* argued that continuous tracking of a car's movements for 28 days provided such a significant quantity of data about a person's life that it was qualitatively different from tracking the car for just one trip. Likewise, the *Riley* court observed that the vast breadth of data available on cell phones exposed too much information to law enforcement. Among other things, the Court noted that "[t]he average smart phone user has installed 33 apps, which together can form a revealing montage of the user's life."[41] Thus, the search of digital files in *Riley* was seen as qualitatively different from the search of physical items because of the sheer quantity and breadth of information that was revealed.

Taken together, *Riley* and *Jones* can be seen as the Court's first steps towards recognizing the potential for new technologies to fundamentally change the way the Fourth Amendment restricts law enforcement surveillance. It is too soon to know where this will lead, but it is clear that the Court is willing to be aggressive in adapting its Fourth Amendment jurisprudence to the modern age.

D. Policy Debate. As we have seen, the SILA doctrine has evolved in a number of ways since the Supreme Court officially adopted it a hundred years ago in *Weeks*. The recent cases of *Gant* and *Riley* maybe the beginning of another stage in this evolution. Recall that in *Robinson*, the Supreme Court held that the power to conduct a search incident to an arrest was automatic, even if there was no danger of weapons and no chance of recovering evidence of the crime of the arrest. Justice Thurgood Marshall dissented in *Robinson,* arguing that the touchstone of the Fourth Amendment is reasonableness, and therefore the Court was wrong to create an automatic right to search the arrestee and his possessions without demonstrating that such a search was reasonable under the circumstances:

[41] Id. at 20.

> There is no formula for the determination of reasonableness. Each case is to be decided on its own facts and circumstances. . . . And the intensive, at times painstaking, case-by-case analysis characteristic of our Fourth Amendment decisions bespeaks our jealous disregard for maintaining the integrity of individual rights.[42]

Justice Marshall also argued that the case Court might have been more willing to protect the arrestee's privacy rights if the container being searched had been something less humble than a cigarette pack:

> One wonders if the result in this case would have been the same were respondent a businessman who was lawfully taken into custody for driving without a license and whose wallet was taken from him by the police. Would it be reasonable for the police officer, because of the possibility that a razor blade was hidden somewhere in the wallet, to open it, remove all the contents, and examine each item carefully? Or suppose a lawyer lawfully arrested for a traffic offense is found to have a sealed envelope on his person. Would it be permissible for the arresting officer to tear open the envelope in order to make sure that it did not contain a clandestine weapon—perhaps a pin or a razor blade?[43]

Finally, Justice Marshall brought up the danger of pretextual arrests, noting that "there is always the possibility that a police officer, lacking probable cause to obtain a search warrant, will use as traffic arrest as a pretext to conduct a search... case-by-case adjudication will always be necessary to determine whether a full arrest was effected for purely legitimate reasons, or, rather, as a pretext for searching the arrestee."[44]

The majority in *Robinson* favored a simpler rule which would not require (or allow) the courts to second-guess the judgment made by the officer on the scene, and emphasized the fact that the arrestee had already suffered a loss of liberty from the very fact of the arrest:

> A police officer's determination as to how and where to search the person of a suspect whom he has arrested is necessarily a quick *ad hoc* judgment which the Fourth Amendment does not require to be broken down in each instance into an analysis of each step in the search. The authority to search the person incident to a lawful custodial arrest, while based upon the need to disarm and to discover evidence, does not depend on what a court may later decide was the probability in a particular arrest situation

[42] United States v. Robinson, 414 U.S. 218, 238 (1973) (Marshall, J., dissenting) (internal quotations and citations omitted).

[43] Id. at 257 (Marshall, J,, dissenting).

[44] Id. at 248 (Marshall, J., dissenting).

> that weapons or evidence would in fact be found upon the person of the suspect. A custodial arrest of a suspect based on probable cause is a reasonable intrusion under the Fourth Amendment; that intrusion being lawful, a search incident to the arrest requires no additional justification.[45]

Of course, in *Robinson*, the simpler, bright-line rule won the day. But *Gant* calls this "automatic right to search" into question. *Gant* only allows a search of the area around the arrestee (the passenger compartment of the car) if the police have reason to believe there is a weapon or evidence of the arrest. As Justice Alito wrote when he dissented in *Gant*, this rule conflicts with *Robinson*'s automatic right to search:

> The . . . new rule . . . raises doctrinal and practical problems that the Court makes no effort to address. Why, for example, is the standard for this type of evidence-gathering search "reason to believe" rather than probable cause? And why is this type of search restricted to evidence of the offense of arrest? It is true that an arrestee's vehicle is probably more likely to contain evidence of the crime of arrest than of some other crime, but if reason-to-believe is the governing standard for an evidence-gathering search incident to arrest, it is not easy to see why an officer should not be able to search when the officer has reason to believe that the vehicle in question possesses evidence of a crime other than the crime of arrest.[46]

The Court's recent decision in *Riley* adds even more doubt to *Robinson*'s automatic right to search. The Court's justification for its decision in *Riley* focuses on the two *Chimel* factors—danger to the police officers and the risk of the suspect destroying evidence. Since those two factors were absent (or at least diminished) in the context of cell phone data, the Court refused to extend the *Robinson* doctrine into the digital universe. Granted, the amount and breadth of data present in cell phones was also an important element of the *Riley* decision, but the Court also pointedly noted that "*Robinson* is the only decision from this Court applying *Chimel* to a search of the contents of an item found on an arrestee's person."[47]

Robinson is still good law—neither *Gant* nor *Riley* overrule it, and the *Riley* Court went out of its way to state that "*Robinson*'s categorical rule strikes the appropriate balance in the context of physical objects."[48] However, given the growing prevalence of cell phones and other digital methods of storing data, it is possible—perhaps even likely—that the *Robinson* doctrine will simply fade into

---

[45] Id. at 235.

[46] United States v. Gant, 556 U.S. 332, 364 (2009) (Alito, J., dissenting).

[47] Id. at 16.

[48] Id. at 9.

insignificance. Currently there is one rule for searching physical containers and one rule for searching digital "containers." In the future, we will carry more and more information—documents, datebooks, contact lists, and so on—inside of digital containers.

Gant also potentially creates an even more significant conflict with *Chimel* itself. Recall that *Chimel* allowed police to conduct a search incident to lawful arrest for any area within the "wingspan" of the arrestee in order to prevent the arrestee from grabbing a nearby weapon or destroying evidence. But this rationale seems to assume that the search is taking place while the arrestee is still present in that location and free to grab any item within his wingspan. *Gant* pointed out how unrealistic that assumption is in the automobile context, holding that there is no justification for a warrantless search of the car if the arrestee is safely secured and has been removed from the location. Dissenting in *Gant*, Justice Alito pointed out that *Gant's* holding calls the *Chimel* wingspan rule into question:

> [I]n the great majority of cases, an officer making an arrest is able to handcuff the arrestee and remove him to a secure place before conducting a search incident to the arrest. [And] because it is safer for an arresting officer to secure an arrestee before searching, it is likely that this is what arresting officers do in the great majority of cases. . . . Thus, if the area within an arrestee's reach were assessed, not at the time of arrest, but at the time of the search, the *Chimel* rule would rarely come into play.
>
> Moreover, if the applicability of the Chimel rule turned on whether an arresting officer chooses to secure an arrestee prior to conducting a search, rather than searching first and securing the arrestee later, the rule would "create a perverse incentive for an arresting officer to prolong the period during which the arrestee is kept in an area where he could pose a danger to the officer."[49]

The result, according to Justice Alito "leaves the law relating to searches incident to arrest in a confused and unstable state."[50] *Gant* allows a search of the arrestee's wingspan only if the arrestee is still present at the site and unsecured. This limitation "applies, at least for now, only to vehicle occupants and recent occupants, but there is no logical reason why the same rule should not apply to all arrestees."[51]

For now *Gant*'s special rules apply only to searches incident to an arrest in the automobile context. Future cases will determine whether the rationale of *Gant* will further weaken *Robinson* or *Chimel.*

---

[49] Id. at 362 (Alito, J., dissenting) (internal quotations and citations omitted).

[50] Id. at 362 (Alito, J., dissenting).

[51] Id. at 363–4 (Alito, J., dissenting) (internal quotations and citations omitted).

Quick Summary

When police officers make a lawful arrest of an individual, they have an automatic right to search the individual and the accessible area immediately surrounding him, known as his "wingspan." Originally these searches were justified by the need to preserve evidence that the arrestee may be able to destroy, and the need to locate weapons which the arrestee could use to threaten the officer's safety, but the doctrine evolved to allow officers to search even if there was no chance of finding evidence of the crime and the defendant posed no threat to officers.

Recently, the Supreme Court has altered this test in the context of arresting the occupant of an automobile: police may only search the automobile as part of a search incident to a lawful arrest if they have "reason to believe" that the automobile contains weapons which could threaten the officer or evidence of the crime of arrest. Therefore, if the arrestee is already secured and removed from the car, the police would not automatically be allowed to search the car under the search incident to a lawful arrest exception.

Review Questions

1. Purse Full of Contraband. Police officers noticed that a car's license plate was obstructed by snow, and so they pulled the car over and ran the name of the driver through the database. The driver had an active warrant, and so the police officers ordered him out of the car and placed him under arrest. The officers ordered the passenger, Emma Coffee, out of the car in order to search the car. Coffee tried to take her purse with her, but officers instructed her to leave it in the car. The officers found nothing in the car, but they found pills, syringes, marijuana, two scales, and various plastic baggies in Coffee's purse.

Officers then searched Coffee's person and found crystal meth. Coffee was arrested for possession of drugs and drug paraphernalia. She is challenging the search of her purse and her person. Was this a legal search under the search incident to a legal arrest doctrine?

2. The Killer Hitchhiker. John Orner was a taxi cab driver in Columbia, South Carolina. After his shift was over, he would frequently stay in his cab for a few extra hours and give free rides to soldiers to and from Fort Jackson. One night, Orner did not return home at his normal time, and his family reported him missing. His cab was found one hour later with significant blood stains, and John was found dead inside the cab.

The police began fanning out through the area and found a man dressed in soldier fatigues named Tom Frieburg hitchhiking a couple of miles away from the taxicab. Hitchhiking is against the law in South Carolina, punishable by a $100 fine. The police officers pulled up alongside Freiburg and exited their car with their weapons drawn, ordering him to put his hands on his head. Freiburg complied. While one officer kept his gun out, the other one searched Freiburg and his bag. Inside his bag was a wallet, and inside the wallet the police found credit cards and identification belonging to Orner. Freiburg was arrested and charged with Orner's murder.

Did the police officers violate Freiburg's Fourth Amendment rights?

3. Stock Fraud and Cocaine. The Securities and Exchange Commission suspected that James Strasser, a stockbroker at a major New York investment bank, was committing securities fraud by anonymously spreading false information about stocks that he held and then selling his shares just before the information was revealed to be false. After a short investigation, they developed probable cause to arrest Strasser for the crime. Shortly after 9:00 AM in the morning, three SEC agents entered Strasser's office and arrested him as he sat at his desk. They handcuffed him and took him just outside his office to stand next to his secretary's cubicle.

One agent guarded Strasser while the other two went back inside his officer and searched through his desk, where they found dozens of papers relating to his fraudulent transactions. Strasser also had a gym bag underneath his desk, and the officers opened up the gym bag and looked through its contents. Inside a pocket of the gym bag, they found a plastic bag containing cocaine. One of the officers also sat at Strasser's computer and browsed through his e-mail and document files. Strasser had logged into his computer using his password just before his arrest, and so his email account and all of his files were accessible to the agent. The agent found a number of emails and files that incriminated Strasser. She printed them out on Strasser's computer in order to use them as evidence.

The officers did not have an arrest warrant or a search warrant.

Did the agents violate Strasser's rights when they searched:

(a) his desk?

(b) his gym bag?

(c) his computer?

FROM THE COURTROOM

ARIZONA v. GANT

United States Supreme Court, 2009
556 U.S. 332

[Justice STEVENS delivered the opinion of the Court.]

[Justices SCALIA concurred in the decision.]

[Justice BREYER filed a dissenting opinion.]

[Justice ALITO filed a dissenting opinion, in which he was joined by Chief Justice ROBERTS and Justice KENNEDY and by Justice BREYER in part.]

I

On August 25, 1999, acting on an anonymous tip that the residence at 2524 North Walnut Avenue was being used to sell drugs, Tucson police officers Griffith and Reed knocked on the front door and asked to speak to the owner. Gant answered the door and, after identifying himself, stated that he expected the owner to return later. The officers left the residence and conducted a records check, which revealed that Gant's driver's license had been suspended and there was an outstanding warrant for his arrest for driving with a suspended license.

When the officers returned to the house that evening, they found a man near the back of the house and a woman in a car parked in front of it. After a third officer arrived, they arrested the man for providing a false name and the woman for possessing drug paraphernalia. Both arrestees were handcuffed and secured in separate patrol cars when Gant arrived. The officers recognized his car as it entered the driveway, and Officer Griffith confirmed that Gant was the driver by shining a flashlight into the car as it drove by him. Gant parked at the end of the driveway, got out of his car, and shut the door. Griffith, who was about 30 feet away, called to Gant, and they approached each other, meeting 10–to–12 feet from Gant's car. Griffith immediately arrested Gant and handcuffed him.

Because the other arrestees were secured in the only patrol cars at the scene, Griffith called for backup. When two more officers arrived, they locked Gant in the backseat of their vehicle. After Gant had been handcuffed and placed in the back of a patrol car, two officers searched his car: One of them found a gun, and the other discovered a bag of cocaine in the pocket of a jacket on the backseat.

Gant was charged with two offenses—possession of a narcotic drug for sale and possession of drug paraphernalia (*i.e.,* the plastic bag in which the cocaine was found). He moved to suppress the evidence seized from his car on the ground that the warrantless search violated the Fourth Amendment.

. . .

II

Consistent with our precedent, our analysis begins, as it should in every case addressing the reasonableness of a warrantless search, with the basic rule that "searches conducted outside the judicial process, without prior approval by judge or magistrate, are *per se* unreasonable under the Fourth Amendment—subject only to a few specifically established and well-delineated exceptions." Among the exceptions to the warrant requirement is a search incident to a lawful arrest. The exception derives from interests in officer safety and evidence preservation that are typically implicated in arrest situations.

In *Chimel,* we held that a search incident to arrest may only include "the arrestee's person and the area 'within his immediate control'—construing that phrase to mean the area from within which he might gain possession of a weapon or destructible evidence." That limitation, which continues to define the boundaries of the exception, ensures that the scope of a search incident to arrest is commensurate with its purposes of protecting arresting officers and safeguarding any evidence of the offense of arrest that an arrestee might conceal or destroy. If there is no possibility that an arrestee could reach into the area that law enforcement officers seek to search, both justifications for the search-incident-to-arrest exception are absent and the rule does not apply.

In *Belton,* we considered *Chimel's* application to the automobile context. A lone police officer in that case stopped a speeding car in which Belton was one of four occupants. While asking for the driver's license and registration, the officer smelled burnt marijuana and observed an envelope on the car floor marked "Supergold"—a name he associated with marijuana. Thus having probable cause to believe the occupants had committed a drug offense, the officer ordered them out of the vehicle, placed them under arrest, and patted them down. Without handcuffing the arrestees, the officer "'split them up into four separate areas of the Thruway . . . so they would not be in physical touching area of each other'" and searched the vehicle, including the pocket of a jacket on the backseat, in which he found cocaine.

The New York Court of Appeals found the search unconstitutional, concluding that after the occupants were arrested the vehicle and its contents were "safely within the exclusive custody and control of the police." The State asked this Court to consider whether the exception recognized in *Chimel* permits an officer to search "a jacket found inside an automobile while the automobile's four occupants, all under arrest, are standing unsecured around the vehicle." We granted certiorari because "courts ha[d] found no workable definition of 'the area within the immediate control of the arrestee' when that area arguably includes the interior of an automobile."

In its brief, the State argued that the Court of Appeals erred in concluding that the jacket was under the officer's exclusive control. Focusing on the number of arrestees and their proximity to the vehicle, the State asserted that it was reasonable for the officer to believe the arrestees could have accessed the vehicle and its contents, making the search permissible under *Chimel.* The United States, as *amicus curiae* in support of the State, argued for a more permissive standard, but it maintained that any search incident to arrest must be "'substantially contemporaneous'" with the arrest—a requirement it deemed "satisfied if the search occurs during the period in which the arrest is being consummated and before the situation has so stabilized that it could be said that the arrest was completed." There was no suggestion by the parties or *amici* that *Chimel* authorizes a vehicle search incident to arrest when there is no realistic possibility that an arrestee could access his vehicle.

After considering these arguments, we held that when an officer lawfully arrests "the occupant of an automobile, he may, as a contemporaneous incident of that arrest, search the passenger compartment of the automobile" and any containers therein. That holding was based in large part on our assumption "that articles inside the relatively narrow compass of the passenger compartment of an automobile are in fact generally, even if not inevitably, within 'the area into which an arrestee might reach.'"

The Arizona Supreme Court read our decision in *Belton* as merely delineating "the proper scope of a search of the interior of an automobile" incident to an arrest. That is, *when* the passenger compartment is within an arrestee's reaching distance, *Belton* supplies the generalization that the entire compartment and any containers therein may be reached. On that view of *Belton,* the state court concluded that the search of Gant's car was unreasonable because Gant clearly could not have accessed his car at the time of the search. It also found that no other exception to the warrant requirement applied in this case.

Gant now urges us to adopt the reading of *Belton* followed by the Arizona Supreme Court.

III

Despite the textual and evidentiary support for the Arizona Supreme Court's reading of *Belton,* our opinion has been widely understood to allow a vehicle search incident to the arrest of a recent occupant even if there is no possibility the arrestee could gain access to the vehicle at the time of the search. This reading may be attributable to Justice Brennan's dissent in *Belton,* in which he characterized the Court's holding as resting on the "fiction . . . that the interior of a car is *always* within the immediate control of an arrestee who has recently been in the car." Under the majority's approach, he argued, "the result would presumably be the same even if [the officer] had handcuffed Belton and his companions in the patrol car" before conducting the search.

. . .

Under this broad reading of *Belton,* a vehicle search would be authorized incident to every arrest of a recent occupant notwithstanding that in most cases the vehicle's passenger compartment will not be within the arrestee's reach at the time of the search. To read *Belton* as authorizing a vehicle search incident to every recent occupant's arrest would thus untether the rule from the justifications underlying the *Chimel* exception—a result clearly incompatible with our statement in *Belton* that it "in no way alters the fundamental principles established in the *Chimel* case regarding the basic scope of searches incident to lawful custodial arrests." Accordingly, we reject this reading of *Belton* and hold that the *Chimel* rationale authorizes police to search a vehicle incident to a recent occupant's arrest only when the arrestee is unsecured and within reaching distance of the passenger compartment at the time of the search.

Although it does not follow from *Chimel,* we also conclude that circumstances unique to the vehicle context justify a search incident to a lawful arrest when it is "reasonable to believe evidence relevant to the crime of arrest might be found in the vehicle." In many cases, as when a recent occupant is arrested for a traffic violation, there will be no reasonable basis to believe the vehicle contains relevant evidence. But in others, including *Belton* and *Thornton,* the offense of arrest will supply a basis for searching the passenger compartment of an arrestee's vehicle and any containers therein.

Neither the possibility of access nor the likelihood of discovering offense-related evidence authorized the search in this case. Unlike in *Belton,* which involved a single officer confronted with four unsecured arrestees, the five officers in this case outnumbered the three arrestees, all of whom had been handcuffed and secured in separate patrol cars before the officers searched Gant's car. Under those circumstances, Gant clearly was not within reaching distance of his car at the time of the search. An evidentiary basis for the search was also lacking in this case. Whereas Belton and Thornton were arrested for drug offenses, Gant was arrested for driving with a suspended license—an offense for which police could not expect to find evidence in the passenger compartment of Gant's car. Because police could not reasonably have believed either that Gant could have accessed his car at the time of the search or that evidence of the offense for which he was arrested might have been found therein, the search in this case was unreasonable.

IV

The State does not seriously disagree with the Arizona Supreme Court's conclusion that Gant could not have accessed his vehicle at the time of the search, but it nevertheless asks us to uphold the search of his vehicle under the broad reading of *Belton* discussed above. The State argues that *Belton* searches are reasonable regardless of the possibility of access in a given case because that expansive rule correctly balances law enforcement interests, including the interest in a bright-line rule, with an arrestee's limited privacy interest in his vehicle.

For several reasons, we reject the State's argument. First, the State seriously undervalues the privacy interests at stake. Although we have recognized that a motorist's privacy interest in his vehicle is less substantial than in his home, the former interest is nevertheless important and deserving of constitutional protection. It is particularly significant that *Belton* searches authorize police officers to search not just the passenger compartment but every purse, briefcase, or other container within that space. A rule that gives police the power to conduct such a search whenever an individual is caught committing a traffic offense, when there is no basis for believing evidence of the offense might be found in the vehicle, creates a serious and recurring threat to the privacy of countless individuals. Indeed, the character of that threat implicates the central concern underlying the Fourth Amendment—the concern about giving police officers unbridled discretion to rummage at will among a person's private effects.

At the same time as it undervalues these privacy concerns, the State exaggerates the clarity that its reading of *Belton* provides. Courts that have read *Belton* expansively are at odds regarding how close in time to the arrest and how proximate to the arrestee's vehicle an officer's first contact with the arrestee must be to bring the encounter within *Belton*'s purview and whether a search is reasonable when it commences or continues after the arrestee has been removed from the scene. The rule has thus generated a great deal of uncertainty, particularly for a rule touted as providing a "bright line."

Contrary to the State's suggestion, a broad reading of *Belton* is also unnecessary to protect law enforcement safety and evidentiary interests. Under our view, *Belton* and *Thornton* permit an officer to conduct a vehicle search when an arrestee is within reaching distance of the vehicle or it is reasonable to believe the vehicle contains evidence of the offense of arrest. . . .

Construing *Belton* broadly to allow vehicle searches incident to any arrest would serve no purpose except to provide a police entitlement, and it is anathema to the Fourth Amendment to permit a warrantless search on that basis. For these reasons, we are unpersuaded by the State's arguments that a broad reading of *Belton* would meaningfully further law enforcement interests and justify a substantial intrusion on individuals' privacy.

V

. . .

The experience of the 28 years since we decided *Belton* has shown that the generalization underpinning the broad reading of that decision is unfounded. We now know that articles inside the passenger compartment are rarely "within 'the area into which an arrestee might reach,'" and blind adherence to *Belton*'s faulty assumption would authorize myriad unconstitutional searches. The doctrine of *stare decisis* does not require us to approve routine constitutional violations.

VI

Police may search a vehicle incident to a recent occupant's arrest only if the arrestee is within reaching distance of the passenger compartment at the time of the search or it is reasonable to believe the vehicle contains evidence of the offense of arrest. When these justifications are absent, a search of an arrestee's vehicle will be unreasonable unless police obtain a warrant or show that another exception to the warrant requirement applies. The Arizona Supreme Court correctly held that this case involved an unreasonable search. Accordingly, the judgment of the State Supreme Court is affirmed.

It is so ordered.

[The concurrences of Justice SCALIA and Justice BREYER are omitted.]

Justice ALITO, with whom THE CHIEF JUSTICE and Justice KENNEDY join, and with whom Justice BREYER joins except as to Part II–E, dissenting.

Twenty-eight years ago, in *New York v. Belton,* this Court held that "when a policeman has made a lawful custodial arrest of the occupant of an automobile, he may, as a contemporaneous incident of that arrest, search the passenger compartment of that automobile." Five years ago, in *Thornton v. United States*—a case involving a situation not materially distinguishable from the situation here—the Court not only reaffirmed but extended the holding of *Belton,* making it applicable to recent occupants. Today's decision effectively overrules those important decisions, even though respondent Gant has not asked us to do so.

To take the place of the overruled precedents, the Court adopts a new two-part rule under which a police officer who arrests a vehicle occupant or recent occupant may search the passenger compartment if (1) the arrestee is within reaching distance of the vehicle at the time of the search or (2) the officer has reason to believe that the vehicle contains evidence of the offense of arrest. The first part of this new rule may endanger arresting officers and is truly endorsed by only four Justices; Justice Scalia joins solely for the purpose of avoiding a "4–to–1–to–4 opinion." The second part of the new rule is taken from Justice Scalia's separate opinion in *Thornton* without any independent explanation of its origin or justification and is virtually certain to confuse law enforcement officers and judges for some time to come. The Court's decision will cause the suppression of evidence gathered in many searches carried out in good-faith reliance on well-settled case law, and although the Court purports to base its analysis on the landmark decision in *Chimel v. California,* the Court's reasoning undermines *Chimel.* I would follow *Belton,* and I therefore respectfully dissent.

. . .

II

Because the Court has substantially overruled *Belton* and *Thornton,* the Court must explain why its departure from the usual rule of *stare decisis* is justified. I recognize that stare decisis is not an "inexorable command,", and applies less rigidly in constitutional cases. But the Court has said that a constitutional precedent should be followed unless there is a "'special justification'" for its abandonment. Relevant factors identified in prior cases include whether the precedent has engendered reliance, whether there has been an important change in circumstances in the outside world, whether the precedent has proved to be unworkable, whether the precedent has been undermined by later decisions, and whether the decision was badly reasoned. These factors weigh in favor of retaining the rule established in *Belton.*

A

Reliance. While reliance is most important in "cases involving property and contract rights," the Court has recognized that reliance by law enforcement officers is also entitled to weight. . . . [T]here certainly is substantial reliance here. The *Belton* rule has been taught to police officers for more than a quarter century. Many searches—almost certainly including more than a few that figure in cases now on appeal—were conducted in scrupulous reliance on that precedent. It is likely that, on the very day when this opinion is announced, numerous vehicle searches will be conducted in good faith by police officers who were taught the *Belton* rule.

The opinion of the Court recognizes that "*Belton* has been widely taught in police academies and that law enforcement officers have relied on the rule in conducting vehicle searches during the past 28 years." But for the Court, this seemingly counts for nothing. The Court states that "[w]e have never relied on *stare decisis* to justify the continuance of an unconstitutional police practice," but of course the Court routinely relies on decisions sustaining the constitutionality of police practices without doing what the Court has done here—*sua sponte* considering whether those decisions should be overruled. And the Court cites no authority for the proposition that *stare decisis* may be disregarded or provides only lesser protection when the precedent that is challenged is one that sustained the constitutionality of a law enforcement practice.

. . .

B

Changed circumstances. Abandonment of the *Belton* rule cannot be justified on the ground that the dangers surrounding the arrest of a vehicle occupant are different today than they were 28 years ago. The Court claims that "[w]e now know that articles inside the passenger compartment are rarely 'within "the area into which an arrestee might reach,"'" but surely it was well known in 1981 that a person who is taken from a vehicle, handcuffed, and placed in the back of a patrol car is unlikely to make it back into his own car to retrieve a weapon or destroy evidence.

C

Workability. The *Belton* rule has not proved to be unworkable. On the contrary, the rule was adopted for the express purpose of providing a test that would be relatively easy for police officers and judges to apply. The Court correctly notes that even the *Belton* rule is not perfectly clear in all situations. Specifically, it is sometimes debatable whether a search is or is not contemporaneous with an arrest, but that problem is small in comparison with the problems that the Court's new two-part rule will produce.

The first part of the Court's new rule—which permits the search of a vehicle's passenger compartment if it is within an arrestee's reach at the time of the search—reintroduces the same sort of case-by-case, fact-specific decisionmaking that the *Belton* rule was adopted to avoid. As the situation in *Belton* illustrated, there are cases in which it is unclear whether an arrestee could retrieve a weapon or evidence in the passenger compartment of a car.

Even more serious problems will also result from the second part of the Court's new rule, which requires officers making roadside arrests to determine whether there is reason to believe that the vehicle contains evidence of the crime of arrest. What this rule permits in a variety of situations is entirely unclear.

D

Consistency with later cases. The *Belton* bright-line rule has not been undermined by subsequent cases. On the contrary, that rule was reaffirmed and extended just five years ago in *Thornton.*

E

Bad reasoning. The Court is harshly critical of *Belton* 's reasoning, but the problem that the Court perceives cannot be remedied simply by overruling *Belton. Belton* represented only a modest—and quite defensible—extension of *Chimel,* as I understand that decision.

Prior to *Chimel,* the Court's precedents permitted an arresting officer to search the area within an arrestee's "possession" and "control" for the purpose of gathering evidence. Based on this "abstract doctrine," the Court had sustained searches that extended far beyond an arrestee's grabbing area.

The *Chimel* Court, in an opinion written by Justice Stewart, overruled these cases. Concluding that there are only two justifications for a warrantless search incident to arrest—officer safety and the preservation of evidence—the Court stated that such a search must be confined to "the arrestee's person" and "the area from within which he might gain possession of a weapon or destructible evidence."

Unfortunately, *Chimel* did not say whether "the area from within which [an arrestee] might gain possession of a weapon or destructible evidence" is to be measured at the time of the arrest or at the time of the search, but unless the *Chimel* rule was meant to be a specialty rule, applicable to only a few unusual cases, the Court must have intended for this area to be measured at the time of arrest.

This is so because the Court can hardly have failed to appreciate the following two facts. First, in the great majority of cases, an officer making an arrest is able to handcuff the arrestee and remove him to a secure place before conducting a search incident to the arrest (stating that it is "the rare case" in which an arresting officer cannot secure an arrestee before conducting a search). Second, because it is safer for an arresting officer to secure an arrestee before searching, it is likely that this is what arresting officers do in the great majority of cases. (And it appears, not surprisingly, that this is in fact the prevailing practice.) Thus, if the area within an arrestee's reach were assessed, not at the time of arrest, but at the time of the search, the *Chimel* rule would rarely come into play.

Moreover, if the applicability of the *Chimel* rule turned on whether an arresting officer chooses to secure an arrestee prior to conducting a search, rather than searching first and securing the arrestee later, the rule would "create a perverse incentive for an arresting officer to prolong the period during which the arrestee is kept in an area where he could pose a danger to the officer." If this is the law, the D.C. Circuit observed, "the law would truly be, as Mr. Bumble said, 'a ass.'"

I do not think that this is what the *Chimel* Court intended. Handcuffs were in use in 1969. The ability of arresting officers to secure arrestees before conducting a search—and their incentive to do so—are facts that can hardly have escaped the Court's attention. I therefore believe that the *Chimel* Court intended that its new rule apply in cases in which the arrestee is handcuffed before the search is conducted.

The *Belton* Court, in my view, proceeded on the basis of this interpretation of *Chimel.* Again speaking through Justice Stewart, the *Belton* Court reasoned that articles in the passenger compartment of a car are "generally, even if not inevitably" within an arrestee's reach. This is undoubtedly true at the time of the arrest of a person who is seated in a car but plainly not true when the person has been removed from the car and placed in handcuffs. Accordingly, the *Belton* Court must have proceeded on the assumption that the *Chimel* rule was to be applied at the time of arrest. And that is why the *Belton* Court was able to say that its decision "in no way alter[ed] the fundamental principles established in the *Chimel* case regarding the basic scope of searches incident to lawful custodial arrests." Viewing *Chimel* as having focused on the time of arrest, *Belton* 's only new step was to eliminate the need to decide on a case-by-case basis whether a particular person seated in a car actually could have reached the part of the passenger compartment where a weapon or evidence was hidden. For this reason, if we are going to reexamine *Belton,* we should also reexamine the reasoning in *Chimel* on which *Belton* rests.

F

The Court, however, does not reexamine *Chimel* and thus leaves the law relating to searches incident to arrest in a confused and unstable state. The first part of the Court's new two-part rule—which permits an arresting officer to search the area within an arrestee's reach at the time of the search—applies, at least for now, only to vehicle occupants and recent occupants, but there is no logical reason why the same rule should not apply to all arrestees.

The second part of the Court's new rule, which the Court takes uncritically from Justice Scalia's separate opinion in *Thornton,* raises doctrinal and practical problems that the Court makes no effort to address. Why, for example, is the standard for this type of evidence-gathering search "reason to believe" rather than probable cause? And why is this type of search restricted to evidence of the offense of arrest? It is true that an arrestee's vehicle is probably more likely to contain evidence of the crime of arrest than of some other crime, but if reason-to-believe is the governing standard for an evidence-gathering search incident to arrest, it is not easy to see why an officer should not be able to search when the officer has reason to believe that the vehicle in question possesses evidence of a crime other than the crime of arrest.

Nor is it easy to see why an evidence-gathering search incident to arrest should be restricted to the passenger compartment. The *Belton* rule was limited in this way because the passenger compartment was considered to be the area that vehicle occupants can generally reach, but since the second part of the new rule is not based on officer safety or the preservation of evidence, the ground for this limitation is obscure.

III

Respondent in this case has not asked us to overrule *Belton,* much less *Chimel.* Respondent's argument rests entirely on an interpretation of *Belton* that is plainly incorrect, an interpretation that disregards *Belton*'s explicit delineation of its holding. I would therefore leave any reexamination of our prior precedents for another day, if such a reexamination is to be undertaken at all. In this case, I would simply apply *Belton* and reverse the judgment below.

FROM THE COURTROOM

RILEY v. CALIFORNIA
UNITED STATES v. WURIE

United States Supreme Court
573 U.S. ___, 134 S.Ct. 2473 (2014)

[Chief Justice ROBERTS delivered the opinion of the Court.]

[Justice ALITO filed a concurring opinion.]

These two cases raise a common question: whether the police may, without a warrant, search digital information on a cell phone seized from an individual who has been arrested.

I

A

In the first case, petitioner David Riley was stopped by a police officer for driving with expired registration tags. In the course of the stop, the officer also learned that Riley's license had been suspended. The officer impounded Riley's car, pursuant to department policy, and another officer conducted an inventory search of the car. Riley was arrested for possession of concealed and loaded firearms when that search turned up two handguns under the car's hood.

An officer searched Riley incident to the arrest and found items associated with the "Bloods" street gang. He also seized a cell phone from Riley's pants pocket. According to Riley's uncontradicted assertion, the phone was a "smart phone," a cell phone with a broad range of other functions based on advanced computing capability, large storage capacity, and Internet connectivity. The officer accessed information on the phone and noticed that some words (presumably in text messages or a contacts list) were preceded by the letters "CK"—a label that, he believed, stood for "Crip Killers," a slang term for members of the Bloods gang.

At the police station about two hours after the arrest, a detective specializing in gangs further examined the con- tents of the phone. The detective testified that he "went through" Riley's phone "looking for evidence, because . . . gang members will often video themselves with guns or take pictures of themselves with the guns." Although there was "a lot of stuff " on the phone, particular files that "caught [the detective's] eye" included videos of young men sparring while someone yelled encouragement using the moniker "Blood." The police also found photographs of Riley standing in front of a car they suspected had been involved in a shooting a few weeks earlier.

Riley was ultimately charged, in connection with that earlier shooting, with firing at an occupied vehicle, assault with a semiautomatic firearm, and attempted murder. The State alleged that Riley had committed those crimes for the benefit of a criminal street gang, an aggravating factor that carries an enhanced sentence.

Prior to trial, Riley moved to suppress all evidence that the police had obtained from his cell phone. He contended that the searches of his phone violated the Fourth Amendment, because they had been performed without a warrant and were not otherwise justified by exigent circumstances. The trial court rejected that argument. At Riley's trial, police officers testified about the photographs and videos found on the phone, and some of the photographs were admitted into evidence.

Riley was convicted on all three counts and received an enhanced sentence of 15 years to life in prison. The court relied on the California Supreme Court's decision in *People v. Diaz*, 51 Cal. 4th 84, (2011), which held that the Fourth Amendment permits a warrantless search of cell phone data incident to an arrest, so long as the cell phone was immediately associated with the arrestee's person.

The California Supreme Court denied Riley's petition for review, and we granted certiorari.

B

In the second case, a police officer performing routine surveillance observed respondent Brima Wurie make an apparent drug sale from a car. Officers subsequently arrested Wurie and took him to the police station. At the station, the officers seized two cell phones from Wurie's person. The one at issue here was a "flip phone," a kind of phone that is flipped open for use and that generally has a smaller range of features than a smart phone. Five to ten minutes after arriving at the station, the officers noticed that the phone was repeatedly receiving calls from a source identified as "my house" on the phone's external screen. A few minutes later, they opened the phone and saw a photograph of a woman and a baby set as the phone's wallpaper. They pressed one button on the phone to access its call log, then another button to determine the phone number associated with the "my house" label. They next used an online phone directory to trace that phone number to an apartment building.

When the officers went to the building, they saw Wurie's name on a mailbox and observed through a window a woman who resembled the woman in the photograph on Wurie's phone. They secured the apartment while obtaining a search warrant and, upon later executing the warrant, found and seized 215 grams of crack cocaine, marijuana, drug paraphernalia, a firearm and ammunition, and cash.

Wurie was charged with distributing crack cocaine, possessing crack cocaine with intent to distribute, and being a felon in possession of a firearm and ammunition. He moved to suppress the evidence obtained from the search of the apartment, arguing that it was the fruit of an unconstitutional search of his cell phone. The District Court denied the motion. Wurie was convicted on all three counts and sentenced to 262 months in prison.

A divided panel of the First Circuit reversed the denial of Wurie's motion to suppress and vacated Wurie's convictions for possession with intent to distribute and possession of a firearm as a felon. The court held that cell phones are distinct from other physical possessions that may be searched incident to arrest with- out a warrant, because of the amount of personal data cell phones contain and the negligible threat they pose to law enforcement interests. We granted certiorari.

II

The Fourth Amendment provides:

"The right of the people to be secure in their persons, houses, papers, and effects, against unreasonable searches and seizures, shall not be violated, and no Warrants shall issue, but upon probable cause, supported by Oath or affirmation, and particularly describing the place to be searched, and the persons or things to be seized."

As the text makes clear, "the ultimate touchstone of the Fourth Amendment is 'reasonableness.' " Our cases have deter- mined that "[w]here a search is undertaken by law enforcement officials to discover evidence of criminal wrong- doing, . . . reasonableness generally requires the obtaining of a judicial warrant. Such a warrant ensures that the inferences to support a search are "drawn by a neutral and detached magistrate instead of being judged by the officer engaged in the often competitive enterprise of ferreting out crime." In the absence of a warrant, a search is reasonable only if it falls within a specific exception to the warrant requirement.

The two cases before us concern the reasonableness of a warrantless search incident to a lawful arrest. In 1914, this Court first acknowledged in dictum "the right on the part of the Government, always recognized under English and American law, to search the person of the accused when legally arrested to discover and seize the fruits or evidences of crime." Since that time, it has been well accepted that such a search constitutes an exception to the warrant requirement. Indeed, the label "exception" is something of a misnomer in this context, as warrantless searches incident to arrest occur with far greater frequency than searches conducted pursuant to a warrant.

Although the existence of the exception for such searches has been recognized for a century, its scope has been debated for nearly as long. That debate has focused on the extent to which officers may search property found on or near the arrestee. Three related precedents set forth the rules governing such searches:

The first, *Chimel v. California*, 395 U. S. 752 (1969), laid the groundwork for most of the existing search incident to arrest doctrine. Police officers in that case arrested Chimel inside his home and proceeded to search his entire three-bedroom house, including the attic and garage. In particular rooms, they also looked through the contents of drawers.

The Court crafted the following rule for assessing the reasonableness of a search incident to arrest:

"When an arrest is made, it is reasonable for the arresting officer to search the person arrested in order to remove any weapons that the latter might seek to use in order to resist arrest or effect his escape. Otherwise, the officer's safety might well be endangered, and the arrest itself frustrated. In addition, it is entirely reasonable for the arresting officer to search for and seize any evidence on the arrestee's person in order to prevent its concealment or destruction .... There is ample justification, therefore, for a search of the arrestee's person and the area 'within his immediate control'—construing that phrase to mean the area from within which he might gain possession of a weapon or destructible evidence." The extensive warrantless search of *Chimel's* home did not fit within this exception, because it was not needed to protect officer safety or to preserve evidence.

Four years later, in *United States v. Robinson*, 414 U. S. 218 (1973), the Court applied the *Chimel* analysis in the context of a search of the arrestee's person. A police officer had arrested Robinson for driving with a revoked license. The officer conducted a patdown search and felt an object that he could not identify in Robinson's coat pocket. He removed the object, which turned out to be a crumpled cigarette package, and opened it. Inside were 14 capsules of heroin.

The Court of Appeals concluded that the search was unreasonable because Robinson was unlikely to have evidence of the crime of arrest on his person, and because it believed that extracting the cigarette package and opening it could not be justified as part of a protective search for weapons. This Court reversed, rejecting the notion that "case-by-case adjudication" was required to determine "whether or not there was present one of the reasons supporting the authority for a search of the person incident to a lawful arrest." As the Court explained, "[t]he authority to search the person incident to a lawful custodial arrest, while based upon the need to disarm and to discover evidence, does not depend on what a court may later decide was the probability in a particular arrest situation that weapons or evidence would in fact be found upon the person of the suspect." Instead, a "custodial arrest of a suspect based on probable cause is a reasonable intrusion under the Fourth Amendment; that intrusion being lawful, a search incident to the arrest requires no additional justification."

The Court thus concluded that the search of Robinson was reasonable even though there was no concern about the loss of evidence, and the arresting officer had no specific concern that Robinson might be armed. In doing so, the Court did not draw a line between a search of Robinson's person and a further examination of the cigarette pack found during that search. It merely noted that, "[h]aving in the course of a lawful search come upon the crumpled package of cigarettes, [the officer] was entitled to inspect it." A few years later, the Court clarified that this exception was limited to "personal property . . . immediately associated with the person of the arrestee."

The search incident to arrest trilogy concludes with *Gant*, which analyzed searches of an arrestee's vehicle. *Gant*, like *Robinson*, recognized that the *Chimel* concerns for officer safety and evidence preservation underlie the search incident to arrest exception. As a result, the Court concluded that *Chimel* could authorize police to search a vehicle "only when the arrestee is unsecured and within reaching distance of the passenger compartment at the time of the search." *Gant* added, however, an independent exception for a warrantless search of a vehicle's passenger compartment "when it is 'reasonable to believe evidence relevant to the crime of arrest might be found in the vehicle.'" That exception stems not from *Chimel*, the Court explained, but from "circumstances unique to the vehicle context."

III

These cases require us to decide how the search incident to arrest doctrine applies to modern cell phones, which are now such a pervasive and insistent part of daily life that the proverbial visitor from Mars might conclude they were an important feature of human anatomy. A smart phone of the sort taken from Riley was unheard of ten years ago; a significant majority of American adults now own such phones. Even less sophisticated phones like Wurie's, which have already faded in popularity since Wurie was arrested in 2007, have been around for less than 15 years. Both phones are based on technology nearly inconceivable just a few decades ago, when *Chimel* and *Robinson* were decided.

Absent more precise guidance from the founding era, we generally determine whether to exempt a given type of search from the warrant requirement "by assessing, on the one hand, the degree to which it intrudes upon an individual's privacy and, on the other, the degree to which it is needed for the promotion of legitimate governmental interests." Such a balancing of interests supported the search incident to arrest exception in *Robinson*, and a mechanical application of *Robinson* might well support the warrantless searches at issue here.

But while *Robinson's* categorical rule strikes the appropriate balance in the context of physical objects, neither of its rationales has much force with respect to digital content on cell phones. On the government interest side, *Robinson* concluded that the two risks identified in *Chimel*—harm to officers and destruction of evidence—are present in all custodial arrests. There are no comparable risks when the search is of digital data. In addition, *Robinson* regarded any privacy interests retained by an individual after arrest as significantly diminished by the fact of the arrest itself. Cell phones, however, place vast quantities of personal information literally in the hands of individuals. A search of the information on a cell phone bears little resemblance to the type of brief physical search considered in *Robinson*.

We therefore decline to extend *Robinson* to searches of data on cell phones, and hold instead that officers must generally secure a warrant before conducting such a search.

A

We first consider each *Chimel* concern in turn. In doing so, we do not overlook *Robinson's* admonition that searches of a person incident to arrest, "while based upon the need to disarm and to discover evidence," are reasonable regardless of "the probability in a particular arrest situation that weapons or evidence would in fact be found." Rather than requiring the "case-by-case adjudication" that *Robinson* rejected, we ask instead whether application of the search incident to arrest doctrine to this particular category of effects would "untether the rule from the justifications underlying the *Chimel* exception,"

1

Digital data stored on a cell phone cannot itself be used as a weapon to harm an arresting officer or to effectuate the arrestee's escape. Law enforcement officers remain free to examine the physical aspects of a phone to ensure that it will not be used as a weapon—say, to determine whether there is a razor blade hidden between the phone and its case. Once an officer has secured a phone and eliminated any potential physical threats, however, data on the phone can endanger no one.

Perhaps the same might have been said of the cigarette pack seized from Robinson's pocket. Once an officer gained control of the pack, it was unlikely that Robinson could have accessed the pack's contents. But unknown physical objects may always pose risks, no matter how slight, during the tense atmosphere of a custodial arrest. The officer in *Robinson* testified that he could not identify the objects in the cigarette pack but knew they were not cigarettes. Given that, a further search was a reasonable protective measure. No such unknowns exist with respect to digital data. As the First Circuit explained, the officers who searched Wurie's cell phone "knew exactly what they would find therein: data. They also knew that the data could not harm them."

The United States and California both suggest that a search of cell phone data might help ensure officer safety in more indirect ways, for example by alerting officers that confederates of the arrestee are headed to the scene. There is undoubtedly a strong government interest in warning officers about such possibilities, but neither the United States nor California offers evidence to suggest that their concerns are based on actual experience. The proposed consideration would also represent a broadening of *Chimel's* concern that an arrestee himself might grab a weapon and use it against an officer "to resist arrest or effect his escape." And any such threats from outside the arrest scene do not "lurk[ ] in all custodial arrests." Accordingly, the interest in protecting officer safety does not justify dispensing with the warrant requirement across the board. To the extent dangers to arresting officers may be implicated in a particular way in a particular case, they are better addressed through consideration of case-specific exceptions to the warrant requirement, such as the one for exigent circumstances.

2

The United States and California focus primarily on the second *Chimel* rationale: preventing the destruction of evidence.

Both Riley and Wurie concede that officers could have seized and secured their cell phones to prevent destruction of evidence while seeking a warrant. That is a sensible concession. And once law enforcement officers have secured a cell phone, there is no longer any risk that the arrestee himself will be able to delete incriminating data from the phone.

The United States and California argue that information on a cell phone may nevertheless be vulnerable to two types of evidence destruction unique to digital data—remote wiping and data encryption. Remote wiping occurs when a phone, connected to a wireless network, receives a signal that erases stored data. This can happen when a third party sends a remote signal or when a phone is preprogrammed to delete data upon entering or leaving certain geographic areas (so-called "geofencing"). Encryption is a security feature that some modern cell phones use in addition to password protection. When such phones lock, data becomes protected by sophisticated encryption that renders a phone all but "unbreakable" unless police know the password.

. . .

We have . . . been given little reason to believe that either problem is prevalent. The briefing reveals only a couple of anecdotal examples of remote wiping triggered by an arrest. Similarly, the opportunities for officers to search a password-protected phone before data becomes encrypted are quite limited. Law enforcement officers are very unlikely to come upon such a phone in an unlocked state because most phones lock at the touch of a button or, as a default, after some very short period of inactivity. This may explain why the encryption argument was not made until the merits stage in this Court, and has never been considered by the Courts of Appeals.

Moreover, in situations in which an arrest might trigger a remote-wipe attempt or an officer discovers an unlocked phone, it is not clear that the ability to conduct a warrant- less search would make much of a difference. The need to effect the arrest, secure the scene, and tend to other pressing matters means that law enforcement officers may well not be able to turn their attention to a cell phone right away.

Cell phone data would be vulnerable to remote wiping from the time an individual anticipates arrest to the time any eventual search of the phone is completed, which might be at the station house hours later. Likewise, an officer who seizes a phone in an unlocked state might not be able to begin his search in the short time remaining before the phone locks and data becomes encrypted.

In any event, as to remote wiping, law enforcement is not without specific means to address the threat. Remote wiping can be fully prevented by disconnecting a phone from the network. There are at least two simple ways to do this: First, law enforcement officers can turn the phone off or remove its battery. Second, if they are concerned about encryption or other potential problems, they can leave a phone powered on and place it in an enclosure that isolates the phone from radio waves. Such devices are commonly called "Faraday bags," after the English scientist Michael Faraday. They are essentially sandwich bags made of aluminum foil: cheap, light- weight, and easy to use. They may not be a complete answer to the problem, but at least for now they provide a reasonable response. In fact, a number of law enforcement agencies around the country already encourage the use of Faraday bags. To the extent that law enforcement still has specific concerns about the potential loss of evidence in a particular case, there remain more targeted ways to address those concerns. If "the police are truly confronted with a 'now or never' situation,"—for example, circumstances suggesting that a defendant's phone will be the target of an imminent remote-wipe attempt—they may be able to rely on exigent circumstances to search the phone immediately. Or, if officers happen to seize a phone in an unlocked state, they may be able to disable a phone's automatic-lock feature in order to prevent the phone from locking and encrypting data. Such a preventive measure could be analyzed under the principles set forth in our decision in *McArthur*, 531 U. S. 326, which approved officers' reasonable steps to secure a scene to preserve evidence while they awaited a warrant.

B

The search incident to arrest exception rests not only on the heightened government interests at stake in a volatile arrest situation, but also on an arrestee's reduced privacy interests upon being taken into police custody. *Robinson* focused primarily on the first of those rationales. But it also quoted with approval then-Judge Cardozo's account of the historical basis for the search incident to arrest exception: "Search of the person becomes lawful when grounds for arrest and accusation have been discovered, and the law is in the act of subjecting the body of the accused to its physical dominion. Put simply, a patdown of Robinson's clothing and an inspection of the cigarette pack found in his pocket constituted only minor additional intrusions compared to the substantial government authority exercised in taking Robinson into custody.

The fact that an arrestee has diminished privacy interests does not mean that the Fourth Amendment falls out of the picture entirely. Not every search "is acceptable solely because a person is in custody." To the contrary, when "privacy-related concerns are weighty enough" a "search may require a warrant, notwithstanding the diminished expectations of privacy of the arrestee." One such example, of course, is *Chimel. Chimel* refused to "characteriz[e] the invasion of privacy that results from a top-to-bottom search of a man's house as 'minor.'" Because a search of the arrestee's entire house was a substantial invasion beyond the arrest itself, the Court concluded that a warrant was required.

The United States asserts that a search of all data stored on a cell phone is "materially indistinguishable" from searches of these sorts of physical items. That is like saying a ride on horseback is materially indistinguishable from a flight to the moon. Both are ways of getting from point A to point B, but little else justifies lumping them together. Modern cell phones, as a category, implicate privacy concerns far beyond those implicated by the search of a cigarette pack, a wallet, or a purse. A conclusion that inspecting the contents of an arrestee's pockets works no substantial additional intrusion on privacy beyond the arrest itself may make sense as applied to physical items, but any extension of that reasoning to digital data has to rest on its own bottom.

1

Cell phones differ in both a quantitative and a qualitative sense from other objects that might be kept on an arrestee's person. The term "cell phone" is itself misleading shorthand; many of these devices are in fact minicomputers that also happen to have the capacity to be used as a telephone. They could just as easily be called cameras, video players, rolodexes, calendars, tape recorders, libraries, diaries, albums, televisions, maps, or newspapers.

One of the most notable distinguishing features of modern cell phones is their immense storage capacity. Before cell phones, a search of a person was limited by physical realities and tended as a general matter to constitute only a narrow intrusion on privacy. Most people cannot lug around every piece of mail they have received for the past several months, every picture they have taken, or every book or article they have read—nor would they have any reason to attempt to do so. And if they did, they would have to drag behind them a trunk of the sort held to require a search warrant in *Chadwick*, rather than a container the size of the cigarette package in *Robinson*.

But the possible intrusion on privacy is not physically limited in the same way when it comes to cell phones. The current top-selling smart phone has a standard capacity of 16 gigabytes (and is available with up to 64 gigabytes). Sixteen gigabytes translates to millions of pages of text, thousands of pictures, or hundreds of videos.

. . .

Finally, there is an element of pervasiveness that characterizes cell phones but not physical records. Prior to the digital age, people did not typically carry a cache of sensitive personal information with them as they went about their day. Now it is the person who is not carrying a cell phone, with all that it contains, who is the exception. According to one poll, nearly three-quarters of smart phone users report being within five feet of their phones most of the time, with 12% admitting that they even use their phones in the shower. A decade ago police officers searching an arrestee might have occasion- ally stumbled across a highly personal item such as a diary. But those discoveries were likely to be few and far between. Today, by contrast, it is no exaggeration to say that many of the more than 90% of American adults who own a cell phone keep on their person a digital record of nearly every aspect of their lives— from the mundane to the intimate. Allowing the police to scrutinize such records on a routine basis is quite different from allowing them to search a personal item or two in the occasional case.

Although the data stored on a cell phone is distinguished from physical records by quantity alone, certain types of data are also qualitatively different. An Internet search and browsing history, for example, can be found on an Internet-enabled phone and could reveal an individual's private interests or concerns—perhaps a search for certain symptoms of disease, coupled with frequent visits to WebMD. Data on a cell phone can also reveal where a person has been. Historic location information is a standard feature on many smart phones and can reconstruct someone's specific movements down to the minute, not only around town but also within a particular building.

Mobile application software on a cell phone, or "apps," offer a range of tools for managing detailed information about all aspects of a person's life. There are apps for Democratic Party news and Republican Party news; apps for alcohol, drug, and gambling addictions; apps for sharing prayer requests; apps for tracking pregnancy symptoms; apps for planning your budget; apps for every conceivable hobby or pastime; apps for improving your romantic life. There are popular apps for buying or selling just about anything, and the records of such transactions may be accessible on the phone indefinitely. There are over a million apps available in each of the two major app stores; the phrase "there's an app for that" is now part of the popular lexicon. The average smart phone user has installed 33 apps, which together can form a revealing montage of the user's life.

In 1926, Learned Hand observed (in an opinion later quoted in *Chimel*) that it is "a totally different thing to search a man's pockets and use against him what they contain, from ransacking his house for everything which may incriminate him."

If his pockets contain a cell phone, however, that is no longer true. Indeed, a cell phone search would typically expose to the government far more than the most exhaustive search of a house: A phone not only contains in digital form many sensitive records previously found in the home; it also contains a broad array of private information never found in a home in any form— unless the phone is.

. . .

2

To further complicate the scope of the privacy interests at stake, the data a user views on many modern cell phones may not in fact be stored on the device itself. Treating a cell phone as a container whose contents may be searched incident to an arrest is a bit strained as an initial matter.

But the analogy crumbles entirely when a cell phone is used to access data located elsewhere, at the tap of a screen. That is what cell phones, with increasing frequency, are designed to do by taking advantage of "cloud computing." Cloud computing is the capacity of Internet-connected devices to display data stored on remote servers rather than on the device itself. Cell phone users often may not know whether particular information is stored on the device or in the cloud, and it generally makes little difference. Moreover, the same type of data may be stored locally on the device for one user and in the cloud for another.

. . .

The United States concedes that the search incident to arrest exception may not be stretched to cover a search of files accessed remotely—that is, a search of files stored in the cloud. Such a search would be like finding a key in a suspect's pocket and arguing that it allowed law enforcement to unlock and search a house. But officers searching a phone's data would not typically know whether the information they are viewing was stored locally at the time of the arrest or has been pulled from the cloud.

C

Apart from their arguments for a direct extension of *Robinson*, the United States and California offer various fallback options for permitting warrantless cell phone searches under certain circumstances. Each of the proposals is flawed and contravenes our general preference to provide clear guidance to law enforcement through categorical rules. "[I]f police are to have workable rules, the balancing of the competing interests . . . 'must in large part be done on a categorical basis—not in an ad hoc, case-by-case fashion by individual police officers.'"

The United States first proposes that the *Gant* standard be imported from the vehicle context, allowing a warrantless search of an arrestee's cell phone whenever it is reasonable to believe that the phone contains evidence of the crime of arrest. But *Gant* relied on "circumstances unique to the vehicle context" to endorse a search solely for the purpose of gathering evidence. Justice Scalia's *Thornton* opinion, on which *Gant* was based, explained that those unique circumstances are "a reduced expectation of privacy" and "heightened law enforcement needs" when it comes to motor vehicles. For reasons that we have explained, cell phone searches bear neither of those characteristics.

At any rate, a *Gant* standard would prove no practical limit at all when it comes to cell phone searches. In the vehicle context, *Gant* generally protects against searches for evidence of past crimes. In the cell phone context, however, it is reasonable to expect that incriminating information will be found on a phone regardless of when the crime occurred. Similarly, in the vehicle context *Gant* restricts broad searches resulting from minor crimes such as traffic violations.

That would not necessarily be true for cell phones. It would be a particularly inexperienced or unimaginative law enforcement officer who could not come up with several reasons to suppose evidence of just about any crime could be found on a cell phone. Even an individual pulled over for something as basic as speeding might well have locational data dispositive of guilt on his phone. An individual pulled over for reckless driving might have evidence on the phone that shows whether he was texting while driving. The sources of potential pertinent information are virtually unlimited, so applying the *Gant* standard to cell phones would in effect give "police officers unbridled discretion to rummage at will among a person's private effects."

. . .

Finally, at oral argument California suggested a different limiting principle, under which officers could search cell phone data if they could have obtained the same information from a pre-digital counterpart. But the fact that a search in the pre-digital era could have turned up a photograph or two in a wallet does not justify a search of thousands of photos in a digital gallery. The fact that someone could have tucked a paper bank statement in a pocket does not justify a search of every bank statement from the last five years. And to make matters worse, such an analogue test would allow law enforcement to search a range of items contained on a phone, even though people would be unlikely to carry such a variety of information in physical form. In Riley's case, for example, it is implausible that he would have strolled around with videotapes, photo albums, and an address book all crammed into his pockets. But because each of those items has a pre-digital analogue, police under California's proposal would be able to search a phone for all of those items—a significant diminution of privacy.

In addition, an analogue test would launch courts on a difficult line-drawing expedition to determine which digital files are comparable to physical records. Is an e-mail equivalent to a letter? Is a voicemail equivalent to a phone message slip? It is not clear how officers could make these kinds of decisions before conducting a search, or how courts would apply the proposed rule after the fact. An analogue test would "keep defendants and judges guessing for years to come."

IV

We cannot deny that our decision today will have an impact on the ability of law enforcement to combat crime. Cell phones have become important tools in facilitating coordination and communication among members of criminal enterprises, and can provide valuable incriminating information about dangerous criminals. Privacy comes at a cost.

Our holding, of course, is not that the information on a cell phone is immune from search; it is instead that a warrant is generally required before such a search, even when a cell phone is seized incident to arrest. Our cases have historically recognized that the warrant requirement is "an important working part of our machinery of government," not merely "an inconvenience to be somehow 'weighed' against the claims of police efficiency."

Recent technological advances similar to those discussed here have, in addition, made the process of obtaining a warrant itself more efficient.

. . .

Modern cell phones are not just another technological convenience. With all they contain and all they may reveal, they hold for many Americans "the privacies of life," The fact that technology now allows an individual to carry such information in his hand does not make the information any less worthy of the protection for which the Founders fought. Our answer to the question of what police must do before searching a cell phone seized incident to an arrest is accordingly simple—get a warrant.

14

Exceptions to the Warrant Requirement: Plain View

Key Concepts

- Lawful Vantage Point
- Lawful Access
- Readily Apparent Incriminating Nature
- Plain Feel (!) and Plain Smell (?)

A. Introduction and Policy. The second exception to the warrant requirement—the "P" in S-P-A-C-E-S—is the plain view exception. As its name implies, this exception at its core allows police officers to search or seize, without a warrant, evidence that is clearly visible. The best way to understand the plain view exception is to keep in mind the two divergent interests that the Fourth Amendment protects. The first—the freedom from unreasonable searches—protects against violations of one's reasonable expectation of privacy. The second—the freedom from unreasonable seizures—protects against violations of one's rightful possessory interests. The plain view exception to the warrant requirement is based on the theory that the search or seizure of a plainly visible item of contraband implicates neither of these interests. Let's take that apart.

When an item can clearly be seen by officers from a lawful vantage point, the mere viewing of that item occasions no further intrusion upon privacy interests than the officers' authorized presence alone. Thus, while the Court has accepted that the Constitution frowns upon police officers foraging about for evidence without a warrant, it has determined that items already in plain view simply do not, as a practical matter, convert otherwise authorized police presence into forbidden general rummaging. Moreover, when the item is obviously contraband, the seizure of that item implicates no invasion of rightful possessory interests, for the owner's interests are defeated by the item's illegal nature. As the Court stated in *Payton v. New York*, "[t]he seizure of property in plain view involves no invasion of privacy and is presumptively reasonable assuming that there is probable cause to associate the property with criminal activity."[1]

The plain view exception is also rooted in the very practical observation that "it would often be a needless inconvenience, and sometimes dangerous—to the evi-

---

[1] Payton v. New York, 445 U.S. 573, 587 (1980).

dence or to the police themselves—to require them to ignore [contraband] until they have obtained a warrant particularly describing it."[2] Imagine for a moment that the police lawfully enter a suspect's home to execute an arrest warrant. Lying on the floor in the entryway is an open basket containing the Crown Jewels. It would make little sense to require the police to leave the Jewels there and return with a warrant before they could seize them. The plain view exception to the warrant requirement attempts to create space in the constitutional landscape for addressing these sorts of practical concerns.

B. The Law. Long-recognized by the Court, plain view is the second of six carefully delineated exceptions to the warrant requirement.[3] Described simply, this exception recognizes that "objects falling in the plain view of an officer who has a right to be in the position to have that view are subject to seizure and may be introduced in evidence."[4]

Since the early years of its articulation, the Court has gradually refined the precise contours of the plain view exception. As currently defined, the doctrine permits warrantless seizures once three conditions are satisfied. Specifically, pursuant to the plain view exception:

> A law enforcement officer may conduct observations and seize items without implicating the Fourth Amendment if:
>
> 1. The police did not violate the Fourth Amendment to arrive at the place from which they observed the item to be searched or seized;
> 2. The police were not only able to observe the item, but also had a lawful means of access to the items; and
> 3. It was immediately apparent to the police that the item they were viewing was evidence of a crime or other contraband.

Though often characterized as an "exception" to the warrant requirement, plain view is perhaps more accurately described as an extension of the authority granted by some other Fourth Amendment rule.[5] This is because the exception's first requirement—that the officer be at a lawful vantage point—requires that officers first demonstrate they had a right to be wherever they were at the time they made their observations. As a practical matter, officers most often establish their right

[2] Coolidge v. New Hampshire, 403 U.S. 443, 468 (1971).
[3] See, e.g., Hester v. United States, 265 U.S. 57 (1924).
[4] Harris v. United States, 390 U.S. 234, 236 (1968).
[5] Texas v. Brown, 460 U.S. 730, 738–39 (1983).

to be present by pointing to a valid warrant or applicable exception to the warrant requirement.

For example, assume an officer chases an armed and fleeing felon through the front door of a house. The officer tackles the felon to the floor in the dining room. Just as he is handcuffing the suspect, the officer looks up and notices Rembrandt's *The Storm on the Sea of Galilee* leaning against the wall. To justify his presence in the home, the officer would most likely point to the exigent circumstances—his pursuit of the fleeing felon (**Chapter 17**). The plain view exception would then extend the officer's lawful authority in the home (originally created by the exigency) to permit the warrantless seizure of the stolen painting (a matter unrelated to the initial justification for the intrusion).

In addition to the three conditions listed above, for many years, the Court also required satisfaction of a fourth prerequisite—inadvertence. Specifically, for plain view to apply, the Court once required that law enforcement's discovery of the seized evidence be unintended. However, the Court has abolished that requirement. Thus, an officer can use this exception even if she intentionally gains access to an area for the sole purpose of using the plain view exception to conduct surveillance. We will consider the abolition of the inadvertence requirement in greater detail below.

C. Applying the Law. As noted, application of the plain view exception requires that the police establish three things—their lawful vantage point, their lawful access, and the "immediately apparent" illicit nature of the item(s) seized. The first two elements of plain view are fairly straightforward and thus have generated relatively little discussion in the Court. They warrant only brief additional coverage here. The "immediately apparent" requirement is a bit more complicated and thus deserves a more lengthy discussion.

First, however, we will examine the abolished "inadvertence" requirement, and consider whether it may still play a factor in the plain view analysis.

1. Inadvertance Is (Probably) No Longer a Factor. As noted above, for many years the Supreme Court held that that a police office could not use the plain view doctrine if she intentionally gained access to a protected area in order to look for contraband. In other words, the observation of the illegal items had to be inadvertent:

> **Example—*Coolidge v. New Hampshire*, 403 U.S. 443 (1971):** Edward Coolidge was suspected in the murder of his fourteen-year-old neighbor, Pamela Mason. Police officers arrested Coolidge at home and then seized two cars parked in his drive

way. Vacuum sweepings taken from one of the cars were introduced into evidence at Coolidge's trial to establish that Mason had been in Coolidge's car prior to her death. The initial seizure (and ensuing search) of the car were initially authorized by a warrant, but the warrant was later invalidated, so the government argued that the seizure of the car was authorized under the plain view doctrine. The police were validly on the property to make the arrest, and the car was openly visible as a known instrument of the crime, so the plain view exception was at least potentially applicable. [6]

Analysis: The Supreme Court rejected the application of the plain view exception in *Coolidge* because the police already knew about the car and its relationship to the case before they made the arrest. "[W]here the discovery is anticipated, where the police know in advance the location of the evidence and intend to seize it, the situation is altogether different. The requirement of a warrant to seize imposes no inconvenience whatever." [7]

The Court explained that the inadvertence requirement advanced two complementary constitutional goals. First, the Constitution requires that warrants particularly describe the things to be seized. Consequently, if the initial police intrusion is based upon a warrant, allowing the seizure of items that are known by the police but not named in the warrant would violate the constitutional demand for particularity. Second, if the initial intrusion is based instead upon some exception to the warrant requirement, allowing the seizure of items that the police "know in advance they will find in plain view and intend to seize, would fly in the face of the basic rule that no amount of probable cause can justify a warrantless seizure [in the absence of exigency]." [8]

Inadvertence remained a requirement for over two decades until the *Horton* case in 1990:

Example—*Horton v. California*, 496 U.S. 128 (1990): The police suspected Terry Brice Horton of robbing the treasurer of the San Jose Coin Club one evening when the treasurer returned home from a coin show. The sergeant in charge of the investigation obtained a warrant to search Horton's home. In his affidavit in support of the warrant, the sergeant described probable cause to believe that both the proceeds of the crime and weapons associated with the offense—stun guns, a machine gun, and a revolver—would be found in Horton's home. For reasons not

[6] Id. at 453.

[7] Id. at 470.

[8] Id. at 471.

explained, the warrant that ultimately issued authorized a search for the proceeds of the crime but not any weapons. However, while executing the warrant, the sergeant not surprisingly came upon the weapons he had anticipated would be found in the house. The sergeant seized the weapons, which were later introduced as evidence during the prosecution's case-in-chief against Horton. Horton argued that the affidavit in support of the search warrant made clear that the discovery of the weapons was not inadvertent—*i.e.*, the sergeant expected to find the weapons during the search. For this reason, Horton argued that the inadvertence requirement was not met and that the plain view exception should not apply.

Analysis: The Supreme Court rejected Horton's arguments and upheld the admission of the weapons pursuant to the plain view doctrine. Reversing its earlier demand that plain view seizures be inadvertent, the Court found the "fact that an officer is interested in an item of evidence and fully expects to find it in the course of a search should not invalidate its seizure if the search is confined in area and duration by the terms of a warrant or a valid exception to the warrant requirement."[9]

The Court rejected its earlier arguments in *Coolidge*. In response to the argument that abolishing the inadvertence requirement would violate the particularity requirement of the warrant clause, the Court professed disbelief that an officer with knowledge of an item would deliberately omit it from an application for a warrant. With regard to *Coolidge*'s second assertion that this change would essentially allow warrantless searches and seizures, the Court found that the interest in preventing general rummaging was already served by the terms of the warrant or the particular contours of the authorizing exception, both of which placed limits on where police officers could look.[10]

Thus, as construed post-*Horton*, the plain view exception requires only the three conditions noted above—lawful vantage point, lawful access, and immediately apparent contraband nature. However, although the *Horton* Court rejected the necessity of inadvertence, the possibility of the concept's continued relevance was left open by that Court's language: "We conclude that even though inadvertence is a characteristic of most legitimate 'plain-view' seizures, it is not a necessary condition." Exactly what the *Horton* Court was hoping to signal regarding the continued relevance of inadvertence, however, is not entirely clear. Depending upon where the emphasis is placed in the sentence, the *Horton* Court could have been saying two very different things.

---

[9] Horton v. California, 496 U.S. 128, 138 (1990).

[10] Id. at 138–139.

First, the Court might simply have been describing the practical reality that police officers do not generally anticipate the discovery of most evidence that is seized because it is in plain view. In other words, the language in *Horton* might be read as nothing more than historically descriptive. Alternatively, the *Horton* Court's language might be read prescriptively. Specifically, the Court may have been signaling that the legitimacy of a discovery is buttressed by its inadvertence. Under this reading, while inadvertence is no longer needed, it would remain relevant to whether warrantless police seizures are excused by the plain view exception. Unfortunately, the *Horton* Court offered no guidance as to which of the two interpretations it intended. In the absence of such direction, the lower federal appellate courts have come to differing conclusions.

At least one federal Court of Appeals has found that the *Horton* Court's language should be understood prescriptively. In *United States v. Carey*,[11] the Tenth Circuit, after acknowledging that inadvertence is no longer a mandatory precondition to application of the plain view exception, went on to exclude evidence that was not discovered inadvertently. Citing the *Horton* Court's conclusion that "inadvertence is a characteristic of most legitimate 'plain-view' seizures," the Tenth Circuit rejected a warrantless search where the investigating detective fully expected to find child pornography on the computer files he opened—"the fact that Detective Lewis did not inadvertently come across the pornographic files is certainly relevant to our inquiry." Twenty years after the Tenth Circuit's *Carey* decision, a second federal circuit affirmed that court's continued embrace of inadvertence. However, that same year, a third federal appellate court explicitly rejected the Tenth Circuit's approach as "inconsistent with *Horton*."

There is no question that inadvertence is not constitutionally required before a warrantless search can be authorized by the plain view exception to the warrant requirement. However, without additional guidance from the Court, practitioners in the field would be wise to carefully review the precedent in their jurisdiction to determine whether inadvertence is, nonetheless, a factor that must be weighed when evaluating the propriety of purported plain view seizures.

2. Lawful Vantage Point. The first step toward establishing that a warrantless search or seizure was justified by the plain view exception requires an officer to demonstrate that his observation of the item was made from a lawful vantage point. There are some lawful vantage points that require little justification. For example, the lawfulness of the officer's vantage point can always be established if the officer is standing in a public space that enjoys no Fourth Amendment protection. Any unaided observations the officer makes from such a place will always satisfy the first element of the plain view exception. Indeed, even if the officer standing in a public space makes unaided observations of a private enclosure, the first element of the plain view exception will still be satisfied.

---

[11] 172 F.3d 1268 (10th Cir. 1999).

Lawful vantage point can also be established if the presence of the police officer in a private space is justified by a warrant or an exception to the warrant requirement. For example, if an officer is executing a valid search warrant in a home and happens upon evidence not mentioned in the warrant, the lawful vantage point element of plain view will be satisfied. Similarly, if an officer responds to a home to settle a violent domestic dispute, observations that the officer makes while lawfully inside the home in response to the call will most typically satisfy the first element of plain view.

The fact that the observed conduct is plainly illegal does not affect the lawful vantage point analysis. Consequently, even the observation of patently criminal conduct will not obviate the need for the lawful vantage point inquiry:

> **Example:** Officer Chris Curious had been assigned the beat in Derek City, Missouri for nearly twenty years. As a result of his many years in the community, Officer Curious knew many of the residents by name. Of late, however, Officer Curious had become concerned by a lot of new faces in the area. Officer Curious noticed that the new people all wore the same style of purple mesh fishing cap and tie-dye t-shirt featuring a logo of dancing kittens. Fearing gang activity, Officer Curious determined to step up his routine surveillance.
>
> The next weekend, while walking the beat, Officer Curious saw two women wearing the "dancing kitten" attire described above. Suspecting they were gang members, Officer Curious followed the women for several blocks until they entered a ground-level garden apartment. After the two entered and closed the door behind them, Officer Curious tiptoed up the public walk that passed along one side of the residence. Several feet up the walk, Officer Curious tested a window at the rear of the apartment. Finding it open, Curious climbed through and found himself in the apartment's bathroom. Peeking through the partially opened bathroom door, Curious clearly observed the two women sitting at a table. Resting on the table was a large trash bag filled with a white powder Officer Curious immediately recognized as cocaine. The women were dividing the cocaine into small baggies using razor blades, a triple beam scale, and a large mirror. Curious could also clearly see a pile of twenty dollar bills on the floor between the two women. Behind them was a photocopier that appeared to be printing sheets of money. Paper and other materials that Officer Curious knew to be necessary to counterfeiting were scattered on a nearby dresser.

Furious that gang members and their criminal enterprises were invading his nice community, Officer Curious drew his service revolver. Slamming the bathroom door open, Curious ordered both women to the ground and placed them under arrest. He then collected all the evidence on the table and brought it to the local prosecutor, demanding that charges be filed.

Analysis: The prosecutor will refuse to file charges. Officer Curious violated the Constitution when he effected a warrantless seizure of the evidence. Accordingly, all of the evidence will ultimately be suppressed.

Though Officer Curious plainly viewed ample evidence of obvious criminal activity, his warrantless seizure of that evidence cannot be justified under the plain view exception to the warrant requirement. The first element of plain view requires that an officer's observation of the evidence be made from a lawful vantage point. Because Officer Curious violated the Fourth Amendment when he crawled through an unlocked window, the lawful vantage point factor cannot be satisfied, and the plain view exception will not apply.

3. Lawful Access. In addition to viewing the evidence from a place where she has a right to be, a police officer also must have lawful access to the evidence before its warrantless search or seizure will be excused under the plain view exception. Lawful access means that the officer must be able to make **lawful contact** with the evidence in order to search or seize it:

Example: Assume we are again dealing with Officer Chris Curious from the example above. This time however, after seeing the two suspected gang members enter the ground-level garden apartment, Officer Curious tiptoed up the walk and looked through a side window of the apartment. From his position on the public walk, Officer Curious was able to see directly into the living room of the apartment, and he again clearly saw the two women dividing the cocaine and counterfeiting money. After twenty minutes, the women finished the task. Leaving the bagged drugs on the table and the money on the floor, the women left the apartment without ever noticing Curious' presence. Waiting fifteen minutes, Officer Curious then crawled through the window of the now-empty apartment, collected the drugs and other evidence, and transported it directly to the local prosecutor demanding that charges be filed.

Analysis: Again the evidence seized by Officer Curious should be suppressed. Without question, Officer Curious' conduct in this second example satisfied the first element of plain view. The public walk from which Officer Curious made his observations was a "lawful vantage point." However, this time the warrantless seizure must fall because Curious cannot satisfy the second element of plain view—lawful access. Though Officer Curious could clearly see the criminal activity occurring in the apartment, and although his observations provided him with probable cause to enter the apartment, he had no justifiable basis for that entry—neither a warrant nor an applicable exception to the warrant requirement.

Rather than surreptitiously entering the apartment, Officer Curious should have documented his observations and applied for search and arrest warrants based upon probable cause.

4. "Immediately Apparent" Nature of the Contraband. Finally, the plain view exception requires that the incriminating character of the seized items be "immediately apparent." This third and final component has received far greater treatment by the Court than the relatively straightforward elements discussed above—lawful vantage point and lawful access. This is in part because it is not at all clear what it means for the illicit nature of an item to be "immediately apparent."

We discussed the "immediately apparent" requirement in the context of seizures in **Chapter 9.** Recall that we said that the term was a bit misleading. Certainly the "immediacy" aspect (sometimes referred to as "readily" apparent), suggests that an officer must fairly quickly be able to ascertain what she is looking at. However, "immediately apparent" does not mean that the officer must unequivocally **know** that she is looking at an illicit item. Instead, the officer must have something like probable cause to believe that the item is contraband or evidence of a crime. In trying to determine whether the item is contraband or evidence, the officer cannot conduct any type of search beyond what has been already been authorized by a warrant or what is allowed under some other exception to the warrant requirement:

> **Example—*Texas v. Brown,* 460 U.S. 730 (1983):** During the summer of 1979, the Fort Worth Police Department set up a vehicle checkpoint on East Allen Street to inspect the driver's licenses of passing motorists. Just after midnight, an officer stopped the car driven by Clifford Brown. The officer asked Brown for his license. At the same time, the officer shone a flashlight into Brown's car. With the interior of the vehicle so illuminated, the officer was able to see Brown remove his hand from his right front pants pocket. Between Brown's fingers was a green party balloon. The balloon was opaque. Accordingly, the officer could not determine what if anything was inside it. But, the officer could see that the balloon was knotted just past

its tip, suggesting that it contained something. As Brown reached over to open the glove compartment, he dropped the balloon onto the seat.

As Brown rummaged about in the glove compartment, the officer leaned down to get a better view into the car. From this vantage point, he saw small plastic vials, a loose white powder, and an opened bag of party balloons inside of the open glove box.

After several minutes, Brown admitted that he did not have a license. The officer ordered Brown out of the car. As Brown was walking to the rear of the vehicle, the officer reached into the car and removed the green knotted balloon from the front seat. It appeared to the officer that the balloon contained some sort of a powdery substance. Brown was placed under arrest. An inventory search of his car turned up several plastic bags of a green leafy substance and a large bottle of milk sugar, which is often used as a cutting agent in the production of cocaine.

Prior to trial, Brown challenged the seizure of the evidence. At the suppression hearing, the government called a chemist who testified that the substance inside the balloon was heroin. The chemist also testified that party balloons were commonly used in the packaging of illegal drugs. In addition to the chemist, the arresting officer testified at the hearing. He testified that in his experience party balloons were frequently used to package drugs.

The trial court denied Brown's request for suppression, and the case proceeded to trial. Following Brown's conviction, the case was eventually appealed to the Supreme Court.

Analysis: The officer's warrantless seizure of the balloon was constitutionally permissible as it fell within the plain view exception to the warrant requirement.

Turning to the three required plain view factors, the Court quickly resolved the first two in the government's favor. First, the stop of Brown's car was a concededly lawful result of the checkpoint. Moreover, the officer's observations as he stood just outside the car also presented no Fourth Amendment concerns. Consequently, the first factor in a plain view seizure was established—the officer observed the balloon from a lawful vantage point. Turning next to the question of lawful access, the Court found that the officer's retrieval of the balloon from the interior of the car was also appropriate under the automobile exception to the warrant requirement (**Chapter 15**)—"While seizure of the balloon required a warrantless, physical intrusion into Brown's automobile, this was proper."

Having thus resolved the first two issues relevant to a plain view seizure, the Court next turned to consider the question of whether the balloon's incriminating nature was "immediately apparent" to the officer. The Texas appellate court had agreed to suppress the evidence because it found this factor required the officer "to know that 'incriminatory evidence was before him when he seized the balloon.'"[12] Because the police officer could not possibly have known for certain that the balloon had drugs in it, the state court excluded the balloon and the drugs found in it. The Supreme Court, however, rejected the state court's construction of "immediately apparent."

The Court found that the third element of plain view required not absolute certainty but rather a belief akin to probable cause. The "seizure of property in plain view . . . is presumptively reasonable, assuming that there is probable cause to associate the property with criminal activity."[13]

Applying this standard to the case before it, the *Brown* Court found it evident that the officer "possessed probable cause to believe the balloon in Brown's hand contained an illicit substance."[14] In particular, the Court found probable cause was established by the officer's testimony about his experience with the packaging of drugs coupled with the officer's other observations of the material in the glove compartment. Because the warrantless seizure of the balloon fell within a recognized exception to the warrant requirement, the admission of the evidence was appropriate.

What happens when the police officer making the observation strongly suspects the incriminating nature of evidence, but cannot establish probable cause for her suspicions without a little bit of additional investigation? Should such evidence satisfy the demand for incriminating evidence that is "immediately apparent?" The case of *Arizona v. Hicks*, which we first discussed in the context of what conduct constitutes a seizure, also helps to demonstrate what is considered "immediately apparent":

> **Example—*Arizona v. Hicks*, 480 U.S. 321 (1987):** Recall in *Hicks*, a bullet was fired through the floor of James Hicks' apartment. The bullet entered the apartment below and struck the man who lived there. Thereafter, the police entered Hicks' apartment looking for the shooter, other victims, and weapons.

---

[12] Texas v. Brown, 460 U.S. 730, 735 (1983).

[13] Id. at 741–42.

[14] Id. at 742.

One of the searching officers noticed two expensive stereo sets in the living room. The officer thought the equipment looked out of place in the apartment. The officer walked over to the equipment and moved it slightly so that he could read the serial numbers off of the backs. When he reported the numbers to headquarters by telephone, he learned that at least one of the components had been stolen during a recent armed robbery.

At trial, Hicks conceded that the initial entry into his apartment was justified by the need for emergency aid created by the recent shooting. However, he maintained that though the police were lawfully in his apartment to investigate the shooting, the further search of the stereo equipment could not be justified by the plain view exception to the warrant requirement.

Analysis: The Court agreed with Hicks and rejected application of the plain view exception in connection with the stereo equipment.

There was no question that the officers were lawfully in the apartment and had a right to look around for weapons. Thus, the first factor of the plain view exception—lawful vantage point—was established. Indeed, if the officer had simply looked at those parts of the stereo equipment he could see without moving it, such an inspection would have been entirely lawful. So too, the Court determined that if the officer had probable cause to believe the equipment was stolen he could have searched or seized it under the plain view exception. The state conceded, however, that the officer did not have probable cause until after headquarters reported that the serial numbers on the components were registered as stolen.

The officers were in the apartment to look for the shooter, other victims, and weapons. Moving the stereo equipment was unrelated to this original justification for the intrusion into the apartment. The Court explained that "taking action, unrelated to the objectives of the authorized intrusion, which exposed to view concealed portions of the apartment or its contents, did produce a new invasion of respondent's privacy unjustified by the exigent circumstances that validated the entry."[15] Accordingly, the reversal of Hicks' conviction was affirmed.

As the above discussion reveals, the third element of the plain view analysis requires police officers to demonstrate they had probable cause to believe the item they were looking at was contraband or evidence of a crime. In the absence of such certainty, the "immediately apparent" aspect of plain view will not be met.

What about evidence that an officer perceives through other senses? What if an officer is standing outside of a stopped car and detects the odor of burning

[15] Arizona v. Hicks, 480 U.S. 321, 325 (1987).

marijuana? Or what if he lawfully touches the suspect (or his property) and immediately senses that what he feels is contraband? Do the principles underlying the plain view exception naturally encompass these situations as well? We explore these questions in the following section.

5. Is Touch a Natural Corollary of Sight? As described above, if a police officer has lawfully engaged with a suspect, the Court has consistently found that plain view permits the officer to seize any plainly incriminating evidence that he perceives through his sense of sight and to which he has lawful access. With regard to touch and smell, however, the Court has reached more mixed results. While the Court has expressly endorsed the seizure of items immediately detected as contraband during a lawful pat-down, it has not provided correspondingly clear guidance with regard to evidence perceived through an officer's sense of smell. Let us consider first what the Court has said in connection with plain feel:

> **Example—*Minnesota v. Dickerson*, 508 U.S. 366 (1992):** Minneapolis police officers patrolling the north side of the city saw Timothy Dickerson leaving an apartment building that the officers knew to be a "crack house." Dickerson started out walking toward the police. However, after making eye contact with one of the officers, Dickerson turned on his heel and headed in the opposite direction. The officers decided to pursue Dickerson when he turned into a nearby alley.
>
> Pulling the squad car into the alley behind Dickerson, the officers instructed him to stop and subjected him to a pat-down search. The searching officer felt no weapons, but did feel a small lump in the front pocket of Dickerson's jacket. The officer was unable to immediately determine what the item was. Accordingly, he "examined it with [his] fingers and it slid and it felt to be a lump of crack cocaine in cellophane."[16] The officer reached into Dickerson's pocket and pulled out a small plastic bag. Inside the baggie was one fifth of a gram of crack cocaine.
>
> Dickerson moved to suppress the drugs before trial. However, his motion was denied, based upon the trial court's determination that the seizure was justified by an extension of plain view to the sense of touch—*i.e.*, plain feel. Following his conviction, Dickerson appealed.

[16] Minnesota v. Dickerson, 508 U.S. 366, 369 (1992).

Analysis: On review, the Court assumed that plain feel was a viable basis for warrantless seizures under some circumstances. However, the Court found that the officer's conduct exceeded the lawful scope of any such authority.

As to the abstract question of the viability of plain feel, the Court looked first for guidance to its decisions in *Terry v. Ohio*,[17] and its progeny (see **Chapter 19**). As the Court noted, it had, in another context, already determined that where an officer is conducting a lawful frisk and comes across evidence that he recognizes as contraband, he is not required to ignore it. "If, while conducting a legitimate *Terry* search of the interior of the automobile, the officer should . . . discover contraband other than weapons, he clearly cannot be required to ignore the contraband, and the Fourth Amendment does not require its suppression in such circumstances."[18]

The Court acknowledged that *Terry*'s creation of the frisk authority was rooted in a concern for officer safety—and thus, was intended as an exploration for weapons. However, the Court further concluded that if during a lawful pat-down an officer felt something that he immediately recognized as contraband, "there has been no invasion of the suspect's privacy beyond that already authorized by the officer's search for weapons."[19] Consequently, forcing an officer to ignore the item and obtain a warrant would not only be impractical but would advance no meaningful Fourth Amendment goal.

The logical extension of *Terry* that was recognized in *Dickerson* was seen as justified by the plain view doctrine. As noted, the detection of non-contraband items during a protective frisk entails no greater infringement of the suspect's privacy interests than the search for weapons alone. Moreover, where an officer feels an object that he immediately perceives as incriminating, "its warrantless seizure would be justified by the same practical considerations that inhere in the plain-view context."[20]

The Court also noted that the standards applied to plain view are similarly imposed upon plain feel. Consequently, before seizing a felt item the officer must have probable cause to believe that the item is contraband. In addition, just as plain view is limited by the legitimacy of the police conduct that put the officer in the position to make observations, plain feel is likewise limited by the legitimacy of the police conduct that allowed the officer to feel the contraband.

Applying these lessons to the case before it, the *Dickerson* Court found that the officer's warrantless seizure of the drugs in Dickerson's pocket could not be justified. The officer knew that the item he felt was not a weapon, but could not tell what else it might be. To identify the small hard lump, the officer had to manipulate the item between his fingers, and "the officer's continued exploration

[17] 392 U.S. 1 (1968).

[18] Id. at 374.

[19] Id. at 375.

[20] Id. at 376.

of [Dickerson's] pocket after having concluded that it contained no weapon was unrelated to the sole justification of the search under *Terry*: the protection of the police officer and others nearby."[21]

In so finding, the *Dickerson* Court compared the facts before it to the holding in *Arizona v. Hicks*. There a challenged search failed to fall within the plain view exception because an officer had to move stereo equipment to ascertain its illicit nature. In *Dickerson*, the same sort of excessive exploration by the police resulted in the constitutional violation.

Like plain view, plain feel is simply an extension of otherwise justified police authority. The doctrine thereby authorizes the search or seizure of items that have already been lawfully perceived through an officer's sense of touch. The doctrine creates no independent authority for the perception in the first instance. Put somewhat differently, for plain feel to apply, the police must already have the authority to make physical contact.

In light of the above limitation, many plain feel cases arise in the context of *Terry* stops or in the context of contemporaneous searches of arrestees. Both of these exceptions to the warrant requirement authorize the police to touch the suspect under certain circumstances. For example, in the context of *Terry*, when the police have a justified belief that the suspect they have approached is armed and presently dangerous, they have the authority to conduct a protective frisk of the suspect's outer clothing. So too, in the context of a lawful arrest, the police may typically search the person of the arrestee (and the immediately surrounding area) for evidence and weapons. In both these contexts, items that the police feel and immediately recognize to be contraband may be seized. However, as the Court found in *Dickerson*, the plain feel doctrine does not afford the police an independent authority to touch. If, for example, police engaged in a *Terry* stop have no justifiable reason to believe the person they are dealing with is armed, plain feel would **not** provide an alternate form of authority for the frisk. Moreover, as in *Dickerson*, if the police have the lawful authority to frisk, but exceed the outer boundaries of that authority, plain feel will not justify a subsequent seizure.

6. A "Plain Smell" Doctrine? Most federal appellate courts have deemed plain smell a natural extension of the plain view doctrine.[22]

[21] Id. at 378.

[22] See, e.g., United States v. Charles, 29 Fed. Appx. 892, 6 (3d Cir. 2002). But see United States v. Dien, 609 F.2d 1038, 1045 (2d Cir. 1979).

Example—*United States v. Angelos*, 433 F.3d 738 (10th Cir. 2006): A woman named Chelsea Davenport contacted the FBI and told them that her boyfriend Weldon Angelos was a drug dealer and that he kept drugs, guns, and money in a safe in the basement of a house in Salt Lake City. FBI Agent Becerra used this information to obtain a search warrant, which authorized him to seize "the personal safe located in the basement of the residence containing drugs, firearms, and money."

When Agent Becerra and his team executed the warrant, they entered the house and proceeded downstairs. While in the basement, the agents detected a strong smell of marijuana emanating from eighteen large duffel bags in the room. They seized those bags in addition to the safe. When they opened up the bags, they found large quantities of marijuana.

Angelos was arrested, and he challenged the seizure of the bags from his home, arguing that the warrant only authorized the seizure of his safe, and so the officers exceeded the scope of the warrant when they seized the duffel bags. His motion was denied, and he appealed the case to the Tenth Circuit.

Analysis: The Tenth Circuit affirmed the trial court's ruling denying suppression. The court agreed that the FBI exceeded the scope of the warrant when they seized the bags. However, the FBI agents had lawful access to the basement. Therefore, if the agents saw anything in plain view in the basement whose contraband nature was "immediately apparent," they would be authorized to seize that item pursuant to the plain view doctrine. In this case, the plain smell of the items indicated that the duffel bags were contraband, and so the agents were authorized to seize the bags pursuant to the plain smell doctrine.

Although this is the majority view, a few circuits have rejected the "plain smell" doctrine. The Second Circuit, in a case similar to *Angelos*, held that officers who went beyond the scope of the warrant to open boxes that smelled of marijuana were **not** justified. Under the Second Circuit view's, even if police officers are lawfully in a location and they smell marijuana coming from a closed container, they cannot open the container without a warrant.[23]

The Supreme Court itself has never expressly recognized plain smell as an exception to the warrant requirement, but it has decided a number of cases that have implicitly approved of the plain smell doctrine. For example, in, *Taylor v.*

[23] United States v. Dien, 609 F.2d 1038, 1045 (2d Cir. 1979).

United States,[24] prohibition officers responding to a call smelled the strong odor of whisky coming from a private garage. Using a flashlight, the officers peered into the building and observed cardboard boxes that might be used to store jars of alcohol. Acting without a warrant, the officers then broke into the building and found 122 cases of whisky. Following the defendant's arrest and conviction, he appealed the case to the Supreme Court. Although the Court found that "the action of the agents was inexcusable and the seizure unreasonable,"[25] it noted that "officers may rely on a distinctive odor as a physical fact indicative of possible crime. The officers' conduct in this case was unconstitutional because "[the odor] alone does not strip the owner of a building of constitutional guaranties . . . against unreasonable search."[26]

The Court also mentioned the "plain smell" doctrine in passing in its recent decision in *Florida v. Jardines*.[27] There, the Court noted as a purely descriptive matter that "a drug-detection dog is a specialized device for discovering objects not in plain view (or plain smell)."[28]

Thus, the Supreme Court has implicitly recognized the plain smell doctrine, but has held that smell, standing alone, can never justify a warrantless search or seizure. Of course, this conclusion is no different than the rule applied to plain view: the initial intrusion upon a suspect's privacy interests must first be justified by some other Fourth Amendment principle before plain view becomes viable. It is possible the Court will one day officially approve the plain smell doctrine in light of the existing circuit split. In the interim, however, practitioners should be careful to review the applicable rules in the relevant jurisdiction before assuming the viability of a "plain smell" exception.

7. Does Pretext Matter? Finally, let us consider whether the motivation of the searching officer makes any difference to the plain view analysis. As noted above, the Court in *Horton* made clear that the inadvertent discovery of an item is not constitutionally required to establish the legitimacy of that item's seizure under the plain view exception to the warrant requirement. However, there is a narrow corollary to the Court's conclusion in *Horton* that has yet to be resolved.

Post-*Horton*, police observation clearly need not be "accidental" for plain view to apply. However, standing opposite "accident" on the intentionality continuum is "pretext." What if a police officer's discovery of evidence wasn't simply "not

[24] 286 U.S. 1 (1932).

[25] Id. at 6.

[26] Id.

[27] 133 S.Ct. 1409 (2013).

[28] Id. at 1418.

an accident," but was instead quite deliberate? If the officer obtained his "lawful vantage point" through pretext, will his conduct still fall within the ambit of the plain view exception? The best answer to this question is "perhaps."

As noted above, plain view operates as an extension of police authority that is otherwise justified by a warrant or exception to the warrant requirement. The first plain view factor—lawful vantage point—thus, depends almost entirely upon the validity of the justification offered for the original intrusion. If the police see child pornography lying on the passenger seat of your car following a traffic stop, the lawfulness of their vantage point for purposes of plain view will depend upon the lawfulness of the stop itself. Similarly, if the police run into a house and see a pile of illegal guns on the table, the lawfulness of this observation will depend upon whether the officers can justify the initial intrusion into the home. Consequently, though the Court has not squarely resolved the issue, the relevance of pretext to plain view appears to depend upon the extent to which the Court has found pretext to be relevant to the initial police intrusion. In some contexts, the Court has suggested that pretext is relevant to the Fourth Amendment analysis. In others, it has said pretext matters not at all.

For example, the Court has said plainly that pretext is irrelevant under the Fourth Amendment to the lawfulness of police behavior that is based on probable cause.[29] Accordingly, a police officer is permitted to stop your car for an observed traffic infraction even if the only reason she did so was because she expected to make incriminating observations of the car's interior after the stop.[30] Any immediately recognizable, incriminating evidence that is seen by the officer can be seized within the parameters of plain view.

On the other hand, if the justification for the original intrusion is an inventory or administrative search, the Court has intimated that pretext might be relevant to the legitimacy of these police actions.[31] We will discuss inventory searches in detail in **Chapter 18**, but for now it is important to know that they are recognized as an exception to the warrant requirement only because they are conducted for a non-law enforcement purpose. Thus, if the court finds that the real reason behind an inventory search is to gather evidence for a crime using the plan view doctrine, it will hold that the search is unconstitutional.

---

[29] Whren v. United States, 517 U.S. 806, 814 (1996).

[30] Id.

[31] See, e.g., Florida v. Wells, 495 U.S. 1 (1990) (finding that an inventory search may not be used as a pretext for a more general search intended to uncover incriminating evidence); New York v. Burger, 482 U.S. 691 (1987) (upholding a warrantless administrative inspection where it was not being used as a pretext to uncover evidence of violations of criminal laws).

Quick Summary

The second recognized exception to the warrant requirement is plain view. Officers making a warrantless search or seizure can justify their actions under the plain view exception if they can establish three things. First, the officers must have made their observations from a lawful vantage point. Second, the officers must have lawful access to the item to execute the search or seizure. And, finally, the incriminating nature of the evidence must be immediately (or readily) apparent.

With regard to the final factor, the Court has found the police must possess only probable cause that an item is contraband, evidence of a criminal offense, or otherwise subject to seizure. Absolute certainty is **not** required.

Though termed an exception to the warrant requirement, plain view is more properly conceived as an extension of a police officer's otherwise lawful authority. Thus, the police must first have a right to be where they are before the plain view analysis will become a factor in justifying their warrantless conduct.

The Court has recognized that the principles underlying the plain view doctrine can be naturally and logically extended to the sense of touch as well. Thus, plain feel allows officers to search or seize evidence that they immediately recognize as contraband during the conduct of an otherwise lawful pat-down or search.

Moreover, while a majority of the federal circuits have recognized the further extension of plain view to the sense of smell, the Supreme Court has yet to formally recognize plain smell as a viable exception to the warrant requirement.

Review Questions

1. Calling the Robber. Rennata Faraday was a high school student waiting at a bus stop on her way to visit friends when a man approached her from behind carrying a knife. He demanded: "Gimme all your stuff or I'll cut you." The man held his knife against her arm while she gave him her school bag, wallet, and cell phone. He then ran away.

When police arrived on the scene, they got a description of the perpetrator and information about the victim's cell phone provider. With the victim's consent, they used the information to locate the cell phone, and narrowed its location down to the 3000 block of Round Road, a neighborhood about two miles from the robbery.

The police officers then went from door to door in that stretch of Round Road, telling the residents that they were looking for a fictitious child molester named "Leroy Smalls." At 3055 Round Road, a man opened the door who matched the description that the victim gave them. The man invited the police into the front room of his home to talk. While one of the officers began explaining the search for Leroy Smalls, the other surreptitiously dialed the victim's cell phone number. They heard the cell phone ring on the second floor of the defendant's home, and they immediately ran upstairs and found the phone under the defendant's bed in a bag, along with the victim's other belongings.

After his arrest, the defendant moved to suppress the evidence that the police found in the home as a result of the warrantless search The government argues that the police officers were lawfully in the defendant's home and heard the cell phone ringing, and so their search was justified by the "plain sight" doctrine—or in this case, the "plain hearing" doctrine. Was the police search justified?

2. A Bucket Full of Heroin. Narcotics detectives suspected that Norris Klymer was selling heroin out of his home, so they sat in their car on the street observing his house. After an hour or so, they observed a man, later identified as Greg Lowis, walk on to the porch and drop three small rectangular packages wrapped in newspaper into bucket on the house's porch. The detectives suspected that the rectangular packages were bricks of heroin. As Lowis began to walk off the porch, the detectives got out of the car and asked Lowis to wait. Lowis complied. The detectives looked in the bucket and unwrapped the packages, confirming that the packages were indeed bricks of heroin. They then arrested Lowis.

While they were on the porch, the officers detected a distinctive vinegar-type smell emanating from inside the home. As experienced narcotics detectives, they recognized that the smell was produced by the processing of pure heroin into "street heroin." They looked inside the screen door and saw paraphernalia associated with processing heroin. The detectives left the home and obtained a warrant based on the information they had learned. When they executed the warrant, they found more heroin inside the house, and they arrested Klymer for heroin possession.

Both Lowis and Klymer are challenging the police action.

a. Did the police violate Lowis' rights when they looked inside the bucket and unwrapped the heroin?

b. Did the police violate Klymer's rights when they smelled the heroin production and then looked inside his house and saw the heroin processing paraphernalia?

3. The Stolen Rings. Baltimore police responded to a 911 call from a parking lot where a woman said she had been sexually assaulted. The woman told the police that she had gotten into her car and the defendant had come up behind her with a knife, pushed her into the back seat of the car, and raped her. He then took two rings off her fingers and her necklace, and fled on foot. The victim described the man as wearing a red shirt, jeans, and a baseball cap. The police fanned out through the neighborhood, looking for the suspect.

A few blocks away, they found Ronald Sherman walking on the sidewalk. He was wearing a reddish-brown shirt, jeans, and a baseball cap. They stopped him and asked him a few questions. When he appeared nervous in answering, they decided to frisk him. They found no weapons, but they did feel what appeared to be two rings in his left front pocket. They pulled out the items and saw that the two rings matched the description of the rings that were stolen from the victim after the rape.

The victim ultimately identified Sherman as the perpetrator, and he was charged with rape and robbery. He is now challenging the seizure of the rings as a violation of his Fourth Amendment rights. Assume (correctly) that the initial stop of Sherman was legal, and that under *Terry* the police were allowed to conduct a brief pat-down for the sole purpose of looking for weapons. Did the police violate Sherman's rights when they pulled the rings out of his pocket?

FROM THE COURTROOM

HORTON v. CALIFORNIA

United States Supreme Court, 1990
496 U.S. 128

[Justice STEVENS delivered the opinion of the Court.]

[Justices BRENNAN filed a dissenting opinion, in which he was joined by Justice MARSHALL.]

In this case we revisit an issue that was considered, but not conclusively resolved, in *Coolidge v. New Hampshire,* 403 U.S. 443 (1971): Whether the warrantless seizure of evidence of crime in plain view is prohibited by the Fourth Amendment if the discovery of the evidence was not inadvertent. We conclude that even though inadvertence is a characteristic of most legitimate "plain-view" seizures, it is not a necessary condition.

I

Petitioner was convicted of the armed robbery of Erwin Wallaker, the treasurer of the San Jose Coin Club. When Wallaker returned to his home after the Club's annual show, he entered his garage and was accosted by two masked men, one armed with a machine gun and the other with an electrical shocking device, sometimes referred to as a "stun gun." The two men shocked Wallaker, bound and handcuffed him, and robbed him of jewelry and cash. During the encounter sufficient conversation took place to enable Wallaker subsequently to identify petitioner's distinctive voice. His identification was partially corroborated by a witness who saw the robbers leaving the scene and by evidence that petitioner had attended the coin show.

Sergeant LaRault, an experienced police officer, investigated the crime and determined that there was probable cause to search petitioner's home for the proceeds of the robbery and for the weapons used by the robbers. His affidavit for a search warrant referred to police reports that described the weapons as well as the proceeds, but the warrant issued by the Magistrate only authorized a search for the proceeds, including three specifically described rings.

Pursuant to the warrant, LaRault searched petitioner's residence, but he did not find the stolen property. During the course of the search, however, he discovered the weapons in plain view and seized them. Specifically, he seized an Uzi machine gun, a .38-caliber revolver, two stun guns, a handcuff key, a San Jose Coin Club advertising brochure, and a few items of clothing identified by the victim. LaRault testified that while he was searching for the rings, he also was interested in finding other evidence connecting petitioner to the robbery. Thus, the seized evidence was not discovered "inadvertently."

The trial court refused to suppress the evidence found in petitioner's home and, after a jury trial, petitioner was found guilty and sentenced to prison.

. . .

II

The Fourth Amendment provides:

> The right of the people to be secure in their persons, houses, papers, and effects, against unreasonable searches and seizures, shall not be violated, and no Warrants shall issue, but upon probable cause, supported by Oath or affirmation, and particularly describing the place to be searched, and the persons or things to be seized.

The right to security in person and property protected by the Fourth Amendment may be invaded in quite different ways by searches and seizures. A search compromises the individual interest in privacy; a seizure deprives the individual of dominion over his or her person or property. The "plain-view" doctrine is often considered an exception to the general rule that warrantless searches are presumptively unreasonable, but this characterization overlooks the important difference between searches and seizures. If an article is already in plain view, neither its observation nor its seizure would involve any invasion of privacy. A seizure of the article, however, would obviously invade the owner's possessory interest. If "plain view" justifies an exception from an otherwise applicable warrant requirement, therefore, it must be an exception that is addressed to the concerns that are implicated by seizures rather than by searches.

The criteria that generally guide "plain-view" seizures were set forth in *Coolidge v. New Hampshire,* 403 U.S. 443 (1971). The Court held that the police, in seizing two automobiles parked in plain view on the defendant's driveway in the course of arresting the defendant, violated the Fourth Amendment. Accordingly, particles of gunpowder that had been subsequently found in vacuum sweepings from one of the cars could not be introduced in evidence against the defendant. The State endeavored to justify the seizure of the automobiles, and their subsequent search at the police station, on four different grounds, including the "plain-view" doctrine. The scope of that doctrine as it had developed in earlier cases was fairly summarized in these three paragraphs from Justice Stewart's opinion:

> It is well established that under certain circumstances the police may seize evidence in plain view without a warrant. But it is important to keep in mind that, in the vast majority of cases, *any* evidence seized by the police will be in plain view, at least at the moment of seizure. The problem with the 'plain view' doctrine has been to identify the circumstances in which plain view has legal significance rather than being simply the normal concomitant of any search, legal or illegal.
>
> An example of the applicability of the 'plain view' doctrine is the situation in which the police have a warrant to search a given area for specified objects,

and in the course of the search come across some other article of incriminating character. (Stewart, J., concurring in result).

Where the initial intrusion that brings the police within plain view of such an article is supported, not by a warrant, but by one of the recognized exceptions to the warrant requirement, the seizure is also legitimate. Thus the police may inadvertently come across evidence while in 'hot pursuit' of a fleeing suspect. And an object that comes into view during a search incident to arrest that is appropriately limited in scope under existing law may be seized without a warrant. Finally, the 'plain view' doctrine has been applied where a police officer is not searching for evidence against the accused, but nonetheless inadvertently comes across an incriminating object.

"What the 'plain view' cases have in common is that the police officer in each of them had a prior justification for an intrusion in the course of which he came inadvertently across a piece of evidence incriminating the accused. The doctrine serves to supplement the prior justification—whether it be a warrant for another object, hot pursuit, search incident to lawful arrest, or some other legitimate reason for being present unconnected with a search directed against the accused-and permits the warrantless seizure. Of course, the extension of the original justification is legitimate only where it is immediately apparent to the police that they have evidence before them; the 'plain view' doctrine may not be used to extend a general exploratory search from one object to another until something incriminating at last emerges."

Justice Stewart then described the two limitations on the doctrine that he found implicit in its rationale: First, that "plain view *alone* is never enough to justify the warrantless seizure of evidence," and second, that "the discovery of evidence in plain view must be inadvertent."

Justice Stewart's analysis of the "plain-view" doctrine did not command a majority, and a plurality of the Court has since made clear that the discussion is "not a binding precedent." Justice Harlan, who concurred in the Court's judgment did not join the plurality's discussion of the "plain-view" doctrine. The decision nonetheless is a binding precedent. Before discussing the second limitation, which is implicated in this case, it is therefore necessary to explain why the first adequately supports the Court's judgment.

It is, of course, an essential predicate to any valid warrantless seizure of incriminating evidence that the officer did not violate the Fourth Amendment in arriving at the place from which the evidence could be plainly viewed. There are, moreover, two additional conditions that must be satisfied to justify the warrantless seizure. First, not only must the item be in plain view; its incriminating character must also be "immediately apparent." Thus, in *Coolidge,* the cars were obviously in plain view, but their probative value remained uncertain until after the interiors were swept and examined microscopically. Second, not only must the officer be lawfully located in a place from which the object can be plainly seen, but he or she must also have a lawful right of access to the object itself. As the United States has suggested, Justice Harlan's vote in *Coolidge* may have rested on the fact that the seizure of the cars was accomplished by means of a warrantless trespass on the defendant's property. In all events, we are satisfied that the absence of inadvertence was not essential to the Court's rejection of the State's "plain-view" argument in *Coolidge.*

III

Justice Stewart concluded that the inadvertence requirement was necessary to avoid a violation of the express constitutional requirement that a valid warrant must particularly describe the things to be seized. He explained:

> The rationale of the exception to the warrant requirement, as just stated, is that a plain-view seizure will not turn an initially valid (and therefore limited) search into a 'general' one, while the inconvenience of procuring a warrant to cover an inadvertent discovery is great. But where the discovery is anticipated, where the police know in advance the location of the evidence and intend to seize it, the situation is altogether different. The requirement of a warrant to seize imposes no inconvenience whatever, or at least none which is constitutionally cognizable in a legal system that regards warrantless searches as '*per se* unreasonable' in the absence of 'exigent circumstances.'
>
> If the initial intrusion is bottomed upon a warrant that fails to mention a particular object, though the police know its location and intend to seize it, then there is a violation of the express constitutional requirement of 'Warrants . . . particularly describing . . . [the] things to be seized.'

We find two flaws in this reasoning. First, evenhanded law enforcement is best achieved by the application of objective standards of conduct, rather than standards that depend upon the subjective state of mind of the officer. The fact that an officer is interested in an item of evidence and fully expects to find it in the course of a search should not invalidate its seizure if the search is confined in area and duration by the terms of a warrant or a valid exception to the warrant requirement. If the officer has knowledge approaching certainty that the item will be found, we see no reason why he or she would deliberately omit a particular description of the item to be seized from the application for a search warrant. Specification of the additional item could only permit the officer to expand the scope of the search. On the other hand, if he or she has a valid warrant to search for one item and merely a suspicion concerning the second, whether or not it amounts to probable cause, we fail to see why that suspicion should immunize the second item from seizure if it is found during a lawful search for the first. The hypothetical case put by Justice White in his concurring and dissenting opinion in *Coolidge* is instructive:

> Let us suppose officers secure a warrant to search a house for a rifle. While staying well within the range of a rifle search, they discover two photographs of the murder victim, both in plain sight in the bedroom. Assume also that the discovery of the one photograph was inadvertent but finding the other was anticipated. The Court would permit the seizure of only one of the photographs. But in terms of the 'minor' peril to Fourth Amendment values there is surely no difference between these two photographs: the interference

> with possession is the same in each case and the officers' appraisal of the photograph they expected to see is no less reliable than their judgment about the other. And in both situations the actual inconvenience and danger to evidence remain identical if the officers must depart and secure a warrant.

Second, the suggestion that the inadvertence requirement is necessary to prevent the police from conducting general searches, or from converting specific warrants into general warrants, is not persuasive because that interest is already served by the requirements that no warrant issue unless it "particularly describ[es] the place to be searched and the persons or things to be seized," and that a warrantless search be circumscribed by the exigencies which justify its initiation. Scrupulous adherence to these requirements serves the interests in limiting the area and duration of the search that the inadvertence requirement inadequately protects. Once those commands have been satisfied and the officer has a lawful right of access, however, no additional Fourth Amendment interest is furthered by requiring that the discovery of evidence be inadvertent. If the scope of the search exceeds that permitted by the terms of a validly issued warrant or the character of the relevant exception from the warrant requirement, the subsequent seizure is unconstitutional without more. Thus, in the case of a search incident to a lawful arrest, "[i]f the police stray outside the scope of an authorized *Chimel* search they are already in violation of the Fourth Amendment, and evidence so seized will be excluded; adding a second reason for excluding evidence hardly seems worth the candle." Similarly, the object of a warrantless search of an automobile also defines its scope:

> The scope of a warrantless search of an automobile thus is not defined by the nature of the container in which the contraband is secreted. Rather, it is defined by the object of the search and the places in which there is probable cause to believe that it may be found. Just as probable cause to believe that a stolen lawnmower may be found in a garage will not support a warrant to search an upstairs bedroom, probable cause to believe that undocumented aliens are being transported in a van will not justify a warrantless search of a suitcase. Probable cause to believe that a container placed in the trunk of a taxi contains contraband or evidence does not justify a search of the entire cab.

In this case, the scope of the search was not enlarged in the slightest by the omission of any reference to the weapons in the warrant. Indeed, if the three rings and other items named in the warrant had been found at the outset—or if petitioner had them in his possession and had responded to the warrant by producing them immediately—no search for weapons could have taken place. Again, Justice White's concurring and dissenting opinion in *Coolidge* is instructive:

> Police with a warrant for a rifle may search only places where rifles might be and must terminate the search once the rifle is found; the inadvertence rule will in no way reduce the number of places into which they may lawfully look.

As we have already suggested, by hypothesis the seizure of an object in plain view does not involve an intrusion on privacy. If the interest in privacy has been invaded, the violation must have occurred before the object came into plain view and there is no need for an inadvertence limitation on seizures to condemn it. The prohibition against general searches and general warrants serves primarily as a protection against unjustified intrusions on privacy. But reliance on privacy concerns that support that prohibition is misplaced when the inquiry concerns the scope of an exception that merely authorizes an officer with a lawful right of access to an item to seize it without a warrant.

In this case the items seized from petitioner's home were discovered during a lawful search authorized by a valid warrant. When they were discovered, it was immediately apparent to the officer that they constituted incriminating evidence. He had probable cause, not only to obtain a warrant to search for the stolen property, but also to believe that the weapons and handguns been used in the crime he was investigating. The search was authorized by the warrant; the seizure was authorized by the "plain-view" doctrine. The judgment is affirmed.

It is so ordered.

Justice BRENNAN, with whom Justice MARSHALL joins, dissenting.

I remain convinced that Justice Stewart correctly articulated the plain-view doctrine in *Coolidge v. New Hampshire,* 403 U.S. 443 (1971). The Fourth Amendment permits law enforcement officers to seize items for which they do not have a warrant when those items are found in plain view and (1) the officers are lawfully in a position to observe the items, (2) the discovery of the items is "inadvertent," and (3) it is immediately apparent to the officers that the items are evidence of a crime, contraband, or otherwise subject to seizure. In eschewing the inadvertent discovery requirement, the majority ignores the Fourth Amendment's express command that warrants particularly describe not only the *places* to be searched, but also the *things* to be seized. I respectfully dissent from this rewriting of the Fourth Amendment.

I

The Fourth Amendment states:

> The right of the people to be secure in their persons, houses, papers, and effects, against unreasonable searches and seizures, shall not be violated, and no Warrants shall issue, but upon probable cause, supported by Oath or affirmation, and particularly describing the place to be searched, and the persons or things to be seized.

The Amendment protects two distinct interests. The prohibition against unreasonable searches and the requirement that a warrant "particularly describ[e] the place to be searched" protect an interest in privacy. The prohibition against unreasonable seizures and the requirement that a warrant "particularly describ[e] . . . the . . . things to be seized" protect a possessory interest in property. The Fourth Amendment, by its terms, declares the privacy and possessory interests to be equally important. As this Court recently stated: "Although the interest protected by the Fourth Amendment injunction against unreasonable searches is quite different from that protected by its injunction against unreasonable seizures, neither the one nor the other is of inferior worth or necessarily requires only lesser protection."

The Amendment protects these equally important interests in precisely the same manner: by requiring a neutral and detached magistrate to evaluate, before the search or seizure, the government's showing of probable cause and its particular description of the place to be searched and the items to be seized. Accordingly, just as a warrantless search is *per se* unreasonable absent exigent circumstances, so too a seizure of personal property is "*per se* unreasonable within the meaning of the Fourth Amendment unless it is accomplished pursuant to a judicial warrant issued upon probable cause and particularly describing the items to be seized . . . ."

The plain-view doctrine is an exception to the general rule that a seizure of personal property must be authorized by a warrant. As Justice Stewart explained in *Coolidge,* we accept a warrantless seizure when an officer is lawfully in a location and inadvertently sees evidence of a crime because of "the inconvenience of procuring a warrant" to seize this newly discovered piece of evidence. But "where the discovery is anticipated, where the police know in advance the location of the evidence and intend to seize it," the argument that procuring a warrant would be "inconvenient" loses much, if not all, of its force. Barring an exigency, there is no reason why the police officers could not have obtained a warrant to seize this evidence before entering the premises. The rationale behind the inadvertent discovery requirement is simply that we will not excuse officers from the general requirement of a warrant to seize if the officers know the location of evidence, have probable cause to seize it, intend to seize it, and yet do not bother to obtain a warrant particularly describing that evidence. To do so would violate "the express constitutional requirement of 'Warrants . . . particularly describing . . . [the] things to be seized,'" and would "fly in the face of the basic rule that no amount of probable cause can justify a warrantless seizure."

. . .

The Court posits two "flaws" in Justice Stewart's reasoning that it believes demonstrate the inappropriateness of the inadvertent discovery requirement. But these flaws are illusory. First, the majority explains that it can see no reason why an officer who "has knowledge approaching certainty" that an item will be found in a particular location "would deliberately omit a particular description of the item to be seized from the application for a search warrant." But to the individual whose possessory interest has been invaded, it matters not *why* the police officer decided to omit a particular item from his application for a search warrant. When an officer with probable cause to seize an item fails to mention that item in his application for a search warrant-for whatever reason-and then seizes the item anyway, his conduct is *per se* unreasonable. Suppression of the evidence so seized will encourage officers to be more precise and complete in future warrant applications.

Furthermore, there are a number of instances in which a law enforcement officer might deliberately choose to omit certain items from a warrant application even though he has probable cause to seize them, knows they are on the premises, and intends to seize them when they are discovered in plain view. For example, the warrant application process can often be time consuming, especially when the police attempt to seize a large number of items. An officer interested in conducting a search as soon as possible might decide to save time by listing only one or two hard-to-find items, such as the stolen rings in this case, confident that he will find in plain view all of the other evidence he is looking for before he discovers the listed items. Because rings could be located almost anywhere inside or outside a house, it is unlikely that a warrant to search for and seize the rings would restrict the scope of the search. An officer might rationally find the risk of immediately discovering the items listed in the warrant—thereby forcing him to conclude the search immediately—outweighed by the time saved in the application process.

The majority also contends that, once an officer is lawfully in a house and the scope of his search is adequately circumscribed by a warrant, "no additional Fourth Amendment interest is furthered by requiring that the discovery of evidence be inadvertent." Put another way, "'the inadvertence rule will in no way reduce the number of places into which [law enforcement officers] may lawfully look.'" The majority is correct, but it has asked the wrong question. It is true that the inadvertent discovery requirement furthers no privacy interests. The requirement in no way reduces the scope of a search or the number of places into which officers may look. But it does protect possessory interests. . . . The inadvertent discovery requirement is essential if we are to take seriously the Fourth Amendment's protection of possessory interests as well as privacy interests. The Court today eliminates a rule designed to further possessory interests on the ground that it fails to further privacy interests. I cannot countenance such constitutional legerdemain.

. . .

FROM THE COURTROOM

MINNESOTA v. DICKERSON

United States Supreme Court, 1993
508 U.S. 366

[Justice WHITE delivered the opinion of the Court.]

[Justice SCALIA filed a concurring opinion.]

[Chief Justice REHNQUIST an opinion concurring in part and dissenting in part, in which he was joined by Justices BLACKMUN and THOMAS.]

In this case, we consider whether the Fourth Amendment permits the seizure of contraband detected through a police officer's sense of touch during a protective patdown search.

I

On the evening of November 9, 1989, two Minneapolis police officers were patrolling an area on the city's north side in a marked squad car. At about 8:15 p.m., one of the officers observed respondent leaving a [twelve]-unit apartment building on Morgan Avenue North. The officer, having previously responded to complaints of drug sales in the building's hallways and having executed several search warrants on the premises, considered the building to be a notorious "crack house." According to testimony credited by the trial court, respondent began walking toward the police but, upon spotting the squad car and making eye contact with one of the officers, abruptly halted and began walking in the opposite direction. His suspicion aroused, this officer watched as respondent turned and entered an alley on the other side of the apartment building. Based upon respondent's seemingly evasive actions and the fact that he had just left a building known for cocaine traffic, the officers decided to stop respondent and investigate further.

The officers pulled their squad car into the alley and ordered respondent to stop and submit to a patdown search. The search revealed no weapons, but the officer conducting the search did take an interest in a small lump in respondent's nylon jacket. The officer later testified:

> [A]s I pat-searched the front of his body, I felt a lump, a small lump, in the front pocket. I examined it with my fingers and it slid and it felt to be a lump of crack cocaine in cellophane.

The officer then reached into respondent's pocket and retrieved a small plastic bag containing one fifth of one gram of crack cocaine. Respondent was arrested and charged in Hennepin County District Court with possession of a controlled substance.

Before trial, respondent moved to suppress the cocaine. The trial court first concluded that the officers were justified under *Terry v. Ohio,* 392 U.S. 1 (1968), in stopping respondent to investigate whether he might be engaged in criminal activity. The court further found that the officers were justified in frisking respondent to ensure that he was not carrying a weapon. Finally, analogizing to the "plain-view" doctrine, under which officers may make a warrantless seizure of contraband found in plain view during a lawful search for other items, the trial court ruled that the officers' seizure of the cocaine did not violate the Fourth Amendment:

> To this Court there is no distinction as to which sensory perception the officer uses to conclude that the material is contraband. An experienced officer may rely upon his sense of smell in DWI stops or in recognizing the smell of burning marijuana in an automobile. The sound of a shotgun being racked would clearly support certain reactions by an officer. The sense of touch, grounded in experience and training, is as reliable as perceptions drawn from other senses. 'Plain feel,' therefore, is no different than plain view and will equally support the seizure here.

His suppression motion having failed, respondent proceeded to trial and was found guilty.

. . .

II

A

The Fourth Amendment, made applicable to the States by way of the Fourteenth Amendment, guarantees "[t]he right of the people to be secure in their persons, houses, papers, and effects, against unreasonable searches and seizures." Time and again, this Court has observed that searches and seizures "'conducted outside the judicial process, without prior approval by judge or magistrate, are *per se* unreasonable under the Fourth Amendment—subject only to a few specifically established and well delineated exceptions.'" One such exception was recognized in *Terry v. Ohio,* which held that "where a police officer observes unusual conduct which leads him reasonably to conclude in light of his experience that criminal activity may be afoot . . . ," the officer may briefly stop the suspicious person and make "reasonable inquiries" aimed at confirming or dispelling his suspicions.

Terry further held that "[w]hen an officer is justified in believing that the individual whose suspicious behavior he is investigating at close range is armed and presently dangerous to the officer or to others," the officer may conduct a patdown search "to determine whether the person is in fact carrying a weapon." "The purpose of this limited search is not to discover evidence of crime, but to allow the officer to pursue his investigation without fear of violence. . . ." Rather, a protective search—permitted without a warrant and on the basis of reasonable suspicion less than probable cause—must be strictly "limited to that which is necessary for the discovery of weapons which might be used to harm the officer or others nearby." If the protective search goes beyond what is necessary to determine if the suspect is armed, it is no longer valid under *Terry* and its fruits will be suppressed.

These principles were settled [twenty-five] years ago when, on the same day, the Court announced its decisions in *Terry* and *Sibron.* The question presented today is whether police officers may seize nonthreatening contraband detected during a protective patdown search of the sort permitted by *Terry.* We think the answer is clearly that they may, so long as the officers' search stays within the bounds marked by *Terry.*

B

We have already held that police officers, at least under certain circumstances, may seize contraband detected during the lawful execution of a *Terry* search. In *Michigan v. Long*, 463 U.S. 1032 (1983), for example, police approached a man who had driven his car into a ditch and who appeared to be under the influence of some intoxicant. As the man moved to reenter the car from the roadside, police spotted a knife on the floorboard. The officers stopped the man, subjected him to a patdown search, and then inspected the interior of the vehicle for other weapons. During the search of the passenger compartment, the police discovered an open pouch containing marijuana and seized it. This Court upheld the validity of the search and seizure under *Terry.* The Court held first that, in the context of a roadside encounter, where police have reasonable suspicion based on specific and articulable facts to believe that a driver may be armed and dangerous, they may conduct a protective search for weapons not only of the driver's person but also of the passenger compartment of the automobile. Of course, the protective search of the vehicle, being justified solely by the danger that weapons stored there could be used against the officers or bystanders, must be "limited to those areas in which a weapon may be placed or hidden." The Court then held: "If, while conducting a legitimate *Terry* search of the interior of the automobile, the officer should, as here, discover contraband other than weapons, he clearly cannot be required to ignore the contraband, and the Fourth Amendment does not require its suppression in such circumstances."

The Court in *Long* justified this latter holding by reference to our cases under the "plain-view" doctrine. Under that doctrine, if police are lawfully in a position from which they view an object, if its incriminating character is immediately apparent, and if the officers have a lawful right of access to the object, they may seize it without a warrant. If, however, the police lack probable cause to believe that an object in plain view is contraband without conducting some further search of the object—*i.e.,* if "its incriminating character [is not] 'immediately apparent,'" the plain-view doctrine cannot justify its seizure.

We think that this doctrine has an obvious application by analogy to cases in which an officer discovers contraband through the sense of touch during an otherwise lawful search. The rationale of the plain-view doctrine is that if contraband is left in open view and is observed by a police officer from a lawful vantage point, there has been no invasion of a legitimate expectation of privacy and thus no "search" within the meaning of the Fourth Amendment—or at least no search independent of the initial intrusion that gave the officers their vantage point. The warrantless seizure of contraband that presents itself in this manner is deemed justified by the realization that resort to a neutral magistrate under such circumstances would often be impracticable and would do little to promote the objectives of the Fourth Amendment. The same can be said of tactile discoveries of contraband. If a police officer lawfully pats down a suspect's outer clothing and feels an object whose contour or mass makes its identity immediately apparent, there has been no invasion of the suspect's privacy beyond that already authorized by the officer's search for weapons; if the object is contraband, its warrantless seizure would be justified by the same practical considerations that inhere in the plain-view context.

The Minnesota Supreme Court rejected an analogy to the plain-view doctrine on two grounds: first, its belief that "the sense of touch is inherently less immediate and less reliable than the sense of sight," and second, that "the sense of touch is far more intrusive into the personal privacy that is at the core of the [F]ourth [A]mendment." We have a somewhat different view. First, *Terry* itself demonstrates that the sense of touch is capable of revealing the nature of an object with sufficient reliability to support a seizure. The very premise of *Terry,* after all, is that officers will be able to detect the presence of weapons through the sense of touch and *Terry* upheld precisely such a seizure. Even if it were true that the sense of touch is generally less reliable than the sense of sight, that only suggests that officers will less often be able to justify seizures of unseen contraband. Regardless of whether the officer detects the contraband by sight or by touch, however, the Fourth Amendment's requirement that the officer have probable cause to believe that the item is contraband before seizing it ensures against excessively speculative seizures. The court's second concern—that touch is more intrusive into privacy than is sight—is inapposite in light of the fact that the intrusion the court fears has already been authorized by the lawful search for weapons. The seizure of an item whose identity is already known occasions no further invasion of privacy. Accordingly, the suspect's privacy interests are not advanced by a categorical rule barring the seizure of contraband plainly detected through the sense of touch.

III

It remains to apply these principles to the facts of this case. Respondent has not challenged the finding made by the trial court and affirmed by both the Court of Appeals and the State Supreme Court that the police were justified under *Terry* in stopping him and frisking him for weapons. Thus, the dispositive question before this Court is whether the officer who conducted the search was acting within the lawful bounds marked by *Terry* at the time he gained probable cause to believe that the lump in respondent's jacket was contraband. The State District Court did not make precise findings on this point, instead finding simply that the officer, after feeling "a small, hard object wrapped in plastic" in respondent's pocket, "formed the opinion that the object . . . was crack . . . cocaine." The District Court also noted that the officer made "no claim that he suspected this object to be a weapon," a finding affirmed on appeal. The Minnesota Supreme Court, after "a close examination of the record," held that the officer's own testimony "belies any notion that he 'immediately'" recognized the lump as crack cocaine. Rather, the court concluded, the officer determined that the lump was contraband only after "squeezing, sliding and otherwise manipulating the contents of the defendant's pocket"—a pocket which the officer already knew contained no weapon.

Under the State Supreme Court's interpretation of the record before it, it is clear that the court was correct in holding that the police officer in this case overstepped the bounds of the "strictly circumscribed" search for weapons allowed under *Terry.* Where, as here, "an officer who is executing a valid search for one item seizes a different item," this Court rightly "has been sensitive to the danger . . . that officers will enlarge a specific authorization, furnished by a warrant or an exigency, into the equivalent of a general warrant to rummage and seize at will." Here, the officer's continued exploration of respondent's pocket after having concluded that it contained no weapon was unrelated to "[t]he sole justification of the search [under *Terry:*] . . . the protection of the police officer and others nearby." It therefore amounted to the sort of evidentiary search that *Terry* expressly refused to authorize, and that we have condemned in subsequent cases.

Once again, the analogy to the plain-view doctrine is apt. In *Arizona v. Hicks,* 480 U.S. 321 (1987), this Court held invalid the seizure of stolen stereo equipment found by police while executing a valid search for other evidence. Although the police were lawfully on the premises, they obtained probable cause to believe that the stereo equipment was contraband only after moving the equipment to permit officers to read its serial numbers. The subsequent seizure of the equipment could not be justified by the plain-view doctrine, this Court explained, because the incriminating character of the stereo equipment was not immediately apparent; rather, probable cause to believe that the equipment was stolen arose only as a result of a further search—the moving of the equipment—that was not authorized by a search warrant or by any exception to the warrant requirement. The facts of this case are very similar. Although the officer was lawfully in a position to feel the lump in respondent's pocket, because *Terry* entitled him to place his hands upon respondent's jacket, the court below determined that the incriminating character of the object was not immediately apparent to him. Rather, the officer determined that the item was contraband only after conducting a further search, one not authorized by *Terry* or by any other exception to the warrant requirement. Because this further search of respondent's pocket was constitutionally invalid, the seizure of the cocaine that followed is likewise unconstitutional.

. . .

[The concurring opinion of Justice SCALIA is omitted.]

[The concurring and dissenting opinion of Chief Justice REHNQUIST, which is joined by Justice BLACKMUN and THOMAS, is omitted.]

15

Exceptions to the Warrant Requirement: Automobile

Key Concepts

- Probable Cause that Car Contains Contraband
- All Containers Therein Are Fair Game
- Car Must Be Functionally Mobile

A. Introduction and Policy. The third exception to the warrant requirement—the "A" in S-P-A-C-E-S—is the automobile exception. The automobile exception allows for the warrantless search of cars and other vehicles when the police have probable cause to believe there is contraband inside.

The automobile exception is based on two very concrete considerations. First, the Court identified the inherent mobility of automobiles as a justification for the exception. When police come upon a car that they reasonably suspect contains contraband, they may not have the time to secure a warrant before it drives away. Accordingly, in the Court's view, strict adherence to a warrant requirement would unduly frustrate law enforcement efforts.

The second justification for the requirement is the Court's observation that most individuals have a reduced expectation of privacy in their cars. Without question, people can reasonably expect some privacy in their cars. However, this expectation is not akin to what is reasonable in connection with a home or office, for two reasons:

1. Much of a car's interior can be seen by passersby; and
2. Cars are subject to governmental oversight, including periodic inspections to ensure compliance with various statutes and rules.

The Court's sense that people do not maintain a substantial interest in privacy in their cars has been the subject of frequent criticism. Many have observed that the necessities of modern life increase the amount of time people spend in their cars. With this development, there has been a commensurate increase in the amount of personal information that cars often contain. Many people treat their cars as quasi-second offices, storing all manner of paperwork and other material inside. Moreover, with near-standard factory installed window tinting in many vehicles coupled with higher, larger cabin sizes, the suggestion that the interior of vehicles is always observable by passersby seems somewhat antiquated. Notwithstanding these modern realities, the Court has been steadfast in concluding that we enjoy only reduced expectations of privacy in our cars.

B. The Law. The automobile exception was first recognized by the Court in 1925 in a case called *Carroll v. United States*.[1] For this reason, you may at times hear the exception referred to as the Carroll Doctrine. The exception states:

> If the police have probable cause to believe a vehicle contains contraband, the automobile exception allows the police to search the car and all containers therein that may hold the object of the search.

There are three significant aspects to this exception:

The first is the nature of its probable cause requirement. The police must have probable cause to believe **the car** contains contraband. Probable cause here may be generated by a belief that 1) the car generally contains contraband or 2) a belief that just a single container inside the car contains contraband. However, you should be careful to clarify the precise nature of the probable cause since, as you will read below, it will define the scope of the warrantless search.

The second significant aspect is the scope of the search that is authorized under this exception. If the police have probable cause to believe generally that a car contains contraband (but don't have particular suspicions about where the evidence might be located), they are entitled to search every single part of the car where the object of the search might be secreted. Consequently, the police may search the trunk and even locked glove compartments. The police may also dissemble door panels and pull apart seats if the item they are looking for might reasonably be found in these places. If, on the other hand, the police have specific knowledge that just a single container in the car contains contraband, the automobile exception will not authorize a search of the entire car. Rather, only the warrantless search of the suspect container will be justified.

Finally, you should note that this exception authorizes a search not only of the car but also of any containers therein that might contain the object of the search. Accordingly, the police may search not only the car but any bags, packages, or other containers that are in the car at the time of the search. This rule applies without regard for ownership. Thus, a passenger's purse or book bag may also be searched once probable cause to search the car is established.

---

[1] 267 U.S. 132 (1925).

The automobile exception will not, however, justify a bodily search of the driver or passengers. Such searches would have to be justified by some other exception to the warrant requirement, such as a search incident to a lawful arrest or a *Terry* stop-and-frisk.

C. A Quick Overview of Automobile Searches. There are four warrantless searches of automobiles that have been recognized by the Supreme Court. The first is governed by the automobile exception. In addition, as noted in **Chapter 13**, the Court has also found that the police may search a car pursuant to the search incident to a lawful arrest exception if the arrestee is a recent occupant of the vehicle, and there is reason to believe the car contains a weapon or evidence of the crime of arrest. Third, if the police have reasonable suspicion to believe a person they have stopped in a car is armed and presently dangerous, the police may conduct a cursory *Terry* frisk of the car's passenger compartment to look for weapons. Finally, police are allowed to conduct an "inventory search" of any car that has been lawfully seized, as long as the search is part of their normal routine for seized cars. The justification for these four searches and their associated scopes have important differences that students should be aware of.

The first important difference concerns the object of police suspicion. With the automobile exception, it is the **car** that is the focus of police scrutiny. In contrast, with the search incident to arrest or the *Terry* frisk, it is the **detainee** who is the target of police suspicion. In those contexts, the search or frisk of the detainee's car is therefore dependent entirely on the validity of the initial seizure of the person.

A second important difference concerns the scope of the search. As noted above, under the automobile exception, the police are entitled to search the entire car, including the trunk, and any containers therein. With the search incident to arrest, however, the scope of the search is more limited. The police are entitled to search only those areas of the car that the recent occupant-arrestee might access. And in the *Terry* context, police may search only those areas in the passenger compartment that may reasonably contain a weapon. Consequently, if the justification for the search of a car is that a recent occupant has been arrested or otherwise detained, the police will not be allowed to search the trunk or a locked gloved compartment.

As noted above, the inherent mobility of automobiles provides one justification for the automobile exception. However, the Court has clarified that the mobility of the vehicle must be judged at the time the automobile is seized, not at the time it is searched. Thus, if police officers have probable cause to believe a vehicle contains contraband, they may seize that vehicle and tow it to the police station. A search of the vehicle at the police station would still be justified under the automobile exception even though a car sitting in the police impound lot is not in danger of driving away in any real sense. Put another way, if the police have probable cause to justify the seizure of a car on a public roadway, they may search the car on the scene or may wait and search the car after they have removed it.

Finally, the "inventory search" exception is a narrowly drawn exception that is closely related to the automobile exception. When the police lawfully seize a car (pursuant to a state impoundment or forfeiture statute, pursuant to their caretaking function, or as a function of probable cause to believe the car contains contraband), the Court has recognized that officer safety, public safety, or the protection of the owner's property may justify a warrantless search of the vehicle.[2] In recognizing this authority, the Court has commented that it "would be unreasonable to hold that the police, having to retain the car in their custody for such a length of time, had no right, even for their own protection, to search it."[3] Accordingly, where such searches are conducted "pursuant to standard police procedures," they will be deemed reasonable.[4]

Warrant Exception	Justification	Scope
Automobile	Probable cause that car or container in car contains contraband.	Entire car including trunk and any containers—anywhere the contraband could reasonably be found.
Search Incident to Lawful Arrest	Police must have "reason to believe" the car contains a weapon or evidence of the crime of arrest.	Only the areas that the suspect may be able to access at the time of the search.
Terry Stop	Reasonable suspicion that criminal activity is afoot and that the suspect may have a weapon.	Anywhere in the passenger compartment that could contain a weapon (not the trunk or locked glove compartment).
Inventory Search	Automatic right after car is lawfully seized as long as it is the standard police practice.	Entire car including trunk and any containers.

D. Applying the Law. The automobile exception to the warrant requirement contains a number of aspects that are relevant to its legitimate application. These include: the nature of the exception's probable cause requirement; the treatment of various containers found in the car; the treatment of people found in the car; and the requirement of inherent mobility. We will consider each below.

---

2 Cady v. Dombrowski, 413 U.S. 433, 447 (1973).

3 Cooper v. California, 386 U.S. 58, 61–62 (1967).

4 South Dakota v. Opperman, 428 U.S. 364, 372 (1976).

1. Probable Cause to Believe the Vehicle Contains Contraband. To establish that a warrantless search was justified by the automobile exception, the police must first establish probable cause to believe the car contained contraband. In 1925, the Court first confronted the question of what sort of evidence will sustain the probable cause requirement in the seminal automobile search case, *Carroll v. United States*:

> **Example—*Carroll v. United States*, 267 U.S. 132 (1925):** Federal prohibition agent Fred Cronenwett was working undercover as "Mr. Stafford" in an apartment in Grand Rapids, Michigan. He was there under the guise of buying cases of illegal alcohol. Three men came to the apartment to facilitate the sale—George Carroll, John Kiro, and a man named Kurska. After conversation, Carroll and Kiro told the undercover that they did not have the liquor on them and would need to go to the other side of Grand Rapids to pick it up. The three men then left. Kruska returned a short time later and told "Mr. Stafford" that the order could not be filled that evening but perhaps could be the following day. The next day, the officer waited as agreed, but the men never returned.
>
> Two weeks later, Cronenwett and his partner were patrolling the road between Grand Rapids and Detroit, which was a known route for transporting bootleg alcohol. Cronenwett saw Carroll and Kiro driving along the road toward Grand Rapids in the same car the two had been in the night of the meeting in the apartment. He gave chase but lost the men just outside of East Lansing.
>
> Two months later, Cronenwett was patrolling the same road between Grand Rapids and Detroit. He again saw Kiro and Carroll and followed them. Eventually Cronenwett stopped the two men just east of Grand Rapids. As he approached the car, Carroll greeted Cronenwett as "Fred," suggesting that he had learned the undercover officer's real identity. Cronenwett and his partner ordered the men out of the car and proceeded to search it thoroughly. They found nothing in the trunk nor under the seats. When Cronenwett began tearing open the upholstery on one of the cushions, Carroll stated, "Don't tear the cushion; we have only got six cases in there."[5] The officers eventually discovered nearly seventy quarts of whisky and gin in the automobile.

---

[5] Carroll, 267 U.S. at 172.

Analysis: The warrantless search of Carroll's car was constitutional.

The Court traced the origin of the automobile exception back to the nation's founding. The Court noted that the first customs laws of this country permitted customs officers to make warrantless searches of ships and vessels and gave them the authority to stop "vehicles, beasts, and persons" if they suspected that they carried contraband. The Court concluded that:

> the guaranty of freedom from unreasonable searches and seizures by the Fourth Amendment has been construed, practically since the beginning of the government, as recognizing a necessary difference between a search of a store, dwelling house, or other structure in respect of which a proper official warrant readily may be obtained and a search of a ship, motor boat, wagon, or automobile for contraband goods, where it is not practicable to secure a warrant, because the vehicle can be quickly moved out of the locality or jurisdiction in which the warrant must be sought.[6]

The facts of the *Carroll* case amply demonstrate probable cause. As a result of their prior dealings with Kiro and Carroll, the officers reasonably believed them to be actively engaged in the sale of bootleg liquor. Detroit, as a result of its international border, was a well-known source for illegally importing alcohol. Moreover, the road between Detroit and Grand Rapids was a causeway known to be used by those engaged in moving alcohol from the border to the interior. Finally, the men were using the same car they used on the night of the aborted liquor sale and were coming from the direction of Detroit.

The Court applied the probable cause standard: "If the facts and circumstances before the officer are such as to warrant a man of prudence and caution in believing that the offense has been committed, it is sufficient."[7] On this record, the evidence was more than sufficient to establish probable cause to believe the car contained contraband.

In *Carroll*, the police had a lengthy history with the suspects and had substantial reason to believe the car they were driving might contain contraband. However, when the information the police have is less substantial, the Court has determined that probable cause should not be found:

Example—*Dyke v. Taylor Implement Mfg. Co.*, 391 U.S. 216 (1968): Employees at the Taylor Implement Manufacturing Company were on strike during the winter of 1966. In connection with the strike, the local chancery court issued an injunction prohibiting anyone from inflicting harm on, among other things, any employee of the company. Lloyd Duckett was a non-striking employee at the company. One evening, an "old make model" car drove past Duckett's home. Shots were fired

---

[6] Id. at 153.

[7] Id. at 161.

from the car as it passed. Duckett's two sons-in-law, who were standing on the front porch at the time, returned fire. A bullet from one of their guns hit the back of the car as it raced away. However, the police were never advised that the men on the porch returned fire or that they believed the car had been hit.

Shortly after the incident at Duckett's house, a two-toned 1960 Dodge was stopped nearby. The officer who stopped the car reported that he stopped the car because 1) it was an old car; 2) it sped up after he began following it; and 3) it had a fresh bullet hole in its trunk. There were three men in the car—Wayne Dyke, Ed McKinney, and John Blackwell. The men were taken to the local jail, and their car was parked just outside. While Dyke and his companions were held, several policemen went outside to the car and searched it. They found an air rifle under the front seat. Dyke and the others were subsequently tried for criminal contempt for violating the standing injunction. The gun was introduced at trial as evidence of the men's guilt.

Dyke objected to the introduction of the gun. He argued that it had not been appropriately seized pursuant to the automobile exception.

Analysis: The Court agreed. The officers who searched the car knew only that the car they were looking for was an "old make model car." This information standing alone was insufficient to establish probable cause to believe the car that was stopped—Dyke's car—was the car in question. Moreover, the observations of the seizing officer—that the car he stopped sped up, was old, and had a bullet hole in it—were insufficient to generate probable cause to believe the car would contain evidence of a crime.[8]

The Court's decision in *Dyke* is just one example of a principle the Court has since repeatedly articulated: Where the police do not have probable cause, the automobile exception cannot justify a warrantless police intrusion.[9] As the Court has said, "the Carroll doctrine does not declare a field day for the police in searching automobiles. Automobile or no automobile, there must be probable cause for the search."[10]

2. Containers Found Therein. Once you determine that police have probable cause to search a car, the question next becomes: What exactly may that search

[8] Dyke, 391 U.S. at 221–22.

[9] Delaware v. Prouse, 440 U.S. 648 (1979).

[10] Almeida-Sanchez v. United States, 413 U.S. 266, 269 (1973).

entail? Will it include the trunk? Does it include closed containers like purses or briefcases? What about paper bags? The Court struggled for many years with this question.

The rule once was that the automobile exception did not justify searches of closed containers found inside the car.[11] The Court's explanation for this rule was that neither of the two exceptions justifying the automobile exception extended to private property found in cars. Specifically, closed containers like suitcases are often the repositories of private items—thus, the Court at one time determined that the reduced expectations rationale was not relevant. Moreover, after "the police have seized a suitcase . . . the extent of its mobility is in no way affected by the place from which it was taken"—thus, the ready mobility of the car in which the suitcase may have been found was also deemed immaterial.[12]

In more recent years, however, the Court has explicitly rejected these earlier conclusions. Since 1991, the Court has clearly expressed the view that the automobile exception authorizes not only the search of the car but also the search of *any* containers found inside the vehicle:

> **Example—*California v. Acevedo*, 500 U.S. 565 (1991):** Police officers in Santa Ana, California came into possession of a redirected package containing marijuana that had been shipped via FedEx. The package was addressed to "J.R. Daza." The police instructed the FedEx office in Santa Ana to hold the package for pickup. The next day, a man who identified himself as Jamie Daza arrived at the FedEx office. After Daza claimed the package, officers followed him to his house, where he took the package inside. About an hour later, Daza left the apartment. He tossed the box and paper that had previously packaged the marijuana into a trashcan.
>
> About twenty minutes after Daza's departure, the officers saw an individual leave the apartment carrying a half-full book bag, get into a car, and drive away. The police stopped the man and searched his car, finding a pound and a half of marijuana in his bag.
>
> A half hour later, Charles Acevedo arrived. He went into the apartment and left about ten minutes later. At the time, he was carrying a full brown paper bag. The officers noted that the bag was approximately the size of one of the packages of marijuana

[11] See, e.g., United States v. Chadwick, 433 U.S. 1 (1977), and Arkansas v. Sanders, 442 U.S. 753 (1979), both abrogated by California v. Acevedo, 500 U.S. 565 (1991).

[12] See Sanders, 442 U.S. at 763–64.

that had been in Daza's original box. Acevedo tossed the bag in the trunk of his car and then got in and began to drive away. The police stopped the car. Opening the trunk and then the bag, they found marijuana.

At his trial for possession with intent to distribute, Acevedo complained that the search of the closed paper bag in his trunk was not authorized by the automobile exception. He conceded that the officers had probable cause to seize the bag under the exception, but contended that a warrant was needed to authorize its search.

Analysis: The Court expressly rejected its earlier holdings on this issue and found that the warrantless search of closed containers is permitted during a lawful search of a car pursuant to the automobile exception.

The Court first traced the historic development of its treatment of closed containers. In prior cases, the Court had opined that the automobile exception did not authorize the warrantless search of "luggage and other closed packages, bags and containers."[13] The rationale for this rule was that "a person expects more privacy in his luggage and personal effects than he does in his automobile."[14]

However, in a case decided just a few years before *Acevedo*, the Court had partially reversed course, for two reasons. First, it determined that once a person places an item in a vehicle, the person's "expectation of privacy in one's vehicle is equal to one's expectation of privacy in the containers" inside the vehicle.[15] Second, the earlier rule did very little to actually protect privacy rights. Under the old rule, if police found an item inside a car and had probable cause to believe it contained contraband, they were allowed to seize it and hold it until a warrant was obtained—and a warrant was invariably issued based on the same probable cause that authorized the seizure. Thus, these containers were eventually searched under the old rule, and forcing the police to obtain a warrant merely impeded law enforcement.

In *Acevedo*, the Court wholeheartedly embraced this reasoning, holding that "the police may search an automobile and the containers within it where they have probable cause to believe contraband or evidence is contained."[16]

There is one important limitation to the *Acevedo* Court's rule. Specifically, while probable cause to believe a car contains contraband will justify a search of the car and all its containers, the related logical proposition is not true. In other words,

[13] Acevedo, 500 U.S. at 573.

[14] Id. at 571.

[15] Id. at 573.

[16] Id. at 580.

where the police have probable cause to believe that only a single container in the car hides contraband, that belief will not authorize a full warrantless exploration: "Probable cause to believe that a container placed into the trunk of a taxi contains contraband or evidence does not justify a search of the entire cab."[17]

But what if the police are quite certain the container that they are searching does not belong to the driver of the car, but instead is the private property of a passenger? Should the police be authorized to conduct warrantless searches of a passenger's things, simply because the passenger happens to be traveling in the car? In a salient illustration of the ages-old admonition "be careful of the company you keep," the Court has found that even a passenger's personal property can be searched so long as it is located in a car that the police have probable cause to believe contains contraband:

> **Example—*Wyoming v. Houghton*, 526 U.S. 295 (1999):** Sandra Houghton was riding in a car with two friends. A Wyoming Highway Patrol officer pulled the car over for speeding and a broken brake light. While talking with the driver, the officer noticed a hypodermic needle in the driver's pocket. When asked why he had the needle, the driver in a paroxysm of honesty responded that he "used it to take drugs."[18] Acting on the driver's admission, officers on the scene then searched the car looking for contraband. During this search, they found a woman's purse on the rear seat. Sandra Houghton informed the officers that the purse was hers. Nonetheless, the officers proceeded to search the purse. Inside they found syringes containing methamphetamine.
>
> Houghton was charged with felony possession of methamphetamine. She moved to suppress the evidence that was found in her purse, arguing that the search was not justified by the automobile exception when the police were clearly informed that the purse did not belong to the driver.

Analysis: The Supreme Court held that the automobile exception allows for the search of all containers in the car, even those containers that police officers know do not belong to the driver.

The Court traced the origins of the automobile exception and found near-unwavering support for the general rule that the automobile exception "justifies the search of every part of the vehicle and its contents that may conceal the object of the search."[19] It was Houghton's contention that an exclusion from this general

---

[17] Id.

[18] Wyoming v. Houghton, 526 U.S. 295, 298 (1999).

[19] Id. at 301.

rule should be carved out for property that the police knew not to belong to the driver. The Court however, declined Houghton's invitation.

First, the Court found that passengers, just like drivers, have reduced expectations of privacy as to the property that they transported in cars. The Court also found that car passengers are often engaged in common pursuits with the driver. Next, the Court noted that even assuming no common enterprise, a driver could hide contraband on an unwitting passenger just as easily as it could be stashed elsewhere in the car. Finally, in an engaging detour into the minds of criminal associates, the Court surmised that "once a 'passenger's property' exception to car searches became widely known, one would expect passenger-confederates to claim everything as their own."[20]

For all of these reasons, the Court found the search of Houghton's purse was entirely lawful.

Thus, the rule applied to containers in cars is clear. Where the police have probable cause to believe generally that a car contains contraband, they may search any and all containers in the car that might hide the items sought. This is true without regard for the actual or putative ownership of the containers searched. But if the logic justifying this rule is that containers might be used to hide contraband, couldn't the same be said for people in the car?

3. Are People Containers? As discussed in the above section, the Court has found that once the police have probable cause to search a car, the scope of that search will extend to all containers in the car. The theory is that contraband could be hidden in a passenger's purse or a suitcase in the trunk just as easily as it could be hidden elsewhere. But what about people? In theory, a driver could shove contraband into a passenger's pocket or his own pocket just as easily as he could stash it in his tote. Does the scope of an automobile search extend to the people in the car as well? The Court answered that question with a resounding "No" in *United States v. Di Re*:

> **Example—*United States v. Di Re*, 332 U.S. 581 (1948):** Recall that Michael Di Re was arrested after being found in a car with two other men who were illegally trading in counterfeit gasoline rations. One of the men was a police informant, who alerted police to the time and location of the planned sale. When the police came upon the car containing the informant, the seller (Buttitta), and Di Re, they saw the informant holding two gas ration coupons in his hand. When asked where he got them, the informant identified Buttitta. All three men were taken into

[20] Id. at 305.

custody and searched. During this search, the police found counterfeit gasoline and fuel oil ration coupons on Di Re.

The government argued that the search of Di Re was justified pursuant to the automobile exception. In particular, the government argued that the police had probable cause to believe the car contained contraband (the counterfeit coupons) and therefore had the authority to search the entire car and its contents (including the people found in it). Di Re countered that the automobile exception should not be read so broadly.

Analysis: The Supreme Court held that the search of Di Re's person could not be justified under the automobile exception.

Without question, automobiles are more vulnerable to warrantless searches than other sorts of property. However, that vulnerability does not provide limitless authorization to law enforcement officers conducting a search.

The same logic that would permit the search of car's occupants under the automobile exception would authorize the search of all persons in a house pursuant to a warranted search of the premises. The Court was unwilling to make this reach. "We see no ground for expanding the ruling in the *Carroll* case to justify this arrest and search as incident to the search of a car. We are not convinced that a person, by mere presence in a suspected car, loses immunities from search of his person to which he would otherwise be entitled."[21]

Thus, while the automobile exception may authorize the search of an occupant's property, it does not authorize the search of the occupants themselves. This is not to say, however, that the police are stripped of any authority to search a car's driver or passengers. Such a search is simply not authorized as a function of the probable cause that justifies the search of the car. To the extent a warrantless search of persons in the car occurs, it would need to be independently justified under some other exception—like *Terry* or search incident to a lawful arrest.

4. The "Inherent Mobility" of Cars. One justification for the automobile exception is the notion that cars are inherently mobile. As the thinking goes, if police were always required to get a warrant before searching cars, in many cases the evidence would drive away before a search could be conducted. But what if as a practical matter the car being searched is not really capable of driving away, either because the occupants have been arrested or because the car is more of a residence than a vehicle? The Court has considered this question and found that the automobile exception still apples:

[21] Di Re, 332 U.S. at 587 (1948).

Example—*Chambers v. Maroney*, 399 U.S. 42 (1970): One evening a Gulf gas station in North Braddock, Pennsylvania, was robbed by two armed men. One man wore a green sweater, and the other wore a trench coat. The men took cash from the station attendant, including coins, which they told the attendant to place in his right-hand glove. Two teenagers who were in the area had noticed a blue station wagon circling the block just before the robbery. After the robbery, the teens saw this same blue station wagon speed off. When the police arrived, the teens told the officers that there were four men in the station wagon, one of whom was wearing a green sweater.

Less than an hour later, a blue station wagon was stopped about two miles from the gas station. There were four men in the car. Frank Chambers was one of them. He was wearing a green sweater. The police also saw a trench coat in the car.

The men were arrested, and their car was driven to the police station by an officer. While the car was parked at the station, officers thoroughly searched it. The officers found two revolvers, a right-hand glove containing coins, and cards bearing the name of a gas station attendant who had been robbed at gunpoint a week earlier in nearby McKeesport, Pennsylvania.

Chambers was charged with both robberies. At trial, both gas station attendants identified Chambers as the man who robbed them. The evidence that was seized from the car during the search at the stationhouse was also introduced as evidence. Chambers argued that the search of the car could not be justified by the automobile exception because the car was in police control at the time of the search, and thus, not in danger of being driven away.

Analysis: The Supreme Court found that the search of the car was legal.

The automobile exception is justified, in part, by the inherent mobility of cars. Thus, where probable cause existed to believe Chambers' car might contain guns and stolen money, there was no question the car could have been searched at the scene. Indeed, that "opportunity to search is fleeting since a car is readily moveable."[22]

---

[22] Chambers, 399 U.S. at 51.

From this starting premise, the Court determined that it was not unreasonable for the officers to wait to conduct the search until after they moved the car to the stationhouse. The car had been stopped originally in a dark parking lot in the middle of the night. A careful search of the car on the scene would have been potentially dangerous to the officers, as well as unfeasible. Moreover, the mobile characteristic of the vehicle did not change simply because the car was in police possession at the time of the search. "[T]he blue station wagon could have been searched on the spot when it was stopped since there was probable cause to search and it was a fleeting target for a search. The probable-cause factor still obtained at the station house and so did the mobility."[23]

Later explaining its holding in *Chambers*, the Court commented, "the police [can] search later whenever they could have searched earlier, had they so chosen."[24] Following its decision in *Chambers*, the Court regularly confirmed that the ready mobility of a car is just one justification for the automobile exception. The parallel justification for the exception is the reduced expectation of privacy. Accordingly, while a car must be functionally mobile, application of the automobile exception will not be strictly limited to cases where true exigency—in the sense of impending flight—exists.[25] In short, "if a car is readily mobile and probable cause exists to believe it contains contraband, the Fourth Amendment thus permits police to search the vehicle without more."[26] But what if a vehicle, while driveable, is really more of a home than a car, including both furnishings and blinds? Will this sort of motor vehicle satisfy the demand for "ready mobility"? The Court confronted precisely this question when the police searched the mobile home of a suspected pedophile and drug dealer:

> **Example—*California v. Carney*, 471 U.S. 386 (1985):** DEA agents working in San Diego received an uncorroborated tip from an informant that a Dodge Mini Motorhome parked in a downtown parking lot was being used by a named individual who was trading drugs for sex. The DEA, accordingly, kept the motorhome under surveillance. One day, an agent saw Charles Carney (not the individual who had been named by the informant) approach a young teenager near the motorhome. Carney and the teen walked back to the motorhome, and once inside closed all of the shades on the windows, including one that covered the front windshield. The two remained inside for more than an hour. When the teenager eventually left, the agent fol-

[23] Chambers, 399 U.S. at 52.

[24] Acevedo, 500 U.S. at 570.

[25] Pennsylvania v. Labron, 518 U.S. 938 (1996).

[26] Id. at 940.

lowed him. The teen told the agent that Carney gave him marijuana in exchange for allowing Carney to touch him sexually.

The agents had the teen return to the motorhome and knock on the door. When Carney answered, the agents entered the motor home and saw marijuana, packaging, and a scale on a table. A more thorough search of the home disclosed more marijuana in the refrigerator, as well as in some cabinets.

Carney argued that the automobile exception could not justify the search of the motorhome, which was more of a house than a car.

Analysis: The Supreme Court held that the search of the motorhome was constitutional.

The two justifications for the automobile exception are by now well known—ready mobility and reduced expectations of privacy. Accordingly, the fact that a vehicle may be stationary at the time of the search will not defeat application of the automobile exception if "a vehicle is being used on the highways, or . . . is readily capable of such use."[27]

Carney's motorhome, though appointed like a residence, was readily mobile with the turn of an ignition key. Moreover the motorhome, because it was a licensed motor vehicle, was subject to a form of police regulation that a regular home would not be. "While it is true that respondent's vehicle possessed some, if not many of the attributes of a home, it is equally clear that the vehicle falls clearly within the scope of the exception laid down in *Carroll* and applied in succeeding cases."[28]

In so holding, the *Carney* Court expressly declined to carve out an exception to the automobile exception for vehicles that were "capable of" functioning as homes.

The Court's language in *Carney* clearly suggests that the automobile exception would not apply if a motor home is in fact being used as a permanent home—for example, if it is on blocks or is otherwise more enduringly attached to the land on which it sits.

---

[27] California v. Carney, 471 U.S. 386, 392 (1985).

[28] Id. at 393.

E. Policy Debate. The Supreme Court created the automobile exception in 1925, under very different economic and social conditions than exist today. Automobiles were relatively uncommon—only about one in seven Americans owned a car—and they were relatively new, giving private individuals an unprecedented way to move quickly around the country. In that context, it is not surprising that the Court created a broad exception to the warrant requirement, based on their "ready mobility" and on the reduced privacy rights that people had in their car.

As *Carney* demonstrates, these two rationales—ready mobility and reduced expectation of privacy—cannot really support a *per se* automobile exception in every case. A plurality of the Supreme Court was concerned about breadth of the automobile exception as far back as 1971, in the case of *Coolidge v. New Hampshire*. In *Coolidge*, the police arrested the defendant at his home and took him to the precinct. Two hours later, they returned to his home and searched his two cars that were parked in his driveway. The police searched one of the cars again two days later, again a year later, and again five months after that. The police had probable cause for all of these searches, but never obtained a warrant. The prosecutor argued that all of these searches were justified under the automobile exception. Four of the justices held that none of the searches were valid, and two more justices agreed that the last two searches were invalid. The plurality expressed its frustration with what it saw as the legal fiction underpinning the automobile exception:

> The word "automobile" is not a talisman in whose presence the Fourth Amendment fades away and disappears. And surely there is nothing in this case to invoke the meaning and purpose of the rule of *Carroll v. United States*—no alerted criminal bent on flight, no fleeting opportunity on an open highway after a hazardous chase, no contraband or stolen goods or weapons, no confederates waiting to move the evidence, not even the inconvenience of a special police detail to guard the immobilized autobile. In short, by no possible stretch of the legal imagination can this be made into a case where "it is not practicable to secure a warrant," and the "automobile exception," despite its label, is simply irrelevant.[29]

Although the defendant in *Coolidge* won his case, *Carney* made it clear that *Coolidge* has little precedential value. Today the automobile exception applies even in cases where the vehicle is not in any realistic sense "readily mobile" (such as the car that was in police custody at the police station in *Chambers*) and where the owner does not in any realistic sense have a lower expectation of privacy than a home (such as the motor home in *Carney*). Thus, the term "automobile" has

[29] Coolidge v. New Hampshire, 403 U.S. 443, 462 (1971).

indeed become a talisman of sorts, giving the police the right to conduct warrantless searches of cars under almost any circumstances, as long as they have probable cause.

Quick Summary

The third recognized exception to the warrant requirement is the automobile exception. The exception provides that officers with probable cause to believe a car contains contraband or other evidence may lawfully search the entire vehicle and any containers therein that might contain the object of the search. Thus, if police officers are looking for a baby elephant, they may not look in the glove compartment. But if they are looking for drugs or other items that may be hidden virtually anywhere, a search of the entire car will be authorized.

A search conducted pursuant to the automobile exception will allow officers to dismantle upholstery and seating if it is reasonable to believe the object of the search might be found in these locations. However, the police are not permitted to search the person of the driver or passengers pursuant to the exception. To the extent that such a warrantless search of a person takes place, it must be independently authorized.

The first rationale for the automobile exception is the inherent mobility of automobiles. The exception is also justified by our reduced expectation of privacy in cars. This reduced expectation is a function of both the highly visible nature of a car's interior and the pervasive government regulation to which cars are subjected.

Review Questions

1. Cocaine in the Trailer. The Drug Enforcement Agency began working with an informant who was part of a cocaine distribution ring. The informant told the DEA that his organization transported drugs from California to New York in tractor trailers hitched to trucks. The trailers contained mundane goods on top, but had a false bottom underneath covering a compartment where the group could store hundreds of kilograms of cocaine.

Acting on information provided by the informant, the DEA began following an individual named Jose Navarro. He was driving a tractor-trailer that the informant said was frequently used for transporting cocaine. Navarro drove the tractor-trailer to a parking garage, where he parked the trailer and unhitched the cab. Officers saw him take two duffel bags from the trailer and placed them in the cab. He then drove the cab out of the parking garage and drove to a nearby McDonald's. Navarro went into the McDonald's carrying the two duffel bags, and the police watched as he handed the duffel bags to a man who the informant had identified as a local marijuana dealer.

The police arrested Navarro and the marijuana dealer, and they searched the duffel bags incident to the arrest. Inside they found two kilograms of cocaine.

The police next went to the parking garage and searched the parked trailer. They removed a few pounds of scrap metal and then pulled back the false bottom, revealing 230 kilograms of cocaine. Navarro was charged with possessing cocaine with the intent to sell.

Was the search of the trailer constitutional under the automobile exception of the Fourth Amendment?

2. Purse Full of Contraband Redux. The police saw a car driving late at night without any headlights. Inside the car was Donald Marshall, his wife Sarah, and their friend Wendell Gibson in the backseat. The police asked for all of their identifications and ran them all through the police database. They learned that Gibson had an outstanding warrant for failure to pay child support, and they ordered Gibson out of the car and placed him under arrest. Once he was secured in their cruiser, they ordered Donald and Sarah out of the car and searched the passenger compartment. Sarah had left her purse in the front seat, and the police searched her purse as well. Inside they found ten grams of heroin. Sarah was arrested and charged with possession of a controlled substance.

At trial, Sarah Marshall challenged the search of the automobile and her purse, arguing that it violated her Fourth Amendment rights. Were her Fourth Amendment rights violated?

(Compare your answer here with your answer using the search incident to a lawful arrest exception in "Purse Full of Contraband" at the end of **Chapter 13**).

3. Avenging His Mother's Death. A woman called the police and told them that her husband had just left the house intending to kill the man whom he believed murdered his mother. She told them he was driving a blue 2003 Ford Taurus, and that he was driving to a home at 2351 Cedar Street. She also told them that he was a Colombian citizen illegally in the United States.

The police drove towards the location, and as they neared the location, they saw a blue 2003 Ford Taurus driving the same route. They waited until the car made a turn without a turn signal, and then they pulled the car over. They asked for the driver's identification and called Immigration and Customs Enforcement (ICE) to verify his status. Within a few minutes they learned that the defendant was in fact illegally in the United States. They arrested the defendant and seized the car, driving it back to the police impound lot. They gave the keys to the manager of the impound lot.

A few hours later, a police sergeant reviewed the case and realized that the defendant might have been carrying a weapon with him when he drove to the house. He ordered the car to be searched in the impound lot. Two police officers went to the impound lot and confirmed that was positioned in a location where it would be possible to start the vehicle and drive it out of the lot. They searched the car and found an illegal shotgun in the trunk.

Was the search of the car's trunk in the impound lot legal?

FROM THE COURTROOM

CALIFORNIA v. CARNEY

United States Supreme Court, 1985
471 U.S. 386

[Chief Justice BURGER delivered the opinion of the Court.]

[Justice STEVENS delivered a dissenting opinion, which was joined by Justices BRENNAN and MARSHALL.]

We granted certiorari to decide whether law enforcement agents violated the Fourth Amendment when they conducted a warrantless search, based on probable cause, of a fully mobile "motor home" located in a public place.

I

On May 31, 1979, Drug Enforcement Agency Agent Robert Williams watched respondent, Charles Carney, approach a youth in downtown San Diego. The youth accompanied Carney to a Dodge Mini Motor Home parked in a nearby lot. Carney and the youth closed the window shades in the motor home, including one across the front window. Agent Williams had previously received uncorroborated information that the same motor home was used by another person who was exchanging marihuana for sex. Williams, with assistance from other agents, kept the motor home under surveillance for the entire one and one-quarter hours that Carney and the youth remained inside. When the youth left the motor home, the agents followed and stopped him. The youth told the agents that he had received marijuana in return for allowing Carney sexual contacts.

At the agents' request, the youth returned to the motor home and knocked on its door; Carney stepped out. The agents identified themselves as law enforcement officers. Without a warrant or consent, one agent entered the motor home and observed marihuana, plastic bags, and a scale of the kind used in weighing drugs on a table. Agent Williams took Carney into custody and took possession of the motor home. A subsequent search of the motor home at the police station revealed additional marihuana in the cupboards and refrigerator.

Respondent was charged with possession of marihuana for sale. At a preliminary hearing, he moved to suppress the evidence discovered in the motor home.

. . .

II

The Fourth Amendment protects the "right of the people to be secure in their persons, houses, papers, and effects, against unreasonable searches and seizures." This fundamental right is preserved by a requirement that searches be conducted pursuant to a warrant issued by an independent judicial officer. There are, of course, exceptions to the general rule that a warrant must be secured before a search is undertaken; one is the so-called "automobile exception" at issue in this case. This exception to the warrant requirement was first set forth by the Court sixty years ago in *Carroll v. United States*. There, the Court recognized that the privacy interests in an automobile are constitutionally protected; however, it held that the ready mobility of the automobile justifies a lesser degree of protection of those interests. The Court rested this exception on a long-recognized distinction between stationary structures and vehicles:

> [T]he guaranty of freedom from unreasonable searches and seizures by the Fourth Amendment has been construed, practically since the beginning of Government, as recognizing a necessary difference between a search of a store, dwelling house or other structure in respect of which a proper official warrant readily may be obtained, and a search of a ship, motor boat, wagon or automobile, for contraband goods, where it is not practicable to secure a warrant because the vehicle can be *quickly moved* out of the locality or jurisdiction in which the warrant must be sought.

The capacity to be "quickly moved" was clearly the basis of the holding in *Carroll,* and our cases have consistently recognized ready mobility as one of the principal bases of the automobile exception. In *Chambers,* for example, commenting on the rationale for the vehicle exception, we noted that "the opportunity to search is fleeting since a car is readily movable." More recently, in *United States v. Ross,* we once again emphasized that "an immediate intrusion is necessary" because of "the nature of an automobile in transit. . . ." The mobility of automobiles, we have observed, "creates circumstances of such exigency that, as a practical necessity, rigorous enforcement of the warrant requirement is impossible."

However, although ready mobility alone was perhaps the original justification for the vehicle exception, our later cases have made clear that ready mobility is not the only basis for the exception. The reasons for the vehicle exception, we have said, are twofold. "Besides the element of mobility, less rigorous warrant requirements govern because the expectation of privacy with respect to one's automobile is significantly less than that relating to one's home or office."

Even in cases where an automobile was not immediately mobile, the lesser expectation of privacy resulting from its use as a readily mobile vehicle justified application of the vehicular exception. In some cases, the configuration of the vehicle contributed to the lower expectations of privacy; for example, we held in *Cardwell v. Lewis,* that, because the passenger compartment of a standard automobile is relatively open to plain view, there are lesser expectations of privacy. But even when enclosed "repository" areas have been involved, we have concluded that the lesser expectations of privacy warrant application of the exception. We have applied the exception in the context of a locked car trunk, a sealed package in a car trunk, a closed compartment under the dashboard, the interior of a vehicle's upholstery, or sealed packages inside a covered pickup truck.

These reduced expectations of privacy derive not from the fact that the area to be searched is in plain view, but from the pervasive regulation of vehicles capable of traveling on the public highways As we explained in *South Dakota v. Opperman,* an inventory search case:

> Automobiles, unlike homes, are subjected to pervasive and continuing governmental regulation and controls, including periodic inspection and licensing requirements. As an everyday occurrence, police stop and examine vehicles when license plates or inspection stickers have expired, or if other violations, such as exhaust fumes or excessive noise, are noted, or if headlights or other safety equipment are not in proper working order.

The public is fully aware that it is accorded less privacy in its automobiles because of this compelling governmental need for regulation. Historically, "individuals always [have] been on notice that movable vessels may be stopped and searched on facts giving rise to probable cause that the vehicle contains contraband, without the protection afforded by a magistrate's prior evaluation of those facts." In short, the pervasive schemes of regulation, which necessarily lead to reduced expectations of privacy, and the exigencies attendant to ready mobility justify searches without prior recourse to the authority of a magistrate so long as the overriding standard of probable cause is met.

When a vehicle is being used on the highways, or if it is readily capable of such use and is found stationary in a place not regularly used for residential purposes—temporary or otherwise—the two justifications for the vehicle exception come into play. First, the vehicle is obviously readily mobile by the turn of an ignition key, if not actually moving. Second, there is a reduced expectation of privacy stemming from its use as a licensed motor vehicle subject to a range of police regulation inapplicable to a fixed dwelling. At least in these circumstances, the overriding societal interests in effective law enforcement justify an immediate search before the vehicle and its occupants become unavailable.

While it is true that respondent's vehicle possessed some, if not many of the attributes of a home, it is equally clear that the vehicle falls clearly within the scope of the exception laid down in *Carroll* and applied in succeeding cases. Like the automobile in *Carroll,* respondent's motor home was readily mobile. Absent the prompt search and seizure, it could readily have been moved beyond the reach of the police. Furthermore, the vehicle was licensed to "operate on public streets; [was] serviced in public places; . . . and [was] subject to extensive regulation and inspection." And the vehicle was so situated that an objective observer would conclude that it was being used not as a residence, but as a vehicle.

Respondent urges us to distinguish his vehicle from other vehicles within the exception because it was *capable of functioning as a home.* In our increasingly mobile society, many vehicles used for transportation can be and are being used not only for transportation but for shelter, *i.e.*, as a "home" or "residence." To distinguish between respondent's motor home and an ordinary sedan for purposes of the vehicle exception would require that we apply the exception depending upon the size of the vehicle and the quality of its appointments. Moreover, to fail to apply the exception to vehicles such as a motor home ignores the fact that a motor home lends itself easily to use as an instrument of illicit drug traffic and other illegal activity. In *United States v. Ross*, we declined to distinguish between "worthy" and "unworthy" containers, noting that "the central purpose of the Fourth Amendment forecloses such a distinction." We decline today to distinguish between "worthy" and "unworthy" vehicles which are either on the public roads and highways, or situated such that it is reasonable to conclude that the vehicle is not being used as a residence.

Our application of the vehicle exception has never turned on the other uses to which a vehicle might be put. The exception has historically turned on the ready mobility of the vehicle, and on the presence of the vehicle in a setting that objectively indicates that the vehicle is being used transportation. These two requirements for application of the exception ensure that law enforcement officials are not unnecessarily hamstrung in their efforts to detect and prosecute criminal activity, and that the legitimate privacy interests of the public are protected. Applying the vehicle exception in these circumstances allows the essential purposes served by the exception to be fulfilled, while assuring that the exception will acknowledge legitimate privacy interests.

III

The question remains whether, apart from the lack of a warrant, this search was unreasonable. Under the vehicle exception to the warrant requirement, "[o]nly the prior approval of the magistrate is waived; the search otherwise [must be such] as the magistrate could authorize."

This search was not unreasonable; it was plainly one that the magistrate could authorize if presented with these facts. The DEA agents had fresh, direct, uncontradicted evidence that the respondent was distributing a controlled substance from the vehicle, apart from evidence of other possible offenses. The agents thus had abundant probable cause to enter and search the vehicle for evidence of a crime notwithstanding its possible use as a dwelling place.

The judgment of the California Supreme Court is reversed, and the case is remanded for further proceedings not inconsistent with this opinion.

It is so ordered.

Justice STEVENS, with whom Justice BRENNAN and Justice MARSHALL join, dissenting.

The character of "the place to be searched" plays an important role in Fourth Amendment analysis. In this case, police officers searched a Dodge/Midas Mini Motor Home. The California Supreme Court correctly characterized this vehicle as a "hybrid" which combines "the mobility attribute of an automobile . . . with most of the privacy characteristics of a house."

The hybrid character of the motor home places it at the crossroads between the privacy interests that generally forbid warrantless invasions of the home, and the law enforcement interests that support the exception for warrantless searches of automobiles based on probable cause. By choosing to follow the latter route, the Court errs in three respects: it has entered new territory prematurely, it has accorded priority to an exception rather than to the general rule, and it has abandoned the limits on the exception imposed by prior cases.

. . .

II

The Fourth Amendment guarantees the "right of the people to be secure in their persons, houses, papers, and effects against unreasonable searches and seizures." We have interpreted this language to provide law enforcement officers with a bright-line standard: "searches conducted outside the judicial process, without prior approval by judge or magistrate, are *per se* unreasonable under the Fourth Amendment—subject only to a few specifically established and well delineated exceptions."

In *United States v. Ross*, the Court reaffirmed the primary importance of the general rule condemning warrantless searches, and emphasized that the exception permitting the search of automobiles without a warrant is a narrow one. We expressly endorsed "the general rule," stated in *Carroll v. United States*, that "'[i]n cases where the securing of a warrant is reasonably practicable, it must be used.'" Given this warning and the presumption of regularity that attaches to a warrant, it is hardly unrealistic to expect experienced law enforcement officers to obtain a search warrant when one can easily be secured.

The ascendancy of the warrant requirement in our system of justice must not be bullied aside by extravagant claims of necessity:

> The warrant requirement . . . is not an inconvenience to be somehow "weighed" against the claims of police efficiency. It is, or should be, an important working part of our machinery of government, operating as a matter of course to check the "well-intentioned but mistakenly overzealous executive officers" who are a part of any system of law enforcement.
>
> . . . By requiring that conclusions concerning probable cause and the scope of a search be drawn by a neutral and detached magistrate instead of being judged by the officer engaged in the often competitive enterprise of ferreting out crime, we minimize the risk of unreasonable assertions of executive authority.

If the motor home were parked in the exact middle of the intersection between the general rule and the exception for automobiles, priority should be given to the rule rather than the exception.

III

The motor home, however, was not parked in the middle of that intersection. Our prior cases teach us that inherent mobility is not a sufficient justification for the fashioning of an exception to the warrant requirement, especially in the face of heightened expectations of privacy in the location searched. Motor homes, by their common use and construction, afford their owners a substantial and legitimate expectation of privacy when they dwell within. When a motor home is parked in a location that is removed from the public highway, I believe that society is prepared to recognize that the expectations of privacy within it are not unlike the expectations one has in a fixed dwelling. As a general rule, such places may only be searched with a warrant based upon probable cause. Warrantless searches of motor homes are only reasonable when the motor home is traveling on the public streets or highways, or when exigent circumstances otherwise require an immediate search without the expenditure of time necessary to obtain a warrant.

As we explained in *Ross*, the automobile exception is the product of a long history:

> [S]ince its earliest days Congress had recognized the impracticability of securing a warrant in cases involving the transportation of contraband goods. It is this impracticability, viewed in historical perspective, that provided the basis for the *Carroll* decision. Given the nature of an automobile in transit, the Court recognized that an immediate intrusion is necessary if police officers are to secure the illicit substance. In this class of cases, the Court held that a warrantless search of an automobile is not unreasonable.

The automobile exception has been developed to ameliorate the practical problems associated with the search of vehicles that have been stopped on the streets or public highways because there was probable cause to believe they were transporting contraband. Until today, however, the Court has never decided whether the practical justifications that apply to a vehicle that is stopped in transit on a public way apply with the same force to a vehicle parked in a lot near a court house where it could easily be detained while a warrant is issued.

In this case, the motor home was parked in an off-the-street lot only a few blocks from the courthouse in downtown San Diego where dozens of magistrates were available to entertain a warrant application. The officers clearly had the element of surprise with them, and with curtains covering the windshield, the motor home offered no indication of any imminent departure. The officers plainly had probable cause to arrest the respondent and search the motor home, and on this record, it is inexplicable why they eschewed the safe harbor of a warrant.

In the absence of any evidence of exigency in the circumstances of this case, the Court relies on the inherent mobility of the motor home to create a conclusive presumption of exigency. This Court, however, has squarely held that mobility of the place to be searched is not a sufficient justification for abandoning the warrant requirement. In *United States v. Chadwick*, the Court held that a warrantless search of a footlocker violated the Fourth Amendment even though there was ample probable cause to believe it contained contraband. The Government had argued that the rationale of the automobile exception applied to movable containers in general, and that the warrant requirement should be limited to searches of homes and other "core" areas of privacy. We categorically rejected the Government's argument, observing that there are greater privacy interests associated with containers than with automobiles, and that there are less practical problems associated with the temporary detention of a container than with the detention of an automobile.

We again endorsed that analysis in *Ross*:

> The Court in *Chadwick* specifically rejected the argument that the warrantless search was "reasonable" because a footlocker has some of the mobile characteristics that support warrantless searches of automobiles. The Court recognized that "a person's expectations of privacy in personal luggage are substantially greater than in an automobile," and noted that the practical problems associated with the temporary detention of a piece of luggage during the period of time necessary to obtain a warrant are significantly less than those associated with the detention of an automobile.

It is perfectly obvious that the citizen has a much greater expectation of privacy concerning the interior of a mobile home than of a piece of luggage such as a footlocker. If "inherent mobility" does not justify warrantless searches of containers, it cannot rationally provide a sufficient justification for the search of a person's dwelling place.

Unlike a brick bungalow or a frame Victorian, a motor home seldom serves as a permanent lifetime abode. The motor home in this case, however, was designed to accommodate a breadth of ordinary everyday living. Photographs in the record indicate that its height, length, and beam provided substantial living space inside: stuffed chairs surround a table; cupboards provide room for storage of personal effects; bunk beds provide sleeping space; and a refrigerator provides ample space for food and beverages. Moreover, curtains and large opaque walls inhibit viewing the activities inside from the exterior of the vehicle. The interior configuration of the motor home establishes that the vehicle's size, shape, and mode of construction should have indicated to the officers that it was a vehicle containing mobile living quarters.

The State contends that officers in the field will have an impossible task determining whether or not other vehicles contain mobile living quarters. It is not necessary for the Court to resolve every unanswered question in this area in a single case, but common English usage suggests that we already distinguish between a "motor home" which is "equipped as a self-contained traveling home," a "camper" which is only equipped for "casual travel and camping," and an automobile which is "designed for passenger transportation." Surely the exteriors of these vehicles contain clues about their different functions which could alert officers in the field to the necessity of a warrant.

The California Vehicle Code also refutes the State's argument that the exclusion of "motor homes" from the automobile exception would be impossible to apply in practice. In its definitional section, the Code distinguishes campers and house cars from station wagons, and suggests that they are special categories of the more general terms—motor vehicles and passenger vehicles. A "house car" is "a motor vehicle originally designed, or permanently altered, and equipped for human habitation, or to which a camper has been permanently attached." Alcoholic beverages may not be opened or consumed in motor vehicles traveling on the highways, except in the "living quarters of a house car or camper." The same definitions might not necessarily apply in the context of the Fourth Amendment, but they do indicate that descriptive distinctions are humanly possible. They also reflect the California Legislature's judgment that "house cars" entertain different kinds of activities than the ordinary passenger vehicle.

In my opinion, searches of places that regularly accommodate a wide range of private human activity are fundamentally different from searches of automobiles which primarily serve a public transportation function. Although it may not be a castle, a motor home is usually the functional equivalent of a hotel room, a vacation and retirement home, or a hunting and fishing cabin. These places may be as spartan as a humble cottage when compared to the most majestic mansion, but the highest and most legitimate expectations of privacy associated with these temporary abodes should command the respect of this Court. In my opinion, a warrantless search of living quarters in a motor home is "presumptively unreasonable absent exigent circumstances."

I respectfully dissent.

16

Exceptions to the Warrant Requirement: Consent

Key Concepts

- Actual v. Apparent Authority
- Prosecutor's Burden to Demonstrate Voluntariness
- Consent-Once-Removed

A. Introduction and Policy. By now, you are very familiar with the rule that the Fourth Amendment proscribes only **unreasonable** searches and seizures. Therefore, as a general principle, the Fourth Amendment presents no barrier to a police officer approaching an individual in public and putting questions to her so long as the subject of the questioning is willing to listen. This notion of voluntary engagement with the police underlies the fourth exception to the warrant requirement, the consent exception—the "C" in S-P-A-C-E-S. The consent exception states that if you give permission to the police to search property or effects, and you have the authority (actual or apparent) to allow such a search, the warrantless search or seizure of the item will not violate the Fourth Amendment. In carving out the consent exception, the Court has said, "it is no doubt reasonable for the police to conduct a search once they have been permitted to do so."[1]

Consent is an exception to both the warrant and probable cause requirements. Therefore, if the police have legitimate permission to search, they not only do not need a warrant, they also do not need probable cause to believe the search will turn up anything of value.[2] The police are free to ask permission to search anywhere even if they have no reason to believe the search will be fruitful, and even if they have no reason to suspect the target of the search of any wrongdoing. One important caveat to this general rule is the police may not intrude upon other Fourth Amendment rights (for example, by illegally stopping you) before securing your permission.

When the Court discusses the policy underlying other exceptions to the warrant requirement, it often does so by focusing upon the salutary value of the particular exception to law enforcement. For example, when discussing the justification for the automobile exception, the Court often points to law enforcement's need to

---

1 Florida v. Jimeno, 500 U.S. 248, 250–51 (1991).

2 United States v. Drayton, 536 U.S. 194, 210 (2002).

conduct such searches quickly in light of a vehicle's mobility. Similarly, with regard to plain view searches, the Court has frequently described the inconvenience and potential hazards of obtaining a warrant to secure items that have already been observed in plain view. With regard to the consent exception, however, the Court's discussion has a different focus. Rather than concentrating on the benefit to law enforcement, the Court more often has tended to emphasize the collective benefit of consent to the community, stating that "[t]he community has a real interest in encouraging consent, for the resulting search may yield necessary evidence for the solution and prosecution of crime, evidence that may insure that a wholly innocent person is not wrongly charged with a criminal offense."[3] In this regard, the Court has said that consent is a concept that should be afforded "weight and dignity" in a society based on law. In the Court's view, "[i]t reinforces the rule of law for the citizen to advise the police of his or her wishes and for the police to act in reliance on that understanding."[4]

The consent exception is one of the most controversial exceptions to the warrant requirement. Police officers are trained how to ask for consent in a way that stays within the bounds of the law but strongly encourages the suspect to agree. The police officers seeking consent need not inform the suspect that she has the right to refuse, and in asking for consent they can use a commanding tone of voice, imply that they know illegal activity is going on, and (within some limits) intimidate the suspect into agreeing. Thus, many commentators argue that a lot of consent searches are not truly consensual, even though the Court has held that they must be "voluntary." Nonetheless, they are a critical component of police investigations, and are probably the most commonly used exception to the warrant requirement.

B. The Law. The consent exception to the warrant requirement gives police broad authority to search as long as they are given permission:

> Law enforcement officials may conduct a search or a seizure if:
>
> 1. The consenting party has actual or apparent authority to consent; and
>
> 2. The consent was freely and voluntarily given, and was not a product of duress or coercion. Consent is voluntary if it is "the product of an essentially free and unconstrained choice by its maker;"[5] consent is not voluntary if the suspect's "will has been overborne and his capacity for self determination [has been] critically impaired."[6]

---

[3] Jimeno, 500 U.S. at 252.

[4] Drayton, 536 U.S. at 207.

[5] Schneckloth v. Bustamonte, 412 U.S. 218, 225 (1973).

[6] Id.

The government bears the burden of proving both of these elements by a preponderance of the evidence.[7]

The consenting party may expressly limit the scope of the search in any way and may withdraw consent at any time.

If the government does not meet its burden, and the warrantless search of property cannot otherwise be justified, the evidence will be excluded from trial. As the above reflects, the government must show two things before any warrantless search will be deemed a "consent" search: the authority of the consenting party and voluntariness. Let's look first at what the Court has said about authority.

1. The "Authority" to Consent. The government must show that someone gave consent who actually had the right to consent, or at least reasonably appeared to have that right. As a practical matter, there are three types of individuals who may fit this description:

1. Actual owners,
2. Third parties with "common authority" over the premises or other property; and
3. Others whom it is reasonable to believe have the right to consent to a search.

The easiest and most common way to prove consent is to show that the person who consented actually owned the property. With a few exceptions (discussed in detail below), actual owners have the authority to consent to the search of their own property.[8]

Additionally, a party other than the owner may consent to the search if that person has "common authority" over the property.[9] "Common authority" means "mutual use of the property by persons generally having joint access or control for most purposes."[10] This second category includes people like roommates, cohabitating spouses and other domestic partners, and adult children and other family members who live in the home. For personal property (as opposed to dwellings or buildings), anyone who jointly uses the item has common authority to consent to a search.[11] For example, if two individuals share a dresser or a gym bag, either

[7] United States v. Matlock, 415 U.S. 164 (1974).
[8] Schneckloth v. Bustamonte, 412 U.S. 218 (1973).
[9] Matlock, 415 U.S. at 170.
[10] Illinois v. Rodriguez, 497 U.S. 177, 181 (1990).
[11] Frazier v. Cupp, 394 U.S. 731 (1969).

individual has the right to consent to a search of that item, since they are both "joint users" of the item.

Finally, if the police reasonably believe someone has the authority to consent to a search, that person's consent will be deemed to have "apparent authority." Someone with apparent authority can authorize the search even if she does not actually have the authority to consent. As we will see below, the test for assessing apparent authority is one of objective reasonableness—as long as the police officers reasonably believed the consenting individual had authority, the search will be valid

Apparent authority should not be confused with the common authority of joint tenants and users described above. Common authority confers upon an individual the **actual** authority to consent to a search. An apparent authority analysis is triggered only if the consenting party did **not** have actual authority to consent to a search but the police reasonably believed that they did.

2. The Need for Voluntariness. In addition to establishing that permission was given, the government must demonstrate that the consent was voluntary. Consent is voluntarily given if it is "the product of an essentially free and unconstrained choice by its maker."[12] Thus, consent is not voluntary if the giver's "will has been overborne and his capacity for self-determination [was] critically impaired."[13]

The test to assess voluntariness of consent is the traditional totality-of-the-circumstances test. Under this test, courts must consider a variety of factors including "evidence of minimal schooling, low intelligence, and the lack of any effective warnings to a person of his rights."[14] Voluntariness also considers "the nature of the police questioning [and] the environment in which it took place."[15] Generally, no one factor is decisive—for example, the fact that police have visible weapons, or display their badges, or wear uniforms standing alone will not justify a finding that the atmosphere that produced the consent was coercive.[16] Active brandishing of a weapon, however, is probably enough to establish coercion.[17]

If the individual who supposedly gave consent has been illegal seized, the consent will be "tainted by the illegality and . . . ineffective to justify the search."[18] However, if a party has been lawfully seized, the police need not mention that the party is free to go for subsequent consent to be deemed valid. For example, assume the police lawfully pull you over for a traffic stop. At the conclusion of the stop,

[12] Schneckloth v. Bustamonte, 412 U.S. 218, 225 (1973).

[13] Id. at 225.

[14] Id. at 248.

[15] Id. at 248.

[16] United States v. Drayton, 536 U.S. 194, 204–05 (2002).

[17] Id. at 205.

[18] Florida v. Royer, 460 U.S. 491, 508 (1983).

the police need not tell you that you are free to go before asking for permission to search your car.[19] In evaluating voluntariness, the question is not whether the person acted against their own interests, but whether they acted of their own free will.[20]

The police cannot falsely claim that they have the right to search in order to obtain consent from the suspect. [21] Accordingly, if an officer falsely announces that she has a search warrant and then receives consent for the search, the consent will be deemed involuntary.[22] However, if the police actually do possess probable cause to search and **could** use it to obtain a warrant, they can tell the suspect that they have this ability in order to obtain consent.

Not every instance of police trickery will invalidate the voluntariness of consent. For example, the Court has found that voluntariness is not nullified if the police deception concerns only the true identity of an officer or informant.[23] In other words, a person may voluntarily invite someone into their home who turns out to be a false friend, either because the guest is an undercover police officer or is otherwise working with the police. The consent to that person's entry is valid, notwithstanding that it was obtained by fraud.[24] While inside, the guest cannot take tangible property or use stealth to listen in on otherwise private conversations.[25] But if the false friend only "seizes" statements by engaging in conversation with the occupants, those conversations will not be illegal because they were engaged in voluntarily.[26] "The use of informers, accessories, accomplices, false friends, or any of the other betrayals which are 'dirty business' may raise serious questions of credibility. . . . [but] such disapproval must not be thought to justify a social policy of the magnitude necessary to arbitrarily exclude otherwise relevant evidence."[27]

The scope of a consent search is limited by the terms of its authorization.[28] When police exceed the terms of that authorization, what may have begun as a consensual encounter will mature into an investigatory seizure that is governed by standard Fourth Amendment principles. In determining the scope of authorization, the question is one of objective reasonableness. You must ask what an objectively

[19] Ohio v. Robinette, 519 U.S. 33 (1996).

[20] United States v. Mendenhall, 446 U.S. 544, 555–56 (1980).

[21] Bumper v. North Carolina, 391 U.S. 543, 549 (1968); see also Kaupp v. Texas, 538 U.S. 626 (2003).

[22] Go-Bart v. United States, 282 U.S. 344 (1931).

[23] Hoffa v. United States, 385 U.S. 293 (1966).

[24] On Lee v. United States, 343 U.S. 747, 752 (1952).

[25] Hoffa, 385 U.S. at 302–03.

[26] On Lee, 343 U.S. at 753–54.

[27] Id. at 757.

[28] Walter v. United States, 447 U.S. 649 (1980).

reasonable person would have understood the exchange between the police officer and the individual to mean.[29]

Let's see how these rules are applied in the real world.

C. Applying the Law. As noted, application of the consent exception requires that the police establish two things—consent by a person with actual or apparent authority to do so; and the voluntariness of the consent. We will consider first the question of actual authority, which affects who can consent to a search and raises questions of how competing assertions of right should be handled.

1. Landlords, Roommates and Spouses: Assessing the Actual Authority to Consent When Property is "Shared". The most straightforward way to prove actual authority is to demonstrate that the owner of the property consented to its search. But what if the actual owner has turned over possession of the property to another? Does the owner, by virtue of her legal title, retain any actual authority to consent to warrantless police entry? This depends on **the degree to which the owner has agreed to "share" use and control of the premises with others.**

When an owner completely turns over use and control to another (as a landlord might do with a tenant), the owner's retained authority to consent is typically very limited. On the other hand, when a person agrees to share use and control of the property with others (as roommates or cohabitating domestic partners might do), the owner will retain far greater rights. Let's consider first what the Court has said in the context of landlords and tenants:

> **Example—*Chapman v. United States*, 365 U.S. 610 (1961):** Bridgaman and a friend owned a house in the woods near Macon, Georgia and rented the house out to tenants. One February Bridgaman learned that a new tenant had just moved into the house, and so he went to the house to invite the new tenant to church. When he arrived, he immediately noticed the smell of alcohol. He knocked on the door, but no one answered, and he was unable to see into the house because the shades were pulled. Bridgaman went home and called the police. He then returned to the property with two officers, Harbin and Chance.
>
> When they arrived at the property, the officers also noticed the very strong smell of liquor. The officers then repeated Bridgaman's efforts—knocking on the door and peering into windows, but they were also unsuccessful. The officers did not have a warrant.

[29] Florida v. Jimeno, 500 U.S. 248 (1991).

However, when they located an unlocked bathroom window, Bridgaman invited them to enter, telling the officers either "[G]o in the window and see what's what in there," or "If it's what I think it is, what it smells like, yes, you can have my permission to go in."

Officer Harbin climbed in and saw a large distillery in the living room and more than one thousand gallons of whiskey. Chapman was arrested when he returned home.

At trial, Chapman contended that the warrantless entry and search of the house violated the Fourth Amendment. In response, the government contended that the warrantless entry was sanctioned by the owner Bridgaman's unequivocal consent to the search.

Analysis: The Supreme Court held that the warrantless entry into the home violated the Fourth Amendment. Though as a landlord Bridgaman retained the authority to enter the home for some purposes, he did not retain a right to authorize a general search by the police for evidence of criminal misconduct.

The Court first reaffirmed that probable cause alone does not authorize entry into a home. A "[b]elief, however well founded, that an article sought is concealed in a dwelling house furnishes no justification for a search of that place without a warrant."[30] The Court found that the pervasive odor of whiskey mash emanating from the house may have provided the officers with probable cause to believe that an illegal distillery was inside, but it did not relieve the officers of the obligation to first obtain a warrant before entering.

Moreover, the consent of the landlord did not justify the officers' action. Georgia law authorized landlords to enter leased premises to take an accounting of the property's condition. However, the common law right to enter to "view waste" did not carry with it a right to forcibly enter without the tenant's permission. The Court found the purpose of the forced entry in Chapman's case was not to view waste. Rather the officers were looking for distilling equipment. "[T]o uphold such an entry, search and seizure without a warrant would reduce the Fourth Amendment to a nullity and leave tenants' homes secure only in the discretion of landlords."[31]

Finally, the Court found that while Chapman's use of the property may work to forfeit his right to the home, the statutory process for ascertaining such forfeiture required legal action on the part of the landlord before forfeiture would be recognized.

[30] Chapman v. United States, 365 U.S. 610, 613 (1961).

[31] Id. at 616–17.

Because the search of the rented house was unlawful, the evidence seized during the search was excluded.

Unlike landlords, who generally cede use of the property to the tenant during the term of the lease, a different rule applies in the context of shared spaces. Where two or more people share mutual use and enjoyment of a space, the Court has found each co-tenant has broad authority to consent to searches of any jointly used areas:

> **Example—*United States v. Matlock*, 415 U.S. 164 (1974):** William Matlock lived with his girlfriend, Gayle Graff, and her young son. They stayed in a house rented by Graff's parents. Graff's mother also lived in the home along with several of Graff's siblings.
>
> Matlock was arrested in the yard of the home after he was indicted for bank robbery. Following Matlock's arrest, three officers knocked on the door of the house. Graff, dressed in a robe and carrying her three-year old son, allowed the police inside. The police asked Graff for permission to search the house, explaining that they were looking for money and a gun. Graff consented to the search, including the search of Matlock's upstairs bedroom, which she shared.
>
> During the search, the police found nearly $5,000 in cash stuffed into a diaper bag in the closet of the room. This evidence was admitted against Matlock at trial. Matlock argued that he had not authorized the search and that the money was seized during an unlawful search of his bedroom. The government replied that Graff had the actual authority to consent to the search on her own. The Court accepted the case to resolve whether Graff's relationship to the bedroom was sufficient to confer upon her the actual authority to consent to the search.

Analysis: The warrantless entry of the bedroom was constitutional as it was grounded in Graff's actual consent. The Court held that the "voluntary consent of any joint occupant of a residence to search the premises jointly occupied is valid against the co-occupant."[32] Where the co-owner is not present to object, the consent of another occupant will be deemed valid. To rely on the consent of a co-tenant, the government need only establish that the person "possessed

---

[32] United States v. Matlock, 415 U.S. 164, 170 (1974).

common authority over or other sufficient relationship to the premises or effects sought to be inspected."[33]

In the *Matlock* case, the following statements from Graff demonstrated her common authority over the bedroom: 1) Graff told the police that she shared the bedroom with Matlock; 2) after leading officers to the bedroom, Graff explained that she and Matlock shared the single dresser in the room; and 3) Graff told the officers that she and Matlock regularly slept in the bedroom together. In addition, there was evidence corroborating Graff's statements. For example, the room contained both a man's and a woman's clothing. Moreover, there was evidence that Matlock referred to Graff as his wife. There was also evidence that the two lived together in Florida before moving in with Graff's mother. And finally, testimony from those in the house confirmed that the couple was often seen heading up to the bedroom together in the evenings. On this record, the Court found that Graff had the actual authority to consent to the search of the room. Therefore, the money seized from the diaper bag was admissible.

The shared space rule only applies to areas of a building that are jointly used by both the suspect and the consenting party. In *Matlock*, the defendant and Graff shared the bedroom and the closet where the contraband was found. However, many times co-tenants may share common areas such as the living room and the kitchen, but maintain their own separate bedrooms. Similarly, a co-tenant may have personal property such as a computer or journal which she does not share with her co-tenants. A co-tenant's authority to consent does not extend to those non-shared areas.

Matlock also involved a co-tenant's permission when the suspect was absent. However, what if the suspect is present and objects to the search? Can the consent of one co-tenant override the objection of another? In 2006, the Court answered this question in the negative:

> **Example—*Georgia v. Randolph*, 547 U.S. 103 (2006):** Scott and Janet Randolph were married and had a son together. The couple separated in 2001. Janet moved out of the house she and Scott shared and moved into her parents' home in Canada, taking their son with her. Several months after the separation, Janet returned. However, just days later, she called the police and complained that Scott had taken their son following an argument. When the police arrived, Janet immediately advised them that Scott was a cocaine user. When Scott returned a short while later, he advised the police that he had taken his son to a neighbor's house to prevent Janet from leaving the country with him again. After retrieving the boy, Janet restated her claims of

[33] Matlock, 415 U.S. at 171.

Scott's drug use. She also told police there was evidence of that drug use in the house.

The police asked Scott for permission to search the house, but he refused. The officer then turned to Janet and asked for her permission to search. She led the police into the house and upstairs to Scott's bedroom. In the room, the officer saw a portion of a drinking straw covered with a powdery substance he believed to be cocaine. The officer seized the straw as evidence. A subsequent search of the house based upon a warrant revealed additional evidence of drug use.

Scott was indicted for drug possession and moved to suppress the evidence. He argued that Janet's consent to the search could not override his explicit objection.

Analysis: The search was unlawful. The Supreme Court affirmed that co-tenants have actual authority to consent to the search of jointly shared spaces. As a general rule, the "consent of one who possesses common authority over premises or effects is valid as against the absent, nonconsenting person with whom that authority is shared."[34] However, when both tenants are present and there is no applicable social hierarchy (such as a parent/child relationship), there is generally no common understanding that one co-tenant may override the express wishes of another.

Against this background, the Court determined that "a warrantless search of a shared dwelling for evidence over the express refusal of consent by a physically present resident cannot be justified as reasonable as to him on the basis of consent given to the police by another resident."[35] Where Scott Randolph's objection to the search was clear, and there was no basis for the warrantless intrusion beyond Janet Randolph's consent, the Court determined that the search violated the Fourth Amendment.

Thus, a co-tenant can consent to a search of shared areas if the suspect is absent, but if the suspect is physically present and objects, the co-tenant's consent is not sufficient to overcome that objection. But what if the police remove the suspect from the scene and then ask the co-tenant for permission to search? This was the situation in *Matlock*, in which the suspect was sitting in the squad car when the police asked his girlfriend for permission to search their joint bedroom. The *Randolph* Court was careful to note that it was not overruling *Matlock*; thus creating a relatively formalist rule: "if a potential defendant with self-interest in objecting is in fact at the door and objects, the co-tenant's permission does not suffice

[34] Georgia v. Randolph, 547 U.S. 103, 110 (2006).

[35] Id. at 120.

for a reasonable search, whereas the potential objector, nearby but not invited to take part in the threshold colloquy, loses out."[36]

But what if the police know that the suspect objects to the search, but the co-tenant consents, and so they remove the suspect from the scene with the **purpose** of making the co-tenant's permission valid? In other words, what if the police officers know they are facing a *Randolph* situation, and so they arrest the suspect in order to transform it into a *Matlock* situation? In 2014, the Supreme Court determined that the *Randolph* rule "applies only when the objector is standing in the door saying 'stay out' when officers propose to make a consent search."[37] The Court further concluded that so long as an occupant has been lawfully detained, that occupant "stands in the same shoes as an occupant who is absent for any other reason," without regard for the subjective motivations of the police in making the arrest.[38]

2. Children, Hotel Night Clerks and Former Lovers: Determining Apparent Authority When Third Parties Consent to Searches. Sometimes it turns out that the person telling the police they can search does not actually have the right to do so. For example, young children are not generally considered to have the authority to authorize a search of their parents' bedroom.[39] When the police rely on the consent of one who ultimately has no authority, does their warrantless conduct violate the Constitution? The answer to the question depends upon whether the police have a reasonable basis for believing the consenting party actually had a right to grant permission. If so, their reliance upon that consent will justify their warrantless conduct. On the other hand, if the police should not reasonably believe the consenting party has authority, reliance upon the consent will not insulate warrantless conduct from constitutional scrutiny:

> **Example—*Stoner v. California*, 376 U.S. 483 (1964):** One night in October, a supermarket in Monrovia, California, was robbed at gunpoint. One of the robbers wore horn-rimmed glasses and a grey sports coat. Following the robbery, Joseph Stoner's checkbook was found in the parking lot. Two witnesses to the robbery identified Stoner as one of the assailants after police obtained a photograph of him.
>
> Records in Stoner's checkbook reflected that checks had been drawn on the account to the Mayfair Hotel in Pomona, California. Accordingly, the police went to the hotel one night and

[36] Id. at 121.

[37] Fernandez v. California, 134 S.Ct. 1126, 1136 (2014).

[38] Id. at 1134.

[39] Randolph, 547 U.S. at 112.

asked the night clerk if Stoner was staying there. The clerk gave the officers Stoner's room number and further explained that Stoner was out. The clerk knew this information because hotel policy required guests to leave their room key with the front desk whenever they left. The officers told the clerk that they suspected Stoner in connection with a recent armed robbery. They did not have a warrant, but instead asked the clerk for permission to search the room. The clerk responded, "In this case, I will be more than happy to give you permission and I will take you directly to the room."[40]

At the room, the clerk placed the key in the door, unlocked the room and told the officers, "Be my guest." The officers entered and thoroughly searched the room. They found a pair of horn-rimmed glasses, a grey jacket, a gun, and ammunition. At trial, these items was offered by the prosecution as evidence of Stoner's guilt. Stoner objected arguing that the warrantless search of his room was unlawful. The government responded that the consent of the night clerk provided adequate justification for the intrusion.

Analysis: The police officers could not reasonably have believed that the night clerk had the authority to consent to the search of the room.

The Court agreed that the night clerk clearly and unambiguously consented to the search by police officers. However, "there [was] nothing in the record to indicate that the police had any basis whatsoever to believe that the night clerk had been authorized by [Stoner] to permit the police to search [his] room"[41]

The Court noted that twice before it had refused to recognize the authority of a hotel proprietor to consent to the warrantless search of hotel guests' rooms.[42] The Court did not dispute that the renter of a hotel room should assume entry into the room by maids and other hotel staff to perform necessary duties like cleaning and repairs. However, as in *Chapman*, the entry into Stoner's hotel room was not for one of these authorized purposes. Accordingly, it could not be excused on these grounds.

Because the police could not reasonably have believed the night clerk had the right to consent to the search, apparent authority did not exist. The warrantless search based on the consent of the clerk was therefore unlawful and Stoner's conviction was reversed.[43]

---

40 Stoner v. California, 376 U.S. 483, 485 (1964).

41 Id. at 489.

42 See Lustig v. United States, 338 U.S. 74 (1949); United States v. Jeffers, 342 U.S. 48 (1951).

43 Stoner, 376 U.S. at 893.

Because the Court had repeatedly found that a hotel clerk does not have the authority to consent to an evidentiary search of a guest's room, it was unreasonable for the police in *Stoner* to assume that the clerk had that authority. But not all cases of apparent authority are as clear cut. What if police reliance on a third party's assertion of authority to consent is admittedly erroneous but nonetheless reasonable? The Court has determined that this type of reasonable reliance will insulate the otherwise illegal police action:

> **Example—*Illinois v. Rodriguez*, 497 U.S. 177 (1990):** Edward Rodriguez and Gail Fischer lived together for several months. Fischer had a key to the apartment and kept most of her things there, although her name was not on the lease. Eventually, Fischer moved out of the apartment taking many of her things with her and relocated to her mother's apartment nearby.
>
> Several weeks later, Fischer's mother called the police. When the police arrived at the mother's apartment, Fischer was there. She showed signs of being violently assaulted. Fischer told the police that Rodriguez had beaten her earlier that day. Fischer repeatedly referred to Rodriguez's apartment as "our" apartment, and mentioned that she had both clothes and furniture there. Fischer did not mention that she and Rodriguez had separated, nor that she had moved some of her things out of the apartment weeks earlier.
>
> The police drove Fischer to Rodriguez's apartment. Fischer unlocked the door with her key and invited the police to enter. The police saw drugs and drug paraphernalia in plain view. They found Rodriguez asleep in the bedroom. He was arrested and the evidence was seized. At trial, Rodriguez challenged the warrantless search of his home. He presented evidence that Fischer's name was not on the lease, that she did not pay rent, that she had no access to the apartment when Rodriguez was away and that she had moved some of her things out.

Analysis: The Supreme Court held that the police did not violate the Fourth Amendment when they entered Rodriguez's apartment without a warrant.

The Court agreed that Fischer did not have actual authority to consent to the search of Rodriguez's apartment. However, the Court held that the Fourth Amendment did not require "factual accuracy." Where Fischer's statements coupled with the surrounding circumstances made it reasonable for the police to rely upon her consent, Fischer had apparent authority to permit the search.

The Court made clear that not all searches based upon a simple assertion of authority will be found legitimate. "Even when the invitation is accompanied by an explicit assertion that the person lives there, the surrounding circumstances could conceivably be such that a reasonable person would doubt the truth and not act upon it without further inquiry."[44] Under such circumstances, the failure to further investigate would yield any warrantless intrusion unlawful. However, in the case before it, the Court found no reason for the police to question Fischer's claims. Accordingly, the warrantless search of Rodriguez's apartment based upon Fischer's apparent authority was as lawful as a warrantless search based upon actual authority to consent.

3. Voluntariness and the Totality of the Circumstances. Once a court has confirmed that the person who gave consent had the actual or apparent authority to do so, it then moves to the next inquiry: whether the consent was "voluntary." As noted above, the Court has determined that the voluntariness of any consent to search should be judged by considering the totality of the circumstances. These include a variety of factors like the consenter's age, her level of education and the environment in which consent is given. However, the Court has held that the suspect does not need to know that he has the right to refuse consent, and consequently the police do not need to inform the suspect of that right:

> **Example—*Schneckloth v. Bustamonte*, 412 U.S. 218 (1973):** An officer on routine patrol in Sunnyvale, California, stopped a car for driving with one headlight and a burned out license plate light. Inside of the car were six men. Three of the men were in the front seat—Joe Alcala, Robert Bustamonte, and the driver, Joe Gonzalez. When the officer asked Gonzalez for identification, he was unable to produce a driver's license. Of the remaining five men, only Alcala could produce identification when asked. Alcala advised the officer that the car belonged to his brother. After two additional police officers arrived, the first officer asked Alcala if he could search the car. Alcala responded, "Sure, go ahead." During the search, Alcala opened the trunk for the officers, as well as the glove box. In the left rear seat, the police found three checks that had been stolen from a car wash. Ultimately, Bustamonte was connected to the stolen checks, and they were admitted over objection as evidence at his trial.
>
> Bustamonte contended that the checks were seized in violation of his constitutional rights. In particular, Bustamonte claimed that the state had not met its burden of demonstrating the

[44] Illinois v. Rodriguez, 497 U.S. 177, 188 (1990).

voluntariness of Alcala's consent where it had not established that Alcala was advised of his right to refuse consent. The trial court rejected Bustamonte's claim and found that the checks were properly admitted pursuant to the consent exception. The case was ultimately appealed to the Supreme Court.

Analysis: The burden is on the prosecution to establish the voluntariness of consent where it seeks to use the consent exception to insulate a warrantless search from constitutional prohibition. However, the government's burden does not include an obligation to prove that police provided notice of the right to refuse consent.

The values underlying notions of voluntariness recognize "that the criminal law cannot be used as an instrument of unfairness, and that the possibility of unfair and even brutal police tactics poses a real and serious threat to civilized notions of justice."[45] The most extensive judicial discussions of voluntariness arise in the context of custodial confessions. However, the same principles that apply to voluntariness in that context apply to the context of consent searches.

The test to be used in assessing voluntariness requires examination of the totality of the circumstances. Age, education, intelligence, advice regarding constitutional rights, the length of detention, the nature of the police inquiry, and the use of physical punishment are all relevant to the question of voluntariness. However, no one of these factor is more relevant than another. "While knowledge of the right to refuse consent is one factor to be taken into account, the government need not establish such knowledge as the *sine qua non* of an effective consent."[46]

Though the Court acknowledged that consent is often referred to as "a 'waiver' of a person's rights under the Fourth and Fourteenth Amendments," the Court further found that "knowing and intelligent waiver" is generally only required for those rights guaranteed by the Constitution in order to protect a fair criminal trial.[47] Because Fourth Amendment rights are not "trial rights," a knowing and intelligent waiver is not needed. "The Fourth Amendment is not an adjunct to the ascertainment of truth. The guarantees of the Fourth Amendment stand as a protection of quite different constitutional values—values reflecting the concern of our society for the right of each individual to be let alone."[48]

Cases like *Schneckloth* have come under some criticism for ignoring the realities of police/citizen encounters. In *Schneckloth*, the suspects had been seized, there were three police officers present, and it was late at night on the side of a road. When one of the officers asked for permission to search—without telling him he had the

[45] Schneckloth v. Bustamonte, 412 U.S. 218, 225 (1973).

[46] Id. at 227.

[47] Id. at 235–36.

[48] Id. at 242.

right to refuse—did the suspect really make a "free and unconstrained" choice? Recall the *Drayton* case from **Chapter 9**, in which three police officers boarded a bus, and one of them approached the suspect and stood only a foot away and asked to search the suspect's bag and person. In that case, Drayton "consented" to the search even though he knew he had over a quarter of a kilogram of heroin strapped to his leg, and even though he had just seen the officers search his friend, find heroin, and arrest him. If Drayton felt free to refuse consent, why did he give his consent?

One problem is that the Supreme Court has used relatively extreme language in their definitions of "voluntary" and "involuntary," Consent is voluntary when it is the product of a "free and unconstrained choice," but it is involuntary if the suspect's "will has been overborne and his capacity for self-determination was critically impaired." Obviously there is a large amount of middle ground between these two alternatives, and most of the consent cases decided by courts fall within this vast middle ground. However, as *Schenckloth* and *Drayton* demonstrate, the Court will usually lean towards finding consent unless it determines that the consent was in fact involuntary—that is, as long as the defendant's will was not overborne and his capacity for self-determination was not critically impaired.

4. Police Declarations of Authority and Their Effect on Voluntariness. The consent exception requires that the consent be voluntarily given. Some forms of police conduct affect voluntariness, while others do not. For example, if the police threaten to **get** a warrant (and actually have the probable cause to do so), this threat will not affect the voluntariness of consent. However, if the police claim that they **have** a warrant when they do not actually have one, and secure your consent in this manner, that consent will be deemed involuntary.

> **Example—*Bumper v. North Carolina*, 391 U.S. 543 (1968):** A young man and his girlfriend were parked on a country road in rural North Carolina not far from where Wayne Bumper lived with his widowed grandmother. The evidence at trial showed that Bumper approached the couple's car armed with a rifle. Over the course of an hour and a half in a remote section of the woods, Bumper twice raped the woman; bound and blindfolded the couple; and shot each through their left breast in an effort to hit their hearts. Bumper then left, assuming both were dead. However, the couple managed to free themselves and sought help from a nearby homeowner who took them to the hospital.
>
> While investigating the crime, the local sheriff, two of his deputies, and a state investigator visited Bumper's grandmother's house, where Bumper's stayed. Bumper's grandmother Hattie

Leath was at home, babysitting two or three young children. Mrs. Leath met the officers at the door, where one of them falsely announced, "I have a search warrant to search your house." Leath further testified that the officer "said he was the law and had a search warrant to search the house, why I thought he could go ahead."[49] Ms. Leath told the officers to "come on in and go ahead and search."[50]

On cross examination during the suppression hearing, Mrs. Leath appeared to testify more emphatically about her decision to give consent and suggested that she had not felt coerced. Leath testified, "He did tell me he had a search warrant. I don't know if [the sheriff] was with him. I was not paying much attention. I told [the officer] after he had come upon the porch to go ahead and look all over the house. I had no objection to them making a search of my house. I was willing to let them look in any room or drawer in my house they wanted to. Nobody threatened me with anything. Nobody told me they were going to hurt me if I didn't let them search my house. Nobody told me they would give me any money if I would let them search. I let them search, and it was all my own free will. Nobody forced me at all."[51]

During the search of Mrs. Leath's home, the officers recovered a .22 caliber rifle that was introduced as evidence against Bumper at trial. Bumper objected to the admission of the rifle, arguing that the warrantless search of the home violated his Fourth Amendment right to be free of unreasonable searches and seizures. The government countered that the warrantless intrusion was authorized by Leath's consent.

Analysis: The Supreme Court held that the warrantless search of the home could not be justified by Mrs. Leath's consent. The Court established a bright-line rule regarding consent that is granted only after a police officer asserts warrant authority. "When a law enforcement officer claims authority to search a home under a warrant, he announces in effect that the occupant has no right to resist the search. The situation is [ripe] with coercion. . . . Where there is coercion there cannot be consent."[52]

[49] Bumper v. North Carolina, 391 U.S. 543, 547 (1968).

[50] Bumper, 391 U.S. at 546.

[51] Id. at 556.

[52] Id. at 550.

The dissent questioned the Court's determination that Mrs. Leath's consent was not voluntary in light of her seemingly unequivocal suppression hearing testimony that she had "no objection" to the search. However, under the majority's bright line test, Mrs. Leath's statements were irrelevant.

The majority did note that issues of race and gender might have influenced Leath's decision to allow the officers in. In particular, the Court noted that Mrs. Leath was an elderly widowed black woman, living on a remote country road in rural North Carolina in 1968. The Court also noted that she gave consent only after being confronted by four white male police officers, who arrived at her doorstep and announced their authority to enter and search. Interestingly, notwithstanding its comment on the particular facts, the Court did not establish a rule requiring case-by-case evaluation of putative consent. Rather, without particular regard for the facts of any case, the Court held that where a police officer says he has a warrant, "there can be no consent under such circumstances."[53]

5. The Scope of Consent Searches and the Terms of Authorization. One final question the Court has considered in connection with consent searches involves their scope. As a general matter, the scope of a consent search is limited by the terms of its authorization. Thus, if an individual tells a police officer she may search his house, the officer is not also entitled to search the car parked in the driveway. A person who gives consent can limit it in any way she wants to, and the police must honor that limitation. For example, if the suspect only gives permission to look in certain rooms of the house, or if she only allows the police to search for five minutes, or allows them to look around but tells them not to open any drawers or cabinets, the police officers may not exceed the scope of the search given.

An interesting question arises when a person tells the police officer that she can search his car and there are closed containers inside the car. If the consenting individual does not mention the containers, does the consent extend to the closed containers inside the car?

> **Example—*Florida v. Jimeno*, 500 U.S. 248 (1991):** Enio Jimeno was using a public pay phone to discuss what sounded like a drug transaction. Officer Frank Trujillo was standing nearby and overheard Jimeno's discussion. When Jimeno got in his car and pulled off, Trujillo followed. A short distance down the road, Trujillo saw Jimeno make a right turn at a red light without first stopping. Trujillo pulled Jimeno over to issue a traffic citation.

[53] Bumper, 391 U.S. at 548.

During the stop, Trujillo told Jimeno that he believed he was in possession of drugs. Trujillo told Jimeno that he did not have to consent, but asked for Jimeno's permission to search the vehicle. Jimeno said he had nothing to hide and gave Trujillo permission to search the car. On the floor of the car in front of the passenger's seat, Trujillo saw a folded brown paper bag. He picked it up and looked inside and found a kilo of cocaine.

Jimeno sought to suppress the drugs at trial. He argued that Trujillo's search of the bag exceed the scope of the consent to search that had been granted. Specifically, Jimeno argued that consent to search a car could not reasonably be interpreted as consent to search all closed containers inside of the car.

Analysis: The Supreme Court held that because Jimeno did not explicitly exclude closed containers when he gave the officer consent to search the car, the search was legal. The "standard for measuring the scope of a suspect's consent under the Fourth Amendment is that of objective reasonableness—what would the typical reasonable person have understood by the exchange between the officer and the suspect?"[54] In other words, the question to be asked is "what would the average person have understood the consent to include?"

Where a party explicitly limits on the scope of their consent, the consent will obviously be circumscribed by these specified boundaries. However, where a party does not place express limits on the scope of the consent granted, the scope of the consent will be guided by the police officer's stated interests at the outset. "The scope of a search is generally defined by its expressed object."[55]

In *Jimeno*, the officer indicated that he believed Jimeno was transporting drugs. Drugs are frequently carried in containers, and are not often found strewn about the interior of a car. Accordingly, when Jimeno generally consented to the search of his car, the Court found "it was objectively reasonable for the police to conclude that the general consent to search [the] car included consent to search containers within that car which might bear drugs."[56]

Significantly, though the Court has previously stated that the quality of the container is irrelevant to the amount of protection it receives under the Fourth Amendment, the Court's language in *Jimeno* did suggest some distinction with regard to consent searches. Specifically, the Court intimated that it is "unreasonable to think that a suspect, by consenting to the search of his trunk, has agreed to the breaking open of a locked briefcase within the trunk, but it is otherwise with respect to a closed paper bag."[57]

---

[54] Id. at 251.

[55] Id. at 251.

[56] Id.

[57] Id. at 252.

Just as the scope of consent can be explicitly limited by the individual who gives consent, it can also be withdrawn at any time. As soon as the consenting individual communicates her withdrawal to the police officer, he no longer has the authority to conduct the search and anything he finds after that point cannot be justified under the consent exception. Of course, at that point the police may have already developed the authority to search under a different exception, such as the automobile exception or (if they have probable cause to arrest the individual) the search incident to a lawful arrest exception.

6. Consent-Once-Removed. In addition to the question of co-tenants who have been removed to avoid objection, there is one other aspect of consent searches that the Court has not yet resolved: the doctrine of consent-once-removed. Consent-once-removed involves a specific fact pattern: when an individual with actual or apparent authority voluntarily invites an undercover officer into a house, and the officer develops probable cause to arrest or to conduct a search, and immediately calls other officers into the house. On the one hand, the first police officer is already legitimately inside the house, and is allowed to seize any contraband in plain view or make an arrest based on probable cause, and so allowing more officers into the house does not significantly impact the suspect's rights. On the other hand, the initial officer does not technically have the authority—actual or apparent—to consent to others entering the house.

Consent-once-removed is thus described as a legal fiction that allows consent as to one party to transfer to another affiliated party to authorize their warrantless entry or search. There is currently a circuit split regarding this question that will have to be resolved by the Supreme Court.[58]

[58] See, e.g., United States v. Diaz, 814 F.2d 454, 459 (7th Cir. 1987); United States v. Bramble, 103 F.3d 1475 (9th Cir. 1996); United States v. Pollard, 215 F.3d 643 (6th Cir. 2000); State v. Henry, 133 N.J. 104 (1993); State v. Johnson, 184 Wis.2d 794 (1994); United States v. Paul, 808 F.2d 645 (1986); United States v. Yoon, 398 F.3d 802 (2005); Pearson v. Callahan, 555 U.S. 223, 244–45 (2009).

Quick Summary

The fourth recognized exception to the warrant requirement is consent. Police officers are generally allowed to engage in consensual encounters with people. The consent exception to the warrant requirement is just an extension of this general principle.

Police seeking to justify warrantless conduct under the consent exception must establish two things. First, they must show that a person with actual or apparent authority consented to the search. Next, the police must prove that the consent was voluntary. The burden is on the government to establish both elements, and they must do so by a preponderance of the evidence.

Property owners and others with common authority have the actual authority to consent to searches. Warrantless searches may also be justified by the consent exception if police officers reasonably believe the person consenting had the authority to do so. This will be true even if the police reliance is erroneous—the only requirement is that the reliance be objectively reasonable.

When evaluating the voluntariness of consent, the question is analyzed by looking to the totality of the circumstances. Factors like age, education, intelligence, advice regarding constitutional rights, the length of detention, the nature of the police inquiry, and the use of physical punishment are all relevant to the question of voluntariness. No one factor is decisive. Thus, there is no requirement that the police advise the suspect of her right to refuse consent the consent to be deemed voluntary.

The individual giving consent can limit the scope of the consent in any way, and the police are bound by those limitations.

Review Questions

1. Searching the Bedroom Closet. The police responded to a call of domestic violence inside the home. At the scene, officers found Karen Winslow standing just outside of the garage next to her teenage son Charles. Karen was bleeding from her forehead and was being attended to by two paramedics. She told the police that her husband Andrew, who was still inside, had choked her and hit her in the head with the butt of a gun. The paramedics then escorted her to the ambulance and the ambulance drove away.

The police entered the house and found Andrew Winslow sitting at the kitchen table. The police asked him if he had a gun, and Andrew said: "You can't be in here without a warrant; you have to leave." At that point Charles came up behind the police and said: "He keeps the gun in his bedroom closet." Andrew responded: "Don't you all go into my bedroom; you have to leave my house." The police arrested Andrew for aggravated assault and put him in their squad car.

After Andrew was arrested, an officer turned to Charles and asked if he could search the house. Charles said yes, led the police into the master bedroom, and pointed out the closet. The police then went to the searched inside the closet and found a shoebox on the top shelf that contained a pistol.

The defendant was indicted on aggravated assault and illegal possession of a firearm, and he is now challenging the search. Did the police violate his rights when they searched his bedroom closet?

2. The Nervous Train Passenger. Two uniformed police officers were walking through the train station when they saw an individual, later known to be Drew Hammond, sitting alone in the waiting room with a red suitcase next to him. They thought Hammond "looked suspicious"—he checked his watch every minute or so, and very few seconds he would look over his shoulder and around the room apprehensively. He was also unshaven and dressed in sweatpants and a hoodie. Although the officers did not know this at the time, Hammond was nineteen years old and never completed high school.

The two officers approached Hammond and stood about two feet away from him, one on each side. One of them stood between Hammond and the suitcase. The officer next to his suitcase said: "Good afternoon. Could you answer a few questions for us?" Hammond shook his head and replied: "No, thanks, I'd like to be left alone." The officer nodded and placed his hand on the suitcase and said: "OK, but we're going to look in your suitcase before we go, is that OK?" Hammond paused and then nodded, saying: "Yeah, OK." The police opened the suitcase and searched through the contents and found a small paper bag with heroin inside. Hammond was arrested, and he now challenges the search of his suitcase. Did the police violate his rights?

3. Searching the Brother-In-Law's Room. The Austin police department received a telephone call from David Gruden, who claimed that his brother-in-law Thomas Childs was selling drugs. Gruden asked police to come out to his house, where Childs and his wife (Gruden's sister) were staying as guests. When the police arrived, Gruden invited them into the house and told him they could search it for drugs.

Childs was present at the house, and when he saw the police, he immediately ran to the door and said: "We have no problems here," and physically barred the police from entering the house. The police told Childs they were here to search the house for drugs and Childs said: "I know my rights. You can't do that without a warrant." The police ignored Childs and searched the house. In the basement they found chemicals and paraphernalia used to manufacture methamphetamine. Childs was arrested and charged with possession of chemicals with the intent to manufacture illegal drugs.

Childs moved to suppress the drugs, arguing that the search was illegal. At the suppression hearing, there was uncontroverted testimony that Gruden owned the house and that neither Childs nor his wife paid any rent to him. Gruden testified that Childs and his wife had lived in the house for six months, and that during that time he had respected Childs' privacy and treated his bedroom as though it were Childs' apartment. Childs and his wife almost always kept their bedroom door locked, and Gruden would infrequently enter or spend time in the bedroom in Childs' absence. When defendant was present, the brother-in-law would not enter without knocking on the door. Gruden also testified that he, Childs, and Childs' wife had "equal access" to the rest of the house, except for Gruden's own bedroom.

Was the search of Gruden's home constitutional?

FROM THE COURTROOM

SCHNECKLOTH v. BUSTAMONTE

United States Supreme Court, 1973
93 U.S. 2041

[Justice STEWART delivered the opinion of the Court.]

[Justice BLACKMUN filed a concurring opinion.]

[Justices POWELL filed a concurring opinion, which was joined by Justice REHNQUIST and CHIEF JUSTICE BURGER]

[Justice DOUGLAS filed a dissenting opinion.]

[Justice BRENNAN filed a dissenting opinion.]

[Justice MARSHALL filed a dissenting opinion.]

It is well settled under the Fourth and Fourteenth Amendments that a search conducted without a warrant issued upon probable cause is per se unreasonable . . . subject only to a few specifically established and well-delineated exceptions. It is equally well settled that one of the specifically established exceptions to the requirements of both a warrant and probable cause is a search that is conducted pursuant to consent. The constitutional question in the present case concerns the definition of "consent" in this Fourth and Fourteenth Amendment context.

I

. . .

While on routine patrol in Sunnyvale, California, at approximately 2:40 in the morning, Police Officer James Rand stopped an automobile when he observed that one headlight and its license plate light were burned out. Six men were in the vehicle. Joe Alcala and the respondent, Robert Bustamonte, were in the front seat with Joe Gonzales, the driver. Three older men were seated in the rear. When, in response to the policeman's question, Gonzales could not produce a driver's license, Officer Rand asked if any of the other five had any evidence of identification. Only Alcala produced a license, and he explained that the car was his brother's. After the six occupants had stepped out of the car at the officer's request and after two additional policemen had arrived, Officer Rand asked Alcala if he could search the car. Alcala replied, "Sure, go ahead." Prior to the search no one was threatened with arrest and, according to Officer Rand's uncontradicted testimony, it "was all very congenial at this time." Gonzales testified that Alcala actually helped in the search of the car, by opening the trunk and glove compartment. In Gonzales' words: "(T)he police officer asked Joe (Alcala), he goes, 'Does the trunk open?' And Joe said, 'Yes.' He went to the car and got the keys and opened up the trunk." Wadded up under the left rear seat, the police officers found three checks that had previously been stolen from a car wash.

The trial judge denied the motion to suppress, and the checks in question were admitted in evidence at Bustamonte's trial. On the basis of this and other evidence he was convicted . . .

II

It is important to make it clear at the outset what is not involved in this case. The respondent concedes that a search conducted pursuant to a valid consent is constitutionally permissible. In *Katz v. United States*, and more recently in *Vale v. Louisiana*, we recognized that a search authorized by consent is wholly valid. And similarly the State concedes that "(w)hen a prosecutor seeks to rely upon consent to justify the lawfulness of a search, he has the burden of proving that the consent was, in fact, freely and voluntarily given."

The precise question in this case, then, is what must the prosecution prove to demonstrate that a consent was "voluntarily" given. And upon that question there is a square conflict of views between the state and federal courts that have reviewed the search involved in the case before us. The Court of Appeals for the Ninth Circuit concluded that it is an essential part of the State's initial burden to prove that a person knows he has a right to refuse consent. The California courts have followed the rule that voluntariness is a question of fact to be determined from the totality of all the circumstances, and that the state of a defendant's knowledge is only one factor to be taken into account in assessing the voluntariness of a consent.

A

The most extensive judicial exposition of the meaning of "voluntariness" has been developed in those cases in which the Court has had to determine the "voluntariness" of a defendant's confession for purposes of the Fourteenth Amendment. Almost 40 years ago, in *Brown v. Mississippi*, the Court held that a criminal conviction based upon a confession obtained by brutality and violence was constitutionally invalid under the Due Process Clause of the Fourteenth Amendment. In some 30 different cases decided during the era that intervened between *Brown* and *Escobedo v. Illinois*, the Court was faced with the necessity of determining whether in fact the confessions in issue had been "voluntarily" given. It is to that body of case law to which we turn for initial guidance on the meaning of "voluntariness" in the present context.

Those cases yield no talismanic definition of "voluntariness," mechanically applicable to the host of situations where the question has arisen. "The notion of 'voluntariness,'" Mr. Justice Frankfurter once wrote, "is itself an amphibian." It cannot be taken literally to mean a "knowing" choice. "Except where a person is unconscious or drugged or otherwise lacks capacity for conscious choice, all incriminating statements—even those made under brutal treatment—are 'voluntary' in the sense of representing a choice of alternatives. On the other hand, if 'voluntariness' incorporates notions of 'but for' cause, the question should be whether the statement would have been made even absent inquiry or other official action. Under such a test, virtually no statement would be voluntary because very few people give incriminating statements in the absence of official action of some kind." It is thus evident that neither linguistics nor epistemology will provide a ready definition of the meaning of "voluntariness."

Rather, "voluntariness" has reflected an accommodation of the complex of values implicated in police questioning of a suspect. At one end of the spectrum is the acknowledged need for police questioning as a tool for the effective enforcement of criminal laws. Without such investigation, those who were innocent might be falsely accused, those who were guilty might wholly escape prosecution, and many crimes would go unsolved. In short, the security of all would be diminished. At the other end of the spectrum is the set of values reflecting society's deeply felt belief that the criminal law cannot be used as an instrument of unfairness, and that the possibility of unfair and even brutal police tactics poses a real and serious threat to civilized notions of justice. "(I)n cases involving involuntary confessions, this Court enforces the strongly felt attitude of our society that important human values are sacrificed where an agency of the government, in the course of securing a conviction, wrings a confession out of an accused against his will."

This Court's decisions reflect a frank recognition that the Constitution requires the sacrifice of neither security nor liberty. The Due Process Clause does not mandate that the police forgo all questioning, or that they be given carte blanche to extract what they can from a suspect. "The ultimate test remains that which has been the only clearly established test in Anglo-American courts for two hundred years: the test of voluntariness. Is the confession the product of an essentially free and unconstrained choice by its maker? If it is, if he has willed to confess, it may be used against him. If it is not, if his will has been overborne and his capacity for self-determination critically impaired, the use of his confession offends due process."

In determining whether a defendant's will was overborne in a particular case, the Court has assessed the totality of all the surrounding circumstances—both the characteristics of the accused and the details of the interrogation. Some of the factors taken into account have included the youth of the accused, his lack of education, or his low intelligence, the lack of any advice to the accused of his constitutional rights, the length of detention, the repeated and prolonged nature of the questioning, and the use of physical punishment such as the deprivation of food or sleep. In all of these cases, the Court determined the factual circumstances surrounding the confession, assessed the psychological impact on the accused, and evaluated the legal significance of how the accused reacted.

The significant fact about all of these decisions is that none of them turned on the presence or absence of a single controlling criterion; each reflected a careful scrutiny of all the surrounding circumstances. In none of them did the Court rule that the Due Process Clause required the prosecution to prove as part of its initial burden that the defendant knew he had a right to refuse to answer the questions that were put. While the state of the accused's mind, and the failure of the police to advise the accused of his rights, were certainly factors to be evaluated in assessing the "voluntariness" of an accused's responses, they were not in and of themselves determinative.

B

Similar considerations lead us to agree with the courts of California that the question whether a consent to a search was in fact "voluntary" or was the product of duress or coercion, express or implied, is a question of fact to be determined from the totality of all the circumstances. While knowledge of the right to refuse consent is one factor to be taken into account, the government need not establish such knowledge as the sine qua non of an effective consent. As with police questioning, two competing concerns must be accommodated in determining the meaning of a "voluntary" consent—the legitimate need for such searches and the equally important requirement of assuring the absence of coercion.

In situations where the police have some evidence of illicit activity, but lack probable cause to arrest or search, a search authorized by a valid consent may be the only means of obtaining important and reliable evidence. In the present case for example, while the police had reason to stop the car for traffic violations, the State does not contend that there was probable cause to search the vehicle or that the search was incident to a valid arrest of any of the occupants. Yet, the search yielded tangible evidence that served as a basis for a prosecution, and provided some assurance that others, wholly innocent of the crime, were not mistakenly brought to trial. And in those cases where there is probable cause to arrest or search, but where the police lack a warrant, a consent search may still be valuable. If the search is conducted and proves fruitless, that in itself may convince the police that an arrest with its possible stigma and embarrassment is unnecessary, or that a far more extensive search pursuant to a warrant is not justified. In short, a search pursuant to consent may result in considerably less inconvenience for the subject of the search, and, properly conducted, is a constitutionally permissible and wholly legitimate aspect of effective police activity.

But the Fourth and Fourteenth Amendments require that a consent not be coerced, by explicit or implicit means, by implied threat or covert force. For, no matter how subtly the coercion was applied, the resulting 'consent' would be no more than a pretext for the unjustified police intrusion against which the Fourth Amendment is directed. In the words of the classic admonition in Boyd v. United States, 116 U.S. 616, 635:

> It may be that it is the obnoxious thing in its mildest and least repulsive form; but illegitimate and unconstitutional practices get their first footing in that way, namely, by silent approaches and slight deviations from legal modes of procedure. This can only be obviated by adhering to the rule that constitutional provisions for the security of person and property should be liberally construed. A close and literal construction deprives them of half their efficacy, and leads to gradual depreciation of the right, as if it consisted more in sound than in substance. It is the duty of courts to be watchful for the constitutional rights of the citizen, and against any stealthy encroachments thereon.

The problem of reconciling the recognized legitimacy of consent searches with the requirement that they be free from any aspect of official coercion cannot be resolved by any infallible touchstone. To approve such searches without the most careful scrutiny would sanction the possibility of official coercion; to place artificial restrictions upon such searches would jeopardize their basic validity. Just as was true with confessions, the requirement of a "voluntary" consent reflects a fair accommodation of the constitutional requirements involved. In examining all the surrounding circumstances to determine if in fact the consent to search was coerced, account must be taken of subtly coercive police questions, as well as the possibly vulnerable subjective state of the person who consents. Those searches that are the product of police coercion can thus be filtered out without undermining the continuing validity of consent searches. In sum, there is no reason for us to depart in the area of consent searches, from the traditional definition of "voluntariness."

The approach of the Court of Appeals for the Ninth Circuit finds no support in any of our decisions that have attempted to define the meaning of "voluntariness." Its ruling, that the State must affirmatively prove that the subject of the search knew that he had a right to refuse consent, would, in practice, create serious doubt whether consent searches could continue to be conducted. There might be rare cases where it could be proved from the record that a person in fact affirmatively knew of his right to refuse—such as a case where he announced to the police that if he didn't sign the consent form, "you (police) are going to get a search warrant;" or a case where by prior experience and training a person had clearly and convincingly demonstrated such knowledge. But more commonly where there was no evidence of any coercion, explicit or implicit, the prosecution would nevertheless be unable to demonstrate that the subject of the search in fact had known of his right to refuse consent.

The very object of the inquiry—the nature of a person's subjective understanding—underlines the difficulty of the prosecution's burden under the rule applied by the Court of Appeals in this case. Any defendant who was the subject of a search authorized solely by his consent could effectively frustrate the introduction into evidence of the fruits of that search by simply failing to testify that he in fact knew he could refuse to consent. And the near impossibility of meeting this prosecutorial burden suggests why this Court has never accepted any such litmus-paper test of voluntariness. It is instructive to recall the fears of then Justice Traynor of the California Supreme Court:

> (I)t is not unreasonable for officers to seek interviews with suspects or witnesses or to call upon them at their homes for such purposes. Such inquiries, although courteously made and not accompanied with any assertion of a right to enter or search or secure answers, would permit the criminal to defeat his prosecution by voluntarily revealing all of the evidence against him and then contending that he acted only in response to an implied assertion of unlawful authority.

One alternative that would go far toward proving that the subject of a search did know he had a right to refuse consent would be to advise him of that right before eliciting his consent. That, however, is a suggestion that has been almost universally repudiated by both federal and state courts, and, we think, rightly so. For it would be thoroughly impractical to impose on the normal consent search the detailed requirements of an effective warning. Consent searches are part of the standard investigatory techniques of law enforcement agencies. They normally occur on the highway, or in a person's home or office, and under informal and unstructured conditions. The circumstances that prompt the initial request to search may develop quickly or be a logical extension of investigative police questioning. The police may seek to investigate further suspicious circumstances or to follow up leads developed in questioning persons at the scene of a crime. These situations are a far cry from the structured atmosphere of a trial where, assisted by counsel if he chooses, a defendant is informed of his trial rights. And, while surely a closer question, these situations are still immeasurably, far removed from "custodial interrogation" where, in *Miranda v. Arizona*, we found that the Constitution required certain now familiar warnings as a prerequisite to police interrogation. Indeed, in language applicable to the typical consent search, we refused to extend the need for warnings:

> Our decision is not intended to hamper the traditional function of police officers in investigating crime. . . . When an individual is in custody on probable cause, the police may, of course, seek out evidence in the field to be used at trial against him. Such investigation may include inquiry of persons not under restraint. General on-the-scene questioning as to facts surrounding a crime or other general questioning of citizens in the fact-finding process is not affected by our holding. It is an act of responsible citizenship for individuals to give whatever information they may have to aid in law enforcement.

Consequently, we cannot accept the position of the Court of Appeals in this case that proof of knowledge of the right to refuse consent is a necessary prerequisite to demonstrating a "voluntary" consent. Rather it is only by analyzing all the circumstances of an individual consent that it can be ascertained whether in fact it was voluntary or coerced. It is this careful sifting of the unique facts and circumstances of each case that is evidenced in our prior decisions involving consent searches.

For example in *Davis v. United States*, federal agents enforcing wartime gasoline-rationing regulations, arrested a filling station operator and asked to see his rationing coupons. He eventually unlocked a room where the agents discovered the coupons that formed the basis for his conviction. The District Court found that the petitioner had consented to the search—that although he had at first refused to turn the coupons over, he had soon been persuaded to do so and that force or threat of force had not been employed to persuade him. Concluding that it could not be said that this finding was erroneous, this Court, in an opinion by Mr. Justice Douglas that looked to all the circumstances surrounding the consent, affirmed the judgment of conviction: "The public character of the property, the fact that the demand was made during business hours at the place of business where the coupons were required to be kept, the existence of the right to inspect, the nature of the request, the fact that the initial refusal to turn the coupons over was soon followed by acquiescence in the demand—these circumstances all support the conclusion of the District Court."

Conversely, if under all the circumstances it has appeared that the consent was not given voluntarily—that it was coerced by threats or force, or granted only in submission to a claim of lawful authority—then we have found the consent invalid and the search unreasonable. See, e.g., *Bumper v. North Carolina,* 391 U.S., at 548–549. In Bumper, a [sixty-six]-year-old Negro widow, who lived in a house located in a rural area at the end of an isolated mile-long dirt road, allowed four white law enforcement officials to search her home after they asserted they had a warrant to search the house. We held the alleged consent to be invalid, noting that "(w)hen a law enforcement officer claims authority to search a home under a warrant, he announces in effect that the occupant has no right to resist the search. The situation is instinct with coercion—albeit colorably lawful coercion. Where there is coercion there cannot be consent."

. . .

In short, neither this Court's prior cases, nor the traditional definition of "voluntariness" requires proof of knowledge of a right to refuse as the sine qua non of an effective consent to a search.

C

It is said, however, that a "consent" is a "waiver" of a person's rights under the Fourth and Fourteenth Amendments. The argument is that by allowing the police to conduct a search, a person 'waives' whatever right he had to prevent the police from searching. It is argued that under the doctrine of *Johnson v. Zerbst,* to establish such a 'waiver' the State must demonstrate "an intentional relinquishment or abandonment of a known right or privilege."

But these standards were enunciated in *Johnson* in the context of the safeguards of a fair criminal trial. Our cases do not reflect an uncritical demand for a knowing and intelligent waiver in every situation where a person has failed to invoke a constitutional protection.

. . .

Almost without exception, the requirement of a knowing and intelligent waiver has been applied only to those rights which the Constitution guarantees to a criminal defendant in order to preserve a fair trial. Hence, and hardly surprisingly in view of the facts of *Johnson* itself, the standard of a knowing and intelligent waiver has most often been applied to test the validity of a waiver of counsel, either at trial, or upon a guilty plea. And the Court has also applied the *Johnson* criteria to assess the effectiveness of a waiver of other trial rights such as the right to confrontation, to a jury trial, and to a speedy trial, and the right to be free from twice being placed in jeopardy. Guilty pleas have been carefully scrutinized to determine whether the accused knew and understood all the rights to which he would be entitled at trial, and that he had intentionally chosen to forgo them. And the Court has evaluated the knowing and intelligent nature of the waiver of trial rights in trial-type situations, such as the waiver of the privilege against compulsory self-incrimination before an administrative agency or a congressional committee, or the waiver of counsel in a juvenile proceeding.

The guarantees afforded a criminal defendant at trial also protect him at certain stages before the actual trial, and any alleged waiver must meet the strict standard of an intentional relinquishment of a "known" right. But the "trial" guarantees that have been applied to the "pretrial" stage of the criminal process [such as identification procedures and interrogations] are similarly designed to protect the fairness of the trial itself.

. . .

There is a vast difference between those rights that protect a fair criminal trial and the rights guaranteed under the Fourth Amendment. Nothing, either in the purposes behind requiring a "knowing" and "intelligent" waiver of trial rights, or in the practical application of such a requirement suggests that it ought to be extended to the constitutional guarantee against unreasonable searches and seizures.

A strict standard of waiver has been applied to those rights guaranteed to a criminal defendant to insure that he will be accorded the greatest possible opportunity to utilize every facet of the constitutional model of a fair criminal trial. Any trial conducted in derogation of that model leaves open the possibility that the trial reached an unfair result precisely because all the protections specified in the Constitution were not provided. A prime example is the right to counsel. For without that right, a wholly innocent accused faces the real and substantial danger that simply because of his lack of legal expertise he may be convicted. As Mr. Justice Harlan once wrote: "The sound reason why (the right to counsel) is so freely extended for a criminal trial is the severe injustice risked by confronting an untrained defendant with a range of technical points of law, evidence, and tactics familiar to the prosecutor but not to himself." The Constitution requires that every effort be made to see to it that a defendant in a criminal case has not unknowingly relinquished the basic protections that the Framers thought indispensable to a fair trial.

The protections of the Fourth Amendment are of a wholly different order, and have nothing whatever to do with promoting the fair ascertainment of truth at a criminal trial. Rather, as Mr. Justice Frankfurter's opinion for the Court put it in *Wolf v. Colorado*, the Fourth Amendment protects the "security of one's privacy against arbitrary intrusion by the police . . . ." In declining to apply the exclusionary rule of *Mapp v. Ohio*, to convictions that had become final before rendition of that decision, the Court emphasized that "there is no likelihood of unreliability or coercion present in a search-and-seizure case," *Linkletter v. Walker*, 381 U.S. 618, 638. In *Linkletter*, the Court indicated that those cases that had been given retroactive effect went to "the fairness of the trial—the very integrity of the fact-finding process. Here . . . the fairness of the trial is not under attack." The Fourth Amendment "is not an adjunct to the ascertainment of truth." The guarantees of the Fourth Amendment stand "as a protection of quite different constitutional values—values reflecting the concern of our society for the right of each individual to be let alone. To recognize this is no more than to accord those values undiluted respect."

Nor can it even be said that a search, as opposed to an eventual trial, is somehow "unfair" if a person consents to a search. While the Fourth and Fourteenth Amendments limit the circumstances under which the police can conduct a search, there is nothing constitutionally suspect in a person's voluntarily allowing a search. The actual conduct of the search may be precisely the same as if the police had obtained a warrant. And, unlike those constitutional guarantees that protect a defendant at trial, it cannot be said every reasonable presumption ought to be indulged against voluntary relinquishment. We have only recently stated: "(I)t is no part of the policy underlying the Fourth and Fourteenth Amendments to discourage citizens from aiding to the utmost of their ability in the apprehension of criminals." Rather, the community has a real interest in encouraging consent, for the resulting search may yield necessary evidence for the solution and prosecution of crime, evidence that may insure that a wholly innocent person is not wrongly charged with a criminal offense.

Those cases that have dealt with the application of the *Johnson v. Zerbst* rule make clear that it would be next to impossible to apply to a consent search the standard of "an intentional relinquishment or abandonment of a known right or privilege." To be true to *Johnson* and its progeny, there must be examination into the knowing and understanding nature of the waiver, an examination that was designed for a trial judge in the structured atmosphere of a courtroom. . . .

It would be unrealistic to expect that in the informal, unstructured context of a consent search, a policeman, upon pain of tainting the evidence obtained, could make the detailed type of examination demanded by *Johnson*. And, if for this reason a diluted form of "waiver" were found acceptable, that would itself be ample recognition of the fact that there is no universal standard that must be applied in every situation where a person foregoes a constitutional right.

. . .

D

. . .

In this case, there is no evidence of any inherently coercive tactics—either from the nature of the police questioning or the environment in which it took place. Indeed, since consent searches will normally occur on a person's own familiar territory, the specter of incommunicado police interrogation in some remote station house is simply inapposite. There is no reason to believe, under circumstances such as are present here, that the response to a policeman's question is presumptively coerced; and there is, therefore, no reason to reject the traditional test for determining the voluntariness of a person's response. *Miranda*, of course, did not reach investigative questioning of a person not in custody, which is most directly analogous to the situation of a consent search, and it assuredly did not indicate that such questioning ought to be deemed inherently coercive.

It is also argued that the failure to require the Government to establish knowledge as a prerequisite to a valid consent, will relegate the Fourth Amendment to the special province of "the sophisticated, v. knowledgeable and the privileged." We cannot agree.

The traditional definition of voluntariness we accept today has always taken into account evidence of minimal schooling, low intelligence, and the lack of any effective warnings to a person of his rights; and the voluntariness of any statement taken under those conditions has been carefully scrutinized to determine whether it was in fact voluntarily given.

E

Our decision today is a narrow one. We hold only that when the subject of a search is not in custody and the State attempts to justify a search on the basis of his consent, the Fourth and Fourteenth Amendments require that it demonstrate that the consent was in fact voluntarily given, and not the result of duress or coercion, express or implied. Voluntariness is a question of fact to be determined from all the circumstances, and while the subject's knowledge of a right to refuse is a factor to be taken into account, the prosecution is not required to demonstrate such knowledge as a prerequisite to establishing a voluntary consent. Because the California court followed these principles in affirming the respondent's conviction, and because the Court of Appeals for the Ninth Circuit in remanding for an evidentiary hearing required more, its judgment must be reversed.

[The concurring opinions of Justice BLACKMUN and Justices POWELL, REHNQUIST, and the CHIEF JUSTICE are omitted.]

[The dissenting opinion of Justice DOUGLAS is omitted.]

Mr. Justice BRENNAN, dissenting.

. . .

The Court holds today that an individual can effectively waive this right even though he is totally ignorant of the fact that, in the absence of his consent, such invasions of his privacy would be constitutionally prohibited. It wholly escapes me how our citizens can meaningfully be said to have waived something as precious as a constitutional guarantee without ever being aware of its existence. In my view, the Court's conclusion is supported neither by "linguistics," nor by "epistemology," nor, indeed, by "common sense." I respectfully dissent.

Mr. Justice MARSHALL, dissenting.

Several years ago, Mr. Justice Stewart reminded us that "(t)he Constitution guarantees . . . a society of free choice. Such a society presupposes the capacity of its members to choose." I would have thought that the capacity to choose necessarily depends upon knowledge that there is a choice to be made. But today the Court reaches the curious result that one can choose to relinquish a constitutional right—the right to be free of unreasonable searches—without knowing that he has the alternative of refusing to accede to a police request to search. I cannot agree, and therefore dissent.

I

I believe that the Court misstates the true issue in this case. That issue is not, as the Court suggests whether the police overbore Alcala's will in eliciting his consent, but rather, whether a simple statement of assent to search, without more, should be sufficient to permit the police to search and thus act as a relinquishment of Alcala's constitutional right to exclude the police. This Court has always scrutinized with great care claims that a person has forgone the opportunity to assert constitutional rights. I see no reason to give the claim that a person consented to a search any less rigorous scrutiny. Every case in this Court involving this kind of search has heretofore spoken of consent as a waiver. Perhaps one skilled in linguistics or opistemology can disregard those comments, but I find them hard to ignore.

. . .

B

. . . [T]his case deals not with "coercion," but with "consent," a subtly different concept to which different standards have been applied in the past. Freedom from coercion is a substantive right, guaranteed by the Fifth and Fourteenth Amendments. Consent, however, is a mechanism by which substantive requirements, otherwise applicable, are avoided. In the context of the Fourth Amendment, the relevant substantive requirements are that searches be conducted only after evidence justifying them has been submitted to an impartial magistrate for a determination of probable cause. There are, of course, exceptions to these requirements based on a variety of exigent circumstances that make it impractical to invalidate a search simply because the police failed to get a warrant. But none of the exceptions relating to the overriding needs of law enforcement are applicable when a search is justified solely by consent. On the contrary, the needs of law enforcement are significantly more attenuated, for probable cause to search may be lacking but a search permitted if the subject's consent has been obtained. Thus, consent searches are permitted, not because such an exception to the requirements of probable cause and warrant is essential to proper law enforcement, but because we permit our citizens to choose whether or not they wish to exercise their constitutional rights. Our prior decisions simply do not support the view that a meaningful choice has been made solely because no coercion was brought to bear on the subject.

For example, in *Bumper v. North Carolina*, four law enforcement officers went to the home of Bumper's grandmother. They announced that they had a search warrant, and she permitted them to enter. Subsequently, the prosecutor chose not to rely on the warrant, but attempted to justify the search by the woman's consent. We held that consent could not be established "by showing no more than acquiescence to a claim of lawful authority." We did not there inquire into all the circumstances, but focused on a single fact, the claim of authority, even though the grandmother testified that no threats were made. It may be that, on the facts of that case, her consent was under all the circumstances involuntary, but it is plain that we did not apply the test adopted by the Court today. And, whatever the posture of the case when it reached this Court, it could not be said that the police in *Bumper* acted in a threatening or coercive manner, for they did have the warrant they said they had; the decision not to rely on it was made long after the search, when the case came into court.

That case makes it clear that police officers may not courteously order the subject of a search simply to stand aside while the officers carry out a search they have settled on. Yet there would be no coercion or brutality in giving that order. No interests that the Court today recognizes would be damaged in such a search. Thus, all the police must do is conduct what will inevitably be a charade of asking for consent. If they display any firmness at all, a verbal expression of assent will undoubtedly be forthcoming. I cannot believe that the protections of the Constitution mean so little.

II

My approach to the case is straight-forward and, to me, obviously required by the notion of consent as a relinquishment of Fourth Amendment rights. I am at a loss to understand why consent "cannot be taken literally to mean a 'knowing' choice." In fact, I have difficulty in comprehending how a decision made without knowledge of available alternatives can be treated as a choice at all.

If consent to search means that a person has chosen to forgo his right to exclude the police from the place they seek to search, it follows that his consent cannot be considered a meaningful choice unless he knew that he could in fact exclude the police. The Court appears, however, to reject even the modest proposition that, if the subject of a search convinces the trier of fact that he did not know of his right to refuse assent to a police request for permission to search, the search must be held unconstitutional. For it says only that "knowledge of the right to refuse consent is one factor to be taken into account." I find this incomprehensible. I can think of no other situation in which we would say that a person agreed to some course of action if he convinced us that he did not know that there was some other course he might have pursued. I would therefore hold, at a minimum, that the prosecution may not rely on a purported consent to search if the subject of the search did not know that he could refuse to give consent. That, I think, is the import of *Bumper v. North Carolina*. Where the police claim authority to search yet in fact lack such authority, the subject does not know that he may permissibly refuse them entry, and it is this lack of knowledge that invalidates the consent.

. . .

I must conclude with some reluctance that when the Court speaks of practicality, what it really is talking of is the continued ability of the police to capitalize on the ignorance of citizens so as to accomplish by subterfuge what they could not achieve by relying only on the knowing relinquishment of constitutional rights. Of course it would be "practical" for the police to ignore the commands of the Fourth Amendment, if by practicality we mean that more criminals will be apprehended, even though the constitutional rights of innocent people also go by the board. But such a practical advantage is achieved only at the cost of permitting the police to disregard the limitations that the Constitution places on their behavior, a cost that a constitutional democracy cannot long absorb.

I find nothing in the opinion of the Court to dispel my belief that, in such a case, as the Court of Appeals for the Ninth Circuit said, "(u)nder many circumstances a reasonable person might read an officer's 'May I' as the courteous expression of a demand backed by force of law." Most cases, in my view, are akin to *Bumper v. North Carolina*: consent is ordinarily given as acquiescence in an implicit claim of authority to search. Permitting searches in such circumstances, without any assurance at all that the subject of the search knew that, by his consent, he was relinquishing his constitutional rights, is something that I cannot believe is sanctioned by the Constitution.

17

Exceptions to the Warrant Requirement: Exigent Circumstance

Key Concepts

- Exigency Needn't Involve "Hue and Cry" in Streets
- Even "Police-Manufactured" Exigency May Qualify
- No *Per Se* Exigency: Totality of Circumstances Should Be Examined in Each Case

A. Introduction and Policy. A suspected felon running from pursuing police officers. A suspected drug dealer flushing drugs down the toilet. A drunken teenager engaging in a violent fistfight with an adult relative. These are the sorts of circumstances the Court has confronted in defining the exigent circumstances exception to the warrant requirement—the "E" in S-P-A-C-E-S. Exigent circumstances will allow the police to effect a warrantless search or seizure (including entry into a private dwelling) if they reasonably conclude that quick action is necessary to prevent harm to people or the destruction of evidence. In a nod to one of the earliest exigent circumstances cases, you may sometimes hear the exception referred to as the "hot pursuit" or "fleeing felon" doctrine.

The exigent circumstances exception is justified in part by the recognition that police officers must be able to "protect or preserve life or avoid serious injury."[1] The exception is also justified by the police interest in avoiding the destruction of property. Thus, courts will allow police officers to act without a warrant when they come upon a scene where immediate action seems reasonably necessary to accomplish one of these goals.

Of the many exceptions to the warrant requirement, the exigent circumstances exception is perhaps the least closely examined. The Court has said often that many of the warrant exceptions contain some aspect of urgency. For example, the warrantless conduct authorized by a search incident to a lawful arrest is motivated in part by the police need to act quickly to avoid harm to themselves or others or to prevent the destruction of evidence. Similarly, the automobile exception imports notions of urgency based on the inherent mobility of cars. For this reason, many cases contain the language of "exigency". But the exigent circumstances

[1] Mincey v. Arizona, 437 U.S. 385, 392 (1978).

exception is different in that it recognizes a free-standing exemption from the warrant requirement that is not conditionally justified.

B. The Law. The exigent circumstances exception to the warrant requirement states:

> If the police have a reasonable and objective basis for believing that immediate action is required to prevent harm to persons or the destruction of evidence, they may effect a warrantless entry and limited search aimed at accomplishing the goals of the initial intrusion.

The first step in applying this rule is determining whether an exigency exists—that is, whether "immediate action is required to prevent harm to persons or the destruction of evidence." The Court has repeatedly declined to find *per se* exigency for different categories of cases. Instead, the exigency test is fact-dependent, requiring the reviewing court to consider the following factors:

1. The gravity or violent nature of the offense with which the suspect is to be charged;
2. Whether the suspect is reasonably believed to be armed;
3. A clear showing of probable cause to believe that the suspect committed the crime;
4. Strong reason to believe that the suspect is in the premises being entered;
5. A likelihood that the suspect will escape (or that evidence will be destroyed) if the suspect is not swiftly apprehended; and
6. The peaceful circumstances of the entry.[2]

The Court has applied the exigent circumstances exception to a number of emergency conditions:

- When police officers are in hot pursuit of a fleeing felon[3]
- When the destruction of evidence is imminent[4]

---

[2] United States v. MacDonald, 916 F.2d 766, 769–70 (2d Cir. 1990) (internal quotations omitted).

[3] United States v. Santana, 427 U.S. 38 (1976).

[4] Schmerber v. California, 384 U.S. 757 (1966).

- To render emergency aid[5]
- In the face of an ongoing fire[6]

The exigent circumstances exception applies even if the police engage in conduct—such as banging loudly on the door or chasing a suspect in the streets—that helps to create the urgent conditions. However, this does not mean the police may behave however they like. If police officers engage in unlawful conduct, they may not then rely upon exigent circumstances to justify a warrantless intrusion. In much the same way that plain view requires a lawful vantage point, police officers must be engaged in lawful conduct at the time the exigency arises for this exception to apply.

The second step in applying the rule is to determine the **scope** of the warrantless search that is authorized. When police are acting under the exigent circumstances exception, they may only act in ways that are a response to the initial exigency. For example, if the police enter a house looking only for a fleeing felon, they may not open drawers and peek in cabinets if the suspect could not be hiding therein.

C. Applying the Law. The Court has decided relatively few cases that discuss directly the exigent circumstances exception. However, those few decisions have provided a rather clear understanding of the precise contours of the doctrine. The exigent circumstances exception to the warrant requirement has been applied in a number of situations including the pursuit of fleeing felons, the prevention of evidence destruction, and the rendering of emergency aid, to name just a few. We will examine these below.

1. Fleeing Felons and "Hot" Pursuit. One of the first cases in which the Court weighed the exigent circumstances exception involved the police pursuit of an armed robber who retreated into his home to avoid capture. As a result of the case, the Court established the principle that the "hot pursuit" of a criminal suspect will justify police officers in entering a home, even without a warrant.

This rule, though ostensibly straightforward, leaves many questions unanswered. For example, how "hot" must the pursuit be? Do the officers have to be right on the heels of the suspect who eludes police only by dashing into a nearby home and slamming the door in the officers' faces? What about the suspect's behavior—must he actually be *running* away, or will a suspect's decision to *walk* away justify a finding of exigency as well? Finally, does it matter what crime the police suspect the retreating party of? Should the high speed foot chase of a suspected jaywalker

---

5 Arizona v. Hicks, 480 U.S. 321 (1987).

6 Michigan v. Tyler, 436 U.S. 499 (1978).

justify relaxing the warrant requirement to the same degree that a meandering pursuit of a mass murder and suspected terrorist might?

Let us consider the case of the fleeing armed robber first:

> **Example—*Warden v. Hayden*, 387 U.S. 294 (1967):** Early one morning an armed robber entered the Baltimore business offices of Diamond Cab company and robbed the establishment of $363. Two of the company's drivers happened to be nearby. When those inside the business yelled out, the two drivers followed the fleeing robber and saw him run into a residence at 2111 Cocoa Lane. One of the drivers radioed back to the dispatcher that the man had entered the stated address. The driver also mentioned that the man was approximately five feet, eight inches tall, and had been wearing a light colored cap and a dark colored jacket. The dispatcher conveyed this information to the police.
>
> Less than five minutes after the drivers saw the man run into the home, a number of police cars descended upon the Cocoa Lane address. The officers completely searched all of the floors. They found Bennie Joe Hayden upstairs in bed, pretending to be asleep. At the same time officers were upstairs arresting Hayden, other officers were searching the house. One officer found a shotgun and a pistol in the flush tank of the toilet located in the adjoining bathroom. Downstairs in the basement, another officer found clothing that matched the description of what the robber was wearing. The officers also found ammunition and a cap in the room where Hayden was found.
>
> Hayden was arrested and charged with armed robbery. The evidence found in his home was introduced over objection by the prosecution. Hayden contended that the evidence should have been suppressed because the warrantless entry into his home was unconstitutional. The government countered that entry was justified by the exigent circumstances.

Analysis: The police had the right to enter Hayden's home without a warrant. Without question, the privacy of the home is at the heart of the Fourth Amendment's protection. But the amendment "does not require police officers to delay in the course of an investigation if to do so would gravely endanger their lives or the lives of others."[7] At times in police work, the speed of the investigation will be of the essence. In such cases, if officers do not act swiftly they run the risk of not

[7] Warden v. Hayden, 387 U.S. 294, 298–99 (1967).

being able to act at all—either because the evidence will be destroyed or because people will already have been injured.

In Hayden's case, police officers knew they were close on the trail of an armed robber who had entered the home just minutes before the police arrived. "[O]nly a thorough search of the house for persons and weapons could have insured that Hayden was the only man present and that the police had control of all weapons which could be used against them or to effect an escape."[8]

The Court's decision in *Hayden* makes clear that the exigent circumstances exception may apply even if the police were not chasing the suspect at the time he fled into his home. Recall in *Hayden*, it was the two cab drivers, not the police, who pursued Hayden and saw him enter the house. The police came onto the scene several minutes **after** Hayden retreated behind closed doors. Nonetheless, the Court found that exigent circumstances justified the warrantless entry.[9] The Court only requires that there be "immediate or continuous pursuit of the [suspect] from the scene of the crime."[10]

Putting aside the question of who was chasing Hayden at the time he retreated into his home, the evidence in *Hayden* unequivocally indicated that Hayden actually ran out of the taxicab office following the robbery, and then ran home. But what if the "hot pursuit" alleged entails only a suspect walking away or stepping back a few feet into her home? Does the same constitutional rule apply if the suspect is not engaged in headlong, breathless flight, but rather is engaged in a more disciplined mode of departure?

Example—*United States v. Santana*, 427 U.S. 38 (1976): Michael Gilletti, working as an undercover officer, arranged to buy $115 in heroin from a woman named Patricia McCafferty. McCafferty and Gilletti then drove in Gilletti's car to "Mom Santana's" house, where McCafferty told the officer she had to go to pick the drugs up. At Mom Santana's house, Gilletti watched as McCafferty walked into the house with the money he had given her. A few moments later, McCafferty returned and got back into the car. In the car, McCafferty retrieved a quantity of glassine envelopes from her brassiere and handed them to Gilletti. Each envelope contained heroin.

---

8 Hayden, 387 U.S. at 299.

9 Though not directly relevant to the instant discussion, students should note that while the *Hayden* decision discusses exigent circumstances, the case is perhaps best known for its express rejection of what had long been called the Fourth Amendment's "mere evidence" rule. That rule was based on the notion that the Fourth Amendment forbade the collection of "mere evidence." In *Hayden*, the Court determined that there was no constitutional reason to distinguish between "intrusions to secure 'mere evidence' from intrusions to secure fruits, instrumentalities, or contraband." Hayden, 387 U.S. at 310.

10 Welsh v. Wisconsin, 466 U.S. 740, 753 (1984).

Gilletti drove a short distance away and then placed McCafferty under arrest. When Gilletti asked McCafferty about the money he had given her, she responded "Mom has the money." Gilletti relayed this information to a nearby backup team of officers who proceeded to Santana's address. When the officers arrived, Santana was standing in her open doorway. The officers disembarked from their van yelling "police," and flashing their badges. Santana immediately took several steps back into the entrance hall of her house. The pursuing officer followed her through the open door and grabbed her arm. When Santana attempted to twist away, the contents of the brown paper bag that she was holding spilled onto the floor. Those contents were bundles of glassine envelopes containing white powder. Santana was searched and, in addition to the drugs, the officers found money, some of which was the buy money provided by Gilletti for the earlier sale.

At her trial for heroin distribution, Santana moved to suppress the money and drugs that were found. Santana argued that the warrantless seizure in her front hallway could not be justified by any exception to the warrant requirement. The prosecution responded that the evidence was admissible pursuant to the exigent circumstances exception to the warrant requirement.

Analysis: The Court held that the entry into the house was constitutional.

The police arrived at the house with the intention of arresting Santana, and were pursuing her with this aim in mind. The police had probable cause for Santana's arrest based on the undercover buy, but, they did not have a warrant. Accordingly, as you read in **Chapter 11**, for the pursuit of Santana to be lawful, the intended warrantless arrest had to begin in a public place. This is because as a general matter the arrest of an individual in her home must be authorized by a warrant.

Turning first to this question of the lawfulness of the initial police conduct, the Court determined that Santana was in a "public" place when she stood in her doorway. As one of the officers testified, "she was standing directly in the doorway; one step forward would have put her outside, one step backward would have put her in the vestibule of her residence."[11] Finding that she was not inside of her home at the point when the police first engaged her, the Court found the initial police involvement with Santana to be entirely lawful.

The Court then turned to the question of whether Santana's retreat into her home rendered unconstitutional the police decision to follow her inside without a war-

[11] United States v. Santana, 427 U.S. 38, 40 n.1 (1976).

rant. The Court found not. Specifically, the Court found that the warrantless intrusion was justified by notions of hot pursuit. "'[H]ot pursuit means some sort of a chase, but it need not be an extended hue and cry 'in and about the public streets.'" The fact that the "pursuit" ended almost immediately did not, in the Court's view, alter the determination that the police were in "hot pursuit" at the time they seized her. "Once Santana saw the police, there was likewise a realistic expectation that any delay would result in the destruction of evidence."[12]

Because Santana's arrest was "set in motion" in a public place, the Court found she should could not defeat that arrest by retreating into her home. The exigent circumstances exception made her warrantless arrest and search in the front hallway of her house fully consistent with the Fourth Amendment.

In *Santana*, the initial arrest of McCafferty took place just a block and a half from Santana's home. During the suppression hearing, officers testified that the prompt arrest of Santana was critical because word of McCafferty's arrest might quickly get back to those in Santana's house and thereby result in the destruction of evidence. Writing in dissent, Justice Marshall concluded that this sort of police-generated exigency should not justify an exception to the warrant requirement: "Had officer Gilletti driven McCafferty to a more remote location before arresting her, it appears that no exigency would have been created by the arrest."[13] The *Santana* Court did not address head-on the notion of police-manufactured exigency that had been flagged by the dissent. However, in coming years, the issue was presented squarely to the Court.

2. Police-Manufactured Exigency. As noted, the police must engage in lawful conduct before the exigent circumstances exception will justify their warrantless actions. However, what if that lawful conduct is what makes the circumstances surrounding an arrest urgent? One line of thinking, as articulated by the dissent in *Santana*, urges that police-manufactured exigency should not work to relieve officers of the duty to obtain a warrant. However, this view is not shared by a majority of the Court. Indeed, only recently, the Court confirmed that even a police-manufactured exigency will excuse the warrant requirement, so long as the police conduct is constitutional:

> **Example—*Kentucky v. King*, 131 S.Ct. 1849 (2011):** Police officers set up a controlled purchase of crack cocaine outside of an apartment complex in Lexington, Kentucky. An undercover officer watched the deal take place from a nearby parking lot. When the deal was complete, the officer radioed to a uniformed back up team to report that they should move in. The under

[12] Id. at 43.

[13] Id. at 48.

cover warned the backup units to move quickly because the suspect was heading toward a breezeway in the complex.

When the uniformed units moved in, they ran into the breezeway just as a door was slamming. They could not tell though which side of the breezeway the slamming door came from, but they smelled a strong odor of marijuana from the door on the left. Accordingly, they banged loudly on the door and yelled out to announce their presence. Immediately the officers could hear movement inside of the apartment, and it sounded like "things were being moved around inside the apartment."[14] Based on this, the officers concluded that the occupants of the apartment were attempting to destroy evidence.

The officers again yelled out, this time announcing that they were coming in. One of the officers then kicked the front door of the apartment in. During a protective sweep of the apartment, the police saw marijuana and a powder that appeared to be cocaine in plain view. Hollis King, who was inside the apartment with his girlfriend and a friend, was charged with marijuana and cocaine distribution. At his trial, King echoed the arguments first advanced by Justice Marshall in his dissent in *Santana*, arguing that the police should not be permitted to seek refuge in the exigent circumstances exception when it was their own conduct that created the exigency.

Analysis: The Court rejected King's claim and held that the police did not violate the Fourth Amendment.

The Court noted that the exigent circumstances exception is a well recognized and long-standing exception to the warrant requirement. So too, the need to prevent the destruction of evidence has long been recognized as a justification for the exception. The Court acknowledged that several lower courts had embraced a "police-created exigency" exception to the exigent circumstances exception. However, the Court found that "a rule that precludes the police from making a warrantless entry to prevent the destruction of evidence whenever their conduct causes the exigency would unreasonably shrink the reach of this well-established exception to the warrant requirement."[15]

A more fitting limitation, the Court found, was that police must simply act reasonably in creating any exigency. This was consistent with similar limitations the Court had imposed in the context of plain view and consent searches. Accord-

[14] Kentucky v. King, 131 S.Ct. 1849, 1854 (2011).

[15] Id. at 1857.

ingly, so long as "the police did not create the exigency by engaging or threatening to engage in conduct that violates the Fourth Amendment, warrantless entry to prevent the destruction of evidence is reasonable and thus allowed."[16] The Court also found that the exigent circumstances exception is not dependent upon a lack of foreseeability nor upon whether the police had probable cause and the time to obtain a warrant.

In an interesting aside in the *King* case, the Court noted that this particular exigency was entirely within the control of the occupant. In the Court's view, if King had simply answered the door, no exigency would have existed and the police would not have been entitled to enter without a warrant. "Occupants who choose not to stand on their constitutional rights but instead elect to attempt to destroy evidence have only themselves to blame for the warrantless exigent-circumstances search that may ensue."[17] In other words, occupants who do not promptly open the door to a police demand could be found to have invited a warrantless intrusion of their home.

3. Categorical Exigency? A handful of exceptions to the warrant requirement impose *per se* rules. For example, one can justify application of the search incident to a lawful arrest exception by establishing membership in the category of lawful arrests. Similarly, the automobile exception applies categorically to all automobiles once a litigant can establish there was probable cause to believe the particular car at issue contained contraband. The exigent circumstances exception, though, has never been subject to a *per se* rule. Rather, the Court has repeatedly said that the exigency in any case must be evaluated by looking at the totality of the circumstances in that case. Whether exigency exists will depend entirely on a close review of that case's facts, not on an assertion that the case falls within some *per se* class of exigency.

For many years, however, there did appear to be a singular exception to this general approach. In the context of drunken driving, the Court at one time appeared to suggest that evidence of drunkenness was, by its very nature, fleeting in existence. A drunk driver's blood alcohol content disappears through natural metabolism with nothing more than the passage of time. When the police are confronted with such evidence does its evanescent nature alone justify a categorical exigency exception to the warrant requirement? The Court once appeared to answer this question in the affirmative, but more recently has said that *per se* "exigency" even for the most ephemeral evidence is inappropriate:

---

[16] Id. at 1858.

[17] Id. at 1862.

Example—*Schmerber v. California*, 384 U.S. 757 (1966): Armando Schmerber was arrested in a Los Angeles hospital for drunk driving. Schmerber was in the hospital receiving treatment for injuries he sustained in a car accident. Without the authorization of a warrant, a police officer who was present at the hospital with Schmerber instructed a doctor, over Schmerber's objection, to draw blood. A chemical analysis of the sample was conducted, and Schmerber's blood alcohol content ("BAC") was found to exceed the legal limit. This evidence was subsequently introduced against Schmerber at trial.

Schmerber argued that the forced blood draw violated his Fourth Amendment rights.

Analysis: The Court found the forced blood draw was constitutional.

There is no question that the Fourth Amendment protects not only against government interference with houses, papers, and effects, but also with a person's body. Here, the police acted without a warrant. The question, therefore, is whether the police conduct was justified by application of some exception to the warrant requirement. It was.

The percentage of alcohol in an individual's blood stream begins to decrease once the consumption of alcohol ends. As the body processes the alcohol consumed, the blood alcohol level continues to drop naturally with the passage of time. The officer in the instant case was occupied immediately after the accident with bringing Schmerber to the hospital and investigating the scene of the accident. Under these circumstances he "might reasonably have believed that he was confronted with an emergency, in which the delay necessary to obtain a warrant, under the circumstances, threatened 'the destruction of evidence.'"[18]

The method for securing the blood sample was entirely reasonable, and the test chosen for evaluating it was likely to produce the precise sort of evidence the government needed.

On these facts, the Court determined that the warrantless extraction of Schmerber's blood did not offend the Fourth Amendment.

The *Schmerber* Court closed its opinion with the observation, "we reach this judgment only on the facts of the present record."[19] Nonetheless, the Court had noted that those facts included a realization that "the percentage of alcohol in the blood begins to diminish shortly after drinking stops, as the body functions to eliminate it from the system."[20] Consequently, for many years the *Schmerber* decision was

[18] Schmerber v. California, 384 U.S. 757, 770 (1966).

[19] Id. at 772.

[20] Id. at 770.

understood to establish the *per se* exigency of securing evidence of blood alcohol content.[21]

More than four decades after its decision in *Schmerber*, the Court considered a second blood draw case in which it explained that categorical exigency was not intended by the *Schmerber* holding:

> **Example—*Missouri v. McNeely*, 133 S.Ct. 1552 (2013):** Early one morning a Missouri police officer pulled over Tyler McNeely. The stop was prompted by the officer's observation that McNeely was driving above the speed limit, and repeatedly crossed the center line. Once McNeely got out of his car, the officer noticed tell-tale signs of intoxication. McNeely's eyes were bloodshot, his speech was slurred, and his breath smelled of alcohol. McNeely also appeared unsteady on his feet.
>
> The officer administered a number of field sobriety test, all of which McNeely performed poorly on. The officer then asked McNeely to submit to a breath test to measure his blood alcohol content, but McNeely refused. At that point, the officer placed McNeely under arrest. On the way to the stationhouse, McNeely again refused the breath test. The officer then transported McNeely to a nearby hospital for a blood draw. At the hospital, a lab technician withdrew McNeely's blood over McNeely's objection. The results established that McNeely's blood alcohol content was nearly twice the legal limit for driving.
>
> McNeely challenged the forced blood draw, arguing that there were no exigent circumstances to justify the state's warrantless action. The state responded that the evanescent nature of blood alcohol content created a *per se* exigency justifying the warrantless police conduct.

Analysis: Limiting its holding in *Schmerber* to the particular facts of that case, the Court found that the forced blood draw in McNeely's case violated his rights.

Where the exigencies of a situation warrant it, the police are exempted from the warrant requirement. However, in assessing exigency, the Court must consider the totality of the circumstances. A case specific inquiry is required.

The Court in *Schmerber* considered the totality of the circumstances before it and concluded that exigency existed on those facts. However, *Schmerber* cannot

---

[21] See, e.g., State v. Shriner, 751 N.W.2d 538 (Minn. 2008); State v. Bohling, 494 N.W.2d 399 (Wisc. 1993); State v. Woolery, 775 P.2d 1210 (Idaho 1989).

be read to establish *per se* exigency any time there is a need to secure evidence of a suspect's blood alcohol content. "[I]t does not follow that we should depart from careful case-by-case assessment of exigency and adopt the categorical rule proposed by the State and its *amici*. In those drunk-driving investigations where police officers can reasonably obtain a warrant before a blood sample can be drawn without significantly undermining the efficacy of the search, the Fourth Amendment mandates that they do so."[22]

"[T]he natural dissipation of alcohol in the bloodstream does not constitute an exigency in every case sufficient to justify conducting a blood test without a warrant." However, the government in *McNeely* could not point to any exigencies beyond the natural dissipation of blood alcohol levels. The warrantless blood draw was therefore rejected as unconstitutional.

If the inherent impermanence of the evidence sought will not justify a specific category of exigency, what about the seriousness of the offense under investigation? Police officers are responsible for solving crimes both big and small. Of the countless offenses investigated by police departments everyday, it goes without saying that some of those investigations are more weighty than others. At the outer limit of this continuum, are some offenses so serious that exigent circumstances should be assumed? Put somewhat differently, is the swift resolution of some criminal enquiries so pressing that courts should assume an automatic finding of exigent circumstances for that category of investigations? This was the government's argument in *Mincey v. Arizona*:

> **Example—*Mincey v. Arizona*, 437 U.S. 385 (1978):** Officer Barry Headricks of the police narcotics squad in Tucson, Arizona, was working undercover. In this capacity, he arranged to buy heroin from Rufus Mincey. After setting up the deal, Headricks told Mincey that he needed to go get money, but promised to return. Later that day, Headricks returned to Mincey's apartment with a team of back-up officers and knocked on the door. John Hodgman, a friend of Mincey's, opened the door. Pandemonium followed.
>
> Before Hodgman could slam the door, Headricks slipped into the apartment and proceeded directly to the back bedroom. Other officers forced the door open and pinned Hodgman against a wall. Several rounds of gunfire erupted from the back bedroom. Headricks staggered out and collapsed. He died days later. Several officers ran into the bedroom and found Mincey lying on the floor, semi-conscious and suffering from multiple gunshot wounds.

[22] Missouri v. McNeely, 133 S.Ct. 1552, 1561 (2013).

Officers on the scene conducted a quick search of the premises looking for other victims. They found a young woman in the bedroom closet who had been shot. Another of Mincey's friends was found shot in the front room.

Approximately ten minutes after all the shooting ended, homicide detectives arrived on the scene. They conducted a warrantless search of the apartment that lasted four days. During the four-day search, the police collected a wealth of evidence: "the entire apartment was searched, photographed, and diagrammed. The officers opened drawers, closets, and cupboards, and inspected their contents; they emptied clothing pockets; they dug bullet fragments out of the walls and floors; they pulled up sections of the carpet and removed them for examination. Every item in the apartment was closely examined and inventoried, and two hundred to three hundred objects were seized."[23]

Mincey was charged with murder, assault, and a number of drug offenses. Prior to trial, Mincey challenged the warrantless search of his apartment as a violation of his Fourth Amendment right to be free of unreasonable searches and seizures. The government argued that the search was justified because a possible homicide "presents an emergency situation demanding immediate action."[24]

Analysis: The Court rejected the state's request to recognize a categorical "murder scene" exception within the exigent circumstances doctrine.

The Court did not dispute the authority of police officers to respond to emergency situations. However, that authority could not be extended to the entire category of homicide investigations. When the police arrive at a homicide scene, they may of course search the area for other victims as well as for the perpetrator, if he may still be on the premises. But the scope of any such search is necessarily defined by the exigency that originally justified it. Thus, if a search does not specifically advance the pressing goal that justified warrantless action in the first place, it will exceed the appropriate limits of the exigent circumstances exception.

The four-day search of Mincey's apartment clearly exceeded appropriate limits, because it did not advance the police need to preserve life or avoid further injury. All of the victims in the apartment had been located by the time the homicide detectives arrived. The suspect, too, had been identified and was in police custody. There was no danger that evidence would be destroyed or otherwise mislaid. A

23 Mincey v. Arizona, 437 U.S. 385, 389 (1978).

24 Id. at 392.

police guard had even been posted at the apartment at all times until the completion of the search. On these facts, the Court declined "to hold that the seriousness of the offense under investigation itself creates exigent circumstances of the kind that under the Fourth Amendment justify a warrantless search."[25]

The Court found in *Mincey* that the extreme seriousness of a crime would not justify an absolute finding of exigency. But this does not mean the seriousness of the crime is not at all relevant to the exigency finding. As noted above, "the nature of the underlying offense is an important factor to be considered in the exigent-circumstances calculus."[26] In other words, a reviewing court should consider, but not be bound by, the seriousness of the crime when deciding whether exigent circumstances existed. The Court has also suggested, but never held, that it is unlikely a warrantless home arrest could ever be justified under the exigent circumstances exception "when the underlying offense is extremely minor."[27]

4. Securing the Premises. As you have read above, the exigent circumstances exception allows the police to conduct a warrantless entry onto premises for the purpose of preventing the destruction of evidence. In addition, the police are allowed to secure premises (and exclude lawful residents), if the surrounding circumstances objectively suggest that this step is needed to avoid the destruction of evidence. Police may not undertake indefinite seizures pursuant to the exception, but seizures that are reasonably related to police efforts to obtain a search warrant have routinely been approved:

> **Example—*Illinois v. McArthur*, 531 U.S. 326 (2001):** Tera McArthur was in the process of leaving her husband, Charles. She enlisted the help of the local police while she removed her belongings from the marital home. Two officers met Mrs. McArthur at the couple's trailer and waited outside while she collected her things. When she left, she told the officers they should check out the trailer because her estranged husband "had dope in there."[28]
>
> One of the officers knocked on the door and reported to Charles McArthur what his wife said. The officer also asked for permission to search the trailer. McArthur refused. The officer then sent his partner to obtain a search warrant based upon Mrs. McArthur's representations.

---

[25] Mincey, 437 U.S. at 394.
[26] Welsh v. Wisconsin, 466 U.S. 740, 751 (1984).
[27] Id. at 753.
[28] Illinois v. McArthur, 531 U.S. 326, 329 (2001).

McArthur was standing on his porch as the two drove away. The first officer then turned to McArthur and advised him that he would not be allowed to reenter his home unless a police officer went with him.

Approximately two hours later, the second officer returned with the warrant. McArthur had been prevented from entering his home without a police escort during this entire period. When the search warrant was executed, the officers found marijuana and related paraphernalia. McArthur was charged with misdemeanor drug offenses. He challenged the two hour "seizure" of his home.

Analysis: The two-hour seizure of McArthur's home was justified by "a plausible claim of specially pressing or urgent law enforcement need."[29]

The Court conducted a fact-based analysis to determine whether an exigency existed:

1. Mrs. McArthur had provided the police with information that her husband kept drugs in their home. She also provided details about the location of the drugs. Because Mrs. McArthur personally informed the police, they were able to make at least a general assessment of the reliability of her claims.
2. There was also substantial reason to believe that if Mr. McArthur were allowed to reenter the home on his own, that he would destroy the evidence before the police had a chance to obtain the warrant.
3. The restrictions placed on McArthur were reasonable—he could reenter his home (and did so on at least three occasions); he just couldn't do so without an officer standing just inside the door.
4. McArthur was excluded from his home for only a brief period.

Under these circumstances, the brief seizure of McArthur's trailer was entirely reasonable.[30]

Thus, the exigent circumstances exception to the warrant requirement justifies not only the warrantless entry or search of property, but as the Court has made clear, also its limited seizure.[31]

---

[29] Id. at 331.

[30] Id. at 337.

[31] Cf. Segura v. United States, 468 U.S. 796 (1984).

Quick Summary

The fifth recognized exception to the warrant requirement is the exigent circumstances exception. The exception provides that police officers may engage in warrantless conduct if they reasonably believe that prompt action is required to avoid the destruction of property or harm to persons. The authorized police conduct includes both warrantless entry, warrantless search and warrantless seizure.

The existence of exigency in any case must be evaluated on a case by case basis. The test is one of the totality of the circumstances. In determining whether exigency exists, the Court has resisted findings of *per se* exigency. Rather, the factors of each case must be considered. These factors include: 1) the type of crime that the individual is suspected of; 2) the reasonableness of a belief that the suspect is armed; 3) probable cause to believe that the suspect committed the crime; 4) the suspect's likely presence in the premises being entered; (5) the likelihood of escape if a prompt arrest is not made; and (6) the peacefulness of the police entry.

As with plain view or search incident to a lawful arrest, the police conduct prior to the exigency must comport with the strictures of the Fourth Amendment. Thus, if the police engage in unlawful conduct from which an exigency arises, the exigency exception will not apply. However, if the police conduct is lawful, even police-manufactured exigency will excuse the need to obtain a warrant.

Review Questions

1. The Child Molester Hides in His House. Early one morning, a couple in a car saw a small girl standing by the side of the road holding her throat. They pulled over and saw that the girl's throat had been cut and she was bleeding from the throat. They took her to the hospital, where they called the police and the girl's mother. The girl told the police that a man named "Ray" who was a friend of her mother had kidnapped her from her home around midnight that night, taken her into the woods, sexually assaulted her, and then cut her throat and left her to die. The girl's mother confirmed that she knew a man named Ray Wike, and gave them his address.

When the police arrived at Wike's house later that morning, they saw a car parked out front that matched the description of the car that the girl said was used to kidnap her. The police went to the front door and knocked, but nobody answered. Fearing that Wike might be destroying evidence of his crime, they broke down the door and entered the house. They heard a person moving upstairs and ran up to find Wike in the bedroom, dressed only in his underwear, trying to crawl out of the window. A pile of clothes was sitting next to the bed. As Wike was being arrested, the officers saw bloodstains on some of the clothes and they seized the clothes as well.

Wike was charged with rape and attempted murder, and he moved to exclude the evidence the police recovered when they engaged in a warrantless entry of his house. Was the police conduct lawful?

2. Informant in Danger. Lawrence Truman was a small-time drug dealer who had been arrested and convinced to cooperate with the police. The police told him to set up a purchase of heroin from his supplier, a man named Albert Capps. Truman was then supposed to carry out the transaction while wearing a wire and under police observation. Truman arranged the sale with Capps at Capps' home in the suburbs. The day before the transaction, Truman told police that he would not wear a wire after all, since Capps always searched everyone who came into his house and Truman feared for his life if Capps learned he was wearing a wire. In order to ensure that they had an audio record of the transaction, the police entered Capps' home that night at a time when they knew he was absent and installed a listening device in the kitchen and the living room. The left the listening devices off until the next day.

The next day Truman entered Capps' house. As soon as he was inside, the police activated the electronic listening devices. The first thing they heard was Capps saying: "Someone told me you were arrested a few weeks ago. If you are working for the police now, I won't let you leave this house alive."

Fearing for the safety of their informant, the police stormed the house and arrested Capps. As part of a search incident to arrest, they found a Styrofoam cooler containing one hundred grams of heroin.

Capps challenged the warrantless arrest inside his home. Does the exigent circumstances exception apply to immunize the police conduct?

3. The Drug Dealer Hides in His House. Police on routine patrol downtown saw a man later identified as Vinson Jones on the sidewalk talking to a woman. The police saw the woman hand Jones some money. Jones then took a small plastic bag out of a paper bag sitting on the sidewalk next to him and gave the woman the plastic bag. At that point Jones looked up and saw the police and said something to the woman, who ran away. Jones picked up his paper bag and began walking away from the police in the other direction. He walked ten feet and then entered a house, closing the door behind him.

The police exited their patrol car and knocked on the door of the home. When a young boy opened the door, they ran into the house and searched for Jones. They found him in the kitchen at the table, with the paper bag next to him. They arrested him and seized the bag incident to his arrest. Inside the bag were eleven small plastic baggies with cocaine inside.

Jones is now challenging the police entry into his home, arguing that the police did not have probable cause to arrest him and that no exigent circumstances existed. Did the police violate Jones' Fourth Amendment rights?

FROM THE COURTROOM

KENTUCKY v. KING

United States Supreme Court, 2011
131 S.Ct. 1849

[Justice ALITO delivered the opinion of the Court.]

[Justice GINSBURG filed a dissenting opinion.]

It is well established that "exigent circumstances," including the need to prevent the destruction of evidence, permit police officers to conduct an otherwise permissible search without first obtaining a warrant. In this case, we consider whether this rule applies when police, by knocking on the door of a residence and announcing their presence, cause the occupants to attempt to destroy evidence. The Kentucky Supreme Court held that the exigent circumstances rule does not apply in the case at hand because the police should have foreseen that their conduct would prompt the occupants to attempt to destroy evidence. We reject this interpretation of the exigent circumstances rule. The conduct of the police prior to their entry into the apartment was entirely lawful. They did not violate the Fourth Amendment or threaten to do so. In such a situation, the exigent circumstances rule applies.

I

A

This case concerns the search of an apartment in Lexington, Kentucky. Police officers set up a controlled buy of crack cocaine outside an apartment complex. Undercover Officer Gibbons watched the deal take place from an unmarked car in a nearby parking lot. After the deal occurred, Gibbons radioed uniformed officers to move in on the suspect. He told the officers that the suspect was moving quickly toward the breezeway of an apartment building, and he urged them to "hurry up and get there" before the suspect entered an apartment.

In response to the radio alert, the uniformed officers drove into the nearby parking lot, left their vehicles, and ran to the breezeway. Just as they entered the breezeway, they heard a door shut and detected a very strong odor of burnt marijuana. At the end of the breezeway, the officers saw two apartments, one on the left and one on the right, and they did not know which apartment the suspect had entered. Gibbons had radioed that the suspect was running into the apartment on the right, but the officers did not hear this statement because they had already left their vehicles. Because they smelled marijuana smoke emanating from the apartment on the left, they approached the door of that apartment.

Officer Steven Cobb, one of the uniformed officers who approached the door, testified that the officers banged on the left apartment door "as loud as [they] could" and announced, "'This is the police'" or "'Police, police, police.'" Cobb said that "[a]s soon as [the officers] started banging on the door," they "could hear people inside moving," and "[i]t sounded as [though] things were being moved inside the apartment." These noises, Cobb testified, led the officers to believe that drug-related evidence was about to be destroyed.

At that point, the officers announced that they "were going to make entry inside the apartment." Cobb then kicked in the door, the officers entered the apartment, and they found three people in the front room: respondent Hollis King, respondent's girlfriend, and a guest who was smoking marijuana. The officers performed a protective sweep of the apartment during which they saw marijuana and powder cocaine in plain view. In a subsequent search, they also discovered crack cocaine, cash, and drug paraphernalia.

Police eventually entered the apartment on the right. Inside, they found the suspected drug dealer who was the initial target of their investigation.

B

In the Fayette County Circuit Court, a grand jury charged respondent with trafficking in marijuana, first-degree trafficking in a controlled substance, and second-degree persistent felony offender status. Respondent filed a motion to suppress the evidence from the warrantless search, but the Circuit Court denied the motion. . . . Respondent then entered a conditional guilty plea, reserving his right to appeal the denial of his suppression motion. The court sentenced respondent to [eleven] years' imprisonment.

. . .

II

A

The Fourth Amendment provides:

> The right of the people to be secure in their persons, houses, papers, and effects, against unreasonable searches and seizures, shall not be violated, and no Warrants shall issue, but upon probable cause, supported by Oath or affirmation, and particularly describing the place to be searched, and the persons or things to be seized.

The text of the Amendment thus expressly imposes two requirements. First, all searches and seizures must be reasonable. Second, a warrant may not be issued unless probable cause is properly established and the scope of the authorized search is set out with particularity.

Although the text of the Fourth Amendment does not specify when a search warrant must be obtained, this Court has inferred that a warrant must generally be secured. "It is a 'basic principle of Fourth Amendment law,'" we have often said, "'that searches and seizures inside a home without a warrant are presumptively unreasonable.'" But we have also recognized that this presumption may be overcome in some circumstances because "[t]he ultimate touchstone of the Fourth Amendment is 'reasonableness.'" Accordingly, the warrant requirement is subject to certain reasonable exceptions.

One well-recognized exception applies when "'the exigencies of the situation' make the needs of law enforcement so compelling that [a] warrantless search is objectively reasonable under the Fourth Amendment."

This Court has identified several exigencies that may justify a warrantless search of a home. Under the "emergency aid" exception, for example, "officers may enter a home without a warrant to render emergency assistance to an injured occupant or to protect an occupant from imminent injury." Police officers may enter premises without a warrant when they are in hot pursuit of a fleeing suspect. And—what is relevant here—the need "to prevent the imminent destruction of evidence" has long been recognized as a sufficient justification for a warrantless search.

B

Over the years, lower courts have developed an exception to the exigent circumstances rule, the so-called "police-created exigency" doctrine. Under this doctrine, police may not rely on the need to prevent destruction of evidence when that exigency was "created" or "manufactured" by the conduct of the police. . . .

In applying this exception for the "creation" or "manufacturing" of an exigency by the police, courts require something more than mere proof that fear of detection by the police caused the destruction of evidence. An additional showing is obviously needed because, as the Eighth Circuit has recognized, "in some sense the police always create the exigent circumstances." That is to say, in the vast majority of cases in which evidence is destroyed by persons who are engaged in illegal conduct, the reason for the destruction is fear that the evidence will fall into the hands of law enforcement. Destruction of evidence issues probably occur most frequently in drug cases because drugs may be easily destroyed by flushing them down a toilet or rinsing them down a drain. Persons in possession of valuable drugs are unlikely to destroy them unless they fear discovery by the police. Consequently, a rule that precludes the police from making a warrantless entry to prevent the destruction of evidence whenever their conduct causes the exigency would unreasonably shrink the reach of this well-established exception to the warrant requirement.

Presumably for the purpose of avoiding such a result, the lower courts have held that the police-created exigency doctrine requires more than simple causation, but the lower courts have not agreed on the test to be applied. Indeed, the petition in this case maintains that "[t]here are currently five different tests being used by the United States Courts of Appeals," and that some state courts have crafted additional tests.

III

A

Despite the welter of tests devised by the lower courts, the answer to the question presented in this case follows directly and clearly from the principle that permits warrantless searches in the first place. As previously noted, warrantless searches are allowed when the circumstances make it reasonable, within the meaning of the Fourth Amendment, to dispense with the warrant requirement. Therefore, the answer to the question before us is that the exigent circumstances rule justifies a warrantless search when the conduct of the police preceding the exigency is reasonable in the same sense. Where, as here, the police did not create the exigency by engaging or threatening to engage in conduct that violates the Fourth Amendment, warrantless entry to prevent the destruction of evidence is reasonable and thus allowed.[4]

We have taken a similar approach in other cases involving warrantless searches. For example, we have held that law enforcement officers may seize evidence in plain view, provided that they have not violated the Fourth Amendment in arriving at the spot from which the observation of the evidence is made. See *Horton v. California,* 496 U.S. 128 (1990). As we put it in *Horton,* "[i]t is . . . an essential predicate to any valid warrantless seizure of incriminating evidence that the officer did not violate the Fourth Amendment in arriving at the place from which the evidence could be plainly viewed." So long as this prerequisite is satisfied, however, it does not matter that the officer who makes the observation may have gone to the spot from which the evidence was seen with the hope of being able to view and seize the evidence. See *id.,* at 138 ("The fact that an officer is interested in an item of evidence and fully expects to find it in the course of a search should not invalidate its seizure"). Instead, the Fourth Amendment requires only that the steps preceding the seizure be lawful.

Similarly, officers may seek consent-based encounters if they are lawfully present in the place where the consensual encounter occurs. If consent is freely given, it makes no difference that an officer may have approached the person with the hope or expectation of obtaining consent.

B

Some lower courts have adopted a rule that is similar to the one that we recognize today. But others, including the Kentucky Supreme Court, have imposed additional requirements that are unsound and that we now reject.

Bad faith. Some courts, including the Kentucky Supreme Court, ask whether law enforcement officers "'deliberately created the exigent circumstances with the bad faith intent to avoid the warrant requirement.'"

This approach is fundamentally inconsistent with our Fourth Amendment jurisprudence. "Our cases have repeatedly rejected" a subjective approach, asking only whether "the circumstances, viewed *objectively,* justify the action." Indeed, we have never held, outside limited contexts such as an "inventory search or administrative inspection . . . , that an officer's motive invalidates objectively justifiable behavior under the Fourth Amendment."

The reasons for looking to objective factors, rather than subjective intent, are clear. Legal tests based on reasonableness are generally objective, and this Court has long taken the view that "evenhanded law enforcement is best achieved by the application of objective standards of conduct, rather than standards that depend upon the subjective state of mind of the officer."

Reasonable foreseeability. Some courts, again including the Kentucky Supreme Court, hold that police may not rely on an exigency if "'it was reasonably foreseeable that the investigative tactics employed by the police would create the exigent circumstances.'" Courts applying this test have invalidated warrantless home searches on the ground that it was reasonably foreseeable that police officers, by knocking on the door and announcing their presence, would lead a drug suspect to destroy evidence.

Contrary to this reasoning, however, we have rejected the notion that police may seize evidence without a warrant only when they come across the evidence by happenstance. In *Horton,* as noted, we held that the police may seize evidence in plain view even though the officers may be "interested in an item of evidence and fully expec[t] to find it in the course of a search."

Adoption of a reasonable foreseeability test would also introduce an unacceptable degree of unpredictability. For example, whenever law enforcement officers knock on the door of premises occupied by a person who may be involved in the drug trade, there is *some* possibility that the occupants may possess drugs and may seek to destroy them. Under a reasonable foreseeability test, it would be necessary to quantify the degree of predictability that must be reached before the police-created exigency doctrine comes into play.

A simple example illustrates the difficulties that such an approach would produce. Suppose that the officers in the present case did not smell marijuana smoke and thus knew only that there was a 50% chance that the fleeing suspect had entered the apartment on the left rather than the apartment on the right. Under those circumstances, would it have been reasonably foreseeable that the occupants of the apartment on the left would seek to destroy evidence upon learning that the police were at the door? Or suppose that the officers knew only that the suspect had disappeared into one of the apartments on a floor with [three, five, ten, or even twenty] units? If the police chose a door at random and knocked for the purpose of asking the occupants if they knew a person who fit the description of the suspect, would it have been reasonably foreseeable that the occupants would seek to destroy evidence?

We have noted that "[t]he calculus of reasonableness must embody allowance for the fact that police officers are often forced to make split-second judgments—in circumstances that are tense, uncertain, and rapidly evolving." The reasonable foreseeability test would create unacceptable and unwarranted difficulties for law enforcement officers who must make quick decisions in the field, as well as for judges who would be required to determine after the fact whether the destruction of evidence in response to a knock on the door was reasonably foreseeable based on what the officers knew at the time.

Probable cause and time to secure a warrant. Some courts, in applying the police-created exigency doctrine, fault law enforcement officers if, after acquiring evidence that is sufficient to establish probable cause to search particular premises, the officers do not seek a warrant but instead knock on the door and seek either to speak with an occupant or to obtain consent to search.

This approach unjustifiably interferes with legitimate law enforcement strategies. There are many entirely proper reasons why police may not want to seek a search warrant as soon as the bare minimum of evidence needed to establish probable cause is acquired. Without attempting to provide a comprehensive list of these reasons, we note a few.

First, the police may wish to speak with the occupants of a dwelling before deciding whether it is worthwhile to seek authorization for a search. They may think that a short and simple conversation may obviate the need to apply for and execute a warrant. Second, the police may want to ask an occupant of the premises for consent to search because doing so is simpler, faster, and less burdensome than applying for a warrant. A consensual search also "may result in considerably less inconvenience" and embarrassment to the occupants than a search conducted pursuant to a warrant. Third, law enforcement officers may wish to obtain more evidence before submitting what might otherwise be considered a marginal warrant application. Fourth, prosecutors may wish to wait until they acquire evidence that can justify a search that is broader in scope than the search that a judicial officer is likely to authorize based on the evidence then available. And finally, in many cases, law enforcement may not want to execute a search that will disclose the existence of an investigation because doing so may interfere with the acquisition of additional evidence against those already under suspicion or evidence about additional but as yet unknown participants in a criminal scheme.

We have said that "[l]aw enforcement officers are under no constitutional duty to call a halt to criminal investigation the moment they have the minimum evidence to establish probable cause." Faulting the police for failing to apply for a search warrant at the earliest possible time after obtaining probable cause imposes a duty that is nowhere to be found in the Constitution.

Standard or good investigative tactics. Finally, some lower court cases suggest that law enforcement officers may be found to have created or manufactured an exigency if the court concludes that the course of their investigation was "contrary to standard or good law enforcement practices (or to the policies or practices of their jurisdictions)." This approach fails to provide clear guidance for law enforcement officers and authorizes courts to make judgments on matters that are the province of those who are responsible for federal and state law enforcement agencies.

C

Respondent argues for a rule that differs from those discussed above, but his rule is also flawed. Respondent contends that law enforcement officers impermissibly create an exigency when they "engage in conduct that would cause a reasonable person to believe that entry is imminent and inevitable." In respondent's view, relevant factors include the officers' tone of voice in announcing their presence and the forcefulness of their knocks. But the ability of law enforcement officers to respond to an exigency cannot turn on such subtleties.

Police officers may have a very good reason to announce their presence loudly and to knock on the door with some force. A forceful knock may be necessary to alert the occupants that someone is at the door. Furthermore, unless police officers identify themselves loudly enough, occupants may not know who is at their doorstep. Officers are permitted—indeed, encouraged—to identify themselves to citizens, and "in many circumstances this is cause for assurance, not discomfort." Citizens who are startled by an unexpected knock on the door or by the sight of unknown persons in plain clothes on their doorstep may be relieved to learn that these persons are police officers. Others may appreciate the opportunity to make an informed decision about whether to answer the door to the police.

If respondent's test were adopted, it would be extremely difficult for police officers to know how loudly they may announce their presence or how forcefully they may knock on a door without running afoul of the police-created exigency rule. And in most cases, it would be nearly impossible for a court to determine whether that threshold had been passed. The Fourth Amendment does not require the nebulous and impractical test that respondent proposes.

D

For these reasons, we conclude that the exigent circumstances rule applies when the police do not gain entry to premises by means of an actual or threatened violation of the Fourth Amendment. This holding provides ample protection for the privacy rights that the Amendment protects.

When law enforcement officers who are not armed with a warrant knock on a door, they do no more than any private citizen might do. And whether the person who knocks on the door and requests the opportunity to speak is a police officer or a private citizen, the occupant has no obligation to open the door or to speak. When the police knock on a door but the occupants choose not to respond or to speak, "the investigation will have reached a conspicuously low point," and the occupants "will have the kind of warning that even the most elaborate security system cannot provide." And even if an occupant chooses to open the door and speak with the officers, the occupant need not allow the officers to enter the premises and may refuse to answer any questions at any time.

Occupants who choose not to stand on their constitutional rights but instead elect to attempt to destroy evidence have only themselves to blame for the warrantless exigent-circumstances search that may ensue.

* * *

Like the court below, we assume for purposes of argument that an exigency existed. Because the officers in this case did not violate or threaten to violate the Fourth Amendment prior to the exigency, we hold that the exigency justified the warrantless search of the apartment.

The judgment of the Kentucky Supreme Court is reversed, and the case is remanded for further proceedings not inconsistent with this opinion.

It is so ordered.

Justice GINSBURG, dissenting.

The Court today arms the police with a way routinely to dishonor the Fourth Amendment's warrant requirement in drug cases. In lieu of presenting their evidence to a neutral magistrate, police officers may now knock, listen, then break the door down, nevermind that they had ample time to obtain a warrant. I dissent from the Court's reduction of the Fourth Amendment's force.

The Fourth Amendment guarantees to the people "[t]he right . . . to be secure in their . . . houses . . . against unreasonable searches and seizures." Warrants to search, the Amendment further instructs, shall issue only upon a showing of "probable cause" to believe criminal activity is afoot. These complementary provisions are designed to ensure that police will seek the authorization of a neutral magistrate before undertaking a search or seizure. Exceptions to the warrant requirement, this Court has explained, must be "few in number and carefully delineated," if the main rule is to remain hardy.

This case involves a principal exception to the warrant requirement, the exception applicable in "exigent circumstances." "[C]arefully delineated," the exception should govern only in genuine emergency situations. Circumstances qualify as "exigent" when there is an imminent risk of death or serious injury, or danger that evidence will be immediately destroyed, or that a suspect will escape. The question presented: May police, who could pause to gain the approval of a neutral magistrate, dispense with the need to get a warrant by themselves creating exigent circumstances? I would answer no, as did the Kentucky Supreme Court. The urgency must exist, I would rule, when the police come on the scene, not subsequent to their arrival, prompted by their own conduct.

I

Two pillars of our Fourth Amendment jurisprudence should have controlled the Court's ruling: First, "whenever practical, [the police must] obtain advance judicial approval of searches and seizures through the warrant procedure," second, unwarranted "searches and seizures inside a home" bear heightened scrutiny. The warrant requirement, Justice Jackson observed, ranks among the "fundamental distinctions between our form of government, where officers are under the law, and the police-state where they are the law." The Court has accordingly declared warrantless searches, in the main, "*per se* unreasonable." "[T]he police bear a heavy burden," the Court has cautioned, "when attempting to demonstrate an urgent need that might justify warrantless searches."

That heavy burden has not been carried here. There was little risk that drug-related evidence would have been destroyed had the police delayed the search pending a magistrate's authorization. As the Court recognizes, "[p]ersons in possession of valuable drugs are unlikely to destroy them unless they fear discovery by the police." Nothing in the record shows that, prior to the knock at the apartment door, the occupants were apprehensive about police proximity.

In no quarter does the Fourth Amendment apply with greater force than in our homes, our most private space which, for centuries, has been regarded as "'entitled to special protection.'" Home intrusions, the Court has said, are indeed "the chief evil against which . . . the Fourth Amendment is directed." How "secure" do our homes remain if police, armed with no warrant, can pound on doors at will and, on hearing sounds indicative of things moving, forcibly enter and search for evidence of unlawful activity?

II

As above noted, to justify the police activity in this case, Kentucky invoked the once-guarded exception for emergencies "in which the delay necessary to obtain a warrant . . . threaten[s] 'the destruction of evidence.'" To fit within this exception, "police action literally must be [taken] 'now or never' to preserve the evidence of the crime."

The existence of a genuine emergency depends not only on the state of necessity at the time of the warrantless search; it depends, first and foremost, on "actions taken by the police *preceding* the warrantless search."

Under an appropriately reined-in "emergency" or "exigent circumstances" exception, the result in this case should not be in doubt. The target of the investigation's entry into the building, and the smell of marijuana seeping under the apartment door into the hallway, the Kentucky Supreme Court rightly determined, gave the police "probable cause . . . sufficient . . . to obtain a warrant to search the . . . apartment." As that court observed, nothing made it impracticable for the police to post officers on the premises while proceeding to obtain a warrant authorizing their entry. Before this Court, Kentucky does not urge otherwise.

In *Johnson*, the Court confronted this scenario: standing outside a hotel room, the police smelled burning opium and heard "some shuffling or noise" coming from the room. Could the police enter the room without a warrant? The Court answered no. Explaining why, the Court said:

> The right of officers to thrust themselves into a home is . . . a grave concern, not only to the individual but to a society which chooses to dwell in reasonable security and freedom from surveillance. When the right of privacy must reasonably yield to the right of search is, as a rule, to be decided by a judicial officer, not a policeman. . . .
>
> * * * * * *
>
> If the officers in this case were excused from the constitutional duty of presenting their evidence to a magistrate, it is difficult to think of [any] case in which [a warrant] should be required.

I agree, and would not allow an expedient knock to override the warrant requirement. Instead, I would accord that core requirement of the Fourth Amendment full respect. When possible, "a warrant must generally be secured," the Court acknowledges. There is every reason to conclude that securing a warrant was entirely feasible in this case, and no reason to contract the Fourth Amendment's dominion.

18

Exceptions to the Warrant Requirement: Special Needs Searches

Key Concepts

- "Special Needs" Searches Serve an Interest Other Than Crime Control
- Usually No Individualized Suspicion is Required
- Categories Include Administrative Searches, Border Searches, Searches of Schoolchildren, Drug Testing, Vehicular Checkpoints, and Anti-Terrorism Searches

A. Introduction and Policy. The final "S" in S-P-A-C-E-S is the final exception to the Warrant Requirement. This final "S" represents what are known as "Special Needs" searches. These are searches that are motivated by some "special need" beyond traditional crime control.

Up to this point, all of the surveillance methods we have discussed have involved law enforcement officers gathering evidence to be used in identifying or convicting a suspected perpetrator: that is, law enforcement officers acting with a purely law enforcement purpose. But sometimes law enforcement officers take actions unrelated (or only tangentially related) to their law enforcement function. For example, they may assist a person whose car has broken down on the highway, or they may respond to a neighbor's complaints of excessive noise from a party. And law enforcement officers are not the only type of government officials who conduct searches. For example, city electrical inspectors enter stores to ensure the wiring is safe; prison guards search prisoners' cells for prohibited items; public agencies require their employees to undergo regular drug tests; and immigration officials search vehicles at the United States border. Should the courts interpret the Fourth Amendment to impose the same strict probable cause and warrant requirements on every government action that gathers information?

There are at least two arguments in favor of a consistent, one-size-fits-all interpretation of the Fourth Amendment. First, the plain language of the Amendment itself does not distinguish between gathering information for law enforcement purposes and gathering information for other purposes. The Amendment merely states that "[t]he right of the people to be secure in their persons, houses, papers, and effects, against unreasonable searches and seizures, shall not be violated."

Second, if the purpose of the Fourth Amendment is to protect the privacy of individuals from government surveillance, why should the purpose of the surveillance matter? Although an individual is only facing a fine or a civil citation for faulty wiring in his store, his privacy is still violated when the electrical inspector enters the store and examines all of the wiring.

The Court has rejected both of these arguments. As a result, the Court has refused to apply the strict probable cause and warrant requirements to searches that are conducted for a purpose other than law enforcement. Instead, the Court has applied a different, more relaxed standard to these searches. There are a number of reasons justifying this different standard:

First, although the plain language of the Fourth Amendment makes no mention of the purpose of surveillance, the Amendment has always been interpreted as a check on the powers of law enforcement, not a general restriction on all government activity. For example, government safety inspectors have traditionally had the right to enter onto private property and conduct whatever search is necessary to perform their duties.

Second, even if one accepts the premise that the Fourth Amendment should be broadly interpreted to protect privacy against all governmental intrusion, as a practical matter, the purpose of the surveillance frequently affects the **extent** of the privacy invasion. Although electrical inspectors conducting a routine search for faulty wiring and police officers conducting a search for contraband both infringe on a citizen's right to privacy, the level of intrusion is not the same. Law enforcement officers attempting to gather evidence of a crime will likely conduct extremely comprehensive searches, while government employees in other contexts are often more narrowly focused on their specific purpose.

Third, administrative searches apply to broad segments of the population, and so are less likely to be abused by government officials. As Justice Jackson commented in an early administrative search case: "there is no more effective practical guaranty against arbitrary and unreasonable government than to require that the principles of law which officials would impose upon a minority must be imposed generally."[1]

The final reason for a different standard is a practical one: safety inspectors, prison guards, public employers, border guards, and similar government employees would find it difficult if not impossible to do their jobs if they had to show probable cause or acquire a warrant before they could conduct employment-related surveillance. Police officers are well-versed in the probable cause standard and the procedures for obtaining a warrant, but most other government employees are not. Furthermore, police officers investigating a crime are reactive: they are

[1] Railway Express Agency v. New York, 336 U.S. 106, 112 (1949) (Jackson, J., concurring).

targeting certain individuals or locations which have fallen under suspicion. Under these circumstances, it is usually easier to demonstrate probable cause. In contrast, non-law-enforcement searches are proactive. By their nature, they apply generally to a large number of people, almost none of whom are suspicious in any way. Requiring a warrant before each instance of a widespread preventative search would be impractical, if not impossible.

Of course, distinguishing between surveillance with a law enforcement purpose and surveillance with a non-law enforcement purpose creates significant problems of line-drawing. How do we know whether a search is being conducted primarily for "law enforcement" purposes? What if the search has multiple purposes, only one of which is enforcing the criminal law? How do you decide which purpose is the primary one? And if law enforcement officers conduct the search, can we presume that the search has a law enforcement purpose? Before we answer these questions, let us examine the general rule.

B. The Law. Searches that are conducted for a purpose other than general law enforcement arise in many different contexts: searches by inspectors or administrative agencies; drug tests of public employees or school children; vehicular checkpoints looking for intoxicated drivers; and anti-terrorism searches at airports, public buildings, and public transportation sites. These types of searches are generally known as "special needs" searches, meaning that the search fulfills a primary need other than general crime control.

I. A "special needs search" is a search with the following characteristics:

(A) The search must primarily serve a special need beyond mere enforcement of the criminal law.[2] The search may ultimately serve a law enforcement purpose in addition to the special need, but the law enforcement need cannot be its "immediate objective"[3] or its "primary purpose."[4]

(B) The search is (usually) not targeted at a specific individual, but rather is broadly applicable to every member of society or everyone engaged in a specific activity.

---

[2] The search may not be solely "aimed at the discovery of evidence of crime." New Jersey v. T.L.O., 469 U.S. 325 (1985) (Brennan, J., dissenting); or it must fulfill a purpose other than "general crime control," City of Indianapolis v. Edmond, 531 U.S. 32, 43 (2000).

[3] Ferguson v. City of Charleston, 532 U.S. 67, 83-84 (2001).

[4] City of Indianapolis v. Edmond, 531 U.S. 31, 41-42 (2000).

II. When a government official conducts a "special needs search," the usual requirements of a warrant and/or probable cause do not apply. Instead, a reviewing court will apply a balancing test to ensure that the search is reasonable. There are four factors in the balancing test:

(A) The significance of the government need;

(B) The efficiency of the search in meeting this need;

(C) The intrusiveness of the search; and

(D) The privacy interest of the individuals being searched.

The trickiest issue in deciding whether a search qualifies as a special needs search is determining whether the immediate objective or primary purpose of the search is to serve the goals of law enforcement. As we will see in the next section, many special needs searches serve dual purposes: both a non-law enforcement purpose and a law enforcement purpose. In some cases, the special needs purpose is far enough removed from a law enforcement purpose that the application of the rule is straightforward. For example, when police officers search an abandoned car before impounding it, their goal is to ensure that it does not contain a bomb or any other items that could pose a danger to officer safety.

In other cases, however, the line can become blurry. Courts have approved special needs searches whose purported purpose is to "protect the safety of the public" but that do little more than search for criminal (though admittedly dangerous) activity. For example, the police are allowed to stop cars on the highway to look for drunk drivers. Similarly, they are allowed to search everyone getting onboard an airplane for weapons. These searches have the dual purpose of keeping the public safe and detecting criminal activity, but it may be hard to untangle one purpose from the other.

The other critical aspect of special needs searches is that they are usually not targeted at a specific individual, but rather are almost always applied to an entire class of people who are engaged in a certain activity. The individual officer who is conducting the search cannot exercise any discretion about whom to search. For example, a police officer cannot simply pull over one driver for no reason and conduct a sobriety test. However, the police officer is allowed to set up a checkpoint and stop every car (or every fifth car, or every tenth car) to conduct a sobriety test. There are a few categories of special needs searches which do permit the government agent to single out a specific target, but they involve individuals who have a reduced expectation of privacy, such as individuals on probation or students being searched in school.

Once a search regime has been categorized as a special needs search, the standard requirements of a warrant and/or probable cause are relaxed. There are two different types of special needs searches: those that still require some level of individualized suspicion (such as reasonable suspicion) and those that are permissible even if the government agent has no individualized suspicion of the target of the search.

Regardless of whether a special needs search requires some level of individualized suspicion, the search must be "reasonable." "Reasonableness" is a much more flexible test in this context than it is for traditional law-enforcement searches. As you read in earlier chapters, with other Fourth Amendment activity the "reasonableness" of the search or seizure usually turns on whether the police have acquired a warrant or whether the search fit into one of the pre-defined exceptions to the warrant requirement. Further inquiry into the precise manner in which the search or seizure was conducted is rare. For "special needs searches" in contrast, whether a search is reasonable depends on a court's careful consideration of the four factors listed in the rule. We will see how the Supreme Court has applied these factors in various contexts in the next section.

C. Applying the Law. The special needs doctrine was first recognized by courts in two different contexts: regulatory searches (known as "administrative searches") and searches at border checkpoints. These are also the areas in which the doctrine is the least controversial because searches in these contexts have an obvious primary purpose beyond law enforcement. Later, the Supreme Court extended the doctrine to other areas, in which the line between the special need and law enforcement need became more and more blurry. We will begin with the easier cases before turning to examine the more challenging ones.

1. Administrative Searches. The growth of the regulatory state in the twentieth century led to a corresponding growth of inspections to ensure that citizens were complying with the new administrative rules. This was especially true in large cities, where buildings sit so close to each other that unsafe conditions in one structure might easily endanger those in the surrounding area. Cities began instituting inspections for fire hazards and unsanitary conditions. As the century progressed, they began conducting inspections for proper ventilation, lighting, electrical wiring, plumbing, and a wide variety of other conditions.

City and state codes gave these inspectors the right to enter and search private residences and commercial establishments to ensure that the structures complied with the regulations. But what if an owner refuses access to the inspector? Does the inspector have a right to enter over her objection notwithstanding the Fourth Amendment's constraint on unreasonable searches?

Example—*Camara v. Municipal Court*, 387 U.S. 523 (1967): Roland Camara leased a ground floor unit in an apartment complex in San Francisco. A city housing inspector entered the building to conduct a routine annual inspection for possible violations of the city's housing code. The inspector was relying on a provision of the city code which granted employees of city agencies the right to enter any building in the city without a warrant to perform necessary inspections. Camara refused entry to the housing inspector, arguing that under the Fourth Amendment the inspector needed a warrant in order to enter his property without his consent.

Analysis: The Supreme Court agreed with Camara that the government agent needed prior judicial authorization before he could enter Camara's home. In the Court's view, the administrative search constituted a "significant intrusion" into Camara's privacy interests. However, the Court rejected Camara's contention that this prior judicial approval was governed by the same probable cause requirement as a warrant in the criminal context: "[I]n a criminal investigation, the police may undertake to recover specific stolen or contraband goods. But that public interest would hardly justify a sweeping search of an entire city conducted in the hope that these goods might be found." In contrast, inspection programs by their nature are searching for hidden defects in homes that government agents would not suspect before the search took place. Instead, these programs require "city-wide compliance" with "routine periodic inspections of all structures."

The Court held that, given these different goals, the administrative search program before it should be governed by a different definition of "probable cause" than is found in the criminal search context. In the context of regional home safety inspection programs, probable cause is determined by evaluating the reasonableness of the legislative or administrative standards governing the search protocol. These standards may be based upon "the passage of time, the nature of the building (e. g., a multi-family apartment house), or the condition of the entire area, but **they will not necessarily depend upon specific knowledge of the condition of the particular dwelling.**"[5]

The *Camara* decision merits two additional bits of discussion. First, though the Court required prior judicial approval (*i.e.*, a warrant) for the search at issue there, *Camara* is nevertheless best understood as one of the Court's earliest forays into the special needs exception to the warrant requirement. As the *Camara* Court noted, it was not requiring a warrant as traditionally understood in the context of criminal investigations. Rather, the "warrant" contemplated in *Camara* was

---

[5] Camara v. Municipal Court, 387 U.S. 523 (1965).

simply prior judicial approval that might be based on something as insubstantial as the mere passage of time since the last inspection.

Second, students should note that the *Camara* case was decided in 1967. As you will read in **Chapter 19**, this was a year before *Terry v. Ohio* revolutionized Fourth Amendment law by holding that something less than probable cause might justify a police search, as long as that search is merely a "frisk" necessary to ensure the officer's safety. *Camara* was a less dramatic case, but in many ways it was no less revolutionary. Both *Terry* and *Camara* used the Fourth Amendment's "reasonableness" language to modify the protections of the Fourth Amendment in a specific context. In *Terry*, those protections were modified in connection with a police officer's pre-arrest activity based on reasonable suspicions. In *Camara*, those protections were modified in connection with area-wide building safety inspections. However, as with *Terry*, the real impact of the case was not truly felt until subsequent cases—like *Terry*, *Camara* was only the beginning.

The shift in Fourth Amendment doctrine authorized in both cases opened the gates to an ongoing modification of standards. The shift in Fourth Amendment protection post-*Terry* is discussed in full in **Chapter 19**. Similar shifts can be seen post-*Camara*. Following its decision in *Camara*, the Supreme Court extended its approval of administrative searches well beyond inspections for building code violations. Inspections were approved for heavily regulated businesses such as liquor stores,[6] firearms sellers,[7] and mines.[8] Moreover, as noted, though the *Camara* Court did not do away entirely with the need for a warrant, it was nonetheless one of the Court's earliest forays into the special needs exception to the warrant requirement. In later cases, the Court moved well past *Camara*'s first tentative steps and fully embraced the "exception" aspect of the doctrine. Rather than require the meager warrant seen in *Camara*, the Court in these later cases simply abolished the warrant requirement altogether. Under modern doctrine, government inspectors do not need a warrant at all to conduct these types of administrative searches because the individuals engaged in those industries are fully aware of the pervasive regulation in their field, and thus they have a reduced expectation of privacy, at least with regard to workplace inspections.[9]

Moving past business inspections, the Supreme Court also has applied the administrative search doctrine to other types of searches conducted by police officers, as long as the search is conducted for a reason other than crime control. For example, police officers frequently conduct what is known as **inventory searches.** This type of search occurs when a police officer takes custody of personal property, either in the aftermath of criminal activity (for example, when they arrest an intoxicated

---

[6] Collonade Catering Corp. v. United States, 397 U.S. 72, 77 (1970).

[7] United States v. Biswell, 406 U.S. 311, 317 (1972).

[8] Donovan v. Dewey, 452 U.S. 594, 606 (1981).

[9] See, e.g., Biswell, 406 U.S. at 315–16.

driver and impound the car),[10] or pursuant to other duties (for example, when they tow a car in violation of parking regulations, or find an abandoned bag in a public place).[11] When police officers take custody of such property, they routinely search the property, for three reasons: (1) to protect the owner's property, (2) to avoid false claims of lost or stolen property by the owner, and (3) to protect the police from potential danger.[12] Because none of these purposes have to do with the police officers' law enforcement function, the Court has concluded that inventory searches are part of the "routine, administrative caretaking" functions of the police.[13] Consequently, these searches are permitted without a warrant or any individualized suspicion.[14]

By definition, an administrative search furthers a purpose other than crime control. However, many special needs searches may also end up furthering a law enforcement purpose. For example, a government regulator inspecting a liquor store may find an unlicensed gun hidden in the storeroom. Or, a police officer conducting an inventory search of a car may find illegal drugs in the glove compartment. The Supreme Court has ruled that as long as the "immediate objective" of the search was not crime control, the search will qualify as an administrative search and the traditional warrant rules will not apply.

However, it can sometimes be difficult to determine what the "immediate objective" of the search is. Furthermore, some "administrative" purposes are very difficult to distinguish from law enforcement purposes. Drawing the appropriate constitutional line in these sorts of cases can be difficult. One important factor courts consider is whether the target of the challenged search has a reduced expectation of privacy. If so, the search's compound purpose will tip the balance in favor of an administrative search finding, so long as such searches are imposed on everyone within the target class. In contrast, where the target of the challenged search enjoys full privacy expectations, a compound purpose will tip the balance in favor of Fourth Amendment protection. The Supreme Court emphasized the importance of this factor in an administrative search case involving a junkyard:

> **Example—*New York v. Burger*, 482 U.S. 691 (1987):** Joseph Burger owned a junkyard in New York City, and made money dismantling old automobiles and selling off their parts. Under state law, police officers have the right to inspect "any vehicles or parts of vehicles . . . which are on the premises" of automobile junkyard dealers. One day five plainclothes police officers, all members of the Auto Crimes Division of the New York Police

[10] See, e.g., People v. Trusty, 516 P.2d 423, 424 (Colo. 1973).

[11] See, e.g., People v. Sullivan, 272 N.E.2d 464, 466 (N.Y. 1971).

[12] South Dakota v. Opperman, 428 U.S. 364, 378 (1976).

[13] Id. at 370 n.5.

[14] Id. at 375–76; Colorado v. Bertine, 479 U.S. 367, 376 (1987).

Department, entered Burger's junkyard to inspect the automobiles and automobile parts that he owned. The Auto Crimes Division conducted between five and ten such inspections on any given day. The officers copied down the Vehicle Identification Numbers (VINs) of automobiles in Burger's junkyard, checked them against a police database, and concluded that they were stolen vehicles. The police then arrested Burger for possession of stolen property. Burger challenged the inspection as an unconstitutional search.

The trial court denied Burger's motion, applying the administrative search doctrine and finding that the automobile junkyard business was a "pervasively regulated industry" and that under the *Camara* line of cases, a warrantless inspection was a reasonable protocol given the legitimate goals of the state. New York's highest court disagreed, however, pointing out that "the only purpose of such searches is to determine whether a junkyard owner is storing stolen property on business premises." The New York court stated that although the law appeared on its face to be a comprehensive regulatory scheme, it was "in reality, designed simply to give the police an expedient means of enforcing penal sanctions for possession of stolen property." The government appealed the case to the United States Supreme Court.

Analysis: The Supreme Court upheld the inspection as a valid administrative search because it furthered a regulatory, not a criminal law enforcement purpose. The Court determined that the search was reasonable because (1) the State had a substantial interest in preventing junkyards from selling stolen vehicle parts; (2) only unannounced, warrantless searches of junkyards would be effective in preventing the re-sale of stolen automobiles; (3) the inspections were limited in scope because they only allowed inspectors to examine the VINs of automobile parts, not conduct a general search; and (4) commercial establishments in a heavily regulated industry receive a lower level of protection under the Fourth Amendment.

Finally, the Court said there was no constitutional significance to the fact that the inspectors were police officers. Police officers have many duties other than law enforcement, and a search which is by its nature part of a regulatory scheme does not lose its administrative nature merely because the state has not set up a specialized agency to enforce the regulation.[15]

[15] New York v. Burger, 482 U.S. 691 (1987).

Although the Supreme Court did not present it as such, *Burger* extended the administrative search doctrine. Prior to *Burger*, the doctrine had only been applied to non-law enforcement regulators who were seeking to enforce administrative regulations. The Court tried to present New York's inspection system as fitting into this mold, arguing that the inspectors merely had the regulatory goal of "seeking to ensure that vehicle dismantlers are legitimate businesspersons and that stolen vehicles and vehicle parts passing through automobile junkyards can be identified."[16] However, the "inspectors" in *Burger* were police officers, and an underlying purpose of the search was unquestionably to detect individuals who were committing crimes. In order to justify this extension, the Court also emphasized another significant difference between administrative statutes and criminal laws:

> An administrative statute establishes how a particular business in a "closely regulated" industry should be operated, setting forth rules to guide an operator's conduct of the business and allowing government officials to ensure that those rules are followed. Such a regulatory approach contrasts with that of the penal laws, a major emphasis of which is the punishment of individuals for specific acts of behavior.

Because the regulatory search at issue in *Burger* was routinely conducted on all similar businesses, because it was limited in scope to checking vehicle identification numbers, and because it was conducted on a very heavily regulated industry (whose members therefore had a diminished expectation of privacy in the workplace), the search was considered to be an administrative search.

2. Emergency Aid and Other Public Administration Functions of Law Enforcement. Police officers routinely take actions that are unrelated to their primary purpose of crime control. For example, they are frequently the first responders to emergencies which have nothing to do with criminal activity. They may respond to reports of a fire, a public safety hazard, or a seriously injured person. Police are also involved in many non-emergency activities that have little to do with crime control: they may be contacted when a drunk person passes out on a street corner, if a neighbor's party is too loud, when a mentally ill person needs to be committed, or simply to serve a subpoena or an eviction notice. Any of these activities may require the police to enter private residences or conduct a cursory search of an area, and while doing so, the police might find evidence of criminal activity.

The Supreme Court has held that when police are engaged in these activities, the special needs exception applies and the police need not acquire a warrant nor demonstrate probable cause. Courts occasionally call this the "emergency aid" doctrine or the "community caretaking" doctrine. It applies to both emergency

---

[16] Id. at 713–14 (emphasis added).

and non-emergency situations, as long as the police are responding to a situation with a reason other than crime control. Like other types of special needs searches, the Court has held that this type of police activity will be judged on the objective reasonableness scale, regardless of the police officer's actual state of mind:

> **Example—*Brigham City v. Stuart*, 547 U.S. 398 (2006):** At three o' clock in the morning, police in Brigham City, Utah responded to a noise complaint about a loud party at a residence. When the police officers arrived, they heard shouting from inside the house, and moved into the backyard of the home, where they observed two underage individuals drinking beer. From the backyard, they could see the kitchen of the home through a screen door and some windows. Inside, four adults were trying to restrain an agitated juvenile. After a moment, the juvenile broke free and attacked one of the adults, punching him in the face. The victim of the assault began to spit up blood into a sink, while the other adults pushed the juvenile up against a refrigerator, still trying to restrain him. The police officers then announced their presence and entered the home. The individuals inside the home stopped fighting. The police ultimately charged some of the people inside the home, including Charles Stuart, with contributing to the delinquency of a minor.
>
> At trial the prosecutor sought to admit evidence that the police found after they entered the home. Stuart sought to suppress the evidence. Relying on the Court's decision in *Payton v. New York*, Stuart argued that a warrantless entry of a home is presumptively unreasonable.[17] The prosecutor argued that the police entered the home legitimately under the emergency aid doctrine, in order to help a person with a serious injury and to prevent further injury to him or anyone else.

Analysis: The Supreme Court confirmed that the police officers acted reasonably and the Court upheld the warrantless entry into the home. The Court acknowledged that the police arguably had two different reasons for entering the home. First, the police had witnessed crimes (such as assault and contributing to the delinquency of a minor) and may have intended to arrest those who were guilty of the crimes. Second, the police may have intended to provide assistance to the injured adult and prevent the juvenile from causing him any further harm. Stuart argued that the first purpose—the law enforcement purpose—was the actual reason that the police officers entered the home. In his view, the desire to render

[17] See **Chapter 9**.

emergency aid was merely a pretext that the officers used to justify their actions. But, the Court ruled that the actual subjective motivations of the police were irrelevant. Even if these particular officers entered the home with the sole purpose of making an arrest, the objective facts of the situation supported an application of the emergency aid doctrine.

The Court also dismissed Stuart's argument that the danger to the victim was not sufficient to justify entry into the home:

> [T]he officer had an objectively reasonable basis for believing both that the injured adult might need help and that the violence in the kitchen was just beginning. Nothing in the Fourth Amendment required them to wait until another blow rendered someone "unconscious" or "semi-conscious" or worse before entering. The role of a peace officer includes preventing violence and restoring order, not simply rendering first aid to casualties.[18]

Note that even if the Court had not applied the emergency aid doctrine in the *Stuart* case above, the actions of the police officers could arguably have been justified by the "exigent circumstances" exception to the warrant requirement, discussed in **Chapter 17**. Under that exception, police entry is justified if the police have probable cause to believe that a crime has been committed, and entry is necessary to prevent physical harm to the police officer or to others.

In the *Stuart* case, the lower court held that exigent circumstances did not exist because the police could have prevented further harm merely by making their presence known outside the home.[19] The Supreme Court, however, did not reach the question of whether the exigent circumstances exception applied. Instead, it used the *Stuart* case to reinforce the principle that an officer's subjective belief is irrelevant to almost every Fourth Amendment analysis. We will discuss that point further in Section 9, below.

3. Border Checkpoints. The special needs exception to the warrant requirement also authorizes warrantless searches at our nation's borders. Government agents at international borders have always had the authority to search individuals and baggage that is entering the United States.[20] The same holds true for international mail that enters the country.[21] These searches are necessary to maintain the integrity of our borders—to prevent illegal immigration, to block contraband from

---

[18] Brigham City v. Stuart, 547 U.S. 398, 406 (2006).

[19] Brigham City v. Stuart, 2005 UT 13, 28-29 (2005).

[20] Carroll v. United States, 267 U.S. 132, 154 (1925). At least one federal appellate court has found that even files on laptop computers can be read by border agents. United States v. Arnold, 533 F.3d 1003, 1008 (9th Cir. 2008).

[21] See, e.g., United States v. Ramsey, 431 U.S. 606, 623 (1977); United States v. Seljan, 547 F.3d 993, 1008 (9th Cir. 2008) (en banc).

entering the country, and to ensure that proper customs duties are collected on items subject to tariffs.[22]

Indeed, the Supreme Court has even approved immigration checkpoints that are set up well inside the international border.[23] Like searches at a border crossing, interior immigration checkpoints do not require a warrant or any level of individualized suspicion. This is because, like border checkpoints, such interior checkpoints deny illegal aliens "a quick and safe route to the interior" of our country.[24] In testing the validity of interior checkpoints, the Court has considered a number of different factors, including:

1. The degree of the government interest at issue;
2. The need for the government action taken;
3. The severity of the intrusion; and
4. The privacy interests of the targeted population.

Applying these considerations to a border checkpoint that was set up sixty miles inside the border, the Court held the checkpoint was constitutional. In so finding, the Court determined that reasonableness balancing justified approval for the following reasons:

1. Border security is a significant government interest;
2. Interior checkpoints are necessary to prevent the influx of illegal aliens because illegal immigration cannot be controlled effectively with border searches alone;
3. Interior checkpoints involve only a low level of intrusion (merely a brief detention, a few questions, production of documents, and a visual inspection of the car), much like *Terry* stops; and
4. Individuals have a diminished expectation of privacy in automobiles.[25]

The Court has never determined precisely how far within the interior a permissible immigration checkpoint may be.

The Court has also only approved of **fixed location** immigration checkpoints; so-called "roving patrols" inside the border are not covered by the special needs doctrine. A roving patrol involves a much higher level of government intrusion, since (unlike the case of a fixed immigration checkpoint) the driver will not know

---

22 United States v. Robles, 45 F.3d 1, 5 (1st Cir. 1995).

23 United States v. Martinez-Fuerte, 428 U.S. 543 (1976).

24 Id. at 557.

25 Id. at 561.

why he is being pulled over. Also, a roving patrol gives law enforcement officers more discretion as to who is pulled over. Thus, if immigration officials want to pull over an automobile as part of a roving patrol, their conduct will be governed by the automobile exception to the warrant requirement; thus, they must demonstrate that at the time of the stop they had probable cause to believe a crime was being committed. [26]

4. Searches of Prisoners, Parolees, and Probationers. Prisoners can be searched at any time, with no need for individualized suspicion. Individuals on probation or parole are also subject to suspicionless searches, sometimes as a condition of their parole and probation. At first, the Supreme Court justified these searches at least partially under the special needs exception to the warrant requirement. Such searches were seen, in the context of prisoners, as necessary to maintain order within a prison and to protect the safety of the prison administrators. In the context of parolees and probationers, such searches were deemed necessary to ensure that people in the neighborhood were not harmed by a former inmate who was transitioning back to the community without supervision.

Throughout the 1990s and early 2000s, however, it became increasingly common for searches of prisoners, parolees and probationers to be conducted for primarily law enforcement purposes. For example, many states began enacting laws allowing government agents to forcibly extract DNA from prisoners, parolees, and probationers in order to add it to a law enforcement database. Such databases were (and are) maintained for purely crime control purposes (to more easily identify these individuals if they commit future crimes and to assist in the resolution of "cold" cases). Consequently, the special needs exception to the warrant requirement could no longer feasibly justify these searches.

The Supreme Court ultimately justified these searches on other grounds. It is a common condition of parole and probation that law enforcement officers are allowed to search parolees and probationers at any time for any reason. Thus, the Court held that probationers and parolees have such a low expectation of privacy in their homes and their belongings that there is no need to justify these searches with a special need beyond a law enforcement purpose.[27] Consequently, any search of their homes, belongings, or persons is not legally a "search" because it does not violate the *Katz* test.

5. DNA Tests of Arrestees. With increasing frequency, police will take a DNA sample from individuals who have been arrested in order to determine their true identity and to see if there is any match with DNA from unsolved crimes.

[26] Almeida-Sanchez v. United States, 413 U.S. 266 (1973).

[27] United States v. Knights, 534 U.S. 112, 119 (2001) (probationers); Samson v. California, 547 U.S. 843, 846, 855 n.4 (2006) (parolees).

We have already seen that prisoners, probationers, or parolees have such a low expectation of privacy that police are allowed to conduct mandatory DNA tests of them without violating the Fourth Amendment. But arrestees are not quite in the same category—because they have not yet been convicted of a crime, taking their DNA is only permissible if there is a non-law-enforcement purpose to the search. The Supreme Court recently considered this issue:

> **Example—*Maryland v. King*, 133 S.Ct. 1958 (2013):** In 2003 a man broke into a woman's home in Salisbury, Maryland and raped her. Because his face was covered, she was unable to identify the man, but the police were able to recover some of the man's DNA from the victim's body.
>
> In 2009, Alonzo King was arrested for menacing a crowd of people with a shotgun. Maryland law required the police to take a DNA sample from every individual who was arrested for a serious crime, and so the police swiped the inside of King's cheek with a cotton swab and sent the DNA sample to the laboratory for analysis. Nearly four months later, the lab matched his DNA with the DNA from the perpetrator of the 2003 rape. The State of Maryland indicted King for the rape, and he challenged the taking of the DNA sample as an unconstitutional search. The trial court rejected his challenge, and King was convicted and sentenced to life in prison without parole. He appealed the Fourth Amendment ruling all the way to the Supreme Court.

Analysis: The Court held that the police did not violate the Fourth Amendment when they took King's DNA sample. The Court agreed that the DNA test was a Fourth Amendment search, but noted that the police did not exercise any discretion when carrying out this search, because it was statutorily required of all those who were arrested for a serious crime. Thus, no individualized suspicion was required and the search should be evaluated by whether it was reasonable.[28] This means the court must balance the legitimate government interest in conducting the search against the level of intrusiveness of the search.

In this case, the state has a strong interest in "a safe and accurate way to process and identify the persons and possessions they . . . take into custody." This is necessary so that the corrections officers know if they have a dangerous criminal in custody, and so that bail can be set based on accurate information about the arrestee's criminal history (which is relevant to both the question of the suspect's flight risk and the question of his dangerousness to the community).

[28] Skinner v. Ry. Labor Executives Ass'n, 489 U.S. 602 (1989).

On the other hand, the intrusion into privacy interests is minimal: an arrestee has a lower expectation of privacy than the general population. By their very nature, arrests result in a "brief period of detention" in which the police may "take the administrative steps incident to arrest," such as fingerprinting and photographing the suspect. The taking of the DNA sample only consists of a "gentle rub along the inside of the cheek [which] does not break the skin, and...involves virtually no risk, trauma, or pain." And the segment of the DNA that is tested consists of "junk DNA"—that is, sets of chromosomes that are uniquely identifiable but which have no known purpose or effect. Thus, the DNA cannot reveal anything personal about the arrestee other than whether it matches DNA already in the crime database. Thus, the taking of the DNA sample was reasonable.[29]

Although the Supreme Court analogized DNA testing to other "administrative" parts of the arrest, it never specifically stated that these DNA tests were a "special needs" search. Writing for a four-Justice dissent, Justice Scalia emphasized this omission: "Whenever this Court has allowed a suspicionless search, it has insisted upon a justifying motive apart from the investigation of crime. It is obvious that no such noninvestigative motive exists in this case."[30] According to the dissent, the DNA sample was not taken to identify those who had been arrested—particularly because the DNA was not processed until four months after the arrest, at which point King had already been arraigned and was awaiting trial. Instead, the dissent argued that the sole purpose of the test was to help solve cold cases, which is a law enforcement purpose.

As of now, the *King* holding only applies to those who have been arrested for "serious offenses," but the dissent correctly points out that there is nothing in the reasoning of the majority's opinion to limit the holding to arrests for serious crimes. Thus, we will have to see if later courts expand the holding to all arrestees.

6. Searches of Students. The warrantless search of students has also been approved under the special needs exception to the warrant requirement. Searches of students serve the special need of maintaining discipline in the classroom and deterring drug use among the nation's children. Thus, warrants may not be required when a school is searching a student or her possessions. However, you should be careful to note the difference between **warrantless** searches and **suspicionless** searches. Though warrantless searches of students are permitted in a number of different contexts, suspicionless searches are only rarely permitted. Depending on the intrusiveness of the search, courts will require the government to show some level of individualized suspicion before the search is found to be reasonable.

---

[29] Maryland v. King, 133 S.Ct. 1958 (2013).

[30] Id. at 1980 (Scalia, J., dissenting).

In the landmark case of *New Jersey v. T.L.O.*,[31] for example, a high school assistant principal searched the purse of a student (T.L.O.), whom he suspected of smoking in school. The search, which was conducted without a warrant in the assistant principal's office, turned up evidence of drug activity. The Supreme Court upheld the search, noting that it was "impracticable" to require school teachers and administrators to acquire a warrant before conducting such searches. More importantly, the Court noted that students in school have reduced expectations of privacy, as compared with adults. Finding that the school's interest in ferreting out drug use was substantial, the Court determined that the search of T.L.O.'s purse was permissible as long as the school administrator had "reasonable grounds" to believe the student had broken a law or a school rule. The search approved in *T.L.O.* was thus warrantless, but not suspicionless. The school had reasons directly related to T.L.O. to believe a search of her property was necessary.

A similar warrantless search was considered by the Court twenty years after its decision in *T.L.O.*, in *Safford Unified School District #1 v. Redding.* This time, however, the Court refused to sanction the school's conduct. In *Redding*, school officials had reasonable suspicion that a thirteen-year-old student possessed prescription drugs in violation of school rules. In an effort to locate the pills, school officials ordered the student to strip to her underwear in the presence of a school nurse. The nurse then ordered the student to stretch out her bra and underpants. Though recognizing that *T.L.O.* established the propriety of warrantless searches of school students, the Court nonetheless determined that the search of Redding went too far. The more intrusive search at issue in *Redding* required greater suspicion than the school administrators possessed. Finding that "the content of the suspicion failed to match the degree of intrusion," the Court held the strip search was unconstitutional.[32]

The Court has also found that the special needs exception to the warrant requirement will in some instances justify **suspicionless** searches of school students. Supsicionless searches, unlike the ones in *T.L.O.* and *Redding*, are those in which the school administrators have no reason to suspect any wrongdoing on the part of the students being searched. The Court has considered and approved suspicionless searches on two occasions. First, the Court approved random drug testing of all student athletes.[33] Shortly, thereafter, the Supreme Court expanded this holding to approve mandatory blanket drug testing of all school children who participate in extracurricular activities.[34] The Court not only found that there was a significant administrative need for such searches, but also that the searches were reasonable. Applying the standard balancing test for special needs searches, the Court found that (1) the state had a strong interest in preventing its high school

[31] 469 U.S. 325 (1985).

[32] Safford Unified School District #1 v. Redding, 557 U.S. 364, 366 (2009).

[33] Vernonia School Dist. 47J v. Acton, 515 U.S. 646 (1995).

[34] Board of Education v. Earls, 536 U.S. 822, 825 (2002).

students from using drugs; (2) there was no other effective way of deterring drug use in schools, (3) the level of intrusion was not significant because the search was limited in scope (a urinalysis which could only reveal evidence of drug use), and (4) high school students have a reduced expectation of privacy compared to the population at large. The Court has to date never extended permissible suspicionless searches of students beyond the two contexts noted above.

7. Drug Testing of Employees. Mandatory drug tests have also been upheld for certain types of employees. For example, in the context of heavily regulated industries, as long as the Court finds an administrative purpose beyond standard law enforcement, drug tests have usually been found to be justified because they are so limited in scope:

> **Example—*Skinner v. Railway Labor Association*, 489 U.S. 602 (1989):** The Federal Railroad Administration ("FRA") is a regulatory agency with a mandate to promulgate and enforce rules that ensure the safety of railroads. After determining that alcohol and drug abuse by railroad employees posed a serious threat to safety, the FRA created a rule that required railroad companies to administer alcohol and drug tests to every railroad operator involved in an accident that caused injury or significant property damage. The results of the tests had to be reported to the FRA. Labor unions representing railroad workers challenged these rules, arguing that mandatory tests without any individualized suspicion violated their members' Fourth Amendment rights. The Ninth Circuit agreed that the special needs exception to the warrant requirement justified the warrantless nature of the searches. However, the Ninth Circuit further determined that **suspicionless** searches were not defensible. In that court's view the drug tests were unreasonable unless the company had reasonable suspicion to believe an individual worker was under the influence of alcohol or drugs.

Analysis: The Supreme Court overruled the Ninth Circuit and held that suspicionless drug tests required by the regulation were reasonable. The easy question was in determining that the drug tests were in fact "special needs" searches. The Supreme Court, like the Ninth Circuit, found that the tests were administered "not to assist in the prosecution of employees, but rather to 'prevent accidents and casualties in railroad operations that result from impairment of employees by alcohol or drugs.'" Thus, as required for application of the special needs exception, the purpose of the tests was not to further law enforcement goals. The Court then held that the drug tests were reasonable even though they were suspicionless, because a urine test involved a relatively low level of intrusion and the railway workers were involved in a heavily regulated industry and thus enjoyed a reduced expectation of privacy.[35]

The Court also upheld mandatory suspicionless drug tests for customs workers who carry a firearm or are engaged in drug interdiction efforts. These tests serve the special need of "deter[ring] drug use among those eligible for promotion to sensitive positions within the [Customs] Service and . . . prevent[ing] the promotion of drug users to those positions."[36]

However, the Court has been extremely reluctant to embrace mandatory drug testing programs in other contexts. The Court's holdings suggest that before approving such programs there must be a particular risk posed by drug use in the specific group of people being tested. For example, the Court held that a Georgia law requiring drug testing of all candidates for elected office could not be justified under the special needs exception because the officials did not "perform high risk, safety-sensitive tasks."[37]

Even if the state offers a legitimate argument that the specific group of people being tested pose a significant risk to others, excessive involvement by law enforcement officials can transform a special needs search into a law enforcement search.

> **Example—*Ferguson v. City of Charleston*, 532 U.S. 67 (2001):** A public hospital in Charleston, South Carolina began mandatory drug testing of all pregnant mothers who sought treatment. Initially, women who tested positive for cocaine use were given treatment and counseling. However, because the program seemed ineffective in reducing the use of cocaine by pregnant women, the hospital reached an agreement with the local prosecutor which stated that the hospital officials would send the positive drug results to the police if the women missed a counseling session or received a second positive test. Hospital officials would also send a positive test result to the police if the woman tested positive for cocaine use after giving birth.
>
> Once the police received the proof of cocaine use, they would charge the women with a crime—possession of narcotics if the woman was twenty-seven weeks pregnant or less; and possession plus distribution of narcotics to a minor if the woman was over twenty-seven weeks pregnant.
>
> Ten women who had tested positive and were subsequently arrested brought a civil suit against the city of Charleston, arguing

[35] 489 U.S. 602.

[36] Nat'l Treasury Employees Union v. Von Raab, 489 U.S. 656, 666 (1989).

[37] Chandler v. Miller, 520 U.S. 305, 321–22 (1997).

that the drug testing violated their Fourth Amendment rights. In defending the procedure, the government presented what seemed to be a relatively strong special needs argument: the drug tests furthered the purpose of protecting the health of the mother and the unborn child.

Analysis: The Supreme Court rejected the city's argument, holding that the primary purpose of the searches was crime control rather than protecting the health of the mother or the fetus.

The Court first noted that the entity conducting the tests was a public hospital, so state action existed. The Court then distinguished these tests from drug testing of railway workers, customs officers, and high school students, noting that all of those tests were conducted for a purpose other than law enforcement. In this case, however, the "central and indispensable feature of the policy from its inception was the use of law enforcement to coerce the patients into substance abuse treatment."[38] The Court pointed out that law enforcement officials were closely involved in the testing procedures—they set up the testing protocols and worked with the hospital officials on a daily basis to implement the program. Thus, although the ultimate goal of the testing program was to encourage women to seek treatment and protect the health of the fetus, the "immediate objective" and the "primary purpose" of the program was to gather evidence for prosecution.[39]

Although the Court does not highlight the point in *Ferguson*, another factor in determining whether the Court will approve of a drug test as a "special needs" search is whether the group of individuals being tested are already subject to a high degree of regulation. Railroad operators and customs agents are in highly regulated industries; likewise, school students are subject to a high degree of government oversight during the school day. But the state ran into trouble when it attempted to require drug tests of ordinary citizens who possess a full, robust expectation of privacy.

The degree to which the subjects of the search are already subject to government regulation is relevant for many different types of special needs searches. Recall the *Burger* case from Section 1, in which the Court held that a police search of an automobile junkyard for evidence of both violations and criminal activity was held to be a special needs search in part because junkyards were a heavily regulated industry.

8. Vehicular Checkpoints. You have read that warrantless, suspicionless checkpoints meant to detect illegal immigration are legal, even if they take place miles from the border. The Court's approval of such checkpoints turns on the fact

[38] Ferguson v. City of Charleston, 532 U.S. 67, 80 (2001).

[39] Id. at 83–4.

that their primary purpose is not to detect illegal activity but instead to further secure our borders. However, immigration checkpoints are not the only types of vehicular checkpoints that the Court has approved.

> **Example—*Michigan v. Sitz*, 496 U.S. 444 (1990):** The Sheriff's Department in Saginaw County, Michigan set up a "sobriety checkpoint" on a public road. From midnight until just past 1:00 AM, every car that passed through the checkpoint was stopped, and a Deputy Sheriff briefly examined the driver for signs of intoxication. In all, one hundred and twenty-six cars were stopped at the checkpoint and the average delay for each vehicle was twenty-five seconds. If the checkpoint officer detected signs of intoxication, the officer directed the driver to pull to the side of the road for further sobriety testing. Two drivers were detained in this manner, and one of them was ultimately arrested for driving while intoxicated. A third driver attempted to drive through the checkpoint. He was pulled over, tested, and also arrested for driving while intoxicated.
>
> Residents of Saginaw County, including Rick Sitz, sued the county, seeking an injunction against the future use of the checkpoint. In the plaintiffs view, the checkpoint violated their rights under the Fourth and Fourteenth Amendments.

Analysis: The Supreme Court held that the sobriety checkpoint was constitutional. The Court agreed that a seizure occurred every time the police stopped a car at a checkpoint. The Court further agreed that these seizures took place without any kind of individualized suspicion. However, the Court placed the sobriety checkpoints in the same category as the immigration checkpoint cases and the approved drug testing cases.

The Fourth Amendment intrusion occasioned by the sobriety checkpoint served a "special governmental need" beyond normal law enforcement. The purpose of the sobriety checkpoint was not to detect and apprehend criminals, but to prevent drunk driving and the deaths, injury, and property damage associated with it. Given this special need, the government did not necessarily have to show any individualized suspicion before conducting these seizures. Instead the government's only burden was to demonstrate that the checkpoint program was reasonable.

In conducting its reasonableness analysis, the Court found (1) a very strong state interest in combating drunk driving, which was responsible for twenty-five thousand deaths, one million injuries and more than five billion dollars in property damage each year; (2) checkpoints were a reasonably effective method of preventing drunk driving, as statistics showed that approximately 1% of all drivers who were stopped were arrested for drunk driving (3) the level of intrusion was minimal, consisting of only a short stop; and (4) drivers receive a lower level of protection under the Fourth Amendment. Thus, the checkpoint program was reasonable.[40]

Beyond its general consideration of the special needs question, the Court in *Sitz* also added a new wrinkle to the analysis. When the Supreme Court measured the "level of intrusion" of the stops, it broke the analysis into two parts: the "objective" level of intrusion, and the "subjective" level. The Court found the objective intrusion was small—merely a twenty-five second stop, including a few questions. The Court found this objective level of intrusion indistinguishable from the level of intrusion present for the immigration checkpoints that the Court had already approved. In determining the subjective intrusiveness of the seizure, the Court considered the question from the perspective of an **innocent** driver. "The 'fear and surprise' to be considered are not the natural fear of one who has been drinking over the prospect of being stopped at a sobriety checkpoint but, rather, the fear and surprise engendered in law abiding motorists by the nature of the stop."[41]

As the above discussion of *Sitz* demonstrates, a critical issue in determining whether the special needs exception to the warrant requirement applies is the preliminary inquiry: did the government action further a need beyond the normal needs of law enforcement? In *Sitz*, the Court determined that drunk drivers pose a sufficiently serious threat to public safety to justify a conclusion that the eradication of drunk driving is a "special need" separate and apart from general law enforcement.

In an earlier case, the Court stated in dicta that it would approve of checkpoints designed to inspect driver's licenses and vehicle registrations because they furthered the special need of maintaining safety on public roads.[42] Law enforcement agencies then decided (unsuccessfully) to try to use checkpoints to find illegal drugs:

> **Example—*Indianapolis v. Edmond*, 531 U.S. 32 (2000):** Indianapolis created "drug checkpoints" at six different locations throughout the city. Officers stationed at the checkpoints stopped a predetermined number of cars and then briefly investigated them while the rest of traffic flowed unimpeded. After the first set of cars was released, the officers would flag down a new group and investigate them.

---

[40] Michigan v. Sitz, 496 U.S. 444 (1990).

[41] Id. at 452.

[42] Delaware v. Prouse, 440 U.S. 648 (1979).

> The investigation of the stopped cars lasted approximately two to three minutes. An officer would check the driver's license and registration, ask her questions, and look for signs of intoxication. In addition, a drug dog was used to sniff around the outside of the car to see if narcotics might be present inside the car. The city conceded that the primary purpose of the checkpoint was to detect illegal drugs.
>
> A total of 1,161 drivers were stopped at the checkpoints, and the police made fifty-five arrests for drug offenses and forty-nine arrests for other offenses, for a "hit rate" of nine percent.
>
> After being stopped (and cleared) at one of the checkpoints, James Edmond and others sued the Indianapolis Police Department, claiming that the checkpoint violated their rights under the Fourth and Fourteenth Amendments.

Analysis: The Court held that the drug checkpoint was unconstitutional. The primary purpose of the checkpoint program was the discovery and interdiction of illegal narcotics, which the Court decided was indistinguishable from a general interest in crime control. The Court distinguished the drug checkpoint from the sobriety checkpoint in *Sitz*:

> The detection and punishment of almost any criminal offense serves broadly the safety of the community, and our streets would no doubt be safer but for the scourge of illegal drugs. Only with respect to a smaller class of offenses, however, is society confronted with the type of immediate, vehicle-bound threat to life and limb that the sobriety checkpoint in *Sitz* was designed to eliminate.[43]

Comparing *Sitz* and *Edmond* leaves us with two questions:

First, how do we know if the purpose for the roadblock is to further a "general interest in crime control" (such as detecting the presence of illegal narcotics) or to further a "special need beyond the normal need for law enforcement" (such as detecting illegal immigrants, finding intoxicated drivers, or checking for invalid driver's licenses)? All four of these checkpoints are detecting evidence of criminal activity, but the Court has explained that the latter three also have a direct effect on another interest: border security or safety on the road. The Supreme Court alluded to this when it mentioned that the *Sitz* roadblocks involved preventing an "immediate, vehicle-bound threat to life and limb."

---

[43] City of Indianapolis v. Edmond, 531 U.S. 32, 43 (2000).

Second, how do we determine what the purpose of a roadblock actually is? The dissent in *Edmond* pointed out that the police at the Indianapolis roadblocks also checked for signs of intoxication and asked for licenses and registration, thus furthering the goal of keeping the roadways safe. Thus, the *Edmond* roadblock had multiple purposes: detecting illegal narcotics, detecting intoxicated drivers, and detecting unlicensed drivers. Two of these purposes had already been approved as serving a special need beyond the normal need for law enforcement, yet the majority in *Edmond* characterized the checkpoints as having a "primary purpose" of detecting illegal narcotics. In *Edmond*, this was an easy call for the Court to make. Indianapolis consistently referred to the checkpoints as "drug checkpoints," and conceded in its pleadings that narcotics interdiction was their primary purpose. But future checkpoints may not be so easily categorized. A court may categorize a checkpoint in different ways depending on how the facts of the checkpoint are presented by the parties.

9. Anti-terrorism Searches. A developing area of special needs searches arises in the context of anti-terrorism measures. These searches are especially prevalent for passengers of airplanes, ferries, and subways. The Ninth Circuit has approved searches prior to airplane flight as permissible under the special needs exception. As that court explained, the searches were "part of a general regulatory scheme in furtherance of an administrative purpose, rather than as part of a criminal investigation to secure evidence of crime."

> **Example:** In 1970, in response to a massive increase in the number of airplane hijackings, President Nixon directed the Department of Transportation to extend its program of searching airplane passengers to every airport in the nation. A few months later, Charles Davis was boarding a flight from San Francisco to Los Angeles when an airline employee informed him that his belongings had to be searched. The airline employee examined his briefcase and found a loaded gun inside. Davis then challenged the search of his briefcase.

Analysis: The Ninth Circuit held that airport searches satisfy a special need because they are "conducted as part of a general regulatory scheme in furtherance of an administrative purpose, namely, to prevent the carrying of weapons or explosives aboard aircraft, and thereby to prevent hijackings."

Applying the same factors so often considered in the context of special needs searches, the Ninth Circuit found the search was reasonable because (1) the need to prevent airline hijacking was "unquestionably grave and urgent; (2) mandatory searches are "necessary" to detect hijackers, and the purpose of the search would be frustrated if courts imposed a warrant requirement or even an individualized suspicion requirement; and (3) the searches were limited in scope to those who wished to board an airplane.[44]

Given the supposed rationale for special needs searches, airport searches intended to "prevent hijackings" may be difficult to distinguish from a general purpose of crime control. However, in theory the same could be said for the purpose of some other special needs searches, such as drunk driving checkpoints or drug testing in schools. And from a practical standpoint, airport searches are now more firmly entrenched in our society than most other forms of special needs searches.

The same anti-terrorism rationale also supports indiscriminate searches of all individuals who enter a courthouse or many other public buildings. And, since 9/11, the government has expanded its anti-terrorism searches to contexts far beyond airplanes and public buildings. Local police have conducted suspicionless searches at subway entrances,[45] on ferries,[46] near political conventions,[47] near reservoirs,[48] at protest rallies,[49] at hockey arenas,[50] and at football stadiums.[51]

The reaction of courts to these attempts by law enforcement to expand the special needs doctrine has been mixed. For example, the Eleventh Circuit refused to allow suspicionless searches at sports arenas and political protests, finding that the government made no showing that there was a specific threat of terrorism in those contexts. On the other hand, the Second Circuit allowed suspicionless searches at ferry terminals and subway stops, saying that there need not be a specific threat of terrorist activity, merely a "substantial and real" possibility that a terrorist attack will occur.[52]

In other words, the government, in the name of the "War on Terror", has become more aggressive in seeking to use the special needs doctrine to empower warrantless (and at times suspicionless) police conduct aimed at preventing terrorist attacks. At the same time, courts are beginning to push back. Some courts are refusing to apply the doctrine to every case in which the government claims such wide-ranging authority is necessary. Other courts are beginning to require a more

---

44 United States v. Davis, 482 F.2d 893 (9th Cir. 1973).

45 MacWade v. Kelly, 460 F.3d 260 (2d Cir. 2006).

46 Cassidy v. Chertoff, 471 F.3d 67, 72 (2d Cir. 2006).

47 Stauber v. City of New York, Nos. 03 Civ. 9162, 03 Civ. 9163, 03 Civ. 9164, 2004 U.S. Dist. LEXIS 13350 (S.D.N.Y. July 19, 2004).

48 Commonwealth v. Carkhuff, 804 N.E.2d 317, 318 (Mass. 2004).

49 Bourgeois v. Peters, 387 F.3d 1303, 1307 (11th Cir. 2004).

50 State v. Seglen, 700 N.W.2d 702, 705 (N.D. 2005).

51 Johnston v. Tampa Sports Auth., 442 F. Supp. 2d 1257, 1259–60 (M.D. Fla. 2006), rev'd per curiam, 490 F.3d 820 (11th Cir. 2007), vacated and superseded on reh'g, 530 F.3d 1320 (11th Cir. 2008) (per curiam).

52 MacWade v. Kelly, 460 F.3d 260 (2d Cir. 2006); Cassidy v. Chertoff, 471 F.3d 67, 72 (2d Cir. 2006).

tangible threat of terrorism before a "special needs" search will be justified. As the nature of the terrorist threat and the methods used by police to combat that threat continue to evolve, courts will have to make difficult choices about when to suspend the usual Fourth Amendment requirements and apply the special needs exception to the warrant requirement.

10. The Problem of Pretext. Application of the special needs exception to the warrant requirement presents a concern for pretext when the police may have multiple reasons for wanting to conduct a search. Courts are confirming that an officer's actual motivations are irrelevant to most Fourth Amendment inquiries—thus, even if the police officer is intentionally conducting a special needs search with the subjective intent of gathering evidence of a crime, the search will be constitutional as long as the police conduct objectively meets the special needs criteria.

This is by now a familiar aspect to Fourth Amendment doctrine: courts will look to whether the police officer's actions were objectively reasonable and not inquire into the state of mind of the police officer who actually conducted the search or seizure. A brief review:

Traffic Stops (Chapter 9). In *Whren*, the Supreme Court held that a traffic stop is permissible if there was probable cause to make the stop, even if the officer had other motivations for pulling over the car.

Arrest Warrants (Chapter 9). In *Steagald*, the Court held that police may not enter your home to effectuate an arrest pursuant to a warrant against a third party, even if they legitimately are only trying to arrest the third party.

Search Incident to Arrest (Chapter 13). In *Chimel* and *Robinson*, the Court allowed a search incident to an arrest as long as officers could reasonably have been looking for a weapon or evidence of crime, regardless of what they were actually looking for.

Plain View (Chapter 14). In *Horton*, the Court held that police are allowed to obtain a warrant as long as they have probable cause to believe some contraband is present, even if they are actually looking for something else.

Exigent Circumstances (Chapter 17). In *Hayden*, the Court held that where exigent circumstances exist, police are allowed to look anywhere they might find a weapon or a suspect, regardless of the actual reason they were searching.

The Court's unwillingness to inquire into an officer's subjective motivations in the above contexts has caused many to raise cautionary warnings of pretext. A similar, and perhaps even greater, concern exists in special needs searches that are conducted on a broad scale without individualized suspicion. In such cases, the problem of pretext is a significant one. A government agency could design a broad search regime for the purpose of detecting criminal activity, yet claim that it was serving a non-law-enforcement purpose. This was the government's approach in *Edmonds*, the vehicle checkpoint meant to find illegal drugs, and *Ferguson*, the drug testing of pregnant women. Both of these programs were squarely rejected by the Court.

To avoid the concern for pretext in the context of special needs searches, the Supreme Court has held that for "programmatic searches" conducted without individualized suspicion, it is necessary for the reviewing courts to inquire into the purpose of the search. The object of the inquiry is to ensure that the search regime is designed to accomplish the non-law enforcement purpose—keeping the streets safe from drunk drivers, or ensuring the safety of officers who are searching a car that is about to be impounded. As we have seen, one of the ways the government can convince a court that the search regime serves a non-law-enforcement purpose is to ensure that the searches are governed by standardized criteria and follow an established routine, leaving no discretion to the individual officers who are conducting the search.

It is important to note that this inquiry into the purpose of the search regime is still distinguishable from an examination into the subjective state of mind of the individual officer conducting the search. In this sense, the courts are trying to ensure that the special needs search doctrine prevents pretextual searches while still remaining faithful to the principle that individual motivations are irrelevant in Fourth Amendment analysis.[53]

---

[53] See Brigham City v. Stuart, 547 U.S. 398, 405 (2006).

Quick Summary

The special needs exception to the warrant requirement is the final exception that we have covered. The special needs exception applies when the immediate objective or the primary reason for the search is other than a law enforcement purpose. The doctrine began with a narrowly defined group of cases involving truly routine and administrative procedures, such as searches for public health dangers by regulatory agents and inventory searches of property by police officers. It has since evolved to cover a wide range of searches—drunk driving checkpoints, searches in schools, drug tests of public employees, and searches for weapons at public buildings, airports, and other potential terrorist targets. Many of these searches ultimately do reveal evidence of criminal activity, and under the plain view doctrine, this evidence can be used in a subsequent prosecution of the individual who was searched.

If the special needs doctrine is applicable, the usual Fourth Amendment requirement of a warrant backed by probable cause will not apply. Instead, courts apply a reasonableness test to determine whether the search is constitutional. On one side of the balance, a reviewing court must consider the importance of the non-law-enforcement purpose and the degree to which the search regime fulfills that purpose. As part of this calculation, reviewing courts must determine whether enforcing the warrant requirement or an individualized suspicion requirement would frustrate the purpose of the search regime. On the other side of the balance, reviewing courts must consider the intrusiveness of the search and the privacy interest of the individuals being searched. Certain individuals, such as school children, motorists, businesses in heavily regulated industries, and (above all) prisoners and probationers enjoy reduced expectations of privacy as compared with the population at large.

Many special needs searches are permitted even though the government agent conducting the search has no individualized suspicion of the target being searched. In these situations, the government agent cannot exercise his or her discretion as to who should be searched.

Review Questions

1. Keeping the Peace? Police officers responded to a call that a man was "going crazy" and thereby causing a disturbance in his home. The officers arrived at the address and saw a pickup truck in the driveway with its front smashed in. There was blood on the hood of the pickup and on clothes inside the pickup. They also noticed three of the house windows were broken, and there was blood on one of the doors to the house. The back door of the house was locked, and the front door had been blocked by a sofa.

Through an open window the officers saw a man later identified as Jeremy Fontaine, screaming and throwing things. They also noticed that Fontaine had a cut on his hand. They asked him if he wanted medical assistance, and he yelled profanities back at them, demanding that they get a warrant. At this point one of the officers pushed his way through the front door and entered Fontaine's house. Immediately upon entry he saw Fontaine point a gun at him, and he hastily left the house.

Fontaine was eventually arrested and charged with assault with a dangerous weapon for pointing a gun at the police officer. He is now challenging the police officer's warrantless entry into his home.

Did the police violated his Fourth Amendment rights when they entered his house without a warrant?

2. Theft During Gym Class. During second period gym class at Evergreen High School, a girl reported to one of the gym teachers that her prom money, amounting to $300, had been stolen out of her locker. The gym teacher contacted the acting principal, who in turn called the police and then went to the gymnasium with two more teachers.

During second period, there were twenty boys and five girls participating in the gym class. The boys were taken into the boys' locker room by two male teachers, who searched their lockers and backpacks. The boys were then called individually into the shower area of the locker room, where each boy was ordered to take off his shirt, pull down his shorts, and pull down his underwear. The boys were never touched during the search.

Meanwhile, the girls were taken into the girls' locker room, where the acting principal (who was a woman) and a female teacher searched their lockers and backpacks. They were then ordered to stand in a large circle and lift up their shirts, though they were not asked to remove their shorts or underwear. The girls were also not touched.

At that point two police officers arrived on the scene. When they were advised of the situation, one of the officers told the acting principal that a strip search was a good idea for the girls as well as the boys, but that the teachers should conduct the searches because "you all have a lot more leeway than police officers do." The acting principal and the female teacher then went back into the girls' locker room and called the girls into the shower area one at a time, ordering each girl to lift up her shirt and remove her underwear. The money was never discovered.

The students and their parents sued the school district, the individual teachers, and the police department in a § 1983 action, arguing that the defendants violated the students' Fourth Amendment rights. Was there a violation for:

a. The search of the boys?

b. The search of the girls before the police arrived?

c. The search of the girls after the police arrived?

3. Full Service Roadblock. The Utah Highway Patrol established a checkpoint on a two lane highway leading out of Salt Lake City. Police at the checkpoint stopped every car that passed, and had the authority to check any or all of the following: license plates, registration certificates, insurance certificates, driver's licenses, compliance with seat belt and child restraint laws; drivers that may be under the influence of alcohol and/or other substances; other alcohol and/or controlled substance violations; vehicle equipment violations; and compliance with commercial vehicle regulations. Based on the officers' discretion, some cars were only stopped for a few seconds while the police officers checked driver's licenses, while others were stopped for a few minutes for a full check of the automobile's equipment and a sobriety check of the driver.

Thomas DeBrine was stopped at the checkpoint and was held for five minutes while the police checked the equipment on his car, ran his license plate, checked his driver's license and registration, and conducted a sobriety check. DeBrine was arrested for drunk driving after he failed the sobriety check, and he was also cited for a broken turn signal. He is challenging the initial stop, arguing that it violated his Fourth Amendment rights. Was the roadblock constitutional?

4. Laptop Search at the Border. Steve Kotter, an American citizen, was re-entering the United States at a border stop near Tuscon. As he pulled up to the border, a customs agent stopped him and asked for his identification. The officers at the border learned that Kotter had been convicted of possession of child pornography eight years before. One of the officers turned to Kotter and said he was going to search the car. Kotter was asked to step out of the car and three different officers began to search the car and the trunk. After a few minutes, one of the officers emerged from the car with Kotter's laptop computer. The officer opened up the computer and skimmed through all the files on his laptop. He found nothing incriminating, but did find a photo file which was password protected. He asked Kotter to provide the password, but Kotter refused. "O.K.," the officer said, "but there is something funny going on around here. We're going to keep this computer until we can see every file you ever put on it."

The officer took the laptop and sent it to a government forensic lab in Phoenix. Kotter was allowed to continue on to his home in Minnesota. The police kept his laptop for ten days, until a forensic expert broke into the password protection and found twelve pictures of naked underage girls. The forensic expert then looked for files which had already been deleted, and found over three hundred photos of naked underage girls.

The customs officers contacted the FBI in Minnesota, who arrested Kotter outside his home. Kotter is now challenging the search of his computer at the border, arguing that the police violated his Fourth Amendment rights.

When (if ever) did the officers violate Kotter's rights?

a. When they stopped him at the roadblock?

b. When they searched his car?

c. When they skimmed through his files on the scene?

d. When they seized the laptop and kept it for ten days?

e. When they looked at his password protected files?

f. When they recovered and examined his deleted files?

FROM THE COURTROOM

CITY OF INDIANAPOLIS v. EDMOND

United States Supreme Court, 2000
531 U.S. 32

[Justice O'CONNOR delivered the opinion of the Court.]

[Chief Justice REHQUIST filed a dissenting opinion, which was joined by Justice THOMAS and in part by Justice SCALIA.]

[Justice THOMAS filed a dissenting opinion.]

In *Michigan Dept. of State Police v. Sitz,* 496 U.S. 444 (1990), and *United States v. Martinez—Fuerte,* 428 U.S. 543 (1976), we held that brief, suspicionless seizures at highway checkpoints for the purposes of combating drunk driving and intercepting illegal immigrants were constitutional. We now consider the constitutionality of a highway checkpoint program whose primary purpose is the discovery and interdiction of illegal narcotics.

I

In August 1998, the city of Indianapolis began to operate vehicle checkpoints on Indianapolis roads in an effort to interdict unlawful drugs. The city conducted six such roadblocks between August and November that year, stopping 1,161 vehicles and arresting 104 motorists. Fifty-five arrests were for drug-related crimes, while [forty-nine] were for offenses unrelated to drugs. The overall "hit rate" of the program was thus approximately nine percent.

The parties stipulated to the facts concerning the operation of the checkpoints by the Indianapolis Police Department (IPD) for purposes of the preliminary injunction proceedings instituted below. At each checkpoint location, the police stop a predetermined number of vehicles. Approximately [thirty] officers are stationed at the checkpoint. Pursuant to written directives issued by the chief of police, at least one officer approaches the vehicle, advises the driver that he or she is being stopped briefly at a drug checkpoint, and asks the driver to produce a license and registration. The officer also looks for signs of impairment and conducts an open-view examination of the vehicle from the outside. A narcotics-detection dog walks around the outside of each stopped vehicle.

The directives instruct the officers that they may conduct a search only by consent or based on the appropriate quantum of particularized suspicion. The officers must conduct each stop in the same manner until particularized suspicion develops, and the officers have no discretion to stop any vehicle out of sequence. The city agreed in the stipulation to operate the checkpoints in such a way as to ensure that the total duration of each stop, absent reasonable suspicion or probable cause, would be five minutes or less.

The affidavit of Indianapolis Police Sergeant Marshall DePew, although it is technically outside the parties' stipulation, provides further insight concerning the operation of the checkpoints. According to Sergeant DePew, checkpoint locations are selected weeks in advance based on such considerations as area crime statistics and traffic flow. The checkpoints are generally operated during daylight hours and are identified with lighted signs reading, "'NARCOTICS CHECKPOINT ___ MILE AHEAD, NARCOTICS K–9 IN USE, BE PREPARED TO STOP.'" Once a group of cars has been stopped, other traffic proceeds without interruption until all the stopped cars have been processed or diverted for further processing. Sergeant DePew also stated that the average stop for a vehicle not subject to further processing lasts two to three minutes or less.

Respondents James Edmond and Joell Palmer were each stopped at a narcotics checkpoint in late September 1998. Respondents then filed a lawsuit on behalf of themselves and the class of all motorists who had been stopped or were subject to being stopped in the future at the Indianapolis drug checkpoints. Respondents claimed that the roadblocks violated the Fourth Amendment of the United States Constitution and the search and seizure provision of the Indiana Constitution. Respondents requested declaratory and injunctive relief for the class, as well as damages and attorney's fees for themselves.

. . .

II

The Fourth Amendment requires that searches and seizures be reasonable. A search or seizure is ordinarily unreasonable in the absence of individualized suspicion of wrongdoing. While such suspicion is not an "irreducible" component of reasonableness, we have recognized only limited circumstances in which the usual rule does not apply. For example, we have upheld certain regimes of suspicionless searches where the program was designed to serve "special needs, beyond the normal need for law enforcement." See, *e.g., Vernonia School Dist. 47J v. Acton,* 515 U.S. 646 (1995) (random drug testing of student-athletes); *Treasury Employees v. Von Raab,* 489 U.S. 656 (1989) (drug tests for United States Customs Service employees seeking transfer or promotion to certain positions); *Skinner v. Railway Labor Executives' Assn.,* 489 U.S. 602 (1989) (drug and alcohol tests for railway employees involved in train accidents or found to be in violation of particular safety regulations). We have also allowed searches for certain administrative purposes without particularized suspicion of misconduct, provided that those searches are appropriately limited. See, *e.g., New York v. Burger,* 482 U.S. 691 (1987) (warrantless administrative inspection of premises of "closely regulated" business); *Michigan v. Tyler,* 436 U.S. 499 (1978) (administrative inspection of fire-damaged premises to determine cause of blaze); *Camara v. Municipal Court of City and County of San Francisco,* 387 U.S. 523 (1967) (administrative inspection to ensure compliance with city housing code).

We have also upheld brief, suspicionless seizures of motorists at a fixed Border Patrol checkpoint designed to intercept illegal aliens, *Martinez–Fuerte, supra,* and at a sobriety checkpoint aimed at removing drunk drivers from the road, *Michigan Dept. of State Police v. Sitz,* 496 U.S. 444 (1990). In addition, in *Delaware v. Prouse,* 440 U.S. 648, 663 (1979), we suggested that a similar type of roadblock with the purpose of verifying drivers' licenses and vehicle registrations would be permissible. In none of these cases, however, did we indicate approval of a checkpoint program whose primary purpose was to detect evidence of ordinary criminal wrongdoing.

In *Martinez–Fuerte,* we entertained Fourth Amendment challenges to stops at two permanent immigration checkpoints located on major United States highways less than 100 miles from the Mexican border. We noted at the outset the particular context in which the constitutional question arose, describing in some detail the "formidable law enforcement problems" posed by the northbound tide of illegal entrants into the United States. . . . [W]e found that the balance tipped in favor of the Government's interests in policing the Nation's borders. In so finding, we emphasized the difficulty of effectively containing illegal immigration at the border itself. We also stressed the impracticality of the particularized study of a given car to discern whether it was transporting illegal aliens, as well as the relatively modest degree of intrusion entailed by the stops. . . . Although the stops in *Martinez–Fuerte* did not occur at the border itself, the checkpoints were located near the border and served a border control function made necessary by the difficulty of guarding the border's entire length.

In *Sitz,* we evaluated the constitutionality of a Michigan highway sobriety checkpoint program. The *Sitz* checkpoint involved brief, suspicionless stops of motorists so that police officers could detect signs of intoxication and remove impaired drivers from the road. Motorists who exhibited signs of intoxication were diverted for a license and registration check and, if warranted, further sobriety tests. This checkpoint program was clearly aimed at reducing the immediate hazard posed by the presence of drunk drivers on the highways, and there was an obvious connection between the imperative of highway safety and the law enforcement practice at issue. The gravity of the drunk driving problem and the magnitude of the State's interest in getting drunk drivers off the road weighed heavily in our determination that the program was constitutional.

In *Prouse,* we invalidated a discretionary, suspicionless stop for a spot check of a motorist's driver's license and vehicle registration. The officer's conduct in that case was unconstitutional primarily on account of his exercise of "standardless and unconstrained discretion." We nonetheless acknowledged the States' "vital interest in ensuring that only those qualified to do so are permitted to operate motor vehicles, that these vehicles are fit for safe operation, and hence that licensing, registration, and vehicle inspection requirements are being observed." Accordingly, we suggested that "[q]uestioning of all oncoming traffic at roadblock-type stops" would be a lawful means of serving this interest in highway safety.

We further indicated in *Prouse* that we considered the purposes of such a hypothetical roadblock to be distinct from a general purpose of investigating crime. The State proffered the additional interests of "the apprehension of stolen motor vehicles and of drivers under the influence of alcohol or narcotics" in its effort to justify the discretionary spot check. We attributed the entirety of the latter interest to the State's interest in roadway safety. We also noted that the interest in apprehending stolen vehicles may be partly subsumed by the interest in roadway safety. We observed, however, that "[t]he remaining governmental interest in controlling automobile thefts is not distinguishable from the general interest in crime control." Not only does the common thread of highway safety thus run through *Sitz* and *Prouse,* but *Prouse* itself reveals a difference in the Fourth Amendment significance of highway safety interests and the general interest in crime control.

III

It is well established that a vehicle stop at a highway checkpoint effectuates a seizure within the meaning of the Fourth Amendment. The fact that officers walk a narcotics-detection dog around the exterior of each car at the Indianapolis checkpoints does not transform the seizure into a search. See *United States v. Place,* 462 U.S. 696, 707 (1983). Just as in *Place,* an exterior sniff of an automobile does not require entry into the car and is not designed to disclose any information other than the presence or absence of narcotics. Like the dog sniff in *Place,* a sniff by a dog that simply walks around a car is "much less intrusive than a typical search." Rather, what principally distinguishes these checkpoints from those we have previously approved is their primary purpose.

As petitioners concede, the Indianapolis checkpoint program unquestionably has the primary purpose of interdicting illegal narcotics. In their stipulation of facts, the parties repeatedly refer to the checkpoints as "drug checkpoints" and describe them as "being operated by the City of Indianapolis in an effort to interdict unlawful drugs in Indianapolis." In addition, the first document attached to the parties' stipulation is entitled "DRUG CHECKPOINT CONTACT OFFICER DIRECTIVES BY ORDER OF THE CHIEF OF POLICE." These directives instruct officers to "[a] dvise the citizen that they are being stopped briefly at a drug checkpoint." The second document attached to the stipulation is entitled "1998 Drug Road Blocks" and contains a statistical breakdown of information relating to the checkpoints conducted. Further, according to Sergeant DePew, the checkpoints are identified with lighted signs reading, "'NARCOTICS CHECKPOINT ___ MILE AHEAD, NARCOTICS K–9 IN USE, BE PREPARED TO STOP.'" Finally, both the District Court and the Court of Appeals recognized that the primary purpose of the roadblocks is the interdiction of narcotics.

We have never approved a checkpoint program whose primary purpose was to detect evidence of ordinary criminal wrongdoing. Rather, our checkpoint cases have recognized only limited exceptions to the general rule that a seizure must be accompanied by some measure of individualized suspicion. We suggested in *Prouse* that we would not credit the "general interest in crime control" as justification for a regime of suspicionless stops. Consistent with this suggestion, each of the checkpoint programs that we have approved was designed primarily to serve purposes closely related to the problems of policing the border or the necessity of ensuring roadway safety. Because the primary purpose of the Indianapolis narcotics checkpoint program is to uncover evidence of ordinary criminal wrongdoing, the program contravenes the Fourth Amendment.

Petitioners propose several ways in which the narcotics-detection purpose of the instant checkpoint program may instead resemble the primary purposes of the checkpoints in *Sitz* and *Martinez–Fuerte.* Petitioners state that the checkpoints in those cases had the same ultimate purpose of arresting those suspected of committing crimes. Securing the border and apprehending drunk drivers are, of course, law enforcement activities, and law enforcement officers employ arrests and criminal prosecutions in pursuit of these goals. If we were to rest the case at this high level of generality, there would be little check on the ability of the authorities to construct roadblocks for almost any conceivable law enforcement purpose. Without drawing the line at roadblocks designed primarily to serve the general interest in crime control, the Fourth Amendment would do little to prevent such intrusions from becoming a routine part of American life.

Petitioners also emphasize the severe and intractable nature of the drug problem as justification for the checkpoint program. There is no doubt that traffic in illegal narcotics creates social harms of the first magnitude. The law enforcement problems that the drug trade creates likewise remain daunting and complex, particularly in light of the myriad forms of spin-off crime that it spawns. The same can be said of various other illegal activities, if only to a lesser degree. But the gravity of the threat alone cannot be dispositive of questions concerning what means law enforcement officers may employ to pursue a given purpose. Rather, in determining whether individualized suspicion is required, we must consider the nature of the interests threatened and their connection to the particular law enforcement practices at issue. We are particularly reluctant to recognize exceptions to the general rule of individualized suspicion where governmental authorities primarily pursue their general crime control ends.

Nor can the narcotics-interdiction purpose of the checkpoints be rationalized in terms of a highway safety concern similar to that present in *Sitz.* The detection and punishment of almost any criminal offense serves broadly the safety of the community, and our streets would no doubt be safer but for the scourge of illegal drugs. Only with respect to a smaller class of offenses, however, is society confronted with the type of immediate, vehicle-bound threat to life and limb that the sobriety checkpoint in *Sitz* was designed to eliminate.

Petitioners also liken the anticontraband agenda of the Indianapolis checkpoints to the antismuggling purpose of the checkpoints in *Martinez–Fuerte.* Petitioners cite this Court's conclusion in *Martinez–Fuerte* that the flow of traffic was too heavy to permit "particularized study of a given car that would enable it to be identified as a possible carrier of illegal aliens," and claim that this logic has even more force here. The problem with this argument is that the same logic prevails any time a vehicle is employed to conceal contraband or other evidence of a crime. This type of connection to the roadway is very different from the close connection to roadway safety that was present in *Sitz* and *Prouse.* Further, the Indianapolis checkpoints are far removed from the border context that was crucial in *Martinez–Fuerte.* While the difficulty of examining each passing car was an important factor in validating the law enforcement technique employed in *Martinez–Fuerte,* this factor alone cannot justify a regime of suspicionless searches or seizures. Rather, we must look more closely at the nature of the public interests that such a regime is designed principally to serve.

The primary purpose of the Indianapolis narcotics checkpoints is in the end to advance "the general interest in crime control." We decline to suspend the usual requirement of individualized suspicion where the police seek to employ a checkpoint primarily for the ordinary enterprise of investigating crimes. We cannot sanction stops justified only by the generalized and ever-present possibility that interrogation and inspection may reveal that any given motorist has committed some crime.

Of course, there are circumstances that may justify a law enforcement checkpoint where the primary purpose would otherwise, but for some emergency, relate to ordinary crime control. For example, as the Court of Appeals noted, the Fourth Amendment would almost certainly permit an appropriately tailored roadblock set up to thwart an imminent terrorist attack or to catch a dangerous criminal who is likely to flee by way of a particular route. The exigencies created by these scenarios are far removed from the circumstances under which authorities might simply stop cars as a matter of course to see if there just happens to be a felon leaving the jurisdiction. While we do not limit the purposes that may justify a checkpoint program to any rigid set of categories, we decline to approve a program whose primary purpose is ultimately indistinguishable from the general interest in crime control.

Petitioners argue that our prior cases preclude an inquiry into the purposes of the checkpoint program. For example, they cite *Whren v. United States,* 517 U.S. 806 (1996) . . . to support the proposition that "where the government articulates and pursues a legitimate interest for a suspicionless stop, courts should not look behind that interest to determine whether the government's 'primary purpose' is valid." [This case], however, do[es] not control the instant situation.

In *Whren,* we held that an individual officer's subjective intentions are irrelevant to the Fourth Amendment validity of a traffic stop that is justified objectively by probable cause to believe that a traffic violation has occurred. We observed that our prior cases "foreclose any argument that the constitutional reasonableness of traffic stops depends on the actual motivations of the individual officers involved." In so holding, we expressly distinguished cases where we had addressed the validity of searches conducted in the absence of probable cause.

Whren therefore reinforces the principle that, while "[s]ubjective intentions play no role in ordinary, probable-cause Fourth Amendment analysis," programmatic purposes may be relevant to the validity of Fourth Amendment intrusions undertaken pursuant to a general scheme without individualized suspicion. Accordingly, *Whren* does not preclude an inquiry into programmatic purpose in such contexts. It likewise does not preclude an inquiry into programmatic purpose here.

. . .

Petitioners argue that the Indianapolis checkpoint program is justified by its lawful secondary purposes of keeping impaired motorists off the road and verifying licenses and registrations. If this were the case, however, law enforcement authorities would be able to establish checkpoints for virtually any purpose so long as they also included a license or sobriety check. For this reason, we examine the available evidence to determine the primary purpose of the checkpoint program. While we recognize the challenges inherent in a purpose inquiry, courts routinely engage in this enterprise in many areas of constitutional jurisprudence as a means of sifting abusive governmental conduct from that which is lawful. As a result, a program driven by an impermissible purpose may be proscribed while a program impelled by licit purposes is permitted, even though the challenged conduct may be outwardly similar. While reasonableness under the Fourth Amendment is predominantly an objective inquiry, our special needs and administrative search cases demonstrate that purpose is often relevant when suspicionless intrusions pursuant to a general scheme are at issue.

Because the primary purpose of the Indianapolis checkpoint program is ultimately indistinguishable from the general interest in crime control, the checkpoints violate the Fourth Amendment. The judgment of the Court of Appeals is, accordingly, affirmed.

It is so ordered.

Chief Justice REHNQUIST, with whom Justice THOMAS joins, and with whom Justice SCALIA joins as to Part I, dissenting.

The State's use of a drug-sniffing dog, according to the Court's holding, annuls what is otherwise plainly constitutional under our Fourth Amendment jurisprudence: brief, standardized, discretionless, roadblock seizures of automobiles, seizures which effectively serve a weighty state interest with only minimal intrusion on the privacy of their occupants. Because these seizures serve the State's accepted and significant interests of preventing drunken driving and checking for driver's licenses and vehicle registrations, and because there is nothing in the record to indicate that the addition of the dog sniff lengthens these otherwise legitimate seizures, I dissent.

I

As it is nowhere to be found in the Court's opinion, I begin with blackletter roadblock seizure law. "The principal protection of Fourth Amendment rights at checkpoints lies in appropriate limitations on the scope of the stop." Roadblock seizures are consistent with the Fourth Amendment if they are "carried out pursuant to a plan embodying explicit, neutral limitations on the conduct of individual officers." Specifically, the constitutionality of a seizure turns upon "a weighing of the gravity of the public concerns served by the seizure, the degree to which the seizure advances the public interest, and the severity of the interference with individual liberty."

. . .

This case follows naturally from *Martinez–Fuerte* and *Sitz.* Petitioners acknowledge that the "primary purpose" of these roadblocks is to interdict illegal drugs, but this fact should not be controlling. Even accepting the Court's conclusion that the checkpoints at issue in *Martinez–Fuerte* and *Sitz* were not primarily related to criminal law enforcement, the question whether a law enforcement purpose could support a roadblock seizure is not presented in this case. The District Court found that another "purpose of the checkpoints is to check driver's licenses and vehicle registrations," and the written directives state that the police officers are to "[l]ook for signs of impairment." The use of roadblocks to look for signs of impairment was validated by *Sitz,* and the use of roadblocks to check for driver's licenses and vehicle registrations was expressly recognized in *Delaware v. Prouse.* That the roadblocks serve these legitimate state interests cannot be seriously disputed, as the [forty-nine] people arrested for offenses unrelated to drugs can attest. And it would be speculative to conclude—given the District Court's findings, the written directives, and the actual arrests—that petitioners would not have operated these roadblocks but for the State's interest in interdicting drugs.

Because of the valid reasons for conducting these roadblock seizures, it is constitutionally irrelevant that petitioners also hoped to interdict drugs. In *Whren v. United States,* we held that an officer's subjective intent would not invalidate an otherwise objectively justifiable stop of an automobile. The reasonableness of an officer's discretionary decision to stop an automobile, at issue in *Whren,* turns on whether there is probable cause to believe that a traffic violation has occurred. The reasonableness of highway checkpoints, at issue here, turns on whether they effectively serve a significant state interest with minimal intrusion on motorists. The stop in *Whren* was objectively reasonable because the police officers had witnessed traffic violations; so too the roadblocks here are objectively reasonable because they serve the substantial interests of preventing drunken driving and checking for driver's licenses and vehicle registrations with minimal intrusion on motorists.

Once the constitutional requirements for a particular seizure are satisfied, the subjective expectations of those responsible for it, be it police officers or members of a city council, are irrelevant. It is the objective effect of the State's actions on the privacy of the individual that animates the Fourth Amendment. Because the objective intrusion of a valid seizure does not turn upon anyone's subjective thoughts, neither should our constitutional analysis.

With these checkpoints serving two important state interests, the remaining prongs of the *Brown v. Texas* balancing test are easily met. The seizure is objectively reasonable as it lasts, on average, two to three minutes and does not involve a search. The subjective intrusion is likewise limited as the checkpoints are clearly marked and operated by uniformed officers who are directed to stop every vehicle in the same manner. The only difference between this case and *Sitz* is the presence of the dog. We have already held, however, that a "sniff test" by a trained narcotics dog is not a "search" within the meaning of the Fourth Amendment because it does not require physical intrusion of the object being sniffed and it does not expose anything other than the contraband items. And there is nothing in the record to indicate that the dog sniff lengthens the stop. Finally, the checkpoints' success rate—[forty-nine] arrests for offenses unrelated to drugs—only confirms the State's legitimate interests in preventing drunken driving and ensuring the proper licensing of drivers and registration of their vehicles.

These stops effectively serve the State's legitimate interests; they are executed in a regularized and neutral manner; and they only minimally intrude upon the privacy of the motorists. They should therefore be constitutional.

. . .

[The dissenting opinion of Justice THOMAS is omitted.]

FROM THE COURTROOM

MARYLAND v. KING

United States Supreme Court, 2013
133 S.Ct. 1958

[Justice KENNEDY delivered the opinion of the Court.]

[Justice SCALIA filed a dissenting opinion, which was joined by Justices GINSBURG, SOTOMAYOR, and KAGAN.]

In 2003 a man concealing his face and armed with a gun broke into a woman's home in Salisbury, Maryland. He raped her. The police were unable to identify or apprehend the assailant based on any detailed description or other evidence they then had, but they did obtain from the victim a sample of the perpetrator's DNA.

In 2009 Alonzo King was arrested in Wicomico County, Maryland, and charged with first- and second-degree assault for menacing a group of people with a shotgun. As part of a routine booking procedure for serious offenses, his DNA sample was taken by applying a cotton swab or filter paper—known as a buccal swab—to the inside of his cheeks. The DNA was found to match the DNA taken from the Salisbury rape victim. King was tried and convicted for the rape. Additional DNA samples were taken from him and used in the rape trial, but there seems to be no doubt that it was the DNA from the cheek sample taken at the time he was booked in 2009 that led to his first having been linked to the rape and charged with its commission.

The Court of Appeals of Maryland, on review of King's rape conviction, ruled that the DNA taken when King was booked for the 2009 charge was an unlawful seizure because obtaining and using the cheek swab was an unreasonable search of the person. It set the rape conviction aside. This Court granted certiorari and now reverses the judgment of the Maryland court.

I

When King was arrested on April 10, 2009, for menacing a group of people with a shotgun and charged in state court with both first- and second-degree assault, he was processed for detention in custody at the Wicomico County Central Booking facility. Booking personnel used a cheek swab to take the DNA sample from him pursuant to provisions of the Maryland DNA Collection Act (or Act).

On July 13, 2009, King's DNA record was uploaded to the Maryland DNA database, and three weeks later, on August 4, 2009, his DNA profile was matched to the DNA sample collected in the unsolved 2003 rape case. Once the DNA was matched to King, detectives presented the forensic evidence to a grand jury, which indicted him for the rape. . . . King pleaded not guilty to the rape charges but was convicted and sentenced to life in prison without the possibility of parole.

. . .

Both federal and state courts have reached differing conclusions as to whether the Fourth Amendment prohibits the collection and analysis of a DNA sample from persons arrested, but not yet convicted, on felony charges. This Court granted certiorari to address the question. . . .

II

The advent of DNA technology is one of the most significant scientific advancements of our era. The full potential for use of genetic markers in medicine and science is still being explored, but the utility of DNA identification in the criminal justice system is already undisputed. Since the first use of forensic DNA analysis to catch a rapist and murderer in England in 1986, law enforcement, the defense bar, and the courts have acknowledged DNA testing's "unparalleled ability both to exonerate the wrongly convicted and to identify the guilty. It has the potential to significantly improve both the criminal justice system and police investigative practices."

A

The current standard for forensic DNA testing relies on an analysis of the chromosomes located within the nucleus of all human cells. "The DNA material in chromosomes is composed of 'coding' and 'noncoding' regions. The coding regions are known as *genes* and contain the information necessary for a cell to make proteins. . . . Non-protein-coding regions . . . are not related directly to making proteins, [and] have been referred to as 'junk' DNA." The adjective "junk" may mislead the layperson, for in fact this is the DNA region used with near certainty to identify a person. The term apparently is intended to indicate that this particular noncoding region, while useful and even dispositive for purposes like identity, does not show more far-reaching and complex characteristics like genetic traits.

Many of the patterns found in DNA are shared among all people, so forensic analysis focuses on "repeated DNA sequences scattered throughout the human genome," known as "short tandem repeats" (STRs). The alternative possibilities for the size and frequency of these STRs at any given point along a strand of DNA are known as "alleles," and multiple alleles are analyzed in order to ensure that a DNA profile matches only one individual. Future refinements may improve present technology, but even now STR analysis makes it "possible to determine whether a biological tissue matches a suspect with near certainty."

. . .

Respondent's DNA was collected in this case using a common procedure known as a "buccal swab." "Buccal cell collection involves wiping a small piece of filter paper or a cotton swab similar to a Q-tip against the inside cheek of an individual's mouth to collect some skin cells." The procedure is quick and painless. The swab touches inside an arrestee's mouth, but it requires no "surgical intrusio[n] beneath the skin," and it poses no "threa[t] to the health or safety" of arrestees.

B

Respondent's identification as the rapist resulted in part through the operation of a national project to standardize collection and storage of DNA profiles. Authorized by Congress and supervised by the Federal Bureau of Investigation, the Combined DNA Index System (CODIS) connects DNA laboratories at the local, state, and national level. Since its authorization in 1994, the CODIS system has grown to include all [fifty] States and a number of federal agencies. CODIS collects DNA profiles provided by local laboratories taken from arrestees, convicted offenders, and forensic evidence found at crime scenes. To participate in CODIS, a local laboratory must sign a memorandum of understanding agreeing to adhere to quality standards and submit to audits to evaluate compliance with the federal standards for scientifically rigorous DNA testing.

One of the most significant aspects of CODIS is the standardization of the points of comparison in DNA analysis. The CODIS database is based on [thirteen] loci at which the STR alleles are noted and compared. These loci make possible extreme accuracy in matching individual samples, with a "random match probability of approximately [one in one hundred] trillion (assuming unrelated individuals)." The CODIS loci are from the non-protein coding junk regions of DNA, and "are not known to have any association with a genetic disease or any other genetic predisposition. Thus, the information in the database is only useful for human identity testing." STR information is recorded only as a "string of numbers"; and the DNA identification is accompanied only by information denoting the laboratory and the analyst responsible for the submission. In short, CODIS sets uniform national standards for DNA matching and then facilitates connections between local law enforcement agencies who can share more specific information about matched STR profiles.

All [fifty] States require the collection of DNA from felony convicts, and respondent does not dispute the validity of that practice. Twenty-eight States and the Federal Government have adopted laws similar to the Maryland Act authorizing the collection of DNA from some or all arrestees. Although those statutes vary in their particulars, such as what charges require a DNA sample, their similarity means that this case implicates more than the specific Maryland law. At issue is a standard, expanding technology already in widespread use throughout the Nation.

III

A

Although the DNA swab procedure used here presents a question the Court has not yet addressed, the framework for deciding the issue is well established. The Fourth Amendment, binding on the States by the Fourteenth Amendment, provides that "[t]he right of the people to be secure in their persons, houses, papers, and effects, against unreasonable searches and seizures, shall not be violated." It can be agreed that using a buccal swab on the inner tissues of a person's cheek in order to obtain DNA samples is a search. Virtually any "intrusio[n] into the human body," will work an invasion of "'cherished personal security' that is subject to constitutional scrutiny." The Court has applied the Fourth Amendment to police efforts to draw blood, scraping an arrestee's fingernails to obtain trace evidence, and even to "a breathalyzer test, which generally requires the production of alveolar or 'deep lung' breath for chemical analysis."

A buccal swab is a far more gentle process than a venipuncture to draw blood. It involves but a light touch on the inside of the cheek; and although it can be deemed a search within the body of the arrestee, it requires no "surgical intrusions beneath the skin." The fact than an intrusion is negligible is of central relevance to determining reasonableness, although it is still a search as the law defines that term.

B

To say that the Fourth Amendment applies here is the beginning point, not the end of the analysis. "[T]he Fourth Amendment's proper function is to constrain, not against all intrusions as such, but against intrusions which are not justified in the circumstances, or which are made in an improper manner." "As the text of the Fourth Amendment indicates, the ultimate measure of the constitutionality of a governmental search is 'reasonableness.'" In giving content to the inquiry whether an intrusion is reasonable, the Court has preferred "some quantum of individualized suspicion . . . [as] a prerequisite to a constitutional search or seizure. But the Fourth Amendment imposes no irreducible requirement of such suspicion."

In some circumstances, such as "[w]hen faced with special law enforcement needs, diminished expectations of privacy, minimal intrusions, or the like, the Court has found that certain general, or individual, circumstances may render a warrantless search or seizure reasonable." Those circumstances diminish the need for a warrant, either because "the public interest is such that neither a warrant nor probable cause is required," or because an individual is already on notice, for instance because of his employment, or the conditions of his release from government custody, that some reasonable police intrusion on his privacy is to be expected. The need for a warrant is perhaps least when the search involves no discretion that could properly be limited by the "interpo[lation of] a neutral magistrate between the citizen and the law enforcement officer."

The instant case can be addressed with this background. The Maryland DNA Collection Act provides that, in order to obtain a DNA sample, all arrestees charged with serious crimes must furnish the sample on a buccal swab applied, as noted, to the inside of the cheeks. The arrestee is already in valid police custody for a serious offense supported by probable cause. The DNA collection is not subject to the judgment of officers whose perspective might be "colored by their primary involvement in 'the often competitive enterprise of ferreting out crime.'" As noted by this Court in a different but still instructive context involving blood testing, "[b]oth the circumstances justifying toxicological testing and the permissible limits of such intrusions are defined narrowly and specifically in the regulations that authorize them.... Indeed, in light of the standardized nature of the tests and the minimal discretion vested in those charged with administering the program, there are virtually no facts for a neutral magistrate to evaluate." Here, the search effected by the buccal swab of respondent falls within the category of cases this Court has analyzed by reference to the proposition that the "touchstone of the Fourth Amendment is reasonableness, not individualized suspicion."

Even if a warrant is not required, a search is not beyond Fourth Amendment scrutiny; for it must be reasonable in its scope and manner of execution. Urgent government interests are not a license for indiscriminate police behavior. To say that no warrant is required is merely to acknowledge that "rather than employing a *per se* rule of unreasonableness, we balance the privacy-related and law enforcement-related concerns to determine if the intrusion was reasonable." This application of "traditional standards of reasonableness" requires a court to weigh "the promotion of legitimate governmental interests" against "the degree to which [the search] intrudes upon an individual's privacy." An assessment of reasonableness to determine the lawfulness of requiring this class of arrestees to provide a DNA sample is central to the instant case.

IV

The legitimate government interest served by the Maryland DNA Collection Act is one that is well established: the need for law enforcement officers in a safe and accurate way to process and identify the persons and possessions they must take into custody. It is beyond dispute that "probable cause provides legal justification for arresting a person suspected of crime, and for a brief period of detention to take the administrative steps incident to arrest." Also uncontested is the "right on the part of the Government, always recognized under English and American law, to search the person of the accused when legally arrested." "The validity of the search of a person incident to a lawful arrest has been regarded as settled from its first enunciation, and has remained virtually unchallenged." Even in that context, the Court has been clear that individual suspicion is not necessary, because "[t]he constitutionality of a search incident to an arrest does not depend on whether there is any indication that the person arrested possesses weapons or evidence. The fact of a lawful arrest, standing alone, authorizes a search."

The "routine administrative procedure[s] at a police station house incident to booking and jailing the suspect" derive from different origins and have different constitutional justifications than, say, the search of a place, for the search of a place not incident to an arrest depends on the "fair probability that contraband or evidence of a crime will be found in a particular place." The interests are further different when an individual is formally processed into police custody. Then "the law is in the act of subjecting the body of the accused to its physical dominion." When probable cause exists to remove an individual from the normal channels of society and hold him in legal custody, DNA identification plays a critical role in serving those interests.

First, "[i]n every criminal case, it is known and must be known who has been arrested and who is being tried." An individual's identity is more than just his name or Social Security number, and the government's interest in identification goes beyond ensuring that the proper name is typed on the indictment. Identity has never been considered limited to the name on the arrestee's birth certificate. In fact, a name is of little value compared to the real interest in identification at stake when an individual is brought into custody. "It is a well recognized aspect of criminal conduct that the perpetrator will take unusual steps to conceal not only his conduct, but also his identity. Disguises used while committing a crime may be supplemented or replaced by changed names, and even changed physical features." An "arrestee may be carrying a false ID or lie about his identity," and "criminal history records . . . can be inaccurate or incomplete."

A suspect's criminal history is a critical part of his identity that officers should know when processing him for detention. It is a common occurrence that "[p]eople detained for minor offenses can turn out to be the most devious and dangerous criminals. Hours after the Oklahoma City bombing, Timothy McVeigh was stopped by a state trooper who noticed he was driving without a license plate. Police stopped serial killer Joel Rifkin for the same reason. One of the terrorists involved in the September 11 attacks was stopped and ticketed for speeding just two days before hijacking Flight 93." Police already seek this crucial identifying information. They use routine and accepted means as varied as comparing the suspect's booking photograph to sketch artists' depictions of persons of interest, showing his mugshot to potential witnesses, and of course making a computerized comparison of the arrestee's fingerprints against electronic databases of known criminals and unsolved crimes. In this respect the only difference between DNA analysis and the accepted use of fingerprint databases is the unparalleled accuracy DNA provides.

The task of identification necessarily entails searching public and police records based on the identifying information provided by the arrestee to see what is already known about him. The DNA collected from arrestees is an irrefutable identification of the person from whom it was taken. Like a fingerprint, the [thirteen] CODIS loci are not themselves evidence of any particular crime, in the way that a drug test can by itself be evidence of illegal narcotics use. A DNA profile is useful to the police because it gives them a form of identification to search the records already in their valid possession. In this respect the use of DNA for identification is no different than matching an arrestee's face to a wanted poster of a previously unidentified suspect; or matching tattoos to known gang symbols to reveal a criminal affiliation; or matching the arrestee's fingerprints to those recovered from a crime scene. DNA is another metric of identification used to connect the arrestee with his or her public persona, as reflected in records of his or her actions that are available to the police. Those records may be linked to the arrestee by a variety of relevant forms of identification, including name, alias, date and time of previous convictions and the name then used, photograph, Social Security number, or CODIS profile. These data, found in official records, are checked as a routine matter to produce a more comprehensive record of the suspect's complete identity. Finding occurrences of the arrestee's CODIS profile in outstanding cases is consistent with this common practice. It uses a different form of identification than a name or fingerprint, but its function is the same.

Second, law enforcement officers bear a responsibility for ensuring that the custody of an arrestee does not create inordinate "risks for facility staff, for the existing detainee population, and for a new detainee." DNA identification can provide untainted information to those charged with detaining suspects and detaining the property of any felon. For these purposes officers must know the type of person whom they are detaining, and DNA allows them to make critical choices about how to proceed.

"Knowledge of identity may inform an officer that a suspect is wanted for another offense, or has a record of violence or mental disorder. On the other hand, knowing identity may help clear a suspect and allow the police to concentrate their efforts elsewhere. Identity may prove particularly important in [certain cases, such as] where the police are investigating what appears to be a domestic assault. Officers called to investigate domestic disputes need to know whom they are dealing with in order to assess the situation, the threat to their own safety, and possible danger to the potential victim."

Recognizing that a name alone cannot address this interest in identity, the Court has approved, for example, "a visual inspection for certain tattoos and other signs of gang affiliation as part of the intake process," because "[t]he identification and isolation of gang members before they are admitted protects everyone."

Third, looking forward to future stages of criminal prosecution, "the Government has a substantial interest in ensuring that persons accused of crimes are available for trials." A person who is arrested for one offense but knows that he has yet to answer for some past crime may be more inclined to flee the instant charges, lest continued contact with the criminal justice system expose one or more other serious offenses. For example, a defendant who had committed a prior sexual assault might be inclined to flee on a burglary charge, knowing that in every State a DNA sample would be taken from him after his conviction on the burglary charge that would tie him to the more serious charge of rape. In addition to subverting the administration of justice with respect to the crime of arrest, this ties back to the interest in safety; for a detainee who absconds from custody presents a risk to law enforcement officers, other detainees, victims of previous crimes, witnesses, and society at large.

Fourth, an arrestee's past conduct is essential to an assessment of the danger he poses to the public, and this will inform a court's determination whether the individual should be released on bail. "The government's interest in preventing crime by arrestees is both legitimate and compelling." DNA identification of a suspect in a violent crime provides critical information to the police and judicial officials in making a determination of the arrestee's future dangerousness. This inquiry always has entailed some scrutiny beyond the name on the defendant's driver's license. For example, Maryland law requires a judge to take into account not only "the nature and circumstances of the offense charged" but also "the defendant's family ties, employment status and history, financial resources, reputation, character and mental condition, length of residence in the community." Knowing that the defendant is wanted for a previous violent crime based on DNA identification is especially probative of the court's consideration of "the danger of the defendant to the alleged victim, another person, or the community."

This interest is not speculative. In considering laws to require collecting DNA from arrestees, government agencies around the Nation found evidence of numerous cases in which felony arrestees would have been identified as violent through DNA identification matching them to previous crimes but who later committed additional crimes because such identification was not used to detain them.

Present capabilities make it possible to complete a DNA identification that provides information essential to determining whether a detained suspect can be released pending trial. Regardless of when the initial bail decision is made, release is not appropriate until a further determination is made as to the person's identity in the sense not only of what his birth certificate states but also what other records and data disclose to give that identity more meaning in the whole context of who the person really is. And even when release is permitted, the background identity of the suspect is necessary for determining what conditions must be met before release is allowed. If release is authorized, it may take time for the conditions to be met, and so the time before actual release can be substantial. For example, in the federal system, defendants released conditionally are detained on average for 112 days; those released on unsecured bond for [thirty-seven] days; on personal recognizance for [thirty-six] days; and on other financial conditions for [twenty-seven] days. During this entire period, additional and supplemental data establishing more about the person's identity and background can provide critical information relevant to the conditions of release and whether to revisit an initial release determination. The facts of this case are illustrative. Though the record is not clear, if some thought were being given to releasing the respondent on bail on the gun charge, a release that would take weeks or months in any event, when the DNA report linked him to the prior rape, it would be relevant to the conditions of his release. The same would be true with a supplemental fingerprint report.

Even if an arrestee is released on bail, development of DNA identification revealing the defendant's unknown violent past can and should lead to the revocation of his conditional release. Pretrial release of a person charged with a dangerous crime is a most serious responsibility. It is reasonable in all respects for the State to use an accepted database to determine if an arrestee is the object of suspicion in other serious crimes, suspicion that may provide a strong incentive for the arrestee to escape and flee.

Finally, in the interests of justice, the identification of an arrestee as the perpetrator of some heinous crime may have the salutary effect of freeing a person wrongfully imprisoned for the same offense. "[P]rompt [DNA] testing . . . would speed up apprehension of criminals before they commit additional crimes, and prevent the grotesque detention of . . . innocent people."

Because proper processing of arrestees is so important and has consequences for every stage of the criminal process, the Court has recognized that the "governmental interests underlying a station-house search of the arrestee's person and possessions may in some circumstances be even greater than those supporting a search immediately following arrest." Thus, the Court has been reluctant to circumscribe the authority of the police to conduct reasonable booking searches. For example, "[t]he standards traditionally governing a search incident to lawful arrest are not . . . commuted to the stricter *Terry* standards." Nor are these interests in identification served only by a search of the arrestee himself. "[I]nspection of an arrestee's personal property may assist the police in ascertaining or verifying his identity."

. . .

B

DNA identification represents an important advance in the techniques used by law enforcement to serve legitimate police concerns for as long as there have been arrests, concerns the courts have acknowledged and approved for more than a century. Law enforcement agencies routinely have used scientific advancements in their standard procedures for the identification of arrestees. "Police had been using photography to capture the faces of criminals almost since its invention." Courts did not dispute that practice, concluding that a "sheriff in making an arrest for a felony on a warrant has the right to exercise a discretion ..., [if] he should deem it necessary to the safe-keeping of a prisoner, and to prevent his escape, or to enable him the more readily to retake the prisoner if he should escape, to take his photograph." By the time that it had become "the daily practice of the police officers and detectives of crime to use photographic pictures for the discovery and identification of criminals," the courts likewise had come to the conclusion that "it would be [a] matter of regret to have its use unduly restricted upon any fanciful theory or constitutional privilege."

Beginning in 1887, some police adopted more exacting means to identify arrestees, using the system of precise physical measurements pioneered by the French anthropologist Alphonse Bertillon. Bertillon identification consisted of 10 measurements of the arrestee's body, along with a "scientific analysis of the features of the face and an exact anatomical localization of the various scars, marks, &c., of the body." . . .

Perhaps the most direct historical analogue to the DNA technology used to identify respondent is the familiar practice of fingerprinting arrestees. From the advent of this technique, courts had no trouble determining that fingerprinting was a natural part of "the administrative steps incident to arrest." In the seminal case of *United*

States v. Kelly, 55 F.2d 67 (2nd Cir. 1932), Judge Augustus Hand wrote that routine fingerprinting did not violate the Fourth Amendment precisely because it fit within the accepted means of processing an arrestee into custody:

"Finger printing seems to be no more than an extension of methods of identification long used in dealing with persons under arrest for real or supposed violations of the criminal laws. It is known to be a very certain means devised by modern science to reach the desired end, and has become especially important in a time when increased population and vast aggregations of people in urban centers have rendered the notoriety of the individual in the community no longer a ready means of identification.

. . .

"We find no ground in reason or authority for interfering with a method of identifying persons charged with crime which has now become widely known and frequently practiced."

By the middle of the 20th century, it was considered "elementary that a person in lawful custody may be required to submit to photographing and fingerprinting as part of routine identification processes."

DNA identification is an advanced technique superior to fingerprinting in many ways, so much so that to insist on fingerprints as the norm would make little sense to either the forensic expert or a layperson. The additional intrusion upon the arrestee's privacy beyond that associated with fingerprinting is not significant, and DNA is a markedly more accurate form of identifying arrestees. A suspect who has changed his facial features to evade photographic identification or even one who has undertaken the more arduous task of altering his fingerprints cannot escape the revealing power of his DNA.

. . .

In sum, there can be little reason to question "the legitimate interest of the government in knowing for an absolute certainty the identity of the person arrested, in knowing whether he is wanted elsewhere, and in ensuring his identification in the event he flees prosecution." To that end, courts have confirmed that the Fourth Amendment allows police to take certain routine "administrative steps incident to arrest—*i.e.*, . . . book[ing], photograph[ing], and fingerprint[ing]." DNA identification of arrestees, of the type approved by the Maryland statute here at issue, is "no more than an extension of methods of identification long used in dealing with persons under arrest." In the balance of reasonableness required by the Fourth Amendment, therefore, the Court must give great weight both to the significant government interest at stake in the identification of arrestees and to the unmatched potential of DNA identification to serve that interest.

V

A

By comparison to this substantial government interest and the unique effectiveness of DNA identification, the intrusion of a cheek swab to obtain a DNA sample is a minimal one. . . .

The expectations of privacy of an individual taken into police custody "necessarily [are] of a diminished scope." . . . In this critical respect, the search here at issue differs from the sort of programmatic searches of either the public at large or a particular class of regulated but otherwise law-abiding citizens that the Court has previously labeled as "special needs" searches. When the police stop a motorist at a checkpoint, or test a political candidate for illegal narcotics, they intrude upon substantial expectations of privacy. So the Court has insisted on some purpose other than "to detect evidence of ordinary criminal wrongdoing" to justify these searches in the absence of individualized suspicion. Once an individual has been arrested on probable cause for a dangerous offense that may require detention before trial, however, his or her expectations of privacy and freedom from police scrutiny are reduced. DNA identification like that at issue here thus does not require consideration of any unique needs that would be required to justify searching the average citizen. The special needs cases, though in full accord with the result reached here, do not have a direct bearing on the issues presented in this case, because unlike the search of a citizen who has not been suspected of a wrong, a detainee has a reduced expectation of privacy.

The reasonableness inquiry here considers two other circumstances in which the Court has held that particularized suspicion is not categorically required: "diminished expectations of privacy [and] minimal intrusions." This is not to suggest that any search is acceptable solely because a person is in custody. Some searches, such as invasive surgery, or a search of the arrestee's home, involve either greater intrusions or higher expectations of privacy than are present in this case. In those situations, when the Court must "balance the privacy-related and law enforcement-related concerns to determine if the intrusion was reasonable," the privacy-related concerns are weighty enough that the search may require a warrant, notwithstanding the diminished expectations of privacy of the arrestee.

Here, by contrast to the approved standard procedures incident to any arrest detailed above, a buccal swab involves an even more brief and still minimal intrusion. A gentle rub along the inside of the cheek does not break the skin, and it "involves virtually no risk, trauma, or pain." "A crucial factor in analyzing the magnitude of the intrusion . . . is the extent to which the procedure may threaten the safety or health of the individual," and nothing suggests that a buccal swab poses any physical danger whatsoever. A brief intrusion of an arrestee's person is subject to the Fourth Amendment, but a swab of this nature does not increase the indignity already attendant to normal incidents of arrest.

. . .

In light of the context of a valid arrest supported by probable cause respondent's expectations of privacy were not offended by the minor intrusion of a brief swab of his cheeks. By contrast, that same context of arrest gives rise to significant state interests in identifying respondent not only so that the proper name can be attached to his charges but also so that the criminal justice system can make informed decisions concerning pretrial custody. Upon these considerations the Court concludes that DNA identification of arrestees is a reasonable search that can be considered part of a routine booking procedure. When officers make an arrest supported by probable cause to hold for a serious offense and they bring the suspect to the station to be detained in custody, taking and analyzing a cheek swab of the arrestee's DNA is, like fingerprinting and photographing, a legitimate police booking procedure that is reasonable under the Fourth Amendment.

The judgment of the Court of Appeals of Maryland is reversed.

It is so ordered.

Justice SCALIA, with whom Justice GINSBURG, Justice SOTOMAYOR, and Justice KAGAN join, dissenting.

The Fourth Amendment forbids searching a person for evidence of a crime when there is no basis for believing the person is guilty of the crime or is in possession of incriminating evidence. That prohibition is categorical and without exception; it lies at the very heart of the Fourth Amendment. Whenever this Court has allowed a suspicionless search, it has insisted upon a justifying motive apart from the investigation of crime.

It is obvious that no such noninvestigative motive exists in this case. The Court's assertion that DNA is being taken, not to solve crimes, but to *identify* those in the State's custody, taxes the credulity of the credulous. And the Court's comparison of Maryland's DNA searches to other techniques, such as fingerprinting, can seem apt only to those who know no more than today's opinion has chosen to tell them about how those DNA searches actually work.

I

A

. . .

Although there is a "closely guarded category of constitutionally permissible suspicionless searches," that has never included searches designed to serve "the normal need for law enforcement." Even the common name for suspicionless searches—"special needs" searches—itself reflects that they must be justified, *always,* by concerns "other than crime detection." We have approved random drug tests of railroad employees, yes—but only because the Government's need to "regulat[e] the conduct of railroad employees to ensure safety" is distinct from "normal law enforcement." So too we have approved suspicionless searches in public schools—but only because there the government acts in furtherance of its "responsibilities . . . as guardian and tutor of children entrusted to its care."

So while the Court is correct to note that there are instances in which we have permitted searches without individualized suspicion, "[i]n none of these cases . . . did we indicate approval of a [search] whose primary purpose was to detect evidence of ordinary criminal wrongdoing." That limitation is crucial. It is only when a governmental purpose aside from crime-solving is at stake that we engage in the free-form "reasonableness" inquiry that the Court indulges at length today. To put it another way, both the legitimacy of the Court's method and the correctness of its outcome hinge entirely on the truth of a single proposition: that the primary purpose of these DNA searches is something other than simply discovering evidence of criminal wrongdoing. As I detail below, that proposition is wrong.

B

The Court alludes at several points of the fact that King was an arrestee, and arrestees may be validly searched incident to their arrest. But the Court does not really *rest* on this principle, and for good reason: The objects of a search incident to arrest must be either (1) weapons or evidence that might easily be destroyed, or (2) evidence relevant to the crime of arrest. Neither is the object of the search at issue here.

The Court hastens to clarify that it does not mean to approve invasive surgery on arrestees or warrantless searches of their homes.. That the Court feels the need to disclaim these consequences is as damning a criticism of its suspicionless-search regime as any I can muster. And the Court's attempt to distinguish those hypothetical searches from this real one is unconvincing. We are told that the "privacy-related concerns" in the search of a home "are weighty enough that the search may require a warrant, notwithstanding the diminished expectations of privacy of the arrestee." But why are the "privacy-related concerns" not also "weighty" when an intrusion into the *body* is at stake? (The Fourth Amendment lists "persons" *first* among the entities protected against unreasonable searches and seizures.) And could the police engage, without any suspicion of wrongdoing, in a "brief and . . . minimal" intrusion into the home of an arrestee—perhaps just peeking around the curtilage a bit? Obviously not.

At any rate, all this discussion is beside the point. No matter the degree of invasiveness, suspicionless searches are *never* allowed if their principal end is ordinary crime-solving. A search incident to arrest either serves other ends (such as officer safety, in a search for weapons) or is not suspicionless (as when there is reason to believe the arrestee possesses evidence relevant to the crime of arrest).

Sensing (correctly) that it needs more, the Court elaborates at length the ways that the search here served the special purpose of "identifying" King. But that seems to me quite wrong—unless what one means by "identifying" someone is "searching for evidence that he has committed crimes unrelated to the crime of his arrest." At points the Court does appear to use "identifying" in that peculiar sense—claiming, for example, that knowing "an arrestee's past conduct is essential to an assessment of the danger he poses." If identifying someone means finding out what unsolved crimes he has committed, then identification is indistinguishable from the ordinary law-enforcement aims that have never been thought to justify a suspicionless search. Searching every lawfully stopped car, for example, might turn up information about unsolved crimes the driver had committed, but no one would say that such a search was aimed at "identifying" him, and no court would hold such a search lawful. I will therefore assume that the Court means that the DNA search at issue here was useful to "identify" King in the normal sense of that word—in the sense that would identify the author of Introduction to the Principles of Morals and Legislation as Jeremy Bentham.

1

The portion of the Court's opinion that explains the identification rationale is strangely silent on the actual workings of the DNA search at issue here. To know those facts is to be instantly disabused of the notion that what happened had anything to do with identifying King.

King was arrested on April 10, 2009, on charges unrelated to the case before us. That same day, April 10, the police searched him and seized the DNA evidence at issue here. What happened next? Reading the Court's opinion, particularly its insistence that the search was necessary to know "who [had] been arrested," one might guess that King's DNA was swiftly processed and his identity thereby confirmed—perhaps against some master database of known DNA profiles, as is done for fingerprints. After all, was not the suspicionless search here crucial to avoid "inordinate risks for facility staff" or to "existing detainee population"? Surely, then—*surely*—the State of Maryland got cracking on those grave risks immediately, by rushing to identify King with his DNA as soon as possible.

Nothing could be further from the truth. Maryland officials did not even begin the process of testing King's DNA that day. Or, actually, the next day. Or the day after that. And that was for a simple reason: Maryland law forbids them to do so. A "DNA sample collected from an individual charged with a crime . . . *may not* be tested or placed in the statewide DNA data base system prior to the first scheduled arraignment date." And King's first appearance in court was not until three days after his arrest. (I suspect, though, that they did not wait three days to ask his name or take his fingerprints.)

This places in a rather different light the Court's solemn declaration that the search here was necessary so that King could be identified at "every stage of the criminal process." I hope that the Maryland officials who read the Court's opinion do not take it seriously. Acting on the Court's misperception of Maryland law could lead to jail time. . . . Does the Court really believe that Maryland did not know whom it was arraigning? The Court's response is to imagine that release on bail could take so long that the DNA results are returned in time, or perhaps that bail could be revoked if the DNA test turned up incriminating information. That is no answer at all. If the purpose of this Act is to assess "whether [King] should be released on bail," why would it *possibly* forbid the DNA testing process to *begin* until King was arraigned? Why would Maryland resign itself to simply hoping that the bail decision will drag out long enough that the "identification" can succeed before the arrestee is released? The truth, known to Maryland and increasingly to the reader: this search had nothing to do with establishing King's identity.

It gets worse. King's DNA sample was not received by the Maryland State Police's Forensic Sciences Division until April 23, 2009—two weeks after his arrest. It sat in that office, ripening in a storage area, until the custodians got around to mailing it to a lab for testing on June 25, 2009—two months after it was received, and nearly *three* since King's arrest. After it was mailed, the data from the lab tests were not available for several more weeks, until July 13, 2009, which is when the test results were entered into Maryland's DNA database, *together with information identifying the person from whom the sample was taken*. Meanwhile, bail had been set, King had engaged in discovery, and he had requested a speedy trial—presumably not a trial of John Doe. It was not until August 4, 2009—four months after King's arrest—that the forwarded sample transmitted (*without* identifying information) from the Maryland DNA database to the Federal Bureau of Investigation's national database was matched with a sample taken from the scene of an unrelated crime years earlier.

A more specific description of exactly what happened at this point illustrates why, by definition, King could not have been *identified* by this match. The FBI's DNA database (known as CODIS) consists of two distinct collections. One of them, the one to which King's DNA was submitted, consists of DNA samples taken from known convicts or arrestees. I will refer to this as the "Convict and Arrestee Collection." The other collection consists of samples taken from crime scenes; I will refer to this as the "Unsolved Crimes Collection." The Convict and Arrestee Collection stores "no names or other personal identifiers of the offenders, arrestees, or detainees." Rather, it contains only the DNA profile itself, the name of the agency that submitted it, the laboratory personnel who analyzed it, and an identification number for the specimen. This is because the submitting state laboratories are expected *already* to know the identities of the convicts and arrestees from whom samples are taken. (And, of course, they do.)

Moreover, the CODIS system works by checking to see whether any of the samples in the Unsolved Crimes Collection match any of the samples in the Convict and Arrestee Collection. That is sensible, if what one wants to do is solve those cold cases, but note what it requires: that the identity of the people whose DNA has been entered in the Convict and Arrestee Collection *already be known*. If one wanted to identify someone in custody using his DNA, the logical thing to do would be to compare that DNA against the Convict and Arrestee Collection: to search, in other words, the collection that could be used (by checking back with the submitting state agency) to identify people, rather than the collection of evidence from unsolved crimes, whose perpetrators are by definition unknown. But that is not what was done. And that is because this search had nothing to do with identification.

In fact, if anything was "identified" at the moment that the DNA database returned a match, it was not King—his identity was already known. (The docket for the original criminal charges lists his full name, his race, his sex, his height, his weight, his date of birth, and his address.) Rather, what the August 4 match "identified" was *the previously-taken sample from the earlier crime.* That sample was genuinely mysterious to Maryland; the State knew that it had probably been left by the victim's attacker, but nothing else. King was not identified by his association with the sample; rather, the sample was identified by its association with King. The Court effectively destroys its own "identification" theory when it acknowledges that the object of this search was "to see what [was] already known about [King]." King was who he was, and volumes of his biography could not make him any more or any less King. No minimally competent speaker of English would say, upon noticing a known arrestee's similarity "to a wanted poster of a previously unidentified suspect," that the *arrestee* had thereby been identified. It was the previously unidentified suspect who had been identified—just as, here, it was the previously unidentified rapist.

. . .

So, to review: DNA testing does not even begin until after arraignment and bail decisions are already made. The samples sit in storage for months, and take weeks to test. When they are tested, they are checked against the Unsolved Crimes Collection—rather than the Convict and Arrestee Collection, which could be used to identify them. The Act forbids the Court's purpose (identification), but prescribes as its purpose what our suspicionless-search cases forbid ("official investigation into a crime"). Against all of that, it is safe to say that if the Court's identification theory is not wrong, there is no such thing as error.

II

The Court also attempts to bolster its identification theory with a series of inapposite analogies.

Is not taking DNA samples the same, asks the Court, as taking a person's photograph? No—because that is not a Fourth Amendment search at all. It does not involve a physical intrusion onto the person, and we have never held that merely taking a person's photograph invades any recognized "expectation of privacy." Thus, it is unsurprising that the cases the Court cites as authorizing photo-taking do not even mention the Fourth Amendment.

But is not the practice of DNA searches, the Court asks, the same as taking "Bertillon" measurements—noting an arrestee's height, shoe size, and so on, on the back of a photograph? No, because that system was not, in the ordinary case, used to solve unsolved crimes. It is possible, I suppose, to imagine situations in which such measurements might be useful to generate leads. (If witnesses described a very tall burglar, all the "tall man" cards could then be pulled.) But the obvious primary purpose of such measurements, as the Court's description of them makes clear, was to verify that, for example, the person arrested today is the same person that was arrested a year ago. Which is to say, Bertillon measurements were *actually* used as a system of identification, and drew their primary usefulness from that task.

It is on the fingerprinting of arrestees, however, that the Court relies most heavily. The Court does not actually say whether it believes that taking a person's fingerprints is a Fourth Amendment search, and our cases provide no ready answer to that question. Even assuming so, however, law enforcement's post-arrest use of fingerprints could not be more different from its post-arrest use of DNA. Fingerprints of arrestees are taken primarily to identify them (though that process sometimes solves crimes); the DNA of arrestees is taken to solve crimes (and nothing else).

. . .

Today, it can fairly be said that fingerprints really are used to identify people—so well, in fact, that there would be no need for the expense of a separate, wholly redundant DNA confirmation of the same information. What DNA adds—what makes it a valuable weapon in the law-enforcement arsenal—is the ability to solve unsolved crimes, by matching old crime-scene evidence against the profiles of people whose identities are already known. That is what was going on when King's DNA was taken, and we should not disguise the fact. Solving unsolved crimes is a noble objective, but it occupies a lower place in the American pantheon of noble objectives than the protection of our people from suspicionless law-enforcement searches. The Fourth Amendment must prevail.

. . .

The Court disguises the vast (and scary) scope of its holding by promising a limitation it cannot deliver. The Court repeatedly says that DNA testing, and entry into a national DNA registry, will not befall thee and me, dear reader, but only those arrested for "serious offense[s]." I cannot imagine what principle could possibly justify this limitation, and the Court does not attempt to suggest any. If one believes that DNA will "identify" someone arrested for assault, he must believe that it will "identify" someone arrested for a traffic offense. This Court does not base its judgments on senseless distinctions. At the end of the day, *logic will out.* When there comes before us the taking of DNA from an arrestee for a traffic violation, the Court will predictably (and quite rightly) say, "We can find no significant difference between this case and *King*." Make no mistake about it: As an entirely predictable consequence of today's decision, your DNA can be taken and entered into a national DNA database if you are ever arrested, rightly or wrongly, and for whatever reason.

The most regrettable aspect of the suspicionless search that occurred here is that it proved to be quite unnecessary. All parties concede that it would have been entirely permissible, as far as the Fourth Amendment is concerned, for Maryland to take a sample of King's DNA as a consequence of his conviction for second-degree assault. So the ironic result of the Court's error is this: The only arrestees to whom the outcome here will ever make a difference are those who *have been acquitted* of the crime of arrest (so that their DNA could not have been taken upon conviction). In other words, this

Act manages to burden uniquely the sole group for whom the Fourth Amendment's protections ought to be most jealously guarded: people who are innocent of the State's accusations.

Today's judgment will, to be sure, have the beneficial effect of solving more crimes; then again, so would the taking of DNA samples from anyone who flies on an airplane (surely the Transportation Security Administration needs to know the "identity" of the flying public), applies for a driver's license, or attends a public school. Perhaps the construction of such a genetic panopticon is wise. But I doubt that the proud men who wrote the charter of our liberties would have been so eager to open their mouths for royal inspection.

. . .

19

Reasonable Suspicion and *Terry*'s "Stop and Frisk"

Key Concepts

- Reasonable Suspicion
- Investigatory Stop
- Protective Frisk

A. Introduction and Policy. A police officer on the street may see something that leads her to believe an individual is engaged in criminal behavior. As you learned earlier in **Chapter 9**, if the strength of the officer's belief rises to the level of probable cause, the officer may lawfully arrest the target of her suspicion. But what if the officer sees something that doesn't quite rise to the level of probable cause but nonetheless suggests that criminal activity is afoot? In such a case, must the officer allow the suspect to walk away? The simple answer is "No." Though lacking probable cause, an officer may temporarily detain a target for further investigation if what the officer sees establishes reasonable suspicion. This sort of brief investigatory stop has come to be known as a "***Terry* stop**"—so named for the case that first authorized it.[1]

During a *Terry* stop, the detaining officer is permitted to ensure her safety by conducting a limited search of the detained person. If the officer has an objectively reasonable belief that the person she is dealing with might be armed, the officer may pat down the target's outer clothing to look for weapons. Not surprisingly, this superficial examination has come to be known as a "***Terry* frisk.**"

Reasonable suspicion is an intermediate level of suspicion that amounts to something less than probable cause. In keeping with its less stringent demands, reasonable suspicion justifies police seizures that are less than full-blown arrests. Like arrests, however, stops justified by reasonable suspicion are governed by the mandates of the Fourth Amendment because they are more than voluntary encounters (from which the public is free to walk away).

The Court created this intermediate level of suspicion for several reasons. First, the Court was concerned that not doing so would "isolate from constitutional scrutiny the initial stages of the contact between the policeman and the citizen."[2] In other words, the Court realized that many of the encounters between police

---

1 Terry v. Ohio, 392 U.S. 1 (1968).

2 Id.

officers and citizens was occurring below the radar, unregulated by rules and unmonitored by the courts. Second, the Court determined that the government had significant interests in effective crime prevention and detection that were furthered by allowing investigatory stops and frisks. Finally, with particular regard for the frisk component of the intrusion, the Court found officer safety to be of paramount importance.

As a matter of policy, the intermediate level of suspicion recognized in *Terry* has countless supporters (including the current composition of the Court). For *Terry*'s adherents, the doctrine affords law enforcement the discretion needed on the streets to effectively combat crime. Indeed, the Court unanimously affirmed its commitment to the doctrine only recently.[3] However, the *Terry* doctrine also faces mounting critics who contend it gives law enforcement enormous discretion which is too often deployed in ways that unjustifiably impact racial minorities and the poor.[4]

B. The Law. In **Chapter 9**, we examined the threshold question of how to evaluate whether a stop was made. If a stop was not made, the encounter will be deemed consensual and the Fourth Amendment will not apply. If a stop was made, the question becomes whether the stop was constitutional. To focus more directly on the question of *Terry*'s limits, we do not discuss the threshold question of whether a stop occurred in most of the examples below. However, you should not make the same leap in practice. Anytime you are faced with determining the constitutionality of a police/citizen interaction, go through three steps:

1. Did a stop occur?
2. What level of suspicion existed?
3. What degree of intrusion did the level of suspicion justify?

Prior to 1968, police stops fell into just two categories. The first category was characterized as entirely consensual encounters that were unregulated by the Fourth Amendment. At the opposite end of the spectrum, the second category included full searches or seizures requiring a warrant or probable cause. In 1968, however, the Court determined that a break from this binary system was warranted. As the Court explained in the landmark case *Terry v. Ohio*,[5] an intermediate level of interaction that lay somewhere between the two poles was needed. This intermediate level would allow the police to act on suspicion amounting to less than probable cause, but also would limit the authorized intrusion commensurate with the reduced showing required. As the *Terry* Court explained, not creating an

[3] Arizona v. Johnson, 129 S.Ct. 781 (2009).

[4] See, e.g., Adams v. Williams, 407 U.S. 143 (1972) (Marshall, J., dissenting).

[5] Terry, 392 U.S. 1.

intermediate level would leave wholly ungoverned the early, face-to-face interactions with police that often precede actual arrests. So the *Terry* doctrine was born:

1. If a police officer has **reasonable suspicion** that a suspect is involved in criminal activity, she may briefly detain the suspect in order to confirm or dispel the suspicion. The reasonable suspicion must be supported **by specific and articulable facts**, and rational inferences from those facts.[6]

2. If a police officer has reason to believe she is dealing with an armed and dangerous individual, she is permitted to conduct a **reasonable search for weapons** in order to **ensure her own safety**.[7]

The two-part *Terry* doctrine permits police officers to briefly detain targets suspected of wrongdoing. This authority extends to targets who are reasonably suspected of criminal activity that is imminent or in-progress. The power to stop also extends to targets who are reasonably suspected of completed felonies. For the moment it is unclear whether the *Terry* right to stop extends further to cover suspicion for any past crime no matter how serious.[8]

The principles of *Terry* do not just authorize the brief detention of people. The Court has determined that *Terry* also permits the brief investigatory detention of personal effects, like luggage.[9]

The purpose of a *Terry* stop is to give police officers a chance to investigate further the basis of their suspicions. To justify a stop, the officer's belief must be more than a mere hunch or intuition; it must be based on "reasonable suspicion." As noted in the introduction, reasonable suspicion is a lower standard than probable cause. Though the Supreme Court has consistently declined to quantify either standard, many trial judges have suggested they find it useful to understand probable cause and reasonable suspicion in terms of numeric probabilities. For example, if probable cause is slightly less than a 50% likelihood the suspect is guilty of a crime, reasonable suspicion is somewhere around a 30% likelihood. Moreover, the officer's suspicion must be supported by "specific and articulable facts." Thus, when the police officer is called on to justify her stop in a suppression hearing, she must be able to list the specific details that gave rise to her suspicion. We will investigate the concept of "reasonable suspicion" further in the next section.

---

[6] Terry, 392 U.S. at 21.

[7] Terry, 392 U.S. at 27.

[8] United States v. Hensley, 469 U.S. 221, 229 (1985).

[9] United States v. Place, 462 U.S. 696 (1983).

In creating the intermediate level in interaction that it recognized in *Terry*, the Court acknowledged that it was deviating from the traditional warrant requirement. However, in justifying that departure, the Court commented:

> [W]e deal here with an entire rubric of police conduct . . . which historically has not been, and as a practical matter could not be, subjected to the warrant procedure. Instead, the conduct involved . . . must be tested by the Fourth Amendment's general proscription against unreasonable searches and seizures.

Accordingly, where a stop is justified only by reasonable suspicion, the question becomes whether the police conducted the stop in a reasonable manner under the circumstances. Reasonableness requires the balancing of the government's interests in investigating crime against the individual's right to be free from arbitrary intrusions by law enforcement.[10] To assist in striking the proper balance, the Court in cases since *Terry* has provided basic guidelines for assessing an investigatory stop's reasonableness. These guidelines require that *Terry* stops be limited in duration.[11] Consequently, police questioning may not stray significantly from the original purpose of the detention if such tangential inquiry significantly extends the duration of the stop. Stops also must be limited in geographic scope. For an investigatory stop to retain its constitutional nature, suspects may not involuntarily be moved great distances. And, though the police may frame their questions in a way designed to encourage answers, they may not lawfully compel a response.[12] Assuming probable cause does not develop during the stop based upon the additional information gathered, after a short time, the target must be allowed to leave.[13] As the Court has said, the detention must be conducted in a manner that is no more intrusive than is necessary to establish or dispel the officer's suspicions.[14]

In addition to authorizing the limited seizure just described, the *Terry* doctrine also authorizes a limited search of the target. The purpose of this limited search is officer safety. The right to conduct a *Terry* frisk does **not** automatically follow from the reasonable suspicion that gave rise to the stop. Rather, any frisk must be independently justified by legitimate concerns for officer safety:

> When an officer is justified in believing that the individual whose suspicious behavior he is investigating at close range is armed and pres-

---

[10] Brown v. Texas, 443 U.S. 47, 50 (1979).

[11] United States v. Place, 462 U.S. 696 (1983).

[12] Though the Fourth Amendment does not require a lawfully detained person to answer police questions during a *Terry* stop, state law—in the form of stop-and-identify statutes—may require that same person to identify themselves upon request. Hiibel v. Sixth Judicial Dist. Ct., 542 U.S. 177 (2004).

[13] Kolender v. Lawson, 461 U.S. 352, 364-65 (1983) (Brennan, J., concurring).

[14] Florida v. Royer, 460 U.S. 491 (1983).

> ently dangerous to the officer or to others, it would appear to be clearly unreasonable to deny the officer the power to take necessary measures to determine whether the person is in fact carrying a weapon and to neutralize the threat of physical harm.[15]

The *Terry* frisk also must be limited in scope to its protective purpose—that is, an officer is only permitted to conduct a superficial search for weapons, not a comprehensive search for contraband or other evidence of a crime. A *Terry* frisk that amounts to more than a superficial exploration for weapons will be treated as a search and subject to the more stringent probable cause, warrant, or warrant exception requirements. In terms of physical boundaries, a subject stopped on the street may have his outer clothing patted down. If the subject is stopped inside of a car, the physical reach of a *Terry* frisk will include the entire passenger compartment of a car, and any containers in it that might contain a weapon. If the target is stopped in a house, the reach of the frisk extends to any areas were a person might be lurking waiting to launch an attack.

C. Applying the Law. As noted, reasonableness is at the core of any stop-and-frisk analysis. Consequently, once a judge has established that a non-consensual stop occurred, she will next consider the level of justification the police officers possessed. The Court has provided some guidance to help determine whether particular facts amount to reasonable suspicion. That guidance is discussed below in Section 1.

Moving past the question of whether reasonable suspicion existed, a judge will next consider whether the officers conducted the stop or frisk in a manner that was consistent with the limited authority granted by the intermediate suspicion they possessed. While the Court has resisted articulating precisely when an investigatory stop moves beyond its appropriate boundaries and becomes an arrest, the Court has articulated a number of factors relevant to the inquiry. The Court has also addressed factors that affect the legitimacy of the frisk:

- The duration of the stop
- Changes in location of the stop
- The method of the frisk
- The physical area of the search

Each of these factors is discussed in detail in the sections below.

---

15 Terry, 392 U.S. at 25.

1. When Does a Police Officer Have "Reasonable Suspicion"? To establish reasonable suspicion, law enforcement must point to specific facts from which one can infer a person is engaged in criminal activity (for the stop), and is armed and dangerous (for the frisk). Mere hunches or inarticulate intuitions will not suffice. Likewise, an officer may not establish reasonable suspicion by recounting a conclusory assertion that "the target looked suspicious."[16] Facts that would seemingly incriminate large swathes of a community or that amount to nothing more than presence do not establish reasonable suspicion.[17] In the same vein, a target's refusal to listen or answer, without more, will not establish reasonable suspicion.[18]

In assessing whether reasonable suspicion existed, the subjective beliefs of the detaining officer are irrelevant. However, the officer's experience may be considered when assessing the reasonable inferences that may be drawn from the information known.

So what **can** establish reasonable suspicion? We know that information forming the basis of reasonable suspicion does not have to be as substantial or as reliable as the type of information required to establish probable cause. Indeed, the Court has acknowledged that information it accepted to establish reasonable suspicion, likely would not survive a probable cause challenge.[19]

When assessing the reasonableness of an officer's suspicion, it is rare that any singular factor, standing alone, will be sufficient. Rather, it is the collection of facts available to officers in each case that determine whether reasonable suspicion exists. For example, in one case, paying for a one-way airline ticket in cash, traveling and checking bags under an assumed name, and having an appearance and mannerisms that fit a drug courier profile were found collectively to establish reasonable suspicion.

Even though ignoring the police does not establish reasonable suspicion, **running** from the police can be an important factor contributing to reasonable suspicion:[20]

> **Example—*Illinois v. Wardlow*, 528 U.S. 119 (2000):** Officers Nolan and Harvey of the Chicago Police Department were in uniform driving through an area of town known for heavy narcotics trafficking. Officer Nolan spotted an individual named William "Sam" Wardlow standing next to a building holding an opaque bag. When Wardlow saw the officers, he immediately

[16] Brown, 443 U.S. at 52.

[17] United States v. Brignoni-Ponce, 422 U.S. 873 (1975); Brown, 443 U.S. at 52.

[18] Florida v. Royer, 460 U.S. 491, 498 (1983).

[19] Adams v. Williams, 407 U.S. 143, 147 (1972); see also Royer, 460 U.S. at 507.

[20] Illinois v. Wardlow, 528 U.S. 119 (2000).

fled. The officers gave chase and eventually caught him. In Officer Nolan's experience, "it was common for there to be weapons in the near vicinity of narcotics transactions," so Officer Nolan frisked Wardlow and felt a heavy, hard object shaped like a gun in Wardlow's bag. He retrieved the item and found a loaded .38 caliber handgun. Wardlow was arrested for unlawful possession of a firearm as a felon. He moved to suppress the handgun, arguing that the police did not have sufficient cause to chase him and seize him.

Analysis: The Supreme Court held that the police officers had reasonable suspicion to conduct a *Terry* stop of Wardlow.[21] The Court noted there were two factors that would not constitute reasonable suspicion if considered separately, but which were sufficient when taken together.

First, "an individual's presence in an area of expected criminal activity, standing alone, is not enough to support a reasonable, particularized suspicion that the person is committing a crime," but "officers are not required to ignore the relevant characteristics of a location in determining whether the circumstances are sufficiently suspicious to warrant further investigation."

Second, it is true that an individual who is approached by the police has the right to ignore the police and go about his business, but "unprovoked flight is simply not a mere refusal to cooperate. Flight, by its very nature, is not 'going about one's business;' in fact, it is just the opposite." In other contexts the Court had held that "nervous, evasive behavior is a pertinent factor in determining reasonable suspicion," and "[h]eadlong flight—wherever it occurs—is the consummate act of evasion."

Thus, the Court held that in a high-crime area, unprovoked flight from the police provides the police with reasonable suspicion.

There were four dissenters in the case, and they argued that it was improper to create a *per se* rule that unprovoked fight could even be a factor for reasonable suspicion, noting that "[a]mong some citizens, particularly minorities and those residing in high crime areas, there is . . . the possibility that the fleeing person is entirely innocent, but, with or without justification, believes that contact with the police can itself be dangerous, apart from any criminal activity associated with the officer's sudden presence." The dissenters argued that police (and courts) should look to the "totality of the circumstances" to determine whether, in this specific case, the unprovoked flight was indicative of criminal activity.

Note that once the *Terry* stop had occurred, the police still had to establish that the frisk of Wardlow was proper—that they had reason to believe that Wardlow

[21] Wardlow, 528 U.S. at 125.

was carrying a weapon. The Court did not reach that question in this case. We will discuss the propriety of a frisk below in Section 4.

To establish reasonable suspicion, an officer does not have to rely exclusively upon his own observations.[22] Reasonable suspicion can also be established with information provided by others, including a reliable informant, an ordinary victim or a fellow officer. To be properly considered, however, such "external" information must bear at least some indicia of reliability:

> **Example—*Florida v. J.L.*, 529 U.S. 266 (2000):** One October afternoon, an anonymous caller contacted the Miami Dade Police Department and reported that a young black man wearing a plaid shirt was standing at a particular bus stop. The caller also reported that this young man was carrying a gun.
>
> At some point after the call, two officers responded to the bus stop. They saw three young men standing there. One of the young men, J.L., was wearing a plaid shirt. However, from what they observed the officers had no reason to suspect J.L. or the other two teens were engaged in any criminal activity. Nonetheless, approaching the three young men, one of the officers ordered J.L. to raise his hands and place them on the bus stop structure. The officer then frisked J.L. and retrieved a gun from his pocket. J.L., who was a juvenile, was charged with possession of a firearm while under the age of eighteen. He challenged the stop, arguing that the police did not possess reasonable suspicion to detain him under *Terry.*

Analysis: The Supreme Court held that the stop of J.L. was unconstitutional. At the time of the stop, the officers had no personal basis for suspecting J.L. of any wrongdoing. The anonymous tip was the only information suggesting that J.L. might be engaged in criminal activity. While police officers may rely upon external sources of information to develop reasonable suspicion, in this case the external source of information was wholly lacking in any indicia of reliability.

Most critically, the source was entirely unknown to police. Anonymous sources, like the tipster in this case, are often deemed less reliable than other sources of external information for there is seldom any way to test their basis of knowledge or veracity. In cases where information from an anonymous tipster is deemed reliable (and thus sufficient to establish reasonable suspicion), it is often because the tipster has provided predictive information about future events, which can be tested for accuracy through independent police investigation.[23] In contrast,

---

[22] Adams v. Williams, 407 U.S. 143, 147 (1972).

[23] Alabama v. White, 496 U.S. 325 (1990).

information about a subject's readily observable characteristics—like location or appearance—is not the sort of predictive data that lends credibility to an anonymous accusation.

In the case of J.L., the anonymous source provided information that only described J.L.'s appearance and location. No predictive information was provided by the tipster and officers did nothing to test the reliability of the information before acting on it. Under such circumstances, a stop is unsupported by reasonable suspicion and thereby unconstitutional.[24]

Thus, before they may rely upon information from an unknown source to justify an investigative stop, officers must provide some independent corroboration of the anonymous tip.

A different rule applies when a detaining officer relies upon information provided by a fellow officer. In such a case, the detaining officer need not know the specific facts that led her fellow officer to reasonably suspect the target. Rather, she need only be informed that reasonable suspicion for the investigatory detention exists:

> **Example—*United States v. Hensley*, 469 U.S. 221 (1985):** One evening patrons in a tavern in St. Bernard, a suburb of Cincinnati, Ohio, were robbed by two armed men. During the investigation of the robbery, St. Bernard police officers interviewed an informant who was familiar with the crime. She advised the police that her boyfriend, Thomas Hensley, drove the getaway car during the robbery. Based on this tip, St. Bernard police distributed a "wanted flyer" to police departments in surrounding jurisdictions. The flyer indicated that Hensley was wanted for questioning in connection with the ongoing robbery investigation. The flyer also provided a description of Hensley and of the robbery. Finally, the flyer asked officers in the neighboring departments to pick Hensley up and "hold him" if he was located.
>
> Approximately two weeks after the tavern robbery, Hensley was spotted driving a white convertible in a neighboring jurisdiction. The officer was familiar with the wanted flyer, and knew Hensley from prior contacts unrelated to the robbery. However, the officer was wholly unfamiliar with any specifics of the St. Bernard investigation.
>
> The officer stopped Hensley's car, and ordered both Hensley and his passenger out. A second officer on the scene saw through the

[24] Florida v. J.L., 529 U.S. 266 (2000).

open passenger door a gun tucked beneath the passenger's seat. The passenger of the car was arrested and a more complete search for weapons was conducted. After two other guns were found, Hensley was arrested. He moved to suppress the gun, arguing that the initial stop of the car was not supported by reasonable suspicion.

Analysis: The Court held that the initial stop of Hensley's car was constitutional even though the detaining officer did not personally suspect Hensley of any involvement in criminal activity. Another police department issued a flyer that announced reasonable suspicion to believe Hensley was involved in an armed robbery. This suspicion was based upon articulable facts that, while unknown to the detaining officer, nonetheless supported a reasonable belief that Hensley had committed a serious offense. Consequently, the detaining officer's reliance on the flyer justified a brief stop to check identification, to pose questions, or to detain Hensley temporarily while attempting to obtain further information.[25]

2. Scope: Duration of the Stop. Once police establish reasonable suspicion, they are permitted to conduct a brief investigatory stop. However, the manner in which that stop is carried out may convert something that was lawful at its inception into an unconstitutional seizure. An investigatory stop allows the police to briefly detain a person for the purpose of limited questioning. The questioning can only take place for a "short period of time."[26] When police officers exceed the scope of this authorized limit, the investigatory stop will evolve into a seizure (or, if they are detaining a person, an arrest) requiring a warrant or probable cause.

Several factors are critical to the determination of whether the length of a challenged stop was excessive:

1. The law enforcement purpose that is served by the stop;
2. The amount of time reasonably needed to accomplish that purpose;
3. Whether the police diligently pursued a mode of inquiry that would quickly accomplish the confirmation or refutation of suspicion; and
4. The nature of the on-the-ground encounter—for example, if police are faced with a rapidly evolving investigation scenario, courts are discouraged from second-guessing their judgments by placing tight temporal limits on their investigatory authority.[27]

---

[25] United States v. Hensley, 469 U.S. 221, 232 (1985).

[26] Florida v. Royer, 460 U.S. 491, 500 (1983); Kolender v. Lawson, 461 U.S. 352, 365 (1983) (Brennan, J., concurring).

[27] United States v. Sharpe, 470 U.S. 675 (1985).

Applying these guidelines, the Court has consistently refused to define a maximum time limit for lawful *Terry* stops. While a bright-line rule would be easy to apply, it would not allow law enforcement to vary its response to account for the particular characteristics of individual investigatory stops. In light of the Court's refusal to adopt a clear rule, it is unclear when precisely a stop becomes too lengthy to retain its constitutional character as a "brief investigatory detention." We do know, however, that a stop lasting just twenty minutes falls clearly within the allowable limits.[28] On the other hand, a stop lasting ninety minutes has been rejected as falling well outside any appropriate temporal constraints:[29]

> **Example—*United States v. Place*, 462 U.S. 696 (1983):** While traveling from Miami to New York by plane, Raymond Place attracted the attention of law enforcement as he stood on line in the Miami International Airport. The officers approached Place and briefly questioned him. When they learned that his flight was about to depart, the officers decided not to search Place's luggage. The Miami agents did, however, call ahead to the Drug Enforcement Administration in New York. The Miami agents alerted New York to be on the look out for Place.
>
> DEA agents waiting at LaGuardia Airport in New York observed Place for a short time after the arrival of his flight. They found his behavior suspicious. After he claimed his checked baggage and while he was waiting on a car service, the agents approached him and identified themselves as law enforcement. After a brief conversation, Place refused to consent to a search of his luggage. The agents then seized the bags, telling Place they were going to obtain a warrant to search them. Place declined to accompany the officers.
>
> The agents took Place's bags to Kennedy Airport. At Kennedy, the bags were subjected to a dog sniff. The dog alerted to one of the two bags. At the time of this alert, approximately an hour and a half had passed since the bags were first seized from Place. Ultimately a large quantity of cocaine was found inside the bag and Place was charged with possession with intent to distribute. He challenged the seizure of himself and his bag.

Analysis: The agents' conduct was unconstitutional because the police held the defendant's bag for an unreasonable amount of time. The initial stop of Place was supported by reasonable suspicion and was therefore justified under *Terry*.

[28] United States v. Sharpe, 470 U.S. 675 (1985).

[29] United States v. Place, 462 U.S. 696 (1983).

In addition, the initial seizure of Place's luggage was appropriate. This is because the principles of *Terry* authorize the brief detention of personal effects if an officer's observations cause him to reasonably believe a person's luggage contains contraband.

However, notwithstanding these initial conclusions, the encounter violated the Constitution. In much the same way that *Terry* requires officers to limit the length of time they detain a person, so too must the detention of personal effects be limited.

The Court has never defined a maximum time limit for valid *Terry* stops. However, wherever that outer limit may be, a detention of ninety minutes is clearly beyond it. The police officers' decision to detain Place's luggage for as long as they did converted what began as a legitimate *Terry* stop into an unlawful seizure.

In some cases, the length of time that a suspect is held is directly related to the substance of the police inquiry. The Court has made clear that, during this time, brief inquiry into matters unrelated to the initial purpose of the detention will not convert a lawful *Terry* stop into an impermissible detention. However, if the unrelated inquiries measurably extend the length of the detention a contrary conclusion might be merited.[30]

3. Scope: Change in Location of the Stop. In addition to the duration of a stop, *Terry* also limits the scope of the stop with regard to location. Under some circumstances the movement of a suspect from one location to another will transform an investigatory stop that was legitimate at its inception into an impermissible intrusion upon the target's rights.[31]

Not every change of location converts a lawful *Terry* stop into an illegal seizure. Law enforcement is allowed to move the target of a *Terry* stop from one location to another if such a move is necessary for security reasons or out of concern for officer safety. For example, both drivers and passengers may be ordered out of a car following a lawful traffic stop.[32] However, in the absence of safety concerns, moving a target from the original location of the stop to a separate, more remote location may trigger a finding that the limited intrusion authorized by *Terry* has been exceeded.

The Court has not identified with precision the minimum distance required to convert a stop from permissible to impermissible. Nor has the Court determined exactly how remote the second location must be before it is disallowed. The Court has identified as significant, however, the appearance of the space to which the subject is moved:

---

[30] Arizona v. Johnson, 555 U.S. 323 (2009).

[31] Dunaway v. New York, 442 U.S. 200 (1979).

[32] Pennsylvania v. Mimms, 434 U.S. 106 (1977); Maryland v. Wilson, 519 U.S. 408 (1997).

Example—*Florida v. Royer*, 460 U.S. 491 (1983): Undercover narcotics detectives in Miami approached Mark Royer in the Miami International Airport. At the time of the approach, the detectives had already observed Royer buying a one-way ticket that he paid for in cash. One of the detectives who stood behind Royer in the ticketing line also noticed that the only information Royer included on the tags for his two checked suitcases was a last name (Holt) and the arrival airport (LaGuardia). It was also the detectives' belief that Royer's appearance and mannerisms fit a drug courier profile used by the police department.

After approaching Royer on the concourse, the detectives asked for his identification and plane tickets. Retaining both, the detectives asked Royer to accompany them to an interview room. The room was approximately forty feet from where the three men stood, and was essentially a "large closet" containing a desk and two chairs. Using Royer's baggage claim stubs, the detectives retrieved Royer's luggage from the airline. A subsequent search of the two bags revealed marijuana. Royer was arrested and ultimately convicted of narcotics offenses. He challenged his seizure as unconstitutional.

Analysis: The Supreme Court agreed with Royer and held that the detectives exceeded their *Terry* authority to seize Royer.

Royer's interaction with the police can be divided into two stages. The first stage of the interaction involved the initial questioning on the airport concourse. The second stage of the interaction occurred after Royer was moved approximately forty feet from the concourse to the interview room. The first stage of engagement was constitutional. The second was not.

Considering the first stage of the interaction, the information known to the detectives at the time they approached Royer was sufficient to warrant an investigatory stop under *Terry*. Royer's appearance and conduct, the fact that he was traveling under an assumed name, and the fact that he paid cash for a one-way ticket were sufficient, considered collectively, to establish reasonable suspicion. However, this suspicion justified only a temporary detention "while [the officers] attempted to verify or dispel their suspicions in a manner that did not exceed the limits of an investigative detention."

During the second stage of the interaction, the detectives asked Royer to accompany them to an interview room after confiscating his ticket and identification. There was no suggestion that the move was prompted by concern for the detectives' safety or by any legitimate need related to the limited purpose of the initial stop. The room to which Royer was moved was approximately forty feet away, and resembled a confined interrogation room. For all of these reasons, the restraint to which Royer was ultimately subjected exceeded the bounds of *Terry*.[33]

When evaluating any *Terry* stop to determine if it exceeds the scope of the limited authority granted, a change in location is significant, but may not be definitive:

Example—*United States v. Mendenhall*, 446 U.S. 544 (1980): While on duty at the Detroit Airport, two DEA agents observed a woman named Sylvia Mendenhall, who arrived on a flight from Los Angeles, and concluded that her behavior fit the profile of a drug courier. They approached her, identified themselves as federal agents, and asked to see her ticket and identification. The name in the ticket did not match the name on her identification, and Mendenhall revealed that she had only been in Los Angeles for two days. When the agents identified themselves specifically as narcotics agents, Mendenhall became "extremely nervous," to the point where she had a "hard time speaking."

The agents returned Mendenhall's identification and ticket to her and then asked her if she would come with them to the DEA office, approximately fifty feet away and up a flight of stairs. She was asked if she would consent to a search of her person and her bag and she agreed. A search of her bag revealed her ticket to Los Angeles, which had been issued under a different name.

A female officer arrived to conduct the search of Mendenhall's person, and informed Mendenhall that she would have to take her clothes off for the search. Mendenhall was reluctant, saying that she had a plane to catch, but eventually agreed. As she took her clothes off, Mendenhall removed two small packets of heroin from her underwear. She was arrested and charged with possession of heroin.

Mendenhall moved to suppress the heroin, arguing that (1) she was seized when the DEA agents approached her in the airport, and that seizure was not supported by reasonable suspicion; and (2) even if reasonable suspicion had existed at the time of the stop, the subsequent actions of the DEA agents transformed the stop into an arrest.

[33] Florida v. Royer, 460 U.S. 491 (1983).

Analysis: The Supreme Court held that the encounter between Mendenhall and the DEA agents was entirely consensual, and therefore she was never seized by the agents.

There were four potential steps to the analysis in this case. First, was Mendenhall seized at any point during this encounter, and if so, when? Second, if she was seized, did reasonable suspicion exist at the point at which she was seized? Third, at any point did the seizure become so intrusive that it transformed into an arrest? And finally, if it did transform into an arrest, was there probable cause to believe that she was guilty of a crime at that time?

In this case, the Court had no need to proceed past the first step. Remember from **Chapter 9** that a suspect is seized when, in view of all of the circumstances surrounding the incident, a reasonable person would have believed that he or she was not free to leave. The Court noted that the agents received consent from Mendenhall for every stage of the encounter, and also noted that the agents returned her ticket and identification to her before they asked her to accompany them to the office. Thus, unlike the situation in *Royer*, the Court concluded that a reasonable person in her situation would have felt free to leave.

The point at which a seizure becomes an arrest (or even the point at which a seizure occurs at all) is a very fact-intensive question. The Supreme Court has repeatedly stated that it will not adopt a "litmus-paper test for . . . determining when a seizure exceeds the bounds of an investigative stop."

4. Traffic Stops. One of the most common type of *Terry* stops is the routine traffic stop, in which the police temporarily seize a car (and all of its occupants) because of a traffic violation. In the context of traffic stops, there is usually no question that the initial stop is justified—the officer usually has personally observed a violation of the traffic laws, so there is no problem proving reasonable suspicion. Instead, the question is what police officers are allowed to do during the traffic stop. As it turns out, the officer can do quite a lot: ask to see the driver's license, registration, and proof of insurance; conduct a check for outstanding warrants or any other prior criminal record;[34] question the occupants of the car about whether the car contains any contraband;[35] and bring a trained dog to sniff the car for the presence of drugs.[36] The general rule is that police can engage in any or all of this conduct as long as it does not unreasonably increase the length of the seizure. In other words, the police officer is allowed to detain the individual for as long as is necessary to complete the initial purpose of the stop—to issue a ticket and check the driver's license and registration. If the officer delays the occupants

[34] United States v. Holloway, 962 F.2d 451 (5th Cir. 1992).

[35] United States v. Long, 532 F.3d 791 (8th Cir. 2008).

[36] Illinois v. Caballes, 543 U.S. 405 (2005).

for a significant amount of time beyond that point for questioning or to wait for a drug dog, the seizure becomes unconstitutional.

Police officers are also permitted to order the driver and all passengers out of the automobile in order to protect themselves during the stop:

> **Example—*Pennsylvania v. Mimms*, 434 U.S. 106 (1977):** Two police officers pulled over Harry Mimms for driving with an expired license plate. One of the officers approached the car and asked Mimms to step out of the vehicle. When Mimms get out of the car, the officer noticed a large bulge under his jacket. The officer believed that Mimms might be armed, and so he frisked Mimms and found a gun in his jacket pocket.
>
> Mimms was arrested for two firearms violations. He moved to exclude the firearm, arguing that the police officer had no right to order him out of the car during a routine traffic stop for a minor traffic infraction.

Analysis: The Supreme Court held the police officer was legally allowed to order Mimms out of the car, and therefore found Mimms's motion was properly denied.

The Court weighed the legitimate law enforcement need to protect the safety of the officer against the liberty interest of a driver who is forced to get out of his car. The Court conceded that at the time of the stop, the officer had no reason to suspect that Mimms might be armed or pose any risk to the police officer. However, the Court noted that in general, all traffic stops pose serious risks to the officer—a "significant percentage" of all murders of police officers occur during traffic stops. Also, in some situations it could be hazardous for the officer to stand by the driver's side door exposed to passing traffic—thus "the officer prudently may prefer to ask the driver of the vehicle to step out of the car and off onto the shoulder of the road where the inquiry may be pursued with greater safety to both."[37]

On the other side of the equation, the Court found that the added deprivation of liberty suffered by a driver who is ordered out of the car is *de minimis.* The driver has already been legitimately seized and must spend the next ten or twenty minutes waiting by the side of the road; whether she must wait in her car or standing next to it is not constitutionally significant. At most, the majority found that being required to get out of the car is a "mere inconvenience."[38]

---

[37] Pennsylvania v. Mimms, 434 U.S. 106, 111 (1977).

[38] Id.

As we will see in the next section, once the officer observed the large bulge in Mimms' jacket, the officer had reason to believe that Mimms was armed, and thus the frisk was also constitutional.

The *Mimms* doctrine was later extended to apply to the passengers in an automobile as well. Passengers could also pose a threat to the officer, and (according to the Court) they suffer very little extra loss of liberty by being ordered to get out of the car.[39]

5. When are Officers Permitted to Frisk the Suspect? We know that the police can briefly detain a suspect if they have reasonable suspicion to believe the suspect was involved in criminal activity. But the authority to make the stop does not automatically allow the police to frisk every suspect. A frisk is only permitted if the police have reason to believe that the suspect may be armed, which will not be true every time the police make a stop.

An officer can develop a reasonable belief that a suspect may be armed in a number of different ways. Probably the most common way is if the initial stop is made for a crime of violence (such as murder, rape armed robbery, or assault with a deadly weapon) or some other crime which implies that the suspect may be armed (such as gun possession or car theft). The government often contends that narcotics trafficking should always be included in this "weapons presumption" category, arguing that so many drug dealers are armed that anyone they stop on reasonable suspicion of being a drug dealer can be frisked. Courts have been reluctant to permit this *per se* presumption, however. Many courts only allow the police to presume someone may be armed if there is a large amount of narcotics involved.

If the crime for which the suspect is stopped does not carry a "weapons presumption," the police officer must point to other facts which gave her a reasonable belief that the suspect was armed. Such factors include:

- A "suspicious bulge" in a pocket;
- The defendant making a sudden or unexpected move for her pocket;
- Refusal or reluctance to remove a hand from her pocket or to show her hands; and
- Knowledge that this suspect had previously been armed or previously committed a crime of violence.

Essentially, anything the suspect does which is consistent with having a weapon can be offered by the police as a factor justifying the need for a frisk. Ultimately,

[39] Maryland v. Wilson, 519 U.S. 408 (1997).

of course, it is up to the magistrate or judge reviewing the frisk to determine whether these factors add up to a reasonable belief.

6. Scope: Method of the Frisk. As discussed in Sections 2 and 3, the limited authority granted by *Terry* imposes temporal and spatial limits on the police. Accordingly, the primary ways in which law enforcement exceeds the scope of a legitimate *Terry* stop is by detaining a person for too long or by moving the person without justification from one location to another.

Law enforcement may also exceed the authorized scope of a *Terry* frisk. The only purpose of a *Terry* frisk is to protect officer safety—thus, the police are only allowed to search using methods and in places where the suspect may have a weapon.

The Supreme Court has found a number of factors to be relevant to whether a challenged protective frisk was appropriately limited. Specifically, the Court has considered the manner in which the frisk was conducted and the physical areas that were the subject of sweeps. We know that *Terry* permits a superficial exploration for weapons of the suspect's outer clothing upon suspicion that the person the officer has lawfully detained is armed and dangerous. If a pat down is more probing than superficial, it may transform that lawful exploration into a search requiring probable cause:

> **Example–*Minnesota v. Dickerson*, 508 U.S. 366 (1993):** One evening, police officers patrolling on the north side of Minneapolis saw Timothy Dickerson leave a building the officers knew to be a notorious crack house. Dickerson started walking toward the officers, but upon seeing the marked police car and making eye contact with the officers, he immediately turned and walked in the opposite direction into an alley. The officers pulled their car into the alley behind Dickerson and ordered him to stop.
>
> One of the officers conducted a pat-down search to establish if Dickerson was armed. The officer detected no weapons. However, he did feel a small lump in the pocket of Dickerson's jacket. Moving the lump around between his fingers, the officer felt what he thought was a piece of crack cocaine wrapped in cellophane. The officer reached into the pocket and retrieved the object. It was a small plastic bag containing crack cocaine.
>
> Dickerson was arrested and charged with drug possession, and he challenged the search of his jacket, arguing that the officers went beyond the "frisk" that is authorized by *Terry*.

Analysis: The Supreme Court held that the officer's search went beyond what was necessary to verify whether Dickerson had a weapon, and therefore exceeded the bounds of *Terry*.

Assuming the initial stop and frisk of Dickerson were supported by reasonable suspicion, the central question for consideration is whether the manner in which the frisk was conducted exceeded the bounds of *Terry*. *Terry* authorizes only a limited pat-down. The sole purpose of that pat-down is to determine whether a suspect is armed.

The officer's manipulation of the object in Dickerson's pocket was not necessary to determine that Dickerson was unarmed. Though the officer could not at first tell what the lump in Dickerson's pocket was, he certainly could tell what it was not. Because the officer had determined the item was not a weapon, his continued exploration of the object went beyond the limited authorization found in *Terry*.

Recall, as you read in **Chapter 14**, if the officer immediately recognized the lump in Dickerson's pocket as contraband, he could have appropriately seized the item under what has come to be known as the "plain feel" doctrine, even though it was not a weapon. However, the above facts reflect that the officer did not know what he was feeling. It was only upon his further manipulation of the lump that he realized it to be drugs. Because the officer had only reasonable suspicion that Dickerson was engaged in wrongdoing, this sort of exploratory search is not permitted.[40]

7. *Terry* "Frisk" of a Location. We have seen that if law enforcement officers reasonably believe the person they are questioning is armed and presently dangerous, they may conduct a protective frisk of the individual. But does *Terry* also authorize protective frisks of areas beyond the person herself? The short answer is "Yes." The location of the suspect at the time of the stop determines the spatial limits of such a protective frisk.

For example, if the occupant of a vehicle is lawfully detained, and police can articulate a reasonable belief that the person is dangerous and is (or could quickly become) armed, law enforcement may not only frisk the person but may also conduct a protective sweep of the passenger compartment of the car. This protective sweep includes exploring any areas where a weapon may be hidden. It also includes exploration of containers (open or closed) that might conceal a weapon. The expansion of the *Terry* frisk to areas beyond the body is grounded in the notion that "suspects may injure police officers and others by virtue of their access to weapons, even though they may not themselves be armed."[41]

---

40 Minnesota v. Dickerson, 508 U.S. 366 (1993).

41 Michigan v. Long, 463 U.S. 1032, 1048 (1983).

Example—*Michigan v. Long*, 463 U.S. 1032 (1983): Sheriff's Deputies Howell and Lewis were patrolling a rural highway just after midnight one evening when a car sped past them going in the opposite direction. The deputies made a U-turn and began following the vehicle. After a few moments, the car swerved into a shallow ditch, coming to rest with its back tires still in the roadway. The deputies stopped behind the car and got out of their vehicle. The driver of the car, David Long, also got out of his vehicle and walked back to meet the deputies. He left his driver's door open.

Long appeared to be under the influence of drugs or alcohol. It took two requests before Long handed over his driver's license. Upon request for his registration, Long turned and began walking back toward his open driver's door. The deputies followed him and saw a large folding hunting knife lying closed on the floorboard in front of the driver's seat. At that point, the deputies stopped Long and conducted a pat-down. Finding no weapons on Long's person, the deputies then searched the interior of the car looking for weapons other than the knife. Kneeling into the car, Deputy Howell lifted an armrest that divided the front seat, and saw an open pouch. Howell shone his flashlight into the pouch and found marijuana. Long was arrested immediately. Following Long's arrest, the deputies decided to impound his car and thus searched the car more thoroughly. A search of the trunk revealed another seventy-five pounds of marijuana.

At his trial on narcotics charges, Long did not contest the initial investigatory stop and protective frisk of his person. However, Long argued that the search under the armrest exceeded the limited scope authorized by *Terry*.

Analysis: Long was incorrect. The initial search of Long's car, which revealed the marijuana in the pouch, was justified by the same principles first announced in *Terry*. *Terry* is not to be understood as narrowly limiting the scope of a protective frisk "to the person of the detained suspect." Indeed, a suspect who might quickly become armed poses as great a risk to officers as a suspect who is presently armed.

As you read in **Chapter 13**, incident to the arrest of a car's occupant, the police have a right to search the car, and this right is grounded in part in concerns for officer safety. The Supreme Court extended this principle to *Terry* stops, noting that "[i]f a suspect is dangerous, he is no less dangerous simply because he is not arrested." Consequently, in the context of *Terry* stops involving cars, an appropriate *Terry* frisk encompasses not only the body of the detainee but also the car's passenger compartment. This search is limited to those areas in the passenger compartment of a car where "a weapon may be placed or hidden . . . if the police officer possesses a reasonable belief based on 'specific and articulable facts which, taken together with the rational inferences from those facts, reasonably warrant' [a belief] that the suspect is dangerous and . . . may gain immediate control of weapons."[42]

If, instead of a car, the suspect is lawfully detained inside a dwelling, spatial limits on the protective frisk are somewhat broader. A protective frisk of a house—also known as a **protective sweep**—encompasses all areas of the home from which an attack on police officers might be launched by another person. The Court has recognized the authority of the police to engage in protective sweeps as an adjunct to their lawful presence in a home while executing an arrest warrant. However, though the protective sweep has been described by the Court as being "incident to an arrest,"[43] it is justified entirely by the reasonableness balancing principles articulated in *Terry*. In *Terry*, interests in officer safety gave birth to the protective frisk. In the context of the home, similar interests justify a corresponding intrusion—"there is an analogous interest of the officers in taking steps to assure themselves that the house in which a suspect is being, or has just been, arrested is not harboring other persons who are dangerous and could unexpectedly launch an attack."[44]

A protective sweep is justified if the police can articulate specific facts that reasonably give rise to the belief that particular areas of the home may be hiding individuals who pose a threat to the officers or others.[45] The protective sweep is not a full search. It is limited to a cursory visual inspection and extends only to those areas where a person may hide. In addition, any sweep must be conducted quickly, and certainly may take no longer that the time it takes to actually complete the arrest and leave the property.

Finally, with regard to police officers and arrestees inside a home, make sure you are able to distinguish between the two similar types of search authority we have discussed to this point. Immediately above, you read about the *Terry*-like right to engage in a protective sweep during the lawful arrest of a home's occupant. In **Chapter 13**, you learned that police officers also have the authority to search some areas of a home incident to a warrantless in-home arrest. Though seemingly comparable, the two types of search authority actually differ in important ways.

---

[42] Michigan v. Long, 463 U.S. 1032, 1049 (1983).

[43] Maryland v. Buie, 494 U.S. 325, 327 (1990).

[44] Id. at 333.

[45] Id. at 334.

A search incident to a warrantless in-home arrest is limited to the arrestee's person and "wingspan"—any areas from which the arrestee might obtain a weapon.[46] The threat being guarded against in that instance is the danger posed by the arrestee himself. The authority for this type of search automatically flows from the arrest itself. In contrast, the *Terry*-like protective sweep of a home allows for the search of any area in the home which may reasonably harbor an attacker. And, though the protective sweep enjoys a broader geographic reach, substantively it is limited to a cursory visual scan. Finally, unlike the search incident, the protective sweep does not flow automatically from the lawful arrest. Rather, it is permissible only if it is justified "by a reasonable articulable suspicion that the house is harboring a person posing a danger to those on the arrest scene."[47]

D. Policy Debate. Since 1968, the police have been allowed to briefly detain suspects even if they do not have probable cause to make an arrest. It has also been settled that attendant to this lawful stop, the police may frisk the suspect for weapons if they reasonably believe the suspect is armed and dangerous. Since its inception, the *Terry* doctrine has been the subject of frequent criticism. The attacks lodged against *Terry* usually fall into one of two categories. First, many commentators question the soundness of the theory underlying the doctrine. Second, a number of critics have voiced concern about the potentially discriminatory impact of the *Terry* rules in application.

Critique of the *Terry* doctrine was first seen in the case itself. In his dissent to *Terry*, Justice Douglas noted that magistrates are not permitted to issue warrants to search or seize on less than probable cause. Yet, the Court in *Terry* allowed police officers to search and seize (albeit in limited ways) on just reasonable suspicion. In Justice Douglas' view, this inconsistency was a strong indicator that the standard the *Terry* Court adopted stood on shaky constitutional ground:

> To give the police greater power than a magistrate is to take a long step down the totalitarian path. Perhaps such a step is desirable to cope with modern forms of lawlessness. But if it is taken, it should be the deliberate choice of the people through a constitutional amendment. Until the Fourth Amendment, which is closely allied with the Fifth, is rewritten, the person and the effects of the individual are beyond the reach of all government agencies until there are reasonable grounds to believe (probable cause) that a criminal venture has been launched or is about to be launched.

---

[46] Chimel v. California, 395 U.S. 752 (1969).

[47] Maryland v. Buie, 494 U.S. 325, 336 (1990).

> There have been powerful hydraulic pressures throughout our history that bear heavily on the Court to water down constitutional guarantees and give the police the upper hand. That hydraulic pressure has probably never been greater than it is today.
>
> Yet if the individual is no longer to be sovereign, if the police can pick him up whenever they do not like the cut of his jib, if they can 'seize' and 'search' him in their discretion, we enter a new regime. The decision to enter it should be made only after a full debate by the people of this country.[48]

Since 1968, the concerns expressed by Justice Douglas have been echoed by other members of the Court. These post-*Terry* critiques have moved beyond a direct attack on the constitutional soundness of the doctrine, and instead have focused on the continued expansion of the *Terry* doctrine. For example, Justice Brennan wrote in the *Michigan v. Long* decision (which extended the *Terry* frisk from the suspect's person to the area around him):

> Today the Court discards . . . basic principles and employs the very narrow exception established by *Terry* to swallow the general rule that Fourth Amendment searches of cars are reasonable only if based on probable cause. Today's decision disregards the Court's warning in *Almeida-Sanchez*: "The needs of law enforcement stand in constant tension with the Constitution's protections for the individual against certain exercises of official power. It is precisely the predictability of these pressures that counsels a resolute loyalty to constitutional safeguards.[49]

The second criticism of *Terry* is the concern that police are deploying the discretion it affords in discriminatory ways. For example, the stop-and-frisk practices of the New York City Police Department have come under heated attack as being racially motivated. A federal judge recently agreed, and narrowly banned the practice as it was being implemented in a particular section of the Bronx. A class action lawsuit attacking the practice city-wide reached a similar conclusion, though the final outcome of that case remains uncertain at the moment as it is currently pending on appeal.

The evidence introduced in the New York City suit raises troubling questions about both the basic efficacy of aggressive *Terry* policing, and the extent to which the broad discretion granted the police under *Terry* disparately impacts racial

[48] Terry v. Ohio, 391 U.S. 1, 39-40 (1968).

[49] Michigan v. Long, 463 U.S. 1032, 1064 (1983) (Brennan, J., dissenting).

minorities. In the New York City suit, the plaintiffs introduced evidence that between 2004 and 2012, the NYPD stopped 4.4 million people. Of these millions of stops, however, a very high percentage proved to be ultimately pointless. In almost 90% of the stops the person stopped was released at the scene because no evidence of criminality was found.[50] In terms of contraband actually seized, the evidence introduced at the trial suggested that the stops did not advance law enforcement interests in any meaningful way. In 2009, for example, the evidence reflected that drugs or other illegal items were found in just 1.6% of the more than 500,000 stops made that year.[51] The police had even less success with guns, which were found in just 1.1% of the stops.[52] There was also evidence that men of color were subjected to stops far more than any other demographic group. The evidence documented more than 700,000 *Terry* stops by the NYPD in 2012 alone.[53] Nearly 85% of those stops were of young black and Latino men.[54]

Notwithstanding the statistics noted above, the plaintiffs in the New York lawsuit do **not** attack the basic soundness of the *Terry* doctrine. Instead, they argued that the stops and frisks engaged in by the NYPD exceeded the scope of legitimate *Terry* stops and frisks because they were not actually based on reasonable suspicion. Consequently, despite the law suits filed in cities like New York and the occasional objection of dissenting justices, *Terry* seems secure. The criticisms of the doctrine noted above have never been embraced by a majority of the Court, and the Court unanimously upheld the reasonable suspicion doctrine as recently as 2009.[55]

---

[50] Floyd v. City of New York, 959 F.Supp.2d 541 (S.D.N.Y. 2013).

[51] Bob Herbert, Op-Ed., Jim Crow Policing, N.Y. Times, Feb. 2, 2010, at A27.

[52] Id. Readers interested in the arguments made in defense of aggressive Terry stops should see generally Lawrence Rosenthal, The Crime Drop and the Fourth Amendment: Toward an Empirical Jurisprudence of Search and Seizure, 29 N.Y.U. Rev. L. & Soc. Change 641 (2005).

[53] Ctr. for Constitutional Rights, STOP AND FRISK: THE HUMAN IMPACT at 3 (2012), available at http://stopandfrisk.org/the-human-impact-report.pdf.

[54] Id.

[55] Arizona v. Johnson, 555 U.S. 323 (2009).

Quick Summary

There are three levels of police interaction with the public. The lowest level is entirely consensual and requires no justification by law enforcement. Subjects of such encounters are free to terminate the discussion at any time and simply walk away. At the opposite end of the spectrum are arrests and full searches. Between these two extremes lies an intermediate encounter that first was recognized by the Court in 1968 in *Terry v. Ohio*. This intermediate interaction can be justified with less than probable cause and allows the police only a limited intrusion.

Pursuant to *Terry*, police are allowed to briefly detain a person for questioning if they reasonably suspect the person has engaged in or is about to engage in criminal conduct. "Reasonable suspicion" is the term applied to the strength of the belief officers must possess before conducting a *Terry* stop. Officers must be able to point to specific facts to establish reasonable suspicion. Accordingly, the reasons articulated for a stop must amount to more than mere hunches. All of the information available to the officer—including informant's tips and information from other officers—is relevant to the question of whether reasonable suspicion existed. However, information that is wholly lacking in any indicia of reliability will not provide an adequate foundation.

In addition to briefly detaining a person, *Terry* also allows an officer to frisk the subject of the lawful detention for weapons if the officer reasonably believes the person she is dealing with is armed and dangerous.

If challenged, a *Terry* stop may fail for two reasons. First, a *Terry* stop may be invalidated if the stop was not justified by reasonable suspicion at its inception. Second, a *Terry* stop that was lawful at inception may nonetheless lose its lawful nature if the stop or frisk go beyond the limited intrusions that are authorized.

Review Questions

1. Reasonable Suspicion in a High-Crime Neighborhood. Officers in plain clothes driving an unmarked car were patrolling in a Boston neighborhood that was known as a high-crime area. The officers saw a car that was parked with its front extending out into the intersection blocking a handicapped ramp, and with its license plate improperly displayed inside the windshield. The officers testified that the driver looked "startled" and "began to look from side to side, not looking back in our direction" after making eye contact with the police.

The officers left their vehicle and approached the driver, whose name was Leonard McElroy. As they approached, the officers saw McElroy move his arm as though he were putting something down. One of the officers ordered McElroy out of the car and frisked him. The officer did not feel any weapons, but he felt something that he believed to be a bag of marijuana. He asked McElroy if he had marijuana on him, and McElroy answered yes.

The police searched McElroy, finding a bag of marijuana and over five grams of cocaine. McElroy was arrested and charged with possession of marijuana and cocaine.

Did the police violate McElroy's Fourth Amendment rights when:

a. They ordered him out of the car?

b. They frisked him?

c. They searched him after the arrest?

2. Taking Drugs to Alaska. Police officers at the Cincinnati airport were watching travelers exit a plane that had just landed from New York. They noticed that every traveler on this particular plane wore a business suit except for one, who wore blue jeans and a leather jacket. They followed this individual to the baggage claim, and noticed that he repeatedly looked behind him as he waited for his luggage. After he picked up his luggage, he went to one of the ticket counters, conducted a transaction, checked his bag, and then walked into the gift shop. One of the officers went to the ticket counter and asked the flight agent about the transaction and learned that the suspect's name was Ralph Alicia and that he had just bought a one-way ticket from Cincinnati to Anchorage in cash forty minutes before takeoff. Anchorage was a known destination for New York drug dealers.

Based on their suspicion that the suspect was carrying drugs, the police decided to approach him. They stopped him and asked if he would answer some questions. He agreed. The police asked for identification and he produced a certified identification with the name of Ralph Alicia. The police officer looked at the ID and believed it to be a fake. The officer then asked for the suspect's ticket, which Alicia handed over. They then asked to search his carry-on. The suspect consented, and the police asked if he would move into a less busy, more secure hallway of the airport to carry out the search. The suspect agreed. The search of the carry-on revealed clothes and children's toys. Police then asked the suspect if they could search his person. The suspect consented, and police found his wallet in his pants. When the police looked in the wallet, they found a New York driver's license with the suspect's photo and the name Jose Bueno. Police then advised the suspect that state law prohibited giving a false name to a police officer. The suspect admitted his name was Jose Bueno.

Police then asked to search the bag he had just checked, and the suspect consented. The suspect asked if he could leave and go board his flight, and the police officers told him he had to stay until his bag was searched. They retrieved the bag and searched it and found a detergent box with approximately five pounds of cocaine inside. They arrested the suspect and charged him with possession of cocaine with intent to sell.

Defendant Bueno is now challenging the search, arguing that the police violated his rights during the encounter. Did the police violate his Fourth Amendment rights, and if so, when?

3. Frisking a Robbery Suspect. Officer Anthony Bowman of the D.C. police department was on patrol when he received a radio report of an armed robbery in the neighborhood. The victim described the suspect as a Asian male, six feet three inches tall, with a moustache, wearing a blue sweatshirt and blue jeans. A few minutes later Officer Bowman saw Paul Ashen walking down the street, approximately two blocks from where the robbery occurred. Ashen was Asian, approximately six feet three inches tall, had a moustache and was wearing a blue jacket over a blue fleece and blue sweatpants. When Ashen saw Officer Bowman's police car, he turned away and walked in a different direction. Officer Bowman stopped Ashen, ordered him to put his hands on his head, conducted a pat-down of his clothing, and then asked for identification. Officer Bowman found no weapons in the pat-down of the clothing.

Other officers arrived at the scene and decided to take Ashen to the victim for a "show-up" identification. They walked him two blocks to where the victim was sitting in a patrol car. Officer Bowman realized that Ashen had probably put the second blue jacket on over the fleece, and since the victim had described him as wearing a blue sweatshirt, Officer Bowman reached over and unzipped Ashen's jacket so that the victim could get a look at the fleece he was wearing. When Officer Bowman unzipped the jacket down to Ashen's waist, he felt a "hard object" tucked into Ashen's waistband. He reached in and pulled out a gun.

The victim was unable to identify Ashen, but police still charged him with possession of an unlicensed firearm. Ashen moved to suppress the gun, arguing:

a. The initial stop was illegal because it was not based on reasonable suspicion;

b. Even if the initial stop was legal, the police exceeded the legal scope of the stop when they moved Ashen to a different location for the show-up; and

c. Even if the initial stop was legal, the officers exceeded the legal scope of the search when they unzipped his jacket.

Did the police violate Ashen's Fourth Amendment rights? If so, at what point?

4. The Evasive Speeder. At two o'clock in the morning, state troopers saw a pickup truck traveling at approximately seventy miles per hour on a country road with a fifty-five mph speed limit. The troopers decided to stop the truck and cite the driver for speeding. As the troopers began to pursue the truck, it turned onto a narrow dirt trail that intersected with the road and seemingly disappeared. The troopers followed down the trail and found the pickup parked in the middle of the trail with its lights off.

The troopers shone a light inside the car and saw a young adult male in the driver's seat and a fourteen-year-old girl in the passenger's seat. They asked the driver, whose name was Darren Horton, why he had driven his car down the trail into the woods. Horton said that he pulled onto the trail so that he could stop to look at a map and get directions home. However, there were no lights on in the truck, Horton was not holding a map, and the troopers did not see any map in the truck.

The troopers asked Horton to step out of the truck and asked him if he had any weapons on his person. Horton answered no. The troopers also asked him if he had any weapons in his vehicle. He hesitated, and then responded, "Not that I know of." The troopers then decided to search the truck. Behind the seat, beneath the floorboard, the troopers recovered a shotgun with an unlawfully short barrel. Horton was convicted of third-degree weapons misconduct.

At trial, Horton argued that the police violated his Fourth Amendment rights when they searched his truck. Was the search valid, and if so, under what warrant exception?

FROM THE COURTROOM

TERRY v. OHIO

United States Supreme Court, 1968
392 U.S. 1

[Chief Justice WARREN delivered the opinion of the Court.]

[Justices BLACK, HARLAN, and WHITE concurred in the decision.]

[Justice DOUGLAS filed a dissenting opinion.]

This case presents serious questions concerning the role of the Fourth Amendment in the confrontation on the street between the citizen and the policeman investigating suspicious circumstances.

Petitioner Terry was convicted of carrying a concealed weapon and sentenced to the statutorily prescribed term of one to three years in the penitentiary. Following the denial of a pretrial motion to suppress, the prosecution introduced in evidence two revolvers and a number of bullets seized from Terry and a codefendant, Richard Chilton, by Cleveland Police Detective Martin McFadden. At the hearing on the motion to suppress this evidence, Officer McFadden testified that while he was patrolling in plain clothes in downtown Cleveland at approximately 2:30 in the afternoon of October 31, 1963, his attention was attracted by two men, Chilton and Terry, standing on the corner of Huron Road and Euclid Avenue. He had never seen the two men before, and he was unable to say precisely what first drew his eye to them. However, he testified that he had been a policeman for [thirty-nine] years and a detective for [thirty-five] and that he had been assigned to patrol this vicinity of downtown Cleveland for shoplifters and pickpockets for [thirty] years. He explained that he had developed routine habits of observation over the years and that he would "stand and watch people or walk and watch people at many intervals of the day." He added: "Now, in this case when I looked over they didn't look right to me at the time."

His interest aroused, Officer McFadden took up a post of observation in the entrance to a store [three hundred] to [four hundred] feet away from the two men. "I get more purpose to watch them when I seen their movements," he testified. He saw one of the men leave the other one and walk southwest on Huron Road, past some stores. The man paused for a moment and looked in a store window, then walked on a short distance, turned around and walked back toward the corner, pausing once again to look in the same store window. He rejoined his companion at the corner, and the two conferred briefly. Then the second man went through the same series of motions, strolling down Huron Road, looking in the same window, walking on a short distance, turning back, peering in the store window again, and returning to confer with the first man at the corner. The two men repeated this ritual alternately between five and six times apiece—in all, roughly a dozen trips. At one point, while the two were standing together on the corner, a third man approached them and engaged them briefly in conversation. This man then left the two others and walked west on Euclid Avenue. Chilton and Terry resumed their measured pacing, peering and conferring. After this had gone on for [ten] to [twelve] minutes, the two men walked off together, heading west on Euclid Avenue, following the path taken earlier by the third man.

By this time Officer McFadden had become thoroughly suspicious. He testified that after observing their elaborately casual and oft-repeated reconnaissance of the store window on Huron Road, he suspected the two men of "casing a job, a stick-up," and that he considered it his duty as a police officer to investigate further. He added that he feared "they may have a gun." Thus, Officer McFadden followed Chilton and Terry and saw them stop in front of Zucker's store to talk to the same man who had conferred with them earlier on the street corner. Deciding that the situation was ripe for direct action, Officer McFadden approached the three men, identified himself as a police officer and asked for their names. At this point his knowledge was confined to what he had observed. He was not acquainted with any of the three men by name or by sight, and he had received no information concerning them from any other source. When the men "mumbled something" in response to his inquiries, Officer McFadden grabbed petitioner Terry, spun him around so that they were facing the other two, with Terry between McFadden and the others, and patted down the outside of his clothing. In the left breast pocket of Terry's overcoat Officer McFadden felt a pistol. He reached inside the overcoat pocket, but was unable to remove the gun. At this point, keeping Terry between himself and the others, the officer ordered all three men to enter Zucker's store. As they went in, he removed Terry's overcoat completely, removed a .38-caliber revolver from the pocket and ordered all three men to face the wall with their hands raised. Officer McFadden proceeded to pat down the outer clothing of Chilton and the third man, Katz. He discovered another revolver in the outer pocket of Chilton's overcoat, but no weapons were found on Katz. The officer testified that he only patted the men down to see whether they had weapons, and that he did not put his hands beneath the outer garments of either Terry or Chilton until he felt their guns. So far as appears from the record, he never placed his hands beneath Katz' outer garments. Officer McFadden seized Chilton's gun, asked the proprietor of the store to call a police wagon, and took all three men to the station, where Chilton and Terry were formally charged with carrying concealed weapons.

On the motion to suppress the guns the prosecution took the position that they had been seized following a search incident to a lawful arrest. The trial court rejected this theory, stating that it "would be stretching the facts beyond reasonable comprehension" to find that Officer McFadden had had probable cause to arrest the men before he patted them down for weapons. However, the court denied the defendants' motion on the ground that Officer McFadden, on the basis of his experience, "had reasonable cause to believe . . . that the defendants were conducting themselves suspiciously, and some interrogation should be made of their action." Purely for his own protection, the court held, the officer had the right to pat down the outer clothing of these men, who he had reasonable cause to believe might be armed. The court distinguished between an investigatory "stop" and an arrest, and between a "frisk" of the outer clothing for weapons and a full-blown search for evidence of crime. The frisk, it held, was essential to the proper performance of the officer's investigatory duties, for without it "the answer to the police officer may be a bullet, and a loaded pistol discovered during the frisk is admissible."

After the court denied their motion to suppress, Chilton and Terry waived jury trial and pleaded not guilty. The court adjudged them guilty, and the Court of Appeals for the Eighth Judicial District, Cuyahoga County, affirmed. The Supreme Court of Ohio dismissed their appeal on the ground that no "substantial constitutional question" was involved. We granted certiorari, to determine whether the admission of the revolvers in evidence violated petitioner's rights under the Fourth Amendment, made applicable to the States by the Fourteenth. We affirm the conviction.

I.

The Fourth Amendment provides that "the right of the people to be secure in their persons, houses, papers, and effects, against unreasonable searches and seizures, shall not be violated . . . ." This inestimable right of personal security belongs as much to the citizen on the streets of our cities as to the homeowner closeted in his study to dispose of his secret affairs. For, as this Court has always recognized,

> No right is held more sacred, or is more carefully guarded, by the common law, than the right of every individual to the possession and control of his own person, free from all restraint or interference of others, unless by clear and unquestionable authority of law.

We have recently held that "the Fourth Amendment protects people, not places," *Katz v. United States*, and wherever an individual may harbor a reasonable "expectation of privacy," he is entitled to be free from unreasonable governmental intrusion. Of course, the specific content and incidents of this right must be shaped by the context in which it is asserted. For "what the Constitution forbids is not all searches and seizures, but unreasonable searches and seizures." Unquestionably petitioner was entitled to the protection of the Fourth Amendment as he walked down the street in Cleveland. The question is whether in all the circumstances of this on-the-street encounter, his right to personal security was violated by an unreasonable search and seizure.

We would be less than candid if we did not acknowledge that this question thrusts to the fore difficult and troublesome issues regarding a sensitive area of police activity—issues which have never before been squarely presented to this Court. Reflective of the tensions involved are the practical and constitutional arguments pressed with great vigor on both sides of the public debate over the power of the police to "stop and frisk" —as it is sometimes euphemistically termed—suspicious persons.

On the one hand, it is frequently argued that in dealing with the rapidly unfolding and often dangerous situations on city streets the police are in need of an escalating set of flexible responses, graduated in relation to the amount of information they possess. For this purpose it is urged that distinctions should be made between a "stop" and an "arrest" (or a "seizure" of a person), and between a "frisk" and a "search." Thus, it is argued, the police should be allowed to "stop" a person and detain him briefly for questioning upon suspicion that he may be connected with criminal activity. Upon suspicion that the person may be armed, the police should have the power to "frisk" him for weapons. If the "stop" and the "frisk" give rise to probable cause to believe that the suspect has committed a crime, then the police should be empowered to make a formal "arrest," and a full incident "search" of the person. This scheme is justified in part upon the notion that a "stop" and a "frisk" amount to a mere "minor inconvenience and petty indignity," which can properly be imposed upon the citizen in the interest of effective law enforcement on the basis of a police officer's suspicion.

On the other side the argument is made that the authority of the police must be strictly circumscribed by the law of arrest and search as it has developed to date in the traditional jurisprudence of the Fourth Amendment. It is contended with some force that there is not—and cannot be—a variety of police activity which does not depend solely upon the voluntary cooperation of the citizen and yet which stops short of an arrest based upon probable cause to make such an arrest. The heart of the Fourth Amendment, the argument runs, is a severe requirement of specific justification for any intrusion upon protected personal security, coupled with a highly developed system of judicial controls to enforce upon the agents of the State the commands of the Constitution. Acquiescence by the courts in the compulsion inherent in the field interrogation practices at issue here, it is urged, would constitute an abdication of judicial control over, and indeed an encouragement of, substantial interference with liberty and personal security by police officers whose judgment is necessarily colored by their primary involvement in "the often competitive enterprise of ferreting out crime." This, it is argued, can only serve to exacerbate police-community tensions in the crowded centers of our Nation's cities.

In this context we approach the issues in this case mindful of the limitations of the judicial function in controlling the myriad daily situations in which policemen and citizens confront each other on the street. The State has characterized the issue here as "the right of a police officer . . . to make an on-the-street stop, interrogate and pat down for weapons (known in street vernacular as 'stop and frisk')." But this is only partly accurate. For the issue is not the abstract propriety of the police conduct, but the admissibility against petitioner of the evidence uncovered by the search and seizure. Ever since its inception, the rule excluding evidence seized in violation of the Fourth Amendment has been recognized as a principal mode of discouraging lawless police conduct. Thus its major thrust is a deterrent one, and experience has taught that it is the only effective deterrent to police misconduct in the criminal context, and that without it the constitutional guarantee against unreasonable searches and seizures would be a mere "form of words." The rule also serves another vital function—"the imperative of judicial integrity."

Courts which sit under our Constitution cannot and will not be made party to lawless invasions of the constitutional rights of citizens by permitting unhindered governmental use of the fruits of such invasions. Thus in our system evidentiary rulings provide the context in which the judicial process of inclusion and exclusion approves some conduct as comporting with constitutional guarantees and disapproves other actions by state agents. A ruling admitting evidence in a criminal trial, we recognize, has the necessary effect of legitimizing the conduct which produced the evidence, while an application of the exclusionary rule withholds the constitutional imprimatur.

The exclusionary rule has its limitations, however, as a tool of judicial control. It cannot properly be invoked to exclude the products of legitimate police investigative techniques on the ground that much conduct which is closely similar involves unwarranted intrusions upon constitutional protections. Moreover, in some contexts the rule is ineffective as a deterrent. Street encounters between citizens and police officers are incredibly rich in diversity. They range from wholly friendly exchanges of pleasantries or mutually useful information to hostile confrontations of armed men involving arrests, or injuries, or loss of life. Moreover, hostile confrontations are not all of a piece. Some of them begin in a friendly enough manner, only to take a different turn upon the injection of some unexpected element into the conversation. Encounters are initiated by the police for a wide variety of purposes, some of which are wholly unrelated to a desire to prosecute for crime. Doubtless some police "field interrogation" conduct violates the Fourth Amendment. But a stern refusal by this Court to condone such activity does not necessarily render it responsive to the exclusionary rule. Regardless of how effective the rule may be where obtaining convictions is an important objective of the police, it is powerless to deter invasions of constitutionally guaranteed rights where the police either have no interest in prosecuting or are willing to forgo successful prosecution in the interest of serving some other goal.

Proper adjudication of cases in which the exclusionary rule is invoked demands a constant awareness of these limitations. The wholesale harassment by certain elements of the police community, of which minority groups, particularly Negroes, frequently complain, will not be stopped by the exclusion of any evidence from any criminal trial. Yet a rigid and unthinking application of the exclusionary rule, in futile protest against practices which it can never be used effectively to control, may exact a high toll in human injury and frustration of efforts to prevent crime. No judicial opinion can comprehend the protean variety of the street encounter, and we can only judge the facts of the case before us. Nothing we say today is to be taken as indicating approval of police conduct outside the legitimate investigative sphere. Under our decision, courts still retain their traditional responsibility to guard against police conduct which is over-bearing or harassing, or which trenches upon personal security without the objective evidentiary justification which the Constitution requires. When such conduct is identified, it must be condemned by the judiciary and its fruits must be excluded from evidence in criminal trials. And, of course, our approval of legitimate and restrained investigative conduct undertaken on the basis of ample factual justification should in no way discourage the employment of other remedies than the exclusionary rule to curtail abuses for which that sanction may prove inappropriate.

Having thus roughly sketched the perimeters of the constitutional debate over the limits on police investigative conduct in general and the background against which this case presents itself, we turn our attention to the quite narrow question posed by the facts before us: whether it is always unreasonable for a policeman to seize a person and subject him to a limited search for weapons unless there is probable cause for an arrest. Given the narrowness of this question, we have no occasion to canvass in detail the constitutional limitations upon the scope of a policeman's power when he confronts a citizen without probable cause to arrest him.

II.

Our first task is to establish at what point in this encounter the Fourth Amendment becomes relevant. That is, we must decide whether and when Officer McFadden "seized" Terry and whether and when he conducted a "search." There is some suggestion in the use of such terms as "stop" and "frisk" that such police conduct is outside the purview of the Fourth Amendment because neither action rises to the level of a "search" or "seizure" within the meaning of the Constitution. We emphatically reject this notion. It is quite plain that the Fourth Amendment governs "seizures" of the person which do not eventuate in a trip to the station house and prosecution for crime—"arrests" in traditional terminology. It must be recognized that whenever a police officer accosts an individual and restrains his freedom to walk away, he has "seized" that person. And it is nothing less than sheer torture of the English language to suggest that a careful exploration of the outer surfaces of a person's clothing all over his or her body in an attempt to find weapons is not a "search." Moreover, it is simply fantastic to urge that such a procedure performed in public by a policeman while the citizen stands helpless, perhaps facing a wall with his hands raised, is a "petty indignity." It is a serious intrusion upon the sanctity of the person, which may inflict great indignity and arouse strong resentment, and it is not to be undertaken lightly.

The danger in the logic which proceeds upon distinctions between a "stop" and an "arrest," or "seizure" of the person, and between a "frisk" and a "search" is twofold. It seeks to isolate from constitutional scrutiny the initial stages of the contact between the policeman and the citizen. And by suggesting a rigid all-or-nothing model of justification and regulation under the Amendment, it obscures the utility of limitations upon the scope, as well as the initiation, of police action as a means of constitutional regulation. This Court has held in the past that a search which is reasonable at its inception may violate the Fourth Amendment by virtue of its intolerable intensity and scope. The scope of the search must be "strictly tied to and justified by" the circumstances which rendered its initiation permissible.

The distinctions of classical "stop-and-frisk" theory thus serve to divert attention from the central inquiry under the Fourth Amendment—the reasonableness in all the circumstances of the particular governmental invasion of a citizen's personal security. "Search" and "seizure" are not talismans. We therefore reject the notions that the Fourth Amendment does not come into play at all as a limitation upon police conduct if the officers stop short of something called a "technical arrest" or a "full-blown search."

In this case there can be no question, then, that Officer McFadden "seized" petitioner and subjected him to a "search" when he took hold of him and patted down the outer surfaces of his clothing. We must decide whether at that point it was reasonable for Officer McFadden to have interfered with petitioner's personal security as he did. And in determining whether the seizure and search were "unreasonable" our inquiry is a dual one—whether the officer's action was justified at its inception, and whether it was reasonably related in scope to the circumstances which justified the interference in the first place.

III.

If this case involved police conduct subject to the Warrant Clause of the Fourth Amendment, we would have to ascertain whether "probable cause" existed to justify the search and seizure which took place. However, that is not the case. We do not retreat from our holdings that the police must, whenever practicable, obtain advance judicial approval of searches and seizures through the warrant procedure, or that in most instances failure to comply with the warrant requirement can only be excused by exigent circumstances. But we deal here with an entire rubric of police conduct—necessarily swift action predicated upon the on-the-spot observations of the officer on the beat—which historically has not been, and as a practical matter could not be, subjected to the warrant procedure. Instead, the conduct involved in this case must be tested by the Fourth Amendment's general proscription against unreasonable searches and seizures.

Nonetheless, the notions which underlie both the warrant procedure and the requirement of probable cause remain fully relevant in this context. In order to assess the reasonableness of Officer McFadden's conduct as a general proposition, it is necessary "first to focus upon the governmental interest which allegedly justifies official intrusion upon the constitutionally protected interests of the private citizen," for there is "no ready test for determining reasonableness other than by balancing the need to search (or seize) against the invasion which the search (or seizure) entails." And in justifying the particular intrusion the police officer must be able to point to specific and articulable facts which, taken together with rational inferences from those facts, reasonably warrant that intrusion. The scheme of the Fourth Amendment becomes meaningful only when it is assured that at some point the conduct of those charged with enforcing the laws can be subjected to the more detached, neutral scrutiny of a judge who must evaluate the reasonableness of a particular search or seizure in light of the particular circumstances. And in making that assessment it is imperative that the facts be judged against an objective standard: would the facts available to the officer at the moment of the seizure or the search "warrant a man of reasonable caution in the belief" that the action taken was appropriate? Anything less would invite intrusions upon constitutionally guaranteed rights based on nothing more substantial than inarticulate hunches, a result this Court has consistently refused to sanction. And simple "good faith on the part of the arresting officer is not enough. . . . If subjective good faith alone were the test, the protections of the Fourth Amendment would evaporate, and the people would be "secure in their persons, houses, papers and effects,' only in the discretion of the police."

Applying these principles to this case, we consider first the nature and extent of the governmental interests involved. One general interest is of course that of effective crime prevention and detection; it is this interest which underlies the recognition that a police officer may in appropriate circumstances and in an appropriate manner approach a person for purposes of investigating possibly criminal behavior even though there is no probable cause to make an arrest. It was this legitimate investigative function Officer McFadden was discharging when he decided to approach petitioner and his companions. He had observed Terry, Chilton, and Katz go through a series of acts, each of them perhaps innocent in itself, but which taken together warranted further investigation. There is nothing unusual in two men standing together on a street corner, perhaps waiting for someone. Nor is there anything suspicious about people in such circumstances strolling up and down the street, singly or in pairs. Store windows, moreover, are made to be looked in. But the story is quite different where, as here, two men hover about a street corner for an extended period of time, at the end of which it becomes apparent that they are not waiting for anyone or anything; where these men pace alternately along an identical route, pausing to stare in the same store window roughly [twenty-four] times; where each completion of this route is followed immediately by a conference between the two men on the corner; where they are joined in one of these conferences by a third man who leaves swiftly; and where the two men finally follow the third and rejoin him a couple of blocks away. It would have been poor police work indeed for an officer of [thirty] years' experience in the detection of thievery from stores in this same neighborhood to have failed to investigate this behavior further.

The crux of this case, however, is not the propriety of Officer McFadden's taking steps to investigate petitioner's suspicious behavior, but rather, whether there was justification for McFadden's invasion of Terry's personal security by searching him for weapons in the course of that investigation. We are now concerned with more than the governmental interest in investigating crime; in addition, there is the more immediate interest of the police officer in taking steps to assure himself that the person with whom he is dealing is not armed with a weapon that could unexpectedly and fatally be used against him. Certainly it would be unreasonable to require that police officers take unnecessary risks in the performance of their duties. American criminals have a long tradition of armed violence, and every year in this country many law enforcement officers are killed in the line of duty, and thousands more are wounded. Virtually all of these deaths and a substantial portion of the injuries are inflicted with guns and knives.

In view of these facts, we cannot blind ourselves to the need for law enforcement officers to protect themselves and other prospective victims of violence in situations where they may lack probable cause for an arrest. When an officer is justified in believing that the individual whose suspicious behavior he is investigating at close range is armed and presently dangerous to the officer or to others, it would appear to be clearly unreasonable to deny the officer the power to take necessary measures to determine whether the person is in fact carrying a weapon and to neutralize the threat of physical harm.

We must still consider, however, the nature and quality of the intrusion on individual rights which must be accepted if police officers are to be conceded the right to search for weapons in situations where probable cause to arrest for crime is lacking. Even a limited search of the outer clothing for weapons constitutes a severe, though brief, intrusion upon cherished personal security, and it must surely be an annoying, frightening, and perhaps humiliating experience. Petitioner contends that such an intrusion is permissible only incident to a lawful arrest, either for a crime involving the possession of weapons or for a crime the commission of which led the officer to investigate in the first place. However, this argument must be closely examined.

Petitioner does not argue that a police officer should refrain from making any investigation of suspicious circumstances until such time as he has probable cause to make an arrest; nor does he deny that police officers in properly discharging their investigative function may find themselves confronting persons who might well be armed and dangerous. Moreover, he does not say that an officer is always unjustified in searching a suspect to discover weapons. Rather, he says it is unreasonable for the policeman to take that step until such time as the situation evolves to a point where there is probable cause to make an arrest. When that point has been reached, petitioner would concede the officer's right to conduct a search of the suspect for weapons, fruits or instrumentalities of the crime, or "mere" evidence, incident to the arrest.

There are two weaknesses in this line of reasoning however. First, it fails to take account of traditional limitations upon the scope of searches, and thus recognizes no distinction in purpose, character, and extent between a search incident to an arrest and a limited search for weapons. The former, although justified in part by the acknowledged necessity to protect the arresting officer from assault with a concealed weapon, is also justified on other grounds, and can therefore involve a relatively extensive exploration of the person. A search for weapons in the absence of probable cause to arrest, however, must, like any other search, be strictly circumscribed by the exigencies which justify its initiation. Thus it must be limited to that which is necessary for the discovery of weapons which might be used to harm the officer or others nearby, and may realistically be characterized as something less than a 'full' search, even though it remains a serious intrusion.

A second, and related, objection to petitioner's argument is that it assumes that the law of arrest has already worked out the balance between the particular interests involved here—the neutralization of danger to the policeman in the investigative circumstance and the sanctity of the individual. But this is not so. An arrest is a wholly different kind of intrusion upon individual freedom from a limited search for weapons, and the interests each is designed to serve are likewise quite different. An arrest is the initial stage of a criminal prosecution. It is intended to vindicate society's interest in having its laws obeyed, and it is inevitably accompanied by future interference with the individual's freedom of movement, whether or not trial or conviction ultimately follows. The protective search for weapons, on the other hand, constitutes a brief, though far from inconsiderable, intrusion upon the sanctity of the person. It does not follow that because an officer may lawfully arrest a person only when he is apprised of facts sufficient to warrant a belief that the person has committed or is committing a crime, the officer is equally unjustified, absent that kind of evidence, in making any intrusions short of an arrest. Moreover, a perfectly reasonable apprehension of danger may arise long before the officer is possessed of adequate information to justify taking a person into custody for the purpose of prosecuting him for a crime. Petitioner's reliance on cases which have worked out standards of reasonableness with regard to "seizures" constituting arrests and searches incident thereto is thus misplaced. It assumes that the interests sought to be vindicated and the invasions of personal security may be equated in the two cases, and thereby ignores a vital aspect of the analysis of the reasonableness of particular types of conduct under the Fourth Amendment.

Our evaluation of the proper balance that has to be struck in this type of case leads us to conclude that there must be a narrowly drawn authority to permit a reasonable search for weapons for the protection of the police officer, where he has reason to believe that he is dealing with an armed and dangerous individual, regardless of whether he has probable cause to arrest the individual for a crime. The officer need not be absolutely certain that the individual is armed; the issue is whether a reasonably prudent man in the circumstances would be warranted in the belief that his safety or that of others was in danger. And in determining whether the officer acted reasonably in such circumstances, due weight must be given, not to his inchoate and unparticularized suspicion or "hunch," but to the specific reasonable inferences which he is entitled to draw from the facts in light of his experience.

IV.

We must now examine the conduct of Officer McFadden in this case to determine whether his search and seizure of petitioner were reasonable, both at their inception and as conducted. He had observed Terry, together with Chilton and another man, acting in a manner he took to be preface to a "stick-up." We think on the facts and circumstances Officer McFadden detailed before the trial judge a reasonably prudent man would have been warranted in believing petitioner was armed and thus presented a threat to the officer's safety while he was investigating his suspicious behavior. The actions of Terry and Chilton were consistent with McFadden's hypothesis that these men were contemplating a daylight robbery—which, it is reasonable to assume, would be likely to involve the use of weapons—and nothing in their conduct from the time he first noticed them until the time he confronted them and identified himself as a police officer gave him sufficient reason to negate that hypothesis. Although the trio had departed the original scene, there was nothing to indicate abandonment of an intent to commit a robbery at some point. Thus, when Officer McFadden approached the three men gathered before the display window at Zucker's store he had observed enough to make it quite reasonable to fear that they were armed; and nothing in their response to his hailing them, identifying himself as a police officer, and asking their names served to dispel that reasonable belief. We cannot say his decision at that point to seize Terry and pat his clothing for weapons was the product of a volatile or inventive imagination, or was undertaken simply as an act of harassment; the record evidences the tempered act of a policeman who in the course of an investigation had to make a quick decision as to how to protect himself and others from possible danger, and took limited steps to do so.

The manner in which the seizure and search were conducted is, of course, as vital a part of the inquiry as whether they were warranted at all. . . . The sole justification of the search in the present situation is the protection of the police officer and others nearby, and it must therefore be confined in scope to an intrusion reasonably designed to discover guns, knives, clubs, or other hidden instruments for the assault of the police officer.

The scope of the search in this case presents no serious problem in light of these standards. Officer McFadden patted down the outer clothing of petitioner and his two companions. He did not place his hands in their pockets or under the outer surface of their garments until he had felt weapons, and then he merely reached for and removed the guns. He never did invade Katz' person beyond the outer surfaces of his clothes, since he discovered nothing in his patdown which might have been a weapon. Officer McFadden confined his search strictly to what was minimally necessary to learn whether the men were armed and to disarm them once he discovered the weapons. He did not conduct a general exploratory search for whatever evidence of criminal activity he might find.

V.

We conclude that the revolver seized from Terry was properly admitted in evidence against him. At the time he seized petitioner and searched him for weapons, Officer McFadden had reasonable grounds to believe that petitioner was armed and dangerous, and it was necessary for the protection of himself and others to take swift measures to discover the true facts and neutralize the threat of harm if it materialized. The policeman carefully restricted his search to what was appropriate to the discovery of the particular items which he sought. Each case of this sort will, of course, have to be decided on its own facts. We merely hold today that where a police officer observes unusual conduct which leads him reasonably to conclude in light of his experience that criminal activity may be afoot and that the persons with whom he is dealing may be armed and presently dangerous, where in the course of investigating this behavior he identifies himself as a policeman and makes reasonable inquiries, and where nothing in the initial stages of the encounter serves to dispel his reasonable fear for his own or others' safety, he is entitled for the protection of himself and others in the area to conduct a carefully limited search of the outer clothing of such persons in an attempt to discover weapons which might be used to assault him. Such a search is a reasonable search under the Fourth Amendment, and any weapons seized may properly be introduced in evidence against the person from whom they were taken.

Affirmed.

[The concurring opinions of Justices BLACK, HARLAN, and WHITE are omitted.]

Mr. Justice DOUGLAS, dissenting.

I agree that petitioner was "seized" within the meaning of the Fourth Amendment. I also agree that frisking petitioner and his companions for guns was a "search." But it is a mystery how that "search" and that "seizure" can be constitutional by Fourth Amendment standards, unless there was "probable cause" to believe that (1) a crime had been committed or (2) a crime was in the process of being committed or (3) a crime was about to be committed.

The opinion of the Court disclaims the existence of "probable cause." If loitering were in issue and that was the offense charged, there would be 'probable cause' shown. But the crime here is carrying concealed weapons; and there is no basis for concluding that the officer had "probable cause" for believing that that crime was being committed. Had a warrant been sought, a magistrate would, therefore, have been unauthorized to issue one, for he can act only if there is a showing of "probable cause." We hold today that the police have greater authority to make a "seizure" and conduct a "search" than a judge has to authorize such action. We have said precisely the opposite over and over again.

In other words, police officers up to today have been permitted to effect arrests or searches without warrants only when the facts within their personal knowledge would satisfy the constitutional standard of probable cause. At the time of their "seizure" without a warrant they must possess facts concerning the person arrested that would have satisfied a magistrate that "probable cause" was indeed present. The term "probable cause" rings a bell of certainty that is not sounded by phrases such as "reasonable suspicion." Moreover, the meaning of "probable cause" is deeply imbedded in our constitutional history. As we stated in *Henry v. United States*:

> The requirement of probable cause has roots that are deep in our history. The general warrant, in which the name of the person to be arrested was left blank, and the writs of assistance, against which James Otis inveighed, both perpetuated the oppressive practice of allowing the police to arrest and search on suspicion. Police control took the place of judicial control, since no showing of "probable cause" before a magistrate was required.
>
> That philosophy (rebelling against these practices) later was reflected in the Fourth Amendment. And as the early American decisions both before and immediately after its adoption show, common rumor or report, suspicion, or even "strong reason to suspect" was not adequate to support a warrant for arrest. And that principle has survived to this day.
>
> . . . It is important, we think, that this requirement (of probable cause) be strictly enforced, for the standard set by the Constitution protects both the officer and the citizen. If the officer acts with probable cause, he is protected even though it turns out that the citizen is innocent. . . . And while a search without a warrant is, within limits, permissible if incident to a lawful arrest, if an arrest without a warrant is to support an incidental search, it must be made with probable cause. . . . This immunity of officers cannot fairly be enlarged without jeopardizing the privacy or security of the citizen.

The infringement on personal liberty of any "seizure" of a person can only be "reasonable" under the Fourth Amendment if we require the police to possess "probable cause" before they seize him. Only that line draws a meaningful distinction between an officer's mere inkling and the presence of facts within the officer's personal knowledge which would convince a reasonable man that the person seized has committed, is committing, or is about to commit a particular crime. "In dealing with probable cause, . . . as the very name implies, we deal with probabilities. These are not technical; they are the factual and practical considerations of everyday life on which reasonable and prudent men, not legal technicians, act."

To give the police greater power than a magistrate is to take a long step down the totalitarian path. Perhaps such a step is desirable to cope with modern forms of lawlessness. But if it is taken, it should be the deliberate choice of the people through a constitutional amendment. Until the Fourth Amendment, which is closely allied with the Fifth, is rewritten, the person and the effects of the individual are beyond the reach of all government agencies until there are reasonable grounds to believe (probable cause) that a criminal venture has been launched or is about to be launched.

There have been powerful hydraulic pressures throughout our history that bear heavily on the Court to water down constitutional guarantees and give the police the upper hand. That hydraulic pressure has probably never been greater than it is today.

Yet if the individual is no longer to be sovereign, if the police can pick him up whenever they do not like the cut of his jib, if they can "seize" and "search" him in their discretion, we enter a new regime. The decision to enter it should be made only after a full debate by the people of this country.

FROM THE COURTROOM

ILLINOIS v. WARDLOW

United States Supreme Court, 2000
528 U.S.119

[Chief Justice REHNQUIST delivered the opinion of the Court.]

[Justice STEVENS concurred in part and dissented in part, in an opinion joined by Justices SOUTER, GINSBURG, and BREYER.]

Respondent Wardlow fled upon seeing police officers patrolling an area known for heavy narcotics trafficking. Two of the officers caught up with him, stopped him and conducted a protective patdown search for weapons. Discovering a .38–caliber handgun, the officers arrested Wardlow. We hold that the officers' stop did not violate the Fourth Amendment to the United States Constitution.

On September 9, 1995, Officers Nolan and Harvey were working as uniformed officers in the special operations section of the Chicago Police Department. The officers were driving the last car of a four car caravan converging on an area known for heavy narcotics trafficking in order to investigate drug transactions. The officers were traveling together because they expected to find a crowd of people in the area, including lookouts and customers.

As the caravan passed 4035 West Van Buren, Officer Nolan observed respondent Wardlow standing next to the building holding an opaque bag. Respondent looked in the direction of the officers and fled. Nolan and Harvey turned their car southbound, watched him as he ran through the gangway and an alley, and eventually cornered him on the street. Nolan then exited his car and stopped respondent. He immediately conducted a protective patdown search for weapons because in his experience it was common for there to be weapons in the near vicinity of narcotics transactions. During the frisk, Officer Nolan squeezed the bag respondent was carrying and felt a heavy, hard object similar to the shape of a gun. The officer then opened the bag and discovered a .38–caliber handgun with five live rounds of ammunition. The officers arrested Wardlow.

. . .

This case, involving a brief encounter between a citizen and a police officer on a public street, is governed by the analysis we first applied in *Terry*. In *Terry*, we held that an officer may, consistent with the Fourth Amendment, conduct a brief, investigatory stop when the officer has a reasonable, articulable suspicion that criminal activity is afoot. While "reasonable suspicion" is a less demanding standard than probable cause and requires a showing considerably less than preponderance of the evidence, the Fourth Amendment requires at least a minimal level of objective justification for making the stop. The officer must be able to articulate more than an "inchoate and unparticularized suspicion or 'hunch'" of criminal activity.

Nolan and Harvey were among eight officers in a four-car caravan that was converging on an area known for heavy narcotics trafficking, and the officers anticipated encountering a large number of people in the area, including drug customers and individuals serving as lookouts. It was in this context that Officer Nolan decided to investigate Wardlow after observing him flee. An individual's presence in an area of expected criminal activity, standing alone, is not enough to support a reasonable, particularized suspicion that the person is committing a crime. But officers are not required to ignore the relevant characteristics of a location in determining whether the circumstances are sufficiently suspicious to warrant further investigation. Accordingly, we have previously noted the fact that the stop occurred in a "high crime area" among the relevant contextual considerations in a *Terry* analysis.

In this case, moreover, it was not merely respondent's presence in an area of heavy narcotics trafficking that aroused the officers' suspicion, but his unprovoked flight upon noticing the police. Our cases have also recognized that nervous, evasive behavior is a pertinent factor in determining reasonable suspicion. Headlong flight—wherever it occurs—is the consummate act of evasion: It is not necessarily indicative of wrongdoing, but it is certainly suggestive of such. In reviewing the propriety of an officer's conduct, courts do not have available empirical studies dealing with inferences drawn from suspicious behavior, and we cannot reasonably demand scientific certainty from judges or law enforcement officers where none exists. Thus, the determination of reasonable suspicion must be based on commonsense judgments and inferences about human behavior. We conclude Officer Nolan was justified in suspecting that Wardlow was involved in criminal activity, and, therefore, in investigating further.

Such a holding is entirely consistent with our decision in *Florida v. Royer*, where we held that when an officer, without reasonable suspicion or probable cause, approaches an individual, the individual has a right to ignore the police and go about his business. And any "refusal to cooperate, without more, does not furnish the minimal level of objective justification needed for a detention or seizure." But unprovoked flight is simply not a mere refusal to cooperate. Flight, by its very nature, is not "going about one's business"; in fact, it is just the opposite. Allowing officers confronted with such flight to stop the fugitive and investigate further is quite consistent with the individual's right to go about his business or to stay put and remain silent in the face of police questioning.

Respondent and *amici* also argue that there are innocent reasons for flight from police and that, therefore, flight is not necessarily indicative of ongoing criminal activity. This fact is undoubtedly true, but does not establish a violation of the Fourth Amendment. Even in *Terry*, the conduct justifying the stop was ambiguous and susceptible of an innocent explanation. The officer observed two individuals pacing back and forth in front of a store, peering into the window and periodically conferring. All of this conduct was by itself lawful, but it also suggested that the individuals were casing the store for a planned robbery. *Terry* recognized that the officers could detain the individuals to resolve the ambiguity.

In allowing such detentions, *Terry* accepts the risk that officers may stop innocent people. Indeed, the Fourth Amendment accepts that risk in connection with more drastic police action; persons arrested and detained on probable cause to believe they have committed a crime may turn out to be innocent. The *Terry* stop is a far more minimal intrusion, simply allowing the officer to briefly investigate further. If the officer does not learn facts rising to the level of probable cause, the individual must be allowed to go on his way. But in this case the officers found respondent in possession of a handgun, and arrested him for violation of an Illinois firearms statute. No question of the propriety of the arrest itself is before us.

The judgment of the Supreme Court of Illinois is reversed, and the cause is remanded for further proceedings not inconsistent with this opinion.

It is so ordered.

Justice STEVENS, with whom Justice SOUTER, Justice GINSBURG, and Justice BREYER join, concurring in part and dissenting in part.

The State of Illinois asks this Court to announce a "bright-line rule" authorizing the temporary detention of anyone who flees at the mere sight of a police officer. Respondent counters by asking us to adopt the opposite *per se* rule—that the fact that a person flees upon seeing the police can never, by itself, be sufficient to justify a temporary investigative stop of the kind authorized by *Terry v. Ohio*.

The Court today wisely endorses neither *per se* rule. Instead, it rejects the proposition that "flight is . . . necessarily indicative of ongoing criminal activity," adhering to the view that "[t]he concept of reasonable suspicion . . . is not readily, or even usefully, reduced to a neat set of legal rules," but must be determined by looking to "the totality of the circumstances—the whole picture." Abiding by this framework, the Court concludes that "Officer Nolan was justified in suspecting that Wardlow was involved in criminal activity."

Although I agree with the Court's rejection of the *per se* rules proffered by the parties, unlike the Court, I am persuaded that in this case the brief testimony of the officer who seized respondent does not justify the conclusion that he had reasonable suspicion to make the stop. Before discussing the specific facts of this case, I shall comment on the parties' requests for a *per se* rule.

I

. . .

The question in this case concerns "the degree of suspicion that attaches to" a person's flight—or, more precisely, what "commonsense conclusions" can be drawn respecting the motives behind that flight. A pedestrian may break into a run for a variety of reasons—to catch up with a friend a block or two away, to seek shelter from an impending storm, to arrive at a bus stop before the bus leaves, to get home in time for dinner, to resume jogging after a pause for rest, to avoid contact with a bore or a bully, or simply to answer the call of nature—any of which might coincide with the arrival of an officer in the vicinity. A pedestrian might also run because he or she has just sighted one or more police officers. In the latter instance, the State properly points out "that the fleeing person may be, *inter alia,* (1) an escapee from jail; (2) wanted on a warrant; (3) in possession of contraband, (i.e. drugs, weapons, stolen goods, etc.); or (4) someone who has just committed another type of crime." In short, there are unquestionably circumstances in which a person's flight is suspicious, and undeniably instances in which a person runs for entirely innocent reasons.

Given the diversity and frequency of possible motivations for flight, it would be profoundly unwise to endorse either *per se* rule. The inference we can reasonably draw about the motivation for a person's flight, rather, will depend on a number of different circumstances. Factors such as the time of day, the number of people in the area, the character of the neighborhood, whether the officer was in uniform, the way the runner was dressed, the direction and speed of the flight, and whether the person's behavior was otherwise unusual might be relevant in specific cases. This number of variables is surely sufficient to preclude either a bright-line rule that always justifies, or that never justifies, an investigative stop based on the sole fact that flight began after a police officer appeared nearby.

Still, Illinois presses for a *per se* rule regarding "unprovoked flight upon seeing a clearly identifiable police officer." The phrase "upon seeing," as used by Illinois, apparently assumes that the flight is motivated by the presence of the police officer. Illinois contends that unprovoked flight is "an extreme reaction," because innocent people simply do not "flee at the mere sight of the police," To be sure, Illinois concedes, an innocent person—even one distrustful of the police—might "avoid eye contact or even sneer at the sight of an officer," and that would not justify a *Terry* stop or any sort of *per se* inference. But, Illinois insists, unprovoked flight is altogether different. Such behavior is so "aberrant" and "abnormal" that a *per se* inference is justified.

Even assuming we know that a person runs because he sees the police, the inference to be drawn may still vary from case to case. Flight to escape police detection, we have said, may have an entirely innocent motivation:

> [I]t is a matter of common knowledge that men who are entirely innocent do sometimes fly from the scene of a crime through fear of being apprehended as the guilty parties, or from an unwillingness to appear as witnesses. Nor is it true as an accepted axiom of criminal law that "the wicked flee when no man pursueth, but the righteous are as bold as a lion." Innocent men sometimes hesitate to confront a jury—not necessarily because they fear that the jury will not protect them, but because they do not wish their names to appear in connection with criminal acts, are humiliated at being obliged to incur the popular odium of an arrest and trial, or because they do not wish to be put to the annoyance or expense of defending themselves.

In addition to these concerns, a reasonable person may conclude that an officer's sudden appearance indicates nearby criminal activity. And where there is criminal activity there is also a substantial element of danger—either from the criminal or from a confrontation between the criminal and the police. These considerations can lead to an innocent and understandable desire to quit the vicinity with all speed.

Among some citizens, particularly minorities and those residing in high crime areas, there is also the possibility that the fleeing person is entirely innocent, but, with or without justification, believes that contact with the police can itself be dangerous, apart from any criminal activity associated with the officer's sudden presence. For such a person, unprovoked flight is neither "aberrant" nor "abnormal." Moreover, these concerns and fears are known to the police officers themselves, and are validated by law enforcement investigations into their own practices. Accordingly, the evidence supporting the reasonableness of these beliefs is too pervasive to be dismissed as random or rare, and too persuasive to be disparaged as inconclusive or insufficient. In any event, just as we do not require "scientific certainty" for our commonsense conclusion that unprovoked flight can sometimes indicate suspicious motives, see neither do we require scientific certainty to conclude that unprovoked flight can occur for other, innocent reasons.

. . .

"Unprovoked flight," in short, describes a category of activity too broad and varied to permit a *per se* reasonable inference regarding the motivation for the activity. While the innocent explanations surely do not establish that the Fourth Amendment is always violated whenever someone is stopped solely on the basis of an unprovoked flight, neither do the suspicious motivations establish that the Fourth Amendment is never violated when a *Terry* stop is predicated on that fact alone. For these reasons, the Court is surely correct in refusing to embrace either *per se* rule advocated by the parties. The totality of the circumstances, as always, must dictate the result.

II.

Guided by that totality-of-the-circumstances test, the Court concludes that Officer Nolan had reasonable suspicion to stop respondent. In this respect, my view differs from the Court's. The entire justification for the stop is articulated in the brief testimony of Officer Nolan. Some facts are perfectly clear; others are not. This factual insufficiency leads me to conclude that the Court's judgment is mistaken.

Respondent Wardlow was arrested a few minutes after noon on September 9, 1995. Nolan was part of an eight-officer, four-car caravan patrol team. The officers were headed for "one of the areas in the 11th District [of Chicago] that's high [in] narcotics traffic." The reason why four cars were in the caravan was that "[n]ormally in these different areas there's an enormous amount of people, sometimes lookouts, customers." Officer Nolan testified that he was in uniform on that day, but he did not recall whether he was driving a marked or an unmarked car.

Officer Nolan and his partner were in the last of the four patrol cars that "were all caravaning eastbound down Van Buren." Nolan first observed respondent "in front of 4035 West Van Buren." Wardlow "looked in our direction and began fleeing." Nolan then "began driving southbound down the street observing [respondent] running through the gangway and the alley southbound," and observed that Wardlow was carrying a white, opaque bag under his arm. After the car turned south and intercepted respondent as he "ran right towards us," Officer Nolan stopped him and conducted a "protective search," which revealed that the bag under respondent's arm contained a loaded handgun.

This terse testimony is most noticeable for what it fails to reveal. Though asked whether he was in a marked or unmarked car, Officer Nolan could not recall the answer. He was not asked whether any of the other three cars in the caravan were marked, or whether any of the other seven officers were in uniform. Though he explained that the size of the caravan was because "[n]ormally in these different areas there's an enormous amount of people, sometimes lookouts, customers," Officer Nolan did not testify as to whether *anyone* besides Wardlow was nearby 4035 West Van Buren. Nor is it clear that that address was the intended destination of the caravan. As the Appellate Court of Illinois interpreted the record, "it appears that the officers were simply driving by, on their way to some unidentified location, when they noticed defendant standing at 4035 West Van Buren." Officer Nolan's testimony also does not reveal how fast the officers were driving. It does not indicate whether he saw respondent notice the other patrol cars. And it does not say whether the caravan, or any part of it, had already passed Wardlow by before he began to run.

Indeed, the Appellate Court thought the record was even "too vague to support the inference that . . . defendant's flight was related to his expectation of police focus on him." Presumably, respondent did not react to the first three cars, and we cannot even be sure that he recognized the occupants of the fourth as police officers. The adverse inference is based entirely on the officer's statement: "He looked in our direction and began fleeing."

No other factors sufficiently support a finding of reasonable suspicion. Though respondent was carrying a white, opaque bag under his arm, there is nothing at all suspicious about that. Certainly the time of day—shortly after noon—does not support Illinois' argument. Nor were the officers "responding to any call or report of suspicious activity in the area." Officer Nolan did testify that he expected to find "an enormous amount of people," including drug customers or lookouts, and the Court points out that "[i]t was in this context that Officer Nolan decided to investigate Wardlow after observing him flee," This observation, in my view, lends insufficient weight to the reasonable suspicion analysis; indeed, in light of the absence of testimony that anyone else was nearby when respondent began to run, this observation points in the opposite direction.

The State, along with the majority of the Court, relies as well on the assumption that this flight occurred in a high crime area. Even if that assumption is accurate, it is insufficient because even in a high crime neighborhood unprovoked flight does not invariably lead to reasonable suspicion. On the contrary, because many factors providing innocent motivations for unprovoked flight are concentrated in high crime areas, the character of the neighborhood arguably makes an inference of guilt less appropriate, rather than more so. Like unprovoked flight itself, presence in a high crime neighborhood is a fact too generic and susceptible to innocent explanation to satisfy the reasonable suspicion inquiry.

It is the State's burden to articulate facts sufficient to support reasonable suspicion. In my judgment, Illinois has failed to discharge that burden. I am not persuaded that the mere fact that someone standing on a sidewalk looked in the direction of a passing car before starting to run is sufficient to justify a forcible stop and frisk.

I therefore respectfully dissent from the Court's judgment to reverse the court below.

20

More Than a Search

Key Concepts

- Statutes Can Create Greater Protections than the Fourth Amendment Provides
- Wiretapping Requires a "Title III Order"
- Courts Set More Stringent Standards for Other Highly Intrusive Surveillance Methods

A. Overview. As a general rule, the more intrusive a surveillance method, the greater the legal requirements law enforcement must meet to conduct that surveillance. So far, we have seen a number of examples of this principle: non-intrusive surveillance (such as following a car on a public street) is unregulated by the Fourth Amendment; brief stops and frisks require reasonable suspicion; and searches of a home require probable cause and prior judicial approval. But as it turns out, a "search" is not the most intrusive category of surveillance. There are certain types of surveillance that are even more intrusive, and are, therefore, given even greater protection than the warrant requirement.

Frequently the Supreme Court is the source of these higher standards—for example, the Court has set high standards for searches that violate a person's bodily integrity, such as performing surgery to remove a bullet. Sometimes, however, these higher standards are set by Congress or by a state legislature, such as the rules governing electronic bugging and wiretapping.

Up until now, we have not discussed the legislative role in regulating government surveillance. Instead, our discussion of search and seizure law has focused almost exclusively on the Fourth Amendment. Thus, the rules and tests we have explored to this point have all been created by courts, based on their interpretation of the Constitution. However, the Fourth Amendment is not the only source of search and seizure law. Over the past few decades, legislatures have taken a much more aggressive role in regulating surveillance. The next two chapters will discuss some of these legislative restrictions.

Today there are dozens of federal provisions that regulate surveillance. For example, federal law limits the interception of oral, telephonic, and electronic communications;[1] controls government access to stored wire and electronic communications held by internet service providers;[2] and sets out rules for electronic surveillance of agents of foreign powers.[3] These statutes create a complex regime of surveillance regulation. When courts are evaluating the legality of a surveillance method—particularly if the surveillance method involves a relatively new technology—the court will frequently apply statutory rules rather than the Fourth Amendment.

Although legislative rules are becoming more common, they are always limited in one significant way—because the Constitution is the supreme law of the land, statutory rules cannot provide **fewer** protections than the Fourth Amendment affords. In this sense, the Fourth Amendment creates a minimum floor of individual rights that cannot be affected by legislative action.

This is sometimes a source of confusion in the popular media. For example, in 2001 Congress passed the Uniting and Strengthening America by Providing Appropriate Tools Required to Intercept and Obstruct Terrorism (known as the "PATRIOT Act") in response to the terrorist attacks that occurred that year. Many commentators criticized the PATRIOT Act for allowing government agents to violate basic constitutional rights. However, no act of Congress can authorize conduct that is prohibited by the Constitution. Consequently, when certain provisions of the Act were found to be in violation of the Fourth Amendment, courts ultimately invalidated those provisions. Other provisions of the PATRIOT Act that were also critiqued as unconstitutional were not. These sections did not remove previously recognized constitutional protections, but rather merely removed previously existing **statutory** protections (such as restrictions on when the government could access stored voicemail).

Though statutes may not afford fewer protections than the Constitution allows, statutes can always provide **more** protection than the Fourth Amendment. Thus, there are two categories of statutory search and seizure rules:

1. Statutes that apply to extremely intrusive types of surveillance for which the Fourth Amendment already requires probable cause and a warrant. These statutes create standards for the government that go above and beyond Fourth Amendment standards.

2. Statutes that apply to surveillance that is not covered by the Fourth Amendment. These statutes create a minimal level of protection in the absence of the Constitutional protection.

---

[1] See Title III of the Omnibus Crime Control and Safe Streets Act of 1968 (18 U.S.C. §§ 2516–2518 (2006)); 1986 Electronic Communications Privacy Act (Pub. L. No., 99-508, 100 Stat. 1848 (1986)).

[2] See Stored Communications Act (18 U.S.C. §§ 2701–2712 (2006)).

[3] See Foreign Intelligence Surveillance Act of 1978 (Pub.L. 95-511, 92 Stat. 1783 (1978)).

In this chapter, we will examine the first category of statutory restrictions, where Congress has exceeded the Fourth Amendment's warrant requirement by creating even stricter standards for the government to meet. Specifically, we will discuss the Wiretap Act, as amended by the Electronic Communications Privacy Act ("ECPA"), which governs the rules for electronic bugging, wiretapping telephones, and interception of emails and other electronic transmissions. We will also examine the instances when the Supreme Court has held that a search is so intrusive that the Fourth Amendment requires more than a warrant. In **Chapter 21**, we will consider the second category of statutory restrictions—those instances in which Congress has stepped in to create minimal statutory protections regarding government actions that are unregulated by the Fourth Amendment.

B. Introduction and Policy. As we will see below, there are many examples of "hyper-intrusive" searches that require more than a warrant: real-time video surveillance of private homes; interception of digital communications while in-transit; searches that involve substantial bodily intrusions; or officers executing a search warrant without first knocking and announcing their presence. But perhaps the most prominent of these hyper-intrusive searches is wiretapping a telephone.

Monitoring telephone conversations is more intrusive than a traditional physical search for a number of reasons:

1. Wiretapping is necessarily more secretive because the target does not know the surveillance is occurring.

2. The surveillance is not a one-time search but is ongoing and continuous, analogous to a law enforcement officer taking up residence in a house and constantly searching all of its rooms.

3. The surveillance is almost certain to be overbroad, because eavesdropping officers often hear many different types of conversations, only a few of which may be pertinent to the crime being investigated. In fact, it is impossible to know whether a specific conversation is pertinent until it has already been "seized" (that is, listened to by the investigating officer). In contrast, the particularity requirements of warrants means that a physical search must be limited to a location and to areas in that location where the specific item being sought might be hidden, and law enforcement may not seize any item unless it has been specified in the warrant and thus pre-approved by a court.

The Supreme Court was the first to recognize that wiretapping is more intrusive than a traditional search. In 1967, the same year that the Supreme Court decided the *Katz* case, it addressed the issue of wiretapping in *Berger v. New York*.[4] The Supreme Court held that intercepting a telephone call was a "search" that required at least a warrant—but its language implied that this type of surveillance was so intrusive that it might require a greater showing than mere probable cause. The *Berger* Court did not specify what that showing might be. In fact, a few Justices on the Court expressed doubt that any standard would be sufficient to justify a search that was so intrusive.[5]

Congress responded to this challenge the next year by passing the Wiretap Act, officially known as Title III of the Omnibus Crime Control and Safe Streets Act of 1968. As we will see below, the Wiretap Act sets out strict requirements for the government to meet before it intercepts oral or telephone communications. Nearly twenty years later, as people began using computers to communicate with each other, Congress passed the ECPA, which amended the Wiretap Act to include electronic communications in addition to oral and telephone communications. The resulting law is ubiquitously known as "Title III," after the provision that created the law in the original legislation. The Supreme Court has never officially ruled on the constitutionality of Title III, but its tacit acceptance of Title III's rules have made it clear that Title III provides at least as much protection as the Fourth Amendment requires. Whether it provides **more** protection than what is required by the Fourth Amendment—that is, whether Congress could loosen its requirements and still satisfy the Constitution—is unclear.

C. The Law. Here are the major provisions of Title III:

> In order to electronically monitor a private conversation or intercept wire or electronic transmissions as they are being transmitted, the government must obtain a "Title III order."
>
> An application for a Title III order must be authorized by a prosecuting attorney in the Department of Justice (on the federal level) or by the primary prosecuting attorney of the state, county, or city that is conducting the investigation (on the local level).
>
> To receive a Title III order, the government must demonstrate the following:
>
> 1. "Normal investigative procedures" have been tried and failed, are unlikely to succeed, or are dangerous (known as the "least intrusive means" requirement);

[4] 388 U.S. 41 (1967).

[5] Id. at 70 (Black., J., dissenting).

2. The surveillance will be conducted in a way that minimizes the interception of irrelevant information (known as the "minimization" requirement);

3. There is probable cause that the target is committing, has committed, or is about to commit an offense on Title III's limited list of specified crimes; and

4. There is probable cause to believe that the interception will reveal evidence of that offense.

The government must specify the type of facilities from which the communications will be intercepted and a particular description of the type of communication sought to be intercepted.

The Title III order only authorizes monitoring for as long as is necessary to achieve the objective and can never authorize monitoring for more than thirty days. The government can request an extension, but it must meet the same requirements as it did for the original order.[6]

Note that Title III only applies to surveillance that intercepts transmissions **as they are happening.** Once the transmission reaches its destination, it is no longer covered by the Wiretap Act. Thus, telephone messages stored in voicemail, e-mails, or texts stored on cell phones, computers, or remote accounts do not receive protection from the Wiretap Act. If the received communications are stored on the recipient's cell phone or hard drive, the government must obtain a warrant to search the cell phone or hard drive. If the received communications are stored on a remote server, the Fourth Amendment does not apply, but the Stored Communications Act (discussed in **Chapter 21**) provides some statutory protection.

Also note that under Supreme Court's current interpretation of the law neither Title III nor the Fourth Amendment applies to address information, such as dialed telephone numbers or the address line of an e-mail. Those are considered "non-content" information, and they receive the lowest level of statutory protection under the Pen Register Act (also discussed in **Chapter 21**). However, the 2013 revelation of the NSA's mass collection of telephone call metadata has caused increased public discussion of the issue. Moreover, with two lower court opinions on the practice coming to divergent conclusions about its likely legality,[7] it is probable the issue will ultimately need to be resolved by the Supreme Court.

---

[6] See 18 U.S.C. § 2518.

[7] Compare ACLU v. Clapper, 13 Civ. 3994 (S.D.N.Y. Dec. 27, 2013) with Klayman v. Obama, Civil Action 13-0851 (D.D.C. Dec. 16, 2013).

Many of the specific Title III requirements are meant to address the necessarily overbroad nature of this type of surveillance. The minimization requirement makes the surveillance more targeted towards conversations that are actually pertinent to the crime being investigated. For example, law enforcement might fulfill the minimization requirement by instructing the case agent who is listening in on the communication to make a determination at the beginning of each conversation as to whether the conversation is pertinent to the crime being investigated. If it is not, the case agent must shut off the recording device and stop listening. Likewise, forcing the government to specify the type of facilities being used and the particular type of communication being intercepted limits the potential for abuse by law enforcement.

Other requirements, such as the thirty-day time limit, exist in order to counteract the continuous nature of electronic eavesdropping. Still other provisions are meant to ensure that the surveillance is reasonable. For example, the least intrusive means requirement ensures that the government does not conduct this type of intrusive surveillance unless it has no other option. Similarly, authorized electronic eavesdropping can only be used for relatively serious crimes, which are listed in the statute.[8] Of the dozens of crimes listed, for the most part they are serious felonies, such as murder, terrorism, or counterfeiting, which could lead to potential sentences of ten years or more.

If the government wants to use the information gained through this surveillance in a criminal trial, the defendant gets a chance to challenge the legality of the Title III order just as she would have a right to challenge a standard warrant. However, even a successful challenge will not necessarily lead to suppression of the evidence. By historical accident, Title III provides a suppression remedy only for illegally obtained oral and wire transmissions, not for illegally obtained electronic transmissions. This is because when the Wiretap Act was amended by the ECPA in 1986 to include electronic transmissions, e-mail was in its infancy, texting, instant messaging, and social media sites were unknown, and "electronic transmissions" essentially meant computers sharing data with each other. Thus, when Congress passed the ECPA it decided that electronic communications deserved less protection than communications using the human voice. As a result, violations of the Wiretap Act involving electronic transmissions can lead to criminal or civil liability on the part of the government, but not suppression of the evidence.

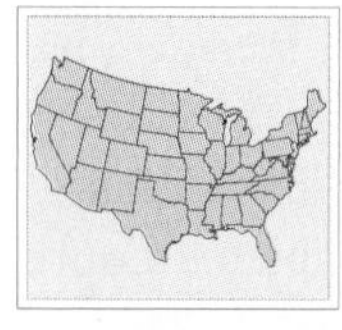

Finally, the Wiretap Act has a consent exception. Third parties (including the government) are permitted to intercept any oral, wire, or electronic transmission if one of the parties to the transmission knowingly consents to the interception.[9] However, different rules may apply under state law. This was true

[8] 18 U.S.C. § 2516.

[9] 18 U.S.C. § 2511(2)(c).

in the case of Linda Tripp, the woman who recorded her conversations with Bill Clinton paramour Monica Lewinsky. Though Tripp was immune from federal prosecution, she was indicted in Maryland for violating a state law that prohibited the recording of telephone conversations unless all parties consented.

D. Applying the Law.

1. How to Get a Title III Order. When a law enforcement officer needs to get a warrant, she writes out an affidavit setting forth the facts that support probable cause and stating with particularity the area to be searched and the items to be seized. She then takes that affidavit to a magistrate or judge, who will (almost always) approve the application and issue a warrant. As we saw in **Chapter 11,** the process does not take very long, and an officer can usually procure a warrant within a few hours.

As might be expected, the process for getting a Title III order is somewhat more onerous. A law enforcement officer can acquire a search warrant without having to consult with a prosecuting attorney. But in order to apply for a Title III order, a law enforcement official must get authorization from an Assistant United States Attorney, who is supposed to review the application to ensure it is sufficient. Of course, frequently the prosecutor and the law enforcement official are already working together on the case, and they will work together on the application.

At the state and local levels, Title III allows for law enforcement to get authorization from the head prosecuting attorney in the relevant jurisdiction—the City Attorney, the District Attorney, the State's Attorney or the Attorney General.

Another more practical limit on acquiring Title III orders is the cost of conducting a wiretap. After a police officer gets a warrant for a traditional search, she simply heads to the location specified in the warrant with a few other officers, secures the location, and conducts the search. Depending on the breadth of the warrant, the search will probably take less than an hour and will not require an enormous amount of resources.

In contrast, conducting a wiretap can be a costly and lengthy endeavor. In 2011, the average wiretap cost over $49,000 and lasted for forty-two days.[10] Moreover, executing the wiretap frequently requires law enforcement to work with third parties. For example, they may be required to consult with your landlord to physically enter your apartment to install a bug, or more commonly, they may be called upon to work with your ISP or telephone service provider to guarantee their help with monitoring your communications.

---

[10] Administrative Office of the U.S. Courts, Applications for Orders Authorizing or Approving the Interception of Wire, Oral, or Electronic Communications (2011), at http://www.uscourts.gov/uscourts/Statistics/WiretapReports/2011/2011WireTapReport.pdf.

How common are wiretaps? In 2011, there were 792 federal wiretaps and 1,940 state wiretaps across the country. The average wiretap intercepted the communications of 113 people, and intercepted a total of 3,716 conversations, of which 868 (or 23%) were considered "incriminating." Ninety-eight percent of wiretaps were conducted on portable devices such as cell phones. Title III also allows the government to request so-called "roving" wiretaps, which target a specific person as opposed to a specific device. Only eleven of the 2,732 total wiretaps were roving wiretaps.

When do police resort to wiretapping? Overwhelmingly police use wiretaps to assist investigations into drug crimes. Eighty-five percent of the wiretaps in the country were used to investigate drug offenses. Homicide cases were a distant second at 4%.[11]

2. Minimization Requirement. One of the most important requirements of real-time telephone or electronic surveillance is the demand that surveillance be conducted in a way that "minimizes the interception of irrelevant information."[12] In theory, this means that the eavesdropping agents must stop listening to any conversation that is not covered by the Title III order. In practice, however, it is very difficult for a defendant to prevail on a claim that the minimization requirements were not met. Courts have emphasized that the minimization requirement is not violated merely because the officers listen to some conversations which are not pertinent. Indeed, there are many cases in which officers listened to complete conversations that were not relevant to the investigation, but were nonetheless found not to have violated the minimization requirement. In reviewing whether the officers have sufficiently "minimized" their surveillance, courts should consider:

a. The nature, scope, and complexity of alleged criminal activities under investigation;

b. The extent to which the government has the information it needs to screen out conversations that are not within the scope of the alleged offenses under investigation; and

c. The degree of judicial supervision over the challenged surveillance practices.[13]

Indeed, because many criminals might begin incriminatory conversations with thirty seconds or a minute of innocent small talk—perhaps with the very purpose

[11] Administrative Office of the U.S. Courts, Applications for Orders Authorizing or Approving the Interception of Wire, Oral, or Electronic Communications (2011), at http://www.uscourts.gov/uscourts/Statistics/WiretapReports/2011/2011WireTapReport.pdf.

[12] 18 U.S.C. § 2518.

[13] United States v. Angiulo, 847 F.2d 956 (1st Cir. 1988).

of encouraging an eavesdropping officer to give up—the officer is allowed to listen to the initial minute of every conversation until she can be certain that the call is not pertinent to the investigation. Once the officers have been listening long enough, they can establish patterns to know for certain which telephone calls are not pertinent (*e.g.*, calls from parents; calls to certain legitimate businesses). Under such circumstances, the officers may be expected to cease eavesdropping on those specific calls:

> **Example:** FBI agents suspected that David Hull, a leader of the White Knights of the Ku Klux Klan, was stockpiling explosives and other weaponry at his house. They applied for a Title III order to monitor his telephone conversations, and in the affidavit for the order they promised to minimize the interceptions by screening out (1) calls under two minutes (2) calls not involving Hull or any other named interceptee; and (3) conversations "non-criminal in nature." In the affidavit the agents explained that they may have to "spot-check" any of these excluded calls to "ensure that the conversations have not turned to criminal matters."
>
> The Title III order was granted, and the agents began monitoring Hull's telephone calls. Every call was initially intercepted to determine the identity and subject of the conversation. If the conversation fell into one of the above three excluded categories, the agents would cease monitoring for one minute, then monitor for two minutes as a "spot check." The agents repeated this pattern for the rest of the telephone conversation until the call was completed. Some of these non-pertinent phone calls were conversations with Hull's girlfriends or with commercial establishments; many of them were sexually explicit. At trial, Hull argued that the agents failed to comply with the minimization requirements of the order.

Analysis: The Third Circuit denied the defendant's motion, holding that the minimization was "reasonable" under the totality of the circumstances. In this case, the government was investigating "a wide-ranging conspiracy between parties known for their penchant for secrecy." Consequently, the government was permitted to conduct a relatively broad surveillance.[14]

---

[14] United States v. Hull, 456 F.3d 133, 142 (3d Cir. 2006).

Although the minimization requirement actually offers little protection to suspects, it is often used by courts to justify close judicial supervision of the wiretap. For example, the authorizing judge may require the law enforcement agents to prepare a report every week or ten days during the wiretap, describing the conversations which they listened in on and the steps taken to minimize the intrusion. In this way, the courts can play a much more active role in overseeing the surveillance and preventing abuses by the government.

3. Least Intrusive Means Requirement. The government agent applying for the warrant must also certify that normal investigative procedures have been tried and failed, are unlikely to succeed, or are likely to be too dangerous. This requirement is meant to ensure that the government only resorts to wiretapping if there is no feasible alternative for conducting the investigation. As with the minimization requirement, courts tend to interpret the least intrusive means requirement broadly. The government need not prove definitively that there is no other way of gathering this information. Rather, the government need only establish that it is reasonable to assume other methods would not work or would be dangerous. Courts do require details in the affidavit that are specific to the case. Boilerplate language about, for example, the general difficulty of using informants in narcotics cases will not suffice. Instead, the affidavit must explain why using an informant in this specific case would be dangerous or unlikely to succeed:

> **Example:** A number of confidential informants notified the FBI that a man named Nicholas Gregorio was stealing items that had traveled or were traveling in interstate commerce. After confirming these tips, the FBI sought and obtained a Title III warrant to wiretap Gregorio's telephone. By listening to the wiretap, the FBI learned that Gregorio was also trafficking in methamphetamine. At the end of the wiretap period, government agents acquired a search warrant for Gregorio's home and found six ounces of methamphetamine. Gregorio was then arrested for various narcotics crimes.
>
> At trial, the prosecutor played over fifty conversations from the wiretap on Gregorio's telephone. The defendant challenged the validity of the Title III order, arguing that the government had other avenues for investigating the crime, including more extensive visual surveillance of Gregorio's house or forcing the informants to testify.

Analysis: The court held that the Title III order had been properly issued. The court emphasized that there are three prongs to the minimization test—either "normal investigative procedures have been tried and have failed" **or** they "reasonably appear to be unlikely to succeed if tried or to be too dangerous." Although Gregorio was correct in arguing that the government had not tried all possible investigative procedures, the government made a sufficient showing in its affidavit that (1) the informants would have refused to testify, even if given immunity; and (2) Gregorio would likely have become aware of more extensive visual surveillance. Furthermore, although other investigative methods would probably have produced evidence of some criminal activity, the wiretapping was necessary to establish the true scope of the conspiracy.[15]

In general, courts follow the broad legislative intent of Title III, preventing law enforcement from using wiretapping for routine crimes, but issuing (and upholding) Title III orders if the government is using them to conduct a long-term investigation of a complicated conspiracy. The Fourth Circuit summed up the courts' general attitude towards the Title III requirements:

> Wiretaps are extraordinary investigative means. Their intrusiveness mandates that courts, in authorizing them, exercise great care in protecting individual privacy. They are necessary tools of law enforcement, however, particularly where crimes are committed by large and sophisticated organizations. Reading the requirements [of Title III] in an overly restrictive manner would hamper unduly the investigative powers of law enforcement agents.[16]

E. Other Hyper-Intrusive Searches. Wiretapping is the most prominent example of hyper-intrusive searches. It also serves as an example of surveillance regulation that was created by Congress rather than the courts. However, there are many other types of hyper-intrusive searches that are regulated by courts rather than the legislature.

1. Covert Video Surveillance of Private Areas. Oddly enough, the statutory language of Title III does not cover video surveillance. Perhaps this is because the last major Congressional action in this area (the ECPA) occurred in 1986, when covert video surveillance was not very common. However, in 1986, the Seventh Circuit was faced with the question of how to regulate such searches in the *Torres* case.[17]

The *Torres* court first noted that although there were no statutory restrictions on covert video surveillance, the activity clearly implicated the Fourth Amendment. The court held that because videotaping violates the suspect's reasonable expectation of privacy, it constitutes a search under *Katz*. *Torres* also acknowledged a

---

[15] United States v. Vento, 533 F.2d 838 (3d Cir. 1976).

[16] United States v. Leavis, 853 F.2d 215 (4th Cir. 1988).

[17] United States v. Torres, 751 F.2d 875, 885 (7th Cir. 1984).

strong similarity between covert video surveillance and wiretapping. Both are kept secret from the suspect; both are ongoing and continuous; and both are overbroad in that they will likely collect a large amount of private information unrelated to the case being investigated. Based on these similarities, the *Torres* court found that covert video surveillance, like wiretapping, should not be permitted unless the government can meet a higher standard than mere probable cause.

The Seventh Circuit then turned to the question of what that higher standard should be, and in setting that standard, it took an unusual step. The *Torres* court decided to "borrow the warrant procedure of Title III, a careful legislative attempt to solve a very similar problem, and hold that it provides the measure of the government's constitutional obligation of particular description in using television to investigate crime."[18] In other words, the *Torres* court found that the higher standards required by the Fourth Amendment for a video surveillance warrant are **identical** to the higher standards set by Title III for an order authorizing a wiretap.

Since *Torres* was decided, every circuit court that has considered this question has followed suit, importing the Title III standards and using them as the requirement for a video surveillance warrant under the Fourth Amendment. (The Supreme Court itself has not yet considered this question). This decision makes the procedure simple when the government intends to conduct electronic and video surveillance (since the government can satisfy both by acquiring a Title III order). It is also a sign of the amount of deference courts are beginning to give to Congress in search and seizure law, especially when new surveillance technologies are involved.

One final reminder: these standards only apply for covert video surveillance of a **private** area—that is, surveillance of an area in which the suspect has a reasonable expectation of privacy. Video surveillance of public areas—whether covert or overt—is not considered a search and is therefore wholly unregulated by the Fourth Amendment.

2. Bodily Intrusions. As we saw in **Chapter 13,** the police are permitted to conduct a full search of the suspect's person incident to a lawful arrest in order to look for evidence of the crime and in order to ensure their own safety. However, the courts have set some restrictions on how intrusive these searches can be. Specifically, police cannot routinely conduct warrantless searches that intrude on the bodily integrity of the suspect, such as extracting blood or performing an invasive medical procedure. Unlike the formalist statutory-based rules which govern video surveillance, the Court applies a subjective balancing test for this type of search. Specifically, the Court set out the following rule:

[18] Torres, 751 F.2d at 885.

Unlike other searches, searches that violate the bodily integrity of the suspect may not be justified based on the search-incident-to-a-lawful-arrest exception. In order to perform such a search after arrest, the government must have probable cause to believe that the search will in fact reveal incriminating evidence and that exigent circumstances exist. In the alternative, the government may obtain a warrant for the search.

For extremely intrusive searches, the government must also demonstrate that the specific search they wish to conduct is "reasonable." The court will consider three factors in determining whether such a search is reasonable:

1. The extent to which the procedure may threaten the safety or health of the individual;

2. The extent of intrusion upon the individual's dignitary interests in personal privacy and bodily integrity; and

3. The community's interest in fairly and accurately determining guilt or innocence.[19]

The Supreme Court applied this test in a famous case involving a forced surgery:

Example—*Winston v. Lee*, 470 U.S. 753 (1985): Late one night a shopkeeper named Ralph Watkinson was the victim of an attempted armed robbery. During the attempted robbery, Watkinson pulled out his own gun, and fired at his assailant. At the same time, the assailant fired at Watkinson. Watkinson was hit in the leg, while the assailant was hit in the left shoulder and promptly fled the scene. Watkinson called the police and was taken to the hospital.

About a half an hour later, a man named Rudolph Lee called the police from a nearby location. Lee had a gunshot wound in his left shoulder, and he claimed he had been shot when two men tried to rob him. When the police brought Lee to the hospital, Watkinson (who was still waiting in the emergency room) identified Lee as the man who tried to rob him. The police realized that the bullet lodged in Lee's body would be strong evidence against him. If the ballistics matched those of Watkinson's gun, the police would be able to conclusively

[19] Winston v. Lee, 470 U.S. 753 (1985).

identify Lee as the perpetrator. However, Lee refused to consent to surgery. The state then applied for a search warrant ordering Lee to undergo surgery. The lower court granted the warrant, and Lee appealed all the way to the Supreme Court.

Analysis: The Supreme Court denied the request for the search warrant, holding that although the government plainly had probable cause to conduct the search, allowing the search would be unreasonable under the circumstances. Expert testimony revealed that the proposed search might have had serious effects on Lee's health, as there was a chance of permanent damage to his muscles and nerves. Moreover, the extent of the intrusion was extreme, representing "virtually total divestment of respondent's ordinary control over surgical probing beneath his skin." [20] The Court also found that the government could not demonstrate a compelling need for this evidence, since (1) the government already possessed strong evidence of Lee's guilt, and (2) the bullet might have corroded so much inside Lee's body that forensic identification would be impossible.

Ever since the Supreme Court set out this test, lower courts have applied the test in numerous circumstances, setting up a continuum for the level of intrusion for different types of bodily intrusion, from hair on one end through breath, saliva, urine, and blood on the other.[21] The Court itself has found that the forced removal of blood, for example, must be examined on a case-by-case basis. At a minimum, such procedures are only allowed if there is a "clear indication" that incriminating evidence will be found.[22] Many courts have indicated that this "clear indication" standard is a higher standard than mere probable cause because "any compelled intrusion into the human body implicates significant, constitutionally protected privacy interests."[23] Greater intrusions, such as pumping the suspect's stomach without his consent, will be even harder to justify. On the infrequent occasions when courts do allow forced medical intrusions, the government must demonstrate that the search must be virtually certain to reveal contraband and that the evidence is likely to be destroyed unless the search is carried out immediately.[24]

It should be noted, however, that courts will very rarely second-guess police activity in this area. The rule merely prevents the police from conducting such intrusive tests on a routine basis. Thus, police will only conduct an invasive search when they have a specific reason for doing so. The police have greater latitude when they engage in less invasive bodily intrusions; for example, police may scrape underneath the defendant's fingernails if the victim claims that he

[20] Lee, 470 U.S. at 765.

[21] See, e.g., United States v. Nicolosi, 885 F. Supp. 50 (E.D.N.Y. 1995).

[22] Schmerber v. California, 384 U.S. 757, 771 (1966).

[23] Missouri v. McNeely, 133 S.Ct. 1552, 1565 (2013).

[24] See, e.g., State v. Strong, 493 N.W.2d 834 (Iowa 1992).

scratched her during the assault, or swab the suspect's penis in a sexual assault case if they believe it is likely that the victim's DNA may be recovered.

What rulings apply to intrusive visual searches that fall just short of invading bodily integrity, such as strip searches or visual body cavity searches? The Supreme Court recently upheld the routine use of these searches for all arrests, at least if the defendant is going to be placed in a detention facility with other inmates.[25] The Court did state that its holding did not cover a "manual bodily cavity search" in which the suspect was physically touched by the law enforcement officer. Furthermore, at least ten states have passed laws forbidding routine strip searches for all arrestees, instead requiring law enforcement to show reasonable suspicion that the suspect has contraband. This provides another example of legislatures stepping in to create heightened standards for highly-intrusive searches.

A few caveats to keep in mind. First, as with covert video surveillance, these heightened rules do not apply to searches of a person's bodily fluids or fragments that are left behind in a public place—hair that has dropped off of the suspect in a public place, for example, or saliva that is left on a coffee cup at Starbucks. Analysis of these "abandoned" pieces of bodily tissue is not considered to be a search under *Katz.*

Second, when police do conduct these searches on individuals in custody, they frequently do so under the consent exception. An individual suspected of drunk driving has the right to refuse a breathalyzer test, for example (although almost every state has a law which states that such a refusal will result in a suspension of the suspect's license). However, there is nothing objectionable about the police administering the test if the suspect consents.

Finally, some of the most intrusive searches of this kind are not considered searches at all, because they are reasonably necessary to protect the health and safety of the suspect. For example, if police suspect that an unconscious suspect has overdosed on drugs, they may seek to have the individual's stomach pumped as part of their "community caretaker" function. If the stomach pumping is not medically necessary, but the police are merely using it as a way to recover evidence, the courts will find that the procedure was too intrusive.[26]

3. "No-Knock" Search Warrants. The final type of hyper-intrusive search we will discuss occurs when police officers seek to execute a search warrant without first knocking on the door of the target location and announcing their presence. As discussed in **Chapter 11**, police officers executing a warrant generally must give notice to the occupants of the premises before they enter. This means they must announce that they are law enforcement and that they seek to search the property. They then must wait a "reasonable" period of time before forcing entry into the premises—generally around fifteen or twenty seconds.[27]

---

[25] Florence v. Board of Chosen Freeholders, 132 S.Ct. 1510 (2012).

[26] Rochin v. California, 342 U.S. 165 (1952) (decided on Due Process grounds).

[27] See United States v. Banks, 540 U.S. 31 (2003).

Entering the premises without prior notice constitutes a more intrusive search, and thus also requires a greater showing on the part of law enforcement officials. In this context, that greater showing involves proving that providing notice would likely lead to danger to the officers or destruction of the evidence being sought.

As you might imagine, the vast majority of these cases are searches pursuant to narcotics investigations, where fifteen or twenty seconds may be sufficient for the suspect to flush the drugs down the toilet, or wash them down the drain, or perhaps even swallow them. Given the increased likelihood of this danger in narcotics cases, many jurisdictions at one time adopted blanket rules permitting no-knock search warrants in every narcotics case, regardless of the specific facts involved. The Supreme Court considered the constitutionality of such blanket rules in the following case from Wisconsin:

> **Example—*Richards v. Wisconsin*, 520 U.S. 385 (1997):** Police officers in Madison, Wisconsin, obtained a warrant to search Steiney Richards' hotel room after demonstrating to a magistrate that there was probable cause to believe that Richards was selling narcotics from the room. Although they requested a "no-knock" warrant in their application, the magistrate deleted that portion of the warrant.
>
> When the police arrived, one of the officers (dressed as a maintenance man) knocked on Richards' door. When Richards opened the door, he saw the uniformed police standing behind the undercover officer, and he slammed the door shut. Two or three seconds later, the officers battered down the door and gained entry to the hotel room, where they found drugs and cash.
>
> After Richards was convicted, he appealed to the Wisconsin Supreme Court, claiming that the no-knock search was unauthorized. The Wisconsin Supreme Court disagreed, finding that it is reasonable to assume that all felony drug crimes will involve "an extremely high risk of serious if not deadly injury to the police as well as the potential for the disposal of drugs by the occupants prior to entry by the police." Therefore, the state high court found, "exigent circumstances justifying a no-knock entry are *always* present in felony drug cases."[28]
>
> Richards appealed to the United States Supreme Court, arguing that the police must demonstrate reasonable suspicion justifying a no-knock search warrant based on the specific facts of his case.

[28] State v. Richards. 201 Wis. 2d 845, 847–848 (1996).

Analysis: The United States Supreme Court found for Richards and rejected the state's proposed "blanket rule" for narcotics cases as unconstitutional.

First, the Court held that such a rule is overbroad, since not every search for drugs poses special risks of destruction of evidence. For example, the officers may know that the only individuals present at the time of the search have no relation to the drug activity, or it may be impossible to destroy the evidence in the specific location being searched.

Second, if blanket rules were allowed, they could conceivably be applied to almost any type of crime—those suspected of armed robbery could destroy their weapons or the contraband they stole, for example. "If a *per se* exception were allowed for each category of criminal investigation that included a considerable—albeit hypothetical—risk of danger to officers or destruction of evidence, the knock-and-announce element of the Fourth Amendment's reasonableness requirement would be meaningless."[29]

The *Richards* Court concluded that trial judges must make case-by-case determinations, based on the specific facts of the proposed entry by the police, that there is "reasonable suspicion that knocking and announcing their presence . . . would be dangerous or futile, or that it would inhibit the effective investigation of the crime by, for example, allowing the destruction of evidence."

Types of Hyper-Intrusive Searches
(Surveillance that requires more than merely probable cause and a warrant)

Type of Surveillance	Source of Law	Showing Required by Government
Real-time interception of oral, telephone, or digital communication	Congress through Title III of the Wiretap Act.	Obtain a Title III order by establishing probable cause, least intrusive means, and minimization. Must be approved by prosecutor and must be re-authorized every 30 days.
Covert video surveillance of a private location	Circuit Courts (e.g., *United States v. Torres*, 751 F.2d 875 (7th Cir. 1984)).	Identical to those required to obtain a Title III Order (see above).
Infringements on bodily integrity	Supreme Court (*Winston v. Lee*, 470 U.S. 753 (1985)).	Search incident to lawful arrest is insufficient; must have probable cause to believe contraband or evidence will be found and exigent circumstances must exist. For more intrusive searches, courts also apply a balancing test which considers the safety of the suspect, the extent of the intrusion, and the community's interest in solving the crime.
"No-knock" search warrants	Supreme Court (*Richards v. Wisconsin*, 520 U.S. 385 (1997)).	Facts specific to the case demonstrating reasonable suspicion that the usual notice would be dangerous to the police or would lead to the destruction of evidence.

[29] Richards v. Wisconsin, 520 U.S. 385, 394 (1997).

Quick Summary

Generally, if a form of surveillance is classified as a "search," the government must establish probable cause and either obtain a warrant or demonstrate that the search fits into one of the warrant exceptions. However, some searches are so intrusive that courts or legislatures create even higher standards for law enforcement to meet.

The most prominent example of these hyper-intrusive searches is real-time interception of oral, telephone, or digital communication (otherwise known as bugging, wiretapping, and intercepting e-mails or texts). This surveillance is regulated by the Wiretap Act, or Title III. In order to obtain a Title III order, the government must establish probable cause that one of the specific enumerated crimes has occurred and that the interception will lead to evidence of that crime. The government must also demonstrate that a wiretap is the least intrusive means of gathering this information, and that steps will be taken to minimize the interception of non-pertinent information. Also, the order must be approved by a prosecutor (rather than a law enforcement official) and must be re-authorized every thirty days.

Other types of hyper-intrusive searches are regulated by courts instead of by Congress. In order to obtain a warrant under the Fourth Amendment to conduct video surveillance of a private premises, the government must meet the same standard that is required to obtain a Title III order under the Wiretap Act. Searches which violate a suspect's bodily integrity are not routinely allowed as a search incident to arrest. Instead, the government must demonstrate exigent circumstances and probable cause that contraband or evidence will be found. Finally, in order to execute a search warrant without giving the traditional fifteen or twenty seconds of notice, the government must specifically demonstrate that notice would be dangerous to the police or would lead to the destruction of evidence.

Review Questions

1. Answering Defendant's Cell Phone. Detective Saul Marsh arrested Tommy Sanderson for selling marijuana. While Sanderson was in custody, Detective Marsh noticed that his cell phone kept ringing. Finally Detective Marsh answered the cell phone with "What's up?" and the caller responded "Can I get some bud?" Detective Marsh posed as the owner of the cell phone for the entire phone call and arranged a meeting with the caller to sell drugs. The meeting took place, and the caller (Francis Gonzalez) gave Detective Marsh over $1,000 for a quantity of marijuana. Gonzalez was immediately arrested.

Gonzalez is now on trial, and he argues that Detective Marsh violated his Fourth Amendment rights when he "intercepted" the cell phone call without a warrant. Did Detective Marsh violate Gonzalez's Fourth Amendment rights?

2. The Vigilante Hacker. A Florida police detective received an anonymous e-mail from an informant that a man named Fred Wendell possessed photos on his computer which showed a young girl being sexually abused and molested. The detective asked the informant to identify himself. The informant refused, but explained that he "was not a cop" and he had very strong evidence of Wendell's guilt. The detective responded, saying: "Send us everything you have." The informant responded with a long e-mail that included Wendell's IP address, internet service provider, home phone, and mailing address. The informant also described the photos in graphic detail and described in which folders in which directories they were stored on Wendell's computer.

The detectives procured a search warrant based on the informant's evidence, and Wendell's computer was seized and searched. The police found multiple images of a girl being sexually abused, and Wendell was arrested and charged with possession and distribution of child pornography.

Before trial, the detectives tried again to find out who the informant was and how he came about the information he gave to the detectives. When asked, the informant responded that he regularly checked the internet for sexual abusers by monitoring chat rooms where he believed child predators might visit. When he noticed someone suspicious, he would send an e-mail to their computer with a "Trojan horse" virus attached. That virus would infect the suspect's computer and allow the informant to remotely look through the defendant's hard drive. When he found evidence of child pornography, he would notify the authorities in that suspect's jurisdiction.

When defendant Wendell heard about the informant's activities, he moved in his criminal case to suppress the evidence the informant provided as a violation of his (Wendell's) Fourth Amendment rights. Wendell also sued the informant in a separate civil case, arguing that the informant violated the Wiretap Act. The Wiretap Act applies to private parties as well as government officials. The remedy for a private violation is monetary damages. Accordingly, Wendell argued even if there was no state action, the informant was liable under the Wiretap Act because the informant engaged in conduct that was forbidden by the Act.

This case raises three issues:

a. Did the informant violate the defendant's Fourth Amendment rights when he obtained the information?

b. Given what the police knew from the informant, did they have probable cause to obtain a warrant?

c. Did the informant violate the defendant's rights under the Wiretap Act?

3. Spying on the Hospital Room. Gloria Butler was a young mother with a history of bringing her young child into the hospital for treatment. Medical professionals suspected that Butler suffered from Munchausen syndrome by proxy ("MSP")—a medical disease that causes mothers to fabricate or cause sickness in or injury to their children to attract attention to themselves. On one hospital visit, Butler reported that her child, Ryley, was having seizure-like symptoms, but the symptoms could not be explained by the doctors. Suspecting MSP, the doctors contacted the local police to ask how to proceed. The police suggested that the hospital set up a secret video camera in the room in which Ryley was staying in order to monitor the mother's interactions with the child when she thought no one was watching. Thereafter, the nurses encouraged Butler to stay in the room with Ryley at night. Later that night, nurses monitoring the video feed saw Butler placing something over Ryley's nose and mouth. The hospital staff entered the room, stopped her, and called the police. Butler was arrested for child endangerment.

Were Butler's Fourth Amendment rights violated when the hospital videotaped her in the hospital room?

4. The Forced Urine Test. Defendant Lockney was pulled over for traveling at a high rate of speed and failing to stop at two stoplights. When the officer made contact with Lockney, he observed that Lockney had slurred speech, bloodshot eyes, and smelled of liquor. The officer performed a breathalyzer, which returned a .07% BAC, just below the legal limit. Suspecting that Lockney was under the influence of something other than alcohol, the officer requested that Lockney submit to a chemical test. Lockney refused.

The officer arrested Lockney for reckless driving. The officer then requested a search warrant, which he was granted. The warrant specified that the officer retrieve the necessary blood and urine samples with "necessary and proper authority."

While at the hospital, Lockney stated that he could not give a urine sample. The police then ordered the doctors to use a catheter on Lockney to extract urine. The insertion of the catheter was quite painful, and it carried a significant risk of causing a urinary tract infection (though ultimately Lockney was not infected). The doctors extracted Lockney's urine and tested it, and the test was positive for "benzodiazepines, opiates, marijuana, oxycodone, opioids, and MDMA (i.e. ecstacy)." He was convicted of driving under the influence, and sentenced to 180 days in jail.

Did the police violate Lockney's rights when they ordered the doctors to use a catheter on him?

21

Statutory Requirements: Less Than a Search

Key Concepts

- The Pen Register Act Applies to Obtaining "Address" Information
- The Stored Communications Act Regulates How the Government Obtains Most Data Stored by Third Parties
- The Foreign Intelligence Surveillance Act Applies to Electronic Surveillance Whose Primary Purpose is Gathering Foreign Intelligence

A. Introduction and Policy.

As noted in the previous chapter, statutes form a layer of protection both in the absence of and in addition to the Fourth Amendment rules. In this chapter, we will examine the second category of statutory restrictions—places where legislatures have stepped in to create minimal statutory protections regarding government actions that are unregulated by the Fourth Amendment.

We will discuss the three most significant statutes in this category that regulate government surveillance: the Pen Register statute, which regulates surveillance of "address" information for telephonic and electronic communication; the Stored Communications Act ("SCA"), which regulates surveillance of e-mails and voicemails which are stored by third parties; and the Foreign Intelligence Surveillance Act ("FISA"), which governs the gathering of information for national intelligence purposes.

The Pen Register Act

B. The Law. The term "pen register" describes the technology that law enforcement once employed to record the outgoing phone numbers that were dialed from a specific telephone. Though named after and created during an era of this once dominant technology, the Pen Register Act now applies to all "dialing, routing, addressing, or signaling" information for any wire or electronic communication, including incoming phone numbers, outgoing phone numbers, and the "To:" and "From:" line on e-mails. The devices currently used are often referred to as "pen/trap" devices.

The Pen Register Act fills in the gap created by the Supreme Court's decision in *Smith v. Maryland.*[1] In *Smith*, the Court found that tracing the telephone numbers a suspect dials is not a search because the suspect has shared the numbers with a third party (the telephone company) and therefore has no reasonable expectation of privacy in the information. In the absence of such an expectation, the Court found the Fourth Amendment places no restrictions on law enforcement when they seek to acquire this information. The Pen Register Act steps into this void. However, though the Pen Register Act creates some protection, it is not a very robust protection. The Act provides a low standard that law enforcement officers must meet before they can lawfully acquire address information. Significantly, the Act requires a court to grant permission if the government overcomes this burden:

> A government agent seeking dialing, routing, addressing, or signaling information must apply *ex parte* for an order from a court. The application must include: (1) the identity of the attorney for the government; (2) the identity of the law enforcement agency conducting the investigation; and (3) a certification that the information likely to be obtained is relevant to an ongoing criminal investigation.
>
> The court **must** grant the order authorizing the surveillance upon receiving this application. The authorization will last for sixty days, and can be renewed every sixty days through the same procedure. The target of the surveillance will not be notified that the surveillance is taking place.[2]

Under this statute, the court is not meant to conduct any independent inquiry as to whether the government agent's certification of relevance is accurate. Rather, the court's role is merely "ministerial" in nature. The purpose of the law is merely to create accountability for the government agent (usually an Assistant United States Attorney), who can be charged with a crime if she makes a false representation to the court. This low standard and lack of any functional judicial screening provides only the slightest protection to targets. But, Congress believed this to be the proper balance between the needs of law enforcement and what it saw as the minimal privacy interest that individuals may have in their dialing, routing, signaling, or addressing information.

C. Applying the Law. The primary issue in applying the Pen Register Act is deciding whether a certain piece of information is "address" information or "con-

---

[1] Smith v. Maryland, 442 U.S. 735 (1979).

[2] See 18 U.S.C. §§ 3122, 3123.

tent" information, a question we discussed in **Chapter 8.** Generally, to make this determination courts will look to the purpose for which the information is used.

1. Post-Cut-Through Dialed Digits. This inelegant name describes the numbers that a telephone user presses after having dialed the phone number and made a connection. These numbers may be used to navigate a phone tree or to input PINs or account numbers. Since they are the functional equivalent of speaking to the party on the other end of the telephone line, these numbers are considered content information and are given the highest level of protection.

> **Example:** The police suspect Barry Young has been stealing bank account numbers, credit card numbers, and customer passwords from various banks and then using them to make withdrawals and purchases over the telephone. The FBI files an application to install a pen/trap device on his telephone line by certifying that the information is likely to be relevant to their investigation of the thefts.
>
> Once the FBI agents have installed the pen/trap device, they learn that on a given day Young called six different banks and fifteen different commercial establishments. They also learn that each time he called one of the banks, he input someone else's account number and access code for that account number, and then used the telephone's automated system to transfer thousands of dollars into his own personal account. When he called the commercial establishments, he used the phone tree to buy items and then input stolen credit card numbers in order to pay for the items.
>
> The FBI agents use all of this information to obtain a warrant and search Young's home, where they find more incriminating evidence. Young challenges the warrant, arguing that the agents used information that was improperly gained from the pen/trap device.

Analysis: The pen/trap device was properly used to obtain the phone numbers that Young dialed. The FBI agents can use the evidence that Young called six different banks and fifteen different commercial establishments to assist in further investigations. For example, they can subpoena the records of each of those banks and companies and connect Young's calls to the transfers and purchases that were made.

However, the agents cannot use—and should never have learned—the numbers that Young dialed once a connection had been established (that is, the digits he dialed after the call "cut through" and made a connection with another telephone). The numbers that were dialed to place the call are routing and signaling data, used only to ensure the telephone call gets to the proper "address." However, the numbers that were dialed after the calls made their connections—the post-cut-through dialed digits—are **content** information: they are functionally and legally identical to statements that Young might have made on the telephone. The court should find that the account numbers, access codes, and credit card numbers were all illegally obtained, and thus the search warrant was improperly granted and all the evidence found pursuant to the search warrant should be suppressed. [3]

2. E-mail Headers. When you send an e-mail, you begin by typing in the address(es) of the recipients and then filling in a subject line. After you write the e-mail and send it, the entire message is converted into "packets" and sent through various internet service providers until it arrives at its destination. Under the rules set out by the Fourth Amendment and the Pen Register Act, a pen/trap order allows the government to intercept the address information of that e-mail in transit—that is, the "To" and "From" line of the message. However, the pen/trap order does not allow the government to access the subject line or the message itself, since this represents content information. Thus, the government (or the ISP responding the government's pen/trap order) must be careful when intercepting and decoding the packets to only access the address information and not the entire e-mail header (or the message itself). Access to this latter form of information is regulated by the Stored Communications Act.

The Stored Communications Act ("SCA")

D. The Law. Like the Pen Register Act, the Stored Communications Act (the "SCA") also fills in the gap in constitutional protection that was left by *Smith v. Maryland*. Unlike the Pen Register Act, the SCA applies primarily to **content** information stored by third parties, and it sets out different levels of protection depending on the type of information the government is seeking to acquire. The third parties regulated by the SCA are internet service providers ("ISP's"), who save e-mails, store documents, and process data for their customers. As you read above, according to *Smith v. Maryland*, the Fourth Amendment does not apply to information that an individual has voluntarily entrusted to a third party, and so, as a constitutional matter, government agents need nothing more than a subpoena to force ISP's to disclose this information. The SCA creates higher standards for government agents seeking to compel this disclosure. The SCA also creates a new legal standard. This standard applies to what is known as a "2703(d) order,"

[3] See In the Matter of Applications for Pen Registers and Trap and Trace Devices, 515 F.Supp. 2d 325, 328 (E.D. NY 2007).

after the provision in the code that creates the standard. The SCA protects three different types of data held by ISP's:

1. "Electronic communication service" data, defined as "any temporary, intermediate storage of a wire or electronic communication incidental to [its] electronic transmission." This includes sent e-mail or other electronic communications which have not yet been opened by the consumer and have been stored for 180 days or less.

   In order to gain access to "electronic communication service" data, the government must obtain a search warrant.

2. "Remote computing service" data, defined as any "computer storage or processing services." This includes:

   a. Unopened e-mail that has been stored for over 180 days;

   b. Opened e-mail or sent e-mail that is still being stored on the ISP; and

   c. Documents or data that are being stored or processed by the ISP.

   In order to gain access to "remote computing service" data, the government must either

   a. Obtain a search warrant;

   b. Obtain a "2703(d)" order and provide notice to the suspect; or

   c. Obtain a subpoena and provide notice to the suspect.

   To obtain a "2703(d)" order, the government must prove to the court that it has "specific and articulable facts showing that there are reasonable grounds to believe" that the information being sought is "relevant and material to an ongoing investigation."

3. "Customer records," defined as "information pertaining to a subscriber or to a customer" (not including the contents of a communications).

   The government can acquire this non-content information (such as the identity of the consumer and information about when and how they use the ISP) with nothing more than a subpoena and without providing notice to the consumer. For other non-content records, the government can use a 2703(d) order without providing notice to the consumer.[1]

[4] 18 U.S.C. §§ 2702-2703.

Thus, the SCA sets up two different standards. For recent, unopened e-mail ("electronic communication service" data), it requires the government to obtain a warrant—that is, to prove to a court that probable cause exists. For other content information ("remote computing service" data), it gives the government a choice. First, the government may obtain a traditional warrant supported by probable cause. Alternatively, the government may elect to inform the target of the surveillance and obtain a 2703(d) order by meeting the lower standard of demonstrating with "specific and articulable facts" that there is reasonable grounds to believe the information is relevant to an ongoing investigation. Finally, the government may inform the suspect of the surveillance and obtain a subpoena by meeting the even lower standard of proving a "reasonable possibility that the information will be relevant to the investigation."

Note that the SCA does not apply to communications **in transit**—that is, when the government is attempting real-time interception of electronic or digital transmission. As we saw in the last chapter, real-time transmission is accorded very robust protection by Title III.

Once the digital message has reached its destination and is in temporary storage waiting to be opened, it is classified as "electronic communications services data." This is analogous to a physical letter sitting in a post office box—it has been "delivered," and it is now being "stored," but this type of temporary storage is a necessary aspect of the delivery process. Thus, just like a physical letter in a post office box, the government would need to obtain a warrant to obtain the information.

After the message has been opened, if the user continues to store the opened mail on the ISP, the message (probably) will be categorized as "remote computer services" data. As we will see in the next section, there is a circuit split on the question of when exactly an opened message transforms from electronic communications services data to remote computer services data.

Also note that the SCA only applies to data that is remotely stored by third party ISP's—it does **not** apply to stored e-mails or computer files that are stored on the suspect's personal hard drive. Those are fully protected by the Fourth Amendment, since they have not been voluntarily turned over to a third party; thus, any government search or seizure of the information on the hard drive requires a warrant or must fit into an exception to the warrant requirement.

However, many internet service providers also keep a copy of sent messages on their server, so that customers have a record of these records. These are covered by the SCA, and they are generally treated like "opened" e-mails and other remote computing services data—that is, courts have held that sent e-mails are not stored "incident to transmission" but instead as part of a long-term data storage.

Furthermore, the SCA does not apply to any other kind of data that may be stored or transmitted electronically. For example, if an individual visits a commercial website like Amazon.com and leaves some customer reviews and then makes some purchases, none of the information transmitted to the website is covered by the SCA, because neither the customer reviews nor the financial data is electronic communication service data or remote computing service data. Likewise, the SCA does not apply when an individual makes payments with PayPal, describes an item they are putting up for bid on e-Bay, or leaves a comment about a story on the Washington Post website. Although a broad definition of "electronic communication" or "computer storage" could conceivably encompass this information, the courts have interpreted the statutory language in such a way that publically available information and commercial transactions are not covered by the SCA.[5] This information is also not covered by the Fourth Amendment as it has been voluntarily disclosed, and thus may be freely accessed by others, subject only to the internal rules of the online company.

The SCA also severely limits the ability of ISP's to **voluntarily** disclose information they are storing for their customers that is covered by the Act. Generally, an ISP cannot voluntarily disclose protected information without the customer's consent unless such disclosure is required because of a dangerous emergency or the ISP has inadvertently discovered evidence of a crime.[6]

Finally, you should know that violations of the Stored Communications Act are not remedied via the exclusionary rule. Just as with electronic communications under the Wiretap Act, Congress did not consider all stored data to require the same level of protection as other types of evidence. Instead, violations of the Stored Communications Act are punished through criminal or civil liability.

E. Applying the Law. The key to applying the SCA is determining whether the stored information is either "electronic communication service" data or "remote computing service" data. When the law was originally passed in 1986, ISP's were conveniently divided into these two different categories: those that transmitted e-mail from one customer to another, and those that stored or processed large amounts of data for customers (a practice that was more common when personal computers had limited memories and slower processors). At that time, it was relatively easy to distinguish between data being held by electronic communication service providers, which received maximum protection under the SCA, and data held by remote computing service providers, which received a lower level of protection.

[5] See In re Jetblue Airways Corp. Privacy Litigation, 379 F. Supp.2d 299 (E.D.N.Y. 2005).

[6] 18 U.S.C. § 2702(b).

Today, however, most ISP's perform both roles. Thus, the amount of protection given to any particular piece of data depends not on the type of ISP that holds the data, but on how the data itself is categorized by the court.

1. What Kind of Data is Covered? Some types of data are easy to categorize; others are not. Consider the following hypothetical:

> **Example:** Devon decides to send a message to his friend Wendy. He types out an e-mail message and before he sends it, he saves a copy of it on his laptop computer. Then he sends it to her through his G-mail account. G-mail saves a copy of the message in his "Sent" folder, and then sends the message to Wendy, where it is stored—unopened—in her stanford.edu e-mail account.
>
> Devon then receives an invitation to an online survey regarding his recent experience with AT&T customer service. He clicks on the invitation, which takes him to a website where he types in his opinion as to how helpful the service was.
>
> Finally, Devon opens up his Facebook page and posts a photo of himself smoking marijuana. The photo can now be seen by all thirty-five of his Facebook "friends."
>
> The government wants to gain access to his e-mail, his statements to AT&T, and the picture that Devon posted on Facebook. What legal requirements, if any, do they need to meet in order to compel production of this information?

Analysis: The SCA and the Fourth Amendment will provide different levels of protection for each of these forms of information.

The message to Wendy was first stored on Devon's personal laptop computer. The SCA does not apply to this copy of the message, because it is not being held by a third party. But that does not mean that no protection is afforded. Under the Fourth Amendment, the government would need to obtain a warrant to search Devon's computer.

The e-mail message that Devon sent is also stored on Wendy's stanford.edu account. The SCA applies here, and because the message is being stored as part of an electronic communications service, the highest level of SCA protection will apply and the government will need a warrant to access the message.

Finally, the message was also stored in the "sent" folder of Devon's Gmail account. Although it may seem counter-intuitive, the message stored in Devon's "Sent" folder may be treated differently than the same message stored in Wendy's

"Inbox." Recall, the SCA provides different levels of protection to different types of information. Information which is stored incident to transmission ("electronic communications services" data) is given a higher level of protection, while information which is stored for a longer period of time ("remote computer services data") is given a lower level of transmission. If the court determines that a message saved in a sent e-mail folder is the former—a form of electronic communications service data—the e-mail will get the same high level of protection as it does in Wendy's Inbox. But if—as is likely—the court determines that this storage is a form of remote computing service data, the message will receive the lower level of SCA protection. In that case, the government can obtain the message merely with notice and a subpoena or a 2703(d) order. For the 2703(d) order, the government need only provide "specific and articulable facts" that demonstrate there are reasonable grounds to believe the message is relevant to their investigation.

The message that Devon posted on the AT&T survey webpage is not covered by the SCA—in this context, AT&T is not acting as an electronic communication service or a remote computing service, and under *Smith v. Maryland,* Devon has no reasonable expectation of privacy in this information that he has chosen to share with third parties.

The same conclusion regarding a lack of protection is probably also true for the photo that Devon posted on Facebook. Although Facebook is both disseminating the photo to others and storing it remotely, a court will probably not conclude that Facebook is acting as a remote computing service or an electronic communication service.

2. Determining the Rule for Stored E-mails. In the last example, we saw that the unopened e-mail in Wendy's inbox is categorized as electronic communication service data. All courts agree that e-mail messages which are stored by an ISP and have not yet been opened fall into this category, since they are electronic communications which are being stored "incidental to [its] electronic transmission." If this storage is "temporary"—which is defined by the SCA as being 180 days or less—the unopened e-mails receive the highest level of protection under the SCA: the government must obtain a warrant. But many consumers continue to store e-mail messages on their ISP even after they have read the message. When (if ever) does stored e-mail transform from "electronic communication service" data into "remote computing service" data?

The traditional view is that once the user has opened the e-mail, the e-mail is transformed from electronic communication service data into remote computing service data. In other words, the e-mail is no longer being held in a virtual mailbox, where the storage is merely incident to its transmission. Instead, the user has opened and (presumably) read the e-mail, and is now merely storing it on the server as she might store any other data file. Thus, most courts have held that opened e-mail is remote computing service data.

But not all courts agree with this analysis. The Ninth Circuit reached a different conclusion when interpreting the SCA in a civil context:

> **Example:** Alwyn Farey-Jones was suing Integrated Capital Associates ("ICA") regarding a commercial dispute. Farey-Jones issued a subpoena to NetGate, ICA's internet service provider, seeking "all copies of e-mails sent or received by anyone" at ICA. A magistrate later reviewed the subpoena and concluded that it was "massively overbroad" and "patently unlawful." ICA then responded by suing Farey-Jones for violating ICA's rights under the SCA.
>
> The SCA provides for civil damages against any private party that gains unauthorized access to electronic communication service data, but there is no remedy for private parties that merely gain unauthorized access to remote computing services data. Thus, ICA argued that the e-mails stored by NetGate were electronic communication service data.

Analysis: The Ninth Circuit held that ICA's opened e-mails that were stored on NetGate's servers were electronic communications service data, even though they had already been opened by ICA. The court found that the copy stored by NetGate was "incidental to its electronic transmission" because the copy was being stored "for purposes of backup protection." In other words, NetGate wanted to have two copies of all their received e-mail: one on their own computers and one on the server. This way, NetGate would be assured of having a copy of the e-mail even if the user accidentally deleted it from his or her computer. The Ninth Circuit decided that the purpose of backup protection was "incidental to [the e-mail's] electronic transmission, and therefore gave the opened, stored e-mails the highest level of SCA protection.[7]

Under the Ninth Circuit's rationale, **all** recent e-mail being stored by an ISP—whether opened or unopened—would qualify as electronic communication service data. However, the 180-day limit, which is written into the statute, would still apply, so after that time period all stored e-mails revert to the lower level of protection afforded remote computing services data.

[7] Theofel v. Farey-Jones, 359 F.3d 1066 (9th Cir. 2004).

So far, no other court has followed the Ninth Circuit's interpretation of the SCA,[8] and this interpretation has not been applied in a criminal context. Thus, the "opened/unopened" distinction still remains the majority rule.

3. Using a Cell Phone to Track Its Owner. One recent issue to arise under the SCA involves "historical cell site information"—that is, information subpoenaed from the cell phone company about the location of a cell phone at a time when a call is placed. The government has argued that this is merely non-content "consumer information," and thus should be obtainable with merely a 2703(d) order, which only requires a showing of "specific and articulable facts" that there are reasonable grounds to believe the message is relevant to their investigation. The government's argument has some logical appeal when the government seeks information about the location of a cell phone one week ago, or even one day ago. But what if the government wants to know the location of the cell phone one minute ago, or perhaps one second ago? Should information so immediately in the past be treated the same way?

A District Court magistrate recently rejected the government's SCA request for "historical cell cite information" on precisely these grounds:

> In reality, the Government is seeking the issuance of an order that would technically permit the Government access to cell site information as early as one second prior to the Court's issuance of the order . . . it is unrealistic to believe that in the explosive world of technological advancement, the Government would not some day (if not now) be able to receive a signed order at 4:00 p.m., e-mail or fax the order to a telecommunication service provider by 4:05 p.m., and receive a cell phone's "historical" cell site information from 3:59 p.m., dramatically narrowing if not pinpointing a location. If this example is not *de jure* "real time" tracking, it is certainly *de facto* "real time" tracking.[9]

Although the user has no reasonable expectation of privacy in her location when she is travelling through a public space, the real time tracking effectively allowed by cell site information would be indiscriminate—that is, it would provide information about the user's location in private areas as well as public areas. The Supreme Court found this sort of indiscriminate tracking violates the Fourth Amendment in the absence of a warrant.[10] Thus, the magistrate held that the government had to meet the higher standard of probable cause and a warrant before obtaining this

---

[8] See United States v. Warshak, 631 F.3d 266, 291 (6th Cir. 2010).

[9] In re Application for Historical Cell Cite Information, 509 F.Supp. 2d 64, 75 (D. MA. 2007).

[10] United States v. Karo, 468 U.S. 705 (1984).

information.[11] Other courts have similarly rejected government attempts to use the Pen Register Act to obtain a cell phone's physical location.[12]

Foreign Intelligence Service Act ("FISA")

F. The Law. Electronic surveillance is not only a valuable tool for law enforcement, but is also critical for espionage and counter-espionage. We have already seen in **Chapter 18** that certain types of surveillance are classified as "special needs" searches if their primary purpose is other than crime control, and that these searches are exempt from the usual probable cause/warrant requirement. But a particular problem arises when government agents carry out domestic surveillance for national security purposes. On the one hand, national security is a special need, and it is an area where courts may be more willing to defer to the government's expertise. On the other hand, allowing government agents to spy on their own citizens without any judicial oversight will likely lead to an abuse of power by the Executive Branch.

When the Supreme Court created the modern rules for government surveillance in *Katz v. United States,* it specifically deferred the question of what rules would apply in cases involving national security.[13] In fact, the Supreme Court has only once addressed how the Fourth Amendment regulates national security surveillance. This was in 1972 in a case called *United States v. United States District Court* (known as the "Keith Case" after now-senior-Sixth Circuit Court of Appeals Judge Damon Keith, the then-federal district court judge who first heard the case).

In the Keith Case, the defendant was charged with a terrorist action. Specifically, he was charged with conspiracy to destroy government property involving the planned bombing of a CIA office in Michigan. In order to gather evidence against the defendant, federal agents installed wiretaps on the defendant's telephone. The government did not obtain any court permission before installing the wiretaps, arguing that in order to protect its citizens from foreign attacks or domestic terrorism, agents frequently had to act quickly and rely on sensitive, classified information. In the government's view, these factors meant that it would be difficult if not impossible to obtain a warrant. The government argued that the Attorney General should be allowed to authorize national security wiretaps without any judicial oversight. Judge Keith denied the government's claims and suppressed the evidence. The Supreme Court affirmed.

---

[11] The magistrate also held that the physical location of the cell phone is protected under another federal statute: the Communications Assistance for Law Enforcement Act of 1994 (47 U.S.C. §§ 1001-1002).

[12] See, e.g., In re Application of the United States for an Order Authorizing the Disclosure of Prospective Cell Site Information, 412 F. Supp. 2d 947, 958 (E.D. Wis. 2006).

[13] Katz v. United States, 389 U.S. 347, 358 n.23 (1967).

The Supreme Court rejected this broad vision of executive power, and held that independent judicial review and the issuance of a warrant were necessary requirements for national security wiretaps. However, the Court acknowledged that national security surveillance is distinct from standard law enforcement surveillance in a number of ways:

> The gathering of security intelligence is often long range and involves the interrelation of various sources and types of information. The exact targets of such surveillance may be more difficult to identify than in surveillance operations [conducted for law enforcement purposes]. Often, too, the emphasis of domestic intelligence gathering is on the prevention of unlawful activity or the enhancement of the Government's preparedness for some possible future crisis or emergency. Thus, the focus of domestic surveillance [for purposes of security intelligence] may be less precise than that directed against more conventional types of crime.[14]

Thus, the Court invited Congress to create a new kind of warrant specifically for national security surveillance, one which would be "reasonable both in relation to the legitimate need of Government for intelligence information and the protected rights of our citizens" and which could set out its own definition of probable cause.

As we saw in the last chapter, Congress had already created a special kind of warrant for wiretapping and electronic surveillance when it passed the Wiretap Act in 1968. The Wiretap Act, however, specifically excluded all surveillance conducted for national security purposes, leaving a gap in the law that the Supreme Court refused to address in the Keith Case. It was not until 1978, six years after the Keith Case was decided, that Congress responded to the Court's invitation by passing the Foreign Intelligence Surveillance Act ("FISA"). FISA sets out broad rules for national security surveillance. For purposes of this discussion, we will focus only on FISA's rules for real-time electronic or telephonic surveillance—essentially, wiretapping phones and intercepting e-mail transmissions.

Even in simplified terms, FISA is a complex statute. To be able to understand its provisions, we first have to define a few terms:

> "Foreign intelligence information" is defined as "information that relates to, and if concerning a United States person is necessary to, the ability of the United States to protect against:
>
> a. actual or potential attack . . . by a foreign power . . . , or
>
> b. sabotage or international terrorism by a foreign power . . . , or

[14] United States v. United States District Court, 407 U.S. 297, 322 (1972).

c. clandestine intelligence activities by an intelligence service or network of a foreign power . . . "

An "agent of a foreign power" is defined in part as anyone who acts on behalf of a foreign power and

a. "knowingly engages in clandestine intelligence gathering activities" which may involve violation of criminal statutes; or

b. knowingly engages in or prepares for acts of sabotage or international terrorism; or

c. uses a false or fraudulent identity.

A "United States person" is a United States citizen or a legal permanent resident of the United States.[14]

And now for the electronic and telephonic surveillance provisions of the statute. Broadly stated, these portions of the statute establish varying degrees of protection depending upon the geographic target of the threat, the citizenship status and location of the suspected target, and the site of the surveillance:

1. When the government is investigating a domestic national security threat, it must comply with all criminal law requirements under the Fourth Amendment and the Wiretap Act.

2. When the government is gathering foreign intelligence information, and the target is not a United States person and is not currently within the United States, the surveillance is not regulated by the Fourth Amendment or FISA.

3. When the government is gathering foreign intelligence information, and the target is not a United States person but is currently within the United States, the Fourth Amendment requires that such monitoring be "reasonable."[15]

4. When the government is gathering foreign intelligence information, and the target is a United States person currently outside the United States, the government must obtain a warrant by demonstrating probable cause that:

[15] 50 U.S.C. § 1801.

[16] United States v. Butenko, 494 F.2d 593 (3d Cir. 1974); United States v. Truong Dinh Hung, 629 F.2d 908 (4th Cir. 1980).

a. the target is reasonably believed to be located outside the country; and

b. the target is an agent of a foreign power.

5. When the government is gathering foreign intelligence information, and the target is a United States person within the United States, the government must obtain a warrant. To obtain this warrant:

a. the Attorney General of the United States must personally review the warrant application;

b. the application must demonstrate probable cause that the target is an agent of a foreign power;

c. the application must demonstrate probable cause that the place at which the surveillance is directed is being used by an agent of a foreign power;

d. the application must contain a description of the nature of information sought and type of communications being monitored;

e. the surveillance must include "minimization procedures" to minimize the chance that the government will intercept non-pertinent information;

f. the application must certify that the information sought cannot reasonably be obtained by normal investigative techniques;

g. the information being sought is foreign intelligence information; and

h. a "significant purpose" of the surveillance must be to gather foreign intelligence information.[16]

The first question to ask when approaching a potential FISA issue is: what is the purpose of the surveillance? As Section (1) of the above discussion reflects, FISA treats an investigation into a domestic national security threat in a manner identical to the treatment of a standard criminal investigation—in both cases, the government must comply with the stringent requirements of the Fourth Amendment and the Wiretap Act. The only exception to this general rule is if a "significant purpose" of the surveillance is to gather foreign intelligence information. Under such circumstances, the special FISA rules might apply.

[17] 50 U.S.C. §1801-11; 1881b(c)(1)(B).

The next step is to determine the citizenship status of the target and the location of the surveillance. Individuals who are neither American citizens nor legal permanent residents of the United States receive the least amount of protection. If such individuals are being monitored overseas, the government faces no restriction on surveillance of them. If they are being monitored within the United States, the government need only prove that at the time of the surveillance, the surveillance was "reasonable."

If the target is a United States citizen or legal permanent resident, the government must obtain a FISA warrant in order to conduct electronic or telephonic surveillance. The standards for this warrant are relatively low if the surveillance is being conducted overseas, but they are much higher if the surveillance is being conducted within the borders of the United States.

The following table simplifies the different requirements:

	NOT a United States person	**United States person**
Outside the United States	No protections under FISA or the Fourth Amendment.	Reasonable belief target is located outside the country and that target is agent of foreign power.
Within the United States	Surveillance must be reasonable.	FISA warrant required.

When government agents seek to obtain a FISA warrant, they do not go to a standard federal court. Instead, they head to a special court—the Foreign Intelligence Surveillance Court (commonly known as the "FISA Court.") The FISA Court is not really a "court" in the traditional sense. It consists of eleven different Federal District Court judges who have been appointed by the Chief Justice of the Supreme Court to a seven year term, during which they hear FISA applications in addition to their normal duties as trial court judges. In order to get a FISA warrant approved, the government must go to one of these eleven judges and present their application. The judge—acting in his or her capacity as a FISA judge—will review the application and then either issue the warrant or deny the application. But there is usually very little suspense, since the FISA judge almost always issues the warrant. From the ten year period between 1999 and 2008, the FISA judges heard over thirteen thousand applications for warrants and denied only eleven of them. Also, the FISA judges work in secret—although their identity is publically known, the warrant applications and the issuance of warrants are kept confidential.

Recently a number of surveillance programs run by the National Security Administration ("NSA") have come to light. Through its "PRISM" program, the NSA was able to collect massive amounts of data stored by third party internet providers. This surveillance was authorized by FISA and approved by the FISA court. Another NSA program involved gathering non-content information such as phone logs and e-mail records; since this was merely "address" information, the NSA only needed to meet the low standards of the Pen Register Act.

The strict requirements for monitoring the communications of a United States citizen or permanent resident in the United States are similar to the requirements set out under Title III. There is a minimization requirement to limit the breadth of the surveillance, and the government must certify that there are no less intrusive means available that will provide the necessary information. There is also a particularity requirement similar to Title III, requiring the government to describe the nature of the information sought and the type of communication being monitored.

However, FISA has a number of important differences from Title III. First, the proceedings are even more secret than a Title III order. In fact, if the information that is gathered is used only for foreign intelligence purposes, the target will probably never learn that the surveillance has taken place. (As explained in the next paragraph, if the government wants to use the information to support a criminal case, the government must notify the defendant that a FISA warrant was used to gather the information).

The focus of FISA's "probable cause" requirement is also somewhat different than Title III. To obtain a Title III order, as with obtaining a standard warrant, the government must demonstrate probable cause to believe the target is committing, has committed, or is about to commit an offense, and that the surveillance will likely provide evidence of that crime. To obtain a FISA warrant, in contrast, the government need only demonstrate probable cause to believe that the target is an agent of a foreign power and that the information being sought is foreign intelligence information. There is no need to support any suspicion that criminal activity is likely present.

Finally, FISA creates one more theoretical check on the government: the Attorney General himself or herself must review the application before it is submitted to the court. Of course, requiring a member of the executive branch to review its own FISA application will not strike many people as a particularly robust way of preventing law enforcement abuses. This is especially true given the fact that the Department of Justice submits over two thousand FISA applications per year, so the level of review cannot be very stringent. Nevertheless, the fact that a cabinet-level official must sign off on the warrant application may deter lower level law enforcement officials from making, at least in the government's view, completely frivolous or unsubstantiated requests.

All of this procedure only allows government agents to obtain information they can use for foreign intelligence purposes. However, what if the government wants to prosecute individuals it was monitoring, and seeks to admit evidence obtained from surveillance conducted pursuant to a FISA warrant? The government must go through several steps to "convert" its FISA information into evidence for a criminal case:

1. The government must notify the trial judge and the defendant that certain information came from a FISA warrant (either directly or indirectly).

2. The defendant then makes a motion to suppress the evidence.

3. If the government does not want to reveal details about the surveillance, it files an affidavit explaining that disclosure of how the information was obtained would damage the national security interests of the United States.

4. The trial judge will then review the affidavit and any other relevant materials *in camera* and determine whether the surveillance was lawful under the Fourth Amendment. The trial judge can make this determination *ex parte* based solely on the materials the government provides, or she may make any or all of the information available to the defendant and conduct an adversary hearing.

At the end of this process, if the trial judge determines that the evidence was obtained in violation of the Fourth Amendment, the judge will apply the exclusionary rule and preclude the evidence as appropriate.

Finally, you should be aware that FISA also sets out its own standards for using pen registers and accessing stored communications. In a (perhaps fruitless) attempt to keep the discussion simple, we will leave those provisions for a more advanced course in computer surveillance.

G. Applying the Law. A critical issue for FISA warrants is how much cooperation is allowed between counterintelligence officers and law enforcement officials. In the wake of the attacks on 9/11, Congress passed the Uniting and Strengthening America by Providing Appropriate Tools Required to Intercept and Obstruct Terrorism Act (the "PATRIOT" Act), which (among other things) made some changes in FISA. For example, before the PATRIOT Act, a FISA warrant was only allowed if the purpose of the surveillance was to gather foreign intelligence information. Under the amended law, as we have seen, the government need only demonstrate that a "significant purpose" was foreign intelligence gathering. The PATRIOT Act also instructed counter-intelligence officers to consult and coordinate with law enforcement officers to prevent violent acts of terrorism.

Although there is a FISA appellate court, it is almost never used due to the secretive nature of FISA warrants. Thus, FISA warrants are only challenged if the information they provide is used in a subsequent criminal case. Even then, the trial judge reviewing the warrant will frequently make her determination without divulging the details of the warrant or the application that led to the warrant. The secrecy of the process has led to a dearth of case law to guide us in understanding how FISA actually works. However, now that counter-intelligence and law enforcement are permitted to coordinate their efforts, the following scenario would be feasible:

> **Example:** The Taliban is a group in Afghanistan that, among other things, funds terrorist operations around the world, including attacks on Americans. The FBI suspects that ten different Afghan immigrants living in Los Angeles are selling heroin made from Afghan opium and then sending the money to members of the Taliban who live in Afghanistan. Therefore, the FBI applies for a FISA warrant to allow them to wiretap the telephones of the suspected Afghan-Americans. The application contains the following information:
>
> 1. The targets of the surveillance are agents of a foreign power because through their drug sales they are "knowingly aiding and abetting" those who were "engaged in sabotage or international terrorism."
>
> 2. Pen/trap surveillance has indicated that the targets of the surveillance have each called individuals in Afghanistan at least once in the last month.
>
> 3. The government is seeking information as to how Taliban leaders in Afghanistan coordinate their heroin distribution network—for example, the exact time and location of shipments leaving the country. This information will be passed along to American intelligence officers in Afghanistan, who will use the information to disrupt the heroin distribution network and capture or kill those involved.
>
> 4. American troops and intelligence officers in Afghanistan have been attempting to acquire this information for years, but have been unable to penetrate the tightly-knit Afghani heroin market with informants or undercover officers. Furthermore, technical problems with the Afghan cell phone infrastructure make any electronic monitoring within Afghanistan extremely unreliable.

5. In order to ensure that translators and intelligence officers have the ability to review all the information received, continuous monitoring and recording of all communications is necessary. However, the case agents working on each suspect would not disseminate any information to law enforcement or to soldiers or agents overseas unless the information provided clear and unequivocal evidence of criminal conduct in the United States or actionable intelligence in Afghanistan.

The targets of the electronic surveillance are all American citizens. The application was reviewed by the Attorney General, and then it was approved by a designated FISA judge. After thirty days, the FBI case agents monitoring the telephone calls turned over to the Drug Enforcement Agency ("DEA") hundreds of pages of transcripts from the telephone conversations which provided unequivocal evidence that all ten of the targets were engaged in heroin trafficking. The DEA arrested all ten individuals and now seeks to use the transcripts in a criminal trial in federal court. The targets (now criminal defendants) object. How should the court rule?

Analysis: The first question is whether the court will even conduct a hearing on the issue or decide the case *ex parte*. The government will probably respond to the defense motions by filing an affidavit that explains how any public disclosure about the FISA warrant or the application which led to the warrant would harm the national interest of the United States. It is likely the trial judge will then privately review the affidavit, along with the FISA warrant, the application, and all other relevant information. If she decides that a hearing is necessary, she has the authority to turn over necessary information to the defense counsel and conduct a hearing. Otherwise, she can decide the question herself without a hearing.

Either way, the trial judge will have to decide whether the surveillance violated the Fourth Amendment. A FISA judge has already determined that there was probable cause to believe the defendants were "agents of a foreign power," which (in this case) meant that they were violating criminal statutes on behalf of a foreign power. The criminal trial judge, however, must conduct her own analysis to ensure that probable cause of a crime existed before the FISA warrant was issued.

H. Overview: The "Spectrum" of Search and Seizure Standards. Over the past few chapters, we have seen how the courts and Congress together have created a complex hierarchy of surveillance regulation, in which the standard the government must meet in order to conduct the surveillance increases as the intrusiveness of the surveillance method increases. Here is a brief summary of the various types of surveillance and the legal requirements for each:

Type of Surveillance	Legal Requirement	Source of Law
Information knowingly exposed to the public	None	*California v. Greenwood* (garbage put out for collection); *Florida v. Riley* (visible from helicopter); *Oliver v. United States* (open fields); etc.
Any search conducted after the suspect has given consent	Consent must be voluntary; no prior judicial review	*Schenckloth v. Bustamonte*
"Address" information (phone numbers, e-mail addresses)	Certified relevance; must be "certified" to a court, but no judicial review	Pen Register Act
"Historic" information (subscriber records, stored, opened e-mail)	Specific and articulable facts that there are reasonable grounds to believe the information is relevant to investigation; prior judicial review required	Stored Communications Act
Contraband or evidence in "plain view"	Police must be legally in the area where they see the item and legally able to access it; the fact that the item is contraband or evidence must be "immediately apparent;" no prior judicial review	*Texas v. Brown*
Exigency	Police must have a reasonable and objective basis for believing that immediate action is required to prevent harm to persons or the destruction of evidence; no prior judicial review	*Warden v. Hayden*
"Special needs" searches	Surveillance must have a primary purpose other than law enforcement; surveillance must be reasonable; no prior judicial approval required	*Camara v. Municipal Court* (administrative searches); *Michigan v. Sitz* (drunk driving checkpoints)
Brief seizure/ Frisk of person	Reasonable suspicion/ Reasonable suspicion of immediate danger to officer; no prior judicial review required	*Terry v. Ohio*
Search incident to arrest, or of automobile	Authority to search flows entirely from the lawfulness of the arrest or from probable cause to believe evidence of the crime will be found in the vehicle; no prior judicial review required required	*United States v. Robinson; Carroll v. United States*
Search with no warrant exception	Warrant issued by court, supported by probable cause	*United States v. Katz*
Contemporaneous interception of telephonic or electronic communications for foreign intelligence purposes	FISA warrant (evidence to show that target is agent of foreign power, plus minimization requirement, least intrusive means requirement)	FISA
Contemporaneous interception of telephone communications or electronic communications for law enforcement purposes; Covert video surveillance	Title III order (probable cause plus minimization requirement, least intrusive means requirement, time limit)	Wiretap Act, ECPA (oral, wire, and electronic surveillance), *United States v. Torres* (covert video surveillance)

Quick Summary

Modern surveillance law is a patchwork of Fourth Amendment restrictions, as set out by the Supreme Court, and statutory restrictions, as passed by Congress and state legislatures. In this chapter we focused on statutes that regulate surveillance in contexts where the Fourth Amendment provides no protection or very minimal protection.

For example, under *Smith v. Maryland*, the Fourth Amendment does not provide any protection for "address" information that is turned over to third parties, such as telephone numbers dialed in order to direct a phone call, or the To/From lines on an e-mail message. The **Pen Register Act** creates a very low standard for government agents seeking to obtain this information. The government must merely certify that the information they seek is relevant to an ongoing investigation, and the court's role is simply to record the certification without conducting any independent review.

Information stored by third party servers such as internet service providers is also not protected under the Fourth Amendment under *Smith*. The **Stored Communications Act**, however, creates three different categories for this data. In order to obtain "Electronic Communications Services" data, such as unopened e-mail that is stored incidental to its delivery, the government must acquire a warrant. In order to obtain "Remote Computing Services" data, such as documents or e-mails that have been stored for over 180 days, the government only need provide notice and either get a subpoena or acquire a 2703(d) order by showing "specific and articulable facts showing that there are reasonable grounds to believe" that the information being sought is "relevant and material to an ongoing investigation." In order to obtain any non-content data, the government need only obtain a subpoena or a 2703(d) order and need not provide notice.

Finally, government surveillance for national security purposes conducted within the United States is only lightly regulated by the Fourth Amendment because it is categorized as a "special need" search. But the **Foreign Intelligence Surveillance Act** sets out a hierarchy of protections for this type of surveillance. If the government is monitoring communications pursuant to a domestic security threat, it must obtain a standard warrant. If the government is monitoring communications of American citizens or legal permanent residents in order to gather foreign intelligence, the government must obtain a "FISA warrant" from a special judge who has been appointed to sit on the FISA court.

Review Questions

1. Tracing the Knife-Wielding Assailant. In a dispute outside a bar, Gary Travers was stabbed in the stomach. As he was being taken to the hospital, he told the police that he knew the person who stabbed him only by the nickname "Ace." However, Ace had been texting Travers threats all night, so Travers knew Ace's cell phone number, which he provided to the police.

The police Googled the number and discovered that Sprint wireless company serviced that number. They called Sprint and asked for the subscriber information, including the name of the subscriber and the address, saying it was an "emergency" and "official police business." Sprint complied and gave the police a name and address. The officers set up a surveillance of the address in question and within a few hours they saw a man emerge from the house who fit the description of "Ace" as provided by Travers. They arrested the man and charged him with assault.

Ace moved to suppress the evidence of his identity from the surveillance, arguing that information the police officer's acquired from Sprint was protected by the Fourth Amendment. Were defendant's rights violated?

2. Locating Osama Bin Laden. In pursuit of the "War on Terror," the intelligence community began to specifically target members of Al-Qaeda, and including Osama Bin Laden, who the intelligence community believed was the spearhead of the terrorist group. The United States intelligence community became aware that persons associated with Bin Laden's organization had established an al Qaeda presence in Kenya. They sought to wiretap the cell phone belonging to Wadih el-Hage,a Lebanese citizen living in Kenya known to have a close connection with Bin Laden.

After listening to his conversations for a few weeks, they learned the names of a number of other Bin Laden associates, including Yusef Kassem, an American citizen who also lived in Kenya and sometimes drove Bin Laden to meetings. The CIA applied for a FISA warrant to wiretap Kassem's phone. They presented the FISA court with eyewitness evidence that Kassem was currently in Kenya, and then evidence from el-Hage's phone to show that Kassem worked for Al-Qaeda and that he was participating in a meeting where violent terrorist attacks were being planned. The FISA court approved the warrant and the CIA began wiretapping Kassem's phone.

One week later, Kassem returned home to the United States. Fearing that Kassem was going to recruit for Al Qaeda, the CIA continued the wiretapping while he was in the United States. This wiretapping provided them with plenty of evidence to arrest him before he left the country.

Kassem now is challenging the wiretapping of his cell phone. Did the police act illegally when they conducted this wiretap?

3. Investigating Medicaid Fraud. The Medicaid Fraud Unit of the Department of Justice received an anonymous tip that Dr. Hallie Gerber was billing the Medicaid program for procedures that she never performed. The informant claimed that Dr. Gerber was working with Terry Huber, an administrator at Riverside Hospital, who would approve Dr. Gerber's imaginary procedures and then receive a share of the Medicaid reimbursement. The informant listed three different procedures that Dr. Gerber claimed to have performed but did not, as well as the dates that Dr. Gerber received reimbursements. Investigators checked their records and confirmed that Dr. Gerber had in fact received reimbursements for those procedures on the specified dates.

In order to investigate this allegation, the prosecutor went to a federal magistrate and requested a 2703(d) order to read Huber's opened e-mail that was stored on Huber's Gmail account. The prosecutor argued that the informant's tip provided "specific and articulable facts showing that there are reasonable grounds to believe" that the information being sought is "relevant and material to an ongoing investigation." The magistrate granted the order, and the prosecutor delivered the order to Google, who dutifully turned over all of Huber's opened e-mails that were stored on Google's server. Huber was notified of the investigation.

The opened e-mails on the Gmail server were helpful to the investigation, but investigators noticed that there were no stored e-mails over five days old, and concluded that Huber had deleted all of her older e-mails from the server. They then took the same 2703(d) order to Huber and told her they needed to look at the e-mails stored on her hard drive. Huber turned over her computer. They learned that Huber had deleted all of her stored e-mails, but their technical experts were able to recover the deleted e-mails, going back five months. They proved to be incriminating against but Huber and Gerber.

At trial, Huber moved to suppress both the e-mails obtained from Google, and the e-mails recovered from her computer. Should this evidence be suppressed?

22

Standing

Key Concepts

- Defendant Must Be "Victim" of Illegal Police Conduct
- Overnight Guests Have Standing
- Short Term Guests May Have Standing
- Standing to Challenge a Seizure

A. Introduction and Policy. You are probably already familiar with the general concept of standing. In civil cases, a litigant must demonstrate a sufficient stake in the outcome in order to proceed with the case. This requirement is usually met if the litigant can prove she has suffered (or imminently will suffer) injury; that the injury was caused by the defendant's conduct; and that the court can remedy the injury. Under this broad definition of standing, every criminal defendant would be able to challenge any illegal government action that turned up evidence that was going to be used against her.

Unfortunately for criminal defendants, in the context of the Fourth Amendment standing requirements are a bit stricter—and unfortunately for students, they are a good deal more complicated. To assert standing in a suppression hearing, a criminal defendant must demonstrate not just that the potentially illegal government action will cause her injury, but also that the government action violated *her* rights at the time it occurred. This is because, in the words of the Supreme Court, Fourth Amendment rights are "personal in nature," and therefore the question of standing is "properly placed within the purview of substantive Fourth Amendment law."[1]

In practice, this means that even if the police undertake an obviously illegal search, a defendant will have no way to challenge that search in his criminal case unless he was in some way the direct victim of that search. For example, assume the police illegally wiretap David's phone and hear him making incriminating statements about the drugs he has just bought from Russell. The police then illegally enter David's house and recover all the drugs, which have Russell's fingerprints all over them. If the police then arrest David for possessing the drugs, the prosecutor will not be allowed to use David's statements or the drugs in David's criminal trial. However, if the police also arrest Russell for selling the drugs, the prosecution at

---

[1] Rakas v. Illinois, 439 U.S. 128, 140 (1978).

Russell's criminal trial would be allowed to admit David's statements from the illegal wiretap (assuming they are otherwise admissible under the rules of evidence) and the drugs found in David's house. Even though the police repeatedly violated the law when investigating the case against Russell, they did not violate any of **Russell's** rights, and so therefore he has no recourse.

As you will read in the next chapter, the primary recourse for an individual whose Fourth Amendment rights have been violated is to challenge the admission of any fruits of that search in a suppression hearing. If the defendant can prove that the police conducted an illegal search or seizure, the court will typically suppress the evidence or contraband recovered from the search. But not all searches and seizures result in incriminating evidence—the police may illegally pull over a car or illegally stop and frisk a person on the street hundreds of times without finding any evidence of criminal activity—either because their suspicions were unfounded or perhaps because they were engaged in harassment.

However, for the most part, Fourth Amendment doctrine does not provide meaningful remedies for illegal police activity that does not uncover potential evidence. As you will read in **Chapter 23**, the primary mechanism for addressing violations of the Fourth Amendment is suppression of the evidence. Consequently, unless the police recover evidence that they intend to use against the target in a criminal case there is very little a person can do to challenge an illegal search. Thus, in the prior example, if the police chose not to charge David with any crime, he would have little chance of a successful challenge.

This is not to say that an innocent person who is the victim of illegal police conduct has no recourse at all. As **Chapter 23** discusses, she could sue the police department in a civil proceeding, arguing that she has suffered damages because her civil rights have been violated. Compared to suppression hearings, however, these lawsuits are relatively rare. Moreover, notwithstanding the recent success of the New York plaintiffs in the stop-and-frisk cases, as a general rule, such cases are also fairly difficult to win. Consequently, they do little to deter police conduct. Suppression hearings occur as a matter of due course in any criminal case, and the defendant will have an attorney to challenge the police action even if he cannot afford one. In contrast, most private lawsuits against the police require the victim of the search to be pro-active—she must hire her own attorney and then initiate litigation. The lawsuits also face an uphill battle: the police enjoy partial immunity for their actions, and the damages for relatively minor police misconduct—an improper stop and frisk, for example—are likely to be small. We will discuss this and other alternatives to the exclusionary rule in the next chapter.

B. The Law. As we saw in **Chapter 6,** the term "reasonable expectation of privacy" is the key to determining whether government surveillance violates the

Fourth Amendment. But even before the court can reach that question, the court must confront the issue of whether the defendant can make an argument that **his** reasonable expectation of privacy has been violated. This latter question is the core of standing.

> An individual has standing and can challenge an alleged Fourth Amendment violation only if:
>
> 1. the police conduct involved an intrusion into his reasonable expectation of privacy;[2] and
>
> 2. the individual is a defendant in the criminal action in which the illegally seized evidence is going to be introduced.[3]

With regard to the first prong—determining whether the defendant's reasonable expectation of privacy has been infringed—the court will undertake a purely objective inquiry into the facts. In other words, it is irrelevant what the police officer believed at the time of the search or what the defendant believed at the time of the search. It is even irrelevant what a **reasonable** police officer or defendant might have believed at the time of the search. Instead, the court will look at all of the facts of the case and determine whether the defendant's rights extended to a reasonable expectation of privacy in the area that was searched.

To help answer this question, the Court has suggested several relevant factors. The considerations useful to determining whether the defendant has a privacy right in the area searched are:

1. Does the defendant have any interest in the location that was searched;

2. Does the defendant have any interest in the items that were seized;

3. Did the search take place in an area where the defendant was lawfully present?

We will consider these specific questions in the following section.

The second prong of the standing test merely reaffirms the limits on the remedy available within the Fourth Amendment for illegal police conduct that does not result in incriminating evidence against the victim of the conduct. In other words, the defendant must be seeking to preclude specific evidence that the prosecutor seeks to use against him in his criminal trial.

---

[2] Mancusi v. DeForte, 392 U.S. 364 (1968).

[3] Rakas v. Illinois, 439 U.S. 128 (1978).

C. Applying the Law.

1. Basic Principles. The first step in determining standing is to isolate each instance of police conduct and then determine which individuals suffered an intrusion into their reasonable expectation of privacy as a result of that conduct. Sometimes this is a straightforward determination: suspect #1's home or car or person is searched, leading to information that incriminates suspect #2. Suspect #2 has no standing to challenge any of the searches that affected suspect #1, unless suspect #2 also had her own possessory interest in the car or the home.

But frequently resolving this first step in the question of standing is a bit more complicated. For example, how should we treat visitors who have no actual ownership interest in the property being searched? And how should we treat owners who are not in possession of the property at the time of the search? The Court has given guidance in both of these areas. Overnight guests in a home (or hotel) have a sufficient possessory interest in the residence to claim standing, even if they are not present at the time of the search.[4] In contrast, an owner of a piece of property who has leased it to a third party and retains no right of possession during the lease will not have standing.

What about individuals who are guests in a home for only a few hours? The law is not completely clear on this point. The Court has stated that being "legitimately on the premises" is **not** enough on its own to confer standing. However, notwithstanding this proclamation, when the Court affirmed that overnight guests have standing, it used language that implied a shorter-term guest would receive the same privilege.[5] In accord with this language, almost all lower courts to consider the question have agreed that short-term social visitors do receive the same Fourth Amendment protections as overnight guests.

Thus, the current rule is (probably) that such guests have standing to challenge a search of that home, at least if their own possessions are seized. We recognize that the ambiguity of this rule may cause some readers concern. But, we must keep the "probably" in the sentence because the Supreme Court has never directly ruled on the issue.

> **Example:** Sarah invites her friend Kathy over for the evening to watch television and have dinner. As Kathy is leaving her apartment to go to Sarah's house, one of Kathy's roommates sees her put a bag containing crack cocaine in her purse and then leave the house. The roommate goes to the police and tells them what she saw and where Kathy was going.

---

[4] Jones v. United States, 362 U.S. 257 (1960) (home); Stoner v. California, 376 U.S. 483 (1964) (hotel).

[5] Minnesota v. Olson, 495 U.S. 91, 98-99 (1990).

Believing (probably correctly) that they now have probable cause to arrest Kathy, the police go to Sarah's house and knock on the door to ask for permission to enter. When nobody answers, they break down the door and (illegally) enter the house without a warrant, finding Kathy and Sarah in the living room. They search the living room and find a bag with crack cocaine stuffed under the couch cushions. Kathy tells the police that the bag belongs to her and that Sarah had nothing to do with it. Kathy is arrested and charged with possession of narcotics. She then challenges the police entry and search of Sarah's house.

Analysis: Kathy (probably) has standing to challenge the search. Even though she was only present in Sarah's house for a few hours to watch television and eat dinner (and smoke crack), while she was there she had the right to assume that her possessions in the area would not be subject to a search by law enforcement.

The Court has limited the short-term guest doctrine in three specific ways. First, the Court has held that that a short-term "guest" in a **car**—*i.e.*, a passenger—does not have standing to challenge a search of the vehicle:

Example—*Rakas v. Illinois*, 439 U.S. 128 (1978): A police officer received a radio call reporting a bank robbery and describing the car the suspects were driving. A few minutes later, the officer saw a car fitting the description he had just received. The officer followed the car for a few minutes, and then he and a few other officers pulled the car over. There were four occupants of the car, two females (one of whom owned the car and was driving) and two males. The officers ordered all four occupants out of the car before searching it. They recovered a box of rifle shells in the locked glove compartment and a sawed-off shotgun under the front seat.

The police arrested the two males and charged them with bank robbery. The defendants challenged the search of the car, arguing that the police lacked probable cause. The government argued that if the defendants did not own the car and claimed not to own the guns and ammunition, they had no standing to challenge the search.

Analysis: The Supreme Court held that the defendants did not have standing to challenge the search. The Court contrasted the defendants' position with that of the defendant in *Jones v. United States*. In *Jones*, the Court held that an overnight guest would be allowed to challenge a search of his host's home. As the *Rakas*

Court explained, a similar rule would not be applied to automobile passengers. "[T]he holding in *Jones* can best be explained by the fact that Jones had a legitimate expectation of privacy in the premises he was using and therefore could claim the protection of the Fourth Amendment with respect to a governmental invasion of those premises." In the *Rakas* case, the defendants "asserted neither a property nor a possessory interest in the automobile, nor an interest in the property seized." Cars "are not to be treated identically with houses or apartments for Fourth Amendment purposes."

In short, the Court held that passengers in a car do not have a reasonable expectation of privacy in the car.[6]

The second limitation on the short-term guest doctrine comes from dictum in the *Rakas* case. Discussing the traditional treatment of visitors in homes, the *Rakas* Court noted that even though an individual may have the right to object to a search of **some portion** of the premises, she does not necessarily have the right to object to a search of the **entire** premises. A contrary rule, the Court found would lead to illogical results. "[A] casual visitor who has never seen, or been permitted to visit, the basement of another's house [would have standing] to object to a search of the basement if the visitor happened to be in the kitchen of the house at the time of the search." Allowing such a challenge would "advance no purpose served by the Fourth Amendment." Applying this logic to the facts before it, the *Rakas* Court noted that the defendants' claim there would have failed even if the car were treated in the same way as a house. Because the defendants "made no showing that they had any legitimate expectation of privacy in the glove compartment or area under the seat of the car in which they were merely passengers" they could not assert a viable Fourth Amendment claim.[7]

This implies (reasonably enough) that a short-term visitor in a home does not have standing to challenge a search of **every** part of the home—for example, a search of the basement, the attic, or the medicine cabinet in the master bathroom. Instead, a short-term visitor in a home would only have standing to challenge a search of the areas in which a guest would reasonably be expected to be present. Thus, in the previous example involving Sarah and Kathy, Kathy could challenge the search of the living room where she and Sarah were watching TV, but not of a more remote part of the house such as a basement closet.

The third limitation on the short-term guest doctrine restricts application of the doctrine to **social** guests. The doctrine does not apply to individuals who are briefly on the premises for commercial or other non-social business purposes:

---

[6] Rakas v. Illinois, 439 U.S. 128 (1978).

[7] Id. at 148-49.

Example—*Minnesota v. Carter*, 525 U.S. 83 (1998): Officer Thielen of the Eagan Police Department received an anonymous tip that cocaine was being packaged in a nearby ground floor apartment. One window in the apartment fronted onto a public street. Accordingly, Officer Thielen walked up to the window, and peeked down into the apartment through a gap in the closed blinds. He saw three individuals putting white powder into small sandwich bags. Officer Thielen notified headquarters, and more police were sent to the location while a search warrant application was prepared. Before the warrant could be issued, however, the police saw two of the individuals, who had been packaging cocaine leave the apartment and get into a car. The police pulled the car over and found a gun in plain view. The two individuals, named Carter and Johns, were arrested. A later search of the car turned up thirty-seven grams of cocaine packaged in small sandwich bags.

When the officers searched the apartment, they found cocaine residue on the kitchen table and plastic bags that matched the ones in the car. They arrested the occupant of the apartment. She informed the police that she was the lessee of the apartment and that Carter and Johns, who had never been to the apartment before, were in town from Chicago and had come to the apartment for the sole purpose of packaging the drugs. In exchange for the use of her apartment, they paid her one-eighth of an ounce of cocaine. They were present in the apartment for just two and a half hours.

Carter and Johns moved to suppress the gun and the drugs found in the car, as well as the drugs and paraphernalia found in the apartment. They also moved to suppress certain incriminating statements they made after their arrest. They argued that Officer Thielen conducted an illegal search when he peeked through the closed blinds of the apartment. The government responded that Carter and Johns did not have standing to object to the search of the apartment. The government further argued that even if they did have standing, Officer Thielen's initial investigation did not constitute a "search."

Analysis: The United States Supreme Court agreed with the government's first contention, and held that Carter and Johns did not have standing to object to Officer Thielen's surveillance of the apartment. The Court noted that the fact pattern fell somewhere between *Jones*, which held that overnight guests had standing, and *Rakas*, which noted that those who were merely "legitimately present" on the property did not have standing.

In *Carter*, the defendants were only in the apartment for a "commercial purpose." The Court has held that the workplace receives less Fourth Amendment protection than a residence. Moreover, the defendants' connection to the apartment was even more tenuous than most individuals' connection to their own workplace—they were only present for two and a half hours and had never been to the apartment before.

The Court concluded that "the purely commercial nature of the transaction engaged in here, the relatively short period of time on the premises, and the lack of any previous connection between respondents and the householder, all lead us to conclude that respondents' situation is closer to that of one simply permitted on the premises." Therefore, the defendants did not have a sufficient privacy interest to challenge the surveillance. Based on its conclusion that Carter and Johns had no authority to challenge the officer's conduct, the Court did not reach the question of whether Officer Thielen's surveillance was a Fourth Amendment Search.[8]

In short, the rule on standing for short-term guests in homes is still evolving. Some of the dicta in *Rakas* appeared to call the right into question. But later cases, including *Carter*, restated the right of some short-term guests while at the same time rejecting application of the rule to individuals who were only using the premises briefly for commercial activity.

Another factor in determining whether the short-term guest has a reasonable expectation of privacy in a home is whether she has a possessory interest in the item searched. We turn to this question next.

2. Possessory Interest in an Item. In general, if an individual has a possessory interest in an item, she can object to a search of that item. For example, if an individual stores his possessions in a suitcase and leaves the suitcase in the basement of a friend's house, he has standing to contest a later search of the suitcase. Note that in practice this rule only applies to closed containers—if an individual leaves an item out in plain view, whether in a public place or inside someone else's home, he has no reasonable expectation of privacy that the item will not be seen. (However, as you read in **Chapter 9**, he still has a right to challenge the **seizure** of that item. As a general rule, items in plain view may only be seized if the contraband nature of the items is immediately apparent).

However, placing your item in **someone else's** closed container is not sufficient to establish standing. You must be able to assert a possessory interest in both the closed container and the item inside:

[8] Minnesota v. Carter. 525 U.S. 83, 91 (1998).

Example—*Rawlings v. Kentucky*, 448 U.S. 98 (1980): David Rawlings arrived in the city of Bowling Green looking for a job. At the time, he was carrying 1,800 tablets of LSD in a jar. He stayed at the house of a friend named Michael Swank, and after a few days he met a woman named Vanessa Cox at a party. Over the next few days, he spent a couple of nights at Cox's house and a couple of nights at Swank's house.

After Rawlings had been in the city for about a week, he, Cox, and a few other individuals were sitting in Swank's house. Rawlings, who had been carrying the jar of LSD on his person for the entire week, turned to Cox and asked her if she would carry the jar in her purse. He then left to go to the bathroom. Moments later, police officers burst into the house with a warrant to arrest one of Swank's housemates. The housemate was not present. But the police smelled marijuana and so believed they had probable cause to search the house. While several of the officers left to secure a warrant to search the house, the other officers remained.

After about forty-five minutes, the first group of officers returned with the warrant and began searching the house. In the process of the search, they asked Cox to empty her purse. She did so, revealing the jar with the LSD in it. Cox turned to Rawlings and asked him to "take what was his." Rawlings immediately claimed possession of the LSD. He was arrested and charged with possession of a controlled substance.

At his suppression hearing, Rawlings moved to suppress the drugs found in Cox's purse and the statements he made about the drugs. He claimed that the search of Cox's purse was illegal.

Analysis: The Supreme Court held that Rawlings did not have standing to object to the search of Cox's purse because he did not have a reasonable expectation of privacy in its contents. He had only known Cox for a few days, he had never before had access to her purse, he had no right to exclude others from the purse, and he took no privacy precautions with respect to the purse.

Rawlings claimed that even though he may not have had a reasonable expectation of privacy in the purse, he had a reasonable expectation of privacy in the drugs that were recovered. The Court acknowledged that his ownership of the drugs was "a fact to be considered." But, this fact alone did not mean he had a reasonable expectation of privacy in the location where the drugs were recovered. For example, if the jar of LSD had been sitting in plain view in a public location, he would have had no basis for challenging police observation of the drugs. In a similar fashion, though Rawlings indisputably had a possessory interest in the drugs themselves, he had no reason to challenge their discovery in Cox's purse.

In the end, the question of standing is a fact-based inquiry in which good advocacy may be able to sway the court. The judge must decide whether the defendant's connection to the location being searched is strong enough that he can assert a reasonable expectation of privacy in the space. If the location of the search is the purse of a friend the defendant met a few days ago, and into which he dumped his drugs a few seconds before the police barged into the room, the connection will be too tenuous. However, if the area being searched is a locked briefcase carried by the defendant's spouse to which only the defendant and his spouse have a key, the connection will probably be sufficient to establish standing.

3. Who Is the "Victim" of the Police Conduct? In resolving the question of standing, the court must next determine whether the person seeking to challenge police conduct was actually the "victim" of that conduct. Sometimes the police engage in a series of illegal actions against a number of different individuals. In these cases it is important to analyze each defendant individually to determine whether each defendant is the "victim" of the specific instance(s) of police misconduct they complain about. You will read more about the Supreme Court's decision in *Wong Sun v. United States* in **Chapter 23**'s discussion of the Exclusionary Rule. However, the case also provides one useful example for exploring the standing issue more closely:

> **Example—*Wong Sun v. United States*, 371 U.S. 471 (1963):** Federal law enforcement agents illegally entered James Wah Toy's home and illegally arrested him. They found no contraband in his home, but during a subsequent interrogation, Toy told the agents that a man named Johnny Yee possessed heroin.
>
> The agents went to Yee's house and illegally entered and searched his house. There they found heroin. Yee was also arrested and interrogated. He told the police that a man named Wong Sun brought him the heroin. The police located Wong Sun's house and illegally entered and searched his home. No drugs were found, but Wong Sun was also arrested. Toy, Yee, and Wong Sun were all charged with possession of narcotics, and then released on their own recognizance after their arraignment.

At a suppression hearing, Wong Sun moved to suppress the heroin found in Yee's house.

Analysis: Wong Sun was the victim of two illegal police actions: the unconstitutional entry and search of his house, and his unconstitutional arrest. However, the illegal activity that Wong Sun suffered was not the direct source of the evidence he sought to suppress. No contraband was found during the search of Wong Sun's home, and he made no statements at the time of his arrest. The heroin recovered from Yee's apartment was a result of the police's illegal conduct against Toy and Yee, but Wong Sun had no standing to challenge those actions. Thus, the drugs that were illegally found at Yee's house were admissible against Wong Sun (though they would be inadmissible against Yee).

The ramifications of the standing requirement are especially evident in a case like *Wong Sun.* Nearly every action the police took was illegal, but evidence was admissible against Wong Sun if the police only violated **someone else's** rights when they obtained the evidence against him.

4. Standing to Object to a Seizure. The rules regulating seizures are very similar to the rules regulating searches. A defendant can only challenge a seizure if the police violated his own liberty interests. Therefore, a defendant cannot challenge the seizure or arrest of another individual. Likewise, a defendant cannot challenge the seizure of an item—even an item that belongs to him—unless his own possessory interest in that item has been affected. If the defendant has loaned the item to someone else for an extended period of time, and the police illegally seize the item from that third party for a short period of time and then return it, the defendant cannot object to the seizure.

Example: Patrick was importing marijuana from Mexico into the United States with plans to sell it in his hometown of Chicago. He sent his friend Debra down to Houston in his car to pick up the marijuana and drive it back to Chicago. On the way back, the police illegally stopped Debra's car (thus seizing Debra, the car, and all of its contents). As the police officer spoke to Debra, he smelled a strong odor of marijuana. This gave him probable cause to legally search the car. When he conducted the search, he found ten pounds of marijuana, along with a handwritten note from Patrick telling Debra where to deliver the cargo. Both Debra and Patrick were arrested and charged with conspiring to distribute marijuana.

Analysis: Debra has standing to challenge the illegal stop and subsequent search. The stop of the car was an intrusion into her justifiable liberty interests, and though she did not own the car, she was driving it at the time of the search and therefore also had a reasonable expectation of privacy in the location that was searched. Her challenge of the stop will be successful because the stop was illegally made. Moreover, everything the police learned as a result of that stop will be excluded from evidence as fruit of the poisonous tree (discussed in greater detail in **Chapter 23**). Thus, the marijuana and the note will be excluded from any trial against Debra, which means that the prosecutor will likely be forced to drop charges against her.

Unlike Debra, Patrick does not have standing to challenge the **stop** of the car. He had no liberty interests which were infringed by the illegal police action. Because Patrick loaned his car to Debra for several days, the fact that the car was stopped for a few minutes by the police did not intrude upon any of his protected rights.

On the other hand, Patrick does have standing to challenge the **search** of the car. As the owner of the car, Patrick maintained a possessory interest in the car that was violated by the search. Therefore, Patrick has standing to challenge the legality of the search. For Patrick this is something of a Pyrrhic victory. Because the search itself was legal (as you read in **Chapter 15**, police officers may lawfully conduct a warrantless search of a vehicle that they have probable cause to believe contains contraband), Patrick will lose the suppression hearing and the marijuana and note will be admissible against him.

In other words, Debra was a "victim" of both the stop and the search, and so is allowed to challenge both. The only police action that Patrick was a "victim" of was the search, and since the search was legal, the evidence is admissible against him.[9]

Similarly, although we know that passengers in a car do not have standing to object to a search of a car, they **do** have standing to object to the stop of the car because their liberty interests are infringed when the car they are riding in is detained.[10]

5. Solving the Standing "Dilemma." The standing requirements can potentially create a difficult choice for defendants. If they want to challenge the allegedly illegal actions by the government, they must admit to some possessory interest in the area or items searched or the items seized—which frequently means they must admit to ownership of the contraband. Consider for example the defendants in *Rakas*, who denied owning the gun and ammunition recovered in the car, or the defendant in *Rawlings*, who admitted to owning the drugs that were recovered in an (unsuccessful) attempt to gain standing to object to the search of his friend's purse.

[9] This hypothetical was adapted from United States v. Powell, 929 F.2d 1190 (7th Cir. 1991).

[10] Brendlin v. California, 551 U.S. 249 (2007).

The Supreme Court (partially) solved this dilemma in a case called *Simmons v. United States.*[11] *Simmons* held that when a defendant testifies during his suppression hearing, that testimony cannot be admitted against him at trial to prove his guilt. However, the Court has not yet ruled as to whether the defendant's suppression hearing testimony can be used to **impeach** his testimony if he takes the stand and testifies contrary to his suppression hearing testimony.

Based on Supreme Court jurisprudence in the Fifth Amendment context, the Court is likely to hold that the defendant's suppression hearing testimony *can* be used as impeachment evidence. If so, the standing dilemma is not really solved; it is only mitigated. When a defendant chooses to challenge the search in a suppression hearing, he may have to take the stand and claim ownership of the item or area that was searched in order to gain standing. If he loses the hearing and the case goes to trial, one of his potential defenses at trial is effectively unavailable to him: if he claims at trial that he did not own the contraband, he can be impeached with his own prior testimony to the contrary.

[11] Simmons v. United States, 390 U.S. 377 (1968).

Quick Summary

The concept of "standing" in the context of the Fourth Amendment is somewhat different than it is in other areas of the law—the court must determine whether the defendant had a reasonable expectation of privacy in the area searched or the item seized. Thus, if the police illegally search a third party's house and find incriminating evidence against the defendant, the defendant has no recourse in his criminal case (though she may be able to sue the police in a civil action for violating her civil rights).

Courts have held that an overnight guest has standing to challenge the search of the residence where they are staying. However, merely being legally present in an area does not automatically confer standing. Occupants of a car or individuals who show up in a house briefly for a commercial purpose only will not have standing to challenge a subsequent search. The Supreme Court has not yet squarely resolved that short-term social guests have standing to challenge the search of the home they are visiting. However, every lower court to consider the question has found that they do, as long as they only challenge the search of the areas where they were present.

If a defendant has a sufficient possessory interest in a container, then he has standing to challenge a search of that container.

A defendant's testimony in a suppression hearing is not admissible at trial as evidence of guilt. However, it may be admissible against him at trial for impeachment purposes.

Review Questions

1. Receiving Mystery Packages. Postal inspectors opened a suspicious package in the mail addressed to Kurt Humphrey and found LSD inside. Federal law enforcement officers then went to Humphrey's house and arrested him. Humphrey denied ownership and called his friend Larry Allen. Soon after, Allen arrived at the house and told the officers that the package was in fact his, and he explained that he had made a business arrangement with Humphreys: Allen's correspondents would send packages to Humphrey's house with Humphrey's name as the addressee, and Humphrey would then personally deliver the packages to Allen. Allen had agreed to pay Humphrey $50 for every such package, and he was never told about what was inside. Humphreys had already received and then delivered two such packages pursuant to this agreement.

Based on Humphrey's explanation, the officers released Humphrey and arrested Allen instead. Allen subsequently challenged the search of the package by the postal inspectors. Does he have standing to challenge this search?

2. Tracking the Getaway Car. Police officers in Seattle were watching surveillance video from a string of convenience store robberies and saw that a white Ford Expedition was driving away from the scene in two of the incidents. They traced the car to its owner, George Middleton. Lacking probable cause to obtain a search warrant, they installed a GPS tracking device on the vehicle while it was parked in a public parking lot. After another robbery matching the same M.O., police activated the GPS and located the vehicle as it drove down a public highway. An unmarked cruiser used the GPS to find the car and began to follow it. When the car failed to make a complete stop at a stop sign, the police pulled the car over and found a man named Darryl Harcourt driving the car. They searched the car and found $770 in cash, which matched the amount stolen from the convenience store. The police later learned that Harcourt was a friend of Middleton, and that Middleton let Harcourt borrow the vehicle from time to time.

Harcourt was arrested for the robbery, and he challenged (a) the installation of the GPS; (b) the use of the GPS to track him; and (c) the search of the car after he was pulled over. Does he have standing to bring any of these challenges?

3. Stashing the Cocaine in Your Girlfriend's Attic. Jimmy Watterson was a cocaine dealer in Nashville. In February of 2014, he started dating Debra Stevens. He stayed over at her house three or four times over the course of the next two months, and he visited her home at least once a week. When he did visit, he spent almost all of his time in her kitchen or bedroom. Without Stevens' knowledge, he also chose to store his stash of cocaine in her attic.

In April, Watterson sold cocaine to an undercover officer and was arrested. The police, who had been watching Watterson's movements for some time, suspected that he might be keeping his stash at his girlfriend's house, and they showed up at Stevens' house a few hours later without a warrant. When Stevens answered the door, they asked for permission to search her house, and she refused. Worried that she would locate and destroy the cocaine before they could get a warrant, they pushed inside the house and, over Stevens' strenuous objections, they searched the entire house, eventually finding five hundred grams of cocaine in the attic.

Through chemical analysis, the police were able to trace the cocaine in the attic to the cocaine that Watterson sold to the undercover, and Watterson was charged with the cocaine sale and with possession of the five hundred grams of cocaine. At the suppression hearing, he testified that he owned the cocaine. On cross-examination, he admitted that he had only been in Stevens' attic twice—once to hide the stash and once to retrieve some for his sale.

Does Watterson have standing to challenge the search of Stevens' home? If not, and the case goes to trial, can the government use his statements during the suppression hearing against him at trial to prove his ownership of the cocaine?

FROM THE COURTROOM

RAWLINGS v. KENTUCKY

United States Supreme Court, 1980
448 U.S. 98

[Chief Justice REHNQUIST delivered the opinion of the Court.]

[Justices BLACKMUN concurred in the decision.]

[Justice WHITE filed an opinion concurring in part and dissenting in part, which Justice STEWART joined.]

[Justice MARSHALL filed a dissenting opinion, in which he was joined by Justice BRENNAN.]

I

In the middle of the afternoon on October 18, 1976, six police officers armed with a warrant for the arrest of one Lawrence Marquess on charges of drug distribution arrived at Marquess' house in Bowling Green, Ky. In the house at the time the police arrived were one of Marquess' housemates, Dennis Saddler, and four visitors, Keith Northern, Linda Braden, Vanessa Cox, and petitioner David Rawlings. While searching unsuccessfully in the house for Marquess, several police officers smelled marihuana smoke and saw marihuana seeds on the mantel in one of the bedrooms. After conferring briefly, Officers Eddie Railey and John Bruce left to obtain a search warrant. While Railey and Bruce were gone, the other four officers detained the occupants of the house in the living room, allowing them to leave only if they consented to a body search. Northern and Braden did consent to such a search and were permitted to depart. Saddler, Cox, and petitioner remained seated in the living room.

Approximately [forty-five] minutes later, Railey and Bruce returned with a warrant authorizing them to search the house. Railey read the warrant to Saddler, Cox, and petitioner, and also read "*Miranda*" warnings from a card he carried in his pocket. At that time, Cox was seated on a couch with petitioner seated to her left. In the space between them was Cox's handbag.

After Railey finished his recitation, he approached petitioner and told him to stand. Officer Don Bivens simultaneously approached Cox and ordered her to empty the contents of her purse onto a coffee table in front of the couch. Among those contents were a jar containing [eighteen hundred] tablets of LSD and a number of smaller vials containing benzphetamine, methamphetamine, methyprylan, and pentobarbital, all of which are controlled substances under Kentucky law.

Upon pouring these objects out onto the coffee table, Cox turned to petitioner and told him "to take what was his." Petitioner, who was standing in response to Officer Railey's command, immediately claimed ownership of controlled substances. At that time, Railey searched petitioner's person and found $4,500 in cash in petitioner's shirt pocket and a knife in a sheath at petitioner's side. Railey then placed petitioner under formal arrest.

Petitioner was indicted for possession with intent to sell the various controlled substances recovered from Cox's purse. At the suppression hearing, he testified that he had flown into Bowling Green about a week before his arrest to look for a job and perhaps to attend the local university. He brought with him at that time the drugs later found in Cox's purse. Initially, petitioner stayed in the house where the arrest took place as the guest of Michael Swank, who shared the house with Marquess and Saddler. While at a party at that house, he met Cox and spent at least two nights of the next week on a couch at Cox's house.

On the morning of petitioner's arrest, Cox had dropped him off at Swank's house where he waited for her to return from class. At that time, he was carrying the drugs in a green bank bag. When Cox returned to the house to meet him, petitioner dumped the contents of the bank bag into Cox's purse. Although there is dispute over the discussion that took place, petitioner testified that he "asked her if she would carry this for me, and she said, 'yes'. . . ." Petitioner then left the room to use the bathroom and, by the time he returned, discovered that the police had arrived to arrest Marquess.

. . .

II

In this Court, petitioner challenges three aspects of the judgment below. First, he claims that he did have a reasonable expectation of privacy in Cox's purse so as to allow him to challenge the legality of the search of that purse.

. . .

A

In holding that petitioner could not challenge the legality of the search of Cox's purse, the Supreme Court of Kentucky looked primarily to our then recent decision in *Rakas v. Illinois,* where we abandoned a separate inquiry into a defendant's "standing" to contest an allegedly illegal search in favor of an inquiry that focused directly on the substance of the defendant's claim that he or she possessed a "legitimate expectation of privacy" in the area searched. In the present case, the Supreme Court of Kentucky looked to the "totality of the circumstances," including petitioner's own admission at the suppression hearing that he did not believe that Cox's purse would be free from governmental intrusion, and held that petitioner "[had] not made a sufficient showing that his legitimate or reasonable expectations of privacy were violated" by the search of the purse.

We believe that the record in this case supports that conclusion. Petitioner, of course, bears the burden of proving not only that the search of Cox's purse was illegal, but also that he had a legitimate expectation of privacy in that purse. At the time petitioner dumped thousands of dollars worth of illegal drugs into Cox's purse, he had known her for only a few days. According to Cox's uncontested testimony, petitioner had never sought or received access to her purse prior to that sudden bailment. Nor did petitioner have any right to exclude other persons from access to Cox's purse. In fact, Cox testified that Bob Stallons, a longtime acquaintance and frequent companion of Cox's, had free access to her purse on the very morning of the arrest and had rummaged through its contents in search of a hairbrush. Moreover, even assuming that petitioner's version of the bailment is correct and that Cox did consent to the transfer of possession, the precipitous nature of the transaction hardly supports a reasonable inference that petitioner took normal precautions to maintain his privacy. In addition to all the foregoing facts, the record also contains a frank admission by petitioner that he had no subjective expectation that Cox's purse would remain free from governmental intrusion, an admission credited by both the trial court and the Supreme Court of Kentucky.

Petitioner contends nevertheless that, because he claimed ownership of the drugs in Cox's purse, he should be entitled to challenge the search regardless of his expectation of privacy. We disagree. While petitioner's ownership of the drugs is undoubtedly one fact to be considered in this case, *Rakas* emphatically rejected the notion that "arcane" concepts of property law ought to control the ability to claim the protections of the Fourth Amendment. Had petitioner placed his drugs in plain view, he would still have owned them, but he could not claim any legitimate expectation of privacy. Prior to *Rakas*, petitioner might have been given "standing" in such a case to challenge a "search" that netted those drugs but probably would have lost his claim on the merits. After *Rakas*, the two inquiries merge into one: whether governmental officials violated any legitimate expectation of privacy held by petitioner.

In sum, we find no reason to overturn the lower court's conclusion that petitioner had no legitimate expectation of privacy in Cox's purse at the time of the search.

. . .

[The concurring decision of Justice BLACKMUN and the concurring decision of Justice WHITE, and Justice STEWART is omitted].

Mr. Justice MARSHALL, with whom Mr. Justice BRENNAN joins, dissenting.

The vials of pills found in Vanessa Cox's purse and petitioner's admission that they belonged to him established his guilt conclusively. The State concedes, as it must, that the search of the purse was unreasonable and in violation of the Fourth Amendment, and the Court assumes that the detention which led to the search, the seizure, and the admissions also violated the Fourth Amendment. Nevertheless, the Court upholds the conviction. I dissent.

I

The Court holds first that petitioner may not object to the introduction of the pills into evidence because the unconstitutional actions of the police officers did not violate his personal Fourth Amendment rights. To reach this result, the Court holds that the Constitution protects an individual against unreasonable searches and seizures only if he has "a 'legitimate expectation of privacy' in the area searched." This holding cavalierly rejects the fundamental principle, unquestioned until today, that an interest in either the place searched or the property seized is sufficient to invoke the Constitution's protections against unreasonable searches and seizures.

The Court's examination of previous Fourth Amendment cases begins and ends—as it must if it is to reach its desired conclusion—with *Rakas v. Illinois*. Contrary to the Court's assertion, however, *Rakas* did not establish that the Fourth Amendment protects individuals against unreasonable searches and seizures only if they have a privacy interest in the place searched. The question before the Court in *Rakas* was whether the defendants could establish their right to Fourth Amendment protection simply by showing that they were "legitimately on [the] premises" searched. Overruling that portion of *Jones v. United States*, 362 U.S. 257 (1960), the Court held that when a Fourth Amendment objection is based on an interest in the place searched, the defendant must show an actual invasion of his personal privacy interest. The petitioners in *Rakas* did not claim that they had standing either under the *Jones* automatic standing rule for persons charged with possessory offenses, which the Court overrules today, or because their possessory interest in the items seized gave them "actual standing." No Fourth Amendment claim based on an interest in the property seized was before the Court, and, consequently, the Court did not and could not have decided whether such a claim could be maintained. In fact, the Court expressly disavowed any intention to foreclose such a claim ("This is not to say that such [casual] visitors could not contest the lawfulness of the seizure of evidence or the search if their own property were seized during the search,") and suggested its continuing validity ("[P]etitioners' claims must fail. They asserted neither a property nor a possessory interest in the automobile, *nor an interest in the property seized*.").

The decision today, then, is not supported by the only case directly cited in its favor. Further, the Court has ignored a long tradition embodying the opposite view. *United States v. Jeffers*, for example, involved a seizure of contraband alleged to belong to the defendant from a hotel room occupied by his two aunts. The Court rejected the Government's argument that because the search of the room did not invade Jeffers' privacy he lacked standing to suppress the evidence. It held that standing to object to the seizure could not be separated from standing to object to the search, for "[t]he search and seizure are . . . incapable of being untied." The Court then concluded that Jeffers "unquestionably had standing . . . unless the contraband nature of the narcotics seized precluded his assertion, for purposes of the exclusionary rule, of *a property interest therein*."

Similarly, *Jones* is quite plainly premised on the understanding that an interest in the seized property is sufficient to establish that the defendant "himself was the victim of an invasion of privacy." The Court observed that the "conventional standing requirement," required the defendant to "claim either to have *owned or possessed the seized property* or to have had a substantial possessory interest in the premises searched." The Court relaxed that rule for defendants charged with possessory offenses because "[t]he same element . . . which has caused a dilemma, *i. e.*, that *possession both convicts and confers standing*, eliminates any necessity for a preliminary showing of an interest in the premises searched *or the property seized*, which ordinarily is required when standing is challenged." Instead, "[t]he possession on the basis of which petitioner is to be and was convicted suffices to give him standing."

Simmons v. United States, 390 U.S. 377, (1968), proceeded upon a like understanding. The Court there reiterated that prior to *Jones* "a defendant who wished to assert a Fourth Amendment objection was required to show that he was the owner or possessor *of the seized property* or that he had a possessory interest in the searched premises." *Jones* had changed that rule only with respect to defendants charged with possessory offenses, so the defendant Garrett, who was charged with armed robbery, had to establish standing. Because he was not "legitimately on [the] premises" at the time of the search, "[t]he only, or at least the most natural, way in which he could [have] found standing to object to the admission of the suitcase was to testify that he was its owner."

The Court's decision today is not wrong, however, simply because it is contrary to our previous cases. It is wrong because it is contrary to the Fourth Amendment, which guarantees that "[t]he right of the people to be secure in their persons, houses, papers, and effects, against unreasonable searches and seizures, shall not be violated." The Court's reading of the Amendment is far too narrow. The Court misreads the guarantee of security "*in* their persons, houses, papers, and effects, *against* unreasonable searches and seizures" to afford protection only against unreasonable searches and seizures *of* persons and places.

The Fourth Amendment, it seems to me, provides in plain language that if one's security in one's "effects" is disturbed by an unreasonable search and seizure, one has been the victim of a constitutional violation; and so it has always been understood. Therefore the Court's insistence that in order to challenge the legality of the search one must also assert a protected interest in the premises is misplaced. The interest in the item seized is quite enough to establish that the defendant's personal Fourth Amendment rights have been invaded by the government's conduct.

The idea that a person cannot object to a search unless he can show an interest in the premises, even though he is the owner of the seized property, was squarely rejected almost [thirty] years ago in *Jeffers*. There the Court stated:

> The Government argues . . . that the search did not invade respondent's privacy and that he, therefore, lacked the necessary standing to suppress the evidence seized. The significant act, it says, is the seizure of the goods of the respondent without a warrant. We do not believe the events are so easily isolable. Rather they are bound together by one sole purpose—to locate and seize the narcotics of respondent. The search and seizure are, therefore, inca-

> pable of being untied. To hold that this search and seizure were lawful as to the respondent would permit a quibbling distinction to overturn a principle which was designed to protect a fundamental right.

When the government seizes a person's property, it interferes with his constitutionally protected right to be secure in his effects. That interference gives him the right to challenge the reasonableness of the government's conduct, including the seizure. If the defendant's property was seized as the result of an unreasonable search, the seizure cannot be other than unreasonable.

In holding that the Fourth Amendment protects only those with a privacy interest in the place searched, and not those with an ownership or possessory interest in the things seized, the Court has turned the development of the law of search and seizure on its head. The history of the Fourth Amendment shows that it was designed to protect property interests as well as privacy interests; in fact, until *Jones* the question whether a person's Fourth Amendment rights had been violated turned on whether he had a property interest in the place searched or the items seized. *Jones* and *Katz v. United States*, 389 U.S. 347 (1967), expanded our view of the protections afforded by the Fourth Amendment by recognizing that privacy interests are protected even if they do not arise from property rights. But that recognition was never intended to exclude interests that had historically been sheltered by the Fourth Amendment from its protection. Neither *Jones* nor *Katz* purported to provide an exclusive definition of the interests protected by the Fourth Amendment. Indeed, as *Katz* recognized: "That Amendment protects individual privacy against certain kinds of governmental intrusion, but its protections go further, and often have nothing to do with privacy at all." Those decisions freed Fourth Amendment jurisprudence from the constraints of "subtle distinctions, developed and refined by the common law in evolving the body of private property law which, more than almost any other branch of law, has been shaped by distinctions whose validity is largely historical." Rejection of those finely drawn distinctions as irrelevant to the concerns of the Fourth Amendment did not render property rights wholly outside its protection, however. Not every concept involving property rights, we should remember, is "arcane."

In fact, the Court rather inconsistently denies that property rights may, by themselves, entitle one to the protection of the Fourth Amendment, but simultaneously suggests that a person may claim such protection only if his expectation of privacy in the premises searched is so strong that he may exclude all others from that place. Such a harsh threshold requirement was not imposed even in the heyday of a property rights oriented Fourth Amendment. . . .

FROM THE COURTROOM

MINNESOTA v. CARTER

United States Supreme Court, 1998
525 U.S. 83

[Chief Justice REHNQUIST delivered the opinion of the Court.]

[Justices SCALIA filed a concurring opinion, in which he was joined by Justice THOMAS.]

[Justice KENNEDY filed a concurring opinion.]

[Justice BREYER filed a concurring opinion.]

[Justice GINSBURG filed a dissenting opinion, in which she was joined by Justices STEVENS and SOUTER.]

Respondents and the lessee of an apartment were sitting in one of its rooms, bagging cocaine. While so engaged they were observed by a police officer, who looked through a drawn window blind. The Supreme Court of Minnesota held that the officer's viewing was a search that violated respondents' Fourth Amendment rights. We hold that no such violation occurred.

James Thielen, a police officer in the Twin Cities' suburb of Eagan, Minnesota, went to an apartment building to investigate a tip from a confidential informant. The informant said that he had walked by the window of a ground-floor apartment and had seen people putting a white powder into bags. The officer looked in the same window through a gap in the closed blind and observed the bagging operation for several minutes. He then notified headquarters, which began preparing affidavits for a search warrant while he returned to the apartment building. When two men left the building in a previously identified Cadillac, the police stopped the car. Inside were respondents Carter and Johns. As the police opened the door of the car to let Johns out, they observed a black, zippered pouch and a handgun, later determined to be loaded, on the vehicle's floor. Carter and Johns were arrested, and a later police search of the vehicle the next day discovered pagers, a scale, and [forty-seven] grams of cocaine in plastic sandwich bags.

After seizing the car, the police returned to Apartment 103 and arrested the occupant, Kimberly Thompson, who is not a party to this appeal. A search of the apartment pursuant to a warrant revealed cocaine residue on the kitchen table and plastic baggies similar to those found in the Cadillac. Thielen identified Carter, Johns, and Thompson as the three people he had observed placing the powder into baggies. The police later learned that while Thompson was the lessee of the apartment, Carter and Johns lived in

Chicago and had come to the apartment for the sole purpose of packaging the cocaine. Carter and Johns had never been to the apartment before and were only in the apartment for approximately [two and a half] hours. In return for the use of the apartment, Carter and Johns had given Thompson one-eighth of an ounce of the cocaine.

Carter and Johns were charged with conspiracy to commit a controlled substance crime in the first degree and aiding and abetting in a controlled substance crime in the first degree, in violation of Minn.Stat. §§ 152.021, subds. 1(1), 3(a), 609.05 (1996). They moved to suppress all evidence obtained from the apartment and the Cadillac, as well as to suppress several post-arrest incriminating statements they had made. They argued that Thielen's initial observation of their drug packaging activities was an unreasonable search in violation of the Fourth Amendment and that all evidence obtained as a result of this unreasonable search was inadmissible as fruit of the poisonous tree.

. . .

The Minnesota courts analyzed whether respondents had a legitimate expectation of privacy under the rubric of "standing" doctrine, an analysis that this Court expressly rejected [twenty] years ago in *Rakas v. Illinois*. In that case, we held that automobile passengers could not assert the protection of the Fourth Amendment against the seizure of incriminating evidence from a vehicle where they owned neither the vehicle nor the evidence. Central to our analysis was the idea that in determining whether a defendant is able to show the violation of his (and not someone else's) Fourth Amendment rights, the "definition of those rights is more properly placed within the purview of substantive Fourth Amendment law than within that of standing." Thus, we held that in order to claim the protection of the Fourth Amendment, a defendant must demonstrate that he personally has an expectation of privacy in the place searched, and that his expectation is reasonable; *i.e.,* one that has "a source outside of the Fourth Amendment, either by reference to concepts of real or personal property law or to understandings that are recognized and permitted by society."

The Fourth Amendment guarantees: "The right of the people to be secure in their persons, houses, papers, and effects, against unreasonable searches and seizures, shall not be violated, and no Warrants shall issue, but upon probable cause, supported by Oath or affirmation, and particularly describing the place to be searched, and the persons or things to be seized." The Amendment protects persons against unreasonable searches of "their persons [and] houses" and thus indicates that the Fourth Amendment is a personal right that must be invoked by an individual. ("[T]he Fourth Amendment protects people, not places"). But the extent to which the Fourth Amendment protects people may depend upon where those people are. We have held that "capacity to claim the protection of the Fourth Amendment depends . . . upon whether the person who claims the protection of the Amendment has a legitimate expectation of privacy in the invaded place."

The text of the Amendment suggests that its protections extend only to people in "their" houses. But we have held that in some circumstances a person may have a legitimate expectation of privacy in the house of someone else. In *Minnesota v. Olson,*

495 U.S. 91(1990), for example, we decided that an overnight guest in a house had the sort of expectation of privacy that the Fourth Amendment protects. We said:

> To hold that an overnight guest has a legitimate expectation of privacy in his host's home merely recognizes the every day expectations of privacy that we all share. Staying overnight in another's home is a longstanding social custom that serves functions recognized as valuable by society. We stay in others' homes when we travel to a strange city for business or pleasure, when we visit our parents, children, or more distant relatives out of town, when we are in between jobs or homes, or when we house-sit for a friend. . . .
>
> From the overnight guest's perspective, he seeks shelter in another's home precisely because it provides him with privacy, a place where he and his possessions will not be disturbed by anyone but his host and those his host allows inside. We are at our most vulnerable when we are asleep because we cannot monitor our own safety or the security of our belongings. It is for this reason that, although we may spend all day in public places, when we cannot sleep in our own home we seek out another private place to sleep, whether it be a hotel room, or the home of a friend.

In *Jones v. United States,* 362 U.S. 257 (1960), the defendant seeking to exclude evidence resulting from a search of an apartment had been given the use of the apartment by a friend. He had clothing in the apartment, had slept there "'maybe a night,'" and at the time was the sole occupant of the apartment. But while the holding of *Jones*—that a search of the apartment violated the defendant's Fourth Amendment rights—is still valid, its statement that "anyone legitimately on the premises where a search occurs may challenge its legality," was expressly repudiated in *Rakas*. Thus, an overnight guest in a home may claim the protection of the Fourth Amendment, but one who is merely present with the consent of the householder may not.

Respondents here were obviously not overnight guests, but were essentially present for a business transaction and were only in the home a matter of hours. There is no suggestion that they had a previous relationship with Thompson, or that there was any other purpose to their visit. Nor was there anything similar to the overnight guest relationship in *Olson* to suggest a degree of acceptance into the household. While the apartment was a dwelling place for Thompson, it was for these respondents simply a place to do business.

Property used for commercial purposes is treated differently for Fourth Amendment purposes from residential property. "An expectation of privacy in commercial premises, however, is different from, and indeed less than, a similar expectation in an individual's home." And while it was a "home" in which respondents were present, it was not their home. Similarly, the Court has held that in some circumstances a worker can claim Fourth Amendment protection over his own workplace. But there is no indication that respondents in this case had nearly as significant a connection to Thompson's apartment as the worker in *O'Connor v. Ortega*, 480 U.S. 709 (1987) had to his own private office.

If we regard the overnight guest in *Minnesota v. Olson* as typifying those who may claim the protection of the Fourth Amendment in the home of another, and one merely "legitimately on the premises" as typifying those who may not do so, the present case is obviously somewhere in between. But the purely commercial nature of the transaction engaged in here, the relatively short period of time on the premises, and the lack of any previous connection between respondents and the householder, all lead us to conclude that respondents' situation is closer to that of one simply permitted on the premises. We therefore hold that any search which may have occurred did not violate their Fourth Amendment rights.

Because we conclude that respondents had no legitimate expectation of privacy in the apartment, we need not decide whether the police officer's observation constituted a "search." The judgments of the Supreme Court of Minnesota are accordingly reversed, and the cause is remanded for proceedings not inconsistent with this opinion.

It is so ordered.

[The concurring opinions of Justices SCALIA (in which he is joined by Justice THOMAS), KENNEDY, and BREYER are omitted.]

Justice GINSBURG, with whom Justice STEVENS and Justice SOUTER join, dissenting.

The Court's decision undermines not only the security of short-term guests, but also the security of the home resident herself. In my view, when a homeowner or lessee personally invites a guest into her home to share in a common endeavor, whether it be for conversation, to engage in leisure activities, or for business purposes licit or illicit, that guest should share his host's shelter against unreasonable searches and seizures.

I do not here propose restoration of the "legitimately on the premises" criterion stated in *Jones v. United States*, for the Court rejected that formulation in *Rakas v. Illinois*, as it did the "automatic standing rule" in *United States v. Salvucci*. First, the disposition I would reach in this case responds to the unique importance of the home—the most essential bastion of privacy recognized by the law. . . . Second, even within the home itself, the position to which I would adhere would not permit "a casual visitor who has never seen, or been permitted to visit, the basement of another's house to object to a search of the basement if the visitor happened to be in the kitchen of the house at the time of the search." Further, I would here decide only the case of the homeowner who chooses to share the privacy of her home and her company with a guest, and would not reach classroom hypotheticals like the milkman or pizza deliverer.

My concern centers on an individual's choice to share her home and her associations there with persons she selects. Our decisions indicate that people have a reasonable expectation of privacy in their homes in part because they have the prerogative to exclude others. . . .

A homedweller places her own privacy at risk, the Court's approach indicates, when she opens her home to others, uncertain whether the duration of their stay, their purpose, and their "acceptance into the household" will earn protection. It remains textbook law that "[s]earches and seizures inside a home without a warrant are presumptively unreasonable absent exigent circumstances." The law in practice is less secure. Human frailty suggests that today's decision will tempt police to pry into private dwellings without warrant, to find evidence incriminating guests who do not rest there through the night. *Rakas* tolerates that temptation with respect to automobile searches. . . . I see no impelling reason to extend this risk into the home. . . . As I see it, people are not genuinely "secure in their . . . houses . . . against unreasonable searches and seizures," if their invitations to others increase the risk of unwarranted governmental peering and prying into their dwelling places.

Through the host's invitation, the guest gains a reasonable expectation of privacy in the home. *Minnesota v. Olson*, so held with respect to an overnight guest. The logic of that decision extends to shorter term guests as well. . . . Visiting the home of a friend, relative, or business associate, whatever the time of day, "serves functions recognized as valuable by society." One need not remain overnight to anticipate privacy in another's home, "a place where [the guest] and his possessions will not be disturbed by anyone but his host and those his host allows inside." In sum, when a homeowner chooses to share the privacy of her home and her company with a short-term guest, the twofold requirement "emerg[ing] from prior decisions" has been satisfied: Both host and guest "have exhibited an actual (subjective) expectation of privacy"; that "expectation [is] one [our] society is prepared to recognize as 'reasonable.'"

As the Solicitor General acknowledged, the illegality of the host-guest conduct, the fact that they were partners in crime, would not alter the analysis. In *Olson,* for example, the guest whose security this Court's decision shielded stayed overnight while the police searched for him. The Court held that the guest had Fourth Amendment protection against a warrantless arrest in his host's home despite the guest's involvement in grave crimes (first-degree murder, armed robbery, and assault). Other decisions have similarly sustained Fourth Amendment pleas despite the criminality of the defendants' activities. Indeed, it must be this way. If the illegality of the activity made constitutional an otherwise unconstitutional search, such Fourth Amendment protection, reserved for the innocent only, would have little force in regulating police behavior toward either the innocent or the guilty.

. . .

The Court's decision in this case veers sharply from the path marked in *Katz.* I do not agree that we have a more reasonable expectation of privacy when we place a business call to a person's home from a public telephone booth on the side of the street, than when we actually enter that person's premises to engage in a common endeavor.

For the reasons stated, I dissent from the Court's judgment, and would retain judicial surveillance over the warrantless searches today's decision allows.

23

Remedies for Violations of the Fourth Amendment: Exclusion, Civil Suits and Criminal Actions

Key Concepts

- The Exclusionary Rule
- Deterrence and Judicial Integrity
- Civil Law Suits and Criminal Prosecution

A. Introduction and Policy. As you learned in **Chapters 6** and **9**, the Fourth Amendment is violated whenever the police engage in an unreasonable search or an unreasonable seizure. Once you have established such a violation, the question next becomes "what should we do about it?" Theoretically, any number of responses might be imagined. In the real world, the Court has identified just three. The foremost remedy used to address unlawful Fourth Amendment intrusions is "exclusion" of the evidence. This remedy is commonly referred to as the exclusionary rule.[1] The exclusionary rule applies not only to violations of the Fourth Amendment, but also to violations of the Fifth and Sixth Amendments, such as illegally obtained confessions and improper identifications.

Under the exclusionary rule, any unlawfully obtained evidence is excluded at trial. This includes physical evidence, spoken statements, and any observations made by the police. The government is then left to make its case with whatever lawfully obtained evidence it has on hand. Often the government's case will be impossible to prove without the tainted evidence—for example, if the defendant successfully excludes the drugs that were found in his pocket or the confession he made during an interrogation.

As you will read later in this chapter, in addition to the remedy of exclusion, the Court has recognized that private civil suits, criminal prosecution, and administrative punishment are, in theory, potential alternatives to the exclusionary rule.[2] However, each of these alternatives presents significant drawbacks. Accordingly, though the exclusionary rule shoulders its own share of considerable criticism, it

---

1 Mapp v. Ohio, 367 U.S. 643 (1961).

2 Id. at 670.

remains the dominant mechanism for enforcement of Fourth Amendment violations.

The text of the Fourth Amendment prohibits unreasonable searches and seizures. However, the text says nothing about the **use** of evidence that is unconstitutionally secured. Thus, the exclusionary rule is not mandated by the text of the Fourth Amendment. It is also debatable whether the authors or ratifiers of the Amendment intended such a remedy. What can be said for certain is the rule was the product of the 1914 Supreme Court case *Weeks v. United States*.[3] In *Weeks*, the Court offered two distinct rationales for the rule:

1. The principle of **judicial integrity** makes it inappropriate for courts to rely upon evidence that has been unconstitutionally obtained. The *Weeks* Court, noted that "[t]he tendency of those who execute the criminal laws of the country to obtain conviction by means of unlawful seizures and enforced confessions . . . should find no sanction in the judgments of the courts."[4] In other words, if courts accept illegally obtained evidence, they become vehicles for violation of the Constitution.

2. Excluding evidence that was obtained in violation of the Constitution **deters unlawful police conduct**.[5] As the *Weeks* Court stated: "[i]f letters and private documents can . . . be seized and held and used in evidence against a citizen accused of an offense, the protection of the 4th Amendment, declaring his right to be secure against such searches and seizures, is of no value."[6] In other words, the best way to give the limitation on law enforcement "force and effect" is to exclude illegally obtained evidence from trial. To the extent the police violate the Fourth Amendment because of a desire to build a case against the accused, we can deter those violations by preventing the government from using the evidence at trial, thus destroying the value of the seized material.

The *Weeks* Court made clear that the Fourth Amendment is a limitation not only upon law enforcement but also upon the federal court system. For decades after *Weeks*, however, the Court was reluctant to extend the remedy of exclusion to state courts. In fact, when the Court first considered the question directly, in the 1949 case of *Wolf v. Colorado*,[7] it held the exclusionary rule should not apply to the states. In *Wolf*, the Court noted that a majority of the states had refused to adopt the rule and that other remedies existed for Fourth Amendment violations. The *Wolf* Court also stated that the exclusionary rule was merely a judicial creation

---

3 232 U.S. 383 (1914).

4 Weeks v. United States, 232 U.S. 383, 392 (1914); see also Terry v. Ohio, 392 U.S. 1, 12–13 (1968).

5 United States v. Calandra, 414 U.S. 338, 347 (1974).

6 Weeks, 232 U.S. at 393.

7 338 U.S. 25 (1949).

and was not "derived from the explicit requirements of the Fourth Amendment."[8] As we will see below, although *Wolf* was eventually overruled, the question of whether the exclusionary rule is mandated by the Constitution is still a significant question today.

Twelve years after *Wolf*, a more liberal Court re-considered the issue in *Mapp v. Ohio* and held that the exclusionary rule did apply to the states.[9] The *Mapp* Court announced that "use of the seized evidence involved 'a denial of the constitutional rights of the accused,'"[10] thus establishing that the exclusionary rule was in fact rooted in the Fourth Amendment. In the years immediately following *Mapp*, a Fourth Amendment violation almost automatically led to exclusion of the evidence as the presumptive "cure" for the illegal police conduct.[11]

As it turns out, however, *Mapp* was the high-water mark for the exclusionary rule. Since then, numerous Supreme Court cases have limited the rule in different ways. Exclusion is no longer an automatic consequence of unconstitutional police conduct.[12] Instead "exclusion is appropriate only if the remedial objectives of the rule are thought most efficaciously served."[13]

Even more troubling for those who support the rule, the rationale for the rule has subtly shifted away from the dual purposes the Court set out in *Weeks*. Although the Court has never expressly disavowed the original "judicial integrity" rationale for exclusion,[14] in recent years it has become more explicit in characterizing deterrence as the "sole" justification for the exclusion of evidence.[15]

Consistent with this understanding of the rule, the Court has repeatedly stated that the rule was never intended to redress the victim of the unlawful search, noting that"[t]he rule was calculated to prevent, not to repair."[16] The contemporary view of deterrence as the **only** justification for suppression has significantly impacted the Court's interpretation of both the value and reach of the exclusionary rule.

B. The Law. The exclusionary rule is usually presented relatively simply in popular culture: "If the police break the law when obtaining evidence, then the evidence they find is inadmissible in court." Unfortunately, the actual exclusionary rule is somewhat more complicated:

---

[8] Id. at 28.

[9] 367 U.S. 643 (1961).

[10] Id. at 648.

[11] Whiteley v. Warden, 401 U.S. 560 (1971).

[12] See, e.g., Illinois v. Krull, 480 U.S. 340 (1987).

[13] Arizona v. Evans, 514 U.S. 1, 13–14 (1995).

[14] See, e.g., Brown v. Illinois, 422 U.S. 590, 599 (1975); see also Arizona v. Evans, 514 U.S. 1, 18 (Stevens, J., dissenting).

[15] Davis v. United States, 131 S.Ct. 2419, 2426 (2011).

[16] United States v. Calandra, 414 U.S. 338, 347 (1974).

If law enforcement officers violate the Constitution when conducting a search or seizure (or when eliciting a confession or conducting an identification procedure), any evidence or information that they gather either directly or indirectly as a result of the unconstitutional conduct is inadmissible at a criminal trial as substantive evidence against the person whose rights were violated, unless:

1. The law enforcement officers legally re-discover the evidence or information at a later date based on an independent source that is independent of the constitutional violation;

2. The law enforcement officers would have inevitably discovered the evidence or information through legal means if they had not already discovered it illegally;

3. The link between the unconstitutional conduct and the discovery of the information is so indirect that there is an attenuation of the taint; or

4. The law enforcement officers who discovered the information or evidence were acting in good faith at the time of the discovery in that they reasonably and honestly believed their actions were constitutional.

As the above reflects, the exclusionary rule is subject to a number of different qualifications, details and exceptions. Most of these function to narrow the rule's application. However, one—the "fruit of the poisonous tree" doctrine—**broadens** the exclusionary rule's scope. The fruit of the poisonous tree doctrine requires exclusion of not only evidence found as a **direct** result of unconstitutional conduct but also any evidence that the unconstitutional conduct ultimately leads to. For example, assume the police illegally search your home and read a passage of your diary in which you admit to killing your Tax Professor. They also read that you buried the professor's body next to an old oak tree in a nearby public park, so they drive to the park and dig up the body. The body has your DNA evidence on it, and bullets in the body match the ballistics on your gun. Because the original search was illegal, the diary itself is inadmissible. And, because the diary (the "poisonous tree") led the police to the body, the DNA evidence and the bullets (the "fruit"), all of that evidence is also inadmissible. We will discuss this doctrine in more detail below.

All of the other important points to note about the exclusionary rule are **limitations** and **exceptions** to its application. The first is that the rule only applies when law enforcement officers violate the **Constitution**. Thus, evidence obtained when a police officer merely violates statutory law (such as trespassing) or internal police regulations (such as clearing a surveillance with a supervisor) is not subject to the exclusionary rule.

Second, the exclusionary rule only precludes evidence from **criminal trials**.[17] Thus, the rule does not apply to pre-trial or post-trial proceedings, such as grand jury questioning,[18] preliminary hearings, parole revocation hearings,[19] and sentencing proceedings. It also does not apply to any civil case, even those to which the government is a party, such as a civil tax proceeding[20] or a deportation hearing.[21] The rationale for this limitation is that adequate deterrence is accomplished through exclusion at the criminal trial itself.

A further qualification is that even in criminal trials, the illegally obtained evidence is only barred if the government seeks to use it as **substantive evidence against the defendant**. If the defendant takes the stand, the exclusionary rule does not bar the prosecution's use of the tainted evidence to impeach the defendant's testimony on cross-examination. We will discuss this "impeachment exception" in Section 3.

As we saw in **Chapter 22**, only the person whose rights have allegedly been violated can challenge the admissibility of the evidence. Thus, the exclusionary rule will not bar use of illegally obtained evidence if the prosecutor wants to use the evidence against a third party whose rights were not violated when the evidence was obtained. [22]

In addition to all of these limitations, there are also four exceptions to the exclusionary rule. Under the "independent source" exception, the rule does not apply if the prosecution demonstrates an independent source for the illegally obtained evidence. The "inevitable discovery" exception states that evidence need not be precluded if the government can demonstrate it would have obtained the evidence even if the police had not carried out the illegal search. The "attenuation of the taint" exception allows for admission of evidence if the government can prove that the link between the evidence and the constitutional violation is so tenuous that applying the exclusionary rule no longer serves the purpose of deterring police misconduct. Fourth, and finally, the "good faith" exception applies if the police officers acted in good faith reliance on 1) a facially valid warrant, 2) information contained in an official warrant database, 3) a later-invalidated statute, or 4) binding appellate precedent. Each of these exceptions to exclusion is discussed more fully below.

---

17 Pennsylvania Bd. of Prob. v. Scott, 524 U.S. 357, 363 (1998).

18 United States v. Calandra, 414 U.S. 338 (1974).

19 Pennsylvania Bd. of Prob., 524 U.S. at 357.

20 United States v. Janis, 428 U.S. 433 (1976).

21 INS v. Lopez-Mendoza, 468 U.S. 1032 (1984).

22 Alderman v. United States, 394 U.S. 165, 174 (1969).

Interestingly, the most significant potential limitation defining the exclusionary rule may be yet to come. In 2011, the Court intimated in dicta that future application of the exclusionary rule should be governed in a case-by-case weighing of its costs and benefits. This would be a radical re-framing of the exclusionary rule, and would constitute a substantial constriction of its applicability.[23] We will discuss the ramifications of this potential change in Section C.8.

C. Applying the Law. In the years after *Mapp*, the Court began a process of applying that mandate to individual cases. These post-*Mapp* rulings articulate some important refinements to the doctrine. As discussed in Section 1, the rule was in one sense broadened. However, in countless other ways, the Court's post-*Mapp* cases have resulted in restriction of the Rule's expanse.

1. Both Tangible and Intangible Evidence May Be Excluded. We have spent many chapters discussing how to determine when law enforcement officers have conducted an illegal search or an illegal seizure. But obviously you cannot actually "suppress" a search or an arrest—by the time they are challenged in court, they have already happened. Consequently, the exclusionary rule is imposed not upon the government's illegal conduct, but upon the product of that illegal activity. The rule attaches to any product of that illegal conduct, including tangible items, like drugs and guns, and intangible items, like oral statements and identifications.

For example, if the police carry out an unreasonable search of your house, and find a gun, it is the gun and not the search that is subject to suppression. In addition to the direct physical product of a constitutional violation, testimony about facts directly acquired during the search is also disallowed.[24] Thus, in the above hypothetical, the law enforcement officer would not even be allowed to testify that she found a gun.

The exclusion of tangible items is exemplified by the *Mapp* case itself, which is noteworthy not only for its holding but also for the colorful facts and cast of characters:

> **Example—*Mapp v. Ohio,* 367 U.S. 643 (1961):** Dollree Mapp, a middle-aged divorcée, lived on the top floor of a two-family home in Cleveland with her fifteen-year-old daughter. Three Cleveland police officers received a tip from a confidential informant that Mapp was providing shelter to a person who the police wanted to question about a recent bombing. (The source of the tip was none other than future boxing promoter Don King. King, a teenager at the time, was a low-level delinquent,

[23] Id. at 2439 (Breyer, J., dissenting).

[24] Silverman v. United States, 365 U.S. 505 (1961).

who was known to police as "The Kid." King apparently implicated Mapp in a self-serving attempt to free himself of the competition generated by a small-time gambling operation that Mapp operated).

When the police arrived at Mapp's door, she called an attorney she had retained for an unrelated civil matter. After speaking with the attorney, Mapp refused to allow the three officers to enter her home without a warrant. Approximately three hours later, four additional officers joined the first three on the scene. The police again attempted entry into the house. When Mapp did not immediately answer their knock, the officers first tried to kick in the door, and then smashed a window on the door and reached through the broken pane to open it. As the officers were entering the hallway, they came upon Mapp, who demanded to see a warrant. When one of the officers waved a piece of paper in front of her, Mapp grabbed it and stuffed it down the front of her dress. Following a struggle, the police arrested Mapp, searched her entire home and found pornographic material. Mapp was charged with and ultimately convicted of possession of obscene material.

The government was unable to prove that the police had a warrant to enter the house. However, they argued that even if the police conduct violated the Fourth Amendment, under *Wolf v. Colorado* there was no need to preclude the evidence that was recovered. The case was appealed all the way to the Supreme Court.

Analysis: The Supreme Court overruled *Wolf* and held that the exclusionary rule applied to the states as well, arguing that "[s]ince the Fourth Amendment's right of privacy has been declared enforceable against the States through the Due Process Clause of the Fourteenth, it is enforceable against them by the same sanction of exclusion as is used against the Federal Government."[25] Thus, all of the pornographic material recovered by the police were inadmissible at Mapp's trial. Without this evidence, the prosecutor had no case against Mapp, and the case against her was dismissed.

Two years after *Mapp*, the Court confirmed that the exclusionary rule applied to **intangible** evidence as well, in a case involving a hopscotching drug investigation

[25] Id. at 655.

that moved in a single morning from a primary target to a second, and then third, and then fourth person:

Example—*Wong Sun v. United States*, 371 U.S. 471 (1963): The initial target of the investigation was a man by the name of Hom Way. Federal narcotics agents in San Francisco came to suspect Hom Way of drug activity. After conducting surveillance of Way for a period of approximately six weeks, the agents arrested him early one morning. During a search of Way's person, the agents found heroin. Way told the officers he had purchased heroin the night before from a person named "Blackie Toy." As far as Way knew, Toy owned a laundry on a nearby street. Toy thus became the second target of that morning's investigation.

Agents visited the street Way described, and after about an hour located a laundry named "Oye's Laundry," which was owned by James Wah Toy. An agent knocked on the door of the laundry. When Toy answered, the agent first asserted that he needed laundry done. However, when Toy told him to come back later in the morning, the agent revealed himself as a federal narcotics agent. Toy slammed the door shut, and ran down the hall. Several agents broke the door in, chased Toy down the hall and arrested him in a back bedroom. A search of the laundry revealed nothing illegal. When Toy was told he had been implicated by Way, Toy denied the allegations. However, Toy then gave the agents the third target of the morning's investigation.

Toy directed the agents to a man named "Johnny," who lived in a house Toy described on a particular street. Toy claimed that "Johnny" had heroin, and further claimed that he had smoked some with "Johnny" the night before. Agents traveled to the house described by Toy. There they found a man by the name of Johnny Yee. Following questioning by the agents, Yee produced a small quantity of heroin. Yee told the agents he had obtained the heroin from Toy and a man he knew only as "Sea Dog." Toy later advised the agents that "Sea Dog" was a man by the name of Wong Sun. Wong Sun thus became the fourth and final target of the investigation that morning.

In the final leg of their investigation, agents visited Wong Sun's house. On the strength of Yee and Toy's allegations alone, Sun was arrested in a back bedroom. However, a full search of Sun's home revealed nothing illegal.

Targets Two, Three and Four—Yee, Toy and Sun—were all charged with conspiracy to violate the narcotics laws, and with the substantive drug offense. The men were interrogated separately, and statements were taken from Toy and Sun. However, both men refused to sign the written statements.

Toy and Sun were ultimately convicted of illegally transporting heroin. They appealed, and the case found its way to the Supreme Court.

Analysis: The information known about Toy and Sun prior to their arrests was not sufficient to establish probable cause. Their arrests were therefore illegal, warrantless seizures within the meaning of the Fourth Amendment. The arrests produced several pieces of evidence that were later used against each man at trial. For example, Toy's arrest resulted 1) in his statement at the time of his arrest (directing the agents to Target Number Three, Johnny Yee) and 2) his statement to the officers following the stationhouse interrogation. Sun's arrest similarly produced a statement to the officers at the stationhouse. These statements were thus direct and derivative results of the agents' original illegality.

Unlike in *Wong Sun*, both *Weeks* and *Mapp* involved the illegal seizure of tangible items. In *Weeks*, it was private papers and letters. In *Mapp*, it was pamphlets and sketches. However, in *Wong Sun* the Court clarified that the reach of the Exclusionary Rule extended to more than just tangible evidence. Explaining the new contours of the rule, the Court announced, "verbal evidence which derives so immediately from an unlawful entry and an unauthorized arrest as the officers' action in the present case is no less the 'fruit' of official illegality than the more common tangible fruits of the unwarranted intrusion."[26]

2. Indirect Evidence Is Also Excluded as "Fruit of the Poisonous Tree." As the Supreme Court has explained, "the exclusionary rule reaches not only primary evidence obtained as a direct result of an illegal search or seizure, but also evidence later discovered and found to be derivative of an illegality."[27] For example, assume the police illegally search your house based on a mere hunch. During the search, they come upon a neon green plastic water gun. The officers, determined to "stick it to you," unreasonably conclude that the gun is a real weapon and arrest you. During questioning at the stationhouse, you protest that the gun is just a toy saying, "Of course it's a toy! It wouldn't even scratch the last guy I killed. I ended up having to stab him." In this instance, your murder confession would be derivative of the initial unlawful entry and illegal arrest.

[26] Wong Sun v. United States, 371 U.S. 471, 485 (1963).

[27] Segura v. United States, 468 U.S. 796, 804 (1984).

As discussed above, derivative evidence uncovered by illegal Fourth Amendment activity is sometimes referred to as the "fruit of the poisonous tree," or more succinctly, as the "fruit."[28] Describing the causal connection between suppressible "fruit" and violation of the Fourth Amendment, the Court has said, "evidence will not be excluded as 'fruit' unless the illegality is at least the 'but for' cause of the discovery of the evidence."[29] Students should note that the "fruit of the poisonous tree" doctrine is not limited to violations of the Fourth Amendment. As you will read in **Chapters 25** and **26**, the Court has also recognized the doctrine in connection with violations of the Fifth and Sixth Amendments.[30]

The application of the exclusionary rule to both direct and derivative evidence would seemingly suggest a remedy of wide-ranging practical reach. However, the fruit of the poisonous tree doctrine is limited by the "attenuation of the taint" exception, which we will discuss in Section 6, below.

3. The Impeachment Exception to the Exclusionary Rule. The exclusionary rule prevents the prosecutor from using illegally obtained evidence in her case-in-chief when she is trying to submit evidence to the jury to establish the defendant's guilt. But what if, after the prosecutor rests, the defendant takes the stand and lies to the jury. If the prosecutor can prove the defendant is lying by referring to the tainted evidence, should she be allowed to do so? Under the "impeachment exception," the Supreme Court has held that the government can use illegally obtained evidence to impeach the defendant:

> **Example:** McElroth and Havens, two attorneys from Indiana, concocted a plan to import cocaine from Peru into the United States. They cut up a tee-shirt and made small "bandages" from the strips, which they sewed into the inside of McElroth's clothing. They then flew to Peru and inserted cocaine into the new pockets they had made.
>
> McElroth was stopped and searched by customs officials in Miami, and the police found the cocaine. Upon questioning, McElroth immediately identified Havens (who had already cleared customs) as his partner in crime. Havens was arrested, and the police seized and searched Havens' suitcase without a warrant. Inside the suitcase they found the tee-shirt with holes cut into it that matched the strips of clothing sewn inside McElroth's clothes.

---

[28] Nardone v. United States, 308 U.S. 338, 341 (1939).

[29] Segura v. United States, 468 U.S. 796, 815 (1984).

[30] See, e.g., United States v. Wade, 388 U.S. 218 (1967); Murphy v. Waterfront Comm'n of New York Harbor, 378 U.S. 52, 79 (1964).

Before trial, Havens successfully moved to suppress the contents of his suitcase, since the customs officials violated his Fourth Amendment rights when they conducted a warrantless search. At trial, McElroth testified against Havens, describing the plan to the jury. Pursuant to the exclusionary rule, however, the prosecutor was unable to admit or even mention the sliced-up tee-shirt found in Havens' suitcase.

After the prosecutor rested, Havens took the stand and testified that he had nothing to do with the plan and that he never owned nor had in his possession the tee-shirt described by Havens.

In his rebuttal case, the prosecutor sought to call the customs official who searched the suitcase in order to testify about the tee-shirt. The prosecutor argued that he was not offering this evidence to prove that Havens actually possessed the tee-shirt (which would be barred by the exclusionary rule), but only to show that Havens was lying to the jury when he claimed that he did not possess it. The trial court allowed the evidence for that limited purpose. Havens was convicted, and he appealed the case. [31]

Analysis: The Supreme Court upheld the ruling of the trial court, holding that a prosecutor can use illegally obtained evidence to impeach the defendant's testimony. The exclusionary rule exists to ensure that the government does not benefit from illegal conduct by using illegally obtained evidence to prove a defendant's guilt. However, the rule is not intended to make it easier for a defendant to lie to the jury: "there is hardly justification for letting the defendant affirmatively resort to perjurious testimony in reliance on the Government's disability to challenge his credibility."[32]

The impeachment exception is based on a tricky concept: that a jury is capable of using tainted evidence for one purpose but not another. In the above case, for example, the jury could not use the evidence about the tee-shirt as proof that the defendant actually **possessed** the tee-shirt, but could use it as evidence that the defendant was lying to them on the stand about possessing the tee-shirt.

The impeachment exception applies only to impeachment of the **defendant's** testimony. The government still may not use tainted evidence to impeach any other defense witness:

[31] The hypothetical is based on United States v. Havens, 446 U.S. 620 (1980). In the actual case, the defendant did not deny owning the tee-shirt until he was cross-examined by the prosecutor, but the Supreme Court held that the cross-examination was within the scope of his direct testimony.

[32] Walder v. United States, 347 U.S. 62, 65 (1954).

Example—*James v. Illinois,* 593 U.S. 307 (1990): One night in Chicago, a group of three boys approached a group of eight boys returning from a party. One of the boys in the smaller group pulled out a gun and shot into the larger group, killing one of the boys and injuring another.

The next evening, Chicago police arrested fifteen-year-old Darryl James in connection with the shooting. The police found James at his mother's beauty parlor under a hair dryer, and when they arrested him, his hair was black and curly. While in custody, James admitted to the police that his hair used to be reddish brown and straight.

James claimed his arrest was unconstitutional because the police lacked probable cause, and the trial court agreed. Thus, the court ruled that all of the statements James made while in custody were inadmissible under the exclusionary rule.

The prosecutor called five witnesses at trial, each of whom testified that the shooter had straight reddish brown hair at the time of the incident, and they identified James in court as the shooter, although his hair was black and curly during the trial.

James himself did not testify, but he called a friend to the stand named Jewel Henderson. Henderson testified that she had taken James to high school early on the day of the shooting, and at the time his hair was black. The government then sought to impeach Henderson's testimony by introducing James' illegally obtained statements about the color of his hair on the day of the shooting. The trial court admitted the statement under the impeachment exception, and the prosecutor successfully impeached the witness. James was convicted of murder and attempted murder and sentenced to thirty years in prison. He appealed his conviction, arguing that the impeachment exception should only apply to the defendant, not to all defense witnesses.

Analysis: The Supreme Court agreed, and overruled the trial court. The Court held that illegally obtained evidence may not be used to impeach defense witnesses other than the defendant.

The Court distinguished between impeaching a defense witness and impeaching the defendant in two ways. First, a defendant may be tempted to perjure himself in order to exculpate himself from a crime, but most other defense witnesses will be unwilling to lie on the stand to help out the defendant. In other words, "the mere threat of a subsequent criminal prosecution for perjury is far more likely to deter a witness from intentionally lying on a defendant's behalf than to deter a defendant, already facing conviction for the underlying offense, from lying on his own behalf."[33]

Second, expanding the impeachment exception to include all defense witnesses would make defendants reluctant to call any witness, and therefore make it too difficult for defendants to put on an effective defense. "Whenever police obtained evidence illegally, defendants would have to assess prior to trial the likelihood that the evidence would be admitted to impeach the otherwise favorable testimony of any witness they call. Defendants might reasonably fear that one or more of their witnesses, in a position to offer truthful and favorable testimony, would also make some statement in sufficient tension with the tainted evidence to allow the prosecutor to introduce that evidence for impeachment."[34] A defense witness, through "insufficient care and attentiveness," may exaggerate or make a mistake in testimony which could open the door to very damaging evidence

The Court has repeatedly said that the various exceptions to the exclusionary rule are meant to strike a balance between the truth-seeking function of trials and the need to deter police officers from violating the Constitution. Applying the impeachment exception to the defendant's testimony furthers the truth-seeking function because it allows the defendant to freely testify as long as he testifies truthfully. But, expanding the exception to other defense witnesses would infringe on the truth-seeking function too much, because a defendant would be reluctant to call any witnesses on his behalf.

4. Exception to Exclusion: Independent Source. The next two exceptions to the exclusionary rule—independent source and inevitable discovery—are easier to understand if you remember that the primary justification for the rule is to ensure that the government cannot profit from police illegality. On the flip side of this coin, the courts have held that the government should not be placed in a **worse** position than it would have been absent the illegal conduct.[35] Thus, the "independent source" doctrine states that evidence discovered following a violation of the Fourth Amendment is **not** subject to suppression if the discovery of that evidence has an alternate source that is independent of the constitutional violation:[36]

---

[33] James v. Illinois, 593 U.S. 307, 314 (1990).

[34] Id. at 315.

[35] Nix v. Williams, 467 U.S. 431, 443 (1984).

[36] Silverthorne Lumber Co. v. United States, 251 U.S. 385 (1920).

Example—*Segura v. United States*, 468 U.S. 796 (1984): Agents with the New York Drug Enforcement Task Force ("NYDEA") received information that Andres Segura and Luz Colon were running a drug operation out of their apartment. During surveillance of the two, the agents observed a meeting at a fast-food restaurant in Queens between Segura, Colon and two others—Esther Parra and Enrique Rivudalla-Vidal. During the meeting, agents watched Colon hand a package to Parra. When Parra and Rivudalla-Vidal were later stopped and searched, the agents found cocaine on Parra, and Rivudalla-Vidal disclosed that Segura was his regular supplier. Based on this information, the agents applied for a search warrant of Segura's apartment. While the warrant application was pending, the agents staked out Segura's apartment.

After several hours, Segura was seen entering the lobby of the building and was immediately arrested. Using Segura as a decoy, the agents knocked on the door of the apartment. When Colon answered, the agents walked in and conducted a brief "security sweep" of the apartment. During this sweep, they saw several items that were consistent with drug trafficking, including a triple beam scale, jars of lactose, and small cellophane baggies. Two agents remained in the apartment awaiting the search warrant while Colon and Segura were transported to NYDEA headquarters.

Nineteen hours later, a search warrant was issued and a full search of the apartment was conducted. During this search, agents discovered cocaine, ammunition and more than $50,000 in cash.

At trial, Segura sought suppression of this evidence. Segura alleged it was "fruit of the poisonous tree" as it was a product of the illegal entry into his home.

Analysis: The Supreme Court held that the evidence discovered pursuant to the search warrant was not subject to suppression. The Court agreed with Segura that the initial entry into his home violated the Fourth Amendment, since neither a warrant nor exigent circumstances justified the intrusion. This constitutional violation required suppression of the scale, lactose, and baggies that agents observed during the initial protective sweep.

However, suppression was not similarly required for the items found during execution of the search warrant. The search warrant was issued based upon information known to the officers well before their illegal entry into Segura's apartment. None of the facts learned by the agents as a result of the illegal entry were used to help secure the warrant. Consequently, the warrant constituted an independent source for the discovery of the cocaine, ammunition and cash. Where such an independent source exists, suppression is not warranted.[37]

Four years after *Segura* the Court decided a second "independent source" case. In this case, the Court was asked to rule upon the scope of the independent source doctrine. The Court found that the doctrine is properly applied not only in cases where evidence was obtained for the first time during a lawful search, but also in cases where evidence is uncovered first during an unlawful search, but then independently "re-discovered" during a lawful search:

> **Example—*Murray v. United States*, 487 U.S. 533 (1988):** Federal agents conducted surveillance of Michael Murray and his partner, James Carter, based on a suspicion that the two men were conspiring to sell illegal narcotics. One afternoon, the agents watched as Murray and Carter drove separate vehicles into a warehouse in south Boston. Approximately twenty minutes later, two different drivers drove away in the vehicles. The cars were followed and then lawfully stopped and searched. Both cars contained marijuana.
>
> Upon learning that the two cars had drugs in them, agents who were still watching the warehouse broke in and saw a number of bales wrapped in burlap. They left the warehouse and returned later with a search warrant. When obtaining the warrant, the agents did not mention their illegal entry into the warehouse, and did not mention what they had seen inside. Once the warrant was issued, the agents searched the warehouse and found 270 bales of marijuana and records documenting a drug trafficking operation.
>
> At trial, Murray and Carter moved to suppress the evidence found in the warehouse. They argued both that the warrant was tainted by the illegal entry, and that the warrant was invalid because it did not mention the illegal entry.

Analysis: The Supreme Court ruled that the evidence discovered during execution of the search warrant was not subject to suppression even though it had been

[37] Segura v. United States, 468 U.S. 796, 814 (1984).

originally observed during an unconstitutional entry into the warehouse. So long as later seized evidence is lawfully obtained in a fashion that is truly independent of an initial illegality, there is no reason for the evidence to be suppressed. Such a conclusion is only appropriate in the case of a later issued warrant if the reviewing court can confidently declare that the unlawful conduct played no part in the decision either to obtain or to issue the warrant.

In this case, the warrant application only mentioned the marijuana found in the cars after they were (lawfully) stopped and searched. The information learned during the agents' unlawful access to the warehouse played no part in the magistrate's decision to issue a warrant.

However, the record was less conclusive on the question of whether the agents' discovery of the bales in the warehouse influenced their decision to seek a warrant in the first instance. On this record, the Court was unwilling to conclude that the warranted "discovery" of the bales was truly independent of the earlier unconstitutional conduct. Accordingly, the case was remanded for the lower court to determine whether "the agents would have sought a warrant if they had not earlier entered the warehouse."[38]

5. Exception to Exclusion: Inevitable Discovery. The inevitable discovery exception provides that evidence discovered following a violation of the Fourth Amendment need not be suppressed if it would have been discovered anyway, absent the unconstitutional official conduct. Put somewhat differently, "unconstitutionally obtained evidence may be admitted at trial if it inevitably would have been discovered in the same condition by an independent line of investigation that was already being pursued when the constitutional violation occurred:"[39]

Example—*Nix v. Williams* ("*Williams II*"), 468 U.S. 431 (1984):[40] One Christmas Eve, a ten-year-old girl disappeared while attending an event at the Des Moines YMCA with her family. Later that evening, a teenage boy reported he had helped open the car door for a man subsequently learned to be Robert Williams. The teen described Williams as carrying a "bundle" wrapped in a blanket. The teen also stated that he saw "two legs" protruding from the bundle.

Several pieces of evidence linking Williams to the girl's disappearance were found the next day. Items of the girl's clothing and Williams' clothing were found at a rest stop approximately

[38] Murray v. United States, 487 U.S. 533, 543 (1988).

[39] Nix v. Williams ("Williams II"), 467 U.S. 431, 459 (1984) (Brennan, J., dissenting).

[40] The original appeal in Williams' case was heard under the name Brewer v. Williams, 430 U.S. 387 (1977). At times referred to as *Williams I*, the original appeal is described in detail in **Chapter 32** in connection with the right to defense counsel during interrogation.

eighty miles east of Des Moines, along with a blanket that matched the description of the bundle that Williams was seen loading into his car. Williams' car was found in a rest stop approximately eighty miles further on. The day after Christmas, a massive manhunt was begun. Working on the assumption that the girl (or her body) had been left somewhere between the Des Moines YMCA and the first rest area (where the clothing was found), searchers divided the relevant area into a grid. More than two hundred searchers, moving from east to west, then searched each square in the grid, looking in and along "all roads, abandoned farm buildings, ditches, culverts, and any other place in which the body of a small child could be hidden."[41]

While the search was underway, Williams turned himself in to the police in a neighboring town. As Williams was being transported back to the Des Moines police station, officers subjected him to custodial interrogation in violation of his constitutional rights. As a product of this interrogation, Williams, among other things, agreed to direct the police to the place where he had hidden the girl's body. The search was called off. With Williams' direction, the corpse was found in a ditch approximately two and a half miles from where the search disbanded.

At Williams' first trial, the prosecutor introduced evidence of Williams' statements in the car, as well as the details of the body as it was found. Williams was convicted of first-degree murder. The Supreme Court overturned this conviction after determining that the statements Williams made during the car ride back to Des Moines were obtained in violation of his right to counsel. A new trial was ordered.

At his second trial, evidence of Williams' statements to police and his pivotal role in locating the body were not introduced. However, the prosecutor again admitted evidence of the condition of the body and the medical examiner's findings. Williams again objected to the admission of this evidence, arguing that the discovery of the body was a direct product of Williams' unconstitutional interrogation and therefore should be precluded as fruit of the poisonous tree.

[41] Williams II, 467 U.S. at 435.

Analysis: The Supreme Court held that evidence of the body's location and condition were not subject to suppression because the girl's body would have been inevitably discovered as a result of the extensive manhunt.

The inevitable discovery exception ensures that the prosecution is placed in no better, nor no worse, a position that it would have been without the illegal police conduct. When evidence is challenged, the government may therefore avoid suppression if it can show by a preponderance of the evidence that "the information ultimately or inevitably would have been discovered by lawful means."[42]

The facts in *Williams* compelled a conclusion that the discovery of the young victim's body was inevitable. The agent in charge of the manhunt testified that he divided the area along the highway between the rest stop and the Des Moines YMCA into a grid. He then assigned four- to six-person search teams to each square of the grid. As a team completed the search of each square, the square was marked and the team was assigned a new section. Though the agent had not yet subdivided the area where the girl's body was ultimately found, he had obtained a map of the county and was planning to break it up as he had done with the areas already searched. The manhunt was suspended after Williams agreed to cooperate. Had it not been suspended, it would have taken the teams another three to five hours to reach the body. "On this record, it is clear that the search parties were approaching the actual location of the body, . . . that the volunteer teams would have resumed the search had Williams not earlier led the police to the body and the body inevitably would have been found."[43]

6. Exception to Exclusion: Attenuation of the Taint. As the name suggests, "attenuation of the taint" allows evidence to be admitted if the connection between the challenged evidence and the "taint" of the illegal conduct is so attenuated as to make suppression illogical. Courts will apply this doctrine when there is a weak connection between the evidence and the official illegality. There is no precise metric for how weak the connection needs to be; instead, the trial judge should ask "whether, granting establishment of the primary illegality, the evidence to which instant objection is made has been come at by exploitation of the illegality or instead by means sufficiently distinguishable to be purged of the primary taint."[44] Another way to think about attenuation is to envision a chain tethering the challenged evidence to the initial Fourth Amendment violation. If the chain is short (consisting of just a few links), there is unlikely to be attenuation. However, if the chain is long (consisting of many links) or if the links are insubstantial, a court will find attenuation. Describing the attenuation doctrine, Justice Powell once explained, "'dissipation of the taint' attempts to mark the point at which the

[42] Nix v. Williams, 467 U.S. 431, 444 (1984).
[43] Id. at 449–50.
[44] Wong Sun, 371 U.S. 471, 487.

detrimental consequences of illegal police action become so attenuated that the deterrent effect of the exclusionary rule no longer justifies its cost."[45]

As you read in the discussion above, the Court's decision in *Wong Sun* is notable for its extension of the exclusionary rule to intangible evidence. The *Wong Sun* decision also offers two useful examples of the attenuation doctrine.

The first example illustrates what attenuation might look like. Recall in *Wong Sun*, the fourth and final target of the investigation at issue in that case was Wong Sun himself. He was arrested at his home illegally but made no statements and no evidence was found. Several days after his arrest, arraignment, and release on his own recognizance, Wong Sun voluntarily returned to the stationhouse to provide a statement. The statement amounted to a confession, and was introduced against him at trial. The Court found the admission permissible. On the record before it, the Court held that "the connection between the [illegal] arrest and the statement had 'become so attenuated as to dissipate the taint.'"

In contrast, the second example in *Wong Sun* illustrates the type of connection that should **not** be considered attenuated. The second target of the police investigation in *Wong Sun* was a man by the name of James Wah Toy. Toy made statements following his illegal arrest that led the police to a third man, Johnny Yee. When Yee was arrested, the police found heroin. The government argued in *Wong Sun* that the heroin should be admitted into evidence because there was sufficient "attenuation" between Toy's illegal arrest and the discovery of the heroin on Yee. The Court disagreed, holding that Toy's illegal arrest led directly to his statements implicating Yee, which led directly to the discovery of the drugs. The Court found "it clear that the narcotics were 'come at by the exploitation of that illegality' and hence that they may not be used against Toy."[46]

The Court has also found the provision of *Miranda* warnings (discussed fully in **Chapter 26**) will not necessarily attenuate the connection between an illegal arrest and subsequent statements:

> **Example—*Brown v. Illinois*, 442 U.S. 590 (1975):** Chicago police detectives William Nolan and William Lenz suspected Richard Brown of being involved in the murder of a man named Roger Corpus. Acting on their suspicions and without a warrant, Nolan and Lenz broke into Brown's apartment while he was out, searched it, and arrested him upon his return. The detectives then transported Brown to the stationhouse for questioning.

[45] Brown v. Illinois, 422 U.S. 590, 609 (Powell, J., concurring in part).

[46] Wong Sun, 371 U.S. at 488.

At the stationhouse, Lenz and Nolan questioned Brown. Prior to this questioning, they provided *Miranda* warnings. The result of the questioning was a two-page statement. In the statement, Brown blamed the shooting on a man named Jimmy Claggett. However, Brown admitted helping Claggett by tying up the victim. Brown was next questioned by an Assistant State's Attorney, who also advised Brown of his *Miranda* rights. Following this questioning, Brown gave a second statement that was largely consistent with the statement he gave the detectives.

Brown was arraigned approximately fourteen hours after his arrest. He was later convicted and sentenced to an indeterminate term of fifteen to thirty years in prison.

On appeal, the reviewing court accepted that Brown's arrest was illegal. However, the Supreme Court of Illinois found that the *Miranda* warnings given broke the causal chain between the statements and the original illegality. The Illinois court therefore found no error in the admission of the two confessions.

Analysis: The United States Supreme Court ruled that the statements were not attenuated from the illegal arrest. The admission of Brown's confessions implicated separately both the Fourth and Fifth Amendments. The Court quickly resolved the Fifth Amendment question, finding Brown's statements were voluntary. However, as the Court explained, resolution of the Fifth Amendment question in the government's favor did not resolve the Fourth Amendment inquiry.

Turning to the Fourth Amendment issue, the Court found that the state court erred when it determination that the *Miranda* warnings categorically disrupted any connection between Brown's illegal arrest and his two confessions. "*Miranda* warnings, alone and per se, cannot always make the act sufficiently a product of free will [that] break[s], for Fourth Amendment purposes, the causal connection between the illegality and the confession."[47]

No single factor determines whether the causal connection between an illegal arrest and a defendant's statements is adequately attenuated. Rather, the question of attenuation must be answered by examining a variety of factors, including 1) the temporal proximity of the confession to the arrest; 2) the existence of intervening circumstances; and 3) the officer's purpose and flagrancy in violating the Fourth Amendment. Applying these factors to the case before it, the *Brown* Court found that the government failed to meet its burden. Brown's conviction was therefore overturned.

---

[47] Brown v. Illinois, 422 U.S. 590, 603 (1975).

7. Exception to Exclusion: Good Faith. At its core, the good faith exception to the exclusionary rule prevents suppression of evidence if the prosecution can demonstrate that the officers conducting the challenged search did not willfully violate the Fourth Amendment. This exception was expressly adopted by the Court in *United States v. Leon*.[48] In *Leon*, officers executed a facially valid search warrant issued by a neutral and detached magistrate. After it was executed, the warrant was found to be invalid, though its invalidity was not on account of any mistake on the part of the officers. Leon moved for suppression of all the evidence recovered. However, the Court rejected his claim. In the Court's view, deterrence—the primary goal of exclusion—was not effectively advanced by suppressing evidence uncovered due to the officers' good faith reliance on a seemingly legitimate search warrant.[49]

Since *Leon*, the Court has extended the good faith exception to include a number of other scenarios, such as when the police rely on an inaccurate warrant database maintained by a court clerk:

> **Example—*Arizona v. Evans,* 541 U.S. 1 (1995):** A Phoenix police officer saw Isaac Evans driving the wrong way down a one-way street in front of the local police station. The officer stopped Evans and asked for a driver's license. When Evans indicated that his license had been suspended, the officer asked for his name. Punching Evans' name into an onboard computer in his squad car, the officer learned that Evans' license had in fact been suspended. The computer also indicated Evans had an outstanding arrest warrant for a misdemeanor.
>
> Acting on this information, the officer ordered Evans out of the car and handcuffed him. As Evans was being cuffed, he dropped a hand-rolled cigarette to the ground. The cigarette smelled of marijuana. A subsequent search of Evans's car revealed a baggie of marijuana under the passenger's seat.
>
> The officer later reported Evans' arrest to the Justice Court and learned that the information contained in the onboard computer system was inaccurate. The warrant for Evans' arrest had been quashed approximately seventeen days earlier. Due to a court clerk's error, however, this information had never been relayed to the Sheriff's Office. Evans thereafter moved to suppress all of the marijuana seized pursuant to his arrest.

---

48 United States v. Leon, 468 U.S. 897 (1984).

49 Id. at 919–20.

Analysis: The Supreme Court held that suppression was inappropriate. The question of whether a Fourth Amendment violation has occurred is separate from the question of the appropriate remedy for that violation. The remedy of exclusion should only be applied when that remedy's primary goal—deterrence—is advanced.

In Evans' case, the inaccurate computer database was the result of a court clerk's error. Consequently, the goal of deterring police misconduct would not be advanced by suppressing the challenged evidence. There was also no reason to believe that excluding the evidence would have particularly salutary effects with regard to the conduct of the court's employees. "Because court clerks are not adjuncts to the law enforcement team engaged in the often competitive enterprise of ferreting out crime, they have no stake in the outcome of particular criminal prosecutions."[50]

Most recently, the Court in 2011 determined that the "good faith" exception to exclusion should apply to a yet another circumstance of police officers acting "with an objectively 'reasonable good-faith belief' that their conduct is lawful."[51] The case was *Davis v. United States*. Echoing the now-dominant bifurcated logic of *Wolf*—violation and then remedy—the *Davis* Court found that the search conducted was invalid under the Fourth Amendment. However, turning to the question of remedy, the Court concluded that suppression was not a foregone consequence of the admittedly unconstitutional search at issue in the case:

> **Example—*Davis v. United States* (2011):** One evening in 2007, officers in Greenville, Alabama, conducted a routine traffic stop of a car driven by Stella Owens. Owens was subsequently arrested for drunk driving. The passenger in her car, Willie Davis, was also arrested when he gave the police a false name. After Owens and Davis were handcuffed and placed in the back of separate squad cars, the police returned to Owens' car. During a search of the passenger compartment, the officers located a gun in a pocket in Davis' jacket.
>
> Davis was charged and convicted of being a felon in possession of a weapon. Prior to trial and on appeal, Davis challenged the search that resulted in the discovery of the gun. Davis acknowledged that binding case law rendered the search lawful at the time it was conducted, since the Supreme Court's 1981 decision in *Belton v. New York* established a bright-line rule allowing officers a contemporaneous search of the passenger compartment of a car incident to the arrest of its recent occupants. Nonetheless,

[50] Arizona v. Evans, 514 U.S. 1, 15 (1995).

[51] Davis v. United States, 131 S.Ct. 2419, 2427.

Davis raised the issue to preserve it for review. Predictably, he lost the motion and the gun that was uncovered in the search was admitted at trial.

Following his conviction, and while Davis' case was pending on appeal, the Supreme Court decided *Arizona v. Gant*. The Court's ruling in *Gant* substantially narrowed the authority of officers to conduct a warrantless search of the passenger compartment of a car incident to the recent arrest of its occupants. Davis contended that *Gant* rendered the challenged search in his case a violation of his Fourth Amendment rights. He therefore sought suppression of the gun.

Analysis: The Supreme Court rejected Davis' claim. In the Court's view, the exclusionary rule was intended only "to deter future Fourth Amendment violations."[52] If suppression would not advance this goal, the Court found its application inappropriate.

The Court determined that the officers' conduct in Davis' case was not deliberate, reckless or grossly negligent. Accordingly, the Court found no reason to exclude the gun. "We have stated before, and we reaffirm today, that the harsh sanction of exclusion should not be applied to deter objectively reasonable law enforcement activity."[53]

In addition to police reliance upon a search warrant (*Leon*), police reliance on a court-maintained database (*Evans*), and police reliance upon binding appellate precedent (*Davis*), the Court has also applied the good-faith exception to avoid exclusion of evidence when police execute a search in objectively reasonable reliance upon a later-invalidated statute.[54] And in another recent case, the Court has held that an officer's good faith reliance on information from a police-maintained database is also covered by the exception. As we will see, this most recent case has the potential to dramatically change the way the exclusionary rule is applied.

8. The Future of the Exclusionary Rule: Case-by-Case Analysis? *Davis* was a significant case not only for its holding, but also for the language the majority used in reaching that holding. In *Davis*, the majority stated that "[f]or exclusion to be appropriate, the deterrence benefits of suppression must outweigh its heavy costs."[55] If fully implemented, this approach would require suppression only in

---

52 Id. at 2426.

53 Id. at 2429.

54 Illinois v. Krull, 480 U.S. 340 (1987).

55 Davis v. United States, 131 S.Ct. 2419, 2427 (2011).

those cases where the police act recklessly, deliberately, or with gross negligence.[56] This doctrine finds its strongest support in the case of *Herring v. United States*:

> **Example—*Herring v. United States*, 555 U.S. 586 (2009):** Investigator Mark Anderson learned that Bennie Herring was coming down to the sheriff's office to retrieve an item from his impounded truck. Investigator Anderson knew that Herring had been involved in criminal activity before, and so he checked to see if Herring had any outstanding arrest warrants. Upon learning that Herring had an arrest warrant in the neighboring county, Anderson pulled Herring over and arrested him pursuant to the warrant. A search incident to arrest revealed methamphetamine on Herring's person and an illegal firearm in his car.
>
> As it turns out, the outstanding arrest warrant had been withdrawn by the court five months earlier, but the police employee in the neighboring county had failed to correct her database. The police employee immediately called Anderson to tell him of the mistake, but by then at least ten minutes had passed and Anderson had already made the arrest and searched Herring. When Herring was charged with possession of methamphetamine and the firearm, he challenged his arrest and subsequent search, arguing that even though Anderson acted in good faith, the information he relied upon was erroneous due to an error of another law enforcement official, and therefore the exclusionary rule should apply. The trial judge denied the motion to suppress and admitted the evidence and Herring ultimately appealed to the Supreme Court.

Analysis: The Supreme Court applied the good faith exception and upheld admission of the evidence. The Court first noted that "the exclusionary rule is not an individual right and applies only where it result[s] in appreciable deterrence" and explained that the application of the exclusionary rule depends on "the efficacy of the rule in deterring Fourth Amendment violations in the future."[57]

The Court then repeated that "the benefits of deterrence must outweigh the costs,"[58] and stated that, consistent with that doctrine, the exclusionary rule had historically been applied when the police engaged in flagrant and willful illegal behavior, as in *Mapp*. Thus, if the police knowingly entered false information into their warrant database or were reckless in maintaining it, the exclusionary rule should be applied to deter such intentional or reckless behavior. However, "when

56 Id.

57 Id. at 141 (internal quotations and citations omitted).

58 Id.

police mistakes are the result of negligence such as that described here, rather than systemic error or reckless disregard of constitutional requirements, any marginal deterrence does not 'pay its way.' In such a case, the criminal should not go free because the constable has blundered."[59]

The four dissenters in *Herring* argued that the exclusionary rule has traditionally served other functions as well, such as maintaining the integrity of the courts. But even if deterrence were the only goal, the dissenters argued that the rule should be interpreted in such a way as to place "the government in the position it would have been in had there been no unconstitutional arrest and search." Thus, the dissent argued that the rule should apply for any police mistake, including negligent mistakes, so that it will "strongly encourage[] police compliance with the Fourth Amendment in the future."[60]

As *Herring* makes clear, the focus on deterrence as the sole purpose of the exclusionary rule has led to a case-by-case cost/benefit analysis of its application. The cost/benefit analysis in turn has led to a broadening of the good faith exception so that the exclusionary rule only applies to reckless or knowing mistakes by law enforcement. Since *Herring*, a number of lower courts have begun to implement the cost-benefit interpretation of the exclusionary rule.[61]

Thus, we should no longer think of the exclusionary rule as providing near-automatic suppression of illegally obtained evidence. Instead, the future of the exclusionary rule may involve case-by-case adjudications in which prosecutors and defense attorneys try to persuade the trial court that in their specific case the deterrence benefit outweighs (or does not outweigh) the cost to the truth-seeking process. For now, though, that future remains in flux.

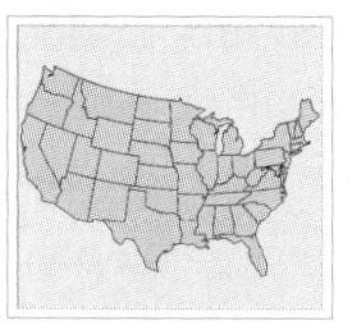

You should note that the Supreme Court's broadening of the good-faith exception to the rule has been expressly rejected by some state courts. Looking to their own constitutions, state courts have found the good-faith exception was originally intended to encourage official reliance upon warrants. These courts have concluded that extending the doctrine beyond this narrow circumstance does little to advance the exception's primary goal. Consequently, these courts have found the good-faith exception should not be called into service beyond its original mission.[62]

---

59 Id. at 147–148.

60 Id. at 148 (Ginsburg, J., dissenting).

61 See, e.g., United State v. Julius, 610 F.3d 60, 66–67 (2d Cir. 2010); United States v. Master, 614 F.3d 236, 243 (6th Cir. 2010).

62 See, e.g., Herbert v. State, 766 A.2d 190, 206 (Md. Ct. Spec. App. 2001).

D. The Mechanics. Knowing that you **can** exclude evidence obtained in violation of the Fourth Amendment is only half of the battle. You must also know, as a practical matter, **how** to ask for such exclusion. The answer is a suppression motion. A sample motion is reproduced at the end of this chapter. You should familiarize yourself with it. Suppression motions are a staple in any criminal practice.

To summarize very briefly, the process of seeking suppression is a fairly straightforward one. Suppression motions are written legal documents that are filed in advance of trial. Some courts require the motion itself to be a very short, straightforward document stating little more than the relief requested, and containing very little substantive argument. In these courts, the detailed substantive argument is provided in a companion document called a "Memorandum of Law." This memorandum is attached to and filed with the motion. In other jurisdictions, however, the requested relief and the legal reasons justifying that relief are all presented in a single document. As you move out into practice you should be sure to familiarize yourself with the preferred method of pleading in your jurisdiction.

In suppression motions, the defense asks the trial judge to exclude certain evidence from the trial. The defense explains the grounds for the requested suppression. For example, the defense might argue that physical evidence was obtained during an unlawful search, or the defense might argue that statements were taken following an unlawful arrest. The prosecution then has an opportunity to offer reasons why suppression is not required. Following the submission of the paper filings, the court will receive evidence during a suppression hearing. Oftentimes, one or more of the police officers engaged in the challenged conduct will testify to what happened. At times, the defense will also present witnesses. The prosecution bears the burden of demonstrating by a preponderance of the evidence that the challenged conduct was lawful or should not otherwise result in the suppression of the evidence. If the prosecution satisfies its burden, the motion will be denied and evidence will be admitted. If the prosecution does not satisfy its burden, the motion will be granted and the evidence will be suppressed.

The lower court's ruling on a suppression motion is appealable. However, to avoid piecemeal litigation, if the ruling denies suppression, the defendant will have to wait until the conclusion of trial to raise the issue on appeal.

Be sure to review the sample suppression motion that is reproduced at the end of this chapter. It is not the only way to present a suppression motion, but it will give you a sense of the structure and flow of such motions.

E. Alternatives to Exclusion. One of the weaknesses of the exclusionary rule is that it offers a remedy only to those who are actually prosecuted. If your Fourth Amendment rights are violated and the police find nothing (or they find something but the state declines to prosecute), the remedy of exclusion is of little assistance. This reality has led the Court and commentators to question what other remedies there might be.

In addition to the exclusionary rule, there are two other primary remedies for violations of the Fourth Amendment: either civil lawsuits or criminal prosecution/ administrative punishment of the police officers. Each of these alternatives has benefits and drawbacks. We will discuss each of these alternatives below, but you should remember that as a practical matter the exclusionary rule for now remains the primary mechanism for enforcing the Fourth Amendment's protections.

1. Civil Lawsuits. In a civil lawsuit, the aggrieved party brings a private cause of action against the state actors who violated the party's Fourth Amendment rights. Civil lawsuits in this context are usually called *Bivens* actions (if they are brought against federal agents) or § 1983 actions (if they are brought against state or local authorities). These names are based on the source of law for these suits: the Supreme Court recognized a cause of action against federal agents in a case called *Bivens v. Six Unknown Names Agents*,[63] while a federal statute—42 U.S.C. § 1983—provides for a similar private action against state and local authorities. Under a § 1983 action, an aggrieved party whose Fourth Amendment rights have been violated may sue both the municipal employer and the individual law enforcement officers responsible for the constitutional violation.

The remedy of private action has been recognized by the Supreme Court and championed by legal academics,[64] but they present a number of their own specific challenges:

a. They can generally only be brought against law enforcement agents, not prosecutors or judges.

b. The public employer is frequently not liable for the actions of its law enforcement officers, leaving the plaintiffs to sue only the "shallow pockets" of the law enforcement officers themselves.

c. Law enforcement officers enjoy a qualified immunity from such suits, which a plaintiff must overcome in order to proceed.

d. In order to obtain injunctive relief, the plaintiff must establish a likelihood of future violations of the Fourth Amendment.

e. Private lawsuits are expensive, and the monetary damages for most violations of the Fourth Amendment are not extensive.

---

[63] 403 U.S. 388 (1971).

[64] See, e.g., Akhil Amar, Fourth Amendment First Principles, 107 Harv. L. Rev. 757 (1994).

We will discuss each of these limitations in turn.

First, the judge who admitted such evidence or the prosecutor who introduced it would typically not be subject to suit. This is true for two reasons. Judicial, quasi-judicial and prosecutorial actors in the criminal justice system are generally afforded absolute immunity from suit for acts performed in the exercise of their official duties.[65] In addition, these lawsuits are based on violations of the Fourth Amendment, and the Court has determined that the **use** of illegally obtained evidence does not constitute an independent violation of the Fourth Amendment. Consequently, the introduction or admission of illegally obtained evidence would not itself violate the Constitution—leaving no basis for a § 1983 claim against prosecutors or judges.

Second, to establish municipal liability, the litigant must establish that "the conduct complained of is attributable to an unconstitutional official policy or custom."[66] Such direct evidence of the municipality's role is necessary because § 1983 does not permit a finding of liability based on the doctrine of *respondeat superior*—under which a city might automatically be responsible for the unconstitutional acts of its workers even if the workers were not acting out the official command or practice of their employer.

Third, although police officers do not enjoy the same absolute immunity afforded judges and prosecutors, before suit can be brought against them the complainant must be able to overcome their claim of qualified immunity. Qualified immunity is not simply a defense to liability; it can preclude the lawsuit from even being filed. This doctrine provides that government officials are immune from civil claims if their challenged conduct did "not violate clearly established statutory or constitutional rights of which a reasonable person would have known."[67] Overcoming an assertion of qualified immunity can be difficult, for officers can point to legal developments in external jurisdictions to establish that the law in their jurisdiction was less than "clearly established:"

> **Example—*Pearson v. Callahan*, 555 U.S. 223 (2009):** Afton Callahan sold methamphetamine to an informant who was working with the police. When the informant gave a signal indicating the sale had taken place, officers of the Central Utah Narcotics Task Force stormed his house without a warrant.
>
> The Utah courts had not recognized any exception to the warrant requirement that might justify the officers' conduct. Nonetheless, the officers asserted a claim of qualified immunity on the

[65] Mitchell v. Forsyth, 472 U.S. 511, 520 (1985).

[66] Polk City v. Dodson, 454 U.S. 312, 326 (1981).

[67] Pearson v. Callahan, 555 U.S. 223, 231 (2009).

theory that the law was not clear. They pointed to decisions in New Jersey and Wisconsin, as well as in the Sixth, Seventh and Ninth Circuits. These cases recognized the doctrine of consent-once-removed, which allows warrantless entry into a home after entry has been granted to an informant or undercover officer who observes contraband in plain view. Callahan argued that adoption of the doctrine by other jurisdictions did not render his claimed Fourth Amendment violation any less clear in Utah.

Analysis: The Supreme Court held that the Utah law enforcement officers deserved qualified immunity for their actions because the law in their jurisdiction was not clearly established. "The officers here were entitled to rely on these cases, even though their own Federal Circuit had not yet ruled on 'consent-once-removed' entries."[68]

Fourth, assuming a litigant can overcome an assertion of qualified immunity, the remedies available pursuant to a § 1983 action include both damages and injunctive relief. However, a litigant seeking injunctive relief would have to establish a likelihood of future violation of the Fourth Amendment, which is a substantial hurdle:

Example—*City of Los Angeles v. Lyons*, 461 U.S. 95 (1983): Adolph Lyons was pulled over for a traffic violation because the rear taillight on his car was out. Two officers approached Lyons with guns drawn and ordered him out of his car. The officers ordered Lyons to face his car and spread his legs. Lyons did so. They next ordered him to clasp his hands on his head. Lyons again did as requested. After one of the officers finished a pat-down search, Lyons dropped his hands to his sides. The officer ordered Lyons to put his hands back on his head. The officer simultaneously grabbed Lyons hands and slammed them against the back of his skull. When Lyons complained that the key ring in his hand was being pressed against his scalp and causing pain, the officer applied a chokehold. Lyons eventually blacked out. When he awoke, he was lying face down on the ground, spitting up blood and dirt. He had lost control of his bladder and bowels. The officers wrote a traffic citation and sent Lyons on his way. Lyons brought suit pursuant to 42 U.S.C. § 1983.

Lyons alleged violation of his Fourth, Eighth, and Fourteenth Amendment rights. He introduced the evidence of his own stop. Lyons also introduced undisputed evidence that the chokehold

[68] Id. at 244.

applied to him was authorized by police department policy. Finally, Lyons introduced evidence that over the course of approximately a five-year period, such chokeholds had resulted in the deaths of sixteen people, the overwhelming majority of whom were (like Lyons) black men. Lyons asked for damages as a result of his treatment on the night of the traffic stop. Citing concern that he may again be stopped for a traffic violation and subjected to similar treatment, Lyons also sought injunctive relief seeking to bar future use of chokeholds by the Los Angeles Police Department.

Analysis: The Supreme Court rejected Lyons' request for injunctive relief. In the Court's view, Lyons had not alleged a case or controversy sufficient to confer jurisdiction upon the federal courts.

The Court agreed that Lyons had been illegally choked by the officers. However, the Court refused to find that Lyons had also adequately complained of "a real and immediate threat that he would again be stopped for a traffic violation, or for any other offense, by an officer or officers who would illegally choke him into unconsciousness without any provocation or resistance on his part."[69] Although Lyons had presented evidence that Los Angeles police officers routinely (and consistent with department policy) applied chokeholds in situations where they did not face the threat of deadly force, this was not sufficient to establish a "real and immediate threat."

Describing the substantial hurdle to be overcome, the Court maintained, "to establish an actual controversy in this case, Lyons would have had not only to allege that he would have another encounter with the police but also to make the incredible assertion either (1) that all police officers in Los Angeles always choke any citizen with whom they happen to have an encounter, whether for the purpose of arrest, issuing a citation or for questioning, or (2) that the City ordered or authorized police officers to act in such a manner."[70]

As the *Lyons* case reflects, there are significant evidentiary hurdles to success in private actions alleging violations of the Fourth Amendment. Indeed, in the last few years only a handful of successful § 1983 claims alleging violation of the Fourth Amendment have been brought. The class action lawsuit challenging New York City's stop and frisk policy is perhaps the most newsworthy private action to date.[71]

Fifth, in addition to the question of likely success, a private cause of action brings with it the significant question of financial burden. Private lawsuits are expensive.

---

[69] City of Los Angeles v. Lyons, 461 U.S. 95, 105 (1983).

[70] Id. at 105–06.

[71] See generally Floyd v. City of New York, 959 F.Supp.2d 541 (S.D.N.Y. 2013).

Unless the case involves an egregious violation resulting in substantial damage, private litigants have little incentive to undertake the cost of a private law suit. A potential litigant would likely conclude that a violation of Fourth Amendment rights that resulted in little to no quantifiable damage was not worth the time and money.

2. Internal Police Discipline or Criminal Prosecution of Violators. As with private suits, this remedy applies even if there is no criminal prosecution of the individual whose rights have been violated. However, unlike private actions, this option relies upon self-policing to enforce the Fourth Amendment. As Justice Murphy noted in his dissent in *Wolf*, "[s]elf-scrutiny is a lofty ideal, but its exaltation reaches new heights if we expect a District Attorney to prosecute himself or his associates for well-meaning violations of the search and seizure clause."[72] This observation has proven accurate. Available records reflect only a handful of prosecutions for violation of the Fourth Amendment.

F. Policy Debate. Perhaps no aspect of criminal procedure is more controversial than the exclusionary rule. The United States is the only country in the world with a rule that excludes evidence from trial when the police officers violate the defendants' rights. Some countries apply a balancing test, weighing the severity of the crime against the severity of the government misconduct, while others simply reject any connection between police misconduct and admission of the resulting evidence. Supporters of the rule argue that (at least in its original, robust form), it provided a strong deterrent against police misconduct. Critics of the rule point to its detrimental effect on the truth-seeking process, which occasionally allows defendants who are obviously guilty—sometimes of horrendous crimes—to walk free because the police officer made a mistake.

The current controversy surrounding the exclusionary rule focuses on two related questions. The first is doctrinal: what is the legal basis of the rule? The second, broader question is a question of policy: is the exclusionary rule a good idea, and is there a better way of enforcing the Fourth Amendment?

1. What Is the Legal Basis for the Rule? Since its creation, the source of authority for the exclusionary rule has been hotly debated.[73] The rule has been described alternately as a "constitutional mandate" and a "judicially created remedy." The Supreme Court's original decision in *Wolf* not to extend the exclusionary rule to the states was grounded in part on its understanding that the exclusionary rule was not mandated by the Constitution. The text of the Fourth Amendment

---

[72] 338 U.S. 25, 42 (1949).

[73] Arizona v. Johnson, 555 U.S. 323 (2009).

clearly proscribes illegal searches and seizures, but the text says nothing about the actual **use** of evidence obtained during such illegal official conduct. The *Wolf* Court's view was that "the government's use of evidence obtained in violation of the Fourth Amendment does not itself violate the Constitution."[74] This is not, however, the only way to understand the Fourth Amendment.

Notionally, you could argue that the Fourth Amendment is offended not only when evidence is **obtained** by illegal search or seizure but also when such evidence is **used** by the government (for example in a trial). Indeed, this is precisely what the Court found approximately a decade after *Wolf* was decided. In the *Mapp* case, Court distanced itself from its rationale in *Wolf* and declared:

> Having once recognized that the right to privacy embodied in the Fourth Amendment is enforceable against the States, and that the right to be secure against rude invasions of privacy by state officers is, therefore, constitutional in origin, we can no longer permit that right to remain an empty promise. Because it is enforceable in the same manner and to like effect as other basic rights secured by the Due Process Clause, we can no longer permit it to be revocable at the whim of any police officer who, in the name of law enforcement itself, chooses to suspend its enjoyment. Our decision, founded on reason and truth, gives to the individual no more than that which the Constitution guarantees him, to the police officer no less than that to which honest law enforcement is entitled, and, to the courts, that judicial integrity so necessary in the true administration of justice.[75]

There is logical appeal to the *Mapp* Court's judgment that the exclusionary rule is a constitutional mandate. For one, the Supreme Court does not have supervisory authority over the administration of state courts. Consequently, if the remedy of exclusion is not constitutionally based, the *Mapp* Court would (as the dissenters in that case argued) have had no authority to impose it upon the states. Absent a constitutional foundation, the Court is free to limit (or even eliminate) the rule as it sees fit. Indeed, as the above discussion reflects, this is precisely what the Court has done in recent years.

However, just over a decade after the decision in *Mapp*, the Court began to describe the rule as a judicial creation. In *United States v. Calandra*, decided some thirteen years after *Mapp*, the Court speaking of the exclusionary rule wrote "the rule is a judicially created remedy designed to safeguard Fourth Amendment rights generally through its deterrent effect, rather than a personal constitutional right of

---

[74] Pennsylvania Bd. of Prob. v. Scott, 524 U.S. 357, 362 (1998).

[75] Id. at 660.

the party aggrieved."[76] Most recently, in 2011, the Court reaffirmed the *Calandra* Court's understanding of the exclusionary rule as a remedy "of this Court's own making." Thus, for now, the modern Court has completely removed the rule's constitutional imprimatur.

At the same time that the Court has reframed the rule as a judicial creation, it has also shifted the narrative used to describe the rule's effect. In the early years, the exclusionary rule was seen as a necessary check on official lawlessness. However, more recently, the rule has been described as a solution whose "bottom-line effect, in many cases, is to suppress the truth and set the criminal loose in the community without punishment."[77] The Court has consequently increasingly declined to impose the remedy of exclusion in cases where it does not feel deterrence will be achieved through suppression. As the Court explained in *Davis*, "[r]eal deterrent value is a 'necessary condition for exclusion.'"[78]

For now there is no question that the exclusionary rule is viewed with increased disfavor by the Court, and has been stripped of its constitutional underpinnings. However, this latter understanding of the rule calls into question the legitimacy of the continued imposition of the rule upon the states. We will have to wait to see which view of the rule will control in the future, and what the Court will do to resolve any attendant questions about the extent of its reach.

2. Should the Court Abolish the Rule? Many commentators believe that it is only a matter of time before the conservatives on the Supreme Court are able to abolish the exclusionary rule altogether. The path for doing so has already been cleared in a number of ways: for example, by declaring that the sole purpose of the rule is to deter police misconduct, and then to portray the rule as a balancing test between its deterrence function and the need to convict the guilty. In order to tip the balancing scales against exclusion, the modern Court has emphasized the costs of the rule, stating that the rule exacts "an enormous price from society and our system of justice[] to further 'protect' criminal activity."[79]

As we have seen, however, the other options for enforcing the Fourth Amendment are unlikely to be effective. Many commentators note that the particularly decentralized aspect of the United States law enforcement system require a blanket rule enforced by the courts, because no one administrative rule could possibly regulate all of the police departments and officers in the country.[80] Others argue

[76] United States v. Calandra, 414 U.S. 338, 348 (1974).

[77] Davis v. United States, 131 S.Ct. 2419, 2427 (2011).

[78] Id.

[79] Segura v. United States, 468 U.S. 796 at 816.

[80] See Adam Liptak, U.S. is Alone on Rejecting All Evidence if Police Err, N.Y. Times (July 19, 2008), available at http://www.nytimes.com/2008/07/19/us/19exclude.html?pagewanted=all&_r=0.

that given the increased professionalism of modern police forces, such a drastic remedy is no longer required—that the instances of flagrant violations such as what happened in the *Mapp* case are now rare. When such abuses do occur, critics of the rule point out that a civil lawsuit will punish those who actually committed the misconduct (the police officers and perhaps their departments) and benefit those who actually suffered (the plaintiffs in the lawsuit).

Perhaps the most troubling aspect of the exclusionary rule is that it appears on its face to only protect the guilty, while leaving the innocent with no effective remedy. Of course, if it were applied consistently, it would in theory deter all illegal police misconduct, thus protecting the guilty and innocent alike.

The debate will continue for many years, and even if the Supreme Court makes a definitive ruling, the debate will continue on the state level as different legislators and state supreme court justices come to different decisions about the wisdom of the rule.

Quick Summary

Violations of the Fourth Amendment are addressed primarily with the exclusionary rule. The rule allows an aggrieved party to seek suppression of evidence that is discovered following a violation of the party's Fourth Amendment rights. The "fruit of the poisonous tree" doctrine means that even evidence indirectly linked to the illegal conduct could potentially be suppressed.

The exclusionary rule is subject to a number of limitations. As a threshold matter, the rule does not apply to grand jury or parole proceedings, and cannot be invoked by anyone other than the victim of the Fourth Amendment violation. It also does not prevent the government from using the tainted evidence to impeach the defendant if the defendant testifies. In addition, the exclusionary rule is subject to several notable exceptions. The independent source doctrine provides that suppression is unnecessary if the evidence was discovered through a source independent of the constitutional violation. The inevitable discovery exception allows admission of evidence, notwithstanding a Fourth Amendment violation, if discovery of the evidence was a foregoing conclusion. The attenuation of the taint doctrine excuses suppression if there is only a weak connection between the illegal government conduct and the Fourth Amendment violation. Finally, the good faith exception provides that an officer's good faith reliance upon a facially valid warrant, an official warrant database, a later-invalidated statute, or then-binding appellate precedent will each render suppression unfitting.

Review Questions

1. Drugs in the Parking Lot. Police officers got an anonymous tip that a worker at the Ford Auto plant was receiving drugs through the mail at work and storing the packages in his car. Since the police had no other identifying information about the suspect, they took a drug detection dog to the parking lot of the Ford Auto plant and began walking the dog next to the cars parked there. Meanwhile some other police officers went to the mail room at Ford and looked for "suspicious" packages. Whenever they found a package that had no return address, they opened it and looked inside. After about an hour, one of the officers opened a package addressed to a worker at the plant named Greg Stamos. Inside the package was a small box containing two ounces of cocaine. The police looked up Greg Stamos on their DMV database and learned that he drove a 2008 Ford Camry, license plate FG-6455. They radioed the officer with the drug dog to look for that specific car. After a few minutes, the officer with the drug dog located that car and brought his dog to examine it. The dog immediately alerted to the trunk of the car. The officers opened the trunk and found three identical packages, each containing some amount of cocaine.

Stamos was arrested and moved to suppress the evidence found against him. The police conceded that the search of the mail was unconstitutional, but they argue that the drug dog sniff of his car was not a search, and that the positive alert from the drug dog was sufficient to give them probable cause to believe the car had cocaine inside. Should the drugs found in the car trunk be excluded?

2. Legalizing Marijuana. Assume that on February 5, 2014, the Governor of the State of Rhode Island signs a law legalizing marijuana. The law takes effect on February 15th.

On February 16th, Samantha Kay is sitting in a lawn chair in her front yard, celebrating the new law by smoking a marijuana cigarette. Officer Harold Marsh, a member of the Providence Police Narcotics Division, drives past her house. Officer Marsh has been on sick leave for the past two months because he was recovering from a gunshot wound sustained in the course of duty. He recuperated with his family in Massachusetts, and so he was unaware that marijuana was now legal. When he saw Kay smoking a marijuana cigarette, he pulled over and placed her under arrest, ignoring her protests about the new law. When he searched her, he found one small bag of marijuana and another bag containing heroin (which is still illegal in Rhode Island).

Kay is charged with possession of heroin. She moves to exclude the evidence, arguing that her arrest was unlawful and therefore the search incident to arrest was also unlawful. Should the bag of heroin be excluded?

3. Looking for Racketeering, Finding Tax Evasion. The police obtained a Title III order to set up a wiretap on William Goldberg, whom they suspected was involved in various racketeering crimes, including coercing "protection money" out of local businesses. The Title III order only authorized a wiretap on Goldberg's office phone, and the police soon realized that Goldberg only made incriminating phone calls from his home phone. After one week, they began wiretapping his home phone as well, even though that was beyond the scope of the Title III order. The home wiretap was much more fruitful, and the government overheard Goldberg talking about receiving payments and depositing them in various bank accounts.

The police turned this information over to the Internal Revenue Service, who subpeonaed Goldberg's records from those banks and compared his actual income to the income he declared on his past year's income taxes. When it turned out that Goldberg had been hiding hundreds of thousands of dollars of income, federal prosecutors charged him with income tax evasion.

Goldberg moved to suppress the bank records as the fruit of the poisonous tree. The government argued that the independent investigation by the IRS attenuated the taint of the illegal wiretap, and that the wiretap had only been intended to investigate rackateering charges, not income tax evasion.

Should the bank records be excluded from the trial?

FROM THE COURTROOM

MAPP v. OHIO

United States Supreme Court, 1961
367 U.S. 643

[Justice CLARK delivered the opinion of the Court.]

[Justice BLACK and Justice DOUGLAS filed concurring opinions.]

[Justice HARLAN filed a dissenting opinion, in which Justice FRANK and Justice WHITTAKER joined.]

. . .

On May 23, 1957, three Cleveland police officers arrived at appellant's residence in that city pursuant to information that "a person (was) hiding out in the home, who was wanted for questioning in connection with a recent bombing, and that there was a large amount of policy paraphernalia being hidden in the home." Miss Mapp and her daughter by a former marriage lived on the top floor of the two-family dwelling. Upon their arrival at that house, the officers knocked on the door and demanded entrance but appellant, after telephoning her attorney, refused to admit them without a search warrant. They advised their headquarters of the situation and undertook a surveillance of the house.

The officers again sought entrance some three hours later when four or more additional officers arrived on the scene. When Miss Mapp did not come to the door immediately, at least one of the several doors to the house was forcibly openedand the policemen gained admittance. Meanwhile Miss Mapp's attorney arrived, but the officers, having secured their own entry, and continuing in their definance of the law, would permit him neither to see Miss Mapp nor to enter the house. It appears that Miss Mapp was halfway down the stairs from the upper floor to the front door when the officers, in this highhanded manner, broke into the hall. She demanded to see the search warrant. A paper, claimed to be a warrant, was held up by one of the officers. She grabbed the "warrant" and placed it in her bosom. A struggle ensued in which the officers recovered the piece of paper and as a result of which they handcuffed appellant because she had been "belligerent" in resisting their official rescue of the "warrant" from her person. Running roughshod over appellant, a policeman "grabbed" her, "twisted (her) hand," and she "yelled (and) pleaded with him" because "it was hurting." Appellant, in handcuffs, was then forcibly taken upstairs to her bedroom where the officers searched a dresser, a chest of drawers, a closet and some suitcases. They also looked into a photo album and through personal papers belonging to the appellant. The search spread to the rest of the second floor including the child's bedroom, the living room, the kitchen and a dinette. The basement of the building and a trunk found therein were also searched. The obscene materials for possession of which she was ultimately convicted were discovered in the course of that widespread search.

At the trial no search warrant was produced by the prosecution, nor was the failure to produce one explained or accounted for. At best, "There is, in the record, considerable doubt as to whether there ever was any warrant for the search of defendant's home." The Ohio Supreme Court believed a "reasonable argument" could be made that the conviction should be reversed "because the 'methods' employed to obtain the (evidence) were such as to offend 'a sense of justice,'" but the court found determinative the fact that the evidence had not been taken "from defendant's person by the use of brutal or offensive physical force against defendant."

The State says that even if the search were made without authority, or otherwise unreasonably, it is not prevented from using the unconstitutionally seized evidence at trial, citing *Wolf v. People of State of Colorado*, in which this Court did indeed hold "that in a prosecution in a State court for a State crime the Fourteenth Amendment does not forbid the admission of evidence obtained by an unreasonable search and seizure." On this appeal, of which we have noted probable jurisdiction, it is urged once again that we review that holding.

I

Seventy-five years ago, in *Boyd v. United States*, considering the Fourth and Fifth Amendments as running "almost into each other" on the facts before it, this Court held that the doctrines of those Amendments

> apply to all invasions on the part of the government and its employes of the sanctity of a man's home and the privacies of life. It is not the breaking of his doors, and the rummaging of his drawers, that constitutes the essence of the offence; but it is the invasion of his indefeasible right of personal security, personal liberty and private property. Breaking into a house and opening boxes and drawers are circumstances of aggravation; but any forcible and compulsory extortion of a man's own testimony or of his private papers to be used as evidence to convict him of crime or to forfeit his goods, is within the condemnation (of those Amendments).

The Court noted that "constitutional provisions for the security of person and property should be liberally construed. It is the duty of courts to be watchful for the constitutional rights of the citizen, and against any stealthy encroachments thereon."

In this jealous regard for maintaining the integrity of individual rights, the Court gave life to Madison's prediction that "independent tribunals of justice will be naturally led to resist every encroachment upon rights expressly stipulated for in the Constitution by the declaration of rights." Concluding, the Court specifically referred to the use of the evidence there seized as "unconstitutional."

Less than [thirty] years after *Boyd*, this Court, in *Weeks v. United States*, stated that

> the 4th Amendment put the courts of the United States and Federal officials, in the exercise of their power and authority, under limitations and restraints (and) forever secure(d) the people, their persons, houses, papers, and effects, against all unreasonable searches and seizures under the guise of law and the duty of giving to it force and effect is obligatory upon all entrusted under our Federal system with the enforcement of the laws.

Specifically dealing with the use of the evidence unconstitutionally seized, the Court concluded:

> If letters and private documents can thus be seized and held and used in evidence against a citizen accused of an offense, the protection of the Fourth Amendment declaring his right to be secure against such searches and seizures is of no value, and, so far as those thus placed are concerned, might as well be stricken from the Constitution. The efforts of the courts and their officials to bring the guilty to punishment, praiseworthy as they are, are not to be aided by the sacrifice of those great principles established by years of endeavor and suffering which have resulted in their embodiment in the fundamental law of the land.

Finally, the Court in that case clearly stated that use of the seized evidence involved "a denial of the constitutional rights of the accused." Thus, in the year 1914, in the *Weeks* case, this Court "for the first time" held that "in a federal prosecution the Fourth Amendment barred the use of evidence secured through an illegal search and seizure." This Court has ever since required of federal law officers a strict adherence to that command which this Court has held to be a clear, specific, and constitutionally required—even if judically implied—deterrent safeguard without insistence upon which the Fourth Amendment would have been reduced to "a form of words." It meant, quite simply, that "conviction by means of unlawful seizures and enforced confessions should find no sanction in the judgments of the courts," and that such evidence "shall not be used at all."

. . .

II

In 1949, [thirty-five] years after *Weeks* was announced, this Court, in *Wolf v. People of State of Colorado*, again for the first time, discussed the effect of the Fourth Amendment upon the States through the operation of the Due Process Clause of the Fourteenth Amendment. It said:

> (W)e have no hesitation in saying that were a State affirmatively to sanction such police incursion into privacy it would run counter to the guaranty of the Fourteenth Amendment.

Nevertheless, after declaring that the "security of one's privacy against arbitrary intrusion by the police" is "implicit in 'the concept of ordered liberty' and as such enforceable against the States through the Due Process Clause," and announcing that it "stoutly adhere(d)" to the *Weeks* decision, the Court decided that the *Weeks* exclusionary rule would not then be imposed upon the States as 'an essential ingredient of the right.' The Court's reasons for not considering essential to the right to privacy, as a curb imposed upon the States by the Due Process Clause, that which decades before had been posited as part and parcel of the Fourth Amendment's limitations upon federal encroachment of individual privacy, were bottomed on factual considerations.

. . .

III

Some five years after *Wolf*, in answer to a plea made here Term after Term that we overturn its doctrine on applicability of the *Weeks* exclusionary rule, this Court indicated that such should not be done until the States had "adequate opportunity to adopt or reject the (*Weeks*) rule. . . ."

Today we once again examine *Wolf*'s constitutional documentation of the right to privacy free from unreasonable state intrusion, and, after its dozen years on our books, are led by it to close the only courtroom door remaining open to evidence secured by official lawlessness in flagrant abuse of that basic right, reserved to all persons as a specific guarantee against that very same unlawful conduct. We hold that all evidence obtained by searches and seizures in violation of the Constitution is, by that same authority, inadmissible in a state court.

IV

Since the Fourth Amendment's right of privacy has been declared enforceable against the States through the Due Process Clause of the Fourteenth, it is enforceable against them by the same sanction of exclusion as is used against the Federal Government. Were it otherwise, then just as without the *Weeks* rule the assurance against unreasonable federal searches and seizures would be "a form of words", valueless and undeserving of mention in a perpetual charter of inestimable human liberties, so too, without that rule the freedom from state invasions of privacy would be so epemeral and so neatly severed from its conceptual nexus with the freedom from all brutish means of coercing evidence as not to merit this Court's high regard as a freedom "implicit in the concept of ordered liberty." At the time that the Court held in *Wolf* that the Amendment was applicable to the States through the Due Process Clause, the cases of this Court, as we have seen, had steadfastly held that as to federal officers the Fourth Amendment included the exclusion of the evidence seized in violation of its provisions. Even *Wolf* "stoutly adhered" to that proposition. The right to privacy, when conceded operatively enforceable against the States, was not susceptible of destruction by avulsion of the sanction upon which its protection and enjoyment had always been deemed dependent under the *Boyd*, *Weeks* and *Silverthorne* cases. Therefore, in extending the substantive protections of due process to all constitutionally unreasonable searches—state or federal—it was logically and constitutionally necessary that the exclusion doctrine—an essential part of the right to privacy—be also insisted upon as an essential ingredient of the right newly recognized by the *Wolf* case. In short, the admission of the new constitutional right by *Wolf* could not consistently tolerate denial of its most important constitutional privilege, namely, the exclusion of the evidence which an accused had been forced to give by reason of the unlawful seizure. To hold otherwise is to grant the right but in reality to whthhold its privilege and enjoyment. Only last year the Court itself recognized that the purpose of the exclusionary rule "is to deter—to compel respect for the constitutional guaranty in the only effectively available way—by removing the incentive to disregard it."

Indeed, we are aware of no restraint, similar to that rejected today, conditioning the enforcement of any other basic constitutional right. The right to privacy, no less important than any other right carefully and particularly reserved to the people, would stand in marked contrast to all other rights declared as "basic to a free society." This Court has not hesitated to enforce as strictly against the States as it does against the Federal Government the rights of free speech and of a free press, the rights to notice and to a fair, public trial, including, as it does, the right not to be convicted by use of a coerced confession, however logically relevant it be, and without regard to its reliability. And nothing could be more certain than that when a coerced confession is involved, "the relevant rules of evidence" are overridden without regard to "the incidence of such conduct by the police," slight or frequent. Why should not the same rule apply to what is tantamount to coerced testimony by way of unconstitutional seizure of goods, papers, effect, documents, etc.? We find that, as to the Federal Government, the Fourth and Fifth Amendments and, as to the States, the freedom from unconscionable invasions of privacy and the freedom from convictions based upon coerced confessions do enjoy an "intimate relation" in their perpetuation of "principles of humanity and civil liberty (secured) . . . only after years of struggle." They express "supplementing phases of the same constitutional purpose—to maintain inviolate large areas of personal privacy." The philosophy of each Amendment and of each freedom is complementary to, although not dependent upon, that of the other in its sphere of influence—the very least that together they assure in either sphere is that no man is to be convicted on unconstitutional evidence.

. . .

V

. . .

There are those who say, as did Justice (then Judge) Cardozo, that under our constitutional exclusionary doctrine "(t)he criminal is to go free because the constable has blundered." In some cases this will undoubtedly be the result. But, as was said in *Elkins*, "there is another consideration—the imperative of judicial integrity." The criminal goes free, if he must, but it is the law that sets him free. Nothing can destroy a government more quickly than its failure to observe its own laws, or worse, its disregard of the charter of its own existence. As Mr. Justice Brandeis, dissenting, said in *Olmstead v. United States*, "Our government is the potent, the omnipresent teacher. For good or for ill, it teaches the whole people by its example. . . . If the government becomes a lawbreaker, it breeds contempt for law; it invites every man to become a law unto himself; it invites anarchy." Nor can it lightly be assumed that, as a practical matter, adoption of the exclusionary rule fetters law enforcement. Only last year this

Court expressly considered that contention and found that "pragmatic evidence of a sort" to the contrary was not wanting. The Court noted that

> The federal courts themselves have operated under the exclusionary rule of *Weeks* for almost half a century; yet it has not been suggested either that the Federal Bureau of Investigation has thereby been rendered ineffective, or that the administration of criminal justice in the federal courts has thereby been disrupted. Moreover, the experience of the states is impressive. . . . The movement towards the rule of exclusion has been halting but seemingly inexorable.

The ignoble shortcut to conviction left open to the State tends to destroy the entire system of constitutional restraints on which the liberties of the people rest. Having once recognized that the right to privacy embodied in the Fourth Amendment is enforceable against the States, and that the right to be secure against rude invasions of privacy by state officers is, therefore, constitutional in origin, we can no longer permit that right to remain an empty promise. Because it is enforceable in the same manner and to like effect as other basic rights secured by the Due Process Clause, we can no longer permit it to be revocable at the whim of any police officer who, in the name of law enforcement itself, chooses to suspend its enjoyment. Our decision, founded on reason and truth, gives to the individual no more than that which the Constitution guarantees him, to the police officer no less than that to which honest law enforcement is entitled, and, to the courts, that judicial integrity so necessary in the true administration of justice.

The judgment of the Supreme Court of Ohio is reversed and the cause remanded for further proceedings not inconsistent with this opinion.

Reversed and remanded.

[The concurring opinions of Justice BLACK and Justice DOUGLAS are omitted.]

[Memorandum of Mr. Justice STEWART is omitted.]

Mr. Justice HARLAN, whom Mr. Justice FRANKFURTER and Mr. Justice WHITTAKER join, dissenting.

. . .

II

Essential to the majority's argument against *Wolf* is the proposition that the rule of *Weeks*, excluding in federal criminal trials the use of evidence obtained in violation of the Fourth Amendment, derives not from the 'supervisory power' of this Court over the federal judicial system, but from Constitutional requirement. This is so because no one, I suppose, would suggest that this Court possesses any general supervisory power over the state courts. Although I entertain considerable doubt as to the soundness of this foundational proposition of the majority, I shall assume, for present purposes, that the *Weeks* rule "is of constitutional origin."

At the heart of the majority's opinion in this case is the following syllogism: (1) the rule excluding in federal criminal trials evidence which is the product of all illegal search and seizure is a "part and parcel" of the Fourth Amendment; (2) *Wolf* held that the "privacy" assured against federal action by the Fourth Amendment is also protected against state action by the Fourteenth Amendment; and (3) it is therefore "logically and constitutionally necessary" that the *Weeks* exclusionary rule should also be enforced against the States.

This reasoning ultimately rests on the unsound premise that because *Wolf* carried into the States, as part of "the concept of ordered liberty" embodied in the Fourteenth Amendment, the principle of "privacy" underlying the Fourth Amendment,it must follow that whatever configurations of the Fourth Amendment have been developed in the particularizing federal precedents are likewise to be deemed a part of "ordered liberty," and as such are enforceable against the States. For me, this does not follow at all.

. . .

I would not impose upon the States this federal exclusionary remedy. The reasons given by the majority for now suddenly turning its back on *Wolf* seem to me notably unconvincing.

First, it is said that "the factual grounds upon which *Wolf* was based" have since changed, in that more States now follow the *Weeks* exclusionary rule than was so at the time *Wolf* was decided. While that is true, a recent survey indicates that at present one-half of the States still adhere to the common-law non-exclusionary rule, and one, Maryland, retains the rule as to felonies. But in any case surely all this is beside the point, as the majority itself indeed seems to recognize. Our concern here, as it was in *Wolf*, is not with the desirability of that rule but only with the question whether the States are Constitutionally free to follow it or not as they may themselves determine, and the relevance of the disparity of views among the States on this point lies simply in the fact that the judgment involved is a debatable one. Moreover, the very fact on which the majority relies, instead of lending support to what is now being done, points away from the need of replacing voluntary state action with federal compulsion.

The preservation of a proper balance between state and federal responsibility in the administration of criminal justice demands patience on the part of those who might like to see things move faster among the States in this respect. Problems of criminal law enforcement vary widely from State of State. One State, in considering the totality of its legal picture, may conclude that the need for embracing the *Weeks* rule is pressing because other remedies are unavailable or inadequate to secure compliance with the substantive Constitutional principle involved. Another, though equally solicitous of Constitutional rights, may choose to pursue one purpose at a time, allowing all evidence relevant to guilt to be brought into a criminal trial, and dealing with Constitutional infractions by other means. Still another may consider the exclusionary rule too rough-and-ready a remedy, in that it reaches only unconstitutional intrusions which eventuate in criminal prosecution of the victims. Further, a State after experimenting with the *Weeks* rule for a time may, because of unsatisfactory experience with it, decide to revert to a non-exclusionary rule. And so on. From the standpoint of Constitutional permissibility in pointing a State in one direction or another, I do not see at all why "time has set its face against" the considerations which led Mr. Justice Cardozo, then chief judge of the New York Court of Appeals, to reject for New York in *People v. Defore*, 242 N.Y. 13 (1926), the *Weeks* exclusionary rule. For us the question remains, as it has always been, one of state power, not one of passing judgment on the wisdom of one state course or another. In my view this Court should continue to forbear from fettering the States with an adamant rule which may embarrass them in coping with their own peculiar problems in criminal law enforcement.

Further, we are told that imposition of the *Weeks* rule on the States makes "very good sense," in that it will promote recognition by state and federal officials of their "mutual obligation to respect the same fundamental criteria" in their approach to law enforcement, and will avoid "needless conflict between state and federal courts." Indeed the majority now finds an incongruity in *Wolf*'s discriminating perception between the demands of "ordered liberty" as respects the basic right of "privacy" and the means of securing it among the States. That perception, resting both on a sensitive regard for our federal system and a sound recognition of this Court's remoteness from particular state problems, is for me the strength of that decision.

An approach which regards the issue as one of achieving procedural symmetry or of serving administrative convenience surely disfigures the boundaries of this Court's functions in relation to the state and federal courts. Our role in promulgating the *Weeks* rule and its extensions in such cases as *Rea*, *Elkins*, and *Rios* was quite a different one than it is here. There, in implementing the Fourth Amendment, we occupied the position of a tribunal having the ultimate responsibility for developing the standards and procedures of judicial administration within the judicial system over which it presides. Here we review state procedures whose measure is to be taken not against the specific substantive commands of the Fourth Amendment but under the flexible contours of the Due Process Clause. I do not believe that the Fourteenth Amendment empowers this Court to mould state remedies effectuating the right to freedom from 'arbitrary intrusion by the police' to suit its own notions of how things should be done, as, for instance, the California Supreme Court did in *People v. Cahan*, with reference to procedures in the California courts or as this Court did in *Weeks* for the lower federal courts.

A state conviction comes to us as the complete product of a sovereign judicial system. Typically a case will have been tried in a trial court, tested in some final appellate court, and will go no further. In the comparatively rare instance when a conviction is reviewed by us on due process grounds we deal then with a finished product in the creation of which we are allowed no hand, and our task, far from being one of over-all supervision, is, speaking generally, restricted to a determination of whether the prosecution was Constitutionally fair. The specifics of trial procedure, which in every mature legal system will vary greatly in detail, are within the sole competence of the States. I do not see how it can be said that a trial becomes unfair simply because a State determines that evidence may be considered by the trier of fact, regardless of how it was obtained, if it is relevant to the one issue with which the trial is concerned, the guilt or innocence of the accused. Of course, a court may use its procedures as an incidental means of pursuing other ends than the correct resolution of the controversies before it. Such indeed is the *Weeks* rule, but if a State does not choose to use its courts in this way, I do not believe that this Court is empowered to impose this much-debated procedure on local courts, however efficacious we may consider the *Weeks* rule to be as a means of securing Constitutional rights.

. . .

The point, then, must be that in requiring exclusion of an involuntary statement of an accused, we are concerned not with an appropriate remedy for what the police have done, but with something which is regarded as going to the heart of our concepts of fairness in judicial procedure. The operative assumption of our procedural system is that "Ours is the accusatorial as opposed to the inquisitorial system. Such has been the characteristic of Anglo-American criminal justice since it freed itself from practices borrowed by the Star Chamber from the Continent whereby an accused was interrogated in secret for hours on end." The pressures brought to bear against an accused leading to a confession, unlike an unconstitutional violation of privacy, do not, apart from the use of the confession at trial, necessarily involve independent Constitutional violations. What is crucial is that the trial defense to which an accused is entitled should not be rendered an empty formality by reason of statements wrung from him, for then "a prisoner . . . (has been) made the deluded instrument of his own conviction." That this is a procedural right, and that its violation occurs at the time his improperly obtained statement is admitted at trial, is manifest. For without this right all the careful safeguards erected around the giving of testimony, whether by an accused or any other witness, would become empty formalities in a procedure where the most compelling possible evidence of guilt, a confession, would have already been obtained at the unsupervised pleasure of the police.

. . .

This, and not the disciplining of the police, as with illegally seized evidence, is surely the true basis for excluding a statement of the accused which was unconstitutionally obtained. In sum, I think the coerced confession analogy works strongly against what the Court does today.

I regret that I find so unwise in principle and so inexpedient in policy a decision motivated by the high purpose of increasing respect for Constitutional rights. But in the last analysis I think this Court can increase respect for the Constitution only if it rigidly respects the limitations which the Constitution places upon it, and respects as well the principles inherent in its own processes. In the present case I think we exceed both, and that our voice becomes only a voice of power, not of reason.

FROM THE COURTROOM

HERRING v. UNITED STATES

United States Supreme Court, 2009
555 U.S. 135

[Chief Justice ROBERTS delivered the opinion of the Court.]

[Justice GINSBURG filed a dissenting opinion, which was joined by Justices SOUTER, BREYER, and STEVENS.]

[Justice BREYER filed a dissenting opinion, which was joined by Justice SOUTER.]

The Fourth Amendment forbids "unreasonable searches and seizures," and this usually requires the police to have probable cause or a warrant before making an arrest. What if an officer reasonably believes there is an outstanding arrest warrant, but that belief turns out to be wrong because of a negligent bookkeeping error by another police employee? The parties here agree that the ensuing arrest is still a violation of the Fourth Amendment, but dispute whether contraband found during a search incident to that arrest must be excluded in a later prosecution.

Our cases establish that such suppression is not an automatic consequence of a Fourth Amendment violation. Instead, the question turns on the culpability of the police and the potential of exclusion to deter wrongful police conduct. Here the error was the result of isolated negligence attenuated from the arrest. We hold that in these circumstances the jury should not be barred from considering all the evidence.

I

On July 7, 2004, Investigator Mark Anderson learned that Bennie Dean Herring had driven to the Coffee County Sheriff's Department to retrieve something from his impounded truck. Herring was no stranger to law enforcement, and Anderson asked the county's warrant clerk, Sandy Pope, to check for any outstanding warrants for Herring's arrest. When she found none, Anderson asked Pope to check with Sharon Morgan, her counterpart in neighboring Dale County. After checking Dale County's computer database, Morgan replied that there was an active arrest warrant for Herring's failure to appear on a felony charge. Pope relayed the information to Anderson and asked Morgan to fax over a copy of the warrant as confirmation. Anderson and a deputy followed Herring as he left the impound lot, pulled him over, and arrested him. A search incident to the arrest revealed methamphetamine in Herring's pocket, and a pistol (which as a felon he could not possess) in his vehicle.

There had, however, been a mistake about the warrant. The Dale County sheriff's computer records are supposed to correspond to actual arrest warrants, which the office also maintains. But when Morgan went to the files to retrieve the actual warrant to fax to Pope, Morgan was unable to find it. She called a court clerk and learned that the warrant had been recalled five months earlier. Normally when a warrant is recalled the court clerk's office or a judge's chambers calls Morgan, who enters the information in the sheriff's computer database and disposes of the physical copy. For whatever reason, the information about the recall of the warrant for Herring did not appear in the database. Morgan immediately called Pope to alert her to the mixup, and Pope contacted Anderson over a secure radio. This all unfolded in [ten] to [fifteen] minutes, but Herring had already been arrested and found with the gun and drugs, just a few hundred yards from the sheriff's office.

Herring was indicted in the District Court for the Middle District of Alabama for illegally possessing the gun and drugs, violations of 18 U.S.C. § 922(g)(1) and 21 U.S.C. § 844(a). He moved to suppress the evidence on the ground that his initial arrest had been illegal because the warrant had been rescinded.

. . .

II

When a probable-cause determination was based on reasonable but mistaken assumptions, the person subjected to a search or seizure has not necessarily been the victim of a constitutional violation. The very phrase "probable cause" confirms that the Fourth Amendment does not demand all possible precision. And whether the error can be traced to a mistake by a state actor or some other source may bear on the analysis. For purposes of deciding this case, however, we accept the parties' assumption that there was a Fourth Amendment violation. The issue is whether the exclusionary rule should be applied.

A

The Fourth Amendment protects "[t]he right of the people to be secure in their persons, houses, papers, and effects, against unreasonable searches and seizures," but "contains no provision expressly precluding the use of evidence obtained in violation of its commands." Nonetheless, our decisions establish an exclusionary rule that, when applicable, forbids the use of improperly obtained evidence at trial. We have stated that this judicially created rule is "designed to safeguard Fourth Amendment rights generally through its deterrent effect."

In analyzing the applicability of the rule, *Leon* admonished that we must consider the actions of all the police officers involved. ("It is necessary to consider the objective reasonableness, not only of the officers who eventually executed a warrant, but also of the officers who originally obtained it or who provided information material to the probable-cause determination"). The Coffee County officers did nothing improper. Indeed, the error was noticed so quickly because Coffee County requested a faxed confirmation of the warrant.

The Eleventh Circuit concluded, however, that somebody in Dale County should have updated the computer database to reflect the recall of the arrest warrant. The court also concluded that this error was negligent, but did not find it to be reckless or deliberate. That fact is crucial to our holding that this error is not enough by itself to require "the extreme sanction of exclusion."

B

1. The fact that a Fourth Amendment violation occurred—*i.e.,* that a search or arrest was unreasonable—does not necessarily mean that the exclusionary rule applies. Indeed, exclusion "has always been our last resort, not our first impulse," and our precedents establish important principles that constrain application of the exclusionary rule.

First, the exclusionary rule is not an individual right and applies only where it "'result[s] in appreciable deterrence.'" We have repeatedly rejected the argument that exclusion is a necessary consequence of a Fourth Amendment violation. Instead we have focused on the efficacy of the rule in deterring Fourth Amendment violations in the future.

In addition, the benefits of deterrence must outweigh the costs. "We have never suggested that the exclusionary rule must apply in every circumstance in which it might provide marginal deterrence." "[T]o the extent that application of the exclusionary rule could provide some incremental deterrent, that possible benefit must be weighed against [its] substantial social costs." The principal cost of applying the rule is, of course, letting guilty and possibly dangerous defendants go free—something that "offends basic concepts of the criminal justice system." "[T]he rule's costly toll upon truth-seeking and law enforcement objectives presents a high obstacle for those urging [its] application."

These principles are reflected in the holding of *Leon*: When police act under a warrant that is invalid for lack of probable cause, the exclusionary rule does not apply if the police acted "in objectively reasonable reliance" on the subsequently invalidated search warrant. We (perhaps confusingly) called this objectively reasonable reliance "good faith." In a companion case, *Massachusetts v. Sheppard*, we held that the exclusionary rule did not apply when a warrant was invalid because a judge forgot to make "clerical corrections" to it.

Shortly thereafter we extended these holdings to warrantless administrative searches performed in good-faith reliance on a statute later declared unconstitutional. Finally, in *Evans*, we applied this good-faith rule to police who reasonably relied on mistaken information in a court's database that an arrest warrant was outstanding. We held that a mistake made by a judicial employee could not give rise to exclusion for three reasons: The exclusionary rule was crafted to curb police rather than judicial misconduct; court employees were unlikely to try to subvert the Fourth Amendment; and "most important, there [was] no basis for believing that application of the exclusionary rule in [those] circumstances" would have any significant effect in deterring the errors. *Evans* left unresolved "whether the evidence should be suppressed if police personnel were responsible for the error," an issue not argued by the State in that case, but one that we now confront.

2. The extent to which the exclusionary rule is justified by these deterrence principles varies with the culpability of the law enforcement conduct. As we said in *Leon,* "an assessment of the flagrancy of the police misconduct constitutes an important step in the calculus" of applying the exclusionary rule. Similarly, in *Krull* we elaborated that "evidence should be suppressed 'only if it can be said that the law enforcement officer had knowledge, or may properly be charged with knowledge, that the search was unconstitutional under the Fourth Amendment.'"

Anticipating the good-faith exception to the exclusionary rule, Judge Friendly wrote that "[t]he beneficent aim of the exclusionary rule to deter police misconduct can be sufficiently accomplished by a practice . . . outlawing evidence obtained by flagrant or deliberate violation of rights."

Indeed, the abuses that gave rise to the exclusionary rule featured intentional conduct that was patently unconstitutional. In *Weeks,* 232 U.S. 383, a foundational exclusionary rule case, the officers had broken into the defendant's home (using a key shown to them by a neighbor), confiscated incriminating papers, then returned again with a U.S. Marshal to confiscate even more. Not only did they have no search warrant, which the Court held was required, but they could not have gotten one had they tried. They were so lacking in sworn and particularized information that "not even an order of court would have justified such procedure." *Silverthorne Lumber Co. v. United States,* 251 U.S. 385 (1920), on which petitioner repeatedly relies, was similar; federal officials "without a shadow of authority" went to the defendants' office and "made a clean sweep" of every paper they could find. Even the Government seemed to acknowledge that the "seizure was an outrage."

Equally flagrant conduct was at issue in *Mapp v. Ohio,* which . . . extended the exclusionary rule to the States. Officers forced open a door to Ms. Mapp's house, kept her lawyer from entering, brandished what the court concluded was a false warrant, then forced her into handcuffs and canvassed the house for obscenity. An error that arises from nonrecurring and attenuated negligence is thus far removed from the core concerns that led us to adopt the rule in the first place. And in fact since *Leon,* we have never applied the rule to exclude evidence obtained in violation of the Fourth Amendment, where the police conduct was no more intentional or culpable than this.

3. To trigger the exclusionary rule, police conduct must be sufficiently deliberate that exclusion can meaningfully deter it, and sufficiently culpable that such deterrence is worth the price paid by the justice system. As laid out in our cases, the exclusionary rule serves to deter deliberate, reckless, or grossly negligent conduct, or in some circumstances recurring or systemic negligence. The error in this case does not rise to that level.

. . .

The pertinent analysis of deterrence and culpability is objective, not an "inquiry into the subjective awareness of arresting officers." We have already held that "our good-faith inquiry is confined to the objectively ascertainable question whether a reasonably well trained officer would have known that the search was illegal" in light of "all of the circumstances." These circumstances frequently include a particular officer's knowledge and experience, but that does not make the test any more subjective than the one for probable cause, which looks to an officer's knowledge and experience, but not his subjective intent.

4. We do not suggest that all recordkeeping errors by the police are immune from the exclusionary rule. In this case, however, the conduct at issue was not so objectively culpable as to require exclusion. In *Leon,* we held that "the marginal or nonexistent benefits produced by suppressing evidence obtained in objectively reasonable reliance on a subsequently invalidated search warrant cannot justify the substantial costs of exclusion." The same is true when evidence is obtained in objectively reasonable reliance on a subsequently recalled warrant.

If the police have been shown to be reckless in maintaining a warrant system, or to have knowingly made false entries to lay the groundwork for future false arrests, exclusion would certainly be justified under our cases should such misconduct cause a Fourth Amendment violation. We said as much in *Leon,* explaining that an officer could not "obtain a warrant on the basis of a 'bare bones' affidavit and then rely on colleagues who are ignorant of the circumstances under which the warrant was obtained to conduct the search." Petitioner's fears that our decision will cause police departments to deliberately keep their officers ignorant, are thus unfounded.

Justice Ginsburg's dissent also adverts to the possible unreliability of a number of databases not relevant to this case. In a case where systemic errors were demonstrated, it might be reckless for officers to rely on an unreliable warrant system. But there is no evidence that errors in Dale County's system are routine or widespread. Officer Anderson testified that he had never had reason to question information about a Dale County warrant, and both Sandy Pope and Sharon Morgan testified that they could remember no similar miscommunication ever happening on their watch. That is even less error than in the database at issue in *Evans,* where we also found reliance on the database to be objectively reasonable. Because no such showings were made here, the Eleventh Circuit was correct to affirm the denial of the motion to suppress.

. . .

Petitioner's claim that police negligence automatically triggers suppression cannot be squared with the principles underlying the exclusionary rule, as they have been explained in our cases. In light of our repeated holdings that the deterrent effect of suppression must be substantial and outweigh any harm to the justice system, we conclude that when police mistakes are the result of negligence such as that described here, rather than systemic error or reckless disregard of constitutional requirements, any marginal deterrence does not "pay its way." In such a case, the criminal should not "go free because the constable has blundered."

The judgment of the Court of Appeals for the Eleventh Circuit is affirmed.

It is so ordered.

Justice GINSBURG, with whom Justice STEVENS, Justice SOUTER, and Justice BREYER join, dissenting.

Petitioner Bennie Dean Herring was arrested, and subjected to a search incident to his arrest, although no warrant was outstanding against him, and the police lacked probable cause to believe he was engaged in criminal activity. The arrest and ensuing search therefore violated Herring's Fourth Amendment right "to be secure . . . against unreasonable searches and seizures." The Court of Appeals so determined, and the Government does not contend otherwise. The exclusionary rule provides redress for Fourth Amendment violations by placing the government in the position it would have been in had there been no unconstitutional arrest and search. The rule thus strongly encourages police compliance with the Fourth Amendment in the future. The Court, however, holds the rule inapplicable because careless recordkeeping by the police—not flagrant or deliberate misconduct—accounts for Herring's arrest.

I would not so constrict the domain of the exclusionary rule and would hold the rule dispositive of this case: "[I]f courts are to have any power to discourage [police] error of [the kind here at issue], it must be through the application of the exclusionary rule." The unlawful search in this case was contested in court because the police found methamphetamine in Herring's pocket and a pistol in his truck. But the "most serious impact" of the Court's holding will be on innocent persons "wrongfully arrested based on erroneous information [carelessly maintained] in a computer data base."

. . .

II

A

The Court states that the exclusionary rule is not a defendant's right; rather, it is simply a remedy applicable only when suppression would result in appreciable deterrence that outweighs the cost to the justice system.

The Court's discussion invokes a view of the exclusionary rule famously held by renowned jurists Henry J. Friendly and Benjamin Nathan Cardozo. Over [eighty] years ago, Cardozo, then seated on the New York Court of Appeals, commented critically on the federal exclusionary rule, which had not yet been applied to the States. He suggested that in at least some cases the rule exacted too high a price from the criminal justice system. words often quoted, Cardozo questioned whether the criminal should "go free because the constable has blundered."

Judge Friendly later elaborated on Cardozo's query. "The sole reason for exclusion," Friendly wrote, "is that experience has demonstrated this to be the only effective method for deterring the police from violating the Constitution." He thought it excessive, in light of the rule's aim to deter police conduct, to require exclusion when the constable had merely "blundered"—when a police officer committed a technical error in an on-the-spot judgment, or made a "slight and unintentional miscalculation." As the Court recounts, Judge Friendly suggested that deterrence of police improprieties could be "sufficiently accomplished" by confining the rule to "evidence obtained by flagrant or deliberate violation of rights."

B

Others have described "a more majestic conception" of the Fourth Amendment and its adjunct, the exclusionary rule. Protective of the fundamental "right of the people to be secure in their persons, houses, papers, and effects," the Amendment "is a constraint on the power of the sovereign, not merely on some of its agents. I share that vision of the Amendment.

The exclusionary rule is "a remedy necessary to ensure that" the Fourth Amendment's prohibitions "are observed in fact." The rule's service as an essential auxiliary to the Amendment earlier inclined the Court to hold the two inseparable.

Beyond doubt, a main objective of the rule "is to deter—to compel respect for the constitutional guaranty in the only effectively available way—by removing the incentive to disregard it." But the rule also serves other important purposes: It "enabl[es] the judiciary to avoid the taint of partnership in official lawlessness," and it "assur[es] the people—all potential victims of unlawful government conduct—that the government would not profit from its lawless behavior, thus minimizing the risk of seriously undermining popular trust in government."

The exclusionary rule, it bears emphasis, is often the only remedy effective to redress a Fourth Amendment violation. Civil liability will not lie for "the vast majority of [F]ourth [A]mendment violations—the frequent infringements motivated by commendable zeal, not condemnable malice." Criminal prosecutions or administrative sanctions against the offending officers and injunctive relief against widespread violations are an even farther cry.

III

The Court maintains that Herring's case is one in which the exclusionary rule could have scant deterrent effect and therefore would not "pay its way." I disagree.

A

The exclusionary rule, the Court suggests, is capable of only marginal deterrence when the misconduct at issue is merely careless, not intentional or reckless. The suggestion runs counter to a foundational premise of tort law—that liability for negligence, *i.e.,* lack of due care, creates an incentive to act with greater care. The Government so acknowledges.

That the mistake here involved the failure to make a computer entry hardly means that application of the exclusionary rule would have minimal value. "Just as the risk of *respondeat superior* liability encourages employers to supervise . . . their employees' conduct [more carefully], so the risk of exclusion of evidence encourages policymakers and systems managers to monitor the performance of the systems they install and the personnel employed to operate those systems."

Consider the potential impact of a decision applying the exclusionary rule in this case. As earlier observed, the record indicates that there is no electronic connection between the warrant database of the Dale County Sheriff's Department and that of the County Circuit Clerk's office, which is located in the basement of the same building. When a warrant is recalled, one of the "many different people that have access to th[e] warrants," must find the hard copy of the warrant in the "two or three different places" where the Department houses warrants, return it to the Clerk's office, and manually update the Department's database, The record reflects no routine practice of checking the database for accuracy, and the failure to remove the entry for Herring's warrant was not discovered until Investigator Anderson sought to pursue Herring five months later. Is it not altogether obvious that the Department could take further precautions to ensure the integrity of its database? The Sheriff's Department "is in a position to remedy the situation and might well do so if the exclusionary rule is there to remove the incentive to do otherwise."

. . .

IV

Negligent recordkeeping errors by law enforcement threaten individual liberty, are susceptible to deterrence by the exclusionary rule, and cannot be remedied effectively through other means. Such errors present no occasion to further erode the exclusionary rule. The rule "is needed to make the Fourth Amendment something real; a guarantee that does not carry with it the exclusion of evidence obtained by its violation is a chimera." In keeping with the rule's "core concerns," suppression should have attended the unconstitutional search in this case.

For the reasons stated, I would reverse the judgment of the Eleventh Circuit.

[The dissent of Justice BREYER, joined by Justice SOUTER, is omitted.]

24

An Introduction to Interrogations

Key Concepts

- "Involuntary" v. "Unwarned" Statements
- Involuntary Statements (and Their Fruit) Are Not Admissible for Any Purpose
- Unwarned (*i.e.*, un-*Mirandized*) Statements May Be Used to Impeach, and Their Fruit May Be Admitted
- Voluntariness and Miranda Requirements Are Complementary, But Distinct, Measures of the Coerciveness of a Statement

During the investigation of crimes, interrogation is frequently used by police officers to secure statements from the accused. The admissibility of these statements at trial is subject to two different tests—voluntariness and compliance with *Miranda*. We will discuss these measures of coerciveness separately in the next two chapters. But first we will briefly discuss the ways in which the two measures are similar and the very important ways in which they differ.

The voluntariness inquiry is driven by the Due Process guarantees of the Fifth Amendment in federal trials and by the Due Process guarantees of the Fourteenth Amendment in state cases. In contrast, the *Miranda* rules are grounded in the Self-Incrimination Clause of the Fifth Amendment. Both tests—voluntariness and compliance with *Miranda*—are used to measure whether a suspect's statement has been coerced. However, though both tests affect the admissibility of confessions, you should remember that they are separate analyses.

The **voluntariness inquiry**, which is discussed in **Chapter 25**, evaluates the totality of the circumstances to determine whether a statement was made **"freely, voluntarily, and without compulsion or inducement."**[1] In contrast, the ***Miranda*** **inquiry**, which is discussed in **Chapter 26**, looks to **whether appropriate warnings were given** regarding the right to remain silent and the right to counsel. The *Miranda* inquiry also considers whether the suspect invoked or waived these rights.

The Fifth Amendment to the Constitution prohibits the use of coerced confessions in criminal trials. As the Court has repeatedly said, the Amendment was adopted with a backward looking gaze at history:

[1] Haynes v. Washington, 373 U.S. 503, 513 (1963).

> The rack, the thumbscrew, the wheel, solitary confinement, protracted questioning and cross questioning, and other ingenious forms of entrapment of the helpless or unpopular had left their wake of mutilated bodies and shattered minds along the way to the cross, the guillotine, the stake and the hangman's noose. And they who have suffered most from secret and dictatorial proceedings have almost always been the poor, the ignorant, the numerically weak, the friendless and the powerless.[2]

The protections of the Fifth Amendment are intended to avoid repeating that history. The Amendment prohibits deprivations of life, liberty or property without appropriate legal procedures. Specifically, the Amendment provides:

> No person shall be held to answer for a capital, or otherwise infamous crime, unless on a presentment or indictment of a Grand Jury, except in cases arising in the land or naval forces, or in the Militia, when in actual service in time of War or public danger; nor shall any person be subject for the same offence to be twice put in jeopardy of life or limb; <u>[1] nor shall be compelled in any criminal case to be a witness against himself, [2] nor be deprived of life, liberty, or property, without due process of law;</u> nor shall private property be taken for public use, without just compensation.[3]

The first relevant clause of the Amendment is the Self-Incrimination Clause [1], which strictly prohibits the practice of forced self-accusation. The second relevant clause is the Due Process Clause [2], which provides in more general terms that the state must follow fair procedures in criminal trials.

The Fifth Amendment's ban on coerced confessions is applied against the States by the provisions of the Fourteenth Amendment's Due Process clause. That amendment provides in relevant part:

> All persons born or naturalized in the United States and subject to the jurisdiction thereof, are citizens of the United States and of the State wherein they reside. No State shall make or enforce any law which shall abridge the privileges or immunities of citizens of the United States; <u>nor shall any State deprive any person of life, liberty, or property, without due process of law;</u> nor deny to any person within its jurisdiction the equal protection of the laws.[4]

---

[2] Chambers v. Florida, 309 U.S. 227, 237–38 (1940).

[3] U.S. Const. amend. V.

[4] U.S. Const. amend. XIV, § 1.

Thus, though states are largely free to manage their own affairs within their borders, the Court has said that the Constitution "severely restricted the States in their administration of criminal justice."[5] The limitation on the use of coerced confessions is one such restriction. As you read above, coerced confessions include both involuntary confessions and unwarned (*i.e.*, un-*Mirandized*) confessions. However, as you will read in greater detail in the coming chapters, the limitations that apply to each type of coerced confession are different.

The limitations that apply to involuntary confessions are the more restrictive of the two. Involuntary confessions are statements that are the product of the subject's will being overborne by her official questioners. Such confessions may not be used for any reason at trial. This means that they may not be introduced as direct evidence of guilt, and also may not be introduced as impeachment evidence. In addition, the so-called "fruit" of involuntary confessions may not be used. Such fruit includes evidence that is derived from the involuntary confession. Consider the involuntariness rules in the following example:

> **Example:** Suzie Suspect is arrested and brought to the police station for questioning in connection with the murder of her partner, Jessica. At the station, the police question Suzie continuously for 48 hours. However, when she fails to provide a statement, the police decide more pressure is needed. They tie Suzie to a chair and water-board her eight times until she agrees to make a statement.
>
> Suzie tells the police that she killed Jessica with a meat tenderizer following a fight. She admits that she then staged the scene to make it look like Jessica slipped and hit her head in the shower. The police take Suzie to the couple's apartment. At the officers' request, Suzie silently re-enacts the fight in the kitchen, showing them how she hit Jessica fourteen times in the back of the head with the meat tenderizer. The officers videotape the silent re-enactment. Suzie then shows the police the hallway she dragged Jessica's body down. While she is doing this, she points out a place where Jessica's sweater caught on a nail in the carpeting and tore. In addition to a small piece of the sweater, upon closer inspection, the police also find Jessica's blood on the carpet. Suzie also retrieves the meat tenderizer from the hamper in her bedroom. The tenderizer is bloody and still has clumps of Jessica's hair in it.

[5] Watts v. Indiana, 338 U.S. 49, 50 (1949).

Analysis: At trial, the constitutional limitations on involuntary confessions (the Due Process Clause of the Fifth Amendment in federal cases, and the Due Process Clause of the Fourteenth Amendment in state cases) would preclude the admission of Suzie's confession, which was rendered involuntary by the physical abuse prompting it. In addition, the constitutional limits would prohibit admission of the evidence secured in the apartment—the videotaped re-enactment, the piece of sweater, the blood on the carpet, and the meat tenderizer—since this evidence would be considered the "fruit" of the involuntary confession.

In addition to considering the voluntariness of confessions, the Supreme Court in 1966 in *Miranda* also determined that the potentially coercive environment of custodial interrogations presented cause for concern. To guard against the potential for coercion, the Court required that suspects be given a series of warnings. These warnings are familiar to any American who has watched television crime dramas:

- You have the right to remain silent;
- If you do not exercise this right anything you say may be used against you;
- You have the right to an attorney; and
- If you cannot afford an attorney one will be provided for you.

The warnings are intended to combat any potential coercion that may be created by the atmosphere of custodial interrogation. As a general rule, unwarned statements are not admissible as direct evidence of guilt. However, a number of pre-conditions and exceptions apply to this general rule:

1. *Miranda* warnings are only required if the suspect is subject to **custodial interrogation**. Thus, both custody and interrogation are necessary pre-conditions before *Miranda* warnings will be required. In **Chapter 26**, we will consider in detail what is required before each of these preconditions is met.

2. Moreover, unlike involuntary statements, all use of unwarned statements is not strictly prohibited under the *Miranda* rules. Put simply, unwarned statements may be used to impeach a defendant. In addition, the fruit of unwarned statements is admissible. Note that these results stand in opposition to the results that would attach if a statement was involuntary.

There is a reason for the differential treatment: the source of the *Miranda* rule. The *Miranda* rule is grounded in the Fifth Amendment's Self-Incrimination Clause, which governs compelled statements. With regard to fruit, therefore, the rationale is that admission of non-testimonial fruit, *i.e.*, physical evidence, in no way implicates this constitutional provision. Similarly, the Court has reasoned that *Miranda*'s protection is appropriately intended as a shield to protect against compelled confessions. However, that protection is not also available as a sword that will enable a defendant to testify unimpeded by the introduction of prior statements that may impeach him.

In application, the limits on unwarned statements thus function quite differently from the limits on involuntary statements. Return for a moment to the saga of Suzie Suspect and her murdered partner Jessica. Suppose again that Suzie is arrested and brought to the police station for questioning. Rather than water-boarding Suzie and questioning her continuously, the police instead simply interrogate her over the span of about thirty minutes. However, the police do not warn Suzie of her *Miranda* rights prior to this interrogation.

Suzie quickly confesses to murdering Jessica and staging the scene to make it look like an accident. As in the above example, Suzie also takes the officers to her apartment where they find the evidence mentioned, including the re-enactment of the fight, the scrap of Jessica's sweater caught on the nail, the bloodstains on the carpet, and the murder weapon. As we saw earlier, if her confession had been deemed "involuntary," all of this evidence would be precluded. In this case, her confession was "voluntary;" but it was taken in violation of her *Miranda* rights. Thus, the law would preclude only Suzie's initial confession at the station. The evidence found at the apartment would all be admissible. Moreover, should Suzie take the stand at trial and testify in conflict with her earlier confession, the prosecution would be allowed to introduce her confession to impeach her contrary trial testimony.

In other words, it is more accurate to think of the protections of *Miranda* not as an affirmative and compulsory duty to warn imposed on the police, but rather as a limitation on what may be done with a statement elicited in the absence of warnings. Put somewhat differently, *Miranda* does not require the police to warn anyone of anything. Rather, *Miranda* only limits what may be done with statements taken during custodial interrogation in the absence of required warnings. You should also note that there is an "emergency exception" to the *Miranda* rule—so that under some circumstances, even statements that are elicited in violation of *Miranda* can still be used to prove guilt.

As you read over the next two chapters, remember that voluntariness and compliance with *Miranda* are rules that work in tandem. When the Court acknowledged the protections afforded under the Fifth Amendment in *Miranda* it did **not** replace or abolish the existing rules regarding voluntariness.. Some readers may question why confessions must be governed by two sets of rules with different limitations. The simplest answer is that they apply in different contexts. Below is a short outline that may help you think through the interplay between the voluntariness and *Miranda* inquiries:

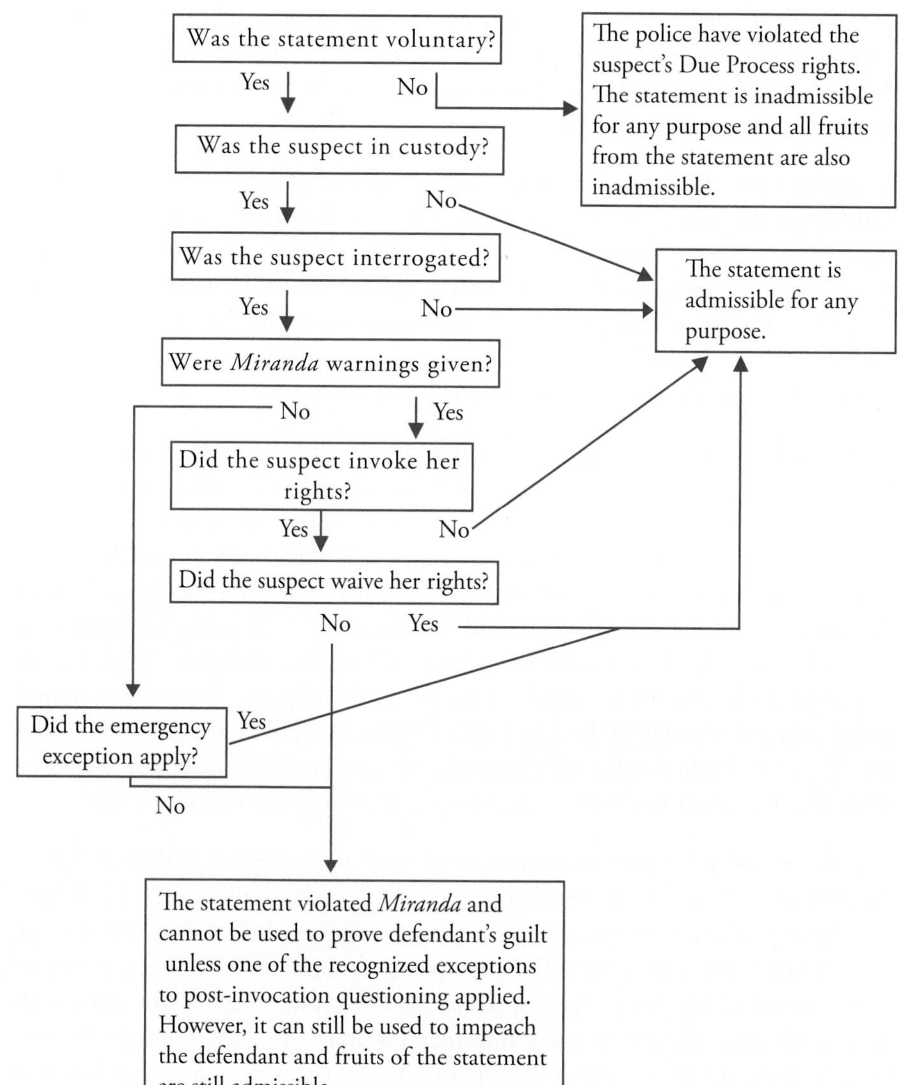
Was the statement voluntary?
Yes
No
The police have violated the suspect's Due Process rights. The statement is inadmissible for any purpose and all fruits from the statement are also inadmissible.
Was the suspect in custody?
Yes
No
Was the suspect interrogated?
Yes
No
The statement is admissible for any purpose.
Were Miranda warnings given?
No
Yes
Did the suspect invoke her rights?
Yes
No
Did the suspect waive her rights?
No
Yes
Did the emergency exception apply?
Yes
No
The statement violated Miranda and cannot be used to prove defendant's guilt unless one of the recognized exceptions to post-invocation questioning applied. However, it can still be used to impeach the defendant and fruits of the statement are still admissible.

25

Interrogations and Voluntariness

Key Concepts

- Voluntariness Inquiry Is Grounded in the Due Process Clause of the Fourteenth Amendments
- The Test Is Whether the Statement Was Made Freely, Voluntarily and Without Compulsion or Inducement
- Involuntary Statements and Their Fruit May Not Be Used for Any Purpose

A. Introduction and Policy. At a most basic level, confessions may not be beaten, cajoled, tortured, or wrung out of suspects. These tactics are abhorrent to notions of justice, though they have been regular features of totalitarian regimes and, for too many, the American criminal justice system until the mid-1900s. In our modern adversarial criminal system, the prosecution must build its case through its own labors, not by forcing the evidence from the mouth of the accused. These principles are what guide the command that voluntariness is the basic requirement for the admissibility of confessions.

As you will read, some of the Court's early voluntariness cases were decided in an era of brutal official violence targeting black Americans. However, while the case law was born in part out of a concern for historic instances of extreme physical abuse, it has long since outgrown its narrow beginnings. The modern Court has said in no uncertain terms that where a confession is elicited through sleep deprivation, or mental and emotional abuses, a finding of involuntariness may be warranted.

B. The Law.

The Due Process Clause of the Fourteenth Amendment (or that same clause of the Fifth Amendment in federal cases) requires that any statement used against the accused must be "voluntary":

> A defendant's statement is inadmissible at trial if it is involuntary. An involuntary statement is one made when the will of the suspect was overborne. To be admissible, the statement must be made "freely, voluntarily, and without compulsion."[1]

[1] Haynes v. Washington, 373 U.S. 503, 513 (1963).

Voluntariness is determined by examining the totality of the circumstances. This test asks a reviewing court to consider factors such as violence; threats of violence; sleep deprivation; the withholding of food; the suspect's age, intelligence and education; the provision of warnings; the nature of the police questioning; whether the suspect was held incommunicado for an extended period; and the suspect's access to counsel.

There are three reasons for excluding coerced confessions. The first is purely practical: a confession which is forced out of a suspect is not very reliable. Improper inducements create a significant risk that a suspect has confessed only to avoid negative (or to secure favorable) consequences.[2] If the purpose of an interrogation is to determine the truth about what happened, the interrogator must take great care to ensure that the suspect is confessing of his own free will, not merely to please the interrogator by saying whatever he thinks the interrogator wants to hear.

The second reason for excluding coerced confessions is that they are seen as corrosive to our adversarial system. Our criminal justice system is based on the theory that the prosecutor bears the burden of **proving** the defendant's guilt beyond a reasonable doubt. The balance of the system is undermined if the prosecution can simply force a defendant to admit his own guilt through strong-arm tactics and intimidation. As the Supreme Court has said "[l]aw triumphs when the natural impulses aroused by a shocking crime yield to the safeguards which our civilization has evolved for an administration of criminal justice at once rational and effective."[3]

Finally, the exclusion of coerced confessions supports the most basic concerns of morality and the proper role of law enforcement, under the theory that the police should obey the law while enforcing the law.[4] Highlighting this notion of fair play, the Court said in *Lisenba*, "[t]he aim of the requirement of due process is not to exclude presumptively false evidence, but to prevent fundamental unfairness in the use of evidence, whether true or false."[5]

The test for determining voluntariness is a totality of the circumstances test. Relevant circumstances to be considered include things like violence or threats of violence; whether the suspect was allowed to sleep;[6] and whether adequate meals were provided.[7] The "age, intelligence, and education" of the suspect are also

[2] Lisenba v. California, 314 U.S. 219, 235 (1941).
[3] Watts v. Indiana, 338 U.S. 49, 55 (1949).
[4] Spano v. New York, 360 U.S. 315, 320–21 (1959).
[5] Lisenba, 314 U.S. at 236.
[6] Ashcraft v. Tennessee, 322 U.S. 143, 152 (1944).
[7] Watts, 338 U.S. at 53.

relevant.[8] A reviewing court may also consider whether warnings were given;[9] the relentless nature of police questioning;[10] and the suspect's access to counsel.[11] A reviewing court then must determine whether under all of the circumstances, the statement was freely and voluntarily given.

Without question, evidence of physical abuse is one hallmark of a coerced confession. But, under the totality of the circumstances test, it is not the only one. The Court has said it will also more closely consider records that show evidence of a prisoner held "incommunicado [who] is subjected to questioning by officers for long periods and deprived of the advice of counsel."[12] Thus, for example, where a suspect was held for days without outside contact, and was told he would not be allowed to communicate with his wife until he provided a statement, the Court rejected his confession as involuntary.[13]

On the other hand, the Court has also made clear that the mere fact of police detention and in-private questioning does not force a conclusion that the confession obtained thereby was involuntary.[14] Thus, a defendant cannot establish involuntariness if there is no evidence of coercive police conduct. Furthermore, if the defendant is, unknown to the police, coerced by someone or something other than law enforcement, the statements will not be deemed "involuntary" under the Constitution. For example, the Court has found that a suspect who was told to confess by "the voice of God" made a "voluntary" statement.[15]

The use of police trickery also will not necessarily render a confession involuntary. For example, if police officers falsely tell a suspect that his co-defendant has confessed, a subsequent confession from the suspect prompted by that false assertion will not necessarily be excluded if the other surrounding circumstances do not suggest coercion.[16]

Finally, the Court has suggested that sufficiently egregious police conduct may give rise to a claim of involuntariness under the Fourteenth Amendment. However, the Court has been careful to note that such conduct would need to be particularly shocking to the conscience before it gave rise to such a claim—"the official conduct most likely to rise to the conscience-shocking level is the conduct intended to injure in some way unjustifiable by any government interest."[17]

---

8 Crooker v. California, 357 U.S. 433, 438 (1958).

9 Frazier v. Cupp, 394 U.S. 731, 739 (1969).

10 Lisenba, 314 U.S. at 239.

11 Crooker, 357 U.S. at 437.

12 Lisenba, 314 U.S. at 240.

13 Haynes v. Washington, 373 U.S. 503 (1963).

14 Crooker, 357 U.S. at 437.

15 Colorado v. Connelly, 479 U.S. 157 (1986).

16 Frazier v. Cupp, 394 U.S. 731, 739 (1969).

17 Chavez v. Martinez, 538 U.S. 760, 775 (2003) (internal quotations and citations omitted).

C. Applying the Law. Since the early 1900s, the Court has decided numerous cases that directly address the voluntariness of confessions. However, unlike some of its other jurisprudence, what the Court has said in its voluntariness cases has been fairly consistent. The rules of voluntariness are therefore relatively easy to remember and apply.

1. Physical Abuse and Torture as Coercion. The most obvious form of coercion involves the violent mistreatment of suspects at the hands of government officials in an attempt to secure a confession. Many readers will no doubt associate such methods with bygone eras primarily (though not exclusively) on foreign soil—historic events like the Inquisition, the Star Chamber, and the Salem Witch Trials. However, until the mid-1900s such abuses were also a not-infrequent tactic of many state law enforcement officers. The Court's seminal coerced confession case—*Brown v. Mississippi*—was one of these. Decided in 1936, it involved three black farmers' horrific tales of abuse at the hands of white police officers in Mississippi:

> **Example—*Brown v. Mississippi*, 297 U.S. 278 (1936):** A white plantation owner by the name of Raymond Stewart was murdered in March of 1934. Within hours of the killing, the police arrested Ed Brown, Henry Shields, and Yank Ellington, three black tenant farmers who worked Stewart's land. Four days later, the three men were indicted and arraigned. A day later, trial was begun. And, by the following day, all three men had been convicted and sentenced to death. The evidence against the men consisted entirely of their confessions. However, there was substantial evidence that the confessions were the product of brutal torture.
>
> Stewart's body was discovered at about one o'clock in the afternoon on the day of his death. That night, the deputy sheriff visited the tenant farmer Ellington's house and carried him to Stewart's home. It is unclear what led the deputy to Ellington other than the fact that Ellington was a tenant farmer on Stewart's land. Ellington and the deputy were met at the house by a small mob of white men. These men immediately accused Ellington of the crime. When he denied any role in the offense, the men placed a noose around his neck and hung him from a tree limb. Before he could choke to death, they let him down and demanded a confession. When Ellington refused, they again hung him from his neck. They let him down a second time and repeated the demand for a confession. Ellington continued to profess his innocence. The men then tied Ellington to a tree and whipped him. Eventually, Ellington was left to make his way

home. Two days later, the deputy and another man returned to Ellington's home to arrest him. As the two were transporting Ellington to the jail, the deputy stopped the car and hauled Ellington out. He whipped Ellington and told him the beating would continue until Ellington confessed. A short time later, the deputy dictated a statement to which Ellington confessed.

Following Ellington's arrest, Brown and Shields were arrested. As with Ellington, apart from their work on Stewart's farm, it is unclear why official scrutiny became focused on the two men. The same deputy who tortured Ellington participated in the interrogation of Brown and Shields. In an interview room at the jail, the deputy accompanied by another police officer and a group of men, all of whom were white, removed Brown and Shields's shirts and strapped the men over the backs of chairs. The officer and the group of men then took turns beating Brown and Shields with the buckle end of a belt until the flesh on their backs was ripped to shreds. Throughout the beating, the deputy advised both men that the cruelty would continue until the men confessed to the murder in precisely the detail the group demanded. When satisfactory confessions had been provided, the men were told if they recanted at any future point, they would be beaten again.

The next day the local sheriffs came to the jail along with a small group to hear the "voluntary" confessions of all three prisoners. At the time of this meeting, the marks on Ellington's neck from his aborted lynching were clearly visible, and either Brown or Shields was limping and unable to sit because of injuries sustained during the interrogation. Nonetheless, the two sheriffs received the confessions, which they later testified to at trial. At trial, those who participated in the beatings admitted that the men had been whipped. However, when asked about the severity of the beatings, the deputy declared, "Not too much for a negro; not as much as I would have done if it were left to me."[18]

Following their conviction and death sentences, all three men appealed. They maintained that the admission of their purported confessions violated the Due Process Clause.

[18] Brown v. Mississippi, 297 U.S. 278, 284 (1936).

Analysis: The admission of the confession was a clear violation of the Fourteenth Amendment. Therefore, reversal of the convictions was required.

Because this case was decided in 1936, most sections of the Bill of Rights had not yet been incorporated—that is, the Court had not yet determined that the various rights guaranteed in the Bill of Rights applied against the states in the same manner that they applied against the federal government. Thus, the Court noted there were many aspects of the criminal process that the state was able to decide for itself—whether to have a jury trial, for example. However, even this early in the evolution of the incorporation doctrine, the Court was unwilling to let a state use such extreme measures as were found in this case: "[b]ecause a state may dispense with a jury trial, it does not follow that it may substitute trial by ordeal."[19]

The Court held that a criminal trial is a "mere pretense" if the conviction is based "solely upon confessions obtained by violence." The Due Process Clause of the Fourteenth Amendment requires that all state actions must be "consistent with the fundamental principles of liberty and justice which lie at the base of all our civil and political institutions." The Court concluded that "it would be difficult to conceive of methods more revolting to the sense of justice than those taken to procure the confessions of these petitioners, and the use of the confessions thus obtained as the basis for conviction and sentence was a clear denial of due process."[20]

Accordingly, all three convictions were reversed.

2. Threats and Psychological Ploys as Coercion. The horrific physical abuse suffered by the petitioners in *Brown* presented an obvious example of official coercion. However, the flagrant savagery seen in that case is not the only manner in which a defendant's statement might be rendered involuntary. Just four years after its *Brown* decision, the Court considered the voluntariness of statements in a case with disputed evidence of physical abuse, but an incontestable record of extreme sleep deprivation and relentless police questioning:

> **Example—*Chambers v. Florida*, 309 U.S. 227 (1940):** On a Saturday evening in May 1933, an elderly white man in Pompano, Florida was killed during the course of a robbery. Within twenty-four hours of the murder, forty black men who lived in the surrounding community were arrested for the offense and taken to the jail in Fort Lauderdale. Over the course of the next week, the forty men being held were subjected to police interrogation. At no point were the prisoners allowed to speak with a lawyer or with family or friends. After five days of continuous questioning, however, no one had confessed. Accordingly, the

[19] Id. at 285.

[20] Id. at 286.

officers selected a smaller group of men upon which to focus their efforts.

On the Saturday after the murder, beginning at approximately 3:30 p.m., Chambers and three other men—Woodward, Williamson and Davis—were subjected to round-the-clock questioning. At about 2:30 Sunday morning, after thirty-six hours of continuous interrogation, Woodward confessed. However, when the prosecutor was called to the jail to witness the confession, he found it to be insufficient. He told the officers, "tear this paper up, this isn't what I want, when you get something worthwhile call me."[21] Another round of questioning then commenced. Around sunrise, confessions were obtained from each of the men, Chambers included. Shortly thereafter, the three men other than Chambers pled guilty. Chambers proceeded to trial. The evidence against him consisted of his confession and the testimony of Woodward, Williamson, and Davis. Following conviction, all four men filed a petition for writ of error coram nobis challenging the legality of their confessions.

Analysis: The Supreme Court held that even though there was no clear evidence of physical abuse, the psychological pressure brought to bear against the defendants was coercive.

The Court began by re-stating the principle from *Brown* that a state using an "improperly obtained confession" may violate the Due Process Clause of the Fourteenth Amendment. In elaborate language the Court explained the importance of the Due Process clause: "From the popular hatred and abhorrence of illegal confinement, torture and extortion of confessions of violations of the 'law of the land' evolved the fundamental idea that no man's life, liberty or property be forfeited as criminal punishment for violation of that law until there had been a charge fairly made and fairly tried in a public tribunal free of prejudice, passion, excitement and tyrannical power."[22]

In this case, the police conduct began with mass arrests on no suspicion and ended with the drawn-out, isolated, and ceaseless questioning of the suspects, who were throughout without access to family or legal counsel. Though there was not clear evidence of physical violence of the sort seen four years earlier in *Brown*, the facts nevertheless clearly supported the conclusion that "compulsion was applied."[23]

Moreover, contrary to the state's claim, the police conduct in this case could not be justified by the pressing law enforcement need to solve the murder. "We are

---

[21] Chambers v. Florida, 309 U.S. 227, 232 (1940).

[22] Id. at 236–37.

[23] Id. at 239.

not impressed by the argument that law enforcement methods such as those under review are necessary to uphold our laws. The Constitution proscribes such lawless means irrespective of the end."[24]

It is not difficult to understand why sleep deprivation and relentless questioning should be treated, like physical abuse, as obvious methods of coercion that we cannot allow police officers to employ. But, *Brown* and *Chambers* involved conduct that was so egregious the two cases are, in a sense, not very useful in determining where the actual line should be drawn between coerced confessions and voluntary confessions. What of more subtle pressure tactics or milder forms of official compulsion? In 1959, the Court held that even in the absence of physical brutality or deprivation, some coercive psychological ploys are impermissible as well:

> **Example—*Spano v. New York*, 360 U.S. 315 (1959):** Vincent Spano was the prime suspect following the shooting death of a man after a bar fight. Spano had been drinking in the bar earlier in the evening. When the victim took Spano's money off the bar, Spano followed him outside and a fight began. The victim, who was a former professional boxer, quickly got the better of Spano. After the fight was over, the victim left while the bartender helped Spano ice his wounds. Shortly thereafter, Spano went home, retrieved his gun, and went to find the victim at a local candy store where he was known to hang out. Spano fired five shots, two of which hit the victim, killing him. Of the people in the candy store, the shooting was witnessed only by a boy who worked there.
>
> Spano was indicted for the murder and a warrant was issued for his arrest. Before turning himself in on the warrant, Spano called a childhood friend, Gaspar Bruno, for advice. Bruno was in the police academy and relayed his conversation with Spano to his senior officers.
>
> The next day, Spano turned himself in. He was accompanied by his attorney. Just before Spano was taken into custody, his attorney warned him not to answer any questions. Spano was then taken back, and his interrogation began at around 7:15 in the evening. For approximately five hours, Spano followed his attorney's advice and refused to answer any questions. Sensing that the interrogation was going nowhere, the officers took a break. Spano was fed and then transferred to another stationhouse.

[24] Id. at 240–41.

At around 12:40 a.m., the interrogation continued in the new location. Over the course of the next three hours, the police used Spano's friend Bruno as the interrogator. Bruno was instructed to tell Spano that his job as a police officer was in jeopardy and consequently his ability to care for his family was being threatened because of Spano's initial call to Bruno. These claims were not true. After three unsuccessful attempts to cajole Spano into confessing using these ploys, Spano finally told Bruno he would make a statement. At approximately 3:30 that morning, the local prosecutor came to the stationhouse to take Spano's statement.

At trial, Spano's statements were introduced into evidence. A jury convicted him of murder and he was sentenced to death. Spano then appealed challenging the voluntariness of his statements.

Analysis: The Supreme Court held that the circumstances surrounding Spano's confession rendered it involuntary. Its admission at his trial therefore violated the Fourteenth Amendment.

The rejection of coerced confessions in the American justice system has as much to do with a fear of false evidence as it does with a sense that the police should not break the law while enforcing it. The kind of appalling violence and physically abusive interrogations that were seen in earlier cases were not at issue here. "But as law enforcement officers become more responsible, and the methods used to extract confessions more sophisticated, [the Court's] duty to enforce federal constitutional protections does not cease."[25]

Given the totality of the circumstances surrounding Vincent Spano's confession, the Court concluded that it was involuntary. Spano was a young man with only six months of high school education. He also had a history of emotional problems. More than fifteen police officers or other officials participated in his interrogation. His confession was produced after eight hours of near-continuous overnight questioning. During this questioning the police took deliberate advantage of Spano's predicted "slowly mounting fatigue."[26] Another factor which must be considered in evaluating the totality of the circumstances is the use of Spano's childhood friend, Gaspar Bruno, to elicit the confession. "There was a bond of friendship between them going back a decade into adolescence. It was with this material that the officers felt that they could overcome petitioner's will."[27] Moreover, the police interrogation continued even though Spano repeatedly refused to answer

---

[25] Spano v. New York, 360 U.S. 315, 321 (1959).

[26] Id. at 322.

[27] Id. at 323.

questions on the advice of counsel, and made repeated requests to meet with his attorney, which were denied.

Under the totality of these circumstances, Spano's confession must be rejected as involuntary.[28]

The Court has also considered cases in which it found the police tactics used were not coercive. For example in 1941 in the case of *Lisenba v. California*,[29] the Court considered the voluntariness of a murder confession. The confession was obtained after two successive rounds of police questioning separated by eleven days. During the first round of questioning, which focused on an unrelated incest charge, the police questioned Lisenba for a period of two or three days. During this period, Lisenba was given very little sleep, but he was provided with meals. Lisenba did not make any incriminating statements during this interrogation. Approximately eleven days later Lisenba was again questioned. Prior to this questioning, Lisenba consulted with his lawyer. The lawyer told Lisenba he was a suspect in his wife's murder and should not make any statements. During the second round of questioning, Lisenba was confronted with the confession of his co-defendant. Lisenba's requests for counsel were dismissed. The prosecutor then questioned Lisenba throughout the day and into the nighttime. The Court found that sometime around midnight, Lisenba turned to one of the officers and said, "Why can't we go out and get something to eat; if we do, I'll tell you the story." After the meal, Lisenba confessed.

The Court acknowledged that during Lisenba's interrogation the police violated procedures required under state law. However, the Court found the constitutional question to be a separate inquiry. Comparing Lisenba's questioning with the sort of cases it had previously considered, the Court noted:

> We have not hesitated to set aside convictions based in whole or in substantial part upon confessions extorted in graver circumstances. These were secured by protracted and repeated questioning of ignorant and untutored persons, in whose minds the power of officers was greatly magnified; who sensed the adverse sentiment of the community and the danger of mob violence; who had been held incommunicado, without the advice of friends or of counsel; some of whom had been taken by officers at night from the prison into dark and lonely places for questioning. This case is outside the scope of those decisions.[30]

---

[28] Id. at 324.

[29] Lisenba v. California, 314 U.S. 219 (1941).

[30] Id. at 239–40.

The Court found that the police tactics used on Lisenba came "close to the line." But on balance, the Court concluded that his statements were voluntary and therefore admissible.[31]

As you will read in the next chapter (**Chapter 26**), if *Lisenba* and *Spano* were decided today, their unheeded requests for counsel would have violated their *Miranda* rights—under *Miranda*, the police must generally cease all questioning once a suspect requests an attorney. However, both cases were decided before the Court created the *Miranda* rule. In the absence of *Miranda*'s prophylactic warning requirement, the cases were therefore resolved entirely on the question of voluntariness. In *Spano*, the Court held that the continuous questioning and use of a childhood friend to deceive the suspect failed that more lenient standard. In *Lisenba*, the Court reached the opposite conclusion.

3. Exploitation of Coercion from Non-Police Sources. In addition to banning torture, relentless questioning coupled with sleep deprivation, and psychologically coercive tactics, the Court has also found that the police may not **knowingly** exploit external threats to accomplish a confession that would have been prohibited had the threat been communicated by an officer:

> **Example—*Arizona v. Fulminante*, 499 U.S. 279 (1991):** Oreste Fulminante was suspected in the murder of his eleven-year-old step daughter, Jeneane. Fulminante had been caring for the child while her mother, Fulminante's wife, was in the hospital. While in Fulminante's care, the girl disappeared. In the early hours of September 14, 1982, Fulminante called the police to report the child missing. Two days later, the girl's body was found in the desert. The child was found partially undressed with a rope around her neck, and she had been shot twice in the head. The condition in which the body was found suggested sexual abuse, but it was impossible to confirm this fact because of extreme decomposition.
>
> Fulminante quickly became a suspect in the killing, but the police could not marshal sufficient evidence to charge him. Thereafter, Fulminante left town. He was subsequently arrested in New Jersey on federal gun charges and was incarcerated at the federal correctional institution in Raybrook, New York.
>
> Anthony Sarivola was an inmate at Raybrook with Fulminante. Unbeknownst to Fulminante, Sarivola was an FBI informant and convicted police officer who was posing as a member of the

[31] Id. at 240–41.

mafia. As rumors of Fulminante's suspected involvement in his stepdaughter's death spread, Fulminante began to receive threats from other inmates. Under instructions from the FBI, Sarivola told Fulminante he could offer protection—but Sarivola conditioned this protection on Fulminante telling Sarivola the truth about the girl's death. Fulminante then confessed to Sarivola that he had taken the child to the desert, raped and beaten her, choked her with a rope, made her beg for her life, and then shot her. According to Sarivola's wife, Donna, Fulminante allegedly repeated this confession to her in a car after his release from prison.

Fulminante was thereafter charged with Jeneane's murder. Prior to trial, he moved to exclude his confessions. The trial court denied the motion and the statements were admitted. A jury convicted Fulminante of murder and he was sentenced to death. On appeal, Fulminante argued that his confession to Sarivola had been coerced.

Analysis: The Supreme Court agreed with Fulminante, and held that the trial court improperly admitted his confession to Sarivola.

At the time he elicited the confession from Fulminante, Sarivola was aware that other inmates in the prison had been threatening Fulminante. "The confession was obtained as a direct result of extreme coercion and was tendered in the belief that the defendant's life was in jeopardy if he did not confess."[32] A statement made under this sort of threat of physical violence is the quintessential coerced confession. Actual violence committed by a government agent is not needed for coercion to be found. Rather, because coercion can be either mental or physical, a threat of physical violence (if credible) will suffice.

In this case, Fulminante confessed because he reasonably feared he would be assaulted by other inmates if Sarivola did not protect him. Under these circumstances, his confession was the product of coercion, and was therefore unconstitutionally admitted as evidence.[33]

In contrast, where the police are unaware of the external pressures that are causing a suspect to speak, statements taken from the suspect will not be excluded from evidence. The Court reached this conclusion in a case involving a suspect who confessed because he was told to do so by "the voice of God:"

---

32 Arizona v. Fulminante, 499 U.S. 279, 286 (1991).

33 Id. at 302.

Example—*Colorado v. Connelly*, 479 U.S. 157 (1986): Francis Connelly walked up to a uniformed police officer and announced that he wanted to confess to murder. The officer immediately advised Connelly of his *Miranda* rights. Connelly denied drinking or using any drugs, but admitted that he had in the past been a patient at a mental health facility. When a supervisor arrived on the scene, he again advised Connelly of his rights. Connelly informed the officers that he had come all the way from Boston to confess. The officer then transported Connelly to the police station where Connelly gave a full confession detailing the murder, including identifying the murder scene. The police were able to match up Connelly's confession with an unsolved murder case from the previous year.

Connelly was held overnight, and the next morning was interviewed by a public defender. During this interview, Connelly became disoriented. He told the lawyer that he had been instructed to confess by "voices" that he heard. An initial evaluation found that Connelly was incompetent to stand trial. However, some time later he was found competent. The prosecutor introduced his confession against him at trial, and Connelly was thereafter convicted. On appeal, defense counsel argued that Connelly's confession was involuntary and should have been excluded from evidence where it was compelled by Connelly's belief that he was hearing "the voice of God."

Analysis: The Supreme Court found the statements were properly admitted. "Absent police conduct causally related to the confession, there is simply no basis for concluding that any state actor has deprived a criminal defendant of due process of law."[34]

The mental condition of the suspect is a critical factor in deciding whether statements obtained were voluntary. But mental health standing alone will never be sufficient for a finding of involuntariness. In addition, there must be some evidence of police overreaching. In Connelly's case, there simply was no such evidence.

In reaching its conclusion, the Court noted that the purpose of excluding evidence is to deter future misconduct by the police. Where the police have not acted improperly in the first instance, there is no bad behavior to deter. Consequently, exclusion would serve little purpose.

[34] Colorado v. Connelly, 479 U.S. 157, 164 (1986).

4. Interrogations that "Shock the Conscience." There are times when official misconduct during an interrogation does not fall neatly within one of the categories described above—*e.g.*, physical torture, sleep deprivation, or psychological ploys. In such cases, the tactics used by the police, though defying easy categorization, may nonetheless be distasteful. The question for the reviewing court thus becomes whether the police tactics were sufficiently distasteful to rise to the level of a constitutional violation.

Though not an interrogation case, one of the early cases offering guidance on this question involved police officers who forced a suspect to undergo a medical procedure to empty his stomach after they saw him swallow what they thought to be drugs. Finding that the Due Process Clause of the Fourteenth Amendment had been violated, the Court wrote, "the proceedings by which this conviction was obtained do more than offend some fastidious squeamishness or private sentimentalism about combatting crime too energetically. This is conduct that **shocks the conscience.**"[35]

Many decades later, the Court returned to the question of official misconduct that "shocks the conscience." In *Chavez v. Martinez*, the police officer conducted the interrogation while the suspect lay in the emergency room being treated for serious gunshot wounds. The Court had earlier found in *Mincey v. Arizona* that similar hospital-bed-questioning violated the Due Process Clause.[36] However, in *Chavez v. Martinez*, the Court made clear that to qualify as impermissibly conscience-shocking, the police misconduct in question must be fairly substantial:

> **Example—*Chavez v. Martinez*, 538 U.S. 760 (2003):** Two police officers were in a vacant lot investigating suspected drug activity, when Oliverio Martinez approached them on a bicycle. The officers detained Martinez, and one of the officers conducted a pat-down. He found a knife. When the officer conducting the pat-down yelled, "He's got my gun," his partner pulled her weapon and fired at Martinez, hitting him several times. Martinez was seriously wounded and was transported to the emergency room. While he was awaiting treatment, an officer named Ben Chavez interrogated him for about ten minutes over the course of a forty-five minute period.
>
> Martinez's early answers during the interview largely consisted of his statements, "I'm dying," "I'm choking," and "I don't know." However, later in the interview, Martinez admitted to taking the first officer's gun and pointing it at him. Martinez

[35] Rochin v. California, 342 U.S. 165, 172 (1952).

[36] Mincey v. Arizona, 437 U.S. 385 (1978).

also admitted to using heroin regularly. During the interview, Martinez complained to Chavez that he was not going to answer any more questions until he was treated. However, Chavez ignored this statement and persisted with the questioning. Because Martinez was never charged with any crime, his answers to Officer Chavez's questions were never introduced against him at a criminal trial. However, Martinez, who was left paralyzed and blind as a result of the shooting, filed a civil suit seeking compensation for his injuries. In the § 1983 action, Martinez alleged that Chavez's questioning violated both the Fifth and Fourteenth Amendments. The trial and intermediate appellate courts granted judgment in Martinez's favor. Chavez then appealed the case to the Supreme Court.

Analysis: The Supreme Court found that neither the Fifth Amendment nor the Fourteenth Amendment were violated by Chavez's conduct.

The Fifth Amendment states that no person can be compelled in any criminal case to be a witness against himself. Consequently, there must be at least the initiation of a criminal proceeding before a violation of the amendment will be found. Moreover, though "[s]tatements compelled by police interrogations of course may not be used against a defendant at trial, . . . it is not until their use in a criminal case that a violation of the Self-Incrimination Clause occurs."[37] Certainly, as he lay in his hospital bed, Martinez did not know the answers he was giving would not be used against him. But that is irrelevant to the Fifth Amendment calculus. The reality is that Martinez's statements were not used against him and so the compulsive questioning techniques did not, standing alone, give rise to a violation of the Fifth Amendment.[38]

However, the finding that the Fifth Amendment provided no remedy did not resolve the case. "Our views on the proper scope of the Fifth Amendment's Self-Incrimination Clause do not mean that police torture or other abuse that results in a confession is constitutionally permissible so long as the statements are not used at trial; it simply means that the Fourteenth Amendment's Due Process Clause, rather than the Fifth Amendment's Self-Incrimination Clause, would govern the inquiry in those cases and provide relief in appropriate circumstances."[39]

On the facts before it though, the Court found that Chavez's conduct was not sufficiently egregious to trigger a violation of the Fourteenth Amendment. Chavez had not interfered with the delivery of medical care and had stopped questioning

---

[37] Chavez v. Martinez, 538 U.S. 760, 767 (2003).

[38] But see Mincey, 437 U.S. at 385 (finding that similar questioning of a hospitalized suspect rendered the statements involuntary under the Fifth Amendment, and thus inadmissible in his subsequent criminal trial).

[39] Chavez, 538 U.S. at 773.

at points to allow the doctors to act. The Court also noted that there was a risk that Martinez's statement would be lost if he died without being questioned. In dictum, the Court described the sort of police interrogation tactic that might constitute a violation of the Fourteenth Amendment: when police officers act in a manner that is intended to injure the suspect and that is not justified by any government interest. Such conduct would "most likely . . . rise to the conscience-shocking level."[40]

5. Fruit of the Poisonous Interrogation Tree. In **Chapter 23**, you read that under certain circumstances the fruit of an unreasonable search or seizure will be suppressed. A similar rule applies to involuntary statements. As you read above, unlike un-Mirandized statements, involuntary statements may not be admitted for any purpose. Moreover, where the police are lead to additional evidence ("fruit") by such involuntary statements ("the poisonous tree") that additional evidence will be suppressed along with the statement.[41] In *United States v. Patane*, the Court recognized that the fruit of un-Mirandized statements and the fruit of involuntary statements would receive radically different treatment—"statements taken without *Miranda* warnings (though not actually compelled) can be used to impeach a defendant's testimony at trial, though the fruits of actually compelled testimony cannot."[42]

From *Brown* to *Fulminante* the Court thus laid out the rules governing voluntary confessions that are described above. Keep these rules in mind as you turn to consider in the next chapter the additional layer of protection against coerced confessions that the Court created in *Miranda*.

[40] Id. at 775.

[41] Cf. Wong Sun v. United States, 371 U.S. 471, 485–86 (1963).

[42] United States v. Patane, 542 U.S. 630, 639 (2004); see also New Jersey v. Portash, 440 U.S. 450, 458–59 (1979).

Quick Summary

Coerced confessions may not be used in criminal trials. Their use is banned by the Due Process Clauses of the Fifth and Fourteenth Amendments. Though confessions that are secured through physical violence are clearly prohibited by the demand for voluntariness, the protections afforded are broader than that. Confessions that are secured through mental or psychological torment also are excluded.

Coerced confessions are excluded for three reasons—concern for false evidence, concern about system legitimacy, and a sense that law enforcement should not be allowed to use certain interrogation tactics in the process of enforcing the law.

To be voluntary, the will of the suspect in making the statement may not be overborne. Rather, the statement must be made "freely, voluntarily, and without compulsion."[43] Courts should consider the totality of the circumstances, including violence; threats of violence; sleep deprivation; the withholding of food; the suspect's age; intelligence and education; the provision of warnings; the nature of the police questioning; whether the suspect was held incommunicado for an extended period; and the suspect's access to counsel.

Not all coerced statements will be deemed "involuntary"—if the police did not create the coercive pressures or intentionally use them to elicit a confession, the statement will still be admissible. Thus, if the suspect is operating due to some internal compulsion (like mental illness), his statement may still be "voluntary" within the meaning of the Due Process clause.

Shocking police conduct may give rise to a claim under the Due Process Clause of the Fourteenth Amendment if the police conduct is sufficiently egregious. Finally, the rule regarding alternate uses of involuntary statements is different from the rule that applies to unwarned statements. Involuntary statements not only are excluded as direct evidence of guilt, they are also excluded for impeachment purposes and the non-testimonial fruit of the statements is similarly inadmissible.

[43] Haynes v. Washington, 373 U.S. 503, 513 (1963).

Review Questions

1. The Stash of Guns. James Braxton bought approximately thirty guns during an eight-week period. The purchases came to the attention of the Bureau of Alcohol, Tobacco & Firearms ("ATF"), which began an investigation. The lead agent on the case asked a local trooper to help her find Braxton, who was eventually found at his mother's home. The agent and the trooper met with Braxton at the house. They told him they "needed to talk with him about his gun purchases." Both officers wore uniforms and showed Braxton their badges. The officers never told Braxton he had a right to remain silent, but they also did not tell him he had to answer their questions. The agents were armed, but they kept their weapons holstered throughout the interview. During the hour-long interview, which was conducted around the kitchen table, the ATF agent accused Braxton of "not coming clean." She also told him that his failure to cooperate might result in a five-year prison sentence. Braxton eventually confessed. At the agent's request, Braxton gave her a photo of himself. He also took the officers to his bedroom to show them the cache of weapons, which they seized.

Prior to trial, Braxton moves to suppress 1) his kitchen table confession, 2) the photograph, 3) the identification of Braxton by the gun dealer (based on the photo), and 4) the weapons. Braxton asserted that his statement was involuntary. He also alleged that the photo, the identification, and the weapons were the fruit of his involuntary statements and should be suppressed. Assuming that there is no *Miranda* claim being raised or considered, how is a court likely to decide each of Braxton's claims?

2. Killing the Boss. Phoebe Henry was arrested for killing her supervisor, Bill Withrow. Following her arrest, Henry was questioned for several hours by Detectives White and Machen. The questioning began with Henry being advised of her *Miranda* rights. Within seconds of this warning, Henry asked for a lawyer. However, the detectives ignored the request. Immediately after Henry's request for an attorney, one of the detectives asked, "Why did you shoot him anyway?" Henry responded "Pardon?" The detective then repeated his question. Henry answered that she had written a bunch of checks to her boss and couldn't figure out how much money her boss owed her. Henry also said that she thought her boss had cheated her out of money and that due to her financial problems she was losing her home. Henry then immediately asked if she was "supposed to keep talking without an attorney." At that point, one of the detectives interrupted, saying "Listen, what you tell us we can't use against you right now . . . We'd just would like to know." Henry then launched into an incoherent and rambling statement about her divorce, her head injury during a recent car accident, her boss, her kids, guns, hunting, her time in the war, her desire to be a police officer, and her love of the woods. Over the course of questioning, Henry appeared to be disoriented, scared, and emotional. She also repeatedly asked the detectives to forgive her. Eventually, Henry made a detailed confession.

Prior to trial, Henry challenged the admissibility of her statements. The prosecution conceded that the *Miranda* violation (continuing to question after the invocation of the right to counsel) rendered the statements inadmissible during the prosecution's case-in-chief. However, the prosecution maintained that because the statements were otherwise voluntary, they were admissible for impeachment purposes.

If you are the trial judge considering Henry's motion, how will you find?

3. Interrogations in the Hospital. Early one morning, James Wolfrath checked into the emergency room complaining of a gunshot wound to his arm. Per hospital procedure, the injury was reported to the police and a detective came to the emergency room to take a report. Wolfrath told the detective that he had almost been robbed, and as he was fighting with his assailant, the gun went off. Later that morning, by happenstance, the detectives stopped a car in the area where Wolfrath claimed he had been assaulted. They arrested the two occupants of the car after seeing a gun on the backseat. During the arrest, one of the occupants tossed a note on the ground that had Wolfrath's name on it. During questioning of the two arrestees, the police learned that Wolfrath was not shot while fighting off an assailant, but instead was the would-be robber (along with one of the arrestees). The next day, the police again visited Wolfrath at the hospital. They brought with them the two arrestees and the gun that was found.

Wolfrath was sitting up in bed. His arm was in a sling, and he had undergone surgery approximately an hour earlier to remove the bullet. After reading Wolfrath his *Miranda* rights, the officers told Wolfrath that his confederate had been arrested and was presently waiting outside of the hospital room door. Wolfrath responded, "Yes, I was telling a lie." He then confessed in detail to participating in the attempted robbery. Wolfrath also told the detectives that he had something else to tell them. At that point, Wolfrath confessed to robbing a beauty salon days earlier. When the police brought Wolfrath's confederate into the room a short time later, Wolfrath lunged at him in an unsuccessful attempt to hit him. But, the hospital equipment that he was hooked up to prevented him from leaving the bed.

The detectives relayed the information about the beauty salon robbery to colleagues who were working that case. One of these detectives then visited Wolfrath who was still in the hospital several days later. The detective brought with him the two salon employees. Wolfrath was sitting in a wheelchair in the hallway when the detective arrived. After the two employees identified Wolfrath as their assailant, the detective again read Wolfrath his rights. Wolfrath told the detective that he "wanted to tell him what happened." Wolfrath then provided a detailed statement confessing to the robbery at the salon. He told the detective that he committed the crime with his confederate from the attempted robbery. He also said, "the reason I am telling you this is I want to see him get caught, because he stuck his wife with the gun charge and he has gotten away scot-free."

Wolfrath was charged with both offenses, and he challenged the statements, arguing that they were involuntary. How should the court rule?

4. Hungry, Cold, and Barefoot. After a week-long investigation into a string of cell phone store burglaries, police arrested Samuel Sanders, a nineteen-year-old with a ninth-grade education and two prior convictions for theft. The police arrested him in the middle of the afternoon in an apartment he shared with his girlfriend and took him down to the station in a t-shirt and sweatpants, but with no shoes or socks. He was interrogated off and on for the next five hours by two detectives, Detective Mack and Detective Jones. The police officers properly gave Sanders his *Miranda* warnings, and Sanders waived his *Miranda* rights. After a couple of hours of interrogation, Sanders was shivering and he told the detective he was cold and complained about being barefoot. The police brought him boots and a blanket. After four hours, he told the detective he had been hungry for the entire interrogation, and the police brought him pizza.

After four and a half hours, Sanders began to scream at the detectives, and Detective Mack screamed back at him. Detective Mack told Sanders (falsely) that the police had found his fingerprints at the scene of two of the burglaries and that if he did not confess now, he was facing a lot of time in prison. Then Detective Mack left the room, and Detective Jones sat close to Sanders and began speaking in a sympathetic tone. Jones told Sanders that he understood that Sanders' girlfriend was pregnant and that Sanders was just trying to do the right thing to support her and their unborn child. "These are victimless crimes," Jones said. "The cell phone stores are all insured, so nobody really loses any money." Jones then said: "I know you love your girlfriend and you want her to love you back. A real man would admit to his mistakes, and I know that women like men who can man up and own up to their mistakes."

At that point, Sanders started crying and he admitted to breaking into the cell phone stores, saying "You already have my fingerprints; I might as well come clean." A few minutes later Sanders signed a written statement confessing to all the burglaries.

Sanders now moves to suppress his confession, arguing that although he waived his *Miranda* rights, his statement was involuntarily made. How should the court rule?

FROM THE COURTROOM

ARIZONA v. FULMINANTE

United States Supreme Court, 1991
499 U.S. 279

[Justice WHITE delivered an opinion, part of which was the opinion of the Court (on the issue of voluntariness), and part of which was a dissenting opinion (on the issue of harmless error, which is omitted here). The dissenting opinion was joined by Justices MARSHALL, BLACKMUN, and STEVENS.]

[Chief Justice REHNQUIST delivered an opinion, part of which was the opinion of the Court, (on the issue of harmless error, which is omitted here), and part of which was a dissenting opinion (on the issue of voluntariness). Justices O'CONNOR , KENNEDY, SOUTER, and SCALIA joined his dissenting opinion in part.]

[Justice KENNEDY filed a concurring opinion on the issue of harmless error.]

I

Justice WHITE delivered the majority opinion of the Court for this issue.

Early in the morning of September 14, 1982, Fulminante called the Mesa, Arizona, Police Department to report that his [eleven]-year-old stepdaughter, Jeneane Michelle Hunt, was missing. He had been caring for Jeneane while his wife, Jeneane's mother, was in the hospital. Two days later, Jeneane's body was found in the desert east of Mesa. She had been shot twice in the head at close range with a large caliber weapon, and a ligature was around her neck. Because of the decomposed condition of the body, it was impossible to tell whether she had been sexually assaulted.

Fulminante's statements to police concerning Jeneane's disappearance and his relationship with her contained a number of inconsistencies, and he became a suspect in her killing. When no charges were filed against him, Fulminante left Arizona for New Jersey. Fulminante was later convicted in New Jersey on federal charges of possession of a firearm by a felon.

Fulminante was incarcerated in the Ray Brook Federal Correctional Institution in New York. There he became friends with another inmate, Anthony Sarivola, then serving a [sixty]-day sentence for extortion. The two men came to spend several hours a day together. Sarivola, a former police officer, had been involved in loansharking for organized crime but then became a paid informant for the Federal Bureau of Investigation. While at Ray Brook, he masqueraded as an organized crime figure. After becoming friends with Fulminante, Sarivola heard a rumor that Fulminante was suspected of killing a child in Arizona. Sarivola then raised the subject with Fulminante in several conversations, but Fulminante repeatedly denied any involvement in Jeneane's death. During one conversation, he told Sarivola that Jeneane had been killed by bikers looking for drugs; on another occasion, he said he did not know what had happened. Sarivola passed this information on to an agent of the Federal Bureau of Investigation, who instructed Sarivola to find out more.

Sarivola learned more one evening in October 1983, as he and Fulminante walked together around the prison track. Sarivola said that he knew Fulminante was "starting to get some tough treatment and whatnot" from other inmates because of the rumor. Sarivola offered to protect Fulminante from his fellow inmates, but told him, "'You have to tell me about it,' you know. I mean, in other words, 'For me to give you any help.'" Fulminante then admitted to Sarivola that he had driven Jeneane to the desert on his motorcycle, where he choked her, sexually assaulted her, and made her beg for her life, before shooting her twice in the head.

Sarivola was released from prison in November 1983. Fulminante was released the following May, only to be arrested the next month for another weapons violation. On September 4, 1984, Fulminante was indicted in Arizona for the first-degree murder of Jeneane.

Prior to trial, Fulminante moved to suppress the statement he had given Sarivola in prison, as well as a second confession he had given to Donna Sarivola, then Anthony Sarivola's fiancée and later his wife, following his May 1984 release from prison. He asserted that the confession to Sarivola was coerced, and that the second confession was the "fruit" of the first. Following the hearing, the trial court denied the motion to suppress, specifically finding that, based on the stipulated facts, the confessions were voluntary. The State introduced both confessions as evidence at trial, and on December 19, 1985, Fulminante was convicted of Jeneane's murder. He was subsequently sentenced to death.

Fulminante appealed, arguing, among other things, that his confession to Sarivola was the product of coercion and that its admission at trial violated his rights to due process under the Fifth and Fourteenth Amendments to the United States Constitution. [The Arizona Supreme Court held that the statement was coerced, and ultimately remanded the case with orders to re-try the case wihout Fulminante's statements.]

. . .

II

We deal first with the State's contention that the court below erred in holding Fulminante's confession to have been coerced. The State argues that it is the totality of the circumstances that determines whether Fulminante's confession was coerced, but contends that rather than apply this standard, the Arizona court applied a "but for" test, under which the court found that but for the promise given by Sarivola, Fulminante would not have confessed. In support of this argument, the State points to the Arizona court's reference to *Bram v. United States*. Although the Court noted in *Bram* that a confession cannot be obtained by "'any direct or implied promises, however slight, nor by the exertion of any improper influence,'" it is clear that this passage from *Bram,* which under current precedent does not state the standard for determining the voluntariness of a confession, was not relied on by the Arizona court in reaching its conclusion. Rather, the court cited this language as part of a longer quotation from an Arizona case which accurately described the State's burden of proof for establishing voluntariness. Indeed, the Arizona Supreme Court stated that a "determination regarding the voluntariness of a confession . . . must be viewed in a totality of the circumstances," and under that standard plainly found that Fulminante's statement to Sarivola had been coerced.

In applying the totality of the circumstances test to determine that the confession to Sarivola was coerced, the Arizona Supreme Court focused on a number of relevant facts. First, the court noted that "because [Fulminante] was an alleged child murderer, he was in danger of physical harm at the hands of other inmates." In addition, Sarivola was aware that Fulminante had been receiving "'rough treatment from the guys.'" Using his knowledge of these threats, Sarivola offered to protect Fulminante in exchange for a confession to Jeneane's murder, and "[i]n response to Sarivola's offer of protection, [Fulminante] confessed." Agreeing with Fulminante that "Sarivola's promise was 'extremely coercive,'" the Arizona court declared: "[T]he confession was obtained as a direct result of extreme coercion and was tendered in the belief that the defendant's life was in jeopardy if he did not confess. This is a true coerced confession in every sense of the word."[2]

We normally give great deference to the factual findings of the state court. Nevertheless, "the ultimate issue of 'voluntariness' is a legal question requiring independent federal determination."

Although the question is a close one, we agree with the Arizona Supreme Court's conclusion that Fulminante's confession was coerced. The Arizona Supreme Court found a credible threat of physical violence unless Fulminante confessed. Our cases have made clear that a finding of coercion need not depend upon actual violence by a government agent; a credible threat is sufficient. As we have said, "coercion can be mental as well as physical, and . . . the blood of the accused is not the only hallmark of an unconstitutional inquisition." As in *Payne,* where the Court found that a confession was coerced because the interrogating police officer had promised that if the accused confessed, the officer would protect the accused from an angry mob outside the jailhouse door, so too here, the Arizona Supreme Court found that it was fear of

[2] There are additional facts in the record, not relied upon by the Arizona Supreme Court, which also support a finding of coercion. Fulminante possesses low average to average intelligence; he dropped out of school in the fourth grade. He is short in stature and slight in build. Although he had been in prison before, he had not always adapted well to the stress of prison life. While incarcerated at the age of [twenty-six], he had "felt threatened by the [prison] population," and he therefore requested that he be placed in protective custody. Once there, however, he was unable to cope with the isolation and was admitted to a psychiatric hospital. The Court has previously recognized that factors such as these are relevant in determining whether a defendant's will has been overborne. . . .

physical violence, absent protection from his friend (and Government agent) Sarivola, which motivated Fulminante to confess. Accepting the Arizona court's finding, permissible on this record, that there was a credible threat of physical violence, we agree with its conclusion that Fulminante's will was overborne in such a way as to render his confession the product of coercion. . . .

Chief Justice REHNQUIST, delivered a dissenting opinion on this issue, joined by Justices O'CONNOR, KENNEDY, and SOUTER.

I

The question whether respondent Fulminante's confession was voluntary is one of federal law. "Without exception, the Court's confession cases hold that the ultimate issue of 'voluntariness' is a legal question requiring independent federal determination." In *Mincey v. Arizona*, we overturned a determination by the Supreme Court of Arizona that a statement of the defendant was voluntary, saying "we are not bound by the Arizona Supreme Court's holding that the statements were voluntary. Instead, this Court is under a duty to make an independent evaluation of the record."

The admissibility of a confession such as that made by respondent Fulminante depends upon whether it was voluntarily made. "The ultimate test remains that which has been the only clearly established test in Anglo–American courts for two hundred years: the test of voluntariness. Is the confession the product of an essentially free and unconstrained choice by its maker? If it is, if he has willed to confess, it may be used against him. If it is not, if his will has been overborne and his capacity for self-determination critically impaired, the use of his confession offends due process."

In this case the parties stipulated to the basic facts at the hearing in the Arizona trial court on respondent's motion to suppress the confession. Anthony Sarivola, an inmate at the Ray Brook Prison, was a paid confidential informant for the FBI. While at Ray Brook, various rumors reached Sarivola that Oreste Fulminante, a fellow inmate who had befriended Sarivola, had killed his stepdaughter in Arizona. Sarivola passed these rumors on to his FBI contact, who told him "to find out more about it." Sarivola, having already discussed the rumors with respondent on several occasions, asked him whether the rumors were true, adding that he might be in a position to protect Fulminante from physical recriminations in prison, but that "[he] must tell him the truth." Fulminante then confessed to Sarivola that he had in fact killed his stepdaughter in Arizona, and provided Sarivola with substantial details about the manner in which he killed the child. At the suppression hearing, Fulminante stipulated to the fact that "[a]t no time did the defendant indicate he was in fear of other inmates nor did he ever seek Mr. Sarivola's 'protection.'" The trial court was also aware, through an excerpt from Sarivola's interview testimony which respondent appended to his reply memorandum, that Sarivola believed Fulminante's time was "running short" and that he would "have went out of the prison horizontally." The trial court found that respondent's confession was voluntary.

The Supreme Court of Arizona stated that the trial court committed no error in finding the confession voluntary based on the record before it. But it overturned the trial court's finding of voluntariness based on the more comprehensive trial record before it, which included, in addition to the facts stipulated at the suppression hearing, a statement made by Sarivola at the trial that "the defendant had been receiving 'rough treatment from the guys, and if the defendant would tell the truth, he could be protected.'" It also had before it the presentence report, which showed that Fulminante was no stranger to the criminal justice system: He had six prior felony convictions and had been imprisoned on three prior occasions.

On the basis of the record before it, the Supreme Court stated:

> Defendant contends that because he was an alleged child murderer, he was in danger of physical harm at the hands of other inmates. Sarivola was aware that defendant faced the possibility of retribution from other inmates, and that in return for the confession with respect to the victim's murder, Sarivola would protect him. Moreover, the defendant maintains that Sarivola's promise was "extremely coercive" because the "obvious" inference from the promise was that his life would be in jeopardy if he did not confess. We agree.

Exercising our responsibility to make the independent examination of the record necessary to decide this federal question, I am at a loss to see how the Supreme Court of Arizona reached the conclusion that it did. Fulminante offered no evidence that he believed that his life was in danger or that he in fact confessed to Sarivola in order to obtain the proffered protection. Indeed, he had stipulated that "[a]t no time did the defendant indicate he was in fear of other inmates nor did he ever seek Mr. Sarivola's 'protection.'" Sarivola's testimony that he told Fulminante that "if [he] would tell the truth, he could be protected," adds little if anything to the substance of the parties' stipulation. The decision of the Supreme Court of Arizona rests on an assumption that is squarely contrary to this stipulation, and one that is not supported by any testimony of Fulminante.

The facts of record in the present case are quite different from those present in cases where we have found confessions to be coerced and involuntary. Since Fulminante was unaware that Sarivola was an FBI informant, there existed none of "the danger of coercion result[ing] from the interaction of custody and official interrogation." The fact that Sarivola was a Government informant does not by itself render Fulminante's confession involuntary, since we have consistently accepted the use of informants in the discovery of evidence of a crime as a legitimate investigatory procedure consistent with the Constitution. The conversations between Sarivola and Fulminante were not lengthy, and the defendant was free at all times to leave Sarivola's company. Sarivola at no time threatened him or demanded that he confess; he simply requested that he speak the truth about the matter. Fulminante was an experienced habitue of prisons, and presumably able to fend for himself. In concluding on these facts that Fulminante's confession was involuntary, the Court today embraces a more expansive definition of that term than is warranted by any of our decided cases.

. . .

[The concurring opinion of Justice KENNEDY is omitted.]

FROM THE COURTROOM

CHAVEZ v. MARTINEZ

United States Supreme Court, 2003
538 U.S. 760

[Justice THOMAS announced the judgment of the Court and delivered an opinion, part of which is the opinion of the Court.]

[Justice SOUTER'S opinion, representing the opinion of the Court in part and concurring in part is omitted.]

[Justice SCALIA filed a concurring opinion.]

[Justice STEVENS filed an opinion concurring in part and dissenting in part.]

[Justice KENNEDY, filed an opinion concurring in part and dissenting in part, which was joined by Justice STEVENS and joined in part by Justice GINSBURG.]

[Justice GINSBURG filed an opinion concurring in part and dissenting in part.]

Justice THOMAS announced the judgment of the Court and delivered an opinion.

This case involves a 42 U.S.C. § 1983 suit arising out of petitioner Ben Chavez's allegedly coercive interrogation of respondent Oliverio Martinez. The United States Court of Appeals for the Ninth Circuit held that Chavez was not entitled to a defense of qualified immunity because he violated Martinez's clearly established constitutional rights. We conclude that Chavez did not deprive Martinez of a constitutional right.

I

On November 28, 1997, police officers Maria Peña and Andrew Salinas were near a vacant lot in a residential area of Oxnard, California, investigating suspected narcotics activity. While Peña and Salinas were questioning an individual, they heard a bicycle approaching on a darkened path that crossed the lot. They ordered the rider, respondent Martinez, to dismount, spread his legs, and place his hands behind his head. Martinez complied. Salinas then conducted a patdown frisk and discovered a knife in Martinez's waistband. An altercation ensued.

There is some dispute about what occurred during the altercation. The officers claim that Martinez drew Salinas' gun from its holster and pointed it at them; Martinez denies this. Both sides agree, however, that Salinas yelled, "'He's got my gun!'" Peña then drew her gun and shot Martinez several times, causing severe injuries that left

Martinez permanently blinded and paralyzed from the waist down. The officers then placed Martinez under arrest.

Petitioner Chavez, a patrol supervisor, arrived on the scene minutes later with paramedics. Chavez accompanied Martinez to the hospital and then questioned Martinez there while he was receiving treatment from medical personnel. The interview lasted a total of about [ten] minutes, over a [forty-five]-minute period, with Chavez leaving the emergency room for periods of time to permit medical personnel to attend to Martinez.

At first, most of Martinez's answers consisted of "I don't know," "I am dying," and "I am choking." Later in the interview, Martinez admitted that he took the gun from the officer's holster and pointed it at the police. He also admitted that he used heroin regularly. At one point, Martinez said "I am not telling you anything until they treat me," yet Chavez continued the interview. At no point during the interview was Martinez given warnings under *Miranda* v.*Arizona*.

Martinez was never charged with a crime, and his answers were never used against him in any criminal prosecution. Nevertheless, Martinez filed suit under Rev. Stat. §1979, 42 U.S.C. §1983, maintaining that Chavez's actions violated his Fifth Amendment right not to be "compelled in any criminal case to be a witness against himself," as well as his Fourteenth Amendment substantive due process right to be free from coercive questioning. The District Court granted summary judgment to Martinez as to Chavez's qualified immunity defense on both the Fifth and Fourteenth Amendment claims. Chavez took an interlocutory appeal to the Ninth Circuit, which affirmed the District Court's denial of qualified immunity. Applying *Saucier* v. *Katz*, the Ninth Circuit first concluded that Chavez's actions, as alleged by Martinez, deprived Martinez of his rights under the Fifth and Fourteenth Amendments. The Ninth Circuit did not attempt to explain how Martinez had been "compelled in any criminal case to be a witness against himself." Instead, the Ninth Circuit reiterated the holding of an earlier Ninth Circuit case, *Cooper* v.*Dupnik*, that "the Fifth Amendment's purpose is to prevent coercive interrogation practices that are destructive of human dignity," and found that Chavez's "coercive questioning" of Martinez violated his Fifth Amendment rights, "[e]ven though Martinez's statements were not used against him in a criminal proceeding," As to Martinez's due process claim, the Ninth Circuit held that "a police officer violates the Fourteenth Amendment when he obtains a confession by coercive conduct, regardless of whether the confession is subsequently used at trial."

The Ninth Circuit then concluded that the Fifth and Fourteenth Amendment rights asserted by Martinez were clearly established by federal law, explaining that a reasonable officer "would have known that persistent interrogation of the suspect despite repeated requests to stop violated the suspect's Fifth and Fourteenth Amendment right to be free from coercive interrogation."

We granted certiorari.

II

In deciding whether an officer is entitled to qualified immunity, we must first determine whether the officer's alleged conduct violated a constitutional right. If not, the officer is entitled to qualified immunity, and we need not consider whether the asserted right was "clearly established." We conclude that Martinez's allegations fail to state a violation of his constitutional rights.

A

1

The Fifth Amendment, [made applicable to the States] by the Fourteenth Amendment, requires that "[n]o person . . . shall be compelled *in any criminal case* to be a *witnesss* against himself." We fail to see how, based on the text of the Fifth Amendment, Martinez can allege a violation of this right, since Martinez was never prosecuted for a crime, let alone compelled to be a witness against himself in a criminal case.

Although Martinez contends that the meaning of "criminal case" should encompass the entire criminal investigatory process, including police interrogations, we disagree. In our view, a "criminal case" at the very least requires the initiation of legal proceedings. We need not decide today the precise moment when a "criminal case" commences; it is enough to say that police questioning does not constitute a "case" any more than a private investigator's pre-complaint activities constitute a "civil case." Statements compelled by police interrogations of course may not be used against a defendant at trial, but it is not until their use in a criminal case that a violation of the Self-Incrimination Clause occurs.

Here, Martinez was never made to be a "witness" against himself in violation of the Fifth Amendment's Self-Incrimination Clause because his statements were never admitted as testimony against him in a criminal case. Nor was he ever placed under oath and exposed to "'the cruel trilemma of self—accusation, perjury or contempt." The text of the Self—Incrimination Clause simply cannot support the Ninth Circuit's view that the mere use of compulsive questioning, without more, violates the Constitution.

2

Nor can the Ninth Circuit's approach be reconciled with our case law. It is well established that the government may compel witnesses to testify at trial or before a grand jury, on pain of contempt, so long as the witness is not the target of the criminal case in which he testifies. Even for persons who have a legitimate fear that their statements may subject them to criminal prosecution, we have long permitted the compulsion of incriminating testimony so long as those statements (or evidence derived from those statements) cannot be used against the speaker in any criminal case. We have also recognized that governments may penalize public employees and government contractors (with the loss of their jobs or government contracts) to induce them to respond to inquiries, so long as the answers elicited (and their fruits) are immunized from use in any criminal case against the speaker. By contrast, no "penalty" may ever be imposed on someone who exercises his core Fifth Amendment right not to be a "witness" against himself in a "criminal case." Our holdings in these cases demonstrate that, contrary to the Ninth Circuit's view, mere coercion does not violate the text of the Self-Incrimination Clause absent use of the compelled statements in a criminal case against the witness.

We fail to see how Martinez was any more "compelled in any criminal case to be a witness against himself" than an immunized witness forced to testify on pain of contempt. One difference, perhaps, is that the immunized witness *knows* that his statements will not, and may not, be used against him, whereas Martinez likely did not. But this does not make the statements of the immunized witness any less "compelled" and lends no support to the Ninth Circuit's conclusion that coercive police interrogations, absent the use of the involuntary statements in a criminal case, violate the Fifth Amendment's Self-Incrimination Clause. Moreover, our cases provide that those subjected to coercive police interrogations have an *automatic* protection from the use of their involuntary statements (or evidence derived from their statements) in any subsequent criminal trial. This protection is, in fact, coextensive with the use and derivative use immunity mandated by *Kastigar* when the government compels testimony from a reluctant witness. Accordingly, the fact that Martinez did not *know* his statements could not be used against him does not change our view that no violation of the Fifth Amendment's Self-Incrimination Clause occurred here.

. . .

Our views on the proper scope of the Fifth Amendment's Self-Incrimination Clause do not mean that police torture or other abuse that results in a confession is constitutionally permissible so long as the statements are not used at trial; it simply means that the Fourteenth Amendment's Due Process Clause, rather than the Fifth Amendment's Self-Incrimination Clause, would govern the inquiry in those cases and provide relief in appropriate circumstances.

B

The Fourteenth Amendment provides that no person shall be deprived "of life, liberty, or property, without due process of law." Convictions based on evidence obtained by methods that are "so brutal and so offensive to human dignity" that they "shoc[k] the conscience" violate the Due Process Clause. Although *Rochin* did not establish a civil remedy for abusive police behavior, we recognized in *County of Sacramento* v.*Lewis*, 523 U.S. 833, 846 (1998), that deprivations of liberty caused by "the most egregious official conduct" may violate the Due Process Clause. While we rejected, in *Lewis*, a § 1983 plaintiff's contention that a police officer's deliberate indifference during a high-speed chase that caused the death of a motorcyclist violated due process, we left open the possibility that unauthorized police behavior in other contexts might "shock the conscience" and give rise to § 1983 liability.

We are satisfied that Chavez's questioning did not violate Martinez's due process rights. Even assuming, *arguendo*, that the persistent questioning of Martinez somehow deprived him of a liberty interest, we cannot agree with Martinez's characterization of Chavez's behavior as "egregious" or "conscience shocking." As we noted in *Lewis*, the official conduct "most likely to rise to the conscience—shocking level" is the "conduct intended to injure in some way unjustifiable by any government interest." Here, there is no evidence that Chavez acted with a purpose to harm Martinez by intentionally interfering with his medical treatment. Medical personnel were able to treat Martinez throughout the interview, and Chavez ceased his questioning to allow tests and other procedures to be performed. Nor is there evidence that Chavez's conduct exacerbated Martinez's injuries or prolonged his stay in the hospital. Moreover, the need to investigate whether there had been police misconduct constituted a justifiable government interest given the risk that key evidence would have been lost if Martinez had died without the authorities ever hearing his side of the story.

The Court has held that the Due Process Clause also protects certain "fundamental liberty interest[s]" from deprivation by the government, regardless of the procedures provided, unless the infringement is narrowly tailored to serve a compelling state interest. Only fundamental rights and liberties which are "'deeply rooted in this Nation's history and tradition"' and "'implicit in the concept of ordered liberty'" qualify for such protection. Many times, however, we have expressed our reluctance to expand the doctrine of substantive due process, in large part "because guideposts for responsible decisionmaking in this unchartered area are scarce and open-ended."

. . .

We . . . must take into account the fact that Martinez was hospitalized and in severe pain during the interview, but also that Martinez was a critical nonpolice witness to an altercation resulting in a shooting by a police officer, and that the situation was urgent given the perceived risk that Martinez might die and crucial evidence might be lost. In these circumstances, we can find no basis in our prior jurisprudence, or in our Nation's history and traditions to suppose that freedom from unwanted police questioning is a right so fundamental that it cannot be abridged absent a "compelling state interest." We have never required such a justification for a police interrogation, and we decline to do so here. The lack of any "guideposts for responsible decisionmaking" in this area, and our oft—stated reluctance to expand the doctrine of substantive due process, further counsel against recognizing a new "fundamental liberty interest" in this case.

We conclude that Martinez has failed to allege a violation of the Fourteenth Amendment, and it is therefore unnecessary to inquire whether the right asserted by Martinez was clearly established.

. . .

[Justice SOUTER'S opinion, representing the opinion of the Court in part and concurring in part is omitted.]

[Justice SCALIA'S concurring opinion is omitted.]

Justice STEVENS, concurring in part and dissenting in part.

As a matter of fact, the interrogation of respondent was [the functional equivalent of an attempt to obtain an involuntary confession from a prisoner by torturous methods.] As a matter of law, that type of brutal police conduct constitutes an immediate deprivation of the prisoner's constitutionally protected interest in liberty. Because these propositions are so clear, the District Court and the Court of Appeals correctly held that petitioner is not entitled to qualified immunity.

I

What follows is an English translation of portions of the tape—recorded questioning in Spanish that occurred in the emergency room of the hospital when, as is evident from the text, both parties believed that respondent was about to die:

"Chavez: What happened? Olivero, tell me what happened.

"O[liverio] M[artinez]: I don't know.

"Chavez: I don't know what happened (sic)?

"O.M.: Ay! I am dying. Ay! What are you doing to me?

"No, …! (unintelligible scream).

"Chavez: What happened, sir?

"O.M.: My foot hurts …

"Chavez: Olivera. Sir, what happened?

"O.M.: I am choking.

"Chavez: Tell me what happened.

"O.M.: I don't know.

"Chavez: 'I don't know.'

"O.M.: My leg hurts.

"Chavez: I don't know what happened (sic)?

"O.M.: It hurts …

"Chavez: Hey, hey look.

"O.M.: I am choking.

"Chavez: Can you hear? Look listen, I am Benjamin Chavez with the police here in Oxnard, look.

"O.M.: I am dying, please.

"Chavez: OK, yes, tell me what happened. If you are going to die, tell me what happened. Look I need to tell (sic) what happened.

"O.M.: I don't know.

"Chavez: You don't know, I don't know what happened(sic)? Did you talk to the police?

"O.M.: Yes.

"Chavez: What happened with the police?

"O.M.: We fought.

"Chavez: Huh? What happened with the police?

"O.M.: The police shot me.

"Chavez: Why?

"O.M.: Because I was fighting with him.

"Chavez: Oh, why were you fighting with the police?

"O.M.: I am dying ...

"Chavez: OK, yes you are dying, but tell me why you are fighting, were you fighting with the police?

. . . . .

"O.M.: Doctor, please I want air, I am dying.

"Chavez: OK, OK. I want to know if you pointed the gun [to yourself] at the police.

"O.M.: Yes.

"Chavez: Yes, and you pointed it [to yourself]? (sic) at the police pointed the gun? (sic) Huh?

"O.M.: I am dying, please ...

. . . . .

"Chavez: OK, listen, listen I want to know what happened, ok ? ?

"O.M.: I want them to treat me.

"Chavez: OK, they are do it (sic), look when you took out the gun from the tape (sic) of the police ...

"O.M.: I am dying ...

"Chavez: Ok, look, what I want to know if you took out (sic) the gun of the police?

"O.M.: I am not telling you anything until they treat me.

"Chavez: Look, tell me what happened, I want to know, look well don't you want the police know (sic) what happened with you?

"O.M.: Uuuggghhh! my belly hurts …

. . . . .

"Chavez: Nothing, why did you run (sic) from the police?

"O.M.: I don't want to say anything anymore.

"Chavez: No?

"O.M.: I want them to treat me, it hurts a lot, please.

"Chavez: You don't want to tell (sic) what happened with you over there?

"O.M.: I don't want to die, I don't want to die.

"Chavez: Well if you are going to die tell me what happened, and right now you think you are going to die?

"O.M.: No.

"Chavez: No, do you think you are going to die?

"O.M.: Aren't you going to treat me or what?

"Chavez: Look, think you are going to die, (sic) that's all I want to know, if you think you are going to die? Right now, do you think you are going to die?

"O.M.: My belly hurts, please treat me.

"Chavez: Sir?

"O.M.:If you treat me I tell you everything, if not, no.

"Chavez: Sir, I want to know if you think you are going to die right now?

"O.M.: I think so.

"Chavez: You think (sic) so? Ok. Look, the doctors are going to help you with all they can do, Ok?. That they can do.

"O.M.: Get moving, I am dying, can't you see me? come on.

"Chavez: Ah, huh, right now they are giving you medication."

The sound recording of this interrogation, which has been lodged with the Court, vividly demonstrates that respondent was suffering severe pain and mental anguish throughout petitioner's persistent questioning.

II

The Due Process Clause of the Fourteenth Amendment protects individuals against state action that either "'shocks the conscience,' or interferes with rights 'implicit in the concept of ordered liberty,'" [Not] every violation of the Fifth Amendment satisfied the second standard. In a host of other cases, however, the Court has held that unusually coercive police interrogation procedures do violate that standard.

By its terms, the Fifth Amendment itself has no application to the States. It is, however, one source of the protections against state actions that deprive individuals of rights "implicit in the concept of ordered liberty" that the Fourteenth Amendment guarantees. Indeed, as I pointed out in my dissent in *Oregon* v. *Elstad*, it is the most specific provision in the Bill of Rights "that protects all citizens from the kind of custodial interrogation that was once employed by the Star Chamber, by 'the Germans of the 1930's and early 1940's,' and by some of our own police departments only a few decades ago." Whenever it occurs, as it did here, official interrogation of that character is a classic example of a violation of a constitutional right "implicit in the concept of ordered liberty."

. . .

Justice KENNEDY, with whom Justice STEVENS joins, and with whom Justice GINSBURG joins as to Parts II and III, concurring in part and dissenting in part.

. . .

III

In my view [the Self- Incrimination Clause is applicable at the time and place police use compulsion to extract a statement from a suspect.] The Clause forbids that conduct. A majority of the Court has now concluded otherwise, but that should not end this case. It simply implicates the larger definition of liberty under the Due Process Clause of the Fourteenth Amendment. Turning to this essential, but less specific, guarantee, it seems to me a simple enough matter to say that use of [torture or its equivalent in an attempt to induce a statement] violates an individual's fundamental right to liberty of the person. The Constitution does not countenance the official imposition of severe pain or pressure for purposes of interrogation. This is true whether the protection is found in the Self-Incrimination Clause, the broader guarantees of the Due Process Clause, or both.

That brings us to the interrogation in this case. Had the officer inflicted the initial injuries sustained by Martinez (the gunshot wounds) for purposes of extracting a statement, there would be a clear and immediate violation of the Constitution, and no further inquiry would be needed. That is not what happened, however. The initial injuries and anguish suffered by the suspect were not inflicted to aid the interrogation. The wounds arose from events preceding it. True, police officers had caused the injuries, but they had not done so to compel a statement or with the purpose of facilitating some later interrogation. The case can be analyzed, then, as if the wounds had been inflicted by some third person, and the officer came to the hospital to interrogate.

There is no rule against interrogating suspects who are in anguish and pain. The police may have legitimate reasons, borne of exigency, to question a person who is suffering or in distress. Locating the victim of a kidnaping, ascertaining the whereabouts of a dangerous assailant or accomplice, or determining whether there is a rogue police officer at large are some examples. That a suspect is in fear of dying, furthermore, may not show compulsion but just the opposite. The fear may be a motivating factor to volunteer information. The words of a declarant who believes his death is imminent have a special status in the law of evidence. A declarant in Martinez's circumstances may want to tell his story even if it increases his pain and agony to do so. The Constitution does not forbid the police from offering a person an opportunity to volunteer evidence he wishes to reveal.

There are, however, actions police may not take if the prohibition against the use of coercion to elicit a statement is to be respected. The police may not prolong or increase a suspect's suffering against the suspect's will. That conduct would render government officials accountable for the increased pain. The officers must not give the impression that severe pain will be alleviated only if the declarant cooperates, for that, too, uses pain to extract a statement. In a case like this one, recovery should be available under § 1983 if a complainant can demonstrate that an officer exploited his pain and suffering with the purpose and intent of securing an incriminating statement. That showing has been made here.

The transcript of the interrogation set out by Justice Stevens, and other evidence considered by the District Court demonstrate [that the suspect thought his treatment would be delayed, and thus his pain and condition worsened, by refusal to answer questions.]

It is true that the interrogation was not continuous. Ten minutes of questions and answers were spread over a [fourty-five]-minute interval. Treatment was apparently administered during those interruptions. The pauses in the interrogation, however, do not indicate any error in the trial court's findings and conclusions.

The District Court found that Martinez ["had been shot in the face, both eyes were injured; he was screaming in pain, and coming in and out of consciousness while being repeatedly questioned about details of the encounter with the police."] His blinding facial wounds made it impossible for him visually to distinguish the interrogating officer from the attending medical personnel. The officer made no effort to dispel the perception that medical treatment was being withheld until Martinez answered the questions put to him. There was no attempt through *Miranda* warnings or other assurances to advise the suspect that his cooperation should be voluntary.

Martinez begged the officer to desist and provide treatment for his wounds, but the questioning persisted despite these pleas and despite Martinez's unequivocal refusal to answer questions.

The standards governing the interrogation of suspects and witnesses who suffer severe pain must accommodate the exigencies that law enforcement personnel encounter in circumstances like this case. It is clear enough, however, that the police should take the necessary steps to ensure that there is neither the fact nor the perception that the declarant's pain is being used to induce the statement against his will. In this case no reasonable police officer would believe that the law permitted him to prolong or increase pain to obtain a statement. The record supports the ultimate finding that the officer acted with the intent of exploiting Martinez's condition for purposes of extracting a statement.

Accordingly, I would affirm the decision of the Court of Appeals that a cause of action under § 1983 has been stated.

26

Interrogations and *Miranda*

Key Concepts

- Both "Custody" and "Interrogation" Are Needed
- Not Just a Prophylactic Rule, a Constitutional Requirement
- Invocation of Rights Must Be Clear and Unambiguous
- But Waiver of Rights Need Only Be Voluntary, Knowing and Intelligent

A. Introduction and Policy. As you read in the prior chapter, the admissibility of any statement that a suspect makes while in police custody is evaluated using a voluntariness test. Was the confession beaten out of the suspect? Was the suspect threatened before providing the statement? These are the sort of questions the voluntariness inquiry under the Fifth and Fourteenth Amendment requires, and voluntariness remains an essential part of a trial court's admissibility determination.

In 1966, however, the Supreme Court determined that something beyond the voluntariness inquiry was required. In the Court's words, "the blood of the accused is not the only hallmark of an unconstitutional inquisition."[1] The Court considered the modern forms of coercion inherent in police-dominated custodial interrogations in *Miranda v. Arizona* and decided that additional protections were needed. There, the Court articulated a four-part recitation to be provided in advance of any custodial interrogation. This four-part recitation has come to be known popularly as "Miranda rights."

In the days following *Miranda*, many thought the required recitation of warnings would so handicap police investigations as to make custodial confessions a thing of the past. The dire predictions of *Miranda*'s impact, however, were vastly overstated. Recent studies suggest that even after being told they need not talk, most suspects waive their rights and agree to speak with investigating officers.[2] As the Court has noted, "*Miranda* has become embedded in routine

---

[1] Miranda v. Arizona, 384 U.S. 436, 448 (1966).

[2] Kit Kinports, The Supreme Court's Love-Hate Relationship with Miranda, 101 J. of Crim. L. and Criminology 375, 379–80 (2011); Richard Leo, Miranda's Irrelevance: Questioning the Relevance of Miranda in the Twenty-First Century, 99 Mich. L. Rev. 1000, 1009 (2001) (noting that as many

police practice to the point where the warnings have become part of our national culture."[3] A Google search for the term "*Miranda* warning" calls up nearly a half-million results; warning cards can be purchased on the internet for as little as $2.00 or printed free; and the *Miranda* litany is a familiar part of virtually every nighttime police drama. In short, *Miranda* has earned an enduring place in the legal landscape of confessions. Let's take a look at the decisions that created and shaped those protections.

B. The Law. The Fifth Amendment to the United States Constitution prohibits **compelled** self-incrimination. Prior to 1966, the question of compulsion was evaluated exclusively using a voluntariness test that considered the totality of the circumstances surrounding the taking of the suspect's statement. But in 1966, the Court determined that simply screening for voluntariness was not enough, and an additional layer of protection was added. In *Miranda v. Arizona*, the Court required that warnings be given to help dissipate the coercion inherent in police-dominated interrogations. As a consequence, when ruling on the admissibility of a challenged statement, a court now must consider not only whether the statement was "voluntary," but also whether police officials complied with *Miranda*. Stated simply:

> Any statements made by a defendant during <u>custodial interrogation</u> by the police are precluded from use in the prosecutor's <u>case-in-chief</u> unless the prosecutor can prove that the defendant understood his rights against self-incrimination and knowingly, voluntarily, and intelligently waived those rights.[5]

Since the *Miranda* warnings were first created in 1966, there have been questions about the source of legal authority for the *Miranda* warnings. In 2000, however, the Court determined once and for all that the decision is firmly grounded in the Constitution. Accordingly, while state legislatures and Congress may amplify *Miranda*'s protections, they may not undercut them. As the Court explained: "*Miranda* being a constitutional decision . . . may not be in effect overruled by an Act of Congress."[5]

The safeguards of *Miranda* are triggered by "custodial interrogation." If a suspect is either not in custody or is not being interrogated, *Miranda*'s protections do not

as 80% of those being interrogated waive their rights). But see generally Paul Cassell, Richard Fowles, Handcuffing the Cops? A Thirty-Year Perspective on Miranda's Harmful Effects on Law Enforcement, 50 STAN. L. REV. 1055 (1998) (arguing that Miranda negatively impacts the rate of crime clearance).

[3] Dickerson v. United States, 530 U.S. 428, 443 (2000).

[4] Miranda, 384 U.S. at 444.

[5] Dickerson, 530 U.S. at 432.

apply. Thus, a court must consider first whether the suspect was "in custody," and second whether the statement was the product of an "interrogation":

1. A suspect is "**in custody**" if there has been a formal arrest or if he is otherwise deprived of his freedom of movement in a **significant** way. However, brief, public detentions (like *Terry* stops or traffic stops) will not constitute *Miranda* custody. This is because these sorts of "comparatively nonthreatening" detentions do not exert the type of pressure that "sufficiently impairs [the detainee's] free exercise of his privilege against self-incrimination."[6] Thus, the question is "was there a formal arrest or restraint on freedom of movement of the degree associated with formal arrest."[7]

2. A suspect is "**interrogated**" when the police directly question him. However, this is not the exclusive test for interrogation. A suspect is also interrogated when the police use "words or actions . . . that they should have known were reasonably likely to elicit an incriminating response."[8]

If a suspect was both in custody and interrogated, the court next must consider whether the government can establish that "procedural safeguards" were provided. In *Miranda*, the Court found that such safeguards include a series of four warnings. Those warnings, which have come to be known as a suspect's *Miranda* rights are:

- You have the right to remain silent;
- If you choose to speak, anything you say may be used as evidence against you;
- You have the right to consult with an attorney before answering any questions and to have the attorney with you during questioning;
- If you cannot afford an attorney, one will be provided for you.[10]

A police department is not required to use the language of *Miranda* verbatim. The privilege against self-incrimination can also be safeguarded by alternate methods so long as those methods convey with equal strength the message of protection provided by the above warnings. For example, the Court recently found sufficient a notice that the suspect, among other things, had "the right to talk to a lawyer

[6] Berkemer v. McCarty, 468 U.S. 420, 437 (1984).

[7] Yarborough v. Alvarado, 541 U.S. 652, 663 (2004) (quoting Thompson v. Keohane, 516 U.S. 99, 112 (1995)).

[8] Rhode Island v. Innis, 446 U.S. 291, 302 (1980).

[9] Id. at 444–45.

before answering any questions," and could exercise the right "at any time during the interview."[10]

However, as the Court has made clear, "unless other **fully effective** means are devised to inform accused persons of their right of silence and to assure a continuous opportunity to exercise it,"[11] the precise warnings articulated by the Court in *Miranda* are required. The Court relied upon this rule when rejecting a proposed alternate that required only that statements be voluntary.[12]

If the suspect has been subjected to custodial interrogation, and if that custodial interrogation was not preceded by adequate warnings, any statements that are the product of the interrogation may not be used in the prosecution's case-in-chief. However, the Court has determined that physical evidence that is recovered as a result of such unwarned statements need **not** be suppressed as "fruit of the poisonous tree" so long as the statements are otherwise voluntary.[13]

If the suspect was subject to custodial interrogation and was given the necessary warnings, the next step in the analysis is to determine whether the suspect invoked his rights. To be effective, invocation of the right to remain silent or the right to counsel must be clearly articulated. Ambiguous statements are not sufficient to activate *Miranda* rights. For example, the Court has held that a suspect's statement, "Maybe I should talk to a lawyer," is not a clear and unambiguous invocation of the right to counsel.[14] In this same vein, the Court has found that a suspect may not invoke the right to remain silent by merely remaining silent.[15] Instead, a clear and direct assertion is needed to trigger *Miranda*'s protections.

Depending upon which right is clearly invoked, differing responses are triggered. The most stringent limits on questioning are imposed following the invocation of the **right to counsel**. Specifically, once a suspect legitimately invokes her right to counsel, all questioning about any subjects must cease until counsel is provided. There are only two exceptions to this categorical rule. The first exception permits police to resume questioning, even after invocation of the right to counsel, if the suspect is the one who reinitiates communication. The second exception allows for renewed questioning after a fourteen-day break in custody. Consequently, even after a suspect invokes the right to counsel, the police may reinitiate questioning and again seek a waiver of the suspect's *Miranda* rights if the suspect has been released from custody for at least fourteen days.

---

[10] Florida v. Powell, 130 S. Ct. 1195 (2010).

[11] Id. at 444.

[12] Dickerson v. United States, 530 U.S. 428 (2000).

[13] United States v. Patane, 542 U.S. 530, 537 (2004).

[14] Davis v. United States, 512 U.S. 452, 462 (1994).

[15] Berghuis v. Thompkins, 560 U.S. 370 (2010).

The invocation of the **right to remain silent** does not trigger similar categorical exclusion of official inquiry. If a suspect legitimately invokes his right to remain silent, the police must simply "scrupulously honor" that request. Unlike with invocation of the right to counsel, this does not mean that all further interrogation on any subject is precluded. While police may not question a suspect about the subject matter of any offense for which a desire to remain silent has been announced, the police may, under certain circumstances, question the suspect about other matters. If the police do resume questioning, the reviewing court will consider a variety of factors in deciding whether the initial invocation was fully respected. For example, changes in police personnel, lengthy breaks between questioning, changes in physical location, the precise language used by the suspect when invoking, and the lack of overlap between offenses will all support that the suspect's articulated desire to remain silent has been scrupulously honored.

If a suspect has invoked his rights, then the police must cease questioning him about that crime. However, if he does **not** invoke his rights, the statements are not automatically admissible. In order to admit the statements, the prosecutor must prove that the suspect has validly **waived** his rights. Waiver is evaluated by looking to the totality of the surrounding circumstances. These circumstances may include things like the suspect's age, education, experience, background, and raw intelligence. The waiver analysis must also consider whether the suspect's ability to understand the warnings and consequences of waiver was in any way impaired. Explicit waiver is not required. Instead, a court must consider all of the facts and circumstances, including the defendant's words and actions to determine if waiver should be found.[16] Waiver exists if a suspect's choice to forgo the protections of *Miranda* is **voluntary, knowing, and intelligent**. In other words, the waiver may not be forced out of the suspect by intimidation, coercion, or deception. In addition, the prosecutor must demonstrate that the suspect was aware of his rights and was aware of the consequences of forsaking them.

Since its 1966 decision, the Court has adjusted the *Miranda* doctrine in many ways. A few of these adjustments were expansions of *Miranda*'s protections: for example, the Court has found that *Miranda* warnings must be given prior to custodial interrogations even if it is not yet certain a criminal prosecution will commence.[17] The Court has also found, as noted above, that interrogation must be defined to include not just direct questioning, but also any words or actions by the police that reasonably should be expected to elicit a response.

---

[16] Fare v. Michael C., 442 U.S. 707 (1979).

[17] Mathis v. United States, 391 U.S. 1, 4 (1968).

However, most of the Court's modifications of *Miranda* have gone in the opposite direction. For example, the Court has narrowly construed the meaning of "custody" for purposes of *Miranda*. Similarly, although the Court has established a fairly low threshold for finding a waiver of rights, it has set a much higher evidentiary bar for invocation to be established. For example, while many would view the statement, "Maybe I should talk to a lawyer," as a relatively clear indication of a suspect's desire for legal assistance, the Court has found this statement is not sufficient to invoke the right to counsel.[18] Similarly, though the Court has agreed that waiver may be found based upon a suspect's behavior, the same is not true with regard to invocation. Invocation of the right to remain silent will not be found simply because the suspect remains silent.[19] The Court has also limited the reach of *Miranda*'s protection. For example, *Miranda* warnings need not be provided to an individual who is being questioned, unbeknownst to her, by an undercover police officer. This rule applies even if the person being interrogated is in custody.[20] In the Court's view, "*Miranda* was not meant to protect suspects from boasting about their criminal activities in front of persons whom they believe to be their cellmates."[21]

A similar limit on the reach of *Miranda* applies to the related exclusion it affords. Though statements taken in violation of *Miranda* may not be used during the prosecution's **case-in-chief**, prosecutors can still use the statements in at least three other ways:

1. The prosecutor can use the statements to impeach the defendant.[22]

2. The statement may lead the prosecutor to other witnesses, who will be allowed to testify in the prosecution's case-in-chief. In other words, if the police question a suspect without *Miranda* warnings and the suspect names another person, the police are free to investigate the named individual. If that investigation ultimately results in the named individual being called as a witness for the prosecution, the witness' testimony is admissible even though disclosure of her identity was the product of a *Miranda* violation.[23]

3. The statement may lead the prosecutor to **physical** evidence, and that physical evidence is admissible against the defendant. This is because the *Miranda* rule only protects against violations of the Fifth Amendment's Self-Incrimination Clause. As the Court has found, the Self-Incrimi-

---

[18] Davis v. United States, 512 U.S. 452, 462 (1994).
[19] Berghuis v. Thompkins, 560 U.S. 370 (2010).
[20] Illinois v. Perkins, 496 U.S. 292 (1990).
[21] Id. at 298.
[22] Harris v. New York, 401 U.S. 222 (1971).
[23] Michigan v. Tucker, 417 U.S. 433 (1974).

> nation Clause cannot be violated by the admission of non-testimonial evidence that is the product of otherwise voluntary statements.[24]

Finally, while *Miranda* warnings must generally be given to any suspect in custody who is being interrogated, the Court has recognized a "public safety" exception to this general rule. Pursuant to this exception, warnings need not be given in advance of custodial interrogation if the police inquiry is directly aimed at mitigating an imminent threat to safety (either the officer's or the public's more broadly).[25] "[T]he doctrinal underpinnings of *Miranda* [do not] require that it be applied in all its rigor to a situation in which police officers ask questions reasonably prompted by a concern for the public safety."[26] For example, if the police arrest a suspect who they believe was recently armed, a question aimed at locating and securing the weapon would be permissible even in the absence of *Miranda* warnings. Along these same lines, the Court indicated in a plurality opinion that *Miranda* warnings need not be given in advance of questions that seek routine biographical data necessary to complete booking procedures. This is sometimes referred to as the "routine booking question" exception to *Miranda*.[27] We will discuss this exception in more detail in **Section 7** below.

Because of all of these exceptions, it is inaccurate to say that *Miranda* warnings are "legally required," as is popularly believed. Instead, it is better to think of *Miranda* warnings as necessary if the police want the statements elicited during custodial interrogation **to be admissible** as part of the prosecutor's case-in-chief. Of course, usually the police **do** want the statements to be admissible, so usually the police do attempt to comply with *Miranda*. But if police officers violate *Miranda* during a custodial interrogation, they are not breaking the law—they are simply limiting the ways in which any statement they elicit can be used. This can be contrasted with violations of the Due Process Clause that we discussed in **Chapter 25**, which are illegal acts that can result not just in exclusion of evidence but also lawsuits and sanctions against the offending police officers. Below is a chart that may help you think through the application of the *Miranda* analysis:

---

[24] United States v. Patane, 542 U.S. 630 (2004).

[25] New York v. Quarles, 467 U.S. 649 (1984).

[26] Id. at 656.

[27] Pennsylvania v. Muniz, 496 U.S. 582, 601–02 (1990).

Was the suspect in custody? (formal arrest or other substantial interference with freedom)	
If the answer to this question is "no," stop here. There was no need for *Miranda* warnings.	If the answer to this question is "yes," move to the next step.

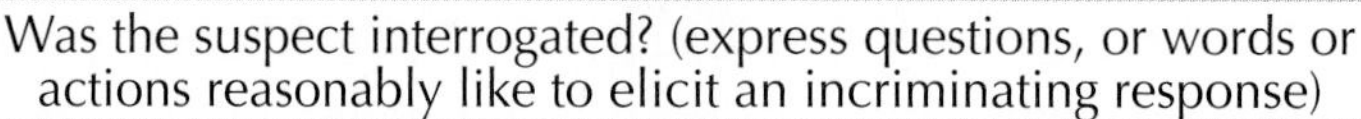

Was the suspect interrogated? (express questions, or words or actions reasonably like to elicit an incriminating response)	
If the answer to this question is "no," stop here. There was no need for *Miranda* warnings.	If the answer to this question is "yes," move to the next step.

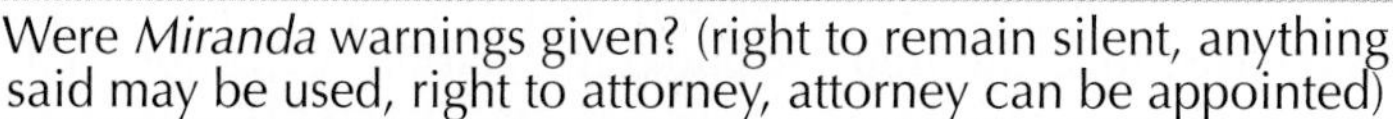

Were *Miranda* warnings given? (right to remain silent, anything said may be used, right to attorney, attorney can be appointed)	
If the answer to this question is "no," statements elicited from the suspect during custodial interrogation are inadmissible during the prosecution's case-in-chief. Such statements may, however, be admitted as impeachment.	If the answer to this question is "yes," move to the next step.

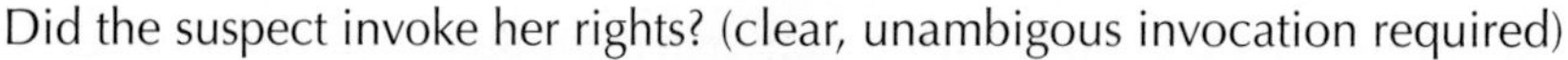

Did the suspect invoke her rights? (clear, unambigous invocation required)		
If the answer to this question is "no," you still must move to the next step to consider whether the suspect waived her rights.	If right to counsel invoked, questioning must cease until counsel is provided, unless suspect indicates desire to renew communication or there is a 14-day break in custody.	If right to remain silent invoked, questioning must cease, unless suspect reinitiates or questioning is about other crimes and police "scrupulously honor" original silence.

Did the suspect waive her rights? (voluntary, knowing and intelligent waiver is required)	
If the answer to this question is "no," statements elicited from the suspect during custodial interrogation are inadmissible during the prosecution's case-in-chief. Such statements may, however, be admitted as impeachment evidence.	If the answer to this question is "yes," any statements elicited from the suspect may be introduced into evidence provided they were voluntarily made.

C. Applying the Law. The familiar litany of *Miranda* rights that police officers read to custodial suspects is now viewed as relatively uncontroversial in most quarters. But when the required warnings were first announced in 1966, the dissenting justices anticipated disaster—"[i]n some unknown number of cases the Court's rule will return a killer, a rapist or other criminal to the streets and to the environment which produced him, to repeat his crime whenever it pleases him."[28] In the late 1960's, crime rates were increasing around the country, and many cities were experiencing severe civil unrest in response to our national legacy of racial inequality. Against this historic backdrop, the *Miranda* decision was seen in some quarters as an inexplicable gift to criminals. In terms of legal doctrine, the case represented a radical departure from the then-prevailing determination that the admissibility of a suspect's statement turned only on its voluntariness.

By most accounts, however, the disaster predicted in the *Miranda* dissent never came to pass. Since 1966, the Court has sometimes expanded but more often contracted the reach of *Miranda.* Meanwhile, law enforcement has largely learned to investigate cases within its confines. Let us now consider the case that started it all:

> **Example—*Miranda v. Arizona*, 384 U.S. 436 (1966):** In the early spring of 1963, an eighteen-year-old girl in Phoenix, Arizona was kidnapped and raped. Ten days after the assault, Ernesto Miranda was arrested and taken to the police station for questioning. At the time he was twenty-three years old, had not completed the ninth grade, and was indigent.
>
> At the station, the victim picked Miranda out of a line-up. Miranda was then interrogated by two police officers. The interrogation lasted approximately two hours. During the course of the interrogation, Miranda confessed and provided officers with a signed, written statement detailing the crime. The police did not threaten Miranda, nor was there any evidence that he had been physically abused. However, prior to giving the statement, Miranda was not provided counsel and was not advised that he had the right to counsel or the right to remain silent.
>
> At trial, the state introduced Miranda's confession into evidence. Based primarily upon the confession and the victim's identification, Miranda was convicted and sentenced to thirty years imprisonment. Following conviction, Miranda challenged the admission of the confession, arguing that the statement violated his Fifth Amendment right against compelled self-incrimination.

[28] Miranda, 384 U.S. at 542.

Analysis: The statement that Miranda provided to the police should have been excluded from evidence.

The privilege against self-incrimination is a foundational thread in the fabric of our nation's constitutional protections. The privilege is an "essential mainstay of our adversary system,"[29] and helps to ensure that a proper balance is struck between the state and the individual. This proper balance also requires that the state shoulder the entire burden in criminal prosecutions. Traditionally, the privilege against self-incrimination was thought to apply primarily in the context of court proceedings. However, there are other settings in which the right must also be enforced if the privilege is to be adequately protected. One such setting is custodial interrogations. Therefore, if the privilege against self-incrimination is to retain value, it must be as jealously guarded in the context of custodial interrogations as it is in the courts.

In the early half of the twentieth century, police interrogations were too often marred by violence, and an aggressive form of questioning known as the third degree. "[T]he police resorted to physical brutality—beatings, hanging, whipping—and to sustained and protracted questioning incommunicado in order to extort confessions."[30] Confessions that were the product of such obvious forms of abuse—and thus violated the privilege against self-incrimination—were deemed "involuntary" and excluded from trial. However, by the latter half of the century, these blatantly corrupt investigatory methods had evolved; "the modern practice of in-custody interrogation is psychologically rather than physically oriented."[31] But even if a confession of the modern era is not "involuntary" in the traditional sense, it may nonetheless be a product of compulsion if steps are not taken to ensure that statements are truly the product of free choice.

One way to combat this psychological pressure and to ensure that the defendant's confession is truly voluntary is to "adequately and effectively apprise [the defendant] of his rights" and then "fully honor" the exercise of those rights. Otherwise the in-custody interrogation process "contains inherently compelling pressures which work to undermine the individual's will to resist and to compel him to speak where he would not otherwise do so freely."

Consequently, before any custodial interrogation occurs, the accused must be provided with adequate warnings. These warnings include four cautions. First, the police must advise the suspect of his right to remain silent. Next, the suspect must be told that if he chooses to speak, anything he says can be used as evidence against him. Third, the suspect must be told that he has a right to an attorney both prior to and during questioning. Finally, if the accused cannot afford an attorney, he must be informed that one will be provided. The specific language of the warnings is not talismanic. If local jurisdictions craft other fully effective

[29] Id. at 460.

[30] Id. at 446.

[31] Id. at 448.

means for notifying a suspect of her rights and assuring that the rights will be scrupulously honored, those jurisdictions are free to use those alternate measures.

Once adequate warnings have been given, the suspect may either invoke his rights—to remain silent and/or to counsel—or may waive them. If the suspect invokes his rights, questioning must cease. If the suspect waives his rights, the government must demonstrate that this waiver was knowingly and intelligently made.

Ernesto Miranda's confession should have been suppressed because he was not provided with any warnings before confessing to the kidnapping and rape of the victim.[32]

The Supreme Court's decision in *Miranda* simultaneously resolved three other criminal appeals (*Vignera v. New York*, *Westover v. United States*, and *California v. Stewart*). In each of these cases, the Court determined that reversal of the conviction was required either because warning had not been given in advance of the interrogation or because the suspect had not waived his rights before confessing.[33]

After *Miranda*, the Court began the process of fine-tuning the new rules as it applied them to different fact patterns. In these subsequent cases, the Court teased out the meaning of "custody" and the definition of "interrogation." The Court also evaluated what precisely a suspect needs to do to invoke her rights, along with what is required to waive them. The Court has carefully considered how police can resume questioning after rights have been invoked. Finally, the Court has determined when warnings given midway (as opposed to at the beginning) of questioning are sufficient.

1. Custody. The *Miranda* warnings must be given only if a suspect is being interrogated while "in custody." If the suspect is not in custody, the *Miranda* Court's concerns about inherent coercion are substantially reduced, and protective counter-measures are not required.[34] But what does it mean to be "in custody"? At one extreme, custody could entail the mere presence of a police officer at the time of questioning. At the other extreme, custody might only be accomplished if the suspect is locked behind bars. The Court has found that custody for *Miranda* purposes falls somewhere between these poles. Thus, the presence of law enforcement agents is insufficient to trigger *Miranda*, and the fact that an interview takes place at the stationhouse is neither necessary nor sufficient to trigger *Miranda*.[35] It is also not enough that the suspect has become the focus of the investigation.[36] Instead, the test for custody is **whether an individual's freedom has been suf-**

---

[32] Miranda, 384 U.S. at 492.

[33] Id. at 494, 496–98.

[34] Beckwith v. United States, 425 U.S. 341, 347 (1976).

[35] Oregon v. Mathiason, 429 U.S. 492 (1977).

[36] Id. at 345.

ficiently restricted. Such restriction may happen at the stationhouse, but it also may happen at one's home:

> **Example—*Orozco v. Texas*, 394 U.S. 324 (1969):** Reyes Arias Orozco was at a restaurant in Dallas, Texas with a female friend. At the restaurant, a man made advances to Orozco's companion. Later outside of the restaurant, Orozco and the man got into a fight. The man hit Orozco repeatedly in his face and referred to him by an ethnic slur. A single shot was then fired, killing Orozco's assailant. Orozco left the scene and returned to the boardinghouse where he was staying. At around 4:00 that morning four police officers arrived at the boardinghouse to arrest Orozco.
>
> After being admitted to the house by a woman who lived there, the police entered Orozco's bedroom and started questioning him. Without first advising Orozco of his rights, the police asked if he had been at the restaurant in question earlier in the evening. The police then asked if Orozco owned a gun. Orozco at first did not answer the question, but when the police asked again, Orozco told them that the gun was in a washing machine located in another room in the house. The gun was linked to the killing by a ballistics match.
>
> At trial, one of the officers who was present at the boardinghouse was allowed to testify to Orozco's admission that he had been at the restaurant, and to his statements regarding the location of the gun. Following conviction, Orozco challenged the admission of his uncounseled statements.

Analysis: Orozco was in custody at the time of the police questioning. Therefore, *Miranda* warnings were required before he could be interrogated. In the absence of such warnings, the admission of the statements was error.

The law does not require that a suspect be confined to a police station before custody will be found. In addition, custody may be found if a suspect's freedom is otherwise significantly restricted.

Orozco was in his own bed in the familiar space of his own room at the time of his questioning. However, he was also "under arrest and not free to leave when he was questioned in his bedroom in the early hours of the morning."[37] For this reason, he was in custody for purposes of *Miranda*, and warnings were required before he was interrogated. In the absence of these warnings, reversal of his conviction was required.

[37] Orozco, 394 U.S. at 327.

Not only does custody not require that the suspect be confined at the police station or local jail, custody also does not require that the suspect's confinement be for the offense under investigation. The warnings required by *Miranda* are not dependent upon the reason for a suspect's custody. Rather, the only relevant concern is whether custody exists.[38]

Official restraint on a suspect's movement is an important factor in the analysis. But, the Court has further explained that "the freedom-of-movement test identifies only a necessary and not a sufficient condition for *Miranda* custody."[39] For example, when a driver is stopped for a traffic violation, the officer exercises control over the driver's freedom of movement. Nonetheless, the Court has refused to extend *Miranda* protections to ordinary traffic stops because "the temporary and relatively nonthreatening detention involved in a traffic stop or *Terry* stop . . . does not constitute *Miranda* custody."[40] Similarly, a probation officer may require a probationer to regularly appear for scheduled meetings. However, as with traffic stops, these encounters do not constitute "custody" for purposes of *Miranda*.[41] In addition to the existence of restrictions on freedom of movement, the Court considers whether the restrictions exert so much pressure upon the detained person that she might be unwilling (or unable) to freely exercise her privilege against self incrimination. If such pressure exists, *Miranda* warnings will be required.[42]

A closer question is presented by the case of incarcerated individuals. But here too, the Court has found that members of the general prison population are not automatically in custody within the meaning of *Miranda*, stating "without minimizing the harsh realities of incarceration, we think lawful imprisonment imposed upon conviction of a crime does not create the coercive pressures identified in *Miranda*."[43] The Court has likewise declined to find that all prisoners who are removed from the general population for questioning are categorically "in custody."[44]

As you have read, putting aside "comparatively non-threatening" seizures like *Terry* stops or traffic stops, the test for custody is whether a reasonable person would have felt free to terminate the contact with the police. But should this test account at all for the characteristics of the accused? For example, in determining whether an individual was "in custody" at the time of questioning, should a court acknowledge that a teenager will likely experience an interaction with the police differently than a middle-aged adult? The Court first considered this

---

[38] Mathis, 391 U.S. at 4–5.

[39] Maryland v. Shatzer, 559 U.S. 98, 112 (2010).

[40] Id. at 113; see also Berkemer v. McCarty, 468 U.S. 420 (1984).

[41] Minnesota v. Murphy, 465 U.S. 420 (1984).

[42] Berkemer, 468 U.S. at 437.

[43] Shatzer, 559 U.S. at 113.

[44] Howes v. Fields, 132 S. Ct. 1181 (2012).

question in *Yarborough v. Alvarado*, and found that the test was a purely objective one. Accordingly, the Court determined that the age and inexperience of the seventeen-year-old suspect in *Alvarado* were not necessarily relevant to the question of whether he was in custody for purposes of *Miranda*.[45] Several years later, however, the Court revisited the question. Considering the questioning of a thirteen-year-old suspect, the Court clarified that while the *Miranda* custody test is an objective one, it should nonetheless account for the age of the detainee to the extent that such is known or reasonably knowable to the police:

> **Example—*J.D.B. v. North Carolina*, 131 S. Ct. 2394 (2011):** J.D.B was a thirteen-year-old seventh grader in Chapel Hill, North Carolina. He was also a suspect in several recent home burglaries in the area. After property from one of the break-ins was found at the school, a police officer investigating the crimes came to J.D.B.'s school to question him. The officer removed J.D.B. from his afternoon social studies class and brought him to a conference room. The uniformed police officer then questioned J.D.B. for approximately thirty minutes in the presence of another police officer and two school administrators. The door to the conference room was closed throughout the questioning, and J.D.B. was not told that he was free to leave. J.D.B. also was not told he could speak to his grandmother, who was his legal guardian. Prior to the questioning, the police did not advise J.D.B. of his *Miranda* rights. After J.D.B. confessed that he and a friend were responsible for the break-ins, the officer advised J.D.B. that he could refuse to answer any questions and told him that he was free to leave. J.D.B. continued to answer questions and ultimately submitted a written statement at the officer's request.
>
> Subsequently, J.D.B. was charged in juvenile court with the burglaries. Prior to trial, defense counsel moved to suppress J.D.B.'s statements, alleging that he had been subject to a custodial interrogation without the benefit of *Miranda* warnings. The trial court found that J.D.B. was not in custody and therefore denied suppression. On appeal, the North Carolina Supreme Court specifically found that J.D.B.'s age was not a relevant factor in making the custody determination. The Supreme Court then granted certiorari to review the issue.

[45] Yarborough v. Alvarado, 541 U.S. 652 (2004).

Analysis: The Supreme Court held that a child's age is a relevant factor in assessing *Miranda* custody. The Court agreed that the test for custody under *Miranda* is an objective one. In particular the Court noted:

> [b]y limiting analysis to the objective circumstances of the interrogation, and asking how a reasonable person in the suspect's position would understand his freedom to terminate questioning and leave, the objective test avoids burdening police with the task of anticipating the idiosyncrasies of every individual suspect and divining how those particular traits affect each person's subjective state of mind.[46]

However, the Court further noted that in applying the objective standard, reviewing courts should not be blind to the fact that "children are not adults."[47] Unlike other personal traits, a child's age provides a reviewing court with information that does not require any inquiry into the subjective understanding of the particular child in question. Children, as a demographic group, will often feel coercive pressure in situations where adults do not. Accordingly, "[n]either officers nor courts can reasonably evaluate the effect of objective circumstances that, by their nature, are specific to children without accounting for the age of the child subjected to those circumstances."[48]

The *J.D.B.* Court was careful to note that a child's age is not determinative of the *Miranda* custody question, and indeed may not even be a significant factor in every case. However, so long as a child's age is known to the officer at the time of the interrogation or would have been objectively apparent to any reasonable officer, it is properly considered in the *Miranda* custody analysis.

2. Interrogation. Custody is not the sole triggering condition for *Miranda* warnings; the suspect must also be under "interrogation" by the police. When is an interrogation taking place? Again, there are extreme cases on either end which are simple to resolve: voluntary, spontaneous statements by an individual are not protected by the language of *Miranda*, while statements made in response to a direct question from the police are clearly within its scope. But what about situations that are in between these extremes?

In *Miranda*, the Court stated that it intended custodial interrogation to mean "questioning initiated by law enforcement officers."[49] Certainly, this language could be construed to extend only to explicit queries directly addressed to the suspect by a police officer. However, the Court has decided that this is too limited an interpretation of the *Miranda* holding. Instead, interrogation includes not just express questioning but also its **"functional equivalent."** The functional

[46] J.D.B. v. North Carolina, 131 S. Ct. 2394, 2402 (2011).

[47] Id. at 2404.

[48] Id. at 2405.

[49] Miranda, 384 U.S. at 444.

equivalent of direct questioning includes "any words or actions on the part of the police (other than those normally attendant to arrest and custody) that the police should know are reasonably likely to elicit an incriminating response from the suspect."[50]

So what counts as the "functional equivalent" of interrogation? The Court evaluated this question in a case in which police officers engaged each other in a conversation in the suspect's presence, eventually resulting in the suspect's confession:

> **Example—*Rhode Island v. Innis*, 446 U.S. 291 (1980):** A cab driver in Providence, Rhode Island contacted the police just after midnight and said that he had just been robbed by a man carrying a shotgun. The driver told the police that he discharged the man who robbed him near the campus of Rhode Island College. While the driver was waiting at the police station to give a statement, he coincidentally saw a picture of Thomas Innis on a bulletin board and identified him as the robber.
>
> A few hours later an officer on routine patrol saw Innis on the street. The officer arrested him and searched him, but did not find a shotgun. As additional officers arrived on the scene, they advised Innis of his *Miranda* rights numerous times. In response to the last advisement, Innis said that he wanted to talk to a lawyer. A police captain who was present instructed three officers to take Innis to the stationhouse and told them not to ask him any questions.
>
> En route to the police station, two of the officers began talking about the missing shotgun. One officer said to the other "there's a lot of handicapped children running around in this area, and God forbid one of them might find a weapon with shells and they might hurt themselves."[51] The other officer responded that it would be a shame if a little girl found the gun and accidentally killed herself. As the officers were talking, Innis interrupted and told them to turn the car around so that he could show them where to find the weapon. Innis was again advised of his rights, but responded that while he understood, he wanted to help them find the gun so that children in the area wouldn't get hurt. Innis drove the officers to a field and showed them where they could find the gun.

---

[50] Rhode Island v. Innis, 446 U.S. 291, 301 (1980).

[51] Id. at 294–95.

When Innis was later charged with kidnapping, robbery, and murder in a related case, he moved to suppress his statements and the weapon. Innis maintained that he expressly invoked his right to counsel and therefore should not have been further interrogated. The trial court rejected his challenged, and Innis was subsequently convicted. However, the Rhode Island Supreme Court agreed and reversed Innis's convictions. The Supreme Court granted certiorari to define "interrogation" for purposes of *Miranda.*

Analysis: The conversation between the two police officers in Innis' presence did not constitute interrogation as contemplated by *Miranda* because it was not reasonably likely to elicit a response.

There was no question that Innis was fully informed of his rights. There was also no question that Innis invoked his right to counsel by telling the police captain he wished to speak with an attorney. Finally, there was no question that Innis was "in custody" as he was being transported to the police station. The only question was whether the conversation between the two police officers amounted to the "functional equivalent" of the interrogation of the suspect.

Though something other than direct questioning may constitute interrogation on the right facts, the conversation between the patrol officers in *Innis* did not amount to the functional equivalent of interrogation. In the Court's view, because the officers had no reason to believe that Innis might be particularly susceptible to an expressed concern about the safety of handicapped children, their conversation could not be said to be deliberately aimed at eliciting a response. Innis was neither disoriented nor particularly upset when he was arrested. And, the conversation between the officers was not a "lengthy harangue." Innis was certainly subject to subtle compulsion. But, a finding of interrogation requires more. Under these circumstances, Innis "was not subjected by the police to words or actions that the police should have known were reasonably likely to elicit an incriminating response from him."[52]

The police can be quite creative in devising tactics to persuade a suspect to "spontaneously" begin talking about a crime. In one case, a suspect accused of killing a woman and stealing furs from her apartment was read his *Miranda* rights and refused to make a statement. The police put him back in his cell and then dumped the stolen furs (which they had recovered) in front of his cell without comment. He then agreed to speak. The New York Court of Appeals ruled that the dumping of the furs was an "interrogation."[53] However, other techniques have been deemed **not** to be interrogation, such as: discussing in front of the suspect the

[52] Id. at 303.

[53] People v. Ferro, 63 N.Y.2d 316 (1984).

possibility that the investigation may have to involve his girlfriend and family;[54] explaining the extent of the incriminating evidence against the defendant;[55] and showing the defendant a surveillance photo of himself committing the crime.[56]

The Court has also held that *Miranda* warnings do not have to be provided to an individual who is interrogated by an undercover officer, even if the individual is in custody. However, readers should note that once the individual is charged with the crime, this interrogation technique will violate the Sixth Amendment:

> **Example—*Illinois v. Perkins*, 496 U.S. 292 (1990):** An inmate at an Illinois prison told the police that fellow inmate Lloyd Perkins talked to him about an unsolved murder. During these conversations, Perkins admitted responsibility for the killing. The police found the reported confession credible because Perkins was said to have mentioned details of the murder that had not been publicized. Consequently, an undercover officer was sent into the facility where Perkins was being held to gather additional information. Posing as an inmate, the undercover, with the help of the original inmate, engaged Perkins in conversations. When the undercover asked Perkins if he had ever "done" anybody, Perkins answered that he had. He then provided the undercover with details of the murder under investigation. Perkins was not advised of his *Miranda* rights prior to making these statements.
>
> When Perkins was later charged with the murder, he moved to suppress the statements he made to the undercover officer.

Analysis: The Supreme Court found that *Miranda* warnings were not required before the undercover agent questioned Perkins. *Miranda* warnings are intended to mitigate some of the compulsion that is present in the police-dominated atmosphere of traditional custodial interrogation. "When a suspect considers himself in the company of cellmates and not officers, the coercive atmosphere is lacking."[57] Put somewhat differently, if a person does not know he is talking with police officers, the concerns identified in *Miranda* are irrelevant. There is no question that once a suspect has been charged with a crime, the Sixth Amendment prevents the use of undercover agents to interrogate that suspect. But here, the case was still under investigation, and Perkins had not yet been charged. On these facts, the absence of *Miranda* warnings had no effect on the admissibility of the confession the undercover officer elicited from Perkins.[58]

[54] United States v. Thierman, 678 F.2d 1331 (9th Cir. 1982).

[55] United States v. Hodge, 487 F.2d 945 (5th Cir. 1973).

[56] United States v. Davis, 527 F.2d 1110 (9th Cir. 1976).

[57] Illinois v. Perkins, 496 U.S. 292, 296 (1990).

[58] Id.

3. Invocation of Rights. The *Miranda* Court held that custodial questioning must cease if the suspected offender indicates "in any manner . . . that he wishes to consult with an attorney."[59] The Court likewise found that questioning should cease "if the individual is alone and indicates in any manner that he does not wish to be interrogated."[60] However, despite the relatively broad language of *Miranda* ("in any manner"), subsequent Courts have declined to give the plain text the liberal application it suggests. Since *Miranda*, the Court has determined that an invocation of rights must be relatively specific to be effective. For example, in *United States v. Davis*, discussed below, the Court found that a suspect's statement "Maybe I should talk to a lawyer," was insufficient to qualify as an invocation of the right to counsel:

> **Example—*Davis v. United States*, 512 U.S. 452 (1994):** Davis, a sailor in the United States Navy, was playing pool with another sailor. A bet on the game resulted in the other sailor owing Davis thirty dollars. The other sailor refused to pay. His body was later found on a loading dock behind the commissary. He had been beaten to death with a pool cue. Davis eventually became a suspect in the murder.
>
> Davis was questioned by Navy investigators. As required by naval law, they advised Davis that he was a suspect in the killing. They also advised him of his right to counsel, of his right to silence, and of the fact that his statements could be used against him. Initially Davis waived his rights both in writing and orally. However, after about an hour and a half of questioning Davis said, "Maybe I should talk to a lawyer."[61] The interrogating officers responded that they did not wish to violate Davis's rights and asked if he was requesting a lawyer or was instead just making a comment about a lawyer. At that point, Davis responded, "No, I'm not asking for a lawyer. . . . No, I don't want a lawyer." The questioning then continued for about another hour, at which point Davis said, "I think I want a lawyer before I say anything else." Questioning then ceased.
>
> Davis was subsequently tried in military court for the murder. His motion to suppress some of the statements made during the interrogation was denied. Davis was found guilty of unpremeditated murder and sentenced to confinement for life. The reviewing military court found that Davis's statement was ambiguous

[59] Miranda, 384 U.S. at 444.

[60] Id. at 445. See also Edwards v. Arizona, 451 U.S. 477 (1981).

[61] Davis v. United States, 512 U.S. 452, 455 (1994).

and therefore was properly rejected as an invocation of his right to counsel. The Supreme Court then took the case up to resolve the question of how ambiguous statements should be treated for purposes of *Miranda* invocation.

Analysis: The Supreme Court held that Davis had not invoked his right to counsel.

As a general rule, if a suspect properly invokes the right to counsel during custodial interrogation, questioning must cease until counsel is provided or the suspect reinitiates questioning. However, to properly invoke the right, it is not enough that a suspect make some vague mention of counsel. At a minimum, proper invocation of the right requires a statement that can at least reasonably be understood as a clear assertion of the desire for a lawyer. If all that can be said is that the suspect "might" be invoking the right, questioning need not cease. "Although a suspect need not speak with the discrimination of an Oxford don, he must articulate his desire to have counsel present sufficiently clearly that a reasonable police officer in the circumstances would understand the statement to be a request for an attorney."[62]

Davis's statement, "Maybe I should talk to a lawyer," was not a clear request for counsel. Therefore it did not require the immediate cessation of questioning. The motion to suppress was therefore properly denied.

Indeed, the Court has imposed its demand for a clear invocation of the right to counsel even on children being questioned by the police:

Example—*Fare v. Michael C.*, 442 U.S. 707 (1979): Michael C., a sixteen-year-old from Van Nuys, California, was implicated in the murder of a man named Robert Yeager. Yeager was killed during a robbery of his home. Michael C. became implicated in the crime after a witness reported seeing a truck that was registered to Michael C.'s mother near the scene. Another witness reported that a teen fitting Michael C.'s description was seen in the area at the time of the killing.

At the time of his arrest, Michael C. was on probation for an unrelated offense. He had been on probation since he was twelve years old.

At the stationhouse, two police officers began the interrogation by advising the teen of his *Miranda* rights. After they advised Michael C. of his right to the presence of an attorney, he asked

[62] Id. at 459 (internal citations and quotations omitted).

"Can I have my probation officer here?"[63] The officer indicated that he would not be able to track down the probation officer, but reiterated that Michael C. had the right to counsel—"Well I can't get a hold of your probation officer right now. You have the right to an attorney."[64] Thereafter, one of the officers asked if Michael C. was willing to talk with them without an attorney present. Michael C. said that he was. During the ensuing interrogation, Michael C. made statements and drew sketches that were incriminating.

A case was then filed in juvenile court accusing Michael C. of the murder. Prior to the trial, Michael C. moved to suppress his statements and sketches. Specifically, he argued that his request for the presence of his probation officer should have been treated as a request for counsel. In support of this theory, Michael C. introduced evidence of a very close relationship with his probation officer. Michael C.'s probation officer testified at the hearing and explained that he had warned Michael C. to immediately contact him if Michael was ever involved with the police. The probation officer also testified that he had chastised Michael C. on past occasions when the teen had come into contact with the police and had not immediately notified him. The California Supreme Court found that because Michael C. was a minor his request to have his probation officer present should have been treated as an invocation of his rights. The court therefore found that the statements the teen made after that invocation should have been suppressed.

Analysis: The California Supreme Court was wrong. Michael C.'s request for the presence of his probation officer was not tantamount to a request for counsel. Accordingly, questioning did not need to cease once this request was made.

In *Miranda*, the Court imposed a bright line rule that requires questioning to cease when an accused requests an attorney. The rigidity of *Miranda* serves a very specific purpose: "the lawyer is the one person to whom society looks as the protector of the legal rights of that person in his dealings with the police and the courts."[65] In contrast, a probation officer does not share this same unique space. A probation officer is an arm of law enforcement, and as such oftentimes will not zealously and single-mindedly protect the rights of the accused. It is therefore inappropriate to impose a *per se* rule that every juvenile's request for their proba-

[63] Fare v. Michael C., 442 U.S. 707, 710 (1979).

[64] Id.

[65] Id. at 720.

tion officer should be treated as an invocation of rights. Moreover, the fact that a particular youth might share a close relationship with his probation officer also does not justify likening the request for the officer to a request for counsel under *Miranda*. If the closeness of the relationship alone were sufficient, a request for any trusted adult figure would suffice to trigger *Miranda* protections. This result cannot be squared with the specific logic of *Miranda*.

The request for the officer also should not be treated as a request to remain silent. The request for a probation officer is a factor a reviewing court may consider in evaluating whether *Miranda* rights have been waived. But, it is not, standing alone, an invocation of those rights. Even in the absence of a *per se* rule, the burden remains on the prosecution to establish that an accused has waived his rights. However, on this record it is clear that Michael C. was adequately advised of his rights and thereafter knowingly and voluntarily chose to waive them.[66]

The Court has imposed a similarly restrictive view on the type of conduct that will successfully constitute invocation of the right to remain silent:

Example—*Berghuis v. Thompkins*, 560 U.S. 370 (2010): During the winter of 2000, two men were shot outside of a mall in Southfield, Michigan. One of the men died. The other lived and testified against his attacker. Van Thompkins, who quickly became a suspect in the shooting, fled the state. A year later, he was found and arrested in Ohio. While Thompkins was in Ohio awaiting extradition to Michigan, two police officers from Southfield traveled to Ohio to question Thompkins.

At the outset of the interview, the officers provided Thompkins with *Miranda* warnings. When asked to sign the form to indicate that he understood his rights, Thompkins refused. Even so, over the course of the next three hours, the officers questioned Thompkins. Though he provided two or three one-word responses, Thompkins largely sat silent during the questioning. Toward the end of the interview, one of the officers asked Thompkins if he believed in God. Thompkins responded that he did. The officer then asked Thompkins, "Do you pray to God to forgive you for shooting that boy down?" Thompkins responded, "Yes."

Thereafter, Thompkins was charged with first degree murder. He moved to suppress the statement he made during interrogation. Thompkins's argument was that his persistent silence over

[66] Id. at 726.

the course of some two and three-quarter hours constituted an invocation of his right to remain silent and therefore required the police to end questioning.

Analysis: A suspect may not invoke his right to remain silent by remaining silent. Rather, an invocation of rights must be definite. "If an accused makes a statement concerning the right to counsel 'that is ambiguous or equivocal' or makes no statement, the police are not required to end the interrogation or ask questions to clarify whether the accused wants to invoke his or her *Miranda* rights."[67] A similar rule is appropriate in the context of the right to remain silent.

Thompkins could have said he did not want to talk with the police. He also could have said he wanted to remain silent. However, where he did neither of these, he should not be deemed to have invoked his rights.

In the absence of an invocation, Thompkins's statement was admissible if it could be found that he waived his rights. Unlike the invocation of rights, the waiver of rights needn't be explicit. "As a general proposition, the law can presume that an individual who, with a full understanding of his or her rights, acts in a manner inconsistent with their exercise has made a deliberate choice to relinquish the protection those rights afford."[68] Thompkins was provided with full warning of his *Miranda* rights. Thereafter, he behaved in a manner that was inconsistent with the exercise of those rights. It matters not at all that this behavior came only after an extended period of ambiguous conduct. "The fact that Thompkins made a statement about three hours after receiving a *Miranda* warning does not overcome the fact that he engaged in a course of conduct indicating waiver."[69]

4. Waiver of Rights. As the above discussion demonstrates, if a suspect does not expressly invoke her rights, the next question is whether she may be deemed to have waived them. The waiver of *Miranda* rights must be voluntary, knowing, and intelligent.[70] More fully describing what this requires, the Court has said that voluntariness means the waiver is "the product of a free and deliberate choice rather than intimidation, coercion, or deception."[71] To establish the knowing and intelligent aspect of the waiver, it "must have been made with a full awareness both of the nature of the right being abandoned and the consequences of the decision to abandon it."[72] Mere silence on the part of the police as to the true scope of the interrogation will not constitute deception sufficient to override the legitimacy of a waiver:

---

[67] Berghuis v. Thompkins, 560 U.S. 370, 380 (2010).

[68] Id. at 2262.

[69] Id. at 2263.

[70] Colorado v. Spring, 479 U.S. 564 (1987).

[71] Id. at 573.

[72] Id.

> a suspect's awareness of all the possible subjects of questioning in advance of interrogation is not relevant to determining whether the suspect voluntarily, knowingly, and intelligently waived his Fifth Amendment privilege.[73]

Certainly, if a suspect states plainly, "I wish to waive my rights. I don't want a lawyer. I would like to speak with you," there is no question that any subsequent interrogation complies with the strictures of *Miranda*. But what if the suspect is not as direct? What if the suspect says nothing or says something ambiguous? How should a court resolve such uncertainty? The Supreme Court addressed precisely this question in a North Carolina robbery case:

> **Example—*North Carolina v. Butler*, 441 U.S. 369 (1979):** Willie Butler was accused of robbing a gas station in Goldsboro, North Carolina with a friend named Elmer Lee. The station attendant was shot by his assailants, and though he was paralyzed, he survived to identify his attackers.
>
> Thereafter, a fugitive warrant was issued in North Carolina, and Butler was arrested in the Bronx by FBI agents acting on the warrant. The agent who arrested Butler immediately advised him of his *Miranda* rights. Butler was then transported to a nearby FBI office in New Rochelle, NY. There, the agents presented Butler with an advice-and-waiver-of-rights form. Butler, who had an eleventh-grade education and could read, reviewed the form and told the agents he understood his rights. He then said: "I will talk to you but I am not signing any form." Thereafter, Butler was questioned by the police and made statements that connected him to the Goldsboro robbery and shooting. Butler never requested counsel and never made any effort to end the interrogation.
>
> At trial, the prosecution offered the testimony of the injured station attendant. The prosecution also offered Butler's inculpatory statements made during the FBI interrogation. The jury convicted Butler of kidnapping, armed robbery, and felony assault. On appeal, Butler argued that his statements were improperly admitted. Specifically, Butler maintained that waiver of *Miranda* rights should be strictly interpreted. Accordingly, because he refused to sign the waiver form and failed to provide a specific oral waiver of his right to counsel, Butler asserted that any statements taken in the absence of an express waiver of his

[73] Id. at 577.

rights had to be excluded. The North Carolina Supreme Court agreed, and the State appealed to the Supreme Court.

Analysis: The North Carolina court erred in suggesting custodial statements could be admitted only if a specific and express waiver of rights was proven.

There is no question that an individual may waive her rights by providing police with a specific statement to that effect. There is also no question that mere silence will not constitute a waiver of rights. However, waiver may be found when a person who has not expressly waived her rights nonetheless engages in a course of conduct from which waiver may be clearly inferred.

When evaluating waiver, courts must consider all of the suspect's words and actions to determine if waiver can be clearly inferred therefrom. On the record in this case, there is no reason that Willie Butler must be presumed not to have waived his right to counsel simply because he did not do so expressly.[74]

In the years after *Butler*, the Court provided more explicit guidance on the evaluation of waivers. The Court explained that the assessment of waiver is an assessment of the totality of the circumstances. The relevant circumstances include:

1. the age of the suspect;
2. her experience;
3. her education;
4. her background;
5. her intelligence; and
6. her actual capacity to understand both any warnings that have been given and the consequences of waiver.[75]

The Court deployed this totality analysis in *Moran v. Burbine* when it considered whether a suspect's waiver of his rights should be deemed valid even if he was unaware, at the time of the waiver, that a family member had already taken steps to secure counsel:

Example—*Moran v. Burbine*, 475 U.S. 412 (1986): Moran was arrested for burglary in Cranston, Rhode Island. During the course of the interrogation, the police officer learned that Moran's nickname was "Butch." The officer knew that the suspect in an unsolved murder in nearby Providence was nicknamed "Butch," and he contacted the Providence police department,

[74] North Carolina v. Butler, 441 U.S. 369 (1979).

[75] Fare v. Michael C., 442 U.S. 707, 726 (1979).

That same evening, Moran's sister contacted the public defender's officer to obtain representation for her brother in connection with the burglary. In response, an assistant public defender called the police station, indicated that she was acting as Moran's lawyer, and notified the officer that she would like to be present for any questioning. The police told the attorney that they were through with Moran for the night and that he would not be placed in a line up or questioned further. They did not tell her that the Providence police had arrived to question Moran about the unsolved murder, and Moran himself was not notified of his sister's efforts to secure counsel or of the call by the attorney.

About an hour later, Moran was questioned by the Providence police officers about the murder. On three separate occasions during this questioning, Moran was advised of his rights by the Providence police, and he waived in writing his right to remain silent or his right to an attorney. Moran eventually signed three written statements confessing to the murder.

Prior to trial, Moran moved to suppress these statements, alleging that his waiver of his rights was not knowing and voluntary. The trial court denied the motion, finding that the call by the attorney had absolutely no bearing on the validity of Moran's waiver. The case eventually worked its way up to the Supreme Court.

Analysis: The validity of Moran's waiver of his rights was not affected by his lack of awareness that an attorney called to make her services available.

The waiver of *Miranda* rights must be voluntary, knowing, and intelligent. The voluntariness aspect of waiver demands that the waiver be the product of a free and deliberate choice instead of the product of coercion or intimidation. The knowing and intelligent aspect requires that a suspect understand both the nature of the right being abandoned and the consequences of that abandonment. Thus, the waiver is valid if the totality of the circumstances surrounding an interrogation reflects the requisite absence of coercion and the required comprehension. Moran's waiver reflected both an absence of coercion and the necessary level of comprehension on his part.

There was no suggestion that Moran's waiver was the product of physical or psychological pressure. Accordingly, there was no suggestion that his waiver was anything but voluntary. Instead, Moran's only claim was that his waiver had not been knowing and intelligent because he was deprived of the information that an attorney willing to represent him had called the station prior to his waiver. Moran's lack of information did not affect his understanding of the rights he held or his appreciation for the consequence of relinquishing those rights. Accordingly, the police officer's failure to inform him of the attorney's call had no affect on the legitimacy of his waiver. "Events occurring outside of the presence of the suspect and entirely unknown to him surely can have no bearing on the capacity to comprehend and knowingly relinquish a constitutional right."[76]

Remember, even a finding of valid waiver does not relieve the prosecution of its obligation to establish that the suspect's statements were also **voluntary** within the tradition Fifth Amendment construction of that term. However, "cases in which a defendant can make a colorable argument that a self-incriminating statement was 'compelled' despite the fact that the law enforcement authorities adhered to the dictates of *Miranda* are rare."[77]

5. Can Communication with a Suspect Be Resumed After Invocation of Rights? After a suspect has invoked either the right to remain silent or the right to counsel, the next question is what happens from there. With regard to invocation of the right to remain silent, the *Miranda* Court said, "[i]f the individual indicates in any manner, at any time prior to or during questioning, that he wishes to remain silent, **the interrogation must cease**."[78] With regard to invocation of the right to counsel, the Court said, "[i]f . . . he indicates in any manner and at any stage of the process that he wishes to consult with an attorney before speaking **there can be no questioning**."[79] Read literally, these instructions might be understood to mean that upon invocation the police must leave the subject alone forever after. However, that is not the way the Court has interpreted the rules.

If a suspect invokes the right to remain silent, the legality of resumed communication will turn first on whether the police or the individual resumes conversation. In cases where the individual resumes the conversation, standard inquiries by the suspect that are a simple function of the custodial relationship—a request to use the bathroom, for example—**will not** authorize resumed questioning. However, a statement by the suspect that indicates a renewed desire to explore the underlying substance of the investigation **will** empower the police to renew their interrogation in full.

A different rule applies if the police resume the conversation. After an appropriate break, the police may reopen questioning on their own initiative only if they "scrupulously honor" the suspect's articulated desire to remain silent. In other words, when the police resume questioning, they, as a general rule, may question the suspect about a new or unrelated offense if they do not inquire in any man-

[76] Moran v. Burdine, 475 U.S. 412, 422 (1986).

[77] Dickerson, 530 U.S. at 444.

[78] Miranda, 384 U.S. at 473.

[79] Id. at 444–5.

ner about the substantive offense for which the right to remain silent has been invoked:

> **Example—*Michigan v. Mosley*, 423 U.S. 96 (1975):** Richard Mosley was arrested based upon his suspected involvement in two robberies. After transporting Mosley to the police station, the arresting detective fully advised him of his *Miranda* rights. The detective then began to interrogate Mosley about the robberies. After Mosley indicated that he did not want to answer any questions about the robberies, the interrogation ended, and Mosley was taken to a holding cell on a separate floor.
>
> Approximately two hours later, a second detective retrieved Mosley from the cell block and brought him to a new interrogation room on yet another floor of the station. This second detective again fully advised Mosley of his *Miranda* rights. This detective also provided Mosley with written notification of his rights, which Mosley read aloud and signed. This second detective then proceeded to question Mosley about a murder that had occurred some months earlier. The murder was wholly unconnected to the robberies that were the subject of Mosley's arrest.
>
> Mosley initially claimed that he had nothing to do with the shooting. However, after the second detective advised Mosley that the other person present at the shooting had implicated him, Mosley made some comments that connected him to the murder. The entire interrogation regarding the murder took no more than fifteen minutes. During the interview, Mosley never invoked his right to remain silent, nor did he request a lawyer. Mosley was subsequently indicted for murder.
>
> Prior to trial, Mosley sought to suppress his statement. Mosley maintained that the second interrogation regarding the murder was inadmissible because he had invoked his right to remain silent while he was with the first detective. Mosley argued that the initial invocation completely precluded any and all additional questioning.

Analysis: Mosley's statements to the second detective were properly admitted at his murder trial. The language in *Miranda* indicating that questioning must cease once a suspect has invoked his right to remain silent cannot be read to foreclose forever any further interrogation by the police. "[Nothing] in the *Miranda* opinion can sensibly be read to create a *per se* proscription of indefinite duration upon any further questioning by any police officer on any subject, once the person in custody has indicated a desire to remain silent."[80] Instead any resumption of questioning must be evaluated by considering whether the suspect's right to cut off questioning was "scrupulously honored."

Mosley's request to cut off questioning in connection with the robbery investigation was scrupulously honored. The first detective immediately ended the interrogation after Mosley said he did not want to talk about the robberies. After his invocation, Mosley was removed from the interrogation room and returned to the cell block. He remained in the cellblock for more than two hours before he was approached by the second detective. This second detective questioned Mosley in a different physical location from the first interrogation, and Mosley was fully Mirandized before the second interrogation began. Moreover, the second interrogation focused completely on the murder investigation and never returned to the initial subject of the robberies.

Because the police fully respected Mosley's stated desire not to talk about the robberies, his invocation of the right to remain silent was scrupulously honored, and the subsequent questioning about the murder was permissible.[81]

The rule regarding resumption of questioning following a request for **counsel** is somewhat different. Once an accused expresses a desire for counsel, he may not be "subject[ed] to further interrogation by the authorities until counsel has been made available to him, unless the accused himself initiates further communication, exchanges, or conversations with the police."[82] Thus, while this rule is more stringent than the rule governing invocation of the right to remain silent, the rule poses no impediment if an accused requests counsel and then volunteers information without further prompting or otherwise suggests a desire to resume communications with the police:

> **Example—*Oregon v. Bradshaw*, 462 U.S. 1039 (1983):** A teenager named Lowell Reynolds was found dead in a pickup truck that had swerved off the road, hit a tree, and flipped into a creek. The truck was lying on its passenger side, with Reynolds still inside, when it was found. Reynolds, the passenger in the truck, was determined to have been killed by a combination of the physical trauma of the accident and drowning. The police eventually came to suspect James Bradshaw as having some role in the accident. He was questioned at the stationhouse shortly after Reynolds's death.

80 Michigan v. Mosley, 423 U.S. 96, 102–03 (1975).

81 Id. at 107.

82 Edwards v. Arizona, 451 U.S. 477, 484–85 (1981).

After he was advised of his rights at the station, Bradshaw admitted that he had given Reynolds alcohol for a party that Reynolds was throwing. Bradshaw, however, disclaimed any knowledge of the accident. Based on his confession, the police arrested Bradshaw for supplying liquor to a minor. They also repeated his *Miranda* warnings. When a police detective advised Bradshaw of his theory—that Bradshaw had been driving the truck at the time of Reynolds's death—Bradshaw stated, "I do want an attorney before it goes very much further."[83] The officer did not ask Bradshaw any further questions.

Shortly thereafter, Bradshaw was transported from the police station to the local jail. During the ride, Bradshaw asked the transporting officer, "Well, what is going to happen to me now?" The officer informed Bradshaw that he did not have to talk to him. The officer also suggested that Bradshaw might help his cause if he agreed to take a polygraph test. The next day, Bradshaw was advised of his rights for a third time. He took the polygraph test, but failed. Bradshaw then admitted that he had been driving the truck but was drunk, and he passed out, causing the truck to crash into the creek.

Bradshaw was charged with first degree manslaughter and other related charges. He challenged the use of his confession at trial. The trial court found the confession was admissible. However, the Oregon appellate court disagreed. The Supreme Court granted certiorari to determine whether Bradshaw's query—"What is going to happen to me now?"—was sufficient to authorized renewed questioning by the police after he had invoked his right to counsel.

Analysis: Bradshaw's statement constituted a generalized re-initiation of communication with the police. Accordingly, the subsequent interrogation of Bradshaw, which produced his confession, was entirely permissible.

Once an accused has invoked the right to counsel, generally all questioning must cease. Under such circumstances, even if the accused re-initiates communication, the burden remains on the prosecution to demonstrate that the totality of the circumstances evince a knowing and voluntary waiver of the suspect's rights.

---

[83] Oregon v. Bradshaw, 462 U.S. 1039, 1041–42 (1983).

There are some perfunctory inquiries or statements by an accused that will never be reasonably viewed as inviting renewed interrogation. These sorts of entreaties might include asking for a glass of water or asking to use the telephone. However, other inquiries do in fact suggest a desire for fuller engagement with the police. The question that reviewing courts must ask is whether the suspect's statements "represent a desire on the part of an accused to open up a more generalized discussion relating directly or indirectly to the investigation."[84] If the statements can be interpreted in this fashion, renewed interrogation will be permissible, assuming waiver is also found.

In the Court's view, Bradshaw demonstrated a desire for continued discussion about the investigation when he asked the transporting officer, "What's going to happen to me now?" Because the police did not improperly resume questioning after an invocation of the right to counsel, the only question was one of legitimate waiver. Waiver was appropriately found on this record where Bradshaw was properly advised of his rights, requested an attorney, and then shortly thereafter engaged in a course of conduct that, without improper influence from the police, clearly suggested he had changed his mind.[85]

The dissent in *Bradshaw* harshly rebuked the majority decision. The defense did not quibble with the majority's determination that a suspect might re-initiate communication even after invoking the right to counsel. However, the defense criticized the further conclusion that the question "What's going to happen to me now?" could be viewed as representing Bradshaw's generalized desire to discuss the investigation of Reynolds' death. Bradshaw had just been moved from the interview room to the back of a police car. He was en route somewhere but had not yet been told where. Accordingly, in the dissent's view, "under the circumstances of this case, it is plain that respondent's only desire was to find out where the police were going to take him."[86]

Since its decision in *Bradshaw*, the Court has also found that an invocation of the right to counsel does not exist into perpetuity to ward off all future attempts at questioning. If there is a sufficient break in custody, the invocation will no longer prohibit future interrogation. In the Court's view a **"sufficient break" is a period of at least fourteen days**. In short, if a suspect is subject to custodial interrogation and requests a lawyer, the police must terminate the questioning. However, if the suspect is then released from custody for a period of fourteen days, the police are free to re-approach the suspect and attempt to secure a waiver of the suspect's *Miranda* rights. In the Court's view, when "a suspect has been released from his pretrial custody and has returned to his normal life for some time before

84 Id. at 1045.

85 Id. at 1046.

86 Id. at 1055.

the later attempted interrogation, there is little reason to think that his change of heart regarding interrogation without counsel has been coerced."[87]

6. Midstream *Miranda* Warnings. Yet another issue raised by *Miranda* is the timing of the warnings. *Miranda* indicated that warnings need to be given "prior to any questioning."[88] However, on occasion, the police will have some conversation with an accused before warnings are given. While the pre-*Miranda* statements are almost always deemed inadmissible, a question exists as to the treatment of statements provided **after** warnings were given. In 1985, the Court considered this question for the first time, and found that *Miranda* warnings given after a brief period of initial questioning were sufficient to insulate the second phase of questioning from the first uncounseled stage:

> **Example—*Oregon v. Elstad*, 470 U.S. 298 (1985):** Nearly $150,000 worth of property was taken from the home of the Gross family during a burglary. A witness identified Michael Elstad as the thief. Elstad was eighteen at the time and was friends with one of the Gross children. Police officers went to Elstad's home. There, they spoke briefly with his mother in the kitchen to explain what was happening. At the same time, a second officer sat with Elstad in the living room. This second officer asked Elstad if he knew why the officers were there. Elstad said he did not. The officer then asked if Elstad knew the Gross family or knew that their home had been broken into. The officer also told Elstad that he thought Elstad was involved. At that point, Elstad turned to the officer and admitted he had been there. There was no dispute that Elstad was in custody at the time.
>
> Elstad was then transported to the station. At the station two different officers read Elstad his rights. After waiver, Elstad gave a full confession. Prior to trial on the burglary charges, Elstad moved to suppress his statement. The trial court denied the motion, and Elstad was convicted and sentenced to five years.

Analysis: Though the brief preliminary questioning that occurred in the living room was inadmissible, Elstad's subsequent statement was properly admitted because it was secured following notice and a valid waiver of his *Miranda* rights. Elstad's subsequent confession was not tainted by his earlier statement to the

[87] Maryland v. Shatzer, 559 U.S. 98, 107 (2010).

[88] Miranda, 384 U.S. at 444.

police officer in his parents' living room. Without question, the unwarned statement had to be suppressed in accordance with *Miranda*. And if the first statement had been coerced (rather than just taken in violation of *Miranda*), the improper police conduct would have precluded any future statement as well. However, "absent deliberately coercive or improper tactics in obtaining the initial statement, the mere fact that a suspect has made an unwarned admission does not warrant a presumption of compulsion [as to the second statement]."[89]

On this record, the Court found Elstad's second statement was free of compulsion. He was fully advised of his rights before giving the statement and provided a valid waiver before confession. Moreover, though Elstad's earlier statement was taken in violation of *Miranda*, there was no suggestion that this statement was "involuntary" within the meaning of the Fifth Amendment. In short, "a suspect who has once responded to unwarned yet uncoercive questioning is not thereby disabled from waiving his rights and confessing after he has been given the requisite *Miranda* warnings."[90]

The Court's decision in *Elstad* appeared to be driven at least in part by its determination that the initial error of not providing Elstad with *Miranda* warnings was not a deliberate police strategy. Several years later, police officers—no doubt aware of the *Elstad* holding—decided to deliberately conduct a two-stage interrogation. They conducted the first stage without *Miranda* warnings and the second stage after *Miranda* warnings. In this case, the Court found the belated provision of *Miranda* warnings could not insulate the second confession given:

Example—*Missouri v. Seibert*, 542 U.S. 600 (2004): Twelve year old Jonathan Seibert died in his sleep. Jonathan had cerebral palsy, and his death seemingly was of natural causes. However, Jonathan's mother feared that his physical condition—bedsores—would lead to charges of neglect. Accordingly, Jonathan's mother, Patrice Seibert, devised a plan with her teenaged sons and their friends to burn the family trailer down. To avoid an accusation that Jonathan was left unattended, Seibert instructed the teens to burn the trailer while Donald Rector, a mentally disabled teenager who lived with the family, was at the home sleeping. The teens proceeded with the scheme as planned, and Donald Rector was killed.

Several days after the fire, a police officer took Seibert in for questioning. Pursuant to department practice, the officer did not advise Seibert of her rights. He then questioned her for more than thirty minutes. During this questioning, Seibert admitted

89 Oregon v. Elstad, 470 U.S. 298, 314 (1985).

90 Id. at 318.

that she knew Donald Rector would likely die in the fire. After a short break, the officer turned on a tape recorder and gave Seibert *Miranda* warnings. After obtaining a signed waiver, he walked Seibert back through her earlier confession. During this second half of the interview, the officer repeatedly referred back to things Seibert said before warnings were given.

In her first degree murder trial, Seibert moved to suppress the pre- and post-warning statements. The trial court agreed that the pre-warning statements should be suppressed. However, it found that the post-warning statements were admissible. The case was ultimately appealed to the Supreme Court.

Analysis: The deliberate practice of pre-warning questioning used on Patrice Seibert violated both the letter and spirit of *Miranda.*

The practice of "question first, warn later" must be evaluated with an eye toward its effect on a suspect's practical ability to later exercise her rights. In the instant case, there can be no question that the police engaged in the practice to render pointless the *Miranda* warnings eventually provided to Seibert. "By any objective measure . . . it is likely that if the interrogators employed the technique of withholding warnings until after interrogation succeeds in eliciting a confession, the warnings will be ineffective in preparing the suspect for successive interrogation, close in time and similar in content."[91] Once the police have obtained the first confession, it will take little effort to secure the second even if warnings are provided between the two.

In evaluating whether midstream *Miranda* warning will be deemed effective, a court should consider a series of factors:

1. The completeness and detail of the questions and answers in the first round of interrogation;
2. The overlapping content of the two statements;
3. The timing and setting of the first and the second rounds of questioning;
4. The continuity of police personnel;
5. The degree to which the interrogator's questions treated the second round as continuous with the first.

Applying these considerations to Seibert's interrogation, the Court found that the midstream warnings did not insulate the later statements. The two statements were taken in the same physical location and were interrupted by just a twenty-minute break. Seibert was never told that her first statement could not be used, and the same officer conducted both phases of the interrogation. The questioning

[91] Missouri v. Seibert, 542 U.S. 600, 613 (2004).

officer also encouraged an impression that the two phases were interconnected by repeatedly referring back to the first session during the second. "It would have been reasonable to regard the two sessions as part of a continuum . . . a reasonable person in the suspect's shoes would not have understood [the belated warnings that were given] to convey a message that she retained a choice about continuing to talk."[92]

The Court's decisions in *Elstad* and *Seibert* can arguably be understood as defining two extremes of mid-stream *Miranda* warnings. However, that is also an oversimplification of the two decisions. In *Elstad*, the provision of midstream warnings was permissible (and insulated the later confession) because the two stages of interrogation did not appear to be a conscious stratagem employed by the police to undermine the effectiveness of *Miranda*. In some sense, *Seibert* then appeared to modify this rule by suggesting that the effectiveness of mid-stream *Miranda* warnings would turn not simply on intentionality, but instead on a multi-factor analysis. However, the extent to which *Seibert* truly modifies *Elstad* remains something of an open question. The opinion in *Seibert* was a plurality, since no one rule in the case garnered a majority of votes. Thus, while the *Seibert* plurality suggested adoption of the multi-factor test to assess the effectiveness of mid-stream *Miranda* warnings, Justice Kennedy wrote in concurrence that post-warning statements should continue to be governed by the *Elstad* rule unless a deliberate two-step process had been employed by the police. For further clarity, we will have to wait for future decisions from the Court.

7. The Public Safety Exception to *Miranda*. Sometimes police officers respond to emergency situations in which they or members of the public might be in imminent peril. In such cases, police may need to obtain information from the suspect quickly in order to alleviate any immediate danger. A strict application of the *Miranda* rule in these situations would force the police to make a difficult choice: either interrogate the suspect quickly without *Miranda* warnings (and be unable to use the answers at trial) or delay questioning in order to read the suspect his rights (and risk the suspect invoking those rights and refusing to cooperate with the police in their attempt to protect the public). The Supreme Court has held that in these situations, the police should not have to make such a choice. Thus, if the police officer's questions are reasonably prompted by a concern for public safety, *Miranda* will not prevent those statements from being admitted at trial:

Example—*New York v. Quarles*, 467 U.S. 649 (1984): Two police officers were on patrol when a woman approached them and told them she had just been raped. She described the perpe-

[92] Id. at 616–17.

trator, informed the police that he had a gun, and told them that she just seen him enter a nearby supermarket. One of the police officers entered the store and saw Benjamin Quarles, who matched the description. Upon seeing the officer, Quarles ran towards the rear of the store, and the officer lost sight of him for a few seconds. The officer then caught up with Quarles and ordered him at gunpoint to freeze and put his hands over his head. The officer then frisked Quarles and found he was wearing an empty shoulder holster. He handcuffed Quarles and then asked him where the gun was. Quarles nodded towards some empty cartons on the shelf and said, "The gun is over there." The officer retrieved the gun and then read Quarles his *Miranda* rights.

At trial, the judge excluded the statement leading officers to the gun and the gun itself from evidence because the defendant made the statement in response to a direct question while he was in custody. The prosecutor appealed the ruling.

Analysis: The Supreme Court reversed the trial court's decision and ruled that the gun should have been admitted into evidence. The Court agreed that Quarles was subjected to custodial interrogation when he told the officer about the gun. But the Court noted that most reasonable officers in the situation would ask about the location of the gun not only to gather evidence against the defendant, but also (and perhaps primarily) to ensure that the gun was not picked up by an accomplice or an innocent person who could hurt themselves or others with it.

The Court announced it was creating a "public safety" exception to the *Miranda* rule, which would apply whenever police officers ask questions "reasonably prompted by a concern for the public safety." The Court noted that in most situations the *Miranda* doctrine struck the proper balance between the defendant's constitutional rights and law enforcement's interest in investigating crime. However, when the police need to gather information quickly in order to protect the public from danger, the calculus changes: "The need for answers to questions in a situation posing a threat to the public safety outweighs the need for the prophylactic rule protecting the Fifth Amendment's privilege against self-incrimination."[93] The Court noted that giving a suspect his *Miranda* rights before asking questions to protect the public safety might result in a defendant invoking those rights and refusing to talk:

[93] Id. at 657.

> We decline to place officers such as Officer Kraft in the untenable position of having to consider, often in a matter of seconds, whether it best serves society for them to ask the necessary questions without the *Miranda* warnings and render whatever probative evidence they uncover inadmissible, or for them to give the warnings in order to preserve the admissibility of evidence they might uncover but possibly damage or destroy their ability to obtain that evidence and neutralize the volatile situation confronting them.[94]

The *Quarles* Court stated that the actual subjective intent of the officer is not the controlling factor in determining whether the public safety exception applies. Without question, an officer may be motivated by a desire to protect the public, a desire to protect himself, a desire to gather evidence, or some combination of the three. In reviewing the applicability of the public safety exception, however, a reviewing court should only determine whether the questions were "reasonably prompted" by a concern for public safety.[95]

Some later cases have interpreted *Quarles* narrowly, applying the exception only when police must conduct a limited interrogation to protect themselves or members of the general public from immediate harm. Such courts have found that the exception does not allow officers an "automatic right" to disregard the *Miranda* warnings simply because they have a suspicion that guns are near or at the scene of the arrest.[96] For these courts, police must have a "real basis to believe that weapons are present, and some specific reason to believe that the weapon's undetected presence poses a danger to the police or to the public."[97] However, other courts have applied the case more broadly, finding that it entitles officers to question without warning even when the future harm is at best fairly speculative.

---

[94] Id. at 657–58.

[95] Id. at 656.

[96] See, e.g., United States v. Jones, 154 F.Supp. 2d 617, 629 (S.D.N.Y. 2001).

[97] Id.

Quick Summary

In addition to determining whether a statement is voluntary, courts deciding on admissibility will also determine whether *Miranda* warnings were provided to a suspect in advance of any custodial interrogation. The *Miranda* warnings are: you have the right to remain silent; if you choose to speak, anything you say can be used against you; you have the right to an attorney; and if you cannot afford an attorney, one will be provided.

Miranda is a constitutional decision. It therefore may not be overruled by Congress or undermined by the states.

Miranda warnings are only required if there is "custodial interrogation." Custody exists if there has been a formal arrest or other significant deprivation of a suspect's freedom of movement akin to an arrest. "Comparatively non-threatening" detentions like a *Terry* stop or a traffic stop will not constitute "custody" for *Miranda* purposes. The test for custody is an objective one. Thus, as a general matter, the particular characteristics of the accused are not relevant. However, the Court has found that a child's age may be relevant to the custody analysis.

There is interrogation whenever there is direct questioning or words or actions on the part of the police that are reasonably likely to elicit an incriminating response.

Statements that are taken in violation of *Miranda* are not admissible during the prosecution's case-in-chief. However, such statements may be used for impeachment purposes. The non-testimonial fruit of unwarned statements also may be admitted. As these exceptions make clear, as a practical matter *Miranda* does not require that police officers issue warnings and obtain waivers prior to conducting custodial interrogation. Rather, *Miranda* only means that the state cannot use the statements that are elicited from unwarned custodial interrogation to establish the suspect's guilt.

Invocation and waiver are also essential to any *Miranda* analysis. To trigger the full protection of her *Miranda* rights, a suspect must invoke those rights. Invocation must be clear and unambiguous. In addition, before the prosecution may rely upon statements made during custodial interrogation, it must prove that the suspect waived her rights. Waiver need only be voluntary, knowing, and intelligent. The factors relevant to waiver are the suspect's age, education, experience, background, and raw intelligence. The waiver analysis must also consider whether the suspect's ability to understand the warnings and consequences of waiver was in any way impaired. Express waiver is not required.

Even after a suspect has invoked his rights, questioning may resume if the suspect reinitiates substantive contact with the police and waives her rights. If the right to silence is invoked, the police may resume questioning so long as they scrupulously honor the original request to remain silent. In determining whether the asserted right has been scrupulously honored, the court will consider things like changes in police personnel, lengthy breaks between questioning, changes in physical location, and the lack of overlap between offenses.

If the right to counsel is invoked, all questioning must cease until counsel is provided and present during the interrogation. However, if there is at least a fourteen-day break in custody the asserted invocation will dissipate, and the authorities are free to renew their efforts to seek a waiver.

While *Miranda* warnings must generally be given to any custodial suspect who is being interrogated, the Court has recognized a "public safety" exception to this general rule. This exception allows the police to engage in inquiries that are reasonably prompted by an imminent threat to safety even in the absence of *Miranda* warnings.

Review Questions

1. Two-Step Investigation of Stolen Money Orders: Capers worked as a mail handler for the U.S. Postal Service. Postal inspectors suspected he was stealing cash and money orders from Express Mail envelopes, so they set up a sting to catch him. They planted two Express Mail envelopes at his mail sorting facility and set up surveillance. One of the envelopes contained $30 in cash. The other contained two $80 money orders and was equipped with a hidden alarm. When Capers noticed the envelopes, he put them into a mail bin and carried them into a trailer. While he was inside the trailer the inspectors lost sight of him. However, a short time later the alarm went off and the inspectors rushed in. They arrested Capers and another mail worker who was in the trailer at the time.

Capers was taken to an office. He was handcuffed and surrounded by three inspectors. The lead inspector, Agent Hoti, told Capers "Talk to me or don't, I don't care. But, you should know I'm going to do my best to put you away. I've been watching you all day and I know everything that you did." Hoti asked Capers what he did with the contents of the Express Mail envelopes. Capers pointed to his pants pocket. With Capers' permission, Hoti reached into Capers' pocket and pulled out the money orders. In response to questioning, Capers then told Hoti the money orders were not his, and that he'd stolen them from the Express Mail envelope. At trial, Hoti testified that he did not give Capers *Miranda* warnings because he needed to act quickly to make sure the missing money orders did not get lost in the large mail sorting facility. Hoti said he was also concerned about quickly releasing the other mail worker, who was handcuffed outside of the office, if it turned out he was not involved in the theft.

Inspectors then transported Capers to another Postal Service facility for additional questioning. During transport, Capers asked one of the inspectors if he would be fired. The inspector replied that it was in Capers' best interest to be completely honest. A short time later, Agent Hoti came in. He read Capers his *Miranda* rights and obtained Capers' signature on a waiver of rights form. Hoti then questioned Capers about the events of earlier in the evening. Capers again confessed to taking the money orders. However, when Hoti asked Capers to provide a written statement, Capers refused. In all approximately ninety minutes lapsed between the first and second rounds of questioning. Capers was charged with Theft of Mail by a Postal Employee. At trial, Capers moved to suppress the statements that he made both before and after receiving *Miranda* warnings. Will Capers be successful in his motion?

2. The Search for the Second Gun. Police officers received a report of a disturbance at a home in an upper-middle-class residential neighborhood in Tulsa. The woman who called in the report told officers she had been locked out of her home by her adult son, William Donachy. She also told the officers arriving on the scene that she though her son was intoxicated and may be armed, and that he had two shotguns hidden in the house. Police records indicated that, on past occasions, Donachy had made threats to kill the President of the United States and police officers. A neighbor who arrived on the scene told the police that he had just seen Donachy walk outside of the house. At the time, Donachy announced that he felt like "getting his shotgun to start blasting away." The neighbor said that Donachy also said he might as well kill them, speaking of his mother and the neighbor.

Officers were eventually able to talk Donachy out of the house. He was handcuffed and arrested on several outstanding warrants. The officers then searched the house but found only one rifle. Without giving Donachy *Miranda* warnings, an officer asked him where the other gun was. Donachy launched into a rambling tirade that didn't answer the question. The officer then told Donachy that if he'd hidden the gun outside it might be a danger to children in the neighborhood. The officer asked Donachy three or four times where the second gun was before Donachy finally answered that he'd stashed it in the trunk of his mother's car.

Donachy was charged with a variety of offenses. At trial, the prosecution sought to introduce Donachy's statements regarding the location of the second gun. Donachy moves to suppress his un-Mirandized statements about the location of the second gun. Should the trial court grant Donachy's motion to suppress? Donachy's also moves to suppress the second gun as the "fruit" of his unwarned statements. Should this second motion succeed?

3. Handcuffed for Speeding. William was stopped pursuant to a traffic violation while he was taking his nine-year-old son to football practice. The police officer initiated their encounter with the defendant by removing him from his car, immediately placing him in handcuffs, and moving him to the rear of his car. The officer told William that he was not under arrest; however, the officer did not tell him why he was in handcuffs. The officer then told William that he could return to his car and asked if he could answer a few questions. The officer asked William if he had any contraband in his car. William said no, but that he had a "J" in his pocket. The officer unhandcuffed William and asked him to hand over the marijuana. The officer then arrested Willaim and charged him with misdemeanor possession of marijuana.

William moved to have the statements suppressed because he was not given *Miranda* warnings before answering questions. The government replied by saying that the defendant was stopped temporarily, pursuant to a routine traffic stop, and so he was not "in custody" at the time he made the incriminating statement. How should the judge rule on the motion?

4. Voluntary Waiver? A man called the police and told them that he had not seen his elderly neighbor for over a week, and that she was not answering her phone at home. The police went to the neighbor's house and knocked, and when there was no answer they entered the house. They found the woman's body chopped into pieces, with bloody utensils strewn throughout the house. James Chalmers had been living with the victim at the time of her death, so the police brought him in for questioning. They took him to an interrogation room and locked the door, and two police detectives sat across the table from him. One of the detectives then read Chalmers his *Miranda* warnings. Chalmers replied that he couldn't afford an attorney. The detective said that they would provide one for him if he wanted. The detective then passed the copy of the *Miranda* warnings across to Chalmers and asked him to sign it to indicate that he understood and waived his rights. The rest of the interrogation went as follows:

Chalmers: I don't really have anything to say I mean I don't know.

Detective: OK. I mean do you want to talk to me to see what I got to say to see what you have to say?

Chalmers: Well, I want to hear what you got to say.

Detective: OK then if you don't mind look that over. You want to look that over before you sign it? You welcome to.

Chalmers: You mean I can have an uh an appointed lawyer right now?

Detective: Well, not at this time.

Chalmers: Cause you know uh I know zero about law you know uh.

Grooms: Just like it says, if you want to talk we can talk and you can stop it at any time.

Chalmers: Well if I am not being charged with anything why, why is this even being

Grooms: Because that is policy procedure

Chalmers: Well then if I am not being charged with anything why am I not just cut loose?

Detective: Because I need to get a statement from you for one.

Chalmers: It will probably haunt me for signing this.

Detective: It's up to you.

Chalmers: You can get a statement from me without signing this, can't you?

Detective: Yea, I have to write down you refused to sign. I read your rights to you right you understand, isn't that right?

Chalmers: Yea.

Detective: I just need you to acknowledge that. Is that true?

Chalmers: Well you gave me this and you read me *Miranda*.

Detective: Ok. You don't have to sign it. I do want you to make sure that you understand what I read to you.

Chalmers: I've just always been told, don't . . . . . . don't do anything that'll haunt you later on . . . you know, . . . I, I

Detective: I can't blame you for that

Chalmers: I mean . . . . .

Detective: But you do understand your rights, is that correct?

Chalmers: Yea

Detective: Ok. You have looked over this form.

Chalmers: Yes I did.

Detective: You feel comfortable talking to me?

Chalmers: Well not really I am scared to death man because uh I haven't did anything you know.

After this interaction, the detective got an incriminating statement from the Chalmers. Chalmers then appealed the admission of the confession, arguing that the waiver of *Miranda* was not voluntary, knowing, and intelligent—namely, that nothing based on that interaction suggests that the Chalmers understood his rights well enough to waive them. How should the court rule?

5. Asking for a Phone Call. Lawrence Garrity was arrested for aggravated battery for shooting at an occupied vehicle and injuring the driver. The police arrested him and read him his *Miranda* rights. Garrity said he understood those rights and was willing to talk. The officer said "Good. Now were you trying to kill this guy or just scare him?"

Garrity paused and then said: "Can I make a phone call so I can get a lawyer?"

The police officer replied: "Stop being a stupid asshole. You should be proud you shot that motherfucker's car. Everyone knows he deserved it. But now all your friends are turning on you and saying you were trying to kill this guy. That means we have to charge you with attempted murder if you don't tell us your side of the story."

Garrity responded by admitting that he shot at the car, but adamantly denying that he was aiming for the driver or trying to kill him. The police wrote down his statement and then charged him with aggravated battery.

Later on, Garrity moved to suppress his statement. He argued that he invoked his right to counsel when he asked if he could make a phone call to get a lawyer. How should the court rule?

FROM THE COURTROOM

MIRANDA v. ARIZONA

United States Supreme Court, 1966
384 U.S. 436

[Chief Justice WARREN delivered the opinion of the Court.]

[Justice CLARK filed an opinion concurring in part and dissenting in part.]

[Justice HARLAN filed a dissenting opinion, which was joined by Justices STEWART and WHITE.]

[Justice WHITE filed a dissenting opinion, which was joined by Justices HARLAN and STEWART.]

The cases before us raise questions which go to the roots of our concepts of American criminal jurisprudence: the restraints society must observe consistent with the Federal Constitution in prosecuting individuals for crime. More specifically, we deal with the admissibility of statements obtained from an individual who is subjected to custodial police interrogation and the necessity for procedures which assure that the individual is accorded his privilege under the Fifth Amendment to the Constitution not to be compelled to incriminate himself.

. . .

Over [seventy] years ago, our predecessors on this Court eloquently stated:

> The maxim "Nemo tenetur seipsum accusare," had its origin in a protest against the inquisitorial and manifestly unjust methods of interrogating accused persons, which (have) long obtained in the continental system, and, until the expulsion of the Stuarts from the British throne in 1688, and the erection of additional barriers for the protection of the people against the exercise of arbitrary power, (were) not uncommon even in England. While the admissions or confessions of the prisoner, when voluntarily and freely made, have always ranked high in the scale of incriminating evidence, if an accused person be asked to explain his apparent connection with a crime under investigation, the ease with which the questions put to him may assume an inquisitorial character, the temptation to press the witness unduly, to browbeat him if he be timid or reluctant, to push him into a corner, and to entrap him into fatal contradictions, which is so painfully evident in many of the earlier state trials, notably in those of Sir Nicholas Throckmorton, and Udal, the Puritan minister, made the system so odious as to give rise to a demand for its total abolition. The change in the English criminal procedure

> in that particular seems to be founded upon no statute and no judicial opinion, but upon a general and silent acquiescence of the courts in a popular demand. But, however adopted, it has become firmly embedded in English, as well as in American jurisprudence. So deeply did the iniquities of the ancient system impress themselves upon the minds of the American colonists that the States, with one accord, made a denial of the right to question an accused person a part of their fundamental law, so that a maxim, which in England was a mere rule of evidence, became clothed in this country with the impregnability of a constitutional enactment.

In stating the obligation of the judiciary to apply these constitutional rights, this Court declared in *Weems v. United States*, 217 U.S. 349 (1910):

> . . . our contemplation cannot be only of what has been, but of what may be. Under any other rule a constitution would indeed be as easy of application as it would be deficient in efficacy and power. Its general principles would have little value, and be converted by precedent into impotent and lifeless formulas. Rights declared in words might be lost in reality. And this has been recognized. The meaning and vitality of the Constitution have developed against narrow and restrictive construction.

This was the spirit in which we delineated, in meaningful language, the manner in which the constitutional rights of the individual could be enforced against overzealous police practices. It was necessary . . . to insure that what was proclaimed in the Constitution had not become but a "form of words," in the hands of government officials. And it is in this spirit, consistent with our role as judges, that we adhere to the principles of *Escobedo* today.

Our holding will be spelled out with some specificity in the pages which follow but briefly stated it is this: the prosecution may not use statements, whether exculpatory or inculpatory, stemming from custodial interrogation of the defendant unless it demonstrates the use of procedural safeguards effective to secure the privilege against self-incrimination. By custodial interrogation, we mean questioning initiated by law enforcement officers after a person has been taken into custody or otherwise deprived of his freedom of action in any significant way. As for the procedural safeguards to be employed, unless other fully effective means are devised to inform accused persons of their right of silence and to assure a continuous opportunity to exercise it, the following measures are required. Prior to any questioning, the person must be warned that he has a right to remain silent, that any statement he does make may be used as evidence against him, and that he has a right to the presence of an attorney, either retained or appointed. The defendant may waive effectuation of these rights, provided the waiver is made voluntarily, knowingly and intelligently. If, however, he indicates in any manner and at any stage of the process that he wishes to consult with an attorney before speaking there can be no questioning. Likewise, if the individual is alone and indicates in any manner that he does not wish to be interrogated, the police may not question him. The mere fact that he may have answered some questions or volunteered some statements on his own does not deprive him of the right to refrain from answering any further inquiries until he has consulted with an attorney and thereafter consents to be questioned.

1

The constitutional issue we decide in each of these cases is the admissibility of statements obtained from a defendant questioned while in custody or otherwise deprived of his freedom of action in any significant way. In each, the defendant was questioned by police officers, detectives, or a prosecuting attorney in a room in which he was cut off from the outside world. In none of these cases was the defendant given a full and effective warning of his rights at the outset of the interrogation process. In all the cases, the questioning elicited oral admissions, and in three of them, signed statements as well which were admitted at their trials. They all thus share salient features—incommunicado interrogation of individuals in a police-dominated atmosphere, resulting in self-incriminating statements without full warnings of constitutional rights.

An understanding of the nature and setting of this in-custody interrogation is essential to our decisions today. The difficulty in depicting what transpires at such interrogations stems from the fact that in this country they have largely taken place incommunicado. From extensive factual studies undertaken in the early 1930's, including the famous Wickersham Report to Congress by a Presidential Commission, it is clear that police violence and the "third degree" flourished at that time. In a series of cases decided by this Court long after these studies, the police resorted to physical brutality—beatings, hanging, whipping—and to sustained and protracted questioning incommunicado in order to extort confessions. The Commission on Civil Rights in 1961 found much evidence to indicate that "some policemen still resort to physical force to obtain confessions." The use of physical brutality and violence is not, unfortunately, relegated to the past or to any part of the country. Only recently in Kings County, New York, the police brutally beat, kicked and placed lighted cigarette butts on the back of a potential witness under interrogation for the purpose of securing a statement incriminating a third party.

The examples given above are undoubtedly the exception now, but they are sufficiently widespread to be the object of concern. Unless a proper limitation upon custodial interrogation is achieved—such as these decisions will advance—there can be no assurance that practices of this nature will be eradicated in the foreseeable future. The conclusion of the Wickersham Commission Report, made over [thirty] years ago, is still pertinent:

> To the contention that the third degree is necessary to get the facts, the reporters aptly reply in the language of the present Lord Chancellor of England (Lord Sankey): "It is not admissible to do a great right by doing a little wrong. . . . It is not sufficient to do justice by obtaining a proper result by irregular or improper means." Not only does the use of the third degree involve a flagrant violation of law by the officers of the law, but it involves also the dangers of false confessions, and it tends to make police and prosecutors less zealous in the search for objective evidence. As the New York prosecutor quoted in the report said, "It is a short cut and makes the

> police lazy and unenterprising." Or, as another official quoted remarked: "If you use your fists, you are not so likely to use your wits." We agree with the conclusion expressed in the report, that "The third degree brutalizes the police, hardens the prisoner against society, and lowers the esteem in which the administration of justice is held by the public."

Again we stress that the modern practice of in-custody interrogation is psychologically rather than physically oriented. As we have stated before, "Since *Chambers v. State of Florida*, this Court has recognized that coercion can be mental as well as physical, and that the blood of the accused is not the only hallmark of an unconstitutional inquisition." Interrogation still takes place in privacy. Privacy results in secrecy and this in turn results in a gap in our knowledge as to what in fact goes on in the interrogation rooms. A valuable source of information about present police practices, however, may be found in various police manuals and texts which document procedures employed with success in the past, and which recommend various other effective tactics. These texts are used by law enforcement agencies themselves as guides. It should be noted that these texts professedly present the most enlightened and effective means presently used to obtain statements through custodial interrogation. By considering these texts and other data, it is possible to describe procedures observed and noted around the country.

The officers are told by the manuals that the "principal psychological factor contributing to a successful interrogation is privacy—being alone with the person under interrogation." The efficacy of this tactic has been explained as follows:

> If at all practicable, the interrogation should take place in the investigator's office or at least in a room of his own choice. The subject should be deprived of every psychological advantage. In his own home he may be confident, indignant, or recalcitrant. He is more keenly aware of his rights and more reluctant to tell of his indiscretions of criminal behavior within the walls of his home. Moreover his family and other friends are nearby, their presence lending moral support. In his office, the investigator possesses all the advantages. The atmosphere suggests the invincibility of the forces of the law.

To highlight the isolation and unfamiliar surroundings, the manuals instruct the police to display an air of confidence in the suspect's guilt and from outward appearance to maintain only an interest in confirming certain details. The guilt of the subject is to be posited as a fact. The interrogator should direct his comments toward the reasons why the subject committed the act, rather than court failure by asking the subject whether he did it. Like other men, perhaps the subject has had a bad family life, had an unhappy childhood, had too much to drink, had an unrequited desire for women. The officers are instructed to minimize the moral seriousness of the offense, to cast blame on the victim or on society. These tactics are designed to put the subject in a psychological state where his story is but an elaboration of what the police purport to know already—that he is guilty. Explanations to the contrary are dismissed and discouraged.

The texts thus stress that the major qualities an interrogator should possess are patience and perseverance. One writer describes the efficacy of these characteristics in this manner:

> In the preceding paragraphs emphasis has been placed on kindness and stratagems. The investigator will, however, encounter many situations where the sheer weight of his personality will be the deciding factor. Where emotional appeals and tricks are employed to no avail, he must rely on an oppressive atmosphere of dogged persistence. He must interrogate steadily and without relent, leaving the subject no prospect of surcease. He must dominate his subject and overwhelm him with his inexorable will to obtain the truth. He should interrogate for a spell of several hours pausing only for the subject's necessities in acknowledgment of the need to avoid a charge of duress that can be technically substantiated. In a serious case, the interrogation may continue for days, with the required intervals for food and sleep, but with no respite from the atmosphere of domination. It is possible in this way to induce the subject to talk without resorting to duress or coercion. The method should be used only when the guilt of the subject appears highly probable.

When the techniques described above prove unavailing, the texts recommend they be alternated with a show of some hostility. One ploy often used has been termed the "friendly-unfriendly" or the "Mutt and Jeff" act:

> . . . In this technique, two agents are employed. Mutt, the relentless investigator, who knows the subject is guilty and is not going to waste any time. He's sent a dozen men away for this crime, and he's going to send the subject away for the full term. Jeff, on the other hand, is obviously a kindhearted man. He has a family himself. He has a brother who was involved in a little scrape like this. He disapproves of Mutt and his tactics and will arrange to get him off the case if the subject will cooperate. He can't hold Mutt off for very long. The subject would be wise to make a quick decision. The technique is applied by having both investigators present while Mutt acts out his role. Jeff may stand by quietly and demur at some of Mutt's tactics. When Jeff makes his plea for cooperation, Mutt is not present in the room.

The interrogators sometimes are instructed to induce a confession out of trickery. The technique here is quite effective in crimes which require identification or which run in series. In the identification situation, the interrogator may take a break in his questioning to place the subject among a group of men in a line-up. "The witness or complainant (previously coached, if necessary) studies the line-up and confidently points out the subject as the guilty party. Then the questioning resumes 'as though there were now no doubt about the guilt of the subject." A variation on this technique is called the "reverse line-up":

> The accused is placed in a line-up, but this time he is identified by several fictitious witnesses or victims who associated him with diferent offenses. It is expected that the subject will become desperate and confess to the offense under investigation in order to escape from the false accusations.

The manuals also contain instructions for police on how to handle the individual who refuses to discuss the matter entirely, or who asks for an attorney or relatives. The examiner is to concede him the right to remain silent. "This usually has a very undermining effect. First of all, he is disappointed in his expectation of an unfavorable reaction on the part of the interrogator. Secondly, a concession of this right to remain silent impresses the subject with the apparent fairness of his interrogator." After this psychological conditioning, however, the officer is told to point out the incriminating significance of the suspect's refusal to talk:

> Joe, you have a right to remain silent. That's your privilege and I'm the last person in the world who'll try to take it away from you. If that's the way you want to leave this, O.K. But let me ask you this. Suppose you were in my shoes and I were in yours and you called me in to ask me about this and I told you, "I don't want to answer any of your questions." You'd think I had something to hide, and you'd probably be right in thinking that. That's exactly what I'll have to think about you, and so will everybody else. So let's sit here and talk this whole thing over.

Few will persist in their initial refusal to talk, it is said, if this monologue is employed correctly.

In the event that the subject wishes to speak to a relative or an attorney, the following advice is tendered:

> (T)he interrogator should respond by suggesting that the subject first tell the truth to the interrogator himself rather than get anyone else involved in the matter. If the request is for an attorney, the interrogator may suggest that the subject save himself or his family the expense of any such professional service, particularly if he is innocent of the offense under investigation. The interrogator may also add, "Joe, I'm only looking for the truth, and if you're telling the truth, that's it. You can handle this by yourself."

From these representative samples of interrogation techniques, the setting prescribed by the manuals and observed in practice becomes clear. In essence, it is this: To be alone with the subject is essential to prevent distraction and to deprive him of any outside support. The aura of confidence in his guilt undermines his will to resist. He merely confirms the preconceived story the police seek to have him describe. Patience and persistence, at times relentless questioning, are employed. To obtain a confession, the interrogator must "patiently maneuver himself or his quarry into a position from which the desired objective may be attained." When normal procedures fail to produce the needed result, the police may resort to deceptive stratagems such as giving false legal advice. It is important to keep the subject off balance, for example, by trading on his insecurity about himself or his surroundings. The police then persuade, trick, or cajole him out of exercising his constitutional rights.

Even without employing brutality, the "third degree" or the specific stratagems described above, the very fact of custodial interrogation exacts a heavy toll on individual liberty and trades on the weakness of individuals. . . .

In the cases before us today, given this backgound, we concern ourselves primarily with this interrogation atmosphere and the evils it can bring. In *Miranda v. Arizona*, the police arrested the defendant and took him to a special interrogation room where they secured a confession. In *Vignera v. New York*, the defendant made oral admissions to the police after interrogation in the afternoon, and then signed an inculpatory statement upon being questioned by an assistant district attorney later the same evening. In *Westover v. United States*, the defendant was handed over to the Federal Bureau of Investigation by local authorities after they had detained and interrogated him for a lengthy period, both at night and the following morning. After some two hours of questioning, the federal officers had obtained signed statements from the defendant. Lastly, in *California v. Stewart*, the local police held the defendant five days in the station and interrogated him on nine separate occasions before they secured his inculpatory statement.

In these cases, we might not find the defendant's statements to have been involuntary in traditional terms. Our concern for adequate safeguards to protect precious Fifth Amendment rights is, of course, not lessened in the slightest. In each of the cases, the defendant was thrust into an unfamiliar atmosphere and run through menacing police interrogation procedures. The potentiality for compulsion is forcefully apparent, for example, in *Miranda*, where the indigent Mexican defendant was a seriously disturbed individual with pronounced sexual fantasies, and in *Stewart*, in which the defendant was an indigent Los Angeles Negro who had dropped out of school in the sixth grade. To be sure, the records do not evince overt physical coercion or patent psychological ploys. The fact remains that in none of these cases did the officers undertake to afford appropriate safeguards at the outset of the interrogation to insure that the statements were truly the product of free choice.

It is obvious that such an interrogation environment is created for no purpose other than to subjugate the individual to the will of his examiner. This atmosphere carries its own badge of intimidation. To be sure, this is not physical intimidation, but it is equally destructive of human dignity. The current practice of incommunicado interrogation is at odds with one of our Nation's most cherished principles—that the individual may not be compelled to incriminate himself. Unless adequate protective devices are employed to dispel the compulsion inherent in custodial surroundings, no statement obtained from the defendant can truly be the product of his free choice.

From the foregoing, we can readily perceive an intimate connection between the privilege against self-incrimination and police custodial questioning. It is fitting to turn to history and precedent underlying the Self-Incrimination Clause to determine its applicability in this situation.

II.

. . .

The question in these cases is whether the privilege is fully applicable during a period of custodial interrogation. In this Court, the privilege has consistently been accorded a liberal construction. We are satisfied that all the principles embodied in the privilege apply to informal compulsion exerted by law-enforcement officers during in-custody questioning. An individual swept from familiar surroundings into police custody, surrounded by antagonistic forces, and subjected to the techniques of persuasion described above cannot be otherwise than under compulsion to speak. As a practical matter, the compulsion to speak in the isolated setting of the police station may well be greater than in courts or other official investigations, where there are often impartial observers to guard against intimidation or trickery.

. . .

III.

Today, then, there can be no doubt that the Fifth Amendment privilege is available outside of criminal court proceedings and serves to protect persons in all settings in which their freedom of action is curtailed in any significant way from being compelled to incriminate themselves. We have concluded that without proper safeguards the process of in-custody interrogation of persons suspected or accused of crime contains inherently compelling pressures which work to undermine the individual's will to resist and to compel him to speak where he would not otherwise do so freely. In order to combat these pressures and to permit a full opportunity to exercise the privilege against self-incrimination, the accused must be adequately and effectively apprised of his rights and the exercise of those rights must be fully honored.

It is impossible for us to foresee the potential alternatives for protecting the privilege which might be devised by Congress or the States in the exercise of their creative rule-making capacities. Therefore we cannot say that the Constitution necessarily requires adherence to any particular solution for the inherent compulsions of the interrogation process as it is presently conducted. Our decision in no way creates a constitutional straitjacket which will handicap sound efforts at reform, nor is it intended to have this effect. We encourage Congress and the States to continue their laudable search for increasingly effective ways of protecting the rights of the individual while promoting efficient enforcement of our criminal laws. However, unless we are shown other procedures which are at least as effective in apprising accused persons of their right of silence and in assuring a continuous opportunity to exercise it, the following safeguards must be observed.

At the outset, if a person in custody is to be subjected to interrogation, he must first be informed in clear and unequivocal terms that he has the right to remain silent. For those unaware of the privilege, the warning is needed simply to make them aware of it—the threshold requirement for an intelligent decision as to its exercise. More important, such a warning is an absolute prerequisite in overcoming the inherent pressures of the interrogation atmosphere. It is not just the subnormal or woefully ignorant who succumb to an interrogator's imprecations, whether implied or expressly stated, that the interrogation will continue until a confession is obtained or that silence in the face of accusation is itself damning and will bode ill when presented to a jury. Further, the warning will show the individual that his interrogators are prepared to recognize his privilege should he choose to exercise it.

The Fifth Amendment privilege is so fundamental to our system of constitutional rule and the expedient of giving an adequate warning as to the availability of the privilege so simple, we will not pause to inquire in individual cases whether the defendant was aware of his rights without a warning being given. Assessments of the knowledge the defendant possessed, based on information as to his age, education, intelligence, or prior contact with authorities, can never be more than speculation; a warning is a clearcut fact. More important, whatever the background of the person interrogated, a warning at the time of the interrogation is indispensable to overcome its pressures and to insure that the individual knows he is free to exercise the privilege at that point in time.

The warning of the right to remain silent must be accompanied by the explanation that anything said can and will be used against the individual in court. This warning is needed in order to make him aware not only of the privilege, but also of the consequences of forgoing it. It is only through an awareness of these consequences that there can be any assurance of real understanding and intelligent exercise of the privilege. Moreover, this warning may serve to make the individual more acutely aware that he is faced with a phase of the adversary system—that he is not in the presence of persons acting solely in his interest.

The circumstances surrounding in-custody interrogation can operate very quickly to overbear the will of one merely made aware of his privilege by his interrogators. Therefore, the right to have counsel present at the interrogation is indispensable to the protection of the Fifth Amendment privilege under the system we delineate today. Our aim is to assure that the individual's right to choose between silence and speech remains unfettered throughout the interrogation process. A once-stated warning, delivered by those who will conduct the interrogation, cannot itself suffice to that end among those who most require knowledge of their rights. A mere warning given by the interrogators is not alone sufficient to accomplish that end. Prosecutors themselves claim that the admonishment of the right to remain silent without more "will benefit only the recidivist and the professional." Even preliminary advice given to the accused by his own attorney can be swiftly overcome by the secret interrogation process. Thus, the need for counsel to protect the Fifth Amendment privilege comprehends not merely a right to consult with counsel prior to questioning, but also to have counsel present during any questioning if the defendant so desires.

The presence of counsel at the interrogation may serve several significant subsidiary functions as well. If the accused decides to talk to his interrogators, the assistance of counsel can mitigate the dangers of untrustworthiness. With a lawyer present the likelihood that the police will practice coercion is reduced, and if coercion is nevertheless exercised the lawyer can testify to it in court. The presence of a lawyer can also help to guarantee that the accused gives a fully accurate statement to the police and that the statement is rightly reported by the prosecution at trial.

An individual need not make a pre-interrogation request for a lawyer. While such request affirmatively secures his right to have one, his failure to ask for a lawyer does not constitute a waiver. No effective waiver of the right to counsel during interrogation can be recognized unless specifically made after the warnings we here delineate have been given. The accused who does not know his rights and therefore does not make a request may be the person who most needs counsel. As the California Supreme Court has aptly put it:

> Finally, we must recognize that the imposition of the requirement for the request would discriminate against the defendant who does not know his rights. The defendant who does not ask for counsel is the very defendant who most needs counsel. We cannot penalize a defendant who, not understanding his constitutional rights, does not make the formal request and by such failure demonstrates his helplessness. To require the request would be to favor the defendant whose sophistication or status had fortuitously prompted him to make it.

. . .

Accordingly we hold that an individual held for interrogation must be clearly informed that he has the right to consult with a lawyer and to have the lawyer with him during interrogation under the system for protecting the privilege we delineate today. As with the warnings of the right to remain silent and that anything stated can be used in evidence against him, this warning is an absolute prerequisite to interrogation. No amount of circumstantial evidence that the person may have been aware of this right will suffice to stand in its stead. Only through such a warning is there ascertainable assurance that the accused was aware of this right.

If an individual indicates that he wishes the assistance of counsel before any interrogation occurs, the authorities cannot rationally ignore or deny his request on the basis that the individual does not have or cannot afford a retained attorney. The financial ability of the individual has no relationship to the scope of the rights involved here. The privilege against self-incrimination secured by the Constitution applies to all individuals. The need for counsel in order to protect the privilege exists for the indigent as well as the affluent. In fact, were we to limit these constitutional rights to those who can retain an attorney, our decisions today would be of little significance. The cases before us as well as the vast majority of confession cases with which we have dealt in the past involve those unable to retain counsel. While authorities are not required to relieve the accused of his poverty, they have the obligation not to take advantage of indigence in the administration of justice. . . .

In order fully to apprise a person interrogated of the extent of his rights under this system then, it is necessary to warn him not only that he has the right to consult with an attorney, but also that if he is indigent a lawyer will be appointed to represent him. Without this additional warning, the admonition of the right to consult with counsel would often be understood as meaning only that he can consult with a lawyer if he has one or has the funds to obtain one. The warning of a right to counsel would be hollow if not couched in terms that would convey to the indigent—the person most often subjected to interrogation—the knowledge that he too has a right to have counsel present. As with the warnings of the right to remain silent and of the general right to counsel, only by effective and express explanation to the indigent of this right can there be assurance that he was truly in a position to exercise it.

Once warnings have been given, the subsequent procedure is clear. If the individual indicates in any manner, at any time prior to or during questioning, that he wishes to remain silent, the interrogation must cease. At this point he has shown that he intends to exercise his Fifth Amendment privilege; any statement taken after the person invokes his privilege cannot be other than the product of compulsion, subtle or otherwise. Without the right to cut off questioning, the setting of in-custody interrogation operates on the individual to overcome free choice in producing a statement after the privilege has been once invoked. If the individual states that he wants an attorney, the interrogation must cease until an attorney is present. At that time, the individual must have an opportunity to confer with the attorney and to have him present during any subsequent questioning. If the individual cannot obtain an attorney and he indicates that he wants one before speaking to police, they must respect his decision to remain silent.

This does not mean, as some have suggested, that each police station must have a "station house lawyer" present at all times to advise prisoners. It does mean, however, that if police propose to interrogate a person, they must make known to him that he is entitled to a lawyer and that if he cannot afford one, a lawyer will be provided for him prior to any interrogation. If authorities conclude that they will not provide counsel during a reasonable period of time in which investigation in the field is carried out, they may refrain from doing so without violating the person's Fifth Amendment privilege so long as they do not question him during that time.

If the interrogation continues without the presence of an attorney and a statement is taken, a heavy burden rests on the government to demonstrate that the defendant knowingly and intelligently waived his privilege against self-incrimination and his right to retained or appointed counsel. This Court has always set high standards of proof for the waiver of constitutional rights, and we reassert these standards as applied to in custody interrogation. Since the State is responsible for establishing the isolated circumstances under which the interrogation takes place and has the only means of making available corroborated evidence of warnings given during incommunicado interrogation, the burden is rightly on its shoulders.

An express statement that the individual is willing to make a statement and does not want an attorney followed closely by a statement could constitute a waiver. But a valid waiver will not be presumed simply from the silence of the accused after warnings are given or simply from the fact that a confession was in fact eventually obtained. A statement we made in *Carnley v. Cochran*, 369 U.S. 506 (1962), is applicable here:

> Presuming waiver from a silent record is impermissible. The record must show, or there must be an allegation and evidence which show, that an accused was offered counsel but intelligently and understandingly rejected the offer. Anything less is not waiver.

Moreover, where in-custody interrogation is involved, there is no room for the contention that the privilege is waived if the individual answers some questions or gives some information on his own prior to invoking his right to remain silent when interrogated.

Whatever the testimony of the authorities as to waiver of rights by an accused, the fact of lengthy interrogation or incommunicado incarceration before a statement is made is strong evidence that the accused did not validly waive his rights. In these circumstances the fact that the individual eventually made a statement is consistent with the conclusion that the compelling influence of the interrogation finally forced him to do so. It is inconsistent with any notion of a voluntary relinquishment of the privilege. Moreover, any evidence that the accused was threatened, tricked, or cajoled into a waiver will, of course, show that the defendant did not voluntarily waive his privilege. The requirement of warnings and waiver of rights is a fundamental with respect to the Fifth Amendment privilege and not simply a preliminary ritual to existing methods of interrogation.

The warnings required and the waiver necessary in accordance with our opinion today are, in the absence of a fully effective equivalent, prerequisites to the admissibility of any statement made by a defendant. No distinction can be drawn between statements which are direct confessions and statements which amount to "admissions" of part or all of an offense. The privilege against self-incrimination protects the individual from being compelled to incriminate himself in any manner; it does not distinguish degrees of incrimination. Similarly, for precisely the same reason, no distinction may be drawn between inculpatory statements and statements alleged to be merely 'exculpatory.' If a statement made were in fact truly exculpatory it would, of course, never be used by the prosecution. In fact, statements merely intended to be exculpatory by the defendant are often used to impeach his testimony at trial or to demonstrate untruths in the statement given under interrogation and thus to prove guilt by implication. These statements are incriminating in any meaningful sense of the word and may not be used without the full warnings and effective waiver required for any other statement. In *Escobedo* itself, the defendant fully intended his accusation of another as the slayer to be exculpatory as to himself.

The principles announced today deal with the protection which must be given to the privilege against self-incrimination when the individual is first subjected to police interrogation while in custody at the station or otherwise deprived of his freedom of action in any significant way. It is at this point that our adversary system of criminal proceedings commences, distinguishing itself at the outset from the inquisitorial system recognized in some countries. Under the system of warnings we delineate today or under any other system which may be devised and found effective, the safeguards to be erected about the privilege must come into play at this point.

Our decision is not intended to hamper the traditional function of police officers in investigating crime. When an individual is in custody on probable cause, the police may, of course, seek out evidence in the field to be used at trial against him. Such investigation may include inquiry of persons not under restraint. General on-the-scene questioning as to facts surrounding a crime or other general questioning of citizens in the fact-finding process is not affected by our holding. It is an act of responsible citizenship for individuals to give whatever information they may have to aid in law enforcement. In such situations the compelling atmosphere inherent in the process of in-custody interrogation is not necessarily present.

In dealing with statements obtained through interrogation, we do not purport to find all confessions inadmissible. Confessions remain a proper element in law enforcement. Any statement given freely and voluntarily without any compelling influences is, of course, admissible in evidence. The fundamental import of the privilege while an individual is in custody is not whether he is allowed to talk to the police without the benefit of warnings and counsel, but whether he can be interrogated. There is no requirement that police stop a person who enters a police station and states that he wishes to confess to a crime, or a person who calls the police to offer a confession or any other statement he desires to make. Volunteered statements of any kind are not barred by the Fifth Amendment, and their admissibility is not affected by our holding today.

To summarize, we hold that when an individual is taken into custody or otherwise deprived of his freedom by the authorities in any significant way and is subjected to questioning, the privilege against self-incrimination is jeopardized. Procedural safeguards must be employed to protect the privilege and unless other fully effective means are adopted to notify the person of his right of silence and to assure that the exercise of the right will be scrupulously honored, the following measures are required. He must be warned prior to any questioning that he has the right to remain silent, that anything he says can be used against him in a court of law, that he has the right to the presence of an attorney, and that if he cannot afford an attorney one will be appointed for him prior to any questioning if he so desires. Opportunity to exercise these rights must be afforded to him throughout the interrogation. After such warnings have been given, and such opportunity afforded him, the individual may knowingly and intelligently waive these rights and agree to answer questions or make a statement. But unless and until such warnings and waiver are demonstrated by the prosecution at trial, no evidence obtained as a result of interrogation can be used against him.

IV.

. . .

In announcing these principles, we are not unmindful of the burdens which law enforcement officials must bear, often under trying circumstances. We also fully recognize the obligation of all citizens to aid in enforcing the criminal laws. This Court, while protecting individual rights, has always given ample latitude to law enforcement agencies in the legitimate exercise of their duties. The limits we have placed on the interrogation process should not constitute an undue interference with a proper system of law enforcement. As we have noted, our decision does not in any way preclude police from carrying out their traditional investigatory functions. Although confessions may play an important role in some convictions, the cases before us present graphic examples of the overstatement of the 'need' for confessions. In each case authorities conducted interrogations ranging up to five days in duration despite the presence, through standard investigating practices, of considerable evidence against each defendant. Further examples are chronicled in our prior cases.

It is also urged that an unfettered right to detention for interrogation should be allowed because it will often redound to the benefit of the person questioned. When police inquiry determines that there is no reason to believe that the person has committed any crime, it is said, he will be released without need for further formal procedures. The person who has committed no offense, however, will be better able to clear himself after warnings with counsel present than without. It can be assumed that in such circumstances a lawyer would advise his client to talk freely to police in order to clear himself.

Custodial interrogation, by contrast, does not necessarily afford the innocent an opportunity to clear themselves. A serious consequence of the present practice of the interrogation alleged to be beneficial for the innocent is that many arrests "for investigation" subject large numbers of innocent persons to detention and interrogation. In one of the cases before us, *California v. Stewart*, police held four persons, who were in the defendant's house at the time of the arrest, in jail for five days until defendant confessed. At that time they were finally released. Police stated that there was "no evidence to connect them with any crime." Available statistics on the extent of this practice where it is condoned indicate that these four are far from alone in being subjected to arrest, prolonged detention, and interrogation without the requisite probable cause.

V.

Because of the nature of the problem and because of its recurrent significance in numerous cases, we have to this point discussed the relationship of the Fifth Amendment privilege to police interrogation without specific concentration on the facts of the cases before us. We turn now to these facts to consider the application to these cases of the constitutional principles discussed above. In each instance, we have concluded that statements were obtained from the defendant under circumstances that did not meet constitutional standards for protection of the privilege.

Miranda v. Arizona.

On March 13, 1963, petitioner, Ernesto Miranda, was arrested at his home and taken in custody to a Phoenix police station. He was there identified by the complaining witness. The police then took him to "Interrogation Room No. 2" of the detective bureau. There he was questioned by two police officers. The officers admitted at trial that Miranda was not advised that he had a right to have an attorney present. Two hours later, the officers emerged from the interrogation room with a written confession signed by Miranda. At the top of the statement was a typed paragraph stating that the confession was made voluntarily, without threats or promises of immunity, and "with full knowledge of my legal rights, understanding any statement I make may be used against me."

At his trial before a jury, the written confession was admitted into evidence over the objection of defense counsel, and the officers testified to the prior oral confession made by Miranda during the interrogation. Miranda was found guilty of kidnapping and rape. He was sentenced to [twenty] to [thirty] years' imprisonment on each count, the sentences to run concurrently. On appeal, the Supreme Court of Arizona held that Miranda's constitutional rights were not violated in obtaining the confession and affirmed the conviction. In reaching its decision, the court emphasized heavily the fact that Miranda did not specifically request counsel.

We reverse. From the testimony of the officers and by the admission of respondent, it is clear that Miranda was not in any way apprised of his right to consult with an attorney and to have one present during the interrogation, nor was his right not to be compelled to incriminate himself effectively protected in any other manner. Without these warnings the statements were inadmissible. The mere fact that he signed a statement which contained a typed-in clause stating that he had "full knowledge" of his "legal rights" does not approach the knowing and intelligent waiver required to relinquish constitutional rights.

. . .

[The opinion of Justice CLARK, concurring in part and dissenting in part, is omitted.]

Mr. Justice HARLAN, whom Mr. Justice STEWART and Mr. Justice WHITE join, dissenting.

I believe the decision of the Court represents poor constitutional law and entails harmful consequences for the country at large. How serious these consequences may prove to be only time can tell. But the basic flaws in the Court's justification seem to me readily apparent now once all sides of the problem are considered.

I. INTRODUCTION.

At the outset, it is well to note exactly what is required by the Court's new constitutional code of rules for confessions. The foremost requirement, upon which later admissibility of a confession depends, is that a fourfold warning be given to a person in custody before he is questioned, namely, that he has a right to remain silent, that anything he says may be used against him, that he has a right to have present an attorney during the questioning, and that if indigent he has a right to a lawyer without charge. To forgo these rights, some affirmative statement of rejection is seemingly required, and threats, tricks, or cajolings to obtain this waiver are forbidden. If before or during questioning the suspect seeks to invoke his right to remain silent, interrogation must be forgone or cease; a request for counsel brings about the same result until a lawyer is procured. Finally, there are a miscellany of minor directives, for example, the burden of proof of waiver is on the State, admissions and exculpatory statements are treated just like confessions, withdrawal of a waiver is always permitted, and so forth.

While the fine points of this scheme are far less clear than the Court admits, the tenor is quite apparent. The new rules are not designed to guard against police brutality or other unmistakably banned forms of coercion. Those who use third-degree tactics and deny them in court are equally able and destined to lie as skillfully about warnings and waivers. Rather, the thrust of the new rules is to negate all pressures, to reinforce the nervous or ignorant suspect, and ultimately to discourage any confession at all. The aim in short is toward "voluntariness" in a utopian sense, or to view it from a different angle, voluntariness with a vengeance.

To incorporate this notion into the Constitution requires a strained reading of history and precedent and a disregard of the very pragmatic concerns that alone may on occasion justify such strains. I believe that reasoned examination will show that the Due Process Clauses provide an adequate tool for coping with confessions and that, even if the Fifth Amendment privilege against self-incrimination be invoked, its precedents taken as a whole do not sustain the present rules. Viewed as a choice based on pure policy, these new rules prove to be a highly debatable, if not one-sided, appraisal of the competing interests, imposed over widespread objection, at the very time when judicial restraint is most called for by the circumstances.

. . .

II. CONSTITUTIONAL PREMISES.

. . .

Having decided that the Fifth Amendment privilege does apply in the police station, the Court reveals that the privilege imposes more exacting restrictions than does the Fourteenth Amendment's voluntariness test. It then emerges from a discussion of Escobedo that the Fifth Amendment requires for an admissible confession that it be given by one distinctly aware of his right not to speak and shielded from "the compelling atmosphere" of interrogation. From these key premises, the Court finally develops the safeguards of warning, counsel, and so forth. I do not believe these premises are sustained by precedents under the Fifth Amendment.

The more important premise is that pressure on the suspect must be eliminated though it be only the subtle influence of the atmosphere and surroundings. The Fifth Amendment, however, has never been thought to forbid all pressure to incriminate one's self in the situations covered by it. On the contrary, it has been held that failure to incriminate one's self can result in denial of removal of one's case from state to federal court, in refusal of a military commission, in denial of a discharge in bankruptcy, and in numerous other adverse consequences. This is not to say that short of jail or torture any sanction is permissible in any case; policy and history alike may impose sharp limits. However, the Court's unspoken assumption that any pressure violates the privilege is not supported by the precedents, and it has failed to show why the Fifth Amendment prohibits that relatively mild pressure the Due Process Clause permits.

. . .

III. POLICY CONSIDERATIONS.

Examined as an expression of public policy, the Court's new regime proves so dubious that there can be no due compensation for its weakness in constitutional law. The foregoing discussion has shown, I think, how mistaken is the Court in implying that the Constitution has struck the balance in favor of the approach the Court takes. Rather, precedent reveals that the Fourteenth Amendment in practice has been construed to strike a different balance, that the Fifth Amendment gives the Court little solid support in this context, and that the Sixth Amendment should have no bearing at all. Legal history has been stretched before to satisfy deep needs of society. In this instance, however, the Court has not and cannot make the powerful showing that its new rules are plainly desirable in the context of our society, something which is surely demanded before those rules are engrafted onto the Constitution and imposed on every State and county in the land.

Without at all subscribing to the generally black picture of police conduct painted by the Court, I think it must be frankly recognized at the outset that police questioning allowable under due process precedents may inherently entail some pressure on the suspect and may seek advantage in his ignorance or weaknesses. The atmosphere and questioning techniques, proper and fair though they be, can in themselves exert a tug on the suspect to confess, and in this light "(t)o speak of any confessions of crime made after arrest as being 'voluntary' or 'uncoerced' is somewhat inaccurate, although traditional. A confession is wholly and incontestably voluntary only if a guilty person gives himself up to the law and becomes his own accuser." Until today, the role of the Constitution has been only to sift out undue pressure, not to assure spontaneous confessions.

The Court's new rules aim to offset these minor pressures and disadvantages intrinsic to any kind of police interrogation. The rules do not serve due process interests in preventing blatant coercion since, as I noted earlier, they do nothing to contain the policeman who is prepared to lie from the start. The rules work for reliability in confessions almost only in the Pickwickian sense that they can prevent some from being given at all. In short, the benefit of this new regime is simply to lessen or wipe out the inherent compulsion and inequalities to which the Court devotes some nine pages of description.

What the Court largely ignores is that its rules impair, if they will not eventually serve wholly to frustrate, an instrument of law enforcement that has long and quite reasonably been thought worth the price paid for it. There can be little doubt that the Court's new code would markedly decrease the number of confessions. To warn the suspect that he may remain silent and remind him that his confession may be used in court are minor obstructions. To require also an express waiver by the suspect and an end to questioning whenever he demurs must heavily handicap questioning. And to suggest or provide counsel for the suspect simply invites the end of the interrogation.

How much harm this decision will inflict on law enforcement cannot fairly be predicted with accuracy. Evidence on the role of confessions is notoriously incomplete, and little is added by the Court's reference to the FBI experience and the resources believed wasted in interrogation. We do know that some crimes cannot be solved without confessions, that ample expert testimony attests to their importance in crime control, and that the Court is taking a real risk with society's welfare in imposing its new regime on the country. The social costs of crime are too great to call the new rules anything but a hazardous experimentation.

While passing over the costs and risks of its experiment, the Court portrays the evils of normal police questioning in terms which I think are exaggerated. Albeit stringently confined by the due process standards interrogation is no doubt often inconvenient and unpleasant for the suspect. However, it is no less so for a man to be arrested and jailed, to have his house searched, or to stand trial in court, yet all this may properly happen to the most innocent given probable cause, a warrant, or an indictment. Society has always paid a stiff price for law and order, and peaceful interrogation is not one of the dark moments of the law.

This brief statement of the competing considerations seems to me ample proof that the Court's preference is highly debatable at best and therefore not to be read into the Constitution. However, it may make the analysis more graphic to consider the actual facts of one of the four cases reversed by the Court. *Miranda v. Arizona* serves best, being neither the hardest nor easiest of the four under the Court's standards.

On March 3, 1963, an [eighteen]-year-old was kidnapped and forcibly raped near Phoenix, Arizona. Ten days later, on the morning of March 13, petitioner Miranda was arrested and taken to the police station. At this time Miranda was [twenty-three] years old, indigent, and educated to the extent of completing half the ninth grade. He had "an emotional illness" of the schizophrenic type, according to the doctor who eventually examined him; the doctor's report also stated that Miranda was "alert and oriented as to time, place, and person," intelligent within normal limits, competent to stand trial, and sane within the legal definition. At the police station, the victim picked Miranda out of a lineup, and two officers then took him into a separate room to interrogate him, starting about 11:30 a.m. Though at first denying his guilt, within a short time Miranda gave a detailed oral confession and then wrote out in his own hand and signed a brief statement admitting and describing the crime. All this was accomplished in two hours or less without any force, threats or promises and—I will assume this though the record is uncertain—without any effective warnings at all.

Miranda's oral and written confessions are now held inadmissible under the Court's new rules. One is entitled to feel astonished that the Constitution can be read to produce this result. These confessions were obtained during brief, daytime questioning conducted by two officers and unmarked by any of the traditional indicia of coercion. They assured a conviction for a brutal and unsettling crime, for which the police had and quite possibly could obtain little evidence other than the victim's identifications, evidence which is frequently unreliable. There was, in sum, a legitimate purpose, no perceptible unfairness, and certainly little risk of injustice in the interrogation. Yet the resulting confessions, and the responsible course of police practice they represent, are to be sacrificed to the Court's own finespun conception of fairness which I seriously doubt is shared by many thinking citizens in this country.

. . .

IV. CONCLUSIONS.

All four of the cases involved here present express claims that confessions were inadmissible, not because of coercion in the traditional due process sense, but solely because of lack of counsel or lack of warnings concerning counsel and silence. For the reasons stated in this opinion, I would adhere to the due process test and reject the new requirements inaugurated by the Court.

. . .

Mr. Justice WHITE, with whom Mr. Justice HARLAN and Mr. Justice STEWART join, dissenting.

. . .

IV.

Criticism of the Court's opinion . . . cannot stop with a demonstration that the factual and textual bases for the rule it propounds are, at best, less than compelling. Equally relevant is an assessment of the rule's consequences measured against community values. The Court's duty to assess the consequences of its action is not satisfied by the utterance of the truth that a value of our system of criminal justice is 'to respect the inviolability of the human personality' and to require government to produce the evidence against the accused by its own independent labors. More than the human dignity of the accused is involved; the human personality of others in the society must also be preserved. Thus the values reflected by the privilege are not the sole desideratum; society's interest in the general security is of equal weight.

The obvious underpinning of the Court's decision is a deep-seated distrust of all confessions. As the Court declares that the accused may not be interrogated without counsel present, absent a waiver of the right to counsel, and as the Court all but admonishes the lawyer to advise the accused to remain silent, the result adds up to a judicial judgment that evidence from the accused should not be used against him in any way, whether compelled or not. This is the not so subtle overtone of the opinion—that it is inherently wrong for the police to gather evidence from the accused himself. And this is precisely the nub of this dissent. I see nothing wrong or immoral, and certainly nothing unconstitutional, in the police's asking a suspect whom they have reasonable cause to arrest whether or not he killed his wife or in confronting him with the evidence on which the arrest was based, at least where he has been plainly advised that he may remain completely silent. Until today, "the admissions or confessions of the prisoner, when voluntarily and freely made, have always ranked high in the scale of incriminating evidence." Particularly when corroborated, as where the police have confirmed the accused's disclosure of the hiding place of implements or fruits of the crime, such confessions have the highest reliability and significantly contribute to the certitude with which we may believe the accused is guilty. Moreover, it is by no means certain that the process of confessing is injurious to the accused. To the contrary it may provide psychological relief and enhance the prospects for rehabilitation.

This is not to say that the value of respect for the inviolability of the accused's individual personality should be accorded no weight or that all confessions should be indiscriminately admitted. This Court has long read the Constitution to proscribe compelled confessions, a salutary rule from which there should be no retreat. But I see no sound basis, factual or otherwise, and the Court gives none, for concluding that the present rule against the receipt of coerced confessions is inadequate for the task of sorting out inadmissible evidence and must be replaced by the per se rule which is now imposed. Even if the new concept can be said to have advantages of some sort over the present law, they are far outweighed by its likely undesirable impact on other very relevant and important interests.

The most basic function of any government is to provide for the security of the individual and of his property. These ends of society are served by the criminal laws which for the most part are aimed at the prevention of crime. Without the reasonably effective performance of the task of preventing private violence and retaliation, it is idle to talk about human dignity and civilized values.

The modes by which the criminal laws serve the interest in general security are many. First the murderer who has taken the life of another is removed from the streets, deprived of his liberty and thereby prevented from repeating his offense. In view of the statistics on recidivism in this country and of the number of instances in which apprehension occurs only after repeated offenses, no one can sensibly claim that this aspect of the criminal law does not prevent crime or contribute significantly to the personal security of the ordinary citizen.

Secondly, the swift and sure apprehension of those who refuse to respect the personal security and dignity of their neighbor unquestionably has its impact on others who might be similarly tempted. That the criminal law is wholly or partly ineffective with a segment of the population or with many of those who have been apprehended and convicted is a very faulty basis for concluding that it is not effective with respect to the great bulk of our citizens or for thinking that without the criminal laws, or in the absence of their enforcement, there would be no increase in crime. Arguments of this nature are not borne out by any kind of reliable evidence that I have been to this date.

Thirdly, the law concerns itself with those whom it has confined. The hope and aim of modern penology, fortunately, is as soon as possible to return the convict to society a better and more law-abiding man than when he left. Sometimes there is success, sometimes failure. But at least the effort is made, and it should be made to the very maximum extent of our present and future capabilities.

The rule announced today will measurably weaken the ability of the criminal law to perform these tasks. It is a deliberate calculus to prevent interrogations, to reduce the incidence of confessions and pleas of guilty and to increase the number of trials. Criminal trials, no matter how efficient the police are, are not sure bets for the prosecution, nor should they be if the evidence is not forthcoming. Under the present law, the prosecution fails to prove its case in about 30% of the criminal cases actually tried in the federal courts. But it is something else again to remove from the ordinary criminal case all those confessions which heretofore have been held to be free and voluntary acts of the accused and to thus establish a new constitutional barrier to the ascertainment of truth by the judicial process. There is, in my view, every reason to believe that a good many criminal defendants who otherwise would have been convicted on what this Court has previously thought to be the most satisfactory kind of evidence will now under this new version of the Fifth Amendment, either not be tried at all or will be acquitted if the State's evidence, minus the confession, is put to the test of litigation.

I have no desire whatsoever to share the responsibility for any such impact on the present criminal process.

In some unknown number of cases the Court's rule will return a killer, a rapist or other criminal to the streets and to the environment which produced him, to repeat his crime whenever it pleases him. As a consequence, there will not be a gain, but a loss, in human dignity. The real concern is not the unfortunate consequences of this new decision on the criminal law as an abstract, disembodied series of authoritative proscriptions, but the impact on those who rely on the public authority for protection and who without it can only engage in violent self-help with guns, knives, and the help of their neighbors similarly inclined. There is, of course, a saving factor: the next victims are uncertain, unnamed, and unrepresented in this case.

Nor can this decision do other than have a corrosive effect on the criminal laws as an effective device to prevent crime. A major component in its effectiveness in this regard is its swift and sure enforcement. The easier it is to get away with rape and murder, the less the deterrent effect on those who are inclined to attempt it. This is still good common sense. If it were not, we should posthaste liquidate the whole law enforcement establishment as a useless, misguided effort to control human conduct.

And what about the accused who has confessed or would confess in response to simple, noncoercive questioning and whose guilt could not otherwise be proved? Is it so clear that release is the best thing for him in every case? Has it so unquestionably been resolved that in each and every case it would be better for him not to confess and to return to his environment with no attempt whatsoever to help him? I think not. It may well be that in many cases it will be no less than a callous disregard for his own welfare as well as for the interests of his next victim.

There is another aspect to the effect of the Court's rule on the person whom the police have arrested on probable cause. The fact is that he may not be guilty at all and may be able to extricate himself quickly and simply if he were told the circumstances of his arrest and were asked to explain. This effort, and his release, must now await the hiring of a lawyer or his appointment by the court, consultation with counsel and then a session with the police or the prosecutor. Similarly, where probable cause exists to arrest several suspects, as where the body of the victim is discovered in a house having several residents, it will often be true that a suspect may be cleared only through the results of interrogation of other suspects. Here too the release of the innocent may be delayed by the Court's rule.

Much of the trouble with the Court's new rule is that it will operate indiscriminately in all criminal cases, regardless of the severity of the crime or the circumstances involved. It applies to every defendant, whether the professional criminal or one committing a crime of momentary passion who is not part and parcel of organized crime. It will slow down the investigation and the apprehension of confederates in those cases where time is of the essence, such as kidnapping, those involving the national security, and some of those involving organized crime. In the latter context the lawyer who arrives may also be the lawyer for the defendant's colleagues and can be relied upon to insure that no breach of the organization's security takes place even though the accused may feel that the best thing he can do is to cooperate.

At the same time, the Court's per se approach may not be justified on the ground that it provides a "bright line" permitting the authorities to judge in advance whether interrogation may safely be pursued without jeopardizing the admissibility of any information obtained as a consequence. Nor can it be claimed that judicial time and effort, assuming that is a relevant consideration, will be conserved because of the ease of application of the new rule. Today's decision leaves open such questions as whether the accused was in custody, whether his statements were spontaneous or the product of interrogation, whether the accused has effectively waived his rights, and whether nontestimonial evidence introduced at trial is the fruit of statements made during a prohibited interrogation, all of which are certain to prove productive of uncertainty during investigation and litigation during prosecution. For all these reasons, if further restrictions on police interrogation are desirable at this time, a more flexible approach makes much more sense than the Court's constitutional straitjacket which forecloses more discriminating treatment by legislative or rule-making pronouncements.

FROM THE COURTROOM

NEW YORK v. QUARLES

United States Supreme Court, 1984
467 U.S. 649

[Justice REHNQUIST delivered the opinion of the Court.]

[Justice O'CONNOR filed an opinion concurring in part and dissenting in part.]

[Justice MARSHALL filed a dissenting opinion, which was joined by Justices BRENNAN and STEVENS.]

Respondent Benjamin Quarles was charged in the New York trial court with criminal possession of a weapon. The trial court suppressed the gun in question, and a statement made by respondent, because the statement was obtained by police before they read respondent his "Miranda rights." That ruling was affirmed on appeal through the New York Court of Appeals. We granted certiorari, and we now reverse. We conclude that under the circumstances involved in this case, overriding considerations of public safety justify the officer's failure to provide Miranda warnings before he asked questions devoted to locating the abandoned weapon.

On September 11, 1980, at approximately 12:30 a.m., Officer Frank Kraft and Officer Sal Scarring were on road patrol in Queens, N.Y., when a young woman approached their car. She told them that she had just been raped by a black male, approximately six feet tall, who was wearing a black jacket with the name "Big Ben" printed in yellow letters on the back. She told the officers that the man had just entered an A & P supermarket located nearby and that the man was carrying a gun.

The officers drove the woman to the supermarket, and Officer Kraft entered the store while Officer Scarring radioed for assistance. Officer Kraft quickly spotted respondent, who matched the description given by the woman, approaching a checkout counter. Apparently upon seeing the officer, respondent turned and ran toward the rear of the store, and Officer Kraft pursued him with a drawn gun. When respondent turned the corner at the end of an aisle, Officer Kraft lost sight of him for several seconds, and upon regaining sight of respondent, ordered him to stop and put his hands over his head.

Although more than three other officers had arrived on the scene by that time, Officer Kraft was the first to reach respondent. He frisked him and discovered that he was wearing a shoulder holster which was then empty. After handcuffing him, Officer Kraft asked him where the gun was. Respondent nodded in the direction of some empty cartons and responded, "the gun is over there." Officer Kraft thereafter retrieved a loaded .38-caliber revolver from one of the cartons, formally placed respondent under arrest, and read him his *Miranda* rights from a printed card. Respondent indicated that he would be willing to answer questions without an attorney present. Officer Kraft then asked respondent if he owned the gun and where he had purchased it. Respondent answered that he did own it and that he had purchased it in Miami, Fla.

In the subsequent prosecution of respondent for criminal possession of a weapon, the judge excluded the statement, "the gun is over there," and the gun because the officer had not given respondent the warnings required by our decision in *Miranda v. Arizona*, before asking him where the gun was located. The judge excluded the other statements about respondent's ownership of the gun and the place of purchase, as evidence tainted by the prior *Miranda* violation. . . .

For the reasons which follow, we believe that this case presents a situation where concern for public safety must be paramount to adherence to the literal language of the prophylactic rules enunciated in *Miranda*.

The Fifth Amendment guarantees that "[n]o person . . . shall be compelled in any criminal case to be a witness against himself." In *Miranda* this Court for the first time extended the Fifth Amendment privilege against compulsory self-incrimination to individuals subjected to custodial interrogation by the police. The Fifth Amendment itself does not prohibit all incriminating admissions; "[a]bsent some officially coerced self-accusation, the Fifth Amendment privilege is not violated by even the most damning admissions." The *Miranda* Court, however, presumed that interrogation in certain custodial circumstances is inherently coercive and held that statements made under those circumstances are inadmissible unless the suspect is specifically informed of his *Miranda* rights and freely decides to forgo those rights. The prophylactic *Miranda* warnings therefore are "not themselves rights protected by the Constitution but [are] instead measures to insure that the right against compulsory self-incrimination [is] protected." Requiring *Miranda* warnings before custodial interrogation provides "practical reinforcement" for the Fifth Amendment right.[4]

In this case we have before us no claim that respondent's statements were actually compelled by police conduct which overcame his will to resist. Thus the only issue before us is whether Officer Kraft was justified in failing to make available to respondent the procedural safeguards associated with the privilege against compulsory self-incrimination since *Miranda*.

. . . [R]espondent was in police custody because we have noted that "the ultimate inquiry is simply whether there is a 'formal arrest or restraint on freedom of movement' of the degree associated with a formal arrest." Here Quarles was surrounded by at least four police officers and was handcuffed when the questioning at issue took place. As the New York Court of Appeals observed, there was nothing to suggest that any of the officers were any longer concerned for their own physical safety. The New York Court of Appeals' majority declined to express an opinion as to whether there might be an exception to the *Miranda* rule if the police had been acting to protect the

---

[4] *Miranda* on its facts applies to station house questioning, but we have not so limited it in our subsequent cases, often over strong dissent.

public, because the lower courts in New York had made no factual determination that the police had acted with that motive.

We hold that on these facts there is a "public safety" exception to the requirement that *Miranda* warnings be given before a suspect's answers may be admitted into evidence, and that the availability of that exception does not depend upon the motivation of the individual officers involved. In a kaleidoscopic situation such as the one confronting these officers, where spontaneity rather than adherence to a police manual is necessarily the order of the day, the application of the exception which we recognize today should not be made to depend on post hoc findings at a suppression hearing concerning the subjective motivation of the arresting officer. Undoubtedly most police officers, if placed in Officer Kraft's position, would act out of a host of different, instinctive, and largely unverifiable motives—their own safety, the safety of others, and perhaps as well the desire to obtain incriminating evidence from the suspect.

Whatever the motivation of individual officers in such a situation, we do not believe that the doctrinal underpinnings of *Miranda* require that it be applied in all its rigor to a situation in which police officers ask questions reasonably prompted by a concern for the public safety. The *Miranda* decision was based in large part on this Court's view that the warnings which it required police to give to suspects in custody would reduce the likelihood that the suspects would fall victim to constitutionally impermissible practices of police interrogation in the presumptively coercive environment of the station house. The dissenters warned that the requirement of *Miranda* warnings would have the effect of decreasing the number of suspects who respond to police questioning. The *Miranda* majority, however, apparently felt that whatever the cost to society in terms of fewer convictions of guilty suspects, that cost would simply have to be borne in the interest of enlarged protection for the Fifth Amendment privilege.

The police in this case, in the very act of apprehending a suspect, were confronted with the immediate necessity of ascertaining the whereabouts of a gun which they had every reason to believe the suspect had just removed from his empty holster and discarded in the supermarket. So long as the gun was concealed somewhere in the supermarket, with its actual whereabouts unknown, it obviously posed more than one danger to the public safety: an accomplice might make use of it, a customer or employee might later come upon it.

In such a situation, if the police are required to recite the familiar *Miranda* warnings before asking the whereabouts of the gun, suspects in Quarles' position might well be deterred from responding. Procedural safeguards which deter a suspect from responding were deemed acceptable in *Miranda* in order to protect the Fifth Amendment privilege; when the primary social cost of those added protections is the possibility of fewer convictions, the *Miranda* majority was willing to bear that cost. Here, had *Miranda* warnings deterred Quarles from responding to Officer Kraft's question about the whereabouts of the gun, the cost would have been something more than merely the failure to obtain evidence useful in convicting Quarles. Officer Kraft needed an answer to his question not simply to make his case against Quarles but to insure that further danger to the public did not result from the concealment of the gun in a public area.

We conclude that the need for answers to questions in a situation posing a threat to the public safety outweighs the need for the prophylactic rule protecting the Fifth Amendment's privilege against self-incrimination. We decline to place officers such as Officer Kraft in the untenable position of having to consider, often in a matter of seconds, whether it best serves society for them to ask the necessary questions without the *Miranda* warnings and render whatever probative evidence they uncover inadmissible, or for them to give the warnings in order to preserve the admissibility of evidence they might uncover but possibly damage or destroy their ability to obtain that evidence and neutralize the volatile situation confronting them.

In recognizing a narrow exception to the *Miranda* rule in this case, we acknowledge that to some degree we lessen the desirable clarity of that rule. At least in part in order to preserve its clarity, we have over the years refused to sanction attempts to expand our *Miranda* holding. As we have in other contexts, we recognize here the importance of a workable rule "to guide police officers, who have only limited time and expertise to reflect on and balance the social and individual interests involved in the specific circumstances they confront." But as we have pointed out, we believe that the exception which we recognize today lessens the necessity of that on-the-scene balancing process. The exception will not be difficult for police officers to apply because in each case it will be circumscribed by the exigency which justifies it. We think police officers can and will distinguish almost instinctively between questions necessary to secure their own safety or the safety of the public and questions designed solely to elicit testimonial evidence from a suspect.

The facts of this case clearly demonstrate that distinction and an officer's ability to recognize it. Officer Kraft asked only the question necessary to locate the missing gun before advising respondent of his rights. It was only after securing the loaded revolver and giving the warnings that he continued with investigatory questions about the ownership and place of purchase of the gun. The exception which we recognize today, far from complicating the thought processes and the on-the-scene judgments of police officers, will simply free them to follow their legitimate instincts when confronting situations presenting a danger to the public safety.[8]

---

[8] Although it involves police questions in part relating to the whereabouts of a gun, *Orozco v. Texas*, 394 U.S. 324 (1969), is in no sense inconsistent with our disposition of this case. In *Orozco* four hours after a murder had been committed at a restaurant, four police officers entered the defendant's boardinghouse and awakened the defendant, who was sleeping in his bedroom. Without giving him *Miranda* warnings, they began vigorously to interrogate him about whether he had been present at the scene of the shooting and whether he owned a gun. The defendant eventually admitted that he had been present at the scene and directed the officers to a washing machine in the backroom of the boardinghouse where he had hidden the gun. We held that all the statements should have been suppressed. In *Orozco*, however, the questions about the gun were clearly investigatory; they did not in any way relate to an objectively reasonable need to protect the police or the public from any immediate danger associated with the weapon. In short there was no exigency requiring immediate action by the officers beyond the normal need expeditiously to solve a serious crime. . . .

We hold that the Court of Appeals in this case erred in excluding the statement, "the gun is over there," and the gun because of the officer's failure to read respondent his *Miranda* rights before attempting to locate the weapon. Accordingly we hold that it also erred in excluding the subsequent statements as illegal fruits of a *Miranda* violation. We therefore reverse and remand for further proceedings not inconsistent with this opinion.

It is so ordered.

[The opinion of Justice O'CONNOR concurring in part and dissenting in part is omitted.]

Justice MARSHALL, with whom Justice BRENNAN and Justice STEVENS join, dissenting.

The police in this case arrested a man suspected of possessing a firearm in violation of New York law. Once the suspect was in custody and found to be unarmed, the arresting officer initiated an interrogation. Without being advised of his right not to respond, the suspect incriminated himself by locating the gun. The majority concludes that the State may rely on this incriminating statement to convict the suspect of possessing a weapon. I disagree. The arresting officers had no legitimate reason to interrogate the suspect without advising him of his rights to remain silent and to obtain assistance of counsel. By finding on these facts justification for unconsented interrogation, the majority abandons the clear guidelines enunciated in *Miranda v. Arizona*, and condemns the American judiciary to a new era of post hoc inquiry into the propriety of custodial interrogations. More significantly and in direct conflict with this Court's longstanding interpretation of the Fifth Amendment, the majority has endorsed the introduction of coerced self-incriminating statements in criminal prosecutions. I dissent.

I

. . .

The majority's entire analysis rests on the factual assumption that the public was at risk during Quarles' interrogation. This assumption is completely in conflict with the facts as found by New York's highest court. Before the interrogation began, Quarles had been "reduced to a condition of physical powerlessness." Contrary to the majority's speculations, Quarles was not believed to have, nor did he in fact have, an accomplice to come to his rescue. When the questioning began, the arresting officers were sufficiently confident of their safety to put away their guns. As Officer Kraft acknowledged at the suppression hearing, "the situation was under control." Based on Officer Kraft's own testimony, the New York Court of Appeals found: "Nothing suggests that any of the officers was by that time concerned for his own physical safety." The Court of Appeals also determined that there was no evidence that the interrogation was prompted by the arresting officers' concern for the public's safety.

The majority attempts to slip away from these unambiguous findings of New York's highest court by proposing that danger be measured by objective facts rather than the subjective intentions of arresting officers. Though clever, this ploy was anticipated by the New York Court of Appeals: "[T]here is no evidence in the record before us that there were exigent circumstances posing a risk to the public safety. . . ."

The New York court's conclusion that neither Quarles nor his missing gun posed a threat to the public's safety is amply supported by the evidence presented at the suppression hearing. Again contrary to the majority's intimations, no customers or employees were wandering about the store in danger of coming across Quarles' discarded weapon. Although the supermarket was open to the public, Quarles' arrest took place during the middle of the night when the store was apparently deserted except for the clerks at the checkout counter. The police could easily have cordoned off the store and searched for the missing gun. Had they done so, they would have found the gun forthwith. The police were well aware that Quarles had discarded his weapon somewhere near the scene of the arrest. As the State acknowledged before the New York Court of Appeals: "After Officer Kraft had handcuffed and frisked the defendant in the supermarket, he knew with a high degree of certainty that the defendant's gun was within the immediate vicinity of the encounter. He undoubtedly would have searched for it in the carton a few feet away without the defendant having looked in that direction and saying that it was there."

. . .

II

The majority's treatment of the legal issues presented in this case is no less troubling than its abuse of the facts. . . .

Before today's opinion, the procedures established in *Miranda v. Arizona* had "the virtue of informing police and prosecutors with specificity as to what they may do in conducting custodial interrogation, and of informing courts under what circumstances statements obtained during such interrogation are not admissible." In a chimerical quest for public safety, the majority has abandoned the rule that brought [eighteen] years of doctrinal tranquility to the field of custodial interrogations. As the majority candidly concedes, a public-safety exception destroys forever the clarity of *Miranda* for both law enforcement officers and members of the judiciary. The Court's candor cannot mask what a serious loss the administration of justice has incurred.

This case is illustrative of the chaos the "public-safety" exception will unlease. The circumstances of Quarles' arrest have never been in dispute. After the benefit of briefing and oral argument, the New York Court of Appeals, as previously noted, concluded that there was "no evidence in the record before us that there were exigent circumstances posing a risk to the public safety." Upon reviewing the same facts and hearing the same arguments, a majority of this Court has come to precisely the opposite conclusion: "So long as the gun was concealed somewhere in the supermarket, with its actual whereabouts unknown, it obviously posed more than one danger to the public safety. . . . "

If after plenary review two appellate courts so fundamentally differ over the threat to public safety presented by the simple and uncontested facts of this case, one must seriously question how law enforcement officers will respond to the majority's new rule in the confusion and haste of the real world. . . .

The end result, as Justice O'CONNOR predicts, will be "a finespun new doctrine on public safety exigencies incident to custodial interrogation, complete with the hair-splitting distinctions that currently plague our Fourth Amendment jurisprudence." In the meantime, the courts will have to dedicate themselves to spinning this new web of doctrines, and the country's law enforcement agencies will have to suffer patiently through the frustrations of another period of constitutional uncertainty.

III

Though unfortunate, the difficulty of administering the "public-safety" exception is not the most profound flaw in the majority's decision. The majority has lost sight of the fact that *Miranda v. Arizona* and our earlier custodial-interrogation cases all implemented a constitutional privilege against self-incrimination. The rules established in these cases were designed to protect criminal defendants against prosecutions based on coerced self-incriminating statements. The majority today turns its back on these constitutional considerations, and invites the government to prosecute through the use of what necessarily are coerced statements.

A

The majority's error stems from a serious misunderstanding of *Miranda v. Arizona* and of the Fifth Amendment upon which that decision was based. The majority implies that *Miranda* consisted of no more than a judicial balancing act in which the benefits of "enlarged protection for the Fifth Amendment privilege" were weighed against "the cost to society in terms of fewer convictions of guilty suspects." Supposedly because the scales tipped in favor of the privilege against self-incrimination, the *Miranda* Court erected a prophylactic barrier around statements made during custodial interrogations. The majority now proposes to return to the scales of social utility to calculate whether *Miranda*'s prophylactic rule remains cost-effective when threats to the public's safety are added to the balance. The results of the majority's "test" are announced with pseudoscientific precision:

"We conclude that the need for answers to questions in a situation posing a threat to the public safety outweighs the need for the prophylactic rule protecting the Fifth Amendment's privilege against self-incrimination."

The majority misreads *Miranda*. Though the *Miranda* dissent prophesized dire consequences, the *Miranda* Court refused to allow such concerns to weaken the protections of the Constitution:

"A recurrent argument made in these cases is that society's need for interrogation outweighs the privilege. This argument is not unfamiliar to this Court. The whole thrust of our foregoing discussion demonstrates that the Constitution has prescribed the rights of the individual when confronted with the power of government when it provided in the Fifth Amendment that an individual cannot be compelled to be a witness against himself. That right cannot be abridged."

Whether society would be better off if the police warned suspects of their rights before beginning an interrogation or whether the advantages of giving such warnings would outweigh their costs did not inform the *Miranda* decision. On the contrary, the *Miranda* Court was concerned with the proscriptions of the Fifth Amendment, and, in particular, whether the Self-Incrimination Clause permits the government to prosecute individuals based on statements made in the course of custodial interrogations.

. . .

In fashioning its "public-safety" exception to *Miranda*, the majority makes no attempt to deal with the constitutional presumption established by that case. The majority does not argue that police questioning about issues of public safety is any less coercive than custodial interrogations into other matters. The majority's only contention is that police officers could more easily protect the public if *Miranda* did not apply to custodial interrogations concerning the public's safety. But *Miranda* was not a decision about public safety; it was a decision about coerced confessions. Without establishing that interrogations concerning the public's safety are less likely to be coercive than other interrogations, the majority cannot endorse the "public-safety" exception and remain faithful to the logic of *Miranda v. Arizona*.

B

The majority's avoidance of the issue of coercion may not have been inadvertent. It would strain credulity to contend that Officer Kraft's questioning of respondent Quarles was not coercive. In the middle of the night and in the back of an empty supermarket, Quarles was surrounded by four armed police officers. His hands were handcuffed behind his back. The first words out of the mouth of the arresting officer were: "Where is the gun?" In the majority's phrase, the situation was "kaleidoscopic." Police and suspect were acting on instinct. Officer Kraft's abrupt and pointed question pressured Quarles in precisely the way that the *Miranda* Court feared the custodial interrogations would coerce self-incriminating testimony.

That the application of the "public-safety" exception in this case entailed coercion is no happenstance. The majority's ratio decidendi is that interrogating suspects about matters of public safety will be coercive. In its cost-benefit analysis, the Court's strongest argument in favor of a "public-safety" exception to *Miranda* is that the police would be better able to protect the public's safety if they were not always required to give suspects their *Miranda* warnings. The crux of this argument is that, by deliberately withholding *Miranda* warnings, the police can get information out of suspects who would refuse to respond to police questioning were they advised of their constitutional rights. The "public-safety" exception is efficacious precisely because it permits police officers to coerce criminal defendants into making involuntary statements.

Indeed, in the efficacy of the "public-safety" exception lies a fundamental and constitutional defect. Until today, this Court could truthfully state that the Fifth

Amendment is given "broad scope" "[w]here there has been genuine compulsion of testimony." Coerced confessions were simply inadmissible in criminal prosecutions. The "public-safety" exception departs from this principle by expressly inviting police officers to coerce defendants into making incriminating statements, and then permitting prosecutors to introduce those statements at trial. Though the majority's opinion is cloaked in the beguiling language of utilitarianism, the Court has sanctioned sub silentio criminal prosecutions based on compelled self-incriminating statements. I find this result in direct conflict with the Fifth Amendment's dictate that "[n]o person . . . shall be compelled in any criminal case to be a witness against himself."

The irony of the majority's decision is that the public's safety can be perfectly well-protected without abridging the Fifth Amendment. If a bomb is about to explode or the public is otherwise imminently imperiled, the police are free to interrogate suspects without advising them of their constitutional rights. Such unconsented questioning may take place not only when police officers act on instinct but also when higher faculties lead them to believe that advising a suspect of his constitutional rights might decrease the likelihood that the suspect would reveal life-saving information. If trickery is necessary to protect the public, then the police may trick a suspect into confessing. While the Fourteenth Amendment sets limits on such behavior, nothing in the Fifth Amendment or our decision in *Miranda v. Arizona* proscribes this sort of emergency questioning. All the Fifth Amendment forbids is the introduction of coerced statements at trial.

To a limited degree, the majority is correct that there is a cost associated with the Fifth Amendment's ban on introducing coerced self-incriminating statements at trial. Without a "public-safety" exception, there would be occasions when a defendant incriminated himself by revealing a threat to the public, and the State was unable to prosecute because the defendant retracted his statement after consulting with counsel and the police cannot find independent proof of guilt. Such occasions would not, however, be common. The prosecution does not always lose the use of incriminating information revealed in these situations. After consulting with counsel, a suspect may well volunteer to repeat his statement in hopes of gaining a favorable plea bargain or more lenient sentence. The majority thus overstates its case when it suggests that a police officer must necessarily choose between public safety and admissibility.

But however frequently or infrequently such cases arise, their regularity is irrelevant. The Fifth Amendment prohibits compelled self-incrimination. As the Court has explained on numerous occasions, this prohibition is the mainstay of our adversarial system of criminal justice. Not only does it protect us against the inherent unreliability of compelled testimony, but it also ensures that criminal investigations will be conducted with integrity and that the judiciary will avoid the taint of official lawlessness. The policies underlying the Fifth Amendment's privilege against self-incrimination are not diminished simply because testimony is compelled to protect the public's safety. The majority should not be permitted to elude the Amendment's absolute prohibition simply by calculating special costs that arise when the public's safety is at issue. Indeed, were constitutional adjudication always conducted in such an ad hoc manner, the Bill of Rights would be a most unreliable protector of individual liberties.

27

Identifications

Key Concepts

- Right to Counsel at Identification Procedures
- Due Process Clause Precludes Extremely Unreliable Out-of-Court Identifications
- Unreliability of Certain Witness Identification Procedures

A. Introduction and Policy. Eyewitness identification is one of the most powerful forms of testimony in criminal trials. In many cases there is no forensic or physical evidence to link the defendant to the crime, and the jury must decide guilt or innocence solely on the testimony of the eyewitnesses. Even if there is other evidence of guilt, most jurors will find eyewitness identifications to be the very compelling. More significantly, in cases where there is strong evidence of innocence, eyewitness identification can be nearly overpowering in its ability to persuade jurors that the defendant is guilty. In other words, not only is eyewitness testimony more persuasive than a ballistic match or fingerprint evidence, it is frequently more persuasive than alibi evidence.

There are essentially four types of eyewitness identification that can be admitted in court. The first is a live, **in-court** identification by the witness. This essentially involves the prosecutor asking the witness if she sees the perpetrator of the crime in the courtroom, and if so, if she could point him out and identify him by an article of clothing he is wearing. The witness responds by pointing at the defendant and saying something like: "Yes, he is sitting right there, wearing a blue and white tie." Because the identification of the defendant needs to be recorded in the written transcript, the prosecutor or the trial judge then notes for the record that the witness has identified the defendant.

This is always a very dramatic moment in the trial, and it may persuade many jurors that the defendant is the person who committed the crime, but it is in fact not a particularly reliable identification procedure. The defendant is relatively easy to locate, sitting next to his attorney at the defense table, and the witness is testifying about an event that probably occurred many months before. Therefore, in addition to an in-court identification, prosecutors frequently try to admit one of the three **out-of-court** methods of identification as well. These three methods are:

1. A "show-up," in which the witness points the defendant out to the police officers, usually at or near the scene of the crime. Usually, this involves the police bringing a recently-apprehended suspect to the witness for identification. Show-ups do not involve the witness choosing the defendant out of a pool of other suspects; usually the defendant is the only person that the witness is shown. Courts have recognized that, of the forms of out-of-court identification, show-ups have the greatest potential for improper suggestiveness.

2. A "lineup," in which the police place the defendant alongside four or five other people (known as "fillers") and ask the witness to choose the person who committed the crime. While a show-up typically occurs minutes after the crime, a line-up might take place hours or even days after the event.

3. A "photo array," in which the victim looks at a series of photos and tries to pick out the perpetrator of the crime. Police often use this method when they do not have an individual in custody (perhaps because they do not yet have probable cause), but they have suspicions about a certain person.

Assuming identity is at issue, a criminal investigation will almost always involve one of these three types of out-of-court identifications by a witness; otherwise the state would not know whom to arrest and charge with the offense. And if this out-of-court identification is performed improperly, the prosecution will be barred from admitting evidence of it at trial.

Furthermore, if the trial court excludes an eyewitness' out-of-court identification, the court will also probably preclude the eyewitness from making an in-court identification, assuming the witness has no independent basis for knowing what the defendant looks like. These exclusions will effectively make it impossible to prove the element of identity using that witness. This concept should be familiar to you from the "fruit of the poisonous tree" doctrine that we learned about in the Fourth Amendment context. As applied here, if the original identification is tainted, there is a (rebuttable) presumption that all later identifications by that witness are also tainted.

However, this is the end of the good news for defendants in the realm of identifications. The defendant's ability to challenge out-of-court identifications is extremely limited. Moreover, though out-of-court identifications are very persuasive to jurors, they can also be surprisingly inaccurate.

Psychological evidence has demonstrated that eyewitness identification evidence is notoriously unreliable. For example, in cases in which a defendant was convicted and later exonerated by DNA evidence, by far the most common reason for the false conviction was a mistaken identification by an eyewitness.[1] Witnesses tend to perceive and remember poorly during times of great stress (such as during a crime), and their minds fill in the "gaps" in their memory with their own preconceptions of what they expected to see, or with information they receive after the event. Poorly constructed out-of-court identification procedures can exacerbate these problems.

Social scientists have also learned which methods of conducting identification procedures are most likely to result in accurate identifications. For example, witnesses are far more likely to be accurate in their identifications if they are shown potential suspects one at a time, not all at once (this is known as using sequential presentation rather than simultaneous presentation). A handful of states and some local jurisdictions have imposed stricter and more specific requirements for identification procedures in response to these social science findings. However, under the Constitution, the Supreme Court has recognized only a few general rights to protect suspects during identification procedures. These rights are based on the Sixth Amendment (which guarantees the right to counsel) and the Due Process Clause of the Fourteenth Amendment. We will examine these broader rights first and then consider some of the more modern reforms undertaken by local jurisdictions.

B. The Law. There are four rules of law regarding identification procedures that are mandated by the Constitution:

1. The <u>police can compel</u> the defendant to participate in an identification procedure without infringing on the defendant's right against self-incrimination.
2. A defendant has the right to counsel at any identification procedure which takes place <u>after adversarial criminal proceedings</u> have begun.
3. If the identification procedure used by law enforcement is both

    (a) <u>unnecessarily suggestive;</u> and

    (b) so <u>unreliable</u> there is a <u>very substantial likelihood of misidentification</u> in the procedure,

then the identification will be inadmissible.

---

[1] http://www.innocenceproject.org/understand/. Eyewitness mistakes occurred in 77% of convictions which were later overturned. The second and third most common reasons were improper forensics (52%) and false confessions (23%). (The total number is greater than 100% because many cases had more than one error).

In judging whether the procedure used was unnecessarily suggestive, the court will examine the type of identification procedure that was utilized and whether any exigency existed at the time of the identification.

In judging whether the identification procedure is reliable, courts will look to the following factors:

(i) the opportunity of the witness to view the criminal at the time of the crime;

(ii) the witness' degree of attention;

(iii) the accuracy of the prior description of the criminal;

(iv) the witness' level of certainty at the identification proceeding; and

(v) the time between the event and the identification proceeding.[2]

4. If a witness' out-of-court identification is inadmissible because of 2. or 3., above, then the witness is barred from making an in-court identification unless the government can show the in-court identification was based on observations other than the tainted out-of-court identification.

The first rule merely states that forcing the suspect to appear at a lineup or a show-up does not violate his self-incrimination rights. This is because the suspect is not being forced to testify or provide any evidence of a communicative nature. This is even true if the police force the suspect to say specific words (sometimes referred to as a voice exemplar) in an attempt to have the witness identify the suspect by his or her voice. The same rule applies to forcing the defendant to provide other identifying information, such as fingerprints, a sample of handwriting, or a sample of DNA.[3]

Of course, compelling a suspect to participate in an identification proceeding does constitute a "seizure" under the Fourth Amendment. Accordingly, the necessary degree of suspicion will depend upon whether that seizure is most properly characterized as a "stop" or an "arrest." In the case of show-ups, which often occur on the street and take just minutes, the identification procedure may be brief enough and non-intrusive enough to qualify as a "stop" and thus require only reasonable suspicion. If the police want to conduct a lineup, however, the

[2] Neil v. Biggers, 409 U.S. 188, 199–200 (1972).

[3] Gilbert v. California, 388 U.S. 263 (1967); Maryland v. King, 133 S.Ct. 1958 (2013).

seizure most certainly will constitute an arrest. Under those circumstances, a suspect could ordinarily not be compelled to participate unless there was already probable cause to believe he had committed the crime (or unless the police already had some other reason to have custody over the suspect). Some states create a procedure short of arrest that allows the police to compel a suspect to submit to a line-up, but they require a court order very similar to a warrant.

The second rule is known as the *Wade* rule, after the case that established it.[4] As we will see in **Chapter 30,** the right to counsel, which is guaranteed by the Sixth Amendment, applies to all "critical" stages of the proceeding. An identification procedure counts as a critical stage only if it takes place **after** "adversarial criminal proceedings" have begun. Thus, the defendant has a right to counsel at any identification proceeding which takes place after a formal charge (such as an indictment) or after an arraignment or other preliminary hearing.[5] However, the right to have an attorney present does **not** exist for identification proceedings that occur after a warrantless arrest, and probably not even after an arrest warrant is issued. We will discuss this question in more detail in Section C below.

The third rule sets out two broad (and relatively low) standards for the reliability of the identification procedure. These standards are compelled by due process considerations. First, the procedure may not be **unnecessarily** suggestive—that is, the defendant must demonstrate not just that the identification was suggestive, but also that a more reliable method of identification was feasible at the time. (For example, a show-up is a suggestive method of identification. But frequently the police do not have time to conduct a full-fledged lineup, so a run-of-the-mill show-up is generally not deemed unnecessarily suggestive. Even if the defense attorney can show that an identification procedure was unnecessarily suggestive, she still must demonstrate that there was a "very substantial likelihood" of misidentification in order to preclude the out-of-court identification.

If the defendant is able to establish that the out-of-court identification is improper, this will mean the identification is inadmissible at trial. However, the government can still seek to have the witness identify the defendant in court if the prosecutor can prove that the in-court identification is not based on the improper out-of-court identification. In other words, the prosecutor must prove that although the earlier identification procedure created a very substantial likelihood of misidentification, it did not create a very substantial likelihood of **irreparable** misidentification.

---

[4] United States v. Wade, 388 U.S. 218 (1967).

[5] Kirby v. Illinois, 406 U.S. 682 (1972).

C. Applying the Law.

1. Right to an Attorney. The Sixth Amendment provides that a criminal defendant has a right to "assistance of counsel for his defense." The Supreme Court has ruled that this right applies not just to the trial but to all "critical stages" of the proceeding, including identification procedures that occur after formal charges have been filed in the case:

> **Example—*United States v. Wade*, 388 U.S. 218 (1967):** The police indicted and then arrested Billy Joe Wade for a bank robbery. About a month later, the police conducted a lineup with five or six other individuals standing next to him. During the lineup, Wade and the other individuals in the lineup were each required to say something like "put the money in the bag" in order to help the witnesses with voice identification. Employees of the bank viewing the lineup identified Wade as the robber.
>
> At the time of the lineup, Wade had a lawyer, but the lawyer was not notified that the lineup was occurring and so was not present for the lineup procedures. At trial, the employees identified Wade in the courtroom and also testified about the prior identification of Wade in the lineup. Wade was convicted, and he appealed, arguing that the lineup violated his Fifth Amendment right against self-incrimination and his Sixth Amendment right to counsel.

Analysis: The Supreme Court first held that the lineup did not implicate Wade's Fifth Amendment rights. Wade was not forced to disclose any knowledge that he had about the crime; he was only required to only to appear and make his voice available for identification purposes. Thus, his right against self-incrimination was not intruded upon.

However, the Court found that Wade had a Sixth Amendment right to counsel during the lineup. At the time of our nation's founding, the right to counsel was only significant at the trial stage, since there was no professional police force or any complicated pre-trial hearings. In modern times, however, "law enforcement machinery involves critical confrontations of the accused by the prosecution at pretrial proceedings where the results might well settle the accused's fate and reduce the trial itself to a mere formality."[6]

The Court went on to note that identifications are a particularly critical stage of the pre-trial process, because they are "peculiarly riddled with innumerable dangers and variable factors which might seriously, even crucially, derogate from

---

[6] Id. at 224.

a fair trial."[7] Moreover, once a witness misidentifies a suspect at a pre-trial lineup, she is likely to stick with that identification through trial, so the error could be irreparable.

Having the defense attorney present at the identification procedure remedies these problems. Counsel's presence gives police officers and witnesses an incentive to keep the identification free from prejudice and unnecessary suggestiveness. Moreover, if the defense attorney notices a problem that is not corrected, she can make a note of it and then expose it to the jury by inquiring about it during cross-examination.

Technically, *Wade* did not hold that an attorney was constitutionally required; it held that notice and presence of counsel is required in the absence of "legislative or other regulations" which eliminate the risk of abuse and unintentional suggestion at line-up proceedings.[8] But as of today, no set of regulations has yet been deemed adequate to render the presence of counsel unnecessary. Until such regulations have been promulgated, an attorney is required to be present at all identification procedures after adversary proceedings have begun.

This rule has two significant built-in limitations. First, it only applies to in-person lineups, not to identification proceedings involving photographs.[9] Second, the rule does not apply to any proceeding that occurs before the adversarial process has begun. Thus, there is no right to have an attorney present at a lineup until formal charges have been filed against the defendant—an arrest alone does not begin "adversary proceedings."[10]

Although the defendant does have a limited right to have an attorney present during identification procedures, the defense attorney does not have any explicit power to dictate how the identification process is conducted. Certainly she can observe the procedure, and make a record of all of the potentially suggestive aspects of the identification to be used later, either at a hearing to suppress the identification altogether or at trial to convince a jury that the identification was unreliable. In addition, her presence will likely deter the police and prosecutor from any unethical or overly suggestive tactics. However, she has no ability to control the identification proceeding or to insist on changes before the proceeding can go forward.

2. Out-of-Court Identifications: "Unnecessarily Suggestive." The Supreme Court has set a relatively high standard for defendants to meet when seeking to preclude an out-of-court identification. In order for the defendant to successfully

---

[7] Wade, 388 U.S. at 228.

[8] Id. at 239.

[9] United States v. Ash, 413 U.S. 300 (1973).

[10] Kirby v. Illinois, 406 U.S. 682 (1972).

preclude the identification, he must prove that it is both "unnecessarily suggestive" and unreliable. We will consider the "unreliability" element in the next section. But first, let's talk about suggestiveness:

> **Example—*Stovall v. Denno*, 388 U.S. 293 (1967):** One night a black man broke into the house of the Behrendts, stabbing the husband to death and stabbing the wife eleven times before leaving her to die. Mrs. Behrendt survived, however, and was taken to the hospital for surgery. The day after the surgery, the police brought the defendant, Theodore Stovall, to Behrendt's hospital room. Stovall was handcuffed to a police officer and was the only black person in the room at the time. The police officers ordered Stovall to say a few words and asked Mrs. Behrendt if Stovall was "the man." She said that he was.
>
> At trial, Behrendt both identified the defendant in court and testified about her identification of him in the hospital room. Stovall objected, arguing that the identification had been unduly suggestive. After Stovall was convicted and sentenced to death, he appealed to the Supreme Court.

Analysis: The Court held that the show-up identification procedure used by the police was constitutional. The Court conceded that "the practice of showing suspects singly to persons for the purpose of identification, and not as part of a lineup, has been widely condemned."[11] However, the Court went on to apply a "totality of the circumstances" test and noted that the police did not have the time or the opportunity to conduct a lineup, because Behrendt's critical condition meant they had to conduct the identification procedure immediately. Interestingly, the Court implied that allowing the procedure was beneficial not just for law enforcement, but also for the defendant Stovall:

> Here was the only person in the world who could possibly exonerate Stovall. Her words, and only her words, 'He is not the man' could have resulted in freedom for Stovall. The hospital was not far distant from the courthouse and jail. No one knew how long Mrs. Behrendt might live. Faced with the responsibility of identifying the attacker, with the need for immediate action and with the knowledge that Mrs. Behrendt could not visit the jail, the police followed the only feasible procedure and took Stovall to the hospital room. Under these circumstances, the usual police station line-up, which Stovall now argues he should have had, was out of the question.[12]

---

[11] Stovall v. Denno, 388 U.S. 293, 302 (1967).

[12] Id.

Thus, even extraordinarily suggestive identification procedures—such as the *Stovall* show-up—may be found constitutionally permissible if exigent circumstances particular to the individual case demonstrate the necessity of using them.

In its most recent case involving identification evidence, the Court clarified that a defendant cannot challenge an identification as suggestive unless the identification procedure was arranged by the police:

> **Example—*Perry v. New Hampshire*, 132 U.S. 716 (2012):** Around 3:00 in the morning, the Nashua Police Department received a 911 call stating that someone was trying to break into cars in the parking lot of an apartment building. Officer Nicole Clay responded to the call and found Barion Perry standing in the parking lot between two cars holding two car stereo amplifiers in his hands. Officer Clay asked Perry where he got the amplifiers, and Perry stated that he had just found them on the ground. A man named Alex Clavijo then came down from the apartment building and told Officer Clay that the rear windows of his car were shattered and the amplifiers from his car stereo were missing.
>
> Officer Clay left Perry with another officer and went upstairs to talk to some of the witnesses to the crime. She spoke with Nubia Blandon, who said that around 2:30 that morning she saw a tall black man walking around the parking lot looking into cars. She then saw the man circle Clavijo's car, open the trunk, and remove something. Officer Clay asked Blandon for a more specific description of the man and Blandon pointed out her kitchen window into the parking lot, where Perry was standing next to the other police officer. Perry was arrested and charged with theft and criminal mischief.
>
> One month later, the police showed Blandon a photo array, and Blandon was unable to pick Perry's photo out of the array.
>
> Before trial, Perry moved to suppress Blandon's identification on the night of the crime, arguing that admitting the identification would violate his due process rights. The trial court denied the motion, and Perry was convicted. Perry then appealed the identification question all the way to the United States Supreme Court.

Analysis: Blandon's identification of Perry on the night of the crime did not violate Perry's due process rights. The Court noted that determining the admissibility of an identification procedure is a two-step process. First, the trial court should determine whether the law enforcement officers used an identification procedure that was both suggestive and unnecessary. If so, the trial court should then analyze the facts of the specific case to determine whether the improper police conduct created a "substantial likelihood of misidentification."[13]

In this case, however, the trial court need not have moved past the first step. Even if the identification procedure in this case was unnecessarily suggestive, the suggestive aspect of the procedure was not based on improper police conduct. In every precedent discussing this issue, police officers had arranged the identification procedure. Blandon's identification of Perry, however, was not arranged by the police; it was a spontaneous point-out by the eyewitness. The Court thus confirmed that the purpose of excluding suggestive identifications was not to ensure reliability, but to deter police from "rigging identification procedures."[14]

Perry had argued that the Due Process Clause could be violated by a suggestive or unreliable identification even if there were no state action in obtaining that identification. The Court rejected this theory:

> When no improper law enforcement activity is involved . . . it suffices to test reliability through the rights and opportunities generally designed for that purpose, notably, the presence of counsel at postindictment lineups, vigorous cross-examination, protective rules of evidence, and jury instructions on both the fallibility of eyewitness identification and the requirement that guilt be proved beyond a reasonable doubt.[15]

There are dozens of ways that an identification may be unreliable: for example, passage of time between the crime and the identification, an eyewitness's poor vision, or even the race of the defendant and the witness. There are also dozens of ways that an identification could be suggestive: for example, the witness may have heard a press report linking the defendant to the crime, or may know that the defendant associates with known criminals. None of these indicia of reliability or suggestiveness are the fault of the police, however, and thus none would give rise to a due process challenge. Instead, the defendant must count on the methods that are used to test reliability of every other kind of evidence.

Thus, in order to mount a due process challenge to an identification, the defendant must first establish not only that the identification procedure was unnecessarily suggestive, but also that the suggestive nature of the identification was the result of improper police conduct. But even this showing is not sufficient to exclude the identification. As a final step, the court will consider the inherent reliability of the identification.

---

[13] Perry v. New Hampshire, 132 U.S. 716, 724 (2012).

[14] Id. at 721.

[15] Id.

3. Out-of-Court Identifications: Reliability. The Supreme Court has shown a strong preference for letting the adversarial process work—that is, to let the jury hear about an identification procedure, even if it was flawed, and then on cross-examination to demonstrate those flaws to a jury. This allows the jury to give the appropriate weight (if any) to the identification, rather than precluding the jury from hearing about it at all. Thus, the Court will only exclude identifications entirely if they are so tainted that there is a "very substantial likelihood of irreparable misidentification"—a difficult standard for defendants to meet, and one that allows juries to hear about many poorly executed identification procedures. Nevertheless, there are examples of identification procedures that are unnecessarily suggestive and that result in unreliable identifications:

> **Example—*Foster v. California*, 394 U.S. 440 (1969):** Three men robbed a Western Union office in California. The next day a man named Clay surrendered to the police and told the police that one of his accomplices was a man named Walter Foster. The police arrested Foster and put him in a lineup to be viewed by the clerk at the Western Union office. The lineup consisted of Foster and two other men. Foster was six inches taller than each of the other men, and he was wearing a leather jacket that matched the description of the jacket worn by the perpetrator. The eyewitness could not definitively identify Foster, and so Foster was brought in for a one-to-one meeting with the eyewitness. The eyewitness still could not identify Foster. About ten days later, Foster was brought back for another lineup in front of the same eyewitness. This time the lineup consisted of five people, but Foster was the only one of the five who had been in the prior lineup. At this second lineup, the eyewitness definitively identified Foster as one of the robbers.
>
> At trial, the eyewitness identified Foster in court and also testified about the prior identification procedures, including the three-man lineup and the one-on-one show-up in which he was unable to identify the defendant, and the later lineup in which he did identify the defendant. Foster was convicted, and he challenged the lineup as violating his rights under the Due Process Clause.

Analysis: The Supreme Court agreed with Foster, and held that the identification procedures were fatally flawed. Although generally the credibility and accuracy of a witness' identification is a question for the jury, it is possible for identification procedures to be "so unnecessarily suggestive and conducive to irreparable mistaken identification" as to be a denial of due process of law.[16]

This was just such a case: "The suggestive elements in this identification procedure made it all but inevitable that [the witness] would identify [Foster] whether or not he was in fact 'the man.' In effect, the police repeatedly said to the witness, 'This is the man.'"[17] The Court noted that the initial lineup was unfairly suggestive, and that the show-up was particularly troubling because "the practice of showing suspects singly to persons for the purpose of identification, and not as part of a lineup, has been widely condemned."[18]

As the *Foster* Court noted, one-on-one show-ups are generally disfavored due to the extreme level of suggestiveness they entail. Photo arrays can be equally suggestive, but because they usually occur early in the investigation, and because they are so useful in helping the police narrow their search, they are frequently found to be "necessary." In *Foster*, the identification procedures used were not only "unnecessarily suggestive" but also "conducive to irreparable mistaken identification." However, it is possible for an identification to be "unnecessarily suggestive" yet still not lead to an "irreparably mistaken identification:

Example—*Simmons v. United States*, 390 U.S. 377 (1968): After two men robbed a Chicago savings and loan, one of the witnesses to the crime described in great detail the car that was used by the perpetrators. The police were able to track this car to a man named William Andrews, who borrowed the car from his sister for the afternoon in question. The police further learned that Thomas Simmons was with Andrews for the entire afternoon. The police officers obtained a number of photographs of Andrews and Simmons and took them to the savings and loan to show to the clerks there. There were six photographs, mostly group shots where Andrews or Simmons were present in the groups. The photographs were shown separately to each of the five clerks, and each clerk identified Simmons as one of the robbers. Thereafter, Simmons was arrested and charged with the crime.

At trial, the clerks each testified, identifying Simmons in court as one of the robbers. Simmons argued that the pre-trial photo identification process was, as a categorical matter, so suggestive it tainted any subsequent in-court identifications:

16 Foster v. California, 394 U.S. 440, 442 (1969) (citations omitted).

17 Id. at 443 (citations omitted).

18 Id.

Analysis: The Supreme Court rejected Simmons's arguments and upheld the identification procedure. Although the Court conceded that the photographic identification procedure used "may have in some respects fallen short of the ideal,"[19] the procedure was not so improper that it violated the defendant's Due Process rights.

The Court noted there are certainly times when photographic identification should be considered untrustworthy. For example, a finding of untrustworthiness would be warranted if the witness obtained only a brief glance of the perpetrator under poor lighting conditions and the police showed a photo of only the defendant. Or if the police indicated to the witness during the identification process that they had other evidence linking the defendant to the crime. Moreover, once a witness makes a misidentification, the witness is "thereafter apt to retain in his memory the image of the photograph rather than of the person actually seen."[20]

However, the Court also acknowledged that using photographs early in a criminal investigation is a well-established and effective investigative technique. On the one hand, it helps the police to quickly identify perpetrators, and on the other it can exonerate the innocent without having to arrest them and force them to participate in a lineup in person. The Court also noted that cross-examination can be used to demonstrate to a jury the weaknesses in the identification process. Thus, the Court was unwilling to categorically bar the use of photographic identification procedures, instead holding that they should be evaluated on a case-by-case basis to see if they were "so impermissibly suggestive as to give rise to a very substantial likelihood of irreparable misidentification."

In determining the admissibility of the photographic identification, the *Simmons* Court found the following factors to be dispositive:

1. The procedure was necessary—a serious felony had been committed, and the police needed to use the photos to swiftly determine whether to focus their investigation on Simmons or expand their efforts more broadly.
2. The witnesses had a good chance of identifying the perpetrator: the robbery took place in the daylight, in a well-lighted bank, and the witnesses saw the robbers (who did not wear a mask) for up to five minutes. The police showed the witnesses the photos only one day after the crime occurred.
3. There was no allegation that the police improperly led the witnesses to focus on Simmons when the witnesses viewed the photos.

Note that the *Simmons* Court did not require an "ideal" identification procedure. Instead, all it required is a procedure that was not likely to have resulted in an irreparable misidentification. The Court noted that it would have been better to

---

[19] Simmons v. United States, 390 U.S. 377, 385–6 (1968).

[20] Id. at 383–84.

have only one or two eyewitnesses look at the photos, and then to bring Simmons in to participate in a lineup for the others to view. It also would have been better to show more than six pictures, to have more people in the photos, and for them to be proportionately fewer photos of Simmons. However, these flaws did not make the procedure unconstitutional.

So how do we know whether an identification procedure is "very likely" to lead to an "irreparable misidentification?" In *Neil v. Biggers*, the Supreme Court listed five factors to consider:

1. The opportunity of the witness to view the criminal at the time of the crime;
2. The witness' degree of attention;
3. The accuracy of the prior description of the criminal;
4. The witness' level of certainty at the identification proceeding; and
5. The time between the event and the identification proceeding.[21]

The Court applied these factors in a case involving an undercover narcotics officer to determine whether the officer's unnecessarily suggestive identification of a suspect was nonetheless reliable:

> **Example—*Manson v. Braithwaite*, 432 U.S. 98 (1977):** Trooper Jimmy Glover of the Connecticut State Police was working undercover when he entered an apartment building to purchase heroin. Glover went to the third floor of the building and knocked on the door. A man opened the door 12-18 inches wide, and Glover asked for "two things" of heroin, passing two ten dollar bills through the door. The door closed, and then a few moments later it re-opened and the man handed Glover two bags containing heroin. During these encounters Glover was two feet away from the seller.
>
> Trooper Glover went back to the police headquarters and described the seller to other officers. One of the other officers believed he knew the person Glover was describing, believing him to be a known convict named Nowell Braithwaite. The officer obtained a photo of Braithwaite and left it on Glover's desk. Two days later, when Glover returned to the office, he saw the photo and believed that it was in fact the person who sold him the heroin. Braithwaite was arrested nearly two months later.

[21] Biggers, 409 U.S. at 199–200.

Trooper Glover did not participate in any further identification proceedings. The case came to trial five months later (seven months after the sale), At the trial, Glover saw Braithwaite for the first time since (allegedly) seeing him sell the narcotics. Glover testified about his identification of Braithwaite in the photo two days after the sale and then positively identified Braithwaite on the stand. Braithwaite was convicted and sentenced to six to nine years. He appealed, arguing that Glover's identification was unconstitutional.

Analysis: The Supreme Court upheld the identification and the conviction. The Court agreed with the defendant that the photo identification was suggestive, and that there was no necessity (such as exigency) to justify its suggestive nature. However, notwithstanding such suggestiveness, the ultimate reliability of the identification procedure should be based on the totality of the circumstances in order to "limit the societal costs imposed by a sanction that excludes relevant evidence from consideration and evaluation by the trier of fact."[22] Thus, the Court applied the *Biggers* factors to determine whether the identification was so unreliable as to create a "very substantial likelihood of misidentification:"

1. **The opportunity to view.** Glover was within two feet of the seller, and saw him both times when the door opened. The sun was still out and there was natural light both in the hallway and inside the apartment.
2. **The degree of attention.** Glover was not a "casual or passing observer," but a trained police officer who can be expected to pay "scrupulous attention to detail," especially since he knew he would later have to identify the seller at trial. Glover and the seller were also both African-American, thus heightening Glover's ability to make a positive identification.
3. **The accuracy of the description.** Glover described the seller in great detail to a fellow officer. This description included information about the seller's race, height, build, the color and style of his hair, and his high cheekbone facial features. Brathwaite fit the description that Glover made.
4. **The witness' level of certainty**. Glover testified that "There is no question whatsoever" that the photo of Braithwaite was a photo of the person who sold him drugs.
5. **The time between the crime and the confrontation**. Glover described the seller to a fellow officer minutes after the transaction, and identified the photo only two days later.

Given these factors, the identification, though suspect, was not constitutionally barred. The Court decided that a jury should be able to make its own decision after hearing about the identification and its weaknesses: "We are content to rely

[22] Manson v. Braithwaite, 432 U.S. 98, 110 (1977).

upon the good sense and judgment of American juries, for evidence with some element of untrustworthiness is customary grist for the jury mill. Juries are not so susceptible that they cannot measure intelligently the weight of identification testimony that has some questionable features. . . . The defect, if there be one, goes to weight and not to substance"[23]

As we will see below, the factors set out by the Supreme Court as indicative of reliability are not necessarily supported by social science research. For example, a witness' level of certainty has been proven to have no relationship to the accuracy of the identification. For this reason, some state courts and legislatures have stepped in with their own rules for regulating identification procedures.

4. Eliminating the Taint of an Improper Identification. Assuming the defendant has successfully demonstrated the state's identification procedure was unduly suggestive and that the identification itself was unreliable, the out-of-court identification will be deemed inadmissible. The general rule—consistent with the "fruit of the poisonous tree" doctrine from Fourth Amendment law—is that if the out-of-court identification is precluded, the government is also precluded from having the witness identify the defendant in court. However, as with the poisonous tree doctrine, the prosecutor can still use an in-court identification if she can prove that the in-court identification is based on an "independent source"—that is, that the witness is identifying the defendant based on what the witness saw at the time of the crime, not based on the occasion when she viewed the defendant in a tainted identification procedure.

When making this independent source determination, courts should look to a number of factors, including:

1. The opportunity the witness had to observe the criminal during the crime;
2. Any discrepancy between the witness' pre-lineup descriptions and the defendant's actual description;
3. Whether the witness ever identified another person prior to the lineup;
4. Whether the witness identified the defendant in a photo prior to the lineup;
5. Whether the witness failed to identify the defendant on a prior occasion; and
6. The lapse of time between the crime and the lineup identification.[24]

[23] Id. at 116–117.

[24] Wade, 388 U.S. at 241.

If the prosecutor is able to establish that the in-court identification is not tainted by the improper prior identification, the jury will get to see the in-court identification but will not hear about any prior identification by the witness. It is hard to judge how this will be interpreted by a jury. In-court identifications tend to make a powerful impression on jurors, but they are a relatively suggestive identification procedure, and defense attorneys will be sure to point that out during closing arguments. Occasionally defense attorneys will get creative by placing the defendant in the audience among the spectators before the witness enters the courtroom, and then forcing the witness to identify the defendant from a group of people. This tactic requires the consent of the judge, but most judges will allow it. However, most judges do **not** permit the defense attorney to engage in the more deceptive tactic of moving the defendant into the audience and placing a person other than the defendant at the defense table before the witness enters the courtroom.

5. Fallibility of Identification Evidence and Methods of Combatting It. Recent studies regarding perception and memory have cast significant doubt on the reliability of eyewitness identifications. There is already substantial evidence that mistaken identification is by far the most common reason for false convictions. Other studies have shown that eyewitness identification is less reliable than almost any form of forensic evidence.

Why are eyewitnesses so unreliable? Psychologists who study eyewitness identification break down eyewitness testimony down into three categories: **acquisition** (perceiving an event or individual); **retention**, (processing and storing of the information that was perceived); and **retrieval** (recalling and communicating the information to others).[25] Acquisition can be adversely affected by a number of predictable factors, such as exposure time, frequency of exposure, and how important witnesses thought certain details were at the time of the perception.[26] But acquisition is also affected by some less-understood factors, such as the existence of violence in an event, the presence of a weapon, heightened levels of stress on the witness, and past experiences and cultural biases or prejudices that influence what the witness expects to see. [27] Even under the best circumstances, witnesses are surprisingly inaccurate when identifying an individual after having previously perceived that individual. For example, in one experiment subjects were shown four pictures of an individual for a total of thirty-two seconds. Eight minutes later, they were asked to pick out the individual they had perceived from a group of 150 pictures. Even given a relatively long period for acquisition, a relatively

[25] See Elizabeth F. Loftus, Eyewitness Testimony 20–109 (1996).

[26] Id. at 23–27.

[27] Id. at 31–36.

short time lapse between acquisition and retrieval, and laboratory conditions for the acquisition itself (low stress environment, adequate lighting conditions, etc.), only 58% of the subjects were able to correctly pick out the individual from the series of pictures.[28]

Studies about the retention and retrieval of information have shown that memories of events, even if accurately formed, may not only fade or disappear but also may be altered in numerous ways. For example, witnesses who are given post-event information about an event often begin to incorporate the post-event information into their existing memories, even if the post-event information is inconsistent with their original memory.[29] In other cases, experiments have shown that witnesses become more confident and certain of an identification as time progresses, even as their actual memory of the original perception fades.[30] Studies have shown that the level of certainty a witness has about the accuracy of the identification is unrelated to the actual accuracy of the identification.[31] It has also been well-documented that cross-racial identifications are notoriously flawed.

These natural obstacles to accurate identifications can be exacerbated by improperly suggestive identification techniques. One-on-one show-ups are particularly problematic because the witness may later "remember" the person they are shown in the show-up as the actual perpetrator even though he was not. And, police officers conducting the identification procedures can improperly influence the process, either intentionally or subconsciously. For example, assume an eyewitness is viewing a photo array, and she pauses at photo #3, saying "This might be the one." If photo #3 is not the suspect, the officer overseeing the procedure might respond by trying to move the witness along: "Make sure you look at all of the pictures before you make a decision." If photo #3 is the suspect, the officer may encourage the witness to focus on the suspect: "O.K. Tell me more about #3. Why do you think he is the one who robbed you?" Officers who respond in these ways may not even be aware they are improperly affecting the witness, but these subtle influences can have a significant effect on how witnesses "remember" the identity of the perpetrator.

What can be done to ensure more accurate identifications? Fortunately, the same studies that demonstrate the fallibility of eyewitness identifications provide some suggestions for enhancing the reliability of identification procedures. Three relatively simple techniques are 1) instituting double-blind identifications, 2)

---

[28] See K.R. Laughery, J.E. Alexander, and A.B. Lane, Recognition of Human Faces: Effects of Target Exposure Time, Target Position, Pose Position, and Type of Photograph, 55 J. Applied Psychol. 477, 477–83 (1971).

[29] Loftus, supra note 802, at 54–55.

[30] Id. at 82–84.

[31] Josephson, S. & Holmes, M. (2008). Cross-race recognition deficit and visual attention: do they all look (at faces) alike? Proceeding ETRA '08 Proceedings of the 2008 symposium on Eye tracking research & applications. ACM New York, NY, USA.

conducting lineups (or photo arrays) sequentially, and 3) recording the identification proceeding.

A **double-blind procedure** guarantees that the witness will not receive any cues—explicit or subconscious—from the officer conducting the identification. Essentially this means that the arresting officer (who of course knows the identity of the suspect) sets up the lineup or photo array but does not interact with the witness. Another officer, who has never seen the suspect, then performs the identification procedure with the witness. Because the second officer does not know who the suspect is, she cannot taint the process by encouraging the witness to provide the "correct" response.

Sequential lineups mean that the witness is shown the possible suspects one at a time instead of all at once. Studies have shown that when a witness sees an entire lineup at once, he will assume the suspect is present (even if he is told that may not be the case). Accordingly, the witness will then tend to pick the individual who most closely resembles his description of the perpetrator, even if he is not sure it is the same person. In contrast, if a witness is shown the potential suspects one at a time, she will compare each suspect to the image of the perpetrator in her memory, instead of comparing them to each other.

Finally, **recording the identification procedure** provides the jury with a precise representation of the reliability of the process, so that the jury can more accurately gauge whether the identification was correct. As with the recording of interrogations, this practice serves the dual purpose of giving the prosecution powerful evidence at trial if the identification practice is performed properly, and letting the jury see all of the weaknesses of a poorly conducted identification.

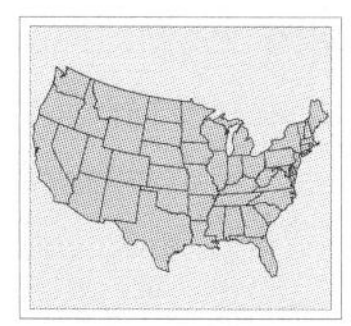

A few law enforcement agencies have chosen to adopt these practices in order to ensure they are pursuing the correct suspect. In some jurisdictions, the legislature has stepped in to mandate these procedures. This is one area in which states and local jurisdictions have made an effort to be more responsive to current social science findings and so differ significantly from the federal constitutional requirements.

A final option for combatting the problems inherent in eyewitness identification is to inform the jury of these problems. These solutions are based on the theory that the real problem is not that eyewitness identifications are unreliable—jurors hear plenty of evidence that may be unreliable, after all—but that jurors **believe** identifications are so much more reliable than they actually are, and therefore give them too much weight. There a couple of ways to respond to this problem. First, a judge could allow the defendant to call expert witnesses who can explain the problems with eyewitness testimony. Almost no judge will allow an expert to evaluate the credibility of a specific eyewitness, but many judges will allow an expert to testify in general terms about issues such as the effect of stress on perception and memory, or the inherent unreliability of cross-racial identifications. Another solution would be to incorporate some of these lessons into the model jury instructions. Some states actually require a jury instruction on the problems with eyewitness testimony, at least in cases where the identification is suspect. The vast majority of states, however, leave the question of whether to give an instruction—and the exact wording of the instruction—to the trial judge. Thus, effective advocacy by the attorneys can be critical in convincing a judge to give—or not to give—these cautionary instructions to the jury.

Quick Summary

Although identification procedures do not implicate the defendant's Fifth Amendment right against self-incrimination, they do at times implicate the Sixth Amendment right to counsel and the Fourteenth Amendment's Due Process Clause. Specifically, a defendant has a right to have an attorney present during any in-person identification procedure that occurs after charges have been formally filed in a case—an identification procedure that violates this rule is inadmissible in court. Also, if the identification procedure is "unnecessarily suggestive" to the point that there is a "very substantial likelihood of misidentification in the procedure," the identification will violate the Due Process Clause and will be inadmissible. However, even identifications secured by very suggestive procedures may be admitted if the procedures were "necessary"—meaning they were justified by the exigent circumstances in the case.

Furthermore, if the earlier, out-of-court identification procedure is inadmissible, the eyewitness will probably be precluded from identifying the defendant in court. If the out-of-court identification was precluded on Due Process grounds, the prosecutor can still seek to have her witness conduct an in-court identification if she can demonstrate that there was not a substantial likelihood of **irreparable** misidentification in the procedure. In other words, the witness can still identify the defendant in court as long as the in-court identification is based on what the witness actually perceived during the crime, rather than based on the improperly suggestive out-of-court identification.

Review Questions

1. Robbery at the Bus Stop. Grant was waiting at a bus stop at 5:00 in the morning when he was approached by a man wearing a hoodie. The man told him: "Don't run away and don't look at me; this is a robbery." Grant complied with the demand and looked down at the ground while the robber stole his wallet. He was only able to see the robber during a few momentary glances, each consisting of a few seconds. He could not remember his clothing; he never saw a gun; and he did not recall if he saw facial hair.

Ten weeks later, the police called Grant into the police department, stating that they believed they had caught the man who robbed him while the man was committing another robbery. The police presented a photo array to Grant. Grant was not sure at first if the perpetrator's photo was in the photo array, so the police officer told him: "We think he's there; just close your eyes and try to remember." Grant obeyed, concentrated, and then five seconds later selected a photo of Garth, who was the individual the police currently had in custody. Garth was charged with the robbery and went to trial. Garth's attorney moved to suppress any evidence of the photo array identification and to preclude Grant from identifying Garth at trial. Should the judge exclude the identifications from evidence?

2. Photo Array in a Computer Database. Defendant went into a beauty salon and robbed a beautician at gunpoint, stealing her purse, rings, and other jewelry. The entire encounter lasted approximately ten minutes. After the defendant left the salon, the victim, a woman named Reed, jumped in her car and followed the defendant while she called the police on her cell phone. Unfortunately, she lost the defendant and returned to the salon just as the police arrived.

When the police asked for a description, Reed described the defendant as a "fair-skinned woman with red hair" with gold teeth, wearing a black flight jacket, black jeans, and a green T-shirt. The police invited Reed to the precinct to look at some photos on a computer database. The database displayed six photographs at a time based on the parameters inputted. The police officer put in "fair-skinned woman with red hair." He then placed Reed in front of the computer, showed her how to page through pictures, and told her to alert him if she saw someone she recognized. After about 15-20 minutes, paging through hundreds of photos, she recognized the defendant, Josephine Nix. When the police asked if she was certain, she said "one hundred percent." The police printed out a number of photos of the suspect, but because their printer was faulty, one of the photos didn't come out very well and they threw it away.

The police told Reed that she could leave, but Reed did not have confidence that the police were going to follow up. As Reed left, she went to the trashcan and took the discarded photo of Nix with her. The photo had Nix's address on it, and she drove to her home and waited. When she saw Nix arrive, she was sure it was the correct person and called the police again. They arrived and arrested Nix and charged her with robbery.

At trial, Nix argued that Reed's identifications from the computer database, at the house, and at trial should all be excluded. Nix pointed out that the police did not keep track of how many photos Reed observed, nor did the database keep track of exactly which photos she saw. Nix also argued that when Reed saw her at the house, the identification was unnecessarily suggestive. Should the judge preclude the identifications?

3. Defense Attorney at the Line-up. Wilbur was arrested and charged with murdering a gas station attendant while robbing the gas station. After his arraignment, he was held without bail at the county jail. In order to obtain an indictment, the prosecutor took two of the eyewitnesses to the precinct and put Wilbur in a line-up. Wilbur's defense attorney was invited to attend. He asked to be placed in the room where the witnesses were going to be when they viewed the line-up, but the police refused, and instead placed him in the room where Wilbur and the rest of the line-up was present, out of view of the witnesses. From this room he could not see nor hear the witnesses who were viewing the line-up, nor could he see or hear the police officers who were talking to the witnesses. The two eyewitnesses successfully chose Wilbur from the line-up, and Wilbur was indicted.

Nix moved to preclude the identification from the trial, arguing that his right to counsel at the line-up had been violated. Should the identification be precluded?

FROM THE COURTROOM

UNITED STATES v. WADE

United States Supreme Court
388 U.S. 218 (1967)

[Justice BRENNAN delivered the opinion of the Court.]

[Justices SCALIA concurred in the decision.]

[Justice BREYER filed a dissenting opinion.]

[Justice ALITO filed a dissenting opinion, in which he was joined by Chief Justice ROBERTS and Justice KENNEDY and by Justice BREYER in part.]

The question here is whether courtroom identifications of an accused at trial are to be excluded from evidence because the accused was exhibited to the witnesses before trial at a post-indictment lineup conducted for identification purposes without notice to and in the absence of the accused's appointed counsel.

The federally insured bank in Eustace, Texas, was robbed on September 21, 1964. A man with a small strip of tape on each side of his face entered the bank, pointed a pistol at the female cashier and the vice president, the only persons in the bank at the time, and forced them to fill a pillowcase with the bank's money. The man then drove away with an accomplice who had been waiting in a stolen car outside the bank. On March 23, 1965, an indictment was returned against respondent, Wade, and two others for conspiring to rob the bank, and against Wade and the accomplice for the robbery itself. Wade was arrested on April 2, and counsel was appointed to represent him on April 26. Fifteen days later an FBI agent, without notice to Wade's lawyer, arranged to have the two bank employees observe a lineup made up of Wade and five or six other prisoners and conducted in a courtroom of the local county courthouse. Each person in the line wore strips of tape such as allegedly worn by the robber and upon direction each said something like "put the money in the bag," the words allegedly uttered by the robber. Both bank employees identified Wade in the lineup as the bank robber.

At trial the two employees, when asked on direct examination if the robber was in the courtroom, pointed to Wade. The prior lineup identification was then elicited from both employees on cross-examination. At the close of testimony, Wade's counsel moved for a judgment of acquittal or, alternatively, to strike the bank officials' courtroom identifications on the ground that conduct of the lineup, without notice to and in the absence of his appointed counsel, violated his Fifth Amendment privilege against self-incrimination and his Sixth Amendment right to the assistance of counsel. The motion was denied, and Wade was convicted. . . .

I.

Neither the lineup itself nor anything shown by this record that Wade was required to do in the lineup violated his privilege against self-incrimination. We have only recently reaffirmed that the privilege "protects an accused only from being compelled to testify against himself, or otherwise provide the State with evidence of a testimonial or communicative nature * * *." *Schmerber v. State of California*, 384 U.S. 757. We there held that compelling a suspect to submit to a withdrawal of a sample of his blood for analysis for alcohol content and the admission in evidence of the analysis report were not compulsion to those ends. That holding was supported by the opinion in *Holt v. United States*, 218 U.S. 245, in which case a question arose as to whether a blouse belonged to the defendant. A witness testified at trial that the defendant put on the blouse and it had fit him. The defendant argued that the admission of the testimony was error because compelling him to put on the blouse was a violation of his privilege. The Court rejected the claim as "an extravagant extension of the Fifth Amendment," Mr. Justice Holmes saying for the Court:

"(T)he prohibition of compelling a man in a criminal court to be witness against himself is a prohibition of the use of physical or moral compulsion to extort communications from him, not an exclusion of his body as evidence when it may be material."

The Court in *Holt*, however, put aside any constitutional questions which might be involved in compelling an accused, as here, to exhibit himself before victims of or witnesses to an alleged crime; the Court stated, "we need now consider how far a court would go in compelling a man to exhibit himself."

We have no doubt that compelling the accused merely to exhibit his person for observation by a prosecution witness prior to trial involves no compulsion of the accused to give evidence having testimonial significance. It is compulsion of the accused to exhibit his physical characteristics, not compulsion to disclose any knowledge he might have. It is no different from compelling Schmerber to provide a blood sample or Holt to wear the blouse, and, as in those instances, is not within the cover of the privilege. Similarly, compelling Wade to speak within hearing distance of the witnesses, even to utter words purportedly uttered by the robber, was not compulsion to utter statements of a "testimonial" nature; he was required to use his voice as an identifying physical characteristic, not to speak his guilt. We held in *Schmerber*, that the distinction to be drawn under the Fifth Amendment privilege against self-incrimination is one between an accused's "communications" in whatever form, vocal or physical, and "compulsion which makes a suspect or accused the source of 'real or physical evidence.'" We recognized that "both federal and state courts have usually held that * * * (the privilege) offers no protection against compulsion to submit to fingerprinting, photography, or measurements, to write or speak for identification, to appear in court, to stand, to assume a stance, to walk, or to make a particular gesture." None of these activities becomes testimonial within the scope of the privilege because required of the accused in a pretrial lineup.

Moreover, it deserves emphasis that this case presents no question of the admissibility in evidence of anything Wade said or did at the lineup which implicates his privilege.

The Government offered no such evidence as part of its case, and what came out about the lineup proceedings on Wade's cross-examination of the bank employees involved no violation of Wade's privilege.

II.

The fact that the lineup involved no violation of Wade's privilege against self-incrimination does not, however, dispose of his contention that the courtroom identifications should have been excluded because the lineup was conducted without notice to and in the absence of his counsel. Our rejection of the right to counsel claim in Schmerber rested on our conclusion in that case that "(n)o issue of counsel's ability to assist petitioner in respect of any rights he did possess is presented." In contrast, in this case it is urged that the assistance of counsel at the lineup was indispensable to protect Wade's most basic right as a criminal defendant-his right to a fair trial at which the witnesses against him might be meaningfully cross-examined.

The Framers of the Bill of Rights envisaged a broader role for counsel than under the practice then prevailing in England of merely advising his client in "matters of law," and eschewing any responsibility for "matters of fact." The constitutions in at least 11 of the 13 States expressly or impliedly abolished this distinction. "Though the colonial provisions about counsel were in accord on few things, they agreed on the necessity of abolishing the facts-law distinction; the colonists appreciated that if a defendant were forced to stand alone against the state, his case was foredoomed." This background is reflected in the scope given by our decisions to the Sixth Amendment's guarantee to an accused of the assistance of counsel for his defense. When the Bill of Rights was adopted, there were no organized police forces as we know them today. The accused confronted the prosecutor and the witnesses against him, and the evidence was marshalled, largely at the trial itself. In contrast, today's law enforcement machinery involves critical confrontations of the accused by the prosecution at pretrial proceedings where the results might well settle the accused's fate and reduce the trial itself to a mere formality. In recognition of these realities of modern criminal prosecution, our cases have construed the Sixth Amendment guarantee to apply to "critical" stages of the proceedings. The guarantee reads: "In all criminal prosecutions, the accused shall enjoy the right * * * to have the Assistance of Counsel for his defence." The plain wording of this guarantee thus encompasses counsel's assistance whenever necessary to assure a meaningful "defence."

As early as *Powell v. State of Alabama*, supra, we recognized that the period from arraignment to trial was "perhaps the most critical period of the proceedings * * *," during which the accused "requires the guiding hand of counsel * * *," if the guarantee is not to prove an empty right. That principle has since been applied to require the assistance of counsel at the type of arraignment-for example, that provided by Alabama-where certain rights might be sacrificed or lost: "What happens there may affect the whole trial. Available defenses may be irretrievably lost, if not then and there asserted * * *." The principle was also applied in *Massiah v. United States*, 377 U.S. 201, where we held that incriminating statements of the defendant should have been excluded from evidence when it appeared that they were overheard by federal agents who, without notice to the defendant's lawyer, arranged a meeting between the defendant and an accomplice turned informant. We said . . . that '(a)nything less * * * might deny a defendant "effective representation by counsel at the only stage when legal aid and advice would help him.' In *Escobedo v. State of Illinois*, 378 U.S. 478, we drew upon the rationale of *Hamilton* and *Massiah* in holding that the right to counsel was guaranteed at the point where the accused, prior to arraignment, was subjected to secret interrogation despite repeated requests to see his lawyer. We again noted the necessity of counsel's presence if the accused was to have a fair opportunity to present a defense at the trial itself:

'The rule sought by the State here, however, would make the trial no more than an appeal from the interrogation; and the 'right to use counsel at the formal trial (would be) a very hollow thing (if), for all practical purposes, the conviction is already assured by pretrial examination". * * * 'One can imagine a cynical prosecutor saying: "Let them have the most illustrious counsel, now. They can't escape the noose. There is nothing that counsel can do for them at the trial."'

Finally in *Miranda v. State of Arizona*, 384 U.S. 436, he rules established for custodial interrogation included the right to the presence of counsel. The result was rested on our finding that this and the other rules were necessary to safeguard the privilege against self-incrimination from being jeopardized by such interrogation.

Of course, nothing decided or said in the opinions in the cited cases links the right to counsel only to protection of Fifth Amendment rights. Rather those decisions "no more than (reflect) a constitutional principle established as long ago as *Powell v. Alabama* * * *." It is central to that principle that in addition to counsel's presence at trial, the accused is guaranteed that he need not stand alone against the State at any stage of the prosecution, formal or informal, in court or out, where counsel's absence might derogate from the accused's right to a fair trial. The security of that right is as much the aim of the right to counsel as it is of the other guarantees of the Sixth Amendment-the right of the accused to a speedy and public trial by an impartial jury, his right to be informed of the nature and cause of the accusation, and his right to be confronted with the witnesses against him and to have compulsory process for obtaining witnesses in his favor. The presence of counsel at such critical confrontations, as at the trial itself, operates to assure that the accused's interests will be protected consistently with our adversary theory of criminal prosecution.

In sum, the principle of *Powell v. Alabama* and succeeding cases requires that we scrutinize any pretrial confrontation of the accused to determine whether the presence of his counsel is necessary to preserve the defendant's basic right to a fair trial as affected by his right meaningfully to cross-examine the witnesses against him and to have effective assistance of counsel at the trial itself. It calls upon us to analyze whether potential substantial prejudice to defendant's rights inheres in the particular confrontation and the ability of counsel to help avoid that prejudice.

III.

The Government characterizes the lineup as a mere preparatory step in the gathering of the prosecution's evidence, not different-for Sixth Amendment purposes-from various other preparatory steps, such as systematized or scientific analyzing of the accused's fingerprints, blood sample, clothing, hair, and the like. We think there are differences which preclude such stages being characterized as critical stages at which the accused has the right to the presence of his counsel. Knowledge of the techniques of science and technology is sufficiently available, and the variables in techniques few enough, that the accused has the opportunity for a meaningful confrontation of the Government's case at trial through the ordinary processes of cross-examination of the Government's expert witnesses and the presentation of the evidence of his own experts. The denial of a right to have his counsel present at such analyses does not therefore violate the Sixth Amendment; they are not critical stages since there is minimal risk that his counsel's absence at such stages might derogate from his right to a fair trial.

IV.

But the confrontation compelled by the State between the accused and the victim or witnesses to a crime to elicit identification evidence is peculiarly riddled with innumerable dangers and variable factors which might seriously, even crucially, derogate from a fair trial. The vagaries of eyewitness identification are well-known; the annals of criminal law are rife with instances of mistaken identification. Mr. Justice Frankfurter once said: "What is the worth of identification testimony even when uncontradicted? The identification of strangers is proverbially untrustworthy. The hazards of such testimony are established by a formidable number of instances in the records of English and American trials. These instances are recent-not due to the brutalities of ancient criminal procedure." The Case of Sacco and Vanzetti 30 (1927). A major factor contributing to the high incidence of miscarriage of justice from mistaken identification has been the degree of suggestion inherent in the manner in which the prosecution presents the suspect to witnesses for pretrial identification. A commentator has observed that '(t)he influence of improper suggestion upon identifying witnesses probably accounts for more miscarriages of justice than any other single factor-perhaps it is responsible for more such errors than all other factors combined." Suggestion can be created intentionally or unintentionally in many subtle ways. And the dangers for the suspect are particularly grave when the witness' opportunity for observation was insubstantial, and thus his susceptibility to suggestion the greatest.

Moreover, '(i)t is a matter of common experience that, once a witness has picked out the accused at the line-up, he is not likely to go back on his word later on, so that in practice the issue of identity may (in the absence of other relevant evidence) for all practical purposes be determined there and then, before the trial."

The pretrial confrontation for purpose of identification may take the form of a lineup, also known as an "identification parade" or "showup," as in the present case, or presentation of the suspect alone to the witness, as in *Stovall v. Denno*, supra. It is obvious that risks of suggestion attend either form of confrontation and increase the dangers inhering in eyewitness identification. But as is the case with secret interrogations, there is serious difficulty in depicting what transpires at lineups and other forms of identification confrontations. "Privacy results in secrecy and this in turn results in a gap in our knowledge as to what in fact goes on * * *." For the same reasons, the defense can seldom reconstruct the manner and mode of lineup identification for judge or jury at trial. Those participating in a lineup with the accused may often be police officers; in any event, the participants' names are rarely recorded or divulged at trial. The impediments to an objective observation are increased when the victim is the witness. Lineups are prevalent in rape and robbery prosecutions and present a particular hazard that a victim's understandable outrage may excite vengeful or spiteful motives. In any event, neither witnesses nor lineup participants are apt to be alert for conditions prejudicial to the suspect. And if they were, it would likely be of scant benefit to the suspect since neither witnesses nor lineup participants are likely to be schooled in the detection of suggestive influences. Improper influences may go undetected by a suspect, guilty or not, who experiences the emotional tension which we might expect in one being confronted with potential accusers. Even when he does observe abuse, if he has a criminal record he may be reluctant to take the stand and open up the admission of prior convictions. Moreover any protestations by the suspect of the fairness of the lineup made at trial are likely to be in vain; the jury's choice is between the accused's unsupported version and that of the police officers present. In short, the accused's inability effectively to reconstruct at trial any unfairness that occurred at the lineup may deprive him of his only opportunity meaningfully to attack the credibility of the witness' courtroom identification.

. . .

The potential for improper influence is illustrated by the circumstances, insofar as they appear, surrounding the prior identifications in the three cases we decide today. In the present case, the testimony of the identifying witnesses elicited on cross-examination revealed that those witnesses were taken to the courthouse and seated in the courtroom to await assembly of the lineup. The courtroom faced on a hallway observable to the witnesses through an open door. The cashier testified that she saw Wade "standing in the hall" within sight of an FBI agent. Five or six other prisoners later appeared in the hall. The vice president testified that he saw a person in the hall in the custody of the agent who "resembled the person that we identified as the one that had entered the bank."

The lineup in *Gilbert* was conducted in an auditorium in which some 100 witnesses to several alleged state and federal robberies charged to Gilbert made wholesale identifications of *Gilbert* as the robber in each other's presence, a procedure said to be fraught with dangers of suggestion. And the vice of suggestion created by the identification in *Stovall*, supra, was the presentation to the witness of the suspect alone handcuffed to police officers. It is hard to imagine a situation more clearly conveying the suggestion to the witness that the one presented is believed guilty by the police.

The few cases that have surfaced therefore reveal the existence of a process attended with hazards of serious unfairness to the criminal accused and strongly suggest the plight of the more numerous defendants who are unable to ferret out suggestive influences in the secrecy of the confrontation. We do not assume that these risks are the result of police procedures intentionally designed to prejudice an accused. Rather we assume they derive from the dangers inherent in eyewitness identification and the suggestibility inherent in the context of the pretrial identification. Williams & Hammelmann, in one of the most comprehensive studies of such forms of identification, said, "(T)he fact that the police themselves have, in a given case, little or no doubt that the man put up for identification has committed the offense, and that their chief pre-occupation is with the problem of getting sufficient proof, because he has not 'come clean,' involves a a danger that this persuasion may communicate itself even in a doubtful case to the witness in some way * * *."

Insofar as the accused's conviction may rest on a courtroom identification in fact the fruit of a suspect pretrial identification which the accused is helpless to subject to effective scrutiny at trial, the accused is deprived of that right of cross-examination which is an essential safeguard to his right to confront the witnesses against him. And even though cross-examination is a precious safeguard to a fair trial, it cannot be viewed as an absolute assurance of accuracy and reliability. Thus in the present context, where so many variables and pitfalls exist, the first line of defense must be the prevention of unfairness and the lessening of the hazards of eyewitness identification at the lineup itself. The trial which might determine the accused's fate may well not be that in the courtroom but that at the pretrial confrontation, with the State aligned against the accused, the witness the sole jury, and the accused unprotected against the overreaching, intentional or unintentional, and with little or no effective appeal from the judgment there rendered by the witness-"that's the man."

Since it appears that there is grave potential for prejudice, intentional or not, in the pretrial lineup, which may not be capable of reconstruction at trial, and since presence of counsel itself can often avert prejudice and assure a meaningful confrontation at trial, there can be little doubt that for Wade the postindictment lineup was a critical stage of the prosecution at which he was "as much entitled to such aid (of counsel) * * * as at the trial itself." Thus both Wade and his counsel should have been notified of the impending lineup, and counsel's presence should have been a requisite to conduct of the lineup, absent an "intelligent waiver." No substantial countervailing policy considerations have been advanced against the requirement of the presence of counsel. Concern is expressed that the requirement will forestall prompt identifications and result in obstruction of the confrontations. As for the first, we note that in the two cases in which the right to counsel is today held to apply, counsel had already been appointed and no argument is made in either case that notice to counsel would have prejudicially delayed the confrontations. Moreover, we leave open the question whether the presence of substitute counsel might not suffice where notification and presence of the suspect's own counsel would result in prejudicial delay. And to refuse to recognize the right to counsel for fear that counsel will obstruct the course of justice is contrary to the basic assumptions upon which this Court has operated in Sixth Amendment cases. We rejected similar logic in Miranda v. State of Arizona, concerning presence of counsel during custodial interrogation.

'(A)n attorney is merely exercising the good professional judgment he has been taught. This is not cause for considering the attorney a menace to law enforcement. He is merely carrying out what he is sworn to do under his oath-to protect to the extent of his ability the rights of his client. In fulfilling this responsibility the attorney plays a vital role in the administration of criminal justice under our Constitution."

In our view counsel can hardly impede legitimate law enforcement; on the contrary, for the reasons expressed, law enforcement may be assisted by preventing the infiltration of taint in the prosecution's indentification evidence. That result cannot help the guilty avoid conviction but can only help assure that the right man has been brought to justice.

Legislative or other regulations, such as those of local police departments, which eliminate the risks of abuse and unintentional suggestion at lineup proceedings and the impediments to meaningful confrontation at trial may also remove the basis for regarding the stage as "critical." But neither Congress nor the federal authorities have seen fit to provide a solution. What we hold today "in no way creates a constitutional straitjacket which will handicap sound efforts at reform, nor is it intended to have this effect."

V.

We come now to the question whether the denial of Wade's motion to strike the courtroom identification by the bank witnesses at trial because of the absence of his counsel at the lineup required, as the Court of Appeals held, the grant of a new trial at which such evidence is to be excluded. We do not think this disposition can be justified without first giving the Government the opportunity to establish by clear and convincing evidence that the in-court identifications were based upon observations of the suspect other than the lineup identification. Where, as here, the admissibility of evidence of the lineup identification itself is not involved, a per se rule of exclusion of courtroom identification would be unjustified. A rule limited solely to the exclusion of testimony concerning identification at the lineup itself, without regard to admissibility of the courtroom identification, would render the right to counsel an empty one. The lineup is most often used, as in the present case, to crystallize the witnesses' identification of the defendant for future reference. We have already noted that the lineup identification will have that effect. The State may then rest upon the witnesses' unequivocal courtroom identifications, and not mention the pretrial identification as part of the State's case at trial. Counsel is then in the predicament in which Wade's counsel found himself-realizing that possible unfairness at the lineup may be the sole means of attack upon the unequivocal courtroom identification, and having to probe in the dark in an attempt to discover and reveal unfairness, while bolstering the government witness' courtroom identification by bringing out and dwelling upon his prior identification. Since counsel's presence at the lineup would equip him to attack not only the lineup identification but the courtroom identification as well, limiting the impact of violation of the right to counsel to exclusion of evidence only of identification at the lineup itself disregards a critical element of that right.

We think it follows that the proper test to be applied in these situations is that quoted in *Wong Sun v. United States*, 371 U.S. 471: "(W)hether, granting establishment of the primary illegality, the evidence to which instant objection is made has been come at by exploitation of that illegality or instead by means sufficiently distinguishable to be purged of the primary taint." Application of this test in the present context requires consideration of various factors; for example, the prior opportunity to observe the alleged criminal act, the existence of any discrepancy between any pre-lineup description and the defendant's actual description, any identification prior to lineup of another person, the identification by picture of the defendant prior to the lineup, failure to identify the defendant on a prior occasion, and the lapse of time between the alleged act and the lineup identification. It is also relevant to consider those facts which, despite the absence of counsel, are disclosed concerning the conduct of the lineup.

We doubt that the Court of Appeals applied the proper test for exclusion of the in-court identification of the two witnesses. The court stated that "it cannot be said with any certainty that they would have recognized appellant at the time of trial if this intervening lineup had not occurred," and that the testimony of the two witnesses "may well have been colored by the illegal procedure (and) was prejudicial." Moreover, the court was persuaded, in part, by the "compulsory verbal responses made by Wade at the instance of the Special Agent." This implies the erroneous holding that Wade's privilege against self-incrimination was violated so that the denial of counsel required exclusion.

On the record now before us we cannot make the determination whether the in-court identifications had an independent origin. This was not an issue at trial, although there is some evidence relevant to a determination. That inquiry is most properly made in the District Court. We therefore think the appropriate procedure to be followed is to vacate the conviction pending a hearing to determine whether the in-court identifications had an independent source, or whether, in any event, the introduction of the evidence was harmless error, and for the District Court to reinstate the conviction or order a new trial, as may be proper..

The judgment of the Court of Appeals is vacated and the case is remanded to that court with direction to enter a new judgment vacating the conviction and remanding the case to the District Court for further proceedings consistent with this opinion. It is so ordered.

[THE CHIEF JUSTICE joins the opinion of the Court except for Part I, from which he dissents for the reasons expressed in the opinion of Mr. Justice FORTAS.]

[Mr. Justice DOUGLAS joins the opinion of the Court except for Part I. . . . On that phase of the case he adheres to the dissenting views in *Schmerber v. State of California*, 384 U.S. 757, 772-779, since he believes that compulsory lineup violates the privilege against self-incrimination contained in the Fifth Amendment.]

[The concurring opinion of Justice CLARK is omitted.]

Mr. Justice BLACK, dissenting in part and concurring in part.

On March 23, 1965, respondent Wade was indicted for robbing a bank; on April 2, he was arrested; and on April 26, the court appointed a lawyer to represent him. Fifteen days later while Wade was still in custody, an FBI agent took him and several other prisoners into a room at the courthouse, directed each to participate in a lineup wearing strips of tape on his face and to speak the words used by the robber at the bank. This was all done in order to let the bank employee witnesses look at Wade for identification purposes. Wade's lawyer was not notified of or present at the lineup to protect his client's interests. At Wade's trial, two bank employees identified him in the courtroom. Wade objected to this testimony, when, on cross-examination, his counsel elicited from these witnesses the fact that they had seen Wade in the lineup. He contended that by forcing him to participate in the lineup, wear strips of tape on his face, and repeat the words used by the robber, all without counsel, the Government had (1) compelled him to be a witness against himself inviolation of the Fifth Amendment, and (2) deprived him of the assistance of counsel for his defense in violation of the Sixth Amendment.

. . .

I.

In rejecting Wade's claim that his privilege against self-incrimination was violated by compelling him to appear in the lineup wearing the tape and uttering the words given him by the police, the Court relies on the recent holding in *Schmerber v. State of California*, 384 U.S. 757. In that case the Court held that taking blood from a man's body against his will in order to convict him of a crime did not compel him to be a witness against himself. I dissented from that holding, and still dissent. The Court's reason for its holding was that the sample of Schmerber's blood taken in order to convict him of crime was neither "testimonial" nor "communicative" evidence. I think it was both. It seems quite plain to me that the Fifth Amendment's Self-incrimination Clause was designed to bar the Government from forcing any person to supply proof of his own crime, precisely what Schmerber was forced to do when he was forced to supply his blood. The Government simply took his blood against his will and over his counsel's protest for the purpose of convicting him of crime. So here, having Wade in its custody awaiting trial to see if he could or would be convicted of crime, the Government forced him to stand in a lineup, wear strips on his face, and speak certain words, in order to make it possible for government witnesses to identify him as a criminal. Had Wade been compelled to utter these or any other words in open court, it is plain that he would have been entitled to a new trial because of having been compelled to be a witness against himself. Being forced by the Government to help convict himself and to supply evidence against himself by talking outside the courtroom is equally violative of his constitutional right not to be compelled to be a witness against himself. Consequently, because of this violation of the Fifth Amendment, and not because of my own personal view that the Government's conduct was "unfair," "prejudicial," or "improper," I would prohibit the prosecution's use of lineup identification at trial.

. . .

Mr. Justice WHITE, whom Mr. Justice HARLAN and Mr. Justice STEWART join, dissenting in part and concurring in part.

The Court has again propounded a broad constitutional rule barring the use of a wide spectrum of relevant and probative evidence, solely because a step in its ascertainment or discovery occurs outside the presence of defense counsel. This was the approach of the Court in *Miranda v. State of Arizona*, 384 U.S. 436. I objected then to what I thought was an uncritical and doctrinaire approach without satisfactory factual foundation. I have much the same view of the present ruling and therefore dissent from the judgment and from Parts II, IV, and V of the Court's opinion.

The Court's opinion is far-reaching. It proceeds first by creating a new per se rule of constitutional law: a criminal suspect cannot be subjected to a pretrial identification process in the absence of his counsel without violating the Sixth Amendment. If he is, the State may not buttress a later courtroom identification, of the witness by any reference to the previous identification. Furthermore, the courtroom identification is not admissible at all unless the State can establish by clear and convincing proof that the testimony is not the fruit of the earlier identification made in the absence of defendant's counsel-admittedly a heavy burden for the State and probably an impossible one. To all intents and purposes, courtroom identifications are barred if pretrial identifications have occurred without counsel being present.

The rule applies to any lineup, to any other techniques employed to produce an identification and a fortiori to a face-to-face encounter between the witness and the suspect alone, regardless of when the identification occurs, in time or place, and whether before or after indictment or information. It matters not how well the witness knows the suspect, whether the witness is the suspect's mother, brother, or long-time associate, and no matter how long or well the witness observed the perpetrator at the scene of the crime. The kidnap victim who has lived for days with his abductor is in the same category as the witness who has had only a fleeting glimpse of the criminal. Neither may identify the suspect without defendant's counsel being present. The same strictures apply regardless of the number of other witnesses who positively identify the defendant and regardless of the corroborative evidence showing that it was the defendant who had committed the crime.

The premise for the Court's rule is not the general unreliability of eyewitness identifications nor the difficulties inherent in observation, recall, and recognition. The Court assumes a narrower evil as the basis for its rule-improper police suggestion which contributes to erroneous identifications. The Court apparently believes that improper police procedures are so widespread that a broad prophylactic rule must be laid down, requiring the presence of counsel at all pretrial identifications, in order to detect recurring instances of police misconduct. I do not share this pervasive distrust of all official investigations. None of the materials the Court relies upon supports it. Certainly, I would bow to solid fact, but the Court quite obviously does not have before it any reliable, comprehensive survey of current police practices on which to base its new rule. Until it does, the Court should avoid excluding relevant evidence from state criminal trials.

The Court goes beyond assuming that a great majority of the country's police departments are following improper practices at pretrial identifications. To find the lineup a "critical" stage of the proceeding and to exclude identifications made in the absence of counsel, the Court must also assume that police "suggestion," if it occurs at all, leads to erroneous rather than accurate identifications and that reprehensible police conduct will have an unavoidable and largely undiscoverable impact on the trial. This in turn assumes that there is now no adequate source from which defense counsel can learn about the circumstances of the pretrial identification in order to place before the jury all of the considerations which should enter into an appraisal of courtroom identification evidence. But these are treacherous and unsupported assumptions resting as they do on the notion that the defendant will not be aware, that the police and the witnesses will forget or prevaricate, that defense counsel will be unable to bring out the truth and that neither jury, judge, nor appellate court is a sufficient safeguard against unacceptable police conduct occurring at a pretrial identification procedure. I am unable to share the Court's view of the willingness of the police and the ordinary citizenwitness to dissemble, either with respect to the identification of the defendant or with respect to the circumstances surrounding a pretrial identification.

There are several striking aspects to the Court's holding. First, the rule does not bar courtroom identifications where there have been no previous identifications in the presence of the police, although when identified in the courtroom, the defendant is known to be in custody and charged with the commission of a crime. Second, the Court seems to say that if suitable legislative standards were adopted for the conduct of pretrial identifications, thereby lessening the hazards in such confrontations, it would not insist on the presence of counsel. But if this is true, why does not the Court simply fashion what it deems to be constitutionally acceptable procedures for the authorities to follow? Certainly the Court is correct in suggesting that the new rule will be wholly inapplicable where police departments themselves have established suitable safeguards.

Third, courtroom identification may be barred, absent counsel at a prior identification, regardless of the extent of counsel's information concerning the circumstances of the previous confrontation between witness and defendant-apparently even if there were recordings or sound-movies of the events as they occurred. But if the rule is premised on the defendant's right to have his counsel know, there seems little basis for not accepting other means to inform. A disinterested observer, recordings, photographs-any one of them would seem adequate to furnish the basis for a meaningful cross-examination of the eyewitness who identifies the defendant in the courtroom.

I share the Court's view that the criminal trial, at the very least, should aim at truthful factfinding, including accurate eyewitness identifications. I doubt, however, on the basis of our present information, that the tragic mistakes which have occurred in criminal trials are as much the product of improper police conduct as they are the consequence of the difficulties inherent in eyewitness testimony and in resolving evidentiary conflicts by court or jury. I doubt that the Court's new rule will obviate these difficulties, or that the situation will be measurably improved by inserting defense counsel into the investigative processes of police departments eyerywhere.

But, it may be asked, what possible state interest militates against requiring the presence of defense counsel at lineups? After all, the argument goes, he may do some good, he may upgrade the quality of identification evidence in state courts and he can scarcely do any harm. Even if true, this is a feeble foundation for fastening an ironclad constitutional rule upon state criminal procedures. Absent some reliably established constitutional violation, the processes by which the States enforce their criminal laws are their own prerogative. The States do have an interest in conducting their own affairs, an interest which cannot be displaced simply by saying that there are no valid arguments with respect to the merits of a federal rule emanating from this Court.

Beyond this, however, requiring counsel at pretrial identifications as an invariable rule trenches on other valid state interests. One of them is its concern with the prompt and efficient enforcement of its criminal laws. Identifications frequently take place after arrest but before an indictment is returned or an information is filed. The police may have arrested a suspect on probable cause but may still have the wrong man. Both the suspect and the State have every interest in a prompt identification at that stage, the suspect in order to secure his immediate release and the State because prompt and early identification enhances accurate identification and because it must know whether it is on the right investigative track. Unavoidably, however, the absolute rule requiring the presence of counsel will cause significant delay and it may very well result in no pretrial identification at all. Counsel must be appointed and a time arranged convenient for him and the witnesses. Meanwhile, it may be necessary to file charges against the suspect who may then be released on bail, in the federal system very often on his own recognizance, with neither the State nor the defendant having the benefit of a properly conducted identification procedure.

Nor do I think the witnesses themselves can be ignored. They will now be required to be present at the convenience of counsel rather than their own. Many may be much less willing to participate if the identification stage is transformed into an adversary proceeding not under the control of a judge. Others may fear for their own safety if their identity is known at an early date, especially when there is no way of knowing until the lineup occurs whether or not the police really have the right man.

Finally, I think the Court's new rule is vulnerable in terms of its own unimpeachable purpose of increasing the reliability of identification testimony.

Law enforcement officers have the obligation to convict the guilty and to make sure they do not convict the innocent. They must be dedicated to making the criminal trial a procedure for the ascertainment of the true facts surrounding the commission of the crime. To this extent, our so-called adversary system is not adversary at all; nor should it be. But defense counsel has no comparable obligation to ascertain or present the truth. Our system assigns him a different mission. He must be and is interested in preventing the conviction of the innocent, but, absent a voluntary plea of guilty, we also insist that he defend his client whether he is innocent or guilty. The State has the obligation to present the evidence. Defense counsel need present nothing, even if he knows what the truth is. He need not furnish any witnesses to the police, or reveal any confidences of his client, or furnish any other information to help the prosecution's case. If he can confuse a witness, even a truthful one, or make him appear at a disadvantage, unsure or indecisive, that will be his normal course. Our interest in not convicting the innocent permits counsel to put the State to its proof, to put the State's case in the worst possible light, regardless of what he thinks or knows to be the truth. Undoubtedly there are some limits which defense counsel must observe[7] but more often than not, defense counsel will cross-examine a prosecution witness, and impeach him if he can, even if he thinks the witness is telling the truth, just as he will attempt to destroy a witness who he thinks is lying. In this respect, as part of our modified adversary system and as part of the duty imposed on the most honorable defense counsel, we countenance or require conduct which in many instances has little, if any, relation to the search for truth.

I would not extend this system, at least as it presently operates, to police investigations and would not require counsel's presence at pretrial identification procedures. Counsel's interest is in not having his client placed at the scene of the crime, regardless of his whereabouts. Some counsel may advise their clients to refuse to make any movements or to speak any words in a lineup or even to appear in one. To that extent the impact on truthful factfinding is quite obvious. Others will not only observe what occurs and develop possibility for later cross-examination but will hover over witnesses and begin their cross-examination then, menacing truthful factfinding as thoroughly as the Court fears the police now do. Certainly there is an implicit invitation to counsel to suggest rules for the lineup and to manage and produce it as best he can. I therefore doubt that the Court's new rule, at least absent some clearly defined limits on counsel's role, will measurably contribute to more reliable pretrial identifications. My fears are that it will have precisely the opposite result. It may well produce fewer convictions, but that is hardly a proper measure of its long-run acceptability. In my view, the State is entitled to investigate and develop its case outside the presence of defense counsel. This includes the right to have private conversations with identification witnesses, just as defense counsel may have his own consultations with these and other witnesses without having the prosecutor present.

Whether today's judgment would be an acceptable exercise of supervisory power over federal courts is another question. But as a constitutional matter, the judgment in this case is erroneous and although I concur in Parts I and III of the Court's opinion I respectfully register this dissent.

[The concurring and dissenting opionion of Justice FORTAS, with whom THE CHIEF JUSTICE and Mr. Justice DOUGLAS join, is omitted.]

FROM THE COURTROOM

NEIL v. BIGGERS

United States Supreme Court
409 U.S. 188 (1972)

[Justice POWELL delivered the opinion of the Court.]

[Justice BRENNAN filed a concurring and dissenting opinion in which, which was joined by Justice DOUGLAS Justice STEWART, in which they declined to reach the merits of the case.]

[Justice MARSHALL took no part in the consideration or decision of this case.]

In 1965, after a jury trial in a Tennessee court, respondent was convicted of rape and was sentenced to 20 years' imprisonment. The State's evidence consisted in part of testimony concerning a station-house identification of respondent by the victim. The Tennessee Supreme Court affirmed. . . .

II

We proceed, then, to consider respondent's due process claim. As the claim turns upon the facts, we must first review the relevant testimony at the jury trial and at the habeas corpus hearing regarding the rape and the identification. The victim testified at trial that on the evening of January 22, 1965, a youth with a butcher knife grabbed her in the doorway to her kitchen:

"A. (H)e grabbed me from behind, and grappled-twisted me on the floor. Threw me down on the floor.

"Q. And there was no light in that kitchen?

"A. Not in the kitchen.

"Q. So you couldn't have seen him then?

"A. Yet, I could see him, when I looked up in his face.

"Q. In the dark?

"A. He was right in the doorway-it was enough light from the bedroom shining through. Yes, I could see who he was.

"Q. You could see? No light? And you could see him and know him then?

"A. Yes."

When the victim screamed, her 12-year-old daughter came out of her bedroom and also began to scream. The assailant directed the victim to "tell her (the daughter) to shut up, or I'll kill you both." She did so, and was then walked at knifepoint about two blocks along a railroad track, taken into a woods, and raped there. She testified that "the moon was shining brightly, full moon." After the rape, the assailant ran off, and she returned home, the whole incident having taken between 15 minutes and half an hour.

She then gave the police what the Federal District Court characterized as "only a very general description," describing him as "being fat and flabby with smooth skin, bushy hair and a youthful voice." Additionally, though not mentioned by the District Court, she testified at the habeas corpus hearing that she had described her assailant as being between 16 and 18 years old and between five feet ten inches and six feet, tall, as weighing between 180 and 200 pounds, and as having a dark brown complexion. This testimony was substantially corroborated by that of a police officer who was testifying from his notes.

On several occasions over the course of the next seven months, she viewed suspects in her home or at the police station, some in lineups and others in showups, and was shown between 30 and 40 photographs. She told the police that a man pictured in one of the photographs had features similar to those of her assailant, but identified none of the suspects. On August 17, the police called her to the station to view respondent, who was being detained on another charge. In an effort to construct a suitable lineup, the police checked the city jail and the city juvenile home. Finding no one at either place fitting respondent's unusual physical description, they conducted a showup instead.

The showup itself consisted of two detectives walking respondent past the victim. At the victim's request, the police directed respondent to say "shut up or I'll kill you." The testimony at trial was not altogether clear as to whether the victim first identified him and then asked that he repeat the words or made her identification after he had spoken. In any event, the victim testified that she had "no doubt" about her identification. At the habeas corpus hearing, she elaborated in response to questioning.

> "A. That I have no doubt, I mean that I am sure that when I-see, when I first laid eyes on him, I knew that it was the individual, because his face-well, there was just something that I don't think I could ever forget. I believe-
>
> "Q. You say when you first laid eyes on him, which time are you referring to?
>
> "A. When I identified him-when I seen him in the courthouse when I was took up to view the suspect."

We must decide whether, as the courts below held, this identification and the circumstances surrounding it failed to comport with due process requirements.

III

We have considered on four occasions the scope of due process protection against the admission of evidence deriving from suggestive identification procedures. In *Stovall v. Denno*, 388 U.S. 293 (1967), the Court held that the defendant could claim that "the confrontation conducted . . . was so unnecessarily suggestive and conductive to irreparable mistaken identification that he was denied due process of law." This we held, must be determined "on the totality of the circumstances." We went on to find that on the facts of the case then before us, due process was not violated, emphasizing that the critical condition of the injured witness justified a showup in her hospital room. At trial, the witness, whose view of the suspect at the time of the crime was brief, testified to the out-of-court identification, as did several police officers present in her hospital room, and also made an in-court identification.

Subsequently, in a case where the witnesses made in-court identifications arguably stemming from previous exposure to a suggestive photographic array, the Court restated the governing test:

"(W)e hold that each case must be considered on its own facts, and that convictions based on eye -witness identification at trial following a pretrial identification by photograph will be set aside on that ground only if the photographic identification procedure was so impermissibly suggestive as to give rise to a very substantial likelihood of irreparable misidentification."

Again we found the identification procedure to be supportable, relying both on the need for prompt utilization of other investigative leads and on the likelihood that the photographic identifications were reliable, the witnesses having viewed the bank robbers for periods of up to five minutes under good lighting conditions at the time of the robbery.

The only case to date in which this Court has found identification procedures to be violative of due process is *Foster v. California*, 394 U.S. 440 (1969). There, the witness failed to identify Foster the first time he confronted him, despite a suggestive lineup. The police then arranged a showup, at which the witness could make only a tentative identification. Ultimately, at yet another confrontation, this time a lineup, the witness was able to muster a definite identification. We held all of the identifications inadmissible, observing that the identifications were "all but inevitable" under the circumstances.

In the most recent case of *Coleman v. Alabama*, 399 U.S. 1, 90 (1970), we held admissible an in-court identification by a witness who had a fleeting but "real good look" at his assailant in the headlights of a passing car. The witness testified at a pretrial suppression hearing that he identified one of the petitioners among the participants in the lineup before the police placed the participants in a formal line. Mr. Justice Brennan for four members of the Court stated that this evidence could support a finding that the in-court identification was "entirely based upon observations at the time of the assault and not at all induced by the conduct of the lineup."

Some general guidelines emerge from these cases as to the relationship between suggestiveness and misidentification. It is, first of all, apparent that the primary evil to be avoided is "a very substantial likelihood of irreparable misidentification." While the phrase was coined as a standard for determining whether an in-court identification would be admissible in the wake of a suggestive out-of-court identification, with the deletion of "irreparable" it serves equally well as a standard for the admissibility of testimony concerning the out-of-court identification itself. It is the likelihood of misidentification which violates a defendant's right to due process, and it is this which was the basis of the exclusion of evidence in *Foster*. Suggestive confrontations are disapproved because they increase the likelihood of misidentification, and unnecessarily suggestive ones are condemned for the further reason that the increased chance of misidentification is gratuitous. But as *Stovall* makes clear, the admission of evidence of a showup without more does not violate due process.

What is less clear from our cases is whether, as intimated by the District Court, unnecessary suggestiveness alone requires the exclusion of evidence. While we are inclined to agree with the courts below that the police did not exhaust all possibilities in seeking persons physically comparable to respondent, we do not think that the evidence must therefore be excluded. The purpose of a strict rule barring evidence of unnecessarily suggestive confrontations would be to deter the police from using a less reliable procedure where a more reliable one may be available, and would not be based on the assumption that in every instance the admission of evidence of such a confrontation offends due process. Such a rule would have no place in the present case, since both the confrontation and the trial preceded *Stovall v. Denno*, when we first gave notice that the suggestiveness of confrontation procedures was anything other than a matter to be argued to the jury.

We turn, then, to the central question, whether under the "totality of the circumstances" the identification was reliable even though the confrontation procedure was suggestive. As indicated by our cases, the factors to be considered in evaluating the likelihood of misidentification include the opportunity of the witness to view the criminal at the time of the crime, the witness' degree of attention, the accuracy of the witness' prior description of the criminal, the level of certainty demonstrated by the witness at the confrontation, and the length of time between the crime and the confrontation. Applying these factors, we disagree with the District Court's conclusion.

In part, as discussed above, we think the District Court focused unduly on the relative reliability of a lineup as opposed to a showup, the issue on which expert testimony was taken at the evidentiary hearing. It must be kept in mind also that the trial was conducted before Stovall and that therefore the incentive was lacking for the parties to make a record at trial of facts corroborating or undermining the identification. The testimony was addressed to the jury, and the jury apparently found the identification reliable. Some of the State's testimony at the federal evidentiary hearing may well have been self-serving in that it too neatly fit the case law, but it surely does nothing to undermine the state record, which itself fully corroborated the identification.

We find that the District Court's conclusions on the critical facts are unsupported by the record and clearly erroneous. The victim spent a considerable period of time with her assailant, up to half an hour. She was with him under adequate artificial light in her house and under a full moon outdoors, and at least twice, once in the house and later in the woods, faced him directly and intimately. She was no casual observer, but rather the victim of one of the most personally humiliating of all crimes. Her description to the police, which included the assailant's approximate age, height, weight, complexion, skin texture, build, and voice, might not have satisfied Proust but was more than ordinarily thorough. She had "no doubt" that respondent was the person who raped her. In the nature of the crime, there are rarely witnesses to a rape other than the victim, who often has a limited opportunity of observation. The victim here, a practical nurse by profession, had an unusual opportunity to observe and identify her assailant. She testified at the habeas corpus hearing that there was something about his face "I don't think I could ever forget."

There was, to be sure, a lapse of seven months between the rape and the confrontation. This would be a seriously negative factor in most cases. Here, however, the testimony is undisputed that the victim made no previous identification at any of the showups, lineups, or photographic showings. Her record for reliability was thus a good one, as she had previously resisted whatever suggestiveness inheres in a showup. Weighing all the factors, we find no substantial likelihood of misidentification. The evidence was properly allowed to go to the jury.

Affirmed in part, reversed in part, and remanded.

[The concurring and dissenting opinion of Justice BRENNAN, with whom Mr. Justice DOUGLAS and Mr. Justice STEWART concur, is omitted.]

28

Screening by Prosecutors

Key Concepts

- The Prosecution's Charging Decision—Exercising Legal Discretion and Equitable Discretion
- Selective Prosecution and Vindictive Prosecution
- Ethical Restrictions on the Charging Power
- Overcharging

A. Overview. In our criminal justice system, the ultimate decision of guilt or innocence is made during the trial, where the finder of fact (usually the jury) evaluates the evidence and decides whether the prosecutor has proven all the elements of the charged crime beyond a reasonable doubt. However, before a criminal case gets to that stage—before the adjudicative process can even begin—the case must go through three or four levels of screening by different institutional actors, each of which independently evaluates the case.

We already saw in **Chapter 2** that individual actors in the criminal justice system have vast amounts of discretion. This discretion is significantly influenced by two things. First, state and federal legislatures have created so many broadly-worded criminal laws it would be impossible to enforce them all. Second, even if it were possible to meaningfully enforce every criminal law it would be undesirable to mechanically pursue each instance of conduct that technically constitutes a crime without taking into account the specific facts and circumstances of each individual case. Therefore, police officers and prosecutors must make choices about which alleged criminal conduct to pursue and which alleged criminal conduct to disregard.

Second, in making decisions about who to arrest and prosecute, actors at the local level can be more responsive to community needs than centralized legislatures in distant state capitals. Thus, the system is built to give discretion to these actors, who (in theory) act in the best interests of the local community, and whose decisions (in theory) are reviewed by the local electorate through democratic processes. As you will read, however, local control of police and prosecutorial decision-making is often more true in theory than in practice.

Screening of criminal cases is a necessary part of the criminal justice system. Some of the screening that occurs involves the exercise of unguided discretion on the part of the screener. Other types of screening are conducted according to strict legal standards. In order, the screening stages (and individuals responsible for making the screening decisions) are:

1. The police officer or officers, who must decide whether there is probable cause to believe that an individual committed a crime; and if so whether this specific crime is worth pursuing;

2. The prosecutor, who must decide whether charges are supported by probable cause, and whether prosecution of the case is appropriate;

3. The judge, who must review the charging document and ensure that the alleged facts, if true, are sufficient to prove all of the elements of the crime;

4. In a felony case and some misdemeanor cases, the magistrate, judge, or grand jury who reviews the evidence to ensure there is probable cause to believe the defendant committed the crime.

Note that while the first two stages of screening involve the exercise of discretion on the part of the screener, the third and (if necessary) the fourth do not. Instead, these latter stages require application of legal standards. We will refer to these different categories as "discretionary screening" and "standard-based screening."

We have already discussed at length the different decisions made by police officers in deciding whether to make an arrest and bring charges. In this chapter we will focus on the screening decision by the prosecutor, who is the primary screener in the criminal justice system. In **Chapter 29,** we will examine the initial appearance (sometimes called the arraignment) and discuss the screening function that the judge plays at that point. In **Chapters 34 and 35,** we will examine the preliminary hearing and the grand jury, two alternate ways in which an independent body reviews the evidence to ensure that the case should move forward.

B. Introduction and Policy. Most criminal cases begin with a police investigation and arrest, at which point the case is turned over to the prosecutor's office.[1] In these cases, the arrest marks a significant turning point in the case: it is the point at which the primary decision-making authority shifts from the police to the prosecutor. The prosecutor must decide whether to bring charges, which charges to bring, whether to offer a plea bargain or other disposition of the case, and (if there is a conviction) what sentence to recommend to the judge. Making these determinations is commonly known as exercising **prosecutorial discretion.**

[1] Occasionally, the prosecutor will conduct her own investigation in conjunction with law enforcement and then make the decision to arrest the defendant.

In addition to these discretionary considerations, the prosecutor must make more mechanical decisions about how to proceed with the case, such as whether to gather more evidence before proceeding, how to respond to suppression and other pre-trial motions from defense attorneys, and what evidence and witnesses to present at trial.

1. Who Are the Prosecutors? Like law enforcement offices, prosecutor's offices come in many shapes and sizes.

Almost all federal crimes are prosecuted by the local United States Attorney's Office. These offices are a part of the United States Department of Justice. There are ninety-three United States Attorneys, one for nearly every federal judicial district. Each United States Attorney works for the United States Attorney General and is theoretically appointed by the President and confirmed by Congress, although in practice the local Senator or Representative will often recommend the candidate. The United States Attorney is almost always a member of the same political party as the President, and when the presidency switches parties, the old United States Attorney often steps down to allow the new President to appoint a member of his or her own party.

Within each U.S. Attorney's Office are a number of other lawyers working as prosecutors. These "line assistants"—the Assistant United States Attorneys who work for each office—are apolitical and typically do not change when the United States Attorney is replaced. Thus, although the United States Attorneys' Offices may receive some political "guidance" from the Attorney General (for example, to recommend tougher sentences on gun crimes, or not to bring cases of marijuana possession), for the most part they are free to pursue individual cases without interference from Washington, D.C., and without concern for political consequences. United States Attorney's Offices range in size based on the population of their district—the largest office, in the District of Columbia, employs approximately 350 attorneys and handles both federal and local crimes. The U.S. Attorney's Office in the District of Columbia is unique in that respect; all other U.S. Attorney's Offices prosecute only federal crimes.

Most state crimes are prosecuted by local offices that bear titles like Office of the District Attorney, Office of the State's Attorney or County Prosecutor's Office. These local prosecutors are typically organized by county. So, in any one state you may have an Office of the State's Attorney for Highland County and an Office of the State's Attorney for Lowland County. Each state also has a statewide Attorney General's Office that takes some responsibility for prosecuting state crimes and generally acts as extra support for county prosecutors on complex cases. Finally, many states have city prosecutors, whose geographic jurisdiction overlaps with the county prosecutors and who prosecute less serious crimes.

Almost all local prosecutors and attorneys generals are elected by the general population of the county or state, though some are appointed by the county executive or the governor. Thus, they are somewhat responsive to public opinion—if they are pursuing policies that are unpopular, they face the possibility that the voters will replace them. In practice, most local prosecutors' campaigns center on the crime rate in the jurisdiction and the conviction rate of the office. As with their federal counterparts, the assistant prosecutors who work in the office and actually try the cases are generally apolitical and stay on the job even if the head prosecutor is replaced. Also similar to their federal counterparts, local prosecutor's offices range in size from approximately one thousand attorneys (in the Los Angeles County office) to small counties with only one prosecutor.

Unlike the members of various police forces, all prosecutors have nearly identical educational backgrounds. However, there is significant variety in the amount of training they receive. As a general rule, the larger prosecutorial offices have more extensive training programs, while prosecutors at smaller officers must do more learning on the job.

The job of a prosecutor can vary dramatically from jurisdiction to jurisdiction. Generally federal prosecutors have a lower caseload, take more serious cases, and spend more time on each case than their state and local counterparts. Local prosecutors usually spend more time in court and have less time to investigate and prepare each case. However, as with any generalization, there are countless exceptions to this rule.

2. The Charging Decision. Typically, the very first decision a prosecutor must make is whether to file charges, and if so, which charges to file. The law enforcement officer has already arrested the suspect for violations of specific provisions of the criminal code, but the prosecutor has an independent duty to review these charges. As with most instances of prosecutorial discretion, there are two aspects to the charging decision: first, do the facts support these charges—that is, does the prosecutor believe that she will ultimately be able to gather and present the evidence necessary to prove this case beyond a reasonable doubt? And second, will pursuing this case be an appropriate use of state resources, or are there reasons why, even though a conviction is likely, the case should not be pursued?

The first aspect of the charging decision—what we will call "**legal discretion**"—is mostly mechanical: given what the prosecutor knows about the case, does she think it is likely she can obtain a conviction? The prosecutor has a greater familiarity with the law than the officer who made the arrest and can better evaluate whether the alleged facts of the case will support a given charge, or perhaps whether another charge should be substituted or added. The prosecutor also knows the rules of evidence and criminal procedure, and can determine which testimony and other types of evidence will be admissible in court. Prosecutors also often have a sense of the make-up of the jury pool in their jurisdiction and might make charging decisions based upon their understanding of the likelihood a jury in the jurisdiction will convict under certain circumstances.

For example, a police officer may make an arrest for grand larceny, alleging the defendant stole a used computer which was worth over $500. The prosecutor may believe that she can prove the defendant stole the computer, but she may realize that there is no way to prove the computer is worth over $500—and therefore the case has to be reduced from a felony grand larceny to a misdemeanor larceny. Or, the prosecutor may review the evidence and realize that a key piece of evidence is inadmissible hearsay, or that the defendant's confession was taken in violation of *Miranda* and so will be suppressed—and therefore the charges must be dropped altogether.

Even after the prosecutor determines that the alleged facts support a criminal charge, she has a broader duty to only pursue a case if it is in the public interest to do so. This is the second aspect of the charging decision—the exercise of "**equitable discretion**." Usually it is consistent with the public interest to pursue any case in which there is a substantial reason to believe the accused committed a crime, but not always. Sometimes the prosecutor will disagree with the assessment of the law enforcement officer and refuse to bring charges. This is a rare occurrence, and usually involves relatively minor crimes and some type of extenuating circumstances. For example, assume a teenager gets drunk in a bar and then goes outside and wanders into traffic, yelling profanities at the drivers. Someone calls the police, but before the police can arrive, the teenager is struck by a car and breaks a leg. The police then arrest the teenager for disorderly conduct, since he unreasonably disrupted traffic and caused a public disturbance. A prosecutor could easily prove this case, but may feel that the teenager has already suffered enough from having a broken leg and that the harm that he caused to others was relatively minor. The prosecutor may also conclude that the teenager's parents will be able to deal with the drinking problem better than the criminal justice system.

The prosecutor is given a great amount of discretion at this stage, but it is not completely unconstrained. We now turn to the legal and ethical restrictions on her charging decisions.

C. The Law. The law regulating prosecutorial discretion at the charging stage is relatively sparse, and the prosecutor's power to make these decisions remains nearly unchallenged. However, there are three narrow limitations that have emerged to curtail that power:

A prosecutor has nearly unreviewable discretion in deciding whether to commence formal criminal charges against a defendant, except:

1. If the local prosecutor decides not to file a charge, the prosecution could still be initiated by:

   (a) The state prosecutor or (if the criminal conduct also involved a violation of federal law) a federal prosecutor;

   (b) The grand jury; or

   (c) A special prosecutor or independent counsel appointed by the executive, Congress, or the courts.

2. If the prosecutor decides to file charges, the prosecutor may not make that charging decision based on a discriminatory standard such as race, religion, or other arbitrary classification. However, it is presumed that a prosecutor's decisions are not motivated by improper considerations, and in order to overcome that presumption the defendant must prove that (a) the prosecutor's charging policy had a discriminatory effect and (b) it was motivated by a discriminatory purpose.[2]

3. The prosecutor may not increase the severity of the charge or file additional charges against a defendant in retaliation for the defendant exercising his right to appeal the case. If the prosecutor increases the severity of the charge or files additional charges after the defendant has been convicted and has successfully challenged his conviction, the defendant enjoys a presumption that the new charges are retaliatory in nature.[3]

The first limitation notes that there are other individuals and institutions that can—in theory, at least—file criminal charges against a defendant. In practice, however, this is a very rare occurrence. Generally, the state-wide prosecutor (the attorney general) will only become involved in a case if she is invited to do so by the local prosecutor—either because there is a conflict of interest with the local prosecutor or because the case is complicated or would require extra resources that are beyond the ability of the county or city. For example, if a member of the prosecutor's staff is arrested, the local prosecutor may ask the attorney general to handle the case to avoid any conflict of interest. Or, if a murder that may be eligible for the death penalty takes place in a small county with only one or two

---

[2] Ah Sin v. Wittman, 198 U.S. 500 (1905).

[3] Blackledge v. Perry, 417 U.S. 21 (1974).

prosecutors, the prosecutor's office may not have the expertise or the resources to try the capital case.

There are infrequent occasions when a local prosecutor will fail or refuse to act, and another prosecutor will step in to bring charges. This will usually happen in a high profile case, in which the attorney general or other state high official is subject to substantial community pressure, or otherwise believes that the local prosecutor is acting in bad faith or with discriminatory motives, or simply has a lack of interest in a certain type of crime.

If the local prosecutor fails to bring charges for alleged criminal conduct that also violated federal law, the local United States Attorney's Office or the Justice Department's Civil Rights Division may step in. This occasionally happened during the Civil Rights Era, when violent crimes committed by white assailants against black victims were ignored by local police and prosecutors, and ultimately prosecuted by the federal government. But federal prosecution of local crime is not limited to the Civil Rights Era. In 1993, the federal government stepped in to prosecute officers from the Los Angeles Police Department for the beating of Rodney King after a jury in a predominately white, politically-conservative suburb of Los Angeles acquitted the officers for the conduct. Even more recently, the Justice Department intervened in a case in Pennsylvania to prosecute several members of the Shenandoah Valley High School football team following the racially-motivated beating death of a Latino man, Luis Ramirez, in a local park. The federal government assumed responsibility for that investigation after it was determined that the local police force obstructed the initial murder investigation.

Although in some jurisdictions grand juries have the right to bring charges without the prosecutor's consent, this almost never happens. As we will see in **Chapter 35**, grand juries are mostly passive bodies that usually follow the prosecutor's lead. When grand juries do exercise independence, it is invariably to **prevent** the prosecutor from going forward with a case rather than to bring charges over the prosecutor's objection. For example, the grand jury may not find the prosecution's witnesses credible enough to establish probable cause and therefore choose to dismiss the case rather than issue an indictment.

Finally, the President, Congress, state governors, state legislatures, or the courts can appoint a special prosecutor or independent counsel to investigate a case and bring charges if necessary. As with the intervention of the attorney general, this is almost always because the local prosecutor has a conflict of interest in the case and so requires an independent prosecutor to evaluate the case and exercise her own discretion. For example, during the 2012 investigation into the shooting death of unarmed Florida teenager Trayvon Martin the original prosecutor removed himself from the case due to mounting community pressure and charges of bias. A prosecutor from a neighboring jurisdiction was assigned by Florida's governor to take over the prosecution of shooter George Zimmerman, who was ultimately acquitted of Martin's murder.

Intervention by the state attorney general is rare, however. An individual seeking to challenge a prosecutor's decision not to bring charges has no real options, because the criminal justice system really does not have a mechanism for moving forward without a prosecutor in charge of the case. Thus, if an individual is frustrated by a prosecutor's lack of interest in a case, she has very few options on her own.

However, once formal charges have been filed against a defendant, most jurisdictions limit the prosecutor's ability to **drop** the charges. For example, in federal courts and many state courts, a prosecutor must obtain court permission before dismissing charges against a defendant.[4] Other states require the prosecutor to file a document explaining the reasons that the charges are being dropped. These rules are meant to prevent the prosecutor from harassing defendants by repeatedly filing charges against an individual and then dismissing them.

The other two legal restrictions on a prosecutor's power to screen cases involve the more traditional situation of the law imposing limits on prosecutorial power to bring a case. One is a bar on **selective prosecution**—ensuring that the charging decision is consistent with the Equal Protection Clause. Defendants face a number of serious obstacles in proving selective prosecution. Proving a discriminatory **effect** is difficult—the defendant must prove not only that members of a certain class are being prosecuted more often than members of the general population, but also that members of a certain class are being prosecuted more often than **similarly situated** members of the general population. Once this has been accomplished, the defendant must also prove that the prosecutor's office had a discriminatory purpose in its actions. As we will see in Section E.1 below, defendants are rarely successful in pursuing these cases.

The final limitation is a bar on **vindictive prosecution**—ensuring that the defendant will not be punished for exercising his rights under the law or the Constitution. This rule does not prohibit the prosecutor from adding additional charges if the defendant does not agree to plead guilty during the plea bargaining process—although that practice may be controversial, it is not illegal or unethical. Vindictive prosecution claims will almost never succeed unless the defendant has been found guilty, successfully challenged his conviction, and then faces additional charges during the re-trial. We will discuss the law surrounding vindictive prosecutions in Section E.2 below.

D. The Ethical Considerations. Given the lack of oversight of the initial charging decision, every prosecutor's office—and every individual prosecutor—has an

---

[4] See, e.g., Fed. R. Crim. Pro. 48(a).

ethical obligation to only pursue charges that can be proven at trial and that are in the public interest. The American Bar Association has promulgated guidelines for prosecutors to follow in making these decisions:

American Bar Association, Standards for Criminal Justice
3-3.9 Discretion in the charging decision

(a) A prosecutor should not institute, or cause to be instituted, or permit the continued pendency of criminal charges when the prosecutor knows that the charges are not supported by probable cause. A prosecutor should not institute, cause to be instituted, or permit the continued pendency of criminal charges in the absence of sufficient admissible evidence to support a conviction.

(b) The prosecutor is not obliged to present all charges which the evidence might support. The prosecutor may in some circumstances and for good cause consistent with the public interest decline to prosecute, notwithstanding that sufficient evidence may exist which would support a conviction. Illustrative or the factors which the prosecutor may properly consider in exercising his or her discretion are:

- **(i)** the prosecutor's reasonable doubt that the accused is in fact guilty;
- **(ii)** the extent of the harm caused by the offense;
- **(iii)** the disproportion of the authorized punishment in relation to the particular offense or the offender;
- **(iv)** possible improper motives of a complainant;
- **(v)** reluctance of the victim to testify;
- **(vi)** cooperation of the accused in the apprehension or conviction of others; and
- **(vii)** availability and likelihood of prosecution by another jurisdiction.

(c) A prosecutor should not be compelled by his or her supervisor to prosecute a case in which he or she has a reasonable doubt about the guilt of the accused.

(d) In making the decision to prosecute, the prosecutor should give no weight to the personal or political advantages or disadvantages which might be involved or to a desire to enhance his or her record of convictions.

(e) In cases which involve a serious threat to the community, the prosecutor should not be deterred from prosecution by the fact that in the jurisdiction juries have tended to acquit persons accused of the particular kind of criminal act in question.

(f) The prosecutor should not bring or seek charges greater in number of degree than can reasonably be supported with evidence at trial or than are necessary to fairly reflect the gravity of the offense.

(g) The prosecutor should not condition a dismissal of charges, nolle prosequi, or similar action on the accused's relinquishment of the right to seek civil redress unless the accused has agreed to the action knowingly and intelligently, freely and voluntarily, and where such waiver is approved by the court.[5]

There are a number of significant aspects to these guidelines. Part (a) sets out the two standards that must be met before a prosecutor can file charges:

1. First, the prosecutor must believe there is **probable cause** that this defendant is guilty of a crime;

2. Second, the prosecutor must believe she has **sufficient evidence to convince a jury** that this defendant is guilty of a crime. In other words, even if the prosecutor is certain that the defendant is guilty she should not file charges against him unless she believes there is sufficient evidence against him that will be admissible at trial.

Part (b) explains that even if the standards in (a) are met, there are certain situations when a prosecutor should not file charges, such as when the authorized punishment is disproportionate to "the particular offense or offender." Although this may sound like an invitation to second-guess the legislature's judgment as to what the authorized punishment for a crime should be, it merely means that the prosecutor should take into account the totality of the circumstances in deciding whether a charge is appropriate. The motive of the crime, the severity of the harm caused, the age of the defendant, the possible collateral consequences—all of these are potential factors that a prosecutor should consider. We will examine this factor in more detail in Section E.3 below.

In part (f), the ABA Guidelines discourage the practice of **overcharging.** Because there are so many criminal laws on the books, many of them overlap and a defendant could conceivably be charged with three or four different crimes for essentially the same criminal behavior. Occasionally, there will also be the possibility of bumping a misdemeanor up to a felony, if certain conditions are met, even though the defendant's conduct does not deserve felony charges or even though it is unlikely a jury will convict on the felony charges. On these occasions, a prosecutor may be tempted to file the multiple charges or more severe charges (even though she does not believe that the defendant deserves the charges) in

[5] American Bar Association, Standards for Criminal Justice, Section 3-3.9.

order to gain leverage in the plea bargaining stage of the proceedings. The Guidelines make it clear that such conduct is unethical. We will discuss the practice of overcharging in Section E.6 below.

E. Applying the Law.

1. Selective Prosecution. The Equal Protection Clauses of the Fifth and Fourteenth Amendment forbid the government from deciding to bring charges based on "unjustifiable standards" such as "race, religion, or other arbitrary standards."[6] However, it is not exactly clear what counts as an "arbitrary standard." On the one hand, prosecutors are given the discretion to focus on specific types of criminal conduct or even specific geographic areas. For example, if a prosecutor wanted to devote extra resources to combatting prostitution, or heroin sales, or terrorist activity, she would be permitted to make that choice even if it resulted in a larger percentage of a certain gender or ethnic group being prosecuted. Or, if a prosecutor wanted to drive drug sales and violent crime out of a certain neighborhood, she would have that power even if the individuals being prosecuted were disproportionately of one race or another. Although a prosecutor is not permitted to explicitly target a group based on their ethnicity, religion, gender, political beliefs, or any other criteria that is unrelated to a legitimate law enforcement purpose, courts will generally defer to prosecutors who argue that a specific type of program (which may have a discriminatory effect) has a legitimate law enforcement purpose.

In order to prevail on a claim of selective prosecution, the defendant must prove that the prosecutorial decisions had not only the **effect** of targeting an arbitrary classification of individuals, but also that the prosecutor had the **intent** to target that group. The Court has held the only way to prove intent is by demonstrating that individuals who are "**similarly situated**" in all ways other than the arbitrary classification were not prosecuted. For example, assume that a defendant is being prosecuted for failure to register for the draft, and this defendant had been indicted immediately after he participated in a legal political protest against United States foreign policy. The defendant could establish that he was the victim of selective prosecution if he could prove that:

1. Every prosecution from that prosecutor's office for failing to register involved a defendant who had participated in political protests (thus proving a discriminatory effect), **and**

2. Many individuals who had not registered for the draft (were "similarly situated") but had not participated in political protests were **not** prosecuted (thus proving a discriminatory purpose).

[6] Oyler v. Boles, 368 U.S. 448 (1962).

The claim would fail, however, if the prosecutor's office could demonstrate that it prosecuted many others who had failed to register and had not engaged in any political protests.[7]

Needless to say, the burden of finding similarly situated individuals who have not been prosecuted for illegal conduct is a very difficult one for defendants to meet. The Supreme Court has acknowledged but nonetheless embraced this difficulty:

> **Example—*United States v. Armstrong*, 517 U.S. 456 (1996):** Federal agents and local police officers in California conducted a three-month investigation into a crack cocaine distribution ring. The investigators had informants purchase a total of over 124 grams of crack on seven different occasions, and eventually raided the hotel room where the sales were transacted. Inside the hotel room, they found more crack and a loaded gun. They arrested numerous individuals as part of the conspiracy, including Christopher Armstrong. Armstrong's case was referred to the federal government for prosecution.
>
> Armstrong and his co-defendants in federal court filed a motion for dismissal, arguing that the government chose to prosecute them in federal court because they were black. They filed an affidavit which noted that during the previous year, every defendant who was prosecuted by this United States Attorney office for a crime involving crack cocaine was black. In response, the trial court ordered the government to provide additional discovery, including a list of all defendants (and their race) who were prosecuted for cocaine or firearms offenses for the last three years, and an explanation of how it decided to prosecute those particular defendants. The government refused to comply with the order, and the court dismissed the charges against Armstrong and his co-defendants. The government then appealed the dismissal.

Analysis: The Supreme Court agreed with the government, and held that the trial court's discovery order was improper. The Court began by stating it was "hesitant" to second-guess the government's decision to prosecute a given case, and that courts should give great deference to the prosecutor's decisions. "Such factors as the strength of the case, the prosecution's general deterrence value, the Government's enforcement priorities, and the case's relationship to the Government's overall enforcement plan are not readily susceptible to the kind of analysis the courts are competent to undertake." Therefore, the criminal defendant must present "clear evidence" that the prosecutor violated his equal protection rights.[8]

[7] See Wayte v. United States, 470 U.S. 598 (1985).

[8] United States v. Armstrong, 517 U.S. 456, 465 (1996) (internal quotations and citations omitted).

A successful selective prosecution claim requires the defendants to prove both discriminatory impact and discriminatory intent. In order to force the government into complying with the discovery order, the defendant had to provide "some evidence" of each of these prongs. The defendant provided some evidence of discriminatory effect, and the lower court believed this would be enough, acting on the presumption "that people of all races commit all types of crimes." The Supreme Court, however, rejected that presumption, noting that some crimes are committed overwhelmingly by certain ethnic groups. For example, "90% of the persons sentenced in 1994 for crack cocaine trafficking were black, [while] 93.4% of convicted LSD dealers were white; and 91% of those convicted for pornography or prostitution were white."[9]

The defendants needed to prove that there were people other than black Americans engaged in the specific criminal conduct with which they had been charged, but who were not prosecuted by this United States Attorney's Office. For example, they could have produced statistics that the State of California prosecuted significant numbers of white crack-cocaine dealers, and that the federal law enforcement officers knew of these dealers but ignored them.[10] Since the defendants presented no such evidence, they had no right to pursue their claim of selective prosecution.

Note that in *Armstrong*, the Court did not even reach the merits of Armstrong's selective prosecution claim. It was merely considering his request for discovery so that he could try to prove the selective prosecution claim. Nonetheless, the Court rejected the request because in the Court's view "the showing necessary to obtain discovery should itself be a significant barrier to the litigation of insubstantial claims."[11]

2. Vindictive Prosecution. The Due Process Clauses of the Fifth and Fourteenth Amendments preclude prosecutors from filing charges based on vindictive motives. In theory, this means that the prosecutor cannot add charges or increase the severity of charges in retaliation for the defendant's exercise of his statutory or constitutional rights. However, in practice, it is nearly impossible to prove a prosecutor's motivation in bringing charges. Thus, unlike its treatment of selective prosecution claims, the Supreme Court has created a **presumption** of vindictive motives whenever the prosecutor adds charges or increases the severity of charges when a defendant is being re-tried after a successful appeal.

In some jurisdictions, a defendant is entitled to two trials—the first is a bench trial, and if he is convicted, the second is a jury trial. (Frequently the defendant will plead guilty after the bench trial in exchange for a slightly reduced sentence, thus saving the state the far greater expense of a jury trial). In those jurisdictions,

---

[9] Id. at 469 (internal citations omitted).

[10] Id. at 470.

[11] Id. at 463-4.

any added charges after the initial conviction will also be subject to the vindictiveness presumption. The presumption also applies in the more traditional case where a defendant successfully seeks review in the appellate courts, and the case is remanded for retrial.

Although this presumption helps the defendant prove vindictiveness in such cases, it only applies on re-trials of prior convictions, and thus is of limited use to defendants. There is no presumption of vindictiveness if the prosecutor adds charges or increases the severity of the charge at any point before the initial trial—in fact, a prosecutor is free to add charges or increase their severity after a plea offer has been rejected. Such behavior is standard practice in many jurisdictions.

Example—*United States v. Goodwin*, 457 U.S. 368 (1982): A United States Park Policeman pulled Learly Goodwin over for speeding on the highway. While processing the ticket, the police officer noticed a clear plastic bag under the armrest, and asked Goodwin to raise the armrest. Goodwin did so, but at the same time put the car into gear and accelerated rapidly. His car struck the officer and knocked him onto the car and then onto the highway.

Goodwin was eventually arrested and charged with various misdemeanor offenses, including assault. He was offered a plea bargain, but he refused. The case was then transferred to a new prosecutor, who conducted further investigation and decided to indict Goodwin on four felony counts, including assaulting a federal officer. The defendant was ultimately convicted after trial on one of the felony counts.

On appeal, Goodwin argued that the government had engaged in vindictive prosecution, since it added significantly more severe charges after he rejected the plea offer. Goodwin claimed that he was being punished for exercising his right to trial, or at the very least the presumption of vindictiveness should apply.

Analysis: The Supreme Court refused to apply the presumption and held that the presumption of vindictiveness will never apply in a pretrial setting. While preparing for trial, it is perfectly reasonable to assume that the prosecutor may learn additional facts or become aware of other legitimate considerations that indicate that more serious charges are appropriate. "At this stage of the proceedings, the prosecutor's assessment of the proper extent of the prosecution may not have crystallized."[12] Moreover, the entire plea bargaining process only works

[12] United States v. Goodwin, 457 U.S. 368, 381 (1982).

because the defendant is offered a discount for pleading guilty—which is in effect the same as a "penalty" for going to trial. "Since charges brought in an original indictment may be abandoned by the prosecutor in the course of plea negotiation—in often what is clearly a 'benefit' to the defendant—changes in the charging decision that occur in the context of plea negotiation are an inaccurate measure of improper prosecutorial 'vindictiveness.' . . . For just as a prosecutor may forgo legitimate charges already brought in an effort to save the time and expense of trial, a prosecutor may file additional charges if an initial expectation that a defendant would plead guilty to lesser charges proves unfounded."[13]

After the trial is over, however, there is almost no legitimate reason that a prosecutor would seek to add additional charges, and thus a presumption is appropriate. "Once a trial begins—and certainly by the time a conviction has been obtained—it is much more likely that the State has discovered and assessed all of the information against an accused and has made a determination, on the basis of that information, of the extent to which he should be prosecuted. Thus, a change in the charging decision made after an initial trial is completed is much more likely to be improperly motivated than is a pretrial decision."[14]

In this case, however, the additional charges were added during the pre-trial process, so no presumption applied. The defendant, of course, could still attempt to prove on his own that the prosecutor was motivated by a vindictive purpose, but there was no evidence of that in this case.

3. Following the Ethical Guidelines—Applying Legal and Equitable Discretion. As we can see from the above discussion, the prosecutorial charging decision is essentially unregulated by the courts. But prosecutors are still bound by an ethical code, and could face judicial sanction or even disbarment if they violate that code.

The most important of the ethical guidelines is that the prosecutor must exercise legal discretion—she must be personally convinced that there is probable cause to believe the defendant is guilty of the crime and to believe there is sufficient evidence to convince a jury of the defendant's guilt. This means that not only must there be sufficient evidence to believe **factually** that the defendant is guilty, but also sufficient **legal** evidence to prove that guilt. If the evidence against the defendant is very strong but is based on inadmissible hearsay, or comes from a witness who will not be available for trial, or from a witness who will have no credibility with the jury, a prosecutor may conclude that there is no way to prove the case in court. Similarly, perhaps the defendant has confessed and the police have found the murder weapon in the defendant's house—but the prosecutor concludes that the confession was taken in violation of *Miranda* and the house

[13] Id. at 380-1.

[14] Id.

was searched in violation of the Fourth Amendment. In such a case there may be no question of the defendant's guilt, but the prosecutor knows that taking the case to trial—or even to a suppression hearing—would be pointless. It would be unethical to bring charges against the defendant under such circumstances.

Even if prosecutors did not feel bound by this ethical duty, strong economic and political pressures often force them to abide by this limitation. Every prosecutor's office has limited resources, and every prosecutor's office is acutely aware of the limited resources of the court system that must process each case that is brought. Thus, a prosecutor who files charges that are not supported by probable cause or which cannot be proven to a jury takes resources away from legitimate criminal cases. Judges will also quickly lose patience with prosecutors who bring charges that cannot be supported, and the resulting loss of credibility will hurt the prosecutors when they are trying to bring more substantial charges. Finally, prosecutors are ultimately accountable to the people—not only will frivolous charges bring poor publicity to the office, but they will interfere with the office's ability to effectively fight crime.

It is worth noting that these economic and political incentives against overcharging are not always effective. Given the extremely high sentences that many defendants face if they are convicted at trial, prosecutors can sometimes bring charges in cases where the evidence is weak and then offer the defendant a much lower sentence if they plead guilty. In these situations, even if the defendant is fairly confident he will win the case at trial, he may face such a high sentence after a jury conviction that it is not worth the risk to take the case to trial. In this way, prosecutors can "get away" with bringing charges with weak evidence—but such practices are unethical and violate the ABA Guidelines.

The second important aspect of the Guidelines—and the hardest to quantify—is the application of equitable discretion. This consideration evaluates both the prioritization of cases—(deciding that some crimes are so trivial or harmless that it is not worth the resources to pursue them) and the evaluation of whether a particular defendant deserves punishment (deciding that certain defendants do not deserve punishment because of their own extenuating circumstances).

When prioritizing cases, prosecutors are urged to give their "greatest attention to those areas of criminal activity that pose the most serious threat to the community."[15] Prosecutors have to make their own judgment calls about which types of criminal activity poses the most serious threat—some prosecutors may aggressively target drug crimes, while others will focus on gun crimes, and still others may crack down on relatively minor "quality of life" offenses. Whatever priorities the prosecutor has will carry through from the charging decision to the offers in the plea bargaining stage to the recommendations at sentencing.

[15] Comments to American Bar Association, Standards for Criminal Justice, Section 3-3.9.

When evaluating whether a specific defendant deserves to be punished, the Guidelines note that the prosecutor is meant to exercise his public duty "not by the unseeing or mechanical application of the 'letter of the law,' but by a flexible and individualized application of its norms through the exercise of a prosecutor's thoughtful discretion."[16] One commentator gives examples of defendants who (perhaps) do not deserve criminal charges even though their conduct clearly violates the criminal law:

> A sixteen-year-old runaway is arrested for prostitution; a mother is arrested for leaving her eleven-year-old home alone for the afternoon; an indigent man is arrested for hopping a turnstile to get to his first day of work; an elderly man is arrested for selling ice pops without a license on a hot summer's day.[17]

Sometimes a prosecutor is able to refer or divert a case to another government agency. A homeless man who is arrested for urinating in the street, for example, does not necessarily deserve punishment from the criminal justice system—nor is it clear that society benefits from imposing punishment. Instead, the man could be referred to social services. Similarly, a heroin junkie with ten prior convictions for possessing small amounts of heroin may not deserve punishment—both she and society might be better off if she could be admitted to a treatment program. Thus, in some cases a prosecutor may agree to delay and then ultimately dismiss criminal charges on condition that the defendant enter into a government-run program or seek private help for his or her problem.

Note that all of these examples involve relatively minor crimes. As crimes increase in severity, prosecutors are less likely to exercise equitable discretion. Serious crimes are routinely given greater resources by a prosecutor's office, and those who commit them are often less likely to have sufficiently sympathetic extenuating circumstances to justify a free pass. But even in the most serious of cases and for the least sympathetic defendants, a prosecutor must always exercise **legal** discretion. For example, although the prosecutor may have probable cause to believe that a murder or rape occurred, if it will not be possible to convince a jury of that fact using admissible evidence that is (or could become) available, a prosecutor should not waste the resources in bringing the case.

4. Failing to Follow the Ethical Guidelines. Most prosecutors make an effort to follow the ethical guidelines when making charging decision, and as we have seen, there are a number of institutional pressures that support the appropriate

---

[16] Id.

[17] Josh Bowers, Legal Guilt, Normative Innocence, and the Equitable Decision Not to Prosecute, 110 Colum. L. Rev. 1655 (2010).

exercise of discretion. However, there are also a number of institutional pressures that influence prosecutors in the other direction.

(a) Professional or Personal Ambition. Many prosecutors believe (with some reason) that they are judged by their supervisors and by the general electorate on the degree to which they are "tough on crime." A prosecutor's office may keep track of the conviction rates of each of its line prosecutors, and those statistics may not take into account the equitable discretion that was legitimately exercised in refusing to bring certain charges. Likewise, a District Attorney who is running for re-election is not likely to campaign on the criminals that were concededly guilty but whom he decided not to prosecute.

Even legal discretion may be skewed by this consideration. If a defendant has committed a serious crime, but the prosecutor knows it cannot be proven in court, it may be politically safer to bring the case anyway, and let the judge (or grand jury or trial jury) take the "blame" for the criminal going free when the inevitable dismissal or acquittal occurs.

For example, assume a defendant is arrested for murder, but the prosecutor knows that the defendant's confession will be thrown out in a suppression hearing, and so refuses to bring charges against him. The defendant is released, and the next week he kills another person. In such a case, the headlines would not be kind to the prosecutor. Assume instead that this same prosecutor fails to exercise the appropriate legal discretion and files charges against the defendant. The defendant is held over on bail for two months for a crime that the prosecutor knows cannot be proven. The resources of the prosecutor's office, the police, and the court system are used to conduct a day-long suppression hearing. At the end of the hearing, the judge suppresses the confession and the defendant is released. Now when he kills another person, the prosecutor can hold a press conference and (unfairly) blame the judge for turning the defendant free, despite the "best efforts" of the prosecutor's office. Given these two potential alternatives, a prosecutor may feel obliged to ignore his best judgment (and the ethical guidelines) and move forward with a case that he knows he cannot win.

(b) Community Pressure. The prosecutor has an unusual relationship with her constituents. On the one hand, most county and state prosecutors are elected, and so they are ultimately accountable to the people who live in their jurisdiction. On the other hand, they are elected to exercise their own professional judgment about which cases to prosecute and how to prosecute them. Usually, individual charging decisions go unnoticed by the electorate; voters often only pay attention to their local prosecutor (to the extent they ever pay them any attention) during the few weeks before the election, at which point they are likely to review the prosecutor's entire record. But occasionally a high-profile case will develop which will create significant community interest—an incident in which a police officer shoots someone during the course of his duties, for example, or a crime in which the suspect or the victim is famous. In those situations, the community may pressure the local prosecutor to take action—and the action is almost always to press charges, not to drop them. Sometimes this community pressure can spur an otherwise indifferent prosecutor's office to bring charges that should have been filed originally. Other times, however, the prosecutor may have originally given the case an appropriate review and correctly determined that no conviction was possible, but then may now feel the need to bring charges nonetheless, to respond to the pressure and placate the community.

The distinction between legal discretion and equitable discretion is critical in evaluating the appropriateness of responding to community calls for prosecution. Such pressure should never overrule the prosecutor's decision not to charge if that decision was made on legal grounds. Even if the public demands that "justice" requires that charges be brought against a suspect, a prosecutor must exercise her expertise to ensure that charges are not filed unless there is sufficient evidence to convince a jury beyond a reasonable doubt. Robust self-defense laws, a lack of first-hand witnesses, illegally obtained evidence that is certain to be excluded—all of these may be factors that convince a prosecutor that filing charges would be pointless and therefore unethical. However, community pressure should arguably be taken into account when the prosecutor exercises equitable discretion. The ethical guidelines state that the prosecutor should take into account the "extent of the harm of the offense" in determining whether to press charges. It could very well be the case that the prosecutor has a different sense of the "extent of the harm of the offense" for certain crimes than the community. The prosecutor must still exercise her own best judgment, but that judgment should be informed by the wishes of the people whom she represents.

(c) Collaboration with the Police. By nature, prosecutors must work closely with law enforcement officials. After the charges are filed, there is no question that the prosecutor has the sole authority to make the decisions. But the prosecutor still needs cooperation from the police officers on the case to help gather evidence, to submit the proper paperwork, and ultimately to testify at suppression hearings and at trial. The prosecutor also knows that she must rely on police officers for pre-charge investigations in future cases. Thus, prosecutors are dependent on law enforcement officers to move their cases forward. Beyond this professional relationship, prosecutors and police officers develop personal friendships from working together closely and from a shared experience as law enforcement officers.

These professional and personal relationships may create a conflict that can at times impede the proper exercise of discretion, especially in cases in which a police officer is a victim or a suspect. If an officer brings charges of resisting arrest or claims that he was attacked by a defendant, the prosecutor may be reluctant to apply the same critical examination of those charges as he would for other cases.

Similarly, if an officer shoots or otherwise injures a citizen, a prosecutor may have an undue amount of sympathy for the officer and fail to aggressively look for witnesses and other evidence that could support charges against him. For this reason, state prosecutors or special prosecutors are frequently brought in to evaluate and ultimately prosecute cases in which the police officer is a potential defendant.

Even in cases in which the officer is not a suspect or a victim, the prosecutor may lose objectivity when assessing whether the evidence gathered by the police officer is admissible. No police officer likes to be told that the prosecutor is refusing to bring charges and the suspect must be turned free because the officer broke the law when conducting a search or taking a statement. Consequently, no prosecutor likes to tell police officers that this must happen. However, the ethical guidelines are clear: if the prosecutor knows that necessary evidence will not survive a suppression hearing, she must refuse to bring charges and order the suspect released.

(d) Indifference Based on Training and Experience. All lawyers are trained from the first day of law school to "think like a lawyer." Among other things, this means that lawyers are taught to ignore how they **feel** about a case, and even to ignore facts which are not legally relevant to resolve the case. This is a critical skill for a lawyer—and especially a prosecutor—if she is to evaluate the strength of a case and pursue the case in court. But this training also tends to suppress the very type of evaluation which is required to wisely exercise equitable discretion. A lawyer who has been trained to disregard legally irrelevant factors may not be sympathetic to arguments that a certain defendant deserves leniency because of his age, or because he needs to feed his family, or because he was egged on by charismatic friends. Law students are usually taught only to see if the *actus reus* and the *mens rea* exist, and to ignore any other "distractions" in the fact pattern.

For prosecutors, this tendency to ignore the "human" aspect of cases is only exacerbated by the experiences they have at their job. In the first few weeks or months, a prosecutor may be moved to exercise equitable discretion by a story of desperate conditions, or by the need to show mercy, or by any number of mitigating circumstances. After many years of hearing defense attorneys use similar arguments and many years of seeing defendants pass through the system, however, many prosecutors will become somewhat jaded. Defendants may no longer appear to be human beings but rather commodities to be processed, while the defense attorney's pleas for leniency may begin to sound repetitive and thus less persuasive. One commentator compares the practice of criminal law to the practice of medicine in emergency rooms:

> The professional's priority is to take care of cases. Lawyers and doctors are not hard-hearted. Rather, callousness is a coping mechanism: Profes-

sionals must detach from the persistent misery surrounding them and engage clinically with technical puzzles.[18]

All four of these institutional pressures can influence the prosecutor's charging decision, sometimes subconsciously. Thus a dedicated prosecutor must work to resist these pressures and keep the ethical guidelines in mind when making charging decisions. A good defense attorney, on the other hand, needs to be aware of these factors when trying to convince a prosecutor not to bring charges against her client.

5. Office-Wide Policies v. Individual Screening. Not all charging decisions are made by the individual prosecutor screening the case. Most prosecutor's offices—especially the larger ones in urban settings—have policies that guide the individual prosecutor in making the charging decision. Sometimes these policies are relatively vague and do little more than re-state the ABA's ethical guidelines. At other times they can be very specific. For example, the head prosecutor may decide to make fighting prostitution one of her highest priorities, and so will issue a memo to all the line assistants forbidding them from dismissing any prostitution cases. (Such a policy is often referred to as a "no-drop policy.") Or, in response to high dismissal rates of domestic violence cases, the head prosecutor may require each individual prosecutor to talk personally with the victim and then get a supervisor's approval before dismissing any case involving domestic violence. Office policies can also be designed to **discourage** individual prosecutors from bringing certain kinds of charges—for example, if the head prosecutor has decided to de-prioritize marijuana cases, he may set out a policy that marijuana possession cases should only be brought if the amount of marijuana is over a certain weight.

As we will see in **Chapter 42** on plea bargaining, many large offices also have guidelines on the type of plea offers that should be made to defendants who commit certain crimes. If a certain crime is usually pled down to a minor misdemeanor or a violation, a prosecutor may be more inclined not to bring charges at all if there are any mitigating circumstances. A defense attorney who is aware of these plea guidelines can even use them to her advantage when arguing for outright dismissal of charges: "Your office usually only gives a day of community service for this crime anyway, and my client doesn't even deserve that because the amount of damage was so low." In other words, the individual prosecutor may use the plea guidelines as indications of the office's official stance on "the extent of harm caused by the offense," and may change his decision about whether to charge a case based on that official stance.

[18] Bowers, supra note 16, at 1689.

Thus, in the same way that legislatures set out broadly applicable laws and depend on prosecutor's offices to exercise judgment in deciding which laws get the most priority, prosecutor's offices set out broadly applicable guidelines and then depend on individual prosecutors to exercise judgment in deciding how the laws and the guidelines should apply to individual cases.

Different offices will give individual prosecutors higher or lower levels of independence, depending on the preference of the chief prosecutor and the caseload the office faces. For example, many United States Attorney's offices (which tend to have more serious cases than their local counterparts) require each of their prosecutors to get a supervisor's approval before charging any suspect with a crime. On the other hand, many large urban county prosecutor offices require a supervisor's approval before deciding **not** to charge a suspect after the police have made an arrest. Thus, in one office, the prosecutor must do extra work to prepare a presentation for a supervisor even before charges can be brought; in the other office, inertia works to encourage charging of every suspect who the police have arrested.

6. Selecting the "Correct" Charge and the Correct Number of Charges. Finally, the ethical guidelines state that prosecutors should not "overcharge" their cases. The term "overcharging" can be used to mean a number of different things. Some practitioners use it to refer to the practice of charging a crime which the prosecutor cannot prove at trial—in other words, an abuse (or poor exercise) of legal discretion. Others use it to describe the practice of charging a greater crime than the defendant normatively deserves—in other words, an abuse of equitable discretion. But the ethical guidelines refer to a very specific type of overcharging, which has to do with the **intent** of the prosecutor in bringing charges. Prosecutors engage in overcharging when:

> prosecutors [bring] charges, not in the good faith belief that they fairly reflect the gravity of the offense, but rather as a harassing and coercive device in the expectation that they will induce the defendant to plead guilty.[19]

In other words, overcharging occurs when a prosecutor brings a charge with the sole purpose of gaining leverage in plea bargaining and without any intention of trying the defendant on that charge (even though there is sufficient evidence to support a conviction). Thus, the focus of the ethical guidelines on overcharging is prosecutorial insincerity, not some normative evaluation of whether the charges are too severe.

There are two types of overcharging.[20] "Vertical" overcharging occurs when the prosecutor brings a charge that is more severe than she believes the defendant

---

[19] Comments to American Bar Association, Standards for Criminal Justice, Section 3-3.9.

[20] See Albert Alschuler, The Prosecutor's Role in Plea Bargaining, 36 U. Chi. L. Rev. 50 (1968).

deserves in order to coerce the defendant into pleading to a lesser crime that the prosecutor believes is a fair reflection of the defendant's conduct. An example of this practice sometimes occurs when prosecutors coerce a plea from a recidivist shoplifter. When a defendant shoplifts from a store for the first time, he is charged with petty larceny (a misdemeanor), and the store will typically require the defendant to sign a form agreeing never to enter the store again—essentially, the store revokes the defendant's privilege to enter the premises. When the defendant returns to the store and shoplifts a second time, he is technically committing a burglary—he is trespassing (entering the store without permission and authority) with the intent to commit a crime (theft). A prosecutor may legally write this crime up as a burglary (a felony) but then tell the defendant he will not indict the felony if the defendant agrees to immediately plead to the theft. In truth, the prosecutor has no intention of ever going forward with the burglary (it would waste the grand jury's time and the felony court's time to indict and then try a case as a felony when all the defendant did was enter a store without permission and steal a relatively inexpensive item). But the defendant, unwilling to take the risk of a felony conviction, agrees to plead to the theft.

"Horizontal" overcharging occurs when the prosecutor brings multiple charges for what is essentially one act of criminal conduct. Again, although the law may **allow** the prosecutor to bring multiple charges, overcharging occurs if the prosecutor never intends to convict the defendant of all the charges but instead intends to dismiss most of the charges in exchange for the defendant pleading guilty to one or two of them. For example, the federal statute against child pornography allows a prosecutor to bring a separate charge of possession for every picture containing child pornography and for every frame of a video that contains child pornography. A typical defendant arrested for possessing child pornography may have hundreds of such pictures on his hard drive, and perhaps a number of three-to-five minute videos. Thus, a prosecutor can legally bring hundreds or thousands of counts of child pornography against the defendant. If the prosecutor honestly intends to bring all of these charges to trial and convict the defendant of each charge, she is not guilty of overcharging—though some may argue that she is not properly exercising her equitable discretion. But frequently prosecutors will bring these hundreds of charges as a tactic to persuade the defendant to plead guilty to one or two charges, in which case she is violating the ethical guidelines.

As the above discussion makes clear, because of the breadth of the criminal code it may be impossible at times to discern whether a prosecutor has brought charges for the improper purpose of gaining leverage or whether instead the lengthy list of charges brought is a true reflection of the prosecutor's assessment of merit. In such cases, the discretion of the prosecutor is almost impossible to police.

Quick Summary

Prosecutors have almost unreviewable legal power to decide whether to charge a defendant and which charges to bring. If a prosecutor decides not to bring charges, charges could theoretically be brought by a federal prosecutor, a state attorney general, a grand jury, or a special prosecutor. But in practice this is extraordinarily rare.

When a prosecutor does bring charges, his discretion is limited by two related concepts. If a defendant brings a claim for **selective prosecution**, she must prove both the prosecutor's discriminatory intent and the discriminatory effect of the charging decision. Alternatively, a defendant can bring a claim for **vindictive prosecution**. Such a claim enjoys a presumption of vindictiveness, but only if a prosecutor brings more charges after the defendant is convicted and the conviction is overturned. While the concepts of selective prosecution and vindictive prosecution provide some limitation on a prosecutor's decision to file a case, in practice these claims are also extremely rare.

Although the prosecutor faces almost no legal restrictions on her charging decisions, the prosecutor's charging decisions are subject to a number of ethical guidelines. When exercising **legal discretion**, a prosecutor should not bring a charge unless there is probable cause to believe that the defendant is guilty and that there is sufficient evidence to convince a jury of his guilt. When exercising **equitable discretion**, a prosecutor should consider what charge (if any) the defendant deserves based on a number of factors, including the extent of the harm caused by the offense, the proportion of the punishment in relation to the offense, and the cooperation of the victim.

Finally, the ethical guidelines indicate that a prosecutor should not engage in **overcharging**, which takes place when a prosecutor seeks to coerce the defendant into pleading guilty by bringing more severe charges than the defendant deserves or multiple charges when the defendant only deserves one charge. However, due to the breadth of the criminal code, actual proof of overcharging is difficult in most cases.

Review Questions

1. The Bar Room "Brawl." Desmond White was in a bar and he punched another man, Steve Grogan, in the face. Grogan suffered a black eye. The bartender called the police and White was arrested for assault. (A person is guilty of assault if he intentionally causes physical injury to another). White was booked and is currently being held at the county jail awaiting formal charges. You are the prosecutor on intake duty, and the arresting officer comes to you with the file and asks you to write up the case. In which of the following scenarios (if any) would you decide to **not** to charge White with assault?

(a) Grogan was drunk and hit White first, giving Grogan a bloody nose. White could have retreated safely, but instead chose to hit White back. Grogan then ran out the back door and has not yet been arrested.

(b) White was in the bar with his girlfriend, and Grogan, who was drunk, approached the girlfriend and grabbed her breast. White's girlfriend did not know Grogan and was extremely offended by Grogan's actions. White told Grogan to apologize and Grogan laughed, so White punched Grogan in the face.

(c) White, who is gay, was at the bar with his boyfriend. Grogan approached the two of them and used an offensive homophobic slur against them. When White and his boyfriend tried to ignore Grogan, Grogan began to yell the slur louder and louder until White finally hit Grogan in the face.

(d) White is an eighty-seven year old man and Grogan is twenty years old. White had asked Grogan to stop smoking (it was illegal to smoke in the bar, and White suffers from asthma) and Grogan replied with a vulgarity and roughly pushed White away, almost causing White to fall down. White responded by punching Grogan in the face.

(e) White and Grogan are old friends who drink together a few times a week. They got into an argument after a few drinks and when the argument got intense, White hit Grogan in the face. Although Grogan suffered a black eye, he laughed after he got hit and he and White reconciled. When the police arrived, Grogan asked them not to arrest White and protested loudly when they did, saying that the punch was no big deal and the police were wasting their time on a minor altercation.

2. Loitering Gangland Style. After a series of high-profile shootings by gangs in Los Angeles, the police department and the county prosecutor announced a joint program to combat the spread of gangs in the city. The police department began making arrests under a brand new "sit-lie" vagrancy law that criminalizes blocking sidewalks and other public thoroughfares. The prosecutor's office states that when they process these arrests, they only file charges if the defendant has a history of gang activity. After one month, the police have made ninety-five arrests under this program, and although most of the suspects have been Hispanic, about a dozen of them were non-Hispanic whites or black Americans. The prosecutor's office has charged over sixty individuals with this crime, and every one of them is Hispanic. Renaldo Lopez, who is Hispanic and has two prior gang-related convictions on his record, has been charged under the new law. He is now moving to dismiss the charges, arguing that the prosecutor's office is engaging in selective prosecution.

You are Lopez's lawyer. Can you successfully get the charges dismissed based only on the facts outline above? If not, what other facts will you need to demonstrate at the pre-trial hearing in order to establish a case of selective prosecution?

29

Initial Appearance

Key Concepts

- Defendant's First Appearance in Court
- Charges Formally Presented to Defendant
- Probable Cause Determination Must Be Made "Promptly" After Arrest

A. Introduction and Policy. Once the prosecutor has decided to file charges, the defendant begins his journey through the criminal court system. The exact route that he takes and the terminology used to describe the stops along the way will vary by jurisdiction, but you can find a general description of his path in **Chapter 1.**

As a brief reminder, the defendant is first brought in front of a judge or a magistrate for his **initial appearance.** Some jurisdictions call this initial appearance the "arraignment;" while others use the term arraignment to refer to a separate proceeding that occurs later in felony cases in which the information or indictment is filed. At the initial appearance, the defendant is informed of his rights and (usually) **bail** is set and (usually) a **defense attorney** is first appointed in the case. If the case is a misdemeanor, the defendant will next proceed to pre-trial motions based on the **complaint** that is filed. If the charge includes a felony, the state must prove that there is probable cause, either in a **preliminary hearing** (in which a judge decides whether there is probable cause) or in a **grand jury** (in which a large jury of lay people decides whether there is probable cause). After probable cause is established, the prosecutor files a new charging document: either an **information** (in the case of a preliminary hearing) or an **indictment** (in the case of a grand jury). Both sides engage in **discovery**, and the prosecutor and/or defendant may then file a number of **pre-trial motions**, such as a motion to suppress evidence, a motion to sever or join defendants, a motion to change venue, a motion to dismiss based on speedy trial rights, or a motion to challenge the competency of the defendant. Finally, the case will proceed to **trial.** If the defendant is convicted, he will be **sentenced** by the judge, and then file an **appeal** in the case. If the defendant is acquitted, the prosecutor cannot appeal the case because of double jeopardy rules. Following an appeal, the convicted person may seek relief in **post-conviction** proceedings.

Unlike the rules governing criminal investigations, which are derived primarily from Supreme Court cases interpreting the Bill of Rights, many of the rules governing pre-trial and trial procedure are statutory. Most of these rules are found in the rules of criminal procedure for the relevant jurisdiction—the federal system applies the Federal Rules of Criminal Procedure, and each state system has its own rules of criminal procedure. Like the Rules of Civil Procedure or the Rules of Evidence, these rules are written and edited by advisory committees appointed by the highest court in the relevant jurisdiction. There are also a series of statutes governing issues like bail, time requirements, and discovery.[1] Finally, some of the rules governing the adjudication of criminal cases are derived from the Constitution.

In this chapter we examine the very first encounter between the defendant and the court system: the initial appearance. (Note that the initial appearance is frequently combined with the bail hearing, which we will discuss in the next chapter). The amount of time between the arrest and the initial appearance varies by jurisdiction, but it is usually around twenty-four hours. During this time, the arresting officer does the following:

1. Transports the arrestee from the place of the arrest to a police precinct;
2. Searches and secures the arrestee in the precinct;
3. Reviews the arrest and charges with a superior officer;
4. Conducts any further interrogation that may be necessary;
5. Fills out paperwork, such as the arrest report and property voucher;
6. Transports the arrestee to central booking (which is usually near the courthouse);
7. Books the arrestee (i.e., takes fingerprints, photographs the arrestee, and transfers the arrestee to the custody of court officers); and
8. While the fingerprints are being processed, draws up a formal complaint to be filed in court (or is interviewed by the prosecutor, who draws up the formal complaint).

It is at this point that the case is formally transferred to the prosecutor, who will then exercise her discretion (as described in **Chapter 28**) to determine what charges, if any, should be filed. The prosecutor may discuss the possible charges with a supervisor, or may need to do additional legal research to ensure that the factual allegations are sufficient to prove the elements of the crime. Once the

[1] See, e.g., 18 U.S.C. § 3142 (bail), 18 U.S.C. § 3161 (time requirements), and 18 U.S.C. § 3500 (discovery).

complaint is filed, it is sent to a member of the court staff to be docketed, and copies are made for the court file, the prosecutor at arraignment, and the soon-to-be-appointed defense attorney.

Meanwhile, a member of the court staff will interview the arrestee to gather information relevant to his bail determination (such as his address, his employment status, and his community ties). In most jurisdictions, a defense attorney will then be appointed, who will review the complaint and then briefly interview the arrestee (now that the charges have been filed, he is known as the "defendant") in order to prepare for the initial appearance.

After all this is done, all of the necessary parties—the defendant, the defense attorney, the prosecutor, and the court—are ready for the initial appearance. At the proceeding, the defendant is formally advised of the charges against him and informed of his various rights. Also at this proceeding, most jurisdictions will conduct a bail hearing to determine if (and under what conditions) the defendant should be released while awaiting trial. If the defendant was arrested without an arrest warrant, many jurisdictions will have the judge or magistrate review the facts to ensure that there was probable cause to make an arrest. Finally, the court will set a trial date and the case will be adjourned until that date.

If the case is a misdemeanor, the defendant has the option of pleading guilty at the initial appearance. Indeed, many minor cases are resolved at this stage. The "plea bargaining" that occurs may be nothing more than the prosecutor making a standard offer in open court and the defense attorney conferring for a few seconds with the defendant and then agreeing to a guilty plea. In less busy courtrooms, the prosecutor and defense attorney may discuss the case for a few minutes before it is called in order to reach a deal, and then the judge will accept the plea and sentence the defendant during the initial appearance.

If the case is a felony, there is usually no option to plead guilty at the initial appearance—the defendant must wait until the formal charging document (the information or indictment) is filed at the next court date.

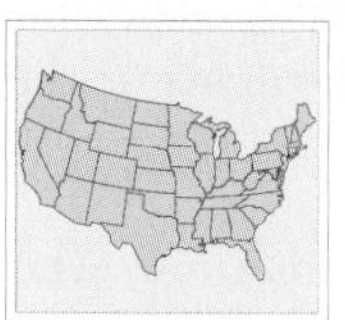

Note that this process will vary widely from jurisdiction to jurisdiction. Sometimes the booking occurs at the local police precinct (smaller jurisdictions, in fact, have no "central booking"—the only police headquarters is located next to the courthouse). Sometimes the police officer draws up the charges without the help of the prosecutor, and the prosecutor does not see the case until just before the initial appearance.

Most of the actions at the initial appearance are a mere formality—the defendant already knows the charges against him, and he has probably already been told about his rights. Also, it is rare (though not impossible) that charges which are not supported by probable cause will reach this stage, since the charges have already been reviewed by a police supervisor and a prosecutor. (Of course, the Constitution requires that a judge or a magistrate review all warrantless arrests for probable cause, so even though this is a formality, it is a mandatory formality). But as we will see in **Chapter 33**, the bail determination is far from a formality—it is a significant decision that impacts not only whether the defendant spends the next few months free or incarcerated, but also how willing he will be to plead guilty and how much he will be able to assist in his own defense.

B. The Law. The law regarding initial appearances is governed mostly by the Rules of Criminal Procedure in each jurisdiction. Federal Rule of Criminal Procedure 5 is a typical such rule, setting out all of the requirements of an initial appearance:

Rule 5–Initial Appearance

(a) In General.

(1) Appearance Upon an Arrest.

(A) A person making an arrest within the United States must take the defendant without unnecessary delay before a magistrate judge . . .

(b) Arrest Without a Warrant. If a defendant is arrested without a warrant, a complaint [that meets] Rule 4(a)'s requirement of probable cause must be promptly filed in the district where the offense was allegedly committed [in order to allow a judge to determine that probable cause existed to make the arrest].

[If the probable cause determination occurs within 48 hours of the arrest, the filing of the complaint will be presumed "prompt" unless the defendant can prove that there was an unreasonable delay. If the probable cause determination occurs over 48 hours after the arrest, the filing of the complaint will be presumed **not** to be prompt unless there is an emergency or extraordinary circumstance.]

. . .

(d) Procedure in a Felony Case.

(1) Advice. If the defendant is charged with a felony, the judge must inform the defendant of the following:

(A) the complaint against the defendant, and any affidavit filed with it;

(B) the defendant's right to retain counsel or to request that counsel be appointed if the defendant cannot obtain counsel;

> **(C)** the circumstances, if any, under which the defendant may secure pretrial release;
>
> **(D)** any right to a preliminary hearing; and
>
> **(E)** the defendant's right not to make a statement, and that any statement made may be used against the defendant.
>
> **(2)** Consulting with Counsel. The judge must allow the defendant reasonable opportunity to consult with counsel.
>
> **(3)** Detention or Release. The judge must detain or release the defendant as provided by statute or these rules.
>
> **(4)** Plea. A defendant [in a felony case] may be asked to plead only under Rule 10 [at the arraignment after indictment or information].
>
> . . .
>
> **(f)** Video Teleconferencing. Video teleconferencing may be used to conduct an appearance under this rule if the defendant consents.

The first thing to notice is that Sections (a) and (b) describe two separate requirements. Section (a) states that the defendant must be brought in front of a magistrate for the initial appearance described in Section (d) "without unnecessary delay." Section (b) adds the requirement that if the defendant has been arrested without a warrant, the prosecutor must "promptly" file a complaint that demonstrates that there is probable cause to believe the defendant is guilty. In practice, this complaint could be filed at the initial appearance, but it need not be—it could be filed in an *ex parte* proceeding, much like the proceeding in which the police obtain an arrest warrant.

Section (a) states that the initial appearance must occur "without unnecessary delay" after the arrest. The courts have consistently refused to set a specific time limit for this process. Instead, courts will conduct a fact-specific inquiry to determine whether the interval between arrest and initial appearance is reasonable, evaluating factors such as the time required to transport the defendant, the availability of a magistrate, and how much evidence gathering took place during the process. We will discuss this question further in Section C.1 below.

In contrast, Section (b) states that a prosecutor must "promptly" file the complaint establishing probable cause. This procedure is required by the Fourth Amendment if the defendant is kept in custody pending trial or if any pretrial release is conditioned on "burdensome conditions that effect a significant restraint on liberty."[2] If a judge has previously issued an arrest warrant in the case, the probable cause determination has already been made by a judicial officer, and so no further confirmation is required. However, if the police arrested the defendant without a warrant, Rule 5(b) and (in most cases) the Fourth Amendment require the prosecutor to file a complaint that demonstrates to the court that probable cause exists.

As with the determination of "unnecessary delay" under section (a), courts apply a flexible standard to the "promptly" standard set forth in section (b). However, since judicial confirmation of probable cause is constitutionally required for cases in which the defendant will be held in pretrial custody, the Supreme Court has provided a little bit more quantitative guidance for this proceeding. Any time period over forty-eight hours will be presumed to violate the Fourth Amendment, while any time period less than forty-eight hours will be presumed to be valid. Since the filing of the complaint coincides with the initial appearance in most jurisdictions, this rule frequently applies to the initial appearance as well. We will examine this further in Section C.2, below.

Jurisdictions will differ as to whether the defendant is appointed an attorney before or after the initial appearance. Subsection (d)(1)(B) of Rule 5 of the Federal Rules states that an individual must be informed of his right to counsel, and subsection (d)(2) of the Rule gives the defendant the right to speak with counsel. However, there is no statutory requirement that counsel be present at this stage. As we will see in **Chapter 30**, the right to defense counsel only applies to "critical stages" of the proceedings, and an initial appearance is not considered to be a critical stage under the Federal Constitution. Some states give a defendant a right to an attorney at the initial appearance under their state constitutions. However, in some states there is neither a statutory nor a constitutional right to an attorney at this stage, and so the defendant may be unrepresented at the initial appearance.

The federal rules, like most of their state counterparts, set out different rules for felony cases than they do for misdemeanor cases. (Note that in the federal system, the "initial appearance" refers to the first time that a defendant appears in court after being arrested, while the term "arraignment" refers to the first time that a defendant appears in court after being indicted).

As noted above, under Federal Rule of Criminal Procedure 5 (and most comparable state rules), a felony defendant cannot plead guilty at the initial appearance. Instead, he must wait until the felony charging instrument (the information or indictment) has been filed at the arraignment. This is partly a question of jurisdiction, since the initial appearance usually takes place in front of a magistrate, who may not have the authority to find a defendant guilty of a felony. It also gives the prosecutor more time to investigate the case to determine the strength of

[2] Gerstein v. Pugh, 420 U.S. 103, 114 (1975).

the case and the severity of the crime—both of which are critical points to know before making a plea offer. **Rule 10** of the Federal Rules of Criminal Procedure deals with the procedure at arraignment, in which the indictment or information is filed, the defendant is formally informed of the substance of the felony charges, and the defendant has his first chance to plead guilty to the felony.

There is another rule (**Rule 58**), which covers the procedure to follow for a misdemeanor case. The procedure is almost identical, except that (1) the defendant is not just informed of the charges against him, but also the "minimum and maximum penalties" of that charge, and (2) the defendant must also be informed of his right to a jury trial in front of a district judge. These additional warnings are required in part because Rule 58 also allows the magistrate to take a plea from the defendant if the defendant agrees in writing to waive his right to a jury trial.

Finally, courts across the country are attempting to save time and money by having defendants appear at their initial court proceedings by way of **video teleconferencing**. It is far easier to bring the defendant to a room inside the detention facility that has a video camera and monitor than it is to transport him all the way to the courtroom. However, some commentators worry that such a procedure makes it more difficult for attorneys to consult with their clients. We will discuss this issue in Section C.3 below.

C. Applying the Law.

1. Timing of the Initial Appearance: the "Unnecessary Delay" Requirement. Courts have been very lenient when reviewing the amount of time it takes to bring a defendant before a magistrate. In case after case, the courts have explained that it is not the **amount** of time that is significant; it is **how** the police and prosecutors have spent that time. If a delay is caused by the need to transport the arrestee a great distance, or a backlog in the administrative task of booking the defendant, then the courts will hold that the delay was valid. Likewise, delays are not impermissible if the police are conducting a line-up, or giving the defendant necessary medical treatment, or are forced to wait through holidays or weekends to find an available magistrate.

The most common reason for a finding of "unnecessary delay" is if the police hold the defendant for an **extended** period of time while conducting an interrogation or while searching for other evidence. Holding the arrestee for a few hours for standard interrogation is permissible, but engaging in "lengthy interrogations" or using "'third degree methods' which are calculated to elicit damaging and incriminating statements" is not.[3] If a court does determine that the delay was unnecessary, the remedy is to exclude any information the police uncovered (such as

[3] Ralph v. Pepersack, 335 F.2d 128, 138 (4th Cir. 1964).

a confession) during the unnecessary part of the delay. However, any information uncovered **before** the delay became unreasonable is not excluded. For example, if the police extract a confession after interrogating a defendant for an hour, and then unreasonably hold him for four days before taking him to a magistrate, the confession will not be barred.[4]

Almost all of the cases that have found the delay to be unreasonable were decided before the more robust protections on interrogation were established. For example, one federal court in 1943 found that keeping two arrestees in a "barren cell" for fourteen hours and then subjecting them to "unremitting questioning" for two days was an unnecessary delay.[5] Today, it is difficult to imagine any delay that would be "unnecessary" under current law that would not also violate an arrestee's rights under the Due Process Clause and *Miranda.*

2. Filing a Complaint. In contrast, the Court has imposed a stricter time limit for the requirement that a complaint be filed establishing probable cause in cases involving warrantless arrest. In *Gerstein v. Pugh*,[6] the Supreme Court held that under the Fourth Amendment, a magistrate or judge must "promptly determine" probable cause as a prerequisite to an extended pretrial detention following a warrantless arrest. In a later case, the Court then explained what it meant by "promptly:"

> **Example— *County of Riverside v. McLaughlin,* 500 U.S. 44 (1991):** Riverside County in California had a procedure by which it combined its probable cause determination with the defendant's initial appearance (which it called the arraignment). The statute required that the initial appearance occur within two days of an arrest, but the two days did not include weekends or holidays, so it was possible for a suspect to be arrested without a warrant and then wait five days (or seven days over the Thanksgiving weekend) before a court reviewed the arrest to ensure there was probable cause.
>
> Donald McLaughlin and the other plaintiffs were prisoners who had been arrested without a warrant and were being held in Riverside County detention awaiting their probable cause determinations. Although the plaintiffs eventually received probable cause hearings within a few days, the court determined that they had standing to pursue this lawsuit, since at the time of their

[4] United States v. Montes-Zarate, 552 F.2d 1330 (9th Cir. 1977).

[5] McNabb v. United States, 318 U.S. 332 (1943).

[6] 420 U.S. 103 (1975).

complaint they were in custody and suffering injury as a result of Riverside County's allegedly unconstitutional action. They brought a class action lawsuit on behalf of themselves and all others similarly situated, demanding prompt probable cause hearings.

Analysis: The Supreme Court held that the county's practice was unconstitutional because it did not comply with *Gerstein*'s requirement that a probable cause determination be "prompt." The Court conceded that the *Gerstein* standard had to be a flexible one, because under the principles of federalism, states were encouraged to experiment with different types of pre-trial procedures, and the Court was reluctant to complicate an already intricate process with specific requirements. The Court also noted that if a county or state decided to combine the probable cause determination with the initial appearance, there will be inevitable delays caused by "paperwork and logistical problems." "In our view, the Fourth Amendment permits a reasonable postponement of a probable cause determination while the police cope with the everyday problems of processing suspects through an overly burdened criminal justice system."[7]

But this flexibility was not meant to give local jurisdictions a "blank check," and unfortunately it had become obvious that *Gerstein*'s vague requirement of "promptness" was providing insufficient guidance to these jurisdictions. This led to a "flurry of systemic challenges to city and county practices" and put the federal courts in the untenable position of making legislative judgments and overseeing local jailhouse operations.[8] Thus, in order to provide some level of guidance, the Supreme Court set forty-eight hours as a soft deadline. Any jurisdiction that provides for a probable cause review within forty-eight hours will be immune from systemic challenges. An arrestee can still challenge a delay of less than forty-eight hours, but the burden will be on the arrestee to prove that the probable cause determination was delayed unreasonably, such as "delays for the purpose of gathering additional evidence to justify the arrest, a delay motivated by ill will against the arrested individual, or delay for delay's sake."[9] However, delays are not unreasonable due to "unavoidable delays in transporting arrested persons from one facility to another, handling late-night bookings where no magistrate is readily available, obtaining the presence of an arresting officer who may be busy processing other suspects or securing the premises of an arrest, and other practical realities."[10]

If the time between arrest and the probable cause determination is over forty-eight hours, the burden of proof shifts to the city or county to prove that there was

[7] County of Riverside v. McLaughlin, 500 U.S. 44, 55 (1991).

[8] Id. at 56.

[9] Id.

[10] Id. at 57.

a "bona fide emergency or other extraordinary circumstance."[11] An intervening weekend or holiday does not qualify as an "extraordinary circumstance," nor does a delay caused by combining the probable cause determination with the initial appearance. A city or county is free to combine these two procedures, but not if it means delaying the probable cause determination by over forty-eight hours.

The Court noted that some jurisdictions conduct a stand-alone probable cause determination immediately after the defendant has been booked, photographed, and fingerprinted, while others (such as Riverside County) choose to combine the probable cause determination with the initial appearance, which creates extra delay. Although the Court said it was "laudable" to conduct a stand-alone probable cause determination (since this would be faster), it allowed cities and counties to combine the probable cause determination with the initial appearance as long as the combined proceeding did not violate the forty-eight-hour limit.

As *County of Riverside* demonstrates, it is difficult for an individual arrestee to gain relief if his right to a prompt probable cause determination is violated. Instead, this right is usually enforced by a class-action lawsuit, and the relief granted is usually an injunction against the city or county which requires the city or county to change their procedures.

It is important to note that the filing of a complaint to establish probable cause is **not** the same as establishing probable cause through a preliminary hearing or grand jury presentation. As you will see in **Chapters 34** and **35**, every felony charge requires that probable cause be determined either by a judge after an adversarial proceeding or by a grand jury. These are both much more formal proceedings which require live testimony—unlike the simple *ex parte* filing of a complaint, which is little more than an after-the-fact request for an arrest warrant. The filing of the complaint is meant to ensure that the police had probable cause to make the arrest and detain the defendant in jail. The preliminary hearing or grand jury presentation is a procedural hurdle required before the prosecutor can formally bring a felony case to trial.

3. Video Appearance. The federal rules were amended in 2002 to allow for the defendant to be "present" at his initial appearance through video teleconferencing, as long as the defendant consents. Many states have followed suit, and using video teleconferencing for initial appearances has become more common. The move towards increased use of video is driven by judicial efficiency—the practice saves money, allows the initial appearance to occur more quickly, and increases security. Also, technological advances have made videoconferencing cheaper. The audio and video quality of the process have also been dramatically improved.

---

[11] Id.

However, video teleconferencing is still somewhat controversial. First of all, the quality of the video transmission is not standardized across jurisdictions. Some courtrooms employ state-of-the-art technology, while others involve a hazy picture or a time delay between the picture and the sound. More substantively, using video surveillance detracts somewhat from the solemnity of the proceeding—the defendant is not brought physically into a courtroom, but is merely staring at a screen in a small room near his jail cell. Similarly, the magistrate does not see the live defendant standing in front of her. If she is making a bail determination, she may need to assess the defendant's credibility. This assessment can be made more difficult by the distance created by teleconferencing. Even if a credibility assessment is not being made, the appearance by video may serve to further "dehumanize" the defendant in the eyes of the court.

Most significantly, using video technology creates a dilemma for the defense attorney regarding where to be physically present. If the defense attorney is present in the courtroom, she can be a more effective advocate during the bail argument and in any plea negotiations. If, however, she is physically present in the room with the defendant, she can more easily establish a rapport with him and can more easily communicate with him confidentially. Whenever video teleconferencing is used, some method of confidential communication needs to be provided—if the defense attorney is physically present in the courtroom, she usually is provided with a private phone line so that she can discuss matters with her client even before and during the initial appearance. But most defense attorneys believe that this is a poor substitute for standing next to the client in person and being able to counsel them throughout the proceeding.

To solve this problem, the American Bar Association has proposed standards which would require both the defense attorney **and** the prosecutor to participate by video—the prosecutor could appear from a teleconferencing location in his office, or be present in the room with the defense attorney and defendant.[12] This way, the defense attorney can be physically with her client and not be at any disadvantage when making arguments to the judge. As of now, however, there are no generally accepted standards with regard to this process.

[12] See ABA Standards for Criminal Justice, Proceedings In and Outside the Courtroom § 6-1.8(d) (3d ed. 1999).

Quick Summary

The initial appearance is the first time that a defendant appears in court after the arrest. The initial appearance must occur "without unnecessary delay" after the arrest, and usually occurs within twenty-four hours. At the initial appearance, the defendant is formally presented with the charges against him, the court informs him of his rights, and usually bail is set. If the case is a misdemeanor, the defendant has the option of pleading guilty.

If the defendant was arrested without a warrant, most jurisdictions require the prosecutor to present a judge or magistrate with evidence demonstrating that the arrest was supported by probable cause. The Supreme Court has held that if there is going to be any significant restraint on the defendant's pre-trial liberty, this probable cause determination must occur "promptly," or within forty-eight hours after the arrest, unless there is an emergency or other extraordinary circumstance. Some jurisdictions combine the probable cause determination with the initial appearance. If this is done, the initial appearance must meet the forty-eight hour time constraint as well.

Finally, the federal courts and many state courts allow the defendant to be present at the initial appearance through video teleconferencing. Although this technique makes it more difficult for the court to assess the defendant's credibility and for the defense attorney to communicate confidentially with her client, it is a cheaper, faster, and safer method of conducting the initial appearance.

Review Question

1. Waiting at the Precinct. Amelia approached a man on the streets of downtown Denver and offered to exchange sex for money. The man was an undercover police officer, and he arrested Amelia and charged her with solicitation. The arrest occurred at 10:00 PM on a Friday night. The police officer frisked Amelia for weapons and then drove her to the police precinct, where he put her in a jail cell while he filled out a police report and made entries in his memo book. Meanwhile a female officer conducted a more thorough search of Amelia and found a glass pipe with crack cocaine residue inside it. The glass pipe was vouchered as evidence. By the time the paperwork was done, it was 2:00 in the morning, and the sergeant at the police precinct decided to have an officer transport Amelia to Central Booking later that morning.

Unfortunately, during the night, another police officer in an unrelated incident shot and killed an unarmed suspect while making an arrest. The incident sparked a spontaneous public protest, and by 8:00 in the morning there were hundreds of people demonstrating in the streets outside the precinct building. The police captain called up every officer he could to help keep order during the protest, ordering them to set up barricades and keep the roads clear for traffic. For this reason, there was no police officer available to drive Amelia to Central Booking until 9:00 that night. When Amelia arrived at Central Booking, the police handed custody over to the court personnel, who logged her into their computer system and then took her fingerprints and her photograph. Meanwhile a prosecutor upstairs wrote up a criminal complaint, charging her with solicitation and possession of cocaine. By the time Amelia was ready to head to arraignment, it was 3:00 AM early Sunday morning, and there was no magistrate available until Monday.

Amelia made her initial appearance at 10:25 AM on Monday morning. The prosecutor on duty filed the complaint, and the magistrate reviewed it to ensure there was probable cause for the arrest. The defense attorney then moved to dismiss the complaint, arguing that Amelia had spent over sixty hours in custody without having been formally charged. How should the court rule?

30

The Sixth Amendment Right to Counsel

Key Concepts

- Attaches Upon Initiation of the Criminal Process
- Enjoyed at All "Critical Stages" of a Criminal Prosecution
- Not Dependent Upon Defendant's Ability to Pay for Counsel
- Waiver Must be Voluntary, Knowing, and Intelligent

A. Introduction and Policy. The right to counsel is governed by rule, by statute, and by state and federal constitutions. For example, in the federal system, Rule 44 of the Federal Rules of Criminal Procedure and 18 U.S.C. § 3006A regulate the appointment of counsel. The statutory provisions proscribe, among other things, the circumstances in which counsel must be appointed, the duration and substitution of counsel, and the rates of pay for appointed attorneys. In almost all other jurisdictions, the appointment of counsel is a matter that is governed by similar statutes and by local rule.

The primary constraint on the right to counsel, however, is provided by the Sixth Amendment. Over the next several chapters, you will read in some detail about the many facets of the Sixth Amendment right to counsel—the constitutional right to counsel, the converse right to self-representation, the right to effective counsel, and the right to counsel during post-indictment interrogations. In this chapter we will cover the right to counsel generally. We will also discuss how that right can be waived and when the right to self-representation must be afforded.

As you will read, the Sixth Amendment right to counsel relates both to retained and appointed counsel. However, the right has been articulated almost exclusively in the context of indigent defendants who seek appointed counsel. It is therefore these cases that most commonly define the contours of the right. Indeed, perhaps the most famous right to counsel case of all—*Gideon v. Wainwright*—involved a poor man's request to have counsel defend him in a burglary case.

In our adversarial system of justice the right to counsel is vital to the fairness of the criminal process because it advances two critical goals.[1] First, the prosecution

---

[1] Maine v. Moulton, 474 U.S. 159, 169 (1985).

of a criminal case can be a confusing and complex process through which an unaided layperson cannot be expected to fare well. The right to counsel therefore "assure[s] that the 'guiding hand of counsel' is available to those in need of its assistance."[2] Second, with the advent of the public prosecutor, a failure to ensure a right to defense counsel would result in the system's imbalance. As the Court has said, "the core purpose of the counsel guarantee was to assure 'Assistance' at trial, when the accused was confronted with both the intricacies of the law and the advocacy of the public prosecutor."[3]

Justice Sutherland explained the magnitude of the right in a frequently cited passage from *Powell v. Alabama*:

> The right to be heard would be, in many cases, of little avail if it did not comprehend the right to be heard by counsel. Even the intelligent and educated layman has small and sometimes no skill in the science of law. If charged with crime, he is incapable, generally, of determining for himself whether the indictment is good or bad. He is unfamiliar with the rules of evidence. Left without the aid of counsel he may be put on trial without a proper charge, and convicted upon incompetent evidence, or evidence irrelevant to the issue or otherwise inadmissible. He lacks both the skill and knowledge adequately to prepare his defense, even though he have a perfect one. He requires the guiding hand of counsel at every stage of the proceedings against him. Without it, though he be not guilty, he faces the danger of conviction because he does not know how to establish his innocence.[4]

B. The Law. As you have read to this point, many aspects of criminal procedure in the adjudication phase are regulated by the Rules of Criminal Procedure. In contrast, the right to counsel is governed primarily by the provisions of the Sixth Amendment to the U.S. Constitution, and by case law that has interpreted that Amendment.

In pertinent part, the Sixth Amendment provides:

> In all criminal prosecutions, the accused shall enjoy the right . . . to have the assistance of counsel for his defense.[5]

---

[2] United States v. Ash, 413 U.S. 300, 308 (1973).

[3] Id. at 39.

[4] Powell v. Alabama, 287 U.S. 45, 68–69 (1932).

[5] U.S. Const. amend. VI.

The Supreme Court has clarified the right in the following ways:

1. The right to counsel does not attach until formal charges have been filed against the defendant.
2. The right to counsel only applies during "critical stages" of the proceeding.
3. Any waiver of the right to counsel must be voluntary, knowing, and intelligent, although the defendant need not first consult with counsel before waiving the right to counsel.

The first clarification is based on the language of the Sixth Amendment which expressly confines the right to "all criminal prosecutions." The Supreme Court has interpreted this to mean "at or after the time that judicial proceedings have been initiated . . . 'whether by way of formal charge, preliminary hearing, indictment, information or arraignment.'"[6] In other words, the actual prosecution of an individual must have begun before the Sixth Amendment right will attach. The Supreme Court has described this point as the point at which "the adverse positions of government and defendant have solidified with respect to a particular alleged crime."[7] Another way to think of it is the point at which the official response to a criminal act moves from investigation to accusation:

> The initiation of judicial criminal proceedings is far from a mere formalism. It is the starting point of our whole system of adversary criminal justice. For it is only then that the government has committed itself to prosecute . . . . It is then that a defendant finds himself faced with the prosecutorial forces of organized society, and immersed in the intricacies of substantive and procedural criminal law. It is this point, therefore, that marks the commencement of the 'criminal prosecutions' to which alone the explicit guarantees of the Sixth Amendment are applicable.[8]

The Court has been fairly stringent in its demand that the Sixth Amendment right does not attach until the adversarial process has begun. Thus, the fact that a suspect or his family has hired an attorney does not trigger the Sixth Amendment right.[9] For similar reasons, in the prison context, the transfer of an inmate to a segregated housing unit during the investigation of a crime committed inside the walls of the facility will not trigger the Sixth Amendment right to counsel.

---

6 Brewer v. Williams, 430 U.S. 387, 398 (1977) (citing Kirby v. Illinois, 406 U.S. 682 (1972)).

7 McNeil v. Wisconsin, 501 U.S. 171 (1991) (citing United States v. Gouveia, 467 U.S. 180, 188 (1984)).

8 Kirby, 406 U.S. 689–90; see also Escobedo v. Illinois, 378 U.S. 478, 492 (1964).

9 Moran v. Burbine, 475 U.S. 412 (1986).

Instead, that right will become activated only upon the formal commencement of adversarial proceedings in connection with the offense.[10]

While initiation of the adversarial process is **necessary** to attachment of the Sixth Amendment right to counsel, it is not **sufficient**—every prosecution does not give rise to the right to counsel. This is because the amendment's language—"all criminal prosecutions"—has not been read as broadly as its plain terms might suggest. An accused has no right to counsel in a misdemeanor case for which a term of imprisonment **is not imposed.**[11] The Supreme Court has never squarely addressed the question of whether imposition of a **suspended** sentence triggers the right to counsel. Moreover, the state and lower federal courts that have taken up the question have come to divergent conclusions. Many of the courts considering the question have concluded that the need for counsel is not triggered in cases where a suspended sentence is imposed because the defendant was not "actually imprisoned."[12] Other courts, in contrast, have determined that counsel in such cases is required because the defendant is sentenced to a "term of imprisonment," even if the execution of that imprisonment is in the end suspended.[13] Until the Supreme Court resolves the question, you should therefore be guided by the relevant rule in your jurisdiction.

The second clarification is that the Amendment guarantees to the accused the presence of counsel not just at the trial itself, but at all "critical stages" of a criminal proceeding. This is because the purpose of the amendment is to provide the untutored layperson with protection at all "critical confrontations with his expert adversary, the government." "Critical stages" include: interrogations that take place after the adversarial process has begun (see **Chapter 32**),[14] post-indictment line-ups,[15] preliminary hearings at which the accused might plead to the charges,[16] preliminary hearings and arraignments at which certain affirmative defenses and substantive claims must be raised or forever waived,[17] examinations by the government's psychiatric experts in capital cases to gather evidence of future dangerousness,[18] and the entry of guilty pleas.[19]

---

[10] United States v. Gouveia, 467 U.S. 180 (1984).

[11] Scott v. Illinois, 440 U.S. 367 (1979); Argersinger v. Hamlin, 407 U.S. 25 (1972).

[12] See, e.g., People v. Reichenbach, 587 N.W.2d 1 (Mich. 1998); United States v. Smith, 56 F.3d 66 (6th Cir. 1995); United States v. Castro-Vega, 945 F.2d 496 (2d Cir. 1991).

[13] See, e.g., United States v. Reilley, 948 F.2d 648 (10th Cir. 1991); United States v. Foster, 904 F.2d 20 (9th Cir. 1994); United States v. Sultani, 704 F.2d 132 (4th Cir. 1991); United States v. White, 529 F.2d 1390 (8th Cir. 1976).

[14] Massiah v. United States, 377 U.S. 201 (1964).

[15] United States v. Wade, 388 U.S. 218 (1967).

[16] White v. Maryland, 373 U.S. 59 (1963).

[17] Hamilton v. Alabama, 368 U.S. 52 (1961); Moore v. Illinois, 434 U.S. 220 (1977).

[18] Estelle v. Smith, 451 U.S. 454 (1981).

[19] Iowa v. Tovar, 541 U.S. 77 (2004).

To determine whether a particular stage is a "critical" one at which an accused is entitled to the assistance of counsel, the Court "scrutinize[s] any pretrial confrontation of the accused to determine whether the presence of his counsel is necessary to preserve the defendant's basic right to a fair trial as affected by his right meaningfully to cross-examine the witnesses against him and to have effective assistance of counsel at the trial itself."[20] For this reason, the appointment must be made sufficiently in advance of trial to allow the attorney time for preparation of a defense.

Relying upon similar analysis, the Court has found the right to counsel is guaranteed to juveniles in delinquency proceedings that may result in the child's institutional commitment.[21] The right is guaranteed as well on the first appeal as a matter of right following a criminal conviction.[22] And, under certain circumstances, counsel is constitutionally required even for a discretionary appeal where that discretionary appeal stands in place of a first appeal and substantively serves a similar function.[23] However, for all other discretionary appeals that do not fall within this narrow category there is no constitutional right to counsel.[24] Nor is there a constitutional right to counsel for the collateral review of a criminal conviction, even in capital cases.[25]

The Court has been reluctant to expand the right to counsel to other stages. Only when the application of the right satisfies the traditional goals of the guarantee—minimizing adversarial imbalance and helping the uninformed lay person navigate a complex system—should expansion be permitted. For example, a prosecutor's pre-trial interview and preparation of witnesses and a prosecutor's post-indictment identification procedure using a photo array are not considered critical stages at which the presence of defense counsel is mandated by the Constitution.[26]

As with other rights, the Sixth Amendment right to counsel may be waived. However, because the Sixth Amendment right to counsel is a fundamental right, the government must prove that the particular waiver in question evinced "an intentional relinquishment or abandonment of a known right or privilege."[27] In other words, the prosecutor must prove that the waiver was voluntary, knowing and intelligent. However, the prosecution does not need to prove that the accused was counseled by an attorney in advance of the waiver.[28]

---

[20] Wade, 388 U.S. at 227.

[21] In re Gault, 387 U.S. 1, 41 (1967).

[22] Douglas v. California, 372 U.S. 353 (1963).

[23] Halbert v. Michigan, 545 U.S. 605 (2005).

[24] Ross v. Moffitt, 417 U.S. 600 (1974).

[25] Murray v. Giarratano, 492 U.S. 1 (1989).

[26] United States v. Ash, 413 U.S. 300 (1973).

[27] Brewer v. Williams, 430 U.S. 387, 404 (1977).

[28] Michigan v. Harvey, 494 U.S. 344, 352–53 (1990).

The voluntary, knowing and intelligent standard is applied differently in different contexts. In the context of post-indictment questioning, an accused individual's valid waiver of her *Miranda* rights will also constitute a valid waiver of her Sixth Amendment right to counsel.[29] With regard to counsel at trial, however, the Court has made clear that it will "require a more searching or formal inquiry before permitting an accused to waive his right to counsel at trial."[30]

Of course, a defendant must also be legally competent in order to validly waive his right to counsel. Courts apply two different standards for competence in connection with the waiver of the right to counsel. If the defendant is waiving his right to counsel and wishes to plead guilty, the court will measure competence using part of the same relatively low standard that is used to assess a defendant's competence to stand trial: whether the defendant has a "rational understanding" of the proceedings.[31]

In contrast, if the defendant is waiving his right to counsel in order to represent himself at trial, courts apply a higher standard of competency: not just that the defendant is competent to stand trial, but also that he is "competent to conduct trial proceedings by [himself]."[32] If a defendant cannot make both showings, the judge may force him to accept counsel at trial.

C. Applying the Law.

1. A Poor Man's Right to a Lawyer. As you read above, the Sixth Amendment provides that an accused shall enjoy the right to the assistance of counsel for his defense. However, the Supreme Court has noted that at the time of our nation's founding the Amendment's language arguably envisioned only "the right of an accused in a criminal prosecution in a federal court to employ a lawyer to assist in his defense."[33] The notion that the right also demands that lawyers be appointed to indigent defendants in criminal cases is a relatively modern interpretation of the language of the Sixth Amendment.

The Court took the first steps toward this modern interpretation of the guarantee in 1932 in a capital case arising out of Alabama. It was not until 1963, however, that the right was extended to include all felony matters. Let's look first at the Court's landmark decision in *Powell v. Alabama*:

[29] Montejo v. Louisiana, 556 U.S. 778, 786 (2009).

[30] Patterson v. Illinois, 487 U.S. 285, 299 (1988).

[31] Godinez v. Moran, 509 U.S. 389 (1993) (citing Dusky v. United States, 362 U.S. 402 (1960)).

[32] Indiana v. Edwards, 554 U.S. 164, 178 (2008).

[33] Scott v. Illinois, 440 U.S. 367, 370 (1979).

Example—*Powell v. Alabama*, 287 U.S. 45 (1932): Ozie Powell was "hoboing" on a freight train through Alabama. Powell, who was black, was sixteen years-old at the time. There were at least eight other black teens on the train. The youngest was twelve or thirteen years old, the oldest was nineteen. A group of young white men was also riding on the freight train, as well as two young white women—Ruby Bates and Victoria Price.

At some point before the train reached Scottsboro, a fight broke out between the white teens and at least some of the black teens on the train. At the end of the fight the white teens either jumped off the train or were thrown off. The white teens immediately reported the fight and a message was sent ahead to stop the train. Instructions were also given "asking that every negro be gotten off the train."[34]

At the time the train was stopped just outside of Scottsboro, Alabama, Powell and several other black teens were found riding in an open gondola car with Bates and Price. At that point, the two women alleged they each had been raped by six different black men. The women further claimed that Powell and the other teens found in the gondola car were among the men who committed the assault.

The boys were taken to Scottsboro for trial, where the militia was called in to avert mob violence. Six days after their arrest, Powell and his co-defendants were indicted and arraigned on the rape charges. For purposes of the arraignment, the trial court "appointed all the members of the bar . . . and then . . . anticipated them to continue to help them if no counsel appears."[35]

Six days after the indictment, the trials were conducted serially in a single courtroom on a single day. On the morning of trial, when asked if the parties were ready for trial, the prosecutor announced that he was. No one answered for the defendants. An out-of-state lawyer, Mr. Roddy, told the court he was not a member of the local bar but had come to watch the trial at the request of people who were interested in the case. When asked if he was appearing on behalf of the defendants, Roddy said he was not but indicated that he would be willing to do so if local

[34] Powell v. Alabama, 287 U.S. 45, 51 (1932).

[35] Id. at 53.

counsel was appointed to assist. Repeatedly insisting that he did not want to "impose" on any member of the local bar, the trial judge then asked the local attorneys who were present in the courtroom if any was willing to assist Roddy. Eventually, one local attorney, Mr. Moody, announced that he was "willing to go ahead and help Mr. Roddy in anything I can do about it, under the circumstances."[36] The judge declared "All right," and with that trial proceeded immediately—presumably with Roddy and Moody intended as defense counsel.

At the conclusion of the trials, each defendant was found guilty and sentenced to death. The convictions and sentences were affirmed by the Alabama state courts. They were then appealed to the Supreme Court.

Analysis: The Supreme Court determined that Powell and the others were denied their Sixth Amendment right to counsel.

Once the right to counsel has attached, at a minimum, the accused should be given a reasonable chance to employ a lawyer of his choosing. In this case, none of the defendants was ever asked if he wished to employ counsel or if he wished to contact family and friends to secure counsel for him.

Moreover, to the extent the trial judge took any steps to appoint counsel, those steps were either too indefinite or too belated to satisfy the accused teens' Sixth Amendment rights. At the time of arraignment, the trial judge appointed the entire local bar to represent the defendants. "Such a designation, even if made for all purposes, would . . . have fallen far short of meeting in any proper sense, a requirement for the appointment of counsel."[37] And, by the time the judge made a more specific designation, it was just moments before the trials commenced. This belated appointment stripped Powell and the others of their "right to have sufficient time to advise with counsel and prepare [their] defense."

The Sixth Amendment as applied through the Fourteenth Amendment to the states demands more than was afforded in this case. The right to counsel is a fundamental right. When an individual is charged with a serious crime, the skill of an attorney is necessary to help him navigate a defense to the prosecution's charges. It was error for the trial court not to afford the defendants an opportunity to secure counsel on their own. It was a further denial of due process for the trial court not to make an effective appointment of counsel in a case such at this where the defendants faced capital charges and were incapable of mounting their own defense.

[36] Id. at 56.

[37] Id.

The holding in *Powell* was limited to capital cases "where the defendant is unable to employ counsel, and is incapable adequately of making his own defense because of ignorance, feeble-mindedness, illiteracy, or the like."[38] But, should the same rule apply in less serious cases? And what if there is no evidence that the defendant is "ignorant" or "feeble-minded?" What if the defendant is not facing capital charges? What if the only punishment anticipated is a term of years? The Court extended the right to counsel for all cases in the federal court system only a few years after *Powell.*[39] But it took another twenty-five years before the Court decided to extend this right to all state prosecutions in what has come to be seen as its seminal "right to counsel" case—*Gideon v. Wainwright*:

> **Example—*Gideon v. Wainwright*, 372 U.S. 335 (1963):** Clarence Earl Gideon was arrested and charged with the felony offense of having broken into a poolroom in Florida with the intention of committing a misdemeanor inside. At the time of trial, Gideon had no money to hire a lawyer and appeared without one.
>
> Gideon asked the trial judge to appoint counsel for him. The judge responded, "I am sorry, but I cannot appoint Counsel to represent you in this case . . . the only time the Court can appoint Counsel to represent a Defendant is when that person is charged with a capital offense." Gideon then proceeded to trial before a jury without a lawyer to assist him.
>
> Gideon made an opening statement, cross-examined the state's witnesses, and presented a few witnesses in his own defense. Gideon also made a brief closing statement advising the jury that he was innocent of the charges. However, at the end of the case, the jury returned a guilty verdict. Gideon was sentenced to five years in prison.
>
> Gideon filed a habeas petition that was rejected by the Florida high court. The Supreme Court then took the case for review.

Analysis: The Sixth Amendment right to enjoy the assistance of counsel includes a mandate that all defendants who cannot afford counsel will be appointed a lawyer to represent them.

[38] Id. at 71.

[39] Johnson v. Zerbst, 304 U.S. 458 (1938).

The Due Process Clause of the Fourteenth Amendment imposes against the states those guarantees in the Bill of Rights that are "fundamental safeguards of liberty."[40] The Sixth Amendment's guarantee of the right to counsel is one such right. Referring back to the language of its decision in *Powell*, the Court noted that lawyers are necessary to help untutored defendants navigate the criminal justice process. "The right of one charged with crime to counsel may not be deemed fundamental and essential to fair trials in some countries, but it is in ours."[41]

Because Gideon was forced to trial without a lawyer, reversal of his conviction was required.

In *Gideon*, the Court observed that the fact "[t]hat government hires lawyers to prosecute and defendants who have the money hire lawyers to defend are the strongest indications of the widespread belief that lawyers in criminal courts are necessities, not luxuries."[42]

Notwithstanding this lofty proclamation, the Court determined many years after *Gideon* that lawyers were not a constitutional necessity for those facing prosecution for misdemeanor charges where a sentence of imprisonment was not imposed:

> **Example—*Scott v. Illinois*, 440 U.S. 367 (1979):** Aubrey Scott was charged with theft after he shoplifted items worth less than $150. Under Illinois law, the maximum penalty for the offense was $500 and/or a year in jail. Following a bench trial, at which Scott was not represented by counsel, he was convicted. The trial judge imposed punishment of a $50 fine.
>
> Scott appealed. He argued that his Sixth Amendment right to counsel was violated. In particular, Scott argued that whenever a term of imprisonment was a potential penalty the appointment of counsel was required. The Illinois courts considered and rejected Scott's argument. The Supreme Court then took the case for review.

Analysis: The Constitution does not require states to appoint counsel for defendants in "petty" cases in which a term of imprisonment is not actually imposed.

The Sixth Amendment as applied against the states through the Fourteenth Amendment is delimited not by the **potential** punishment but the **actual** punishment imposed on a misdemeanor offender. "[A]ctual imprisonment is a penalty different in kind from fines or the mere threat of imprisonment."[43] Accordingly,

---

40 Gideon v. Wainwright, 372 U.S. 335, 341 (1963).

41 Id. at 344.

42 Id.

43 Scott v. Illinois, 440 U.S. 367, 373 (1979).

actual imprisonment is an appropriate place at which to draw the line of the Sixth Amendment's application to the states. The Constitution requires only that an individual not be "sentenced to a term of imprisonment unless the State has afforded him the right to the assistance of appointed counsel in his defense."[44]

2. Initiation of the Adversarial Process. The Court has been extremely consistent in its determination that the Sixth Amendment right to counsel will not attach until the adversarial process has begun. The Court has also noted that the particular mode of that commencement—formal charge, preliminary hearing, indictment, information or arraignment—is not particularly relevant, so long as the official process has moved from investigation to accusation. However, the language of the Sixth Amendment specifically states that the right attaches in "all criminal **prosecutions**." In some jurisdictions, the initial stages of adjudication take place without a prosecutor. Does such a prosecutor-less proceeding still constitute commencement of the adversarial process for the purposes of the Sixth Amendment? The Supreme Court has held that it does:

> **Example—*Rothgery v. Gillespie County, Tex.*, 554 U.S. 191 (2008):** Walter Rothgery was arrested for being a felon in possession of a weapon. Rothgery had never actually been convicted of a felony, but an error in a police database suggested that Rothgery had a record. Because the police did not have a warrant, they brought Rothgery before a magistrate for an initial appearance. At the hearing, the arresting officers presented an affidavit, which was considered by the magistrate. No prosecutor was present at the proceeding. After considering the evidence, the magistrate made an assessment of probable cause. He also set bail and advised Rothgery of the charges against him. Rothgery repeatedly asked for an attorney, but his requests were ignored. The magistrate set bond, and Rothgery was released.
>
> Several months later, Rothgery was indicted and his bail was increased. Rothgery was at first unable to post the increased bail, and was therefore incarcerated for several weeks. Six months later, an attorney was appointed to represent Rothgery. The lawyer immediately sought and obtained a reduction in the bail amount. The lawyer also gathered the appropriate paperwork documenting Rothgery's lack of a criminal record. When these materials were shared with the prosecutor, the charges against Rothgery were dismissed.

[44] Id. at 374.

Rothgery then filed a civil action alleging the violation of his right to counsel at the initial hearing. The trial court granted summary judgment for the defendants. The appellate court affirmed. The Supreme Court then agreed to review the case.

Analysis: The failure to appoint an attorney to represent Rothgery at the initial hearing was a violation of his Sixth Amendment right to counsel.

It is certainly true that the Sixth Amendment right to counsel attaches only upon the initiation of the adversarial process. However, the actual involvement of the prosecutor is not a necessary precondition to the initiation of the adversarial process.

On at least two prior occasions, the Court has found that "the right to counsel attaches at the initial appearance before a judicial officer."[45] At such appearances, the judicial officer will inform the accused of the charges against him, will inform the accused of his rights in the coming stages of the process, and will establish the conditions for pre-trial release. The hearing that Rothgery attended was just such an appearance.

The government's relationship with Rothgery at the time of the initial appearance had "become solidly adversarial."[46] It did not matter that the prosecutor was not actually a participant in the hearing. "[A]n accusation filed with a judicial officer is sufficiently formal, and the government's commitment to prosecute is sufficiently concrete, when the accusation prompts arraignment and restrictions on the accused's liberty to facilitate the prosecution."[47]

3. Critical Stages. Even after the right to counsel has attached, the accused only has the right to representation at a "critical stage" in the process. Through the process of case-by-case analysis, the Court has come to define this constellation of pre-trial interactions that trigger the right to counsel. In defining these stages, the Court is guided by whether the presence of counsel at the preliminary stage in question would preserve the defendant's subsequent right to a fair trial. Thus, if decisions made at the pre-trial stage in question will "affect the whole trial," the Court has suggested that counsel is likely required.[48]

Of course, almost everything that happens prior to trial affects the subsequent trial outcome in some manner. Thus, the Court has interpreted the "critical stage" test rather narrowly, looking to "whether potential **substantial** prejudice

[45] Rothgery v. Gillespie County, Tex., 554 U.S. 191, 199 (2008).

[46] Id. at 202.

[47] Id. at 207.

[48] Hamilton v. Alabama, 368 U.S. 52, 54 (1961).

to the defendant's rights inheres in the particular confrontation and the ability of counsel to help avoid that prejudice."[49]

As we have already seen in **Chapter 27**, the Court in *United States v. Wade* readily concluded that post-indictment line-ups meet this refined definition of a "critical stage" of the prosecution. As a reminder, here is a summary of the *Wade* case:

> **Example—*United States v. Wade*, 388 U.S. 218 (1967):** Several months after a bank robbery in Eustace, Texas, Billy Joe Wade was charged with the offense. After counsel had been appointed, an FBI agent forced Wade to participate in a line-up identification procedure. Wade's attorney was not notified of the line-up, and thus was not present during the procedure. The two bank employees who observed the line-up identified Wade as the robber.
>
> At Wade's trial, both witnesses testified about their earlier identification of Wade, and identified him in the courtroom as their assailant. Wade was convicted. On appeal, he challenged the admission of the identifications as violating his Sixth Amendment right to counsel.

Analysis: The post-indictment line-up identification of Wade in the absence of counsel violated his constitutional rights.

The modern criminal justice system entails a number of confrontations between arraignment and the trial itself that may essentially determine the outcome of the case. To ensure the fairness of the later trial process, it is therefore necessary to ensure that the accused has access to counsel for any of the earlier stages at which "the results might well settle the accused's fate and reduce the trial itself to a mere formality."[50]

There are certain pre-trial confrontations that definitely will not trigger the right to counsel. These include procedures such as the state's scientific analysis of a defendant's fingerprints, blood, hair, or clothing. However, the identification of Wade at the line-up was not a confrontation in the same vein.

Pre-trial identification procedures are fraught with the potential for error. If counsel is absent from these procedures, the opportunity to expose any such errors at the later trial will be substantially hampered. Moreover, any errors in the initial identification may be compounded if that earlier identification also forms the basis for the witness' subsequent identification of the defendant at trial.[51]

---

[49] United States v. Wade, 388 U.S. 218, 227 (1967).

[50] Id. at 224 (1967).

[51] Id. at 235.

The presence of counsel at the pre-trial line-up would achieve the dual goal of discouraging any prejudicial practices in the initial identification procedures and enabling the defense to meaningfully challenge at trial any such practices to the extent they occur. For this reason, the post-indictment line-up is a "critical stage" of trial at which the defendant enjoys a right to counsel.[52]

As was the case in *Wade*, the prosecutor will often have eyewitnesses identify the accused in a post-indictment line-up, and then will have the eyewitness identify the defendant again in court. If the initial identification is done in the absence of counsel, the *Wade* rule requires that testimony about it is excluded. And, this initial illegality calls into question the admissibility of the subsequent in-court identification.

Exclusion of the in-court identification is not, however, a foregone conclusion. The Court has repeatedly determined that the subsequent in-court identification is properly admitted if it is based on a source independent of the uncounseled line-up.[53] An independent source might be something like a witness' past familiarity with the accused. This aspect of identification was discussed at greater length in **Chapter 27.**

The *Wade* Court's decision that the presence of counsel is required at post-indictment line-ups was motivated by serious concern for the reliability of eyewitness identifications. The Court wrote in that case, "[a] major factor contributing to the high incidence of miscarriage of justice from mistaken identification has been the degree of suggestion inherent in the manner in which the prosecution presents the suspect to witnesses for pretrial identification."[54] While the particular identification procedure at issue in *Wade* was a line-up, many of the stated concerns about the potential for error would seemingly apply to other forms of pre-trial identification of the defendant—including, for example, the identification of a suspect in a photo array. However, several years after *Wade* the Court was asked to consider just such a procedure and concluded that it did not constitute a "critical stage" at which the right to counsel was triggered:

> **Example—*United States v. Ash*, 413 U.S. 300 (1973):** A bank in Washington, D.C., was robbed by two masked assailants. The first man walked into the bank waving a gun. The second man grabbed money from the tellers' drawers and stuffed it into a bag. Three or four minutes after they first entered the bank, both men ran out taking the cash with them.

[52] Id. at 241–42.

[53] Id. at 242; Gilbert v. California, 388 U.S. 263, 272 (1967).

[54] Wade, 388 U.S. at 228.

Shortly after the robbery, an informant reported to the FBI that Charles Ash was one of the men involved in the robbery. A photo array that included Ash was shown to the witnesses from the bank, each of whom could only hesitantly identify Ash as the robber. Following additional investigation, Ash and another man, John Bailey, were indicted for the crime.

While preparing for trial, the prosecutor wanted to make sure the witnesses would be able to identify Ash before asking them to do so in front of the jury, so he showed the witnesses a photo array containing Ash's picture along with four others. Three of the witnesses picked Ash's picture from the array. The fourth witness did not identify any of the five as his assailant.

At trial, all four witnesses then made in-court identifications of Ash, testifying that he was one of the men who had robbed the bank. The informant also testified about his conversations with Ash concerning the robbery. Ash was thereafter convicted.

On appeal, Ash challenged the prosecutor's pre-trial use of the photo array in the absence of defense counsel. Relying on the Court's line-up cases, the intermediate appellate court reversed Ash's conviction. The State appealed.

Analysis: The prosecutor's pre-trial use of the post-indictment photo array did not violate Ash's Sixth Amendment right to counsel.

The Sixth Amendment right to counsel is motivated by two concerns. The first is the realization that an untutored person will face significant challenges if she tries to navigate the criminal justice system unaided by an attorney. The second is the recognition that with the advent of the public prosecutor, defense counsel is needed to evenly match the sides in the adversarial criminal process. While these two goals could be said to require counsel only at the time of trial, it has become increasingly clear that there are stages in advance of trial where "the accused [is] confronted, just as at trial, by the procedural system, or by his expert adversary, or by both."[55] For this reason, the right to counsel has not been narrowly limited to the trial itself but has been read to include a number of pre-trial interactions. Each of the pre-trial interactions that has been deemed a "critical stage," however, has been identified as such because counsel was necessary to "act as a spokesman for, or advisor to, the accused."[56]

---

[55] United States v. Ash, 413 U.S. 300, 310 (1973).

[56] Id. at 312.

In this case, Ash asks that the category of cases treated as "critical stages" be expanded to include post-indictment photo array proceedings. Further expansion of the right should happen only in those instances where the original goals of the guarantee are most closely matched. Photo array proceedings are not such an instance.

While the right to counsel recognized in *Wade* did make mention of concerns about the reliability of eyewitness identifications, that was not the core motivation for the holding in that case. Instead, the *Wade* Court was primarily focused on the fact that "the lineup constituted a trial-like confrontation, requiring the 'Assistance of Counsel' to preserve the adversary process by compensating for advantages of the prosecuting authorities."[57] This same concern is not present in the case of photo arrays. The pretrial interviewing of witnesses is an age-old prosecutorial practice. Showing witnesses photos during those interviews does not radically change the character of this particular form of trial preparation. The counterbalance is not to allow defense counsel to be present during the prosecutor's preparations, but instead to allow defense counsel the ability to access the witnesses on her own. Certainly allowing defense access does not eliminate all potential for abuse during the prosecutor's preparation sessions, but access does resolve imbalances in the adversarial process and thereby satisfies the commands of the Sixth Amendment.

For these reasons, "the Sixth Amendment does not grant the right to counsel at photographic displays conducted by the Government for the purpose of allowing a witness to attempt an identification of the offender."[58]

The courts have determined that the following procedures constitute "critical stages" of the process:

- Post-indictment interrogations (see **Chapter 32**)
- Post-indictment line-ups
- Preliminary hearings at which the accused might plead to the charges
- Preliminary hearings and arraignments at which certain affirmative defenses and substantive claims must be raised or forever waived
- Examinations by the government's psychiatric experts to gather evidence of future dangerousness
- Entering a guilty plea

[57] Id. at 314.

[58] Id. at 321.

4. Waiver of Counsel and the Right to Self-Representation. As with all other rights, a defendant may waive his right to counsel. For example, a defendant subject to a post-indictment interrogation may waive his right to counsel and agree to answer questions without the assistance of a lawyer. Similarly, a defendant at trial may determine that he does not wish the aid of an attorney but would rather go it alone.

A defendant's waiver must be voluntary, knowing, and intelligent. However, the actual steps that must be taken to insure a particular waiver meets this standard will vary depending upon the stage of the proceedings at which the right is being waived. In the context of a post-indictment interrogation, the waiver of the Sixth Amendment right to counsel is a relatively straightforward procedure. If a defendant is fully advised of his *Miranda* rights but agrees to waive those rights and speak with the police, that waiver will also constitute valid waiver of the Sixth Amendment right to counsel.

A bit more is required, however, in the context of a waiver of the right to counsel at trial. The standard does not change—a voluntary, knowing, and intelligent choice is still required. But a trial judge must do more than provide the *Miranda* admonitions to ensure the validity of the waiver at this stage. Noting the substantial benefit gained by proceeding to trial with counsel, the Court has "imposed the most rigorous restrictions on the information that must be conveyed to a defendant, and the procedures that must be observed before permitting him to waive his right to counsel at trial."[59] The contours of these procedures were considered by the Court in the case of a defendant who demanded that his public defender be released:

> **Example—*Faretta v. California*, 422 U.S. 806 (1975):** Anthony Faretta was charged with theft. At Faretta's arraignment, the judge appointed counsel from the public defender's office to represent him in the case. Some time before the actual trial date, Faretta advised the court that he wanted to represent himself. Faretta expressed his concern that any attorney from the public defender's office would have a very big caseload and would not be able to devote the time and attention necessary to Faretta's case. The trial judge expressed his opinion that proceeding to trial without counsel was a mistake, but nonetheless initially granted Faretta's request.
>
> Some weeks later, the trial judge held a hearing to assess Faretta's familiarity with certain trial rules and procedures. When Faretta was unable to satisfactorily describe certain rules governing hearsay and voir dire, the trial judge determined that Faretta had

[59] Patterson v. Illinois, 487 U.S. 285 (1988).

not knowingly and voluntarily waived his right to counsel. The court therefore reversed its initial decision, and appointed a public defender to represent Faretta at trial. Faretta was ultimately convicted of the charged offense. On appeal, he challenged the trial judge's decision to force representation upon him. The California courts affirmed. The Supreme Court then took the case for review.

Analysis: Faretta's waiver of his Sixth Amendment right to counsel was valid, and thus his conviction should be reversed.

The Sixth Amendment right to counsel carries with it a companion right to self-representation. That right is also recognized by federal statute, as well as by most state constitutions. The rights enshrined in the Sixth Amendment are rights granted directly to the accused for the purpose of allowing him to mount a defense. In some sense, the right to counsel is no different than, for example, the right to notice and the right to compulsory process—all are designed to "be an aid to a willing defendant."[60] There is no question that most defendants will fare better with the assistance of counsel. But, "[p]ersonal liberites are not rooted in the law of averages."[61] Acknowledging the reality that attorneys are usually better for a defendant therefore does not justify a further conclusion that counsel may always be foisted upon an unwilling client.

If a defendant knowingly and intelligently waives the right to the benefits that accompany the appointment of counsel that choice must be honored. To ensure that a waiver is valid, the defendant "should be made aware of the dangers and disadvantages of self-representation, so that the record will establish that 'he knows what he is doing and his choice is made with eyes open.'"[62]

Faretta knew what he was doing and made his choice with open eyes. He stated clearly several weeks before trial that he did not want a lawyer to be appointed. The record clearly indicates that Faretta was "literate, competent, and understanding."[63] The record is also clear that his decision was voluntary. The trial judge explained to Faretta that it would be a mistake to proceed without an attorney. The trial judge also explained that Faretta would be expected to adhere to standard rules of trial procedure. That Faretta did not completely understand the hearsay rule or the voir dire process was irrelevant to the question of whether his waiver was knowing and intelligent.

On the facts of this case, Faretta's decision to proceed without counsel should have been respected.[64]

---

[60] Faretta v. California, 422 U.S. 806, 820 (1975).

[61] Id. at 834.

[62] Id. at 835.

[63] Id.

[64] Id. at 836.

The Court has also provided guidance on what specific advice the Sixth Amendment requires before a trial court can legitimately accept a guilty plea from a *pro se* defendant. Waiver of the right to counsel will be satisfactory in this context if the court before accepting the plea "informs the accused of the nature of the charges against him, of his right to be counseled regarding the plea, and of the range of allowable punishments attendant upon the entry of the guilty plea."[65]

The right to proceed in the absence of counsel is not only protected by the Constitution. In the federal system, the right to self-representation is also protected by statute.[66] And in most states, the right to self-representation is recognized either by statute, by court decision, or by the state constitution.

However, the right to self-representation is not absolute. A trial judge may terminate self-representation or may appoint standby counsel[67] if a defendant is competent to stand trial, but not competent enough to represent himself.[68] A defendant's disruptive behavior may also be a factor in refusing to allow self-representation.

If standby counsel is appointed, she may participate in the trial, so long as that participation does not wrest control of the case from the defendant and does not destroy the jury's belief that the defendant is acting *pro se*.[69]

Note that although there is a right to counsel on appeal, there is not a parallel right to self-representation at that stage in a criminal case.[70]

Finally, the Supreme Court has yet to resolve whether a defendant has the ability to reassert his Sixth Amendment right to trial counsel once it has been knowingly and intelligently waived.[71] The state and lower federal courts that have considered the question have come to differing conclusions. Some courts have embraced a strong presumption that a request for counsel should not be refused even if it follows a valid waiver of the right; while others have concluded that a trial judge has the discretion to deny such a request based on the totality of the circumstances.[72] In practice, be sure to consult the guidance relevant to your jurisdiction.

[65] Iowa v. Tovar, 541 U.S. 77, 81 (2004).

[66] 28 U.S.C. § 1654.

[67] Martinez v. Court of Appeal of California, 528 U.S. 152, 162 (2000).

[68] Indiana v. Edwards, 554 U.S. 164 (2008).

[69] McKaskle v. Wiggins, 465 U.S. 168 (1984).

[70] Martinez, 528 U.S. at 152.

[71] Marshall v. Rodgers, 133 S.Ct. 1446 (2013).

[72] Compare Robinson v. Ignacio, 360 F.3d 1044, 1058 (9th Cir. 2004) with People v. Lawley, 27 Cal. 4th 102, 147–51 (2002).

5. The Right to Counsel of One's Choosing. One of the only aspects of the right to counsel that deals specifically with defendants who are able to retain paid counsel is the right to counsel of one's choosing. Embedded within the Sixth Amendment right to counsel is the belief that defendants who can afford to hire their own attorneys are entitled to counsel of their choosing. However, this right has significant limitations.

A defendant is not entitled to select the lawyer of his choosing if he cannot afford to pay for the attorney. Thus, a defendant who requires appointed counsel has no right to demand that a particular attorney be assigned to him. The right to counsel of one's choosing also does not allow an accused to seek representation by someone who is not licensed to practice in the jurisdiction. An accused also cannot require a court to accept his willingness to proceed with conflicted counsel.[73]

Commenting broadly on the limits that have been placed on the right, the Court said, "[w]e have recognized a trial court's wide latitude in balancing the right to counsel of choice against the needs of fairness, and against the demands of its calendar. The court has, moreover, an 'independent interest in ensuring that criminal trials are conducted within the ethical standards of the profession and that legal proceedings appear fair to all who observe them.'"[74] The Court discussed the right to counsel of choice in detail in a 2006 decision involving a man accused of a wide-ranging drug conspiracy:

> **Example—*United States v. Gonzalez-Lopez*, 548 U.S. 140 (2006):** Cuauhtemoc Gonzalez-Lopez was charged in a marijuana conspiracy. His family hired an attorney named John Fahle to represent Gonzalez-Lopez at trial. On his own, Gonzalez-Lopez reached out to an out-of-state attorney named Joseph Low. After meeting with Low, Gonzalez-Lopez hired him to work with Fahle.
>
> Low and Fahle appeared together at an evidentiary hearing as defense counsel. The hearing judge agreed to allow Low to act as counsel at the hearing provided he immediately apply for *pro hac vice* admission, a temporary certification that allows an out-of-state attorney to practice for a short time within the state. However, the judge reversed course during the hearing when he saw Low passing notes to Fahle during cross-examination. This conduct violated a local practice rule restricting cross-examination to a single attorney.

[73] Wheat v. United States, 486 U.S. 153 (1988).

[74] United States v. Gonzalez-Lopez, 548 U.S. 140, 152 (2006).

Approximately one week later, Gonzalez-Lopez decided he wanted just Low as counsel. However, the trial court repeatedly denied Low's motions for admission *pro hac vice*. After attorney Fahle withdrew from the case, Gonzalez-Lopez hired another attorney by the name Dickhaus. During trial, Low repeated his request for *pro hac vice* admission and was again denied. The court also refused to allow Low to sit at counsel table with Dickhaus, and prohibited Low from communicating with Dickhaus during the trial proceedings by seating a U.S. Marshall between the two. Low was able to see Gonzalez-Lopez only once, on the last night of trial. Gonzalez-Lopez was ultimately convicted.

On appeal, the Eighth Circuit vacated the conviction. The court found that the trial court improperly read the local rule to prohibit Low's communications in this case and in the separate case to which the trial court referred. Because the trial court's findings regarding the improper communications was the stated basis for denial of the *pro hac vice* motions, the reviewing court found that Gonzalez-Lopez' Sixth Amendment right to paid counsel of his choice was violated. The Supreme Court then granted cert.

Analysis: Gonzalez-Lopez' right to paid counsel of his choosing was violated by the trial court's action in this case, and so Gonzalez-Lopez' conviction was reversed.

The Sixth Amendment grants defendants the right to the assistance of counsel. Part and parcel of this right is the right of defendants with the ability to pay counsel to obtain counsel of their choosing. There are limits on the right to counsel of one's choice, but those limits do not apply in this case.

Establishing a violation of the right does not require a showing that counsel who was ultimately obtained was constitutionally ineffective. There is also no need for the accused to demonstrate that the lawyer he wanted to use would have utilized a strategy different from the one that retained counsel pursued.

The Sixth Amendment right to counsel is intended to advance the goal of a fair trial. But that does not mean the right can be ignored whenever the accused enjoys an otherwise error-free process. "In sum, the right at stake here is the right to counsel of choice, not the right to a fair trial; and that right was violated because the deprivation of counsel was erroneous. No additional showing of prejudice is required to make the violation 'complete.'"[75] Once this error has been established, it is not subject to a harmless error analysis.

[75] Id. at 146.

Some criminal statutes allow the government to freeze any assets that were acquired through the criminal conduct. Usually these assets are frozen prior to the criminal trial in a civil forfeiture action. But what if the defendant intended to use those assets to pay for an attorney? Does the right to counsel of one's choice prevent the prosecutor from freezing the assets prior to the criminal trial? The Court recently confirmed that the Sixth Amendment right to counsel of one's choosing does not prevent asset seizure:

> **Example—*Kaley v. United States*, 134 S.Ct. 1090 (2014):** Keri Kaley and her husband, Brian, were charged with stealing prescription medical devices from Keri's employer and selling them for profit. The Kaleys asserted that the devices they sold were not stolen, but rather were excess inventory that Keri's employer allowed her (and other employees) to take and sell.
>
> After indicting the Kaleys, the government obtained an order freezing their assets. Among the frozen assets was a $500,000 certificate of deposit that the Kaleys were planning to use to pay their attorney's legal fees. At a hearing, the trial court agreed to consider whether the assets could be traced to the alleged criminal conduct. But, the court refused to consider the Kaleys' further claim that the conduct alleged was not criminal.
>
> After the Kaleys conceded that they had engaged in the alleged conduct (while still disputing its criminality) the trial court upheld the restraint on their assets. The appellate court affirmed, and the case then arrived in the Supreme Court for review.

Analysis: A defendant cannot challenge the forfeiture of her assets merely because it will prevent her from hiring the attorney of her choice.

There is no question that our system of criminal justice presumes an accused to be innocent until proven guilty beyond a reasonable doubt. However, the standard for freezing assets that are suspected of being involved with criminal activity is much lower than the reasonable doubt threshold. Freezing assets requires only probable cause to believe the assets will ultimately be deemed forfeitable. Once the grand jury has properly returned an indictment, the necessary probable cause finding has been made and restraint on the assets is appropriate. There is no need to give the accused any further opportunity to be heard other than on the question of whether the assets can be traced to the allegedly criminal conduct. The fact that the accused hoped to use the frozen assets to pay for a lawyer does not alter this analysis.

There is no question that the Kaleys had a vital interest in retaining a lawyer of their own choosing. And the wrongful failure to afford them this right is error of such magnitude that it is not subject to a harmless error analysis. But "'[a] defendant has no Sixth Amendment right to spend another person's money for legal fees—even if that is the only way to hire a preferred lawyer."[76]

Consequently, the seizure of the money that the defendants intended to use to pay for their lawyer was not error where they conceded the connection between the money and the alleged conduct, and where the grand jury had determined there was probable cause to believe they committed the crimes charged.

The Court in *Kaley* was careful to note that deprivation of the right to **counsel of one's choosing** is not a deprivation of the right to **effective counsel** (you will read about the effective assistance of counsel next in **Chapter 31**). The overwhelming majority of people processed through the criminal justice system do so with appointed counsel. Thus, responding to the *Kaley* dissenting justices' suggestion that the Kaleys should have been allowed to pay for counsel because appointed counsel would be less effective, the Court noted, "the Court has never thought, as the dissent suggests today, that [using appointed counsel] risks the 'fundamental fairness of the actual trial.' If it does, the right way to start correcting the problem is not by adopting the dissent's position, but by ensuring that the right to effective counsel is fully vindicated."[77]

---

[76] Kaley v. United States, 134 S.Ct. 1090, 1096 (2014) (citing Caplin & Drysdale v. United States, 491 U.S. 617, 625 (1989)).

[77] Id. at 1102 n.13.

Quick Summary

The right to counsel is governed by rule, by statute, and by the state and federal constitutions. However, the primary regulation of the right to counsel is provided by the Sixth Amendment to the U.S. Constitution. The right is applied against the states through the Fourteenth Amendment's due process guarantee.

The right to counsel is central to the fairness of the trial because of (1) the confusing and complex nature of the criminal justice process, and (2) the need to ensure balance in an adversarial system that employs public prosecutors.

The Sixth Amendment right to counsel does not attach until judicial proceedings in a case have begun—when the official response to a criminal act moves from investigation to accusation. The mere hiring of an attorney cannot force the attachment of the right at an earlier point. Also, an accused has no right to counsel in a misdemeanor case for which a term of imprisonment is not imposed.

The right to counsel is guaranteed not just at the trial itself, but at all "critical stages" of a criminal proceeding, such as post-indictment interrogations, post-indictment line-ups, and the entering of guilty pleas. The question of whether a particular stage is "critical" is answered by considering whether the presence of counsel is required to preserve the defendant's basic right to a fair trial.

As with other rights, the Sixth Amendment right to counsel may be waived. Thus, the right to counsel carries with it a concomitant right to self-representation.

Any waiver must be voluntary, knowing, and intelligent. However, pre-waiver advice by an attorney is not required.[1] In the context of post-indictment questioning, an accused individual's valid waiver of her *Miranda* rights will also constitute valid waiver of her Sixth Amendment right to counsel. However, a waiver of the right to trial counsel requires a more thorough inquiry.

A defendant who is able to pay for counsel also has the right to the counsel of his own choosing, In order to prove that his right to counsel of his choosing was violated, he need not prove that the counsel he was forced to use instead was ineffective or that using that counsel in some way denied him a right to a fair trial.

[1] Michigan v. Harvey, 494 U.S. 344, 352–53 (1990).

Review Questions

1. The Adolescent Arsonist. Gregory Johnstone was accused of breaking into a building and setting it ablaze. At his first trial, Johnstone was represented by counsel. At the close of the evidence there was a hung jury. The government then announced its intention to try Johnstone again. In advance of the second trial, Johnstone asked the court to appoint another attorney. Johnstone was angry with original trial counsel for filing notice of an insanity defense in advance of the first trial without consulting with him. When the trial judge informed Johnstone that new counsel would not be appointed, Johnstone announced that he wished to waive his right to counsel and proceed *pro se*.

The trial judge conducted a lengthy inquiry. She asked Johnstone about his age, education, employment, and experience with the legal process. The judge also compared Johnstone's legal abilities with those of his existing attorney, noting in particular that the attorney had successfully avoided a guilty verdict in the first trial. The trial judge also warned Johnstone about the risk of self-representation. After further conversation with Johnstone, the trial judge concluded "Johnstone is eighteen, he has scarcely any formal education so far as I can ascertain, he has no known occupation and has virtually no previous exposure to legal procedures, except for the first trial." Finding that Johnstone was competent to stand trial, the trial judge nonetheless concluded that Johnstone was not capable of representing himself. For that reason, the judge denied Johnstone's request to discharge counsel.

The case proceeded to trial with appointed counsel. At the conclusion of the case, the jury returned a verdict of guilty on all counts. Johnstone appealed, alleging a violation of his right to self-representation. How should the court rule?

2. The Belligerent Bomber. Eddie Milton Garey attempted to extort money from various sources by threatening to bomb several buildings in the Macon, Georgia area. After police investigators traced one of the calls to Garey's home, he was indicted on 27 counts in connection with these threats. Shortly after his arrest, Garey submitted to a competency evaluation. The psychiatrists conducting the evaluation concluded that Garey suffered from paranoia with antisocial and narcissistic features. However, they found that he was competent to stand trial.

The day after Garey's arrest, the trial court appointed counsel. Three days before trial, Garey indicated that he wanted another lawyer. In Garey's view, his appointed counsel suffered a conflict of interests because his office was in one of the buildings that Garey had threatened to bomb. The trial court advised Garey that he could represent himself or could proceed with assigned counsel. Specifically, the court explained:

> You do not have the right to pick who your appointed attorney is, but you do have the right to proceed without an attorney . . . Just as you have the constitutional right to have an attorney appointed for you, if you cannot afford one, you have the constitutional right to represent yourself.
>
> If you choose to represent yourself, or before making that decision, I would caution you that you should make that decision very carefully. There are advantages to having an attorney trained in the law to represent you, to have someone who is expert on the rules of evidence and the other rules of law applicable to your case. I think it would generally be a disadvantage not to have that experience and expertise available to you. And there are many pitfalls for someone to proceed without an attorney, with regard to various aspects of the trial, including the questioning of witnesses, the decisions on who to put up as witnesses, the decision on whether to testify or not, decisions regarding impeachment, cross-examination. All of those things, in the court's view, it's very important to have an attorney providing you with legal advice.

The court then asked Garey if he wanted to move forward without an attorney. Garey refused to make the choice. He continued to adamantly insist that he did not want assigned counsel, while at the same time steadfastly refusing to waive his right to counsel.

After advising Garey of the potential penalties he might face, and reminding him of the hazards of proceeding *pro se*, the trial court determined that Garey, by his conduct, had knowingly and voluntarily waived his right to counsel. The court removed counsel from the case, and assigned him the role of standby counsel. Garey then proceeded *pro se*. He was convicted on all counts.

On appeal, Garey contended that his Sixth Amendment right to counsel was violated. Is he correct?

3. **The Substitute**. Santos Contreras was charged with cocaine possession and possession of a firearm in connection with a drug offense. Counsel was appointed to represent him. This attorney conducted all of the pretrial hearings and prepared the case for trial. Days before trial was to commence Contreras filed a Motion to Substitute Counsel. In the motion, Contreras complained that new counsel was required because appointed counsel was ill-prepared for trial and was not able to effectively represent him. After being advised by both the prosecution and defense counsel that they were prepared to go forward, the trial court denied Contreras' motion. In denying the motion, the court made no actual inquiry into appointed counsel's preparedness, and did not ask Contreras whether he planned to hire a new attorney.

Contreras was convicted of both counts at trial. On appeal, Contreras maintained that his right to counsel of his choosing had been violated by the denial of his motion. Will Contreras prevail?

4. **Stuck in Traffic**. Curtis Jeffery Benford and Michael Jerome King were indicted jointly on charges related to the robbery of the Bank of America in East Brea, California. Shortly after the indictment was handed down, Benford and King were arrested. Two different attorneys were appointed to separately represent each of the men. At a post-indictment hearing, the trial judge scheduled both a pre-trial status conference and the trial date. On the date of the pre-trial status conference, however, counsel for Benford called the court and advised that he was "on his way." According to counsel, he was stuck in traffic but would be in court shortly. The prosecutor, counsel for co-defendant King, and both King and Benford were present. The court began the status conference with the assumption that Benford's attorney would arrive shortly.

None of the individuals present (counsel nor the co-defendants) identified any pre-trial issues that needed to be resolved. The prosecutor and King's attorney advised the court that the scheduled trial date was still suitable. The prosecutor then mentioned that he heard Benford's lawyer had talked to another prosecutor about possibly moving the trial date. The prosecutor concluded though by saying he "didn't know anything beyond that." Based on the information presented, the trial judge stated, "the matter will proceed to trial on the date of March 8th when it's presently set." The conference then concluded before counsel for Benford arrived.

The trial began on the scheduled date and Benford's attorney at no point sought a continuance. The jury ultimately found Benford guilty as charged. He was sentenced to just over twelve years in prison. Benford appealed. He asserted that his right to counsel at all critical stages of the prosecution had been violated by defense counsel's absence at the post-indictment, pre-trial status conference. Is Benford right?

FROM THE COURTROOM

POWELL. v. ALABAMA

United States Supreme Court, 1932
287 U.S. 45

[Mr. Justice SUTHERLAND delivered the opinion of the Court.]

The petitioners, hereinafter referred to as defendants, are negroes charged with the crime of rape, committed upon the persons of two white girls. The crime is said to have been committed on March 25, 1931. The indictment was returned in a state court of first instance on March 31, and the record recites that on the same day the defendants were arraigned and entered pleas of not guilty. There is a further recital to the effect that upon the arraignment they were represented by counsel. But no counsel had been employed, and aside from a statement made by the trial judge several days later during a colloquy immediately preceding the trial, the record does not disclose when, or under what circumstances, an appointment of counsel was made, or who was appointed. During the colloquy referred to, the trial judge, in response to a question, said that he had appointed all the members of the bar for the purpose of arraigning the defendants and then of course anticipated that the members of the bar would continue to help the defendants if no counsel appeared. Upon the argument here both sides accepted that as a correct statement of the facts concerning the matter.

There was a severance upon the request of the state, and the defendants were tried in three several groups . . . . As each of the three cases was called for trial, each defendant was arraigned, and, having the indictment read to him, entered a plea of not guilty. Whether the original arraignment and pleas were regarded as ineffective is not shown. Each of the three trials was completed within a single day. Under the Alabama statute the punishment for rape is to be fixed by the jury, and in its discretion may be from ten years imprisonment to death. The juries found defendants guilty and imposed the death penalty upon all. The trial court overruled motions for new trials and sentenced the defendants in accordance with the verdicts. The judgments were affirmed by the state supreme court. Chief Justice Anderson thought the defendants had not been accorded a fair trial and strongly dissented.

In this court the judgments are assailed upon the grounds that the defendants, and each of them, were denied due process of law and the equal protection of the laws, in contravention of the Fourteenth Amendment, specifically as follows: (1) They were not given a fair, impartial, and deliberate trial; (2) they were denied the right of counsel, with the accustomed incidents of consultation and opportunity of preparation for trial; and (3) they were tried before juries from which qualified members of their own race were systematically excluded. These questions were properly raised and saved in the courts below.

The only one of the assignments which we shall consider is the second, in respect of the denial of counsel; and it becomes unnecessary to discuss the facts of the case or the circumstances surrounding the prosecution except in so far as they reflect light upon that question.

The record shows that on the day when the offense is said to have been committed, these defendants, together with a number of other negroes, were upon a freight train on its way through Alabama. On the same train were seven white boys and the two white girls. A fight took place between the negroes and the white boys, in the course of which the white boys, with the exception of one named Gilley, were thrown off the train. A message was sent ahead, reporting the fight and asking that every negro be gotten off the train. The participants in the fight, and the two girls, were in an open gondola car. The two girls testified that each of them was assaulted by six different negroes in turn, and they identified the seven defendants as having been among the number. None of the white boys was called to testify, with the exception of Gilley, who was called in rebuttal.

Before the train reached Scottsboro, Ala., a sheriff's posse seized the defendants and two other negroes. Both girls and the negroes then were taken to Scottsboro, the county seat. Word of their coming and of the alleged assault had preceded them, and they were met at Scottsboro by a large crowd. It does not sufficiently appear that the defendants were seriously threatened with, or that they were actually in danger of, mob violence; but it does appear that the attitude of the community was one of great hostility. The sheriff thought it necessary to call for the militia to assist in safeguarding the prisoners. Chief Justice Anderson pointed out in his opinion that every step taken from the arrest and arraignment to the sentence was accompanied by the military. Soldiers took the defendants to Gadsden for safe-keeping, brought them back to Scottsboro for arraignment, returned them to Gadsden for safe-keeping while awaiting trial, escorted them to Scottsboro for trial a few days later, and guarded the courthouse and grounds at every stage of the proceedings. It is perfectly apparent that the proceedings, from beginning to end, took place in an atmosphere of tense, hostile, and excited public sentiment. During the entire time, the defendants were closely confined or were under military guard. The record does not disclose their ages, except that one of them was nineteen; but the record clearly indicates that most, if not all, of them were youthful, and they are constantly referred to as "the boys." They were ignorant and illiterate. All of them were residents of other states, where alone members of their families or friends resided.

However guilty defendants, upon due inquiry, might prove to have been, they were, until convicted, presumed to be innocent. It was the duty of the court having their cases in charge to see that they were denied no necessary incident of a fair trial. With any error of the state court involving alleged contravention of the state statutes or Constitution we, of course, have nothing to do. The sole inquiry which we are permitted to make is whether the federal Constitution was contravened; and as to that, we confine ourselves, as already suggested, to the inquiry whether the defendants were in substance denied the right of counsel, and if so, whether such denial infringes the due process clause of the Fourteenth Amendment.

First. The record shows that immediately upon the return of the indictment defendants were arraigned and pleaded not guilty. Apparently they were not asked whether they had, or were able to employ, counsel, or wished to have counsel appointed; or whether they had friends or relatives who might assist in that regard if communicated with. That it would not have been an idle ceremony to have given the defendants reasonable opportunity to communicate with their families and endeavor to obtain counsel is demonstrated by the fact that very soon after conviction, able counsel appeared in their behalf. This was pointed out by Chief Justice Anderson in the course of his dissenting opinion. "They were nonresidents," he said, "and had little time or opportunity to get in touch with their families and friends who were scattered throughout two other states, and time has demonstrated that they could or would have been represented by able counsel had a better opportunity been given by a reasonable delay in the trial of the cases judging from the number and activity of counsel that appeared immediately or shortly after their conviction."

It is hardly necessary to say that the right to counsel being conceded, a defendant should be afforded a fair opportunity to secure counsel of his own choice. Not only was that not done here, but such designation of counsel as was attempted was either so indefinite or so close upon the trial as to amount to a denial of effective and substantial aid in that regard. This will be amply demonstrated by a brief review of the record.

April 6, six days after indictment, the trials began. When the first case was called, the court inquired whether the parties were ready for trial. The state's attorney replied that he was ready to proceed. No one answered for the defendants or appeared to represent or defend them. Mr. Roddy, a Tennessee lawyer not a member of the local bar, addressed the court, saying that he had not been employed, but that people who were interested had spoken to him about the case. He was asked by the court whether he intended to appear for the defendants, and answered that he would like to appear along with counsel that the court might appoint. The record then proceeds:

"The Court: If you appear for these defendants, then I will not appoint counsel; if local counsel are willing to appear and assist you under the circumstances all right, but I will not appoint them.

"Mr. Roddy: Your Honor has appointed counsel, is that correct?

"The Court: I appointed all the members of the bar for the purpose of arraigning the defendants and then of course I anticipated them to continue to help them if no counsel appears.

"Mr. Roddy: Then I don't appear then as counsel but I do want to stay in and not be ruled out in this case.

"The Court: Of course I would not do that—

"Mr. Roddy: I just appear here through the courtesy of Your Honor.

"The Court: Of course I give you that right * * *."

And then, apparently addressing all the lawyers present, the court inquired:

"* * * Well are you all willing to assist?

"Mr. Moody: Your Honor appointed us all and we have been proceeding along every line we know about it under Your Honor's appointment.

"The Court: The only thing I am trying to do is, if counsel appears for these defendants I don't want to impose on you all, but if you feel like counsel from Chattanooga—

"Mr. Moody: I see his situation of course and I have not run out of anything yet. Of course, if Your Honor purposes to appoint us, Mr. Parks, I am willing to go on with it. Most of the bar have been down and conferred with these defendants in this case; they did not know what else to do.

"The Court: The thing, I did not want to impose on the members of the bar if counsel unqualifiedly appears; if you all feel like Mr. Roddy is only interested in a limited way to assist, then I don't care to appoint—

"Mr. Parks: Your Honor, I don't feel like you ought to impose on any member of the local bar if the defendants are represented by counsel.

"The Court: That is what I was trying to ascertain, Mr. Parks.

"Mr. Parks: Of course if they have counsel, I don't see the necessity of the Court appointing anybody; if they haven't counsel, of course I think it is up to the Court to appoint counsel to represent them.

"The Court: I think you are right about it Mr. Parks and that is the reason I was trying to get an expression from Mr. Roddy.

"Mr. Roddy: I think Mr. Parks is entirely right about it, if I was paid down here and employed, it would be a different thing, but I have not prepared this case for trial and have only been called into it by people who are interested in these boys from Chattanooga. Now, they have not given me an opportunity to prepare the case and I am not familiar with the procedure in Alabama, but I merely came down here as a friend of the people who are interested and not as paid counsel, and certainly I haven't any money to pay them and nobody I am interested in had me to come down here has put up any fund of money to come down here and pay counsel. If they should do it I would be glad to turn it over—a counsel but I am merely here at the solicitation of people who have become interested in this case without any payment of fee and without any preparation for trial and I think the boys would be better off if I step entirely out of the case according to my way of looking at it and according to my lack of preparation for it and not being familiar with the procedure in Alabama * * *."

Mr. Roddy later observed:

"If there is anything I can do to be of help to them, I will be glad to do it; I am interested to that extent.

"The Court: Well gentlemen, if Mr. Roddy only appears as assistant that way, I think it is proper that I appoint members of this bar to represent them, I expect that is right. If Mr. Roddy will appear, I wouldn't of course, I would not appoint anybody. I don't see, Mr. Roddy, how I can make a qualified appointment or a limited appointment. Of course, I don't mean to cut off your assistance in any way—Well gentlemen, I think you understand it.

"Mr. Moody: I am willing to go ahead and help Mr. Roddy in anything I can do about it, under the circumstances.

"The Court: All right, all the lawyers that will; of course I would not require a lawyer to appear if—

"Mr. Moody: I am willing to go ahead and help Mr. Roddy in anything I can do about it, under the circumstances.

"The Court: All right, all the lawyers that will, of course, I would not require a lawyer to appear if—

"Mr. Moody: I am willing to do that for him as a member of the bar; I will go ahead and help do anything I can do.

"The Court: All right."

And in this casual fashion the matter of counsel in a capital case was disposed of.

It thus will be seen that until the very morning of the trial no lawyer had been named or definitely designated to represent the defendants. Prior to that time, the trial judge had "appointed all the members of the bar" for the limited "purpose of arraigning the defendants." Whether they would represent the defendants thereafter, if no counsel appeared in their behalf, was a matter of speculation only, or, as the judge indicated, of mere anticipation on the part of the court. Such a designation, even if made for all purposes, would, in our opinion, have fallen far short of meeting, in any proper sense, a requirement for the appointment of counsel. How many lawyers were members of the bar does not appear; but, in the very nature of things, whether many or few, they would not, thus collectively named, have been given that clear appreciation of responsibility or impressed with that individual sense of duty which should and naturally would accompany the appointment of a selected member of the bar, specifically named and assigned.

That this action of the trial judge in respect of appointment of counsel was little more than an expansive gesture, imposing no substantial or definite obligation upon any one, is borne out by the fact that prior to the calling of the case for trial on April 6, a leading member of the local bar accepted employment on the side of the prosecution and actively participated in the trial. It is true that he said that before doing so he had understood Mr. Roddy would be employed as counsel for the defendants. This the lawyer in question, of his own accord, frankly stated to the court; and no doubt he acted with the utmost good faith. Probably other members of the bar had a like understanding. In any event, the circumstance lends emphasis to the conclusion that during perhaps the most critical period of the proceedings against these defendants, that is to say, from the time of their arraignment until the beginning of their trial, when consultation, thorough-going investigation and preparation were vitally important, the defendants did not have the aid of counsel in any real sense, although they were as much entitled to such aid during that period as at the trial itself.

Nor do we think the situation was helped by what occurred on the morning of the trial. At that time, as appears from the colloquy printed above, Mr. Roddy stated to the court that he did not appear as counsel, but that he would like to appear along with counsel that the court might appoint; that he had not been given an opportunity to prepare the case; that he was not familiar with the procedure in Alabama, but merely came down as a friend of the people who were interested; that he thought the boys would be better off if he should step entirely out of the case. Mr. Moody, a member of the local bar, expressed a willingness to help Mr. Roddy in anything he could do under the circumstances. To this the court responded: "All right, all the lawyers that will; of course I would not require a lawyer to appear if—." And Mr. Moody continued: "I am willing to do that for him as a member of the bar; I will go ahead and help do anything I can do." With this dubious understanding, the trials immediately proceeded. The defendants, young, ignorant, illiterate, surrounded by hostile sentiment, haled back and forth under guard of soldiers, charged with an atrocious crime regarded with especial horror in the community where they were to be tried, were thus put in peril of their lives within a few moments after counsel for the first time charged with any degree of responsibility began to represent them.

It is not enough to assume that counsel thus precipitated into the case thought there was no defense, and exercised their best judgment in proceeding to trial without preparation. Neither they nor the court could say what a prompt and thorough-going investigation might disclose as to the facts. No attempt was made to investigate. No opportunity to do so was given. Defendants were immediately hurried to trial. Chief Justice Anderson, after disclaiming any intention to criticize harshly counsel who attempted to represent defendants at the trials, said: "* * * The record indicates that the appearance was rather pro forma than zealous and active * * *." Under the circumstances disclosed, we hold that defendants were not accorded the right of counsel in any substantial sense. To decide otherwise, would simply be to ignore actualities. This conclusion finds ample support in the reasoning of an overwhelming array of state decisions . . . .

It is true that great and inexcusable delay in the enforcement of our criminal law is one of the grave evils of our time. Continuances are frequently granted for unnecessarily long periods of time, and delays incident to the disposition of motions for new trial and hearings upon appeal have come in many cases to be a distinct reproach to the administration of justice. The prompt disposition of criminal cases is to be commended and encouraged. But in reaching that result a defendant, charged with a serious crime, must not be stripped of his right to have sufficient time to advise with counsel and prepare his defense. To do that is not to proceed promptly in the calm spirit of regulated justice but to go forward with the haste of the mob.

As the court said in *Commonwealth v. O'Keefe*, 298 Pa. 169, 173:

"It is vain to give the accused a day in court, with no opportunity to prepare for it, or to guarantee him counsel without giving the latter any opportunity to acquaint himself with the facts or law of the case. * * *

"A prompt and vigorous administration of the criminal law is commendable and we have no desire to clog the wheels of justice. What we here decide is that to force a defendant, charged with a serious misdemeanor, to trial within five hours of his arrest, is not due process of law, regardless of the merits of the case."

Second. . . . The question . . . which it is our duty, and within our power, to decide, is whether the denial of the assistance of counsel contravenes the due process clause of the Fourteenth Amendment to the Federal Constitution.

. . .

It . . . appears that in at least twelve of the thirteen colonies . . . the right to counsel [was] fully recognized in all criminal prosecutions, save that in one or two instances the right was limited to capital offenses or to the more serious crimes; and this court seems to have been of the opinion that this was true in all the colonies. . . .

The fact that the right involved is of such a character that it cannot be denied without violating those "fundamental principles of liberty and justice which lie at the base of all our civil and political institutions", is obviously one of those compelling considerations which must prevail in determining whether it is embraced within the due process clause of the Fourteenth Amendment, although it be specifically dealt with in another part of the Federal Constitution. . . . While the question has never been categorically determined by this court, a consideration of the nature of the right and a review of the expressions of this and other courts makes it clear that the right to the aid of counsel is of this fundamental character.

It never has been doubted by this court, or any other so far as we know, that notice and hearing are preliminary steps essential to the passing of an enforceable judgment, and that they, together with a legally competent tribunal having jurisdiction of the case, constitute basic elements of the constitutional requirement of due process of law. The words of Webster, so often quoted, that by "the law of the land" is intended "a law which hears before it condemns," have been repeated in varying forms of expression in a multitude of decisions. In *Holden v. Hardy*, 169 U.S. 366, 389, the necessity of due notice and an opportunity of being heard is described as among the "immutable principles of justice which inhere in the very idea of free government which no member of the Union may disregard." And Mr. Justice Field, in an earlier case, *Galpin v. Page*, 18 Wall. 350, 368, said that the rule that no one shall be personally bound until he has had his day in court was as old as the law, and it meant that he must be cited to appear and afforded an opportunity to be heard. "Judgment without such citation and opportunity wants all the attributes of a judicial determination; it is judicial usurpation and oppression, and never can be upheld where justice is justly administered." Citations to the same effect might be indefinitely multiplied, but there is no occasion for doing so.

What, then, does a hearing include? Historically and in practice, in our own country at least, it has always included the right to the aid of counsel when desired and provided by the party asserting the right. The right to be heard would be, in many cases, of little avail if it did not comprehend the right to be heard by counsel. Even the intelligent and educated layman has small and sometimes no skill in the science of law. If charged with crime, he is incapable, generally, of determining for himself whether the indictment is good or bad. He is unfamiliar with the rules of evidence. Left without the aid of counsel he may be put on trial without a proper charge, and convicted upon incompetent evidence, or evidence irrelevant to the issue or otherwise inadmissible. He lacks both the skill and knowledge adequately to prepare his defense, even though he have a perfect one. He requires the guiding hand of counsel at every step in the proceedings against him. Without it, though he be not guilty, he faces the danger of conviction because he does not know how to establish his innocence. If that be true of men of intelligence, how much more true is it of the ignorant and illiterate, or those of feeble intellect. If in any case, civil of criminal, a state or federal court were arbitrarily to refuse to hear a party by counsel, employed by and appearing for him, it reasonably may not be doubted that such a refusal would be a denial of a hearing, and, therefore, of due process in the constitutional sense.

. . . In numerous other cases the court, in determining that due process was accorded, has frequently stressed the fact that the defendant had the aid of counsel. . . .

In the light of the facts outlined in the forepart of this opinion—the ignorance and illiteracy of the defendants, their youth, the circumstances of public hostility, the imprisonment and the close surveillance of the defendants by the military forces, the fact that their friends and families were all in other states and communication with them necessarily difficult, and above all that they stood in deadly peril of their lives—we think the failure of the trial court to give them reasonable time and opportunity to secure counsel was a clear denial of due process.

But passing that, and assuming their inability, even if opportunity had been given, to employ counsel, as the trial court evidently did assume, we are of opinion that, under the circumstances just stated, the necessity of counsel was so vital and imperative that the failure of the trial court to make an effective appointment of counsel was likewise a denial of due process within the meaning of the Fourteenth Amendment. Whether this would be so in other criminal prosecutions, or under other circumstances, we need not determine. All that it is necessary now to decide, as we do decide, is that in a capital case, where the defendant is unable to employ counsel, and is incapable adequately of making his own defense because of ignorance, feeble-mindedness, illiteracy, or the like, it is the duty of the court, whether requested or not, to assign counsel for him as a necessary requisite of due process of law; and that duty is not discharged by an assignment at such a time or under such circumstances as to preclude the giving of effective aid in the preparation and trial of the case. To hold otherwise would be to ignore the fundamental postulate, already adverted to, "that there are certain immutable principles of justice which inhere in the very idea of free government which no member of the Union may disregard." In a case such as this, whatever may be the rule in other cases, the right to have counsel appointed, when necessary, is a logical corollary from the constitutional right to be heard by counsel. . . .

Let us suppose the extreme case of a prisoner charged with a capital offense, who is deaf and dumb, illiterate, and feeble-minded, unable to employ counsel, with the whole power of the state arrayed against him, prosecuted by counsel for the state without assignment of counsel for his defense, tried, convicted, and sentenced to death. Such a result, which, if carried into execution, would be little short of judicial murder, it cannot be doubted would be a gross violation of the guarantee of due process of law; and we venture to think that no appellate court, state or federal, would hesitate so to decide. The duty of the trial court to appoint counsel under such circumstances is clear, as it is clear under circumstances such as are disclosed by the record here; and its power to do so, even in the absence of a statute, can not be questioned. Attorneys are officers of the court, and are bound to render service when required by such an appointment.

The United States by statute and every state in the Union by express provision of law, or by the determination of its courts, make it the duty of the trial judge, where the accused is unable to employ counsel, to appoint counsel for him. In most states the rule applies broadly to all criminal prosecutions, in others it is limited to the more serious crimes, and in a very limited number, to capital cases. A rule adopted with such unanimous accord reflects, if it does not establish the inherent right to have counsel appointed at least in cases like the present, and lends convincing support to the conclusion we have reached as to the fundamental nature of that right.

The judgments must be reversed and the causes remanded for further proceedings not inconsistent with this opinion.

FROM THE COURTROOM

GIDEON v. WAINWRIGHT

Supreme Court of the United States, 1963
372 U.S. 335

[Mr. Justice BLACK delivered the opinion of the Court.]

Petitioner was charged in a Florida state court with having broken and entered a poolroom with intent to commit a misdemeanor. This offense is a felony under Florida law. Appearing in court without funds and without a lawyer, petitioner asked the court to appoint counsel for him, whereupon the following colloquy took place:

"The Court: Mr. Gideon, I am sorry, but I cannot appoint Counsel to represent you in this case. Under the laws of the State of Florida, the only time the Court can appoint Counsel to represent a Defendant is when that person is charged with a capital offense. I am sorry, but I will have to deny your request to appoint Counsel to defend you in this case.

"The Defendant: The United States Supreme Court says I am entitled to be represented by Counsel."

Put to trial before a jury, Gideon conducted his defense about as well as could be expected from a layman. He made an opening statement to the jury, cross-examined the State's witnesses, presented witnesses in his own defense, declined to testify himself, and made a short argument "emphasizing his innocence to the charge contained in the Information filed in this case." The jury returned a verdict of guilty, and petitioner was sentenced to serve five years in the state prison. Later, petitioner filed in the Florida Supreme Court this habeas corpus petition attacking his conviction and sentence on the ground that the trial court's refusal to appoint counsel for him denied him rights "guaranteed by the Constitution and the Bill of Rights by the United States Government." Treating the petition for habeas corpus as properly before it, the State Supreme Court, "upon consideration thereof" but without an opinion, denied all relief. Since 1942, when *Betts v. Brady*, 316 U.S. 455, was decided by a divided Court, the problem of a defendant's federal constitutional right to counsel in a state court has been a continuing source of controversy and litigation in both state and federal courts. To give this problem another review here, we granted certiorari. Since Gideon was proceeding in forma pauperis, we appointed counsel to represent him and requested both sides to discuss in their briefs and oral arguments the following: "Should this Court's holding in *Betts v. Brady*, 316 U.S. 455, be reconsidered?"

I

The facts upon which Betts claimed that he had been unconstitutionally denied the right to have counsel appointed to assist him are strikingly like the facts upon which Gideon here bases his federal constitutional claim. Betts was indicted for robbery in a Maryland state court. On arraignment, he told the trial judge of his lack of funds to hire a lawyer and asked the court to appoint one for him. Betts was advised that it was not the practice in that county to appoint counsel for indigent defendants except in murder and rape cases. He then pleaded not guilty, had witnesses summoned, cross-examined the State's witnesses, examined his own, and chose not to testify himself. He was found guilty by the judge, sitting without a jury, and sentenced to eight years in prison. Like Gideon, Betts sought release by habeas corpus, alleging that he had been denied the right to assistance of counsel in violation of the Fourteenth Amendment. Betts was denied any relief, and on review this Court affirmed. It was held that a refusal to appoint counsel for an indigent defendant charged with a felony did not necessarily violate the Due Process Clause of the Fourteenth Amendment, which for reasons given the Court deemed to be the only applicable federal constitutional provision. The Court said:

"Asserted denial (of due process) is to be tested by an appraisal of the totality of facts in a given case. That which may, in one setting, constitute a denial of fundamental fairness, shocking to the universal sense of justice, may, in other circumstances, and in the light of other considerations, fall short of such denial."

Treating due process as "a concept less rigid and more fluid than those envisaged in other specific and particular provisions of the Bill of Rights," the Court held that refusal to appoint counsel under the particular facts and circumstances in the *Betts* case was not so "offensive to the common and fundamental ideas of fairness" as to amount to a denial of due process. Since the facts and circumstances of the two cases are so nearly indistinguishable, we think the *Betts v. Brady* holding if left standing would require us to reject Gideon's claim that the Constitution guarantees him the assistance of counsel. Upon full reconsideration we conclude that *Betts v. Brady* should be overruled.

II.

The Sixth Amendment provides, "In all criminal prosecutions, the accused shall enjoy the right * * * to have the Assistance of Counsel for his defence." We have construed this to mean that in federal courts counsel must be provided for defendants unable to employ counsel unless the right is competently and intelligently waived. *Betts* argued that this right is extended to indigent defendants in state courts by the Fourteenth Amendment. In response the Court stated that, while the Sixth Amendment laid down "no rule for the conduct of the states, the question recurs whether the constraint laid by the amendment upon the national courts expresses a rule so fundamental and essential to a fair trial, and so, to due process of law, that it is made obligatory upon the states by the Fourteenth Amendment." In order to decide whether the Sixth Amendment's guarantee of counsel is of this fundamental nature, the Court in *Betts* set out and considered "(r)elevant data on the subject * * * afforded by constitutional and statutory provisions subsisting in the colonies and the states prior to the inclusion of the Bill of Rights in the national Constitution, and in the constitutional, legislative, and judicial history of the states to the present date." On the basis of this historical data the Court concluded that "appointment of counsel is not a fundamental right, essential to a fair trial." It was for this reason the *Betts* Court refused to accept the contention that the Sixth Amendment's guarantee of counsel for indigent federal defendants was extended to or, in the words of that Court, "made obligatory upon the states by the Fourteenth Amendment". Plainly, had the Court concluded that appointment of counsel for an indigent criminal defendant was "a fundamental right, essential to a fair trial," it would have held that the Fourteenth Amendment requires appointment of counsel in a state court, just as the Sixth Amendment requires in a federal court.

We think the Court in *Betts* had ample precedent for acknowledging that those guarantees of the Bill of Rights which are fundamental safeguards of liberty immune from federal abridgment are equally protected against state invasion by the Due Process Clause of the Fourteenth Amendment. This same principle was recognized, explained, and applied in *Powell v. Alabama*, 287 U.S. 45 (1932), a case upholding the right of counsel, where the Court held that despite sweeping language to the contrary in *Hurtado v. California*, 110 U.S. 516 (1884), the Fourteenth Amendment "embraced" those "fundamental principles of liberty and justice which lie at the base of all our civil and political institutions," even though they had been "specifically dealt with in another part of the Federal Constitution." In many cases other than *Powell* and *Betts*, this Court has looked to the fundamental nature of original Bill of Rights guarantees to decide whether the Fourteenth Amendment makes them obligatory on the States. Explicitly recognized to be of this "fundamental nature" and therefore made immune from state invasion by the Fourteenth, or some part of it, are the First Amendment's freedoms of speech, press, religion, assembly, association, and petition for redress of grievances. For the same reason, though not always in precisely the same terminology, the Court has made obligatory on the States the Fifth Amendment's command that private property shall not be taken for public use without just compensation, the Fourth Amendment's prohibition of unreasonable searches and seizures, and the Eighth's ban on cruel and unusual punishment. On the other hand, this Court in *Palko v. Connecticut*, 302 U.S. 319 (1937), refused to hold that the Fourteenth Amendment made the double jeopardy provision of the Fifth Amendment obligatory on the States. In so refusing, however, the Court, speaking through Mr. Justice Cardozo, was careful to emphasize that "immunities that are valid as against the federal government by force of the specific pledges of particular amendments have been found to be implicit in the concept of ordered liberty, and thus, through the Fourteenth Amendment, become valid as against the states" and that guarantees "in their origin * * * effective against the federal government alone" had by prior cases "been taken over from the earlier articles of the Federal Bill of Rights and brought within the Fourteenth Amendment by a process of absorption."

We accept *Betts v. Brady*'s assumption, based as it was on our prior cases, that a provision of the Bill of Rights which is "fundamental and essential to a fair trial" is made obligatory upon the States by the Fourteenth Amendment. We think the Court in *Betts* was wrong, however, in concluding that the Sixth Amendment's guarantee of counsel is not one of these fundamental rights. Ten years before *Betts v. Brady*, this Court, after full consideration of all the historical data examined in *Betts*, had unequivocally declared that "the right to the aid of counsel is of this fundamental character." *Powell v. Alabama*. While the Court at the close of its *Powell* opinion did by its language, as this Court frequently does, limit its holding to the particular facts and circumstances of that case, its conclusions about the fundamental nature of the right to counsel are unmistakable. Several years later, in 1936, the Court reemphasized what it had said about the fundamental nature of the right to counsel in this language:

"We concluded that certain fundamental rights, safeguarded by the first eight amendments against federal action, were also safeguarded against state action by the due process of law clause of the Fourteenth Amendment, and among them the fundamental right of the accused to the aid of counsel in a criminal prosecution."

And again in 1938 this Court said:

"(The assistance of counsel) is one of the safeguards of the Sixth Amendment deemed necessary to insure fundamental human rights of life and liberty. * * * The Sixth Amendment stands as a constant admonition that if the constitutional safeguards it provides be lost, justice will not "still be done."

In light of these and many other prior decisions of this Court, it is not surprising that the *Betts* Court, when faced with the contention that "one charged with crime, who is unable to obtain counsel, must be furnished counsel by the state," conceded that "(e)xpressions in the opinions of this court lend color to the argument * * *". The fact is that in deciding as it did—that "appointment of counsel is not a fundamental right, essential to a fair trial"—the Court in *Betts v. Brady* made an abrupt break with its own well-considered precedents. In returning to these old precedents, sounder we believe than the new, we but restore constitutional principles established to achieve a fair system of justice. Not only these precedents but also reason and reflection require us to recognize that in our adversary system of criminal justice, any person haled into court, who is too poor to hire a lawyer, cannot be assured a fair trial unless counsel is provided for him. This seems to us to be an obvious truth. Governments, both state and federal, quite properly spend vast sums of money to establish machinery to try defendants accused of crime. Lawyers to prosecute are everywhere deemed essential to protect the public's interest in an orderly society. Similarly, there are few defendants charged with crime, few indeed, who fail to hire the best lawyers they can get to prepare and present their defenses. That government hires lawyers to prosecute and defendants who have the money hire lawyers to defend are the strongest indications of the wide—spread belief that lawyers in criminal courts are necessities, not luxuries. The right of one charged with crime to counsel may not be deemed fundamental and essential to fair trials in some countries, but it is in ours. From the very beginning, our state and national constitutions and laws have laid great emphasis on procedural and substantive safeguards designed to assure fair trials before impartial tribunals in which every defendant stands equal before the law. This noble ideal cannot be realized if the poor man charged with crime has to face his accusers without a lawyer to assist him. A defendant's need for a lawyer is nowhere better stated than in the moving words of Mr. Justice Sutherland in *Powell v. Alabama*:

"The right to be heard would be, in many cases, of little avail if it did not comprehend the right to be heard by counsel. Even the intelligent and educated layman has small and sometimes no skill in the science of law. If charged with crime, he is incapable, generally, of determining for himself whether the indictment is good or bad. He is unfamiliar with the rules of evidence. Left without the aid of counsel he may be put on trial without a proper charge, and convicted upon incompetent evidence, or evidence irrelevant to the issue or otherwise inadmissible. He lacks both the skill and knowledge adequately to prepare his defense, even though he have a perfect one. He requires the guiding hand of counsel at every step in the proceedings against him. Without it, though he be not guilty, he faces the danger of conviction because he does not know how to establish his innocence."

The Court in *Betts v. Brady* departed from the sound wisdom upon which the Court's holding in *Powell v. Alabama* rested. Florida, supported by two other States, has asked that *Betts v. Brady* be left intact. Twenty-two States, as friends of the Court, argue that *Betts* was "an anachronism when handed down" and that it should now be overruled. We agree.

The judgment is reversed and the cause is remanded to the Supreme Court of Florida for further action not inconsistent with this opinion.

Reversed.

31

The Sixth Amendment Right to Effective Counsel

Key Concepts

- *Strickland v. Washington*'s Two-Pronged Test: Deficient Performance + Prejudice = Constitutionally Ineffective Assistance
- Deficient Performance: Counsel's Performance Fell Below an Objective Standard of Reasonableness as Measured by Prevailing Professional Norms
- Prejudice: Reasonable Probability Exists that But For Counsel's Deficient Performance the Result of the Proceeding Would Have Been Different
- Right to Effective Counsel Includes Within It the Right to Conflict-Free Counsel

A. Introduction and Policy. As you read in the preceding chapter, defendants have a Sixth Amendment right to counsel even if they cannot afford to retain counsel with their own funds. The Court has said this Sixth Amendment right to counsel means something more than that a person with a law degree will be sitting beside you at trial. Instead, the right to counsel means the right to **effective** counsel. Your lawyer must meaningfully engage to ensure the adversarial process results in a fair trial. In speaking of the constitutional guarantee of effective counsel, one jurist has written: "While a criminal trial is not a game in which the participants are expected to enter the ring with a near match in skills, neither is it a sacrifice of unarmed prisoners to gladiators."[1]

In most jurisdictions, a claim of ineffective assistance of counsel will not be available to an accused until after she has completed the initial review of her conviction—*i.e.*, after her direct appeal is over. This is because it is the very rare case in which clear evidence of ineffectiveness actually appears in the trial record. In most cases, proof of counsel's ineffectiveness requires information and evidence beyond that which is available in the transcript. For example, imagine that you are represented by a lawyer who has a raging drinking problem that causes her to nod off in a stupor through most of your trial. Unless someone comments on the record that defense counsel is asleep, the transcript will be silent on this issue. Proof of the lawyer's slumber—a step toward establishing her ineffective-

[1] United States ex rel. Williams v. Twomey, 510 F.2d 634, 640 (7th Cir.), cert. denied sub nom. Sielaff v. Williams, 423 U.S. 876 (1975).

ness—will require a witness either taking the stand or swearing out an affidavit. Efforts to introduce this sort of extra-record evidence on direct appeal will usually be rejected, since direct appeals are generally confined to the four corners of the trial record.

Note that this may not always be the case for technology is changing the way we record trial proceedings. The increased videotaping of trials may have an interesting impact on the timing and consideration of ineffective assistance of counsel claims. For example, if the appellate court can see counsel sleeping during the proceedings on the video recording of the trial, should this alter whether the claim can be presented at that stage? Are there arguments to be made that what looked like slumber was in fact thoughtful contemplation? Proposals regarding the impact of videotaping on the range of issues viable on direct appeal have, for now, been confined to academic writings. However, as the prevalence of videotaping increases courts may become more willing to weigh in on the issue.

For now, most ineffective assistance claims are raised in post-conviction. And at that stage in the case the concern for finality is considerable. For this reason, the Supreme Court has often viewed ineffective assistance of counsel claims with something just shy of open hostility. As the Court wrote recently, "[a]n ineffective-assistance claim can function as a way to escape rules of waiver and forfeiture and raise issues not presented at trial [or in pretrial proceedings], and so the . . . standard must be applied with scrupulous care, lest 'intrusive post-trial inquiry' threaten the integrity of the very adversary process the right to counsel is meant to serve."[2]

Ineffective assistance of counsel claims—which contend that trial counsel's performance was sufficiently substandard to undermine confidence in the results—are a staple in most post-conviction proceedings and often are referred to in shorthand as "IAC" claims. Though pure "right to counsel" claims—*e.g.*, a lawyer was not present—are not often seen in post-conviction, "ineffective assistance of counsel" claims are seen in virtually every collateral attack upon a conviction.

B. The Law. The Supreme Court defined the guarantee of effective counsel in *Strickland v. Washington*.[3] For this reason, ineffective assistance of counsel cases will often involve courts discussing whether an attorney's challenged performance fell below the "*Strickland* standard."[4] The test for effectiveness that was articulated in *Strickland* is a two-prong test:

---

[2] Premo v. Moore, 131 S.Ct. 733, 739–40 (2011).

[3] Strickland v. Washington, 466 U.S. 668 (1984).

[4] As an interesting aside, although the test has come to be known as the *Strickland* standard, Strickland was not the convicted person in the case. Strickland was the warden of the Florida State Prison, the facility where David Leroy Washington was held at the time he filed his habeas claim. It was Washington, not Strickland, who sought relief from a death sentence that he contended was secured due to his lawyer's ineffectiveness.

1. **Deficient Performance:** Was counsel's performance objectively unreasonable?

2. **Prejudice:** Is there a reasonable probability that the result of the proceeding would have been different absent counsel's deficiency?

The *Strickland* standard thus examines both counsel's performance and the likely impact of counsel's performance on the outcome of the proceeding. The burden of proof is on the convicted person. Ineffectiveness will be found if the former client can establish that "counsel's conduct so undermined the proper functioning of the adversarial process that the trial cannot be relied on as having produced a just result."[5] In other words, a convicted person will satisfy the performance prong of *Strickland* if he can show that his lawyer's representation fell below an objective standard of reasonableness. The Court has at times described this standard as requiring proof that counsel was "incompetent," not simply inexpert.[6] This is far from a simple task. While the *Strickland* standard is "by no means insurmountable," it is, as the Court has noted, "highly demanding."[7]

Describing what reasonably effective assistance might look like, the Court has articulated just six general duties for defense counsel in every case:

1. Counsel owes the client a duty of loyalty, which means counsel must avoid conflicts of interests;

2. Counsel must advocate the client's cause;

3. Counsel must consult with the client on important decisions;

4. Counsel must keep the client informed of important developments;

5. Counsel must "bring to bear such skill and knowledge as will render the trial a reliable adversarial testing process;" and

6. "Counsel has a duty to make reasonable investigations or to make a reasonable decision that makes particular investigations unnecessary."[8]

In articulating these general duties, the Court has made clear they do not define the totality of a defense attorney's obligations to a client, nor do they comprise "a checklist for judicial evaluation of attorney performance."[9] Thus, even if counsel is found wanting with regard to one of these duties, a finding of deficient perfor-

[5] Strickland, 466 U.S. at 686.

[6] Premo, 131 S.Ct. at 733.

[7] Kimmelman v. Morrison, 477 U.S. 365, 382 (1986).

[8] Id. at 384.

[9] Strickland, 466 U.S. at 688.

mance is not assured. Instead, counsel's error must be analyzed in light of all the circumstances.

The Court has found that "[n]o particular set of detailed rules for counsel's conduct can satisfactorily take account of the variety of circumstances faced by defense counsel or the range of legitimate decisions regarding how best to represent a criminal defendant."[10] However, while reviewing courts are not guided by a specific list of things that counsel must or must not do, many professional organizations do publish detailed recommendations for best practices in connection with the role of defense counsel. For example, the American Bar Association regularly issues its "Policies and Guidelines on Indigent Defense" as well as its "Guidelines for the Appointment and Performance of Defense Counsel in Death Penalty Cases." In addition, states often have public defender statutes or other ordinances that contain in-depth information about the particular role of defense counsel. The Supreme Court has said that these should be used by courts only as guides in assessing counsel's constitutional effectiveness in any one case.

Though the Court has largely refused to identify particular instances of attorney conduct as examples of *per se* ineffectiveness,[11] there are one or two exceptions. For instance, counsel's disregard of a client's specific instruction to file a notice of appeal is *per se* professionally unreasonable.[12] In the vast majority of other circumstances, though, courts reviewing ineffectiveness claims should simply be guided by the more general prevailing professional norms cited above.

The performance prong of the *Strickland* test is highly deferential to trial counsel and the assessment of performance should be made from the perspective of the lawyer **at the time.**[13] Deference is required, the Court has suggested, because in the absence of deference, the influence of hindsight would too frequently compel reviewing courts to find counsel's performance lacking. Thus, the question is not whether counsel's performance could have been improved. Instead, the question is whether counsel's assistance was reasonably effective. This is because the Court has found that the constitutional right to the effective assistance of counsel is not concerned with improving the quality of legal practice, but instead is intended only to ensure fair trials. As the Court has said, "[t]he Sixth Amendment guarantees reasonable competence, not perfect advocacy judged with the benefit of hindsight."[14]

The second prong of the *Strickland* test is prejudice. You should note, however, that in a handful of instances the Court has found that a showing of prejudice is **not** required. The no-prejudice line of analysis is most frequently traced to

[10] Strickland, 466 U.S. at 688–89.

[11] See, e.g., Kimmelman, 477 U.S. at 384.

[12] Roe v. Flores-Ortega, 528 U.S. 470, 477 (2000).

[13] Strickland, 466 U.S. at 689.

[14] Yarborough v. Gentry, 540 U.S. 1, 8 (2003).

the Court's decision in *United States v. Cronic*.[15] There, the Court held that an inquiry into prejudice is not needed if "the likelihood that any lawyer, even a fully competent one, could provide effective assistance is so small that a presumption of prejudice is appropriate without inquiry into the actual conduct of the trial."[16]

Pursuant to *Cronic*, evidence of deficient performance alone is sufficient for a showing of constitutional ineffectiveness in a narrow band of cases. There are, to date, just three instances in which the *Cronic*-approach applies. First, prejudice is presumed where the right to counsel is completely denied.[17] Next, prejudice will be presumed where counsel is operating under an actual conflict of interests. Third and finally, prejudice is presumed where the government meaningfully interferes with counsel's assistance.[18] In all other ineffective assistance cases, the two-pronged *Strickland* approach applies, and the burden is upon the convicted person to establish a reasonable likelihood that the result in his case would have been different but for counsel's errors.

The question of whether an accused can satisfy the prejudice prong of the test depends in no small part upon the strength of the prosecution's case. Where there is overwhelming evidence of guilt, it will be much more difficult for an accused to establish that counsel's conduct likely impacted the conviction or sentence.[19] That said, the prejudice assessment is not purely outcome determinative. Instead, the reviewing court must consider "whether the result of the proceeding was fundamentally unfair or unreliable."[20]

Moreover, while the assessment of counsel's **performance** must be conducted from the perspective of the lawyer at the time of the trial,[21] the Court has found that no similar temporal constraint operates on the evaluation of **prejudice**. For example, in *Lockhart v. Fretwell*, trial counsel failed to object to a capital sentencing procedure that had been deemed to be unconstitutional by an intermediate appellate court. After being sentenced to death, the condemned client argued that counsel's lack of objection constituted ineffective assistance. However, while this claim was working its way through the courts, the intermediate appellate court's ruling was overturned and the capital sentencing procedure at issue was found valid.

The Supreme Court agreed that Fretwell would not originally have been sentenced to death if trial counsel had entered a timely objection. However, the

[15] 466 U.S. 648 (1984).

[16] Wright v. Van Patten, 552 U.S. 120, 124 (2008) (citing United States v. Cronic, 466 U.S. 648, 659–60 (1984)).

[17] United States v. Cronic, 466 U.S. 648, 659 (1984).

[18] Geders v. United States, 425 U.S. 80 (1976).

[19] Smith v. Spisak, 558 U.S. 139 (2010).

[20] Lockhart v. Fretwell, 506 U.S. 364, 369 (1993).

[21] Bobby v. Van Hook, 558 U.S. 4 (2009).

Court refused to limit its prejudice analysis to the state of affairs at the time of Fretwell's sentencing. Where the basis for the objection to the sentencing procedure had since been eliminated, the court found that Fretwell could not establish prejudice in support of his IAC claim. "In judging prejudice and the likelihood of a different outcome, a defendant has no entitlement to the luck of a lawless decisionmaker."[22]

It is not just trial lawyers who must provide effective assistance. Appellate counsel too must satisfy a constitutional threshold of effectiveness. Appellate counsel's constitutional duty does not require that counsel move forward with an appeal that counsel has determined to be frivolous. But, it does require that counsel function in the role of an advocate.

Ineffective assistance of counsel is also relevant to questions that come up as a case moves from direct appeal into post-conviction. Before a person convicted in state court can ask a federal court for habeas relief, he must establish that he has "exhausted" any claims presented. In other words, the person must show that the issues he is asking the federal habeas court to pass upon have already been presented to the state court for consideration. The failure to first present a claim to the state court constitutes "procedural default," which is a bar to federal relief. This bar, however, can be lifted by the federal habeas court if the petitioner can assert "cause" for the procedural default and can demonstrate "prejudice." The Supreme Court has found that, in some instances, "[i]neffective assistance of counsel . . . is cause for a procedural default."[23] Attorney errors that do not amount to ineffective assistance will not establish "cause" and therefore do not excuse the failure to "exhaust."

Finally, as you will read in **Chapter 48**, Fourth Amendment claims cannot be presented in post-conviction federal habeas claims. But, what if a claim of ineffective assistance of counsel is grounded in counsel's inept handling of the client's Fourth Amendment claim at trial or on appeal? The Court has found that a viable IAC claim will **not** be precluded in habeas simply because it is based upon counsel's ineffectiveness with regard to a suppression motion or other Fourth Amendment matter.[24]

C. Applying the Law.

1. Assessing Ineffectiveness—Generally. Prior to 1984, the Supreme Court considered several cases that dealt with the actual or constructive denial of the Sixth Amendment right to counsel, including state conduct that was said to interfere with an accused's right to effective counsel. But, it was not until 1984

[22] Fretwell, 506 U.S. at 370.

[23] Murray v. Carrier, 477 U.S. 478, 488 (1986).

[24] Kimmelman, 477 U.S. at 365.

that the Court took a case that required the Court to evaluate a direct challenge to the adequacy of counsel's performance. That case was *Strickland v. Washington*:

Example—*Strickland v. Washington*, 466 U.S. 668 (1984): David Leroy Washington and two friends engaged in a ten-day, three-incident crime spree that left three people dead and several others injured. Washington turned himself in and confessed to one of the killings. Because Washington was indigent, counsel was assigned to represent him. Against counsel's advice, Washington confessed to the other two murders and pled guilty to all of the charges against him, accepting full responsibility for his role in the crimes. Washington then had a sentencing hearing to determine whether he should receive the death penalty.

In preparation for the sentencing hearing, counsel successfully moved to exclude Washington's criminal history, and he also talked to Washington's wife and mother by telephone. However, he did no other investigation. At the sentencing hearing, the attorney did not present any witnesses, nor did he have Washington himself testify. Instead, counsel argued that Washington's life should be spared because he had taken responsibility for the crimes, had no prior criminal history, and was stressed at the time of the crime spree. In support of these arguments, counsel relied primarily on the statements Washington made when he pled guilty. The state presented witnesses who testified to the details of the murders. The judge sentenced Washington to death after finding that the aggravating evidence outweighed the mitigating evidence.

Washington later argued that defense counsel was ineffective during the sentencing hearing. His claim was rejected by the state post-conviction court. He then brought the same claim in federal court. In support of this claim, federal habeas counsel secured fourteen affidavits from family and friends who said they would have testified on Washington's behalf if trial counsel had asked them to. Habeas counsel also presented two mental health reports that found Washington committed the crimes while he was "chronically frustrated and depressed." The case ultimately reached the Supreme Court.

Analysis: Defense counsel was not constitutionally ineffective. There is no one checklist that will define appropriate attorney behavior for every case. Courts instead must simply be guided by prevailing professional norms.

When assessing a convicted person's claim that his lawyer was ineffective courts should employ a two-prong test. The first prong requires the convicted person to show that his attorney's performance was "deficient." The second prong requires the convicted person to show that the lawyer's deficient performance "prejudiced" his case. Both prongs are necessary. Consequently, if a reviewing court realizes that either of the prongs cannot be satisfied, rejection of an ineffective assistance claim without review of the remaining prong is appropriate.

Deficiency requires a showing that counsel's performance fell below an objective standard of reasonableness. This assessment must be conducted with appropriate deference to trial counsel's choices. It is all too easy to critique a failed performance with the benefit of hindsight. For that reason, "counsel is strongly presumed to have rendered adequate assistance and made all significant decisions in the exercise of reasonable professional judgment."[25] If counsel makes strategic choices after conducting a thorough investigation of the case, those choices will be "virtually unchallengeable."[26] If counsel conducts a less than thorough investigation, strategic choices may still require deference if the limitations on the investigation were professionally reasonable.

Even if a convicted person establishes that his lawyer performed deficiently, he must also prove that there is "a reasonable probability that, but for counsel's unprofessional errors, the result of the proceeding would have been different. A reasonable probability is a probability sufficient to undermine confidence in the outcome."[27] The strength of the prosecution's case for guilt is relevant to the question of prejudice.

In Washington's case, counsel's representation did not fall below an objective standard of reasonableness and was not prejudicial. Counsel's decision not to conduct further investigation for mitigating evidence was not unreasonable. By relying upon the evidence presented at the plea colloquy, counsel prevented the government from introducing damaging evidence of Washington's criminal record, of his psychological state, and of his bad character. Counsel's decision to rely upon Washington's acceptance of responsibility as mitigation was also reasonable. While counsel admitted to feeling hopeless about the case, this hopelessness did not impact his professional judgment. Moreover, the mitigating evidence that was uncovered by post-conviction counsel would have had little impact had it been discovered by trial counsel. This evidence essentially amounted to the testimony of family and friends that Washington was a good person. The new psychological evidence indicated that Washington was suffering from stress at the time of his offenses but found that this stress did not rise to the level of "extreme emotional distress"—the required statutory mitigator.

---

25 Id. at 689.

26 Id. at 690.

27 Id. at 694.

Because Washington could not prove that counsel's performance was deficient and could not prove any prejudice resulting from counsel's failure to conduct further investigation in advance of the sentencing hearing, his death sentence was affirmed.

As the Court in *Strickland* noted, it is next to impossible to challenge a lawyer's strategic choices if the lawyer makes those choices after a complete review of the law and the facts in a case. Even incomplete investigation of the law or facts may insulate the lawyer's strategic choices as long as "reasonable professional judgments support the limitations on investigation."[28] Counsel's decision to present a limited or incomplete case also will not give rise to an ineffective assistance finding if the restricted presentation is intended to deliberately constrain the State's options.[29]

In a later case, however the Court held that counsel's total failure to engage in any pretrial discovery constitutes deficient performance if that failure is not justified by any plausible explanation.[30] Similarly, counsel's performance will be deemed deficient if counsel unreasonably restricts the defense investigation:

> **Example—*Wiggins v. Smith*, 539 U.S. 510 (2003):** A seventy-seven-year-old woman, Florence Lacs, was found dead in her bathtub. She had been drowned and her apartment was torn apart. Kevin Wiggins was charged with capital murder as well as with robbery. Two public defenders were assigned to represent Wiggins. After a bench trial, Wiggins was convicted. For his capital sentencing hearing, Wiggins choose to proceed before a jury.
>
> Counsel asked the sentencing court to split the sentencing hearing to allow the defense to first present evidence that someone other than Wiggins killed Lacs. At the second phase of the hearing, counsel then intended to present mitigation evidence. The court denied the request to split the sentencing proceeding. But, to preserve the issue for appeal, counsel proffered for the court a summary of the mitigation evidence that the defense would have introduced had the bifurcation motion been granted. This evidence consisted of expert reports that discussed Wiggins's limited intellect (he was borderline mentally retarded), immaturity, empathy and absence of aggression.

[28] Strickland, 466 U.S. at 691.

[29] Wong v. Belmontes, 558 U.S. 15 (2009).

[30] Kimmelman, 477 U.S. at 365.

During opening arguments at the sentencing hearing, counsel told the jurors they would hear evidence of Wiggins' difficult life, his work history, and his lack of a criminal record. During the sentencing proceeding, however, no such evidence was ever introduced. The jury voted to sentence Wiggins to death.

Thereafter, Wiggins collaterally attacked his death sentence arguing that trial counsel had been constitutionally ineffective for failing to investigate or put on a mitigation case. During the post-conviction hearing, Wiggins presented the testimony of a licensed social worker. In preparation for the hearing, the social worker interviewed Wiggins's relatives, and reviewed Wiggins's social services, school and medical records. The social worker's testimony chronicled the horrific physical and sexual abuse that Wiggins had endured.

At the post-conviction hearing, one of Wiggins's trial attorneys testified. Counsel maintained that the defense strategy at sentencing had been to focus on the fact that Wiggins was not directly responsible for Lacs's death. For this reason, counsel explained, the defense chose not to extensively investigate Wiggins's social history. The hearing judge found that the decision not to investigate was a strategic one and thus could not form the basis for ineffective assistance. The case ultimately reached the Supreme Court.

Analysis: Defense counsel's decision not to investigate Wiggins' social history fell below an objective standard of reasonableness and prejudiced the defense. Accordingly, his death sentence was reversed.

Supreme Court precedent does not require a defense attorney to thoroughly investigate every possible line of mitigation as long as the limitations on the investigation were reasonable. But, if the limitations on investigation were not reasonable, counsel's subsequent strategic choices are not immune from critique. In this case, the investigation conducted by defense counsel was unreasonably inadequate.

Prior to the sentencing hearing, defense counsel had a psychologist test Wiggins to assess his intellectual capacity and to identify any mental health issues. However, this examination did not contain any inquiry into Wiggins' life history. Counsel also reviewed the pre-sentence investigation report that contained a one-page summary of Wiggins' life. And, counsel amassed some of Wiggins' social services records. Though there was funding available to hire a forensic social worker, counsel chose not to hire such an expert to prepare a social history report on Wiggins. At the time of Wiggins' sentencing hearing it was standard practice in Maryland (and the recommendation of national guidelines) that such a report be prepared. In fact, the judge who initially heard Wiggins' IAC claim stated that he "could not remember a capital case in which counsel had not compiled a social history of the defendant."

The fact that counsel had **some** information about Wiggins' background did not immunize the tactical decisions that flowed from that limited knowledge. Counsel's knowledge of Wiggins' background was based upon the very "narrow set of sources" they accessed—the pre-sentence report and the Department of Social Services records. Furthermore, what little information counsel did have should have suggested that additional investigation was needed. "In light of what the [pre-sentence investigation] and [Department of Social Services] records actually revealed . . . counsel chose to abandon their investigation at an unreasonable juncture, making a fully informed decision with respect to sentencing strategy impossible."[31]

Moreover, contrary to counsel's testimony at the post-conviction hearing, the record reflected that even as late as the opening statements the defense strategy did not exclude the possibility of presenting a mitigation case. "When viewed in this light, the 'strategic decision' the state courts and respondents all invoke to justify counsel's limited pursuit of mitigating evidence resembles more a post hoc rationalization of counsel's conduct than an accurate description of their deliberations prior to sentencing."[32]

The mitigation evidence that defense counsel did not present was compelling. "[Had] the jury been confronted with this considerable mitigating evidence, there is a reasonable probability that it would have returned with a different sentence."[33] Accordingly, Wiggins demonstrated both necessary prongs of ineffective assistance, and reversal of his death sentence was required.

When a court is evaluating whether an attorney's decision to curtail a particular line of investigation is a "reasonable professional judgment," the court should consider information that is provided by the client. For example, assume a client is accused of murdering her husband. She tells her attorney that she was not at home at the time of the shooting and directs him to witnesses who she contends will provide an alibi. After her conviction, substantial evidence is uncovered that the client was abused by her husband, that he had been beating her with a metal rod just before his death, and that the shooting actually occurred in self-defense. However, none of this evidence was uncovered by trial counsel because the client's claimed alibi led the attorney not to pursue a self-defense strategy. Under these circumstances, the attorney will likely not be deemed constitutionally ineffective

[31] Wiggins v. Smith, 539 U.S. 510, 527–28 (2003).

[32] Id. at 527.

[33] Id. at 536.

for failing to investigate the self-defense claim—the information provided by the client (assuming it was reasonable to believe that information) suggested that there was no factual basis for any claim of self-defense.

Thus, in some instances, information conveyed by the client will affect the choices the attorney makes when investigating and crafting particular lines of defense. In other cases, information conveyed by the client may suggest to the attorney that the client cannot take the stand and testify in her own defense without committing perjury. In such a case, does the Sixth Amendment guarantee of effective assistance require counsel to call a client to the stand if the attorney reasonably expects the client will perjure himself?

Example—*Nix v. Whiteside*, 475 U.S. 157(1986): Emmanuel Charles Whiteside went with two friends to buy marijuana from a dealer, Calvin Love. Love was home with his girlfriend. During the sale, Whiteside and Love got into an argument, and Love told his girlfriend, "Go and get my piece." At a later point, Love went to the bedroom himself. Whiteside testified that he saw Love reach under his pillow and then turn to approach him. At this point Whiteside stabbed Love once in the chest, killing him. Whiteside was charged with murder. Counsel was appointed to represent him.

Whiteside told counsel prior to trial that he never actually saw a gun in Love's hand, but honesty believed Love was pulling a gun from under the pillow. The two people who were with Whiteside also told counsel that they had not seen a gun, and a gun was never found in Love's house. Counsel told Whiteside that a self-defense claim could still be raised so long as Whiteside reasonably believed Love was getting a gun. Thereafter, Whiteside repeatedly advised counsel he actually believed Love had a gun though he had not seen one.

A week before trial, counsel was preparing Whiteside to testify. During this prep session, Whiteside stated for the first time that just before the stabbing, he saw "something metallic" in Love's hand. Explaining his change in testimony, Whiteside told counsel, "If I don't say I saw a gun, I'm dead."

Counsel explained that if Whiteside presented this new narrative at trial, counsel would notify the court that Whiteside perjured himself. Counsel also told Whiteside if he insisted upon committing perjury, he (counsel) would withdraw from the case.

At trial Whiteside took the stand in his own defense. He told the jury he "knew" Love had a gun. He also told the jury he stabbed Love because he thought Love was reaching for a gun. On cross examination, the prosecutor pressed Whiteside on whether he'd actually seen a gun and Whiteside admitted he had not. Whiteside was convicted of murder.

In post-trial proceedings, Whiteside maintained that his right to the effective assistance of counsel was violated when his lawyer prevented him from testifying that he'd seen a gun (or "something metallic") in Love's hand. The Supreme Court took the case to decide whether counsel was ineffective.

Analysis: Whiteside did not have a constitutional right to present perjured testimony. Therefore, defense counsel could not have been constitutionally ineffective for failing to allow Whiteside to engage in such conduct.

This case implicates two separate constitutional considerations. The first is a criminal defendant's right to testify in his own defense. The second is the right to the effective assistance of counsel.

Counsel definitely owed Whiteside a duty of loyalty and a duty to advocate the defense case. However, those duties were "limited to legitimate, lawful conduct compatible with the very nature of a trial as a search for truth." The Model Code of Professional Responsibility and the Model Rules of Professional Conduct both require the disclosure of knowingly perjured testimony. Perjury is also a crime.

In light of the prevailing professional norms, counsel's conduct in this case did not fall below an objective standard of reasonableness. "On this record, the accused enjoyed continued representation within the bounds of reasonable professional conduct and did in fact exercise his right to testify; at most he was denied the right to have the assistance of counsel in the presentation of false testimony."[34]

Whiteside also could not establish any prejudice. Whiteside could not plausibly contend that confidence in the outcome of his trial was undermined because he was not allowed to present the jury with false testimony. Whiteside's murder conviction was therefore affirmed.

The Court's decision in *Nix v. Whiteside* makes clear that a lawyer has an affirmative obligation not to assist a client in presenting testimony that the attorney knows to be false. Perjury statutes and long-standing ethical and court rules contain a similar admonition. However, a more complicated scenario arises when counsel strongly suspects but is not certain the client's version of events is fabricated. Some jurisdictions have adopted a novel approach to dealing with this dilemma

[34] Nix v. Whiteside, 475 U.S. 157, 174 (1986).

that preserves the client's right to testify but does not implicate the lawyer in the suspected perjury. In such jurisdictions, by either common law or court rule, the client is allowed to testify "in narrative format." Typically, the lawyer will ask a single question at the outset of direct examination—e.g., "What would you like to tell the ladies and gentlemen of the jury?" The client then offers his uninterrupted account of the events without any further questioning by counsel.[35]

2. Conceding Guilt. As you read above, the review of trial counsel's performance in an ineffective assistance of counsel case is intentionally deferential. Applying this deference, courts have found a wide range of attorney conduct falls within the constitutional baseline of objective reasonableness. Thus, as a general rule, the Court has declined to identify any specific instance of attorney conduct as *per se* ineffectiveness. But what of a lawyer who admits his client's guilt to the jury? Should such attorney conduct presumptively fall below an objective standard of reasonableness? At least in the context of a capital case, the Supreme Court held that the answer was no:

> **Example—*Florida v. Nixon*, 543 U.S. 175 (2004):** Jeanne Bickner went to a mall in Tallahassee, Florida. As she was leaving, Joe Elton Nixon approached her. He said he was having car trouble. After some conversation, Bickner agreed to give Nixon a ride home.
>
> As Bickner was driving, Nixon punched her in the face. Nixon then forced Bickner into the trunk and drove her to an isolated wooded area. Nixon tied Bickner to a tree using jumper cables. Bickner agreed to give Nixon the car if he did not kill her. However, Nixon was afraid that Bickner would identify him, and so decided to kill her by setting her on fire. Nixon drove away in Bickner's car.
>
> Nixon told his brother and his girlfriend what he had done. The police arrested Nixon the following day after his brother turned him in. Nixon provided the police with a detailed confession to Bickner's kidnapping and murder.
>
> In addition to his confessions, the evidence against Nixon consisted of witnesses who saw him with Bickner in the mall parking lot; witnesses who saw him driving Bickner's car after her murder; Nixon's palm print on the trunk of Bickner's car; the testimony of

[35] See, e.g., Commonwealth v. Mitchell, 438 Mass. 535, 544–545 (2003); People v. Johnson, 62 Cal. App. 4th 608 (1998).

a pawnshop owner who identified Nixon as the man who sold him two of Bickner's rings; and the pawnshop receipt that listed Nixon's driver's license number.

After discovery, Bickner's counsel determined that the State's case was overwhelming. When plea negotiations with the State failed, defense counsel began investigating potential mitigation evidence for use at sentencing. In particular, counsel intended to focus the sentencing jury's attention on the fact that Nixon was mentally unstable. To most effectively advance this evidence, counsel decided that he would best preserve his credibility if he did not contest Nixon's guilt. Counsel explained this trial strategy to Nixon on three separate occasions, but Nixon offered no response.

During opening argument, defense counsel told the jurors that there wouldn't "be any question, none whatsoever, that my client, Joe Elton Nixon, caused Jeannie Bickner's death. That fact will be proved to your satisfaction beyond any doubt."[36] Counsel did not cross examine any of the state's witnesses beyond what was needed to offer clarification. Counsel also presented no defense case.

After the jury convicted Nixon on all counts, the case moved into the sentencing phase. As mitigation, counsel presented eight witnesses. These witnesses described Nixon's emotional difficulties and his unpredictable behavior. Two psychiatric experts testified that Nixon suffered from anti-social personality disorder, a low IQ, a history of mental health treatment, and the possibility of brain damage. After deliberating for three hours, the jury recommended a death sentence.

On appeal, Nixon argued that trial counsel provided ineffective assistance by conceding guilt without first securing Nixon's consent. Nixon claimed that the decision to concede guilt was tantamount to a guilty plea, which could not have been entered without his express consent. Nixon also argued that prejudice should be presumed because the prosecution's case had not been subjected to any meaningful adversarial review. The Supreme Court ultimately agreed to hear the case to decide whether an

[36] Florida v. Nixon, 543 U.S. 175, 183 (2004).

attorney's decision to concede guilt in a capital case is *per se* deficient, and whether a showing of prejudice is required.

Analysis: Defense counsel's decision in this capital case to concede guilt was not automatic evidence of deficient performance. In addition, to succeed on his claim of ineffectiveness Nixon had a duty to establish prejudice.

Defense counsel's duty to consult with the client about important decisions in the case does not translate into a requirement that counsel receive the client's consent for every decision that is made. Certain decisions do require express input by the client. For example, decisions about whether to plead guilty, waive a jury trial, testify, or take an appeal are all decisions upon which "[a] defendant . . . has the ultimate authority." But a decision to concede guilt at trial is not the same as a decision to plead guilty.

By entering a guilty plea, an accused forgoes other rights—*e.g.*, the right to trial by jury, the right not to incriminate oneself, the right of confrontation. The same is not always true in the case of uncontested guilt at trial. Where defense counsel's concession of guilt allows the state to obtain a conviction on something less than full proof beyond a reasonable doubt, equating that concession with a guilty plea is appropriate.[37] However, where counsel's concession does not result in something less than a full presentation to the jury by the prosecutor, the comparison is not appropriate.

Defense counsel repeatedly informed Nixon of his intended approach. Nixon never responded during any of these discussions. Because the trial that followed was not the equivalent of a guilty plea, counsel was not further required to obtain Nixon's consent.

Moreover, counsel's decision to concede guilt did not fall below an objective standard of reasonableness. It was entirely reasonable for counsel to seek to maintain credibility with the jury by not contesting the fact that Nixon was responsible for Bickner's death. Given the overwhelming evidence of guilt, counsel's decision to focus on the mitigation case was imminently reasonable. Because Nixon could not establish the first prong of his *Strickland* claim, he was not entitled to a new trial.

On a close read, you should recognize that the Supreme Court's refusal to find *per se* ineffectiveness after a defense attorney conceded guilt was not as radical as it at first may have seemed. *Nixon* was a capital case. Therefore, the question of guilt and the question of punishment were tried in two separate phases. In many capital cases, the evidence of guilt is overwhelming, and experienced practitioners will tell you that simply avoiding a death sentence is often considered "a win." A concession of guilt under these circumstances therefore is substantially different than a concession of guilt in an ordinary criminal case. For this reason, a broader

[37] See, e.g., Brookhart v. Janis, 384 U.S. 1 (1966).

application of the rule seems unlikely. Indeed, the Court expressly recognized the distinction in *Nixon*. Though not squarely deciding the question, the Court noted: "Although such a concession in a run-of-the-mine trial might present a closer question, the gravity of the potential sentence in a capital trial and the proceeding's two-phase structure vitally affect counsel's strategic calculus."[38]

3. The Question of Prejudice. If an attorney's performance is grossly deficient, some would argue there should be no need to show prejudice at all. After all, the adversarial system is our mechanism for assessing guilt. If one component of that process is found wanting, how can we be confident about the results? Even in cases involving substantial evidence of guilt, there are myriad stories of skillful counsel securing a client's acquittal.

As you have read, however, with the exception of the narrow band of *Cronic*-style cases, the Supreme Court has squarely rejected such arguments. The *Strickland* test is a two-pronged test. Relief on an ineffective assistance of counsel claim is not warranted simply because deficient performance had been established. The accused must also prove prejudice—*i.e.*, that the deficient performance of the lawyer impacted the outcome of the case.

The Court in *Cronic* (and in cases since) has recognized a small minority of cases where a showing of prejudice is unnecessary. In such cases prejudice is presumed. For instance, if the right to counsel is completely denied at a critical stage—an actual or constructive violation of the Sixth Amendment right to a lawyer—prejudice will be presumed.[39] So too, prejudice is presumed if the government meaningfully interferes with the right to counsel.[40] The Court has also noted that prejudice will be presumed if "counsel entirely fails to subject the prosecution's case to meaningful adversarial testing."[41]

The same presumption sometimes applies if the ineffectiveness is caused by an alleged conflict of interests. However, an ineffective assistance of counsel claim that is grounded in a claim of conflicting interests is a complicated undertaking. If an actual conflict of interests exists **and is objected to** prior to the representation, the client will enjoy a presumption of prejudice as a result of the conflict. If the conflict is not objected to, a viable claim of ineffective assistance will lie only if "the defendant demonstrates that counsel actively represented conflicting interests and that an actual conflict of interest adversely affected his lawyer's performance."[42]

[38] Nixon, 543 U.S. at 177.
[39] Cronic, 466 U.S. at 659.
[40] See, e.g., Geders, 425 U.S. 80.
[41] Bell v. Cone, 535 U.S. 685, 696 (2002).
[42] Burger v. Kemp, 483 U.S. 776 (1987); Cuyler v. Sullivan, 446 U.S. 335 (1980).

Example—*Mickens v. Taylor*, 535 U.S. 162 (2002): Walter Mickens was convicted of killing a teenager by the name of Timothy Hall during or after an attempted forcible sodomy. After Mickens was sentenced to death, he contended that defense counsel provided ineffective assistance. In particular, Mickens argued that, unbeknownst to Mickens, trial counsel had been representing the victim, Hall, on unrelated criminal charges at the time Hall was killed by Mickens. Counsel had not disclosed his prior representation of the victim to anyone else, and Mickens only learned of the representation when a clerk accidentally turned over Hall's juvenile court file to post-conviction counsel. The Supreme Court accepted the case for review.

Analysis: Defense counsel's prior representation of the victim did not justify relief in Mickens's case.

Particular challenges are created when an attorney simultaneously represents multiple interests. When such representation results in an ineffective assistance of counsel claim the reviewing court's treatment of the issue will depend in part upon whether an objection was raised below.

When an attorney actively represents conflicting interests over an express objection an additional showing of prejudice is not required to succeed on a claim of ineffective assistance. However, to succeed on an IAC claim where no objection is made, the convicted person must demonstrate the conflict of interests "actually affected the adequacy of his representation."[43] Beyond that, however, no further prejudice need be shown.

With respect to the trial court's duties, the court must inquire into potential conflicts only if the court knew or should have known that a potential conflict existed.

In the instant case, since Mickens did not object to the potential conflict at the trial stage, he was required to make some showing that counsel's prior representation actually affected his defense of Mickens. Mickens could not make this showing. Counsel represented Hall only briefly, and had met with him just once prior to his death. Four days after Hall was killed, counsel was released from the representation with a note that the client was deceased. Counsel did not believe that he owed any further duties to Hall at the time he accepted representation of Mickens.

Because Mickens could not show any actual impact on his defense that flowed from counsel's prior representation, Mickens's conviction and death sentence were affirmed.

---

[43] Mickens v. Taylor, 535 U.S. 162, 168 (2002). Compare Holloway v. Arkansas, 435 U.S. 475 (1978) with Cuyler v. Sullivan, 446 U.S. 335 (1980).

4. The Effectiveness of Appellate Counsel. Just as a defendant is entitled to effective representation at his trial and sentencing, a person seeking direct review of his conviction is entitled to effective representation on appeal. As you read in **Chapter 47**, the Constitution does not compel states to provide an automatic right of appeal in all criminal cases.[44] However, once a state makes an appeal as of right available, there is a constitutional right to counsel to make that review meaningful.[45] Moreover, as with the right to trial counsel, the right to appellate counsel entails a right to effective counsel.

While the Court has declined to offer firm guidelines regarding trial counsel's specific duties, it has been somewhat more forthcoming with regard to the expectations of appellate counsel. Appellate counsel "must be available to assist in preparing and submitting a brief to the appellate court;" and when crafting that brief, counsel "must play the role of an active advocate, rather than a mere friend of the court assisting in a detached evaluation of the appellant's claim."[46]

There is absolutely no requirement that an appellate attorney present **every** meritorious argument that is present in the record. Rather, it is permissible for counsel to winnow the appellate claims to advance only those with the greatest likelihood of success. It is not permissible, however, for counsel to file a brief that fails to conform to basic filing requirements contained in the applicable rules of appellate procedure. Such conduct will result in a finding of ineffective assistance.[47]

A separate issue arises if the appellate attorney carefully reviews the record and concludes that there are no meritorious issues in the case. If the client insists upon presenting appellate claims that the attorney believes to be wholly without merit, the attorney faces a dilemma: proceed with a frivolous appeal, or withdraw from the case. Generally, when an attorney withdraws from the case, she must give an explanation to the court explaining the reason for her withdrawal. As the following case demonstrates, sometimes an explanation which is too conclusory and provides no help to the client will be deemed ineffective assistance of counsel:

> **Example—*Anders v. California*, 386 U.S. 738 (1967):** Charles Anders was convicted of possessing marijuana. He was assigned appellate counsel who reviewed the trial record. Following this review, counsel concluded that Anders had no non-frivolous appellate issues. Accordingly, rather than filing a brief on Anders's behalf counsel sent a letter to the court offering his assessment of the case. Counsel also advised the court that Anders wished to file his own appellate brief.

---

[44] Evitts v. Lucey, 469 U.S. 387 (1985).

[45] Douglas v. California, 372 U.S. 353 (1963).

[46] Evitts, 469 U.S. at 394.

[47] Id.

Anders's request for replacement counsel was denied, and he proceeded *pro se* on the appeal. The state appellate court affirmed his conviction. Anders thereafter sought federal habeas review. Anders contended that his right to the effective assistance of counsel was denied by counsel's failure to file a brief on his behalf. The Supreme Court then reviewed the case to consider what duty an appointed attorney owes his appellate client after counsel concludes that an appeal has no merit.

Analysis: Anders was denied the right to the effective assistance of counsel. There is no question that an appellate attorney may withdraw from an appeal if, after reviewing the record, she concludes that any appellate challenge to the conviction would be frivolous. However, in withdrawing, counsel must do more than offer a bare conclusion that the appeal has no merit.

By filing his bare conclusion about the merit of the case, counsel did not act "in the role of an advocate."[48] Moreover, when the appellate court then affirmed Anders's conviction without making its own independent assessment of frivolity, Anders was not "provide[d] that full consideration and resolution of the matter as is obtained when counsel is acting in that capacity [the capacity of an advocate]."

Once counsel finds an appeal to be wholly without merit, she may notify the court of this conclusion and may seek permission to withdraw. However, counsel must also file a brief "referring to anything in the record that might arguably support the appeal. A copy of counsel's brief should be furnished [to] the indigent and time allowed him to raise any points that he chooses."[49]

Because the no-merit letter that Anders's attorney filed with the appellate court did not meet these requirements, the decision in his case was reversed and the case remanded for an appellate proceeding in which his right to counsel was not denied.

Following its decision in *Anders*, many thought that the procedures it laid out for so-called "no-merit briefs" were mandatory—in particular *Anders*'s requirement that counsel identify the non-meritorious issues in the case. However, three decades later the Court clarified that the *Anders* procedures are not compulsory. In *Smith v. Robbins*, the Court determined that "States are free to adopt different procedures, so long as those procedures adequately safeguard a defendant's right to appellate counsel."[50]

In *Robbins*, counsel determined that an appeal would be frivolous. However, rather than filing a brief that complied with the *Anders* procedures, counsel filed

[48] Anders v. California, 386 U.S. 738, 743 (1967).

[49] Anders, 386 U.S. at 744.

[50] 528 U.S. 259, 265 (2000).

a brief that was silent on the merits but summarized the facts and procedural posture of the case, including citation to the record. The Court found that this brief, which was filed in conformity with the prevailing state procedures, adequately protected Robbins's right to the effective assistance of appellate counsel. "A State's procedure provides [adequate] review so long as it reasonably ensures that an indigent's appeal will be resolved in a way that is related to the merit of that appeal."[51]

5. Effective Assistance and Guilty Pleas. Finally, the Court has considered ineffective assistance of counsel claims in the context of guilty pleas. These cases have evaluated counsel's responsibility in connection with the client's decision to take a plea, as well as counsel's responsibilities if the client forgoes a plea and proceeds to trial.

The first issue involves the duties of an attorney when her client pleads guilty. One of these duties is to ensure that the client is aware of the potential consequences of taking the guilty plea. For example, the attorney should inform the defendant of the maximum possible sentence he could receive or the amount of time he will have to serve before he becomes eligible for parole. If an attorney fails to do so, her performance falls below an objective standard as measured by professional norms, and is therefore constitutionally deficient. However, the client still has the burden of proving the second prong of the *Strickland* standard: that the proper information about his sentence would have caused him to reject the plea offer and proceed to trial, thus causing him prejudice. If the client cannot make this showing relief will be denied.[52]

In modern times, criminal convictions do not just result in the sentence handed down by the court, but also impose a number of "collateral consequences" on the defendant. For example, a defendant convicted of a felony frequently loses his right to vote for some period of time, an individual convicted of domestic violence might lose his right to carry a firearm, or a person convicted of drunk driving may have his driver's license suspended for a number of years. One of the most serious collateral consequences in the criminal justice system involves a defendant's immigration status: if a non-citizen is convicted of certain crimes, he could face deportation in addition to the sentence imposed by the court. The Supreme Court has held that an attorney's failure to inform the defendant of at least the more severe of these collateral consequences fulfills the "constitutionally deficient" prong of the *Strickland* test:

Example—*Padilla v. Kentucky*, 559 U.S. 356 (2010): Jose Padilla was a native of Honduras. He became a lawful permanent resident of the United States who served in the armed

[51] Smith v. Robbins, 528 U.S. 259, 276–77 (2000).

[52] Hill v. Lockhart, 474 U.S. 52 (1985).

forces during the Vietnam War and lived a quiet law abiding life for some forty years. Padilla was working as a truck driver when he was arrested and charged with transporting a large quantity of marijuana in his truck.

Upon the advice of counsel, Padilla pled guilty to drug charges. Prior to entering the plea, Padilla's lawyer assured him that he "did not have to worry about immigration status since he had been in the country so long." However, in direct conflict with counsel's assurance, Padilla almost immediately became subject to deportation proceedings. In a post-conviction challenge to his guilty plea, Padilla sought to withdraw the plea based upon the ineffective assistance provided by counsel. The state court that reviewed his claim found that the right to effective assistance of counsel did not include a right to accurate advice on collateral consequences. Because the court viewed the immigration issue as a collateral consequence of the plea, it found that it did not form a basis for post-conviction relief. The Supreme Court granted cert.

Analysis: Padilla's attorney's performance was constitutionally deficient. Under modern immigration law, there are a host of criminal offenses for which deportation is now an inevitable consequence. Moreover, the range of criminal offenses for which the sanction of automatic deportation now applies has been substantially expanded. "These changes to our immigration laws have dramatically raised the stakes of a noncitizen's criminal conviction. The importance of accurate legal advice for noncitizens accused of crimes has never been more important."[53]

The Sixth Amendment guarantees the effective assistance of counsel to a defendant who is trying to decide whether to plead guilty. In determining how far the reach of that assistance extends, the Supreme Court has never recognized a distinction between the direct and collateral consequences that might flow from a plea. It may be, as the state court suggested, that such a distinction is merited. But, that is a question for another day. For now, it need only be said that deportation is a "particularly severe penalty" that is "intimately related to the criminal process."[54]

Under *Strickland*'s deficient performance prong, counsel should have accurately advised Padilla of the deportation risk associated with his guilty plea. Prevailing professional norms offer near universal endorsement of the notion that defense attorneys should advise their non-citizen clients of the risks of deportation.

---

[53] Padilla v. Kentucky, 559 U.S. 356, 364 (2010).

[54] Padilla, 559 U.S. at 366.

There are aspects of immigration law that are extremely complicated and unclear. In those cases, the obligations of counsel may be different. But, in Padilla's case the immigration consequences were easily identifiable.

Defense counsel's pre-plea conduct in Padilla's case fell below an objective standard of reasonableness. Whether Padilla was entitled to relief on remand depended upon whether he could establish prejudice as a result of counsel's bad advice. Establishing prejudice would require Padilla to demonstrate that he would have rationally rejected the plea had he known of the risk of deportation.

The second issue involving ineffective assistance claims in the plea bargaining contexts occurs when the defendant forgoes a plea offer and proceeds to trial. The Supreme Court recently decided two such cases. In the first case, counsel informed the client of the offer, but suggested that it should be rejected. In the second case, counsel never informed the client of the state's initial offer. In both cases, harsher punishment was ultimately meted out. The question therefore became whether the attorney in either case violated his or her client's right to effective counsel. First, let's consider the case of the attorney who advised the client to reject the prosecution's offer:

Example—*Lafler v. Cooper*, 132 S.Ct. 1376 (2012): For reasons that never became clear, Anthony Cooper pointed a gun at Kali Mundy's head one evening and pulled the trigger. After the shot missed, Cooper ran after Mundy firing at her. Mundy was hit three times but survived. Cooper was charged with a number of offenses including assault with intent to murder.

Prior to trial, the prosecution offered a plea. If Cooper would plead to two of the four charges, the prosecution would drop the other two and recommend a sentence of 51 to 85 months. Defense counsel advised Cooper to reject the plea, stating that the prosecution would not be able to prove intent to murder because Cooper had aimed below Mundy's waist. Cooper followed this advice, rejected the plea, and was subsequently convicted at trial on all counts, including assault with intent to murder. He was sentenced to the mandatory minimum—185 to 360 months in prison.

Cooper then maintained that his lawyer's advice to reject the plea constituted ineffective assistance. The state courts considering the claim found that Cooper knowingly rejected the two plea offers. However, the federal district court hearing the habeas challenge found that counsel had provided ineffective assistance and ordered specific performance of the negotiated sentence. After that finding was upheld by the circuit court, the Supreme Court granted review.

Analysis: Cooper's attorney did provide deficient performance by advising him that he could not be convicted. However, the appropriate remedy is not specific performance of the negotiated sentence, since the trial court still has the discretion to decide whether to accept the plea bargain.

There is no question that the Sixth Amendment right to effective counsel extends to plea negotiations. And, while Cooper did not have a "right' to a plea deal, he was entitled to the effective assistance of counsel where a plea offer was made. By incorrectly instructing Cooper that he should reject that plea because he could not be found guilty, counsel's conduct fell below an objective standard of reasonableness. Moreover, Cooper was prejudiced by counsel's error when he rejected the offer, proceeded to trial, and was sentenced three and half times more harshly than he would been had he accepted the plea.

On remand, the state must reoffer the plea deal. If Cooper accepts, the trial court should then "exercise its discretion in determining whether to vacate the convictions and resentence [Cooper] pursuant to the plea agreement, to vacate only some of the convictions and resentence respondent accordingly, or to leave the convictions and sentence from trial undisturbed."[55]

The same day that the Court decided *Cooper*, it decided a second case challenging the effectiveness of trial counsel's assistance in connection with a guilty plea. In *Missouri v. Frye*, defense counsel failed to inform Frye of a plea offer until after it lapsed. Frye then pled guilty on much less favorable terms. In a post-conviction proceeding, Frye sought relief alleging that counsel's failure to disclose the earlier plea offer constituted ineffective assistance:

Example—*Missouri v. Frye*, 132 S.Ct. 1399 (2012): Galin Frye was charged with driving on a revoked license in the summer of 2007. This charge made him eligible for a maximum sentence of four years upon conviction. The prosecutor offered two potential resolutions of the case: 1) Frye could plead to the felony charge and receive a three year sentence with a recommendation that Frye serve just ten days of this time; or 2) Frye could plead guilty to a misdemeanor and receive a 90-day sentence. The prosecutor communicated the offer in a letter to defense counsel that clearly stated the date on which the offer expired. Trial counsel never informed Frye of the offers, and they expired. Frye was arrested again for driving on a revoked license. Eventually, Frye pled guilty to the original charge and was sentenced to three years in prison.

[55] Lafler v. Cooper, 132 S.Ct. 1376, 1391 (2012).

Frye sought post-conviction relief, arguing that he would have plead guilty to the misdemeanor offense had counsel informed him of the offer. The Supreme Court ultimately accepted the case for review.

Analysis: The Supreme Court determined that Frye had a viable claim for ineffective assistance of counsel and remanded the case for the lower court to determine whether he had been prejudiced by his attorney's deficient performance.

The overwhelming majority of criminal convictions are the product of guilty pleas—97% in the federal system and 94% in the state system. "To a large extent horse trading between prosecutor and defense counsel determines who goes to jail and for how long. That is what plea bargaining is. It is not some adjunct to the criminal justice system; it is the criminal justice system."[56] The prevalence of pleas in our system requires that the right to effective counsel be enforced at this stage of the process. Accordingly, the Court has found that guilty pleas are one of the "critical stages" to which the Sixth Amendment right to counsel attaches.

In assessing counsel's performance in connection with a guilty plea, the two-part *Strickland* test applies. There will be time at some later point to articulate the exact contours of counsel's duties in connection with a guilty plea. At a minimum, it can be said that counsel has performed deficiently if counsel allows a formal, potentially favorable offer from the prosecution to expire without communicating it to the client.

Turning to the question of prejudice, Frye must be able to show both a reasonable probability that he would have accepted the earlier offer **and** a reasonable probability that the prosecutor would not have rescinded and the court would have accepted the plea (if such rejection was authorized by state law).

The case was remanded for the state court to consider whether Frye demonstrated a reasonable probability that his misdemeanor plea would have been accepted, even though he had subsequently been arrested for a new driving offense.

Thus, in the context of a lapsed plea bargain, defendants have a dual prejudice showing—that they would have accepted the offer and that the offer would not have been either rescinded by the prosecutor or rejected by the court. On remand, the state appellate court in Frye's case found that the prosecutor and the trial court had the authority under state law to reject the plea, but the case was again remanded (this time to the trial court) for a determination of whether Frye's plea likely would have been rejected.

---

[56] Missouri v. Frye, 132 S.Ct. 1399, 1407 (2012).

Quick Summary

The Sixth Amendment right to counsel includes within it a right to the **effective** assistance of counsel. *Strickland v. Washington* defines the standards that govern ineffective assistance claims. The two-pronged *Strickland* test requires a showing of deficient performance and a showing of prejudice. The deficient performance prong asks whether counsel's performance fell below an objective standard of reasonableness. The prejudice prong asks whether there is a reasonable probability the result of the proceeding would have been different but for counsel's deficiency.

The burden of proof with regard to any ineffective assistance claim is on the convicted person.

The Court has never defined a precise list of conduct that will or will not constitute ineffectiveness. Rather, the Court has said that reviewing courts should be guided by prevailing professional norms.

To avoid the distorting lens of hindsight, any ineffective assistance claim must afford extreme deference to counsel's choices. The question in IAC cases is not whether counsel's performance could have been improved, but whether counsel's assistance was reasonably effective.

In a handful of cases, the Court has found that the *Strickland* demand for a showing of prejudice is not required. The three instances where the Court has found this "*Cronic* no-prejudice" rule to apply are: 1) where the right to counsel is completely denied; 2) where counsel is operating under an actual conflict of interests that has been objected to; and 3) where the government meaningfully interferes with counsel's assistance. In all other ineffective assistance cases, the two-pronged *Strickland* approach applies, and the burden is upon the convicted person to establish a reasonable likelihood that the result in his case would have been different but for counsel's errors.

In addition to the effective assistance of trial counsel, the Sixth Amendment also confers a right to the effective assistance of appellate counsel.

The right to effective assistance of counsel also applies to the plea bargaining stage of the representation. The right could be violated if the attorney fails to inform the client of the collateral consequences of pleading guilty, if the attorney gives the client incorrect information which leads the client to forgo a plea deal, or if the attorney does not convey a plea offer to the defendant.

Review Questions

1. A Robbery Between Friends. Fred Baty and Leroy Miller were arrested for robbing a grocery store. A single gun was found. Miller maintained that he had been hitchhiking and was picked up by Baty. Miller denied any advance knowledge of the robbery, placed Baty in the store at the time of the robbery, and swore that he (Miller) had not had a gun during the post-robbery shootout with police.

Baty contradicted these claims. Baty asserted that he was not in the store at the time of the robbery and did not have the gun.

Both Baty and Miller retained an attorney by the name of William Smith. Smith notified the trial court of the conflict of interests presented by the joint representation. He asked the court to sever the two cases for purposes of trial. He also asked the court to appoint a second attorney if the severance motion was denied. The severance motion was denied and Smith's partner, Charles Taylor, was assigned to be counsel for Baty.

In preparation for trial, the new attorney Taylor primarily relied upon information gathered during conversations with his partner Smith. He did not interview any witnesses or read the preliminary hearing transcript, and he talked with his client Baty for just a half an hour on the morning of trial. At trial, Smith argued motions on behalf of both defendants and rested the defense for both clients. Taylor did not make an opening argument for his client, and did not cross-examine Miller to challenge his assertion that he was not the one who had the gun. The jury convicted Baty.

At the sentencing hearing, Taylor offered no statement or other evidence, and the judge sentenced Baty to life in prison. On review, Baty alleged ineffective assistance of trial counsel both as a result of Taylor's lack of preparation and the conflict of interests. How should the court rule?

2. My Brother's Keeper. Kenneth Brown was working as a cashier in a convenience store. He and Fred Vela, a customer in the store, got into an argument one evening. The two agreed to "step outside" to settle their differences. As the men were walking out of the store, they encountered Conrado Vela, Fred's brother. Conrado came to his brother's defense and began fighting with Brown. Brown punched Conrado in the face hard enough to knock him to the ground. Brown then returned to the store. Conrado quickly drove home, got his gun, and drove back to the store. The entire trip took him approximately twenty minutes. Conrado shot and killed Brown. He was arrested later that evening in his house.

Conrado Vela chose to plead guilty to murder. Under a Texas sentencing procedure, the jury could then find Vela guilty of murder "with malice," punishable by up to life in prison, or guilty of murder "without malice," punishable by a maximum of five years incarceration. At the sentencing hearing, the State introduced a host of sympathy-inducing evidence, including testimony that Brown was a young father who left behind a wife and a three-year old child. The state also introduced evidence that Brown was in college, working two jobs, and playing football for a championship team at the time of his death. Defense counsel failed to register any objection. After considering this evidence, the jury found Vela to be guilty "with malice" and Vela was sentenced to ninety-nine years in prison.

On appeal, Vela raised a number of claims concerning the improper testimony that had been admitted during sentencing. Though the reviewing court agreed that the testimony was improper, it declined to award relief in light of counsel's failure to object. Vela then sought federal habeas relief, alleging the ineffective assistance of trial counsel. Is he correct?

3. The Enraged Ex. George Porter was a wounded and decorated veteran who fought in the Korean War. His experiences in battle left Porter severely traumatized upon his return from battle. Many years later, Porter became angry after his girlfriend began dating another man. Porter stalked his ex for several days before breaking into her house. Porter shot and killed his ex-girlfriend inside the home and then shot and killed her new boyfriend when the boyfriend came to her defense.

After an aborted attempt at self-representation, Porter decided to plead guilty to both murder charges. The prosecution sought the death penalty. Counsel was appointed for the penalty phase. Counsel introduced one witness to present mitigating evidence. This witness, Porter's ex-wife, testified that Porter had a good relationship with their son. The state put in significant aggravating evidence. The state's witnesses established that the murders were committed after Porter broke into his ex-girlfriend's home; that he had stalked her for days before the shooting; and that Porter had killed more than one person. The jury recommended that Porter be sentenced to death. If Porter challenges the effectiveness of his attorney on direct appeal will he likely be successful? If Porter does not raise an IAC claim on direct appeal, when should it be raised? What sort of evidence would you introduce to establish the two *Strickland* prongs?

4. A Failed Strategy. Jonathan Franklin was charged with a number of very serious charges, including drug distribution, conspiracy, CCE ("Continuing Criminal Enterprise") and murder. Some of the charges subjected Franklin to a mandatory life sentence upon conviction. For other charges, a life sentence was not mandatory but was in the range of punishment that might be imposed by the court.

Prior to trial, the prosecution offered Franklin a plea deal. Pursuant to the deal, Franklin would plead to some of the charges and would cooperate with the government in building cases against his brother and his cousin. In return, Franklin would be sentenced to a minimum prison term of thirty-five years. Trial counsel communicated the offer to Franklin, but advised him to reject it. Instead, counsel suggested that the defense adopt a "concession strategy" at trial. Pursuant to this strategy, the defense would not contest guilt on some of the more minor charges to build credibility with the jury, but would vigorously contest Franklin's guilt on the more serious offenses. The asserted goal of counsel's plan was to secure acquittals on any charges with mandatory life terms. If Franklin was convicted of any other offenses, counsel's plan was then to argue forcefully at sentencing for a period of incarceration less than life.

This strategy was partly effective in that the jury acquitted Franklin on many of the more serious charges, including murder. However, the jury convicted Franklin of conspiracy, which carried a mandatory life term. On collateral review, Franklin maintained that trial counsel's concession strategy and recommendation that he reject the plea offer constituted ineffective assistance of counsel. Franklin maintained that he would have pled guilty and cooperated with the government if he understood that a life sentence remained possible (due to the judge's discretion to impose such a sentence) even if the concession strategy was entirely effective in avoiding a mandatory life sentence. In assessing whether Franklin is entitled to relief, what issues should the reviewing court consider?

FROM THE COURTROOM

STRICKLAND v. WASHINGTON

Supreme Court of the United States, 1984
467 U.S. 1267

[Justice O'CONNOR delivered the opinion of the Court.]

[Justice BRENNAN concurred in part and dissented in part and filed an opinion.]

[Justice MARSHALL dissented and filed opinion.]

This case requires us to consider the proper standards for judging a criminal defendant's contention that the Constitution requires a conviction or death sentence to be set aside because counsel's assistance at the trial or sentencing was ineffective.

I

A

During a 10–day period in September 1976, respondent planned and committed three groups of crimes, which included three brutal stabbing murders, torture, kidnaping, severe assaults, attempted murders, attempted extortion, and theft. After his two accomplices were arrested, respondent surrendered to police and voluntarily gave a lengthy statement confessing to the third of the criminal episodes. The State of Florida indicted respondent for kidnaping and murder and appointed an experienced criminal lawyer to represent him.

Counsel actively pursued pretrial motions and discovery. He cut his efforts short, however, and he experienced a sense of hopelessness about the case, when he learned that, against his specific advice, respondent had also confessed to the first two murders. By the date set for trial, respondent was subject to indictment for three counts of first-degree murder and multiple counts of robbery, kidnaping for ransom, breaking and entering and assault, attempted murder, and conspiracy to commit robbery. Respondent waived his right to a jury trial, again acting against counsel's advice, and pleaded guilty to all charges, including the three capital murder charges.

In the plea colloquy, respondent told the trial judge that, although he had committed a string of burglaries, he had no significant prior criminal record and that at the time of his criminal spree he was under extreme stress caused by his inability to support his family. He also stated, however, that he accepted responsibility for the crimes. The trial judge told respondent that he had "a great deal of respect for people who are willing to step forward and admit their responsibility" but that he was making no statement at all about his likely sentencing decision.

Counsel advised respondent to invoke his right under Florida law to an advisory jury at his capital sentencing hearing. Respondent rejected the advice and waived the right. He chose instead to be sentenced by the trial judge without a jury recommendation.

In preparing for the sentencing hearing, counsel spoke with respondent about his background. He also spoke on the telephone with respondent's wife and mother, though he did not follow up on the one unsuccessful effort to meet with them. He did not otherwise seek out character witnesses for respondent. Nor did he request a psychiatric examination, since his conversations with his client gave no indication that respondent had psychological problems.

Counsel decided not to present and hence not to look further for evidence concerning respondent's character and emotional state. That decision reflected trial counsel's sense of hopelessness about overcoming the evidentiary effect of respondent's confessions to the gruesome crimes. It also reflected the judgment that it was advisable to rely on the plea colloquy for evidence about respondent's background and about his claim of emotional stress: the plea colloquy communicated sufficient information about these subjects, and by forgoing the opportunity to present new evidence on these subjects, counsel prevented the State from cross-examining respondent on his claim and from putting on psychiatric evidence of its own.

Counsel also excluded from the sentencing hearing other evidence he thought was potentially damaging. He successfully moved to exclude respondent's "rap sheet." Because he judged that a presentence report might prove more detrimental than helpful, as it would have included respondent's criminal history and thereby would have undermined the claim of no significant history of criminal activity, he did not request that one be prepared.

At the sentencing hearing, counsel's strategy was based primarily on the trial judge's remarks at the plea colloquy as well as on his reputation as a sentencing judge who thought it important for a convicted defendant to own up to his crime. Counsel argued that respondent's remorse and acceptance of responsibility justified sparing him from the death penalty. Counsel also argued that respondent had no history of criminal activity and that respondent committed the crimes under extreme mental or emotional disturbance, thus coming within the statutory list of mitigating circumstances. He further argued that respondent should be spared death because he had surrendered, confessed, and offered to testify against a codefendant and because respondent was fundamentally a good person who had briefly gone badly wrong in extremely stressful circumstances. The State put on evidence and witnesses largely for the purpose of describing the details of the crimes. Counsel did not cross-examine the medical experts who testified about the manner of death of respondent's victims.

The trial judge found several aggravating circumstances with respect to each of the three murders. He found that all three murders were especially heinous, atrocious, and cruel, all involving repeated stabbings. All three murders were committed in the course of at least one other dangerous and violent felony, and since all involved robbery, the murders were for pecuniary gain. All three murders were committed to avoid arrest for the accompanying crimes and to hinder law enforcement. In the course of one of the murders, respondent knowingly subjected numerous persons to a grave risk of death by deliberately stabbing and shooting the murder victim's sisters-in-law, who sustained severe—in one case, ultimately fatal—injuries.

With respect to mitigating circumstances, the trial judge made the same findings for all three capital murders. First, although there was no admitted evidence of prior convictions, respondent had stated that he had engaged in a course of stealing. In any case, even if respondent had no significant history of criminal activity, the aggravating circumstances "would still clearly far outweigh" that mitigating factor. Second, the judge found that, during all three crimes, respondent was not suffering from extreme mental or emotional disturbance and could appreciate the criminality of his acts. Third, none of the victims was a participant in, or consented to, respondent's conduct. Fourth, respondent's participation in the crimes was neither minor nor the result of duress or domination by an accomplice. Finally, respondent's age (26) could not be considered a factor in mitigation, especially when viewed in light of respondent's planning of the crimes and disposition of the proceeds of the various accompanying thefts.

In short, the trial judge found numerous aggravating circumstances and no (or a single comparatively insignificant) mitigating circumstance. With respect to each of the three convictions for capital murder, the trial judge concluded: "A careful consideration of all matters presented to the court impels the conclusion that there are insufficient mitigating circumstances . . . to outweigh the aggravating circumstances." He therefore sentenced respondent to death on each of the three counts of murder and to prison terms for the other crimes. The Florida Supreme Court upheld the convictions and sentences on direct appeal.

B

Respondent subsequently sought collateral relief in state court on numerous grounds, among them that counsel had rendered ineffective assistance at the sentencing proceeding. Respondent challenged counsel's assistance in six respects. He asserted that counsel was ineffective because he failed to move for a continuance to prepare for sentencing, to request a psychiatric report, to investigate and present character witnesses, to seek a presentence investigation report, to present meaningful arguments to the sentencing judge, and to investigate the medical examiner's reports or cross-examine the medical experts. In support of the claim, respondent submitted 14 affidavits from friends, neighbors, and relatives stating that they would have testified if asked to do so. He also submitted one psychiatric report and one psychological report stating that respondent, though not under the influence of extreme mental or emotional disturbance, was "chronically frustrated and depressed because of his economic dilemma" at the time of his crimes.

The trial court denied relief without an evidentiary hearing, finding that the record evidence conclusively showed that the ineffectiveness claim was meritless.

. . .

C

Respondent next filed a petition for a writ of habeas corpus in the United States District Court for the Southern District of Florida. He advanced numerous grounds for relief, among them ineffective assistance of counsel based on the same errors, except for the failure to move for a continuance, as those he had identified in state court.

. . .

On the legal issue of ineffectiveness, the District Court concluded that, although trial counsel made errors in judgment in failing to investigate nonstatutory mitigating evidence further than he did, no prejudice to respondent's sentence resulted from any such error in judgment. Relying in part on the trial judge's testimony but also on the same factors that led the state courts to find no prejudice, the District Court concluded that "there does not appear to be a likelihood, or even a significant possibility," that any errors of trial counsel had affected the outcome of the sentencing proceeding. The District Court went on to reject all of respondent's other grounds for relief, including one not exhausted in state court, which the District Court considered because, among other reasons, the State urged its consideration. The court accordingly denied the petition for a writ of habeas corpus.

On appeal, ... [t]he full Court of Appeals developed its own framework for analyzing ineffective assistance claims and reversed the judgment of the District Court and remanded the case for new factfinding under the newly announced standards.

. . .

D

Petitioners, who are officials of the State of Florida, filed a petition for a writ of certiorari seeking review of the decision of the Court of Appeals. The petition presents a type of Sixth Amendment claim that this Court has not previously considered in any generality. The Court has considered Sixth Amendment claims based on actual or constructive denial of the assistance of counsel altogether, as well as claims based on state interference with the ability of counsel to render effective assistance to the accused. With the exception of *Cuyler v. Sullivan*, 446 U.S. 335 (1980), however, which involved a claim that counsel's assistance was rendered ineffective by a conflict of interest, the Court has never directly and fully addressed a claim of "actual ineffectiveness" of counsel's assistance in a case going to trial.

In assessing attorney performance, all the Federal Courts of Appeals and all but a few state courts have now adopted the "reasonably effective assistance" standard in one formulation or another. Yet this Court has not had occasion squarely to decide whether that is the proper standard. With respect to the prejudice that a defendant must show from deficient attorney performance, the lower courts have adopted tests that purport to differ in more than formulation.

. . .

For these reasons, we granted certiorari to consider the standards by which to judge a contention that the Constitution requires that a criminal judgment be overturned because of the actual ineffective assistance of counsel.

. . .

II

In a long line of cases that includes *Powell v. Alabama*, 287 U.S. 45 (1932), *Johnson v. Zerbst*, 304 U.S. 458 (1938), and *Gideon v. Wainwright*, 372 U.S. 335 (1963), this Court has recognized that the Sixth Amendment right to counsel exists, and is needed, in order to protect the fundamental right to a fair trial. The Constitution guarantees a fair trial through the Due Process Clauses, but it defines the basic elements of a fair trial largely through the several provisions of the Sixth Amendment, including the Counsel Clause:

"In all criminal prosecutions, the accused shall enjoy the right to a speedy and public trial, by an impartial jury of the State and district wherein the crime shall have been committed, which district shall have been previously ascertained by law, and to be informed of the nature and cause of the accusation; to be confronted with the witnesses against him; to have compulsory process for obtaining witnesses in his favor, and to have the Assistance of Counsel for his defence."

Thus, a fair trial is one in which evidence subject to adversarial testing is presented to an impartial tribunal for resolution of issues defined in advance of the proceeding. The right to counsel plays a crucial role in the adversarial system embodied in the Sixth Amendment, since access to counsel's skill and knowledge is necessary to accord defendants the "ample opportunity to meet the case of the prosecution" to which they are entitled.

Because of the vital importance of counsel's assistance, this Court has held that, with certain exceptions, a person accused of a federal or state crime has the right to have counsel appointed if retained counsel cannot be obtained. That a person who happens to be a lawyer is present at trial alongside the accused, however, is not enough to satisfy the constitutional command. The Sixth Amendment recognizes the right to the assistance of counsel because it envisions counsel's playing a role that is critical to the ability of the adversarial system to produce just results. An accused is entitled to be assisted by an attorney, whether retained or appointed, who plays the role necessary to ensure that the trial is fair.

For that reason, the Court has recognized that "the right to counsel is the right to the effective assistance of counsel." Government violates the right to effective assistance when it interferes in certain ways with the ability of counsel to make independent decisions about how to conduct the defense. See, e.g., *Geders v. United States*, 425 U.S. 80 (1976) (bar on attorney-client consultation during overnight recess); *Herring v. New York*, 422 U.S. 853 (1975) (bar on summation at bench trial); *Brooks v. Tennessee*, 406 U.S. 605, 612–613 (1972) (requirement that defendant be first defense witness); *Ferguson v. Georgia*, 365 U.S. 570, 593–596 (1961) (bar on direct examination of defendant). Counsel, however, can also deprive a defendant of the right to effective assistance, simply by failing to render "adequate legal assistance."

The Court has not elaborated on the meaning of the constitutional requirement of effective assistance in the latter class of cases—that is, those presenting claims of "actual ineffectiveness." In giving meaning to the requirement, however, we must take its purpose—to ensure a fair trial—as the guide. The benchmark for judging any claim of ineffectiveness must be whether counsel's conduct so undermined the proper functioning of the adversarial process that the trial cannot be relied on as having produced a just result.

The same principle applies to a capital sentencing proceeding such as that provided by Florida law. We need not consider the role of counsel in an ordinary sentencing, which may involve informal proceedings and standardless discretion in the sentencer, and hence may require a different approach to the definition of constitutionally effective assistance. A capital sentencing proceeding like the one involved in this case, however, is sufficiently like a trial in its adversarial format and in the existence of standards for decision that counsel's role in the proceeding is comparable to counsel's role at trial—to ensure that the adversarial testing process works to produce a just result under the standards governing decision. For purposes of describing counsel's duties, therefore, Florida's capital sentencing proceeding need not be distinguished from an ordinary trial.

III

A convicted defendant's claim that counsel's assistance was so defective as to require reversal of a conviction or death sentence has two components. First, the defendant must show that counsel's performance was deficient. This requires showing that counsel made errors so serious that counsel was not functioning as the "counsel" guaranteed the defendant by the Sixth Amendment. Second, the defendant must show that the deficient performance prejudiced the defense. This requires showing that counsel's errors were so serious as to deprive the defendant of a fair trial, a trial whose result is reliable. Unless a defendant makes both showings, it cannot be said that the conviction or death sentence resulted from a breakdown in the adversary process that renders the result unreliable.

A

As all the Federal Courts of Appeals have now held, the proper standard for attorney performance is that of reasonably effective assistance. The Court indirectly recognized as much when it stated in McMann v. Richardson, 397 U.S., at 770, that a guilty plea cannot be attacked as based on inadequate legal advice unless counsel was not "a reasonably competent attorney" and the advice was not "within the range of competence demanded of attorneys in criminal cases." When a convicted defendant complains of the ineffectiveness of counsel's assistance, the defendant must show that counsel's representation fell below an objective standard of reasonableness.

More specific guidelines are not appropriate. The Sixth Amendment refers simply to "counsel," not specifying particular requirements of effective assistance. It relies instead on the legal profession's maintenance of standards sufficient to justify the law's presumption that counsel will fulfill the role in the adversary process that the Amendment envisions. The proper measure of attorney performance remains simply reasonableness under prevailing professional norms.

Representation of a criminal defendant entails certain basic duties. Counsel's function is to assist the defendant, and hence counsel owes the client a duty of loyalty, a duty to avoid conflicts of interest. From counsel's function as assistant to the defendant derive the overarching duty to advocate the defendant's cause and the more particular duties to consult with the defendant on important decisions and to keep the defendant informed of important developments in the course of the prosecution. Counsel also has a duty to bring to bear such skill and knowledge as will render the trial a reliable adversarial testing process.

These basic duties neither exhaustively define the obligations of counsel nor form a checklist for judicial evaluation of attorney performance. In any case presenting an ineffectiveness claim, the performance inquiry must be whether counsel's assistance was reasonable considering all the circumstances. Prevailing norms of practice as reflected in American Bar Association standards and the like are guides to determining what is reasonable, but they are only guides. No particular set of detailed rules for counsel's conduct can satisfactorily take account of the variety of circumstances faced by defense counsel or the range of legitimate decisions regarding how best to represent a criminal defendant. Any such set of rules would interfere with the constitutionally protected independence of counsel and restrict the wide latitude counsel must have in making tactical decisions. Indeed, the existence of detailed guidelines for representation could distract counsel from the overriding mission of vigorous advocacy of the defendant's cause. Moreover, the purpose of the effective assistance guarantee of the Sixth Amendment is not to improve the quality of legal representation, although that is a goal of considerable importance to the legal system. The purpose is simply to ensure that criminal defendants receive a fair trial.

Judicial scrutiny of counsel's performance must be highly deferential. It is all too tempting for a defendant to second-guess counsel's assistance after conviction or adverse sentence, and it is all too easy for a court, examining counsel's defense after it has proved unsuccessful, to conclude that a particular act or omission of counsel was unreasonable. A fair assessment of attorney performance requires that every effort be made to eliminate the distorting effects of hindsight, to reconstruct the circumstances of counsel's challenged conduct, and to evaluate the conduct from counsel's perspective at the time. Because of the difficulties inherent in making the evaluation, a court must indulge a strong presumption that counsel's conduct falls within the wide range of reasonable professional assistance; that is, the defendant must overcome the presumption that, under the circumstances, the challenged action "might be considered sound trial strategy." There are countless ways to provide effective assistance in any given case. Even the best criminal defense attorneys would not defend a particular client in the same way.

The availability of intrusive post-trial inquiry into attorney performance or of detailed guidelines for its evaluation would encourage the proliferation of ineffectiveness challenges. Criminal trials resolved unfavorably to the defendant would increasingly come to be followed by a second trial, this one of counsel's unsuccessful defense. Counsel's performance and even willingness to serve could be adversely affected. Intensive scrutiny of counsel and rigid requirements for acceptable assistance could dampen the ardor and impair the independence of defense counsel, discourage the acceptance of assigned cases, and undermine the trust between attorney and client.

Thus, a court deciding an actual ineffectiveness claim must judge the reasonableness of counsel's challenged conduct on the facts of the particular case, viewed as of the time of counsel's conduct. A convicted defendant making a claim of ineffective assistance must identify the acts or omissions of counsel that are alleged not to have been the result of reasonable professional judgment. The court must then determine whether, in light of all the circumstances, the identified acts or omissions were outside the wide range of professionally competent assistance. In making that determination, the court should keep in mind that counsel's function, as elaborated in prevailing professional norms, is to make the adversarial testing process work in the particular case. At the same time, the court should recognize that counsel is strongly presumed to have rendered adequate assistance and made all significant decisions in the exercise of reasonable professional judgment.

These standards require no special amplification in order to define counsel's duty to investigate, the duty at issue in this case. As the Court of Appeals concluded, strategic choices made after thorough investigation of law and facts relevant to plausible options are virtually unchallengeable; and strategic choices made after less than complete investigation are reasonable precisely to the extent that reasonable professional judgments support the limitations on investigation. In other words, counsel has a duty to make reasonable investigations or to make a reasonable decision that makes particular investigations unnecessary. In any ineffectiveness case, a particular decision not to investigate must be directly assessed for reasonableness in all the circumstances, applying a heavy measure of deference to counsel's judgments.

The reasonableness of counsel's actions may be determined or substantially influenced by the defendant's own statements or actions. Counsel's actions are usually based, quite properly, on informed strategic choices made by the defendant and on information supplied by the defendant. In particular, what investigation decisions are reasonable depends critically on such information. For example, when the facts that support a certain potential line of defense are generally known to counsel because of what the defendant has said, the need for further investigation may be considerably diminished or eliminated altogether. And when a defendant has given counsel reason to believe that pursuing certain investigations would be fruitless or even harmful, counsel's failure to pursue those investigations may not later be challenged as unreasonable. In short, inquiry into counsel's conversations with the defendant may be critical to a proper assessment of counsel's investigation decisions, just as it may be critical to a proper assessment of counsel's other litigation decisions.

B

An error by counsel, even if professionally unreasonable, does not warrant setting aside the judgment of a criminal proceeding if the error had no effect on the judgment. The purpose of the Sixth Amendment guarantee of counsel is to ensure that a defendant has the assistance necessary to justify reliance on the outcome of the proceeding. Accordingly, any deficiencies in counsel's performance must be prejudicial to the defense in order to constitute ineffective assistance under the Constitution.

In certain Sixth Amendment contexts, prejudice is presumed. Actual or constructive denial of the assistance of counsel altogether is legally presumed to result in prejudice. So are various kinds of state interference with counsel's assistance. Prejudice in these circumstances is so likely that case-by-case inquiry into prejudice is not worth the cost. Moreover, such circumstances involve impairments of the Sixth Amendment right that are easy to identify and, for that reason and because the prosecution is directly responsible, easy for the government to prevent.

One type of actual ineffectiveness claim warrants a similar, though more limited, presumption of prejudice. In Cuyler v. Sullivan, the Court held that prejudice is presumed when counsel is burdened by an actual conflict of interest. In those circumstances, counsel breaches the duty of loyalty, perhaps the most basic of counsel's duties. Moreover, it is difficult to measure the precise effect on the defense of representation corrupted by conflicting interests. Given the obligation of counsel to avoid conflicts of interest and the ability of trial courts to make early inquiry in certain situations likely to give rise to conflicts, it is reasonable for the criminal justice system to maintain a fairly rigid rule of presumed prejudice for conflicts of interest. Even so, the rule is not quite the per se rule of prejudice that exists for the Sixth Amendment claims mentioned above. Prejudice is presumed only if the defendant demonstrates that counsel "actively represented conflicting interests" and that "an actual conflict of interest adversely affected his lawyer's performance."

Conflict of interest claims aside, actual ineffectiveness claims alleging a deficiency in attorney performance are subject to a general requirement that the defendant affirmatively prove prejudice. The government is not responsible for, and hence not able to prevent, attorney errors that will result in reversal of a conviction or sentence. Attorney errors come in an infinite variety and are as likely to be utterly harmless in a particular case as they are to be prejudicial. They cannot be classified according to likelihood of causing prejudice. Nor can they be defined with sufficient precision to inform defense attorneys correctly just what conduct to avoid. Representation is an art, and an act or omission that is unprofessional in one case may be sound or even brilliant in another. Even if a defendant shows that particular errors of counsel were unreasonable, therefore, the defendant must show that they actually had an adverse effect on the defense.

It is not enough for the defendant to show that the errors had some conceivable effect on the outcome of the proceeding. Virtually every act or omission of counsel would meet that test, and not every error that conceivably could have influenced the outcome undermines the reliability of the result of the proceeding. Respondent suggests requiring a showing that the errors "impaired the presentation of the defense." That standard, however, provides no workable principle. Since any error, if it is indeed an error, "impairs" the presentation of the defense, the proposed standard is inadequate because it provides no way of deciding what impairments are sufficiently serious to warrant setting aside the outcome of the proceeding.

On the other hand, we believe that a defendant need not show that counsel's deficient conduct more likely than not altered the outcome in the case. This outcome-determinative standard has several strengths. It defines the relevant inquiry in a way familiar to courts, though the inquiry, as is inevitable, is anything but precise. The standard also reflects the profound importance of finality in criminal proceedings. Moreover, it comports with the widely used standard for assessing motions for new trial based on newly discovered evidence. Nevertheless, the standard is not quite appropriate.

Even when the specified attorney error results in the omission of certain evidence, the newly discovered evidence standard is not an apt source from which to draw a prejudice standard for ineffectiveness claims. The high standard for newly discovered evidence claims presupposes that all the essential elements of a presumptively accurate and fair proceeding were present in the proceeding whose result is challenged. An ineffective assistance claim asserts the absence of one of the crucial assurances that the result of the proceeding is reliable, so finality concerns are somewhat weaker and the appropriate standard of prejudice should be somewhat lower. The result of a proceeding can be rendered unreliable, and hence the proceeding itself unfair, even if the errors of counsel cannot be shown by a preponderance of the evidence to have determined the outcome.

Accordingly, the appropriate test for prejudice finds its roots in the test for materiality of exculpatory information not disclosed to the defense by the prosecution, and in the test for materiality of testimony made unavailable to the defense by Government deportation of a witness. The defendant must show that there is a reasonable probability that, but for counsel's unprofessional errors, the result of the proceeding would have been different. A reasonable probability is a probability sufficient to undermine confidence in the outcome.

In making the determination whether the specified errors resulted in the required prejudice, a court should presume, absent challenge to the judgment on grounds of evidentiary insufficiency, that the judge or jury acted according to law. An assessment of the likelihood of a result more favorable to the defendant must exclude the possibility of arbitrariness, whimsy, caprice, "nullification," and the like. A defendant has no entitlement to the luck of a lawless decisionmaker, even if a lawless decision cannot be reviewed. The assessment of prejudice should proceed on the assumption that the decisionmaker is reasonably, conscientiously, and impartially applying the standards that govern the decision. It should not depend on the idiosyncracies of the particular decisionmaker, such as unusual propensities toward harshness or leniency. Although these factors may actually have entered into counsel's selection of strategies and, to that limited extent, may thus affect the performance inquiry, they are irrelevant to the prejudice inquiry. Thus, evidence about the actual process of decision, if not part of the record of the proceeding under review, and evidence about, for example, a particular judge's sentencing practices, should not be considered in the prejudice determination.

The governing legal standard plays a critical role in defining the question to be asked in assessing the prejudice from counsel's errors. When a defendant challenges a conviction, the question is whether there is a reasonable probability that, absent the errors, the factfinder would have had a reasonable doubt respecting guilt. When a defendant challenges a death sentence such as the one at issue in this case, the question is whether there is a reasonable probability that, absent the errors, the sentencer—including an appellate court, to the extent it independently reweighs the evidence—would have concluded that the balance of aggravating and mitigating circumstances did not warrant death.

In making this determination, a court hearing an ineffectiveness claim must consider the totality of the evidence before the judge or jury. Some of the factual findings will have been unaffected by the errors, and factual findings that were affected will have been affected in different ways. Some errors will have had a pervasive effect on the inferences to be drawn from the evidence, altering the entire evidentiary picture, and some will have had an isolated, trivial effect. Moreover, a verdict or conclusion only weakly supported by the record is more likely to have been affected by errors than one with overwhelming record support. Taking the unaffected findings as a given, and taking due account of the effect of the errors on the remaining findings, a court making the prejudice inquiry must ask if the defendant has met the burden of showing that the decision reached would reasonably likely have been different absent the errors.

IV

A number of practical considerations are important for the application of the standards we have outlined. Most important, in adjudicating a claim of actual ineffectiveness of counsel, a court should keep in mind that the principles we have stated do not establish mechanical rules. Although those principles should guide the process of decision, the ultimate focus of inquiry must be on the fundamental fairness of the proceeding whose result is being challenged. In every case the court should be concerned with whether, despite the strong presumption of reliability, the result of the particular proceeding is unreliable because of a breakdown in the adversarial process that our system counts on to produce just results.

To the extent that this has already been the guiding inquiry in the lower courts, the standards articulated today do not require reconsideration of ineffectiveness claims rejected under different standards. In particular, the minor differences in the lower courts' precise formulations of the performance standard are insignificant: the different formulations are mere variations of the overarching reasonableness standard. With regard to the prejudice inquiry, only the strict outcome-determinative test, among the standards articulated in the lower courts, imposes a heavier burden on defendants than the tests laid down today. The difference, however, should alter the merit of an ineffectiveness claim only in the rarest case.

Although we have discussed the performance component of an ineffectiveness claim prior to the prejudice component, there is no reason for a court deciding an ineffective assistance claim to approach the inquiry in the same order or even to address both components of the inquiry if the defendant makes an insufficient showing on one. In particular, a court need not determine whether counsel's performance was deficient before examining the prejudice suffered by the defendant as a result of the alleged deficiencies. The object of an ineffectiveness claim is not to grade counsel's performance. If it is easier to dispose of an ineffectiveness claim on the ground of lack of sufficient prejudice, which we expect will often be so, that course should be followed. Courts should strive to ensure that ineffectiveness claims not become so burdensome to defense counsel that the entire criminal justice system suffers as a result.

The principles governing ineffectiveness claims should apply in federal collateral proceedings as they do on direct appeal or in motions for a new trial. As indicated by the "cause and prejudice" test for overcoming procedural waivers of claims of error, the presumption that a criminal judgment is final is at its strongest in collateral attacks on that judgment. An ineffectiveness claim, however, as our articulation of the standards that govern decision of such claims makes clear, is an attack on the fundamental fairness of the proceeding whose result is challenged. Since fundamental fairness is the central concern of the writ of habeas corpus, no special standards ought to apply to ineffectiveness claims made in habeas proceedings.

Finally, in a federal habeas challenge to a state criminal judgment, a state court conclusion that counsel rendered effective assistance is not a finding of fact binding on the federal court to the extent stated by 28 U.S.C. § 2254(d). Ineffectiveness is not a question of "basic, primary, or historical fac[t]." Rather, like the question whether multiple representation in a particular case gave rise to a conflict of interest, it is a mixed question of law and fact. Although state court findings of fact made in the course of deciding an ineffectiveness claim are subject to the deference requirement of § 2254(d), and although district court findings are subject to the clearly erroneous standard of Federal Rule of Civil Procedure 52(a), both the performance and prejudice components of the ineffectiveness inquiry are mixed questions of law and fact.

V

Having articulated general standards for judging ineffectiveness claims, we think it useful to apply those standards to the facts of this case in order to illustrate the meaning of the general principles. The record makes it possible to do so. There are no conflicts between the state and federal courts over findings of fact, and the principles we have articulated are sufficiently close to the principles applied both in the Florida courts and in the District Court that it is clear that the factfinding was not affected by erroneous legal principles.

Application of the governing principles is not difficult in this case. The facts as described above, make clear that the conduct of respondent's counsel at and before respondent's sentencing proceeding cannot be found unreasonable. They also make clear that, even assuming the challenged conduct of counsel was unreasonable, respondent suffered insufficient prejudice to warrant setting aside his death sentence.

With respect to the performance component, the record shows that respondent's counsel made a strategic choice to argue for the extreme emotional distress mitigating circumstance and to rely as fully as possible on respondent's acceptance of responsibility for his crimes. Although counsel understandably felt hopeless about respondent's prospects, nothing in the record indicates, as one possible reading of the District Court's opinion suggests, that counsel's sense of hopelessness distorted his professional judgment. Counsel's strategy choice was well within the range of professionally reasonable judgments, and the decision not to seek more character or psychological evidence than was already in hand was likewise reasonable.

The trial judge's views on the importance of owning up to one's crimes were well known to counsel. The aggravating circumstances were utterly overwhelming. Trial counsel could reasonably surmise from his conversations with respondent that character and psychological evidence would be of little help. Respondent had already been able to mention at the plea colloquy the substance of what there was to know about his financial and emotional troubles. Restricting testimony on respondent's character to what had come in at the plea colloquy ensured that contrary character and psychological evidence and respondent's criminal history, which counsel had successfully moved to exclude, would not come in. On these facts, there can be little question, even without application of the presumption of adequate performance, that trial counsel's defense, though unsuccessful, was the result of reasonable professional judgment.

With respect to the prejudice component, the lack of merit of respondent's claim is even more stark. The evidence that respondent says his trial counsel should have offered at the sentencing hearing would barely have altered the sentencing profile presented to the sentencing judge. As the state courts and District Court found, at most this evidence shows that numerous people who knew respondent thought he was generally a good person and that a psychiatrist and a psychologist believed he was under considerable emotional stress that did not rise to the level of extreme disturbance. Given the overwhelming aggravating factors, there is no reasonable probability that the omitted evidence would have changed the conclusion that the aggravating circumstances outweighed the mitigating circumstances and, hence, the sentence imposed. Indeed, admission of the evidence respondent now offers might even have been harmful to his case: his "rap sheet" would probably have been admitted into evidence, and the psychological reports would have directly contradicted respondent's claim that the mitigating circumstance of extreme emotional disturbance applied to his case.

Our conclusions on both the prejudice and performance components of the ineffectiveness inquiry do not depend on the trial judge's testimony at the District Court hearing. We therefore need not consider the general admissibility of that testimony, although that testimony is irrelevant to the prejudice inquiry. Moreover, the prejudice question is resolvable, and hence the ineffectiveness claim can be rejected, without regard to the evidence presented at the District Court hearing. The state courts properly concluded that the ineffectiveness claim was meritless without holding an evidentiary hearing.

Failure to make the required showing of either deficient performance or sufficient prejudice defeats the ineffectiveness claim. Here there is a double failure. More generally, respondent has made no showing that the justice of his sentence was rendered unreliable by a breakdown in the adversary process caused by deficiencies in counsel's assistance. Respondent's sentencing proceeding was not fundamentally unfair.

We conclude, therefore, that the District Court properly declined to issue a writ of habeas corpus. The judgment of the Court of Appeals is accordingly.

Reversed.

Justice BRENNAN, concurring in part and dissenting in part.

I join the Court's opinion but dissent from its judgment. Adhering to my view that the death penalty is in all circumstances cruel and unusual punishment forbidden by the Eighth and Fourteenth Amendments, I would vacate respondent's death sentence and remand the case for further proceedings.

I

This case and United States v. Cronic present our first occasions to elaborate the appropriate standards for judging claims of ineffective assistance of counsel. In Cronic, the Court considers such claims in the context of cases "in which the surrounding circumstances [make] it so unlikely that any lawyer could provide effective assistance that ineffectiveness [is] properly presumed without inquiry into actual performance at trial." This case, in contrast, concerns claims of ineffective assistance based on allegations of specific errors by counsel—claims which, by their very nature, require courts to evaluate both the attorney's performance and the effect of that performance on the reliability and fairness of the proceeding. Accordingly, a defendant making a claim of this kind must show not only that his lawyer's performance was inadequate but also that he was prejudiced thereby.

I join the Court's opinion because I believe that the standards it sets out today will both provide helpful guidance to courts considering claims of actual ineffectiveness of counsel and also permit those courts to continue their efforts to achieve progressive development of this area of the law. Like all federal courts and most state courts that have previously addressed the matter, the Court concludes that "the proper standard for attorney performance is that of reasonably effective assistance." And, rejecting the strict "outcome-determinative" test employed by some courts, the Court adopts as the appropriate standard for prejudice a requirement that the defendant "show that there is a reasonable probability that, but for counsel's unprofessional errors, the result of the proceeding would have been different," defining a "reasonable probability" as "a probability sufficient to undermine confidence in the outcome." I believe these standards are sufficiently precise to permit meaningful distinctions between those attorney derelictions that deprive defendants of their constitutional rights and those that do not; at the same time, the standards are sufficiently flexible to accommodate the wide variety of situations giving rise to claims of this kind.

With respect to the performance standard, I agree with the Court's conclusion that a "particular set of detailed rules for counsel's conduct" would be inappropriate. Precisely because the standard of "reasonably effective assistance" adopted today requires that counsel's performance be measured in light of the particular circumstances of the case, I do not believe our decision "will stunt the development of constitutional doctrine in this area," post, at 2076 (Marshall, J., dissenting). Indeed, the Court's suggestion that today's decision is largely consistent with the approach taken by the lower courts, simply indicates that those courts may continue to develop governing principles on a case-by-case basis in the common-law tradition, as they have in the past. Similarly, the prejudice standard announced today does not erect an insurmountable obstacle to meritorious claims, but rather simply requires courts carefully to examine trial records in light of both the nature and seriousness of counsel's errors and their effect in the particular circumstances of the case.

II

Because of their flexibility and the requirement that they be considered in light of the particular circumstances of the case, the standards announced today can and should be applied with concern for the special considerations that must attend review of counsel's performance in a capital sentencing proceeding. In contrast to a case in which a finding of ineffective assistance requires a new trial, a conclusion that counsel was ineffective with respect to only the penalty phase of a capital trial imposes on the State the far lesser burden of reconsideration of the sentence alone. On the other hand, the consequences to the defendant of incompetent assistance at a capital sentencing could not, of course, be greater. Recognizing the unique seriousness of such a proceeding, we have repeatedly emphasized that "'where discretion is afforded a sentencing body on a matter so grave as the determination of whether a human life should be taken or spared, that discretion must be suitably directed and limited so as to minimize the risk of wholly arbitrary and capricious action.'"

For that reason, we have consistently required that capital proceedings be policed at all stages by an especially vigilant concern for procedural fairness and for the accuracy of factfinding. As Justice Marshall emphasized last Term:

"This Court has always insisted that the need for procedural safeguards is particularly great where life is at stake. Long before the Court established the right to counsel in all felony cases, it recognized that right in capital cases. Time and again the Court has condemned procedures in capital cases that might be completely acceptable in an ordinary case.

"Because of th[e] basic difference between the death penalty and all other punishments, this Court has consistently recognized that there is 'a corresponding difference in the need for reliability in the determination that death is the appropriate punishment in a specific case.'"

In short, this Court has taken special care to minimize the possibility that death sentences are "imposed out of whim, passion, prejudice, or mistake."

In the sentencing phase of a capital case, "[w]hat is essential is that the jury have before it all possible relevant information about the individual defendant whose fate it must determine." For that reason, we have repeatedly insisted that "the sentencer in capital cases must be permitted to consider any relevant mitigating factor." In fact, as Justice O'Connor has noted, a sentencing judge's failure to consider relevant aspects of a defendant's character and background creates such an unacceptable risk that the death penalty was unconstitutionally imposed that, even in cases where the matter was not raised below, the "interests of justice" may impose on reviewing courts "a duty to remand [the] case for resentencing."

Of course, "[t]he right to present, and to have the sentencer consider, any and all mitigating evidence means little if defense counsel fails to look for mitigating evidence or fails to present a case in mitigation at the capital sentencing hearing." Accordingly, counsel's general duty to investigate takes on supreme importance to a defendant in the context of developing mitigating evidence to present to a judge or jury considering the sentence of death; claims of ineffective assistance in the performance of that duty should therefore be considered with commensurate care.

That the Court rejects the ineffective-assistance claim in this case should not, of course, be understood to reflect any diminution in commitment to the principle that "'the fundamental respect for humanity underlying the Eighth Amendment . . . requires consideration of the character and record of the individual offender and the circumstances of the particular offense as a constitutionally indispensable part of the process of inflicting the penalty of death.'" I am satisfied that the standards announced today will go far towards assisting lower federal courts and state courts in discharging their constitutional duty to ensure that every criminal defendant receives the effective assistance of counsel guaranteed by the Sixth Amendment.

Justice MARSHALL, dissenting.

The Sixth and Fourteenth Amendments guarantee a person accused of a crime the right to the aid of a lawyer in preparing and presenting his defense. It has long been settled that "the right to counsel is the right to the effective assistance. The state and lower federal courts have developed standards for distinguishing effective from inadequate assistance. Today, for the first time, this Court attempts to synthesize and clarify those standards. For the most part, the majority's efforts are unhelpful. Neither of its two principal holdings seems to me likely to improve the adjudication of Sixth Amendment claims. And, in its zeal to survey comprehensively this field of doctrine, the majority makes many other generalizations and suggestions that I find unacceptable. Most importantly, the majority fails to take adequate account of the fact that the locus of this case is a capital sentencing proceeding. Accordingly, I join neither the Court's opinion nor its judgment.

I

The opinion of the Court revolves around two holdings. First, the majority ties the constitutional minima of attorney performance to a simple "standard of reasonableness." Second, the majority holds that only an error of counsel that has sufficient impact on a trial to "undermine confidence in the outcome" is grounds for overturning a conviction. I disagree with both of these rulings.

A

My objection to the performance standard adopted by the Court is that it is so malleable that, in practice, it will either have no grip at all or will yield excessive variation in the manner in which the Sixth Amendment is interpreted and applied by different courts. To tell lawyers and the lower courts that counsel for a criminal defendant must behave "reasonably" and must act like "a reasonably competent attorney" is to tell them almost nothing. In essence, the majority has instructed judges called upon to assess claims of ineffective assistance of counsel to advert to their own intuitions regarding what constitutes "professional" representation, and has discouraged them from trying to develop more detailed standards governing the performance of defense counsel. In my view, the Court has thereby not only abdicated its own responsibility to interpret the Constitution, but also impaired the ability of the lower courts to exercise theirs.

The debilitating ambiguity of an "objective standard of reasonableness" in this context is illustrated by the majority's failure to address important issues concerning the quality of representation mandated by the Constitution. It is an unfortunate but undeniable fact that a person of means, by selecting a lawyer and paying him enough to ensure he prepares thoroughly, usually can obtain better representation than that available to an indigent defendant, who must rely on appointed counsel, who, in turn, has limited time and resources to devote to a given case. Is a "reasonably competent attorney" a reasonably competent adequately paid retained lawyer or a reasonably competent appointed attorney? It is also a fact that the quality of representation available to ordinary defendants in different parts of the country varies significantly. Should the standard of performance mandated by the Sixth Amendment vary by locale? The majority offers no clues as to the proper responses to these questions.

The majority defends its refusal to adopt more specific standards primarily on the ground that "[n]o particular set of detailed rules for counsel's conduct can satisfactorily take account of the variety of circumstances faced by defense counsel or the range of legitimate decisions regarding how best to represent a criminal defendant." I agree that counsel must be afforded "wide latitude" when making "tactical decisions" regarding trial strategy, but many aspects of the job of a criminal defense attorney are more amenable to judicial oversight. For example, much of the work involved in preparing for a trial, applying for bail, conferring with one's client, making timely objections to significant, arguably erroneous rulings of the trial judge, and filing a notice of appeal if there are colorable grounds therefor could profitably be made the subject of uniform standards.

The opinion of the Court of Appeals in this case represents one sound attempt to develop particularized standards designed to ensure that all defendants receive effective legal assistance. By refusing to address the merits of these proposals, and indeed suggesting that no such effort is worthwhile, the opinion of the Court, I fear, will stunt the development of constitutional doctrine in this area.

B

I object to the prejudice standard adopted by the Court for two independent reasons. First, it is often very difficult to tell whether a defendant convicted after a trial in which he was ineffectively represented would have fared better if his lawyer had been competent. Seemingly impregnable cases can sometimes be dismantled by good defense counsel. On the basis of a cold record, it may be impossible for a reviewing court confidently to ascertain how the government's evidence and arguments would have stood up against rebuttal and cross-examination by a shrewd, well-prepared lawyer. The difficulties of estimating prejudice after the fact are exacerbated by the possibility that evidence of injury to the defendant may be missing from the record precisely because of the incompetence of defense counsel. In view of all these impediments to a fair evaluation of the probability that the outcome of a trial was affected by ineffectiveness of counsel, it seems to me senseless to impose on a defendant whose lawyer has been shown to have been incompetent the burden of demonstrating prejudice.

Second and more fundamentally, the assumption on which the Court's holding rests is that the only purpose of the constitutional guarantee of effective assistance of counsel is to reduce the chance that innocent persons will be convicted. In my view, the guarantee also functions to ensure that convictions are obtained only through fundamentally fair procedures. The majority contends that the Sixth Amendment is not violated when a manifestly guilty defendant is convicted after a trial in which he was represented by a manifestly ineffective attorney. I cannot agree. Every defendant is entitled to a trial in which his interests are vigorously and conscientiously advocated by an able lawyer. A proceeding in which the defendant does not receive meaningful assistance in meeting the forces of the State does not, in my opinion, constitute due process.

In *Chapman v. California*, 386 U.S. 18, 23 (1967), we acknowledged that certain constitutional rights are "so basic to a fair trial that their infraction can never be treated as harmless error." Among these rights is the right to the assistance of counsel at trial. In my view, the right to effective assistance of counsel is entailed by the right to counsel, and abridgment of the former is equivalent to abridgment of the latter. I would thus hold that a showing that the performance of a defendant's lawyer departed from constitutionally prescribed standards requires a new trial regardless of whether the defendant suffered demonstrable prejudice thereby.

II

Even if I were inclined to join the majority's two central holdings, I could not abide the manner in which the majority elaborates upon its rulings. Particularly regrettable are the majority's discussion of the "presumption" of reasonableness to be accorded lawyers' decisions and its attempt to prejudge the merits of claims previously rejected by lower courts using different legal standards.

A

In defining the standard of attorney performance required by the Constitution, the majority appropriately notes that many problems confronting criminal defense attorneys admit of "a range of legitimate" responses. And the majority properly cautions courts, when reviewing a lawyer's selection amongst a set of options, to avoid the hubris of hindsight. The majority goes on, however, to suggest that reviewing courts should "indulge a strong presumption that counsel's conduct" was constitutionally acceptable, and should "appl[y] a heavy measure of deference to counsel's judgments."

I am not sure what these phrases mean, and I doubt that they will be self-explanatory to lower courts. If they denote nothing more than that a defendant claiming he was denied effective assistance of counsel has the burden of proof, I would agree. But the adjectives "strong" and "heavy" might be read as imposing upon defendants an unusually weighty burden of persuasion. If that is the majority's intent, I must respectfully dissent. The range of acceptable behavior defined by "prevailing professional norms," seems to me sufficiently broad to allow defense counsel the flexibility they need in responding to novel problems of trial strategy. To afford attorneys more latitude, by "strongly presuming" that their behavior will fall within the zone of reasonableness, is covertly to legitimate convictions and sentences obtained on the basis of incompetent conduct by defense counsel.

The only justification the majority itself provides for its proposed presumption is that undue receptivity to claims of ineffective assistance of counsel would encourage too many defendants to raise such claims and thereby would clog the courts with frivolous suits and "dampen the ardor" of defense counsel. I have more confidence than the majority in the ability of state and federal courts expeditiously to dispose of meritless arguments and to ensure that responsible, innovative lawyering is not inhibited. In my view, little will be gained and much may be lost by instructing the lower courts to proceed on the assumption that a defendant's challenge to his lawyer's performance will be insubstantial.

B

For many years the lower courts have been debating the meaning of "effective" assistance of counsel. Different courts have developed different standards. On the issue of the level of performance required by the Constitution, some courts have adopted the forgiving "farce-and-mockery" standard, while others have adopted various versions of the "reasonable competence" standard. On the issue of the level of prejudice necessary to compel a new trial, the courts have taken a wide variety of positions ranging from the stringent "outcome-determinative" test to the rule that a showing of incompetence on the part of defense counsel automatically requires reversal of the conviction regardless of the injury to the defendant.

The Court today substantially resolves these disputes. The majority holds that the Constitution is violated when defense counsel's representation falls below the level expected of reasonably competent defense counsel, and so affects the trial that there is a "reasonable probability" that, absent counsel's error, the outcome would have been different.

Curiously, though, the Court discounts the significance of its rulings, suggesting that its choice of standards matters little and that few if any cases would have been decided differently if the lower courts had always applied the tests announced today. Surely the judges in the state and lower federal courts will be surprised to learn that the distinctions they have so fiercely debated for many years are in fact unimportant.

The majority's comments on this point seem to be prompted principally by a reluctance to acknowledge that today's decision will require a reassessment of many previously rejected ineffective-assistance-of-counsel claims. The majority's unhappiness on this score is understandable, but its efforts to mitigate the perceived problem will be ineffectual. Nothing the majority says can relieve lower courts that hitherto have been using standards more tolerant of ineffectual advocacy of their obligation to scrutinize all claims, old as well as new, under the principles laid down today.

III

The majority suggests that, "[f]or purposes of describing counsel's duties," a capital sentencing proceeding "need not be distinguished from an ordinary trial." I cannot agree.

The Court has repeatedly acknowledged that the Constitution requires stricter adherence to procedural safeguards in a capital case than in other cases.

"[T]he penalty of death is qualitatively different from a sentence of imprisonment, however long. Death, in its finality, differs more from life imprisonment than a 100–year prison term differs from one of only a year or two. Because of that qualitative difference, there is a corresponding difference in the need for reliability in the determination that death is the appropriate punishment in a specific case."

The performance of defense counsel is a crucial component of the system of protections designed to ensure that capital punishment is administered with some degree of rationality. "Reliability" in the imposition of the death sentence can be approximated only if the sentencer is fully informed of "all possible relevant information about the individual defendant whose fate it must determine." The job of amassing that information and presenting it in an organized and persuasive manner to the sentencer is entrusted principally to the defendant's lawyer. The importance to the process of counsel's efforts, combined with the severity and irrevocability of the sanction at stake, require that the standards for determining what constitutes "effective assistance" be applied especially stringently in capital sentencing proceedings.

It matters little whether strict scrutiny of a claim that ineffectiveness of counsel resulted in a death sentence is achieved through modification of the Sixth Amendment standards or through especially careful application of those standards. Justice Brennan suggests that the necessary adjustment of the level of performance required of counsel in capital sentencing proceedings can be effected simply by construing the phrase, "reasonableness under prevailing professional norms," in a manner that takes into account the nature of the impending penalty. Though I would prefer a more specific iteration of counsel's duties in this special context, I can accept that proposal. However, when instructing lower courts regarding the probability of impact upon the outcome that requires a resentencing, I think the Court would do best explicitly to modify the legal standard itself. In my view, a person on death row, whose counsel's performance fell below constitutionally acceptable levels, should not be compelled to demonstrate a "reasonable probability" that he would have been given a life sentence if his lawyer had been competent; if the defendant can establish a significant chance that the outcome would have been different, he surely should be entitled to a redetermination of his fate.

IV

The views expressed in the preceding section oblige me to dissent from the majority's disposition of the case before us. It is undisputed that respondent's trial counsel made virtually no investigation of the possibility of obtaining testimony from respondent's relatives, friends, or former employers pertaining to respondent's character or background. Had counsel done so, he would have found several persons willing and able to testify that, in their experience, respondent was a responsible, non-violent man, devoted to his family, and active in the affairs of his church. Respondent contends that his lawyer could have and should have used that testimony to "humanize" respondent, to counteract the impression conveyed by the trial that he was little more than a cold-blooded killer. Had this evidence been admitted, respondent argues, his chances of obtaining a life sentence would have been significantly better.

Measured against the standards outlined above, respondent's contentions are substantial. Experienced members of the death-penalty bar have long recognized the crucial importance of adducing evidence at a sentencing proceeding that establishes the defendant's social and familial connections. The State makes a colorable—though in my view not compelling—argument that defense counsel in this case might have made a reasonable "strategic" decision not to present such evidence at the sentencing hearing on the assumption that an unadorned acknowledgment of respondent's responsibility for his crimes would be more likely to appeal to the trial judge, who was reputed to respect persons who accepted responsibility for their actions. But however justifiable such a choice might have been after counsel had fairly assessed the potential strength of the mitigating evidence available to him, counsel's failure to make any significant effort to find out what evidence might be garnered from respondent's relatives and acquaintances surely cannot be described as "reasonable." Counsel's failure to investigate is particularly suspicious in light of his candid admission that respondent's confessions and conduct in the course of the trial gave him a feeling of "hopelessness" regarding the possibility of saving respondent's life.

That the aggravating circumstances implicated by respondent's criminal conduct were substantial does not vitiate respondent's constitutional claim; judges and juries in cases involving behavior at least as egregious have shown mercy, particularly when afforded an opportunity to see other facets of the defendant's personality and life. Nor is respondent's contention defeated by the possibility that the material his counsel turned up might not have been sufficient to establish a statutory mitigating circumstance under Florida law; Florida sentencing judges and the Florida Supreme Court sometimes refuse to impose death sentences in cases "in which, even though statutory mitigating circumstances do not outweigh statutory aggravating circumstances, the addition of nonstatutory mitigating circumstances tips the scales in favor of life imprisonment."

If counsel had investigated the availability of mitigating evidence, he might well have decided to present some such material at the hearing. If he had done so, there is a significant chance that respondent would have been given a life sentence. In my view, those possibilities, conjoined with the unreasonableness of counsel's failure to investigate, are more than sufficient to establish a violation of the Sixth Amendment and to entitle respondent to a new sentencing proceeding.

I respectfully dissent.

32

The Right to Defense Counsel—Interrogations

Key Concepts

- "Deliberate Elicitation" of Statements Is Required, Which Is Not Synonymous With "Custodial Interrogation"
- The Sixth Amendment Right to Counsel Is Offense-Specific
- Even If Statements Are Taken in Violation of the Sixth Amendment Right To Counsel, They May Be Used as Impeachment Evidence

A. Introduction and Policy. As you have read, defendants enjoy a right to counsel under the Sixth Amendment. Up to now, we have discussed this right in the context of actual trial proceedings. However, the Supreme Court has held that this right applies beyond those events that occur inside the walls of a courtroom before the judge; it also applies to all "critical stages" of the process. Pre-trial interrogations are one of these "critical stages." The extension of this right to interrogations was seen as necessary to ensure the robust viability of the right to counsel in later stages of the case. As the Court has said, due process envisions "an indictment . . . followed by a trial, 'in an orderly courtroom, presided over by a judge, open to the public, and protected by all the procedural safeguards of the law.'"[1] If these procedural safeguards, which include the right to counsel, are to be truly effective, then the Constitution must also ensure the aid of counsel for "an indicted defendant under interrogation by the police in a completely extrajudicial proceeding."[2]

It is important to distinguish between *Miranda*'s right to counsel, discussed in **Chapter 26**, and the Sixth Amendment right to counsel during interrogations, which is discussed here. The *Miranda* right finds its footing in the Fifth Amendment's ban on compelled statements. The Sixth Amendment right to counsel during interrogations, in contrast, is grounded in the concern that the defendant should not be deprived of "effective representation by counsel at the only stage when legal aid and advice would help him."[3] As a result, while the Sixth Amendment right to counsel during interrogations shares a number of characteristics

---

[1] Massiah v. United States, 377 U.S. 201, 204 (1964).

[2] Id.

[3] Kansas v. Ventris, 556 U.S. 586, 591 (2009).

with the *Miranda* right, it also differs in significant respects. We will point out these differences as we move through the chapter, and provide a summary chart at the end to review these differences.

B. The Law. Like the *Miranda* rules, the rules governing the right to counsel at interrogation have been developed and refined by the Supreme Court over the past few decades. The right was first established in 1964, and it was given its broadest and strongest interpretation in the mid-1980s. However, since that high-water mark, the Court has interpreted the rule more restrictively.

The right to counsel does not attach in interrogations until:

1. The adversarial process has been initiated (that is, the defendant must be formally charged); and
2. The police are "deliberately eliciting" the statements.

Any statements taken in violation of the right may not be used during State's case-in-chief, but they may be used as impeachment evidence.

In order to invoke the right to counsel, the suspect must clearly assert the right. Once the right has been invoked it may not be waived in counsel's absence unless the suspect initiates communication.

The right to counsel is offense-specific; that is, if the defendant is only charged with one crime, the right to counsel will not exist with regard to other, as-yet uncharged crimes.

As you read in **Chapter 30**, the Sixth Amendment right to counsel attaches once "the adversary judicial process has been initiated."[4] The adversarial process begins once the defendant has been formally charged with an offense; therefore, the accused has the right to the presence of counsel at interrogations only after he has been formally charged with an offense. If the government deliberately elicits statements from a charged defendant in the absence of counsel, the Sixth Amendment is transgressed and evidence regarding the charged offenses will not be admissible at trial.

However, notwithstanding the general rule that formal charges must have been initiated, the Court has identified one very narrow set of circumstances involving interrogations in which the right to counsel attached even though the suspect had not yet been charged. That case, *Escobedo v. Illinois*, involved a young man suspected of murdering his brother-in-law. Acknowledging that Escobedo had not

[4] Montejo v. Louisiana, 556 U.S. 778, 786 (2009).

been charged with murder at the time of his questioning, the Court nonetheless found his Sixth Amendment right to counsel was violated. In the Court's view,

> [once] the investigation is no longer a general inquiry into an unsolved crime but has begun to focus on a particular suspect, the suspect has been taken into police custody, the police carry out a process of interrogations that lends itself to eliciting incriminating statements, the suspect has requested and been denied an opportunity to consult with his lawyer, and the police have not effectively warned him of his absolute constitutional right to remain silent, the accused has been denied 'The Assistance of Counsel' in violation of the Sixth Amendment to the Constitution as 'made obligatory upon the States by the Fourteenth Amendment and . . . no statement elicited by the police during the interrogation may be used against him at a criminal trial.[5]

The *Escobedo* rule has not been extended beyond the particular facts presented in that case. It is possible that the Court's willingness to extend the right to counsel to Escobedo even though he had not been charged was a reaction to the extreme police conduct in that case. An attorney who represented Escobedo came to the police station and repeatedly asked to speak with his client. For more than three hours the police continuously refused the attorney access to Escobedo, until finally at 1:00 in the morning he gave up and went home. During this same period, Escobedo asked the police on several occasions if he could speak with his lawyer. His requests were similarly rebuffed. The Court also was careful to note that the police were determined to get Escobedo to talk, as he was by that time the prime suspect in the case: "Petitioner had become the accused, and the purpose of the interrogation was to 'get him' to confess his guilt despite his constitutional right not to do so."[6] Barring such extreme circumstances, however, the Court has been faithful to its general maxim that a Sixth Amendment right to counsel does not attach until formal charges have been brought.

Unlike the Fifth Amendment right to counsel, a Sixth Amendment violation is not dependent on the suspect being in custody nor is it dependent upon there being an actual interrogation. All that matters is that the defendant has been charged and that the police are deliberately eliciting information from the defendant. Indeed, the suspect need not even be aware of the police involvement. For example, if the police use a cellmate or other informant to deliberately elicit information from the accused that too will constitute a violation of the Sixth Amendment.[7] While deliberate elicitation is not the same as interrogation, some action beyond "mere listening" is required.[8]

---

[5] Escobedo v. Illinois, 378 U.S. 478, 490-91 (1964).

[6] Id. at 485.

[7] Maine v. Moulton, 474 U.S. 159 (1985).

[8] Kuhlmann v. Wilson, 477 U.S. 436, 459 (1986).

The Sixth Amendment right to counsel attaches only to those offenses that have been formally charged. For all other offenses, the accused may enjoy a Fifth Amendment right to counsel, but will not enjoy a Sixth Amendment right to counsel until charges are brought. Indeed, the offense-specific nature of the Sixth Amendment right has been read so restrictively that it does not even encompass charges that are "closely related factually" to the charged offense.

For example, assume Danny Derelict breaks into a home that appears vacant. As he is rifling through the silverware cabinet, the homeowner startles him and Derelict hits him in the head with a heavy candlestick killing the homeowner instantly. Derelict then quickly stashes the body in the attic and resumes his progress through the house, loading everything he can carry into an empty pillowcase. The burglary is soon discovered by neighbors and Derelict, who was observed leaving the scene, is charged. However, because the homeowner's body has not been found and he travels a great deal for work, his absence does not immediately trigger suspicion. Derelict is indicted only for burglary. Under these circumstances, the Sixth Amendment right to counsel would govern any police attempts to deliberately elicit information regarding the burglary. However, it would not limit police questioning regarding the murder, even though the murder is "closely related factually" to the break in.[9]

In addition, the Sixth Amendment right to counsel during interrogations is not self-executing. The accused must actually invoke the right. Thus, it will not be enough that the accused asked for or was appointed a lawyer **at arraignment**. Instead, at the time of interrogation, the accused must clearly assert her right to counsel.[10] If the right is clearly asserted, all questioning must cease and counsel must be present before questioning can resume. These are the same rules that apply in the context of the Fifth Amendment and *Miranda*.

Finally, the Court has held that the Sixth Amendment violation occurs not at the time the statement is admitted at trial, but instead at the time the uncounseled gathering of information happens. Consequently, while the Constitution prohibits the use of statements taken in violation of the Sixth Amendment right to counsel as direct evidence, there is no similar ban on their use as impeachment. Statements taken in violation of an accused's Sixth Amendment right to counsel may be used to impeach any defendant who takes the stand and testifies, assuming his testimony conflicts with the statements he previously made.[11]

---

[9] Moulton, 474 U.S. at 180 n.16.

[10] Montejo v. Louisiana, 556 U.S. 778, 789 (2009).

[11] Kansas v. Ventris, 556 U.S. 586 (2009).

C. Applying the Law.

1. Recognizing Pre-Trial Interrogation as a "Critical Stage" of Trial. As noted in **Chapter 30,** in 1963 the Supreme Court recognized that the Sixth Amendment right to counsel applied to all criminal defendants; attached once the adversarial process was initiated; and extended to all "critical stages" of trial. The next year, in the landmark case of *Massiah v. United States*, the Court further concluded that pre-trial interrogations are a critical stage to which the right to counsel attaches:

> **Example—*Massiah v. United States*, 337 U.S. 201 (1964):** Winston Massiah was a merchant seaman on board the S.S. Santa Maria. He was a member of the crew of a ship that was sailing from South America to the United States. Customs agents in New York received a tip that Massiah was transporting drugs on the ship. Accordingly, when the Santa Maria docked in New York, custom agents boarded, searched it and found three pounds of cocaine. They also received other information that connected the drugs to Massiah.
>
> Thereafter, Massiah was arrested, arraigned and indicted for possessing narcotics aboard a United States vessel. A second man, Colson, was eventually indicted along with Massiah. Massiah obtained counsel and was released on bail.
>
> Unknown to Massiah, several days after their release, Colson decided to cooperate with the police. In particular, he agreed to allow police officers to install a radio transmitter under the seat of his car. One evening prior to trial, Colson and Massiah engaged in a conversation in Colson's car. The entire conversation was monitored by a police officer on the other end of the transmitter. During this conversation, Massiah said several things that suggested his guilt in connection with the drug charges.
>
> At trial, and over the objection of defense counsel, Massiah's statements to Colson were admitted at his trial. Massiah was convicted. After an unsuccessful appeal, the Supreme Court agreed to hear Massiah's claim. Massiah alleged that the use of his statements violated his Sixth Amendment right to counsel.

Analysis: Massiah was correct. The Sixth Amendment guarantees an accused the right to counsel once adversarial proceedings have begun. However, while the assistance of counsel at the actual trial is critical, the aid of a lawyer prior to that point is essential as well. "[F]rom the time of their arraignment until the beginning of their trial, when consultation, thorough-going investigation and preparation are vitally important . . . defendants are as much entitled to such aid of counsel during that period as at the trial itself."[12]

Massiah's Sixth Amendment right to counsel was violated because the police deliberately elicited statements from him after his indictment and in the absence of counsel. The Court found it irrelevant that Massiah was not aware that the police were questioning him (through Colson), or that he was not in custody but was free on bail. In light of the Sixth Amendment violation, Massiah's statements should not have been used as direct evidence against him.

Having determined that the right to counsel attached to pre-trial interrogations, the Court then set about defining the precise contours of that right. In the years following *Massiah*, the Court addressed questions like: whether the right must be affirmatively invoked, whether the right prohibits only actual questioning, and whether statements taken in violation of the right can be introduced into evidence for reasons other than direct evidence of the accused's guilt.

2. Invocation and Waiver of the Right. What, if anything, must an accused do to invoke the right to counsel? If a lawyer has been previously appointed, will that be sufficient to invoke the Sixth Amendment right to counsel during an interrogation? Does the defendant invoke the right if he asked for an attorney during a preliminary hearing? And will a valid waiver of one's *Miranda* rights also constitute waiver of the Sixth Amendment right to counsel, or is something more needed? The Court confronted these questions in a capital murder case arising out of Louisiana and found that the same rules it developed in the context of *Miranda*'s Fifth Amendment protections apply in the context of the Sixth Amendment:

> **Example—*Montejo v. Louisiana*, 556 U.S. 778 (2009):** Lewis Ferrari owned a dry cleaning business. In 2002, he was found dead in his home. Moore, a former employee of the business who had a troubled relationship with Ferrari, was almost immediately suspected of the murder. Jesse Montejo, a known affiliate of Moore's, was brought in for questioning.
>
> After the police gave Montejo the appropriate *Miranda* warnings, he waived his rights and agreed to speak. During the interrogation, Montejo eventually confessed that he and Moore killed Ferrari during a bungled attempt to burglarize his home. Montejo also admitted to discarding the murder weapon in a nearby lake. Three days after the interrogation, in accordance with state law,

[12] Powell v. Alabama, 287 U.S. 45, 57 (1932).

Montejo was brought before a judge for a preliminary hearing where he was advised of the pending first degree murder charges. At the hearing, the court ordered that counsel be appointed to represent Montejo.

After the hearing, two detectives went to see Montejo in jail. They asked him to take them to the lake where he had tossed the gun. They again read Montejo his *Miranda* rights, after which he agreed to accompany them. During the trip, he wrote out an apology to Ferrari's widow. When Montejo and the officers returned from the trip, Montejo met defense counsel for the first time.

At trial, defense counsel moved to suppress the apology note. Counsel argued that the apology was obtained in violation of Montejo's Sixth Amendment right to counsel. To support this contention, counsel pointed to the Supreme Court's decision in *Michigan v. Jackson*,[13] which held that a defendant's request for counsel at arraignment should be treated as an invocation of the right to counsel at every future critical stage—thus barring subsequent police-initiated questioning in the absence of counsel. Defense counsel argued that the *Jackson* decision should also be understood to bar interrogation of defendants, like Montejo, for whom counsel had been assigned at a preliminary hearing. In response, the State urged a much narrower reading of *Jackson* and suggested that it stood only for the proposition that interrogation was prohibited when defendants affirmatively requested counsel at their preliminary hearing, not when (as in this case) the defendant had simply been appointed counsel by the court.

The trial court agreed with the State and denied the motion. Montejo was ultimately convicted and sentenced to death.

The Supreme Court then took the case to determine which interpretation of *Jackson* was more appropriate and to decide whether Montejo's apology letter was properly admitted.

Analysis: The Court not only rejected both interpretations of *Jackson*, but also overruled that decision. The Court then identified a new legal framework for evaluating a claim that police-initiated interrogation violated a suspect's Sixth Amendment rights. Specifically, the Court determined that the rules created in

[13] 475 U.S. 625 (1986) (overruled by Montejo v. Louisiana, 556 U.S. 778 (2009)).

the context of the Fifth Amendment and *Miranda* sufficiently protect a suspect's Sixth Amendment rights as well.

Under these rules, the accused must affirmatively invoke the right to counsel. Once the right is invoked, questioning must cease until counsel is made available, unless the suspect initiates contact. If the accused does not invoke the right, he may waive it without regard for whether he is represented; and the waiver may be valid even if it is not preceded by consultation with counsel. The State must prove only that the "relinquishment of the right is voluntary, knowing, and intelligent."[14] When an accused is given *Miranda* warnings and thereafter waives his rights that waiver will typically be sufficient to waive the Sixth Amendment right to counsel as well.

Turning to the case before it, the Supreme Court first confirmed that the Sixth Amendment guarantees an accused the right to counsel once adversarial proceedings begin. However, the Court refused to find that the appointment of counsel at the arraignment was relevant to the question of invocation or the question of waiver. With regard to invocation, the Court found that the appointment of counsel was insufficient to invoke Montejo's rights in connection with the custodial interrogation. With regard to waiver, the Court declined to presume that Montejo's waiver of his right to counsel at the interrogation was invalid simply because he had been previously assigned an attorney. Instead, the Court held that the assessment of Montejo's Sixth Amendment right to counsel in the interrogation context should focus on "what happens when the defendant is approached for interrogation, and (if he consents) what happens during the interrogation—not what happened at any preliminary hearing."[15]

The appropriate question, therefore, was whether Montejo "made a clear assertion of the right to counsel when the officers approached him about accompanying them on the excursion for the murder weapon."[16] If Montejo made such an assertion, all questioning should have ceased and further interrogation of Montejo would be impermissible until counsel was present. However, if Montejo did not make such an assertion, his waiver only needed to be voluntary, knowing, and intelligent to be valid. The case was remanded to the lower court to make findings on these issues.

As Montejo makes clear, the question of when the Sixth Amendment right to counsel comes into existence and when it has been invoked are separate inquiries. The right comes into existence upon the initiation of the adversary process. To invoke the right, however, the defendant must affirmatively indicate that he wants counsel's assistance.

---

[14] Montejo v. Louisiana, 556 U.S. 778, 786 (2009).

[15] Id. at 797.

[16] Id.

Absent invocation, the inquiry turns to examine whether the defendant validly waived his rights. Valid waiver requires knowing and intelligent action on the part of the defendant. But, the provision of *Miranda* warnings will suffice to adequately inform the accused and automatically make any subsequent waiver "knowing and intelligent." In the Court's view, "an accused who is admonished with the warnings prescribed by this Court in *Miranda*, has been sufficiently apprised of the nature of his Sixth Amendment rights, and of the consequences of abandoning those rights so that his waiver on this basis will be considered a knowing and intelligent one."[17]

3. Deliberate Elicitation of Statements Is Required. What constitutes "deliberate elicitation" of a statement? If the police sit in a room with an indicted inmate while she launches into an unsolicited rant about the crime, are they "deliberately eliciting statements? What if the police talk to the suspect, but don't directly ask him any questions? The Court answered these questions in the 1977 case of *Brewer v. Williams* (a case we discussed in **Chapter 23** in the context of the inevitable discovery exception to the exclusionary rule):

> **Example—*Brewer v. Williams* ("*Williams I*"), 430 U.S. 387 (1977):** One Christmas Eve, a 10-year-old girl accompanied her family to a wrestling tournament at the local YMCA in Des Moines, Iowa. She went to the bathroom and never returned. Robert Williams was a resident at the YMCA who had recently escaped from a mental institution. Attendees at the wrestling event saw Williams in the lobby shortly after the girl's disappearance with clothes and a blanket covering a large bundle. A teenager who helped Williams into his car reported that he saw two "skinny and white" legs protruding from the blanket as Williams loaded it into the car. Williams's car was found the next day about 160 miles east of Des Moines.
>
> The day after Williams's car was found, a lawyer in Des Moines contacted the police and advised them that Williams was going to turn himself in at the police station in the neighboring town of Davenport. After Williams surrendered, he spoke by telephone with his lawyer who was still at the Des Moines police station. Within the hearing of the detectives, the attorney explained that two detectives from Des Moines were coming to pick Williams up to transport him. The attorney also told Williams that the detectives were not going to interrogate him, and that he should not talk

[17] Patterson v. Illinois, 487 U.S. 285 (1988).

to them about the little girl until after he returned to Des Moines and talked to counsel.

Williams was arraigned in Davenport. He spoke with another attorney there, Kelly, who confirmed that Williams should not make any statements until he met with counsel in Des Moines. The attorney Kelly also reminded the detectives when they arrived that Williams was not to be asked about the little girl's disappearance until he arrived in Des Moines and had a chance to talk to counsel there. Kelly asked to accompany Williams on the drive to Des Moines, but the detectives refused his request.

During the approximately three-hour trip, Williams said several times to the officers "when I get to Des Moines and see Mr. McKnight, I am going to tell you the whole story."[18] Not long into the drive, however, one of the detectives delivered a speech often referred to as the "Christian burial" speech. In this speech, the detective commented on the weather and the likelihood that Williams would be unable to find the location where he had dumped the girl's body if it snowed. The detective also talked about how nice it would be if the girl's parents could give her a Christian burial to ease some of their pain. The detective ended by telling Williams, "I do not want you to answer me. I don't want to discuss it any further. Just think about it as we're riding down the road."[19]

Thereafter, Williams directed the police to the location of the little girl's body. At trial, Williams sought to exclude his statements, arguing that they had been taken in violation of his Sixth Amendment right to counsel. The trial court determined that Williams waived his rights, and admitted the statements made in the car. Williams's conviction for murder eventually worked its way to the Supreme Court.

Analysis: Williams's Sixth Amendment right to counsel during interrogation was violated by the detective's conduct in the police car during the trip from Davenport to Des Moines.

There was no question that judicial proceedings had been initiated against Williams before he got into the car with the police to make the trip to Des Moines. Moreover, the detective in the case "deliberately and designedly set out to elicit

[18] Brewer v. Williams, 430 U.S. 387, 392 (1977).

[19] Id. at 393.

information from Williams just as surely as and perhaps more effectively than if he had formally interrogated him."[20] The Court also found that the record did not support a conclusion that Williams waived his right to counsel.

Even though Williams was not affirmatively questioned by the detective, the Court concluded that the case was "constitutionally indistinguishable" from *Massiah*. The Court found it irrelevant that the statements in *Massiah* had been collected secretly (through the use of a recording device and a cooperating co-defendant) but were collected overtly in Williams's case. Because the detective "proceeded to elicit incriminating statements from Williams" in the absence of counsel after judicial proceedings against him had been initiated, Williams's statements should have been suppressed.

On one end of the spectrum, the "deliberate elicitation" standard means that evidence will not be excluded simply because the right to counsel has attached—if the defendant freely chooses to talk to the police, or the police fortuitously acquire inculpatory statements from him, his right to counsel has not been violated.[21] On the other end of the spectrum, the "deliberate elicitation" standard can be met even if the police are not asking direct questions.

A pair of cases involving paid informants nicely illustrates what the Supreme Court means by "deliberate elicitation. In *United States v. Henry*, federal agents planted a paid jailhouse informant in the cell with Billy Gale Henry, who had been indicted for an armed bank robbery. The federal agents instructed the informant not to question Henry. Nonetheless, the informant engaged the defendant in conversations and "developed a relationship of trust and confidence with [Henry] such that [Henry] revealed incriminating information."[22] The Supreme Court held that the government informant "deliberately used his position to secure incriminating information from [the defendant] when counsel was not present."[23] Although the informant had not questioned the defendant, the informant had "stimulated" conversations with the defendant in order to "elicit" incriminating information.[24] Thus, "[b]y intentionally creating a situation likely to induce Henry to make incriminating statements without the assistance of counsel, the Government violated Henry's Sixth Amendment right to counsel."[25]

A few years later, the Court considered a similar case in which police officers placed a paid informant in a cell with Joseph Wilson, who had just been arraigned

---

[20] Id. at 399.

[21] Maine v. Moulton, 474 U.S. 159, 176 (1985).

[22] United States v. Henry, 447 U.S. 264, 269 (1980).

[23] Id. at 270.

[24] Id. at 273.

[25] Id. at 274.

on charges that he robbed a taxicab company. This time, the police told their informant not to ask any questions, but simply to "keep his ears open" in case Wilson made some incriminating statements.[26] The informant did not initiate any conversation at all, and did little more than listen as Wilson gave details about the robbery. The Supreme Court held that these statements were not "deliberately elicited" because "the defendant must demonstrate that the police and their informant took some action, beyond merely listening, that was designed deliberately to elicit incriminating remarks."[27] As Chief Justice Burger said in his concurring opinion: "There is a vast difference between placing an 'ear' in the suspect's cell and placing a voice in the cell to encourage conversation for the 'ear' to record."[28] Finally in 2004, the Court expressly affirmed that there can be "deliberate elicitation" even in the absence of actual interrogation:

> **Example—*Fellers v. United States*, 540 U.S. 519 (2004):** John Fellers was indicted for conspiring to distribute methamphetamine. Local police officers arrested Fellers at his house pursuant to a warrant. The officers told Fellers he had been indicted along with four other people. They also told Fellers they were there to talk to him about his role in the scheme. After the officers named the four others who had been indicted, Fellers admitted knowing them and said he had used methamphetamine with them in the past.
>
> After about fifteen minutes, the officers took Fellers to the local jail. At the jail, he was given *Miranda* warnings for the first time. He signed a waiver and again confirmed that he knew the four others associated with the methamphetamine ring. He also admitted that he suspected a woman in the group was involved in drug sales but had loaned her money anyway.
>
> At trial, Fellers move to suppress the statements he made at his house and the statements he made at the jailhouse. The trial court agreed to suppress the unwarned statements made at Fellers's home. However, the court refused to suppress the statements made at the jailhouse. Fellers was subsequently convicted.
>
> On appeal, Fellers argued that the statements made at the jailhouse were the inadmissible fruit of the uncounseled statements he made at his house. The appellate court disagreed. That court found there was no need to provide Fellers with warnings at his

[26] Kuhlmann v. Wilson, 477 U.S. 436, 439 (1986).

[27] Id. at 459.

[28] Id. at 461 (Burger, C.J., concurring).

house because the police officers had not "interrogated" him. Because the court found the first statements were not improper, it further concluded the second round of statements did not need to be suppressed as fruit. The Supreme Court took the case to decide whether the statements Fellers made at his home were illegally obtained, and whether the subsequent statements should have been suppressed as the fruit of the initial illegality.

Analysis: Fellers' uncounseled statements at his home were properly suppressed because the police "deliberately elicited" statements from Fellers after his Sixth Amendment right to counsel attached.

Describing the "deliberate elicitation" standard in somewhat greater detail than it had previously, the Court noted that the officers "upon arriving at [Fellers'] house, informed him that their purpose in coming was to discuss his involvement in the distribution of methamphetamine and his association with certain charged co-conspirators."[29] The Court found it irrelevant that this conduct at the house could not be characterized as an interrogation. The Fifth Amendment custodial interrogation standard, the Court noted, had been "expressly distinguished" from the Sixth Amendment's "deliberate elicitation" requirement.

Because the police deliberately elicited information from Fellers, the statements he made at this house were properly suppressed.

As you will note from the above discussion, the Court in *Fellers* failed to reach the second question in the case—whether the statements taken after *Miranda* warnings at the jailhouse should have been suppressed as the fruit of the uncounseled statements taken at Fellers's house in violation of his Sixth Amendment rights. The Court acknowledged that it had not yet determined whether "the fruits of previous questioning conducted in violation of the Sixth Amendment deliberate-elicitation standard" had to be suppressed along with the initial statements. Yet, instead of resolving the question, the Court remanded the case to the Eighth Circuit for it to decide.

On remand, the Eighth Circuit determined that suppression of the jailhouse statements was not required. In that court's view, the jailhouse statements followed full and complete *Miranda* warnings, which Fellers validly waived. Moreover, the court found the police had not used the improper questioning conducted at Fellers's house to extract additional statements from him at the jailhouse. In particular, the court found that "the exclusionary rule is inapplicable in Fellers's case because, as with the Fifth Amendment in *Elstad,* the use of the exclusionary

[29] Fellers v. United States, 540 U.S. 519, 524 (2004).

rule in this case would serve neither deterrence nor any other goal of the Sixth Amendment."[30]

The Supreme Court is not likely to conclusively resolve this question until a decided circuit split develops. For now, the best that can be said is that a statement taken subsequent to a violation of the Sixth Amendment may be admissible at trial if, as in *Fellers*, the second statement was insulated by appropriate *Miranda* warnings and the two-step process does not appear to be a deliberate strategy on the part of the police.

4. The Sixth Amendment Right Is Offense Specific. As you read in **Chapter 26**, before the police subject a suspect to custodial interrogation, they must provide the suspect with *Miranda* warnings if they hope to use the product of the interrogation as direct evidence of guilt. If the suspect invokes her *Miranda* right to counsel, the police must end *all* questioning until counsel is provided. However, the Sixth Amendment right is not equally expansive. Even if a suspect invokes his Sixth Amendment right to counsel with regard to one crime, the police are not prohibited from asking about other crimes.

> **Example—*McNeil v. Wisconsin*, 501 U.S. 171 (1991):** Paul McNeil was arrested and charged with an armed robbery in West Allis, Wisconsin. McNeil was arraigned, and counsel from the local public defender's office represented McNeil at the hearing.
>
> Two days later, a detective and two police officers visited McNeil in jail to question him about an unrelated murder investigation in Caledonia. The detective read McNeil *Miranda* warnings. McNeil agreed to waive his rights. He then described his involvement in the Caledonia offense in detail and claimed that two men, Willie Pope and Lloyd Crowley, helped him with the crime. Two days later the detective and officers returned and again gave McNeil *Miranda* warnings. They confronted McNeil with their belief that Pope was not involved. McNeil then admitted that he mentioned Pope in an attempt to deflect attention from himself. McNeil wrote out another statement again detailing the events of the crime, but this time omitting any mention of Pope's alleged involvement.
>
> The next day, McNeil was arraigned for murder and other charges in connection with the Caledonia offense. He moved to suppress his statements. He maintained that his appearance with counsel in

[30] United States v. Fellers, 397 F.3d 1090, 1095 (8th Cir. 2005), abrogated on other grounds by United States v. Thorpe, 447 F.3d 565 (8th Cir. 2006).

connection with the West Allis crimes constituted invocation of his right to counsel, and therefore voided the subsequent statements about the Caledonia crime that were elicited in the absence of counsel. The trial judge ruled that although McNeil's original appearance with counsel in the West Allis case may have constituted an invocation of his right to counsel for the West Allis case, his right to counsel for the Caledonia case had not yet attached and thus could not be invoked until he was arraigned later for the Caledonia offense. [You should note that this case pre-dated the *Montejo* case, described in Section C.2 above. Prior to *Montejo* the law provided that an appearance with counsel at arraignment was sufficient to invoke the defendant's Sixth Amendment right to counsel. Counsel's argument and the trial court's ruling in *McNeil* were, thus, based on that pre-*Montejo* rule]. McNeil appealed, and the case worked its way to the Supreme Court.

Analysis: McNeil's uncounseled statements in connection with the Caledonia offense, which were taken after the provision and valid waiver of *Miranda* warnings, were properly admitted.

The Sixth Amendment right to counsel does not attach until prosecution for a particular crime has begun. The right is offense-specific. The initiation of a prosecution on one set of charges does not trigger the attachment of the right for other uncharged conduct. Consequently, if incriminating statements are made about offenses for which the right has not yet attached admission of those statements is not precluded by the Sixth Amendment.

McNeil had been charged with the West Allis offense and therefore his Sixth Amendment right to counsel in connection with that offense attached. If McNeil chose to invoke that right to counsel, police questioning about the armed robbery would have been prohibited. But the police did not question McNeil about the West Allis armed robbery; they questioned him about the Caledonia murder. The Sixth Amendment right to counsel in the Caledonia case had not yet attached and indeed would not attach until after McNeil was charged with the murder.

It is of course true that if McNeil had invoked his *Miranda* right to counsel when the police first approached him about the Caledonia case the police could not then have re-initiated questioning in the absence of counsel. However, McNeil expressly waived his *Miranda* rights each time he was questioned in connection with the Caledonia murder. The *Miranda* right, which he waived, was the only right to counsel he possessed related to the murder charge. Because attachment of McNeil's offense-specific Sixth Amendment right did not also trigger attachment or invocation of McNeil's offense-neutral *Miranda* rights, McNeil's waiver was valid and his statements were properly admitted.

The armed robbery and murder offenses at issue in *McNeil* were wholly unrelated. Beyond the fact that McNeil was suspected in connection with both crimes, there was no relationship between the Caledonia murder and the West Allis armed robbery. Application of the offense-specific Sixth Amendment right is perhaps easy to analyze in this context.

But the Court has also held that the same rule applies even if the uncharged offense is very, very similar to the charged offense or is factually a part of the same course of conduct as the charged offense. In other words, even if there is a strong factual similarity between the charged and uncharged offenses, the police are not precluded from deliberately eliciting information about the uncharged offense.

> **Example—*Texas v. Cobb*, 532 U.S. 162 (2001):** Lindsey Owings lived in Walker County, Texas, with his wife and sixteen-month old daughter. One evening, Owings called the police to report that his home had been burglarized and his wife and daughter were missing. The police received an anonymous tip implicating Owings' neighbor, Raymond Levi Cobb, in the crime.
>
> A few months later, Cobb was arrested for an unrelated crime, and he confessed to the burglary of the Owings' home. Cobb was charged with the burglary and counsel was appointed to represent Cobb in connection with that charge.
>
> Three months later, Cobb was released on bond for the burglary charge and went to live with his father. Cobb's father contacted the police and told them Cobb admitted to him that he killed Mrs. Owings during the burglary. After his father provided a written statement, Cobb was arrested and read his *Miranda* rights; however, counsel was not consulted. Cobb waived his rights and provided a full confession to the murder of Owings' wife and daughter.
>
> According to Cobb, Mrs. Owings confronted him in the home as he was attempting to take a stereo, and so he fatally stabbed her. He also killed the young daughter and buried them both in a wooded area behind the house. At the police officer's request, Cobb led the officers to the site, where they found both bodies.
>
> Cobb was charged and convicted of capital murder. On appeal, Cobb argued that his confession to the murders should have been suppressed because it was taken in violation of his Sixth

Amendment right to counsel. The appellate court in Texas reversed Cobb's conviction finding that because of the close factual relationship between the burglary charge and the murder charge, Cobb's Sixth Amendment rights attached on the murder charge even though he had not yet been charged with that offense. The State then appealed.

Analysis: The Court meant what it said in *McNeil*—the Sixth Amendment right to counsel is offense-specific. Therefore, the questioning of Cobb about the murder did not violate his Sixth Amendment rights.

An accused person's rights under the Sixth Amendment do not attach until a prosecution has begun. Accordingly, the rights conferred by that amendment relate only to charged conduct.

Certainly, a crime is not necessarily "limited to the four corners of a charging instrument."[31] Consequently it is possible that a later charged crime might be subsumed in charged conduct for Sixth Amendment purposes. However, in deciding whether two offenses are "the same," courts should look to the *Blockburger* test, which asks "whether each provision requires proof of a fact which the other does not."[32] This is the same test that is used for purposes of double jeopardy. [See **Chapter 46** for more detail on the *Blockburger* test].

Applying the *Blockburger* test to Cobb's case makes it clear that his Sixth Amendment right to counsel for the murder charge had not yet attached at the time of questioning. The crime of capital murder and the crime of burglary are not the same under Texas law for each requires proof of a fact that the other does not. Burglary under Texas law requires entry into a building while capital murder requires the murder of more than one person during a single course of criminal conduct. Because the two offenses are not the same under the *Blockburger* test the attachment of Cobb's Sixth Amendment rights for one offense (burglary) did not constitute the attachment of those rights for the other (murder). Cobb had not yet been charged with the murder of Mrs. Owings or her daughter. Therefore, the police questioning about those offenses was entirely permissible upon the provision and waiver of *Miranda*.

5. The Use of Statements as Impeachment Evidence. There is no question that statements taken in violation of a defendant's Sixth Amendment right to counsel may not be used as direct evidence of guilt during the prosecution's case-in-chief. However, the Court has been less restrictive when it comes to the use of such statements for impeachment. This is, in part, because of the Court's view that a violation of the Sixth Amendment occurs at the time the uncounseled interrogation happens, not at the time the statements are introduced at trial:

---

31 Texas v. Cobb, 532 U.S. 162, 173 (2001).

32 Blockburger v. United States, 284 U.S. 299, 304 (1932).

Example—*Kansas v. Ventris,* 556 U.S. 586 (2009): Donnie Ray Ventris and his friend Rhonda Theel went on a two-day drug binge during which they got no sleep. During this period, Ventris and Theel resolved to confront a neighbor, Ernest Hicks, about rumors that he abused children.

During the confrontation, Hicks was shot and killed. It was not clear whether Ventris or Theel or both were responsible for the shooting. After the killing, the two left the scene in Hicks's pickup truck with about $300 in stolen cash and Hicks's cell phone. A friend of Ventris and Theel's tipped the police off and the two were arrested.

Prior to trial, Theel struck a deal with the prosecution. In exchange for her guilty plea to robbery and her testimony identifying Ventris as the shooter, the prosecution agreed to drop the murder charge against her. The government then focused its investigation on Ventris, who had been indicted on counts of felony murder, aggravated robbery, aggravated burglary and misdemeanor theft in connection with the Hicks killing.

Police officers planted an informant in Ventris's holding cell and told him to listen for any incriminating statements Ventris might make. Thereafter, the informant told Ventris that he seemed to have "something more serious weighing in on his mind."[33] In response, Ventris confessed to shooting "this man in his head and his chest" and robbing him.

Ventris took the stand at trial in his own defense. He testified that Theel was entirely responsible for the shooting. The government then introduced the testimony of the informant to impeach Ventris's trial testimony. Ventris was acquitted of the murder count, but was convicted of the aggravated burglary and robbery charges. On appeal, Ventris challenged the admission of the informant's testimony as a violation of his Sixth Amendment right to counsel.

Analysis: The use of Ventris's uncounseled statements as impeachment evidence was entirely permissible.

Some violations of the Constitution demand exclusion of the evidence at trial. For example, the Fifth Amendment is violated when evidence taken in violation of its

[33] Kansas v. Ventris, 556 U.S. 586, 589 (2009).

terms is introduced. Therefore, involuntary statements must be excluded for all purposes. Violations of the Sixth Amendment are not, however, such violations.

The Sixth Amendment right to counsel is primarily concerned with affording defendants "the opportunity . . . to consult with an attorney and to have him investigate the case and prepare a defense for trial."[34] To the extent that right includes interrogations, the amendment is violated when a suspect is denied the assistance of counsel at the interrogation, not at some later point. "It is illogical to say that the right is not violated until trial counsel's task of opposing conviction has been undermined by the statement's admission into evidence."[35]

Because the admission of the evidence did not itself constitute the constitutional violation, the Court then turned to assess the relative value of excluding the evidence. Weighing the cost of admission against the cost of exclusion, the Court concluded that exclusion would provide the accused with both a sword and a shield. Noting that it had allowed unconstitutionally obtained evidence to be introduced as impeachment in other contexts, the Court therefore found that such admission was also proper in Ventris's case.

The *Ventris* Court's conclusion that admission of the evidence was appropriate was primarily driven by its conclusion that the constitutional violation in the case arose at the time of the uncounseled interrogation, not at the point of the admission of the evidence. However, the decision was also driven, at least in part, by the Court's continuing dissatisfaction with the remedy of exclusion (see **Chapter 23**). When balancing the relative cost of excluding the evidence, the Court concluded that "the game of excluding tainted evidence for impeachment purposes is not worth the candle."[36]

6. *Miranda* v. Sixth Amendment Right to Counsel. As we have noted throughout the chapter, the contours of the Sixth Amendment right to counsel during interrogation are slightly different from those of the *Miranda* right. Obviously, the government must comply with both sets of rules when eliciting information from the defendant.

The chart below provides a brief summary of the similarities and differences between the *Miranda* right to counsel and the Sixth Amendment right to counsel during interrogations:

[34] Michigan v. Harvey, 494 U.S. 344, 348 (1990).

[35] Kansas v. Ventris, 556 U.S. 586, 592 (2009).

[36] Id.

Miranda **Right to Counsel**	**Sixth Amendment Right to Counsel**
Suspect must be "in custody"	Adversarial process must have been initiated
Suspect must be "interrogated"	Police must "deliberately elicit" statements
Statements taken in violation of right may not be used in State's case-in-chief	Statements taken in violation of right may not be used during State's case-in-chief
Statements taken in violation of right may be used as impeachment	Statements taken in violation of the right may be used as impeachment
Right is **not** offense-specific	Right **is** offense-specific
Suspect must clearly invoke right	Suspect must clearly invoke right
Once invoked, right may not be waived in counsel's absence unless 1) suspect initiates communication or 2) there is a 14-day break in custody	Once invoked, right may not be waived in counsel's absence unless suspect initiates communications
Fruit of unwarned statements is admissible	Fruit of Sixth Amendment violation may be admissible

Quick Summary

One of the critical stages at which the Sixth Amendment right to counsel attaches is pre-trial interrogations. If the police deliberately elicit information from the accused after the adversarial process has begun, the Sixth Amendment right to counsel will be implicated. Deliberate elicitation requires some action on the part of the government beyond mere listening.

Statements taken during post-indictment questioning in violation of the accused's Sixth Amendment right to counsel may not be used as direct evidence of guilt during the prosecution's case in chief. However, such statements may be used to impeach the defendant at trial.

Unlike the Fifth Amendment right to counsel, the Sixth Amendment right requires neither custody nor interrogation. An awareness of police presence is also not required for the right to attach.

Also unlike the Fifth Amendment right to counsel, the Sixth Amendment right is offense-specific. It attaches only to those charges for which the accusatory process has commenced. In determining whether two offenses should be treated the same for purposes of the Sixth Amendment right, courts should use the same test that is used to assess "sameness" for double jeopardy purposes—the *Blockburger* test.

The Sixth Amendment right to counsel during interrogations is not self-executing. The accused must actually invoke the right. At the time of interrogation, the accused must clearly assert her right to counsel. If the right is clearly asserted, all questioning must cease and counsel must be present before questioning can resume.

On the other hand, if the accused does not invoke her rights, her waiver of them must be only voluntary, knowing and intelligent. If an accused is provided with *Miranda* warnings, and thereafter waives her right to counsel, such waiver will be valid for purpose of both the Fifth and Sixth Amendments.

Review Questions

1. The Homeless Murder. Nineteen-year old Tyreese Hall had an IQ of 65 and could only read at a second grade level. Very early one morning, Hall was out with his cousin and his uncle. The three came upon a homeless man in an alley. The uncle beat and robbed the man, and Hall and his cousin participated marginally. The man, who was horrifically assaulted, slipped into a coma and fifty-three days later died of his injuries. Shortly after the crime was committed and before the victim died, another homeless man who witnessed the beating identified Hall as one of the assailants. Hall was arrested on assault charges and brought in for questioning.

Detective Williamson, who interviewed Hall at the station, read *Miranda* warnings to Hall. Williamson also had Hall initial and sign a waiver of rights form. Hall at first denied any knowledge of the crime. But, after the detective encouraged Hall to "be a man," and "take his part in this," Hall described the beating in detail. Hall confessed to kicking and punching the homeless man because his uncle had done so. Hall also said he begged his uncle to stop hitting the homeless man but didn't actually stop him because he was "scared shitless" of his uncle. The interrogation took about an hour. After Hall's confession, the detective bought him a soda and some potato chips because Hall had not eaten all day.

While Hall was awaiting trial on the assault charge, the victim died. Hall then called Detective Williamson and said he had more things he "needed to tell" Williamson about the crime. Hall was brought to the police station. Williamson did not re-read the *Miranda* warnings, but did remind Hall that he had previously heard the warnings. Williamson also advised Hall that a murder indictment would be handed down shortly in light of the victim's death. Williamson asked Hall if he was still "waiving his rights." Hall indicated that he was. Hall then gave a fuller accounting of the crime, including a clearer description of his cousin's role in the offense and a more detailed accounting of his uncle's actions.

Prior to trial, Hall moved to suppress both statements he gave to Detective Williamson. How should the court rule?

2. One Fateful Delivery. Jesus Rojas lived with his mother and her boyfriend, Carlos Marcelo. Marcelo was a mid-level supplier in a larger cocaine distribution ring. One day, Marcelo asked Rojas to deliver a package containing a kilogram of cocaine to a client. Rojas agreed. This one delivery was Rojas's only involvement in the broader drug operation. A short time later, the government secured an indictment charging all those involved, including Rojas, with conspiracy and other drug offenses. Arrest warrants were issued. Rojas, who had financial resources, hired an experienced criminal defense attorney to represent him. Counsel arranged with the government for Rojas's self-surrender on the outstanding arrest warrant. Rojas's attorney did not, however, accompany him to the station. After Rojas was processed, DEA agents who were working the case interviewed him. Rojas signed a *Miranda* waiver form and gave a written and videotaped statement to the agents detailing his role in the single delivery. After a motion to suppress was denied, Rojas was convicted and sentenced to five years in prison. On appeal, Rojas challenged the admission of his written statement. Will he be successful?

3. Obstruction of Justice. Michael Jacques devised a scheme to sexually abuse J.P., a nine-year old girl. Using a series of email messages from a fake criminal organization he called Breckenridge, Jacques convinced J.P. that the organization would kill her family and pets if she did not have sex with him. Jacques's sexual abuse of J.P. continued for some five years. At one point after her fourteenth birthday, J.P. received an email from Breckenridge indicating that a 12-year-old girl named Brooke had been marked for termination. J.P. was told to invite Brooke to a party to facilitate the murder. J.P. did as she was told and when Brooke accepted, Jacques and J.P. drove to pick Brooke up. Brooke's body was found several days later. She had been drugged, raped and murdered. Eventually, the police connected Jacques to the messages from Breckenridge. He was arrested and charged in one indictment with sexually assaulting J.P. He was charged in a second indictment with the kidnapping and murder of Brooke.

While Jacques was awaiting trial on the two sets of charges, he wrote a letter to his friend Michael Garcia. Jacques asked Garcia to "help" him but said he couldn't explain exactly what he needed over the prison line because it was recorded. Garcia, unbeknownst to Jacques, immediately contacted the FBI. Over the course of the next several weeks, agents recorded all of Garcia's subsequent phone calls and meetings with Jacques. The agents instructed Garcia not to ask Jacques anything about the sexual assault, murder or kidnapping charges—an instruction that Garcia mainly adhered to though at one point he asked Jacques about an unrelated sexual assault from many years ago.

During an initial phone call, Jacques solicited Garcia's help with convincing J.P. to lie to authorities about Jacques's responsibility for her multiple rapes and Brooke's rape and murder. Garcia agreed to help Jacques. Accordingly, over the course of several phone calls and prison visits Jacques told Garcia exactly what he needed him to do. In particular, Jacques asked Garcia to deliver a message to J.P. informing her that the "bad guys" were still out there. He also mailed an instruction packet to Garcia in which he described the steps that J.P. should be instructed to take, including telling the authorities and Jacques's wife that he was innocent. The instruction packet also included suggestions on ways Garcia could avoid being connected to the messages to J.P., like using computers at internet cafes and public libraries.

Jacques was subsequently charged with obstruction of justice. At trial, all of his recorded statements to Garcia and the instruction packet that he sent were introduced during the prosecution's case-in-chief. On appeal, Jacques maintained that the evidence should have been excluded because it was taken in violation of his Sixth Amendment right to counsel. Is he correct?

4. **Keeping Your Friends Close.** Rodney Williamson was indicted on cocaine conspiracy charges. Williamson was unaware of the charges, however, because the December 18, 2006 indictment was sealed. In January of 2007, the police sent a confidential informant out to talk with Williamson about the drug ring. The informant was wearing a wire and the entire conversation was recorded. A short time later, Williamson was arrested. At trial, the government offered a transcript of Williamson's conversation with the informant. The conversation included Williamson's repeated references to the sale and transportation of various weights of drugs. Williamson moved to exclude the transcript. Will he succeed?

FROM THE COURTROOM

MASSIAH v. UNITED STATES

United States Supreme Court, 1964
337 U.S. 201

[Justice STEWART delivered the opinion of the Court.]

[Justice WHITE filed a dissenting opinion, in which Justice CLARK and HARLAN joined.]

. . .

The petitioner, a merchant seaman, was in 1958 a member of the crew of the S. S. Santa Maria. In April of that year federal customs officials in New York received information that he was going to transport a quantity of narcotics aboard that ship from South America to the United States. As a result of this and other information, the agents searched the Santa Maria upon its arrival in New York and found in the afterpeak of the vessel five packages containing about three and a half pounds of cocaine. They also learned of circumstances, not here relevant, tending to connect the petitioner with the cocaine. He was arrested, promptly arraigned, and subsequently indicted for possession of narcotics aboard a United States vessel. In July a superseding indictment was returned, charging the petitioner and a man named Colson with the same substantive offense, and in separate counts charging the petitioner, Colson, and others with having conspired to possess narcotics aboard a United States vessel, and to import, conceal, and facilitate the sale of narcotics. The petitioner, who had retained a lawyer, pleaded not guilty and was released on bail, along with Colson.

A few days later, and quite without the petitioner's knowledge, Colson decided to cooperate with the government agents in their continuing investigation of the narcotics activities in which the petitioner, Colson, and others had allegedly been engaged. Colson permitted an agent named Murphy to install a Schmidt radio transmitter under the front seat of Colson's automobile, by means of which Murphy, equipped with an appropriate receiving device, could overhear from some distance away conversations carried on in Colson's car.

On the evening of November 19, 1959, Colson and the petitioner held a lengthy conversation while sitting in Colson's automobile, parked on a New York street. By prearrangement with Colson, and totally unbeknown to the petitioner, the agent Murphy sat in a car parked out of sight down the street and listened over the radio to the entire conversation. The petitioner made several incriminating statements during the course of this conversation. At the petitioner's trial these incriminating statements were brought before the jury through Murphy's testimony, despite the insistent objection of defense counsel. The jury convicted the petitioner of several related narcotics offenses, and the convictions were affirmed by the Court of Appeals.

The petitioner argues that it was an error of constitutional dimensions to permit the agent Murphy at the trial to testify to the petitioner's incriminating statements which Murphy had overheard under the circumstances disclosed by this record. . . . [I]t is said that the petitioner's Fifth and Sixth Amendment rights were violated by the use in evidence against him of incriminating statements which government agents had deliberately elicited from him after he had been indicted and in the absence of his retained counsel. . . .

In *Spano v. New York*, 360 U.S. 315, this Court reversed a state criminal conviction because a confession had been wrongly admitted into evidence against the defendant at his trial. In that case the defendant had already been indicted for first-degree murder at the time he confessed. The Court held that the defendant's conviction could not stand under the Fourteenth Amendment. While the Court's opinion relied upon the totality of the circumstances under which the confession had been obtained, four concurring Justices pointed out that the Constitution required reversal of the conviction upon the sole and specific ground that the confession had been deliberately elicited by the police after the defendant had been indicted, and therefore at a time when he was clearly entitled to a lawyer's help. It was pointed out that under our system of justice the most elemental concepts of due process of law contemplate that an indictment be followed by a trial, 'in an orderly courtroom, presided over by a judge, open to the public, and protected by all the procedural safeguards of the law.' It was said that a Constitution which guarantees a defendant the aid of counsel at such a trial could surely vouchsafe no less to an indicted defendant under interrogation by the police in a completely extrajudicial proceeding. Anything less, it was said, might deny a defendant 'effective representation by counsel at the only stage when legal aid and advice would help him.'

Ever since this Court's decision in the Spano case, the New York courts have unequivocally followed this constitutional rule. 'Any secret interrogation of the defendant, from and after the finding of the indictment, without the protection afforded by the presence of counsel, contravenes the basic dictates of fairness in the conduct of criminal causes and the fundamental rights of persons charged with crime.'

This view no more than reflects a constitutional principle established as long ago as *Powell v. Alabama*, 287 U.S. 45, where the Court noted that '* * * during perhaps the most critical period of the proceedings * * * that is to say, from the time of their arraignment until the beginning of their trial, when consultation, thorough-going investigation and preparation (are) vitally important, the defendants * * * (are) as much entitled to such aid (of counsel) during that period as at the trial itself.' And since the *Spano* decision the same basic constitutional principle has been broadly reaffirmed by this Court. See *Gideon v. Wainwright*, 372 U.S. 335.

Here we deal not with a state court conviction, but with a federal case, where the specific guarantee of the Sixth Amendment directly applies. We hold that the petitioner was denied the basic protections of that guarantee when there was used against him at his trial evidence of his own incriminating words, which federal agents had deliberately elicited from him after he had been indicted and in the absence of his counsel. It is true that in the *Spano* case the defendant was interrogated in a police station, while here the damaging testimony was elicited from the defendant without his knowledge while he was free on bail. But, as Judge Hays pointed out in his dissent in the Court of Appeals, 'if such a rule is to have any efficacy it must apply to indirect and surreptitious interrogations as well as those conducted in the jailhouse. In this case, Massiah was more seriously imposed upon * * * because he did not even know that he was under interrogation by a government agent.'

The Solicitor General, in his brief and oral argument, has strenuously contended that the federal law enforcement agents had the right, if not indeed the duty, to continue their investigation of the petitioner and his alleged criminal associates even though the petitioner had been indicted. He points out that the Government was continuing its investigation in order to uncover not only the source of narcotics found on the S. S. Santa Maria, but also their intended buyer. He says that the quantity of narcotics involved was such as to suggest that the petitioner was part of a large and well-organized ring, and indeed that the continuing investigation confirmed this suspicion, since it resulted in criminal charges against many defendants. Under these circumstances the Solicitor General concludes that the Government agents were completely 'justified in making use of Colson's cooperation by having Colson continue his normal associations and by surveilling them.'

We may accept and, at least for present purposes, completely approve all that this argument implies, Fourth Amendment problems to one side. We do not question that in this case, as in many cases, it was entirely proper to continue an investigation of the suspected criminal activities of the defendant and his alleged confederates, even though the defendant had already been indicted. All that we hold is that the defendant's own incriminating statements, obtained by federal agents under the circumstances here disclosed, could not constitutionally be used by the prosecution as evidence against him at his trial.

Reversed.

[The dissenting opinion of Justice WHITE, which was joined by Justices CLARK and HARLAN has been omitted].

FROM THE COURTROOM

BREWER v. WILLIAMS

United States Supreme Court, 1977
430 U.S. 387

[Justice STEWART delivered the opinion of the Court.]

[Justices MARSHALL, POWELL and STEVENS filed separate concurring opinions].

[Chief Justice BURGER filed a dissenting opinion].

[Justice WHITE, filed a dissenting opinion, which was joined by Justices BLACKMUN and REHNQUIST].

[Justice BLACKMUN filed a dissenting opinion, which was joined by Justices WHITE and REHNQUIST].

I

On the afternoon of December 24, 1968, a 10-year-old girl named Pamela Powers went with her family to the YMCA in Des Moines, Iowa, to watch a wrestling tournament in which her brother was participating. When she failed to return from a trip to the washroom, a search for her began. The search was unsuccessful.

Robert Williams, who had recently escaped from a mental hospital, was a resident of the YMCA. Soon after the girl's disappearance Williams was seen in the YMCA lobby carrying some clothing and a large bundle wrapped in a blanket. He obtained help from a 14-year-old boy in opening the street door of the YMCA and the door to his automobile parked outside. When Williams placed the bundle in the front seat of his car the boy "saw two legs in it and they were skinny and white." Before anyone could see what was in the bundle Williams drove away. His abandoned car was found the following day in Davenport, Iowa, roughly 160 miles east of Des Moines. A warrant was then issued in Des Moines for his arrest on a charge of abduction.

On the morning of December 26, a Des Moines lawyer named Henry McKnight went to the Des Moines police station and informed the officers present that he had just received a long-distance call from Williams, and that he had advised Williams to turn himself in to the Davenport police. Williams did surrender that morning to the police in Davenport, and they booked him on the charge specified in the arrest warrant and gave him the warnings required by *Miranda v. Arizona*, 384 U.S. 436. The Davenport police then telephoned their counterparts in Des Moines to inform them that Williams had surrendered. McKnight, the lawyer, was still at the Des Moines police headquarters, and Williams conversed with McKnight on the telephone. In the presence of the Des Moines chief of police and a police detective named Leaming, McKnight advised Williams that Des Moines police officers would be driving to Davenport to pick him up, that the officers would not interrogate him or mistreat him, and that Williams was not to talk to the officers about Pamela Powers until after consulting with McKnight upon his return to Des Moines. As a result of these conversations, it was agreed between McKnight and the Des Moines police officials that Detective Leaming and a fellow officer would drive to Davenport to pick up Williams, that they would bring him directly back to Des Moines, and that they would not question him during the trip.

In the meantime Williams was arraigned before a judge in Davenport on the outstanding arrest warrant. The judge advised him of his Miranda rights and committed him to jail. Before leaving the courtroom, Williams conferred with a lawyer named Kelly, who advised him not to make any statements until consulting with McKnight back in Des Moines.

Detective Leaming and his fellow officer arrived in Davenport about noon to pick up Williams and return him to Des Moines. Soon after their arrival they met with Williams and Kelly, who, they understood, was acting as Williams' lawyer. Detective Leaming repeated the Miranda warnings, and told Williams:

"(W)e both know that you're being represented here by Mr. Kelly and you're being represented by Mr. McKnight in Des Moines, and . . . I want you to remember this because we'll be visiting between here and Des Moines."

Williams then conferred again with Kelly alone, and after this conference Kelly reiterated to Detective Leaming that Williams was not to be questioned about the disappearance of Pamela Powers until after he had consulted with McKnight back in Des Moines. When Leaming expressed some reservations, Kelly firmly stated that the agreement with McKnight was to be carried out that there was to be no interrogation of Williams during the automobile journey to Des Moines. Kelly was denied permission to ride in the police car back to Des Moines with Williams and the two officers.

The two detectives, with Williams in their charge, then set out on the 160-mile drive. At no time during the trip did Williams express a willingness to be interrogated in the absence of an attorney. Instead, he stated several times that "(w)hen I get to Des Moines and see Mr. McKnight, I am going to tell you the whole story." Detective Leaming knew that Williams was a former mental patient, and knew also that he was deeply religious.

The detective and his prisoner soon embarked on a wide-ranging conversation covering a variety of topics, including the subject of religion. Then, not long after leaving Davenport and reaching the interstate highway, Detective Leaming delivered what has been referred to in the briefs and oral arguments as the "Christian burial speech." Addressing Williams as "Reverend," the detective said:

"I want to give you something to think about while we're traveling down the road. . . . Number one, I want you to observe the weather conditions, it's raining, it's sleeting, it's freezing, driving is very treacherous, visibility is poor, it's going to be dark early this evening. They are predicting several inches of snow for tonight, and I feel that you yourself are the only person that knows where this little girl's body is, that you yourself have only been there once, and if you get a snow on top of it you yourself may be unable to find it. And, since we will be going right past the area on the way into Des Moines, I feel that we could stop and locate the body, that the parents of this little girl should be entitled to a Christian burial for the little girl who was snatched away from them on Christmas (E)ve and murdered. And I feel we should stop and locate it on the way in rather than waiting until morning and trying to come back out after a snow storm and possibly not being able to find it at all."

Williams asked Detective Leaming why he thought their route to Des Moines would be taking them past the girl's body, and Leaming responded that he knew the body was in the area of Mitchellville a town they would be passing on the way to Des Moines. Leaming then stated: "I do not want you to answer me. I don't want to discuss it any further. Just think about it as we're riding down the road."

As the car approached Grinnell, a town approximately 100 miles west of Davenport, Williams asked whether the police had found the victim's shoes. When Detective Leaming replied that he was unsure, Williams directed the officers to a service station where he said he had left the shoes; a search for them proved unsuccessful. As they continued towards Des Moines, Williams asked whether the police had found the blanket, and directed the officers to a rest area where he said he had disposed of the blanket. Nothing was found. The car continued towards Des Moines, and as it approached Mitchellville, Williams said that he would show the officers where the body was. He then directed the police to the body of Pamela Powers.

Williams was indicted for first-degree murder. Before trial, his counsel moved to suppress all evidence relating to or resulting from any statements Williams had made during the automobile ride from Davenport to Des Moines. After an evidentiary hearing the trial judge denied the motion. He found that "an agreement was made between defense counsel and the police officials to the effect that the Defendant was not to be questioned on the return trip to Des Moines," and that the evidence in question had been elicited from Williams during "a critical stage in the proceedings requiring the presence of counsel on his request." The judge ruled, however, that Williams had "waived his right to have an attorney present during the giving of such information."

The evidence in question was introduced over counsel's continuing objection at the subsequent trial. The jury found Williams guilty of murder, and the judgment of conviction was affirmed by the Iowa Supreme Court, a bare majority of whose members agreed with the trial court that Williams had 'waived his right to the presence of his counsel' on the automobile ride from Davenport to Des Moines. The four dissenting justices expressed the view that 'when counsel and police have agreed defendant is not to be questioned until counsel is present and defendant has been advised not to talk and repeatedly has stated he will tell the whole story after he talks with counsel, the state should be required to make a stronger showing of intentional voluntary waiver than was made here.'

Williams then petitioned for a writ of habeas corpus in the United States District Court for the Southern District of Iowa. . . . The District Court made findings of fact as summarized above, and concluded as a matter of law that the evidence in question had been wrongly admitted at Williams' trial. This conclusion was based on three alternative and independent grounds: (1) that Williams had been denied his constitutional right to the assistance of counsel; (2) that he had been denied the constitutional protections defined by this Court's decisions in *Escobedo v. Illinois*, 378 U.S. 478, and *Miranda v. Arizona*, 384 U.S. 436; and (3) that in any event, his self-incriminatory statements on the automobile trip from Davenport to Des Moines had been involuntarily made. Further, the District Court ruled that there had been no waiver by Williams of the constitutional protections in question.

The Court of Appeals for the Eighth Circuit, with one judge dissenting affirmed this judgment, and denied a petition for rehearing en banc. We granted certiorari to consider the constitutional issues presented.

II

. . .

B

As stated above, the District Court based its judgment in this case on three independent grounds. The Court of Appeals appears to have affirmed the judgment on two of those grounds. We have concluded that only one of them need be considered here.

Specifically, there is no need to review in this case the doctrine of *Miranda v. Arizona*, a doctrine designed to secure the constitutional privilege against compulsory self-incrimination. It is equally unnecessary to evaluate the ruling of the District Court that Williams' self-incriminating statements were, indeed, involuntarily made. For it is clear that the judgment before us must in any event be affirmed upon the ground that Williams was deprived of a different constitutional right the right to the assistance of counsel.

This right, guaranteed by the Sixth and Fourteenth Amendments, is indispensable to the fair administration of our adversary system of criminal justice. Its vital need at the pretrial stage has perhaps nowhere been more succinctly explained than in Mr. Justice Sutherland's memorable words for the Court 44 years ago in *Powell v. Alabama*, 287 U.S. 45]:

"(D)uring perhaps the most critical period of the proceedings against these defendants, that is to say, from the time of their arraignment until the beginning of their trial, when consultation, thorough-going investigation and preparation were vitally important, the defendants did not have the aid of counsel in any real sense, although they were as much entitled to such aid during that period as at the trial itself."

There has occasionally been a difference of opinion within the Court as to the peripheral scope of this constitutional right. But its basic contours, which are identical in state and federal contexts, are too well established to require extensive elaboration here. Whatever else it may mean, the right to counsel granted by the Sixth and Fourteenth Amendments means at least that a person is entitled to the help of a lawyer at or after the time that judicial proceedings have been initiated against him "whether by way of formal charge, preliminary hearing, indictment, information, or arraignment."

There can be no doubt in the present case that judicial proceedings had been initiated against Williams before the start of the automobile ride from Davenport to Des Moines. A warrant had been issued for his arrest, he had been arraigned on that warrant before a judge in a Davenport courtroom, and he had been committed by the court to confinement in jail. The State does not contend otherwise.

There can be no serious doubt, either, that Detective Leaming deliberately and designedly set out to elicit information from Williams just as surely as and perhaps more effectively than if he had formally interrogated him. Detective Leaming was fully aware before departing for Des Moines that Williams was being represented in Davenport by Kelly and in Des Moines by McKnight. Yet he purposely sought during Williams' isolation from his lawyers to obtain as much incriminating information as possible. Indeed, Detective Leaming conceded as much when he testified at Williams' trial:

"Q. In fact, Captain, whether he was a mental patient or not, you were trying to get all the information you could before he got to his lawyer, weren't you?

"A. I was sure hoping to find out where that little girl was, yes, sir.

"Q. Well, I'll put it this way: You was (sic) hoping to get all the information you could before Williams got back to McKnight, weren't you?"

"A. Yes, sir."[6]

The state courts clearly proceeded upon the hypothesis that Detective Leaming's 'Christian burial speech' had been tantamount to interrogation. Both courts recognized that Williams had been entitled to the assistance of counsel at the time he made the incriminating statements. Yet no such constitutional protection would have come into play if there had been no interrogation.

---

[6] Counsel for petitioner, in the course of oral argument in this Court, acknowledged that the "Christian burial speech" was tantamount to interrogation:
"Q: But isn't the point, really, Mr. Attorney General, what you indicated earlier, and that is that the officer wanted to elicit information from Williams
"A: Yes, sir.
"Q: by whatever techniques he used, I would suppose a lawyer would consider that he were pursuing interrogation.
"A: It is, but it was very brief."

The circumstances of this case are thus constitutionally indistinguishable from those presented in *Massiah v. United States*. The petitioner in that case was indicted for violating the federal narcotics law. He retained a lawyer, pleaded not guilty, and was released on bail. While he was free on bail a federal agent succeeded by surreptitious means in listening to incriminating statements made by him. Evidence of these statements was introduced against the petitioner at his trial, and he was convicted. This Court reversed the conviction, holding "that the petitioner was denied the basic protections of that guarantee (the right to counsel) when there was used against him at his trial evidence of his own incriminating words, which federal agents had deliberately elicited from him after he had been indicted and in the absence of his counsel."

That the incriminating statements were elicited surreptitiously in the *Massiah* case, and otherwise here, is constitutionally irrelevant. Rather, the clear rule of *Massiah* is that once adversary proceedings have commenced against an individual, he has a right to legal representation when the government interrogates him. It thus requires no wooden or technical application of the *Massiah* doctrine to conclude that Williams was entitled to the assistance of counsel guaranteed to him by the Sixth and Fourteenth Amendments.

III

The Iowa courts recognized that Williams had been denied the constitutional right to the assistance of counsel. They held, however, that he had waived that right during the course of the automobile trip from Davenport to Des Moines. The state trial court explained its determination of waiver as follows:

"The time element involved on the trip, the general circumstances of it, and more importantly the absence on the Defendant's part of any assertion of his right or desire not to give information absent the presence of his attorney, are the main foundations for the Court's conclusion that he voluntarily waived such right."

In its lengthy opinion affirming this determination, the Iowa Supreme Court applied "the totality-of-circumstances test for a showing of waiver of constitutionally-protected rights in the absence of an express waiver," and concluded that "evidence of the time element involved on the trip, the general circumstances of it, and the absence of any request or expressed desire for the aid of counsel before or at the time of giving information, were sufficient to sustain a conclusion that defendant did waive his constitutional rights as alleged."

In the federal habeas corpus proceeding the District Court, believing that the issue of waiver was not one of fact but of federal law, held that the Iowa courts had "applied the wrong constitutional standards" in ruling that Williams had waived the protections that were his under the Constitution. The court held "that it is the government which bears a heavy burden . . . but that is the burden which explicitly was placed on (Williams) by the state courts." After carefully reviewing the evidence, the District Court concluded:

"(U)nder the proper standards for determining waiver, there simply is no evidence to support a waiver. . . . (T)here is no affirmative indication . . . that (Williams) did waive his rights . . . (T)he state courts' emphasis on the absence of a demand for counsel was not only legally inappropriate, but factually unsupportable as well, since Detective Leaming himself testified that (Williams), on several occasions during the trip, indicated that he would talk after he saw Mr. McKnight. Both these statements and Mr. Kelly's statement to Detective Leaming that (Williams) would talk only after seeing Mr. McKnight in Des Moines certainly were assertions of (Williams') 'right or desire not to give information absent the presence of his attorney . . . .' Moreover, the statements were obtained only after Detective Leaming's use of psychology on a person whom he knew to be deeply religious and an escapee from a mental hospital with the specific intent to elicit incriminating statements. In the face of this evidence, the State has produced no affirmative evidence whatsoever to support its claim of waiver, and, a fortiori, it cannot be said that the State has met its 'heavy burden' of showing a knowing and intelligent waiver of . . . Sixth Amendment rights."

The Court of Appeals approved the reasoning of the District Court:

"A review of the record here . . . discloses no facts to support the conclusion of the state court that (Williams) had waived his constitutional rights other than that (he) had made incriminating statements. . . . The District Court here properly concluded that an incorrect constitutional standard had been applied by the state court in determining the issue of waiver. . . .

"(T)his court recently held that an accused can voluntarily, knowingly and intelligently waive his right to have counsel present at an interrogation after counsel has been appointed. . . . The prosecution, however, has the weighty obligation to show that the waiver was knowingly and intelligently made. We quote agree with Judge Hanson that the state here failed to so show."

The District Court and the Court of Appeals were correct in the view that the question of waiver was not a question of historical fact, but one which, in the words of Mr. Justice Frankfurter, requires "application of constitutional principles to the facts as found . . . ."

The District Court and the Court of Appeals were also correct in their understanding of the proper standard to be applied in determining the question of waiver as a matter of federal constitutional law—that it was incumbent upon the State to prove "an intentional relinquishment or abandonment of a known right or privilege." That standard has been reiterated in many cases. We have said that the right to counsel does not depend upon a request by the defendant, and that courts indulge in every reasonable presumption against waiver. This strict standard applies equally to an alleged waiver of the right to counsel whether at trial or at a critical stage of pretrial proceedings.

We conclude, finally that the Court of Appeals was correct in holding that, judged by these standards, the record in this case falls far short of sustaining petitioner's burden. It is true that Williams had been informed of and appeared to understand his right to counsel. But waiver requires not merely comprehension but relinquishment, and Williams' consistent reliance upon the advice of counsel in dealing with the authorities refutes any suggestion that he waived that right. He consulted McKnight by long-distance telephone before turning himself in. He spoke with McKnight by telephone again shortly after being booked. After he was arraigned, Williams sought out and obtained legal advice from Kelly. Williams again consulted with Kelly after Detective Leaming and his fellow officer arrived in Davenport. Throughout, Williams was advised not to make any statements before seeing McKnight in Des Moines, and was assured that the police had agreed not to question him. His statements while in the car that he would tell the whole story after seeing McKnight in Des Moines were the clearest expressions by Williams himself that he desired the presence of an attorney before any interrogation took place. But even before making these statements, Williams had effectively asserted his right to counsel by having secured attorneys at both ends of the automobile trip, both of whom, acting as his agents, had made clear to the police that no interrogation was to occur during the journey. Williams knew of that agreement and, particularly in view of his consistent reliance on counsel, there is no basis for concluding that he disavowed it.

Despite Williams' express and implicit assertions of his right to counsel, Detective Leaming proceeded to elicit incriminating statements from Williams. Leaming did not preface this effort by telling Williams that he had a right to the presence of a lawyer, and made no effort at all to ascertain whether Williams wished to relinquish that right. The circumstances of record in this case thus provide no reasonable basis for finding that Williams waived his right to the assistance of counsel.

The Court of Appeals did not hold, nor do we, that under the circumstances of this case Williams could not, without notice to counsel, have waived his rights under the Sixth and Fourteenth Amendments. It only held, as do we, that he did not.

IV

The crime of which Williams was convicted was senseless and brutal, calling for swift and energetic action by the police to apprehend the perpetrator and gather evidence with which he could be convicted. No mission of law enforcement officials is more important. Yet "(d)isinterested zeal for the public good does not assure either wisdom or right in the methods it pursues. Although we do not lightly affirm the issuance of a writ of habeas corpus in this case, so clear a violation of the Sixth and Fourteenth Amendments as here occurred cannot be condoned. The pressures on state executive and judicial officers charged with the administration of the criminal law are great, especially when the crime is murder and the victim a small child. But it is precisely the predictability of those pressures that makes imperative a resolute loyalty to the guarantees that the Constitution extends to us all.

The judgment of the Court of Appeals is affirmed.

[The separate concurring opinions of Justices MARSHALL, POWELL and STEVENS are omitted].

[The dissenting opinion of Chief Justice BURGER is also omitted].

[The dissenting opinion of Justice WHITE, which was joined by Justices BLACKMUN and REHNQUIST is also omitted].

[The dissenting opinion of Justice BLACKMUN, with was joined by Justices WHITE and REHNQUIST is also omitted].

33

Bail and Pre-Trial Detention

Key Concepts

- Purpose of Bail Is to Ensure Defendant Returns to Court
- Excessive Bail Prohibited
- Preventive Detention Permissible Under Certain Circumstances

A. Introduction and Policy. The time period between the defendant's initial appearance and the final disposition of his case could be as brief as a period of days or could be as lengthy as several months or even a year or more. During this time, one of the critical questions in the case is whether the defendant should be held in custody. There are two justifications for keeping the defendant in custody while his case is pending: first, to ensure that he makes all of his court appearances; and second, where there is evidence of such risk, to prevent him from committing other crimes while his case makes its way through the court system.

With regard to the first justification the real question is: how can the court ensure that the defendant will appear at all upcoming court appearances including trial? Of course, if guaranteeing presence were the only consideration, the surest method of accomplishing this goal would be to keep the defendant in jail the entire time, thereby assuring his presence in court whenever necessary. However, until the defendant is convicted, he is still presumed innocent of the charges against him. Further, it is a waste of limited resources to pay the relatively high cost of incarcerating someone simply to guarantee his appearance if other less costly restrictions can accomplish an identical result. Pre-conviction incarceration may also impose significant costs upon the defendant in terms of disruptions to family life and employment that are disproportionate to the alleged harm he caused. This is the crux of the bail decision: how to ensure the defendant's future appearance in court while considering the systemic and societal costs and respecting his basic rights as a presumptively innocent citizen.

As we will see, there are two primary tools that courts use to strike this balance. One is the threat of incarceration. Under this approach, the defendant is informed that if he fails to appear at scheduled court appearances, he will be re-arrested and probably forced to stay in jail until his case is over. The other is financial. The judge can require the defendant to pay money (or become liable to pay money) if he fails to appear for a future court date. This is known as "setting bail."

If a judge determines that neither the threat of incarceration nor bail will be sufficient to ensure the defendant's presence in court, she can deny bail altogether—that is, order that the defendant be held in custody until his case is over. In many cases, judges set bail at amounts that are so high defendants are not able to pay it—thus, the effect in these cases is the same as if bail were denied outright.

The second justification for keeping the defendant in custody while the case is pending is to prevent him from committing other crimes while awaiting trial. This is known as "preventive detention." The practice is authorized by most bail statutes, and has been found to be constitutional by the Supreme Court, but it is somewhat controversial. On the one hand, the defendant is presumed innocent, and so it potentially infringes on his rights to lock him up merely because a magistrate determines that he may commit a crime in the future. On the other hand, prosecutors, judges, and legislators seek to avoid the possibility that a defendant who has been arrested, particularly for a crime of violence, might be released into the community only to commit another crime while awaiting trial for the first. In this context, the political pressure to prevent a "known criminal" (or, rather, a known **suspected** criminal) from committing more crimes has influenced legislators to authorize pre-trial detention based on the defendant's potential danger to the community.

Police officers also exercise substantial discretion with regard to pre-trial detention decisions. Remember that the arresting officer has the ability to make the initial decision of whether to keep a suspect in custody after an arrest is made. The officer may (for misdemeanors or other less severe crimes) give the arrestee a summons or citation instead of taking him into custody. The summons requires the arrestee to voluntarily appear in court at a later date for his initial appearance, and although a judge could theoretically set bail at that point, she is unlikely to do so because the arrestee has already demonstrated that he will come to court on his own.

Also, in many jurisdictions police officers have the authority to release a defendant after arrest and before his court appearance by referring to a set "bail schedule" for minor crimes. The bail schedule establishes a fixed cash payment for a given crime that can be paid at the police station. The arrestee is then released and allowed to remain free until his court date.

However, the vast majority of defendants are held in a jail cell following arrest until their initial appearance, and then the question of whether to release them—and if so, under what conditions—rests with the magistrate or judge. If the prosecutor believes the defendant is a flight risk or is a danger to others, she will point out all the relevant factors to the judge and request for bail to be set at a certain amount (or, in very severe cases, for bail to be denied altogether). The defense attorney, of course, will offer all the reasons why the defendant should be released without bail, or why bail should be set at a very low level.

A defendant who is held in custody pending trial (either because he was denied bail or because he cannot afford to pay the level of bail that was set) is at a severe disadvantage. He is unable to participate in his own defense (that is, he cannot assist the defense attorney in tracking down witnesses, gathering evidence, etc.). His attorney will almost certainly spend less time with him preparing for trial (a defense attorney with limited resources cannot go to the jail to interview her client nearly as often as she could meet with him in her office). He is unable to work, and so may lose his job during the months that pass until his trial (which may make it harder for him to pay for an attorney). And, especially for a defendant who is charged with a misdemeanor, he will be much more inclined to take a plea deal and agree to "time served" as a sentence. For example, assume a defendant is arrested for possession of cocaine. If the defendant cannot make bail, he could conceivably wait in custody for two months or more until his trial begins. If a bail is set at an amount higher than the defendant can afford and he is then offered a plea bargain with a thirty-day sentence, he may reasonably decide to take the deal simply to be released more quickly.

Thus, the bail determination is a critical decision in the case. And although the statutes and rules provide magistrates and judges with specific factors to consider as guidelines, the court is given an enormous amount of discretion in this area.

B. The Law. The law regarding bail is mostly based on statutes, but there is one federal constitutional provision regarding bail:

Amendment VIII, United States Constitution

"Excessive bail shall not be required."

As with many other aspects of the Bill of Rights, the language of this restriction is extremely vague. The United States Supreme Court has held that the excessive bail clause means two things: (1) a bail determination must take into account the specific facts and circumstances of the case and the particular defendant; and (2) the amount of bail must be no more than is necessary to meet the legitimate interest of the government (ensuring defendant's attendance at future court appearances and/or preventing the defendant from committing more crimes while the case is pending).[1] The Supreme Court has made it clear that the Eighth

[1] Stack v. Boyle, 342 U.S. 1 (1951).

Amendment does **not** create an absolute right to bail; as long as the judge or magistrate gives the defendant individual attention and focuses on legitimate government interests, she is legally allowed to deny bail altogether.

The Supreme Court has stated in dicta that this part of the Bill of Rights has been incorporated to apply to the states.[2] In addition, many state constitutions have restrictions on excessive bail, and some provide an absolute right to bail, except in capital cases. We will discuss the issue of excessive bail further in Section 4.

As noted, the primary source of law for bail determinations is statutory, and is generally found either in the penal code or in the Criminal Rules of Procedure for the jurisdiction in question. For example, the federal law on bail is governed by the Bail Reform Act of 1984, now codified at 18 U.S.C. §§ 3141-50. (Rule 46 of the Federal Rules of Criminal Procedure covers release from custody generally, and refers to 18 U.S.C. §§ 3141-42 for all pre-trial custody issues).

We will focus on three specific aspects of the Bail Reform Act:

18 U.S.C. § 3142(g)—Factors To Be Considered

The judicial officer shall, in determining whether there are conditions of release that will reasonably assure the appearance of the person as required and the safety of any other person and the community, take into account the available information concerning—

(1) the nature and circumstances of the offense charged, including whether the offense is a crime of violence, a violation of [sex trafficking of children], a Federal crime of terrorism, or involves a minor victim or a controlled substance, firearm, explosive, or destructive device;

(2) the weight of the evidence against the person;

(3) the history and characteristics of the person, including—

- **(A)** the person's character, physical and mental condition, family ties, employment, financial resources, length of residence in the community, community ties, past conduct, history relating to drug or alcohol abuse, criminal history, and record concerning appearance at court proceedings; and
- **(B)** whether, at the time of the current offense or arrest, the person was on probation, on parole, or on other release pending trial, sentencing, appeal, or completion of sentence for an offense under Federal, State, or local law; and

(4) the nature and seriousness of the danger to any person or the community that would be posed by the person's release.

[2] Schlib v. Kuebel, 404 U.S. 357, 365 (1971).

Section 3142(g) first notes that in determining the appropriate conditions for releasing the defendant, the court should try to ensure "the appearance of the person as required" and "the safety of any other person and the community." As noted above, these are the two justifications for requiring bail. The statute then lists the four factors that should guide the court: the type of crime charged, the strength of the evidence, the defendant's individual characteristics (family ties, community ties, prior criminal record, prior record of appearing in court, etc.) and the "danger to the community" the defendant may present if released.

Another section of the Act (18 U.S.C. § 3142(e)) enumerates charges which create a rebuttable presumption that bail should be denied outright, including any sex crime that involves children, any crime of violence, international terrorism, or controlled substance violation which carries a potential punishment of over ten years, any crime involving human trafficking that carries a potential punishment of over twenty years, or any crime at all which carries a potential life sentence or the death penalty. For these types of crimes, the defense bears the burden of proving that he deserves to be released pending trial.

The other important section of the Act explains how and when the bail hearings take place:

18 U.S.C. § 3142(f)—Detention Hearing

The judicial officer shall hold a hearing to determine whether any condition or combination of conditions . . . will reasonably assure the appearance of such person as required and the safety of any other person and the community . . .

The hearing shall be held immediately upon the person's first appearance before the judicial officer unless that person, or the attorney for the Government, seeks a continuance. Except for good cause, a continuance on motion of such person may not exceed five days [not including weekends or holidays], and a continuance on motion of the attorney for the Government may not exceed three days [not including weekends or holidays].

. . .

At the hearing, such person has the right to be represented by counsel, and, if financially unable to obtain adequate representation, to have counsel appointed. The person shall be afforded an opportunity to testify, to present witnesses, to cross-examine witnesses who appear at the hearing, and to present information by proffer or otherwise. The rules concerning admissibility of evidence in criminal trials do not apply to the presentation and consideration of information at the hearing.

The facts the judicial officer uses to support a finding . . . that no condition or combination of conditions will reasonably assure the safety of any other person and the community shall be supported by clear and convincing evidence. The person may be detained pending completion of the hearing.

> The hearing may be reopened, before or after a determination by the judicial officer, at any time before trial if the judicial officer finds that information exists that was not known to the movant at the time of the hearing and that has a material bearing on the issue whether there are conditions of release that will reasonably assure the appearance of such person as required and the safety of any other person and the community.

Thus, under the federal rules the hearing must be held immediately at the initial appearance or a few days thereafter if either side requests a delay. Since the initial appearance must take place "without unnecessary delay," this ensures that a neutral judge or magistrate will promptly review the defendant's case and decide whether (and on what conditions) he should be released pending trial. Although the rules provide for a full-fledged hearing, with witnesses and other evidence, such an occurrence is relatively rare. Usually the bail hearing merely involves arguments by both attorneys citing facts from the arrest report or the defendant's interview with pretrial services. We will discuss the mechanics of the bail hearing in more detail in Section C.2.

At the federal level, the defendant is provided with an attorney at the initial appearance. But this is a matter of federal statute, not constitutional command. Accordingly, some states do not provide for an attorney at this initial stage, in which case the question of bail can be re-opened by the defendant at a later date when he has representation. In these state systems, such a re-opening is know as "bail review."

Federal law (and all state laws) also provide for the possibility of re-opening the bail determination at a later date if relevant, new information comes to light after the initial appearance—that is, if there are "changed circumstances" that are relevant to the question of bail. This may be information that neither side originally knew about because of the short amount of time between the arrest and the initial appearance—for example, the defense attorney may not have been able to confirm that the defendant is employed full-time or has a permanent residence within the jurisdiction. Or the new information may involve material developments in the case itself—for example, the defendant got re-arrested for another crime or violated a condition of his bail.

Note that after the initial appearance, all jurisdictions have statutory speedy trial provisions that require the government to move the case forward within a certain amount of time (for example, an indictment or information must be filed within thirty days, and the trial must commence within ninety days). Often, if the defendant is in custody, the statutes set much shorter speedy trial deadlines, with the goal of ensuring the defendant does not have to wait in custody for an unreasonable amount of time. We will discuss these deadlines further in **Chapter 41.**

C. Applying the Law.

1. Mechanics of Bail. There are many different potential outcomes for a bail determination. The details and the exact terminology will differ from jurisdiction to jurisdiction, but the basic concepts are as follows:

a. Released on Recognizance ("ROR"). This is the best possible outcome for a defendant. The court allows the defendant to be released from custody immediately with just a promise to appear voluntarily at all future court appearances. The defendant will be warned that if he fails to appear an arrest warrant will be issued against him (and of course, once he fails to appear even once, it is unlikely a judge will ROR him for any future appearances). This is a common outcome for first-time offenders who are charged with low-level crimes.

b. Unsecured Bail. The defendant is released immediately and agrees to appear voluntarily at all future appearances, but he agrees that he will pay a fee if he fails to appear. This option is rarely used for indigent defendants, since they are unlikely to be able to pay a fee and so the unsecured bail provides no real incentive for them to return to court.

c. Monitoring. The defendant is released immediately, but must check in periodically with designated court personnel, such as pre-trial services either in person or by phone. The judge may also require the defendant to wear some sort of monitoring device, like an ankle bracelet. For defendants who have geographic restrictions placed on their release (*e.g.*, stay away from schools or stay 500 feet away from your ex-husband's new house) these devices can help ensure the defendant does not stray into prohibited areas.

d. Cash Bond. The defendant must pay a certain amount of money to the court in order to be released from custody while the case proceeds. The defendant will receive the money back when the case is over as long as he shows up at all court appearances throughout the case. If the defendant fails to appear at any time, an arrest warrant is issued and the cash that he put up is forfeited. If the defendant re-appears within a certain amount of time, the magistrate or judge has the option of setting aside the forfeiture and returning the money.

In theory, the amount of the cash bond should be high enough that it ensures the defendant will return, but low enough that he is able to post the bail. Striking this balance can be challenging for a court, as noted in Section C.5 below.

As with all bail options, the actual outcome of the case is irrelevant to whether the defendant gets his bail money back—that is, as long as the defendant makes all appearances, the bail is returned to him at the end of the case regardless of whether he is convicted, acquitted, or the case is dismissed.

However, if the outcome of the case involves any fines or court fees, the money to pay these fines or fees will be deducted from the cash bond before it is returned to the defendant.

e. Percentage Bond. This option combines unsecured bail with a cash bond. Bail is set at a certain amount, and the defendant is required to pay a percentage of that amount up front (usually 10% of the total) in order to secure his immediate release. If the defendant makes all of his court appearances, the deposit is returned to him, minus a small administrative fee (usually 10% of the deposit). If he does not make a court appearance, he could forfeit the deposit and be liable for the rest of the money (and, as always, a warrant is issued for his arrest). For example, if a judge sets a $20,000 10% percentage bond, the defendant must pay $2,000 immediately to be released. If he makes all of his court appearances, then $1,800 will be returned to him and the court keeps $200 as a fee. If he does not make an appearance, the court could order that the bond be forfeited. At that point, the court keeps the entire $2,000 and he is personally liable for the remaining $18,000.

f. Surety Bond. This is similar to a percentage bond, in which the court requires only a small deposit with the rest of the money due only if the defendant does not appear. The difference between a percentage bond and a surety bond is that with the latter the defendant pays the deposit to a third party (the "surety") instead of to the court. Unlike the deposit paid to the court for a percentage bond, the money paid to the surety is usually a non-refundable fee. The surety is then responsible for the entire amount of the bond if the defendant does not appear in court. The surety could be a friend or a family member, but is usually an independent entity known as a bail bondsman—an individual or company who agrees to risk the entire amount of the bond in exchange for the fee from the defendant.

If the defendant makes all of his appearances, the surety merely keeps the fee that it charged the defendant. If the defendant misses a court date, an arrest warrant is issued and the bail money is forfeited. If the surety returns the defendant to the court at a later date, the court has the option of setting aside the forfeiture and giving the surety his or her money back. Once the defendant fails to appear, the surety therefore has a real incentive to bring the defendant back to court. This means that many bail bondsmen occasionally act as modern-day bounty hunters, tracking down absconding defendants and bringing them to court by force. Less colorfully, the surety may require a defendant (or a defendant's family member) to pledge assets as collateral up front which will be turned over to the surety if the defendant does not appear.

For example, if a judge sets a $20,000 10% surety bond, the defendant may choose to pay a $2,000 non-refundable fee to the bail bondsman. The bondsman will then be liable for $20,000 if the defendant fails to appear and the bondsman is unable to hunt him down and return him to court.

Regardless of whether the surety is a family member or a bail bondsman, the court will almost always require some proof of assets to ensure that the surety is able to pay the balance of the bond if the defendant absconds.

g. Property Bond. The defendant—or a family member or friend of the defendant—pledges real property or securities as assets which will be turned over to the court if the defendant does not make his court appearances. Thus, if the defendant fails to appear, the court will foreclose on the property or take possession of the securities.

h. Combining Different Types of Bail. Frequently a court will give different options to a defendant: for example, a court may set a cash bond at $50,000, or a percentage bond of $100,000 with a 10% required deposit. Thus, the defendant has the option of paying $50,000 now or paying $10,000 now but being liable for an additional $90,000 if he fails to appear. Similarly, cash bonds, percentage bonds, or surety bonds could be combined with some kind of monitoring by pre-trial services. For various reasons, a defendant may prefer to have one type of bond or another, and his attorney can request that the judge offer the type of bond he prefers. Ultimately, it is the court's decision as to which type of bond (or options for types of bonds) will best ensure the defendant's attendance at trial.

i. Other Conditions. In almost every case, the judge will attach conditions to the defendant's release. Some of these conditions—for example, not to commit any crimes while awaiting trial—do not create any special obligation on the part of the defendant. But others conditions do, particularly those which are specific to the crime that is charged. For example, the judge may issue an order of protection prohibiting the defendant from interacting with the victim in the case. Or, the judge may order weekly drug testing, or may order the defendant to surrender all firearms. The defendant is warned that any violation of these bail conditions could result in his bail status being re-evaluated, causing him to be taken back into custody. Also, the judge may order other restrictions designed to lower the risk of flight—for example, the judge may require the defendant to surrender his passport or not leave the jurisdiction.

One problem with cash bonds, percentage bonds, or property bonds is that the bond may be posted by the defendant's friend or family member. Unlike a bail bondsman, who fully understand the risk involved in accepting this responsibility, and who is generally equipped to track down absent defendants, private individuals who post bail may be stuck with significant liability if the defendant does not return to court. The defendant also will not have the same incentive to return as he would if it were his own money.

As noted in all of the above scenarios, if a defendant does not appear at any of his court dates, the court issues an arrest warrant (usually called a "bench warrant") for the defendant. Often, the defendant himself will appear in court the next day or in a few weeks to clear the warrant. Depending upon the explanation offered by the defendant for his failure to appear, the judge may decide to change the bail conditions. If the defendant does not return, the outstanding warrant stays on the defendant's record. Depending on the severity of the crime, the police may or may not act on this warrant. For misdemeanors and even less severe felonies, the police may simply put the warrant in the system and wait for the defendant's next contact with law enforcement—usually the next time he is arrested or pulled over. For more serious cases, the police will send out their "warrant squad" to try to track the defendant down and bring him in. In either case, the fact that a bench warrant was issued will be recorded on the defendant's permanent criminal record and will certainly be used by the prosecutor in any bail arguments for future arrests.

2. The Bail Hearing. As noted above, the bail determination usually takes place at the initial appearance. There is no constitutional right to an attorney for the bail hearing, but some states (and the federal government) provide a right to an attorney by statute.

Since the initial appearance is literally the first stage of the adjudication process, the bail hearing is generally a relatively informal affair—there are usually no written briefs or witnesses called or evidence presented. Both sides have probably only had a few hours or perhaps even a few minutes to prepare for the hearing. Nevertheless, in those jurisdictions where counsel is provided, an experienced attorney is often able to quickly assemble a coherent argument for the amount of bail that is appropriate. Most statutes do provide for the possibility of a more formal bail review, which usually takes place a few weeks after the initial appearance. In that case, one of the parties (usually the defendant) is seeking to have the initial bail determination changed, and may then present a more formal case involving witnesses and even written briefs. In most jurisdictions where counsel is not required at the initial bail hearing, counsel will be provided at the bail review.

When the bail argument occurs at the initial appearance, the most critical aspect of the bail hearing occurs before the hearing even begins. Both the prosecutor and the defense attorney will gather as much information as possible about the defendant's flight risk and danger to the community. The defense attorney will interview the defendant himself and also try to reach out to the defendant's friends or family to confirm his ties to the community, ascertain what amount of bail (if any) the defendant would be able to post, and identify who (if anyone) would be willing to act as a surety. The prosecutor will interview the law enforcement officer to learn about the strength of the case and the defendant's level of cooperation during and after the arrest. Usually a member of the court system from the pre-trial services division will interview the defendant before his initial appearance and put together a short report on the defendant's community ties. This report is made available to the prosecutor, the defense attorney, and the judge. Finally, both sides will examine the defendant's prior criminal record (if any), which will include relevant facts such as whether he has ever failed to appear for prior cases, and whether he has ever given false names, birthdates, or social security numbers to the police during prior arrests.

In some cases—for example if the charges are minor and the defendant has no prior criminal record—the prosecutor will consent to a defendant's release on his own recognizance. Otherwise, the bail hearing will usually begin with the prosecutor requesting a certain amount of bail and then justifying the request. The defense attorney will then make her own request, and support her request with her own arguments. The defense attorney cannot, of course, vouch for the defendant personally or guarantee that the defendant will return to court, but like the prosecutor she can refer to facts in the record or facts she has learned from interviewing various individuals. And both sides will be guided by the factors that are listed in the appropriate rule or statute that governs bail in their jurisdiction.

As noted above, the two reasons to set bail or keep a defendant in custody are (1) to ensure that the defendant returns to court for future appearances; and (2) to prevent the defendant from committing more crimes while he is awaiting disposition for the current charges. We will discuss the question of preventive detention in Section C.3 below; for now we will focus on the factors that are relevant to the question of flight risk. These factors vary slightly from state to state, but the federal statute set out in Section B is typical in listing three considerations:

1. The severity of the crime charged;
2. The strength of the evidence against the defendant; and
3. The defendant's specific characteristics relating to his risk of flight if released.

For example, if the defendant is charged with a serious felony, he will potentially face years or decades in prison, which would give him a much stronger incentive to flee than if he were charged with shoplifting or minor cocaine possession. Similarly, if the evidence against the defendant is overwhelming, he will believe that a conviction is unavoidable and therefore have a stronger incentive to flee than if the evidence is weak. And the court will also focus on the defendant's specific characteristics to determine how likely he is to abscond—his family ties, whether he is employed, whether he has missed past court appearances, whether he abuses alcohol or drugs, how many assets he has, and so on. If the defendant is already on parole or probation for a prior conviction, or if he is already released on bail for a prior arrest, the judge will almost certainly deny bail for this new arrest (and the defendant will probably have a probation violation hearing or have his bail revoked on his pre-existing case).

By way of example, a typical bail hearing might proceed along these lines:

> PROSECUTOR: Your honor, the state is requesting bail in the amount of $5,000 cash in this case. The defendant is charged with second-degree robbery; that crime carries a maximum penalty of fifteen years in prison. According to his rap sheet, he already has two prior felony convictions, so he is likely to face something close to the maximum penalty if convicted. This is a strong case: the police interviewed two eyewitnesses at the scene who positively identified him as the robber only a few minutes after the incident. The defendant himself has a history of not showing up for court. He missed a pre-trial hearing date on his last case and a warrant had to be issued for his arrest. Also, the last time he was arrested he gave a false name to the police; indicating an attempt to conceal his past record.
>
> Pre-trial services reports that he has no job and that he has substance abuse problems, and he has been in and out of treatment programs with no success. We can see from his record that he has three prior convictions for possession of cocaine. He told pre-trial services that he lives with his girlfriend at an address on 5th Street. But pre-trial services was unable to reach this girlfriend to confirm this fact. He has been arrested five times over the past five years and each time he has given a different home address, so he does not appear to have a stable home here. He was born in another state and his parents still live there, so given his lack of community ties there is certainly a risk that he would leave this jurisdiction and never come back.
>
> COURT: Thank you. I'll hear from the defense counsel now.
>
> DEFENSE COUNSEL: Thank you, your honor, I would request that my client be released on his own recognizance or if not, that a reasonable bail be set. I would be surprised if this case even went to trial, your honor. The victims claim they were robbed at knifepoint and that the perpetrator stole $27 from them, but when my client was arrested just fifteen minutes after the event, the police did not recover any weapon or money from him. The identification was a very suggestive show-up, and I don't think it will survive a suppression hearing. Even if it does, it is going to be very hard to convince a jury that my client was the perpetrator based on two extremely suggestive identifications made after a nighttime robbery on a dark street.

> As far as my client's prior record, your honor, I know that he does have two prior felonies, but even with those prior felonies we all know there is no way he is going to get 15 years in prison if convicted of this crime. And I would disagree with the prosecutor's characterization of his track record in showing up for court. In his past criminal cases he voluntarily appeared for eight different scheduled appearances for pre-trial hearings and for trials. On the one occasion that he missed he had a very good reason for being late. His car broke down and he was late for the pre-trial hearing. The judge issued a warrant, which is on the record; but my client showed up three hours later and the warrant was quashed.
>
> My client does have strong ties to this community. The reason that pre-trial services was unable to reach my client's girlfriend is that she does not have a cell phone. But, she has been here in the courtroom for the past three hours waiting for this arraignment. I have spoken to her and she has confirmed that she and the defendant live together on 5th Street. They have lived there together for over a year, judge, and although he was born out of state he has maintained a residence in this city for his entire adult life. He did have substance abuse problems, but he assures me he has been clean for over a year, and his record does seem to bear that out—his last arrest for possession was two years ago. Although he does not have a job now, he tells me that he had been working at a moving company for six months and just lost his job last week. But the company apparently told him that they would hire him back in the spring when the business picks up again, so he does have a reason to stick around.
>
> Your honor, I realize this is a serious allegation against my client, and I acknowledge that he has a prior criminal record, and so you may be inclined to set some bail in this case. However, given my client's limited resources, $5,000 is equivalent to denying bail altogether. As I said before, I have spoken to my client's girlfriend and she is able to post a bond of $500. I have tried to reach my client's parents to see if they can act as a surety, but I have been unable to contact them, and at any rate my client is doubtful that they could serve as a surety. So really cash bond is the only option here and $500 is more than sufficient to ensure that my client will return for his court appearances.

In the end, the magistrate or judge is given significant discretion in setting bail. As with sentencing and many other decisions made by trial judges, the judge's personal ideology and other characteristics will be a major factor in determining what level of bail will be set. Some judges have a reputation for setting a high bail in almost every case; others will be known to give defendants the benefit of the doubt more often and seek to set a bail low enough to ensure that the defendant can post it and be released.

3. Preventive Detention. In addition to ensuring a defendant will return for his future court appearances, the federal bail statute and most state statutes also permit a court to set a higher bail amount—or deny bail altogether—if the government can demonstrate that the defendant is dangerous to other individuals or to his community. This raises two constitutional questions. First, does keeping a defendant in jail before he is convicted simply because he may commit more crimes violate his rights under the Due Process Clause of the Fifth Amendment, which states that "No person shall . . . be deprived of life, liberty, or property, without due process of law. . . ."? Second, does the Eighth Amendment's rule that "[e]xcessive bail shall not be required" mean that the court cannot consider a defendant's danger to the community as a factor in setting bail? The Supreme Court considered both these questions in *United States v. Salerno*:

> **Example—*United States v. Salerno,* 481 U.S. 739 (1987):** Anthony Salerno and Vincent Cafaro were charged with twenty-nine crimes, including racketeering, extortion, fraud, and conspiracy to commit murder. At the arraignment, the government argued that no condition of release would ensure the safety of the community, and so argued that the defendant should be detained without bail pursuant to 18 U.S.C. § 3142(e). The trial court ordered a full-fledged bail hearing to decide the issue.
>
> At the bail hearing, the government offered wiretap evidence that showed Salerno was the "boss" of the Genovese crime family of La Cosa Nostra and that Cafaro was a "captain" in the Genovese family. The tapes from the phone calls indicated that the two defendants repeatedly used violence to further their criminal ends. The government also offered the testimony of two live witnesses who testified that Salerno personally participated in two murder conspiracies. Salerno challenged the credibility of these witnesses, and also provided numerous character witnesses on his behalf.
>
> The trial judge agreed with the prosecutor and denied bail for both Salerno and Cafaro. The defendants appealed, arguing that the statute permitting pretrial detention on the ground that the arrestee is likely to commit future crimes was unconstitutional on its face. The defendants argued that the statute violated both the Due Process Clause of the Fifth Amendment and the Excessive Bail Clause of the Eighth Amendment. The case ultimately reached the Supreme Court.

Analysis: The Court upheld the statute as constitutional. The Court first noted that pre-trial detention was not meant as a "punishment" but instead served a "regulatory" purpose. The Court conceded that the Due Process Clause implied a "general rule" that the government may not detain a person prior to a judgment of guilt in a criminal trial, but also noted that there were many exceptions to this general rule. The government is allowed to detain dangerous individuals without trial in times of war. Preventive detention is also allowed if the individual is a dangerous illegal alien pending deportation proceedings; is a mentally unstable individual who may pose a danger to others; or is a dangerous defendant who is incompetent to stand trial. The Court recently authorized detaining juveniles who are arrested pending trial if they pose a danger to the community. And the government has always been allowed to detain arrested individuals for the more traditional reason of ensuring their appearance at court.[3] Given all of these exceptions to the "general rule" against detaining a person prior to a determination of guilt, the Court was willing to approve of preventive detention for adults in order to further the legitimate and compelling government interest in preventing arrestees from committing further crimes. The government must demonstrate "by clear and convincing evidence that no conditions of release can reasonably assure the safety of the community or any person."[4]

The Court also rejected the defendants' Eighth Amendment arguments, mostly on textual grounds. The Court pointed out that "[n]othing in the text of the Bail Clause limits permissible Government considerations solely to questions of flight." Thus, increasing bail (or denying bail altogether) based on the fact that the defendant would be a danger to others or to the community did not violate the defendant's Eighth Amendment rights.

Salerno's case was controversial not only because of the factors that the trial court considered in determining bail, but also because the trial court ultimately denied bail altogether. This raised a separate question in the case: when a court denies bail altogether—either because of risk of flight or because of concerns about the defendant's dangerousness, or because of a combination of the factors—is the court setting "excessive" bail? We turn to that question in the next section.

4. When is Bail "Excessive?" The prohibition against excessive bail is fundamentally linked to the presumption of innocence. The very first federal statute governing criminal procedure provided that anyone arrested for a non-capital offense deserved a bail hearing.[5] As the Supreme Court has stated, this "traditional right to freedom before conviction permits the unhampered preparation of a defense, and serves to prevent the infliction of punishment prior to conviction. Unless this right to bail before trial is preserved, the presumption of innocence,

[3] United States v. Salerno, 481 U.S. 739, 748–49 (1987).

[4] Id. at 750.

[5] See Judiciary Act of 1789, 1 Stat. 73, 91.

secured only after centuries of struggle, would lose its meaning."[6] Thus, in order for this right to be meaningful, bail must not be "excessive."

> **Example—*Stack v. Boyle,* 342 U.S. 1 (1951):** Lorretta Stack and numerous codefendants were arrested for conspiring to overthrow the United States government. The magistrate originally set various amounts of bail for the defendants that ranged from $2,500 to $100,000. However, after a motion from the government, the trial court readjusted the bail amounts for each petitioner to a uniform $50,000.
>
> The defendants challenged the new bail as excessive under the Eighth Amendment, and submitted evidence as to their financial resources, family relationships, health, prior criminal records, and other information. In response, the government offered only a record showing that four individuals previously convicted of conspiring to overthrow the United States government had forfeited bail.
>
> The trial court denied the defendants' motion and the defendants appealed all the way to the Supreme Court.

Analysis: The Court declared the procedures followed in the case were insufficient to ensure that the bail was not excessive. Bail should be set at an amount reasonably calculated to ensure the appearance of the defendant for future court proceedings. If it is set any higher than that amount, it is excessive under the Eighth Amendment. Thus, "the fixing of bail for any individual defendant must be based upon standards relevant to the purpose of assuring the presence of that defendant."[7] In this case, the government asked (and was granted) an amount of bail much greater than would usually be set for a crime of this nature, and asked the trial court to simply assume the defendants were flight risks without offering any individual evidence in support of this assertion. "To infer from the fact of indictment alone a need for bail in an unusually high amount is an arbitrary act."[8]

Do not be misled by the Supreme Court's statement that defendants have a "right to bail." Instead, it is more accurate to say that *Stack v. Boyle* gives defendants the right to an individualized determination of the necessary amount of bail in each case. That "necessary amount" might be infinite; i.e. the court may need to deny bail altogether. As you read above, the Court in *Salerno* approved of the trial court's denial of bail because the trial court, after careful analysis, determined

---

[6] Stack v. Boyle, 342 U.S. 1, 4 (1951) (citations omitted).

[7] Id. at 5.

[8] Id. at 6.

that no amount of bail could prevent the defendant from being a danger to the community. The Court noted that from the very beginning of our legal system, bail was denied to individuals who were accused of capital crimes, so there never was an "absolute right" to bail. The *Salerno* Court concluded:

> Of course, to determine whether the Government's response is excessive, we must compare that response against the interest the Government seeks to protect by means of that response. Thus, when the Government has admitted that its only interest is in preventing flight, bail must be set by a court at a sum designed to ensure that goal, and no more. [But] when Congress has mandated detention on the basis of a compelling interest other than prevention of flight, as it has here, the Eighth Amendment does not require release on bail.[9]

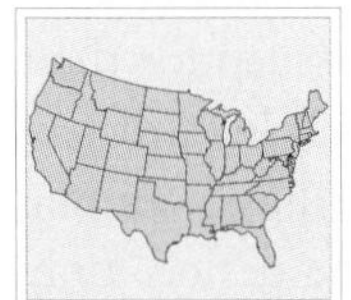

As the above passage notes, the federal bail statute allows for a denial of bail if no amount of bail and/or bail conditions can ensure the defendant's return to court and prevent the defendant from committing more crimes. However, states vary widely in their approach to the bail issue. Many states provide for a right to bail in all non-capital cases. Others broaden the category of non-bailable offenses to all serious felonies, and require the government to demonstrate a significant amount of evidence of guilt. Still others only allow bail to be denied altogether in preventive detention situations; i.e., only if the court finds that the defendant is a danger to others.

For example, California's constitution states that bail may only be denied altogether in certain situations, such as capital crimes or felonies involving violence or sexual assault when the evidence is strong and "the court finds based upon clear and convincing evidence that there is a substantial likelihood the person's release would result in great bodily harm to others."[10] Ohio's Criminal Rule 46(A) states that bail may only denied if the court finds by "clear and convincing evidence" that

1. "The proof is evident and the presumption grate that the accused committed" murder, a first-or-second degree felony, aggravated vehicular homicide or felony driving while impaired;

2. The accused poses a substantial risk of serious physical harm to any person or the community; and

3. No release conditions will reasonably assure the safety of that person and the community.

[9] Salerno, 481 U.S. at 755–56 (citations omitted).

[10] Cal. Constitution, Art. 1, § 12.

Remember that if a magistrate sets bail at an amount higher than the defendant can afford, this is the functional equivalent of a denial of bail—even though the magistrate has technically complied with the rule that bail must be set.

5. Bail by the Numbers.[11] Approximately 32% of felony defendants in state courts nationwide were released on their own recognizance, meaning that 68% of felony defendants had some kind of financial bail set. The median amount of bail was $9,000, and the mean was $35,800. (The mean is much higher than the median because the few defendants who face the most serious charges such as murder and rape frequently have bail set at $50,000 or more.)

How well does the bail system actually function? 62% percent of all felony defendants in state court were released prior to disposition of their case—some because they had no bail set, others because they were able to make bail. Of those, 25% ultimately failed to appear in court, resulting in a warrant being issued for their arrest. This may imply that bail is being set too low, since an ideal level of bail would ensure that the defendant returns to court. On the other hand, among the 38% of defendants who remained in custody during this time period, only one in six had bail denied outright—the other five out of six had bail set but were unable to post their bail. This may imply that bail is being set too high for those five out of six defendants, since an ideal level of bail would be an amount that a defendant could post. In addition, 20% of all defendants who were detained prior to disposition were eventually acquitted or had their cases dismissed. The average amount of time that all detained defendants spent between arrest and detention was forty-five days.

As far as the need for preventive detention, one out of six defendants who was released pending trial was arrested for a new offense during that time period, and half of those arrests were for felonies. For those who approve of the concept of preventive detention, this may be an indication that it should be used more often. Of course, for those who believe that preventive detention violates the presumption of innocence, this number is irrelevant.

There is some evidence that bail actually does provide an incentive for defendants to return: defendants who were required to post bail were more likely to return to court than defendants released on their own recognizance. This number is even more impressive given the fact that defendants who are required to post bail are generally thought to be a greater flight risk than those who are released on their own recognizance.

---

[11] Unless otherwise noted, all of the statistics in this section come from Thomas H. Cohen and Brian A. Reaves, Pretrial Release of Felony Defendants in State Courts, Bureau of Justice Statistics Special Report, United States Department of Justice, November 2007 at http://www.bjs.gov/index.cfm?ty=pbdetail&iid=834.

The effect of pre-trial detention on the outcome of the case is hard to quantify but is certainly negative from the defense perspective. Studies show there is a significant difference in the conviction rates of detained defendants as compared to defendants who are released. If you are a felony defendant and you are released pending trial, you have a 60% chance of being convicted. If you are a felony defendant and you are kept in custody pending trial, you have a 78% chance of being convicted. As we have seen, magistrates and judges will be likely to set a higher level of bail if the evidence against the defendant is strong, so you would expect to see a higher conviction rate for those who are detained. But, some of this difference is probably explained by the fact that a defendant who is kept in custody is less able to assist in his own defense and more likely to accept a plea bargain.

The story is somewhat different on the misdemeanor level. More defendants are released on their own recognizance—approximately 75% in New York City, for example.[12] However, if bail is set and the defendant cannot post bail (a common occurrence in most urban areas), the defendant can expect to be in jail for a number of weeks or months, perhaps more time than the expected sentence for their relatively minor crime. This provides the defendant with a strong—and improper—incentive to plead guilty.

6. Alternatives to Bail. The posting of bail is a tool primarily meant to ensure that the defendant appears in court as his case is pending. It is meant to replace the original method of ensuring the defendant's appearance: keeping the defendant incarcerated until the case was resolved. When compared to incarceration, bail is superior in that it enhances the defendant's liberty interest; is more compatible with the presumption of innocence; reduces employment and familial disruptions for the defendant; and is less expensive for the state. (One study in New York City found that it costs an average of $161 per day to keep a defendant in jail while awaiting trial. Nationwide, the cost to incarcerate those awaiting trial is over a billion dollars per year.)[13] However, bail is at best an imperfect tool. It disadvantages poor defendants compared to wealthier ones, since many indigent defendants cannot meet even the lowest amount of bail and thus stay in jail, unable to meaningfully assist in their own defense and suffering a deprivation of liberty while still presumed innocent. Furthermore, magistrates understandably have a hard time determining exactly the proper amount of bail to set which will ensure the defendant's return—in some cases, bail will be set too low, resulting in defendants who do not return to court and thus have to be tracked down and re-arrested. In other cases, bail will be set unreasonably high and even defendants of moderate means will be unable to secure their freedom.

---

[12] The Price of Freedom, Human Rights Watch (Dec. 3, 2010), at http://www.hrw.org/node/94574/section/2.

[13] Id.

In theory, there are other methods of ensuring the defendant's appearance which may be cheaper, more consistent with the defendant's liberty interest, or even more effective than setting bail. Many of the conditions attached to release could serve the same purpose: for example, the defendant may be required to wear an ankle monitor with a GPS device attached so that law enforcement officials always know where he is. Other, lower-tech solutions include imposing curfews, requiring regular check-ins with probation officers, or forbidding the defendant from leaving his home. Another possibility is to increase the penalties for failure to appear in court—if a defendant knows he will face an additional five or ten years for not showing up on court, he is less likely to abscond.

Of course, in some cases the defendant is kept incarcerated not because of a risk of flight but because he poses a danger to the community. But even in these cases, cheaper and more liberty-enhancing alternatives may exist. Requiring the defendant to provide a DNA sample as a condition of release may help to deter him from committing future crimes. An ankle monitor would also make it difficult for him to commit new crimes, since his whereabouts would always be known. As technology improves, it may even be possible to order the defendant to be under constant video surveillance. While this is a serious infringement on the defendant's liberty, some may find it preferable to spending the time in jail.

Quick Summary

For the period between the defendant's arrest and the disposition of his case, a court has a number of options. The court can release the defendant on his own recognizance and order him to return voluntarily to future court appearances; the court can set some level of bail (either as a cash payment, bond, property, or some combination) and allow the defendant's release only when he posts the bail; or the court can deny bail altogether and keep the defendant in custody.

If the defendant is not released on his own recognizance, the judge must set a bail at a level that is reasonably necessary to (1) ensure that the defendant returns to court and (2) ensure the safety of the community and others. In some cases, particularly capital cases, there may be no amount which is sufficient, in which case the court in most jurisdictions is permitted to deny bail altogether. There is no federal constitutional right to bail. But, defendants do have a constitutional right to not have "excessive" bail set. The Supreme Court has found that the excess bail prohibition means the magistrate must consider the defendant's individual circumstances when setting bail. These circumstances include (1) the severity of the crime charged; (2) the strength of the evidence against the defendant; and (3) the individual characteristics of the defendant that indicate whether he may be a flight risk, including his family ties, employment record, financial resources, length of residence in the community, other community ties, any history relating to drug or alcohol abuse, criminal history, and his prior record concerning appearance at court proceedings. If the prosecutor is asking for the defendant to be held in preventive detention, the court must also take into consideration whether the defendant poses a risk to others or to the community.

Review Questions

1. Bail for Suspected Arsonists? Jack Ferris and his brother Mark were charged with arson, murder, and witness intimidation. The prosecutor alleged that Jack, who owned a building downtown, paid his brother Mark to burn the building down in order to collect insurance money. Although all the residents of the building escaped the fire, a firefighter died while battling the blaze. When the prosecutor subpoenaed residents of the building to testify in the grand jury about how the fire started, Mark allegedly called the residents and told them he would "end them" if they cooperated with the authorities. Most of the residents refused to testify, but two residents came before the grand jury and gave testimony.

At the grand jury, the prosecutor presented an expert witness—a fire marshal with thirty years experience—who testified that empty gas cans were found at the scene and that there was no doubt in his mind the fire was started intentionally. The prosecutor then called the first resident, who testified that at 10:30 PM, half an hour before the fire started, he looked out his window and saw Mark (whom he knows well since he acted as a rent collector for the building) enter the building carrying two large cans of what appeared to be gasoline. The second resident testified that at 11:05 PM, as the fire was burning, he saw Mark's car driving away from the building at a high speed. Both residents testified that they received a threatening phone call from Mark after they received their subpoenas, in which Mark said he would "end them" if they talked to the authorities. The residents reported that Mark also said "if you value the lives of your family, you will stay quiet." Finally, the prosecutor called Terry Ferris, the youngest brother in the family, who testified that he came to see Jack at Jack's office the day after the fire. While he was waiting outside the office, he overheard Mark tell Jack, "There is a chance someone saw me come into the building" and Jack respond: "You just have to make it clear to all of them that talking to anyone about it is a bad idea." Terry will testify that Jack runs their family business and makes all the decisions.

At the initial appearance in federal court, the prosecutor asked that both Jack and Mark be held without bail. Defense counsel objected, arguing that neither defendant had a criminal record. Counsel also noted that both Jack and Mark had lived in the community their entire life, both owned multimillion-dollar properties in the community, and both had families in the community. The defense attorneys argued that the court should set bail at a percentage bond of $250,000 apiece, secured by the defendants' property, with each defendant putting up $25,000 cash. The defendants also offered to surrender their passports and check in with pre-trial services once a week in person and once a day by telephone.

(a) If you were the magistrate, would you agree to the proposed bail conditions or would you deny bail for Mark Ferris? What about for his brother Jack? Is there any further information you would want to know before making your decision?

(b) Assume someone else is the magistrate judge and made the opposite decisions that you made in (a). The defendants seek bail review. You are now a judge reviewing the decision under a clear error standard. Do you reverse the magistrate's decision regarding Mark? What about the decision regarding Jack?

2. Bail for a Bank Robber? Charlie Haskett was arrested for bank robbery. He was then brought before a federal magistrate within 24 hours for his initial appearance. At the initial appearance, the prosecutor asked for a continuance on the bail hearing. The state wanted to run Haskett's DNA through a federal database to see if it matched any unsolved cases. Defense counsel objected to the continuance, but the court granted it. Haskett was held in custody until the bail hearing.

Two days later, the bail hearing was held in front of a federal judge. The prosecutor informed the court that Haskett's DNA did not match any unsolved crimes. Nonetheless, the prosecutor asked for $5,000 in bail, arguing that Haskett was a flight risk because the crime was serious and the evidence was strong—an image of Haskett's face was caught on a surveillance camera. Haskett's attorney asked for him to be released on his own recognizance, since he had only one prior conviction—a misdemeanor, for which he made all of his court appearances. Haskett had lived in the jurisdiction his entire life, and he reported that he had a steady job. Counsel also informed the judge that Haskett had no assets and so could not reasonably post a bail of $5,000. After the arguments, the judge set a cash bail of $5,000.

One week later, Haskett was still in jail, having been unable to raise the $5,000. Haskett's attorney asked for a new bail hearing. She had confirmed that Haskett had a steady job, and wanted to call Haskett's employer to the stand during the hearing to testify that Haskett was a dependable worker and always came to work promptly. The trial judge denied the motion for a new bail hearing.

Were Haskett's rights violated when:

1. The magistrate granted a continuance for the bail hearing?
2. The trial judge set $5,000 bail?
3. The judge refused to grant a new bail hearing?

FROM THE COURTROOM

UNITED STATES v. SALERNO

United States Supreme Court, 1987
481 U.S. 739

[Chief Justice Rehquist delivered the opinion of the Court.]

[Justice MARSHALL filed a dissenting opinion, which was joined by Justice BRENNAN.]

[Justice STEVENS filed a dissenting opinion.]

The Bail Reform Act of 1984 (Act) allows a federal court to detain an arrestee pending trial if the Government demonstrates by clear and convincing evidence after an adversary hearing that no release conditions "will reasonably assure . . . the safety of any other person and the community." The United States Court of Appeals for the Second Circuit struck down this provision of the Act as facially unconstitutional, because, in that court's words, this type of pretrial detention violates "substantive due process." We granted certiorari because of a conflict among the Courts of Appeals regarding the validity of the Act. We hold that, as against the facial attack mounted by these respondents, the Act fully comports with constitutional requirements. We therefore reverse.

I

Responding to "the alarming problem of crimes committed by persons on release," Congress formulated the Bail Reform Act of 1984, 18 U.S.C. § 3141 *et seq.* as the solution to a bail crisis in the federal courts. The Act represents the National Legislature's considered response to numerous perceived deficiencies in the federal bail process. By providing for sweeping changes in both the way federal courts consider bail applications and the circumstances under which bail is granted, Congress hoped to "give the courts adequate authority to make release decisions that give appropriate recognition to the danger a person may pose to others if released."

To this end, § 3141(a) of the Act requires a judicial officer to determine whether an arrestee shall be detained. Section 3142(e) provides that "[i]f, after a hearing pursuant to the provisions of subsection (f), the judicial officer finds that no condition or combination of conditions will reasonably assure the appearance of the person as required and the safety of any other person and the community, he shall order the detention of the person prior to trial." Section 3142(f) provides the arrestee with a number of procedural safeguards. He may request the presence of counsel at the detention hearing, he may testify and present witnesses in his behalf, as well as proffer evidence, and he may cross-examine other witnesses appearing at the hearing. If the judicial officer finds that no conditions of pretrial release can reasonably assure the safety of other persons and the community, he must state his findings of fact in writing, § 3142(i), and support his conclusion with "clear and convincing evidence," § 3142(f).

The judicial officer is not given unbridled discretion in making the detention determination. Congress has specified the considerations relevant to that decision. These factors include the nature and seriousness of the charges, the substantiality of the Government's evidence against the arrestee, the arrestee's background and characteristics, and the nature and seriousness of the danger posed by the suspect's release. § 3142(g). Should a judicial officer order detention, the detainee is entitled to expedited appellate review of the detention order. §§ 3145(b), (c).

Respondents Anthony Salerno and Vincent Cafaro were arrested on March 21, 1986, after being charged in a 29–count indictment alleging various Racketeer Influenced and Corrupt Organizations Act (RICO) violations, mail and wire fraud offenses, extortion, and various criminal gambling violations. The RICO counts alleged 35 acts of racketeering activity, including fraud, extortion, gambling, and conspiracy to commit murder. At respondents' arraignment, the Government moved to have Salerno and Cafaro detained pursuant to § 3142(e), on the ground that no condition of release would assure the safety of the community or any person. The District Court held a hearing at which the Government made a detailed proffer of evidence. The Government's case showed that Salerno was the "boss" of the Genovese crime family of La Cosa Nostra and that Cafaro was a "captain" in the Genovese family. According to the Government's proffer, based in large part on conversations intercepted by a court-ordered wiretap, the two respondents had participated in wide-ranging conspiracies to aid their illegitimate enterprises through violent means. The Government also offered the testimony of two of its trial witnesses, who would assert that Salerno personally participated in two murder conspiracies. Salerno opposed the motion for detention, challenging the credibility of the Government's witnesses. He offered the testimony of several character witnesses as well as a letter from his doctor stating that he was suffering from a serious medical condition. Cafaro presented no evidence at the hearing, but instead characterized the wiretap conversations as merely "tough talk."

The District Court granted the Government's detention motion, concluding that the Government had established by clear and convincing evidence that no condition or combination of conditions of release would ensure the safety of the community or any person:

> The activities of a criminal organization such as the Genovese Family do not cease with the arrest of its principals and their release on even the most stringent of bail conditions. The illegal businesses, in place for many years, require constant attention and protection, or they will fail. Under these circumstances, this court recognizes a strong incentive on the part of its leadership to continue business as usual. When business as usual involves threats, beatings, and murder, the present danger such people pose in the community is self-evident.

Respondents appealed, contending that to the extent that the Bail Reform Act permits pretrial detention on the ground that the arrestee is likely to commit future crimes, it is unconstitutional on its face. Over a dissent, the United States Court of Appeals for the Second Circuit agreed. Although the court agreed that pretrial detention could be imposed if the defendants were likely to intimidate witnesses or otherwise jeopardize the trial process, it found "§ 3142(e)'s authorization of pretrial detention [on the ground of future dangerousness] repugnant to the concept of substantive due process, which we believe prohibits the total deprivation of liberty simply as a means of preventing future crimes." The court concluded that the Government could not, consistent with due process, detain persons who had not been accused of any crime merely because they were thought to present a danger to the community. It reasoned that our criminal law system holds persons accountable for past actions, not anticipated future actions. Although a court could detain an arrestee who threatened to flee before trial, such detention would be permissible because it would serve the basic objective of a criminal system—bringing the accused to trial. The court distinguished our decision in *Gerstein v. Pugh,* 420 U.S. 103 (1975), in which we upheld police detention pursuant to arrest. The court construed *Gerstein* as limiting such detention to the "'administrative steps incident to arrest.'" The Court of Appeals also found our decision in *Schall v. Martin,* 467 U.S. 253 (1984), upholding postarrest, pretrial detention of juveniles, inapposite because juveniles have a lesser interest in liberty than do adults. The dissenting judge concluded that on its face, the Bail Reform Act adequately balanced the Federal Government's compelling interests in public safety against the detainee's liberty interests.

II

A facial challenge to a legislative Act is, of course, the most difficult challenge to mount successfully, since the challenger must establish that no set of circumstances exists under which the Act would be valid. The fact that the Bail Reform Act might operate unconstitutionally under some conceivable set of circumstances is insufficient to render it wholly invalid, since we have not recognized an "overbreadth" doctrine outside the limited context of the First Amendment. We think respondents have failed to shoulder their heavy burden to demonstrate that the Act is "facially" unconstitutional.

Respondents present two grounds for invalidating the Bail Reform Act's provisions permitting pretrial detention on the basis of future dangerousness. First, they rely upon the Court of Appeals' conclusion that the Act exceeds the limitations placed upon the Federal Government by the Due Process Clause of the Fifth Amendment. Second, they contend that the Act contravenes the Eighth Amendment's proscription against excessive bail. We treat these contentions in turn.

A

The Due Process Clause of the Fifth Amendment provides that "No person shall . . . be deprived of life, liberty, or property, without due process of law. . . ." This Court has held that the Due Process Clause protects individuals against two types of government action. So-called "substantive due process" prevents the government from engaging in conduct that "shocks the conscience," *Rochin v. California,* 342 U.S. 165 (1952), or interferes with rights "implicit in the concept of ordered liberty," *Palko v. Connecticut,* 302 U.S. 319 (1937). When government action depriving a person of life, liberty, or property survives substantive due process scrutiny, it must still be implemented in a fair manner. *Mathews v. Eldridge,* 424 U.S. 319 (1976). This requirement has traditionally been referred to as "procedural" due process.

Respondents first argue that the Act violates substantive due process because the pretrial detention it authorizes constitutes impermissible punishment before trial. The Government, however, has never argued that pretrial detention could be upheld if it were "punishment." The Court of Appeals assumed that pretrial detention under the Bail Reform Act is regulatory, not penal, and we agree that it is.

As an initial matter, the mere fact that a person is detained does not inexorably lead to the conclusion that the government has imposed punishment. To determine whether a restriction on liberty constitutes impermissible punishment or permissible regulation, we first look to legislative intent. Unless Congress expressly intended to impose punitive restrictions, the punitive/regulatory distinction turns on "'whether an alternative purpose to which [the restriction] may rationally be connected is assignable for it, and whether it appears excessive in relation to the alternative purpose assigned [to it].'"

We conclude that the detention imposed by the Act falls on the regulatory side of the dichotomy. The legislative history of the Bail Reform Act clearly indicates that Congress did not formulate the pretrial detention provisions as punishment for dangerous individuals. Congress instead perceived pretrial detention as a potential solution to a pressing societal problem. There is no doubt that preventing danger to the community is a legitimate regulatory goal.

Nor are the incidents of pretrial detention excessive in relation to the regulatory goal Congress sought to achieve. The Bail Reform Act carefully limits the circumstances under which detention may be sought to the most serious of crimes. See 18 U.S.C. § 3142(f) (detention hearings available if case involves crimes of violence, offenses for which the sentence is life imprisonment or death, serious drug offenses, or certain repeat offenders). The arrestee is entitled to a prompt detention hearing, and the maximum length of pretrial detention is limited by the stringent time limitations of the Speedy Trial Act. Moreover, as in *Schall v. Martin,* the conditions of confinement envisioned by the Act "appear to reflect the regulatory purposes relied upon by the" Government. As in *Schall,* the statute at issue here requires that detainees be housed in a "facility separate, to the extent practicable, from persons awaiting or serving sentences or being held in custody pending appeal. We conclude, therefore, that the pretrial detention contemplated by the Bail Reform Act is regulatory in nature, and does not constitute punishment before trial in violation of the Due Process Clause.

The Court of Appeals nevertheless concluded that "the Due Process Clause prohibits pretrial detention on the ground of danger to the community as a regulatory measure, without regard to the duration of the detention." Respondents characterize the Due Process Clause as erecting an impenetrable "wall" in this area that "no governmental interest—rational, important, compelling or otherwise—may surmount."

We do not think the Clause lays down any such categorical imperative. We have repeatedly held that the Government's regulatory interest in community safety can, in appropriate circumstances, outweigh an individual's liberty interest. For example, in times of war or insurrection, when society's interest is at its peak, the Government may detain individuals whom the government believes to be dangerous. Even outside the exigencies of war, we have found that sufficiently compelling governmental interests can justify detention of dangerous persons. Thus, we have found no absolute constitutional barrier to detention of potentially dangerous resident aliens pending deportation proceedings. We have also held that the government may detain mentally unstable individuals who present a danger to the public, and dangerous defendants who become incompetent to stand trial. We have approved of postarrest regulatory detention of juveniles when they present a continuing danger to the community. Even competent adults may face substantial liberty restrictions as a result of the operation of our criminal justice system. If the police suspect an individual of a crime, they may arrest and hold him until a neutral magistrate determines whether probable cause exists. Finally, respondents concede and the Court of Appeals noted that an arrestee may be incarcerated until trial if he presents a risk of flight or a danger to witnesses.

Respondents characterize all of these cases as exceptions to the "general rule" of substantive due process that the government may not detain a person prior to a judgment of guilt in a criminal trial. Such a "general rule" may freely be conceded, but we think that these cases show a sufficient number of exceptions to the rule that the congressional action challenged here can hardly be characterized as totally novel. Given the well-established authority of the government, in special circumstances, to restrain individuals' liberty prior to or even without criminal trial and conviction, we think that the present statute providing for pretrial detention on the basis of dangerousness must be evaluated in precisely the same manner that we evaluated the laws in the cases discussed above.

The government's interest in preventing crime by arrestees is both legitimate and compelling. In *Schall,* we recognized the strength of the State's interest in preventing juvenile crime. This general concern with crime prevention is no less compelling when the suspects are adults. Indeed, "[t]he harm suffered by the victim of a crime is not dependent upon the age of the perpetrator." The Bail Reform Act of 1984 responds to an even more particularized governmental interest than the interest we sustained in *Schall.* The statute we upheld in *Schall* permitted pretrial detention of any juvenile arrested on any charge after a showing that the individual might commit some undefined further crimes. The Bail Reform Act, in contrast, narrowly focuses on a particularly acute problem in which the Government interests are overwhelming. The Act operates only on individuals who have been arrested for a specific category of extremely serious offenses. Congress specifically found that these individuals are far more likely to be responsible for dangerous acts in the community after arrest. Nor is the Act by any means a scattershot attempt to incapacitate those who are merely suspected of these serious crimes. The Government must first of all demonstrate probable cause to believe that the charged crime has been committed by the arrestee, but that is not enough. In a full-blown adversary hearing, the Government must convince a neutral decisionmaker by clear and convincing evidence that no conditions of release can reasonably assure the safety of the community or any person. While the Government's general interest in preventing crime is compelling, even this interest is heightened when the Government musters convincing proof that the arrestee, already indicted or held to answer for a serious crime, presents a demonstrable danger to the community. Under these narrow circumstances, society's interest in crime prevention is at its greatest.

On the other side of the scale, of course, is the individual's strong interest in liberty. We do not minimize the importance and fundamental nature of this right. But, as our cases hold, this right may, in circumstances where the government's interest is sufficiently weighty, be subordinated to the greater needs of society. We think that Congress' careful delineation of the circumstances under which detention will be permitted satisfies this standard. When the Government proves by clear and convincing evidence that an arrestee presents an identified and articulable threat to an individual or the community, we believe that, consistent with the Due Process Clause, a court may disable the arrestee from executing that threat. Under these circumstances, we cannot categorically state that pretrial detention "offends some principle of justice so rooted in the traditions and conscience of our people as to be ranked as fundamental."

Finally, we may dispose briefly of respondents' facial challenge to the procedures of the Bail Reform Act. To sustain them against such a challenge, we need only find them "adequate to authorize the pretrial detention of at least some [persons] charged with crimes," whether or not they might be insufficient in some particular circumstances. We think they pass that test. As we stated in *Schall,* "there is nothing inherently unattainable about a prediction of future criminal conduct."

Under the Bail Reform Act, the procedures by which a judicial officer evaluates the likelihood of future dangerousness are specifically designed to further the accuracy of that determination. Detainees have a right to counsel at the detention hearing. They may testify in their own behalf, present information by proffer or otherwise, and cross-examine witnesses who appear at the hearing. The judicial officer charged with the responsibility of determining the appropriateness of detention is guided by statutorily enumerated factors, which include the nature and the circumstances of the charges, the weight of the evidence, the history and characteristics of the putative offender, and the danger to the community. The Government must prove its case by clear and convincing evidence. Finally, the judicial officer must include written findings of fact and a written statement of reasons for a decision to detain. The Act's review provisions, provide for immediate appellate review of the detention decision.

We think these extensive safeguards suffice to repel a facial challenge. The protections are more exacting than those we found sufficient in the juvenile context, see *Schall,* and they far exceed what we found necessary to effect limited postarrest detention in *Gerstein v. Pugh.* Given the legitimate and compelling regulatory purpose of the Act and the procedural protections it offers, we conclude that the Act is not facially invalid under the Due Process Clause of the Fifth Amendment.

B

Respondents also contend that the Bail Reform Act violates the Excessive Bail Clause of the Eighth Amendment. The Court of Appeals did not address this issue because it found that the Act violates the Due Process Clause. We think that the Act survives a challenge founded upon the Eighth Amendment.

The Eighth Amendment addresses pretrial release by providing merely that "[e]xcessive bail shall not be required." This Clause, of course, says nothing about whether bail shall be available at all. Respondents nevertheless contend that this Clause grants them a right to bail calculated solely upon considerations of flight. They rely on *Stack v. Boyle,* 342 U.S. 1 (1951), in which the Court stated that "[b]ail set at a figure higher than an amount reasonably calculated [to ensure the defendant's presence at trial] is 'excessive' under the Eighth Amendment." In respondents' view, since the Bail Reform Act allows a court essentially to set bail at an infinite amount for reasons not related to the risk of flight, it violates the Excessive Bail Clause. Respondents concede that the right to bail they have discovered in the Eighth Amendment is not absolute. A court may, for example, refuse bail in capital cases. And, as the Court of Appeals noted and respondents admit, a court may refuse bail when the defendant presents a threat to the judicial process by intimidating witnesses. Respondents characterize these exceptions as consistent with what they claim to be the sole purpose of bail—to ensure the integrity of the judicial process.

While we agree that a primary function of bail is to safeguard the courts' role in adjudicating the guilt or innocence of defendants, we reject the proposition that the Eighth Amendment categorically prohibits the government from pursuing other admittedly compelling interests through regulation of pretrial release. The above-quoted *dictum* in *Stack v. Boyle* is far too slender a reed on which to rest this argument. The Court in *Stack* had no occasion to consider whether the Excessive Bail Clause requires courts to admit all defendants to bail, because the statute before the Court in that case in fact allowed the defendants to be bailed. Thus, the Court had to determine only whether bail, admittedly available in that case, was excessive if set at a sum greater than that necessary to ensure the arrestees' presence at trial.

. . .

Nothing in the text of the Bail Clause limits permissible Government considerations solely to questions of flight. The only arguable substantive limitation of the Bail Clause is that the Government's proposed conditions of release or detention not be "excessive" in light of the perceived evil. Of course, to determine whether the Government's response is excessive, we must compare that response against the interest the Government seeks to protect by means of that response. Thus, when the Government has admitted that its only interest is in preventing flight, bail must be set by a court at a sum designed to ensure that goal, and no more. We believe that when Congress has mandated detention on the basis of a compelling interest other than prevention of flight, as it has here, the Eighth Amendment does not require release on bail.

III

In our society liberty is the norm, and detention prior to trial or without trial is the carefully limited exception. We hold that the provisions for pretrial detention in the Bail Reform Act of 1984 fall within that carefully limited exception. The Act authorizes the detention prior to trial of arrestees charged with serious felonies who are found after an adversary hearing to pose a threat to the safety of individuals or to the community which no condition of release can dispel. The numerous procedural safeguards detailed above must attend this adversary hearing. We are unwilling to say that this congressional determination, based as it is upon that primary concern of every government—a concern for the safety and indeed the lives of its citizens—on its face violates either the Due Process Clause of the Fifth Amendment or the Excessive Bail Clause of the Eighth Amendment.

The judgment of the Court of Appeals is therefore

Reversed.

Justice MARSHALL, with whom Justice BRENNAN joins, dissenting.

This case brings before the Court for the first time a statute in which Congress declares that a person innocent of any crime may be jailed indefinitely, pending the trial of allegations which are legally presumed to be untrue, if the Government shows to the satisfaction of a judge that the accused is likely to commit crimes, unrelated to the pending charges, at any time in the future. Such statutes, consistent with the usages of tyranny and the excesses of what bitter experience teaches us to call the police state, have long been thought incompatible with the fundamental human rights protected by our Constitution. Today a majority of this Court holds otherwise. Its decision disregards basic principles of justice established centuries ago and enshrined beyond the reach of governmental interference in the Bill of Rights.

. . .

II

The majority approaches respondents' challenge to the Act by dividing the discussion into two sections, one concerned with the substantive guarantees implicit in the Due Process Clause, and the other concerned with the protection afforded by the Excessive Bail Clause of the Eighth Amendment. This is a sterile formalism, which divides a unitary argument into two independent parts and then professes to demonstrate that the parts are individually inadequate.

On the due process side of this false dichotomy appears an argument concerning the distinction between regulatory and punitive legislation. The majority concludes that the Act is a regulatory rather than a punitive measure. The ease with which the conclusion is reached suggests the worthlessness of the achievement. The major premise is that "[u]nless Congress expressly intended to impose punitive restrictions, the punitive/regulatory distinction turns on '"whether an alternative purpose to which [the restriction] may rationally be connected is assignable for it, and whether it appears excessive in relation to the alternative purpose assigned [to it].""" The majority finds that "Congress did not formulate the pretrial detention provisions as punishment for dangerous individuals," but instead was pursuing the "legitimate regulatory goal" of "preventing danger to the community." Concluding that pretrial detention is not an excessive solution to the problem of preventing danger to the community, the majority thus finds that no substantive element of the guarantee of due process invalidates the statute

This argument does not demonstrate the conclusion it purports to justify. Let us apply the majority's reasoning to a similar, hypothetical case. After investigation, Congress determines (not unrealistically) that a large proportion of violent crime is perpetrated by persons who are unemployed. It also determines, equally reasonably, that much violent crime is committed at night. From amongst the panoply of "potential solutions," Congress chooses a statute which permits, after judicial proceedings, the imposition of a dusk-to-dawn curfew on anyone who is unemployed. Since this is not a measure enacted for the purpose of punishing the unemployed, and since the majority finds that preventing danger to the community is a legitimate regulatory goal, the curfew statute would, according to the majority's analysis, be a mere "regulatory" detention statute, entirely compatible with the substantive components of the Due Process Clause.

The absurdity of this conclusion arises, of course, from the majority's cramped concept of substantive due process. The majority proceeds as though the only substantive right protected by the Due Process Clause is a right to be free from punishment before conviction. The majority's technique for infringing this right is simple: merely redefine any measure which is claimed to be punishment as "regulation," and, magically, the Constitution no longer prohibits its imposition. Because, as I discuss in Part III, the Due Process Clause protects other substantive rights which are infringed by this legislation, the majority's argument is merely an exercise in obfuscation.

The logic of the majority's Eighth Amendment analysis is equally unsatisfactory. The Eighth Amendment, as the majority notes, states that "[e]xcessive bail shall not be required." The majority then declares, as if it were undeniable, that: "[t]his Clause, of course, says nothing about whether bail shall be available at all." If excessive bail is imposed the defendant stays in jail. The same result is achieved if bail is denied altogether. Whether the magistrate sets bail at $1 million or refuses to set bail at all, the consequences are indistinguishable. It would be mere sophistry to suggest that the Eighth Amendment protects against the former decision, and not the latter. Indeed, such a result would lead to the conclusion that there was no need for Congress to pass a preventive detention measure of any kind; every federal magistrate and district judge could simply refuse, despite the absence of any evidence of risk of flight or danger to the community, to set bail. This would be entirely constitutional, since, according to the majority, the Eighth Amendment "says nothing about whether bail shall be available at all."

But perhaps, the majority says, this manifest absurdity can be avoided. Perhaps the Bail Clause is addressed only to the Judiciary. "[W]e need not decide today," the majority says, "whether the Excessive Bail Clause speaks at all to Congress' power to define the classes of criminal arrestees who shall be admitted to bail." The majority is correct that this question need not be decided today; it was decided long ago. Federal and state statutes which purport to accomplish what the Eighth Amendment forbids, such as imposing cruel and unusual punishments, may not stand. The text of the Amendment, which provides simply that "[e]xcessive bail shall not be required, nor excessive fines imposed, nor cruel and unusual punishments inflicted," provides absolutely no support for the majority's speculation that both courts and Congress are forbidden to inflict cruel and unusual punishments, while only the courts are forbidden to require excessive bail.

The majority's attempts to deny the relevance of the Bail Clause to this case are unavailing, but the majority is nonetheless correct that the prohibition of excessive bail means that in order "to determine whether the Government's response is excessive, we must compare that response against the interest the Government seeks to protect by means of that response." The majority concedes, as it must, that "when the Government has admitted that its only interest is in preventing flight, bail must be set by a court at a sum designed to ensure that goal, and no more." But, the majority says, "when Congress has mandated detention on the basis of a compelling interest other than prevention of flight, as it has here, the Eighth Amendment does not require release on bail." This conclusion follows only if the "compelling" interest upon which Congress acted is an interest which the Constitution permits Congress to further through the denial of bail. The majority does not ask, as a result of its disingenuous division of the analysis, if there are any substantive limits contained in both the Eighth Amendment and the Due Process Clause which render this system of preventive detention unconstitutional. The majority does not ask because the answer is apparent and, to the majority, inconvenient.

III

The essence of this case may be found, ironically enough, in a provision of the Act to which the majority does not refer. Title 18 U.S.C. § 3142(j) provides that "[n]othing in this section shall be construed as modifying or limiting the presumption of innocence." But the very pith and purpose of this statute is an abhorrent limitation of the presumption of innocence. The majority's untenable conclusion that the present Act is constitutional arises from a specious denial of the role of the Bail Clause and the Due Process Clause in protecting the invaluable guarantee afforded by the presumption of innocence.

"The principle that there is a presumption of innocence in favor of the accused is the undoubted law, axiomatic and elementary, and its enforcement lies at the foundation of the administration of our criminal law." Our society's belief, reinforced over the centuries, that all are innocent until the state has proved them to be guilty, like the companion principle that guilt must be proved beyond a reasonable doubt, is "implicit in the concept of ordered liberty," and is established beyond legislative contravention in the Due Process Clause.

The statute now before us declares that persons who have been indicted may be detained if a judicial officer finds clear and convincing evidence that they pose a danger to individuals or to the community. The statute does not authorize the Government to imprison anyone it has evidence is dangerous; indictment is necessary. But let us suppose that a defendant is indicted and the Government shows by clear and convincing evidence that he is dangerous and should be detained pending a trial, at which trial the defendant is acquitted. May the Government continue to hold the defendant in detention based upon its showing that he is dangerous? The answer cannot be yes, for that would allow the Government to imprison someone for uncommitted crimes based upon "proof" not beyond a reasonable doubt. The result must therefore be that once the indictment has failed, detention cannot continue. But our fundamental principles of justice declare that the defendant is as innocent on the day before his trial as he is on the morning after his acquittal. Under this statute an untried indictment somehow acts to permit a detention, based on other charges, which after an acquittal would be unconstitutional. The conclusion is inescapable that the indictment has been turned into evidence, if not that the defendant is guilty of the crime charged, then that left to his own devices he will soon be guilty of something else. "'If it suffices to accuse, what will become of the innocent?'"

To be sure, an indictment is not without legal consequences. It establishes that there is probable cause to believe that an offense was committed, and that the defendant committed it. Upon probable cause a warrant for the defendant's arrest may issue; a period of administrative detention may occur before the evidence of probable cause is presented to a neutral magistrate. Once a defendant has been committed for trial he may be detained in custody if the magistrate finds that no conditions of release will prevent him from becoming a fugitive. But in this connection the charging instrument is evidence of nothing more than the fact that there will be a trial, and

> release before trial is conditioned upon the accused's giving adequate assurance that he will stand trial and submit to sentence if found guilty. Like the ancient practice of securing the oaths of responsible persons to stand as sureties for the accused, the modern practice of requiring a bail bond or the deposit of a sum of money subject to forfeiture serves as additional assurance of the presence of an accused.

The finding of probable cause conveys power to try, and the power to try imports of necessity the power to assure that the processes of justice will not be evaded or obstructed. "Pretrial detention to prevent future crimes against society at large, however, is not justified by any concern for holding a trial on the charges for which a defendant has been arrested." The detention purportedly authorized by this statute bears no relation to the Government's power to try charges supported by a finding of probable cause, and thus the interests it serves are outside the scope of interests which may be considered in weighing the excessiveness of bail under the Eighth Amendment.

. . .

IV

There is a connection between the peculiar facts of this case and the evident constitutional defects in the statute which the Court upholds today. Respondent Cafaro was originally incarcerated for an indeterminate period at the request of the Government, which believed (or professed to believe) that his release imminently threatened the safety of the community. That threat apparently vanished, from the Government's point of view, when Cafaro agreed to act as a covert agent of the Government. There could be no more eloquent demonstration of the coercive power of authority to imprison upon prediction, or of the dangers which the almost inevitable abuses pose to the cherished liberties of a free society.

"It is a fair summary of history to say that the safeguards of liberty have frequently been forged in controversies involving not very nice people." Honoring the presumption of innocence is often difficult; sometimes we must pay substantial social costs as a result of our commitment to the values we espouse. But at the end of the day the presumption of innocence protects the innocent; the shortcuts we take with those whom we believe to be guilty injure only those wrongfully accused and, ultimately, ourselves.

Throughout the world today there are men, women, and children interned indefinitely, awaiting trials which may never come or which may be a mockery of the word, because their governments believe them to be "dangerous." Our Constitution, whose construction began two centuries ago, can shelter us forever from the evils of such unchecked power. Over 200 years it has slowly, through our efforts, grown more durable, more expansive, and more just. But it cannot protect us if we lack the courage, and the self-restraint, to protect ourselves. Today a majority of the Court applies itself to an ominous exercise in demolition. Theirs is truly a decision which will go forth without authority, and come back without respect.

I dissent.

[The dissenting opinion of Justice STEVENS is omitted].

34

Preliminary Hearings

Key Concepts

- Full Adversarial Hearing to Determine Probable Cause
- Either a Preliminary Hearing or Grand Jury Is Necessary to Move Forward with Felony Case
- Also Provides Discovery, Preserves Testimony, and Generates Written Record of Witness Statements

A. Introduction and Policy.

1. Complaint, Information, or Indictment. So far we have traced the defendant from the point of his arrest through to the initial appearance and the bail hearing. At this point, in order to know what happens to the defendant next, we need to know more about the crime for which he is being charged and the laws of the jurisdiction in which he was arrested.

First, we need to know if the defendant is being charged with a **misdemeanor** or a **felony.** A felony is a crime for which the maximum possible sentence is one year or greater; a misdemeanor is any crime whose maximum sentence is less than one year. (Most jurisdictions classify the least severe misdemeanors as "violations" or "minor misdemeanors," but for the purposes of our current discussion all misdemeanors are treated alike.)

If the defendant is being charged only with misdemeanors, the charging document is called a "**complaint**" and is usually filed at the initial appearance. The complaint merely states the crime(s) that the defendant is charged with committing, and describes the facts of the case in sufficient detail to fulfill the elements of the charged crime(s). The complaint needs to be signed under oath by someone who can attest to the facts. However, the statement of facts can include hearsay allegations, so the witness who signs the complaint need not have first-hand knowledge. Usually the complaint is signed and sworn by the arresting officer and includes language such as "I have been informed by . . . ." The complaint then quotes the actual witnesses in the case in order to establish the elements of the crime.

If the defendant is charged with at least one felony, the prosecutor can begin the case by filing a complaint at the initial appearance, but she cannot move forward with the case until she files an **information** (which is issued after a preliminary hearing) or an **indictment** (which is issued after a grand jury presentation). Different jurisdictions have different requirements. Some jurisdictions require a grand jury presentation, while some allow the case to proceed after only a preliminary hearing. In either case, the primary purpose of this phase is the same: a formal screening of the case in order to ensure there is probable cause to move forward. This formal screening is different in kind from the *Gerstein* hearing to determine probable cause that we discussed in **Chapter 29** and that usually occurs at the initial appearance. The *Gerstein* hearing can be a cursory, *ex parte* examination of the complaint by a magistrate, equivalent to the issuing of an arrest warrant. In contrast, the preliminary hearing is a true hearing—with witnesses testifying under oath and defense attorneys present and able to cross-examine or present their own witnesses. The grand jury also involves live witness testimony in front of a panel of lay people.

In jurisdictions in which a grand jury indictment is required (such as in federal courts), prosecutors can usually bypass the preliminary hearing by obtaining an indictment of the defendant. In some of these jurisdictions, a prosecutor will do both: first conduct a preliminary hearing and then obtain an indictment from the grand jury. This may be because of statutorily imposed deadlines: the prosecutor must formally establish probable cause within a certain period of time, and the grand jury caseload may be so high that the prosecutor cannot obtain an indictment within the required time. The preliminary hearing may have other benefits for the prosecutor as well, which we will explore below.

In jurisdictions where an indictment is not required, prosecutors have the option of obtaining an information via a preliminary hearing instead of an indictment from the grand jury. Most prosecutors choose to use a preliminary hearing in these situations. We will compare preliminary hearings and grand jury presentations in more depth at the end of **Chapter 35**.

Finally, a handful of states permit a felony to move forward without a preliminary hearing or an indictment through a process called "direct filing." In these states the prosecutor simply files an information with a supporting affidavit, and the trial judge reviews the filing *ex parte* to determine whether probable cause exists. Essentially this is a second *Gerstein* hearing, conducted by the trial judge instead of the magistrate. However, in most other jurisdictions, the preliminary hearing will be held before a magistrate.

2. Function of the Preliminary Hearing. A preliminary hearing may also be referred to as a "bindover hearing," a "preliminary examination," or a "probable cause hearing." The primary function of the hearing is for the judge to screen the case to ensure there is sufficient probable cause to move the case to trial. In theory, this step in the process acts as a judicial check on prosecutorial power meant to prevent weak cases from going forward. This saves the state resources and ensures that a defendant need not go through the ordeal of trial (not to mention perhaps remaining in pre-trial custody) if the prosecutor does not have a sufficient case. In reality, only 5%-10% of cases are dismissed at the preliminary hearing stage, but the mere fact that the prosecutor must overcome this hurdle may affect a prosecutor's initial decision to file charges.

The screening function can also have an important effect on the plea bargaining process. By letting the defense attorney and the defendant see a preview of evidence, the preliminary hearing may convince a defense attorney that a certain plea offer is reasonable, or may convince a recalcitrant defendant to accept a plea offer. Similarly, if the evidence ends up looking weaker than the prosecutor expects—a witness does not appear credible on the stand, or cross-examination exposes unexpected weaknesses in the evidence—the prosecutor may make a more reasonable plea demand.

The preliminary hearing also serves at least three other functions:

1. It provides the defense attorney with information about the prosecutor's case, thus acting as a *de facto* discovery tool;

2. It preserves the testimony of witnesses in case they are not available at trial; and

3. For the witnesses who do testify at trial, it creates an official record of their testimony which can be used to impeach them if they change their story at trial.

We will explore these other purposes in more detail in Section C.2 below.

B. The Law. The Constitution never mentions preliminary hearings, but the Fifth Amendment requires an indictment for any "capital or otherwise infamous crime" in all federal courts. For this reason, in almost every federal jurisdiction, the prosecutor will proceed by obtaining an indictment from the grand jury instead of conducting a preliminary hearing. The Federal Rules of Criminal Procedure acknowledge this reality. Although Rule 5.1 sets out the procedure for preliminary hearings, it allows the preliminary hearing to be bypassed for felony charges if the prosecutor has obtained an indictment.

Rule 5.1. Preliminary Hearing

(a) In General. If a defendant is charged with an offense other than a petty offense, a magistrate judge must conduct a preliminary hearing unless:

(1) the defendant waives the hearing;

(2) the defendant is indicted;

(3) the government files an information under Rule 7(b) [after the defendant has waived the indictment requirement] charging the defendant with a felony;

(4) the government files an information charging the defendant with a misdemeanor; or

(5) the defendant is charged with a misdemeanor and consents to trial before a magistrate judge.

. . .

(c) Scheduling. The magistrate judge must hold the preliminary hearing within a reasonable time, but no later than 14 days after the initial appearance if the defendant is in custody and no later than 21 days if not in custody.

(d) Extending the Time. With the defendant's consent and upon a showing of good cause—taking into account the public interest in the prompt disposition of criminal cases—a magistrate judge may extend the time limits in Rule 5.1(c) one or more times. If the defendant does not consent, the magistrate judge may extend the time limits only on a showing that extraordinary circumstances exist and justice requires the delay.

(e) Hearing and Finding. At the preliminary hearing, the defendant may cross-examine adverse witnesses and may introduce evidence but may not object to evidence on the ground that it was unlawfully acquired. If the magistrate judge finds probable cause to believe an offense has been committed and the defendant committed it, the magistrate judge must promptly require the defendant to appear for further proceedings.

(f) Discharging the Defendant. If the magistrate judge finds no probable cause to believe an offense has been committed or the defendant committed it, the magistrate judge must dismiss the complaint and discharge the defendant. A discharge does not preclude the government from later prosecuting the defendant for the same offense.

. . .

Under section (a), the prosecutor can bypass the preliminary hearing if she has indicted the defendant or if the defendant waives the indictment or the preliminary hearing itself. The Rule also notes that preliminary hearings are not required for misdemeanors. Usually the prosecutor will indict the defendant within the time limits set out in section (c), thus obviating the need for a preliminary hearing. (Note that occasionally a defendant will be indicted **before** he is arrested—for example, if he has been the subject of a long-term grand jury investigation. In that case, there is also no need to conduct a preliminary hearing).

Section (c) sets a time limit for the preliminary hearing, which—thanks to the language of section (a)—also sets a time limit for the grand jury indictment. If the defendant is in custody, the prosecutor must either indict the defendant within 14 days of the initial appearance or conduct a preliminary hearing. If the defendant is not in custody, the time limit is twenty-one days. Section (d) notes that these time limits may not be extended without the defendant's consent unless there are "extraordinary circumstances."

Section (e) sets out the procedure for the hearing. A preliminary hearing proceeds very much like a bench trial. Each side may make an opening statement, and then the prosecutor presents witnesses, who the defense has the right to cross-examine. After the prosecution's case, the defendant has the right to present his own witnesses, and the prosecutor can cross-examine them. Then each side has the chance for a brief closing argument, and the judge will make her ruling.

One significant difference between the preliminary hearing and a full trial is that the exclusionary rule does not apply at this stage—that is, the defendant may not challenge the admission of evidence on the grounds that it was unconstitutionally obtained. Furthermore, in many jurisdictions (including the federal courts) the rules of evidence do not apply—thus, the prosecutor can introduce hearsay evidence. However, some states do apply the rules of evidence in preliminary hearings,[1] and even in jurisdictions in which the rules of evidence do not apply, the magistrate or judge may give less weight to evidence that would be inadmissible at trial. Also note that privilege rules always apply, in every jurisdiction, at every stage of the criminal proceeding.[2]

The other significant difference between a preliminary hearing and a trial is that the prosecutor need only prove there is probable cause to believe the defendant committed the crime. In contrast, at a trial, the prosecution's burden is proof beyond a reasonable doubt. We will discuss this probable cause standard in more detail in Section C.1 below. The reasonable doubt standard is discussed in **Chapter 44**.

Finally, section (f) requires that the magistrate dismiss the charges if there is no probable cause. Such a dismissal would not prevent the prosecutor from bringing the charges again if she wants. In reality, though, a prosecutor who has lost a

---

[1] See, e.g., Ohio R. Crim. P. 5(b)(2).

[2] See, e.g., Fed. R. Evid. 1101(c).

preliminary hearing is unlikely to re-file the same charges unless substantial new evidence is uncovered. Even the most zealous prosecutor would face pressure from superiors not to bring the same case with identical evidence, and such an action would cause her to lose credibility with the judge or magistrate.

The federal rule cited above is similar in many respects to state rules for preliminary hearings. The primary difference is that in many states the prosecutor does not have to obtain an indictment from the grand jury and so routinely uses the preliminary hearing to establish probable cause. Thus, the preliminary hearing is far more common in these states (known as "informations states") than it is on the federal level. Although there is no constitutional right to a preliminary hearing, once a state provides for such a hearing, the Constitution mandates that the defendant be represented by counsel at the hearing (see generally **Chapter 30**). And just like on the federal level, most state statutes give the defendant the right to cross-examine witnesses and the right to call his own witnesses at the hearing.

If the defendant's constitutional or statutory rights are violated during the preliminary hearing—for example, if he is denied a right to counsel, or the judge or magistrate commits error in finding probable cause—the defendant's recourse is somewhat limited. If the preliminary hearing were conducted by a trial judge, the defendant can appeal to the trial judge, who could order a new hearing if she determines the initial preliminary hearing was faulty. (Of course, if the prosecutor indicts the defendant at any point, there is no need for a preliminary hearing and so any mistakes in the preliminary hearing are moot). If the trial judge does not find any error in the preliminary hearing, the defendant cannot take an interlocutory appeal to an appellate court. His case will proceed to trial. If he is convicted, almost any mistake made during the preliminary hearing is considered harmless error—after all, a jury has now found that the defendant is guilty beyond a reasonable doubt, so clearly there was probable cause to believe the defendant committed the crime.

C. Applying the Law.

1. "Probable Cause." You should by now be very familiar with the term "probable cause" from other contexts: it is the standard by which quite a lot of law enforcement activity is judged, including the issuance of search warrants and arrest warrants. The same standard is also used at a *Gerstein* hearing if the defendant was arrested without a warrant in order to ensure the arrest was valid. In some states, "probable cause" has essentially the same meaning at the preliminary hearing stage. Those states tend to have the most relaxed evidentiary standards for the hearing, and they also limit the magistrate's role of the magistrate or judge in assessing credibility. If a witness' testimony is completely implausible, the magistrate or judge should disregard it, but otherwise she should leave credibility determinations to the jury at the subsequent trial. Essentially, the preliminary hearing in these jurisdictions is duplicative of the *Gerstein* hearing, except that the procedure is a bit more formalized.

However, in most jurisdictions the term "probable cause" means something slightly different in the context of a preliminary hearing than it does when authorizing (or reviewing) actions by law enforcement. When authorizing or reviewing law enforcement actions, the magistrate or judge is merely deciding whether there is sufficient evidence to lead a reasonable person to believe the suspect may have committed a crime. When reviewing a case at a preliminary hearing under the heightened standard, the magistrate or judge must decide whether there is sufficient evidence of guilt to believe that the defendant should face trial on the charges.

Thus, the probable cause standard in the context of a preliminary hearing is analogous to the standard used by a trial court when deciding a directed verdict motion by the defense: given the amount of credible evidence presented by the state, does it make sense to send the case to a jury, or is there so little evidence that no reasonable jury could find the defendant guilty beyond a reasonable doubt? This is much lower than the reasonable doubt standard, but it is higher than the probable cause standard used by law enforcement. One commentator noted the magistrate or judge at a preliminary hearing must determine "whether the policeman's 'reasonable belief,' when made visible constitutes 'probable cause' to believe a crime has been committed . . . [and] sufficient evidence [exists] to warrant a jury's finding the accused guilty."[3] In this sense, the preliminary hearing looks forward to the trial rather than backward at the law enforcement action.

In states that use this higher standard for probable cause, the preliminary hearing resembles more of a "mini-trial." Some states enforce the hearsay rule, forcing the prosecutor to bring live witnesses to establish probable cause for every element of the crime. In these states, the magistrate or judge will evaluate whether there is sufficient **admissible** evidence to constitute probable cause.

Similarly, because the role of the magistrate or judge in these states is to determine whether a reasonable juror could convict the defendant at a future trial, she must more closely weigh the credibility of the prosecutor's witnesses. As a result, the defense attorney is given more leeway in cross-examining the witnesses. The magistrate or judge may be convinced that probable cause exists after the direct examination of a key witness, but the defense then gets the chance to challenge the credibility of the witness (and thus challenge the probable cause itself) on cross-examination:

---

[3] Abraham S. Goldstein, The State and the Accused: Balance of Advantage in Criminal Procedure, 69 Yale L.J. 1149, 1166 (1960).

Example: Kenneth Myers was arrested for rape. The prosecutor alleged that Myers broke into the victim's home at night carrying a knife and attacked her while she was in bed. At the preliminary hearing, the victim was the only witness in the case, and she testified about the crime and identified Myers as the perpetrator. The defense attorney began his direct examination by asking whether the victim believed in witchcraft. The magistrate cut off questioning, stating that he had heard enough from the direct examination to determine that probable cause existed in the case, and that any cross-examination was unnecessary. The defense attorney then sought to admit evidence of a psychiatric report that diagnosed the victim with a number of mental illnesses. But, the magistrate refused to consider the report and terminated the hearing. The defendant appealed the case to the trial judge, arguing that he had not been permitted to present evidence relevant to the witness' credibility.[4]

Analysis: The trial judge agreed with the defendant and ordered a new preliminary hearing. The judge noted that the magistrate's role was to determine whether it was proper to bind over the defendant and send the prosecution's case to a jury. "The examining magistrate could not have possibly made an informed judgment on the question of whether there was sufficient credible evidence of the defendant's guilt to support a bind over until he had considered all of this evidence."[5]

The trial court noted that most of the time a defendant's evidence—whether it is an attack on the credibility of the state's witnesses or is instead his own witnesses who cast doubt on the prosecution's case—"will do no more than raise a conflict which can best be resolved by a jury at the actual trial."[6] Since the magistrate's job was not to determine ultimate guilt, he should bind those cases over so that a jury can resolve the conflict. But occasionally the evidence elicited by the defendant may be so damaging to the prosecution's case that it may "lead the examining magistrate to disbelieve the prosecution's witnesses,"[7] which would mean that the magistrate should dismiss the case for lack of probable cause. In order to know whether the defendant's evidence was strong enough to reach that point, the magistrate must allow the defendant to cross-examine the prosecution's witnesses and allow him to present his own evidence.[8]

As we will see below, however, magistrates are permitted to limit cross-examination to the issues which are relevant to the probable cause determination. So, for ex-

[4] Myers v. Commonwealth, 298 N.E.2d 819 (Mass. 1973).

[5] Id. at 826.

[6] Id.

[7] Id.

[8] Id. at 825–27.

ample, if the defense attempts to use cross-examination merely as a way to gather more discovery (for example, to elicit names of other witnesses), the magistrate may terminate the cross-examination.

2. Other Functions of the Preliminary Hearing.

a. Discovery. As we will see in **Chapter 39,** formal discovery in a criminal case occurs after the charging document is filed, and is primarily governed by Rule 16 of the Rules of Criminal Procedure, as well as other rules and statutes. However, in addition to the formal discovery process, the preliminary hearing can be a significant early source of discovery for the defendant. The prosecutor must essentially reveal the names of at least some of its witnesses, and these witnesses will make formal statements about what they saw in the case. The preliminary hearing will also reveal useful information about the prosecutor's theory of the case.

Courts have made clear that any discovery the defendant receives in the preliminary hearing is only an ancillary benefit—it is not the true purpose of the hearing. In other words, although the defendant can and frequently does use the preliminary hearing as a discovery tool, his ability to do so is limited by the official purpose of the proceedings:

> **Example**—Michael Hinkle was charged with second degree murder after he allegedly stabbed Alfred Robinson in the throat. At the preliminary hearing the prosecutor called Officer Day, who testified that he responded to an altercation outside a restaurant where he found Robinson bleeding from the throat and then saw Robinson being taken away in an ambulance. He spoke to a number of witnesses at the scene, three of whom were holding down the defendant and told him they had seen the defendant stab Robinson. Officer Day later went to the hospital and spoke to a doctor there who informed him that Robinson was pronounced dead on arrival. On cross-examination, the defense attorney asked Officer Day to name all of the witnesses with whom he spoke. The prosecutor objected to these questions and the magistrate sustained the objection.
>
> The prosecutor next called Paul Posten, who testified that he was in the restaurant eating dinner with two friends when he saw Hinkle and Robinson engaged in an argument. He then saw Hinkle pull out a knife and stab Robinson in the throat. On cross-examination, the defense attorney asked Posten how much he had been drinking that night and about a prior dispute Posten had with Hinkle. The prosecutor objected to these questions and

the objection was sustained. The defense attorney then asked Posten for the names of his two dinner companions, and the prosecutor again objected and the objection was sustained.

The prosecutor rested her case, and the defense attorney sought to call Officer Day. When the magistrate inquired why, the defense attorney explained that he wanted to ask Officer Day the question he had not been allowed to ask on cross—the names of the other witnesses with whom the officer spoke. The magistrate denied the request to call Officer Day. The defendant called no other witnesses.

The magistrate found there was probable cause, and bound the defendant over for trial. The defense attorney appealed the decision to the trial judge and requested a new hearing. The defense attorney argued he was denied the right to cross-examine the prosecution witnesses, and also denied the right to call his own witnesses.

Analysis: The magistrate did not commit error in prohibiting the defense attorney from asking Officer Day about the names of other witnesses. The only official purpose of the preliminary hearing is to establish whether probable cause exists, and the names of the other witnesses were irrelevant to that inquiry. This was true whether the defendant was attempting to elicit the information on cross examination or in his own case-in-chief. The prosecution was only required to bring forward the witnesses who were necessary to establish probable cause. Similarly, the defense attorney's efforts to elicit other names from eyewitness Posten was also beyond the scope of the preliminary hearing.

However, the magistrate did err when it sustained the objections to whether Posten had been drinking or whether Posten and the defendant had an earlier dispute. These questions bore directly on Posten's credibility, and his credibility was relevant to determining whether probable cause existed to believe the defendant committed the crime. However, given the relatively low standard for probable cause, it is likely this mistake was harmless error. Officer Day testified that three witnesses identified Hinkle as the perpetrator. Assuming that hearsay evidence was admissible in preliminary hearings in this jurisdiction, Officer Day's testimony alone established probable cause.[9]

As the trial court said in the above case: "The Government's burden at the preliminary hearing begins and ends with the obligation of producing as much testimony as believed needed to establish probable cause for holding the accused

[9] This example is roughly based on United States v. Hinkle, 307 F.Supp. 117 (D.D.C. 1969).

for possible action of the Grand Jury. The Government does not have to call all its witnesses in order that the defendant may use them to buttress his defense."[10] If the prosecution miscalculates and does not call sufficient witnesses to establish probable cause, the magistrate will find for the defendant and dismiss the charges.

If the defendant puts on a case at the preliminary hearing, the prosecutor may gain some valuable discovery as well—she will learn about defense witness, hear their statements, and get some idea of what defense the defendant will be relying upon at trial. This is one of the reasons why the defendant usually will not put on a case at this stage. The probable cause standard is so low the defendant is unlikely to win the hearing anyway, and so putting up a fight in the hearing only serves to tip the defense hand to the prosecutor. It will also generate recorded statements taken under oath that can be used to impeach the witnesses at trial, as noted below.

b. Preserving Testimony. In some cases, a prosecutor may be concerned that a key witness will not be available to testify at trial. The witness may be ill or may be vulnerable to coercion or persuasion on the part of the defendant or others. Or, if the witness does not have strong community ties, the prosecutor may be concerned that the witness may leave the jurisdiction or that she will lose contact with the witness before the trial occurs. If the witness testifies at the preliminary hearing, where she is subject to cross-examination, the rules of evidence allow the prosecutor to admit her testimony if it can be established that she has become unavailable at trial.[11] And because the defendant had the chance to cross-examine the witness at the preliminary hearing, the prior testimony will probably survive a Confrontation Clause challenge. In contrast, grand jury testimony cannot be used at trial if the witness becomes unavailable; this is one reason why a prosecutor may choose to conduct a preliminary hearing even if the law ultimately requires her to obtain an indictment from the grand jury.

If a witness testifies at the preliminary hearing and then becomes unavailable at trial, the defendant may object that his opportunity to cross-examine the witness at the preliminary hearing was limited in a way that it would not have been at trial. We have already seen that the limited purpose of the preliminary hearing means that the defendant will not necessarily have the same motive to challenge every aspect of the witness' story. At the preliminary hearing, the defendant may not want to reveal too much about the theory of his defense, and so may refrain from a vigorous cross-examination, understanding that he will probably lose the preliminary hearing anyway. Most courts have rejected this argument, however, arguing that the defendant's opportunity to cross-examine the defendant in

---

[10] Id. at 125.

[11] See, e.g., Fed. R. Evid. 804(b)(1).

theory is sufficient to protect the defendant's rights under the hearsay rules and the Confrontation Clause.

c. Creating a Written Record of Witness' Testimony. One of the most effective methods of impeachment is to confront a witness with a prior statement that is inconsistent with his testimony at trial. Even if the inconsistency is relatively minor, or concerns a relatively trivial point, the jury will see that the witness has changed his story—either because his memory is faulty or because he is willingly misleading the jury. Either way, the credibility of the witness is called into question. However, every time a witness tells a story, he will invariably change some details. Thus, every time he tells his story he will increase the number of versions of the story that exist and that can be used to impeach him when he finally takes the stand.

For this reason, many prosecutors avoid making written records of a witness' statements. Some written records are unavoidable—statements made to the police, for example, are almost always recorded, and they must be handed over to the defense attorney, who can use any inconsistencies to impeach the witness when she takes the stand. The preliminary hearing or grand jury presentation is another stage which generates formal written records of witness statements. Thus, the prosecutor generally wants to call the smallest number of witnesses possible in a preliminary hearing in order to avoid creating too much of a record for the defense to use. This consideration will also influence the defense attorney's decision of whether to call witnesses during the preliminary hearing, especially because otherwise many defense witnesses will not have any recorded statements for the prosecutor to use at trial.

Quick Summary

After the initial appearance in a felony case, the prosecutor must conduct a formal proceeding to establish probable cause before the case can proceed to trial. This formal proceeding is either a preliminary hearing or a grand jury presentation seeking an indictment, depending on the jurisdiction and (perhaps) the preference of the prosecutor. There is usually a time limit by which the prosecutor must complete this stage. At the federal level that time limit is fourteen days after the initial appearance if the defendant is in custody, and twenty-one days if he is not.

There is no constitutional right to a preliminary hearing, but once a state law provides for a hearing, the Constitution requires that the defendant be represented by an attorney at the hearing. A preliminary hearing is a full hearing with live witnesses in front of a magistrate. The defendant and his attorney are present, and the defendant has the right to cross-examine the government's witnesses and call his own witnesses. In most jurisdictions neither the rules of evidence nor the exclusionary rule apply.

The hearing is limited in scope to determining whether there is probable cause to believe the defendant committed the crimes charged. "Probable cause" usually means something slightly different in this context than it does in the context of evaluating law enforcement actions. At a preliminary hearing, the inquiry is more forward-looking, since the magistrate is trying to determine whether a reasonable jury could ultimately find the defendant guilty beyond a reasonable doubt.

Furthermore, the hearing serves a number of other subsidiary functions: it provides discovery information to the defendant (and to the prosecutor, if the defendant puts on a case); it can be used by the prosecutor as a tool to preserve testimony of witnesses who may become unavailable for trial; and it generates written records of the witness statements, which can be used by the opposing parties to impeach the witnesses at trial if their preliminary hearing testimony is inconsistent with their trial testimony.

35

Grand Juries

Key Concepts

- In "Indictment States," Grand Jury Indictment Required to Formally Charge in Any Felony Case
- Proceedings and Deliberations are Secret, Although Witnesses May Discuss Testimony
- At Federal Level, No Rules of Evidence, No Exclusionary Rule, No Judicial Review

A. Introduction and Policy. In order to move forward with a felony case, the prosecutor must obtain a charging document: either an information from a preliminary hearing or an indictment from a grand jury. A grand jury is a mysterious institution to most lay people, both because the proceedings are cloaked in secrecy and because the procedure in a grand jury is unlike the procedure found anywhere else in the criminal justice system.

A grand jury is a panel of lay people that usually has between nine and twenty-four members. The grand jury is empaneled by the court and frequently will meet in a location inside of the prosecutor's office. However, the grand jury is technically an independent body that is not part of the court system nor part of the prosecutor's office. A grand jury's members are selected randomly from the community in the same way that trial jurors are. However, unlike the empaneling of a trial jury, grand jurors are not selected after an extensive process of questioning and examination (also known as *voir dire*, as discussed in **Chapter 43**). Another difference between trial jurors and grand jurors is that with grand jury selection there is no way any defendant can argue that a particular grand juror should not be seated—indeed, at the time of empaneling, there is no specific "defendant" to object to the composition of the grand jury. A defendant who has been indicted by a grand jury has the right to challenge its composition only after the fact and only on the grounds that the selection of jurors violated the Equal Protection Clause. For example, if there was evidence that women or Hispanic Americans were systematically excluded from the grand jury, a defendant could make a motion before trial that his indictment should be dismissed. Such challenges, however, are extremely rare, in part because compiling the statistical evidence required to make a prima facie showing of discrimination can be daunting.

A grand jury will stay together for a set length of time (commonly one year or eighteen months). During this period, the grand jury will meet periodically—usually at intervals somewhere between once-a-week and once-a-month. The grand jury may hear dozens or even hundreds of cases while it is convened. Larger jurisdictions will have often have a number of grand juries empaneled at the same time, often meeting on different days.

When a grand jury is first empaneled, a judge from the trial court will swear the jurors in and give them their basic charge—that is, the law that they must follow during their time as jurors. As part of that charge, the judge will provide them with the following (now familiar) definition of probable cause:

> To return an indictment charging an individual with an offense, it is not necessary that you find that individual guilty beyond a reasonable doubt. You are not a trial jury and your task is not to decide the guilt or innocence of the person charged. Your task is to determine whether the government's evidence as presented to you is sufficient to cause you to conclude that there is probable cause to believe that the person being investigated committed the offense charged. To put it another way, you should vote to indict where the evidence presented to you is sufficiently strong to warrant a reasonable person's belief that the person being investigated is probably guilty of the offense charged.[1]

After this initial charge, the judge will leave the grand jury in the hands of the prosecutor and the grand jurors will probably never see the judge again until their term is over and they are officially dismissed.

Cases are presented to the grand jury for consideration by the prosecutor. In each case, the prosecutor and the court reporter will enter the grand jury room. The prosecutor will then provide a brief introduction of the case, call witnesses, and interrogate the witnesses in order to elicit the facts necessary to establish probable cause. In most jurisdictions (including in the federal system), an accused person has no right to appear, call witnesses, present evidence, or cross-examine the prosecutor's witnesses. Indeed, in many cases, the defendant will not even know the grand jury has met until after the indictment is handed down.

After the evidence has been presented, the prosecutor reads the elements of each of the crimes to the grand jurors and may repeat the probable cause charge. The prosecutor will also explain any other relevant law, such as the concept of constructive possession or the law of self-defense. Finally, the prosecutor will answer any questions the grand jurors might have about the law. She (and the court

---

[1] Model Federal Grand Jury Charge, United States Courts (last visited July 20, 2014), available at http://www.uscourts.gov/FederalCourts/JuryService/ModelGrandJuryCharge.aspx (approved by the Judicial Conference of the United States, March 2005).

reporter) will then leave the grand jurors alone to deliberate and vote. More often than not, there is no real "deliberation"—the grand jurors simply vote to indict the case immediately as soon as the prosecutor leaves the room. When the grand jury votes to indict, it marks the indictment "True Bill" and returns it to the court. This simply means the case can move forward because the grand jury has found sufficient evidence to satisfy the probable cause standard. The grand jury's failure to find such evidence will result in a "no true bill."

Historically, the grand jury was an institution of regular citizens that protected individuals from abuses by the prosecutor, ensuring that the government could only bring felony charges against those who deserved them and could not charge individuals on weak evidence or simply to harass political enemies. In the modern era, however, prosecutors tend to be quite successful in obtaining indictments. For example, True Bill rates at the federal level are over 99%. This high rate has led to heavy criticism of the grand jury as a "rubber stamp" for the prosecutor. You have no doubt heard the expression that a grand jury would "indict a ham sandwich." While the modern grand jury theoretically still plays its historic gatekeeper function, in practice the grand jury is so easily controlled by the prosecutor that in most jurisdictions it does not provide a meaningful check on prosecutorial discretion.

The reason that indictments are so easy to obtain is not necessarily because of any bias or lack of objectivity on the part of the individual grand jurors. Instead, it is an inevitable consequence of the grand jury's rules. In most jurisdictions, grand jurors hear only the prosecution's evidence untested by cross examination or rebuttal witnesses. And in order to support an indictment, the evidence need only satisfy the relatively low showing of probable cause. Under these circumstances, it would be difficult to imagine grand juries doing anything other than indicting most cases they review. We will discuss critiques of the grand jury and proposed reforms of the institution in Section C.5 below.

Grand jury proceedings are usually not only *ex parte*, but are also usually beyond judicial review. Although there are some rules limiting what prosecutors can and cannot do in the grand jury, a judge is not present to enforce these rules. In addition, neither the judge nor the defense attorney gets to review the grand jury transcripts unless the case goes to trial and the grand jury witness testifies. Thus, the defense attorney frequently has no chance to ascertain whether there were improprieties in the proceedings.

Broadly speaking, there are two types of grand juries: the indicting grand jury, and the investigative grand jury. Both follow the same procedures, but their purposes are very different. The indicting grand jury exists to review the evidence in a case and determine whether probable cause exists. The prosecutor will come before the indicting grand jury only after all of her evidence is prepared. In these cases, the prosecutor will usually call only one or two witnesses to testify because that is all that will be required to establish probable cause. The entire presentation may only take a few minutes, and the indicting grand jury may hear dozens of cases in a single day.

In contrast, the investigative grand jury is used to **gather** evidence in a case. The prosecutor will issue subpoenas on the authority of the court on behalf of the grand jury, thereby forcing individuals to come forward and answer questions under oath. A prosecutor presenting a case to an investigative grand jury will almost certainly call multiple witnesses over the course of multiple grand jury sessions, and the defendant himself may be called as a witness. At the end of the investigation, the investigative grand jury will almost always be asked to return an indictment. But this request will be made only after the prosecutor has used the grand jury to gather most of the evidence. Investigative grand juries are usually used in more serious or complicated cases.

Most of this chapter will discuss the indicting grand jury. We will discuss the investigative in more detail in Section C.4 below.

B. The Law. The Fifth Amendment to the United States Constitution states that:

> No person shall be held to answer for a capital, or otherwise infamous crime, unless on a presentment or indictment of a Grand Jury. . . .

Thus, in federal courts, a prosecutor must obtain an indictment from a grand jury in order to proceed in a felony case. This is one of the few aspects of the Bill of Rights that has not been incorporated, and therefore no state is constitutionally required to use a grand jury to charge felony cases. As we saw in **Chapter 34,** most states use a preliminary hearing to move cases forward instead of a grand jury.

The Rules of Criminal Procedure for the jurisdiction describe how a grand jury operates. Federal Rule 6 is typical:

> **Federal Rule of Criminal Procedure 6.**
>
> **The Grand Jury**
>
> **(a)** Summoning a Grand Jury.
>
> **(1)** In General. When the public interest so requires, the court must order that one or more grand juries be summoned. A grand jury must have 16 to 23 members, and the court must order that enough legally qualified persons be summoned to meet this requirement.
>
> . . .

(c) Foreperson and Deputy Foreperson. The court will appoint one juror as the foreperson and another as the deputy foreperson. In the foreperson's absence, the deputy foreperson will act as the foreperson. The foreperson may administer oaths and affirmations and will sign all indictments. The foreperson—or another juror designated by the foreperson—will record the number of jurors concurring in every indictment and will file the record with the clerk, but the record may not be made public unless the court so orders.

(d) Who May Be Present.

(1) While the Grand Jury Is in Session. The following persons may be present while the grand jury is in session: attorneys for the government, the witness being questioned, interpreters when needed, and a court reporter or an operator of a recording device.

(2) During Deliberations and Voting. No person other than the jurors, and any interpreter needed to assist a hearing-impaired or speech-impaired juror, may be present while the grand jury is deliberating or voting.

(e) Recording and Disclosing the Proceedings.

. . .

(B) Unless these rules provide otherwise, the following persons must not disclose a matter occurring before the grand jury:

(i) a grand juror;

(ii) an interpreter;

(iii) a court reporter;

(iv) an operator of a recording device;

(v) a person who transcribes recorded testimony;

(vi) an attorney for the government; or

(vii) a person to whom disclosure is made under Rule 6(e)(3)(A)(ii) or (iii).

(3) Exceptions.

(A) Disclosure of a grand-jury matter—other than the grand jury's deliberations or any grand juror's vote—may be made to:

(i) an attorney for the government for use in performing that attorney's duty;

(ii) any government personnel—including those of a state, state subdivision, Indian tribe, or foreign government—that an attorney for the government considers necessary to assist in performing that attorney's duty to enforce federal criminal law;

or

(iii) a person authorized by 18 U.S.C. §3322 [involving specific banking law violations].

(B) A person to whom information is disclosed under Rule 6(e)(3)(A)(ii) may use that information only to assist an attorney for the government in performing that attorney's duty to enforce federal criminal law. An attorney for the government must promptly provide the court that impaneled the grand jury with the names of all persons to whom a disclosure has been made, and must certify that the attorney has advised those persons of their obligation of secrecy under this rule.

(C) An attorney for the government may disclose any grand-jury matter to another federal grand jury.

. . .

(4) Sealed Indictment. The magistrate judge to whom an indictment is returned may direct that the indictment be kept secret until the defendant is in custody or has been released pending trial. The clerk must then seal the indictment, and no person may disclose the indictment's existence except as necessary to issue or execute a warrant or summons.

(5) Closed Hearing. Subject to any right to an open hearing in a contempt proceeding, the court must close any hearing to the extent necessary to prevent disclosure of a matter occurring before a grand jury.

(6) Sealed Records. Records, orders, and subpoenas relating to grand-jury proceedings must be kept under seal to the extent and as long as necessary to prevent the unauthorized disclosure of a matter occurring before a grand jury.

. . .

(f) Indictment and Return. A grand jury may indict only if at least 12 jurors concur. The grand jury—or its foreperson or deputy foreperson—must return the indictment to a magistrate judge in open court. . . .

(g) Discharging the Grand Jury. A grand jury must serve until the court discharges it, but it may serve more than 18 months only if the court, having determined that an extension is in the public interest, extends the grand jury's service. An extension may be granted for no more than 6 months, except as otherwise provided by statute.

. . .

Most of Rule 6 is concerned with maintaining the secrecy of the grand jury. Very few individuals are allowed into the grand jury room, and almost all of those who are allowed in—the prosecutor, the court reporter, the grand jurors themselves—are for the most part prohibited from disclosing the names of any of witnesses who appeared or the content of their testimony. The deliberations that occur inside the grand jury are also confidential, although the secrecy requirement does not apply to the witnesses themselves—they are free to disclose any information they want, from the fact of their appearance to the questions they are asked and answers they gave. Furthermore, other provisions of Rule 6 allow the court to authorize disclosure of grand jury information under certain circumstances. We will discuss the secrecy requirement in greater detail in Section C.2 below.

In addition to the secrecy requirement, the grand jury has a number of other peculiar characteristics. Almost all of these tend to favor the prosecution by making it easier to indict a case. For example, in most jurisdictions (including the federal system):

1. The **rules of evidence** (including the hearsay rule) **do not apply**.[2] Thus, the grand jury proceeding frequently consists of one witness—a law enforcement officer—who will read from the case file, including all of the statements made by the witnesses in the case. The grand jurors frequently do not see the eyewitnesses testify and have no way of evaluating their credibility or asking them follow-up questions.

2. The **exclusionary rule does not apply** in the grand jury, so the prosecutor may present evidence that was obtained in violation of the defendant's constitutional rights.[3] However, witnesses still maintain their Fifth Amendment rights inside the grand jury. Hence, they may not be forced to testify if they believe the information will incriminate them.[4] Unlike at trial, however, the prosecutor can still call the defendant into the grand jury, swear him in, and then ask him a series of incriminating questions and force him to assert his right against self-incrimination in front of the grand jury. Also, if the witness is not the target of the investigation, the prosecutor may grant the witness immunity for anything he might say in the grand jury, in which case the witness must testify or be held in contempt.

3. The **defendant has no right to appear**, to present evidence on his behalf, or to cross-examine witnesses, **and the prosecutor has no duty to dis-**

[2] Costello v. United States, 350 U.S. 359 (1956).

[3] United States v. Calandra, 414 U.S. 338 (1974).

[4] Kastigar v. United States, 406 U.S. 441 (1972).

close any exculpatory evidence.[5] Thus, the grand jury only hears one side of the story.

4. As with the finding of probable cause at the preliminary hearing, once the defendant has been convicted, any errors in the indictment process will be deemed **harmless.**[6]

5. If the grand jury refuses to issue an indictment (issues a "no true bill"), the prosecutor can re-present the same case to a different grand jury.[7] In other words, there is **no double jeopardy** protection at this stage in the process. In practice, most prosecutors will not re-present a case to a grand jury once a no true bill has been issued, but there is no legal bar that prohibits them from doing so.

6. Finally, because the grand jury is independent of the court system, its actions are generally not subject to judicial review. If a prosecutor incorrectly charged the grand jury, or if the grand jury abused its discretion by indicting a case when no reasonable juror could have found probable cause, or if any other irregularity occurred, there will almost **no opportunity for judicial review** of the proceedings. We will discuss the rules for judicial review in Section 3 below.

C. Applying the Law.

1. History of the Grand Jury. The modern grand jury is something of an anachronism, and so the best way to understand its function is to learn something about its history. The grand jury is over 850 years old—older even than the trial jury—and it originated in England as an accusatory body. Long before there was an organized police force, the King established the grand jury as a panel of twelve men who would report any crimes which may have occurred in the community. For centuries the grand jury acted as the prosecutorial machine, usually manipulated by the Crown, and an indictment from the grand jury typically resulted in conviction, since the only trials that existed were trials by ordeal.

Nevertheless, during these centuries the grand jury established a significant principle in the common-law criminal justice system: the belief that lay individuals with no legal training and no formal connection to the government should pass judgment on their fellow citizens in criminal cases. By the seventeenth century, grand jurors were beginning to show some signs of independence from the government. In one famous instance, the King of England tried to indict his politi-

[5] United States v. Williams, 504 U.S. 36 (1992).

[6] United States v. Mechanik 475 U.S. 66 (1986).

[7] Ex parte United States, 287 U.S. 241, 250–51 (1932).

cal enemy the Earl of Shaftesbury for treason. In a then-relatively rare display, the grand jury defied royal pressure and refused to indict the case. The public perception of grand juries began to shift as well—they were increasingly seen as a important check on the otherwise limitless power of the King to bring charges against his enemies.

This public perception was enhanced in colonial times, after another famous instance of a grand jury shielding a citizen from prosecution. In the mid-eighteenth century, the Royal governor of New York brought charges against a newspaper publisher who had criticized him. The grand jury refused to indict the publisher. Cases such as these were in the forefront of the minds of the drafters of the Bill of Rights when they inserted the grand jury clause into the Fifth Amendment as a further protection against government abuse of the prosecutorial power.

The modern grand jury has changed quite dramatically from its early protective role. Grand jurors rarely refuse to indict the cases brought before them, and most practitioners and commentators consider them to do little more than passively accept the evidence presented and dutifully indict when requested to do so. The unique history of the grand jury does, however, help to explain many of the peculiar aspects of the body—from the required secrecy to the lack of judicial oversight of their proceedings.

2. Grand Jury Secrecy. Unlike most other aspects of criminal adjudication, grand jury proceedings are shrouded in secrecy. Traditionally courts have given five justifications for this secrecy:

1. Preventing the escape of defendants who may be indicted;
2. Preventing tampering with grand jurors;
3. Preventing tampering with witnesses who appear before the grand jury;
4. Encouraging witnesses to come forward and be honest while testifying; and
5. Protecting the reputation of an innocent defendant whom the grand jury refuses to indict.[8]

These justifications make sense from a historical standpoint: when the grand jury was primarily an accusatory body investigating suspects and indicting only those for whom sufficient evidence existed, it was important to keep its activities secret to prevent tampering and not let the suspect or the community know who was being investigated.

[8] United States v. Procter & Gamble Co., 356 U.S. 677, 681 n.6 (1958) (citing United States v. Rose, 215 F.2d 617, 628–29 (3d Cir. 1954)).

In modern times, these requirements still make sense with respect to the investigative grand jury. However, in the case of an indicting grand jury, they are less persuasive. The defendant is often already in custody—thus, he cannot flee and his reputation has already been damaged. And because hearsay is allowed, the witnesses tend to be law enforcement officers reporting on their investigation, so the need to prevent witness tampering or encourage honesty in witnesses is less acute.

Nevertheless, the secrecy requirements apply with full force to investigative and indicting grand juries. Ironically, the secrecy of the proceedings—along with the lack of judicial review—now may harm the defendant by effectively shielding the process from public view.

The rules do provide for some disclosures of grand jury activity. Specifically, the prosecutor is permitted to disclose information from grand jury presentations to other government attorneys "for use in performing that attorney's duty," or to any government personnel if necessary to assist the prosecutor in her duty to enforce federal criminal law. Courts have interpreted this provision relatively narrowly, allowing a prosecutor to disclose information to other federal prosecutors[9] or to law enforcement agents who are assisting in their case,[10] but prohibiting disclosure to federal personnel who are conducting a civil investigation[11] and to private employees who are working for the government as consultants.[12]

Also, Rule 6(E) permits the supervising court to authorize disclosure of grand jury matters in connection with a judicial proceeding, in response to a defense request if the defendant can show that there may have been an irregularity in the grand jury, or in response to a prosecutor request to help in an investigation or if the prosecutor can show that the matter may disclose a violation of state law, foreign law, or military criminal law. In reality, it is very difficult for a defendant to make such a request, because the secrecy laws usually prevent him from developing grounds to support the allegation that an irregularity occurred.

Finally, a defendant can access grand jury testimony in a number of ways. If the testimony is exculpatory to the defendant, the prosecutor has a duty to promptly hand it over (along with any other exculpatory evidence) under the *Brady* rule. And in federal court, the Jencks Act forces the prosecutor to turn over all prior statements made by a trial witness—including grand jury testimony—after the

---

[9] United States v. Sells Engineering, Inc., 463 U.S. 418 (1983).

[10] United States v. Anzelmo, 319 F.Supp. 1106 (E.D.La. 1970).

[11] In re Grand Jury Proceedings, 445 F.Supp. 349 (D.R.I. 1978), appeal dismissed 580 F.2d 13 (1st Cir. 1978).

[12] In re Grand Jury Matter, 607 F.Supp.2d 273 (D.Mass. 2009).

witness has testified at trial.[13] We will review these procedures when we discuss discovery in **Chapter 39.**

The defendant can also gain access to the grand jury proceedings when he files a motion to quash the indictment, since such a motion would require a review of the grand jury transcript. However, as we will see in the next section, the Supreme Court has held that such motions are very difficult to bring.

3. Lack of Judicial Review. In theory, a defendant can move to quash an indictment based on a lack of evidence or on improper conduct in the grand jury. In practice, the Supreme Court has so limited the grounds for such a motion they are almost never filed. In a series of cases beginning in 1956, the Supreme Court steadily narrowed the grounds upon which a federal court can review the decisions of a grand jury or the conduct of a prosecutor in the grand jury. First, the Court held that the hearsay rule (and other rules of evidence) did not apply in the grand jury, since the grand jury was meant to be an institution of lay people who could "conduct their inquiry unfettered by technical rules."[14] In the same case, the Court noted that the courts had no power to review a grand jury indictment on the basis of the **quantity** of evidence—that is, if the grand jury determined there was sufficient evidence to constitute probable cause, the courts should not review that decision. Then the Court held that the exclusionary rule did not apply in the grand jury, allowing the prosecutor to present evidence which was acquired in violation of the Constitution.[15] Next, the Court applied a harmless error analysis to any procedural irregularities that occurred in the grand jury, effectively holding that any prosecutorial misconduct in the grand jury proceeding becomes harmless once the defendant is convicted.[16]

The final blow to judicial review came in 1992, when the Court held the prosecutor has no duty to present the grand jury with exculpatory evidence:

> **Example—*United States v. Williams,* 504 U.S. 36 (1992):** After a long investigation, a grand jury indicted John Williams for knowingly providing false financial statements to various banks. In particular, the prosecutor alleged that Williams overvalued his assets and his interest income when applying for bank loans.
>
> Williams moved to dismiss the indictment, arguing that the prosecutor failed to present exculpatory evidence to the grand jury. Specifically, Williams argued that in his private accounting

[13] 18 U.S.C. § 3500.

[14] Costello v. United States, 350 U.S. 359, 364 (1956).

[15] United States v. Calandra, 414 U.S. 338 (1974).

[16] United States v. Mechanik, 475 U.S. 66 (1986).

and on his tax returns, he valued his assets and income in exactly the same way he valued them in his loan application. According to Williams, this demonstrated that he did not intentionally mislead the banks, he merely made an honest accounting error when calculating the numbers. The prosecutor conceded that the evidence could be exculpatory, but argued that the government had no duty to present exculpatory evidence to the grand jury, since the grand jury's role was not to determine ultimate guilt but merely to decide whether there was probable cause to believe the defendant committed a crime.

Analysis: The Court ruled for the government, holding that the prosecutor had no duty to present exculpatory information to the grand jury. The Court's broad language in the decision discouraged federal courts from reviewing grand jury proceedings for any reason. Citing its earlier cases, the Court noted that "over the years, we have received many requests to exercise supervision over the grand jury's evidence-taking process, but we have refused them all."[17]

The *Williams* Court justified this hands-off philosophy by explaining that "the grand jury is an institution separate from the courts, over whose functioning the courts do not preside." Because the grand jury is not mentioned in the body of the Constitution, but only in the Bill of Rights, the Court reasoned that "it has not been textually assigned . . . to any of the branches described in the first three Articles. It is a constitutional fixture in its own right." This "textual" independence allows the federal courts to effectively wash their hands of supervisory review.

Williams effectively forecloses any judicial review of grand jury proceedings, not just because of the broad language the Court used to assert the institutional independence of the grand jury, but also because after the decision there is literally almost nothing left for courts to review. The prosecutor has no duty to present exculpatory evidence and is allowed to use hearsay evidence and illegally obtained evidence, and the grand jury's determination that the evidence is sufficient to establish probable cause is unreviewable.

The Supreme Court has mentioned in dicta that there are some legitimate grounds for a motion to quash an indictment—specifically if there is prosecutorial misconduct that had a "substantial effect on the jury's assessment of the testimony or its decision to indict"[18] this might be a basis for relief. For example, if the prosecutor coerced a witness into testifying falsely by threatening to charge him with a crime if he did not testify as the prosecutor requested, such an action would be misconduct and would likely affect the jury's decision to indict, assuming the witness' testimony was significant. However, because of grand jury secrecy laws (which

---

[17] United States v. Williams, 504 U.S. 36, 50 (1992).

[18] Bank of Nova Scotia v. United States, 487 U.S. 250, 262 (1988).

ensure that the defense attorney knows nothing about what was said in the grand jury), it is very difficult for a defense attorney to learn about such misconduct unless the witness himself comes forward with the information. Other types of prosecutorial misconduct that may occur when there is no witness in the room (such as telling the grand jury they must indict the case because the evidence is overwhelming, or personally vouching for the credibility of a key witness) would be virtually undetectable.

In short, aside from the requirement that she must present the minimal amount of evidence to convince a majority of the jurors to vote for indictment, there is no real check on the quantity or quality of the evidence that a federal prosecutor needs to present to a grand jury.

4. The Investigative Grand Jury. The grand jury has been described as both a "sword" and a "shield," referring to its investigative and indicting responsibilities respectively. In practice, any grand jury can be used to investigate crimes or to issue indictments, though in larger jurisdictions, prosecutors tend to segregate grand jury functions and use some grand juries as investigative tools and others to merely hear evidence and indict. But even if it is the same grand jury fulfilling both functions, the two roles are so distinct that the investigative grand jury should be discussed separately.

The investigative grand jury is essentially a tool the prosecutor uses to issue subpoenas and gather evidence before an indictment is issued. When a prosecutor undertakes an investigation, most witnesses cooperate with the prosecutor and are willing to answer questions or deliver documents, but many witnesses (especially those who may be targets of the investigation) are often not cooperative. Since the prosecutor has no power on her own to compel a witness to speak, or to force a witness to provide documents or other physical evidence, the prosecutor will occasionally "ask" the grand jury to issue subpoenas to compel these witnesses to act. The grand jury will almost always comply and issue the subpoenas. Usually the prosecutor uses the investigative grand jury for complicated cases or long-term investigations.

By using the court's subpoena power, the grand jury (and by extension, the prosecutor acting through the grand jury) has more power than law enforcement officials—a police officer cannot force a suspect to provide information during an interview. Furthermore, the Supreme Court applies a more lenient Fourth Amendment standard to grand jury actions than it does to law enforcement activity:

Example—*United States v. Dioniso*, 410 U.S. 1 (1973): A grand jury in Virginia was investigating potential gambling violations, and the prosecutor submitted wiretap evidence of voice recordings in which various individuals made incriminating statements. In order to determine who was speaking on the wiretap recordings, the prosecutor asked the grand jury to issue subpoenas to twenty different people, including Antonio Dionisio. The subpoenas asked each of the recipients to provide voice exemplars that could be compared with the voices on the wiretaps. Each recipient was asked to go to a local United States Attorney office and read from a transcript into a recording device. A number of witnesses, including Dioniso, refused to comply, arguing that this request was a broad dragnet that constituted an unreasonable seizure.

Dioniso argued that the request was similar to the seizures in *Davis v. Mississippi*,[19] in which a woman told the police she had been raped by a young black man, and the police responded by detaining 24 local young black men, transporting each one to the precinct, taking their fingerprints, interrogating them briefly, and then releasing them. The *Davis* Court held that the police action was an unreasonable seizure and precluded the fingerprint evidence. The District Court rejected Dioniso's comparison to the *Davis* case and held him in contempt until he agreed to comply with the subpoena. Dioniso appealed, and the case reached the Supreme Court.

Analysis: The Supreme Court unanimously upheld the grand jury's action and ordered the defendant to comply with the subpoena. It held that the *Davis* case was inapplicable to the question of whether the grand jury had the power to issue the subpoenas. A subpoena is not a "seizure" within the meaning of the Fourth Amendment.[20] Accordingly, there is no "constitutional immunity" from grand jury subpoenas. In fact, citizens have a duty to appear and give evidence to the grand jury when ordered to do so.

The Court distinguished the compulsion created by a grand jury subpoena from the constraint on liberty caused by an arrest: "The latter is abrupt, is effected with force or the threat of it and often in demeaning circumstances, and, in the case of arrest, results in a record involving social stigma. [In contrast, a] subpoena is served in the same manner as other legal process; it involves no stigma whatever; if the time for appearance is inconvenient, this can generally be altered; and it remains at all times under the control and supervision of a court."[21]

---

[19] 394 U.S. 721 (1969).

[20] Williams, 504 U.S. at 50.

[21] United States v. Dioniso, 410 U.S. 1, 10 (1973) (quoting United States v. Doe (Schwartz) 457 F.2d 895, 898 (2d Cir. 1972)).

The only limits the Court placed on the grand jury's subpoena power arose from the Fifth Amendment—the grand jury cannot force an individual to incriminate himself, or to turn over incriminating documents—and from the First Amendment—the grand jury cannot be used to harass members of the press.

In *Dioniso* and later cases, the Court has described the authority of the grand jury expansively to include "broad investigative powers to determine whether a crime has been committed and who has committed it." In making its assessments, the Court has explained that grand jurors "may act on tips, rumors, evidence offered by the prosecutor, or their own personal knowledge. No grand jury witness is entitled to set limits to the investigation that the grand jury may conduct."[22]

However, the Court has been somewhat schizophrenic in articulating a justification for this sweeping interpretation of the grand jury's authority. In some instances, the Court highlights the grand jury's institutional independence as the rationale. For example, as with the secrecy rules and lack of judicial review that we discussed in the context of the indicting grand jury, the Court has said the grand jury's broad investigative powers are warranted in part because the grand jury is an "independent body," and therefore should not be restrained by the courts from looking at any source in its mission to investigate wrongdoing.

At other times, however, the Court has emphasized judicial oversight as the rationale for the grand jury's great power. For example, in *Dioniso*, the Court justified the wide-ranging use of the subpoena power in part by offering the assurance that that power remained under the control and supervision of a court.

Ironically, at the same time the Supreme Court was touting judicial oversight as a rationale for broad grand jury authority, it was slowly weakening judicial supervision over every aspect of the grand jury. Moreover, as we have seen, the independence of the federal grand jury is little more than a legal fiction—so in reality the Court has given these broad investigative powers not to a body of concerned citizens but to the federal prosecutor. All of these critiques have led some to conclude that reform of the grand jury system is needed.

5. Proposed Grand Jury Reforms. In the federal system, the lack of rules and oversight governing the grand jury process has resulted in a weak institution that essentially follows the lead of the prosecutor by indicting almost every case brought before it. Federal statistics routinely show an indictment rate of over 99% for cases brought to grand juries.[23] The relative impotence of the grand jury has led to various calls to reform the institution. For example, in 2000 the American Bar Association and the National Association of Criminal Defense

---

[22] Dioniso, 410 U.S. at 15.

[23] See, e.g., United States Department of Justice, Compendium of Federal Justice Statistics, 1990-1998.

Lawyers proposed a series of changes that would increase the independence and power of the federal grand jury, including:

- Allowing grand jury witnesses to bring their attorneys into the grand jury room;
- Requiring the prosecutor to disclose exculpatory evidence;
- Giving the accused the right to testify;
- Strengthening the jury instructions that are read to the grand jury, and providing the defendant with a copy afterwards; and
- Prohibiting the prosecutor from calling a witness to the stand if the prosecutor knows the witness will invoke her right against self-incrimination.[24]

For now, the Department of Justice has successfully fended off these (and other) proposals, preferring to keep the federal grand jury in its current form. However, there are a variety of different grand jury rules on the state level.

As we have already seen, the majority of states do not require grand jury indictment at all. In these states, prosecutors proceed with a preliminary hearing instead. But, of the nineteen states that do require grand jury indictments, some have more robust grand jury rules than are found at the federal level. For example, a few states now require the prosecutor to obtain judicial approval before re-presenting a case to the grand jury after a No True Bill has been returned. In addition, some states apply the rules of evidence in the grand jury or give the accused the right to testify. These states also tend to require some form of judicial review of the grand jury proceedings—the prosecutor still runs the grand jury presentation, but after indictment, a judge will review the grand jury transcript to ensure that all of the rules were followed.

Nonetheless, jurisdictions with more liberal grand jury rules like those noted above can be seen are still in the small minority. Of those states that require grand jury indictments, a majority still observe rules similar to those governing the federal grand jury process.

6. Comparing the Preliminary Hearing and the Grand Jury. For both the preliminary hearing and the grand jury, a subsequent conviction will render harmless most irregularity that may have occurred. This means that—on the federal level at least—these procedures are merely a means to an end—a procedural hoop for

[24] See National Association of Criminal Defense Lawyers, Federal Grand Jury Reform Report & "Bill of Rights" (2000), https://www.nacdl.org/criminaldefense.aspx?id=10372&libID=10345.

the prosecutor to jump through in order to advance the case towards trial. As long as the defendant has been convicted at trial, the Supreme Court has determined that most irregularity in the grand jury or the preliminary hearing process will not have caused harm to the defendant because guilt has now been established beyond a reasonable doubt at trial.

This rule stands in stark contrast to the consequences that federal courts attach to other pre-trial errors by law enforcement officers or prosecutors. For instance, if the government acquires evidence illegally, obtains an improper confession, uses an overly suggestive identification procedure, fails to turn over exculpatory evidence, or even fails to comply with discovery rules, there is at least a possibility of sanction against the government even after conviction. In this sense, the preliminary hearing and the grand jury are on the lowest tier of procedural safeguard in the federal system.

Although they serve the same purpose—ensuring that the government possesses probable cause before a defendant can be formally charged with and ultimately tried for a felony—the preliminary hearing and the grand jury bear little resemblance to each other. Statistics show that it is somewhat easier for the government to obtain an indictment from a grand jury than to survive a preliminary hearing, though prosecutors enjoy particularly high success rates in both contexts. Many prosecutors may prefer grand juries because the procedure tends to be faster and the defendant and defense attorney do not get a chance to cross-examine the prosecutor's witnesses or even hear what the witnesses are saying. As we will see later in **Chapter 39,** federal discovery rules do not force the prosecutor to turn over the witness statements from the grand jury until after the witnesses have testified at trial (though in practice, many prosecutors turn over such statements much sooner as a professional courtesy).

However, in the many states in which an indictment is not required prosecutors routinely use a preliminary hearing instead of a grand jury. Though many benefits of a preliminary hearing accrue to the defense in the form of additional discovery, there are also significant reasons why a prosecutor may chose the preliminary hearing process:

1. First and foremost, preliminary hearings can be cheaper and easier for the state. Though the presentation of a case in the grand jury is also relatively straightforward, the process of empaneling as many as twenty-four lay citizens for every grand jury can be a cumbersome one.

2. In addition, a preliminary hearing allows the government to "test-run" its evidence. The prosecutor is able to watch the witnesses present at the hearing and assess weakness in their testimony (either substantive or stylistic) that must be strengthened before the case is heard by a jury. As you

will read in the Double Jeopardy chapter (**Chapter 46**), the prosecution often benefits from the repeat presentation of its evidence. However, by making this presentation at a preliminary hearing, the prosecutor reaps the benefits of repeat presentation without implicating double jeopardy concerns.

3. A third benefit of the preliminary hearing is that it can be used to "lock in" the testimony of reluctant witnesses (in much the same way that grand jury testimony can). For certain types of offenses, a witness might be quite angry with the accused shortly after the crime and therefore willing to cooperate with the prosecution. However, where there is a prior close relationship, the lapse of time between offense and trial may soften the witness' perspective and make him less willing to cooperate. As you read in **Chapter 34**, if by the time of trial a witness refuses to testify (or is unavailable for other reasons), the preliminary hearing testimony, which has been tested by the defense, may under certain circumstances be introduced instead. At minimum, the preliminary hearing testimony could be used to impeach the reluctant witness' contrary trial testimony.

4. A fourth benefit of the preliminary hearing is that it provides the government with some amount of discovery (though certainly not as much as is provided to the defense). In particular, areas of inquiry and specific questions asks on cross will provide the prosecutor with valuable information about the defense theory as well as the probable lines of attack that will be used at trial. Between the time of the hearing and trial, the prosecutor can use this information to shore up these areas with additional evidence or further witness preparation.

5. A final benefit of the preliminary hearing is that it may give the defendant an increased incentive to plead guilty if the evidence presented at the hearing is strong.

Quick Summary

A grand jury is a body of between nine and twenty-four lay individuals who are empaneled by the court but who legally act as an independent entity in gathering and reviewing evidence. The grand jury's ostensible function is to act as a check on the prosecutor to ensure there is probable cause to believe the defendant committed a felony. In reality, the federal grand jury is run by the prosecutor and rarely refuses to indict a case when asked to do so.

In the federal grand jury, the rules of evidence and the exclusionary rule do not apply. In addition, the defendant has no right to call witnesses, to cross-examine the prosecutor's witnesses, to appear himself before the grand jury, or even be present during its proceedings. The prosecutor has no duty to present exculpatory evidence, and the court will not review the proceedings afterward to ensure that the grand jury acted reasonably in determining probable cause. Because so few rules govern the proceedings, there is almost no judicial supervision over the federal grand jury process.

The federal Constitution requires a grand jury indictment in every felony case. However, this is one of the few requirements in the Bill of Rights that has not been incorporated by the Fourteenth Amendment. Accordingly, to date only nineteen states have chosen to also require a grand jury process in criminal cases. The remaining states proceed by information and use a preliminary hearing to establish probable cause. The preliminary hearing process is generally less expensive and provides the defendant with more rights.

Review Questions

1. Not Keeping a Secret. The government is conducting an investigation into cocaine smuggling by two brothers, George and Jonah, who run a shipping company in Albuquerque, New Mexico. The grand jury subpoenas Victor, who works for George and Jonah at their warehouse. Victor testifies in the grand jury that while working at the warehouse he saw a suspicious crate with a return address from San Diego, California. When he opened the crate, he saw a large quantity of white powder.

After his grand jury appearance, Victor went to George and Jonah and told them the questions he was asked and the answers he gave. Meanwhile, the prosecutor in Albuquerque contacted his counterpart in the United States Attorney's Office in the Southern District of California (where San Diego is located) and told her about Victor's testimony, suggesting that she investigate the address Victor described on the crate. Finally, one of the grand jurors went home and told her husband about Victor's testimony, warning him to stay away from the neighborhood where George and Jonah's warehouse is located because there might be violence associated with that quantity of drug dealing.

Which of these three individuals (if any) have violated the grand jury secrecy rules?

2. Domestic Terrorism. You are a federal prosecutor. The FBI comes to you with a terrorism case. One week ago a car bomb went off at a farmer's market downtown—nobody was injured, but there was significant property damage. A few days after the bombing the FBI received an anonymous phone call saying that a man named Kyle Harrison committed the crime and may be planning another attack soon. FBI agents located Kyle's house, but nobody answered the door. Believing that exigent circumstances existed, the agents entered the house and searched it without a warrant. Nobody was home, but the FBI located a number of common household chemicals which could have been used to create the bomb from the farmer's market.

While the agents are searching the home, one of Kyle's brothers (who also lives in the home) returned to the house and sees the agents there. Upon questioning, the brother admits that he saw Kyle mixing some of these chemicals together in the basement. The agent takes a formal statement from the brother. Later when the agent gets back to the office, he checks to see if the brother has a criminal record and learns that the brother has two prior convictions for burglary and also spent six months in a mental hospital for a psychotic disorder.

The FBI agent believes that if Kyle were arrested and formally charged, he would be willing to cooperate and provide more information about terrorist activities in the area. How do you want to proceed? Do you believe you have probable cause that Kyle is guilty of a crime? If so, do you want to arrest him and then give his case to a grand jury, or try to indict him first without his knowledge and arrest him once the indictment is obtained? If you choose to proceed by indictment, what evidence do you want to present to the grand jury? Will you have just the agent testify or will you also subpoena Kyle's brother? If you do force the brother to testify, will you tell the grand jury about his prior convictions and his psychiatric history?

FROM THE COURTROOM

UNITED STATES v. WILLIAMS

United States Supreme Court, 1992
504 U.S. 36

[Justice SCALIA delivered the opinion of the Court.]

[Justices SCALIA concurred in the decision.]

[Justice BREYER filed a dissenting opinion.]

[Justice ALITO filed a dissenting opinion, in which he was joined by Chief Justice ROBERTS and Justice KENNEDY and by Justice BREYER in part.]

The question presented in this case is whether a district court may dismiss an otherwise valid indictment because the Government failed to disclose to the grand jury "substantial exculpatory evidence" in its possession.

I

On May 4, 1988, respondent John H. Williams, Jr., a Tulsa, Oklahoma, investor, was indicted by a federal grand jury on seven counts of "knowingly mak[ing] [a] false statement or report . . . for the purpose of influencing . . . the action [of a federally insured financial institution]," in violation of 18 U.S.C. § 1014. According to the indictment, between September 1984 and November 1985 Williams supplied four Oklahoma banks with "materially false" statements that variously overstated the value of his current assets and interest income in order to influence the banks' actions on his loan requests.

Williams' misrepresentation was allegedly effected through two financial statements provided to the banks, a "Market Value Balance Sheet" and a "Statement of Projected Income and Expense." The former included as "current assets" approximately $6 million in notes receivable from three venture capital companies. Though it contained a disclaimer that these assets were carried at cost rather than at market value, the Government asserted that listing them as "current assets"—*i.e.,* assets quickly reducible to cash—was misleading, since Williams knew that none of the venture capital companies could afford to satisfy the notes in the short term. The second document—the Statement of Projected Income and Expense—allegedly misrepresented Williams' interest income, since it failed to reflect that the interest payments received on the notes of the venture capital companies were funded entirely by Williams' own loans to those companies. The Statement thus falsely implied, according to the Government, that Williams was deriving interest income from "an independent outside source."

Shortly after arraignment, the District Court granted Williams' motion for disclosure of all exculpatory portions of the grand jury transcripts. Upon reviewing this material, Williams demanded that the District Court dismiss the indictment, alleging that the Government had failed to fulfill its obligation under the Tenth Circuit's prior decision in *United States v. Page*, 808 F.2d 723, 728 (1987), to present "substantial exculpatory evidence" to the grand jury. His contention was that evidence which the Government had chosen not to present to the grand jury—in particular, Williams' general ledgers and tax returns, and Williams' testimony in his contemporaneous Chapter 11 bankruptcy proceeding—disclosed that, for tax purposes and otherwise, he had regularly accounted for the "notes receivable" (and the interest on them) in a manner consistent with the Balance Sheet and the Income Statement. This, he contended, belied an intent to mislead the banks, and thus directly negated an essential element of the charged offense.

The District Court initially denied Williams' motion, but upon reconsideration ordered the indictment dismissed without prejudice. It found, after a hearing, that the withheld evidence was "relevant to an essential element of the crime charged," created "'a reasonable doubt about [respondent's] guilt,'" and thus "render[ed] the grand jury's decision to indict gravely suspect." Upon the Government's appeal, the Court of Appeals affirmed the District Court's order, following its earlier decision in *Page*. It first sustained as not "clearly erroneous" the District Court's determination that the Government had withheld "substantial exculpatory evidence" from the grand jury. It then found that the Government's behavior "'substantially influence[d]'" the grand jury's decision to indict, or at the very least raised a "'grave doubt that the decision to indict was free from such substantial influence.'" Under these circumstances, the Tenth Circuit concluded, it was not an abuse of discretion for the District Court to require the Government to begin anew before the grand jury. We granted certiorari.

. . .

III

Respondent does not contend that the Fifth Amendment itself obliges the prosecutor to disclose substantial exculpatory evidence in his possession to the grand jury. Instead, building on our statement that the federal courts "may, within limits, formulate procedural rules not specifically required by the Constitution or the Congress," *United States v. Hasting*, 461 U.S. 499 (1983), he argues that imposition of the Tenth Circuit's disclosure rule is supported by the courts' "supervisory power." We think not. *Hasting*, and the cases that rely upon the principle it expresses, deal strictly with the courts' power to control their **own** procedures. That power has been applied not only to improve the truth-finding process of the trial, but also to prevent parties from reaping benefit or incurring harm from violations of substantive or procedural rules (imposed by the Constitution or laws) governing matters apart from the trial itself. Thus, *Bank of Nova Scotia v. United States*, 487 U.S. 250 (1988), makes clear that the supervisory power can be used to dismiss an indictment because of misconduct before the grand jury, at least where that misconduct amounts to a violation of one of those "few, clear rules which were carefully drafted and approved by this Court and by Congress to ensure the integrity of the grand jury's functions."

We did not hold in *Bank of Nova Scotia*, however, that the courts' supervisory power could be used, not merely as a means of enforcing or vindicating legally compelled standards of prosecutorial conduct before the grand jury, but as a means of **prescribing** those standards of prosecutorial conduct in the first instance—just as it may be used as a means of establishing standards of prosecutorial conduct before the courts themselves. It is this latter exercise that respondent demands. Because the grand jury is an institution separate from the courts, over whose functioning the courts do not preside, we think it clear that, as a general matter at least, no such "supervisory" judicial authority exists, and that the disclosure rule applied here exceeded the Tenth Circuit's authority.

A

"[R]ooted in long centuries of Anglo–American history," the grand jury is mentioned in the Bill of Rights, but not in the body of the Constitution. It has not been textually assigned, therefore, to any of the branches described in the first three Articles. It "'is a constitutional fixture in its own right.'" In fact the whole theory of its function is that it belongs to no branch of the institutional Government, serving as a kind of buffer or referee between the Government and the people. Although the grand jury normally operates, of course, in the courthouse and under judicial auspices, its institutional relationship with the Judicial Branch has traditionally been, so to speak, at arm's length. Judges' direct involvement in the functioning of the grand jury has generally been confined to the constitutive one of calling the grand jurors together and administering their oaths of office.

The grand jury's functional independence from the Judicial Branch is evident both in the scope of its power to investigate criminal wrongdoing and in the manner in which that power is exercised. "Unlike [a] [c]ourt, whose jurisdiction is predicated upon a specific case or controversy, the grand jury 'can investigate merely on suspicion that the law is being violated, or even because it wants assurance that it is not.'" It need not identify the offender it suspects, or even "the precise nature of the offense" it is investigating. The grand jury requires no authorization from its constituting court to initiate an investigation, nor does the prosecutor require leave of court to seek a grand jury indictment. And in its day-to-day functioning, the grand jury generally operates without the interference of a presiding judge. It swears in its own witnesses, and deliberates in total secrecy.

True, the grand jury cannot compel the appearance of witnesses and the production of evidence, and must appeal to the court when such compulsion is required. And the court will refuse to lend its assistance when the compulsion the grand jury seeks would override rights accorded by the Constitution, or even testimonial privileges recognized by the common law. Even in this setting, however, we have insisted that the grand jury remain "free to pursue its investigations unhindered by external influence or supervision so long as it does not trench upon the legitimate rights of any witness called before it." Recognizing this tradition of independence, we have said that the Fifth Amendment's "constitutional guarantee **presupposes** an investigative body 'acting independently of either prosecuting attorney **or judge**' . . . ."

No doubt in view of the grand jury proceeding's status as other than a constituent element of a "criminal prosecutio[n]," we have said that certain constitutional protections afforded defendants in criminal proceedings have no application before that body. The Double Jeopardy Clause of the Fifth Amendment does not bar a grand jury from returning an indictment when a prior grand jury has refused to do so. We have twice suggested, though not held, that the Sixth Amendment right to counsel does not attach when an individual is summoned to appear before a grand jury, even if he is the subject of the investigation. And although "the grand jury may not force a witness to answer questions in violation of [the Fifth Amendment's] constitutional guarantee" against self-incrimination, our cases suggest that an indictment obtained through the use of evidence previously obtained in violation of the privilege against self-incrimination "is nevertheless valid."

Given the grand jury's operational separateness from its constituting court, it should come as no surprise that we have been reluctant to invoke the judicial supervisory power as a basis for prescribing modes of grand jury procedure. Over the years, we have received many requests to exercise supervision over the grand jury's evidence-taking process, but we have refused them all, including some more appealing than the one presented today. In *United States v. Calandra*, a grand jury witness faced questions that were allegedly based upon physical evidence the Government had obtained through a violation of the Fourth Amendment; we rejected the proposal that the exclusionary rule be extended to grand jury proceedings, because of "the potential injury to the historic role and functions of the grand jury." In *Costello v. United States*, 350 U.S. 359 (1956), we declined to enforce the hearsay rule in grand jury proceedings, since that "would run counter to the whole history of the grand jury institution, in which laymen conduct their inquiries unfettered by technical rules."

These authorities suggest that any power federal courts may have to fashion, on their own initiative, rules of grand jury procedure is a very limited one, not remotely comparable to the power they maintain over their own proceedings. It certainly would not permit judicial reshaping of the grand jury institution, substantially altering the traditional relationships between the prosecutor, the constituting court, and the grand jury itself. As we proceed to discuss, that would be the consequence of the proposed rule here.

B

Respondent argues that the Court of Appeals' rule can be justified as a sort of Fifth Amendment "common law," a necessary means of assuring the constitutional right to the judgment "of an independent and informed grand jury." Respondent makes a generalized appeal to functional notions: Judicial supervision of the quantity and quality of the evidence relied upon by the grand jury plainly facilitates, he says, the grand jury's performance of its twin historical responsibilities, i.e., bringing to trial those who may be justly accused and shielding the innocent from unfounded accusation and prosecution. We do not agree. The rule would neither preserve nor enhance the traditional functioning of the institution that the Fifth Amendment demands. To the contrary, requiring the prosecutor to present exculpatory as well as inculpatory evidence would alter the grand jury's historical role, transforming it from an accusatory to an adjudicatory body.

It is axiomatic that the grand jury sits not to determine guilt or innocence, but to assess whether there is adequate basis for bringing a criminal charge. That has always been so; and to make the assessment it has always been thought sufficient to hear only the prosecutor's side. As Blackstone described the prevailing practice in 18th–century England, the grand jury was "only to hear evidence on behalf of the prosecution[,] for the finding of an indictment is only in the nature of an enquiry or accusation, which is afterwards to be tried and determined." So also in the United States. According to the description of an early American court, three years before the Fifth Amendment was ratified, it is the grand jury's function not "to enquire . . . upon what foundation [the charge may be] denied," or otherwise to try the suspect's defenses, but only to examine "upon what foundation [the charge] is made" by the prosecutor. As a consequence, neither in this country nor in England has the suspect under investigation by the grand jury ever been thought to have a right to testify or to have exculpatory evidence presented.

Imposing upon the prosecutor a legal obligation to present exculpatory evidence in his possession would be incompatible with this system. If a "balanced" assessment of the entire matter is the objective, surely the first thing to be done—rather than requiring the prosecutor to say what he knows in defense of the target of the investigation—is to entitle the target to tender his own defense. To require the former while denying (as we do) the latter would be quite absurd. It would also be quite pointless, since it would merely invite the target to circumnavigate the system by delivering his exculpatory evidence to the prosecutor, whereupon it would **have** to be passed on to the grand jury—unless the prosecutor is willing to take the chance that a court will not deem the evidence important enough to qualify for mandatory disclosure.

Respondent acknowledges (as he must) that the "common law" of the grand jury is not violated if the **grand jury itself** chooses to hear no more evidence than that which suffices to convince it an indictment is proper. Thus, had the Government offered to familiarize the grand jury in this case with the five boxes of financial statements and deposition testimony alleged to contain exculpatory information, and had the grand jury rejected the offer as pointless, respondent would presumably agree that the resulting indictment would have been valid. Respondent insists, however, that courts must require the modern prosecutor to alert the grand jury to the nature and extent of the available exculpatory evidence, because otherwise the grand jury "merely functions as an arm of the prosecution." We reject the attempt to convert a nonexistent duty of the grand jury itself into an obligation of the prosecutor. The authority of the prosecutor to seek an indictment has long been understood to be "coterminous with the authority of the grand jury to entertain [the prosecutor's] charges." If the grand jury has no obligation to consider all "substantial exculpatory" evidence, we do not understand how the prosecutor can be said to have a binding obligation to present it.

There is yet another respect in which respondent's proposal not only fails to comport with, but positively contradicts, the "common law" of the Fifth Amendment grand jury. Motions to quash indictments based upon the sufficiency of the evidence relied upon by the grand jury were unheard of at common law in England. And the traditional American practice was described by Justice Nelson, riding circuit in 1852, as follows:

"No case has been cited, nor have we been able to find any, furnishing an authority for looking into and revising the judgment of the grand jury upon the evidence, for the purpose of determining whether or not the finding was founded upon sufficient proof, or whether there was a deficiency in respect to any part of the complaint. . . ."

We accepted Justice Nelson's description in *Costello v. United States*, where we held that "[i]t would run counter to the whole history of the grand jury institution" to permit an indictment to be challenged "on the ground that there was inadequate or incompetent evidence before the grand jury." And we reaffirmed this principle recently in *Bank of Nova Scotia*, where we held that "the mere fact that evidence itself is unreliable is not sufficient to require a dismissal of the indictment," and that "a challenge to the reliability or competence of the evidence presented to the grand jury" will not be heard. It would make little sense, we think, to abstain from reviewing the evidentiary support for the grand jury's judgment while scrutinizing the sufficiency of the prosecutor's presentation. A complaint about the quality or adequacy of the evidence can always be recast as a complaint that the prosecutor's presentation was "incomplete" or "misleading." Our words in *Costello* bear repeating: Review of facially valid indictments on such grounds "would run counter to the whole history of the grand jury institution[,] [and] [n]either justice nor the concept of a fair trial requires [it]."

Echoing the reasoning of the Tenth Circuit in *United States v. Page*, respondent argues that a rule requiring the prosecutor to disclose exculpatory evidence to the grand jury would, by removing from the docket unjustified prosecutions, save valuable judicial time. That depends, we suppose, upon what the ratio would turn out to be between unjustified prosecutions eliminated and grand jury indictments challenged—for the latter as well as the former consume "valuable judicial time." We need not pursue the matter; if there is an advantage to the proposal, Congress is free to prescribe it. For the reasons set forth above, however, we conclude that courts have no authority to prescribe such a duty pursuant to their inherent supervisory authority over their own proceedings. The judgment of the Court of Appeals is accordingly reversed, and the cause is remanded for further proceedings consistent with this opinion.

So ordered.

Justice STEVENS, with whom Justice BLACKMUN and Justice O'CONNOR join, and with whom Justice THOMAS joins as to Parts II and III, dissenting.

. . .

II

Like the Hydra slain by Hercules, prosecutorial misconduct has many heads. Some are cataloged in Justice Sutherland's classic opinion for the Court in *Berger v. United States*, 295 U.S. 78 (1935):

"That the United States prosecuting attorney overstepped the bounds of that propriety and fairness which should characterize the conduct of such an officer in the prosecution of a criminal offense is clearly shown by the record. He was guilty of misstating the facts in his cross-examination of witnesses; of putting into the mouths of such witnesses things which they had not said; of suggesting by his questions that statements had been made to him personally out of court, in respect of which no proof was offered; of pretending to understand that a witness had said something which he had not said and persistently cross-examining the witness upon that basis; of assuming prejudicial facts not in evidence; of bullying and arguing with witnesses; and in general, of conducting himself in a thoroughly indecorous and improper manner. . . .

"The prosecuting attorney's argument to the jury was undignified and intemperate, containing improper insinuations and assertions calculated to mislead the jury."

This, of course, is not an exhaustive list of the kinds of improper tactics that overzealous or misguided prosecutors have adopted in judicial proceedings. The reported cases of this Court alone contain examples of the knowing use of perjured testimony, the suppression of evidence favorable to an accused person, and misstatements of the law in argument to the jury, to name just a few.

Nor has prosecutorial misconduct been limited to judicial proceedings: The reported cases indicate that it has sometimes infected grand jury proceedings as well. The cases contain examples of prosecutors presenting perjured testimony, questioning a witness outside the presence of the grand jury and then failing to inform the grand jury that the testimony was exculpatory, failing to inform the grand jury of its authority to subpoena witnesses, operating under a conflict of interest, misstating the law, and misstating the facts on cross-examination of a witness.

Justice Sutherland's identification of the basic reason why that sort of misconduct is intolerable merits repetition:

"The United States Attorney is the representative not of an ordinary party to a controversy, but of a sovereignty whose obligation to govern impartially is as compelling as its obligation to govern at all; and whose interest, therefore, in a criminal prosecution is not that it shall win a case, but that justice shall be done. As such, he is in a peculiar and very definite sense the servant of the law, the twofold aim of which is that guilt shall not escape or innocence suffer. He may prosecute with earnestness and vigor—indeed, he should do so. But, while he may strike hard blows, he is not at liberty to strike foul ones. It is as much his duty to refrain from improper methods calculated to produce a wrongful conviction as it is to use every legitimate means to bring about a just one." *Berger v. United States*, 295 U.S., at 88.

It is equally clear that the prosecutor has the same duty to refrain from improper methods calculated to produce a wrongful indictment. Indeed, the prosecutor's duty to protect the fundamental fairness of judicial proceedings assumes special importance when he is presenting evidence to a grand jury. As the Court of Appeals for the Third Circuit recognized, "the costs of continued unchecked prosecutorial misconduct" before the grand jury are particularly substantial because there

"the prosecutor operates without the check of a judge or a trained legal adversary, and virtually immune from public scrutiny. The prosecutor's abuse of his special relationship to the grand jury poses an enormous risk to defendants as well. For while in theory a trial provides the defendant with a full opportunity to contest and disprove the charges against him, in practice, the handing up of an indictment will often have a devastating personal and professional impact that a later dismissal or acquittal can never undo. Where the potential for abuse is so great, and the consequences of a mistaken indictment so serious, the ethical responsibilities of the prosecutor, and the obligation of the judiciary to protect against even the appearance of unfairness, are correspondingly heightened."

In his dissent in *United States v. Ciambrone*, 601 F.2d 616 (CA2 1979), Judge Friendly also recognized the prosecutor's special role in grand jury proceedings:

"As the Supreme Court has noted, 'the Founders thought the grand jury so essential to basic liberties that they provided in the Fifth Amendment that federal prosecution for serious crimes can only be instituted by "a presentment or indictment of a Grand Jury."' Before the grand jury the prosecutor has the dual role of pressing for an indictment and of being the grand jury adviser. In case of conflict, the latter duty must take precedence. "The *ex parte* character of grand jury proceedings makes it peculiarly important for a federal prosecutor to remember that, in the familiar phrase, the interest of the United States 'in a criminal prosecution is not that it shall win a case, but that justice shall be done.'"

. . .

In an opinion that I find difficult to comprehend, the Court today repudiates the assumptions underlying these cases and seems to suggest that the court has no authority to supervise the conduct of the prosecutor in grand jury proceedings so long as he follows the dictates of the Constitution, applicable statutes, and Rule 6 of the Federal Rules of Criminal Procedure. The Court purports to support this conclusion by invoking the doctrine of separation of powers and citing a string of cases in which we have declined to impose categorical restraints on the grand jury. Needless to say, the Court's reasoning is unpersuasive.

Although the grand jury has not been "textually assigned" to "any of the branches described in the first three Articles" of the Constitution, it is not an autonomous body completely beyond the reach of the other branches. Throughout its life, from the moment it is convened until it is discharged, the grand jury is subject to the control of the court. As Judge Learned Hand recognized over 60 years ago, "a grand jury is neither an officer nor an agent of the United States, but a part of the court." This Court has similarly characterized the grand jury:

"A grand jury is clothed with great independence in many areas, but it remains an appendage of the court, powerless to perform its investigative function without the court's aid, because powerless itself to compel the testimony of witnesses. It is the court's process which summons the witness to attend and give testimony, and it is the court which must compel a witness to testify if, after appearing, he refuses to do so."

This Court has, of course, long recognized that the grand jury has wide latitude to investigate violations of federal law as it deems appropriate and need not obtain permission from either the court or the prosecutor.

Correspondingly, we have acknowledged that "its operation generally is unrestrained by the technical procedural and evidentiary rules governing the conduct of criminal trials." But this is because Congress and the Court have generally thought it best not to impose procedural restraints on the grand jury; it is not because they lack all power to do so.

To the contrary, the Court has recognized that it has the authority to create and enforce limited rules applicable in grand jury proceedings. Thus, for example, the Court has said that the grand jury "may not itself violate a valid privilege, whether established by the Constitution, statutes, or the common law." And the Court may prevent a grand jury from violating such a privilege by quashing or modifying a subpoena, or issuing a protective order forbidding questions in violation of the privilege. Moreover, there are, as the Court notes, a series of cases in which we declined to impose categorical restraints on the grand jury. In none of those cases, however, did we question our power to reach a contrary result.

Although the Court recognizes that it may invoke its supervisory authority to fashion and enforce privilege rules applicable in grand jury proceedings, and suggests that it may also invoke its supervisory authority to fashion other limited rules of grand jury procedure, it concludes that it has no authority to **prescribe** "standards of prosecutorial conduct before the grand jury," because that would alter the grand jury's historic role as an independent, inquisitorial institution. I disagree.

We do not protect the integrity and independence of the grand jury by closing our eyes to the countless forms of prosecutorial misconduct that may occur inside the secrecy of the grand jury room. After all, the grand jury is not merely an investigatory body; it also serves as a "protector of citizens against arbitrary and oppressive governmental action." Explaining why the grand jury must be both "independent" and "informed," the Court wrote in *Wood v. Georgia*, 370 U.S. 375 (1962):

"Historically, this body has been regarded as a primary security to the innocent against hasty, malicious and oppressive persecution; it serves the invaluable function in our society of standing between the accuser and the accused, whether the latter be an individual, minority group, or other, to determine whether a charge is founded upon reason or was dictated by an intimidating power or by malice and personal ill will."

It blinks reality to say that the grand jury can adequately perform this important historic role if it is intentionally misled by the prosecutor—on whose knowledge of the law and facts of the underlying criminal investigation the jurors will, of necessity, rely.

Unlike the Court, I am unwilling to hold that countless forms of prosecutorial misconduct must be tolerated—no matter how prejudicial they may be, or how seriously they may distort the legitimate function of the grand jury—simply because they are not proscribed by Rule 6 of the Federal Rules of Criminal Procedure or a statute that is applicable in grand jury proceedings. Such a sharp break with the traditional role of the federal judiciary is unprecedented, unwarranted, and unwise. Unrestrained prosecutorial misconduct in grand jury proceedings is inconsistent with the administration of justice in the federal courts and should be redressed in appropriate cases by the dismissal of indictments obtained by improper methods.

III

What, then, is the proper disposition of this case? I agree with the Government that the prosecutor is not required to place all exculpatory evidence before the grand jury. A grand jury proceeding is an *ex parte* investigatory proceeding to determine whether there is probable cause to believe a violation of the criminal laws has occurred, not a trial. Requiring the prosecutor to ferret out and present all evidence that could be used at trial to create a reasonable doubt as to the defendant's guilt would be inconsistent with the purpose of the grand jury proceeding and would place significant burdens on the investigation. But that does not mean that the prosecutor may mislead the grand jury into believing that there is probable cause to indict by withholding clear evidence to the contrary. I thus agree with the Department of Justice that "when a prosecutor conducting a grand jury inquiry is personally aware of substantial evidence which directly negates the guilt of a subject of the investigation, the prosecutor must present or otherwise disclose such evidence to the grand jury before seeking an indictment against such a person."

Although I question whether the evidence withheld in this case directly negates respondent's guilt, I need not resolve my doubts because the Solicitor General did not ask the Court to review the nature of the evidence withheld. Instead, he asked us to decide the legal question whether an indictment may be dismissed because the prosecutor failed to present exculpatory evidence. Unlike the Court and the Solicitor General, I believe the answer to that question is yes, if the withheld evidence would plainly preclude a finding of probable cause. I therefore cannot endorse the Court's opinion.

More importantly, because I am so firmly opposed to the Court's favored treatment of the Government as a litigator, I would dismiss the writ of certiorari as improvidently granted.

36

Charging the Defendant

Key Concepts

- Purposes of the Charging Document
- Sufficiency and Specificity Requirements
- Amending the Charging Document
- Variances

A. Introduction and Policy. At some point in the criminal process, the prosecutor must formally charge the defendant with a crime. As you read in **Chapter 36**, she does so using a document known as a charging instrument—either a complaint (in misdemeanor cases) or an information or indictment (in felony cases). The primary purpose of the charging instrument is to provide the defendant with sufficient notice about the actions he is being accused of committing and the specific laws he has allegedly violated. As we will see, the document serves other purposes as well.

For cases involving only misdemeanor charges, the defendant is usually formally charged at his initial appearance when the prosecutor files a complaint, which has been written up by the arresting officer or the prosecutor. Since the misdemeanor defendant has been charged at the initial appearance, the case can proceed to pre-trial motions and trial directly from the initial appearance. If the defendant wants to plead guilty, most jurisdictions will allow him to do so at the initial appearance.

However, if the case involves a felony, the prosecutor cannot formally charge the defendant until the charges have been approved by a judge through a preliminary hearing or by a grand jury. Once the charges have been officially approved using one of these two methods, the defendant will make a second appearance at an **arraignment**, sometimes called a **felony arraignment**, where the prosecutor files the information or indictment. The judge at the arraignment then has the authority to either accept a guilty plea or send the case on for pre-trial motions.

In either case, the charging instrument is a critical aspect of the proceeding. The filing of the charging instrument is in a very real sense the beginning of the formal criminal case against the defendant. And although many students (and practitioners) see the pleadings in a criminal case as a mere technicality, the charging requirements actually perform a significant substantive role. The rules governing pleadings must balance two significant and competing policy considerations.

First, it is desirable to provide the defendant as much detail as possible about the alleged criminal action in order to provide him with sufficient notice to prepare for trial. Second, because the prosecutor may learn much more detail about the criminal offense between the time the charging instrument is filed and the trial date, there must be some flexibility in allowing the prosecutor to deviate somewhat from the details in the charging instrument when proving her case at trial.

These two policy considerations are in conflict. If the rules require the prosecutor to include significant detail in the original charging instrument, the rules then also must allow for more flexibility between the facts alleged in the charging document and the facts which are proven at trial. But if there is a large deviation between the facts alleged in the charging document and the evidence submitted at trial, the "notice" the defendant originally received from the charging document may become insufficient—in fact, the information contained in the charging document may have misled the defendant rather than provided him with adequate notice. Furthermore, in indictment jurisdictions, the prosecutor is only authorized to try the defendant for the specific charges that were approved by the grand jury. A significant difference between the facts alleged in the indictment and the facts proven at trial would mean the prosecutor has overstepped her legal authority and is *de facto* trying the defendant for acts that were not reviewed by the grand jury.

Thus, the rules surrounding the drafting of the charging instrument are closely tied to the rules surrounding the law of "variances"—when the evidence that is produced at trial is somewhat different from the facts alleged in the charging document. When a variance occurs, the judge must decide whether the difference between the alleged facts and the facts proven prejudiced the defendant.

We have already seen that the charging document provides notice to the defendant so that he can begin preparing his defense. In some ways, the charging document is thus the first step of discovery. However, the charging document also fulfills three other important purposes:

1. **Assisting with the Double Jeopardy Analysis.** The charging document provides protection against double jeopardy. As we will see in **Chapter 46**, generally a defendant cannot be prosecuted twice for the same criminal conduct. For example, assume the state charges the defendant with stealing a car, and the defendant goes to trial and is acquitted. The state will thereafter be barred from bringing charges against the defendant for that same criminal conduct. If after the acquittal the state brings another charge against the defendant for stealing the same car, and the defendant moves to dismiss on double jeopardy grounds, the judge will have to decide whether the motion should be granted.

In making this determination, the judge looks at the charging document from the earlier case and compares it to the charging document from the current case. If the earlier charging document merely states that the defendant "stole a car sometime in September 2015," and the current charging document says the same thing, there is no way of knowing for sure whether the prosecutor is charging the same criminal conduct or not. But if the earlier charging document alleges that the defendant stole "a Toyota Camry from George Donovan at 6:00 PM on September 17, 2014, and the current charging document alleges the same facts, it is clear that the new charges violate the defendant's double jeopardy rights. In other words, an unambiguous, specific set of allegations in the charging document will provide clear guidance for a later double jeopardy challenge.

2. **Providing an Official Record.** If the defendant is ultimately convicted, the charging document provides the formal record of the criminal conduct for which the defendant has been convicted. The formal record will be used for many different purposes: law enforcement officers may use it if they are investigating another crime; if the defendant is convicted of other crimes, the judge in the subsequent case may use the fact of the earlier conviction when deciding on an appropriate sentence; in future trials, the details of the conviction may be used to impeach the defendant; and even future potential employers can access the record to understand exactly what crimes the defendant committed. After conviction, the charging document contains the only facts that we can be certain occurred in the case. Although the witnesses who testify in the case and other evidence in the record may imply many things about what the defendant did, a conviction means only that the defendant admitted to (or the jury concluded beyond a reasonable doubt) the exact allegations that are set out in the charging document.

   For example, assume the information charges that "on October 17, 2013, the defendant stabbed the victim with a knife in the leg, causing serious physical injury." At trial, the prosecution's witnesses testify not only that the defendant stabbed the victim in the leg with a knife and caused serious physical injury, but also that the defendant was drunk; that he tried to stab the victim in the chest and missed; that he referred to the victim using a racial epithet; and that he carried three knives on his person at all times. Even if the defendant is convicted, none of those "extra" facts have formally been proven. In other words, for all we know, the jury did not believe any of that testimony. All we know for certain (or as certain as we can ever be in the law) is that the defendant stabbed the victim with a knife in the leg, causing serious physical injury.

3. **Facilitating the Review of Legal Sufficiency Claims.** The charging document assists the trial judge in determining whether the prosecutor's case is legally sufficient when the defendant makes a motion to dismiss. This motion may come at two different stages. The first opportunity would be just after the charging instrument is filed. At this point in the case, the defendant could argue that the facts alleged in the complaint, even if true, are not sufficient to constitute the crimes charged in the complaint. For example, assume that the information alleges that the defendant committed aggravated assault, which consists of "knowingly causing serious bodily injury to another." The information then alleges the following facts: "At or around 2:00 AM on January 24, 2010, the defendant struck the victim, Debra Hennessy, in the face with a closed fist, causing swelling, bruising, and pain." At the arraignment, the defense attorney can review the information and then point out that the definition of "serious physical injury" is "serious or permanent disfigurement, serious impairment of health or loss or protracted impairment of the function of any bodily organ or limb and that creates a reasonable risk of death." The injuries alleged: "swelling, bruising, and pain," do not rise to the level of serious physical injury. Thus, the information should be dismissed. In this context, immediate review of the pleadings helps all of the parties. The defendant's case is immediately dismissed before it proceeds any further. The prosecutor does not move forward on a charge that cannot be proven (if the case proceeded to a jury trial before the mistake was detected, jeopardy would attach and the charges could not be re-brought even as a misdemeanor). And the court saves time and resources by immediately dismissing a case that has been improperly charged.

   Second, the defendant may use the charging document to move for dismissal of the case after the prosecutor has presented her evidence at trial. For example, assume the prosecutor charges the defendant with grand larceny. The charging document will list the crime charged and the elements of that crime: "the defendant took property valued at $1,000 or more of another individual without consent and with the intent of permanently depriving the legal owner of possession." The charging document would then describe the facts which are alleged: ". . . to wit, at or around 4:30 PM on February 25, 2012, the defendant took an Apple iPhone out of the Best Buy store at 3421 Lane Avenue without paying for it and was apprehended by store security outside the doors after the last possible point of purchase." Assume that at trial the prosecutor presents sufficient evidence to prove these facts beyond a reasonable doubt, but on cross-examination, the manager of the Best Buy store admits that the Apple iPhone sells for $400. The defendant could move to dismiss the case based on the fact that the prosecutor has not proven that the defendant stole property "valued at $1,000 or more," as alleged in the charging document. If the prosecutor instead produces evidence that the defendant stole five iPhones, the defendant would argue improper variance (since the evidence produced at trial was different from the facts alleged in the information).

4. **Ensuring Grand Jury Limits on Prosecutorial Discretion.** Finally, if the defendant is charged with a felony in indictment jurisdictions, the prosecutor is only permitted to move forward with charges for which the grand jury has found probable cause. Thus, the charging document limits the prosecutor to the charges already approved by the grand jury. If the prosecutor were permitted to submit one set of charges to the grand jury but then prove a different set of charges at trial, the protection of the grand jury would be somewhat meaningless. The same problem would arise if the prosecutor obtained an indictment with a vague statement of facts and then filled in the details at trial. As the Supreme Court has stated: "To allow the prosecutor, or the court, to make a subsequent guess as to what was in the minds of the grand jury at the time they returned the indictment would deprive the defendant of a basic protection which the guaranty of a grand jury was designed to secure."[1]

   Of course, since the modern grand jury does not provide much actual protection for defendants, this final purpose is probably the least important in practice. However, from a procedural standpoint, it is important that the prosecutor stays within the bounds of the charges the grand jury approved.

As with many other aspects of law, knowing the purpose behind the charging document will help you understand and remember the various rules that govern this area of law—provisions that may at first seem arbitrary or overly technical will seem sensible (or at least somewhat sensible) if you keep in mind the functions they serve.

B. The Law. The pleading rules are always found in the applicable jurisdiction's Rules of Criminal Procedure. Here are the applicable rules in federal court:

[1] Russell v. United States, 369 U.S. 749, 770 (1962).

Rule 7. The Indictment and the Information

(c) Nature and Contents.

(1) **In General.** The indictment or information must be a plain, concise, and definite written statement of the essential facts constituting the offense charged and must be signed by an attorney for the government. It need not contain a formal introduction or conclusion.

A count may incorporate by reference an allegation made in another count.

A count may allege that the means by which the defendant committed the offense are unknown or that the defendant committed it by one or more specified means.

For each count, the indictment or information must give the official or customary citation of the statute, rule, regulation, or other provision of law that the defendant is alleged to have violated.

. . .

(2) **Citation Error.** Unless the defendant was misled and thereby prejudiced, neither an error in a citation nor a citation's omission is a ground to dismiss the indictment or information or to reverse a conviction.

(d) Surplusage.

Upon the defendant's motion, the court may strike surplusage from the indictment or information.

(e) Amending an Information.

Unless an additional or different offense is charged or a substantial right of the defendant is prejudiced, the court may permit an information to be amended at any time before the verdict or finding.

(f) Bill of Particulars.

The court may direct the government to file a bill of particulars. The defendant may move for a bill of particulars before or within 14 days after arraignment or at a later time if the court permits. The government may amend a bill of particulars subject to such conditions as justice requires.

Rule 12. Pleadings and Pretrial Motions.

(b) Pretrial Motions.

(3) Motions That Must Be Made Before Trial.

The following must be raised before trial:

. . .

(B) a motion alleging a defect in the indictment or information—but at any time while the case is pending, the court may hear a claim that the indictment or information fails to invoke the court's jurisdiction or state an offense;

. . .

Rule 52. Harmless and Plain Error

(a) Harmless Error. Any error, defect, irregularity or variance [between the charging document and the proof presented at trial] that does not affect substantial rights must be disregarded.

The modern pleading rules are best understood in a historic context because the role of the charging instrument has changed dramatically over the past few centuries. Originally, when most of the criminal law was not codified, the charging instrument was necessary to set out the exact contours of the common-law crime of which the defendant was being accused. Since there was no penal code to refer to, the charging instrument had to set out the elements of the crime as well as the specific factual allegations. Up until the middle of the nineteenth century, criminal law pleadings were notoriously technical and arcane, and overly formalistic rules governed the exact wording and phrases that had to be used to properly charge a defendant. Almost any deviation from these strict rules would render the charging instrument invalid, and the prosecutor would have to re-charge the defendant, which usually meant going back to the grand jury and presenting the case again. Also, the rules generally required the prosecutor to state the "means" by which the crime was accomplished. For example, if the crime charged was murder, the prosecutor would have to state the manner in which the murder had been committed and the specific injuries caused. If the prosecutor did not know that information at the time of the charging, he faced a dilemma. If he did not specify the means and the injury, the pleading would be struck for lack of specificity. If he made his best guess as to these details, and the evidence later showed the crime happened in a different way, the defendant could challenge the indictment on those grounds.

The rules usually allowed the defendant to challenge the charging instrument at any point in the proceeding, even after a conviction. This meant that even a minor technical error might void an entire criminal trial and force the prosecutor to begin the case from scratch.

After numerous attempts to reform the pleading requirements, the federal courts created the Federal Rules of Criminal Procedure in 1946, which became a model for almost every state court system as well. Central to the pleading reforms was Rule 7, which set out common-sense requirements for the charging document—stating that the information or indictment need only set out "a plain, concise, and definite written statement of the essential facts constituting the offense charged" and need not contain a "formal introduction or conclusion." The rules also allow the prosecutor to charge a crime without specifying the means, or by listing in the alternative a number of different possible means. Finally, the new rules changed the law regarding the time the defendant had to challenge a defective charging instrument. The defendant now must object before trial to any defect in the indictment other than "critical defects." An example of a critical defect is one which fails to invoke the court's jurisdiction or fails to state an offense.[2]

The rules also allow the prosecutor to amend the charging instrument within certain limits. The type of charging document used—indictment or information—will dictate the ease with which amendment may occur. Under the federal rules, it is easier to amend an information than an indictment. Rule 7(e) of the Federal Rules of Criminal Procedure states that an information can be amended at any time unless:

1. The amendment adds to or changes the offense charged; or

2. The amendment prejudices a substantial right of the defendant.

Generally an amendment will add to or change the offense charged if the new charge involves a different statute or if the crime charged is based on a completely different series of events. If a new or different offense is charged, the defendant does not have to prove any prejudice; the amendment is barred and the prosecutor will have to drop the current charges and formally file a new information.[3]

With regard to the second prong of the rule, courts will only find that an amendment prejudices a defendant's substantial rights if the defendant can prove that he has been surprised by new facts contained in the amendment and the surprise affects his ability to defend himself against the charges. If new facts were already known to the defendant through discovery or the bill of particulars, the defendant will not be able to demonstrate surprise. Even if the defendant is able to demonstrate surprise, an amendment which is made before trial can generally be cured by granting the defendant a continuance to give him sufficient time to prepare and respond to the new evidence. Thus, an amendment will usually be barred based on prejudice only if it references previously undisclosed information and is made during the trial itself.

Amendments to an indictment are less likely to be permitted under the federal rules than amendments to an information. Unlike an information, the exact wording of the indictment has been approved by a supposedly independent grand jury. Thus, aside from very minor changes to fix typographical errors, federal

[2] Fed. R. Crim. Pro. 12(b)(3).

[3] Fed. R. Crim. Pro. 12(b)(3)(B).

indictments cannot be amended. We discuss this in more detail in Section C.4 below. Unlike the federal courts, most states have more lenient rules governing the amendment of indictments that are more analogous to the federal rule for amending informations.

In contrast to an amendment, in which the prosecutor seeks to make changes to the charging instrument, a **variance** occurs when the proof that the prosecutor presents at trial is different from the allegations made in the charging instrument. For example, the information might state that the defendant defrauded the victim on December 10, 2014, but at trial the witness may testify that the fraud occurred on December 12, 2014. Or, the information may allege that the defendant was involved in a conspiracy with Jones and Smith, but at trial there is only proof that the defendant was involved in a conspiracy with Smith. Or, perhaps the information alleges that the defendant committed larceny by deception, but the evidence at trial shows that the defendant committed larceny by stealth, and the prosecutor (realizing that the defendant will be acquitted if the jury is charged only on the law of larceny by deception), requests a jury instruction on larceny by stealth. In any of these cases, the defendant can object that there is a variance between the facts alleged in the charging instrument and those proven at trial.

Once a variance between the prosecutor's charges and the prosecutor's proof becomes apparent, the prosecutor has two options. First, she can seek to amend the charging instrument to conform to the proof offered at trial. If the prosecutor chooses to proceed in this fashion, the defendant can object to the amendment, and the judge will evaluate the amendment based on the standards discussed above. Alternatively, the prosecutor can let the variance stand, in which case the judge applies a slightly different standard to evaluate the validity of the variance. We will discuss the tests for when a variance is permitted in Section C.3. below, but generally you should be aware that a variance will be allowed unless:

1. The variance deprives the defendant of fair notice of the charges against him; or

2. The variance creates the risk of double jeopardy in that a later information or indictment could charge the defendant with the same crime he is being charged with *de facto* in this trial.

In addition to providing the rules that govern amendments and variances, Rule 7 also regulates the additional information that a defendant is entitled to regarding the charges she faces. Rule 7(f) states that a defendant may make a request for a "bill of particulars" after the charging document has been filed in order to obtain more specific details about the crimes alleged. Technically, a bill of particulars is not meant to be a standard discovery device—the defendant's discovery tools are detailed in other rules and statutes which we cover in **Chapter 39.** Instead, the bill of particulars is meant to be used only when the indictment does not provide the defendant with sufficient information to begin preparing his defense.[4] For example, a valid request for a bill of particulars might include a request for the dates of the alleged criminal activity, the names of other individuals involved in the alleged crimes (such as victims or co-conspirators), or the specific items or amounts of money alleged to have been stolen.

C. Applying the Law.

1. Sufficiency and Specificity. The primary requirements for a charging instrument are that it be "sufficient" and "specific." The first requirement—sufficiency—can be thought of as a legal question: does the charging document list the offense or offenses charged and describe conduct that establishes every element of these offenses? The second requirement—specificity—is more of a fact-based question: do the allegations provide the defendant with adequate notice so that he can prepare his defense?

The Supreme Court has set the standards for sufficiency and specificity by stating that (1) the charging document must "contain[] the elements of the offense intended to be charged, and sufficiently apprise[] the defendant of what he must be prepared to meet; and (2) . . . [must] show[] with accuracy to what extent he may plead a former acquittal or conviction."[5]

A charging document that is **insufficient**—that is, one that does not state an offense—is fatally flawed. Federal Rule 12(b)(3) (and the analogous state rules) treat this defect as seriously as if a court lacks jurisdiction. This means that the defendant can bring a motion to dismiss a charging document on sufficiency grounds at any time while the case is pending. If the defendant has not yet been convicted, the case must be dismissed, and if the defendant has already been convicted at trial, the conviction will be reversed—even if the question is being raised for the first time on appeal. (There is a split among courts as to whether a conviction as a result of a guilty plea must be reversed for such a defect. Some courts have found that the defendant waives the right to challenge the sufficiency of the indictment/information when he pleads guilty). Although challenges to the sufficiency of the indictment/information are permitted at the appellate level, a charging document that is the subject of such a challenge must be construed liberally in favor of validity.[6]

In contrast, if the charging document merely lacks **specificity**, the defendant must object before trial or he will waive his right to object altogether. Even if the

---

[4] United States v. Kerik, 615 F.Supp. 2d 256 (S.D.N.Y. 2009).

[5] Russell v. United States, 369 U.S. 749, 763-4 (1962) (internal quotations and citations omitted).

[6] United States v. Sutton, 961 F.2d 476, 478–79 (4th Cir. 1992).

charging document does lack specificity, the defendant must prove that the lack of specificity caused prejudice to him by failing to provide him with enough notice to allow him to prepare his defense. And even if the defendant does demonstrate prejudice, the prosecutor can usually cure that prejudice by filing a bill of particulars which describes the offense with the appropriate level of specificity.

Thus, if a charging document is invalid, it is important to determine whether the invalidity is a result of a lack of sufficiency (failure to allege conduct that establishes every element of an offense) or is instead merely a result of a lack of specificity (failure to provide adequate details of the offense). On the margins, this can be a difficult determination. For example, assume the charging document alleges that the defendant committed burglary by trespassing on someone's property with the intent to commit a crime, but does not specify the crime that the defendant intended to commit. Or assume that the defendant is charged with selling narcotics, but the charging instrument does not specify the type of narcotic he sold. Are these omissions a problem with specificity or a failure to state an element of the offense?

Appellate courts have provided some guidance in making this determination. Usually, in order to be sufficient, the charging document must do more than merely cite the statutory language of the offense; it must explain what the particular defendant did to violate each of the elements of the offense, and it must describe the conduct with an adequate amount of detail. As the United States Court of Appeals for the D.C. Circuit explained:

> The test for sufficiency is whether it is fair to require the accused to defend himself on the basis of the charge as stated in the indictment. In some cases, it is enough if the indictment puts the charge in the words of the statute but this is acceptable only where the statute itself fully, directly, and unambiguously sets forth all of the elements of the offense. The more generally applicable rule is that the indictment may use the language of the statute, but that language must be supplemented with enough detail to apprise the accused of the particular offense with which he is charged.[7]

If the charging document only references a provision of the penal code and does not provide many other details, the charging document runs the risk of being insufficient, especially if the statute itself covers multiple crimes:

> **Example**—Kyong Kim was driving his car on the highway when a police officer ran his license plate and determined that Kim's driver's license had been suspended. Kim was pulled over and given a citation. Eventually a criminal complaint was filed against him, alleging:

[7] United States v. Conlon, 628 F.2d 150,155 (D.C. Cir. 1980).

"On January 4, 2012, Kyong Kim was driving on the Baltimore-Washington Parkway, operating a motor vehicle while suspension of his privilege for doing so was in effect, in violation of Section 16–303 of the Maryland Transportation Code."

The case proceeded to trial, and the prosecutor called the police officer who had observed Kim driving and admitted a copy of his suspended driver's license. Kim then moved to dismiss the case based on the fact that the complaint failed to state the offense, because Section 16-303 of the Maryland Transportation Code includes multiple crimes, and the language in the complaint did not describe which crime the defendant committed.[8]

Analysis: The trial court held the complaint was invalid because it failed to state an offense. Thus, the defendant's motion was timely even though it was filed after the trial began. The court noted the three requirements for the charging document: it must (1) allege the essential facts constituting the offense; (2) allege each element of the offense, so that fair notice is provided; and (3) be sufficiently distinctive that a verdict will bar a second prosecution for the same offense.[9] The court held that the complaint failed in all three respects.

Section 16-303 does not itself specify one crime. Instead, it is a "compilation of nine distinct traffic offenses and one administrative provision."[10] The language in the rest of the complaint narrowed the crime being charged down to three possible offenses in that it accused the defendant of driving "while suspension of privileges was in effect." However, even this narrowing was not sufficient.

Each of the three possible crimes being charged constituted a separate offense—1) driving while his license had been suspended by the state of Maryland; 2) driving while his license had been suspended by a different state for a traffic violation; 3) driving while his license had been suspended by a different state for failure to appear in court or pay a fine. If the prosecutor had simply specified the exact provision of Section 16-303 that the defendant was accused of violating, the complaint would have been valid. However, since each subsection of Section 16-303 has different elements, the "generic charge" found in the complaint "does not allege the essential facts, does not provide fair notice, and is not 'sufficiently distinctive' to bar a second prosecution for the same offense."[11]

As the *Kim* case makes clear, when a complaint alleges **multiple** crimes without specifying **which** crime the defendant is alleged to have committed, it is insuf-

[8] This problem is based on United States v. Kim, 902 F.Supp.2d 763 (D. Md. 2012). In the actual case, the charging document was a "Violation Notice," not a complaint.

[9] Id. at 767 (internal quotations and citations omitted).

[10] Id.

[11] Id. at 768.

ficient because it fails to state an offense. However, if a complaint alleges one crime but does not identify the **means** by which the offense was committed, the complaint merely lacks specificity:

> **Example**—One night Francis Crowley, a midshipman at the Merchant Marine Academy, entered the room of another midshipman, Stacy Vascarro, without permission. Crowley then proceeded to hold Vascarro down, and, ignoring her protests, he fondled her breasts and touched her vagina. Vascarro was able to prevent him from committing any other acts against her, and her protests eventually became so loud that Crowley left the room. Vascarro reported the assault immediately, and Crowley was arrested.
>
> The grand jury charged Crowley with attempted violation of 18 U.S.C § 2241(a)(1), which prohibits "knowingly causing another person to engage in a sexual act . . . by using force against that other person." "Sexual act" is defined by the statute as:
>
> (A) contact between the penis and the vulva or the penis and the anus . . .;
>
> (B) contact between the mouth and the penis, the mouth and the vulva, or the mouth and the anus;
>
> (C) the penetration, however slight, of the anal or genital opening of another by a hand or finger or by any object, with an intent to abuse, humiliate, harass, degrade, or arouse or gratify the sexual desire of any person; or
>
> (D) the intentional touching, not through the clothing, of the genitalia of another person who has not attained the age of 16 years with an intent to abuse, humiliate, harass, degrade, or arouse or gratify the sexual desire of any person.
>
> The indictment read as follows:
>
> "On or about May 14, 2002, Francis Crowley entered Stacy Vascarro's room, forcibly held her down on the bed, and attempted to engage in a sexual act with her."

Before trial began, Crowley filed a boilerplate motion which moved to dismiss the indictment on a number of grounds, including the fact that it was "impermissibly vague." The trial court denied the motion. Crowley was convicted after a jury trial, and he appealed, arguing that the indictment lacked specificity because it did not define what type of sexual act he was alleged to have attempted.[12]

Analysis: The appellate court upheld the conviction. The court noted that because the defendant was challenging a lack of specificity, the objection should have been made before trial began. The defendant's boilerplate motion before trial did not constitute a proper challenge to the indictment, since (unlike the appeal), it did not specify exactly what aspect of the indictment was vague. The court explained:

> The purposes of Rule 12(b)(2) would not be served—indeed, they would be subverted—if a defendant could "raise" a specificity challenge merely by including generic, boilerplate objections to the indictment in his pretrial motion papers. If such were the case, a defendant could baldly assert in a pretrial motion to dismiss that the indictment by which he was charged was insufficiently particular. Assuming that the motion was not granted, the trial would then begin and the defendant would have the luxury of hedging his bets: If he were convicted, he could file a motion for a new trial that fleshed out the objection that he had already "raised" in his pretrial motion, and hope that a new jury (and ultimately a new grand jury) would look more favorably upon his case. Such hedging of bets would cause precisely the mischief that Rule 12(b)(2) seeks to prevent: It would trivialize the criminal justice system by treating juries as tradeable game pieces, and would waste a great deal of time by permitting defendants to substantiate their arguments for the first time after their trial is completed.
>
> Accordingly, we hold that in order to raise a challenge to the specificity of an indictment within the meaning of Fed.R.Crim.P. 12(b)(2) . . . the defendant must apprise the District Court of those particular portions of the indictment that are lacking in the requisite specificity, and explain why, in the circumstances, greater specificity is required.[13]

Thus, not only does a challenge to the specificity of the charging document have to be brought before trial, but it also (somewhat ironically) must be specific

[12] This example is based on United States v. Crowley, 236 F.3d 104 (2d Cir. 2000).

[13] Id. at 108-109.

enough to inform the court and the prosecutor exactly what part of the charging document lacks specificity.

Because the *Crowley* court held that the defendant had not made a timely motion to dismiss the indictment, it did not reach the question of whether the indictment was, in fact, so vague that it prejudiced the defendant because it did not provide adequate notice for him to prepare his defense. This would have been a close call. The definition of "sexual act" that is found in the statute cited in the indictment involves four possible actions, and one of them (an attack on a person under the age of 16) could not possibly apply in this case. The other three are similar acts, but distinct enough that a defendant may conceivably prepare different defenses depending on whether he is accused of using his genitals, his mouth, or his finger to commit the assault.

The *Crowley* case made a persuasive argument in favor of the procedural rule requiring timely motions for challenging the specificity of the charging document. However, as we have seen, this restriction does not apply to motions that attack the sufficiency of the charging document. Your perspective on whether this absence of restriction is a good or bad thing may depend upon who you represent.

From the prosecution's perspective, the absence of restriction allows defense attorneys to engage in the very type of gamesmanship the *Crowley* court discussed. Indeed, in the *Kim* case, there is some indication the defense attorney believed early on the complaint was fatally defective but intentionally refused to make a motion to dismiss before trial. By deliberately waiting until after the trial began (and jeopardy had attached), defense counsel in *Kim* successfully (and permanently) disposed of the case.

From the defense perspective, the result in *Kim* is not the product of gamesmanship but of zealous advocacy. In this view, the defense attorney's obligation to zealously represent her client creates an obligation **not** to raise objections to the sufficiency of the indictment early on. By bringing the matter to the court's attention only after the trial is over, the remedy (as it was in *Kim*) is an automatic dismissal.

Recently some federal and state appellate courts have narrowed the appellate relief that might be afforded in a case where the charging instrument does not state an offense. These courts apply a harmless error analysis (see **Chapter 47**) to such defects if they are not brought to the court's attention until after conviction. Thus, if the failure to properly charge an offense in the charging document did not prejudice the defendant, the conviction will not be overturned on those grounds.[14]

[14] United States v. Prentiss, 256 F.3d 971 (10th Cir. 2001).

2. Duplicitous and Multiplicitous Counts. A **duplicitous charging instrument** contains two or more distinct offenses in a single count. For example: "defendant recklessly caused serious physical injury to George Stevens and Victor Jones." Duplicitous counts are flawed because a trial jury may convict on the count even though half of the jurors found the defendant guilty of one charge (e.g., recklessly causing serious physical injury to George Stevens) and the other half found the defendant guilty of the second charge (e.g., recklessly causing serious physical injury to Victor Jones). Unlike the failure to state a claim, however, this defect can be corrected if the prosecutor simply strikes one of the charges from the count and proceeds on the other charge. The error can also be corrected by giving the jury a limiting instruction in which jurors are told that the jury must unanimously agree on one of the two charges. Once again, however, this correction may not be possible if the duplicitous count is part of an indictment because the prosecutor would be going beyond what was authorized by a grand jury.

Arguments about duplicity occasionally occur in conspiracy cases or complex fraud cases. For example, the prosecutor may charge a conspiracy or fraud in one count, and include in that count a number of other criminal actions that form the basis of the conspiracy or fraud. In such a case, the count is not duplicitous because the other crimes charged in that context are merely elements of the conspiracy or fraud charge itself. However, if multiple conspiracies are charged in a single count (for example, an accountant is charged with conspiracy to defraud both his client and the Internal Revenue Service), the count is duplicitous. Likewise, if one count charges multiple fraudulent schemes against multiple victims, the count is duplicitous. Duplicitous counts are unusual outside of the context of conspiracy and fraud cases because most prosecutors use standardized forms to charge defendants.

A **multiplicitous charging instrument** charges a single offense in multiple counts. For example, assume that there is a federal law making it a crime to file a Medicaid claim that contains a false statement. The statute clearly states that the crime is the filing of the claim with the false statement, not the making of the false statement. The prosecutor then files the following indictment

> Count 1: Defendant intentionally provided false information about his income on a claim for Medicaid benefits filed September 17, 2014.
>
> Count 2: Defendant intentionally provided false information about his physical condition on a claim for Medicaid benefits filed September 17, 2014.

In this example, the defendant has only committed one crime—filing a Medicaid form with a false statement—but the crime has been split up into two counts. It is permissible to charge the defendant this way, but it is not permissible for the defendant to be punished separately for both counts because that would result in the defendant being punished twice for the same criminal conduct in violation of the double jeopardy prohibition against multiple punishment. Thus, if the charging instrument contains two counts for the same criminal conduct, the trial judge will "merge" the two counts at the end of the trial so that the defendant cannot be punished twice.

The issue of multiplicitous counts usually occurs when the statute is ambiguous as to whether a certain criminal action constitutes one crime or two or more crimes. As a rule, as long as each count of the indictment contains some element that is distinct from every other count, the counts are not multiplicitous. Often, this is a question of legislative intent: whether the legislature intended to create multiple punishments for the same criminal conduct.

> **Example—*United States v. Woodward*, 469 U.S. 105 (1985):** Charles Woodward and his wife landed at Los Angeles airport after a flight from Brazil. Upon landing, Woodward was handed a standard customs form asking a number of questions, including whether he was carrying over $5,000 in currency. Woodward checked the "No" box next to that question. After asking Woodward some questions, the customs agents became suspicious and decided to search Woodward and his wife. At that point Woodward admitted that he and his wife were each carrying over $10,000 in cash.
>
> Woodward was charged with two crimes:
>
> > (1) Making a false statement to an agency of the United States in violation of 18 U.S.C. § 1001.
> >
> > (2) Willfully failing to report that he was carrying in excess of $5,000 into the United States, 84 Stat. 1121, 1122, 31 U.S.C. §§ 1058.
>
> Woodward was convicted and sentenced on both counts. On appeal, he sought to dismiss the indictment on the grounds that the two charges were multiplicitous, since they were based on identical criminal conduct.

Analysis: The Supreme Court held that the two counts were not multiplicitous. Although in this case the defendant committed one action which simultaneously violated both laws, there are ways to commit each crime without committing the other. A defendant can clearly make a false statement to a government agency that does not involve carrying currency. And, a defendant could conceivably carry over $5,000 of currency into the country and fail to report that fact merely by remaining silent and thus without making a false statement at all.

Furthermore, there was no evidence that Congress intended only one punishment for the two different crimes, since they were passed to serve different purposes: "The currency reporting statute was enacted to develop records that would 'have a high degree of usefulness in criminal, tax, or regulatory investigations.' The false statement statute, on the other hand, was designed 'to protect the authorized functions of governmental departments and agencies from the perversion which might result from the deceptive practices described.'[15]

3. Variances. Occasionally the evidence submitted by the prosecutor at trial differs somewhat from the allegations contained in the charging document. For example, perhaps the defendant is charged with burglary on November 2, but at trial the evidence shows that the burglary took place on October 31, but was not discovered until November 2. Or, the indictment may state that the defendant committed aggravated assault by knowingly causing serious physical injury. When the witness testifies, however, it is clear that the defendant did not cause serious physical injury, just physical injury; but the defendant used a weapon when causing the injury. Thus, if the prosecutor's witness is credible, the defendant is still guilty of aggravated assault, but by a different means (and under a different subsection of the statute).

All of these are examples of a **variance**. Variances are disfavored for two reasons. First, they obviously subvert the primary purpose of the charging document, which is to provide the defendant with notice of the legal and factual charges against him. Second, variances create double jeopardy problems. Assume, for example, that the defendant has formally been charged with committing a burglary on November 2, and is convicted after the jury hears evidence that he committed the burglary on October 31. His formal record now states that he has been tried and convicted of a November 2 burglary. There would therefore be nothing to stop the prosecutor from bringing a new indictment charging him with committing a burglary on October 31 and then (in theory) presenting the same evidence to a new jury and getting a second conviction for the same crime.

Although variances are disfavored, modern pleading rules such as Rule 52 of the Federal Rules of Criminal Procedure allow for variances as long as they do not affect the substantial rights of the defendant. Therefore, a court will allow a variance unless it deprives the defendant of fair notice or creates the possibility that the defendant will be placed in jeopardy twice.[16] A court will generally find that the defendant had notice if he was made aware of the variance at an early date—for example, through a filing of a bill of particulars or through discovery.

[15] United States v. Woodward, 469 U.S. 105, 109 (1985) (internal citations omitted).

[16] Berger v. United States, 295 U.S. 78 (1935).

Sometimes a variance occurs because a witness changes his or her testimony, or because the prosecutor simply learns more details about the crime as the trial date approaches. Often, however, a variance occurs because the crime being charged is somewhat ambiguous, and the trial court (or an appellate court) interprets the law slightly differently than the prosecutor expected, which forces the prosecutor to submit different evidence in order to obtain a conviction:

> **Example—*Dunn v. United States*, 442 U.S. 100 (1979):** Robert Dunn gave grand jury testimony in June of 1976 implicating a man named Musgrave in various drug crimes. On September 30, 1976, Dunn visited Musgrave's attorney, and gave an oral statement, under oath in the presence of a notary public, in which he stated that his grand jury testimony was false. The prosecutor was notified of Dunn's recantation, and a special hearing was held in Musgrave's case on October 21. At the hearing, Dunn gave sworn testimony in which he repeated his statement that his grand jury testimony was false. The prosecutor duly reduced the charges against Musgrave in response to this new information, and then charged Dunn with perjury for his false statements in the grand jury.
>
> Dunn was charged with violating 18 U.S.C. § 1623, which prohibits false declarations made under oath "in any proceeding before or ancillary to any court or grand jury of the United States." Specifically, the indictment stated that Dunn's testimony before the June 1976 grand jury was inconsistent with statements made "on September 30, 1976, while under oath as a witness in a proceeding ancillary to United States v. Musgrave . . . to the degree that one of said declarations was false."[17]
>
> At the perjury trial, the prosecutor submitted evidence of Dunn's June grand jury testimony, his sworn statements in the attorney's office on September 30, and his sworn statements at the October 21 hearing. Dunn was convicted. On appeal, the Tenth Circuit held that 18 U.S.C. § 1623 only applied to a "proceeding before or ancillary to any court or grand jury," and that the September 30 statements in the attorney's office were not such a proceeding. The October 21 hearing, however, was such a proceeding, and the prosecutor had produced evidence of the October 21 proceeding at trial. Thus, the appellate court found there was a variance between the facts that were charged and the facts that were proven at

[17] Dunn v. United States, 442 U.S. 100, 103-4 (1979).

trial to support the charge. However, the court further concluded that this variance did not prejudice the defendant because the defendant was on notice the October 21 statement would be used:

> This court has consistently held that a variance between the indictment and evidence is not fatal unless the defendant could not have anticipated from the indictment what evidence would be presented at trial or unless the conviction based on an indictment would not bar a subsequent prosecution. Clearly, where Dunn's testimony in the Musgrave motion hearing was inextricably related to his statement [in the attorney's office], that is, affirming the truth of the latter, it cannot be said that Dunn could not have anticipated that such evidence would be presented against him at his perjury trial.[18]

Dunn appealed to the Supreme Court. He argued that he was charged with making an inconsistent statement under oath on September 30, but the only way his conviction was valid was if the jury used the inconsistent statement under oath on October 21. Thus, Dunn argued there was a fatal variance in the proof at trial.

Analysis: The Supreme Court reversed the conviction. The Court held that technically there was no variance between the facts alleged in the indictment and the proof presented at trial because the trial jury was told by the trial judge to follow the indictment and compare the September 30 interview with the June grand jury testimony. However, the September 30 interview could not be a basis for the conviction—only the October 21 hearing could—and although the jury heard evidence of the October 21 hearing, the legal charge they received from the judge was to use the September 30 interview. In the Court's words:

> To uphold a conviction on a charge that was neither alleged in an indictment nor presented to a jury at trial offends the most basic notions of due process. Few constitutional principles are more firmly established than a defendant's right to be heard on the specific charges of which he is accused. There is, to be sure, no glaring distinction between the Government's theory at trial and the Tenth Circuit's analysis on appeal. The jury might well have reached the same verdict had the prosecution built its case on petitioner's October 21 testimony adopting his September 30 statement rather than on the September statement itself. But the offense was not so defined, and appellate courts are not free to revise the basis on which a defendant is convicted simply because the same result would likely obtain on retrial.

[18] United States v. Dunn, 577 F.2d 119, 123-4 (1978).

> . . . [I]t is as much a violation of due process to send an accused to prison following conviction of a charge on which he was never tried as it would be to convict him upon a charge that was never made.[19]

The prosecutor could probably have cured the problem in *Dunn* if he or she acknowledged the variance at trial and asked the trial judge for an instruction telling the jury to compare the October 21 statement with the grand jury testimony instead of the September 30 statement that was charged in the indictment. Under the intermediate appellate court's reasoning, such a variance would have been permitted because the defendant had adequate notice the October 21 statement would be used at trial. But since the trial jury never had a chance to decide the case based on the proper facts, the conviction it handed down was void.

The prosecutor's other possible course of action in *Dunn*—which is probably the most common response to a variance—would be to seek to formally amend the charging instrument during trial. If the amendment had been granted, there would have been no due process problem, and no need for the jury to be charged differently from what was in the indictment. However, as we will see in the next section, formally amending the charging instrument may create another set of problems because a prosecutor is not allowed to add to the charges that were approved by the grand jury.

4. Amending an Information vs. Amending an Indictment. As noted in Section B., Rule 7(e) allows a prosecutor to amend an *information* at any time before the verdict as long as no new offense is added and as long as the defendant is not prejudiced by surprise. If a new offense is added by the amendment, there will be no need for the defendant to show prejudice. We have already seen in our discussion about sufficiency and multiplicity that there may be some dispute as to what constitutes a distinct offense. In the context of amendments, parties will argue over whether the prosecutor has added a "new offense" or merely altered the means by which the defendant is accused of committing the original crime.

For the most part, however, courts are relatively liberal in allowing the prosecutor to amend an information (or, in a misdemeanor case, a complaint). Technical mistakes can be fixed as a matter of course and even substantive changes—as long as they do not add new offenses—will generally be allowed as long as the defendant is given any extra time needed to prepare in response to the change.

The rules are somewhat stricter, however, for amending indictments. This is because the prosecutor is only authorized to move forward on the specific charges approved by the grand jury. Over a century ago, the Supreme Court set out a very high standard in *Ex Parte Bain*.[20] *Bain* involved a defendant who had been

[19] Dunn v. United States, 442 U.S. 100, 106-7 (1979).

[20] Ex parte Bain, 121 U.S. 1 (1887).

charged with making a false report to the federal government about the bank he worked for "with the intent to deceive the Comptroller of the Currency and the agent appointed to examine the affairs" of the bank. The defendant objected to the indictment, and the prosecutor responded to the objection by amending the indictment to remove any reference to the Comptroller. Thus, the new indictment charged the defendant with filing a false report "with the intent to deceive the agent appointed to examine the affairs" of the bank. The trial court that allowed the amendment found the reference to the Comptroller in the indictment was mere surplusage. The defendant appealed this all the way to the Supreme Court, which ruled unanimously for the defendant:

> [H]ow can it be said that, with these words stricken out, it is the indictment which was found by the grand jury? If it lies within the province of a court to change the charging part of an indictment to suit its own notions of what it ought to have been, or what the grand jury would probably have made it if their attention had been called to suggested changes, the great importance which the common law attaches to an indictment by a grand jury, as a prerequisite to a prisoner's trial for a crime, and without which the constitution says 'no person shall be held to answer,' may be frittered away until its value is almost destroyed.[21]

The broadest interpretation of the *Bain* rule would prevent even the most minor of changes to the indictment, since any change could conceivably have altered the way a grand juror might have voted. However, if *Bain* ever stood for such a broad proposition, it no longer does. The Supreme Court modified and limited the *Bain* rule nearly a hundred years later in the context of deciding a variance between the proof presented at trial and the charges that were approved by a grand jury:

> **Example—*United States v. Miller*, 471 U.S. 130 (1985):** James Miller was indicted on three counts of mail fraud. The government alleged in the indictment that Miller consented to a burglary of his business, and then lied to his insurance company about the value of his losses. Miller used the United States mail system to send his false insurance claim. Specifically, Miller was charged with violating 18 U.S.C. § 1341: "Whoever, having devised . . . any scheme or artifice to defraud, or for obtaining money or property by means of false or fraudulent pretenses . . . for the purpose of executing such scheme or artifice . . . places in any post office . . . any matter or thing whatever to be sent or delivered by the Postal Service, shall be fined not more than $1,000 or imprisoned not more than five years, or both."

[21] Id. at 10.

At trial, the prosecutor only submitted evidence to prove that Miller lied to his insurance company about the value of his losses. The government offered no proof that Miller consented to the burglary ahead of time. The prosecutor thus moved to amend the indictment to strike all references to the aspect of the fraud in which Miller consented to the burglary. The trial judge denied the amendment, and the case went to the jury, which convicted Miller.

The defendant appealed his conviction, arguing that under the *Bain* standard, any variance between the facts alleged in the indictment and the facts used to prove his guilt at trial violated his Fifth Amendment right to a grand jury. The appellate court agreed, and the government appealed the case to the Supreme Court.

Analysis: The Supreme Court upheld the defendant's conviction, holding that the variance of the indictment did not prejudice the defendant nor violate his Fifth Amendment rights.

The Court first determined whether the variance violated Rule 52—that is, whether it prejudiced a substantial right of the defendant. The Court noted that the facts proven at trial conformed to one of the means of fraud that was specified in the indictment, so "[c]ompetent defense counsel certainly should have been on notice that that offense was charged and would need to be defended against."[22] Thus, there was no showing of prejudice on the part of the defendant.

The Court then turned to the question of the defendant's Fifth Amendment grand jury rights. The Court conceded that *Bain* would seem to support the defendant's arguments, but then proceeded to dissect the *Bain* decision. In the Court's view, *Bain* could be interpreted in one of two ways. The narrowest application of *Bain* would mean that a defendant cannot be convicted of any offense that was not contained in the original indictment. This aspect of *Bain* is still good law. However, it does not help the defendant in this case because the crime he was ultimately convicted of in light of the variance (fraudulently using the mail to report an inflated loss to his insurance company) was in fact contained in the original indictment.

A broader interpretation of *Bain* would mean that if an amendment or a variance effectively strikes out any part of the indictment, the entire indictment is invalid, because the trial court cannot know whether the grand jury would have indicted if the language were changed. The Court held that this aspect of *Bain* did not survived the intervening century: "To the extent *Bain* stands for the

[22] United States v. Miller, 471 U.S. 130, 134 (1985).

proposition that it constitutes an unconstitutional amendment to drop from an indictment those allegations that are unnecessary to an offense that is clearly contained within it, that case has simply not survived."[23] Thus, because "the variance complained of added nothing new to the grand jury's indictment and constituted no broadening,"[24] the defendant's conviction stands.

Although *Miller* did not overrule *Bain* outright, it certainly made it easier for prosecutors to amend indictments. As long as the original indictment includes the charge for which the defendant is ultimately convicted, the defendant's grand jury rights will not be violated. For example, consider the *Crowley* case involving sexual assault from Section C.1 above. In that case, the defendant argued that the indictment lacked specificity because it did not describe which of the three possible types of sexual assault had been attempted by the defendant. If the defendant brought that motion in a timely fashion, and the trial court agreed the indictment lacked specificity, how could the prosecutor respond? Under the original holding of *Bain*, the prosecutor could not have gone forward with the indictment, since the defendant has a Fifth Amendment right to have the specific words of the indictment approved by a grand jury. However, under the updated *Miller* standard, the prosecution could simply file a bill of particulars describing the exact type of attempted sexual assault that was being alleged, in order to provide the defendant with the necessary notice for the case. The fact that some grand jurors might have originally indicted the case based on a theory of attempted intercourse, while others might have indicted based on a theory of attempted oral sex, would be irrelevant to the analysis. In the same way, it was irrelevant in *Miller* that some grand jurors may only have indicted the defendant because they believed that his only fraud was in consenting to the burglary ahead of time.

Finally, if the court does not allow the prosecutor to amend the information or the indictment—for whatever reason—the prosecutor will usually have to dismiss the charges and then file a new information or obtain a new indictment. This can be more than a mere formality. In an indictment jurisdiction, the prosecutor must bring the case to a new grand jury, which takes time and resources. In any jurisdiction, dismissing and re-filing the charging document could have other repercussions—for example, it may delay the trial further, which could put pressure on the prosecutor to meet the speedy trial deadlines for the case. And if the defendant is being held in custody pending trial, dismissing the case against him may result in his release until new charges can be filed.

---

23 Id. at 144.

24 Id. at 145.

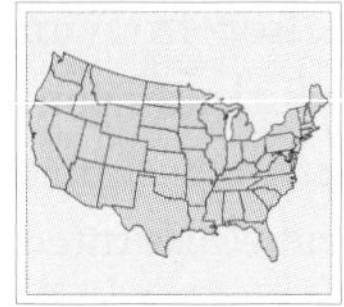

5. State Variations. As alluded to throughout this chapter, different states will vary in their rules and requirements for charging the defendant. Most obviously, some states do not require an indictment in a criminal case and therefore amending the charging document is easier. There are many other differences, such as:

- Some states adhere to a more traditional set of requirements when evaluating the validity of an amendment to the charging document. In the federal system, Rule 7(e) allows an amendment to the charging instrument as long as a new offense is not being added and as long as the defendant does not suffer prejudicial surprise from the change. Some states apply the "form/substance" distinction, which only allows amendments to the "form" of the charging document but not the "substance" of the document. This results in fewer amendments being allowed, since any amendment that changes the description of the crime, the mens rea of the crime, or even the result of the crime could be deemed a substantive amendment, even if it does not cause prejudicial surprise to the defendant.

- Some states put a further limit on variances by applying a "constructive amendment" standard. In other words, they will treat a variance as having the same legal effect as a formal amendment to the charging instrument. In some cases this does not make much difference, since the standards for evaluating the validity of a variance and the validity of an amendment are very similar. However, if the jurisdiction also has stricter rules governing the amendment of the charging instrument (such as the form/substance distinction discussed above, or something closer to the original *Bain* standard for amending an indictment), then courts will be much less likely to allow a constructive variance than they would in the federal system.

- In contrast, some states do not differentiate between amending an information or an indictment—that is, they have disregarded *Bain* entirely. Thus, they have a single standard for amending any charging document—usually the same standard found in Federal Rule 7(e).

As always, it is important to check the rules in your local jurisdiction to see how they may differ from the federal rules.

6. Sample Indictment. Charging documents can run from one page to dozens of pages, depending on the number of crimes being charged and the complexity of the factual background. They will always begin with a caption that includes the jurisdiction, the name of the charging body (e.g. the Commonwealth of Virginia or the People of the State of New York), and the name of the defendant or defendants. For more complex crimes, such as conspiracies or complex criminal schemes, the charging document will usually contain a section entitled "Background" or "Introduction" that introduces the various actors (such as the victims and the defendants) and lays out the basic facts. The charging document will then set out the charge or charges as "Count One," "Count Two," and so on. Each count will typically contain a citation to the specific penal law that has allegedly been violated. At the end of the charging document will be a signature line for the prosecutor who is filing the document, as well as (in the case of an indictment) a signature line for the foreperson of the grand jury.

Below is an example of a short, simple indictment from the Casey Anthony case in 2008. Anthony was charged with murdering her two-year old daughter, and she was also charged with six other counts, including child abuse, manslaughter of a child, and four counts of providing false information to a police officer. As is typical with charging instruments, the most severe charge is listed first:

IN THE CIRCUIT COURT OF THE NINTH JUDICIAL CIRCUIT IN AND FOR ORANGE COUNTY, FLORIDA

SPRING TERM, 2008

THE STATE OF FLORIDA
vs.
CASEY MARIE ANTHONY

INDICTMENT CASE #
DIVISION-

1. FIRST DEGREE MURDER (CAPITAL)
2. AGGRAVATED CHILD ABUSE (F1-L9)
3. AGGRAVATED MANSLAUGHTER OF A CHILD (F1-L10)
4. PROVIDING FALSE INFORMATION TO A LAW ENFORCEMENT OFFICER
5. PROVIDING FALSE INFORMATION TO A LAW ENFORCEMENT OFFICER
6. PROVIDING FALSE INFORMATION TO A LAW ENFORCEMENT OFFICER
7. PROVIDING FALSE INFORMATION TO A LAW ENFORCEMENT OFFICER

IN THE NAME AND BY THE AUTHORITY OF THE STATE OF FLORIDA:

COUNT ONE

The Grand Jurors of the County of Orange, duly called, impaneled and sworn to inquire and true presentment make in and for the body of the County of Orange, upon their oaths do present that CASEY MARIE ANTHONY, between the 15th day of June, 2008, and the 16th day of July, 2008, in said County and State, did, in violation of Florida Statute 782.04(1)(a)(l), from a premeditated design to effect the death of CAYLEE MARIE ANTHONY, a human being, unlawfully kill CAYLEE MARIE ANTHONY.

COUNT TWO

And the Grand Jurors of the County of Orange, duly called, impaneled and sworn to inquire and true presentment make in and for the body of the County of Orange, upon their oaths do present that CASEY MARIE ANTHONY, between the 15th day of June, 2008, and the 16th day of July, 2008, in said County and State, did knowingly or willfully, in violation of Florida Statute 827.03(2) cause great bodily harm, permanent disfigurement or permanent disability to CAYLEE MARIE ANTHONY, a child under 18 years of age, by intentionally inflicting physical injury upon CAYLEE MARIE ANTHONY, or by intentionally committing an act or actively encouraging another person to commit an act which could reasonably be expected to result in physical injury to CAYLEE MARIE ANTHONY.

COUNT THREE

And the Grand Jurors of the County of Orange, duly called, impaneled and sworn to inquire and true presentment make in and for the body of the County of Orange, upon their oaths do present that CASEY MARIE ANTHONY, between the 15th day of June, 2008, and the 16th day of July, 2008, in said County and State, did willfully or by culpable negligence, in violation of Florida Statutes 782.07(3) and 827.03(3), while a caregiver to CAYLEE MARIE ANTHONY, a child under 18 years of age, fail or omit to provide CAYLEE MARIE ANTHONY with the care, supervision and services necessary to maintain CAYLEE MARIE ANTHONY'S physical and mental health, or fail to make a reasonable effort to protect CAYLEE MARIE ANTHONY from abuse, neglect or exploitation by another person, and in so doing caused the death of CAYLEE MARIE ANTHONY.

COUNT FOUR

The Grand Jurors of the County of Orange, duly called, impaneled and sworn to inquire and true presentment make in and for the body of the County of Orange, upon their oaths do present that CASEY MARIE ANTHONY, on the 16th day of July, 2008, in said County and State, did, in violation of Florida Statute 837.055, knowingly and willfully give false information to YURI MELICH, a law enforcement officer with the ORANGE COUNTY SHERIFF, who was conducting a missing person investigation, with the intent to mislead YURI MELICH or impede his investigation, to-wit: that CASEY MARIE ANTHONY was employed at Universal Studios Orlando during the year 2008.

COUNT FIVE

The Grand Jurors of the County of Orange, duly called, impaneled and sworn to inquire and true presentment make in and for the body of the County of Orange, upon their oaths do present that CASEY MARIE ANTHONY, on the 16th day of July, 2008, in said County and State, did, in violation of Florida Statute 837.055, knowingly and willfully give false information to YURI MELICH, a law enforcement officer with the ORANGE COUNTY SHERIFF, who was conducting a missing person investigation, with the intent to mislead YURI MELICH or impede his investigation, to-wit: that CASEY MARIE ANTHONY left the child CAYLEE MARIE ANTHONY at the Sawgrass Apartments, 2863 South Conway Road, Apt. 210, Orlando, Florida with a person identified as ZENAIDA FERNANDEZ-GONZALEZ on June 9, 2008 or any subsequent date.

COUNT
SIX

The Grand Jurors of the County of Orange, duly called, impaneled and sworn to inquire and true presentment make in and for the body of the County of Orange, upon their oaths do present that CASEY MARIE ANTHONY, on the 16th day of July, 2008, in said County and State, did, in violation of Florida Statute 837.055, knowingly and willfully give false information to YURI MELICH, a law enforcement officer with the ORANGE COUNTY SHERIFF, who was conducting a missing person investigation, with the intent to mislead YURI MELICH or impede his investigation, to-wit: that CASEY MARIE ANTHONY informed persons identified as JEFFREY MICHAEL HOPKINS and JULLIETTE LEWIS, former Universal Studios Orlando employees, of the disappearance of the child CAYLEE MARIE ANTHONY between June 9, 2008 and July 16, 2008.

COUNT
SEVEN

The Grand Jurors of the County of Orange, duly called, impaneled and sworn to inquire and true presentment make in and for the body of the County of Orange, upon their oaths do present that CASEY MARIE ANTHONY, on the 16th day of July, 2008, in said County and State, did, in violation of Florida Statute 837.055, knowingly and willfully give false information to YURI MELICH, a law enforcement officer with the ORANGE COUNTY SHERIFF, who was conducting a missing person investigation, with the intent to mislead YURI MELICH or impede his investigation, to-wit: that CASEY MARIE ANTHONY received a phone call from the child CAYLEE MARIE ANTHONY on July 15, 2008 at approximately 12:00 pm.

A TRUE BILL

Foreman of the Grand Jury

As authorized and required by law, I have advised the Grand Jury returning this indictment.

Quick Summary

A formal charging document (usually a complaint, an information, or an indictment) is necessary to give the defendant notice of the charges against him. The document also protects the defendant against double jeopardy, creates a formal record of his crime if he is convicted, ensures the prosecutor's factual allegations are legally sufficient, and (in indictment jurisdictions) guarantees the prosecutor does not move to trial on any crimes which have not been approved by the grand jury. Modern pleading requirements are far more liberal than those which existed under the old common law rules: the charging document merely needs to set out in common sense terms the factual allegations supporting the legal charge. The rules governing the charging document are set out in the Rules of Criminal Procedure for that jurisdiction. Because many jurisdictions have embraced some version of the federal rules, the relevant rule is usually Rule 7.

The charging document must be legally sufficient (it must describe conduct which meets the legal elements of each crime that is charged) and factually specific (by providing the defendant with adequate notice so that he can prepare his defense). The prosecutor can amend the charging document in any way as long as the amendment does not create prejudicial surprise to the defendant and as long as it does not allege a new offense. Some courts have stricter rules for amending an indictment, since the defendant has a Fifth Amendment right in the federal system not to be tried for a crime unless the grand jury has first authorized the prosecution. Courts also sometimes have to deal with a variance, which means that the evidence produced at trial is different from the facts alleged in the charging instrument. A variance will usually be allowed as long as it does not deprive the defendant of the fair notice that the charging document originally provided, and as long as it does not put the defendant in danger of double jeopardy in a later prosecution.

Finally, courts must consider questions of duplicity and multiplicity. A duplicitous indictment is one that charges more than one offense in a single count. In contrast, a multiplicitous indictment is one that charges a single offense in multiple counts.

Review Questions

1. Blocking the Immigration Officers. Victor ran a lumber yard in Texas near the Mexican border and employed six Mexican nationals as workers. None of his employees had proper documentation to work in the United States. One day Louis, an Immigration and Customs Enforcement ("ICE") agent, was driving past the lumber yard and noticed that the employees all ran indoors when they saw his marked van. The ICE agent got out of his van and approached the lumber yard, but Victor came out of the building and said "Go away, there is nothing going on here." When the ICE agent showed him his badge and demanded entry, Victor pushed the agent to the ground and ran into the building, locking the door.

Victor was ultimately arrested and charged with violating 18 U.S.C. § 111, which prohibits forcibly assaulting and interfering with the duties of a federal agent. (Section 111 references a different section of the penal code which lists different federal agents who are protected by the statute, including ICE agents). The indictment read as follows:

> On or about March 13, 1980, within the Western District of Texas, Defendant, Victor Harrison, forcibly assaulted, resisted, opposed, impeded, intimidated and interfered with Louis E. Barragan, while engaged in the performance of his official duties, in violation of Title 18, United States Code, Section 111.

Victor made no objection to the indictment before trial. After he was convicted, he appealed his conviction, arguing that (1) the indictment was defective because it failed to explain exactly what conduct Victor engaged in that constituted "forcibly assaulting, resisting, opposing, impeding, intimidating and interfering" with the agent; and (2) the indictment failed to state that Louis was a federal agent. What should the appellate court do?

2. How Much Cocaine? Nick was arrested after officers pulled over his car and found a bag of cocaine in his trunk. After getting the lab report back from the chemist which stated that the defendant possessed 50 grams of cocaine, the prosecutor presented the grand jury with an indictment that charged Nick with violating 21 U.S.C. § 841(a)(1), possession of cocaine with intent to sell, based on the fact that he possessed 50 grams of cocaine. The penalty for this crime is between zero and 20 years in prison. The grand jury returned the indictment.

(A) Assume that one week before trial, the prosecutor received an amended lab report from the chemist which stated that due to a clerical error, the chemist had mistakenly reported the amount of cocaine as 50 grams when in fact it was 550 grams. The new weight would mean that the defendant was being charged with a more serious crime, and he would now face a penalty of between 5 and 40 years in prison. That same day, the prosecutor moved to amend the indictment to change the weight of the cocaine that the defendant was alleged to have possessed. The defendant objected to the amendment. What should the court do? Would your answer be different if this were an information instead of an indictment?

(B) Assume that one week before the trial, the prosecutor received an amended lab report from the chemist which stated that due to a clerical error, the chemist had mistakenly reported the amount of cocaine as 50 grams when in fact it was 450 grams. This new weight did not change the crime for which the defendant would be charged, and he would face the same sentence. The prosecutor moves to amend the indictment to change the weight of the cocaine the defendant was alleged to have possessed, and the defendant objected. What should the court do? Would your answer be different if this were an information instead of an indictment?

(C) Assume that during the trial, the prosecutor meets with the chemist just before the chemist is about to testify, and the chemist tells the prosecutor that she just realized she wrote the wrong amount of cocaine on the original lab report—the actual amount is 450 grams, not 50 grams. This weight does not affect the charge the defendant is facing. The prosecutor goes ahead and puts the chemist on the stand, and she testifies that the amount was 450 grams. Once the prosecution rests its case, the defendant objects, arguing that the chemist's testimony is different from what was alleged in the indictment. What should the judge do?

3. Conflict of Interest? James Garvey was the Director of the Federal Bureau of Engraving and Printing, which designs and prints United States currency. Beginning in January of 2010, Garvey chaired a task force that was considering ways to improve the security of paper money. After five months of deliberation, in May of 2010, the task force agreed to contract with a private company, the American Bank Note Company ("ABN") to pay them to re-design the currency with improved safeguards against counterfeiting. The contract was worth millions of dollars to ABN.

In June of 2010, Garvey retired from his job as Director of the Bureau of Engraving and was hired as the President of ABN. The FBI began investigating, and determined that Garvey was negotiating for the job with ABN at the same time that he was deciding whether to award ABN the federal contract. The FBI turned this information over to the United States Attorney's Office, and Garvey was indicted under 18 U.S.C. § 208(a), which states in pertinent part:

> Any officer of the executive branch of the United States Government may not participate as a Government officer in evaluating a proposal

> with a company with whom he is negotiating or has arranged prospective employment.

The indictment read, in part:

> In the period from on or about January 2010 through June 2010, in the District of Columbia, JAMES A. GARVEY, the Defendant, being an officer of the executive branch of the United States Government, unlawfully and knowingly did participate as such officer in a proposal of the American Bank Note Company for a Security Signature System for U.S. Currency, a particular matter in which to his knowledge the American Bank Note Company, a company with which he was negotiating and then had arranged prospective employment, had a financial interest.

Garvey moved to dismiss the indictment, arguing that it lacked sufficiency and did not provide him with adequate notice. Specifically, Garvey alleged that the words "participate" and "negotiating" were vague. He also stated that the indictment did not specify any exact dates in which Garvey "participated" in the ABN proposal or when he "negotiated" with them.

How should the court rule? And if there is a defect in the indictment, can the government cure it by filing a bill of particulars, or does the indictment have to be dismissed?

37

Pre-Trial Motions—A Brief Primer

Key Concepts

- Pre-Trial Motions Are Governed Primarily By Rule 12 and Rule 47.
- Magistrates Decide Motions, Usually After Conducting Oral Arguments or Hearings.

A. Overview. At this point in the criminal process both parties have begun to gather and disclose discovery and the case is moving towards trial. Before the trial occurs, however, there are a number of pre-trial proceedings—otherwise known as motion practice—which may take place. There are ten primary types of pre-trial motions that can be filed:

- A motion to dismiss the case based on **improper pleading**;
- A motion to **amend the charging document**;
- A motion to review the status of the defendant's **bail or pre-trial detention status**;
- A motion to change **venue**;
- A motion to **compel discovery** or for a **bill of particulars**;
- A motion to assess the **competency** of the defendant;
- A motion to dismiss because the prosecutor has violated the defendant's right to a **speedy trial**;
- A motion **to sever or join** defendants or charges;
- A motion to **suppress evidence** based on alleged constitutional violations; and
- A motion **in limine to exclude evidence** under the Rules of Evidence.

A motion to dismiss the case for **improper pleading** would be filed by the defense attorney at the very beginning of the case, usually at the initial appearance or arraignment. As you read in **Chapter 36**, there are a number of possible flaws in the charging document that might lead to dismissal. For example, the charging document might not allege the facts with the required **specificity**, or it may not allege facts that make out the elements of the crime and so might lack **sufficiency**. And as we will learn in **Chapter 38,** the case may have been brought in a court which lacks **jurisdiction** over the case, or in a district or county which is an improper **venue.** If a motion to dismiss for improper pleadings is brought on any of these grounds, the prosecutor can always re-file the charges (provided, of course, that jeopardy has not attached and she has fixed the mistake that led to the dismissal—for example, if she adds specificity to the charging document or files the case in a different court if the original court lacked jurisdiction). If the charging instrument is dismissed and the defendant was being held in pre-trial detention, the court will likely release the defendant until new charges are filed.[1] There are also a number of other, less common potential grounds for a motion to dismiss which cannot be fixed and therefore lead to permanent dismissal of the case—for example, if dismissal is requested because the charge is barred by the double jeopardy doctrine, or because the statute of limitations has expired.

In response to a motion to dismiss for improper pleading, the prosecutor can move to **amend the charging document.** Thus, instead of the judge dismissing the charging document and then forcing the prosecutor to re-file it later, the judge will generally allow the prosecutor to make changes to the charging document, as long as the changes do not add a new offense and as long as the defendant is not prejudiced by surprise. If the charging document is an indictment, many jurisdictions will be less likely to allow an amendment, since the grand jury voted to indict based on the specific wording of the original indictment. There are, however, some amendments to an indictment that are not deemed material and that will be permitted.

A motion to review the defendant's **bail or pre-trial detention status** can be brought by either side at any point whenever there are changed circumstances that warrant a reconsideration of the initial bail determination. As discussed in **Chapter 33,** the prosecutor may ask for increased bail (or for bail to be revoked entirely) if the defendant commits another crime; otherwise violates the terms of his release; or fails to make a scheduled appearance. On the other hand, the defendant may ask for a reduction in bail if serious problems are developing with regard to the prosecutor's evidence (such as a key witness dying or becoming uncooperative, or a key piece of evidence being suppressed) or if new information is available concerning the defendant's community ties.

A motion to **change venue**, as we will see in **Chapter 38,** is usually filed by the defense attorney. This motion seeks to move the trial from the current location to a different location. A court will grant a change in venue if pre-trial publicity or some other factor has prejudiced the potential jury pool to the extent that the defendant cannot receive a fair trial or (less commonly) if a different venue would

---

1 Fed. R. Crim. Proc. 4(g).

be more convenient for the parties, the witnesses, or in the interests of justice. A prosecution request to change venue is not permitted by the Federal Rules of Criminal Procedure. It is allowed in some states, but even when it is permitted, it is a relatively rare occurrence.

A motion to **compel discovery**, as will be discussed in **Chapter 39**, can be brought by either side to ask the court to force the opposing party to comply with statutory discovery obligations. Generally, the court does not intervene in the discovery process—the parties file discovery requests with one another and comply with the requests without judicial involvement. However, if one party believes the other is not providing sufficient discovery, she can file a motion with the court. The opposing party can respond by providing the discovery or by showing cause why he does not need to comply with the discovery request (for example, he could argue that the information being sought is privileged or is otherwise not covered by the discovery rules). As described in **Chapter 36**, a motion for a **bill of particulars** is similar in that it seeks to compel the opposing party to reveal information. It is brought by the defendant shortly after the charging document is filed and seeks additional details about the offense.

A motion to assess the **competency of the defendant** can be brought by either side; but it is usually filed by the defendant. This is in part because the defense attorney usually has greater knowledge of the defendant's competency (or lack thereof). If the defendant does not bring a motion to assess competency, most courts will hold that the defendant has waived the right to challenge competency after conviction.[2]

The motion to assess competency is intended to test whether the defendant has the mental capacity to stand trial. This inquiry is distinct from the question of whether the defendant was legally insane at the time of the offense. In assessing whether the defendant is competent to stand trial, the court is evaluating the defendant's mental state at the current time, not at the time he committed the offense. Also, as noted below, the standard for competency to stand trial is different from the standard for legal insanity.

According to the Supreme Court, if the defense attorney files a motion to assess competency, the defendant has a right to a competency evaluation before proceeding to trial. This evaluation usually involves an examination of the defendant by a mental health professional, who will then file a report and testify at a competency hearing. At the hearing, the magistrate will deem the defendant incompetent only if a) the defendant does not have the ability to consult rationally with his attorney and aid in his own defense or b) he does not possess a rational and factual understanding of the charges against him.[3] If the magistrate finds the defendant

[2] United States v. Morin 338 F.3d 838 (8th Cir. 2003).

[3] Dusky v. United States, 362 U.S. 402 (1960).

to be incompetent, the defendant will be committed involuntarily and will receive treatment until he is competent to stand trial.

A motion to dismiss on **speedy trial** grounds is brought by the defense attorney and alleges that the prosecutor has taken too long to bring the case to trial. As will be discussed in **Chapter 41**, there are both statutory and constitutional limits on the amount of time the prosecutor has to bring a case to trial. There are also a number of reasons these limits might be extended by the court. If a motion to dismiss on speedy trial grounds is granted, the prosecutor is usually not allowed to re-file the case.

A motion to **sever or join** defendants or charges is a request by the prosecutor or defendant to amend the charging document by adding or subtracting parties or charges. For example, if the prosecutor has charged two defendants on the same indictment, and one of the defendants believes that he will be unfairly tainted in the jury's mind if the two parties are tried together, he can bring a motion to sever the indictment. If the court grants the motion, it will force the prosecutor to charge (and try) the two defendants separately. We will discuss these motions in more detail in **Chapter 40.**

A motion to **suppress evidence** may be brought by the defense attorney, usually close to the trial date once discovery is completed. With this motion, the defendant alleges that the government (specifically, the law enforcement officers who were involved in the case) broke the law when they obtained the evidence against the defendant. The suppression motion could argue that the police conducted an illegal search or seizure, an illegal identification procedure, or an illegal interrogation. As discussed in the first part of this book, illegally obtained evidence is usually subject to exclusion. Thus, if the defendant wins this motion, any evidence that the police obtained as a result of this illegal conduct (and frequently any "fruit" of the illegality, any evidence that was obtained **indirectly**) is usually inadmissible at trial.

Finally, a motion in limine to **exclude evidence** can be filed by either party in order to argue that certain pieces of evidence that will be offered by the opposing party violate the Rules of Evidence for that jurisdiction. For example, a party can argue that some of the opposing party's proposed evidence violates the hearsay rule, or is unfairly prejudicial, or reveals privileged information. Essentially, motions in limine are pre-emptive objections to trial evidence that are made before the trial begins. The procedure and substantive law surrounding these motions is covered in the standard class on Evidence, so we will not discuss them further here.

B. The Law. Pre-trial motion practice is regulated by the Rules of Criminal Procedure for the appropriate jurisdiction. For the federal government, the format and timing of such motions are governed by Rule 47. Other rules pertaining to pre-trial motions are set out in Federal Rule of Criminal Procedure 12. Each of those rules provides in relevant part:

Rule 47

Motions and Supporting Affidavits

(a) In General. A party applying to the court for an order must do so by motion.

(b) Form and Content of a Motion. A motion—except when made during a trial or hearing—must be in writing, unless the court permits the party to make the motion by other means. A motion must state the grounds on which it is based and the relief or order sought. A motion may be supported by affidavit.

(c) Timing of a Motion. A party must serve a written motion—other than one that the court may hear ex parte—and any hearing notice at least 7 days before the hearing date, unless a rule or court order sets a different period. For good cause, the court may set a different period upon ex parte application.

(d) Affidavit Supporting a Motion. The moving party must serve any supporting affidavit with the motion. A responding party must serve any opposing affidavit at least one day before the hearing, unless the court permits later service.

Rule 12

Pleadings and Pretrial Motions

(a) [Describes Pleadings]

(b) Pretrial Motions.

(1) In General. Rule 47 [see above] applies to a pretrial motion.

(2) Motions That May Be Made Before Trial. A party may raise by pretrial motion any defense, objection, or request that the court can determine without a trial of the general issue.

(3) Motions That Must Be Made Before Trial. The following must be raised before trial:

(A) a motion alleging a defect in instituting the prosecution;

(B) a motion alleging a defect in the indictment or information—but at any time while the case is pending, the court may hear a claim that the indictment or information fails to invoke the court's jurisdiction or to state an offense;

> **(C)** a motion to suppress evidence;
>
> **(D)** a Rule 14 motion to sever charges or defendants; and
>
> **(E)** a Rule 16 motion for discovery.
>
> **(4)** Notice of the Government's Intent to Use Evidence.
>
> **(A) At the Government's Discretion.** At the arraignment or as soon afterward as practicable, the government may notify the defendant of its intent to use specified evidence at trial in order to afford the defendant an opportunity to object before trial under Rule 12(b)(3)(C).
>
> **(B) At the Defendant's Request.** At the arraignment or as soon afterward as practicable, the defendant may, in order to have an opportunity to move to suppress evidence under Rule 12(b)(3)(C), request notice of the government's intent to use (in its evidence-in-chief at trial) any evidence that the defendant may be entitled to discover under Rule 16.
>
> **(c) Motion Deadline.** The court may, at the arraignment or as soon afterward as practicable, set a deadline for the parties to make pretrial motions and may also schedule a motion hearing.
>
> **(d) Ruling on a Motion.** The court must decide every pretrial motion before trial unless it finds good cause to defer a ruling. The court must not defer ruling on a pretrial motion if the deferral will adversely affect a party's right to appeal. When factual issues are involved in deciding a motion, the court must state its essential findings on the record.
>
> **(e) Waiver of a Defense, Objection, or Request.** A party waives any Rule 12(b)(3) defense, objection, or request not raised by the deadline the court sets under Rule 12(c) or by any extension the court provides. For good cause, the court may grant relief from the waiver.
>
> **(f) Recording the Proceedings.** All proceedings at a motion hearing, including any findings of fact and conclusions of law made orally by the court, must be recorded by a court reporter or a suitable recording device.
>
> **(g) Defendant's Continued Custody or Release Status.** If the court grants a motion to dismiss based on a defect in instituting the prosecution, in the indictment, or in the information, it may order the defendant to be released or detained under 18 U.S.C. § 3142 for a specified time until a new indictment or information is filed. This rule does not affect any federal statutory period of limitations.

Most of these rules are self-explanatory. Motions to dismiss for improper pleading are generally made orally at the preliminary hearing or the arraignment. For all other pre-trial motions, the trial court will set a **motion schedule** at the arraignment pursuant to Rule 12(c). The motion schedule will set deadlines for the defendant to file any motions and for the prosecutor to respond, and will set the date for any hearings that will arise. Under Rule 47, all pre-trial motions must be made in writing, and they must be filed at least seven days before the hearing along with any supporting affidavits. If the opposing party files a response, any affidavit in support of that response must be filed at least one day before the hearing. In practice, the motion schedule set by the court will generally require the motions and responses to be filed with more advance notice than required by Rule 47.

The prosecutor has a duty to disclose "at the arraignment or as soon as possible thereafter"[4] any evidence that may be the subject of a suppression hearing. Many state rules are even stricter, requiring the prosecutor to disclose at arraignment any identifications or statements which she intends to admit against the defendant at trial. If an identification or statement is not disclosed promptly, some states will preclude the prosecutor from admitting the evidence at trial unless the prosecutor can show good cause why notice was not given at the proper time.

The requirements for a motion are not extensive; the motion need only set out "the grounds on which it is based and the relief or order sought."[5] Most pre-trial motions are reviewed under a preponderance standard. For example, with motions to suppress, the prosecutor has the burden of proving by a simple preponderance of the evidence that the motion to suppress should be denied.

Most written motions are followed by a hearing during which both sides argue their case. In the federal court system and most state systems, these hearings will take place in front of a magistrate instead of a judge. If the motion involves a question of pure law, such as a motion to change venue or a motion to join or sever defendants, there will be no live witnesses, just oral argument from the attorneys on each side. If there are questions of fact to be resolved, such as a motion challenging the defendant's competency or a motion to suppress evidence, one or both sides may call witnesses to establish those facts.

For example, at a suppression hearing, the prosecutor calls the law enforcement officers who obtained the evidence, and the officers explain their actions. The prosecutor may also introduce tangible evidence, such as a document, a video, or a sound recording. For example, in order to prove the officer had probable cause to pull over the defendant's car, the prosecutor might offer video from the officer's dashboard camera that recorded the defendant's car weaving prior to the stop. Or, to prove a warrantless search was authorized, the prosecutor could offer video showing the defendant consenting to the search. Or, to prove the defendant's

---

4 Fed. R. Crim. Proc. 12(b)(4)(A).

5 Fed. R. Crim. Proc. 47(b).

confession was voluntary, the prosecutor could introduce the signed form or an audiotape of the defendant being given warnings and thereafter waiving his rights.

After the government introduces any such evidence or testimony, the defense attorney will then have the opportunity to cross-examine the witness to challenge the witness' credibility or elicit additional facts that tend to show the officer did not follow the proper procedure in obtaining the evidence. The success rates for suppression motions are generally low; but defendants can benefit from making the motion even if it is unsuccessful because it forces the prosecutor to disclose information about her case and it creates formal testimony by some of the prosecutor's witnesses. This testimony can later be useful during trial if the witness changes his testimony in any way.

After the argument or hearing, the magistrate will make a ruling on the motion. Depending on the jurisdiction and the complexities of the issue, the magistrate may give the ruling orally immediately following the hearing, or she may issue a written rule a few days (or weeks) afterwards. The magistrate must state her findings of fact and conclusions of law on the record so that reviewing court will have a record to evaluate should the losing side appeal the decision.

The consequences of the magistrate's decision will obviously depend on the type of motion being considered. For motions to change venue, compel discovery, join or sever defendants, amend the bail, or amend the charging document, the magistrate simply grants or denies the relief requested and the case moves forward. For motions to dismiss the case based on speedy trial or other grounds, the magistrate could of course dismiss the case entirely.

For suppression motions, the result is a bit more complicated. If the suppression motion is denied, there may be one more round of plea bargaining (with the defendant now more willing to accept the prosecutor's offer, and the prosecutor less willing to make a generous offer). If a deal cannot be reached, the case will proceed to trial usually within a few weeks. If the suppression motion is granted, the consequences are more dramatic. If the suppressed evidence was essential to the case (for example, the contraband that was recovered from the defendant, or a confession in a case where there is not a lot of other compelling evidence), a lost suppression hearing may mean the prosecutor is forced to dismiss the case. If the suppressed evidence was useful but not essential, the prosecutor will probably simply adjust his plea bargain offer accordingly—and the defendant will likewise become less willing to plead.

As we have seen in numerous case examples so far, a suppression motion which is denied can become the basis for an appeal if the defendant is convicted. If the defendant wins the case on appeal, the case is remanded for a new trial, at which the disputed evidence is not admitted (which, again, may mean that the prosecutor is forced to dismiss the case or at least make a more generous plea bargain). On the other hand, if the judge grants the suppression motion and the evidence was critical to the prosecution's case, the prosecutor may take an immediate appeal challenging the suppression ruling. This form of prosecution appeal, which is specifically authorized by 18 U.S.C. § 3731, is discussed in greater detail in **Chapter 47**. If instead of taking an immediate appeal the prosecutor takes her chances and proceeds to trial without the evidence, there will never be another opportunity to challenge the adverse suppression ruling. If the defendant is convicted, there is no need to appeal the suppression ruling; if the defendant is acquitted, double jeopardy will bar any appeal because a second trial would be precluded even if the suppression ruling was in error.

38

Jurisdiction and Venue

Key Concepts

- Personal and Subject Matter Jurisdiction Needed Before Court Can Hear Case
- Subject Matter Jurisdiction of the Federal Courts Is Conferred by Constitution and by Statute
- Venue Is Proper if One of the Elements of the Crime Occurred Within Boundaries of Forum District/State
- Federal and State Jurisdiction May Overlap
- Continuing Crimes May Give Rise to Jurisdiction and Venue in Multiple State and Federal Courts

A. Introduction and Policy. Jurisdiction refers to the power of a court to make legal decisions and judgments in a case. There are two different kinds of jurisdiction necessary in a criminal case: subject matter jurisdiction (which refers to the court's power to hear a particular type of case) and personal jurisdiction (which means the court has power over the defendant himself). In addition to jurisdiction, **venue** and **vicinage** are concepts that will influence the selection of the particular court in which the prosecution is brought:

1. **Subject matter jurisdiction** in the federal courts is conferred by statute or by the Constitution. Jurisdiction for criminal cases will lie in the federal courts if Congress has passed a statute criminalizing conduct. In contrast, the state courts are courts of general subject matter jurisdiction, meaning they have the authority to adjudicate a comprehensive array of issues, assuming another court does not have exclusive jurisdiction over a particular matter. Lack of subject matter jurisdiction cannot be waived, and a challenge to subject matter jurisdiction can be made at any time, even after conviction and sentencing. If a court lacks jurisdiction, the court never had the power to act and all of its actions in the case are legally void.

2. **Personal jurisdiction** is based on whether the defendant has had sufficient minimal contacts with the proposed forum to justify the court's exercise of authority over her. Generally, personal jurisdiction in a criminal case exists if the defendant is physically present in the geographic territory where the court sits. In addition, as you will read below, personal

jurisdiction may exist if the accused's alleged criminal conduct sufficiently affected the forum district/state. Unlike subject matter jurisdiction, problems with personal jurisdiction can be waived by the defendant.

3. **Venue** refers to the location where the court proceedings will be held. A particular court will generally be the appropriate venue for a prosecution if it is the site where at least one of the elements of the crime occurred. In this sense, the concept of venue may at times be closely related to the concept of personal jurisdiction. The primary purpose of the venue requirement is to ensure that the defendant is tried by a jury of his peers—that is, his own community should be the one to judge his conduct. A secondary purpose is mere convenience—the witnesses and evidence that will be used by both sides are likely to be found in the location where the crime occurred. For pragmatic reasons, some state laws allow for venue to extend slightly beyond the community where the offense took place to facilitate the prosecution of crimes that take place at or close to the community's border.

4. Finally, **vicinage** refers to the community from which the jury pool is drawn. In the vast majority of cases, the vicinage and the venue are identical; but, in rare situations, the court will grant a motion to transfer a case to a new venue yet will empanel a jury from the original venue in order to ensure the defendant is judged by a jury of his peers.

Different sovereigns can have overlapping subject matter jurisdiction. For example, bank robbery is both a federal crime and a state crime—so, if the defendant robs a bank in Oklahoma, both the federal government and the state of Oklahoma will have jurisdiction to adjudicate the crime and punish the defendant.

If Congress does not wish there to be this overlapping jurisdiction, it has the authority to grant the federal courts **exclusive jurisdiction** in some criminal cases.[1] Along these lines, you will occasionally see federal laws that explicitly grant the federal courts exclusive jurisdiction over certain crimes or over all crimes committed on federal territory.[2] Alternatively, federal laws regarding a certain subject matter may be so comprehensive that an intent to pre-empt state criminal laws will be read into the statute.[3] In those situations, the federal government has exclusive jurisdiction and the state courts will be precluded from hearing such cases.

Overlapping jurisdiction may also exist between states if a crime takes place in more than one location. There are two ways this could happen. First, a crime

[1] Tafflin v. Levitt, 493 U.S. 455 (1990).

[2] See, e.g., 18 U.S.C. § 1153.

[3] Arizona v. United States, 132 S.Ct. 2492 (2012).

may consist of a single action that has an interstate effect—for example, using a telephone or a computer to place an illegal bet in another state or to transfer child pornography to another state. Second, the defendant could be accused of a **continuing crime**—that is, the defendant may be accused of committing multiple acts in different place, all of which collectively constitute just one crime. For example, if a defendant kidnapped an individual in New York and then transported the victim to New Jersey and held him there, both states would have jurisdiction over the crime. Or if two defendants agree to a conspiracy in Nevada, but carry out their overt act in California, both states would have jurisdiction as well. In both these instances, the federal courts may also have jurisdiction if a federal statute has criminalized the interstate conduct.

As we will see in **Chapter 46**, if different sovereigns have overlapping jurisdiction to adjudicate the same criminal conduct, they can each prosecute the case separately. This is because double jeopardy rules do not apply if a different sovereign is prosecuting the defendant. In our example of concurrent federal and state bank robbery jurisdiction above, after the state prosecutor in Oklahoma tried the defendant, there would be no legal reason why the federal government could not bring its own charges and try the defendant in federal court, regardless of the outcome of the state case. In practice, however, this rarely happens. The one noted exception would be in high-profile cases where an acquittal is handed down in state court; under these circumstances, the federal government may step in to re-try the case. In **Chapter 28**, you read about two such instances—the Los Angeles Police Department assault case for the beating of Rodney King and the Shenandoah Valley Football Team trial for the murder of Luis Ramirez.

In most cases, when state and federal prosecutors both have jurisdiction, they usually come to some agreement as to which one will handle the case. Occasionally the two different sovereigns will have a long-standing arrangement to determine which one should prosecute the crime. For example, in many districts the United States Attorney's Office and the local prosecutor will agree that if a bank robber displays a firearm, the case will be prosecuted in federal court, but otherwise the case will be prosecuted in state court. In other cases involving overlapping jurisdiction between the federal and state governments, the entity that made the arrest will likely be the one to prosecute the case. For example, if federal Drug Enforcement Administration agents conducted the investigation, the defendants will be prosecuted federally, but if the investigation was undertaken by the special narcotics task force of the local Sheriff's Office, the case will be handled by the state prosecutor. Finally, there are times when a state will hand a case to the federal government (or vice-versa) because the defendant will likely receive a higher sentence if prosecuted by the other jurisdiction.

Similarly, in the state systems while the overlapping jurisdiction of a continuing or multi-jurisdiction offense may authorize multiple states to prosecute the crime separately, in practice the prosecutors in each state usually come to an agreement about which state will handle the case. Usually the prosecution will take place in the state which suffered the most harm from the crime—for example, if a computer hacker in Connecticut destroyed millions of dollars worth of data in Massachusetts, the prosecutor in Connecticut would probably defer to the prosecutor in Massachusetts to take the case.

To this point we have focused on the concept of a court's subject matter jurisdiction to hear a case. Before we turn to discuss venue, it is worth taking just a moment to clarify that subject matter jurisdiction and venue—though closely related—are not the same. In thinking about the difference between the two, consider the following: subject matter jurisdiction in the federal system is an analysis of whether **any** federal trial court has the authority to hear a particular case. In comparison, venue is a more localized inquiry that considers **which** federal trial court should hear the case. In the federal system, venue thus refers to the judicial district where the case will be heard—e.g., the U.S. District Court for the District of Maryland or the U.S. District Court for the Southern District of Ohio or the U.S. District Court for the Eastern District of New York, etc. In state courts, as we have noted, subject matter jurisdiction is rarely an issue, since the courts have general jurisdiction. And in state court venue usually refers to the county where the court sits—e.g., Baltimore County Circuit Court or Franklin County Common Pleas Court or the Kings County Supreme Court—Criminal Term.

Finally, as with overlapping jurisdiction in multiple courts, it is also possible for one crime to have multiple venues. If different elements of a crime occur in more than one district or county, then more than one location can be the venue for the trial. Also, many states have laws which expand the venue of a given county to a few hundred yards beyond the county line—thus, if a single act of criminal conduct takes place near the border of two counties, either county could be the venue for the trial. In these situations, the trial will again usually take place where the harm from the criminal conduct was the greatest, or where it is most convenient for the defendant and the witnesses. Unlike the context of overlapping jurisdictions, double jeopardy rules apply in cases with multiple venues—thus, once jeopardy attaches in a trial in one venue, the defendant cannot be tried in any other venue in the same jurisdiction.

B. The Law. The law governing jurisdiction is relatively simple. Article III of the U.S. Constitution provides that the power of the federal courts

> shall extend to all cases, in law and equity, arising under this Constitution, the laws of the United States, and treaties made, or which shall be made, under their authority.[4]

[4] U.S. Const., Art. III, § 2.

Building upon this constitutional language, 18 U.S.C. § 3231 provides:

> The district courts of the United States shall have original jurisdiction, exclusive of the courts of the States, of all offenses against the laws of the United States.

In other words, if Congress has passed a statute criminalizing certain conduct and an individual thereafter engages in that conduct, the federal trial courts will have original jurisdiction over the criminal prosecution.

Section 3231 expressly notes that by conferring jurisdiction on the federal courts, the section does not strip the state courts of their simultaneous authority to hear cases that arise under their own laws: "Nothing in this title shall be held to take away or impair the jurisdiction of the courts of the several States under the laws thereof."[5] In contrast to the federal courts' limited jurisdiction, the state courts are courts of general subject matter jurisdiction that possess broad authority to hear all manner of criminal cases without a specific delegation of authority. Thus, as you read above, it is possible that jurisdiction to adjudicate a particular course of criminal conduct will lie in both state and federal courts.

This is precisely what happened in the case of the "Beltway Sniper." In that case, over the course of three weeks in October 2002, two shooters—John Allen Muhammad and Lee Boyd Malvo—killed ten people and injured three others. Six of the dead were killed in Maryland, three were killed in Virginia, and the final victim was killed in Washington, D.C. When Muhammad and Malvo were eventually caught, a twenty-count criminal complaint was filed in the U.S. Court for the District of Maryland alleging the violation of numerous federal statutes. Charges were also brought in state court in Maryland and Virginia. However, after Muhammad was tried and convicted of capital murder in Virginia state court and convicted of six separate murder charges in Maryland state court, federal prosecutors in Maryland decided not to pursue an indictment in the case.

Congress has broad authority to create federal crimes based on the authority granted to it in the federal Constitution.[6] For example, "Congress routinely exercises its authority to enact criminal laws in furtherance of . . . its enumerated powers to regulate interstate and foreign commerce, to enforce civil rights, to spend funds for the general welfare, to establish federal courts, to establish post offices, to regulate bankruptcy, to regulate naturalization, and so forth."[7] A federal court has subject matter jurisdiction pursuant to § 3231 to hear a criminal prosecution alleging the violation of any such statute that Congress enacted.

---

5 18 U.S.C. § 3231.

6 United States v. Comstock, 560 U.S. 126, 135 (2010).

7 Comstock, 560 U.S. at 136 (citing U.S. Const., Art. I, § 8, cls. 1, 3, 4, 7, 9; Amends. 13–15).

It has long been understood that Congress' authority to enact statutes is constrained by our concept of a federal government with enumerated powers. In certain cases, therefore, an accused may seek to defeat prosecution by challenging Congress' authority to criminalize particular conduct. That question though is separate from the question of whether the federal court had jurisdiction to hear the case. As the Court has said, "[e]ven the unconstitutionality of the statute under which the proceeding is brought does not oust a court of jurisdiction."[8] We will consider this question in closer detail in Section C.1, below.

In addition to subject matter jurisdiction, federal and state courts must also possess personal jurisdiction over the defendant before a case will be properly brought in the court. The demand for personal jurisdiction is mandated by due process concerns.[9] A criminal defendant need not be physically present in the forum state for personal jurisdiction to exist in the local courts. However, the defendant "generally must have 'certain minimum contacts . . . such that the maintenance of the suit does not offend "traditional notions of fair play and substantial justice."'"[10] In defining the minimal demands of the personal jurisdiction requirement, the federal courts "ordinarily follow state law in determining the bounds of their jurisdiction over persons."[11]

As a practical matter, personal jurisdiction exists as long as the defendant is somewhere in the territory of the sovereign or is subject to the reach of its judicial process. This is true even if the defendant has been brought into the territory using force or some illegal action. It is irrelevant whether the defendant is a citizen or a resident of the territory. The only exception is that some foreign diplomats have diplomatic immunity, which makes them immune to personal jurisdiction.

The Nevada statute defining the minimal personal contacts needed to establish personal jurisdiction in its state courts provides a representative example of the sort of minimal contacts with the forum state that will suffice to establish that forum's personal jurisdiction over the accused:

---

[8] United States v. Williams, 341 U.S. 58, 66 (1951).

[9] World–Wide Volkswagen Corp. v. Woodson, 444 U.S. 286, 291 (1980).

[10] Walden v. Fiore, 134 S.Ct. 115, 1121 (2014) (citing International Shoe Co. v. Washington, 326 U.S. 310, 316 (1945) and Milliken v. Meyer, 311 U.S. 457, 463 (1940)).

[11] Walden, 134 S.Ct. at 1121.

N.R.S. 194.020

194.020. Persons liable to punishment

The following persons . . . are liable to punishment:

1. A person who commits in the State any crime, in whole or in part.
2. A person who commits out of the State any act which, if committed within it, would be larceny, and is afterward found in the State with any of the stolen property.
3. A person who, being out of the State, counsels, causes, procures, aids or abets another to commit a crime in this State.
4. A person who, being out of the State, abducts or kidnaps, by force or fraud, any person, contrary to the laws of the place where the act is committed, and brings, sends or conveys such person into this State.
5. A person who commits an act without the State which affects persons or property within the State, or the public health, morals or decency of the State, which, if committed within the State, would be a crime.[12]

As the above example reflects, the question of personal jurisdiction in the criminal context explores questions such as whether the effects of the accused's alleged criminal conduct were felt within the proposed forum, and whether the accused held or enjoyed the products of alleged extra-territorial criminal conduct within the proposed forum. In this sense, the question of personal jurisdiction is thus very much related to the question of venue.

The primary law governing venue in federal court is governed by Article III, Section 2 of the Constitution, and the primary law governing vicinage is governed by the Sixth Amendment.

United States Constitution

Article III, Section 2

Trial of all Crimes . . . shall be held in the State where the said Crimes shall have been committed.

Sixth Amendment

Trial must occur "by an impartial jury of the State and district wherein the crime shall have been committed."

---

[12] Nev. Rev. Statutes 194.020.

The fact that these provisions are in the Constitution and the Bill of Rights is evidence that the Founders believed venue and vicinage were not mere technicalities or matters of convenience, but were instead significant protections for the defendant—the right to be tried in and judged by members of your own community. One of the grievances listed in the Declaration of Independence was that the King transported colonists "beyond Seas to be tried."[13]

In addition to these basic provisions, the details of venue in federal courts are set out in Rule 18 of the Federal Rules of Criminal Procedure:

Rule 18. Place of Prosecution and Trial

Unless a statute or these rules permit otherwise, the government must prosecute an offense in a district where the offense was committed. The court must set the place of trial within the district with due regard for the convenience of the defendant, any victim, and the witnesses, and the prompt administration of justice.

Congress has also provided for overlapping venue for continuing crimes.

18 U.S.C. § 3237(a)

Offenses "begun in one district and completed in another" may be "prosecuted in any district in which [the] offense was begun, continued, or completed."

All states have similar laws linking venue with the location of the offense and providing for overlapping venue.

Finally, the federal rules include a provision that allows the defendant to request a change of venue, either because of unfair prejudice in the original venue or for reasons of convenience. Again, all states have rules which are essentially identical:

Rule 21. Transfer [of Venue] for Trial

(a) For Prejudice. Upon the defendant's motion, the court must transfer the proceeding against that defendant to another district if the court is satisfied that so great a prejudice against the defendant exists in the transferring district that the defendant cannot obtain a fair and impartial trial there.

(b) For Convenience. Upon the defendant's motion, the court may transfer the proceeding, or one or more counts, against that defendant to another district for the convenience of the parties, any victim, and the witnesses, and in the interest of justice.

[13] United States v. Cabrales, 524 U.S. 1, 6 (1998).

A sample Motion to Transfer that was filed in the Scott Peterson murder trial is included at the end of this chapter. Peterson was tried in the Superior Court for Stanislaus County (California) for killing his wife Laci on Christmas Eve 2002 while she was seven and a half months pregnant with their first child. The case generated intense public interest and quite a bit of media attention. Before the trial started, Peterson's attorney successfully moved to transfer venue of the case in light of the mounting public animosity toward Peterson in the Stanislaus County area. However, the change of venue in Peterson's case is not typical. In less sensational criminal prosecutions, motions to change venue are rarely granted.

As you will notice, Rule 21 of the Federal Rules of Criminal Procedure predicates the ability to change venue upon a defense motion. Some states allow prosecutors as well as defendants to request a change of venue, but it is rare for a prosecutor to make such a request. We will discuss change of venue motions in more detail in Section C.4 below.

C. Applying the Law.

1. Ensuring Federal Jurisdiction. As you read above, the jurisdiction of the federal courts is conferred by the Constitution and by statute. With regard to statutory grants of authority, 18 U.S.C. § 3231 provides for federal court jurisdiction in matters alleging violations of federal laws. A related question is thus whether Congress had the authority to pass a particular law. The federal government does not have the authority to criminalize whatever conduct it wishes. Its power to act is granted (and limited) by the Constitution. Under the Constitution, the federal government is a government of enumerated powers; if a power is not specified somewhere in the Constitution, the federal government does not have that power. At the time of the nation's founding, when the concept of federalism was much more robust, federal crimes were relatively rare, and courts would interpret the Constitution strictly to limit the federal government's authority to criminalize certain conduct.

In the twentieth century, however, the power of the federal government vis-à-vis the state governments grew dramatically in almost every realm. Congress' willingness to criminalize conduct that had previously been within the exclusive jurisdiction of the state courts was no exception. For example, in the 1930s, new laws were passed to extend the federal government's power in the economic sphere; and during the Civil Rights Era of the 1960s, new laws were passed to extend the federal government's ability to protect the rights of its citizens. Each of these sets of laws included some criminal statutes, which created new federal crimes.

The authority to create federal crimes has been recognized as a legitimate exercise of the federal government's many enumerated powers including the power to regulate interstate commerce, the power to enforce civil rights, and the federal government's spending powers.[14] Of these, Congress' authority to regulate interstate commerce has been one of the most frequently cited authorities for the creation of new crimes. The Commerce Clause gives Congress the power "[t]o regulate Commerce with foreign Nations, and among the several States, and with the Indian Tribes."[15]

There are three ways the Commerce Clause grants Congress the power to act. First, Congress may regulate "the use of the channels of interstate commerce."[16] Second, Congress is empowered to "regulate and protect the instrumentalities of interstate commerce, or persons or things in interstate commerce."[17] Third, Congress has the power "to regulate those activities that substantially affect interstate commerce."[18]

For many decades in the twentieth century, the Supreme Court allowed Congress to expansively interpret its powers under the Commerce Clause to create new criminal offenses. As long as the newly defined criminal conduct had some "nexus to interstate commerce," the federal government was generally deemed to have the authority to act. This expansion in federal criminal statutes created a commensurate expansion in the jurisdiction of the federal trial courts. Then, in 1995, the Court drew a line as to how tenuous the connection to interstate commerce could be.

> **Example—*United States v. Lopez,* 514 U.S. 549 (1995):** Alphonso Lopez, a 12th grade student, arrived at school in Texas carrying a concealed .38-caliber handgun. Acting on an anonymous tip, school officials confronted Lopez and he admitted he was carrying the gun. Lopez was arrested and charged with violating a Texas law which barred the carrying of a firearm on school grounds. The next day those charges were dropped and Lopez was charged federally with violating 18 U.S.C. § 922(q)(1)(A), which makes it illegal "for any individual knowingly to possess a firearm at a place that the individual knows, or has reasonable cause to believe, is a school zone."
>
> Lopez moved to dismiss the charges, arguing that the statute was unconstitutional because the crime covered an area that was not within the federal government's enumerated powers. The government contended that the law had a nexus with interstate

---

14 Comstock, 560 U.S. at 136.

15 United States Constitution, Art. I, § 8, cl. 3.

16 United States v. Lopez, 514 U.S. 549, 558–9 (1995).

17 Id.

18 Id.

commerce in two ways. First, the law prevents violent crime, which both imposes costs that are spread across the entire population and affects the willingness of citizens to travel to certain parts of the country. Second, the government argued that the law reduced "a substantial threat to the educational process by threatening the learning environment" in public schools, which ultimately results in less economic productivity in the country.[19] The trial court agreed with the government's arguments, and Lopez was convicted and sentenced to six months in jail. Lopez appealed all the way to the Supreme Court.

Analysis: The Supreme Court held that the law exceeded Congress' authority under the Commerce Clause.

As drafted at the time of Lopez' prosecution, the statute contained no requirement that the gun being possessed had traveled in interstate commerce. Accordingly, the law did not regulate the channels or instrumentalities of, nor persons or things involved in interstate commerce. For the Commerce Clause to authorize congressional action, the regulated activity must "substantially affect interstate commerce." But the challenged section, §922, had no direct relation to interstate commerce. And the government's proposed links to interstate commerce—based on preventing violent crime or protecting the learning environment—were too broad:

> The Government admits, under its "costs of crime" reasoning, that Congress could regulate not only all violent crime, but all activities that might lead to violent crime, regardless of how tenuously they relate to interstate commerce. Similarly, under the Government's "national productivity" reasoning, Congress could regulate any activity that it found was related to the economic productivity of individual citizens: family law (including marriage, divorce, and child custody), for example. Under the theories that the Government presents in support of § 922(q), it is difficult to perceive any limitation on federal power, even in areas such as criminal law enforcement or education where States historically have been sovereign. Thus, if we were to accept the Government's arguments, we are hard pressed to posit any activity by an individual that Congress is without power to regulate.

The Court conceded that past cases approving a congressional exercise of authority pursuant to the Commerce Clause hinted that Congress had the power to regulate virtually any activity. For example, the Agricultural Adjustment Act of 1938 regulated how much wheat a farmer was allowed to harvest each year. In one case, a farmer raised twenty-three acres of wheat instead of the eleven acres he was permitted to raise, but he used all of the wheat on his own farm, feeding

---

[19] Id. at 563–4.

his animals, baking bread, and sowing his own fields. However, in that case the Court found his activity was properly regulated under the Commerce Clause because by using too much of his own wheat he was purchasing less wheat from the interstate market, which (however infinitesimally) affected interstate prices.[20] Thus, even in that case, there was some link between the regulated activity and interstate commerce. No such link exists for carrying a firearm into a school.

Although *Lopez* is still good law with regard to its statements about the limits of congressional power, Congress has since amended the specific statute in response to that case's holding. The new § 922 prohibits the knowing possession of "a firearm that has moved in or that otherwise affects interstate or foreign commerce at a place that the individual knows, or has reasonable cause to believe, is a school zone."[21] Thus, Congress added an element to require the prosecutor to prove that the gun had been transported across state lines or otherwise had an effect on interstate commerce. The lower courts have uniformly concluded that this additional element renders the statute constitutional. Accordingly, the jurisdiction of the federal courts to adjudicate prosecutions alleging violations of the section remains intact.[22]

Unlike the federal government, state governments have broad police powers to ensure the health, safety, morals, and general welfare of their citizens. Thus, questions of state jurisdiction do not depend on interpretations of the power granted by state constitutions, but instead are based in questions of subject matter jurisdiction and personal jurisdiction.

2. Determining Venue. As noted in Section B, a "continuing offense" is a crime that begins in one district and is completed in another. In such cases, venue could rest in any district in which the crime began, continued, or was completed. Occasionally, when faced with a question of the appropriate venue for a continuing crime, courts must decide what constitutes the "beginning" of a crime:

> **Example—*United States v. Cabrales*, 524 U.S. 1 (1998):** A group of individuals sold narcotics in Missouri, and then sent the proceeds of the narcotics sales (totaling $40,000) to Florida to a woman named Vickie Cabrales. Cabrales then deposited the $40,000 in a bank in Florida and later withdrew it in amounts of $9,500 or less in order to avoid the mandatory reporting of a financial transaction of more than $10,000. Cabrales was ultimately indicted in the Western District of Missouri and charged with three crimes: (1) conspiracy to avoid a transaction-reporting requirement; (2) conducting a financial transaction to avoid a

---

20 Wickard v. Filburn, 317 U.S. 111 (1942).

21 18 U.S.C. § 922(q)(2)(A).

22 See, e.g., United States v. Dorsey, 418 F.3d 1038 (9th Cir. 2005).

transaction-reporting requirement; and (3) engaging in a monetary transaction in criminally derived property of a value greater than $10,000.

Cabrales moved to dismiss the indictment on the grounds that the Western District of Missouri was not the proper venue for these charges. The District Court denied the motion with respect to the first count (the conspiracy count), stating that the defendant "was present in Missouri during the conspiracy, lived with a conspirator in Missouri, and participated in various activities in Missouri in furtherance of the conspiracy."[23] But the District Court granted the motion to dismiss with regard to the second and third counts (involving the actual money transfers) because "the deposit and withdrawals occurred in Florida and [n]o activity of money laundering . . . occurred in Missouri."[24]

The government appealed the dismissal for lack of venue all the way to the Supreme Court, arguing that because the money was illegally generated in the Western District of Missouri, that district was an appropriate venue for the conspiracy count and for the money laundering prosecution.

Analysis: The Supreme Court unanimously upheld the trial court's decision that there was no venue in the Western District of Missouri for the money laundering counts. The transactions which formed the elements of the money laundering crimes—the depositing of the money, the failure to report the deposit, and the withdrawal of the money with the intent to avoid reporting requirements—all occurred in the state of Florida.

The government argued that one of the elements of the third count was that the money involved in the transaction was "criminally derived property" and therefore the crime that generated the criminally derived property (in this case, the Missouri drug trafficking) was an "essential element" of that money laundering charge. The Court rejected this argument, holding that the only element of the money laundering charge is that the defendant know the money was derived from criminal activity—the location of that original criminal activity is completely irrelevant to the charge.

Money laundering could be a "continuing offense" if the defendant acquired the money in one location and then carried that money into another forum in order to conduct the financial transaction. But in this case the defendant was in Florida when she received the money.

---

[23] United States v. Cabrales, 524 U.S. 1, 4 (1998) (internal quotations and citations omitted).

[24] Id. (internal quotations and citations omitted).

In *Cabrales*, the Court acknowledged that its conclusion that Missouri was an inappropriate venue for the money laundering charges ended up being less efficient for the government and for the court since the government was still going ahead with the conspiracy charges against the defendant in a Missouri court and because all of the evidence of narcotics trafficking (which formed the basis of the money-laundering charge) occurred in Missouri.[25] However, this inconvenience was not sufficient to justify the Western District of Missouri as a venue. Cabrales had the right to be prosecuted for each crime only in the location where the crime occurred.

The year after *Cabrales*, the Court returned to the question of continuing offenses, this time deciding whether a crime "continued" when the defendant committed some of the elements in multiple jurisdictions, but committed all of the elements in only one jurisdiction.

> **Example—*United States v. Rodriquez-Moreno*, 526 U.S. 275 (1999):** During a drug transaction in Texas, a New York drug dealer stole 50 kilograms of cocaine from a Texas distributor. Thereafter, the distributor hired Jacinto Rodriguez–Moreno to track down the New York drug dealer and the stolen drugs. Rodriguez-Moreno kidnaped the middle-man in the transaction, Ephrain Avendano, and took him on a drive from Texas to New Jersey. Rodriguez-Moreno's plan was to use Avendano to help him find the New York dealer. Rodriguez-Moreno kept Avendano in a house in New Jersey for a few days, then took him to an apartment in New York. The two finally ended up in a house in Maryland.
>
> In Maryland, Rodriguez-Moreno obtained a gun and he threatened to shoot Avendano in the head. However, Avendano escaped. The Maryland police ultimately arrested Rodriguez-Moreno.
>
> Rodruiguez-Moreno was charged in the District of New Jersey with multiple crimes, including conspiring to kidnap Avendano and kidnapping Avendano. He was also charged with 18 U.S.C. § 924(c)(1), which states:
>
> "[w]hoever, during and in relation to any crime of violence . . . for which he may be prosecuted in a court of the United States, uses or carries a firearm, shall, in addition to the punishment

[25] Id. at 9.

provided for such crime of violence . . . be sentenced to imprisonment for five years."

Rodriguez-Moreno moved to dismiss this final count for lack of venue, since he only "used or carried a firearm" in relation to his crime of violence (kidnapping) in Maryland. The trial court in the District of New Jersey denied the motion, and Rodriguez-Moreno appealed to the Supreme Court.

Analysis: The District of New Jersey was an appropriate venue for the charge of using a firearm in relation to the crime of violence.

The Supreme Court evaluated the appropriateness of venue by examining whether any element of the crime took place in New Jersey. The first step was to determine the exact elements of 18 U.S.C. § 924(c)(1). The Court concluded there were two elements: "using or carrying a gun" and committing a kidnapping. Although the defendant only used and carried a gun in Maryland, he committed the kidnapping in over a dozen different districts and states, including New Jersey. Thus, instead of being a "point-in-time" offense, in which the using or carrying of the gun only happens at one point in time, 18 U.S.C. § 924(c)(1) is a continuing offense in which the kidnapping occurred across an extended stretch of time. As long as, at some point in that kidnapping, the defendant used or carried a firearm, then he used or carried the firearm "during and in relation to" a kidnapping that occurred in more than a dozen states.

The dissent argued that the crime effectively had just one element: using or carrying a gun. The dissent determined that the kidnapping was not an element, but a predicate offense. Since the act of kidnapping itself was already criminalized separately, the only unique aspect of 18 U.S.C. § 924(c)(1) was the specific act of using or carrying a gun while committing the underlying offense. This specific act only occurred in Maryland, and so Maryland was the only possible venue for this crime. As the dissent noted, the majority reasoning would mean there was "no difference between a statute making it a crime to steal a cookie and eat it (which could be prosecuted either in New Jersey, where the cookie was stolen, or in Maryland, where it was eaten) and a statute making it a crime to eat a cookie while robbing a bakery (which could be prosecuted only where the ingestive theft occurred)."[26]

Note that there was no dispute about venue for the kidnapping charge or the conspiracy to kidnap. The kidnapping was a "continuing offense" which took place in every district in each state in which the defendant held Avendano, including all the districts he drove through from Texas to New Jersey, as well as districts in New York and Maryland. Likewise, although the conspiracy to kidnap the

---

[26] United States v. Rodriquez-Moreno, 526 U.S. 275, 283–4 (1999) (Scalia, J., dissenting).

victim was agreed to in Texas, the overt acts to carry out the conspiracy occurred in all of those districts as well. Thus, venue would be appropriate in any of the districts through which the defendant traveled with the victim. However, as you read in the introduction, despite the potential for multiple prosecutions in multiple jurisdictions, the various prosecutorial authorities reached an agreement as to who would file charges. After consultation with the other United States Attorney's Offices that could potentially prosecute the case, it was agreed the United States Attorney for the District of New Jersey would be given the opportunity to prosecute.

Also note that in both *Cabrales* and *Rodriguez-Moreno*, although the Supreme Court was deciding venue for federal purposes, the same analysis would apply in determining venue for state purposes. In other words, in *Cabrales*, the Court's decision meant that the state of Missouri had no power to prosecute the defendant for her money laundering in Florida. And in *Rodriguez-Moreno,* any state from Texas to Maryland would be an appropriate venue in which to prosecute the defendant for his kidnapping, and (to the extent the state statute criminalized the use of a firearm during such kidnapping) for his use of a firearm in Maryland during the kidnapping as well. The Supreme Court did not discuss the issue of jurisdiction in either case because the federal government had subject matter jurisdiction over the crimes regardless of the state where the defendant committed the crime, since it has jurisdiction over any federal crime committed anywhere in the United States.

3. Conspiracy and Computer Crimes. As noted in the previous sections, conspiracy charges tend to create cases with multiple jurisdictions and multiple venues. As long as any of the overt acts of the conspiracy take place in a different state or district, that state or district will have jurisdiction and venue respectively.

Computer crimes tend to create their own unique problems of jurisdiction and venue. For example, assume a defendant in California logs onto a gambling site that is also located in California, but the internet service provider that he uses routes his signals through a server in Arizona. Does the federal government have jurisdiction, since the signals passed through interstate commerce? Does Arizona have jurisdiction over this crime, since the communication passed through Arizona? According to the current state of the law, the federal government does have jurisdiction, but Arizona might not, since the federal government might pre-empt the field:

> **Example:** Joseph Kammersell, a nineteen-year old living in Riverdale, Utah, sent an e-mail that contained a bomb threat from his home computer to his girlfriend who worked at the local America OnLine ("AOL") service center in Ogden, Utah.

The message was transmitted to the AOL server in Virginia and then back to the service center in Utah.

Kammersell was arrested and charged with violating 18 U.S.C. § 875(c), which prohibits "transmit[ting] in interstate . . . commerce any communication containing any threat . . . to injure the person of another."

Kammersell argued that the federal courts did not have jurisdiction in the case, since § 875(c) had last been amended in 1939, "when the telegraph was the primary form of interstate communication." Since nobody but the recipient in Utah could have actually read the threat, Kammersell argued that in practical terms there was no interstate aspect to his actions.

Analysis: The Court, relying upon the plain meaning of the statute, held that the law clearly covered any interstate transmission of a threat. Furthermore, the statute did not exceed Congress' power under the Commerce Clause because any transmission which crosses state lines affects interstate commerce. Thus, where the crime involved an element of interstate action, the federal statute was constitutional and the federal court had jurisdiction.[27]

In a later case, *United States v. Lewis*, the First Circuit went even further in finding federal jurisdiction. Lewis was caught with child pornography on his computer, and was charged with a federal crime which barred the possession of child pornography that had been "transported in interstate or foreign commerce." However, the government had no evidence that the images recovered from Lewis's computer had crossed state lines. Thus, the defendant argued that the government could not prove the jurisdictional element of "transported in interstate or foreign commerce." The government could, however, prove that the images had been downloaded from the internet. The circuit court held that fact alone was sufficient to establish a nexus with interstate commerce: "the use of the [i]nternet is enough, standing alone, to satisfy the jurisdictional element" of interstate commerce.[28] Thus, according to some courts the federal government essentially gets automatic jurisdiction for any internet crime.

However, the opposite is true for state jurisdiction over internet crimes. A number of federal courts have struck down state laws that cover criminal activity over the internet, on the grounds that the Commerce Clause not only empowers Congress but also has a "negative" effect on state regulation

[27] This example is based on United States v. Kammersell, 196 F.3d 1137 (10th Cir. 1999).

[28] United States v. Lewis, 554 F.3d 208, 216 (1st Cir. 2009).

of interstate commerce. Thus, a state law that criminalizes particular activity over the internet will likely be held invalid in these courts, since the internet is a tool of interstate commerce. However, this is still a developing area of law, and some courts have upheld state laws which ban criminal activity on the internet.

4. Motions to Change Venue. Jurisdiction involves the power of a specific sovereign to try an offense; thus, it cannot be waived by the defendant and it cannot be transferred to another territory that did not originally have jurisdiction. Venue, however, can be waived by the defendant or transferred to a new location at the defendant's request. A motion to change venue is brought on one of two grounds:

1. The defendant cannot receive a fair trial in the original location.
2. The original location is not convenient for the parties or the witnesses.

Under Rule 21(a) of the Federal Rules of Criminal Procedure, a trial court should grant the motion to change venue if "so great a prejudice against the defendant exists in the transferring district that the defendant cannot obtain a fair and impartial trial there." For example, in one case from the 1960s, a man was accused of robbery and murder, and a local television station broadcast footage of the man confessing the crime to the police. The defendant's attorney moved for a change of venue, but his motion was denied, and his client was convicted. The Supreme Court ultimately held that denying the motion to change venue violated the defendant's due process rights.[29]

One of the most famous cases involving a change of venue involved the prosecution of four police officers in southern California who beat a black motorist named Rodney King. The incident was caught on video camera and replayed dozens of times in the media. The defendant police officers successfully argued to the state trial court that they could not receive a fair trial in Los Angeles County, the multi-racial urban county where the incident occurred. The trial was moved to nearby Ventura County, a mostly white suburban county. The defendants were able to choose from a jury pool that was slightly less tainted by pre-trial publicity. They were also able to choose from a jury pool with almost no black potential jurors and almost no potential jurors who understood the dynamics of the police/citizen interactions in Los Angeles County. The resulting jury had no black members and the four defendants were all acquitted. The high-profile case caused a small controversy involving the appropriateness of changes in venue. As we will see in **Chapter 43,** there are other ways to counteract prejudicial pre-trial publicity (such as the use of voir dire) which are less disruptive and less likely to

[29] Rideau v. Louisiana, 373 U.S. 723 (1963).

create unwanted side effects such as changes in the ethnic make-up and shared community values of the jury pool.

In addition to seeking a change in venue for reasons of potential prejudice, under Rule 21(b), the defendant can also request a change in venue "for the convenience of the parties, any victim, and the witnesses, and in the interest of justice." The Supreme Court has held that the following factors are relevant in determining whether a change of venue is appropriate:

- location of the defendant;
- location of possible witnesses;
- location of events likely to be in issue;
- location of documents and records likely to be involved;
- disruption of the defendant's business unless the case is transferred;
- expense of the parties;
- location of counsel;
- relative accessibility of place of trial; and
- any other special elements which might affect a transfer.[30]

The decision of whether to transfer venue on convenience grounds rests within the broad discretion of the trial judge. The defendant has the burden of proving the need to change venue, and the judge should only transfer venue if she is satisfied that the prosecution in the district where the indictment was properly returned will result "in a **substantial balance of inconvenience** to . . . [the Defendant]."[31] A sample motion is attached at the end of this chapter for your review.

---

[30] Platt v. Minnesota Mining and Manufacturing Co., 376 U.S. 240, 243–44 (1964). The Supreme Court originally cited a tenth factor—the docket condition of the various potential districts—but most courts have held that this is no longer a relevant factor. See, e.g., United States v. Oster, 580 F.Supp. 599, 602 (S.D.W.V. 1984).

[31] United States v. B & O Railroad Co., 538 F.Supp. 200, 205 (D.D.C. 1982) (quoting United States v. Jones, 43 F.R.D. 511, 514 (D.D.C. 1967) (emphasis added)).

Quick Summary

In order for a court to have the power to make decisions about a case, the court must have **subject matter jurisdiction.** In the federal system such power is granted by the Constitution and federal statutes. In the state courts, subject matter jurisdiction is somewhat more expansive as most state courts enjoy general subject matter jurisdiction, meaning they do not need an express grant of authority to hear and decide a broad array of legal matters. Courts must also have **personal jurisdiction**, which usually means that the defendant is physically present within the territory or the defendant's alleged criminal conduct caused harm in the proposed forum. Closely related to the concept of personal jurisdiction is the more localized concept of venue. The court must be the proper **venue** for the case in order to ensure that the defendant is tried by a jury of his peers. Venue can be transferred to a different location, while jurisdiction cannot.

Federal courts and state courts frequently have overlapping jurisdiction if the crime violates both federal law and state law. Congress' ability to criminalize conduct (and thereby confer jurisdiction upon the federal courts) is limited by the enumerated powers in the Constitution. This is not a very robust limitation, but the criminal statute must show some nexus to interstate commerce or some other link to an enumerated power. State courts have broad police power and so their jurisdiction is not limited to enumerated powers. Their authority to hear cases is, however, limited by the personal jurisdiction requirement to crimes that occurred within their geographic boundaries. Also, in some areas federal laws either explicitly or implicitly precludes any state court jurisdiction.

If a crime occurs in multiple states, then each state has jurisdiction over the crime and each state could conceivably be a proper venue for that crime. Although the double jeopardy clause does not preclude multiple prosecutions in different sovereigns if each sovereign has jurisdiction, usually only one sovereign will prosecute a given crime.

Review Questions

1. Vandalizing Cemeteries. Carlos, Henry, and John all lived in Virginia. While in Virginia they made a plan to vandalize a series of graveyards where military serviceman were buried in order to protest what they perceived to be an overly militarized United States foreign policy. Their plan was to spray-paint every grave of a veteran who died while overseas with the words "Victims of Imperialism." Carlos drove across the border to West Virginia to purchase ten cases of red spray paint. On the first night, Henry took some of the cans of spray paint and vandalized twenty-five gravestones in Virginia, while John took some of the cans and vandalized thirty gravestones in Maryland. The next day the crimes were detected and Virginia police quickly tracked down and arrested all three individuals.

West Virginia, Virginia, and Maryland each have misdemeanor laws prohibiting vandalism. West Virginia bumps the crime up to a felony, with a maximum punishment of three years, if the vandalism is of a graveyard. There is also a federal law making it a felony, with a maximum punishment of one year, for vandalizing the grave of any American serviceman. All three states and the federal government have conspiracy statutes that make it illegal to plan to commit a crime with someone else as long as any of the conspirators commit some overt act to further the conspiracy. The conspiracy laws carry the same punishment as the criminal act that is being planned.

Carlos, Henry, and John could be charged with vandalism and conspiracy to commit vandalism. Which one or more of the sovereigns has jurisdiction over these crimes? In which of these jurisdictions would venue be proper? If you find that multiple sovereigns have jurisdiction and venue, where should the prosecution take place?

2. Solicitation of a Minor. Kyle saw an advertisement in a magazine for "underage girls who can come to your home and make your fantasies come true." The advertisement had a website address. He went to the website, registered with his name and address, and requested that an underage girl visit him. The website stated that a girl would come to his house that night, and that the cost was $500 in cash, payable to the girl when she arrived. That night, a girl who appeared to be about sixteen arrived at Kyle's home, and Kyle gave her $500 and then asked her to perform certain sexual acts. The girl, who was in fact a 19-year old police officer trainee, radioed to her backup and Kyle was arrested for soliciting sex from a minor.

Kyle lives in Indiana and never left the state of Indiana during the entire incident. The website he visited was designed by state police officers in Indiana, but it was stored on a server in Minnesota.

Kyle potentially violated two statutes:

(a) An Indiana statute makes it a felony for an individual to "solicit sexual conduct from a person who presents himself or herself as under 18 years old." The maximum penalty is one year.

(b) A federal statute makes it a felony to "solicit sexual conduct in any way that involves or affects interstate commerce from a person whom he reasonably believes to be under 18 years old." Under the federal law, the maximum penalty is two years, but it increases to ten years if the defendant pays for the requested sexual conduct.

A day after Kyle was arrested and charged with the Indiana statute, federal agents arrived at the local prosecutor's office and asked the prosecutor to transfer the case to federal court. Does the federal government have jurisdiction over this case? If so, should the local Indiana prosecutor hand the case over to the United States Attorney's Office?

3. Check Forgery. Patricia was driving from Texas to Wyoming. When she was at a diner in Oklahoma, she saw that a customer at another table left her purse behind when she left the restaurant. Patricia stole the purse, which contained a wallet with over $100 and a checkbook. On her next stop, in Colorado, Patricia took out the checkbook and wrote three checks to herself, forging the owner's signature on each check. When she got home to Wyoming, she put the three forged checks in an envelope and mailed them to her bank in California. The bank processed the checks and transferred the money into her account.

Patricia's crime was eventually discovered and she was prosecuted under federal law for mail fraud, which makes it a crime to "use the federal mail system to perpetrate any fraud." Which states have district courts with the proper venue to prosecute this crime?

SAMPLE MOTION FOR CHANGE OF VENUE

This motion was filed in the murder trial for Scott Peterson after there was an intense amount of media coverage surrounding his case. The trial judge granted the motion and the trial was transferred to a different location.

GERAGOS & GERAGOS
A PROFESSIONAL CORPORATION
LAWYERS
39TH FLOOR
350 S. GRAND AVENUE
LOS ANGELES, CA 90071-3480
TELEPHONE (213) 625-3900
FACSIMILE (213) 625-1600
MARK J. GERAGOS SBN 108325
Attorney for Defendant SCOTT LEE PETERSON

FILED
03 DEC 15 AM 9:18
CLERK OF THE SUPERIOR COURT
COUNTY OF STANISLAUS
BY ______ DEPUTY

SUPERIOR COURT OF THE STATE OF CALIFORNIA

FOR THE COUNTY OF STANISLAUS

THE PEOPLE OF THE STATE OF CALIFORNIA, Plaintiff, vs. SCOTT LEE PETERSON, et al., Defendant.	Case No. 1056770 NOTICE OF MOTION AND MOTION FOR CHANGE OF VENUE; MEMORANDUM OF POINTS AND AUTHORITIES IN SUPPORT THEREOF; DECLARATION OF MARK J. GERAGOS DATE: January 8, 2004 TIME: 9:30 a.m. PLACE: Dept. 2

TO: STANISLAUS COUNTY DISTRICT ATTORNEY; and

TO: CLERK OF THE ABOVE-ENTITLED COURT:

PLEASE TAKE NOTICE that on January 8, 2004 at the hour of 9:30 a.m., or as soon thereafter as counsel can be heard, Defendant Scott Lee Peterson ("Mr. Peterson"), through counsel Mark J. Geragos, will move this Court to transfer venue of the pending matter to another County on the grounds that a fair and impartial trial cannot be had in Stanislaus County.

///

///

///

This Motion will be based on this Notice, the attached memorandum of points and authorities, the declaration of Mark J. Geragos, the surveys conducted by Paul J. Strand and Stephen Schoenthaler, the pleadings and records on file herein, and upon such other and further argument as may be presented to the Court at the hearing of this matter.

Dated: December 14, 2003

Respectfully submitted,
GERAGOS & GERAGOS

By: ______________________
MARK J. GERAGOS
Attorney for Defendant
SCOTT LEE PETERSON

MOTION

Defendant Scott Lee Peterson, by and through counsel, hereby moves the Court for an order transferring venue of the pending matter to another County on the grounds that a fair and impartial trial cannot be had in Stanislaus County.

Dated: December 14, 2003

Respectfully submitted,
GERAGOS & GERAGOS

By: ______________________
MARK J. GERAGOS
Attorney for Defendant
SCOTT LEE PETERSON

MEMORANDUM OF POINTS AND AUTHORITIES

I.

INTRODUCTION

The widespread, pervasive and negative nature of the media reports surrounding this case have made it impossible to seat a fair and unbiased jury in Stanislaus County. As such, this Court must transfer venue of the pending matter to another county. The extent and intensity of the publicity in this case is of unprecedented proportions in Northern California. From the date of the underlying incident, this case has been the subject of intense local media interest. More importantly, the community's interest in the story has not diminished. Each and every court appearance in this case has been covered in depth by the local media. The coverage of the Modesto Bee has been almost daily, usually on the front page and often derisive of Mr. Peterson. In fact, the inflammatory and editorial nature of these media reports has steadily increased since Laci Peterson's disappearance, subsequent search and later recovery of her body to the point where public opinion in Stanislaus County has become downright hostile and threatening to Mr. Peterson.[1/]

In applying the appropriate five-factor venue test to the case at hand, it is beyond cavil that a fair trial cannot be had in Stanislaus County. First, Mr. Peterson is facing the gravest of all punishments – the death penalty. Second, the small size of Stanislaus County, coupled with the daily, unremitting, and inflammatory media coverage of this case, militates strongly in favor of a venue change. Further, the victim, Laci Peterson, has become a posthumous celebrity, loved and cherished by the community, whereas Mr. Peterson has been demonized as an evil outsider to the community. Additionally, the fact that political overtones have encompassed this case since the day of Laci Peterson's disappearance constitutes an independent reason for a change of venue.

---

[1] One recent example of the public's continuing anger towards Mr. Peterson, is that on December 12, 2003, after the Court appearance, counsel for Mr. Peterson observed a vehicle parked outside Mr. Peterson's business warehouse which had the words "HANG THE BASTARD" painted across the front windshield.

Finally, studies conducted by two experts in the field of survey research indicate that a significant percentage of Stanislaus County residents (ranging from 39% to 59.3%) have already in their minds convicted Mr. Peterson of these crimes. These figures, reflecting preconceived attitudes, are significantly higher than surveys conducted in other cases in which change of venue are ordered. Accordingly, it is clear that the persistent and negative publicity of this case prevents Mr. Peterson from having a fair trial in Stanislaus County.

II.

STATEMENT OF FACTS

On April 21, 2003 Scott Lee Peterson was charged by criminal complaint with two counts of premeditated murder in connection with the deaths of his wife Laci Peterson and the couple's son, Conner Peterson. Laci Peterson was thirty two weeks pregnant when she was reported missing on Christmas Eve. On or about April 13, 2003, both her body and that of the baby washed up on the shore of San Francisco Bay. On or about April 16, 2003, Stanislaus County District Attorney James Brazelton stated: "I feel pretty strongly it is Peterson." Thereafter, on April 18, 2003 Modesto police arrested Mr. Peterson in San Diego, California on two counts of murder. On April 18, 2003, California State Attorney General Bill Lockyer stated "this is a compellingly strong case. I would call the odds slam-dunk that he is going to be convicted." Mr. Peterson pleaded not guilty to two capital murder charges during his arraignment on April 21, 2003.

On or about April 26, 2003, District Attorney James Brazelton announced that he would seek the death penalty for Mr. Peterson. Additionally, in or about May of 2003, the family of the deceased launched a campaign to recognize and support legislation that would make killing a fetus a distinct federal crime. In fact, the proposed legislation was titled Laci and Conner's Law. At about the same time, there were several concerts and memorial events held in Modesto in honor of Laci and Connor Peterson. Furthermore, state senators pushed for the state to cover Stanislaus County's costs in this case.

Thereafter, on October 29, 2003, the preliminary hearing in the instant case began and lasted until November 18, 2003. On November 18, 2003, this Court held Mr. Peterson to stand trial. Mr. Peterson again pleaded not guilty to the murder charges at his arraignment on December 3, 2003.

The grand-scale media coverage of this case has been undeniably biased against Mr. Peterson. As explained more fully herein, the pre-trial publicity associated with this case has been extensive and inflammatory, and has created more than a reasonable apprehension that a fair trial cannot be had in the current venue. It is undisputable that the majority of potential jurors have formed strong opinions about Mr. Peterson's guilt.[2] Because media reports have also significantly penetrated adjacent counties and as far away as Contra Costa County, Merced County, San Joaquin County, Sacramento County, Tuolumne County and Fresno County, those counties would similarly not be viable alternative locations for seating a fair and unbiased jury. For this same reason, busing in jurors from the counties mentioned above would similarly not be a viable alternative, nor would the defense agree to that proposal. These neighboring counties are in the same media market and are exposed to the same news reports, both print and television as Stanislaus County.

III.

MR. PETERSON IS ENTITLED TO A CHANGE OF VENUE BECAUSE A FAIR AND IMPARTIAL TRIAL CANNOT BE HAD IN STANISLAUS COUNTY.

A. The Right To A Fair Trial Is Guaranteed By Both The United States and California Constitutions.

The Sixth Amendment to the United States Constitution guarantees a criminal defendant the right to a fair trial by an impartial jury. *Duncan v. Louisiana* (1968) 391 U.S. 145, 148-154. This fundamental right includes the right to a trial by a jury free from

---

[2] As evidence of the public's anger towards this case, on May 9, 2003, while defense counsel was visiting Mr. Peterson in jail, the tires on his vehicle were slashed. Additionally, later that month while defense counsel was having breakfast at a local restaurant in Modesto, defense counsel was accosted and yelled at by other patrons for defending a "murderer".

outside influences, such as prejudicial pretrial publicity. *Sheppard v. Maxwell* (1966) 384 U.S. 333, 362-363. If an impartial jury cannot be impaneled, the defendant is entitled to a change of venue. *See Groppi v. Wisconsin* (1971) 400 U.S. 505, 509-511 (the failure to afford an accused a fair hearing violates even the minimal standards of due process).

The Due Process Clause of Article I, Section 16 of the California Constitution also guarantees a criminal defendant the right to a trial by an impartial and unprejudiced jury. *People v. Wheeler* (1978) 22 Cal.3d 258, 265. If no such jury can be impaneled, a change of venue must be granted to ensure the accused a fair trial. *People v. Welch* (1972) 8 Cal.3d 106, 113. Thus, under the California Constitution, a defendant will be denied due process if a change of venue is not granted when an impartial jury, free from outside influences, cannot be obtained.

The California Supreme court has adopted the standard set forth in *Sheppard*, to determine whether a change of venue should be granted in a criminal action. *Maine v. Superior Court* (1968) 68 Cal.2d 375, 383. A criminal action must be transferred if there is a "reasonable likelihood" that, in the absence of a change of venue, the accused will not receive a fair trial. *Ibid.*

Similarly, California Penal Code Section 1033 provides that the court must grant a motion for change of venue if "there is a reasonable likelihood that a fair and impartial trial cannot be had in the county." The phrase "reasonable likelihood" has been interpreted as requiring something less than "more probable than not," and something more than merely "possible." *Powell v. Superior Court* (1991) 232 Cal.App.3d 785. This determination may be based on qualified public opinion surveys or opinion testimony offered by individuals, or on the court's own evaluation of the nature, frequency and timing of the material involved. *Williams v. Superior Court* (1983) 34 Cal.3d 584.

When pre-trial publicity is the grounds upon which prejudice is based, a motion for change of venue must be granted whenever it is determined that because of the dissemination of potentially prejudicial news, there is a reasonable likelihood that in the absence of such relief, a fair trial cannot be had. *Smith v. Superior Court* (1969) 276

CA.2d 145. The test as to the right to a change of venue because of adverse publicity is not actual prejudice, but a reasonable likelihood that a fair trial cannot be had. *Clifton v. Superior Court* (1970) 7 CA.3d 245. In fact, in a pretrial motion for change of venue, because the prejudicial effect of publicity before jury selection is necessarily speculative, it is settled that "any doubt as to the necessity of removal . . . should be resolved in favor of a venue change." *Williams v. Superior Court* (1983) 34 Cal.3d 584, 588.

As demonstrated by the professionally conducted public opinion polls, the prejudicial media coverage that has saturated the potential jury pool in this County established more than a "reasonable likelihood" that Mr. Peterson cannot receive a fair trial in the venue of Stanislaus County.

B. The California Supreme Court's Five Part Test for Change of Venue Requires Venue To Be Moved From Stanislaus County.

Courts have traditionally examined five factors to determine whether to grant a motion for change of venue due to dissemination of potentially prejudicial material. The five factors to be considered are as follows: [1] the nature and gravity of the offense; [2] the size of the community; [3] the status of the victim and accused; [4] the nature and extent of the publicity; and [5] the existence of political overtones in the case. *Martinez v. Superior Court* (1981) 29 Cal.3d 574; *Williams v. Superior Court* (1983) 34 Cal.3d 584. An analysis of the facts of this case, and the publicity it has generated, demonstrates that Mr. Peterson cannot receive a fair and impartial trial in Stanislaus County.

1. <u>The Nature and Gravity of the Offense.</u>

It is well settled that in capital cases "the factor of gravity must weigh heavily in a determination regarding the change of venue." *Martinez v. Superior Court* (1981) 29 Cal.3d 574, 583; *see also Clifton v. Superior Court* (1970) 7 CA.3d 245 (in determining whether the risk of prejudice from publicity warrants a change of venue, the gravity of the charge against defendant is a consideration). The term "gravity" of a crime refers to its seriousness in the law and to the possible consequences to an accused in the event of a guilty verdict. *Martinez v. Superior Court of Placer County* (1981) 29 Cal.3d 574, 582.

In the instant case, Mr. Peterson is charged with two counts of premeditated murder. If convicted, Mr. Peterson faces the gravest of punishments – the death penalty. *See Martinez*, 29 Cal.3d at 583 (murder is a crime of utmost gravity; inasmuch as the state is seeking the death penalty, it is a crime of the gravest consequences to petitioner. Because it carries such grave consequences, a death penalty case inherently attracts press coverage; in such a case the factor of gravity must weigh heavily in a determination regarding the change of venue). Hence, it is manifest that this factor weighs heavily in favor of a change of venue.

2. <u>The Size of the Community.</u>

In determining whether the risk of prejudice from publicity warrants a change of venue, the size of the community is also a consideration. Stanislaus County is a relatively small county by California standards. At the present time, the population is approximately 468,566. In fact, Stanislaus County has been judicially recognized as not being of such size as to disregard or be indifferent to a barrage of publicity detailing a serious crime. *See Fain v. Superior Court* (1970) 2 Cal.3d 46 (Stanislaus County determined too small to dissipate the effects of extensive pretrial publicity); *Griffin v. Superior Court* (1972) 26 Cal.App.3d 672 (size of Stanislaus County inadequate to sufficiently dissipate the impact of adverse publicity surrounding a criminal trial); *People v. Miller* (1973) 33 Cal.App.3d 1005, 1012 (Stanislaus County is a relatively small community); *Frazier v. Superior Court* (1971) 5 Cal.3d 287 (Santa Cruz which had a population of 123,700 too small to dissipate the effects of extensive pretrial publicity); *Steffen v. Municipal Court* (1978) 80 Cal.App.3d 623 (court ordered change of venue from San Mateo County, 11th most populous county in the state with almost 600,000 residents). Yet despite its small population, it is important to note that Stanislaus County is well served by local press. As discussed below, there are several major newspaper and radio companies in Stanislaus County, and each had constant newspaper and radio stories that appeared that were extensive, sensational and inflammatory pretrial publicity. The small size of the community, particularly when viewed in light of the extensive local media attention paid to this case, therefore militates strongly in favor of a change of venue.

3. <u>The Status of The Victim and the Accused.</u>

Another significant factor courts have looked to in determining the appropriateness of transferring venue is the relative status of the victim and the accused. This factor also clearly weighs in favor of transferring venue in the instant case. The victim in this case, Laci Peterson, was the daughter of a local family and was born and raised in Modesto, whereas Mr. Peterson is from San Diego, CA. Furthermore, although almost all media reports about this case emphasized Laci Peterson's good looks, infectious smile and other worthy attributes, Mr. Peterson has consistently been portrayed as an adulterous fertilizer salesman in dire financial difficulty who is an outsider to Modesto.

In *People v. Williams*, the California Supreme Court addressed this issue as follows, "Equally or perhaps even more compelling, however, was the relative status of the victim and the defendant in the community. Aside from the stark brutality of the offenses, the pretrial publicity focused heavily on the fact that the victim was a Placer County resident and the defendant was an outsider. Most articles described the victim as a young 'Roseville woman' and defendant as a "Sacramento man." Moreover, though the victim, Heather Mead, was herself not especially prominent, she came from an extended family with long and extensive ties to the community." *Williams*, 48 Cal.3d at 1129. Moreover, as stated in *Odle v. Superior Court, supra*, the victim's status frequently emerges as a product of the publicity itself. In *Odle*, the Supreme Court noted that "...by virtue of the events and media coverage after the crimes, [the victim] became a posthumous celebrity." *Id.* at 940.

Based on the media's constant depiction of Laci Peterson as a "beautiful daughter" of Modesto, who has even taken on a status of a "celebrity" and Mr. Peterson as being an outsider to their community, coupled with the media's constant barrage of predetermined allegations of guilt towards Mr. Peterson, a grave concern should arise regarding the jury pool in Stanislaus County. *See* Illumen Compact Disc, Modesto Bee, Article # 99, Jury's

Out Whether a Fair Trial Can Be Held Here, April 24, 2003, attached hereto as Exhibit A; *see also* Declaration of Adam Talaat, attached hereto as Exhibit B. As stated in *Williams*,

> "the risk is enormously high that the verdict may be based on a desire for revenge, or the fear of social ostracism as the cost of a mitigated verdict. In such circumstances, as we observed in *Tidwell*, 'the juror may consider himself honored and fortunate to be selected to culminate a community's anger against a stranger accused of killing [a] respected member [] of the community, [and] returning anything less than a death verdict for first degree murder might be viewed as a betrayal of both his trust as a juror and his friendship with witnesses [or the prosecution]. When a juror might reasonably fear that the cost of a mitigated verdict might be . . . the alienation of an entire community, there is a danger that such fears will play a part in his deliberations.'"

Id. at 1131.

4. The Media Coverage Associated with this Case Has Been Extensive and Inflammatory.

In describing the ramifications of extensive and biased media coverage, the Supreme Court in *Williams* stated as follows:

> "'When a spectacular crime has aroused community attention and a suspect has been arrested, the possibility of an unfair trial may originate in widespread publicity describing facts, statements and circumstances which tend to create a belief in his guilt.'" (*Martinez v. Superior Court, supra,* 29 Cal.3d at p.580, quoting *Corona v. Superior Court* (1972) 24 Cal.App.3d 872, 877).

Williams, 48 Cal.3d at 1128.

In granting the defendant's motion to change venue, the court in *Williams* was faced with media coverage that was significantly less inflammatory, sensational, and widespread than the media coverage in the instant case. In *Williams*, the Court was careful to note that more than 50 newspaper and radio reports appeared during the 9-month period between defendant's arrest and motion to change venue. Later news reports in that case also focused on preliminary hearing evidence and sheriff's statements indicating that the defendant was the actual "triggerman" and rapist. *Id.* at 1127; *see also* *People v. Cummings* (1993) 4 Cal.4th 1233, 1275 (extensive coverage found where 51 articles made print; *People v. Jennings* (1991) 53 Cal.3d 334, 361 (six newspaper articles); *People v. Bonin* (1988) 46 Cal.3d 659, 672-679 (extensive coverage noted without mention of exhibits); *Smith v. Superior Court* (1969) 276 Cal.App.2d 145 (290 articles); *F. Williams v. Superior Court* (1983) 34 Cal.3d 584 (157 articles).

In contrast, over eight thousand (8,000) newspaper and radio reports appeared during the 8-month period between Mr. Peterson's arrest and the filing of this motion. Additionally, several hundred media reports focused exclusively on the evidence and testimony introduced at Mr. Peterson's preliminary hearing. This evidence included statements by witnesses who claimed that Mr. Peterson's alleged suspicious actions made him the primary suspect in this case.

Attached hereto is a representative collection of some of the countless newspaper articles that have appeared in the Modesto Bee and other newspapers in Stanislaus County beginning in 2002 on the guilt of Mr. Peterson. As indicated, there are over eight thousand (8,000) articles published in the various newspapers relating to the facts or circumstances of this case. *See* Exhibit A. This coverage includes approximately 500 articles published in the Modesto Bee, approximately 425 articles on the website for KTVU, approximately 99 articles in the Contra Costa Times, approximately 42 articles in the Fresno Bee, approximately 228 in the Sacramento Bee, approximately 155 articles on the website for KCRA Channel 3 [Sacramento/Modesto], approximately 98 articles on the website for KFSN Channel 30 (ABC) [Fresno], over 100 articles on the website for KGPE Channel 47 (CBS) [Fresno], over 50 articles on the website for KRON Channel 4 [San Francisco], approximately 381 articles on the website for KPIX Channel 5 (CBS) [San Francisco], approximately 118 articles on the website for KGO Channel 7 (ABC) [San Francisco/Oakland/San Jose], approximately 620 articles on the website for KNTV Channel 11 (NBC) [San Jose/San Francisco], approximately 200 articles published in the Tri-Valley Herald [Tracey, CA], and approximately 150 articles on the website for KNTV Channel 11 (NBC) [San Jose/San Francisco]. Attached hereto as Exhibit C is a true and correct copy of the search results obtained from the various websites mentioned above; *see also* Declaration of Nareg Gourjian, attached hereto as Exhibit D. This coverage included front page pictures, feature stories, special sections, in depth analyses, editorials, results of numerous polls conducted, timelines, and pictures of key individuals.

In addition to the countless print articles, there has also been extensive television coverage that has also improperly and prematurely convicted Mr. Peterson of the alleged crimes. FOX, CNN, NBC and Court TV, to name a few, have covered this case on a regular basis and have all had television trucks parked outside the court house providing constant reports of the developments of the day. In fact, FOX New's Friday coverage relating to this case was the single most-watched program on cable, with more than 5 million viewers. Thus, day after day, potential jurors in this case have been bombarded with news accounts relating directly to the issue of Mr. Peterson's guilt.

As demonstrated by the surveys conducted by Dr. Paul Strand and Stephen J. Schoenthaler, the effect of this incessant news coverage has been felt most acutely in Stanislaus County, a small rural community, due to the Modesto Bee newspaper articles,[3/] all of which are available both in print and on-line to potential jurors. The tone of these articles has been to prejudice and bias readers against Mr. Peterson, which has destroyed the fairness of the potential jury pool in Stanislaus County.

As is evident from the titles of the articles, these articles have presented a very one-sided, pro-prosecution version of the case. The articles have had only one purpose – to inflame and bias the public against Mr. Peterson. As demonstrated by the following list of titles from amongst the 500 Modesto Bee ("ModBee") articles, the local media has already served as judge, jury and executioner in this case, having already convicted Mr. Peterson.

- "Relative Voices Suspicion: Modesto police told Laci Peterson's family that her husband was having an affair and recently took out a $250,000 life

---

[3] The Modesto Bee ("ModBee") is the major print source in Stanislaus County. The ModBee began over 100 years ago and is delivered to homes from Ripon to Merced, Patterson to Sonora. There are over 800 locations throughout the Valley where the ModBee can be purchased. The ModBee has a daily circulation of 84,000 and an additional 12,000 on Sundays. Furthermore, ModBee is available on-line at ModBee.com. In fact, the website features a special section devoted exclusively to news about the Peterson case, and includes photo galleries available upon payment of a small premium.

insurance policy on her" ModBee, January 17, 2003.

- "Peterson Eyed for Link for Missing Student: San Luis Obispo detectives are looking at Scott Peterson in connection with the disappearance of a college student nearly seven years ago" ModBee, January 18, 2003.
- "Homicide Victims Usually Know Killer: If Laci Peterson has been killed, statistics say she was slain by someone close to her" ModBee, January 28, 2003.
- "Fertilizer Sales Field Tough" ModBee, January 30, 2003.
- "Peterson Suspicious in Eyes of Experts" ModBee, January 31, 2003.
- "Police Search Peterson Home, Confiscate New Truck" ModBee, February 18, 2003.
- "Driver Says that She Saw Something in Back of Scott Peterson's Truck" ModBee, March 20, 2003.
- "Scott Peterson's Life Presents Picture with Conflicts" ModBee, April 19, 2003.
- "Peterson Conferring as Wife, Unborn Son Mourned Nearby: As thousands of people grieved for Laci Peterson and her unborn son Sunday, the man accused of their murders spent the afternoon conferring with his attorney several blocks away" ModBee, May 5, 2003.
- "Skeptics Question Peterson Claims: The image of Scott Peterson fishing alone in San Francisco Bay on Christmas Eve does not sit well with some longtime sturgeon fishermen" ModBee, May 23, 2003.
- "In Memo, Mayor says Peterson Lacked Grief at January 3, Meeting: Modesto Mayor Carmen Sabatino said this week that he did not detect "much grief" from Scott Peterson when the two met 10 days after Peterson's pregnant wife, Laci, was reported missing" ModBee, June 20, 2003.
- "Inmate: Peterson Pursued Kidnap: A jail inmate here says Scott Peterson,

during a November meeting with two members of a neo-Nazi gang, broached the idea of kidnapping his wife" ModBee, September 20, 2003.

- "Few Bites from Fishermen on Peterson Sturgeon Alibi: Details from Scott Peterson's preliminary hearing about his Christmas Eve fishing trip left some already skeptical fishermen with more doubt" ModBee, November 30, 2003.

There can be no question that the media coverage associated with this case has been undeniably biased against Mr. Peterson. The nature and extent of the publicity, including the massive print media coverage, extensive radio coverage, and graphic television coverage has been inflammatory, sensational and highly prejudicial to Mr. Peterson. The dissemination of the prejudicial and biased materials in this case has undoubtedly resulted in a reasonable likelihood that a fair and impartial trial cannot be had in Stanislaus County.

5. <u>The Presence of Political Overtones</u>.

One cannot dispute the existence of vast political overtones in this case. In fact, political overtones encompassed this case even before Mr. Peterson's arrest. As discussed above, even before Mr. Peterson was arraigned, Attorney General Bill Lockyer labeled the odds a "slam-dunk" that Mr. Peterson would be convicted of these crimes. Also, the County Board of Supervisors had a meeting in which they discussed this case at length. Moreover, the family of the deceased entered the political arena to support legislation that would allow the federal government to charge people with killing a fetus. Finally, various state senators pushed for the state to cover Stanislaus County's costs in this case. As stated in *Powell v. Superior Court,* "Political factors have no place in a criminal proceeding, and when they are likely to appear, as here, they constitute an independent reason for a venue change." *Powell v. Superior Court* (1991) 232 Cal.App.3d 785, citing *Maine v. Superior Court* (1968) 68 Cal.2d 375.

///

///

C. Stanislaus County Residents Have Prejudgments About Mr. Peterson According to Expert Surveys.

The results of two surveys demonstrate that a change of venue is necessary to preserve Mr. Peterson's right to an impartial jury and fair trial. A survey conducted by Paul J. Strand, Ph.D. clearly establishes that potential jurors from Stanislaus County cannot view this case with the requisite impartiality. In a random sample of 300 Stanislaus County residents, ninety-eight percent (98%) said they were aware of a criminal case involving Scott Peterson. Additionally, thirty nine percent (39%) had admitted predisposition towards Mr. Peterson's guilt. *See* Declaration of Paul J. Strand, attached hereto as Exhibit E, *see also* Peterson Case Venue Study, attached hereto as Exhibit F. .

Also, a survey conducted by Stephen J. Schoenthaler, Ph.D. demonstrates the impact of the negative publicity on the venire in Stanislaus County. In a random sample of 150 Stanislaus County residents, seventy five percent (75%) said they had decided whether Mr. Peterson was guilty, what his sentence should be or both. Additionally, 59.3 percent (59.3%) thought Mr. Peterson was either "probably guilty" or "guilty beyond a reasonable doubt." Only 2.7 percent (2.7%) believed Mr. Peterson was innocent. The survey also showed that fifty-one percent (51%) favored the death penalty if Mr. Peterson were found guilty. Accordingly, Dr. Schoenthaler believes these results suggest that "there is clear evidence that a fair and impartial trial cannot be had in Stanislaus County."

These figures, reflecting preconceived attitudes, are also significantly higher than those in similar surveys made in *Williams v. Superior Court* (1983) 34 Cal.3d 584, 590, in which a writ of mandate was granted directing the trial court to grant a change of venue. In *Williams*, of the 117 individuals surveyed, 22.4 percent (22.4%) claimed they had formed opinions on the guilt or innocence of the defendant. *Id.*; *see also Martinez v. Superior Court* (1981) 29 Cal.3d 574, 589 (change of venue ordered where less than five percent had formed any opinion of the guilt or innocence of defendant, and fifteen percent believed they could not decide the case solely on the evidence that would be presented in court). Moreover, the United States Supreme Court has held in *Irvin v. Dowd* (1961) 366 U.S. 717 that there is "clear and convincing" evidence that a trial needed to be moved when sixty-two percent (62%) of the jury pool admitted to having prejudgments about a defendant. *Irvin*, 366 U.S. at 728.

In the case at bar, the survey suggests that 98% of the jury pool had some awareness of this case, 75% of the jury pool admitted to having prejudgments about Mr. Peterson, well over the 62% "clear and convincing" standard set forth by the United States Supreme Court. These levels of prejudgment could only suggest that the residents of Stanislaus County have already made up their minds and convicted Mr. Peterson of these crimes. Therefore, it is clear from the above that a fair trial cannot be had in Stanislaus County. Only a change of venue can ensure that Mr. Peterson obtains the fair and impartial trial to which he is constitutionally entitled.

D. Admonitions During the Jury Voir Dire Will Not Cure The Prejudicial Pretrial Publicity In The Present Case.

It is abundantly clear that a change of venue motion is properly made prior to the commencement of jury trial. In fact, given the unnecessary burden on the potential jurors, litigants, and the Court, not to mention, the unnecessary and wasteful use of judicial resources, it is preferable to litigate a motion to change venue prior to trial rather than to risk the possibility of transferring the case after the commencement of *voir dire*.

The preference for litigating issues of venue during pretrial proceedings was first enunciated by the California Supreme Court in *Maine v. Superior Court, supra*, 68 Cal.2d 375. The court held the burden and expense of conducting an entire capital trial only to have it reversed on appeal because of an erroneous denial of a change of venue motion "... often falls short of sufficient protection, since 'the burden, expense and delay involved in a trial render an appeal from an eventual judgment an inadequate remedy.' [Citation omitted.]" (*Id.*, at 378.) This was readily demonstrated by the reversal of the second *Williams* decision (*People v. Williams* [*Kenneth*] (1989) 48 Cal.3d 1112) where the California Supreme Court remanded the capital case for retrial in a new venue, over nine years after the date of the original offense. Virtually every case in recent history has upheld the propriety of litigating a venue motion prior to the commencement of a jury trial and, if necessary, seeking of review of any ruling through a pretrial writ of mandate.

The California Supreme Court's decision in *Odle v. Superior Court* (1982) 32 Cal.3d 932, discusses a corollary to this issue. *Odle* has often been cited for the proposition that a trial court may defer ruling on a venue motion until the time of *voir dire*, to better judge from juror responses the likelihood of a fair trial for the accused. What *Odle* actually says is that when a defendant fails to make an adequate showing at the pretrial motion for change of venue, the defendant may renew the motion during *voir dire*; and the trial court should grant the motion if juror responses indicate the publicity has in fact infected the *venire*:

> "We conclude, therefore, that the extensive publicity of the two-week period that followed the crimes, either alone or in combination with other criteria, does not establish a reasonable likelihood that a fair trial cannot be had in that county[.] Our conclusion is necessarily based on the evidence before us at this time. ... If our perception and conclusions are faulty and the *voir dire* reveals that, in fact, the dissemination of potentially prejudicial material was more widespread than was or could be anticipated, the trial court will have not only the opportunity, but the duty to order a change of venue upon renewed motion of the defendant."

(*Id.*, at p. 943.)

The opinion in *Irvin v. Dowd* (1961) 366 U.S. 717, 727-728, is also instructive. In *Irvin*, the United States Supreme Court held that a verdict of guilty by a jury which was not impartial violated the defendant's constitutional rights. The Supreme Court held that the nature and extent of the media coverage associated with this case, along with the strength of the opinions formed, prevented jurors from setting aside their opinion and rendering a verdict based on the evidence presented in court. The Court stated:

> "Here the build-up of prejudice is clear and convincing. . .With such an opinion permeating their minds, it would be difficult to say that each could exclude this preconception of guilt from his deliberations. The influence that lurks in an opinion once formed is so persistent that it unconsciously fights detachment from the mental processes of the average man. Where one's life is at stake – and accounting for the frailties of human nature – we can only say that in the light of the circumstances here the finding of impartiality does not meet constitutional standards. . .No doubt each juror was sincere when he said that he would be fair and impartial to petitioner, but psychological impact requiring such a

> declaration before one's fellows is often its father. Where so many, so many times, admitted prejudice, such a statement of impartiality can be given little weight. . .With his life at stake, it is not requiring too much that petitioner be tried in an atmosphere undisturbed by so huge a wave of public passion."

Id. at 727-728.

Thus, in an age of extremely powerful pervasive mass communications, trial courts can no longer look to judicial admonitions during *voir dire* as the remedy for continuing and prejudicial pretrial publicity. The conclusion is clear that, despite the sincere expressions by prospective jurors that they can "put aside" prejudgments and hold on to the presumption of a defendant's innocence, it is unrealistic to expect that any individual bombarded by the frenzy of media reports in Stanislaus County would be able to do so. The remedy of a change of venue is available to trial courts precisely to avoid such dilemmas. In the appropriate instances, such as that presented in this case, the remedy must be utilized.

IV.

CONCLUSION

The lynch mob atmosphere that has been created in this case has become so poisonous that the nature of the news coverage has in many instances been reduced to nothing more than vilification. In fact, even former Modesto Mayor Carmen Sabatino stated on numerous occasions that Mr. Peterson cannot get a fair trial in Stanislaus County. One does not have to look further than the public's reaction to Mr. Peterson's arrest. Over 300 people, not including the media, showed up to witness the arrival of Mr. Peterson at the Stanislaus County Jail. Even the spokesman for the Stanislaus County Sheriff's Department, Kelly Huston, was surprised by the intensity of the crowd and was quoted as saying, "We were considering doing a last-minute booking change . . . Our No.1 goal was to make sure he was booked safely, and that included that **he didn't get lynched when he came in the driveway.** There were people out there screaming, 'Murderer.'" "We're here tonight in support of Laci and her baby and her family," one woman said. "We've been waiting a long time for the cops to arrest Scott, and we just wanted to be here when they brought him in. Tonight is a piece of history." (Emphasis supplied) *See* Exhibit A, Modesto Bee, Article # 108, Crowd On Hand to See Scott's Arrival at Jail, April 20, 2003.

For the foregoing reasons, Mr. Peterson respectfully requests that this Court transfer venue of the pending matter to another County.

Dated: December 14, 2003

Respectfully submitted,
GERAGOS & GERAGOS

By: ____________________
MARK J. GERAGOS
Attorney for Defendant
SCOTT LEE PETERSON

39

Discovery

Key Concepts

- *Brady* Rule: Prosecutor Must Disclose Material, Exculpatory Information
- Discovery Regulated by Rules 12.1, 12.2, 12.3, 16, and 26.2 of the Federal Rules of Criminal Procedure
- State Rules Vary Significantly In Terms of Obligations Imposed
- Any Disclosure Rules Imposed on the Defense Must Be Matched by Reciprocal Requirements for the Prosecution

A. Introduction and Policy. Discovery rules deal with the obligation of each side to disclose information about the case to the opposing side. As with most aspects of criminal procedure, crafting the proper discovery rules requires a delicate balancing of many interests. On the one hand, disclosure is critical to the truth-seeking function of a trial. For example, if the defendant does not know what evidence the prosecutor will use against him, the defendant cannot prepare a cross-examination that will effectively test the accuracy of witness testimony; challenge the reliability of expert reports; or conduct his own investigation to explain to the jury his version of the facts. The same is true for disclosure by the defense—the prosecutor cannot effectively rebut an alibi defense or an insanity defense without receiving some information from the defense ahead of time.

Discovery also enhances the fairness of the proceeding. When a criminal case begins, the state generally has more information than the defendant. In a typical street crime case, the police officers are on the scene moments after the event to interview witnesses, collect evidence, and make observations. For longer-term investigations, the detectives and their agents might have been building a case for weeks or months before the defendant is charged. As the case progresses, the prosecutor almost always has greater resources to conduct further investigations, such as the subpoena power to force witnesses to come in and testify in front of the grand jury. Even without that power, most witnesses are, for a variety of reasons, more inclined to cooperate with the prosecutor. Thus, requiring the prosecutor to disclose information to the defendant helps to even the playing field.

Going in the other direction, the defense may have information the prosecutor does not have access to—information about his own activity at the time of the crime, as well as perhaps access to documents and witnesses of his own. Giving the prosecutor this information enhances the fairness of the proceeding, especially if the prosecutor has already been required to turn over her own information.

However, disclosure of information also carries certain costs. In some cases, disclosing the names and addresses of potential witnesses to criminal defendants may increase the risk that the defendant will retaliate against the witnesses or intimidate them to prevent them from testifying. Even if this is only a remote possibility (which it is in almost any case), it may not appear very remote to potential witnesses, and so many of them may be unwilling to cooperate if they are told that the defendant will be given their name and contact information. Giving the defendant information about the prosecutor's case also may increase the risk of perjury by certain defendants—if a guilty defendant learns exactly what the prosecutor's witnesses are going to say, he can tailor his story to exonerate himself without contradicting their testimony.

Finally, there is a question as to how reciprocal the discovery requirements can and should be. Should the prosecutor's discovery obligation be greater than the defendant's? It is true that the state begins the case with more information and greater resources to gather additional information. But the reasoning behind the discovery rules—enhancing the truth-seeking function of the trial, and keeping the trial proceedings fair—applies equally to disclosure by both sides. Nonetheless, most jurisdictions put a greater discovery burden on the prosecutor than on the defense.

Before diving into the specific legal requirements for discovery, you should keep two things in mind. First, this chapter only deals with the formal rules on discovery. As we have seen in past chapters, there are many other ways that parties—particularly defendants—are able to learn information about the case from the opposing side. For example, the pleading rules, discussed in **Chapter 36,** require the prosecutor to specify the basic allegations of the case. If the charging document does not provide sufficient information, the defense attorney can make a motion for a bill of particulars. Also, if the prosecutor conducts a preliminary hearing, as described in **Chapter 34**, the defendant will learn details of the case from the direct and cross-examination of the witnesses.

Second, the rules set out here are merely the minimum requirements for disclosure in criminal cases. Nothing prevents parties from sharing more information with each other. In fact, in some jurisdictions, prosecutors engages in what is known as "open file" discovery—that is, the prosecutor will reveal all the information she knows about the case to the defendant as soon as she knows it (with the exception of truly secret information such as the name of confidential informants). Prosecutors who practice open file discovery gain the benefit of never having to respond to formal discovery requests or to litigate discovery issues. Also, the full disclosure makes plea bargaining more transparent because defense attorneys in the jurisdiction know exactly what information the prosecutor has (good and bad) and so it is easier for both sides to agree on a reasonable resolution. Finally, open file discovery has the intangible but very real benefit of enhancing the relationship between the prosecutor's office and the defense bar; it creates trust, encourages open communication, and can lead to defense attorneys being more willing to share their own information with the government.

Even in jurisdictions without open file discovery, some defense attorneys choose to share more information than legally required. Such a practice though is highly variable and depends heavily upon both the particular defense attorney and the particular case. If a defense attorney believes certain information will lead the prosecutor to dismiss the case or make a more generous plea offer, it is in the defense interest to disclose that information to the prosecutor early rather than require the client to endure the continued anxiety (and possible incarceration) of pending charges.

B. The Law. Perhaps more than any other aspect of criminal procedure, discovery rules vary from state to state. As usual, we will focus on the federal rules here. We will discuss the many state variations in Section C.6, below.

In the federal system, discovery is governed by two different sources of law. First, the Due Process Clause mandates two important principles for discovery rules. Second, Rules 12.1, 12.2, 12.3, 16, and 26.2 of the Federal Rules of Criminal Procedure set out the basic structure for the discovery process.

The Supreme Court has held that the Due Process Clause imposes two discovery requirements. The first is the well-known *Brady* rule, mandating disclosure of exculpatory evidence:

> The prosecutor has a duty to disclose any material evidence favorable to the defendant, including evidence which could be used to impeach the prosecutor's witnesses. If the prosecutor does not disclose this information, the conviction will be reversed if there is a reasonable probability that disclosure of the withheld information would have changed the outcome of the proceeding.[1]

In evaluating an alleged *Brady* violation, a court will focus on two questions: first, whether the withheld evidence was "exculpatory"; and second, whether the

[1] Brady v. Maryland, 373 U.S. 83 (1963); United States v. Bagley, 473 U.S. 667 (1985); Kyles v. Whitley, 514 U.S. 419 (1995); Wood v. Bartholomew, 516 U.S. 1 (1995).

withheld evidence was "material" (that is, did it have a reasonable probability of changing the outcome of the proceeding). You should also note that prosecutors have an **ethical** duty to disclose exculpatory evidence that goes somewhat beyond the constitutional requirements of *Brady.* We will discuss the contours of the *Brady* rule in Section C.2, below.

As long as its prosecutors comply with the *Brady* doctrine, a state is free to set up almost any discovery scheme that it wants, including provisions that require the defendant to disclose information to the prosecutor. When states first created discovery obligations for defendants, many defense attorneys objected to these requirements, arguing that the discovery requirements violated their clients' Fifth Amendment right against self-incrimination. In the 1970 case of *Williams v. Florida*,[2] the Court rejected this argument by upholding a state discovery rule that required the defendant to notify the prosecutor in advance of an alibi defense. We will discuss the scope of *Williams* in Section C.4, below.

However, if the state mandates any disclosure by the defendant, the Supreme Court has held that similar discovery obligations must also be placed on the prosecutor:

> If a rule mandates that a defendant is required to disclose information, there must also be a rule in which the prosecutor is required to disclose reciprocal information to the defendant.[3]

For example, if a state rule requires the defense to turn over the names of all witnesses who will support an alibi defense, the state must bear a countervailing obligation to disclose the names of any witnesses who will refute the alibi defense.

The requirements imposed by the Due Process Clause apply in every criminal court throughout the country, but they represent only a small fraction of the rules that govern the discovery process in any given court. The nuts and bolts of the discovery rules are found in the rules of criminal procedure for that jurisdiction. Rule 16 of the Federal Rules of Criminal Procedure is a lengthy and extremely detailed rule that sets out the basic structure of discovery in federal cases and lists most of the information subject to disclosure. Here is a summary of the rule's key provisions:

> Upon request of the defendant, the government must:
>
> 1. Disclose the substance of any oral statement that the defendant made in response to interrogation by a person the defendant knew was a government agent that the prosecutor intends to introduce at trial;

---

[2] 399 U.S. 78 (1970).

[3] Wardius v. Oregon, 412 U.S. 470 (1973).

2. Disclose any written or recorded statement made by the defendant that is within the government's control and that the prosecutor knows exists or could know exists through due diligence;
3. Disclose the defendant's recorded testimony before a grand jury;
4. Turn over the defendant's prior criminal record that the prosecutor knows about or could know about through due diligence;
5. Allow the defendant to inspect and copy books, papers, documents, data, photographs, tangible objects, buildings or places, or copies or portions of any of these items, if the item is within the government's possession, custody, or control and (a) the item is material to preparing the defense; (b) the government intends to use the item in its case-in-chief at trial; or (c) the item was obtained from or belongs to the defendant;
6. Allow the defendant to inspect and copy results of any physical or mental examination or any scientific test or experiment if (a) the item is within the government's control, (b) the prosecutor knows it exists or could know it exists through due diligence, and (c) the item is material to the defense or the government intends to use it in its case-in-chief at trial; and
7. Disclose a written summary of any expert testimony that the prosecutor seeks to use during its case-in-chief.

Once the prosecutor complies with the defense requests, the defense must (at the request of the prosecutor) do the following:

1. Allow the prosecutor to inspect or copy any books, papers, documents, data, photographs, tangible objects, buildings or places if the item is within the defendant's control and the defendant intends to use the item in the defendant's case-in-chief at trial;
2. Allow the prosecutor to inspect and copy results of any physical or mental examination or any scientific test or experiment if the item is within the defendant's control and the defendant either intends to use the item in his case-in-chief at trial or intends to call the witness who prepared the report; and
3. Disclose a written summary of any expert testimony that the defendant seeks to use during his case-in-chief.

Note that the discovery obligations imposed by Rule 16 are not self-activating. Rather they are triggered by the opposing party's request for disclosure. Once the opposing party makes the request, however, the disclosing party has a continuing duty to turn over any new information that it later obtains that would have been subject to the original request. In practice, both the prosecutor and the defense routinely request all possible discovery material as part of boilerplate motions at the beginning of the motion practice period, and so the "request" requirement is generally not significant in reality.

Rule 16 is divided into two parts: discovery obligations of the government and discovery obligations of the defendant. Both sides are required to turn over documents, objects, reports from tests and examinations, and summaries of prospective expert testimony. Officially the defendant's obligation to disclose much of this information is not triggered unless the defendant first makes a request of the prosecutor, but since these requests are routinely made by defendants, the defendant must be ready to disclose this information.

Rule 16 creates further discovery obligations for the prosecutor with regard to information she has about the defendant. The prosecutor must disclose the defendant's prior criminal record, as well as all records of prior oral or written statements made by the defendant which are under the control of the government and are relevant to the case. Rule 16(b) creates a duty for the prosecutor to exercise due diligence in searching for these statements. Obviously this includes any statements that the defendant made to law enforcement, but it would also include any statements made to various government agencies that are relevant to the case.

Rule 16 also clarifies certain types of information that do not have to be disclosed:

1. Work product created by the attorneys or their agents;[4]
2. Transcripts of grand jury testimony;[5] and
3. Any statement made by a witness, a prospective witness or the defendant himself to anyone on the defense team.[6]

In addition to the requirements of Rule 16, Rules 12.1, 12.2, and 12.3 of the Federal Rules of Criminal Procedure also create special obligations for the defendant to disclose information if he is presenting an alibi defense, an insanity defense, or a defense that he acted on behalf of a law enforcement agency. Additional discovery obligations are also imposed on the government by Rule 12.1 in connection with alibi evidence:

> If the defendant intends to present an alibi defense, the defendant must disclose the place he claims to have been at the time of the offense and the name, address, and telephone numbers of every witness whom he will call to establish the defense. If the government intends to rebut this defense using the victim's testimony, the court can order the government to either provide the defendant with the victim's address and telephone number, or fashion a reasonable procedure that allows the defendant to prepare but also protects the victim's interests.[7]

[4] Fed. R. Crim. Pro. (Rule 16(a)(2)) and 16(b)(2)(A)).

[5] Fed. R. Crim. Pro. (Rule 16(a)(3)).

[6] Fed. R. Crim. Pro. 16(b)(2)(B).

[7] Fed. R. Crim. Pro. 12.1.

If the defendant intends to present an insanity defense or present any expert evidence of a mental condition, he must notify the prosecutor during the time set out for motion practice. He must also then subject himself to a mental examination if requested by the prosecutor and provide the government with a written summary of the expert's testimony.[8]

If the defendant intents to present a defense that he acted on behalf of a law enforcement authority or federal intelligence agency, he must notify the prosecutor during the time set out for motion practice.

Finally, Rule 26.2 sets out the obligation of both sides to disclose previous statements by their witnesses:

Rule 26.2.

Producing a Witness's Statement

(a) Motion to Produce. After a witness other than the defendant has testified on direct examination, the court, on motion of a party who did not call the witness, must order an attorney for the government or the defendant and the defendant's attorney to produce, for the examination and use of the moving party, any statement of the witness that is in their possession and that relates to the subject matter of the witness's testimony.

(b) Producing the Entire Statement. If the entire statement relates to the subject matter of the witness's testimony, the court must order that the statement be delivered to the moving party.

(c) Producing a Redacted Statement. If the party who called the witness claims that the statement contains information that is privileged or does not relate to the subject matter of the witness's testimony, the court must inspect the statement *in camera*. After excising any privileged or unrelated portions, the court must order delivery of the redacted statement to the moving party. If the defendant objects to an excision, the court must preserve the entire statement with the excised portion indicated, under seal, as part of the record.

(d) Recess to Examine a Statement. The court may recess the proceedings to allow time for a party to examine the statement and prepare for its use.

(e) Sanction for Failure to Produce or Deliver a Statement. If the party who called the witness disobeys an order to produce or deliver a statement, the court must strike the witness's testimony from the record. If an attorney for the government disobeys the order, the court must declare a mistrial if justice so requires.

[8] Fed. R. Crim. Pro. 12.2.

(f) "Statement" Defined. As used in this rule, a witness's "statement" means:

> **(1)** a written statement that the witness makes and signs, or otherwise adopts or approves;
>
> **(2)** a substantially verbatim, contemporaneously recorded recital of the witness's oral statement that is contained in any recording or any transcription of a recording; or
>
> **(3)** the witness's statement to a grand jury, however taken or recorded, or a transcription of such a statement.
>
> . . .

Some of the provisions of Rule 26.2 are also contained in 18 U.S.C. § 3500, which was passed as part of the Jencks Act in 1957. For this reason, witness statements are sometimes referred to as "Jencks Act material."

Note that Rule 26.2 differs from the other discovery rules in that the discovery obligation it creates does not arise until after the witness testifies on direct. In practice, however, most attorneys do not wait until this point to turn over relevant material. This is because following the literal timing of Rule 26.2 would be very cumbersome. If the opposing party did not get to see any of the witness's statements until after direct, she would invariably ask for a recess under Rule 26.2(d) to examine the statements and prepare cross-examination strategy. Furthermore, if there is some dispute as to how much of the statement is relevant to the direct testimony, or if the attorney who called the witness is claiming some portion of the statements are privileged, the judge will have to call a recess under Rule 26.2(c) to determine whether the statement needs to be redacted. The jury would have to wait during these recesses, having heard only the direct but not yet the cross-examination. Most judges are not willing to put up with these kinds of delays in the middle of a trial and will pressure parties to disclose a witness's prior statements in advance of trial. Thus, in practice most parties turn over witness statements before trial, either out of courtesy or under pressure from the trial judge.

In the rare case where witness statements have not been disclosed before trial, it is good practice to make a request for such statements on the record after every direct examination. As explained above, the obligations under Rule 26.2 are not triggered until the opposing party makes a formal request and until the witness has testified. Thus, making a renewed request at the close of the witness' testimony re-affirms any obligations arising under Rule 26.2. In addition, this practice helps to ensure that any claimed error flowing from the lack of compliance with the discovery rules is clearly preserved for subsequent review.

Subsection (f) of the rule creates a very broad definition of "statement," which includes not just a formal written statement made by the witness, but also any record of the witness' oral statements, including any record of statements contained in notes taken by police officers or investigators. This rule also overrules the usual secrecy requirement surrounding a witness' grand jury testimony.

Also note that Rule 26.2 does not apply to statements made by a defendant. Requiring the defendant to disclose his own prior statements would raise issues under the self-incrimination clause and would create issues with regard to attorney-client privilege.

There are other disclosure requirements that are not found in the Rules of Criminal Procedure. For example, the Federal Rules of Evidence require advance notice if a party is going to use a prior criminal conviction to impeach an opposing party's witness.[9] Advance notice is also required by the Rules of Evidence if the defendant intends to introduce evidence of a victim's prior sexual history under an exception to the rape shield law.[10]

Before we move on, you should note one important category of information that is not mentioned by any of the rules: the names of and contact information for the witnesses that each side intends to call. Rule 16(a)(1)(G) and 16(b)(1)(C) create special disclosure rules for expert witnesses; and Rules 12.1 creates special disclosure rules for alibi witnesses (and prosecution witnesses used to rebut alibi witnesses), but aside from these requirements, there is no need for either party to tell the other side the names of the witnesses who will be called to the stand.

Many prosecutors have routinely resisted a blanket rule requiring disclosure of the names and addresses of their witnesses, arguing that this may deter witnesses from coming forward and, in some cases, result in witness intimidation. However, in practice, it is not uncommon for this information to be disclosed to the defendant. As noted above, some prosecutors engage in open-file discovery, which involves turning over the witness information; even those that do not have an open-file policy will hand over witness statements (and other witness information) earlier than is required under Rule 26.2. Also, as noted in Section C.6, below, many state rules require the parties to disclose this information prior to trial. Other states give the trial judge discretion to order disclosure of names and contact information, but only if the defendant demonstrates a significant need for the information.

Finally, remember that every court system has its own set of local rules, and those rules may include discovery obligations for either side. For example, many courts have a local rule which requires parties to submit a witness list to the court and

---

[9] Fed. R. Evid. 609(b)(2).

[10] Fed. R. Evid. 412(c)(1).

the opposing party one week before trial begins. Moreover, as a practical matter, the names of witnesses for each side are commonly disclosed during the voir dire process to ensure that none of the potential jurors have any conflicts.

C. Applying the Law.

1. Discovery in Practice. Compared to the discovery process in civil cases, discovery in a criminal case is significantly less comprehensive. A civil case might have months or even years of formal discovery, in which opposing sides set up a discovery schedule, send interrogatories to each other, and ultimately depose each other's witnesses in formal depositions attended by both attorneys and sometimes the opposing parties. In contrast, discovery in a criminal case typically begins with the defendant sending a boilerplate written discovery request to the prosecutor, seeking all the information that is specified in Rule 16(a) (or its state law equivalent). The discovery process usually begins with the defendant's request because under most discovery rules the prosecution does not have any right to make such a request initially. As you read above, most discovery rules do not create any defense obligation to turn over information until after the defendant has requested discovery and the prosecutor has complied with those requests. After the defendant makes a request, the prosecutor will respond with the necessary disclosures and her own boilerplate request seeking all of the information that is specified in Rule 16(b) as well as any notifications as required by Rules 12.1, 12.2, and 12.3. Once the defendant complies with this request, the discovery process is usually finished and the case will proceed to motion practice.

Rule 16 does not set out any specific deadline for the request or for compliance after a request has been made. However, most jurisdictions require that the request and the compliance be done in a timely manner. Also, in many cases the magistrate will set deadlines for discovery requests and responses at the arraignment. Other than this initial scheduling, it is rare for the judge or magistrate to get involved with discovery issues.

However, if a party believes that the opposing party is being uncooperative or non-responsive, the party can bring a **motion to compel discovery**. Rule 16(d) gives the judge broad powers to regulate and enforce the discovery process. If the judge finds that the opposing party has not complied with its discovery obligations, it can order the party to disclose information and can impose additional sanctions as needed to ensure the fairness of the trial, including but not limited to continuances or the exclusion of testimony.

Conversely, if a party believes that it does not need to disclose certain information, Rule 16(d) allows the party to file a **motion for a protective order**. Such a motion must explain why there is good cause not to comply with the discovery request. The motion for a protective order is filed *ex parte* with the magistrate, although notice of the motion is given to the opposing party. In practice, it is almost always the prosecutor who files a motion for a protective order, and the usual reason justifying the motion is a particular risk to the physical safety of a witness or an increased chance of perjury or witness intimidation if the information is revealed. Obviously the prosecutor must do more than make bare assertions of such risks; she must set out specific facts and reasoning to explain why an exception to the rules should be made for this particular information. If the magistrate finds that a sufficient showing has been made, the material will be shielded from disclosure. If the magistrate finds that a sufficient showing has not been made, however, the motion will be denied and disclosure will be required.

2. *Brady* Rule: "Exculpatory" and "Material": Under the *Brady* rule, prosecutors have a duty to disclose all material, exculpatory evidence to the defendant. In the *Brady* case, two defendants were tried separately for committing a murder together, and in the trial of the first defendant, the prosecutor failed to disclose to the defense (and to the jury) that the second defendant had confessed to actually killing the victim. The Supreme Court held that withholding this evidence violated the Due Process Clause: "A prosecution that withholds evidence on demand of an accused which, if made available, would tend to exculpate him or reduce the penalty helps shape a trial that bears heavily on the defendant."[11] The prosecutor's good faith or bad faith has no impact on the prosecutor's *Brady* obligations.

In later cases, the Court has clarified that the *Brady* obligation to disclose exculpatory evidence exists even if the defense does not make a formal demand for such evidence. In addition, two questions left open by *Brady* have since been resolved. The first question left open in the case was a clear definition of what constituted "exculpatory evidence." The second question was the definition of "material"—that is, what is the appropriate standard for determining whether the evidence, if disclosed, would have affected the trial.

As to the first issue, exculpatory evidence obviously includes any evidence of the defendant's actual innocence, such as fingerprint or DNA evidence in a single assailant case that identified someone else as the perpetrator, or eyewitnesses who supported the defendant's alibi defense. Nine years after *Brady*, in *Giglio v. United States*, the Court expanded the category, holding that some information that can be used to impeach a prosecution witness should also be considered exculpatory evidence.[12] Such impeachment evidence includes any evidence that a prosecution witness has changed her story, or received payment or a favorable plea deal from

[11] Brady v. Maryland, 373 U.S. 83, 88 (1963).

[12] Giglio v. United States, 405 U.S. 150 (1972).

the government, or has a past history of dishonest conduct. Thus, evidence that tends to impeach a prosecutor's case is sometimes known as *Giglio* material.

However, the *Giglio* case created a potential problem. Under the Jencks Act (now also codified in Rule 26.2), a witness' prior statements do not need to be turned over to the opposing party until after the witness testifies. However, when the defendant makes a motion for *Brady/Giglio* material before trial, the prosecutor may be unsure of her obligations. If the witness has made a significant number of pre-trial statements, it is likely that some of them conflict with each other in at least some of the details. Thus, the statements may potentially be *Brady* material, and the prosecutor would risk violating *Brady* if she does not immediately turn over those statements

Courts are currently split on the effect of *Giglio* on Jencks Act material. Some argue that Rule 26.2 already requires a prosecutor to reveal all of a witness' prior statements (which of course will include inconsistent statements) after the witness testifies, and that this timing is sufficient to satisfy *Giglio.* Other courts require prosecutors to disclose inconsistent statements prior to trial; this forces prosecutors to comb through their witness' statements and decide whether any of them are so inconsistent as to rise to the level of "exculpatory" evidence—and also whether they are so exculpatory that not disclosing them before trial could change the outcome of the trial.

The second prong of the *Brady* test—materiality—is slightly more complicated, since it requires the reviewing court to determine whether the outcome of the trial would have been different if the exculpatory information had been disclosed. To fulfill this prong, the defendant does not need to prove that it is more likely than not that disclosure of the evidence would have changed the outcome of the trial; only that there is a **reasonable probability** that it would have changed the outcome of the trial. Reasonable probability is defined as "whether in the absence of the disclosure the defendant received a fair trial, understood as a trial resulting in a verdict worthy of confidence."[13]

Example—*United States v. Bagley*, 473 U.S. 667 (1985): Hughes Bagley was indicted in federal court on various counts of narcotics and firearms charges. The government's two primary witnesses were Officers O'Connor and Mitchell, two state law enforcement officers who had been assisting the federal Bureau of Alcohol, Tobacco, and Firearms ("ATF") in investigating Bagley.

[13] Kyles v. Whitley, 514 U.S. 419, 434 (1995).

As part of a routine discovery motion, Bagley requested "[t]he names and addresses of witnesses that the government intends to call at trial. Also the prior criminal records of witnesses, and any deals, promises or inducements made to witnesses in exchange for their testimony."[14] The government responded to the request with a statement that no "deals, promises or inducements" were given to O'Connor or Mitchell. Also, in response to a Jencks Act request for witness statements, the government provided Bagley with affidavits signed by O'Connor and Mitchell, which concluded with the statement "I made this statement freely and voluntarily without any threats or rewards, or promises of reward having been made to me in return for it."[15]

Bagley was convicted of the narcotics charges. Two and a half years later, in response to a request under the Freedom of Information Act, Bagley obtained contracts between O'Connor, Mitchell, and the ATF. In the contracts, the ATF agreed to pay each of the witnesses $300 in exchange for their investigation in the Bagley case, but only if the ATF was satisfied with the result of the investigation. Bagley then moved to vacate his sentence, claiming that the government had violated his *Brady* rights by not disclosing the contracts or the payments before trial.

Analysis: The Supreme Court held that the payments to the witnesses were exculpatory and that the case had to be remanded to the appellate court to determine whether nondisclosure of the payments was material. The Court had little trouble finding that the evidence of the payments was exculpatory: had the defendant known about the payments, he would certainly have used them to impeach the witnesses' credibility.

In discussing materiality, the Court first noted that the defendant made a specific request for this information. A specific request for information will increase its materiality because "the more specifically the defense requests certain evidence, thus putting the prosecutor on notice of its value, the more reasonable it is for the defense to assume from the nondisclosure that the evidence does not exist, and to make pretrial and trial decisions on the basis of this assumption."[16] Thus, the defendant was misled into believing that the witnesses had no inducements offered to them in exchange for their testimony.

The Court stopped short of concluding that the nondisclosure was material, however, and remanded the case to the appellate court to examine the factual record

[14] United States v. Bagley, 473 U.S. 667, 669-70 (1985).

[15] Id. at 670.

[16] Id. at 682-3.

and determine whether there was a reasonable probability that the result might have been different. On remand, the appellate court noted that the government's case rested "solely on the credibility of O'Connor and Mitchell," and that the undisclosed ATF contracts would have proven that the two witnesses perjured themselves in their affidavits when they claimed to have received no inducements from the government.[17] On remand, the appellate court reviewed the facts and concluded that the nondisclosure was material and vacated Bagley's conviction.

When the defendant argues that a reasonable probability of a different outcome exists, he must argue specifically how the undisclosed information would have changed the result at trial. This can be difficult if the evidence against the defendant is particularly strong:

> **Example—*Wood v. Bartholomew*, 516 U.S. 1 (1995):** Dwayne Bartholomew robbed a laundromat and shot and killed the laundromat attendant. He admitted to the robbery and the shooting, but he claimed that the gun went off accidentally. The prosecutor's two witnesses were Dwayne's brother Rodney and Rodney's girlfriend Tracy. They both testified that Dwayne told them he intended to rob the laundromat and "leave no witnesses." They both also denied any participation in the crime. The prosecutor also presented evidence that Dwayne's gun was a single action revolved that had to be manually cocked before each shot, and that Dwayne shot the gun twice during the robbery, casting doubt on his explanation that the shooting was an accident. Finally, the prosecutor produced evidence from Dwayne's cellmate, who testified that Dwayne admitted to intentionally killing the attendant.
>
> During his testimony, Dwayne claimed that his brother Rodney helped him with the robbery by convincing the laundromat attendant to leave the door open even though the laundromat was closed for the night. Dwayne's attorney argued to the jury that Rodney and Tracy were manufacturing testimony to please the prosecutor in order to cover up Rodney's role in the incident.
>
> Before the trial began, the prosecutor asked both Tracy and Rodney to take polygraph examinations. The examiner concluded that Tracy was telling the truth, but that Rodney was lying when he denied assisting Dwayne with the robbery. The prosecutor did not disclose the polygraph results to the defense.

[17] Bagley v. Lumpkin, 798 F.2d 1297, 1301 (1986).

The jury concluded that Dwayne intentionally killed the attendant and convicted him of aggravated first-degree murder. After the polygraph results were discovered, Dwayne appealed his conviction, arguing that the government violated *Brady* when it failed to disclose Rodney's failed polygraph test.

Analysis: The Supreme Court held that Dwayne's *Brady* rights were not violated. There was no reasonable probability that the disclosure of the failed polygraph test would have changed the result at trial. Polygraph tests are inadmissible in court, so the jury could never have heard about the results.

The defendant argued he would have made additional discovery requests had he known that one of the prime witnesses was lying—for example, he might have tried to depose Rodney and ultimately obtained an admission from Rodney that he did participate in the crime. This admission could then have been used to impeach Rodney at trial, since it would show that he initially lied about one aspect of the story.

The Court rejected this argument as speculative. The Court noted that on habeas review, the lower court allowed Dwayne's defense attorney to question Rodney under oath and confront him with the polygraph results, and that Rodney made no admission of guilt during the interrogation. Thus, there was little reason to believe that Rodney would have made such an admission if he had been deposed before the original trial. Furthermore, the Court noted that the evidence against Dwayne was "overwhelming" even without Rodney's testimony.[18]

One important aspect in determining whether a non-disclosure is material is whether the defense attorney made a specific request for the information. In the original *Brady* case, the defendant made a specific request for the statements by the co-defendant, and the prosecutor did not comply with that request. Later cases clarified that the *Brady* obligation exists even if the defendant does not specifically request the information—if the evidence is exculpatory and there is a reasonable probability that it would have affected the outcome of the trial, the prosecutor must turn it over regardless of what discovery requests the defendant has made.[19] However, a reviewing court is much more likely to determine that the non-disclosure could have affected the outcome of the trial if the defendant made a specific request for particular items and was denied. The fact that the defendant made a request is evidence that the defendant believed the information was important to his defense, which makes the information more likely to be "material."

If the defendant does make a motion to compel discovery of exculpatory evidence and the prosecutor denies it, the defendant may seek to inspect the items or information himself in order to determine whether any exculpatory evidence

[18] Wood v. Bartholomew, 516 U.S. 1, 8 (1995).

[19] United States v. Augurs, 427 U.S. 97 (1976).

exists. Obviously the defendant must do more than make a boilerplate request to look through the prosecutor's files; he must make a plausible showing that exculpatory evidence exists in a given set of materials. If the defendant makes this showing, the trial court is still unlikely to turn over potential discovery to the defense directly. Instead, the court will conduct an *in camera* hearing to determine whether any of the information is exculpatory. The Supreme Court has determined that this sort of *in camera* review serves as a compromise between the defendant's right to exculpatory information and the prosecutor's right to protect sensitive information that is not otherwise discoverable:

> Although this rule denies [the defendant] the benefits of an "advocate's eye," we note that the trial court's discretion is not unbounded. If a defendant is aware of specific information contained in the file . . . he is free to request it directly from the court, and argue in favor of its materiality. Moreover, the duty to disclose is ongoing; information that may be deemed immaterial upon original examination may become important as the proceedings progress, and the court would be obligated to release information material to the fairness of the trial.[20]

Once the trial is over and the defendant seeks to vacate his conviction based on a *Brady* violation, the reviewing court should look at the cumulative effect of all of the non-disclosed exculpatory evidence in order to determine whether the omissions were material. This means that although a prosecutor need not turn over every piece of exculpatory evidence, she must exercise her judgment to ensure that the amount of non-disclosed exculpatory evidence never reaches the point where it creates a reasonable probability that disclosure would have created a different result:

> [S]howing that the prosecution knew of a [single] item of favorable evidence unknown to the defense does not amount to a *Brady* violation, without more. But the prosecution, which alone can know what is undisclosed, must be assigned the consequent responsibility to gauge the likely net effect of all such evidence and make disclosure when the point of "reasonable probability" is reached. This in turn means that the individual prosecutor has a duty to learn of any favorable evidence known to the others acting on the government's behalf in the case, including the police. But whether the prosecutor succeeds or fails in meeting this obligation . . . the prosecution's responsibility for [a failure] to disclose known, favorable evidence rising to a material level of importance is inescapable.[21]

Undoubtedly, most prosecutors err on the side of more disclosure in order to ensure they never cross the "reasonable probability" threshold. The Supreme Court

---

[20] Pennsylvania v. Ritchie, 480 U.S. 39, 60 (1987).

[21] Kyles v. Whitley, 514 U.S. 419, 437-8 (1995).

has stated that this is perfectly appropriate, since "[s]uch disclosure will serve to justify trust in the prosecutor as the representative . . . of a sovereignty . . . whose interest . . . in a criminal prosecution is not that it shall win a case, but that justice shall be done."[22] Nonetheless, recent high-profile examples of non-disclosure stubbornly remain despite the clear obligations imposed under *Brady*.[23]

The legal obligations imposed under the *Brady* rule are lenient when compared to a prosecutor's duties under the ethical guidelines. The American Bar Association ("ABA") Standards for Criminal Conduct state that prosecutors "should not intentionally fail to make timely disclosure to the defense, at the earliest feasible opportunity, of the existence of all evidence or information which tends to negate the guilt of the accused or mitigate the offense charged or which would tend to reduce the punishment of the accused."[24] The ABA Model Rules of Professional Conduct require a prosecutor to "make timely disclosure to the defense of all evidence or information known to the prosecutor that tends to negate the guilt of the accused or mitigates the offense."[25] A prosecutor who complies with these ethical standards will have no problem staying within the confines of the *Brady* rule and thus will never have to worry about the "reasonable probability" standard.

On the other side of the spectrum, a prosecutor who intentionally violates the *Brady* rule could face professional consequences far more severe than dismissal of the case. A prosecutor who intentionally withholds evidence of innocence from the defendant (and by extension, from the court) could face disciplinary measures from the state bar, up to and including suspension of her license to practice law. The prosecutor could also theoretically be sued by the criminal defendant, but such cases are rare and difficult to maintain.[26]

3. Extending *Brady*: Duty to Preserve Evidence and Assist the Defendant. The prosecutor's duty to ensure a fair trial goes beyond the need to disclose exculpatory material. The Court has stated that the *Brady* doctrine is properly thought of as a specific type of case that fits into a broader category cases dealing with a defendant's "constitutionally guaranteed access to evidence."[27]

Because the prosecutor is an officer of the court, she owes a duty of fairness to the court and the defendant. For example, if she has reason to believe that evidence may exonerate the defendant, she cannot intentionally destroy or fail to preserve

[22] Id. at 439 (internal quotations and citations omitted).

[23] See, e.g., Smith v. Cain, 132 S.Ct. 627 (2012).

[24] ABA Standards for Criminal Justice, Prosecution Function and Defense Function 3–3.11(a) (3d ed. 1993).

[25] ABA Model Rule of Professional Conduct 3.8(d) (1984).

[26] Connick v. Thompson, 131 S.Ct. 1350 (2011).

[27] United States v. Valenzuela–Bernal, 458 U.S. 858, 867 (1982).

that evidence. However, this duty does not mean that the prosecutor has an **affirmative duty** to preserve all evidence which may be helpful to the defendant:

> **Example—*Arizona v. Youngblood*, 488 U.S. 51 (1988):** After a ten-year-old boy was kidnapped and sexually assaulted, he was taken to a hospital for medical treatment. The doctor used a sexual assault kit to collect saliva, hair, and semen from the victim's body. The samples were stored in a refrigerator. The police also collected the boy's clothes and stored them, though not in a refrigerated space. A police criminologist examined the samples briefly to confirm that a sexual assault occurred, but in accordance with standard police procedure, he did not perform any tests on the samples.
>
> A few days later the police showed the victim a photo array and he selected Larry Youngblood as the perpetrator. Youngblood was arrested for kidnapping and sexual assault. The prosecutor sought a court order to force the defendant to provide blood and saliva samples to compare with the samples recovered from the victim, but the court denied the motion, ruling that the state had such a small sample that it would be impossible to make a valid comparison. The government did perform a basic test on the samples to determine the blood type of the perpetrator, but the test was inconclusive.
>
> Thirteen months later, a police criminologist examined the boy's clothing for the first time and conducted a series of chemical tests on the clothes. However, there was not enough biological evidence on the clothing to reach any conclusions about the identity of the perpetrator.
>
> The defendant claimed mistaken identity and argued that the sample tests might not have been inconclusive if the criminologist had conducted tests on the sample immediately after the attack or if the clothes had been refrigerated. After the defendant was convicted, he argued that the government's failure to preserve the evidence violated his due process rights. The appellate court agreed, stating that "when identity is an issue at trial and the police permit the destruction of evidence that could eliminate the defendant as the perpetrator, such loss is material to the defense and is a denial of due process."[28] The state appealed the decision and it was ultimately heard by the United States Supreme Court.

---

[28] Arizona v. Youngblood, 488 U.S. 51, 54 (1988).

Analysis: The government's failure to preserve evidence that was only potentially useful did not violate Youngblood's due process rights. In order to prevail on a due process claim for failure to preserve potentially useful evidence, a defendant must prove that the police or prosecutor acted in bad faith. In this case, the government conduct was perhaps negligent, but there was no showing of bad faith. There is no indication that the government intentionally failed to preserve the evidence in order to prejudice the defendant's case. The government also did not have an affirmative duty to perform tests that may exonerate the defendant. For example, in a prosecution for drunk driving, the police need not conduct a breathalyzer test if the case can be proven by observation alone: "the defendant is free to argue to the finder of fact that a breathalyzer test might have been exculpatory, but the police do not have a constitutional duty to perform any particular tests."[29]

The Court contrasted the absolute duty under *Brady* to disclose exculpatory evidence with the more lenient duty to preserve evidence which may be helpful to the defense. In evaluating a *Brady* claim, the good faith of the prosecutor is irrelevant—any failure to turn over material, exculpatory evidence results in reversal. But it would be unworkable to "impos[e]on the police an undifferentiated and absolute duty to retain and to preserve all material that might be of conceivable evidentiary significance in a particular prosecution."[30] Requiring bad faith on the part of the government means that a due process violation only occurs in those cases "in which the police themselves by their conduct indicate that the evidence could form a basis for exonerating the defendant."[31]

4. Defendant's Discovery Obligations. Rules 12.1, 12.2, and 12.3 create a discovery obligation for the defendant if he intends to present an alibi defense, an insanity defense, or a defense that he was acting under the authority of a law enforcement agency. The theory behind these rules is that these defenses are nearly impossible to rebut unless the prosecutor has advance notice in order to prepare. When defense-notification rules were first proposed decades ago, defense attorneys initially argued that creating discovery obligations for defendants violated the Self-Incrimination Clause. The Supreme Court rejected these claims, but did put some limit on the use of these provisions:

Example—*Williams v. Florida*, 399 U.S. 78 (1970): Johnny Williams was indicted for robbery in the state of Florida. Florida's rules of criminal procedure required every defendant to give pre-trial notice if he intended to present an alibi defense. The defendant was also required to disclose the name and addresses of any alibi witnesses he intended to call. Williams gave notice

[29] Id. at 59.

[30] Id. at 57.

[31] Id. at 58.

of his alibi defense, but initially refused to furnish the names and addresses of the likely witnesses, arguing that forcing him to reveal this information violated his right against self-incrimination. The trial judge ruled that, under Florida law, if Williams did not disclose the names of the witnesses, he could not call them at trial. Williams relented and gave the prosecutor the name and address of Mary Scotty.

Just before trial began, the prosecutors called Scotty to their office and deposed her about the testimony she was going to give. At the trial, after Scotty testified for the defendant, the prosecutor was able to impeach her with inconsistencies between her testimony and her pre-trial deposition. The prosecutor was also prepared with a rebuttal witness: a police officer who said that at the time Scotty claimed to be in her apartment with Williams, the officer was speaking to her at a different location.

Williams was convicted and he appealed. In the Supreme Court, Williams argued that arguing that the alibi notification rule violated his due process rights and self-incrimination rights under the Fifth and Fourteenth Amendments.

Analysis: The Supreme Court found the alibi notification rule constitutional. The Court quickly disposed of the due process argument. Because alibi defenses can easily be fabricated, the state had an "obvious and legitimate" interest in protecting itself against such fabrications.[32] The Court noted that the ultimate purpose of a trial is to determine the truth, and the adversary system is only a means to that end. Thus, although discovery rules technically run contrary to the theory of an adversarial system, they are acceptable if they serve to enhance the truth-seeking function of the trial.

The Court then turned to Williams's self-incrimination claim. The Court drew an analogy between a prosecutor's traditional right to cross-examine defense witnesses and the alibi-notification requirements at issue in this case. Defendants always have to choose between complete silence at trial and presenting a defense. If they choose to present a defense, they must subject all of their witnesses (including the defendant himself, if he chooses to testify) to potentially incriminating cross-examination by the prosecutor. These cross-examinations are not considered to be "compelled" disclosure, because the defendant has made the choice to present a defense. In other words, a defendant is never required to call any witnesses in his defense, but if he does, the prosecutor has the right to cross-examine them in order to test their credibility.

---

[32] Williams v. Florida, 399 U.S. 78, 81 (1970).

The alibi disclosure provisions are analogous: the defendant is not required to present an alibi defense, but if he does, he is required to disclose the names and addresses of his witnesses ahead of time so the prosecutor can effectively test their credibility. All the alibi notification did was accelerate the timing of the defendant's disclosure, since the prosecutor would ultimately learn the name and address of the witnesses when they testified at trial.

A few years later, the Court returned to the question of discovery rules regarding alibi defenses, and again focused on ensuring that the rules furthered the truth-seeking function of the trial. In *Wardius v. Oregon*,[33] the defendant objected to an Oregon discovery rule that required him to provide the prosecutor with names and addresses of his alibi witnesses, but did not require the prosecutor to provide any reciprocal discovery. The Court reiterated its statement in *Williams* that the Due Process Clause is not violated by a discovery rule that is "designed to enhance the search for truth in the criminal trial by insuring both the defendant and the State ample opportunity to investigate certain facts crucial to the determination of guilt or innocence."[34] In *Williams*, the prosecutor faced reciprocal discovery obligations, and so the alibi notice provision furthered the search for truth. In contrast, Oregon did not give any discovery rights to the defendant at all. The Court noted that, as long as a state complied with its *Brady* obligations, it did not need to give any discovery rights to the defendant. However, the Court did hold

> that in the absence of a strong showing of state interests to the contrary, discovery must be a two-way street. The State may not insist that trials be run as a "search for truth" so far as defense witnesses are concerned, while maintaining "poker game" secrecy for its own witnesses. It is fundamentally unfair to require a defendant to divulge the details of his own case while at the same time subjecting him to the hazard of surprise concerning refutation of the very pieces of evidence which he disclosed to the State.[35]

Thus, under the Due Process Clause, if a discovery scheme does require the defendant to disclose information, it must also require the prosecutor to disclose reciprocal information.

5. Remedies for Discovery Violations. As we saw in Section C.1, above, the court has broad powers to regulate and enforce the discovery process. But what if the court determines that a party has failed to comply with its discovery obligations? If the party has refused a court order to disclose the information, the court should issue an order to show cause, and if the party cannot show good cause, the court can hold the party in contempt until it complies with its discovery obligations.

---

[33] 412 U.S. 470 (1973).

[34] 412 U.S. at 474.

[35] Id. at 475-6.

But such contempt proceedings only apply when a party flatly refuses to comply with a court order, which is extremely rare. Usually a discovery violation has to do with timing: one of the parties fails to disclose necessary information until the eve of trial, or during the trial itself. For example, assume the prosecutor notifies the defendant the day before the trial that she seeks to call an expert witness, and hands over the results of the expert's tests at that time. Or, assume the local rules compel both sides to disclose the names of their witnesses seven days before trial, and the defendant waits until after the prosecutor's case to notify the court and the prosecutor that he intends to call a witness who was not on his list. In these situations, the court has the following options:

1. Grant a continuance;

2. Grant a mistrial;

3. Prohibit the witness from testifying, or (if applicable) prohibit the evidence from being introduced;

4. Instruct the jury that its allowed to presume certain facts adverse to the non-disclosing party;

5. Sanction the attorney; or

6. Make any other order the court deems appropriate, up to and including dismissal of the case.

In general, enforcing discovery obligations against the prosecution is much easier than enforcing them against the defense. The first two sanctions—a continuance or a mistrial—are usually effective deterrents to the prosecutor, who in most cases has a strong interest in moving the trial forward. But delay will not be as effective a deterrent against the defense in a case where a continuance puts pressure on the speedy trial clock or increases the likelihood that prosecution witnesses will become uncooperative or forget details of their testimony. Similarly, depending upon the stage of the case at which the sanction is imposed, the defense also may not be motivated by the potential sanction of a mistrial, which simply forces the prosecutor to start the prosecution over. The third sanction—precluding the witness or the evidence from trial—can certainly be effective against either party, but it runs into constitutional problems when applied against the defendant, who has a right under the Compulsory Process Clause of the Sixth Amendment to call witnesses on his behalf. The Supreme Court has held that witness preclusion is a permitted sanction against the defendant, but that it must be used sparingly:

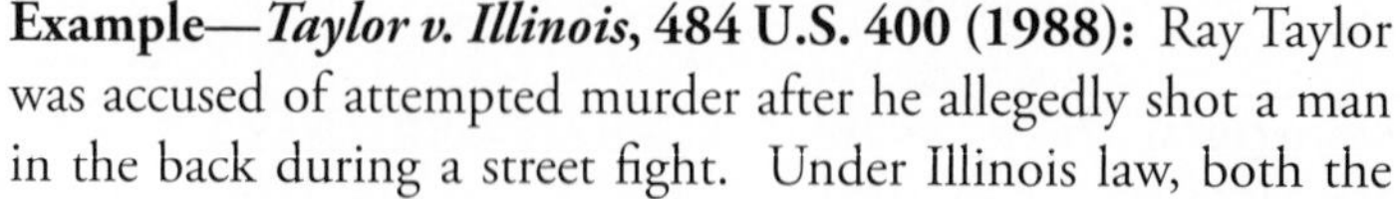

Example—*Taylor v. Illinois*, 484 U.S. 400 (1988): Ray Taylor was accused of attempted murder after he allegedly shot a man in the back during a street fight. Under Illinois law, both the prosecutor and the defendant had a duty to disclose the names, contact information, and any recorded statements of all of the witnesses the party intended to call at trial. The prosecutor made a request for such disclosure well in advance of trial, and the defendant listed four witnesses, two of whom did in fact testify at the trial. After the first day of trial, the defense attorney sought to add two more witnesses to his list, including a man named Alfred Wormley. The defense attorney told the court that he had only recently been informed about the witnesses by his client, and that he had been unable to locate Wormley until that very day. The judge noted on the record that the defense attorney could at least have disclosed Wormley's name at an earlier time even if he did not know Wormley's address.

The court held a special hearing the next day outside the presence of the jury in order to hear what Wormley had to say. Wormley testified that someone other than the defendant had brought guns to the fight. He also testified that he met the defendant four months before the trial, and that—contrary to the defense attorney's representations to the court—the defense attorney had come to Wormley's home to speak with him one week before the trial.

The judge ruled that the defense attorney had committed a blatant and willful violation of the discovery rules, and he precluded Wormley from testifying in front of the jury. The defendant appealed the case to the Supreme Court, arguing that barring Wormley's testimony violated Taylor's Sixth Amendment right to call witnesses in his own defense.

Analysis: The trial court did not abuse its discretion in prohibiting the defense witness from testifying. The Court began its analysis by confirming that "few rights are more fundamental than that of an accused to present witnesses in his own defense,"[36] noting that this right is as important as the right to confront the prosecutor's witnesses. However, the Court noted that the defendant's right to present witnesses is not absolute. For example, "[t]he accused does not have an unfettered right to offer testimony that is incompetent, privileged, or otherwise inadmissible under standard rules of evidence."[37]

The whole point of giving defendants the right to call witnesses is to ensure that the adversary process produces the truth, not merely one version of the truth.

[36] Taylor v. Illinois, 484 U.S. 400 (1988).

[37] Id. at 410.

Discovery rules which require defendants to provide information to the prosecutor in order to allow the prosecutor to effectively plan a cross-examination serve exactly the same function. In other words, "[d]iscovery, like cross-examination, minimizes the risk that a judgment will be predicated on incomplete, misleading, or even deliberately fabricated testimony. The State's interest in protecting itself against an eleventh-hour defense is merely one component of the broader public interest in a full and truthful disclosure of critical facts."[38] This same principle underlies the requirement that a defendant must subject himself to cross-examination if he testifies. In short, "[t]he Sixth Amendment does not confer the right to present testimony free from the legitimate demands of the adversarial system; one cannot invoke the Sixth Amendment as a justification for presenting what might have been a half-truth."[39]

The Court acknowledged that other remedies were available to sanction the defense attorney for his violation of the discovery rules, but held that they were "less effective than the preclusion sanction" and that some of them (such as granting a continuance or a mistrial) might merely increase the prejudice to the government.[40] The Court refrained from setting down specific rules to govern when it is appropriate to prohibit the defendant's witnesses. The Court did provide some guidance, however:

> [A] trial judge may certainly insist on an explanation for a party's failure to comply with a request to identify his or her witnesses in advance of trial. If that explanation reveals that the omission was **willful** and **motivated by a desire to obtain a tactical advantage** that would minimize the effectiveness of cross-examination and the ability to adduce rebuttal evidence, it would be entirely consistent with the purposes of the Compulsory Process Clause simply to exclude the witness' testimony.[41]

In this case, the defense attorney's conduct met this standard, and so preclusion of the defendant's witnesses was an appropriate remedy.

Although the Supreme Court upheld the right of trial judges to preclude defense witnesses as a punishment for discovery violations, it also acknowledged that this is a drastic remedy. In reality, most trial judges are unwilling to go that far to punish a defendant's discovery violations unless they are severe, repeated, and/or there is evidence of bad faith on the part of the defense attorney. In the *Taylor* case, all three of these factors were present: the defense attorney did not disclose the existence of the witness until the day before he was to testify; the trial judge noted that "defense attorneys have been violating discovery in this courtroom in the last three or four cases blatantly and I am going to put a stop to it;"[42] and the

---

[38] Id. at 411-2 (internal quotations and citations omitted).

[39] Id. at 412-3 (quoting United States v. Nobles, 422 U.S. 225, 241 (1975)).

[40] Id. at 413.

[41] Id. at 415 (emphasis added).

[42] Id. at 405.

defense attorney lied to the court about when he learned the witness' address. Even in that situation, the *Taylor* dissent argued that it was unfair to infringe on the defendant's constitutional rights when it was the defense attorney who made the error.[43] Thus, sanctions of the defense attorney are a more common route for discovery violations than actual remedies that affect the outcome of the trial.

The relative impotence of discovery enforcement mechanisms against the defendant is occasionally a source of frustration to prosecutors, leading many prosecutors to conclude that discovery is, in effect, a "one-way street." In practice, judges have very effective methods of punishing a prosecutor's discovery violations, but relatively fewer tools to force a defendant to comply. Defense attorneys respond that this imbalance flows naturally from the defendant's constitutional rights, and that prosecutors already have an enormous advantage in gathering information, given the vast resources of the state.

6. State Variations. As you can see from the *Taylor* case, state discovery rules can vary significantly from the federal rules set out in Section B. Generally speaking, the federal rules on discovery are among the most restrictive of any jurisdiction. On the other side of the spectrum are the model rules proposed by the American Bar Association ("ABA"),[44] which have been adopted as a model (or at least as a starting point) by a number of states. In addition to the information that is listed in the federal discovery rules, the ABA rules require disclosure of the following information by the prosecutor:

1. The names and addresses of everyone "known to the prosecution to have information concerning the offense."

2. All of their written statements which are within the possession and control of the prosecutor.

3. Identification of which people on the list above will actually be called as witnesses.

4. The relationship (if any) between the prosecutor and any prospective witness, including any agreement or representation used for inducement of cooperation.

5. As far as is known by the prosecutor, any criminal record of any potential witness that may be called by either side which could be used to impeach the witness.

---

[43] Id. at 433 (Brennan, J., dissenting).

[44] ABA Standards for Criminal Justice: Discovery and Trial by Jury, 3d ed., 1996 American Bar Association.

6. Any character, reputation or other act evidence the prosecutor intends to use against or in favor of any witness.

7. Whether any electronic surveillance was used in the investigation.

8. If there is any tangible item that the prosecutor intends to admit as evidence that was obtained through search and seizure, all information and documents relating to the search and seizure.[45]

The ABA rules also require the following disclosures by the defense:

1. The names and addresses of everyone (other than the defendant) that the defendant intends to call as a witness. However, any witnesses who are being called with the sole purpose to impeach a prosecution witness need not be disclosed until after the prosecution witness has testified.

2. All of the written statements of those prospective witnesses that are in the possession and control of the defense and that relate to the subject matter of the witness' likely testimony.

3. Any character, reputation or other act evidence the defense intends to use against or in favor of any witness (with the exception of evidence that relates to the defendant).[46]

4. Upon request and reasonable notice, the defendant should be required to appear at a specified time in order to provide "fingerprints, photographs, handwriting exemplars, or voice exemplars from the defendant, or for the purpose of having the defendant appear, move, or speak for identification in a lineup or try on clothing or other articles."[47]

5. The defendant also will be required to appear upon request to provide specimens of blood, urine, saliva, breath, hair, nails, material under the nails, other samples from the body, and "to submit to a reasonable physical or medical inspection of the body."[48]

The ABA rules state that each jurisdiction should develop its own time limits for requiring these disclosures, but that completion of the discovery should be "sufficiently early in the process that each party has sufficient time to use the disclosed information adequately to prepare for trial."[49] In other words, witness statements must be turned over far earlier in the process than what is required under the federal rules.

---

[45] Id. at Standard 11-2.1.

[46] Id. at Standard 11-2.2.

[47] Id. at Standard 11-2.3(a).

[48] Id. at Standard 11-2.3(b).

[49] Id. at Standard 11-4.1.

As is frequently the case with rule or statute-based areas of criminal procedure, different states will have adopted different provisions from either the Federal Rules or the ABA standards. The only universal requirements are the *Brady* rule regarding exculpatory evidence and the rule that the defendant's burden to disclose cannot be greater than the prosecutor's burden.

7. Other Ways of Gathering Information. Viewed broadly, discovery is a very specific method of preparing for trial by gathering information from the opposing party. The majority of information that an attorney gathers in preparation for trial is usually done not through discovery but by gathering information on her own—by using law enforcement agents or private investigators to find witnesses, by interviewing these witnesses, and by gathering and sometimes testing physical items—weapons, narcotics, videos, cell phones—that are relevant to the case.

In an ideal world, all potential witnesses would be completely cooperative with both the prosecutor and the defense attorney, and they would volunteer to be interviewed by each side and also willingly bring any documents or other items in their possession when asked. The reality, of course, is quite different. Some witnesses are willing, even eager to cooperate (at least with the prosecutor); others are reluctant to become involved, and some are hostile and refuse to cooperate. It frequently takes a fair amount of work to track down and interview witnesses and gather physical evidence.

The prosecutor has many advantages in this search for information: she has law enforcement agents who have already gathered names of witnesses and seized evidence, and who are willing (at least in theory) to do more investigation into the case upon request. Furthermore, witnesses—and especially victims—tend to be much more willing to cooperate with prosecutors than defense attorneys. In fact, some witnesses are completely unwilling to talk to defense attorneys or their investigators. Of course, the prosecutor has the burden of proof at trial, and so a greater need to collect evidence. But, most practitioners agree that the prosecutor has an easier job in this stage of trial preparation.

The defense attorney does have at least one distinct advantage in gathering information: she is able to interview the defendant and hear not only his story but also gather names of other witnesses from him. As we have already seen, the defendant has an absolute right not to talk to the prosecutor, and once an attorney is assigned, it is rare that the defendant will agree to talk—unless he is promised immunity or offered a lenient plea agreement, as discussed below. Of course, police officers and prosecutors try to elicit information from the defendant before an attorney is assigned, but if the defendant asserts his right to counsel at any time, the government must stop asking questions.

There are three tools that are available—primarily to prosecutors—to assist in gathering information for trial. The first is the **subpoena power.** Subpoenas are covered by **Rule 17** of the Federal Rules of Criminal Procedure and analogous state rules. The subpoena power technically belongs to the court, but essentially either party can issue a subpoena in the court's name. Pursuant to Rule 17, a party obtains a blank, signed subpoena from the court's clerk and then fills out the name of the witness and the date on which the witness must appear and/or bring the requested documents or items. The attorney then needs to make sure the subpoena is served on the witness. Usually, the prosecutor has law enforcement officers serve the subpoena, while defense attorneys may serve it themselves or assign a member of their office to serve it.

Once a witness has been served, they are legally compelled to come to trial and/or bring the requested documents or items to court. The witness can move to quash the subpoena if she believes it is unreasonable, but most witnesses comply with the order. Technically the subpoena only requires the witness to testify at trial (or bring the item to the court for use at trial), but once the witness has been served, the attorney can usually convince the witness to come to her office a few hours before the trial begins to discuss her testimony. In addition, the threat of a subpoena can frequently persuade otherwise reluctant witnesses to come to the attorney's office and discuss the case in advance of trial.

In felony cases, the prosecutor also has the opportunity to issue a subpoena for the grand jury. The procedure for issuing the subpoena is the same as for trial, but the date on the subpoena is the date of the grand jury presentation (which is usually scheduled by the prosecutor). By subpoenaing witnesses for the grand jury, the prosecutor is able to meet with all her witnesses at a very early stage of the case. As with the trial subpoena, the grand jury subpoena technically only requires the witness to enter the grand jury room and testify, but once a witness has been subpoenaed, they are usually willing to come to the prosecutor's office to discuss the case before their testimony. In most jurisdictions, the defense attorney has no power to call witnesses before the grand jury and so no subpoena power to use (or threaten) until the trial date.

The second tool that facilitates the gathering of information, and one which is available exclusively to prosecutors, is the ability to grant **immunity** to an individual in exchange for their cooperation and/or testimony. Frequently a potential witness is also a participant in the crime who will be unwilling to talk about the case out of fear of incriminating himself. In these situations, the prosecutor essentially enters into a contract with the potential witness, guaranteeing protection from prosecution. There are two kinds of immunity: **use immunity** and **transactional immunity.** "Use immunity" is the weaker of the two; it means that the prosecutor cannot use any of the statements that the witness makes against him in any later prosecution. However, if the prosecutor obtains evidence independent of the statements, the prosecutor is not barred from proceeding with a prosecution using that independent evidence. Most—but not all—grants of use immunity also include "derivative use immunity," which also prevents the prosecutor from using evidence that was derived from the witness' statements—that is, evidence that was found only as a result of the statements being made. "Transactional immunity" is much broader and less common; it guarantees the witness complete immunity from prosecution for the criminal activity under discussion. It essentially is a promise by the government that it will never prosecute the witness for the crimes for which the witness is providing evidence. It is extraordinarily rare for any defense attorney to allow his client to speak to the prosecutor about anything unless some type of immunity is granted first. Thus, before the prosecutor meets with the witness, she and the witness' defense attorney will work out ahead of time which type of immunity is being granted.

The final tool used to encourage witness cooperation, which is also only available to prosecutors, is the use of **plea bargaining.** If a potential witness is a co-participant, or perhaps has been arrested for an unrelated crime, the prosecutor can offer to allow the witness to plead to a reduced charge, or to recommend a light sentence, in exchange for information and testimony.

Of course, offering lenient plea deals in exchange for information and testimony has its risks—the stronger the inducement, the more likely it is that the witness will manufacture information in order to please the prosecutor. And, any deals that are made—whether for immunity or for a better plea bargain—must be disclosed to the defense attorney, so the jury is certain to hear about them. Nevertheless, these remain important tools when a prosecutor is faced with a number of potential witnesses who are all initially unwilling to cooperate because of their own potential criminal liability.

Quick Summary

The *Brady* rule states that the prosecutor must disclose all exculpatory and material information to the defendant. This includes any information that can be used to impeach the prosecutor's witnesses. Exculpatory information will only be deemed "material" if there is a "reasonable probability" that it would have changed the outcome of the trial; or to put it another way, if the defendant did not receive a fair trial in the absence of the disclosure. The prosecutor may not intentionally destroy evidence (such as DNA evidence) that she knows may exonerate the defendant, but she has no affirmative duty to obtain such evidence, and the loss of such evidence through negligence is not a *Brady* violation.

The Supreme Court has held that it does not violate the defendant's right against self-incrimination to require the defendant to disclose some information about his case. However, the Court has stated that the defendant's discovery obligations cannot exceed the prosecutor's discovery obligations.

All other discovery rules are either mandated by the criminal rules and statutes of the applicable jurisdiction, or are found in the local rules of the applicable court.

The federal discovery rules are primarily governed by Rule 16, which requires both sides to disclose expert reports and any tangible items or documents that they intend to admit at trial. In addition, the prosecutor must disclose any of the defendant's statements that are within the control of the prosecutor. Rules 12.1, 12.2, and 12.3 require the defendant to provide information if he is presenting an alibi defense, an insanity defense, or a defense of acting on the authority of law enforcement. Finally, Rule 26.2 requires each side to turn over any prior statements made by their witnesses, although this disclosure is technically not required until after the witnesses have testified on direct.

If a party is found to have violated its discovery obligations, courts have various methods of enforcing the rules. The most common response is to order the party to immediately disclose and to grant the opposing party a continuance in order to give the opposing party a chance to examine and prepare for the newly disclosed information. The court can also bar the non-disclosed evidence from trial, instruct a jury that it can draw a negative inference because of the non-disclosure, and/or sanction the attorney. In egregious cases, the court can grant a mistrial.

Many state disclosure rules are more liberal than the federal rules, and they may require disclosure of all witness names and contact information, early disclosure of all witness statements, and prior criminal records of all witnesses. In addition, the defendant may be required to cooperate with the prosecutor by providing samples from his body or to submit to a medical exam.

Review Questions

1. Drugs in Hartford. Liane Rousseau was arrested by the Drug Enforcement Agency ("DEA") after a long-term investigation into a large drug organization in Hartford, Connecticut. After her arrest, Rousseau was indicted for conspiracy and possession of cocaine with intent to sell. The government alleged that Rousseau was part of a large organization involving ten to twelve individuals who were involved in importing, packaging, and selling cocaine on the streets. After her arraignment, Rousseau filed a request for discovery, seeking the following:

(a) The names of all the cooperating witnesses that the prosecutor intended to call at trial, as well as their prior criminal records;

(b) Copies of the notes that the DEA investigator made during Rousseau's interrogation after her arrest;

(c) Copies of the notes that the investigator made during the interrogation of her co-conspirators after their arrests;

(d) Testimony given by one of the cooperating witnesses in the grand jury in which he explicitly stated that Rousseau had no knowledge of the conspiracy; and

(e) Notification of whether the government used any wiretaps or other electronic surveillance during their investigation.

Which of these (if any) should the government turn over to the defense? If the government refuses to turn over information that the defendant believes she deserves, what should the defendant do?

2. Shortage of Body Armor. Meagan Woodall ran a company which was an independent contractor that provided the United States Army with body armor. In 2012, the Department of Justice conducted an audit of all military contractors and found some irregularities in Woodall's accounts. Specifically, the DOJ audit found evidence that in 2007, Woodall agreed to provide (and was paid for) 50,000 units of body armor, but only delivered 35,000 units. The DOJ also uncovered evidence that Kenny Johnson, an Army employee in charge of acquisition, worked with Woodall to commit this fraud by doctoring official army documents to inflate the number of units of body armor delivered by Woodall's company.

Both Woodall and Johnson were arrested in 2014, and Johnson pled guilty before trial. Woodall's theory of the case was that her company actually did deliver 50,000 units of body armor in 2007, and so she sought discovery of "all inventory records for the storage depots of the United States Army in the years 2007 and 2008." The government attempted to comply with this request, but learned that storage depot inventory records are routinely purged every five years. Consequently, the inventory records for 2007 and 2008 no longer existed. Woodall was eventually convicted, and she appealed the case, arguing that the government's failure to maintain the potentially exculpatory evidence of the storage depot inventories was a *Brady* violation. How should the appellate court rule?

3. Belated Brain Damage Diagnosis. Chris Ballard worked as an insurance broker selling insurance policies to corporations. He was indicted on multiple counts of mail fraud and wire fraud in connection with the alleged theft of over one million dollars from employee benefit plans that he sold and administered. His defense was that he lacked the *mens rea* necessary for a fraud conviction because he had suffered brain damage in an accident three years earlier. After his felony arraignment, Ballard requested discovery from the government under Rule 16(a) and gave notice under Rule 12.2(b) that he intended to present expert evidence of his medical condition. In response, the state requested discovery under Rule 16(b), including disclosure of a written summary of any expert testimony that the defendant sought to introduce. The defendant responded three months later, naming Dr. Grant Spordak as his expert witness and including a one-page report that listed the experiments that Dr. Spordak had conducted on Ballard. The government made another motion asking for more detailed information, but the defendant did not respond.

Two weeks later—and one week before trial—the trial court held a hearing to determine whether Dr. Spordak's scientific methods were reliable enough to be admissible at trial. The prosecutor asked Spordak on cross-examination what his conclusions were, and Spordak testified that he had diagnosed Ballard with a severe mental deficiency which made him unable to formulate complex plans. This was the first time that the prosecutor learned of Spordak's scientific conclusion.

The prosecutor filed a motion under Rule 16 to exclude Dr. Spordak's testimony at trial because his scientific methods were unreliable and because the defendant had failed to comply with Rule 16. Assume the trial court has concluded that Spordak's methods were sufficiently reliable. How should the court respond to the second part of the prosecutor's motion?

FROM THE COURTROOM

UNITED STATES v. BAGLEY

United States Supreme Court, 1985
473 U.S. 667

[Justice BLACKMUN delivered the opinion of the Court.]

[Justice WHITE filed an opinion concurring in part and concurring in the judgment, which was joined by Justice BURGER and Justice REHNQUIST.]

[Justice MARSHALL filed a dissenting opinion, which was joined by Justice BRENNAN.]

[Justice STEVENS filed a dissenting opinion,]

[Justice POWELL took no part in the decision of this case.]

In *Brady v. Maryland*, 373 U.S. 83, 87 (1963), this Court held that "the suppression by the prosecution of evidence favorable to an accused upon request violates due process where the evidence is material either to guilt or punishment." The issue in the present case concerns the standard of materiality to be applied in determining whether a conviction should be reversed because the prosecutor failed to disclose requested evidence that could have been used to impeach Government witnesses.

I

In October 1977, respondent Hughes Anderson Bagley was indicted in the Western District of Washington on 15 charges of violating federal narcotics and firearms statutes. On November 18, 24 days before trial, respondent filed a discovery motion. The sixth paragraph of that motion requested:

"The names and addresses of witnesses that the government intends to call at trial. Also the prior criminal records of witnesses, and any deals, promises or inducements made to witnesses in exchange for their testimony."

The Government's two principal witnesses at the trial were James F. O'Connor and Donald E. Mitchell. O'Connor and Mitchell were state law-enforcement officers employed by the Milwaukee Railroad as private security guards. Between April and June 1977, they assisted the federal Bureau of Alcohol, Tobacco and Firearms (ATF) in conducting an undercover investigation of respondent.

The Government's response to the discovery motion did not disclose that any "deals, promises or inducements" had been made to O'Connor or Mitchell. In apparent reply to a request in the motion's ninth paragraph for "[c]opies of all Jencks Act material," the Government produced a series of affidavits that O'Connor and Mitchell had signed between April 12 and May 4, 1977, while the undercover investigation was in progress. These affidavits recounted in detail the undercover dealings that O'Connor and Mitchell were having at the time with respondent. Each affidavit concluded with the statement, "I made this statement freely and voluntarily without any threats or rewards, or promises of reward having been made to me in return for it."

Respondent waived his right to a jury trial and was tried before the court in December 1977. At the trial, O'Connor and Mitchell testified about both the firearms and the narcotics charges. On December 23, the court found respondent guilty on the narcotics charges, but not guilty on the firearms charges.

In mid-1980, respondent filed requests for information pursuant to the Freedom of Information Act and to the Privacy Act of 1974, 5 U.S.C. §§ 552 and 552a. He received in response copies of ATF form contracts that O'Connor and Mitchell had signed on May 3, 1977. Each form was entitled "Contract for Purchase of Information and Payment of Lump Sum Therefor." The printed portion of the form stated that the vendor "will provide" information to ATF and that "upon receipt of such information by the Regional Director, Bureau of Alcohol, Tobacco and Firearms, or his representative, and upon the accomplishment of the objective sought to be obtained by the use of such information to the satisfaction of said Regional Director, the United States will pay to said vendor a sum commensurate with services and information rendered." Each form contained the following typewritten description of services:

"That he will provide information regarding T–I and other violations committed by Hughes A. Bagley, Jr.; that he will purchase evidence for ATF; that he will cut [sic] in an undercover capacity for ATF; that he will assist ATF in gathering of evidence and testify against the violator in federal court."

The figure "$300.00" was handwritten in each form on a line entitled "Sum to Be Paid to Vendor."

Because these contracts had not been disclosed to respondent in response to his pretrial discovery motion, respondent moved under 28 U.S.C. § 2255 to vacate his sentence. He alleged that the Government's failure to disclose the contracts, which he could have used to impeach O'Connor and Mitchell, violated his right to due process under *Brady v. Maryland.*

The motion came before the same District Judge who had presided at respondent's bench trial. An evidentiary hearing was held before a Magistrate. The Magistrate found that the printed form contracts were blank when O'Connor and Mitchell signed them and were not signed by an ATF representative until after the trial. He also found that on January 4, 1978, following the trial and decision in respondent's case, ATF made payments of $300 to both O'Connor and Mitchell pursuant to the contracts. Although the ATF case agent who dealt with O'Connor and Mitchell testified that these payments were compensation for expenses, the Magistrate found that this characterization was not borne out by the record. There was no documentation for expenses in these amounts; Mitchell testified that his payment was not for expenses, and the ATF forms authorizing the payments treated them as rewards.

. . .

The District Court found beyond a reasonable doubt . . . that had the existence of the agreements been disclosed to it during trial, the disclosure would have had no effect upon its finding that the Government had proved beyond a reasonable doubt that respondent was guilty of the offenses for which he had been convicted. The District Court reasoned: Almost all of the testimony of both witnesses was devoted to the firearms charges in the indictment. Respondent, however, was acquitted on those charges. The testimony of O'Connor and Mitchell concerning the narcotics charges was relatively very brief. On cross-examination, respondent's counsel did not seek to discredit their testimony as to the facts of distribution but rather sought to show that the controlled substances in question came from supplies that had been prescribed for respondent's personal use. The answers of O'Connor and Mitchell to this line of cross-examination tended to be favorable to respondent. Thus, the claimed impeachment evidence would not have been helpful to respondent and would not have affected the outcome of the trial. Accordingly, the District Court denied respondent's motion to vacate his sentence.

The United States Court of Appeals for the Ninth Circuit reversed. . . . The Court of Appeals apparently based its reversal . . . on the theory that the Government's failure to disclose the requested Brady information that respondent could have used to conduct an effective cross-examination impaired respondent's right to confront adverse witnesses.

. . . We granted certiorari . . . and we now reverse.

II

The holding in *Brady v. Maryland* requires disclosure only of evidence that is both favorable to the accused and "material either to guilt or to punishment." The Court explained in *United States v. Agurs*, 427 U.S. 97, 104, "A fair analysis of the holding in *Brady* indicates that implicit in the requirement of materiality is a concern that the suppressed evidence might have affected the outcome of the trial." . . .

The *Brady* rule is based on the requirement of due process. Its purpose is not to displace the adversary system as the primary means by which truth is uncovered, but to ensure that a miscarriage of justice does not occur. Thus, the prosecutor is not required to deliver his entire file to defense counsel, but only to disclose evidence favorable to the accused that, if suppressed, would deprive the defendant of a fair trial:

"For unless the omission deprived the defendant of a fair trial, there was no constitutional violation requiring that the verdict be set aside; and absent a constitutional violation, there was no breach of the prosecutor's constitutional duty to disclose . . . .

"But to reiterate a critical point, the prosecutor will not have violated his constitutional duty of disclosure unless his omission is of sufficient significance to result in the denial of the defendant's right to a fair trial."

In *Brady* and *Agurs*, the prosecutor failed to disclose exculpatory evidence. In the present case, the prosecutor failed to disclose evidence that the defense might have used to impeach the Government's witnesses by showing bias or interest. Impeachment evidence, however, as well as exculpatory evidence, falls within the *Brady* rule. Such evidence is "evidence favorable to an accused," so that, if disclosed and used effectively, it may make the difference between conviction and acquittal.

The Court of Appeals treated impeachment evidence as constitutionally different from exculpatory evidence. According to that court, failure to disclose impeachment evidence is "even more egregious" than failure to disclose exculpatory evidence "because it threatens the defendant's right to confront adverse witnesses." Relying on *Davis v. Alaska*, 415 U.S. 308, (1974), the Court of Appeals held that the Government's failure to disclose requested impeachment evidence that the defense could use to conduct an effective cross-examination of important prosecution witnesses constitutes "'constitutional error of the first magnitude'" requiring automatic reversal.

This Court has rejected any such distinction between impeachment evidence and exculpatory evidence. In *Giglio v. United States*, the Government failed to disclose impeachment evidence similar to the evidence at issue in the present case, that is, a promise made to the key Government witness that he would not be prosecuted if he testified for the Government. This Court said:

"When the 'reliability of a given witness may well be determinative of guilt or innocence,' nondisclosure of evidence affecting credibility falls within th[e] general rule [of *Brady*]. We do not, however, automatically require a new trial whenever 'a combing of the prosecutors' files after the trial has disclosed evidence possibly useful to the defense but not likely to have changed the verdict. . . .' A finding of materiality of the evidence is required under *Brady*. . . . A new trial is required if 'the false testimony could . . . in any reasonable likelihood have affected the judgment of the jury . . . .'"

Thus, the Court of Appeals' holding is inconsistent with our precedents.

Moreover, the court's reliance on *Davis v. Alaska* for its "automatic reversal" rule is misplaced. In Davis, the defense sought to cross-examine a crucial prosecution witness concerning his probationary status as a juvenile delinquent. The defense intended by this cross-examination to show that the witness might have made a faulty identification of the defendant in order to shift suspicion away from himself or because he feared that his probationary status would be jeopardized if he did not satisfactorily assist the police and prosecutor in obtaining a conviction. Pursuant to a state rule of procedure and a state statute making juvenile adjudications inadmissible, the trial judge prohibited the defense from conducting the cross-examination. This Court reversed the defendant's conviction, ruling that the direct restriction on the scope of cross-examination denied the defendant "the right of effective cross-examination which 'would be constitutional error of the first magnitude and no amount of showing of want of prejudice would cure it.'"

The present case, in contrast, does not involve any direct restriction on the scope of cross-examination. The defense was free to cross-examine the witnesses on any relevant subject, including possible bias or interest resulting from inducements made by the Government. The constitutional error, if any, in this case was the Government's failure to assist the defense by disclosing information that might have been helpful in conducting the cross-examination. As discussed above, such suppression of evidence amounts to a constitutional violation only if it deprives the defendant of a fair trial. Consistent with "our overriding concern with the justice of the finding of guilt," a constitutional error occurs, and the conviction must be reversed, only if the evidence is material in the sense that its suppression undermines confidence in the outcome of the trial.

III

A

It remains to determine the standard of materiality applicable to the nondisclosed evidence at issue in this case. Our starting point is the framework for evaluating the materiality of *Brady* evidence established in *United States v. Agurs*. The Court in *Agurs* distinguished three situations involving the discovery, after trial, of information favorable to the accused that had been known to the prosecution but unknown to the defense. The first situation was the prosecutor's knowing use of perjured testimony or, equivalently, the prosecutor's knowing failure to disclose that testimony used to convict the defendant was false. The Court noted the well-established rule that "a conviction obtained by the knowing use of perjured testimony is fundamentally unfair, and must be set aside if there is any reasonable likelihood that the false testimony could have affected the judgment of the jury." Although this rule is stated in terms that treat the knowing use of perjured testimony as error subject to harmless-error review, it may as easily be stated as a materiality standard under which the fact that testimony is perjured is considered material unless failure to disclose it would be harmless beyond a reasonable doubt. The Court in *Agurs* justified this standard of materiality on the ground that the knowing use of perjured testimony involves prosecutorial misconduct and, more importantly, involves "a corruption of the truth-seeking function of the trial process."

At the other extreme is the situation in *Agurs* itself, where the defendant does not make a *Brady* request and the prosecutor fails to disclose certain evidence favorable to the accused. The Court rejected a harmless-error rule in that situation, because under that rule every nondisclosure is treated as error, thus imposing on the prosecutor a constitutional duty to deliver his entire file to defense counsel. At the same time, the Court rejected a standard that would require the defendant to demonstrate that the evidence if disclosed probably would have resulted in acquittal. The Court reasoned: "If the standard applied to the usual motion for a new trial based on newly discovered evidence were the same when the evidence was in the State's possession as when it was found in a neutral source, there would be no special significance to the prosecutor's obligation to serve the cause of justice." The standard of materiality applicable in the absence of a specific *Brady* request is therefore stricter than the harmless-error standard but more lenient to the defense than the newly-discovered-evidence standard.

The third situation identified by the Court in *Agurs* is where the defense makes a specific request and the prosecutor fails to disclose responsive evidence. The Court did not define the standard of materiality applicable in this situation, but suggested that the standard might be more lenient to the defense than in the situation in which the defense makes no request or only a general request. The Court also noted: "When the prosecutor receives a specific and relevant request, the failure to make any response is seldom, if ever, excusable."

The Court has relied on and reformulated the *Agurs* standard for the materiality of undisclosed evidence in two subsequent cases arising outside the *Brady* context. In neither case did the Court's discussion of the *Agurs* standard distinguish among the three situations described in *Agurs*. In *United States v. Valenzuela-Bernal*, 458 U.S. 858 (1982), the Court held that due process is violated when testimony is made unavailable to the defense by Government deportation of witnesses "only if there is a reasonable likelihood that the testimony could have affected the judgment of the trier of fact." And in *Strickland v. Washington*, 466 U.S. 668 (1984), the Court held that a new trial must be granted when evidence is not introduced because of the incompetence of counsel only if "there is a reasonable probability that, but for counsel's unprofessional errors, the result of the proceeding would have been different." The *Strickland* Court defined a "reasonable probability" as "a probability sufficient to undermine confidence in the outcome."

We find the *Strickland* formulation of the *Agurs* test for materiality sufficiently flexible to cover the "no request," "general request," and "specific request" cases of prosecutorial failure to disclose evidence favorable to the accused: The evidence is material only if there is a reasonable probability that, had the evidence been disclosed to the defense, the result of the proceeding would have been different. A "reasonable probability" is a probability sufficient to undermine confidence in the outcome.

The Government suggests that a materiality standard more favorable to the defendant reasonably might be adopted in specific request cases. The Government notes that an incomplete response to a specific request not only deprives the defense of certain evidence, but also has the effect of representing to the defense that the evidence does not exist. In reliance on this misleading representation, the defense might abandon lines of independent investigation, defenses, or trial strategies that it otherwise would have pursued.

We agree that the prosecutor's failure to respond fully to a *Brady* request may impair the adversary process in this manner. And the more specifically the defense requests certain evidence, thus putting the prosecutor on notice of its value, the more reasonable it is for the defense to assume from the nondisclosure that the evidence does not exist, and to make pretrial and trial decisions on the basis of this assumption. This possibility of impairment does not necessitate a different standard of materiality, however, for under the Strickland formulation the reviewing court may consider directly any adverse effect that the prosecutor's failure to respond might have had on the preparation or presentation of the defendant's case. The reviewing court should assess the possibility that such effect might have occurred in light of the totality of the circumstances and with an awareness of the difficulty of reconstructing in a post-trial proceeding the course that the defense and the trial would have taken had the defense not been misled by the prosecutor's incomplete response.

B

In the present case, we think that there is a significant likelihood that the prosecutor's response to respondent's discovery motion misleadingly induced defense counsel to believe that O'Connor and Mitchell could not be impeached on the basis of bias or interest arising from inducements offered by the Government. Defense counsel asked the prosecutor to disclose any inducements that had been made to witnesses, and the prosecutor failed to disclose that the possibility of a reward had been held out to O'Connor and Mitchell if the information they supplied led to "the accomplishment of the objective sought to be obtained . . . to the satisfaction of [the Government]." This possibility of a reward gave O'Connor and Mitchell a direct, personal stake in respondent's conviction. The fact that the stake was not guaranteed through a promise or binding contract, but was expressly contingent on the Government's satisfaction with the end result, served only to strengthen any incentive to testify falsely in order to secure a conviction. Moreover, the prosecutor disclosed affidavits that stated that O'Connor and Mitchell received no promises of reward in return for providing information in the affidavits implicating respondent in criminal activity. In fact, O'Connor and Mitchell signed the last of these affidavits the very day after they signed the ATF contracts. While the Government is technically correct that the blank contracts did not constitute a "promise of reward," the natural effect of these affidavits would be misleadingly to induce defense counsel to believe that O'Connor and Mitchell provided the information in the affidavits, and ultimately their testimony at trial recounting the same information, without any "inducements."

The District Court, nonetheless, found beyond a reasonable doubt that, had the information that the Government held out the possibility of reward to its witnesses been disclosed, the result of the criminal prosecution would not have been different. If this finding were sustained by the Court of Appeals, the information would be immaterial even under the standard of materiality applicable to the prosecutor's knowing use of perjured testimony. Although the express holding of the Court of Appeals was that the nondisclosure in this case required automatic reversal, the Court of Appeals also stated that it "disagreed" with the District Court's finding of harmless error. In particular, the Court of Appeals appears to have disagreed with the factual premise on which this finding expressly was based. The District Court reasoned that O'Connor's and Mitchell's testimony was exculpatory on the narcotics charges. The Court of Appeals, however, concluded, after reviewing the record, that O'Connor's and Mitchell's testimony was in fact inculpatory on those charges. Accordingly, we reverse the judgment of the Court of Appeals and remand the case to that court for a determination whether there is a reasonable probability that, had the inducement offered by the Government to O'Connor and Mitchell been disclosed to the defense, the result of the trial would have been different.

It is so ordered.

[The concurring opinion of Justice WHITE is omitted.]

Justice MARSHALL, with whom Justice BRENNAN joins, dissenting.

When the Government withholds from a defendant evidence that might impeach the prosecution's only witnesses, that failure to disclose cannot be deemed harmless error. Because that is precisely the nature of the undisclosed evidence in this case, I would affirm the judgment of the Court of Appeals and would not remand for further proceedings.

I

. . .

Whenever the Government fails, in response to a request, to disclose impeachment evidence relating to the credibility of its key witnesses, the truth-finding process of trial is necessarily thrown askew. The failure to disclose evidence affecting the overall credibility of witnesses corrupts the process to some degree in all instances, but when "the 'reliability of a given witness may well be determinative of guilt or innocence,'" and when "the Government's case depend[s] almost entirely on" the testimony of a certain witness, evidence of that witness' possible bias simply may not be said to be irrelevant, or its omission harmless. . . .

II

Instead of affirming, the Court today chooses to reverse and remand the case for application of its newly stated standard to the facts of this case. While I believe that the evidence at issue here, which remained undisclosed despite a particular request, undoubtedly was material under the Court's standard, I also have serious doubts whether the Court's definition of the constitutional right at issue adequately takes account of the interests this Court sought to protect in its decision in *Brady v. Maryland*, 373 U.S. 83 (1963).

A

I begin from the fundamental premise, which hardly bears repeating, that "[t]he purpose of a trial is as much the acquittal of an innocent person as it is the conviction of a guilty one." When evidence favorable to the defendant is known to exist, disclosure only enhances the quest for truth; it takes no direct toll on that inquiry. Moreover, the existence of any small piece of evidence favorable to the defense may, in a particular case, create just the doubt that prevents the jury from returning a verdict of guilty. The private whys and wherefores of jury deliberations pose an impenetrable barrier to our ability to know just which piece of information might make, or might have made, a difference.

When the state does not disclose information in its possession that might reasonably be considered favorable to the defense, it precludes the trier of fact from gaining access to such information and thereby undermines the reliability of the verdict. Unlike a situation in which exculpatory evidence exists but neither the defense nor the prosecutor has uncovered it, in this situation the state already has, resting in its files, material that would be of assistance to the defendant. With a minimum of effort, the state could improve the real and apparent fairness of the trial enormously, by assuring that the defendant may place before the trier of fact favorable evidence known to the government. This proposition is not new. We have long recognized that, within the limit of the state's ability to identify so-called exculpatory information, the state's concern for a fair verdict precludes it from withholding from the defense evidence favorable to the defendant's case in the prosecutor's files.

This recognition no doubt stems in part from the frequently considerable imbalance in resources between most criminal defendants and most prosecutors' offices. Many, perhaps most, criminal defendants in the United States are represented by appointed counsel, who often are paid minimal wages and operate on shoestring budgets. In addition, unlike police, defense counsel generally is not present at the scene of the crime, or at the time of arrest, but instead comes into the case late. Moreover, unlike the government, defense counsel is not in the position to make deals with witnesses to gain evidence. Thus, an inexperienced, unskilled, or unaggressive attorney often is unable to amass the factual support necessary to a reasonable defense. When favorable evidence is in the hands of the prosecutor but not disclosed, the result may well be that the defendant is deprived of a fair chance before the trier of fact, and the trier of fact is deprived of the ingredients necessary to a fair decision. This grim reality, of course, poses a direct challenge to the traditional model of the adversary criminal process, and perhaps because this reality so directly questions the fairness of our longstanding processes, change has been cautious and halting. Thus, the Court has not gone the full road and expressly required that the state provide to the defendant access to the prosecutor's complete files, or investigators who will assure that the defendant has an opportunity to discover every existing piece of helpful evidence. Instead, in acknowledgment of the fact that important interests are served when potentially favorable evidence is disclosed, the Court has fashioned a compromise, requiring that the prosecution identify and disclose to the defendant favorable material that it possesses. This requirement is but a small, albeit important; step toward equality of justice.

B

Brady v. Maryland, of course, established this requirement of disclosure as a fundamental element of a fair trial by holding that a defendant was denied due process if he was not given access to favorable evidence that is material either to guilt or punishment. Since *Brady* was decided, this Court has struggled, in a series of decisions, to define how best to effectuate the right recognized. To my mind, the *Brady* decision, the reasoning that underlay it, and the fundamental interest in a fair trial, combine to give the criminal defendant the right to receive from the prosecutor, and the prosecutor the affirmative duty to turn over to the defendant, all information known to the government that might reasonably be considered favorable to the defendant's case. Formulation of this right, and imposition of this duty, are "the essence of due process of law. It is the State that tries a man, and it is the State that must insure that the trial is fair." If that right is denied, or if that duty is shirked, however, I believe a reviewing court should not automatically reverse but instead should apply the harmless-error test the Court has developed for instances of error affecting constitutional rights.

My view is based in significant part on the reality of criminal practice and on the consequently inadequate protection to the defendant that a different rule would offer. To implement *Brady*, courts must of course work within the confines of the criminal process. Our system of criminal justice is animated by two seemingly incompatible notions: the adversary model, and the state's primary concern with justice, not convictions. *Brady*, of course, reflects the latter goal of justice, and is in some ways at odds with the competing model of a sporting event. Our goal, then, must be to integrate the *Brady* right into the harsh, daily reality of this apparently discordant criminal process.

At the trial level, the duty of the state to effectuate *Brady* devolves into the duty of the prosecutor; the dual role that the prosecutor must play poses a serious obstacle to implementing *Brady*. The prosecutor is by trade, if not necessity, a zealous advocate. He is a trained attorney who must aggressively seek convictions in court on behalf of a victimized public. At the same time, as a representative of the state, he must place foremost in his hierarchy of interests the determination of truth. Thus, for purposes of *Brady*, the prosecutor must abandon his role as an advocate and pore through his files, as objectively as possible, to identify the material that could undermine his case. Given this obviously unharmonious role, it is not surprising that these advocates oftentimes overlook or downplay potentially favorable evidence, often in cases in which there is no doubt that the failure to disclose was a result of absolute good faith. Indeed, one need only think of the Fourth Amendment's requirement of a neutral intermediary, who tests the strength of the policeman-advocate's facts, to recognize the curious status *Brady* imposes on a prosecutor. . . .

The prosecutor surely greets the moment at which he must turn over Brady material with little enthusiasm. In perusing his files, he must make the often difficult decision as to whether evidence is favorable, and must decide on which side to err when faced with doubt. In his role as advocate, the answers are clear. In his role as representative of the state, the answers should be equally clear, and often to the contrary. Evidence that is of doubtful worth in the eyes of the prosecutor could be of inestimable value to the defense, and might make the difference to the trier of fact.

Once the prosecutor suspects that certain information might have favorable implications for the defense, either because it is potentially exculpatory or relevant to credibility, I see no reason why he should not be required to disclose it. After all, favorable evidence indisputably enhances the truth-seeking process at trial. And it is the job of the defense, not the prosecution, to decide whether and in what way to use arguably favorable evidence. In addition, to require disclosure of all evidence that might reasonably be considered favorable to the defendant would have the precautionary effect of assuring that no information of potential consequence is mistakenly overlooked. By requiring full disclosure of favorable evidence in this way, courts could begin to assure that a possibly dispositive piece of information is not withheld from the trier of fact by a prosecutor who is torn between the two roles he must play. A clear rule of this kind, coupled with a presumption in favor of disclosure, also would facilitate the prosecutor's admittedly difficult task by removing a substantial amount of unguided discretion.

If a trial will thereby be more just, due process would seem to require such a rule absent a countervailing interest. I see little reason for the government to keep such information from the defendant. Its interest in nondisclosure at the trial stage is at best slight: the government apparently seeks to avoid the administrative hassle of disclosure, and to prevent disclosure of inculpatory evidence that might result in witness intimidation and manufactured rebuttal evidence. Neither of these concerns, however, counsels in favor of a rule of nondisclosure in close or ambiguous cases. To the contrary, a rule simplifying the disclosure decision by definition does not make that decision more complex. Nor does disclosure of favorable evidence inevitably lead to disclosure of inculpatory evidence, as might an open file policy, or to the anticipated wrongdoings of defendants and their lawyers, if indeed such fears are warranted. We have other mechanisms for disciplining unscrupulous defense counsel; hamstringing their clients need not be one of them. I simply do not find any state interest that warrants withholding from a presumptively innocent defendant, whose liberty is at stake in the proceeding, information that bears on his case and that might enable him to defend himself.

Under the foregoing analysis, the prosecutor's duty is quite straightforward: he must divulge all evidence that reasonably appears favorable to the defendant, erring on the side of disclosure.

C

. . .

The standard for disclosure that the Court articulates today enables prosecutors to avoid disclosing obviously exculpatory evidence while acting well within the bounds of their constitutional obligation. . . .

The Court's definition poses other, serious problems. Besides legitimizing the nondisclosure of clearly favorable evidence, the standard set out by the Court also asks the prosecutor to predict what effect various pieces of evidence will have on the trial. He must evaluate his case and the case of the defendant—of which he presumably knows very little—and perform the impossible task of deciding whether a certain piece of information will have a significant impact on the trial, bearing in mind that a defendant will later shoulder the heavy burden of proving how it would have affected the outcome. At best, this standard places on the prosecutor a responsibility to speculate, at times without foundation, since the prosecutor will not normally know what strategy the defense will pursue or what evidence the defense will find useful. At worst, the standard invites a prosecutor, whose interests are conflicting, to gamble, to play the odds, and to take a chance that evidence will later turn out not to have been potentially dispositive. . . .

The Court's standard also encourages the prosecutor to assume the role of the jury, and to decide whether certain evidence will make a difference. In our system of justice, that decision properly and wholly belongs to the jury. The prosecutor, convinced of the guilt of the defendant and of the truthfulness of his witnesses, may all too easily view as irrelevant or unpersuasive evidence that draws his own judgments into question. Accordingly he will decide the evidence need not be disclosed. But the ideally neutral trier of fact, who approaches the case from a wholly different perspective, is by the prosecutor's decision denied the opportunity to consider the evidence. The reviewing court, faced with a verdict of guilty, evidence to support that verdict, and pressures, again understandable, to finalize criminal judgments, is in little better position to review the withheld evidence than the prosecutor.

I simply cannot agree with the Court that the due process right to favorable evidence recognized in *Brady* was intended to become entangled in prosecutorial determinations of the likelihood that particular information would affect the outcome of trial. Almost a decade of lower court practice with *Agurs* convinces me that courts and prosecutors have come to pay "too much deference to the federal common law policy of discouraging discovery in criminal cases, and too little regard to due process of law for defendants." Apparently anxious to assure that reversals are handed out sparingly, the Court has defined a rigorous test of materiality. Eager to apply the "materiality" standard at the pretrial stage, as the Court permits them to do, prosecutors lose sight of the basic principles underlying the doctrine. I would return to the original theory and promise of *Brady* and reassert the duty of the prosecutor to disclose all evidence in his files that might reasonably be considered favorable to the defendant's case. prosecutor can know prior to trial whether such evidence will be of consequence at trial; the mere fact that it might be, however, suffices to mandate disclosure.

D

In so saying, I recognize that a failure to divulge favorable information should not result in reversal in all cases. It may be that a conviction should be affirmed on appeal despite the prosecutor's failure to disclose evidence that reasonably might have been deemed potentially favorable prior to trial. The state's interest in nondisclosure at trial is minimal, and should therefore yield to the readily apparent benefit that full disclosure would convey to the search for truth. After trial, however, the benefits of disclosure may at times be tempered by the state's legitimate desire to avoid retrial when error has been harmless. However, in making the determination of harmlessness, I would apply our normal constitutional error test and reverse unless it is clear beyond a reasonable doubt that the withheld evidence would not have affected the outcome of the trial.

. . .

[The dissenting opinion of Justice STEVENS is omitted.]

40

Joinder and Severance

Key Concepts

- Joinder of Offenses Allowed if Same Character, Same Act, or Common Scheme
- Joinder of Defendants Allowed if Charged with Same Series of Acts or Transactions
- Severance Required if Defendant Demonstrates Severe Prejudice
- *Bruton* Rule Mandates Severance if Prosecutor Admits Co-Defendant's Confession and Co-Defendant Does Not Testify

A. Introduction and Policy. In the most basic charging instrument, the prosecutor charges one defendant with one crime, and the case proceeds to trial on a single charge. However, most cases are not this simple. The defendant may have been arrested for multiple crimes, or there may have been several defendants arrested for committing the same crime. Thus, a question arises as to when a charging instrument can contain multiple counts (known as "joinder of offenses") and/or charge multiple defendants (known as "joinder of defendants.")

As with most pleading issues, this may at first appear to be a mundane technical question. However, there are important policy considerations surrounding the question of joinder. On the one hand, assuming the different charges are related in some way, joining multiple charges or defendants into one charging instrument—and thus being able to try them all together in one proceeding—provides multiple advantages to the prosecution and to the court system:

1. Promoting efficiency and saving court resources;
2. Lessening the chances of inconsistent verdicts for identical conduct; and
3. Decreasing the inconvenience to witnesses who would otherwise have to testify in multiple trials.

On the other hand, including multiple charges and/or defendants in the same charging instrument carries certain risks for the defendants. The potential for prejudice can be divided into the following four categories:

1. **Spillover of Evidence.** In the case of joint charges, this problem arises when evidence admissible as to one of the charges may not be admissible as to another. The judge will give the jurors a limiting instruction, ordering them to ignore the evidence for any charge to which it does not relate; but this is a notoriously difficult instruction for jurors to follow.

   A similar problem arises with joint defendants. Evidence admissible against one defendant may be inadmissible against the other. Again, the jurors will be given a limiting instruction, but they may not be able to comply with it. This is especially true if the incriminating evidence is a confession by one of the defendants, as it will be particularly difficult for a jury to ignore a co-defendant's confession.

2. **Guilt by Association.** In the context of joint charges, a defendant may be charged with dozens of crimes in one charging instrument. A jury who sees all of these charges may assume that the defendant must be guilty of something, since he has been accused of so many crimes. Thus, whereas jurors may be willing to stick to the "beyond a reasonable doubt" standard for a defendant charged with one crime, if they see that an accused has been charged with ten or twelve crimes, they may at least subconsciously be more willing to return a guilty verdict on at least one charge.

   This problem can be even more severe in the context of joint defendants. The evidence of guilt may be very strong as to one of the defendants, but relatively weak with regard to the co-defendant. Even if the jurors are able to follow the limiting instructions and keep the evidence against each defendant separate, once the jurors conclude that one of the defendants is guilty, they may be more inclined to find the co-defendant guilty because of his association with the first defendant.

3. **Inconsistent Defenses.** The defendant may have inconsistent defenses for different charges. For example, the defendant may have an excellent claim of self-defense for one of the charges, but a strong insanity defense for another charge. Because presenting both defenses may weaken the persuasive power of each, the defendant may be forced to choose between the two.

   Once again, this problem can be exacerbated with multiple defendants when the defendants want to use defenses that are inconsistent with one another. For example, both defendants may want to argue that their co-defendant was the primary wrongdoer. Or, one defendant may want to claim self-defense while the other wants to claim mistaken identity for the same incident. If the defendants were together at the time of the crime, the presentation of both defenses will make it difficult for the jury to accept either.

4. Self-Incrimination. Finally, the defendant may want to testify in his own defense for one of the charges, but not for the others. This selective introduction of testimony, however, will not be possible. Generally, a defendant waives his right against self-incrimination entirely once he testifies at trial. If multiple charges are joined together, the defendant would have to persuade the judge that even though he is testifying about one of the charges, he should retain his right against self-incrimination on other charges.

A similar problem arises in the case of joint defendants. The defendant may want to call his co-defendant as a witness to support the defendant's story. However, the co-defendant has a right under the Fifth Amendment not to testify, and so may refuse to take the stand, thus depriving the first defendant of important evidence.

As noted earlier, the prosecutor makes the initial determination of which charges and defendants should be prosecuted together when she draws up the original charging instrument. As the case progresses, however, the prosecutor may seek to join new charges or different defendants to the charging instrument. More commonly, the defendant may seek to alter the charging instrument. He may try to sever charges into different charging instruments, or sever his case from that of his co-defendants so that each defendant is charged separately and tried in separate proceedings. Less commonly, a defendant may move to consolidate charges, so that he does not have to stand trial for similar or related offenses more than once.

B. The Law. The law of joinder and severance is essentially the rules governing when a prosecutor is allowed to include multiple charges or multiple defendants on the same charging instrument, and the rules governing when the defendant is allowed to force the prosecutor to place charges or defendants on separate charging instruments or consolidate separate charges onto the same charging instrument. Joinder and severance law is based almost entirely on the relevant jurisdiction's Rules of Criminal Procedure. However, when two or more defendants are joined, there is also a significant constitutional issue related to the Confrontation Clause.

First, we will look at the Federal Rules of Criminal Procedure:

Rule 8.

Joinder of Offenses or Defendants.

(a) **Joinder of Offenses.** The indictment or information may charge a defendant in separate counts with 2 or more offenses if the offenses charged—whether felonies or misdemeanors or both—are of the same or similar character, or are based on the same act or transaction, or are connected with or constitute parts of a common scheme or plan.

(b) **Joinder of Defendants.** The indictment or information may charge 2 or more defendants if they are alleged to have participated in the same act or transaction, or in the same series of acts or transactions, constituting an offense or offenses. The defendants may be charged in one or more counts together or separately. All defendants need not be charged in each count.

Rule 13.

Joint Trial of Separate Cases

The court may order that separate cases be tried together as though brought in a single indictment or information if all offenses and all defendants could have been joined in a single indictment or information.

Rule 14.

Relief from Prejudicial Joinder.

(a) **Relief.** If the joinder of offenses or defendants in an indictment, an information, or a consolidation for trial appears to prejudice a defendant or the government, the court may order separate trials of counts, sever the defendants' trials, or provide any other relief that justice requires.

(b) **Defendant's Statements.** Before ruling on a defendant's motion to sever, the court may order an attorney for the government to deliver to the court for in camera inspection any defendant's statement that the government intends to use as evidence.

If a defendant brings a motion to sever charges or defendants, the first step in the analysis is to determine whether the prosecutor had the right to join in the first place. For joinder to be appropriate, the charges must be "of the same or similar character, . . . based on the same act or transaction, or . . . connected with or constitut[ing] parts of a common scheme or plan."[1] Multiple defendants must be "alleged to have participated in the same act or transaction or . . . same series of acts or transactions."[2] If the court finds that the initial joinder was improper, the request for severance should be granted.

---

[1] Fed. R. Crim. Proc. 8(a).

[2] Fed. R. Crim. Proc. 8(b).

If the original joinder was proper, the second step is to determine whether the defendant is prejudiced by the joinder. As discussed below in Section C.2., there must be a significant amount of prejudice to justify severance, not merely a greater chance of conviction. The prosecutor can also move to sever offenses or parties based on prejudice, but this is rarely done since the prosecutor was the one who made the initial decision to join when she originally charged the case.

Finally, Rule 13 allows a court to combine multiple cases for trial if the judge determines that the charges or defendants could originally have been charged together on the same charging instrument. In effect, the judge is overruling the prosecutor's decision to bring separate charges. The judge could make this decision in response to a defendant's motion to consolidate or may decide on her own to consolidate. In either case, the decision rests within the broad discretion of the trial court.

The law of joinder and severance also implicates constitutional concerns when two defendants are being tried together:

The *Bruton* Rule

If two defendants are being tried together and one has confessed to the crime, implicating both himself and his co-defendant, the confession is inadmissible in their joint trial unless:

1. The confessing defendant chooses to testify; or
2. The confession can be redacted to remove all mention or implication that the non-confessing co-defendant was involved.[3]

This rule—known as **the *Bruton* rule**—is based on the Confrontation Clause of the Sixth Amendment. If the first defendant's confession is admitted and implicates the second defendant, the second defendant deserves the right to confront the first defendant by cross-examining him about the statement. However, the first defendant has an absolute right under the Fifth Amendment not to testify. If he chooses to exercise this right nobody—neither the prosecutor nor the co-defendant—can force him to take the stand. Thus, admitting the first defendant's statement violates the second defendant's right to confront his accuser. The only solution is either to redact the first defendant's statement to remove all mention or implication of the first defendant or to sever the trials and try each defendant separately. We will explore the *Bruton* rule further in Section C.3, below.

[3] Bruton v. United States, 391 U.S. 123 (1968).

C. Applying the Law.

1. Should Offenses/Defendants Be Joined? Under Rule 8 of the Federal Rules of Criminal Procedure, different offenses may be joined in the same charging instrument if:

1. They are of the same or similar character; or
2. They are based on the same act or transaction; or
3. They are connected with or constitute parts of a common scheme or plan.

The second and third reasons are relatively straightforward: if the defendant commits an assault, a kidnapping, and a rape against the same victim during the course of the same incident, it makes sense to charge all three of those crimes together. Or, if the defendant robs two people at gunpoint at the same time, or detonates a bomb that kills five people, the crimes should be charged and tried together because they are based on the same criminal act or plan. Courts interpret the "same act or transaction" language broadly to encompass even criminal activity that stretches over a number of days. For example, if the prosecutor charges the defendant with conspiracy to commit a crime, and then with the underlying crime itself, the charges are part of the same act or transaction. As one court put it, "transaction" is "generally construed to embrace a series of occurrences or an aggregate of acts which are logically related to a single course of criminal conduct."[4]

Likewise, courts will broadly interpret "common scheme or plan" to include separate crimes, if those crimes share a mutual and distinctive *modus operandi*:

> **Example:** Defendant was charged with two counts of unlawful possession of stolen mail. The evidence showed that on two separate occasions the defendant recruited a teenage girl to help him. Each time he drove a girl to a location where she could get a false identification card, paid for the card, and then drove her to a store, where she used the false identification card to cash a state welfare check that had been stolen from the mail. The defendant admitted that he drove the girls from place to place, but denied providing them with any funds or stolen checks, and denied any knowledge of what they were doing at each location.
>
> The defendant moved to sever the charges, and his motion was denied. After the defendant was convicted of both counts of unlawful possession of stolen mail, he appealed the case, arguing that the counts were improperly joined.

[4] United States v. Baker, 14 M.J. 361 (U.S. Ct. of Mil. App. 1983).

Analysis: The appellate court held that the two crimes were properly joined. The two offenses were identical, and they demonstrated a common plan on the part of the defendant. The court went on to hold that the motion to sever was properly denied because the defendant did not show any prejudice from the joinder (as discussed in Section C.2, below).[5]

Allowing joinder for crimes based merely on the fact that the crimes are of "the same or similar character" (the first reason for joinder noted above) is somewhat more controversial. As we will see in the next section, it can be very prejudicial to a defendant if a jury hears that the defendant is accused of repeatedly committing the same type of crime. And, the usual justifications for joinder—saving resources, convenience to witnesses, and avoiding inconsistent verdicts—do not really apply if the only thing that links the crimes is that they are of the "same or similar character." Thus, most courts have held that joinder is only appropriate under the "same or similar character" provision if the crimes occurred over a relatively short period of time or if there is some amount of overlap in the evidence necessary to prove each crime.[6] For example, if the defendant is accused of multiple counts of transporting women for the purposes of prostitution over a five-month period, the joinder would makes sense if there was some overlap in the witnesses for each of the crimes.[7] Likewise, if a law enforcement team conducted a long-term investigation against the defendant and learned that he engaged in three unrelated instances of extorting money, the charges could be brought in the same charging instrument because the same law enforcement officers would be testifying for each case.

The rules for joinder of defendants, however, are narrower. Defendants can be joined in the same charging instrument only if:

a. The criminal conduct charged for each defendant is based on the same act or transaction; or

b. The criminal conduct charged for each defendant is based on the same series of acts or transactions.

There is no "same or similar character" or "common scheme or plan" provision for joining defendants. However, as long as the defendants' various criminal acts share some facts or participants, a court will likely determine that the initial joinder is proper. One way to ensure all the defendants' actions are based on the same transaction or series of transactions is to charge all the defendants with a conspiracy and then charge the underlying actions. Thus, multiple defendants are most commonly seen in conspiracy cases. However, the crimes need not be con-

[5] United States v. Jordan, 602 F.2d 171 (8th Cir. 1979).

[6] See, e.g., Johnson v. United States, 356 F.2d 680 (8th Cir. 1966).

[7] Id.

nected by a conspiracy count as long as they are part of the same act or series of actions. The general rule is if the defendants committed the crime together, they should be charged together. Thus, joint defendants can be found in any number of cases from robbery and drug sales to white collar crimes and racketeering.

In determining whether separate defendants have engaged in criminal conduct that is part of the same "series of acts or transactions," courts examine the facts underlying each of the charged offenses. If the facts are "so closely connected that proof of such facts is necessary to establish each offense, joinder of defendants and offenses is proper," but "when there is no substantial identity of facts or participants between the two offenses," there is no "series" of acts under the rule.[8] Accordingly, even if the crimes are similar and related in some way, there needs to be some showing that the defendants were acting together in order to join the defendants for trial:

> **Example:** Edward Partin was charged with various crimes of violence. Two individuals, Hugh and Tom, allegedly conspired to prevent an eyewitness from testifying against Partin. The government accused Hugh and Tom of intimidating the witness and threatening him unless he lied on the stand when testifying in Partin's case.
>
> Two other individuals, Harold and Ben, allegedly conspired to prevent a different eyewitness from testifying against Partin. The two of them paid the eyewitness money and then drove him out of the jurisdiction in order to ensure that he did not testify.
>
> Prosecutors learned of the different conspiracies and charged Hugh and Tom with one count of conspiracy and three underlying crimes. On the same indictment they charged Harold and Ben with one count of conspiracy and two underlying crimes. There was no indication that Hugh and Tom were working with Harold and Ben, though there was evidence that Partin ordered both pairs of men to carry out the actions.
>
> Before trial, Harold and Ben moved to sever their charges from Hugh and Tom's charges. The trial court denied the motion and the four men were tried together and convicted. Harold and Ben appealed the conviction and the denial of severance.[9]

[8] United States v. Harrelson. 454 F.2d 1153 (5th Cir. 1985).

[9] This example is roughly based on United States v. Marionneaux, 514 F.2d 1244 (5th Cir. 1975).

Analysis: The two crimes were not properly joined, and so the severance motion should have been granted. Although the crimes were of similar character, and appeared to be part of a common scheme or plan, they were not part of the same "series of transactions," since the two pairs of men did not coordinate with each other or act together.

The appellate court noted that a "'series' of acts . . . is something more than 'similar' acts."[10] The crimes by the two pairs of defendants were similar in that they involved obstructing the prosecution of Partin. It is also the case that both were attempts to prevent witnesses from testifying truthfully. But "the conspiracies [had] different participants and completely different overt actions."[11]

Thus, there was no "substantial identity of facts or participants between the two offenses,"[12] and so the two pairs of defendants did not share the same "series of transactions."

2. Once Joined, Can Offenses/Defendants Ever Be Severed? When a defendant makes a motion to sever offenses or parties, his first line of attack is to argue that the joinder itself was improper under Rule 8. However, this argument usually fails, since most prosecutors only charge multiple offenses or defendants in a single charging document if there is reason to believe they are related to each other. Thus, the defendant must move to the next line of attack, which is to argue that even if the initial joinder was proper, a severance is now necessary under Rule 14 of the Federal Rules of Criminal Procedure because trying the offenses or defendants together will cause prejudice to the defendant.

To establish prejudice, the defendant must do more than merely show that trying the offenses or parties together will make it harder for him to be acquitted. The Supreme Court has held that courts should grant a severance only if "there is a serious risk that a joint trial would compromise a specific trial right of one of the defendants, or prevent the jury from making a reliable judgment about guilt or innocence."[13] If multiple defendants are charged jointly with a conspiracy, many courts will require an even higher standard of prejudice, stating that separate trials should be permitted only upon a showing of "specific and compelling prejudice resulting from a joint trial which can be rectified only by separate trials."[14]

As noted in the introduction, joinder of charges or parties may create prejudice in four different ways: **spillover of evidence, guilt by association**, **inconsistent defenses**, or **problems regarding self-incrimination**.

---

[10] Id. at 1248.

[11] Id.

[12] Id. at 1249.

[13] Zafiro v. United States, 506 U.S. 534 (1993).

[14] United States v. Barrett, 933 F.2d 355 (6th Cir. 1991) (quoting United States v. Howell, 664 F.2d 101, 106 (5th Cir.1981)).

a. The issue of **spillover of evidence** is frequently addressed with a limiting instruction—that is, the jury is instructed to use a certain piece of evidence to decide only one of the charges or when deciding the guilt of only one of the defendants. There is significant dispute as to how well jurors can follow these instructions, but they are routinely used to guide the jury in their use of evidence.

In order to gauge the level of potential prejudice from evidence spillover, it is necessary to first determine which pieces of evidence are admissible for each charge and against each defendant. There are many reasons why a particular piece of evidence may only be admissible for certain charges or against certain defendants. Frequently, the Rules of Evidence dictate that certain pieces of evidence are admissible with regard to some charges or defendants but not others:

> **Example:** Charlie is charged with aggravated assault and menacing. The facts show that Charlie was angry with his co-worker, so he picked up a wrench and said: "How would you like it if I broke your jaw open?" When the co-worker attempted to leave the room, Charlie threw the wrench, striking the co-worker in the back of her head.
>
> The elements of aggravated assault are that the defendant knowingly caused physical injury to another. The elements of menacing are that the defendant knowingly placed another in reasonable fear of serious physical injury. The prosecutor has evidence that on two occasions in the past year, the defendant threw a wrench at co-workers on the job. This evidence is inadmissible for the assault charge—its only relevance to the assault charge would be to demonstrate Charlie has a propensity to act violently, which is an improper rationale for the admission of evidence. However, the evidence is admissible in connection with the menacing charge—assuming the victim knew of the prior violent incidents, it is much more likely that the victim felt a reasonable fear of serious physical injury when Charlie picked up the wrench and threatened her. The defendant thus seeks a severance, arguing that if the jurors hear about his prior acts of violence, they will use that evidence for the improper purpose of concluding he has a violent disposition and is therefore more likely to have committed the assault.

Analysis: The trial court will almost certainly deny the motion to sever. The charges were properly joined, because they are part of the same criminal action. Although there is a risk that the jury will misuse the evidence of the defendant's prior violent conduct, the judge will give the jury a limiting instruction, ordering them to disregard the evidence when considering the aggravated assault charge.

The remaining prejudice is not sufficient to require severance, especially given how closely linked the two charges are.

Note that if the trial judge decides that severance is required, the prosecutor is faced with a choice: she can sever the charges and file two charging instruments—one for the assault and one for the menacing—or she could simply decide not to use the evidence of the prior violent conduct and proceed to try both charges jointly.

An example of evidence spillover with multiple defendants might include evidence recovered after an illegal search in which one defendant has standing to contest the search and the admission of the evidence but the other does not. As we saw in **Chapter 22**, the exclusionary rule will bar evidence only against the defendant with standing, not against any other defendant. In these cases, the judge will again have to decide whether, even with a limiting instruction, there is a serious risk of prejudice to the defendant who had standing to object to the search.

Generally the question of whether it is necessary to grant a severance based on the potential for evidence spillover is a matter left squarely to the discretion of the trial court. However, if the prosecutor wishes to admit a confession by a defendant in a joint trial, and the confession is admissible against the defendant who made it but not against his co-defendant, the issue takes on a constitutional dimension. We discuss that special problem in Section C.3, below.

b. **Guilt by association** is most commonly a problem when the evidence against one defendant is overwhelming, but the evidence against the co-defendant is relatively weak. In those cases, the co-defendant will be concerned about being presumed guilty because of the strong case against the other defendant. Once again, the system relies in part on jury instructions to minimize the prejudice. A standard instruction for this issue will involve the trial judge ordering the jury to "give separate consideration to each individual defendant and to each separate charge against him. Each defendant is entitled to have his or her case determined from his or her own conduct and from the evidence [that] may be applicable to him or to her."[15]

c. **Inconsistent defenses** create a problem in that joinder of charges may force a defendant to abandon his best defense for one charge in order to proceed with an inconsistent defense for another of his charges. In the case of joinder of parties, the defendants may be working at cross-purposes: each defendant may be trying to create reasonable doubt by showing the co-defendant was the one who was truly culpable.

As with any other potential problem with joinder, however, the mere existence of inconsistent defenses does not automatically require severance; the defendant must also demonstrate a serious risk of substantial prejudice based on the inconsistent defenses.

[15] Zafiro v. United States, 506 U.S. 534, 541 (1993).

Example—Zafiro v. United States, 506 U.S. 534 (1993): Law enforcement officers in Chicago saw Salvador Garcia and Alfonso Soto carrying a large box. The men placed the box in the trunk of a car and drove away. The officers were suspicious, and followed the car to an apartment building, where they observed Garcia and Soto carry the box up the stairs. When the officers identified themselves, Garcia and Soto dropped the box and ran into an apartment. The officers opened the box and found 55 pounds of cocaine. They secured the apartment, obtained a search warrant, and then searched the apartment, finding 16 more pounds of cocaine, 25 grams of heroin, 4 pounds of marijuana in a suitcase in the closet, and a bag containing over $22,000 in cash. They also found two other individuals in the apartment: Gloria Zafiro and Jose Martinez. The apartment belonged to Zafiro and Martinez was her boyfriend. All four occupants—Garcia, Soto, Zafiro, and Martinez—were arrested and charged with multiple counts of possession of controlled substances and conspiracy to possess controlled substances with the intent to sell.

Before trial, Garcia and Soto moved to sever their cases, arguing that their defenses were mutually antagonistic. Each of them claimed that he knew nothing about the contents of the box: Garcia argued that Soto knew what was inside the box but Garcia did not, while Soto claimed the reverse. Likewise, Zafiro and Martinez sought to sever their cases. Zafiro claimed that Martinez asked to store a suitcase in her closet, but never told her there were drugs inside; Martinez argued that he was merely visiting Zafiro's apartment at the time and never stored anything there.

The trial court denied all of the motions to sever, and the four were tried together and convicted. On appeal, they argued that the trial court abused its discretion in not severing the cases. The appeal was ultimately heard by the Supreme Court.

Analysis: The Court affirmed the convictions. The Court held both that joinder was proper and that the defendants had not shown the required level of prejudice to justify severance. The Court began by pointing out the preference for joint trials for defendants who are charged together. As a result of this preference, the defendant bears the burden of proving prejudice under Rule 14 of the Federal Rules of Criminal Procedure. To prevail on a severance motion, the showing of prejudice must be substantial: "defendants are not entitled to severance merely because they may have a better chance of acquittal in separate trials."[16]

---

[16] Zafiro, 506 U.S. at 540.

The defendants suggested two ways in which they were prejudiced by the joint trial. First, the defendants argued that the jury might have concluded that each defendant was lying and convicted them on that basis. Alternatively, the defendants suggested the jury might have concluded that at least one of the defendants must have been lying and therefore voted to convict even if the prosecutor had not proven her case beyond a reasonable doubt.

As to the first argument, the Court noted that there was nothing unfairly prejudicial about having co-defendants testify in a way that was damaging to the defendant's case. "A defendant normally would not be entitled to exclude the testimony of a **former** codefendant if the district court did sever their trials, and we see no reason why relevant and competent testimony would be prejudicial merely because the witness is also a [current] codefendant."[17]

With regard to the second argument, the Court examined the facts of the case and determined that the prosecutor offered sufficient evidence to prove all of the defendants' guilt beyond a reasonable doubt. Thus, there was no reason to assume the jury found any of the defendants guilty because of the co-defendants' testimony rather than the government's evidence. Also, the trial judge properly instructed the jury that the prosecutor had the burden of proving each element of each charge against each defendant beyond a reasonable doubt, and jurors are presumed to follow a trial judge's instructions.

As *Zafiro* points out, a defendant must meet a very high standard in order to be granted a severance on the grounds of inconsistent defenses—the prejudice must be so high that proceeding without a severance in effect denies the defendant a fair trial or prevents the jury from making a reliable judgment about guilt or innocence.[18] For example, if one defendant was going to call attention to his co-defendant's refusal to take the stand, the co-defendant's right against self-incrimination would be compromised and the trial court would be forced to sever the trials.[19] The *Bruton* rule, discussed in Section 3, provides another example of a co-defendant's trial rights being violated when he is tried jointly with another defendant.

d. Finally, joinder can create prejudice with regard to the defendant's right against **self-incrimination.** In the context of joint charges, this concern arises when the defendant wants to testify in response to only some of the charges, but not testify (and thus not be cross-examined) about other charges. The general rule is once the defendant testifies about any one of the charges, the prosecutor is permitted to cross-examine him about all of the charges. In order to limit cross-examination to only the crimes about which he testified on direct, the defendant

---

[17] Id.

[18] United States v. Newport, 162 F.R.D. 414 (D. Mass. 1995).

[19] United States v. Aguiar, 610 F.2d 1296 (5th Cir. 1980), rehearing denied 614 F.2d 1299, certiorari denied 449 U.S. 827.

must show that he has "important testimony" to give on one of the charges but a "strong need to refrain from testifying" on the other charges.[20]

> **Example:** Emil Earl Little Dog was originally indicted on three counts of aggravated sexual abuse. Three different girls, ages seven, nine, and fourteen, each claimed that Little Dog had sexually abused them. As the case moved towards trial, Little Dog allegedly wrote a letter to friends of one of the victims, urging them to (falsely) tell the authorities that the victim (referred to as "MRL") bore a grudge against Little Dog and made up the story of sexual abuse in order to harm him. After the letter was discovered, the prosecutor indicted Little Dog for obstruction of justice, and then joined the obstruction charge to the three counts of aggravated sexual abuse.
>
> Little Dog moved to sever the obstruction charge from the sexual abuse charge. He argued in the first instance that joining the charges was improper under Rule 8. In addition, Little Dog claimed that even if the initial joinder was proper, he had compelling testimony to give on the sexual abuse charges but he did not want to have to testify regarding the obstruction charge. The motion for severance was denied, and Little Dog was convicted. He appealed the case.[21]

Analysis: The appellate court upheld the conviction. First, the court held that the initial joinder was proper because the obstruction charge was connected to the sexual abuse charges, and nearly identical evidence would be offered in both cases.

If the district court had severed the charges, evidence of Little Dog's attempt to tamper with or influence witnesses would have been admissible in his sexual abuse trial to show criminal intent and state of mind. In a separate trial for obstruction, evidence of Little Dog's sexual abuse of MRL would be required to show his motive for seeking to influence [MRL's friends] into giving false testimony about MRL. Therefore, the "evidence is such that one crime would be probative and admissible at the defendant's separate trial of the other crime."

The court then determined that the defendant did not suffer the "severe prejudice" necessary to require severance under Rule 14. Little Dog's argument was essentially that he wanted to testify as to the sexual abuse charges but not the obstruction charge. This was presumably because he believed he had a persuasive story to tell regarding the sexual abuse charges, but had no real defense as to the

---

[20] United States v. Little Dog, 398 F.3d 1032 (8th Cir. 2005).

[21] The example is roughly based on the Eighth Circuit's 2005 decision in United States v. Little Dog, 398 F.3d 1032.

obstruction charges. This fell far short of the standard, which would require him to show he had important testimony to give on the sexual abuse offense but a strong need to refrain from testifying on the obstruction count. In order to meet that standard, the defendant must "present enough information regarding the nature of the testimony he wishes to give on one count and his reasons for not wishing to testify on the other to satisfy the court that the claim of prejudice is genuine and to enable [the court] intelligently to weigh the considerations of economy and expedition in judicial administration against the defendant's interest in having a free choice with respect to testifying."[22]

In the context of joined defendants, the problem with self-incrimination arises when the defendant wishes to call his co-defendant to the stand to give exculpatory testimony, but the co-defendant exercises his right against self-incrimination and refuses to testify. Thus, the defendant is unable to present the evidence to the jury. As with the other forms of prejudice, the defendant must meet a relatively high standard: he must prove that the co-defendant's testimony is "crucial to his defense" and that it is "unavailable from any other source."[23]

Example: E. Graydon Shuford was a personal injury attorney in South Carolina, and Herman S. Jordan was a legal investigator who worked for him in his office. In 1963, Shuford partnered with a physical therapist named Gene Long to create the West Ashley Physical Therapy Laboratory to provide physical therapy to Shuford's clients. After a few weeks, Long contacted Shuford and told him that many of the patients referred to the clinic by Shuford were not keeping their appointments. Shuford instructed Long to go ahead and bill the patients for the appointments anyway. Long then reached out to Jordan, Shuford's employee, and Jordan gave Shuford the same instructions. Shuford would ultimately file a claim for these phantom appointments under the Federal Tort Claims Act and request reimbursement even though no therapy was in fact occurring.

Eventually Shuford's scheme was discovered, and Shuford and his employee Jordan were indicted for conspiracy and knowingly submitting false documents as part of a Federal Tort Claims Act prosecution. Long was not charged, and he served as the government's chief witness in the fraud charge.

Before trial, Shuford moved to sever his case from Jordan's case. Shuford's defense was that he instructed Long that it was appropri-

[22] United States v. Jardin, 552 F.2d 216, 220 (8th Cir. 1977) (internal quotations omitted).

[23] United States v. Shuford, 454 F.2d 772 (4th Cir. 1971).

ate to bill the patients for missed appointments, but that these bills must be kept separate from the other bills so they would not later be the basis of a reimbursement claim. Long was set to testify that there was no such instruction. Shuford claimed that if Jordan testified, he would confirm Shuford's specific instructions. However, Jordan was unwilling to testify because he believed the evidence against him was weak and he did not want to give the prosecutor the chance to cross-examine him. Thus, Shuford had no way of confirming his version of events.

The trial judge denied the severance motion, and both Shuford and Jordan were convicted. Shuford appealed the conviction.[24]

Analysis: The appellate court overturned the conviction and held that severance was necessary. The court agreed that the initial joinder was proper, and also conceded that there was a presumption against severance when one crime can be proven against two defendants using the same set of evidence. However, in this case a joint trial denied Shuford's right to a fair trial.

Shuford needed Jordan's testimony with regard to a "crucial fact on which the Government and Shuford were in sharp disagreement."[25] Long's testimony regarding the specific nature of Shuford's instructions to him about the billing procedure was critical. If the jury believed Long, it would have to find Shuford guilty; if it believed Shuford, it would have to acquit him. Thus, "the guilt or innocence of Shuford hinged, in large measure, on the outcome of this credibility dispute."[26] No other witness could possibly testify as to the nature of these instructions.

The court emphasized that it was not creating a blanket rule in which a severance is required every time one defendant wishes to call a co-defendant to testify. In this case, however, Shuford made a number of specific showings:

1. He set out the specifics of Jordan's likely testimony;
2. He demonstrated how that testimony was critical to his defense;
3. He showed that there was no other way to present this evidence to the jury; and
4. He had evidence that Jordan would be willing to testify at Shuford's individual trial if the cases were severed.

Without all four of these factors being met, severance is not necessarily required.

3. Co-Defendant's Confessions. As noted above, one potential problem with simultaneously trying multiple defendants is that evidence which is admissible

[24] This example is roughly based on Shuford, 454 F.2d 772.

[25] Id. at 776.

[26] Id. at 777.

against one may be inadmissible against the others. One solution to this problem is to give the jurors a limiting instruction, ordering them to use the evidence against the proper defendant but to disregard it as to all of the other defendants. In deciding whether a severance is proper, one of the factors the trial court must consider is the danger of jurors ignoring the limiting instruction and improperly using such evidence against all of the defendants.

There is one circumstance, however, where the trial court does not have any discretion. This is when the prosecutor seeks to admit a confession which incriminates not only the defendant who made it but also one or more of his co-defendants. Under the Rules of Evidence, the confession is clearly admissible against the defendant who made it under the "opposing party statement" exception to the hearsay rule. However, the confession is inadmissible hearsay as to the other defendants in the case. Ordinarily the court would conduct a fact-based analysis to decide whether the prejudice to the non-confessing co-defendants would be so great (even with a limiting instruction) that severance was required. However, the Supreme Court has held that in the case of criminal confessions, the potential prejudice is so great that severance will always be required, unless the co-defendants have a chance to cross-examine the defendant who made the statement:

> **Example—*Bruton v. United States*, 391 U.S. 123 (1968):** Bruton and Evans were jointly charged with armed postal robbery. After their arrest, Evans confessed to a postal inspector. Evans's confession was admissible against Evans under an exception to the hearsay rule that allows a party's own statements to be admitted against him. However, Evans's confession was not admissible against Bruton, since there was no hearsay exception to allow it to be used against him. Thus, the trial court admitted Evans's confession at trial but instructed the jury to only use the confession as evidence against Evans and to disregard it when deciding Bruton's guilt. Bruton appealed his conviction, arguing that even with the jury instruction the confession carried an unacceptably high risk of prejudice to Bruton.

Analysis: The Supreme Court overruled the conviction, establishing a rule that when a defendant's confession implicates the co-defendant it cannot be admitted at a joint trial unless the co-defendant has the right to cross-examine the defendant. Admitting Evans's confession was so prejudicial to Bruton that even a limiting instruction was not sufficient to dispel the prejudice. If Bruton had been able to cross-examine Evans about the confession, the cross-examination might have dispelled some of the prejudice. However, Evans had a Fifth Amendment right not to take the stand, so Bruton was unable to call Evans to the stand to challenge the statement. Thus, there was significant "guilt by association" prejudice against

Bruton when Evans's confession was admitted in their joint trial.

Even more problematic was the fact that the admission of Evans's confession violated Bruton's constitutional rights. Evan's confession implicated Bruton, which made Evans a witness against Bruton. Bruton had a Sixth Amendment right to confront all witnesses against him:

> Here the introduction of Evans's confession posed a substantial threat to petitioner's right to confront the witnesses against him, and this is a hazard we cannot ignore. Despite the concededly clear instructions to the jury to disregard Evans's inadmissible hearsay evidence inculpating petitioner, in the context of a joint trial we cannot accept limiting instructions as an adequate substitute for petitioner's constitutional right of cross-examination. The effect is the same as if there had been no instruction at all.

The *Bruton* doctrine comes into play every time the government prosecutes multiple defendants when one of them has confessed and implicated the others. In this situation, *Bruton* gives the prosecutor three primary choices: not to use the confession at all; to sever the trial and try the confessing defendant separately; or to redact the confession so that it makes no mention of the co-defendant whatsoever. Technically, *Bruton* would allow the prosecutor to admit a defendant's confession if the defendant then chooses to testify, since the co-defendant would get a chance to cross-examine the confessing defendant and thereby protect his Sixth Amendment rights. However, in practice at the time the prosecutor presents her case, she cannot know for certain whether the confessing defendant will in fact testify on his own behalf. Thus, the prosecutor usually must choose to either do without the confession, sever the case, or redact the confession.

In theory, the redaction option is the best solution—it removes the prejudice from the evidence since the co-defendant is no longer being implicated, and because the defendant is no longer accusing the co-defendant, it avoids the Confrontation Clause issue. However, in practice redaction ends up being much more difficult than it first appears:

> **Example—*Gray v. Maryland*, 523 U.S. 185 (1998):** Anthony Bell and Kevin Gray were jointly charged in the beating death of Stacey Williams. Bell confessed to the crime, telling police that he, Kevin Gray, and another man committed the crime together. At the joint trial, the prosecutor sought to admit Bell's confession. Aware of the *Bruton* problem, the prosecutor redacted Bell's confession so that the word "deleted" appeared instead of Gray's name. For example, in response to the question "Who was in the group that beat Stacey?" the answer was: "Me, deleted, deleted, and a few other guys."

After the police detective read the redacted confession to the jury, the prosecutor asked the detective "after [Bell] gave you this information, you subsequently were able to arrest Mr. Kevin Gray, is that correct?" The detective responded: "That's correct."

The trial judge instructed the jury that the confession could only be used against Bell and that the jury should disregard it with regard to Gray. Bell and Gray were both convicted, and Gray appealed the *Bruton* issue all the way to the Supreme Court.

Analysis: The Court held that Gray's Sixth Amendment rights were violated and it reversed the conviction. The jury was likely to realize that one of the deleted names was Gray's—in fact, the deletion was likely to call attention to the deleted name, invite juror speculation as to whose name it might be, and thus give extra emphasis to the name of the deleted individual. In other words, "the blank space in an obviously redacted confession . . . points directly to the [other] defendant, and it accuses the defendant in a manner similar to Evans' use of Bruton's name or to a testifying codefendant's accusatory finger."[27] The follow-up question in which the detective stated that the confession led the detective to arrest Gray was also improper, since it called attention to the fact that Gray was mentioned in the confession.

The Court contrasted this case with *Richardson v. Marsh*, another post-*Bruton* case. In *Richardson*, the defendant was jointly tried with a man named Williams. Williams confessed, implicating himself, Richardson, and a third party. In that case, the state redacted Williams's confession so there was no indication anyone other than Williams and the third party was involved. For example, the original confession said that Williams, Richardson, and the third party discussed the murder while they drove to the victim's house. The redacted confession said that Williams and the third party discussed the murder while they drove to the victim's house. Thus, the redacted confession in *Richardson* was not "incriminating on its face," unlike the confession in *Bruton* or the redacted confession in Gray's case.

The Court even suggested that Bell's confession could have been used in Bell and Gray's joint trial if it had been redacted more fully. For example, in response to the question "Who was in the group that beat Stacey," the answer could have been changed to: "Me and a few other guys."[28]

Thus, redaction is possible as long as it does not lead the jury to believe that the co-defendant is implicated in the crime.

---

[27] Gray v. Maryland, 523 U.S. 185, 194 (1998).

[28] Id. at 196.

Quick Summary

The law of joinder and severance governs when a prosecutor is allowed to charge multiple offenses and/or multiple defendants in the same charging document (joinder) and when the defendant is allowed to demand that charges or defendants be split up and charged on different charging instruments (severance).

Rule 8 of the Federal Rules of Criminal Procedure covers joinder. It permits the prosecutor to join offenses if they are of the same or similar character, are based on the same act or transaction, or are a part of a common scheme or plan. It permits the prosecutor to join defendants if they participated in the same act or transaction or series of acts or transactions.

Rule 14 covers severance motions, and it states that even if charges or defendants are properly joined, the court can order severance if there is prejudice to the defendant (or to the prosecutor, though this is rare in practice). There are four types of prejudice: spillover of evidence, guilt by association, inconsistent defenses, and problems with the self-incrimination right. There is a presumption against severance if the original joinder was proper, so courts will require a substantial risk of severe prejudice before ordering a severance.

Finally, there is one critical constitutional issue raised by the law of joinder and severance. The *Bruton* doctrine states if multiple defendants are being tried together, and the prosecutor wants to admit a confession by one of them which implicates another, the prosecutor will have to redact the confessing defendant's statement so that it removes all reference to the co-defendant. If this is not possible, the court must sever the trials.

Review Questions

1. Third Time's the Charm. Phillip Cole was charged with three counts of possession of a firearm as a convicted felon. The first count was for an arrest on April 10, 2013, in which he was pulled over for speeding and the police officer saw a handgun in his car. Cole was originally not charged for that incident. The second count was for an incident on September 25, 2014, in which police officers saw Cole carrying a sawed-off shotgun while chasing three men down the street. Cole evaded apprehension at that time, but one of the police officers recognized him and contacted his probation officer. The probation officer then contacted the local police in her area and they searched Cole's home on October 8, 2014 (no warrant was required for the search because Cole was on probation). The police found a sawed-off shotgun in Cole's bedroom. Cole was home at the time and he was arrested. A few days later, he was indicted on three counts of possession of a firearm—one on April 10, 2013; one on September 25, 2014, and one on October 8, 2014. Cole immediately moved to sever the charges contained in the indictment, arguing (a) that the offenses were improperly joined under Rule 8 and (b) even if they were properly joined that they should be severed under Rule 14. How should the court rule?

2. Selling LSD. Michael Gentry met Susan Parks in a bar and offered to buy some LSD for them to use together. Unbeknownst to Gentry, Parks was actually an undercover police officer who was stationed at the bar because of the high level of drug trafficking there. Parks agreed to accompany Gentry to purchase the LSD. Gentry invited another friend of his named George Martin, and the three left the bar and drove to a nearby house. They told Parks to stay in the car, and she watched from the car as they knocked on the door, exchanged money with the owner, and received two small Ziploc bags in return. Gentry and Martin each took a bag. Gentry then dropped Martin off at the original bar, and took Parks back to his apartment, intending to share the LSD with her there. Backup police officers were waiting at his apartment, where they arrested Gentry. They searched him and found LSD inside of a Ziploc bag. The police charged Gentry with possession of LSD with the intent to sell, under the theory that he intended to give some of the LSD to Parks, because under the law any transfer of LSD to another, whether or not money is exchanged, counted as a "sale."

Meanwhile another pair of undercover police officers watched Martin in the bar. They saw him engage in a transaction with another bar patron, and they followed that patron outside, where they arrested and searched him, finding a small amount of LSD on him. Unfortunately they lost Martin inside the bar. Ten days later, however, the same officers saw Martin in the same bar, and watched him engage in another transaction with another patron. They then immediately arrested Martin and his customer. They searched both individuals and found a small amount of LSD on the customer and one paper bag on Martin containing LSD.

The prosecutor ultimately charged Gentry and Martin in the same indictment. Count One charged Martin and Gentry with possession of LSD with intent to sell, Count Two charged Martin with selling LSD on the night he and Gentry bought the drug, and Count Three charged Martin with selling LSD ten days later.

Before trial, Gentry moved to sever Martin's case from his own, arguing that (a) the defendants were improperly joined under Rule 8 and (b) even if they were properly joined they should be severed under Rule 14. How should the judge rule?

3. Conflicting Defenses. On November 26, Tony Collins and Hugh Bannon allegedly broke into the home of Danielle Travers and beat her with brass knuckles. Bannon was arrested two days after the incident and confessed. He stated that he was high on PCP, entered Travers's home without permission through a window and beat Travers. Bannon's statement did not mention Collins.

The prosecutor charged Collins and Bannon together with burglary (trespass with the intent to commit an assault) and assault. Collins moved to sever his trial from Bannon's on two grounds. First, he claimed that although Bannon's statement did not mention him directly, when combined with other witnesses the statement would incriminate Collins. Since Bannon was not testifying, admitting the statement would violate Collins's Sixth Amendment right to confrontation. Second, he claimed that his defense was incompatible with Bannon's defense because he was going to testify that he and Collins entered Travers's home through the front door after having been invited inside by Travers, and only after the three of them got into an argument did he end up striking Travers. In other words, Collins planned to admit to the assault, but not to the trespass and thus not to the burglary. Based on Bannon's statement, Collins argued that Bannon's defense was going to be lack of *mens rea* based on intoxication.

Should the trial court sever the defendants?

FROM THE COURTROOM

ZAFIRO v. UNITED STATES

United States Supreme Court, 1992
596 U.S. 534

[Justice O'CONNOR delivered the opinion of the Court.]

[Justices STEVENS concurred in the decision.]

Rule 8(b) of the Federal Rules of Criminal Procedure provides that defendants may be charged together "if they are alleged to have participated in the same act or transaction or in the same series of acts or transactions constituting an offense or offenses." Rule 14 of the Rules, in turn, permits a district court to grant a severance of defendants if "it appears that a defendant or the government is prejudiced by a joinder." In this case, we consider whether Rule 14 requires severance as a matter of law when codefendants present "mutually antagonistic defenses."

I

Gloria Zafiro, Jose Martinez, Salvador Garcia, and Alfonso Soto were accused of distributing illegal drugs in the Chicago area, operating primarily out of Soto's bungalow in Chicago and Zafiro's apartment in Cicero, a nearby suburb. One day, Government agents observed Garcia and Soto place a large box in Soto's car and drive from Soto's bungalow to Zafiro's apartment. The agents followed the two as they carried the box up the stairs. When the agents identified themselves, Garcia and Soto dropped the box and ran into the apartment. The agents entered the apartment in pursuit and found the four petitioners in the living room. The dropped box contained 55 pounds of cocaine. After obtaining a search warrant for the apartment, agents found approximately 16 pounds of cocaine, 25 grams of heroin, and 4 pounds of marijuana inside a suitcase in a closet. Next to the suitcase was a sack containing $22,960 in cash. Police officers also discovered 7 pounds of cocaine in a car parked in Soto's garage.

The four petitioners were indicted and brought to trial together. At various points during the proceeding, Garcia and Soto moved for severance, arguing that their defenses were mutually antagonistic. Soto testified that he knew nothing about the drug conspiracy. He claimed that Garcia had asked him for a box, which he gave Garcia, and that he (Soto) did not know its contents until they were arrested. Garcia did not testify, but his lawyer argued that Garcia was innocent: The box belonged to Soto and Garcia was ignorant of its contents.

Zafiro and Martinez also repeatedly moved for severance on the ground that their defenses were mutually antagonistic. Zafiro testified that she was merely Martinez's girlfriend and knew nothing of the conspiracy. She claimed that Martinez stayed in her apartment occasionally, kept some clothes there, and gave her small amounts of money. Although she allowed Martinez to store a suitcase in her closet, she testified, she had no idea that the suitcase contained illegal drugs. Like Garcia, Martinez did not testify. But his lawyer argued that Martinez was only visiting his girlfriend and had no idea that she was involved in distributing drugs.

The District Court denied the motions for severance. The jury convicted all four petitioners of conspiring to possess cocaine, heroin, and marijuana with the intent to distribute. In addition, Garcia and Soto were convicted of possessing cocaine with the intent to distribute, Martinez was convicted of possessing cocaine, heroin, and marijuana with the intent to distribute.

Petitioners appealed their convictions. Garcia, Soto, and Martinez claimed that the District Court abused its discretion in denying their motions to sever. (Zafiro did not appeal the denial of her severance motion, and thus, her claim is not properly before this Court.)

. . .

II

Rule 8(b) states that "[t]wo or more defendants may be charged in the same indictment or information if they are alleged to have participated in the same act or transaction or in the same series of acts or transactions constituting an offense or offenses." There is a preference in the federal system for joint trials of defendants who are indicted together. Joint trials "play a vital role in the criminal justice system." They promote efficiency and "serve the interests of justice by avoiding the scandal and inequity of inconsistent verdicts." For these reasons, we repeatedly have approved of joint trials. But Rule 14 recognizes that joinder, even when proper under Rule 8(b), may prejudice either a defendant or the Government. Thus, the Rule provides:

"If it appears that a defendant or the government is prejudiced by a joinder of . . . defendants . . . for trial together, the court may order an election of separate trials of counts, grant a severance of defendants or provide whatever other relief justice requires."

In interpreting Rule 14, the Courts of Appeals frequently have expressed the view that "mutually antagonistic" or "irreconcilable" defenses may be so prejudicial in some circumstances as to mandate severance. Notwithstanding such assertions, the courts have reversed relatively few convictions for failure to grant a severance on grounds of mutually antagonistic or irreconcilable defenses. The low rate of reversal may reflect the inability of defendants to prove a risk of prejudice in most cases involving conflicting defenses.

Nevertheless, petitioners urge us to adopt a bright-line rule, mandating severance whenever codefendants have conflicting defenses. We decline to do so. Mutually antagonistic defenses are not prejudicial *per se.* Moreover, Rule 14 does not require severance even if prejudice is shown; rather, it leaves the tailoring of the relief to be granted, if any, to the district court's sound discretion. We believe that, when defendants properly have been joined under Rule 8(b), a district court should grant a severance under Rule 14 only if there is a serious risk that a joint trial would compromise a specific trial right of one of the defendants, or prevent the jury from making a reliable judgment about guilt or innocence. Such a risk might occur when evidence that the jury should not consider against a defendant and that would not be admissible if a defendant were tried alone is admitted against a codefendant. For example, evidence of a codefendant's wrongdoing in some circumstances erroneously could lead a jury to conclude that a defendant was guilty. When many defendants are tried together in a complex case and they have markedly different degrees of culpability, this risk of prejudice is heightened. Evidence that is probative of a defendant's guilt but technically admissible only against a codefendant also might present a risk of prejudice. Conversely, a defendant might suffer prejudice if essential exculpatory evidence that would be available to a defendant tried alone were unavailable in a joint trial. The risk of prejudice will vary with the facts in each case, and district courts may find prejudice in situations not discussed here. When the risk of prejudice is high, a district court is more likely to determine that separate trials are necessary, but, as we indicated in *Richardson v. Marsh,* less drastic measures, such as limiting instructions, often will suffice to cure any risk of prejudice.

Turning to the facts of this case, we note that petitioners do not articulate any specific instances of prejudice. Instead they contend that the very nature of their defenses, without more, prejudiced them. Their theory is that when two defendants both claim they are innocent and each accuses the other of the crime, a jury will conclude (1) that both defendants are lying and convict them both on that basis, or (2) that at least one of the two must be guilty without regard to whether the Government has proved its case beyond a reasonable doubt.

As to the first contention, it is well settled that defendants are not entitled to severance merely because they may have a better chance of acquittal in separate trials. Rules 8(b) and 14 are designed "to promote economy and efficiency and to avoid a multiplicity of trials, [so long as] these objectives can be achieved without substantial prejudice to the right of the defendants to a fair trial." While "[a]n important element of a fair trial is that a jury consider *only* relevant and competent evidence bearing on the issue of guilt or innocence," a fair trial does not include the right to exclude relevant and competent evidence. A defendant normally would not be entitled to exclude the testimony of a former codefendant if the district court did sever their trials, and we see no reason why relevant and competent testimony would be prejudicial merely because the witness is also a codefendant.

As to the second contention, the short answer is that petitioners' scenario simply did not occur here. The Government argued that all four petitioners were guilty and offered sufficient evidence as to all four petitioners; the jury in turn found all four petitioners guilty of various offenses. Moreover, even if there were some risk of prejudice, here it is of the type that can be cured with proper instructions, and "juries are presumed to follow their instructions." The District Court properly instructed the jury that the Government had "the burden of proving beyond a reasonable doubt" that each defendant committed the crimes with which he or she was charged. The court then instructed the jury that it must "give separate consideration to each individual defendant and to each separate charge against him. Each defendant is entitled to have his or her case determined from his or her own conduct and from the evidence [that] may be applicable to him or to her." In addition, the District Court admonished the jury that opening and closing arguments are not evidence and that it should draw no inferences from a defendant's exercise of the right to silence. These instructions sufficed to cure any possibility of prejudice.

Rule 14 leaves the determination of risk of prejudice and any remedy that may be necessary to the sound discretion of the district courts. Because petitioners have not shown that their joint trial subjected them to any legally cognizable prejudice, we conclude that the District Court did not abuse its discretion in denying petitioners' motions to sever. The judgment of the Court of Appeals is

Affirmed.

Justice STEVENS, concurring in the judgment.

When two people are apprehended in possession of a container filled with narcotics, it is probable that they both know what is inside. The inference of knowledge is heightened when, as in this case, both people flee when confronted by police officers, or both people occupy the premises in which the container is found.. At the same time, however, it remains entirely possible that one person did not have such knowledge. That, of course, is the argument made by each of the defendants in this case: that he or she did not know what was in the crucial box or suitcase.

Most important here, it is also possible that *both* persons lacked knowledge of the contents of the relevant container. Moreover, that hypothesis is compatible with individual defenses of lack of knowledge. There is no logical inconsistency between a version of events in which one person is ignorant, and a version in which the other is ignorant; unlikely as it may seem, it is at least theoretically possible that both versions are true, in that both persons are ignorant. In other words, dual ignorance defenses do not necessarily translate into "mutually antagonistic" defenses, as that term is used in reviewing severance motions, because acceptance of one defense does not necessarily preclude acceptance of the other and acquittal of the codefendant.

In my view, the defenses presented in this case did not rise to the level of mutual antagonism. First, as to Garcia and Martinez, neither of whom testified, the only defense presented was that the Government had failed to carry its burden of proving guilt beyond a reasonable doubt. Nothing in the testimony presented by their codefendants, Soto and Zafiro, supplemented the Government's proof of their guilt in any way. Soto's testimony that he did not know the contents of the box he delivered with Garcia, as discussed above, could have been accepted *in toto* without precluding acquittal of his codefendant. Similarly, the jury could have accepted Zafiro's testimony that she did not know the contents of the suitcase found in her apartment, and also acquitted Martinez.

It is true, of course, that the jury was unlikely to believe that none of the defendants knew what was in the box or suitcase. Accordingly, it must be acknowledged that if the jury had believed that Soto and Zafiro were ignorant, then it would have been more likely to believe that Garcia and Martinez were not. That, however, is not the standard for mutually antagonistic defenses.

. . .

I would save for another day evaluation of the prejudice that may arise when the evidence or testimony offered by one defendant is truly irreconcilable with the innocence of a codefendant. Because the facts here do not present the issue squarely, I hesitate in this case to develop a rule that would govern the very different situation faced in cases like *People v. Braune*, 363 Ill. 551, 557 (1936), in which mutually exclusive defenses transform a trial into "more of a contest between the defendants than between the people and the defendants." Under such circumstances, joinder may well be highly prejudicial, particularly when the prosecutor's own case in chief is marginal and the decisive evidence of guilt is left to be provided by a codefendant.

The burden of overcoming any individual defendant's presumption of innocence, by proving guilt beyond a reasonable doubt, rests solely on the shoulders of the prosecutor. Joinder is problematic in cases involving mutually antagonistic defenses because it may operate to reduce the burden on the prosecutor, in two general ways. First, joinder may introduce what is in effect a second prosecutor into a case, by turning each codefendant into the other's most forceful adversary. Second, joinder may invite a jury confronted with two defendants, at least one of whom is almost certainly guilty, to convict the defendant who appears the more guilty of the two regardless of whether the prosecutor has proven guilt beyond a reasonable doubt as to that particular defendant. Though the Court is surely correct that this second risk may be minimized by careful instructions insisting on separate consideration of the evidence as to each codefendant, the danger will remain relevant to the prejudice inquiry in some cases.

Given these concerns, I cannot share the Court's enthusiastic and unqualified "preference" for the joint trial of defendants indicted together. The Court correctly notes that a similar preference was announced a few years ago in *Richardson v. Marsh*, and that the Court had sustained the permissibility of joint trials on at least two prior occasions. There will, however, almost certainly be multidefendant cases in which a series of separate trials would be not only more reliable, but also more efficient and manageable than some of the mammoth conspiracy cases which the Government often elects to prosecute. And in all cases, the Court should be mindful of the serious risks of prejudice and overreaching that are characteristic of joint trials, particularly when a conspiracy count is included in the indictment.

. . .

I agree with the Court that a "bright-line rule, mandating severance whenever codefendants have conflicting defenses" is unwarranted. For the reasons discussed above, however, I think district courts must retain their traditional discretion to consider severance whenever mutually antagonistic defenses are presented. Accordingly, I would refrain from announcing a preference for joint trials, or any general rule that might be construed as a limit on that discretion.

Because I believe the District Court correctly decided the severance motions in this case, I concur in the Court's judgment of affirmance.

FROM THE COURTROOM

BRUTON v. UNITED STATES

United States Supreme Court, 1968
391 U.S. 123

[Justice BRENNAN delivered the opinion of the Court.]

[Justice BLACK and Justice STEWART filed concurring opinions.]

[Justice WHITE and Justice Harlan filed dissenting opinions.]

This case presents the question, last considered in *Delli Paoli v. United States*, 352 U.S. 232, whether the conviction of a defendant at a joint trial should be set aside although the jury was instructed that a codefendant's confession inculpating the defendant had to be disregarded in determining his guilt or innocence.

A joint trial of petitioner and one Evans in the District Court for the Eastern District of Missouri resulted in the conviction of both by a jury on a federal charge of armed postal robbery. A postal inspector testified that Evans orally confessed to him that Evans and petitioner committed the armed robbery. The postal inspector obtained the oral confession, and another in which Evans admitted he had an accomplice whom he would not name, in the course of two interrogations of Evans at the city jail in St. Louis, Missouri, where Evans was held in custody on state criminal charges. Both petitioner and Evans appealed their convictions to the Court of Appeals for the Eighth Circuit. That court set aside Evans' conviction on the ground that his oral confessions to the postal inspector should not have been received in evidence against him. However, the court, relying upon *Delli Paoli*, affirmed petitioner's conviction because the trial judge instructed the jury that although Evans' confession was competent evidence against Evans it was inadmissible hearsay against petitioner and therefore had to be disregarded in determining petitioner's guilt or innocence. We granted certiorari to reconsider *Delli Paoli*. . . . We hold that, because of the substantial risk that the jury, despite instructions to the contrary, looked to the incriminating extrajudicial statements in determining petitioner's guilt, admission of Evans' confession in this joint trial violated petitioner's right of cross-examination secured by the Confrontation Clause of the Sixth Amendment. We therefore overrule *Delli Paoli* and reverse.

The basic premise of *Delli Paoli* was that it is 'reasonably possible for the jury to follow' sufficiently clear instructions to disregard the confessor's extrajudicial statement that his codefendant participated with him in committing the crime. If it were true that the jury disregarded the reference to the codefendant, no question would arise under the Confrontation Clause, because by hypothesis the case is treated as if the confessor made no statement inculpating the nonconfessor. But since *Delli Paoli* was decided this Court has effectively repudiated its basic premise. Before discussing this, we pause to observe that in *Pointer v. State of Texas*, 380 U.S. 400, we confirmed 'that the right of cross-examination is included in the right of an accused in a criminal case to confront the witnesses against him' secured by the Sixth Amendment, 'a major reason underlying the constitutional confrontation rule is to give a defendant charged with crime an opportunity to cross-examine the witnesses against him.'

. . .

Delli Paoli assumed that this encroachment on the right to confrontation could be avoided by the instruction to the jury to disregard the inadmissible hearsay evidence. But, as we have said, that assumption has since been effectively repudiated. True, the repudiation was not in the context of the admission of a confession inculpating a codefendant but in the context of a New York rule which submitted to the jury the question of the voluntariness of the confession itself. Nonetheless the message of Jackson for *Delli Paoli* was clear. We there held that a defendant is constitutionally entitled at least to have the trial judge first determine whether a confession was made voluntarily before submitting it to the jury for an assessment of its credibility. More specifically, we expressly rejected the proposition that a jury, when determining the confessor's guilt, could be relied on to ignore his confession of guilt should it find the confession involuntary. Significantly, we supported that conclusion in part by reliance upon the dissenting opinion of Mr. Justice Frankfurter for the four Justices who dissented in *Delli Paoli*.

That dissent challenged the basic premise of *Delli Paoli* that a properly instructed jury would ignore the confessor's inculpation of the nonconfessor in determining the latter's guilt. 'The fact of the matter is that too often such admonition against misuse is intrinsically ineffective in that the effect of such a nonadmissible declaration cannot be wiped from the brains of the jurors. The admonition therefore becomes a futile collocation of words and fails of its purpose as a legal protection to defendants against whom such a declaration should not tell.'. The dissent went on to say, as quoted in the cited note in *Jackson*, 'The Government should not have the windfall of having the jury be influenced by evidence against a defendant which, as a matter of law, they should not consider but which they cannot put out of their minds.' To the same effect, and also cited in the Jackson note, is the statement of Mr. Justice Jackson in his concurring opinion in *Krulewitch v. United States*, 336 U.S. 440: 'The naive assumption that prejudicial effects can be overcome by instructions to the jury * * * all practicing lawyers know to be unmitigated fiction. * * *'

The significance of *Jackson* for *Delli Paoli* was suggested by Chief Justice Traynor in *People v. Aranda*, 63 Cal.2d 518:

'Although *Jackson* was directly concerned with obviating any risk that a jury might rely on an unconstitutionally obtained confession in determining the defendant's guilt, its logic extends to obviating the risks that the jury may rely on any inadmissible statements. If it is a denial of due process to rely on a jury's presumed ability to disregard an involuntary confession, it may also be a denial of due process to rely on a jury's presumed ability to disregard a codefendant's confession implicating another defendant when it is determining that defendant's guilt or innocence.

'Indeed, the latter task may be an even more difficult one for the jury to perform than the former. Under the New York procedure, which Jackson held violated due process, the jury was only required to disregard a confession it found to be involuntary. If it made such a finding, then the confession was presumably out of the case. In joint trials, however, when the admissible confession of one defendant inculpates another defendant, the confession is never deleted from the case and the jury is expected to perform the overwhelming task of considering it in determining the guilt or innocence of the declarant and then of ignoring it in determining the guilt or innocence of any codefendants of the declarant. A jury cannot 'segregate evidence into separate intellectual boxes.' * * * It cannot determine that a confession is true insofar as it admits that A has committed criminal acts with B and at the same time effectively ignore the inevitable conclusion that B has committed those same criminal acts with A.'

In addition to Jackson, our action in 1966 in amending Rule 14 of the Federal Rules of Criminal Procedure also evidences our repudiation of *Delli Paoli's* basic premise. Rule 14 authorizes a severance where it appears that a defendant might be prejudiced by a joint trial. The Rule was amended in 1966 to provide expressly that '(i)n ruling on a motion by a defendant for severance the court may order the attorney for the government to deliver to the court for inspection in camera any statements or confessions made by the defendants which the government intends to introduce in evidence at the trial.' The Advisory Committee on Rules said in explanation of the amendment:

'A defendant may be prejudiced by the admission in evidence against a co-defendant of a statement or confession made by that co-defendant. This prejudice cannot be dispelled by cross-examination if the co-defendant does not take the stand. Limiting instructions to the jury may not in fact erase the prejudice. * * *

'The purpose of the amendment is to provide a procedure whereby the issue of possible prejudice can be resolved on the motion for severance. * * *'

Those who have defended reliance on the limiting instruction in this area have cited several reasons in support. Judge Learned Hand, a particularly severe critic of the proposition that juries could be counted on to disregard inadmissible hearsay, wrote the opinion for the Second Circuit which affirmed *Delli Paoli's* conviction. In Judge Hand's view the limiting instruction, although not really capable of preventing the jury from considering the prejudicial evidence, does as a matter of form provide a way around the exclusionary rules of evidence that is defensible because it 'probably furthers, rather than impedes, the search for truth * * *.' Insofar as this implies the prosecution ought not to be denied the benefit of the confession to prove the confessor's guilt, however, it overlooks alternative ways of achieving that benefit without at the same time infringing the nonconfessor's right of confrontation. Where viable alternatives do exist, it is deceptive to rely on the pursuit of truth to defend a clearly harmful practice.

Another reason cited in defense of *Delli Paoli* is the justification for joint trials in general, the argument being that the benefits of joint proceedings should not have to be sacrificed by requiring separate trials in order to use the confession against the declarant. Joint trials do conserve state funds, diminish inconvenience to witnesses and public authorities, and avoid delays in bringing those accused of crime to trial. But the answer to this argument was cogently stated by Judge Lehman of the New York Court of Appeals, dissenting in *People v. Fisher*, 249 N.Y. 419:

'We still adhere to the rule that an accused is entitled to confrontation of the witnesses against him and the right to cross-examine them * * *. We destroy the age-old rule which in the past has been regarded as a fundamental principle of our jurisprudence by a legalistic formula, required of the judge, that the jury may not consider any admissions against any party who did not join in them. We secure greater speed, economy and convenience in the administration of the law at the price of fundamental principles of constitutional liberty. That price is too high.'

Finally, the reason advanced by the majority in *Delli Paoli* was to tie the result to maintenance of the jury system. 'Unless we proceed on the basis that the jury will follow the court's instructions where those instructions are clear and the circumstances are such that the jury can reasonably be expected to follow them, the jury system makes little sense.' We agree that there are many circumstances in which this reliance is justified. Not every admission of inadmissible hearsay or other evidence can be considered to be reversible error unavoidable through limiting instructions; instances occur in almost every trial where inadmissible evidence creeps in, usually inadvertently. 'A defendant is entitled to a fair trial but not a perfect one.' It is not unreasonable to conclude that in many such cases the jury can and will follow the trial judge's instructions to disregard such information. Nevertheless, as was recognized in *Jackson v. Denno*, there are some contexts in which the risk that the jury will not, or cannot, follow instructions is so great, and the consequences of failure so vital to the defendant, that the practical and human limitations of the jury system cannot be ignored. Such a context is presented here, where the powerfully incriminating extrajudicial statements of a codefendant, who stands accused side-by-side with the defendant, are deliberately spread before the jury in a joint trial. Not only are the incriminations devastating to the defendant but their credibility is inevitably suspect, a fact recognized when accomplices do take the stand and the jury is instructed to weigh their testimony carefully given the recognized motivation to shift blame onto others. The unreliability of such evidence is intolerably compounded when the alleged accomplice, as here, does not testify and cannot be tested by cross-examination. It was against such threats to a fair trial that the Confrontation Clause was directed.

We, of course, acknowledge the impossibility of determining whether in fact the jury did or did not ignore Evans' statement inculpating petitioner in determining petitioner's guilt. But that was also true in the analogous situation in *Jackson v. Denno*, and was not regarded as militating against striking down the New York procedure there involved. It was enough that that procedure posed 'substantial threats to a defendant's constitutional rights to have an involuntary confession entirely disregarded and to have the coercion issue fairly and reliably determined. These hazards we cannot ignore.'.

Here the introduction of Evans' confession posed a substantial threat to petitioner's right to confront the witnesses against him, and this is a hazard we cannot ignore. Despite the concededly clear instructions to the jury to disregard Evans' inadmissible hearsay evidence inculpating petitioner, in the context of a joint trial we cannot accept limiting instructions as an adequate substitute for petitioner's constitutional right of cross-examination. The effect is the same as if there had been no instruction at all.

Reversed.

[The concurring opinions of Justice BLACK and Justice STEWART are omitted.]

Justice WHITE, dissenting.

Whether or not Evans' confession was inadmissible against him, nothing in that confession which was relevant and material to Bruton's case was admissible against Bruton. As to him it was inadmissible hearsay, a presumptively unreliable out-of-court statement of a nonparty who was not a witness subject to cross-examination. Admitting Evans' confession against Bruton would require a new trial unless the error was harmless.

The trial judge in this case had no different view. He admitted Evans' confession only against Evans, not against Bruton, and carefully instructed the jury to disregard it in determining Bruton's guilt or innocence. Contrary to its ruling just a decade ago in *Delli Paoli v. United States*, the Court now holds this instruction insufficient and reverses Bruton's conviction. It would apparently also reverse every other case where a court admits a codefendant's confession implicating a defendant, regardless of cautionary instructions and regardless of the circumstances. I dissent from this excessively rigid rule. There is nothing in this record to suggest that the jury did not follow the trial judge's instructions. There has been no new learning since *Delli Paoli* indicating that juries are less reliable than they were considered in that case to be. There is nothing in the prior decisions of this Court which supports this new constitutional rule.

The Court concedes that there are many instances in which reliance on limiting instructions is justified—'(N)ot every admission of inadmissible hearsay or other evidence can be considered to be reversible error unavoidable through limiting instructions; instances occur in almost every trial where inadmissible evidence creeps in, usually inadvertently.' The Court asserts, however, that the hazards to the defendant of permitting the jury to hear a codefendant's confession implicating him are so severe that we must assume the jury's inability to heed a limiting instruction. This was the holding of the Court with respect to a confession of the defendant himself in *Jackson v. Denno*. There are good reasons, however, for distinguishing the codefendant's confession from that of the defendant himself and for trusting in the jury's ability to disregard the former when instructed to do so.

First, the defendant's own confession is probably the most probative and damaging evidence that can be admitted against him. Though itself an out-of-court statement, it is admitted as reliable evidence because it is an admission of guilt by the defendant and constitutes direct evidence of the facts to which it relates. Even the testimony of an eyewitness may be less reliable than the defendant's own confession. An observer may not correctly perceive, understand, or remember the acts of another, but the admissions of a defendant come from the actor himself, the most knowledgeable and unimpeachable source of information about his past conduct. Certainly, confessions have profound impact on the jury, so much so that we may justifiably doubt its ability to put them out of mind even if told to do so. This was the conclusion of the Court in *Jackson*, and I continue to believe that case to be sound law.

Second, it must be remembered that a coerced confession is not excluded because it is thought to be unreliable. Regardless of how true it may be, it is excluded because specific provisions of the Constitution demand it, whatever the consequences for the criminal trial. In Jackson itself it was stated that '(i)t is now axiomatic that a defendant in a criminal case is deprived of due process of law if his conviction is founded, in whole or in part, upon an involuntary confession, without regard for the truth or falsity of the confession * * *.' In giving prospective effect only to its rules in *Miranda v. State of Arizona* the Court specifically reaffirmed the principle that coerced confessions are inadmissible regardless of their truth or falsity. The Court acknowledged that the rules of Miranda apply to situations 'in which the danger (of unreliable statements) is not necessarily as great as when the accused is subjected to overt and obvious coercion.'

. . .

The situation in this case is very different. Here we deal with a codefendant's confession which is admitted only against the codefendant and with a firm instruction to the jury to disregard it in determining the defendant's guilt or innocence. That confession cannot compare with the defendant's own confession in evidentiary value. As to the defendant, the confession of the codefendant is wholly inadmissible. It is hearsay, subject to all the dangers of inaccuracy which characterize hearsay generally. Furthermore, the codefendant is no more than an eyewitness, the accuracy of whose testimony about the defendant's conduct is open to more doubt than would be the defendant's own account of his actions. More than this, however, the statements of a codefendant have traditionally been viewed with special suspicion. Due to his strong motivation to implicate the defendant and to exonerate himself, a codefendant's statements about what the defendant said or did are less credible than ordinary hearsay evidence. Whereas the defendant's own confession possesses greater reliability and evidentiary value than ordinary hearsay, the codefendant's confession implicating the defendant is intrinsically much less reliable.

The defendant's own confession may not be used against him if coerced, not because it is untrue but to protect other constitutional values. The jury may have great difficulty understanding such a rule and following an instruction to disregard the confession. In contrast, the codefendant's admissions cannot enter into the determination of the defendant's guilt or innocence because they are unreliable. This the jury can be told and can understand. Just as the Court believes that juries can reasonably be expected to disregard ordinary hearsay or other inadmissible evidence when instructed to do so, I believe juries will disregard the portions of a codefendant's confession implicating the defendant when so instructed. Indeed, if we must pick and choose between hearsay as to which limiting instructions will be deemed effective and hearsay the admission of which cannot be cured by instructions, codefendants' admissions belong in the former category rather than the latter, for they are not only hearsay but hearsay which is doubly suspect. If the Court is right in believing that a jury can be counted on to ignore a wide range of hearsay statements which it is told to ignore, it seems very old to me to question its ability to put aside the codefendant's hearsay statements about what the defendant did.

It is a common experience of all men to be informed of 'facts' relevant to an issue requiring their judgment, and yet to disregard those 'facts' because of sufficient grounds for discrediting their veracity or the reliability of their source. Responsible judgment would be impossible but for the ability of men to focus their attention wholly on reliable and credible evidence, and jurymen are no less capable of exercising this capacity than other men. Because I have no doubt that serious-minded and responsible men are able to shut their minds to unreliable information when exercising their judgment, I reject the assumption of the majority that giving instructions to a jury to disregard a codefendant's confession is an empty gesture.

The rule which the Court announces today will severely limit the circumstances in which defendants may be tried together for a crime which they are both charged with committing. Unquestionably, joint trials are more economical and minimize the burden on witnesses, prosecutors, and courts. They also avoid delays in bringing those accused of crime to trial. This much the Court concedes. It is also worth saying that separate trials are apt to have varying consequences for legally indistinguishable defendants. The unfairness of this is confirmed by the common prosecutorial experience of seeing codefendants who are tried separately strenuously jockeying for position with regard to who should be the first to be tried.

In view of the practical difficulties of separate trials and their potential unfairness, I am disappointed that the Court has not spelled out how the federal courts might conduct their business consistent with today's opinion. I would suppose that it will be necessary to exclude all extrajudicial confessions unless all portions of them which implicate defendants other than the declarant are effectively deleted. Effective deletion will probably require not only omission of all direct and indirect inculpations of codefendants but also of any statement that could be employed against those defendants once their identity is otherwise established. Of course, the deletion must not be such that it will distort the statements to the substantial prejudice of either the declarant or the Government. If deletion is not feasible, then the Government will have to choose either not to use the confession at all or to try the defendants separately. To save time, money, and effort, the Government might best seek a ruling at the earliest possible stage of the trial proceedings as to whether the confession is admissible once offending portions are deleted. The failure of the Government to adopt and follow proper procedures for insuring that the inadmissible portions of confessions are excluded will be relevant to the question of whether it was harmless error for them to have gotten before the jury. Oral statements, such as that involved in the present case, will present special problems, for there is a risk that the witness in testifying will inadvertently exceed permissible limits. Except for recommending that caution be used with regard to such oral statements, it is difficult to anticipate the issues which will arise in concrete factual situations.

I would hope, but am not sure, that by using these procedures the federal courts would escape reversal under today's ruling. Even so, I persist in believing that the reversal of Delli Paoli unnecessarily burdens the already difficult task of conducting criminal trials, and therefore I dissent in this case.

[Justice MARSHALL took no part in the consideration or decision of this case.]

41

Speedy Trial

Key Concepts

- Constitutional and Statutory Right to Speedy Trial
- Calculating Speedy Trial Time
- Right to a Speedy Charge—Also Constitutional and Statutory

A. Introduction and Policy. The Sixth Amendment states that "[i]n all criminal prosecutions, the accused shall enjoy the right to a speedy and public trial." Although the Constitution frames this as a right of the defendant, the Supreme Court has noted that the prosecutor and the community also have strong interests in speedy trials. The denial of the speedy trial right has the following negative effects:

- The defendant is denied a prompt resolution of his case, causing him to live with the stigma and anxiety of a pending criminal charge.
- If the defendant is incarcerated awaiting trial, he must endure the incarceration for a longer period of time even though he is presumed to be innocent. This also tends to cause overcrowding in local jails, which must hold the incarcerated defendants until trial.
- If the defendant is not incarcerated, he remains free in the community for an extended period of time, perhaps endangering others or committing crimes.
- If the defendant is not incarcerated, he may be tempted to leave the jurisdiction, thereby making trial on the pending charges more difficult.
- The prosecutor's (and the defendant's) witnesses may become unavailable or begin to forget the facts of the case.
- Courts become backlogged with old cases, overburdening the court system.
- Rehabilitation is less likely to be effective if there is a long period of time between the commission of the offense and the sentence.[1]

[1] Barker v. Wingo, 407 U.S. 514, 520 (1972).

The constitutional right to a speedy trial is one of the most amorphous rights in the criminal justice system because, as a practical matter, it is "impossible to determine with precision when the right has been denied."[2] For example, assume the prosecutor moves for a thirty-day continuance. Does granting that continuance violate the defendant's speedy trial right? What if the prosecutor moved for a sixty-day continuance, or a six-month continuance? The Supreme Court has been unwilling to set out a strict time frame for how long it should take to bring a criminal case to trial, and instead has set out a complicated balancing test. The federal and state legislatures have thus promulgated statutes and rules that set concrete deadlines depending on the severity of the crime, though those deadlines can be extended by various procedural actions.

B. The Law. As with many of the laws in this area of criminal procedure, the rules governing the defendant's speedy trial right are found both in the Constitution and in statutes. The constitutional rule is a balancing test, sometimes known as the *Barker* test after the case in which the Court set out the factors:

In determining whether the defendant's speedy trial rights have been violated, courts will look to four factors:

1. The length of the delay;
2. The reason for the delay;
3. The defendant's assertion of his right; and
4. Any prejudice to the defendant.[3]

The time begins to run when the defendant is arrested or formally charged.

The first factor—length of the delay—has been referred to as a "threshold factor" by a number of courts, since a defendant cannot legitimately claim that his speedy trial right has been violated unless there has been a substantial delay in bringing him to trial. However, the Supreme Court has consistently refused to offer any specific length of time that will trigger the possibility of a constitutional speedy trial claim. Some circuit courts, however, have held that a delay of at least one year between arrest and trial is necessary before the defendant can claim a speedy trial violation.[4] Even in jurisdictions that do not articulate a specific length of time, courts generally will not entertain a constitutional speedy trial claim unless the defendant has been waiting for at least nine months.[5] Most claims involve

[2] Id. at 521.
[3] Id. at 530.
[4] See, e.g., United States v. Zabawa, 719 F.3d 555 (6th Cir. 2013).
[5] See, e.g., United States v. Dixon, 542 Fed.Appx. 273 (4th Cir. 2013).

much longer delays, such as three years or more. For the purposes of calculating the delay, courts will start at the time of arrest or indictment, whichever came first.

Although the length of delay is a threshold factor, it is certainly not dispositive. Once the amount of time has been established, courts will examine the other four factors of the *Barker* test to contrast and compare the conduct of the defense and the prosecution in order to determine if any challenged delay is acceptable. At one end of the continuum, if the court finds that the delay was lengthy and prejudicial and was caused by the prosecution, it more likely will be found to violate the guarantee of a speedy trial. At the other end of the continuum, if the delay was brief, immaterial, and largely caused by the defense, a violation will not be found. The challenge is resolving the countless cases that lie between these two poles.

As to the particular factors that it has identified as being most relevant, the Supreme Court has held that the appropriateness of any **length of delay** will depend on the circumstances of the particular case, specifically the complexity of the crime charged. The delay will also count more or less heavily against the government depending on the **reason for the delay**. If the prosecutor intentionally delays the trial to prejudice the defense, the delay will count heavily against the government. On the other hand, if the delay is due to an overcrowded court system or simple negligence on the part of the prosecutor, it will count only slightly against the government.[6] And, if the delay is for a "legitimate" reason (such as a witness who is missing or ill) or if it is the fault of the defendant, it will not count at all in the balancing test.

If the defendant remains silent or explicitly consents to any part of the delay, that portion of the delay will generally not count against the government. This is because, as with other rights, the defendant generally must **assert his right** in order to get relief under the Constitution. The fourth and final factor, **prejudice to the defendant,** can come in one of three ways: (1) excessive pretrial incarceration; (2) anxiety and concern because of the charge hanging over the defendant's head; and (3) impairment of the defense case due to degradation of evidence or the loss of witnesses.

In contrast with the broad and somewhat vague balancing test required by the Constitution, the statutory rules on speedy trial rights create specific deadlines for the prosecutor to follow. Every jurisdiction has these rules. By way of example, consider the details of the federal speedy trial law, which governs both the time in which charges must be filed and the time in which those charges must be brought to trial:

---

[6] Barker, 407 U.S. at 531.

The indictment or information must be filed within thirty days after the defendant is arrested or served with a summons. This deadline will be extended by thirty days if the jurisdiction has not had a grand jury convene in the first thirty days.[7]

The trial must take place within seventy days of the date the charging instrument is filed or from the date that the defendant first appeared in court on those charges, whichever date comes later.[8]

If a charge against the defendant is dismissed by the prosecutor or is dismissed after a successful motion by the defendant, and the prosecutor later brings a new charge against the defendant based on the same criminal conduct or arising from the same criminal episode, the time elapsed on the original charge will be assessed on the new charge.[9]

If, following a mistrial or reversal on appeal, the government reinstitutes the prosecution, the re-trial must take place within seventy days of the date of the reinstatement. The court may extend this period to one hundred eighty days if witnesses are unavailable or the passage of time has made the seventy-day deadline impractical.[10]

Certain delays will be excluded from calculating the amount of time that has passed. These excludable periods of delay include those that occur for one of the following reasons:

1. Examinations or proceedings to determine the competency of the defendant;[11]
2. The defendant is being tried on other unrelated charges;[12]
3. The case is on interlocutory appeal;[13]
4. A motion that has been filed in the case is still pending;[14]
5. The defendant is being transported to or from another district or a hospital, as long as the time required for that transfer does not exceed twelve days;[15]
6. The court is considering a proposed plea agreement;[16]

---

7 18 U.S.C. § 3161(b).
8 Id. at § 3161(c).
9 Id. at § 3161(d)(1).
10 Id. at § 3161(d)(2).
11 Id. at § 3161(h)(1)(A).
12 Id. at § 3161(h)(1)(B).
13 Id. at § 3161(h)(1)(C).
14 Id. at § 3161(h)(1)(D).
15 Id. at § 3161(h)(1)(E)-(F).
16 Id. at § 3161(h)(1)(G).

7. The court is, for up to thirty days, considering any other proceeding involving the defendant;[17]
8. The defendant has consented to the delay and the court has agreed to the delay in order to allow the defendant a period of time in which to demonstrate his good conduct;[18]
9. The defendant or an essential witness is absent or unavailable;[19]
10. The defendant is mentally incompetent or physically unable to stand trial;[20]
11. If the charge is dismissed and a new charge is then filed for the same criminal conduct, the time period between the dismissal and the new charge being filed;[21]
12. The defendant is joined for trial with a co-defendant who has no time accrued on his speedy trial calculation, up to a reasonable amount of time;[22]
13. Any continuance granted by the judge (whether requested by the prosecutor or defense attorney, or whether granted on the judge's own initiative), if the judge believes that the ends of justice served by granting the continuance outweigh the interests that the public and the defendant have in a speedy trial. The court must set forth its reasoning on the record;[23] and
14. Evidence is located in a foreign country, and a party has made an official request for the evidence, up to one year.[24]

In the parlance of practitioners, every defendant gets a speedy trial "clock," which starts ticking as soon as the defendant is arrested or served with a summons. In the federal system, the initial clock begins with thirty days on it. These thirty days tick down until the defendant is formally charged or until the time on the clock runs out, whichever comes first. Once the defendant is formally charged and makes his court appearance, the clock is reset with seventy days and begins ticking again. It then ticks down until the trial begins or until it runs out.

If the clock runs out at any point, the case can be dismissed. The case can either be dismissed **without prejudice**, which means the charges can be re-filed by the

[17] Id. at § 3161(h)(1)(H).
[18] Id. at § 3161(h)(2).
[19] Id. at § 3161(h)(3)(A).
[20] Id. at § 3161(h)(4).
[21] Id. at § 3161(h)(5).
[22] Id. at § 3161(h)(6).
[23] Id. at § 3161(h)(7).
[24] Id. at § 3161(h)(8).

prosecutor, or **with prejudice**, which means the dismissal is a final disposition of the charges. Whether the court grants a dismissal with prejudice or without prejudice will be discussed in Section C.4, below.

However, the speedy trial clock is not always running. There are numerous conditions—enumerated above as 1 through 14—that can pause or "toll" the speedy trial clock. These conditions can complicate the calculation of how much time remains on the speedy trial clock. We will see examples of how to calculate speedy trial time in Section C.2, below.

Most of the conditions that toll the speedy trial clock are self-explanatory, but two of them deserve some extra attention.

Section 3161(h)(3)(A) (#9 in the above list) states that the speedy trial clock is tolled while the defendant or an essential witness is "absent or unavailable." For the defendant or a witness to be "absent" it first must be true that the person's whereabouts are unknown. In addition, to be "absent" either (a) the person must be attempting to avoid apprehension or prosecution, or (b) his whereabouts must be incapable of discovery through the exercise of due diligence.[25] In contrast, the defendant or a witness will be "unavailable" if their whereabouts are known but either (a) they resist appearing or being returned to trial or (b) their presence cannot be secured with due diligence.[26] A witness is "essential" to the case if the witness is "important to the proceeding" and the government has a good faith belief that it will use that witness' testimony at trial.[27] Finding that a witness is "essential" does not, however, require proof that a conviction can only be secured if the witness testifies.

Section 3161(h)(7) (#13 in the above list) states that any continuance granted by a judge is excludable as long as the judge believes "the ends of justice served by granting the continuance outweigh the interests that the public and the defendant have in a speedy trial." The trial judge is generally given a lot of discretion in deciding whether the "ends of justice" are served by the continuance, but the judge is required to formally state, either orally or in writing, the justification for the continuance, and why it serves the ends of justice. Appellate courts have generally found that routine court congestion is not a sufficient reason under this provision to exclude the time.[28] The statute gives some examples of when the ends of justice will be served by a continuance. These examples include circumstances such as the extreme complexity of the case, the defendant's need for extra time to obtain counsel, or the need for extra time (by either side) to ensure the continuity of counsel.

---

25 Id. at 3161(h)(3)(B).

26 Id.

27 United States v. Marrero, 705 F.2d 652, 656 (2d Cir. 1983).

28 United States v. Ferguson, 565 F.Supp.2d 32 (D.D.C. 2008).

Finally, remember the usual admonition when discussing statutory law: each jurisdiction will have its own specific time limits and its own rules of what conditions will toll the clock. In most states, for example, the amount of time on the speedy trial clock is longer for more serious offenses and shorter for less serious offenses—for example, ninety days for a serious felony, sixty days for a misdemeanor, and thirty days for a petty offense. Also, many jurisdictions have shorter speedy trial times if the defendant is incarcerated while awaiting trial. For example, there may be a provision that every non-excludable day the defendant spends in jail before trial counts as three days on the speedy trial clock.

Although each jurisdiction's speedy trial rules may vary, as a general rule, delays requested or caused by the defendant or the court will toll the clock, while delays requested or caused by the prosecutor will not.

C. Applying the Law.

1. The Balancing Test for a Constitutional Claim. Because the statutory deadlines that are in place tend to set deadlines that are shorter than the constitutional deadlines, speedy trial claims based on the Constitution are relatively rare. The seminal case for constitutional claims is *Barker v. Wingo*, which first set out the four-factor balancing test:

> **Example—*Barker v. Wingo*, 407 U.S. 514 (1972):** On July 20, 1958, an elderly man and woman were beaten to death with a tire iron. Approximately two months later, the grand jury indicted two men, Silas Manning and Willie Barker, for the crime. The government had a strong case against Manning but a somewhat weaker case against Barker. The prosecutor's strategy was to convict Manning first and then offer him a deal on sentencing if he would agree to testify against Barker. Therefore, the government sought multiple continuances in Barker's case while it proceeded against Manning.
>
> It proved difficult—and time consuming—to convict Manning. The first trial ended in a hung jury, the second and third trials ended in convictions but were reversed on appeal, and the fourth trial also resulted in a hung jury. The fifth trial resulted in a conviction for murdering just one victim, and the sixth trial resulted in conviction for the murder of the second victim. By then it was December of 1962, over four years after Barker's indictment.

During this time the prosecutor sought and received fourteen continuances for Barker's case. Barker did not object to these continuances. He was in jail for the first ten months of this period, but then he posted bail and was released.

Barker's trial was set for March of 1962, but on that date the prosecutor sought and was granted another continuance because one of its key witnesses was ill. Barker objected to the continuance, but his objection was denied. The prosecutor received two more continuances due to the illness of the witness, and Barker objected both times. Finally, on October 9, 1963, Barker moved to dismiss his case on speedy trial grounds, and the motion was denied. More than five years after his indictment, Barker's trial then began with Manning as the chief witness against him. Barker was convicted and given a life sentence.

Barker appealed the case to the Supreme Court, arguing that the government had denied his constitutional right to a speedy trial under the Sixth Amendment.

Analysis: The five-year delay in Barker's case did not violate his constitutional right to a speedy trial. The Court set out its four-factor balancing test and applied it to the facts in Barker's case.

On the one hand, the length of the delay was "extraordinary"—over five years between indictment and trial. Furthermore, although the prosecutor had a "strong excuse"—the illness of the sheriff—for seven months of that time,[29] the justification for the rest of the delay was weak. The need to utilize a co-defendant as a witness may justify a short delay, but not one as long as what occurred in this case.

However, the two remaining factors that must be considered overcome the first two factors. The prejudice to Barker was minimal. Although he spent ten months in jail and had to live "for over four years under a cloud of suspicion and anxiety,"[30] none of his witnesses died or became unavailable. Indeed, the record revealed only two very minor and insignificant lapses in the memory of the witnesses. More importantly, Barker did not object to the vast majority of the continuances. Thus, there is no evidence that he actually wanted a speedy trial. The Court implied that Barker was essentially gambling on the outcome of his co-defendant Manning's trial. Barker was hoping that Manning would be acquitted and then the case against Barker would be dismissed. Barker did not begin objecting to the continuances until after Manning was convicted. At that point, however, the state had a legitimate reason for the last few continuances.

---

[29] Barker, 407 U.S. at 534.

[30] Id.

The *Barker* Court implied that the fourth factor in its balancing test—the requirement that the defendant object to the continuances—was a necessary precondition to finding a speedy trial violation. Absent "extraordinary circumstances" such as severe prejudice or incompetent counsel, a defendant who implicitly consents to the continuances cannot later argue that his speedy trial rights were violated.

Twenty years later, the Supreme Court explained that in certain cases it is appropriate to read the "prejudice" factor of the *Barker* test rather liberally. The facts of the case were rather unusual, however, so the actual reach of the holding may be limited:

> **Example—*Doggett v. United States*, 505 U.S. 647 (1992):** In February of 1980, Marc Doggett was indicted for conspiracy to import and distribute cocaine. The Drug Enforcement Agency ("DEA") set out to arrest him at his parents' house. However, when the agents arrived, Doggett's parents told the agents that Doggett had left for Colombia, South America. The DEA put out an alert that would notify the agency when Doggett returned to the United States. This alert expired seven months later without Doggett reentering the country. When the DEA later learned that Doggett had been arrested on drug charges in Panama, it asked the Panamanian authorities to send him to the United States when his case in Panama was finished. However, the Panamanian authorities simply let Doggett go instead, and he returned to Columbia.
>
> In September of 1982, Doggett re-entered the United States without incident. He then settled in Virginia, married, earned a college degree, and got a job as a computer operations manager. He lived in Virginia for six years under his own name and never got into trouble with law enforcement.
>
> For most of this time period, the DEA assumed that Doggett was languishing in a Panamanian prison. Then in September of 1988, eight and a half years after Doggett's indictment, the Federal Marshalls ran a basic credit check on thousands of individuals with outstanding warrants and immediately found Doggett's home address. Doggett was arrested on the 1980 indictment.
>
> Doggett moved to dismiss the indictment on speedy trial grounds. He argued (and the trial court found in its finding of facts) that he had no knowledge of his indictment, and therefore he had no way of objecting to the long delay between indictment and trial. The

government responded that Doggett had shown no prejudice from the delay, since he did not even know that he was under indictment. The trial court denied Doggett's motion, and he entered a conditional guilty plea. Then he appealed his speedy trial claim.

Analysis: The Supreme Court applied the *Barker* four-factor test and held that Doggett's constitutional speedy trial rights were violated.

The first factor—the length of the delay—clearly weighed in favor of the defendant's claim. Eight and a half years is an extraordinarily long time between indictment and trial.

The second factor is the cause of the delay. Although the government claimed that it had been actively seeking Doggett, the trial court found that the government was negligent in not finding Doggett sooner. "For six years, the Government's investigators made no serious effort to test their progressively more questionable assumptions that Doggett was living abroad, and, had they done so, they could have found him within minutes."[31]

The third factor is whether the defendant invoked his right to a speedy trial. The Court held since there was no evidence the defendant knew of his indictment, his failure to demand a speedy trial before his arrest would not be counted against him.

The most complicated question involved the fourth factor—whether the defendant could make any showing of prejudice. The government argued that there were only three possible types of prejudice that the defendant could show: pretrial incarceration, the anxiety of being formally accused, and the impairment of his defense case at trial. Since Doggett was never incarcerated, never knew that he had been accused, and made no showing that his defense would be impaired, the government argued that Doggett was not prejudiced by the delay.

The Court disagreed with the government. Impairment of one's defense is the "most difficult form of speedy trial prejudice to prove because time's erosion of exculpatory evidence and testimony can rarely be shown."[32] Therefore, the Court stated that "excessive delay presumptively compromises the reliability of a trial in ways that neither party can prove or, for that matter, identify."[33] The strength of the presumptive prejudice increases with the length of the delay, and its importance depends to some extent on the second factor of the *Barker* test—the reason for the delay. If the prosecutor intentionally created the delay to get a tactical advantage, the presumptive prejudice from this lengthy delay would be overwhelming. If the prosecutor had diligently been pursuing Doggett for the entire period of time and was not at all to blame for the delay, there would be no presumptive prejudice and Doggett would have had to prove actual prejudice. In

---

[31] Doggett v. United States, 505 U.S. 647, 652-3 (1992).

[32] Id. at 655 (internal citations and quotations omitted).

[33] Id.

this case, the government was merely negligent, and "negligence unaccompanied by particularized trial prejudice [as in this case] must have lasted longer than negligence demonstrably causing such prejudice" in order to support a speedy trial claim.[34] In this case, eight and half years of negligence was more than enough to create a presumption of prejudice.

Since the facts of *Doggett* are so unusual, it is not clear what role "presumptive prejudice" will play in cases involving shorter delays. However, the case is significant in that it broadened the definition of the prejudice factor of the *Barker* test.

2. Calculating the Numbers for a Statutory Claim. If the defendant believes that the statutory speedy trial clock has run out in his case, he may file a motion to dismiss the case on speedy trial grounds. Somewhat ironically, the delay caused by the defendant's speedy trial motion tolls the speedy trial clock, so in order to get the case dismissed for undue delay, the defendant must delay his case even further.

The defendant's speedy trial motion will set out the timeline for the case, explaining which (if any) periods of time are tolled and which are not. Time which is not tolled is "charged to the prosecutor;" time that is tolled is either charged to the defendant or charged to the court. The defendant's argument is essentially that the amount of time charged to the prosecutor exceeds the total amount of speedy trial time allowed for the case (in the federal system, seventy days after the formal charges are filed). The prosecutor then files her response to the motion, in which she makes her own arguments about which periods of time are tolled and then adds up the speedy trial time. The judge then reviews the motion papers and determines how much speedy trial time has run on the case.

For example, assume a defendant is indicted for robbery on January 1. At that point, the seventy-day speedy trial clock starts. At the arraignment a few days later, the magistrate sets a motion schedule, telling the defendant to file all motions by February 1, with the prosecutor's response due February 15 and a hearing on March 1. On February 1, the defendant files a motion to suppress his identification and his statement to the police, and on February 15, the prosecutor files a response. At the March 1 hearing, one of the prosecutor's key law enforcement officers is ill and cannot testify. The officer is not officially "unavailable" under the speedy trial rules, but the prosecutor asks for a continuance. The continuance is granted, and the hearing takes place on April 1 instead. The prosecutor calls her law enforcement officer to testify about the line-up and the interrogation, and the defendant cross-examines him. The magistrate does not issue a decision right away, but instead takes the issue under advisement and issues a written order on April 14. On the same day the magistrate sets a trial date of May 14. On May

[34] Id. at 657.

14, one of the prosecutor's primary civilian witnesses is out of the country on business and so is "unavailable" under the speedy trial rules. The judge grants a continuance until June 14. On that day, the defendant files a motion to dismiss the case based on a violation of his speedy trial rights.

In this case, the court would simply count up the excludable and non-excludable time:

> The time from January 1 to February 1 (thirty-one days) is charged to the prosecutor.
>
> The defendant filed a motion on February 1, which tolled the clock until the hearing on March 1.
>
> When the prosecutor sought a continuance for his sick law enforcement witness on March 1, that delay is non-excludable. Accordingly, the time between the March 1 request and the April 1 hearing adds another thirty-one days to the prosecutor's total.
>
> The time from the hearing on April 1 to the decision on April 14 is excludable because this time was necessary for the court to respond to the defense motion.
>
> The delay from April 14 until May 14 is not excludable, so another thirty days are charged to the prosecutor.
>
> The final delay from May 14 until June 14 is excludable because the witness was officially unavailable.

Unfortunately for the prosecutor, by the time of trial the prosecutor would have been charged with ninety-two days of delay (twenty-two days more than she had on the speedy trial clock). Accordingly, the defendant's motion to dismiss should be granted.

What could the prosecutor have done to prevent this? Many jurisdictions allow the prosecutor to announce that she is ready for trial and thereby stop the speedy trial clock from running as of the date of that announcement. This allows the prosecutor to avoid losing thirty days of speedy trial time every time the judge sets a new court date. In the above example, the magistrate issued her ruling on the suppression motion on April 14 and set a trial date for May 14, thus adding thirty days to the speedy trial clock. If the rules of the jurisdiction allow it, the prosecutor could announce her readiness to go to trial on April 14 and thus ensure that the thirty days from April 14 to May 14 are not counted. Some prosecutor's offices use this technique to ensure that almost no time ever runs on their speedy trial clock—but of course if they formally announce they are ready for trial, they must in good faith believe that they are in fact ready.

Here is a more complicated example of a speedy trial calculation:

> **Example:** Defendant was arraigned on two counts of bank robbery on May 12, 1982. His trial commenced on April 28, 1983, exactly 351 days later. After his conviction, he appealed the case, arguing that his statutory right to a speedy trial was violated. Thus, the issue on appeal was whether 281 of the days between arraignment and trial were excludable.

Analysis: The appellate court must review all of the proceedings that occurred during those 351 days:

On May 12, 1982, the day of the arraignment, the government filed a motion to obtain hair samples from the defendant. This motion was granted by the trial court on June 14, and the appellate court ruled that this thirty-three-day period between the filing of the motion and the disposition of the motion was "prompt" within the meaning of 18 U.S.C. § 3161(h)(1)(D). Thus, thirty-three days were excluded.

On June 25, the defendant filed several motions, including a motion for reduction of bond. A hearing was held on July 15 and the court denied the motion on August 10. The time between the filing of the motion and the hearing is excluded because "a motion that has been filed in the case is still pending."[35] The time between the hearing and the judge's decision is excluded because the court was "considering any other proceeding concerning the defendant, up to thirty days."[36] Thus, a total of forty-six days were excluded.

On August 15, the defendant's attorney filed a motion for leave to withdraw, which once again tolled the speedy trial clock. The new counsel appeared on August 19, so there were four days excluded because of that motion.

On September 22, the new attorney filed a motion to dismiss on speedy trial grounds. The motion was denied on October 21, and again the appellate court ruled that the thirty-day period between the filing of the motion and the disposition was "prompt." Thirty days were excluded because of this motion.

On November 2, the district judge suffered a heart attack and underwent quadruple bypass surgery. As a result, on November 5, the judge ordered a continuance due to his poor health. This continuance remained in place until trial commenced on April 28 of the next year. The appellate court held that severe illness of the trial judge was a legitimate reason for an "ends of justice" continuance under 18 U.S.C.§3161(h)(7)—that is, because of the judge's incapacitation the ends of justice outweighed the prejudice to the defendant and to the public of the delay. This continuance resulted in the exclusion of 169 days.

---

[35] 18 U.S.C. § 3161(h)(1)(D).

[36] Id. at § 3161(h)(1)(H).

The appellate court thus concluded that the total number of excludable days was 33 + 46 + 4 + 30 + 169 = 282 days.[37] This means that only sixty-nine non-excludable days elapsed between arraignment and trial, so the defendant's speedy trial claim was denied.

The above example was unusual in that there was such a long delay—over half a year—allowed for the "ends of justice" continuance due to the judge's heart attack. But it is otherwise typical in a couple of ways. First, there were a number of delays which might or might not be excludable, depending on the court's interpretation of the statutory language. Specifically, the trial court took thirty-three days to decide the prosecutor's motion for hair samples and thirty days to decide the defendant's original speedy trial motion. These delays would not be fully excludable unless the appellate court agreed that the dispositions were "prompt." Likewise, the 169-day continuance because of the judge's heart attack would only be fully excludable if the appellate court agreed that the "ends of justice" outweighed the prejudice to the public and to the defendant. Thus, although speedy trial determinations are in many respects purely mathematical calculations, there is frequently room for legal interpretation in deciding whether the clock has been tolled.

The second way in which the example is typical is that the appellate court resolved these ambiguities in favor of the government. Taking thirty days or more to resolve a motion may not seem "prompt" to some readers. And the 169-day continuance while the judge recovered from the heart attack was arguably not justified by the "ends of justice"—after all, the case could have been transferred to another judge during that time period. But generally appellate courts (and trial courts) are reluctant to dismiss cases on speedy trial grounds and so will tend to interpret the relevant statute broadly to find the delays to be excludable.

In spite of this judicial preference, speedy trial requirements represent a very significant challenge for prosecutors. In urban jurisdictions with many cases, a small but significant number of cases are lost to speedy trial challenges. This is especially true for misdemeanors, because they usually have shorter speedy trial clocks, they are much more numerous (thus overburdening the prosecutors who handle them), and law enforcement agencies and other government agencies tend to devote fewer resources to their prosecution, thus leading to more continuance requests by the prosecutor.

3. Right to a Speedy Arrest and Charge. As noted above, the right to a speedy trial does not attach until the defendant is formally charged or arrested. However,

[37] This example is roughly based on United States v. Savoca, 739 F.2d 220 (6th Cir. 1984). Some of the dates have been changed to simplify the analysis.

the prosecutor does have a duty to avoid undue delay in bringing charges. The reasons for this duty are similar to some of the reasons behind the speedy trial provisions. Statutes of limitation promote efficiency in bringing cases: if the case is charged many years after the event in question, witnesses may have died, moved away, or simply forgotten the facts. Although this is most likely to prejudice the prosecutor, the defendant's ability to present a defense may also be compromised. Statutes of limitations also encourage a prosecutor to bring charges promptly, since a delay means that a potential criminal remains at large and the victim of the crime lacks closure.

The legal duty to bring charges promptly comes from two sources, the **Due Process Clause**, which applies equally to all cases in every jurisdiction, and the **statute of limitations**, which increases in length depending on the severity of the crime and varies depending on the laws of the jurisdiction.

The first source is the **Due Process Clause** of the Fifth and Fourteenth Amendments. The Supreme Court has held that a delay in bringing a charge can be a due process violation if the defendant can show that:

1. The delay resulted in actual prejudice to the defendant's ability to present a case; and

2. The prosecution's conduct was intentional and motivated by an intent to harass the defendant or gain a tactical advantage over him.

As you may expect, the second factor—intentional action on the part of the prosecutor—is particularly hard to prove. Consider the following case:

> **Example—*United States v. Lovasco*, 431 U.S. 783 (1977):** Between July 25 and August 31 of 1973, eight guns were stolen from the post office. The government began an investigation, and within a month of the crime, a man named Eugene Lovasco confessed to having possessed and sold some the guns. However, Lovasco did not confess to stealing them. Instead, he claimed he found the guns in his car after visiting his son, who worked at the post office. The government conducted almost no further investigation during the next seventeen months. Finally, on March 6, 1975, eighteen months after the crime occurred, Lovasco was indicted on eight counts of stealing firearms from the United States mails and one count of selling firearms without a license.
>
> Lovasco argued that his due process rights were violated by the delay. He pointed out that because of the delay he lost two key witnesses. One witness, Tom Stewart died one year after the crime. He would have testified that he was the source of two or

three of the guns. Another witness, Lovasco's brother, died nine months after the crime. He would have testified that he was present for the transactions between Lovasco and Stewart, and could have confirmed that at least some of the guns came from Stewart. In response, the prosecutor offered no reason to explain the delay.

The District Court conducted a hearing and issued findings of fact stating that as of one month after the crime, the prosecutor had all the information relating to the defendant's conduct, and that the seventeen-month delay that followed was "unnecessary and unreasonable."[38] The District Court then found that the undue delay violated the defendant's due process rights and dismissed the case. The government appealed to the Supreme Court.

Analysis: The government did not violate Lovasco's due process rights. Prejudice to the defendant is a necessary but not sufficient element of a due process claim in this context. In this case, the trial court overstepped its bounds when it second-guessed the government's decision to not bring charges immediately.

Prosecutors do not deviate from "fundamental conceptions of justice" when they defer seeking indictments until they have probable cause to believe an accused is guilty; indeed it is unprofessional conduct for a prosecutor to recommend an indictment on less than probable cause.

It should be equally obvious that prosecutors are under no duty to file charges as soon as probable cause exists but before they are satisfied they will be able to establish the suspect's guilt beyond a reasonable doubt. To impose such a duty would have a deleterious effect both upon the rights of the accused and upon the ability of society to protect itself. From the perspective of potential defendants, requiring prosecutions to commence when probable cause is established is undesirable because it would increase the likelihood of unwarranted charges being filed, and would add to the time during which defendants stand accused but untried. . . . From the perspective of law enforcement officials, a requirement of immediate prosecution upon probable cause is equally unacceptable because it could make obtaining proof of guilt beyond a reasonable doubt impossible by causing potentially fruitful sources of information to evaporate before they are fully exploited. And from the standpoint of the courts, such a requirement is unwise because it would cause scarce resources to be consumed on cases that prove to be insubstantial, or that involve only some of the responsible parties or some of the criminal acts. Thus, no one's interests would be well served by compelling prosecutors to initiate prosecutions as soon as they are legally entitled to do so.[39]

---

[38] United States v. Lovasco, 431 U.S. 783, 787 (1977).

[39] Id. at 790-1.

The Court also refused to adopt a rule that required prosecutors to immediately file charges when they had evidence of guilt beyond a reasonable doubt. The prosecutor may still be investigating other illegal acts by the defendant or other individuals who may be involved. Also, it is not always clear at what point the prosecutor has evidence proving guilt beyond a reasonable doubt, and a rule mandating immediate prosecution would cause prosecutors to "resolve doubtful cases in favor of early—and possibly unwarranted—prosecutions."[40] Many times a prosecutor may consider exercising her discretion to not file charges at all, but the prosecutor would need to gather more information to decide whether such forbearance is warranted.

Thus, the only way a defendant can prevail on a due process claim based on a delay in being charged is if he can demonstrate that the prosecutor undertook the delay with the purpose of harassing the defendant or gaining a tactical advantage over him.

The second source of the legal duty to bring charges promptly is statutory. Almost every crime has a **statute of limitations**, which is set out in the penal code of the relevant jurisdiction. The statute of limitations is a specific time limit that runs from the date the crime is committed to the date by which a charge must be formally filed against the defendant.

The federal penal code sets a "default" statute of limitations of five years for any crime unless otherwise specified by the specific criminal provision.[41] Certain crimes then set their own specific statute of limitations. For example, tax crimes have a six year statute of limitation; most fraud crimes have a seven year statute of limitations; and crimes against financial institutions and most immigration crimes have a ten year statute of limitation. Murder and acts of terrorism which result in death have no statute of limitation.

Under state law, the amount of time is generally longer for more serious crimes. The exact deadline varies depending on the jurisdiction, but a typical state statute of limitations would set the following time limits:

- Six months for a minor misdemeanor of violation (a petty offense with minimal or no jail time)
- Two years for a misdemeanor
- Six years for a felony
- No statute of limitations for murder

[40] Id. at 793.

[41] See 18 U.S.C. § 3282.

Under both federal and state rules, the statute of limitations "clock" does not begin to run until the defendant has committed every element of the crime. If one of the elements is a continuing course of conduct (such as participation in a conspiracy), the statute of limitations clock does not begin to run until the continuing course of conduct is over or the defendant withdraws from the conduct. For example, if a defendant is engaging in fraud by applying for government benefits every month while concealing her true income, the statute of limitations clock will not begin to run until the defendant ceases her fraudulent conduct.[42]

There are a number of factors that can delay the commencement of the statute of limitations or that will toll the clock. For example, the clock generally does not begin to run until the harm of the crime has been discovered by a third party[43]—for example, if the defendant commits a theft, but the theft goes unnoticed for three years, the statute of limitations would not begin to run until after the theft is discovered. Also, the clock can be tolled if the defendant is actively avoiding prosecution by concealing his identity or fleeing the jurisdiction.[44] If the defendant committed a crime of physical or sexual abuse against a minor, the speedy trial clock is tolled for as long as the victim is still alive.[45] And finally, the clock is tolled during any time that a charge has actually been filed in the case (though of course the speedy trial clock is running during that time).

Aside from these extensions, the statute of limitations is a bright-line test. The defendant need not prove any negligence or willfulness on the part of the prosecutor, nor does he have to establish prejudice to his own case. As long as the required amount of time has expired, the prosecutor is barred from bringing a charge. If the prosecutor does bring a charge for which the statute of limitations has run, the remedy is dismissal of the charge with prejudice.

Note that the statutory and constitutional deadlines for filing charges are completely separate from the statutory and constitutional deadlines for bringing a defendant to trial once he has been charged. Both "clocks" cannot be ticking at the same time—if the defendant has not yet been charged, or if his charge has been dismissed, then the speedy trial clock is not running. If the defendant is currently charged, then the statute of limitation clock is tolled.

4. Remedy for Violation. As we have seen, if the defendant believes that the prosecutor has violated his speedy trial rights, the defendant should file a motion to dismiss the case. In federal courts and most state courts, the defendant has the burden of production—that is, he must file the motion and show that the total

---

[42] See, e.g., United States v. Banks, 708 F.Supp.2d 622 (E.D. Ky. 2010).

[43] See, e.g., Exploration Co. v. United States, 247 U.S. 435 (1918).

[44] See 18 U.S.C. § 3290.

[45] Id. at § 3283. Even if the child victim dies, the statute of limitations for such a crime is a minimum of ten years.

number of days between the arrest or initial appearance and the trial exceeds the allowable amount. The burden then shifts to the prosecutor to prove there was sufficient excludable time to fit within the deadline.

If the defendant wins the speedy trial motion, the case is dismissed. However, under certain circumstances, the prosecutor will be allowed to bring the identical charges again. Under the federal rules, the court will consider the following factors to decide whether the dismissal is with prejudice:

1. The seriousness of the offense;
2. The facts and circumstances of the case that led to the dismissal; and
3. The impact of a re-prosecution on the administration of justice.[46]

Regarding the first factor, generally the more serious the offense, the more likely the trial court is to allow the prosecutor to re-file the charges. In considering the second factor (the "facts and circumstances of the case which led to the dismissal"), trial courts will use the four factors of the *Barker* test, even if the dismissal was on statutory grounds. Thus, if the original case was two months beyond the speedy trial deadline, the dismissal is more likely to be with prejudice than if it was five days beyond the deadline. Likewise, if the trial court finds the prosecutor engaged in bad faith or was negligent in causing the delay, or if the defendant can show actual prejudice from the delay, the dismissal is more likely to be with prejudice.

The court's decision of whether to dismiss with or without prejudice is very fact-based, and trial courts are given a fair amount of discretion in making the decision. However, the trial court must state on the record which factors led it to decide one way or another.

[46] 18 U.S.C. § 3162.

Quick Summary

Both the Constitution and statutes set out deadlines for the prosecutor to bring a case to trial after the arrest or formal charge. These deadlines exist primarily to protect the defendant's rights, but they also serve the community at large to ensure that cases are resolved promptly and that potentially dangerous criminals are not left at large for an undue period while awaiting trial. The constitutional deadline is evaluated using a four-factor balancing test in which the trial court will consider the length of the delay, the cause of the delay, the assertion of the defendant of his speedy trial rights, and the prejudice to the defendant. If the delay is particularly long, prejudice to the defendant may be presumed.

The statutory deadline is a set amount of time beyond which the case will be dismissed. However, many different types of delay will not be counted in determining whether the deadline has been met. This time is known as "excludable time;" and the speedy trial clock is "tolled" during these delays. Examples of excludable time include time spent on motions filed by the defendant, or time spent on an interlocutory appeal.

The Constitution and statutory law also create deadlines for filing charges after an offense has occurred. Under the Constitution, the defendant must meet the relatively high standard of proving both actual prejudice and that the prosecution's conduct was intentional and motivated by an intent to harass the defendant or gain a tactical advantage. The statutory restrictions are known as statutes of limitations, and they are written into the applicable penal code. Generally more serious crimes have longer statutes of limitations, and murder has no statute of limitations. Like the statutory speedy trial deadline, there are a number of factors that could toll the statute of limitations, such as if the harm of the crime has not yet been discovered, or if the victim is a minor.

If the defendant prevails on his speedy trial claim, the court has the option of dismissing the case with prejudice (thus barring any future re-prosecution for the same criminal conduct) or without prejudice. This is a fact-based analysis that is within the discretion of the trial court.

Review Questions

1. Waiving His Rights Goodbye? Robert Lloyd was charged with first degree assault, and he was arraigned in federal court on June 1, 2012. At his arraignment, he was released on his own recognizance and he waived his statutory right to a speedy trial. The court granted a number of continuances that the prosecutor requested in order to further investigate the case, and at each continuance Lloyd explicitly waived his statutory right to a speedy trial. Finally, when his case came up for a preliminary hearing on September 15, 2014, he reasserted his right to a speedy trial. The state requested two more delays in order to prepare for the preliminary hearing, and the hearing was held on November 15, 2014. After the hearing was over, Lloyd moved to dismiss his case based on his statutory and constitutional right to a speedy trial under *Doggett*. How should the court rule?

2. Waiting for the State. On November 2, 2011, Andy Seltzman was indicted by a federal grand jury on one count of manufacturing counterfeit currency. At the time, he was in jail awaiting trial for an unrelated state crime and so the federal agents did not serve an arrest warrant on him. On April 5, 2012, Seltzman posted bail on his unrelated crime so that he could be released from custody, but he was then informed for the first time that he could not be released because there was a federal detainer on him based on the counterfeit charges.

On May 11, 2012, Seltzman filed a motion to be released from jail which also asserted his right to a speedy trial. The motion was denied because his attorney did not have a license to practice law in the state. On June 6, 2012, he filed a motion to have an attorney appointed to him, since he had no attorney at that time. On July 15, 2012, an attorney was appointed. The attorney made three requests for a felony arraignment on Seltzman's federal charges, and each time the federal prosecutor refused, stating that he intended to wait until Seltzman's state charges were resolved. On November 30, 2012, Seltzman pled guilty to the state charges and on February 5, 2013, he was sentenced to eight years in prison on those charges.

During this entire time, up until August of 2013, the government conducted no investigation into Seltzman's case—it did not conduct any tests on the currency that had been recovered nor interview any witnesses. Finally, after a week of investigation, on August 8, 2013, the government arraigned Seltzman. At the arraignment, Seltzman filed a motion to dismiss his indictment, arguing that the government violated his constitutional right to a speedy trial and his statutory right to a speedy trial. How should the court rule on his motion?

3. Stopping and Re-Starting the Case. On March 5, 2013, Chris Caulfield was indicted on one charge of gross sexual imposition of a minor. He had his felony arraignment on March 10. At his arraignment, he filed a motion for discovery and a motion to suppress the victim's identification. On April 10, the prosecutor filed for reciprocal discovery and filed a response to the motion to suppress. On April 24, the judge held a hearing on Caulfield's motion. On May 10, the judge granted the motion and suppressed the identification. The government appealed the case.

On September 5, the appellate court overruled the lower court and ruled that the identification should be admitted. The case was remanded to the trial court. On October 10, the prosecutor requested a continuance because they could not locate the victim, who was to be a witness in the case. On the next trial date, November 15, the prosecutor requested another continuance because the prosecutor in charge of the case was ill. On the next date, December 20, Caulfield's lawyer moved to withdraw from the case and the motion was granted. On January 5, 2014, a new lawyer was assigned and she requested a continuance until February 15 to prepare for trial. On February 15, the prosecutor moved to dismiss the indictment because it could still not locate the victim. The case was dismissed without prejudice.

On June 10, 2014, the prosecutor re-indicted Caulfield on the same charge. Caulfield was arrested on the same day, and bail was set on his case. He filed a motion to review his bail status, and a hearing was set on that motion for June 17. On June 17, the hearing was held and the judge denied the motion. On that same date, Caulfield moved to dismiss the case, arguing that his statutory speedy trial rights had been violated. Should the court grant the motion?

FROM THE COURTROOM

DOGGETT v. UNITED STATES

United States Supreme Court, 1992
505 U.S. 647

[Justice SOUTER delivered the opinion of the Court.]

[Justice O'CONNOR filed a dissenting opinion]

[Justice THOMAS filed a dissenting opinion, which was joined by CHIEF JUSTICE REHNQUIST and Justice SCALIA.]

. . .

I

On February 22, 1980, petitioner Marc Doggett was indicted for conspiring with several others to import and distribute cocaine. Douglas Driver, the Drug Enforcement Administration's (DEA's) principal agent investigating the conspiracy, told the United States Marshals Service that the DEA would oversee the apprehension of Doggett and his confederates. On March 18, 1980, two police officers set out under Driver's orders to arrest Doggett at his parents' house in Raleigh, North Carolina, only to find that he was not there. His mother told the officers that he had left for Colombia four days earlier.

To catch Doggett on his return to the United States, Driver sent word of his outstanding arrest warrant to all United States Customs stations and to a number of law enforcement organizations. He also placed Doggett's name in the Treasury Enforcement Communication System (TECS), a computer network that helps Customs agents screen people entering the country, and in the National Crime Information Center computer system, which serves similar ends. The TECS entry expired that September, however, and Doggett's name vanished from the system.

In September 1981, Driver found out that Doggett was under arrest on drug charges in Panama and, thinking that a formal extradition request would be futile, simply asked Panama to "expel" Doggett to the United States. Although the Panamanian authorities promised to comply when their own proceedings had run their course, they freed Doggett the following July and let him go to Colombia, where he stayed with an aunt for several months. On September 25, 1982, he passed unhindered through Customs in New York City and settled down in Virginia. Since his return to the United States, he has married, earned a college degree, found a steady job as a computer operations manager, lived openly under his own name, and stayed within the law.

Doggett's travels abroad had not wholly escaped the Government's notice, however. In 1982, the American Embassy in Panama told the State Department of his departure to Colombia, but that information, for whatever reason, eluded the DEA, and Agent Driver assumed for several years that his quarry was still serving time in a Panamanian prison. Driver never asked DEA officials in Panama to check into Doggett's status, and only after his own fortuitous assignment to that country in 1985 did he discover Doggett's departure for Colombia. Driver then simply assumed Doggett had settled there, and he made no effort to find out for sure or to track Doggett down, either abroad or in the United States. Thus Doggett remained lost to the American criminal justice system until September 1988, when the Marshals Service ran a simple credit check on several thousand people subject to outstanding arrest warrants and, within minutes, found out where Doggett lived and worked. On September 5, 1988, nearly 6 years after his return to the United States and 8½ years after his indictment, Doggett was arrested.

He naturally moved to dismiss the indictment, arguing that the Government's failure to prosecute him earlier violated his Sixth Amendment right to a speedy trial. The Federal Magistrate hearing his motion applied the criteria for assessing speedy trial claims set out in *Barker v. Wingo*, 407 U.S. 514 (1972): "[l]ength of delay, the reason for the delay, the defendant's assertion of his right, and prejudice to the defendant." The Magistrate found that the delay between Doggett's indictment and arrest was long enough to be "presumptively prejudicial," that the delay "clearly [was] attributable to the negligence of the government," and that Doggett could not be faulted for any delay in asserting his right to a speedy trial, there being no evidence that he had known of the charges against him until his arrest. The Magistrate also found, however, that Doggett had made no affirmative showing that the delay had impaired his ability to mount a successful defense or had otherwise prejudiced him. In his recommendation to the District Court, the Magistrate contended that this failure to demonstrate particular prejudice sufficed to defeat Doggett's speedy trial claim.

The District Court took the recommendation and denied Doggett's motion. Doggett then entered a conditional guilty plea under Federal Rule of Criminal Procedure 11(a)(2), expressly reserving the right to appeal his ensuing conviction on the speedy trial claim.

A split panel of the Court of Appeals affirmed. Following Circuit precedent, the court ruled that Doggett could prevail only by proving "actual prejudice" or by establishing that "the first three *Barker* factors weigh[ed] heavily in his favor." The majority agreed with the Magistrate that Doggett had not shown actual prejudice, and, attributing the Government's delay to "negligence" rather than "bad faith," it concluded that *Barker*'s first three factors did not weigh so heavily against the Government as to make proof of specific prejudice unnecessary. Judge Clark dissented, arguing, among other things, that the majority had placed undue emphasis on Doggett's inability to prove actual prejudice.

We granted Doggett's petition for certiorari, and now reverse.

II

The Sixth Amendment guarantees that, "[i]n all criminal prosecutions, the accused shall enjoy the right to a speedy . . . trial . . . ." On its face, the Speedy Trial Clause is written with such breadth that, taken literally, it would forbid the government to delay the trial of an "accused" for any reason at all. Our cases, however, have qualified the literal sweep of the provision by specifically recognizing the relevance of four separate enquiries: whether delay before trial was uncommonly long, whether the government or the criminal defendant is more to blame for that delay, whether, in due course, the defendant asserted his right to a speedy trial, and whether he suffered prejudice as the delay's result.

The first of these is actually a double enquiry. Simply to trigger a speedy trial analysis, an accused must allege that the interval between accusation and trial has crossed the threshold dividing ordinary from "presumptively prejudicial" delay, since, by definition, he cannot complain that the government has denied him a "speedy" trial if it has, in fact, prosecuted his case with customary promptness. If the accused makes this showing, the court must then consider, as one factor among several, the extent to which the delay stretches beyond the bare minimum needed to trigger judicial examination of the claim. This latter enquiry is significant to the speedy trial analysis because, as we discuss below, the presumption that pretrial delay has prejudiced the accused intensifies over time. In this case, the extraordinary 8½ year lag between Doggett's indictment and arrest clearly suffices to trigger the speedy trial enquiry; its further significance within that enquiry will be dealt with later.

As for *Barker*'s second criterion, the Government claims to have sought Doggett with diligence. The findings of the courts below are to the contrary, however, and we review trial court determinations of negligence with considerable deference. The Government gives us nothing to gainsay the findings that have come up to us, and we see nothing fatal to them in the record. For six years, the Government's investigators made no serious effort to test their progressively more questionable assumption that Doggett was living abroad, and, had they done so, they could have found him within minutes. While the Government's lethargy may have reflected no more than Doggett's relative unimportance in the world of drug trafficking, it was still findable negligence, and the finding stands.

The Government goes against the record again in suggesting that Doggett knew of his indictment years before he was arrested. Were this true, *Barker*'s third factor, concerning invocation of the right to a speedy trial, would be weighed heavily against him. But here again, the Government is trying to revisit the facts. At the hearing on Doggett's speedy trial motion, it introduced no evidence challenging the testimony of Doggett's wife, who said that she did not know of the charges until his arrest, and of his mother, who claimed not to have told him or anyone else that the police had come looking for him. From this the Magistrate implicitly concluded, and the Court of Appeals expressly reaffirmed, that Doggett had won the evidentiary battle on this point. Not only that, but in the factual basis supporting Doggett's guilty plea, the Government explicitly conceded that it had "no information that Doggett was aware of the indictment before he left the United States in March 1980, or prior to his arrest. His mother testified at the suppression hearing that she never told him, and Barnes and Riddle [Doggett's confederates] state they did not have contact with him after their arrest [in 1980]."

While one of the Government's lawyers later expressed amazement that "that particular stipulation is in the factual basis," he could not make it go away, and the trial and appellate courts were entitled to accept the defense's unrebutted and largely substantiated claim of Doggett's ignorance. Thus, Doggett is not to be taxed for invoking his speedy trial right only after his arrest.

III

The Government is left, then, with its principal contention: that Doggett fails to make out a successful speedy trial claim because he has not shown precisely how he was prejudiced by the delay between his indictment and trial.

A

We have observed in prior cases that unreasonable delay between formal accusation and trial threatens to produce more than one sort of harm, including "oppressive pretrial incarceration," "anxiety and concern of the accused," and "the possibility that the [accused's] defense will be impaired" by dimming memories and loss of exculpatory evidence. Of these forms of prejudice, "the most serious is the last, because the inability of a defendant adequately to prepare his case skews the fairness of the entire system." Doggett claims this kind of prejudice, and there is probably no other kind that he can claim, since he was subjected neither to pretrial detention nor, he has successfully contended, to awareness of unresolved charges against him.

The Government answers Doggett's claim by citing language in three cases for the proposition that the Speedy Trial Clause does not significantly protect a criminal defendant's interest in fair adjudication. In so arguing, the Government asks us, in effect, to read part of *Barker* right out of the law, and that we will not do. In context, the cited passages support nothing beyond the principle, which we have independently based on textual and historical grounds, that the Sixth Amendment right of the accused to a speedy trial has no application beyond the confines of a formal criminal prosecution. Once triggered by arrest, indictment, or other official accusation, however, the speedy trial enquiry must weigh the effect of delay on the accused's defense just as it has to weigh any other form of prejudice that *Barker* recognized.

As an alternative to limiting *Barker*, the Government claims Doggett has failed to make any affirmative showing that the delay weakened his ability to raise specific defenses, elicit specific testimony, or produce specific items of evidence. Though Doggett did indeed come up short in this respect, the Government's argument takes it only so far: consideration of prejudice is not limited to the specifically demonstrable, and, as it concedes, affirmative proof of particularized prejudice is not essential to every speedy trial claim. *Barker* explicitly recognized that impairment of one's defense is the most difficult form of speedy trial prejudice to prove because time's erosion of exculpatory evidence and testimony "can rarely be shown." And though time can tilt the case against either side, one cannot generally be sure which of them it has prejudiced more severely. Thus, we generally have to recognize that excessive delay presumptively compromises the reliability of a trial in ways that neither party can prove or, for that matter, identify. While such presumptive prejudice cannot alone carry a Sixth Amendment claim without regard to the other *Barker* criteria, it is part of the mix of relevant facts, and its importance increases with the length of delay.

B

This brings us to an enquiry into the role that presumptive prejudice should play in the disposition of Doggett's speedy trial claim. We begin with hypothetical and somewhat easier cases and work our way to this one.

Our speedy trial standards recognize that pretrial delay is often both inevitable and wholly justifiable. The government may need time to collect witnesses against the accused, oppose his pretrial motions, or, if he goes into hiding, track him down. We attach great weight to such considerations when balancing them against the costs of going forward with a trial whose probative accuracy the passage of time has begun by degrees to throw into question. Thus, in this case, if the Government had pursued Doggett with reasonable diligence from his indictment to his arrest, his speedy trial claim would fail. Indeed, that conclusion would generally follow as a matter of course however great the delay, so long as Doggett could not show specific prejudice to his defense.

The Government concedes, on the other hand, that Doggett would prevail if he could show that the Government had intentionally held back in its prosecution of him to gain some impermissible advantage at trial. That we cannot doubt. *Barker* stressed that official bad faith in causing delay will be weighed heavily against the government, and a bad-faith delay the length of this negligent one would present an overwhelming case for dismissal.

Between diligent prosecution and bad-faith delay, official negligence in bringing an accused to trial occupies the middle ground. While not compelling relief in every case where bad-faith delay would make relief virtually automatic, neither is negligence automatically tolerable simply because the accused cannot demonstrate exactly how it has prejudiced him. It was on this point that the Court of Appeals erred, and on the facts before us, it was reversible error.

Barker made it clear that "different weights [are to be] assigned to different reasons" for delay. Although negligence is obviously to be weighed more lightly than a deliberate intent to harm the accused's defense, it still falls on the wrong side of the divide between acceptable and unacceptable reasons for delaying a criminal prosecution once it has begun. And such is the nature of the prejudice presumed that the weight we assign to official negligence compounds over time as the presumption of evidentiary prejudice grows. Thus, our toleration of such negligence varies inversely with its protractedness, and its consequent threat to the fairness of the accused's trial. Condoning prolonged and unjustifiable delays in prosecution would both penalize many defendants for the state's fault and simply encourage the government to gamble with the interests of criminal suspects assigned a low prosecutorial priority. The Government, indeed, can hardly complain too loudly, for persistent neglect in concluding a criminal prosecution indicates an uncommonly feeble interest in bringing an accused to justice; the more weight the Government attaches to securing a conviction, the harder it will try to get it.

To be sure, to warrant granting relief, negligence unaccompanied by particularized trial prejudice must have lasted longer than negligence demonstrably causing such prejudice. But even so, the Government's egregious persistence in failing to prosecute Doggett is clearly sufficient. The lag between Doggett's indictment and arrest was 8½ years, and he would have faced trial 6 years earlier than he did but for the Government's inexcusable oversights. The portion of the delay attributable to the Government's negligence far exceeds the threshold needed to state a speedy trial claim; indeed, we have called shorter delays "extraordinary." When the Government's negligence thus causes delay six times as long as that generally sufficient to trigger judicial review, and when the presumption of prejudice, albeit unspecified, is neither extenuated, as by the defendant's acquiescence, nor persuasively rebutted, the defendant is entitled to relief.

IV

We reverse the judgment of the Court of Appeals and remand the case for proceedings consistent with this opinion.

So ordered.

[Justice O'CONNOR's dissent is omitted.],

Justice THOMAS, with whom THE CHIEF JUSTICE and Justice SCALIA join, dissenting.

Just as "bad facts make bad law," so too odd facts make odd law. Doggett's 8½–year odyssey from youthful drug dealing in the tobacco country of North Carolina, through stints in a Panamanian jail and in Colombia, to life as a computer operations manager, homeowner, and registered voter in suburban Virginia is extraordinary. But even more extraordinary is the Court's conclusion that the Government denied Doggett his Sixth Amendment right to a speedy trial despite the fact that he has suffered none of the harms that the right was designed to prevent. I respectfully dissent.

I

We have long identified the "major evils" against which the Speedy Trial Clause is directed as "undue and oppressive incarceration" and the "anxiety and concern accompanying public accusation." The Court does not, and cannot, seriously dispute that those two concerns lie at the heart of the Clause, and that neither concern is implicated here. Doggett was neither in United States custody nor subject to bail during the entire 8½–year period at issue. Indeed, as this case comes to us, we must assume that he was blissfully unaware of his indictment all the while, and thus was not subject to the anxiety or humiliation that typically accompanies a known criminal charge.

Thus, this unusual case presents the question whether, independent of these core concerns, the Speedy Trial Clause protects an accused from two additional harms: (1) prejudice to his ability to defend himself caused by the passage of time; and (2) disruption of his life years after the alleged commission of his crime. The Court today proclaims that the first of these additional harms is indeed an independent concern of the Clause, and on that basis compels reversal of Doggett's conviction and outright dismissal of the indictment against him. As to the second of these harms, the Court remains mum—despite the fact that we requested supplemental briefing on this very point.

I disagree with the Court's analysis. In my view, the Sixth Amendment's speedy trial guarantee does not provide independent protection against either prejudice to an accused's defense or the disruption of his life. I shall consider each in turn.

A

As we have explained, "the Speedy Trial Clause's core concern is impairment of liberty." Whenever a criminal trial takes place long after the events at issue, the defendant may be prejudiced in any number of ways. But "[t]he Speedy Trial Clause does not purport to protect a defendant from all effects flowing from a delay before trial." The Clause is directed not generally against delay-related prejudice, but against delay-related prejudice to a defendant's liberty. "The speedy trial guarantee is designed to minimize the possibility of lengthy incarceration prior to trial, to reduce the lesser, but nevertheless substantial, impairment of liberty imposed on an accused while released on bail, and to shorten the disruption of life caused by arrest and the presence of unresolved criminal charges." Thus, "when defendants are not incarcerated or subjected to other substantial restrictions on their liberty, a court should not weigh that time towards a claim under the Speedy Trial Clause."

A lengthy pretrial delay, of course, may prejudice an accused's ability to defend himself. But, we have explained, prejudice to the defense is not the sort of impairment of liberty against which the Clause is directed. "Passage of time, whether before or after arrest, may impair memories, cause evidence to be lost, deprive the defendant of witnesses, and otherwise interfere with his ability to defend himself. **But this possibility of prejudice at trial is not itself sufficient reason to wrench the Sixth Amendment from its proper context.**" Even though a defendant may be prejudiced by a pretrial delay, and even though the government may be unable to provide a valid justification for that delay, the Clause does not come into play unless the delay impairs the defendant's liberty. "Inordinate delay . . . may impair a defendant's ability to present an effective defense. But the major evils protected against by the speedy trial guarantee exist quite apart from actual or possible prejudice to an accused's defense."

These explanations notwithstanding, we have on occasion identified the prevention of prejudice to the defense as an independent and fundamental objective of the Speedy Trial Clause. In particular, in *Barker v. Wingo*, we asserted that the Clause was "designed to protect" three basic interests: "(i) to prevent oppressive pretrial incarceration; (ii) to minimize anxiety and concern of the accused; and (iii) to limit the possibility that the defense will be impaired." Indeed, the *Barker* Court went so far as to declare that of these three interests, "the most serious is the last, because the inability of a defendant adequately to prepare his case skews the fairness of the entire system."

We are thus confronted with two conflicting lines of authority, the one declaring that "limit[ing] the possibility that the defense will be impaired" is an independent and fundamental objective of the Speedy Trial Clause e.g., *Barker*, and the other declaring that it is not, e.g., *Marion*. The Court refuses to acknowledge this conflict. Instead, it simply reiterates the relevant language from *Barker* and asserts that *Marion* "support[s] nothing beyond the principle . . . that the Sixth Amendment right of the accused to a speedy trial has no application beyond the confines of a formal criminal prosecution." That attempt at reconciliation is eminently unpersuasive.

. . .

In my view, the choice presented is not a hard one. *Barker's* suggestion that preventing prejudice to the defense is a fundamental and independent objective of the Clause is plainly dictum. Never, until today, have we confronted a case where a defendant subjected to a lengthy delay after indictment nonetheless failed to suffer any substantial impairment of his liberty. I think it fair to say that *Barker* simply did not contemplate such an unusual situation.

. . .

Just because the Speedy Trial Clause does not independently protect against prejudice to the defense does not, of course, mean that a defendant is utterly unprotected in this regard. To the contrary, "'the applicable statute of limitations . . . is . . . the primary guarantee against bringing overly stale criminal charges.'" These statutes "represent legislative assessments of relative interests of the State and the defendant in administering and receiving justice; they 'are made for the repose of society and the protection of those who may [during the limitation] . . . have lost their means of defence.'" Because such statutes are fixed by the legislature and not decreed by courts on an ad hoc basis, they "provide predictability by specifying a limit beyond which there is an irrebuttable presumption that a defendant's right to a fair trial would be prejudiced."

Furthermore, the Due Process Clause always protects defendants against fundamentally unfair treatment by the government in criminal proceedings. As we explained in *Marion*, "the Due Process Clause . . . would require dismissal of [an] indictment if it were shown at trial that [a] delay . . . caused substantial prejudice to [a defendant's] rights to a fair trial and that the delay was an intentional device to gain tactical advantage over the accused."

Therefore, I see no basis for the Court's conclusion that Doggett is entitled to relief under the Speedy Trial Clause simply because the Government was negligent in prosecuting him and because the resulting delay may have prejudiced his defense.

B

It remains to be considered, however, whether Doggett is entitled to relief under the Speedy Trial Clause because of the disruption of his life years after the criminal events at issue. In other words, does the Clause protect a right to repose, free from secret or unknown indictments? In my view, it does not, for much the same reasons set forth above.

The common law recognized no right of criminals to repose. "The maxim of our law has always been 'Nullum tempus occurrit regi,' ['time does not run against the king'], and as a criminal trial is regarded as an action by the king, it follows that it may be brought at any time."

That is not to deny that our legal system has long recognized the value of repose, both to the individual and to society. But that recognition finds expression not in the sweeping commands of the Constitution, or in the common law, but in any number of specific statutes of limitations enacted by the federal and state legislatures. Such statutes not only protect a defendant from prejudice to his defense (as discussed above), but also balance his interest in repose against society's interest in the apprehension and punishment of criminals. In general, the graver the offense, the longer the limitations period; indeed, many serious offenses, such as murder, typically carry no limitations period at all. These statutes refute the notion that our society ever has recognized any general right of criminals to repose.

Doggett, however, asks us to hold that a defendant's interest in repose is a value independently protected by the Speedy Trial Clause. He emphasizes that at the time of his arrest he was "leading a normal, productive and law-abiding life," and that his "arrest and prosecution at this late date interrupted his life as a productive member of society and forced him to answer for actions taken in the distant past." However uplifting this tale of personal redemption, our task is to illuminate the protections of the Speedy Trial Clause, not to take the measure of one man's life.

There is no basis for concluding that the disruption of an accused's life years after the commission of his alleged crime is an evil independently protected by the Speedy Trial Clause. Such disruption occurs regardless of whether the individual is under indictment during the period of delay. Thus, had Doggett been indicted shortly before his 1988 arrest rather than shortly after his 1980 crime, his repose would have been equally shattered—but he would not have even a colorable speedy trial claim. To recognize a constitutional right to repose is to recognize a right to be tried speedily after the offense. That would, of course, convert the Speedy Trial Clause into a constitutional statute of limitations—a result with no basis in the text or history of the Clause or in our precedents.

II

Our constitutional law has become ever more complex in recent decades. That is, in itself, a regrettable development, for the law draws force from the clarity of its command and the certainty of its application. As the complexity of legal doctrines increases, moreover, so too does the danger that their foundational principles will become obscured. I fear that danger has been realized here. So engrossed is the Court in applying the multifactor balancing test set forth in *Barker* that it loses sight of the nature and purpose of the speedy trial guarantee set forth in the Sixth Amendment. The Court's error, in my view, lies not so much in its particular application of the *Barker* test to the facts of this case, but more fundamentally in its failure to recognize that the speedy trial guarantee cannot be violated—and thus *Barker* does not apply at all—when an accused is entirely unaware of a pending indictment against him.

I do not mean to question *Barker*'s approach, but merely its scope. We have long recognized that whether an accused has been denied his right to a speedy trial "depends upon circumstances." By setting forth a number of relevant factors, *Barker* provided this contextual inquiry with at least a modicum of structure. But *Barker*'s factors now appear to have taken on a life of their own. Instead of simply guiding the inquiry whether an individual who has been deprived of a liberty protected by the Clause is entitled to relief, *Barker* has become a source for new liberties under the Clause. In my view, application of *Barker* presupposes that an accused has been subjected to the evils against which the Speedy Trial Clause is directed—and, as I have explained, neither pretrial delay nor the disruption of life is itself such an evil.

Today's opinion, I fear, will transform the courts of the land into boards of law enforcement supervision. For the Court compels dismissal of the charges against Doggett not because he was harmed in any way by the delay between his indictment and arrest, but simply because the Government's efforts to catch him are found wanting. Indeed, the Court expressly concedes that "if the Government had pursued Doggett with reasonable diligence from his indictment to his arrest, his speedy trial claim would fail." Our function, however, is not to slap the Government on the wrist for sloppy work or misplaced priorities, but to protect the legal rights of those individuals harmed thereby. By divorcing the Speedy Trial Clause from all considerations of prejudice to an accused, the Court positively invites the Nation's judges to indulge in ad hoc and result-driven second-guessing of the government's investigatory efforts. Our Constitution neither contemplates nor tolerates such a role. I respectfully dissent.

42

Plea Bargaining

Key Concepts

- Plea Bargains Are the Primary Method of Resolving Criminal Cases
- Governed by Rule 11
- Governed by Principles of Contract Law
- Plea Must Be Knowing and Voluntary
- Must Be a Factual Basis for Plea

A. Introduction and Policy. A "plea bargain" occurs when the defendant agrees to plead guilty and forgo a trial, and in exchange the prosecutor agrees to either:

1. Reduce the charges or dismiss some charges against the defendant;
2. Recommend a lenient sentence to the judge or stay silent during sentencing; or
3. Commit to a specific sentence or type of sentence (such as probation).

If the plea bargain requires the prosecutor to commit to a specific sentence, the plea must be conditioned on the judge agreeing to the plea bargain—if the judge does not agree, the agreement is void and the parties either work out a different deal or the defendant proceeds to trial. Some jurisdictions (such as the federal courts) also require judicial approval of any plea bargain in which charges are reduced or dismissed. And in some jurisdictions, judges exert greater influence on the plea bargaining process by telling the parties ahead of time what sentence she is likely to give the defendant if he pleads guilty to a specific charge. In the normal course, though, plea negotiations are conducted solely by the prosecutor and the defense, with little to no input from the bench.

Plea bargaining is now the primary form of resolving criminal cases. As of 2012, over 97% of federal cases and 94% of state cases that result in conviction are resolved through plea bargaining.[1] As a seminal article on plea bargaining explained:

[1] Erica Goode, Stronger Hand for Judges in the 'Bazaar' of Plea Deals, New York Times (Mar. 22, 2012), available at http://www.nytimes.com/2012/03/23/us/stronger-hand-for-judges-after-rulings-on-plea-deals.html?_r=0.

> The criminal process that law students study and television shows celebrate is formal, elaborate, and expensive. It involves detailed examination of witnesses and physical evidence, tough adversarial argument from attorneys for the government and defense, and fair-minded decisionmaking from an impartial judge and jury. For the vast majority of cases in the real world, the criminal process includes none of these things. . . . Most cases are disposed of by means that seem scandalously casual: a quick conversation in a prosecutor's office or a courthouse hallway between attorneys familiar with only the basics of the case, with no witnesses present, leading to a proposed resolution that is then "sold" to both the defendant and the judge. . . . That is what plea bargaining is. It is not some adjunct to the criminal justice system; it is the criminal justice system.[2]

Although most practitioners would agree that plea bargaining is the primary method of resolving criminal cases, it is important not to overstate this position. Plea bargaining, like all negotiations in a legal setting, takes place "in the shadow of the law." The defendant has a right to go to trial. Also, unless the defendant is willing to plead guilty to every count in the indictment, the prosecution has a right to force a trial. Accordingly, both parties will base their negotiation strategy on what they think will happen if the case goes to trial. The admissibility of evidence, the credibility of witnesses, the likely sympathies of the jurors—all of these factors will inform the plea offers that are made by both the prosecutor and defense attorney. In other words, the results of plea bargaining are limited by the reality of the trial process. When a rare case actually does go to trial, the results are used as guidelines for future plea negotiations, since the negotiating parties will look to the decisions of jurors and judges in past cases in determining the likely outcome of their case.

The term "plea bargaining" itself is misleading for a couple of reasons. First, it implies the defendant is getting a discount—a "bargain" on his sentence. Sometimes this is true, but not always. Often the plea bargain represents the expected sentence at trial reduced by the chance of acquittal. For example, if both parties believe the defendant will receive a 5-year sentence if convicted at trial, and both parties believe there is a 20% chance of acquittal, the prosecutor might offer a 4-year sentence. Thus, there is no real "discount"—in economic terms, the defendant is just as well off taking the plea bargain as he would be going to trial; he (and the prosecutor) have simply eliminated the risk. Also, the plea bargaining process may allow the parties to craft a more creative disposition than would be possible after trial—the defendant may work out a restitution schedule, for example; or may be able to find a treatment program that fits his particular circumstances. In

---

[2] Robert E. Scott & William J. Stuntz, Plea Bargaining as Contract, 101 Yale L. J. 1909, 1911-12 (1992).

these cases, the defendant is not receiving a discount as much as he is receiving a more appropriate sentence.

The second reason the term is misleading is that it makes the process sound like haggling at a marketplace. The reality usually involves something either much less involved or much more involved.

For minor crimes, first offenses, or crimes that have relatively simple and common fact patterns (such as drug possession or shoplifting), there is no real "negotiation" at all: the prosecutor's office will generally have a standard deal that is always offered and almost always accepted in every case. For example, simple possession of crack cocaine is usually a high-level misdemeanor, punishable under the statute with any sentence up to twelve months in jail. The prosecutor's office may have a standing offer that any first-time offender is automatically offered 5 days of jail at arraignment. The defense attorney is not able to "haggle" down to a lesser sentence; she knows this is the deal that every defendant receives, and she can either take it or go to trial. These standard offers are usually not written down, but every prosecutor (and every defense attorney and every judge) knows them, and they become the *de facto* law for the jurisdiction.

On the other hand, for repeat offenders, or for more serious crimes, the plea bargaining process involves an intense negotiation, with reasoned arguments on both sides. Here is where the exercise of prosecutorial discretion, first discussed in **Chapter 28**, becomes truly significant. The prosecutor's plea offer will be based on both the law—the expected outcome at trial discounted by the chance of acquittal—and on equity—what the prosecutor believes the defendant deserves given his conduct, his prior record, and any other factor that might influence the prosecutor's decision. Thus, a plea negotiation will involve both sides trying to convince the other of the likely legal outcome at trial and the appropriate equitable outcome in the interest of justice.

For example, assume the defendant was arrested after the police pulled him over, searched his car, and found twelve baggies of crack cocaine in the glove compartment. He was charged under state law with possession with intent to sell, a Class B felony punishable by up to twelve years in prison. He has one prior conviction for simple possession of narcotics from five years ago. The conversation between the prosecutor and the defense attorney might go something like this:

> DEFENSE COUNSEL: What can you give me on this case? You realize you have big problems with the search. My client was allegedly pulled over for a broken taillight, which in itself is ridiculous, and then the officer searched his car without any probable cause. I doubt this will get past the suppression hearing. Even if you do, there is no way you will make out possession with intent to sell to a jury. My client had just

returned to town after being away for six months, and he had borrowed his brother's car for the night. He had no idea what was in the glove compartment. And even if you can prove knowledge, twelve individual baggies is not enough to prove intent to distribute—that could easily be what a person buys for a week of personal use. At best—if you win the suppression hearing, and if you show he somehow knew the baggies were there—you have a misdemeanor drug case. So why not knock this down to a misdemeanor now?

PROSECUTOR: I talked to the police officer and he says your client consented to the search. I realize cops sometimes try to force a consensual search, but I know this police officer and I trust that he did this by the book. And I am pretty confident that the magistrate at the suppression hearing will believe him also.

DEFENSE COUNSEL: Well, if you believe that is true, then that supports my argument that this kid had no idea about what was in the glove compartment. If he freely gave consent to search his car, isn't it more likely that he had no idea the drugs were there?

PROSECUTOR: Defendants consent to searches all the time, even when they know drugs are there. You know that. And your client has a prior conviction for drug possession. I know the jury probably won't hear about that prior conviction, but it at least convinces me that he is not naïve when it comes to the drug trade.

DEFENSE COUNSEL: He was an addict, that is true. That was over five years ago. He went to a program, got clean, and he got a good job in California as a landscaper. He's supporting a girlfriend and a small child. He's even enrolled in community college, learning about computers. He's a success story. If he ends up with a felony conviction of any kind, he will lose his job and be unemployable once he gets out of prison. Is all of that worth twelve bags of cocaine that probably weren't even his?

PROSECUTOR: I may be willing to recommend no jail time because he has no prior felony record and because it was such a small amount of drugs. But I think he was dealing these drugs, and so I need to have a felony conviction. We can knock it down to a Class E felony—simple possession of over 500 miligrams—and I will recommend probation.

This discussion might go on for a while, with each side blending legal arguments with equitable ones. As with any negotiation, both sides may employ strategies to manipulate the process: establishing a bargaining zone, tactically using or withholding information, deflecting questions if the answers are unhelpful, looking for areas of common ground, and so on. Also, both attorneys are usually bargaining as agents: the prosecutor may state that he agrees in principle with the defendant, but that his supervisor will never go for anything less than a certain sentence, while the defense attorney may explain that his client will not agree to anything higher than a certain sentence.

Plea bargaining remains as controversial as it is ubiquitous: many judges and especially academics criticize the process. Most practitioners accept the process as a necessary component of the criminal justice process. Plea bargaining first came into existence as a way to save resources: resolving the case without a trial saves the prosecutor (and the witnesses, and the police, and the court system) a significant amount of time and money. But there are other advantages to plea bargaining as well. As with any method of alternative dispute resolution, plea bargaining allows the parties to craft a more individualized resolution—and perhaps a more fair resolution—than the all-or-nothing result of litigation. The prosecutor can take equitable arguments into consideration, and has more flexibility than a sentencing judge in tailoring the sentence in response to those considerations. And—to the extent that many feel the penal system is too punitive and sentences are too harsh—plea bargaining alleviates the problem somewhat by giving defendants lower sentences than they would receive at trial. (At any rate, for each individual plea bargain, the defendant is better off—or at least believes he is better off—than he would be if he went to trial; otherwise he would not accept the deal.) Finally, there is some potential good in the defendant accepting responsibility for his actions—it can facilitate rehabilitation, it can help to provide closure for the victim, and it may result in the defendant providing valuable information to the prosecutor about other crimes.

Critics of plea bargaining respond that the practice is not really necessary—it is only seen as such because the state is unwilling to spend sufficient money on the criminal justice system to provide all defendants with a proper trial. And a defendant who agrees to a bargained-for guilty plea is giving up valuable rights—the right to a fair trial conducted by a neutral judge, the right to call witnesses and confront witnesses against him, the right to an impartial jury of his peers, and so on. As plea bargaining becomes more widespread, these rights become less and less meaningful in the real world. Trials—and the procedural rights that accompany them—also have a strong symbolic value to society. And there is the concern that a defendant who rejects a plea bargain and then receives a higher sentence at trial has been punished for exercising his right to trial.

But the most common argument against plea bargaining is that it shifts the power base in the criminal justice system from the judge to the prosecutor. The prosecutor already gets to decide whether to bring charges; plea bargaining essentially allows the prosecutor to be the judge in the case as well. Although the prosecutor is ideally always supposed to "do justice" in every case, she is still an advocate representing one side in the adversarial process, and so there may be a temptation to abuse that power and not act in the public interest. (Or, even if the prosecutor believes herself to be acting in the public interest, she may not be the best party to decide what the public interest is.) Faced with this power disparity between the prosecutor and the defense attorney—and faced with ever-increasing maximum potential sentences for their crimes—defendants may be coerced into pleading guilty, even if they are innocent.

Supporters of plea bargaining generally concede that the prosecutor is given more power under this system, but note that the prosecutor knows more about the case—having interviewed the victims, spoken to the defense attorney, investigated the facts—than any sentencing judge would know. And although it is no doubt true that the process leads some innocent defendants to plead guilty, criminal trials also end up convicting innocent people, and there is no way of knowing exactly which process is more accurate.

The debate over plea bargaining will no doubt continue for decades to come. For now, however, it is a fixture of the criminal justice system, and as such, it is incorporated into the rules of criminal procedure.

B. The Law. The process of pleading guilty is regulated by **Rule 11(c)** of the Federal Rules of Criminal Procedure or its corresponding state rule. The Rule expressly authorizes the process of plea bargaining, with the following restrictions:

The court may not participate in plea negotiations.[3]

In exchange for the defendant's plea, the prosecutor can:

1. Promise not to bring charges, or to dismiss existing charges (a "Type A agreement").[4]
2. Recommend a sentence to the court or not oppose the defendant's recommendation (a "Type B agreement"). This recommendation does not bind the court.
3. Agree that a specific sentence is appropriate or that a specific sentencing factor does or does not apply (a "Type C agreement"). This recommendation binds the court if the court accepts the plea agreement.[5]

---

[3] Fed. R. Crim. P. 11(c)(1).

[4] Id.

[5] Id.

A plea agreement described in 1., or 3., above, must ultimately be approved by the court. If the court rejects the plea agreement, it must inform the defendant that the defendant has the right to withdraw his plea and must warn the defendant that if the defendant does not withdraw his plea, the court may give the defendant a harsher sentence than was provided for in the plea agreement.[6]

A plea agreement described in 2., above, need not be approved by the court. However, before the defendant pleads guilty, the court must advise the defendant that he has no right to withdraw the plea if the court does not follow the prosecutor's recommendation.[7]

The plea agreement must be publicly disclosed, unless the court for good cause allows the parties to keep it secret.[8]

As Rule 11 makes clear, a plea bargain is essentially a contract between the prosecutor and the defendant. If the prosecutor fails to fulfill her part of the bargain, the court may either order specific performance of the contract—that is, force the prosecutor to follow through on her agreement—or the court may allow the defendant to withdraw his plea. Prosecutors also have an institutional incentive to follow through on their promises, since they—and the defense attorneys with whom they negotiate—are repeat players in the system.

There is no way to enforce the contract against the defendant—that is, the court cannot force the defendant to plead guilty if he changes his mind before he actually enters his plea. Thus, up until the time when he formally pleads guilty, the defendant always has the right to back out of the agreement and proceed to trial. However, once the plea is taken, Rule 11 does restrict when the defendant can withdraw his guilty plea:

1. Before the court accepts the plea, the defendant can withdraw his plea "for any reason or no reason."[9]

2. After the court accepts the plea but before sentencing, the defendant can withdraw his plea only if the court rejected a plea agreement OR if the defendant can show a "fair and just reason" for withdrawing the plea.[10]

3. After the court sentences the defendant, he may not withdraw his plea under any circumstances. His only choices are to appeal the case to the appellate court or to bring a collateral attack on the conviction.[11]

[6] Id. at (c)(5).
[7] Id. at (c)(1) & (3).
[8] Id. at (c)(2).
[9] Id. at (d)(1).
[10] Id. at (d)(2).
[11] Id. at (e).

We will discuss the contractual nature of plea bargains in Section C.5, below.

Rule 11 prohibits the judge from becoming involved in the actual plea negotiations, but it does specify a role for the judge in the process. The specific role of the judge will vary depending on the type of deal the prosecutor is offering:

> If the prosecutor is merely offering to recommend a light sentence to the judge in exchange for the defendant's guilty plea, the judge has no right to reject the agreement. However, the judge is not bound in such a case by the prosecutor's recommendation.
>
> If the prosecutor is offering to dismiss charges or promises a specific sentence, the judge must agree to the bargain in order for it to be effective. For these two categories of deals, the judge is a third party to the agreement who is not permitted to involve herself in the negotiation. However, the judge does have the right to veto the deal that the parties have struck.

We will examine the role of the judge in more detail in Section C.4, below.

Rule 11 also states that the plea bargain must be made public unless there is good cause to keep it secret. This ensures that secret deals, promises, or threats are not made to the defendant during the process.

The rest of Rule 11 regulates other aspects of pleading guilty unrelated to the negotiation process. For example, if a defendant refuses to enter a plea, the court must enter a not guilty plea on his behalf.[12] The rule also authorizes three types of pleas: not guilty (which means the defendant will proceed to trial unless he changes his plea), guilty, or **nolo contendere.**[13] A plea of nolo contendere (otherwise known as a "no contest" plea), is a distinctive way of settling a case. The defendant does not formally admit guilt, but he admits on the record that the prosecution could prove beyond a reasonable doubt all of the facts that are alleged in the charging instrument. Since these facts are sufficient to convict him, the judge then immediately finds the defendant guilty based on his admissions, and the case proceeds to sentencing just as it would if the defendant had pled guilty.

The only practical difference between a guilty plea and a nolo contendere plea is the effect the plea has for future cases. A guilty plea can be admitted in any future criminal or civil case as evidence that the defendant committed the underlying action, while a nolo contendere plea is inadmissible in any future proceeding in federal court.[14] For example, assume the defendant is charged in criminal court with assaulting the victim with a knife, and the victim has also sued the defendant

---

[12] Id. at (a)(4).

[13] Id. at (a)(1).

[14] See Fed. R. Evid. 410(a)(2).

in civil court for monetary damages. If the defendant pleads guilty (or is found guilty after a trial), the victim can admit that fact against the defendant in the civil trial. But if the defendant pleads nolo contendere and is subsequently found guilty by the court, the victim cannot admit anything about the results of the criminal case in the civil trial.

Sometimes a nolo contendere plea will be part of a plea agreement, because the defendant will be willing to be found guilty only if doing so does not open him up to civil liability. Other times the prosecutor might object to the nolo contendere plea because she believes it means the defendant is not taking full responsibility for his actions. Whether or not the prosecutor consents, the ultimate decision of whether to allow a nolo contendere plea rests with the court, who must "consider the parties' views and the public interest in the effective administration of justice."[15]

The rules also allow the defendant to enter a **conditional plea,** in which he formally pleads guilty but reserves the right to appeal a specific adverse legal decision that was made after a pretrial motion. For example, if the defendant moved to suppress his confession and the trial court denied the motion, the defendant could enter a conditional plea of guilty and then appeal the question of the confession's admissibility. If the defendant loses the appeal, he is then sentenced on his guilty plea. If he wins the appeal, he has the right to withdraw the guilty plea and proceed to trial.[16]

When the defendant pleads guilty, the court must ensure three things:

1. The plea must be <u>knowing</u>.
2. The plea must be <u>voluntary</u>.
3. There must be a <u>factual basis</u> for concluding that the defendant is guilty.

All three of these requirements are usually satisfied during the **plea colloquy**, which is a conversation between the judge and the accused (with input from counsel in some instances). The colloquy occurs just before the defendant formally pleads guilty. Before the conversation takes place, the court places the defendant under oath. The court then will ask questions, provide information, and hear from the defendant to ensure that the plea is **knowing**. The judge will inform the defendant of all of the rights that he is surrendering by pleading guilty (such as the right to trial and the right to cross-examine witnesses). The judge will also inform the penalties associated with being found guilty (such as the

[15] Fed. R. Crim. P. 11(a)(3).

[16] Id. at (a)(2).

maximum potential sentence and the collateral consequences of the conviction).[17] We will discuss these warnings in more detail in Section C.1, below.

Next, the court ensures that the plea is **voluntary**. The rules require the court to address "the defendant personally in open court and determine that the plea is voluntary and did not result from force, threats, or promises (other than promises in a plea agreement)."[18] The judge will also ensure that the defendant is not currently under the influence of alcohol or drugs. We will consider the standard of "voluntariness" in Section C.2, below.

Also in the colloquy, the court will ask the defendant to make (or agree to) a brief statement of facts to support his guilty plea.[19] Essentially, this is an in-court confession of guilt, made on the record under penalties of perjury. The defendant must state sufficient facts to meet all of the elements of the crime. In some jurisdictions, the courts are allowed to accept an "***Alford*** **plea**," in which the defendant pleads guilty but does not admit to any of the facts in the charging instrument—in other words, the defendant formally pleads guilty but maintains that he is factually innocent.[20] We will consider *Alford* pleas and other issues relating to the factual basis of the guilty plea in Section C.3, below.

A defendant can challenge a plea by arguing one of three things:

1. The technical requirements of Rule 11 were not met when he pled guilty. This type of claim will be assessed under the **harmless error** doctrine.[21] Thus, an appellate court will not overturn a guilty plea simply because some minor aspect of Rule 11 has been violated; the error will have to affect the defendant's substantial rights. This means there must be a reasonable probability based on the appellate record as a whole that but for the complained-of error the defendant would not have pled guilty. In addition, if the defendant did not object to the error during the change of plea hearing, the appellate court will apply a **plain error** analysis. This means that he cannot win on appeal unless he proves that the error undermined the integrity of the proceedings and caused a miscarriage of justice.

2. His plea was not knowing or voluntary. In this case, the defendant is arguing that his waiver of his trial rights at the time he took the plea was invalid. As is the case with other situations when the defendant waives his rights, the harmless error rule does not apply. Thus, as long as the defendant can prove that his waiver was invalid, he need not demonstrate actual prejudice.

---

[17] Id. at (b)(1).

[18] Id. at (b)(2).

[19] Id. at (b)(3).

[20] North Carolina v. Alford, 400 U.S. 25 (1970).

[21] Fed. R. Crim. P. 11(h).

3. The prosecutor did not comply with the terms of the deal. As with an invalid waiver, the defendant need not show actual prejudice in order to prevail on this claim; as we will see in Section C.5, the court will apply contract law to the agreement and either grant the defendant specific performance or allow him to withdraw the plea and proceed to trial. However, as with most other issues on appeal, if the defendant does not enter a timely objection to the prosecutor's lack of compliance, a plain error analysis may be employed.

Finally, Rule 11 and Federal Rule of Evidence 410 state that if the plea negotiations break down, the prosecutor may not admit any plea discussions or plea offers at trial. These provisions encourage defendants to freely negotiate and bargain without having to worry that their statements or offers will later be used against them in court.[22] In some cases, the prosecutor will refuse to negotiate with the defendant unless he agrees to waive his Rule 410 rights,[23] but this is relatively unusual, since most defendants are not willing to enter into plea negotiations without the promise of confidentiality.

C. Applying the Law.

1. What Is a "Knowing" Plea? In the landmark case of *Boykin v. Alabama*,[24] the Supreme Court stated that courts accepting a guilty plea must ensure the defendant "has a full understanding of what the plea connotes and of its consequence." The Court explained:

> A plea of guilty is more than a confession which admits that the accused did various acts; it is itself a conviction; nothing remains but to give judgment and determine punishment. Admissibility of a confession must be based on a 'reliable determination on the voluntariness issue which satisfies the constitutional rights of the defendant.' The requirement that the prosecution spread on the record the prerequisites of a valid waiver is no constitutional innovation. In *Carnley v. Cochran*, we dealt with a problem of waiver of the right to counsel, a Sixth Amendment right. We held: 'Presuming waiver from a silent record is impermissible. The record must show, or there must be an allegation and evidence which show, that an accused was offered counsel but intelligently and understandingly rejected the offer. Anything less is not waiver.' We think that the same standard must be applied to determining whether a guilty plea is voluntarily made.[25]

---

[22] Id. at (f); Fed. R. Evid. 410.

[23] United States v. Mezzanato, 513 U.S. 196 (1995).

[24] 395 U.S. 238 (1969).

[25] Id. at 242 (internal citations omitted).

Thus, when a defendant pleads guilty, he must do so "knowingly and understandingly." In practice, this means that the trial judge must inform the defendant of a number of facts before she accepts the defendant's plea. Essentially there are three categories of information that must be imparted to the defendant:

1. The critical elements of each charge to which he is pleading;

2. The rights that the defendant is forfeiting by pleading guilty; and

3. The potential consequences of his guilty plea (the maximum possible sentence and some of the collateral consequences of a conviction).

The first requirement is grounded in the defendant's due process rights: just as a jury can only convict a defendant if it finds that he has committed every element of the crime beyond a reasonable doubt, the judge cannot accept a guilty plea unless she is sure the defendant is aware of every element of the crime.[26] This constitutional right is also codified in Rule 11(b)(1). This requirement is almost always satisfied by the related requirement (discussed in Section C.5, below) that the judge must ensure there is a factual basis for the plea.

Rule 11(b)(1) also states that before accepting the guilty plea, the judge must "address the defendant personally in open court" and "inform the defendant of, and determine that the defendant understands, the following:"[27]

1. The right to plead not guilty, or having already so pleaded, to persist in that plea;

2. The right to a jury trial;

3. The right to be represented by counsel—and if necessary have the court appoint counsel—at trial and at every critical stage of the proceeding; and

4. The right at trial to confront and cross-examine adverse witnesses, to be protected from compelled self-incrimination, to testify and present evidence, and to compel the attendance of witnesses.

The Rule also states that the defendant must be informed that he is waiving these rights by pleading guilty, and (if the plea agreement says so) that he is waiving the right to appeal or collaterally attack the conviction and sentence.

Finally, the defendant must be informed of the potential consequences of his plea. In this regard, Rule 11(b)(1) states that the judge must inform the defendant of:

---

[26] Henderson v. Morgan, 426 U.S. 637 (1976).

[27] Fed. R. Crim. P. 11(b).

1. Any maximum possible penalty, including imprisonment, fine, and term of supervised release;

2. Any mandatory minimum penalty;

3. Any applicable forfeiture;

4. The court's authority to order restitution;

5. The court's obligation to impose a special assessment;

6. In determining a sentence, the court's obligation to calculate the applicable sentencing-guideline range and to consider that range, possible departures under the Sentencing Guidelines, and other relevant sentencing factors; and

7. If the defendant is not a United States citizen, the fact that he may be removed from the United States, denied citizenship, and denied admission to the United States in the future.

If the plea agreement does not bind the judge to a particular sentence, the judge must also inform the defendant that she has no obligation to follow the prosecutor's recommendation and that the defendant will not have the right to withdraw his plea after sentencing.[28]

All of these requirements are intended to ensure that the defendant is fully aware of what he is doing when he pleads guilty. However, neither the Constitution nor the Federal Rules require the judge to explain all of the potential consequences of pleading guilty. Specifically, most criminal convictions carry a number of "collateral consequences"—legal liabilities that are imposed on the defendant above and beyond the specific sentence. Depending on the crime, a defendant could suffer a number of collateral consequences, such as:

- Deportation (if the defendant is not a United States citizen);
- Losing the right to vote, serve on a jury, or hold public office;
- Losing the right to carry a firearm;
- Losing the right to public benefits such as welfare payments;
- Losing the right to hold a driver's license;
- Losing custody of a child;
- Eligibility for a higher sentence if convicted of another crime;

[28] Id. at (c)(3)(B).

- Mandatory registration as a sex offender; or
- Civil liability to individuals harmed by the criminal conduct.

A criminal conviction creates a number of extra-legal consequences as well: A convicted criminal will find it harder to get a job, he will suffer social stigma from his community, and he may become ineligible to enter certain professions. However, with one exception, there is no obligation to inform the defendant of the collateral consequences that he might face. The exception is the possibility of deportation for non-citizen defendants. This collateral consequence is thought to be so severe that Rule 11(b) requires all federal judges to inform the defendant of the chance that he will be deported if he is not a citizen. Furthermore, the Supreme Court has mandated that all defense attorneys—whether in state court or federal court—must inform their clients of the risk of deportation. Failure to do so will give rise to a claim of ineffective assistance of counsel.[29] A fuller discussion of this issue is found in **Chapter 31**.

In practice, some judges will go well beyond Rule 11's mandates during the plea colloquy and advise the defendant of some of the formal and informal collateral consequences of conviction. The American Bar Association has promulgated ethical standards which encourage judges to advise defendants of "additional consequences including but not limited to the forfeiture of property, the loss of certain civil rights, disqualification from certain governmental benefits, enhanced punishment if the defendant is convicted of another crime in the future, and, if the defendant is not a United States citizen, a change in the defendant's immigration status."[30] Even if the judge does not give these warnings, most experienced defense attorneys will do so. Also, a few states have enacted rules which require the judge to inform the pleading defendant of certain collateral consequences. For example, Indiana requires judges to inform defendants who plead guilty to domestic violence that the conviction will restrict their right to carry a firearm;[31] And New Mexico judges must advise defendants pleading to sex crimes that they may have to register as a sex offender.[32]

2. What is a "Voluntary" Plea? The *Boykin* case, mentioned above, states that the defendant's plea must be knowing and voluntary. The "knowing" requirement is actually a necessary component of the voluntariness requirement; a plea cannot be truly voluntary if the defendant does not know what he is pleading to and the consequences of that plea. But voluntariness also requires that the defendant has not been coerced into pleading guilty.

---

29 Padilla v. Kentucky, 559 U.S. 356 (2010).

30 ABA Standards for Criminal Justice, Pleas of Guilty, Standard 14-1.4(c) (3d ed. 1999).

31 Ind. Code Ann. § 35-35-1-2.

32 N.M. R. Metro. Ct. R.C.R.P. 7-502 (B) (7).

The possibility of coercion is one of the main arguments cited by critics of plea bargaining. Many crimes carry high mandatory sentences, and prosecutors can offer to drop or reduce charges in order to avoid those mandatory sentences in exchange for a guilty plea. Thus, a defendant might see no reasonable option other than to plead guilty in order to avoid the possibility of many extra years or even decades in prison. This is obviously a problem if the defendant is innocent of the crime, but it is also a problem for defendants who are guilty and who feel forced to waive their procedural rights.

Nonetheless, the Supreme Court has consistently rejected claims of coercion. In *Bordenkircher v. Hayes*, the Court held that a prosecutor did not engage in coercive behavior when he threatened to bring more serious charges if the defendant did not plead guilty to the original charges:

> **Example—*Bordenkircher v. Hayes*, 434 U.S. 357 (1978).** A Kentucky grand jury indicted Paul Lewis Hayes on one count of uttering a forged instrument, which was punishable by two to ten years in prison. During plea negotiations, the prosecutor offered to recommend a five-year sentence in exchange for a guilty plea. The prosecutor also stated that if Hayes did not plead guilty, the prosecutor would return to the grand jury and indict Hayes under the Kentucky Habitual Criminal Act, which (because of Hayes's two proper felony convictions) would carry a mandatory life sentence upon conviction.
>
> Hayes rejected the deal, and the prosecutor indicted him under the Habitual Criminal Act. Hayes was convicted at trial and sentenced to life in prison. The defendant appealed the case, arguing that the prosecutor's actions were coercive.

Analysis: The Supreme Court rejected Hayes' argument and upheld the life sentence. The Court noted that the prosecutor always had the ability in this case to bring charges under the Habitual Criminal Act, and so this situation was no different than "if the grand jury had indicted Hayes as a recidivist from the outset, and the prosecutor had offered to drop that charge as part of the plea bargain."[33]

The Court noted that it is wrong "[t]o punish a person because he has done what the law plainly allows him to do" and that it is "patently unconstitutional" for a prosecutor to penalize someone for relying on her legal rights.[34] However, "in the 'give-and-take' of plea bargaining, there is no such element of punishment

[33] Bordenkircher v. Hayes, 434 U.S. 357, 361 (1978).

[34] Id. at 363.

or retaliation so long as the accused is free to accept or reject the prosecution's offer."[35] The Court continued:

> [A]cceptance of the basic legitimacy of plea bargaining necessarily implies rejection of any notion that a guilty plea is involuntary in a constitutional sense simply because it is the end result of the bargaining process . . . . While confronting a defendant with the risk of more severe punishment clearly may have a 'discouraging effect on the defendant's assertion of his trial rights, the imposition of these difficult choices [is] an inevitable'—and permissible—'attribute of any legitimate system which tolerates and encourages the negotiation of pleas.' It follows that, by tolerating and encouraging the negotiation of pleas, this Court has necessarily accepted as constitutionally legitimate the simple reality that the prosecutor's interest at the bargaining table is to persuade the defendant to forgo his right to plead not guilty.[36]

The Court concluded by acknowledging that "the breadth of discretion that our country's legal system vests in prosecuting attorneys carries with it the potential for both individual and institutional abuse." However, the Court went on to find that the prosecutor in this case did no more than what is to be expected during a plea negotiation.

In dissent, Justice Powell stated that there was a significant difference between the prosecutor threatening severe charges if the defendant refused to plead guilty and the prosecutor including the severe charges in the original indictment and offering to dismiss them if the defendant pled guilty. In the latter case, the prosecutor is making a reasonable, responsible judgment that the defendant deserves the charges, but is willing to dismiss them if the defendant pleads guilty. In the former case—a case such as *Hayes*—the prosecutor only brings the severe charges with the sole purpose of discouraging the defendant from going to trial.[37]

In *United States v. Goodwin*,[38] discussed in **Chapter 28**, the Supreme Court reached the same conclusion in the context of a vindictive prosecution claim. In that case, the Court held that bringing extra felony charges against the defendant after he rejected the initial plea offers did not constitute vindictive prosecution or even the presumption of vindictive prosecution: "just as a prosecutor may forgo legitimate charges already brought in an effort to save the time and expense of trial, a prosecutor may file additional charges if an initial expectation that a defendant would plead guilty to lesser charges proves unfounded."[39]

---

[35] Id.

[36] Id. at 363–64.

[37] Id. at 370–71.

[38] 457 U.S. 368 (1982).

[39] Id. at 380.

Thus, the fact that the defendant might face more criminal charges or a more severe sentence if he rejects the plea offer does not render the guilty plea involuntary. This inducement aside, however, the court has a duty under Rule 11(b)(2) to ensure that the plea "did not result from force, threats, or promises (other than the promises in the plea agreement)." The court will usually fulfill this duty during the colloquy, simply by asking the defendant whether he has received any inducements or threats other than those associated with the plea bargaining process.

3. What Facts Does the Defendant Need to Admit? Rule 11(b)(3) states that before accepting a plea, the court must determine there is a "factual basis" for the plea. Usually this occurs during the plea colloquy, which may include an **allocution** by the defendant. The allocution is simply a speech by the defendant, under oath, in which he admits to facts sufficient to make out the elements of the charged crime. However, what if the defendant wants to plead guilty but claims that he is factually innocent? In other words, the defendant asserts that he did not commit the crime, but believes that he has a good chance of losing the case at trial and the plea bargain that he has been offered is so generous that he believes pleading guilty is the best course of action. The Supreme Court has approved of this practice, as long as there is sufficient evidence from other sources to support the defendant's guilt:

> **Example—*North Carolina v. Alford*, 400 U.S. 25 (1970).** Henry Alford was indicted for first-degree murder. He maintained he was innocent, and gave his attorney the names of a number of witnesses whom he claimed would support his story. However, when the attorney interviewed these witnesses, none of them supported his story. Meanwhile, the prosecutor stated that he would offer to reduce the charge to second-degree murder if Alford agreed to plead to that charge. Since first-degree murder was a capital offense, and second-degree murder was not, this deal would ensure that Alford would not get the death penalty. Alford agreed to plead guilty.
>
> At the change of plea hearing, the trial court heard sworn testimony from witnesses who testified that Alford left his house with a gun, stating his intention to kill the victim, and he returned home later stating that he had in fact killed the victim. Alford himself then took the stand, and testified that he had not committed the murder but was pleading guilty in order to avoid the death penalty. The court asked Alford if he still wanted to plead guilty even though he claimed innocence, and Alford agreed. He was sentenced to thirty years in prison.

Alford challenged his conviction later, arguing that it was the product of coercion since he only pled guilty to avoid the death penalty. The case reached the United States Supreme Court.

Analysis: The Court upheld Alford's guilty plea. It noted that states and lower federal courts were split on whether a trial judge should accept a guilty plea which "contains only a waiver of trial but no admission of guilt."[40] Many lower courts allowed this practice, because (1) it is wrong to "force any defense on a defendant in a criminal case, particularly when advancement of the defense might end in disaster;" and (2), "since guilt, or the degree of guilt, is at times uncertain and elusive, an accused, though believing in or entertaining doubts respecting his innocence, might reasonably conclude a jury would be convinced of his guilt and that he would fare better in the sentence by pleading guilty."[41]

The Supreme Court agreed with these arguments. In Alford's case, both the prosecutor and the defendant had agreed that the plea deal was a better resolution of the case than a trial, and (critically) notwithstanding the defendant's protestations of innocence, the judge had heard strong evidence of the defendant's actual guilt. If there were not such a strong independent factual basis for the plea, the trial judge would have been wrong to accept it.

As far as Alford's claim that his plea was involuntary, the Supreme Court noted that his decision to plead guilty to avoid a harsher sentence was no different from what happened in every plea bargaining case. A contrary ruling would mean that some defendants would be forced to go to trial even though they preferred to take the plea bargain that was being offered to them. This result would have the perverse effect of harming future defendants in the name of protecting their rights. "The prohibitions against involuntary or unintelligent pleas should not be relaxed, but neither should an exercise in arid logic render those constitutional guarantees counterproductive and put in jeopardy the very human values they were meant to preserve."[42]

This case gave rise to the term "*Alford* plea," which describes a guilty plea made by a defendant who maintains his innocence. Jurisdictions are divided as to whether they will accept an *Alford* plea, but the *Alford* case makes clear that if a court does accept a guilty plea from a defendant who claims to be innocent, there must be a significant amount of other evidence indicating his guilt. The federal rules leave the question up to the trial judge, as long as the judge is ultimately satisfied that there is a factual basis for the plea.

Alford pleas are controversial. On the one hand, it strikes many observers as morally wrong to allow a person to plead guilty and accept a punishment if they

[40] North Carolina v. Alford, 400 U.S. 25, 33 (1970).

[41] Id. at 33 (internal quotations and citations omitted).

[42] Id. at 39.

claim to be innocent. The practice turns the guilty plea into a legal fiction. The defendant is not really confessing to anything; he is merely agreeing to be punished for a crime he claims he did not commit in order to avoid the near-certainty of being punished even more severely after trial. Thus, *Alford* pleas do "serious damage to the symbolic, deterrent, and correctional functions of criminal law."[43]

On the other hand, defendants clearly believe they are better off if they are allowed to enter an *Alford* plea. In one case, for example, a defendant was charged with six felonies and wished to accept the prosecutor's offer to plead to one of the felonies and receive a six-year sentence. The trial court initially accepted the plea, but then refused the plea when the defendant stated during the colloquy that he was innocent of the crime. The defendant was forced to proceed to trial, where he was convicted of all six crimes and sentenced to twenty years in prison.[44]

A more fundamental critique of *Alford* pleas is that their very existence proves that the process of plea bargaining is inherently coercive and unfair—but in reality, this is a critique of plea bargaining itself, not of the practice of allowing *Alford* pleas.

Unlike in *Alford*, most defendants who plead guilty are willing to admit that they are guilty, either because they are in fact guilty or because they want the judge to accept their plea. However, the "factual basis" requirement raises a deeper and more widespread issue: what if the prosecutor and the defendant agree to a deal whereby the defendant will plead to a less severe charge, but the elements of that charge do not correspond to the defendant's actual conduct?

For example, assume the defendant is accused of robbery in the second degree—a Class C felony—based on evidence that he used a firearm to steal money from a convenience store. The Class C felony carries a mandatory minimum of five years in prison because the defendant used a firearm in committing the offense. The prosecutor and the defendant agree to have the defendant plead to a Class E felony, which does not carry any mandatory minimum, and which has a maximum penalty of three years. But there is no Class E felony that matches the defendant's conduct, so the parties both agree that the defendant will plead guilty to grand larceny in the third degree, which states that the defendant stole property by trick or deception rather than force. Can the defendant plead guilty to the charge, even though he used no trick or deception in committing his crime? Is it appropriate to give the prosecutor this much power in crafting a plea bargain? After all, the legislature has made it clear that anyone who uses a firearm to steal money deserves at least five years in prison, and the fictitious charge is a blatant end run around the legislative intent. On the other hand, the prosecutor certainly

---

[43] Abraham S. Goldstein, Converging Criminal Justice Systems: Guilty Pleas and the Public Interest, 49 SMU L. Rev. 567, 573 (1996).

[44] People v. Cabrera, 402 Ill. App. 3d 440, 442–43 (Ill. App. Ct. 2010).

knows the facts of this particular case better than the legislature, and she has made a professional determination that there is a substantial risk of acquittal if the case goes to trial, which would result in no punishment at all for the defendant.

Courts faced with this question have dealt with it in one of three ways.[45] In federal courts and some state courts, the trial judge will accepted the substituted crime as long as it is "reasonably related" to the original charge.[46] (Remember also that in federal courts, any plea bargain which involves dismissing charges is a "Type A" agreement and thus must be approved by the trial court.) In some other state courts, the defendant may not plead guilty unless he can admit under oath to conduct sufficient to establish the exact crime to which he is pleading.[47] And in other state courts, the defendant is allowed to plead to any crime as long as the court determines that the sentence is appropriate to his actual conduct.[48]

4. The Role of the Judge. Rule 11 sets out very strict guidelines regarding the judge's role in the plea bargaining process. Under Rule 11(c)(3), the court has the right to veto certain types of plea agreements—specifically, any agreement in which the prosecutor dismisses charges or commits to a certain sentence or sentencing range. But other than that limited role, the judge is meant to stay out of the process entirely: Rule 11(c)(1) states that the court "may not participate" in plea bargaining discussions. This is primarily intended to prevent judges from coercing defendants into pleading guilty—for example, by threatening a much higher sentence if the defendant takes the case to trial. However, the rule applies even if the trial judge does not make any threats:

> **Example:** Kenneth Baker obtained a blank check from an elderly client and then filled out an amount of $96,000 and deposited it in a friend's account. He withdrew $37,000 of the money in cash and then transferred the rest into the client's account. The client learned about the forgery and theft and reported the crime. Baker was ultimately charged with five counts of fraud.
>
> The day before the trial was set to begin, the trial judge participated in the following conversation:
>
> THE COURT: . . . For the last time, I guess, what's the government offering, anything? No harm in asking.

[45] Goldstein, supra note 43 at 574–75.

[46] See, e.g., Arizona v. Norris, 558 P.2d 903, 905 (Ariz. 1976).

[47] See. e.g., Jones v. State, 505 S.W.2d 903, 907 (Tex. Crim. App. 1974).

[48] See, e.g., People v. Genes, 227 N.W.2d 241, 243 (Mich. Ct. App. 1975).

ASSISTANT UNITED STATES ATTORNEY (AUSA): Your Honor, the offer that we extended last Thursday -

THE COURT: I'm just asking. I don't lean on people. I've given up leaning on people. I don't do that. I'm just asking. I just want to make sure the record is clear.

AUSA: We're offering, and notwithstanding the fact that it had expired, but we would allow the defendant if he takes it today, the same offer we made on Thursday, which I think was 21 to 27 months.

THE COURT: Let me throw something out here. This may have an impact, it may not.

I took a plea about two months ago from a man who pled guilty, first offender, sixty-three years of age, pled guilty to-I don't want to misspeak. The government can check its files. Mr. Krecji, K-R-E-C-J-I. My recollection is he stole $66,000. Maybe it was $166,000. Somewhere around there. He invaded the ERISA plan and made full restitution. And no prior convictions. There was not the vulnerable victim, which I think may be the difference here. The guideline range was twelve to something, twelve to, I can't recall. And he pled guilty and he pled guilty early on and assumed responsibility. I sentenced him to a year and a day, and that's the sentence he'll serve.

Now, judges do try to be consistent. And I sentenced him to a year and a day so he would get 15 percent credit for good time. And had it been punitive I would have sentenced him to one year and he wouldn't have gotten it.

And I just throw that out. I would probably be just as consistent here. There are no prior convictions here, right?

DEFENDANT'S COUNSEL: Correct, Your Honor.

THE COURT: But, again, the difference may well be that there were not vulnerable victims in that case, although there was an abuse of trust.

AUSA: And there's an abuse of trust here, too, Your Honor.

THE COURT: But the range was twelve months to something, and I rejected it on the bases for adjustments and medical. I rejected all of that and I sentenced him to a year and a day. And that's the sentence he's going to serve. That's all I can say.

DEFENDANT'S COUNSEL: Thank you, Your Honor.[49]

Later the court again encouraged the parties to resolve the case, noting that "all bets are off now if we go through this. I'm not making any promise about anything."

The next day, Baker pled guilty. During the colloquy, the court repeatedly asked Baker if he had been promised anything in exchange for his plea, and Baker said no.

Four months later, the pre-sentence report was ready, and it recommended a sentencing range between thirty-three months to forty-one months. During the sentencing hearing, Baker told the court that when he had pled guilty four months earlier, "I was pretty much thinking in relation to a case that you had referenced prior to my making my guilty plea of an individual who, I think you said he took a hundred and some odd thousand dollars and you gave him like a year and a day."[50] The judge sentenced Baker to a total of fifty-one months in prison.

Baker appealed the sentence, arguing that the judge had violated Rule 11 by participating in the plea negotiation.

Analysis: The Ninth Circuit agreed with the defendant, holding that the judge had improperly participated in the plea bargaining session. The appellate court stated that the prohibition on judicial participation was justified for three reasons:

1. "[I]t diminishes the possibility of judicial coercion of a guilty plea, regardless whether the coercion would actually result in an involuntary guilty plea."
2. "[T]he judge's involvement in the negotiations is apt to diminish the judge's impartiality. By encouraging a particular agreement, the judge may feel personally involved, and thus, resent the defendant's rejection of his advice."
3. "[T]he judge's participation creates a misleading impression of his role in the proceedings. The judge's role seems more like an advocate for the agreement than a neutral arbiter if he joins in the negotiations."[51]

---

[49] United States v. Baker, 489 F.3d 366, 368–69 (D.C. Cir. 2007).

[50] Id. at 370.

[51] Id. at 370–71 (citations omitted).

The court noted that courts have interpreted this prohibition very broadly: "the sentencing judge should take no part whatever in any discussion or communication regarding the sentence to be imposed."[52]

The court held that the trial judge's behavior was "plain error" and that the error was not harmless—that is, there was a "reasonable probability" that, but for the error, the defendant would not have entered the plea. "It is difficult to imagine how a defendant, faced with a potential sentence of over four years . . . could fail to be powerfully influenced by the sentencing judge's repeated allusions to his intent to be 'consistent' with a 'year and a day' sentence in another case-especially when the allusions were mentioned precisely because they might "have an impact" on the defendant's plea negotiations."[53]

The *Baker* case involved comments which were "lengthy, repetitive, initiated and pursued by the court, and accompanied by several concurrent suggestions that the parties 'talk again' and 'resolve this case.' This can be contrasted with other cases in which trial judges have permissibly made "impromptu, unemphatic, and unrepeated," or "off-the cuff" remarks that were "initiated and pursued entirely by the defense counsel."[54]

The facts of *Baker* raise yet another problem with federal judges participating in the plea bargaining process—the judge may imply during plea negotiations that she will impose a lenient sentence but then impose a much harsher sentence after the defendant has pled guilty. The rules and the case law provide for a defendant to withdraw his plea if the prosecutor fails to perform her side of the bargain or if the judge rejects the deal that both parties have agreed to, but they provide no remedy for a judge who misleads the defendant prior to a negotiated plea being entered.

5. Plea Bargains as Contracts. In agreeing to a plea bargain, both the prosecutor and the defense attorney are promising to take certain actions, just as with a standard contract. However, the contract does not become enforceable until the moment the defendant formally enters his plea in court. Until that point, the defendant is under no legal obligation to plead guilty, and the prosecutor is under no legal obligation to fulfill her side of the deal. In other words, either side could withdraw from the plea bargain up until the moment the defendant pleads guilty.[55] It should be noted, however, that the prosecutor (and even more so the prosecutor's office) is a repeat player, and so there would be severe reputational effects among the defense bar and the judges if the prosecutor agreed to a plea

[52] Id. at 371 (citations omitted).

[53] Id. at 374.

[54] Id. at 375 (citations omitted).

[55] United States v. Norris, 486 F.3d 1045 (8th Cir. 2007).

deal and then withdrew from the deal without justification before the defendant pled guilty.

Once the defendant pleads guilty, however, the prosecutor is strictly bound to the terms of the plea bargain:

> **Example—*Santobello v. New York*, 404 U.S. 257 (1971):** Prosecutors in New York indicted Rudolph Santobello on two counts of gambling: Promoting Gambling in the First Degree, and Possession of Gambling Records in the First Degree. After plea negotiations, the prosecutor agreed to let the defendant plead guilty to the lesser-included offense of Possession of Gambling Records in the Second Degree. The prosecutor also agreed to make no recommendation as to sentencing. Santobello pled guilty and the case was set for sentencing.
>
> A few weeks later, Santobello hired a new defense attorney, who moved to withdraw the guilty plea and moved to suppress the evidence against him. The judge denied these motions, but these procedures delayed sentencing by three and a half months. At that point, a new prosecutor had been appointed to the case who was unaware of the details of the original plea agreement. At sentencing, the new prosecutor made a recommendation, urging the judge to sentence Santobello to the maximum sentence of one year in prison based on Santobello's long criminal record and alleged ties to organized crime. The defense attorney immediately objected, arguing that by the terms of the plea agreement the prosecutor had promised to remain silent at sentencing.
>
> The sentencing judge rejected the defense attorney's argument, stating:
>
>> I am not at all influenced by what the District Attorney says, so that there is no need to adjourn the sentence, and there is no need to have any testimony. It doesn't make a particle of difference what the District Attorney says he will do, or what he doesn't do.[56]
>
> The judge then noted that according to the pre-sentence report, the defendant was a "professional criminal" who was "unamenable" to community supervision, and that he deserved to be in jail for a long time. Since the maximum penalty for

[56] Santobello v. New York, 404 U.S. 257, 259 (1971).

the crime he pled guilty to was one year, the judge imposed a sentence of one year.

Santobello appealed the decision all the way to the United States Supreme Court.

Analysis: The Court held that the prosecutor's violation of the plea agreement should be treated as a breach of contract. "[W]hen a plea rests in any significant degree on a promise or agreement of the prosecutor, so that it can be said to be part of the inducement or consideration, such promise must be fulfilled."[57]

The Court stated that it was irrelevant that the sentencing judge stated he was not influenced by the prosecutor's arguments at sentencing; the defendant need not prove that the breach of the plea agreement was material. Nor did it matter that the new prosecutor's mistake was inadvertent; there is no intent requirement. Santobello deserved exactly what he was promised in the plea agreement.

The *Santobello* Court remanded the case to state court to determine the appropriate remedy. It saw two possible options: allowing the defendant to withdraw his plea or requiring specific performance by the prosecutor (meaning the case would be sent to a different judge for sentencing, and the prosecutor would have to make no recommendation at sentencing, as originally promised). In the years since *Santobello*, the Court has refused to state which of these two options is preferred. Thus, it is up to the trial court to decide whether to merely allow a withdrawal of the plea or to force specific performance. The trial court should fashion a remedy that insures the defendant "what is reasonably due in the circumstances."[58]

The *Santobello* case is also significant because of the explicit approval that the Court gave to the practice of plea bargaining. It stated that plea bargaining was an "essential component of the administration of justice" and that it should be "encouraged" because it saved resources:[59]

> Disposition of charges after plea discussions is not only an essential part of the process but a highly desirable part for many reasons. It leads to prompt and largely final disposition of most criminal cases; it avoids much of the corrosive impact of enforced idleness during pre-trial confinement for those who are denied release pending trial; it protects the public from those accused persons who are prone to continue criminal conduct even while on pretrial release; and, by shortening the time between charge and

[57] Id. at 262.

[58] Id.

[59] Id. at 260.

> disposition, it enhances whatever may be the rehabilitative prospects of the guilty when they are ultimately imprisoned.[60]

Under *Santobello*, the prosecutor must follow the terms of the plea bargain to the letter—if she does not, the deal may be rescinded by the defendant or specific performance may be demanded. But what of the defendant? Unlike the prosecutor's office, a defendant need not worry about the reputational cost of backing out of a deal before his plea is entered. Accordingly, he is permitted to back out of the deal at any time before he formally pleads guilty. Once he has pled guilty, however, he has committed himself at least partly to the deal and Rule 11 states that he can only withdraw his plea if he provides a "fair and just" reason or if the court rejects the plea agreement.[61] In the *Santobello* case, for example, the new defense attorney initially made a motion to withdraw the defendant's plea because he claimed the defendant did not know that some of the evidence against him was the result of a potentially illegal search. The trial court rejected this motion to withdraw the plea because it noted that the defendant had actually filed a motion to suppress before agreeing to the plea deal, and thus he did in fact know about the potentially illegal search at the time he made the plea agreement.

A defendant's ability to withdraw a guilty plea was discussed further nearly thirty years after *Santobello* in a case involving allegations of fraud:

> **Example—*United States v. Hyde,* 520 U.S. 670 (1997):** Robert Hyde was indicted on eight counts of mail fraud, wire fraud, and related crimes. On the day of his trial, he agreed to a plea bargain with the prosecutor in which he agreed to plead guilty to four of the counts and the prosecutor agreed to drop the other four and to not bring any more charges for related fraudulent conduct.
>
> The parties submitted the agreement to the court. The court questioned Hyde extensively to ensure the plea was knowing and voluntary, and to ensure there was a factual basis for the plea. The court also warned Hyde that the maximum sentence for pleading guilty was thirty years. Hyde then pled guilty and the trial court accepted the plea. The court deferred acceptance of the plea bargain until the judge had a chance to read through Hyde's pre-sentence report.
>
> One month later, the pre-sentence report was completed and Hyde returned to court for the judge to decide whether to accept

[60] Id. at 261.

[61] Fed. R. Crim. P. 11(d)(2)(A)(B).

the plea agreement and for Hyde to be sentenced. At that time, Hyde moved to withdraw his plea, arguing that he had pled guilty under duress and that his admissions to the court at the time had been false. The court held an evidentiary hearing and found no evidence to support Hyde's claim that he had been coerced. The court thus concluded that Hyde had not provided a "fair and just" reason for withdrawing his plea, and denied the motion. The court then accepted the plea bargain and sentenced Hyde to two and a half years.

Hyde appealed the denial of his motion to withdraw his plea. The appellate court reversed the lower court, holding that the "fair and just" standard does not apply until after the trial judge accepts the plea bargain—thus, according to the appellate court, Hyde was still free to withdraw his plea for any reason for the time period between the acceptance of the plea and the acceptance of the plea bargain. The prosecutor appealed the case.

Analysis: The Supreme Court reversed the appellate court's ruling and held that the "fair and just reason" requirement was triggered at the time Hyde pled guilty. The Court reviewed the requirements for accepting a guilty plea that are set out in Rule 11(c): the court must ensure the defendant's actions are voluntary, that he knows the maximum possible punishment, that there is a factual basis for the plea, and that the defendant knows he is waiving a number of constitutional rights. All of this occurred in Hyde's case. If Hyde's argument were correct, it would "debase[] the judicial proceeding in which a defendant pleads and the court accepts his plea"—after that entire colloquy ensuring the plea was proper, the defendant would still be allowed to withdraw his guilty plea "simply on a lark."[62] A guilty plea that is accepted under Rule 11(c) is not "tentative"—it is a "grave and solemn act" which is "accepted only with care and discernment."[63]

Of course, since this was a "Type A agreement"—a plea bargain in which the prosecutor agreed to drop charges in exchange for the defendant's guilty plea—the trial court had the right to reject the plea agreement. If the judge had done so, Rule 11(d) permits the defendant to withdraw his plea. However, in this case, the court accepted the plea agreement, and so Hyde had no absolute right to withdraw his plea.

In determining whether withdrawing the guilty plea is fair and just, the trial court should balance the following factors:

---

[62] United States v. Hyde, 520 U.S. 670, 676 (1997).

[63] Id. at 677.

- Whether the defendant has offered credible evidence that his plea was not knowing or not voluntary;
- Whether the defendant has credibly asserted his legal innocence;
- Whether there has been delay between the entering of the plea and the filing of a motion to withdraw;
- Whether the defendant has had close assistance of competent counsel;
- Whether withdrawal will cause prejudice to government; and
- Whether withdrawal will inconvenience the court and waste judicial resources.[64]

Most courts follow the spirit of the *Hyde* case and set a very high standard for the defendant to meet in proving that his withdrawal would be "fair and just"—generally there needs to be a credible claim of actual innocence or ineffective assistance of counsel to warrant a withdrawal.

The "fair and just" standard only applies to the time period after the defendant has pled guilty but before he has been sentenced. After sentencing, the defendant is fully committed to the plea deal and may not withdraw his plea for any reason (though a valid claim that the plea was not knowing and voluntary will provide a basis for relief).

As the preceding cases have demonstrated, most courts apply contract theory to interpret a plea bargain, using terms like consideration and breach. Occasionally there is some dispute as to whether the prosecutor breached the agreement, and courts will use principles of contract law to decide the case. For example, in *United States v. Benchimol*,[65] the prosecutor agreed to recommend probation at sentencing. At the sentencing hearing, the defense attorney pointed out to the judge that the prosecutor had agreed to recommend probation, and the prosecutor responded: "That is an accurate representation."[66] The sentencing judge, unpersuaded by the prosecutor's "less-than-enthusiastic" recommendation, sentenced the defendant to six years in prison. The defense attorney claimed that the prosecutor breached the agreement, but the Supreme Court disagreed. The Court noted that the plea agreement only required the prosecutor to make the recommendation, and the prosecutor was under no obligation to make the recommendation "enthusiastically" or to explain the reasons for the recommendation. The defendant could have insisted on terms that required a wholehearted recommendation when he was negotiating the plea deal, but he did not. In other words, the Court treated

[64] United States v. Wilson, 81 F.3d 1300 (4th Cir. 1996).
[65] 471 U.S. 453 (1985).
[66] Id. at 454–55.

the case as a contract dispute, and construed the contract literally, refusing to read into the agreement any "implied-in-law" terms.

In contrast with *Benchimal*, consider the Fifth Circuit case *Petition of Geisser.*[67] In *Geisser*, the government promised to "use its best efforts" to prevent the defendant's extradition to Switzerland after her case had been resolved in the United States. In order to fulfill its side of the bargain, the prosecutor wrote a letter to the State Department requesting non-extradition, but the letter only referred to the agreement without giving any persuasive reasons against extradition. The circuit court held that the prosecutor was in breach of the agreement, since it had "obligated itself to serve, in effect, as Geisser's personal advocate on the issue of her extradition. . . . The reasons underlying the original bargain, Geisser's admirable performance in keeping her part of the agreement, her 'intense fear of reprisals,' and the conclusion of Government agents on the case that her fears were well-founded were never presented to the State Department."[68] Since the defendant had already served most of her prison time as a result of the plea agreement, the court decided that allowing her to withdraw her plea would be a meaningless remedy. Thus, it ordered specific performance—that is, that the "vast powers of persuasion at the command of the Departments of Justice and State" be applied to oppose the defendant's s extradition.[69]

6. Right to Counsel in Plea Negotiations. As noted in **Chapter 31**, the Supreme Court has recognized that plea bargaining is such a prominent aspect of the criminal justice system that it is a "critical stage" under the Sixth Amendment. Thus, the defendant's right to effective counsel applies to plea bargaining. In *Lafler v. Cooper*,[70] the defense attorney advised that the defendant reject the plea bargain, erroneously telling his client that the alleged facts could not make out the elements of the charged crime. The defendant followed his lawyer's advice and was convicted at trial. In *Missouri v. Frye*,[71] the defense attorney never communicated the prosecutor's plea offer to his client, and the offer expired. The defendant then pled guilty pursuant to a far less generous plea bargain. In both cases, the Court held that the defendant's attorney provided ineffective assistance. In *Lafler*, the Court held that the prosecutor had to re-offer the original plea deal; in *Frye*, the Court remanded the case so that the lower court could determine whether the defendant was prejudiced by the attorney's mistake.

---

[67] 554 F.2d 698 (1977).

[68] Id. at 703.

[69] Id. at 706.

[70] 132 S.Ct. 1376 (2012).

[71] 132 S.Ct. 1399 (2012).

Quick Summary

Federal Rule of Criminal Procedure 11 regulates guilty pleas, including the plea bargaining process. Plea bargaining occurs when the defendant agrees to plead guilty to at least some of the charges and in return the prosecutor agrees to dismiss some of the charges, agrees to a specific sentence after conviction, or agrees to recommend a specific sentence to the judge after conviction. Under the federal rules, the judge has the right to reject either of the first two types of plea bargains, but has no power to reject (and consequently is not bound by) the third type of plea bargain. Aside from this power to reject certain plea bargains, Rule 11 prohibits the judge from participating in the plea bargaining process.

Plea bargaining is a widespread practice, but it remains somewhat controversial. Supporters of the practice note that it saves significant state resources and also has the advantage of allowing the parties to avoid the risk of a trial and to craft a resolution to the case which meets each of their needs better than the all-or-nothing result of an actual trial. Critics of the practice note that it bypasses critical procedural rights, lacks the symbolic and public virtues of a trial, and shifts too much power into the hands of the prosecutor, who can effectively coerce the defendant into pleading guilty.

Plea bargains are governed by principles of contract law. Once the defendant has pled guilty, the prosecutor is legally bound to fulfill his end of the bargain. If the prosecutor fails to do so, the court may order specific performance or may allow the defendant to withdraw his plea. The defendant is also committed—once he has pled guilty, he will only be able to withdraw his plea if the court rejects the plea bargain or if the defendant can demonstrate a "fair and just reason" for the withdrawal.

When a defendant pleads guilty—whether or not it is pursuant to a plea deal—the trial judge must ensure that the plea is knowing and voluntary, and that there is a factual basis for the plea. The judge usually fulfills all of these obligations during the plea colloquy, in which the defendant is sworn in and the judge then engages in a conversation with the defendant on the record. The judge will advise the defendant of all of the rights that he is waiving, and also will notify him of all of the direct consequences of his conviction, such as the maximum sentence and any mandatory minimum sentences. Neither the rules nor the Constitution require the judge to warn the defendant of any collateral consequences, with the exception of the possibility of deportation if the defendant is not a United States citizen.

The judge will ensure that the defendant is voluntarily taking the plea—that is, that nobody has threatened, induced, or promised him anything in exchange for the plea (other than what is in the plea bargain). The fact that the prosecutor threatened to bring more charges against the defendant if he did not plead guilty does not create any presumption of involuntariness. Finally, the defendant will usually allocute to the crime, admitting to facts which make out the elements of the charges against him. If he denies having committed the crime but still wants to plead guilty, some courts will allow such a plea (this is known as an *Alford* plea). Whether through allocution or through some other means, such as witnesses or a pre-sentence report, the trial judge must have evidence that there is a factual basis for the defendant's guilt.

Review Questions

1. A Prior Here, A Prior There. Richard Lace was charged with price fixing in violation of antitrust laws. A few weeks after he was charged, he and the prosecutor reached an agreement that he would plead guilty to the charge. In exchange for the guilty plea, the prosecutor agreed that Lace's "base offense level" under the sentencing guidelines would be 20; and his criminal history would be I, to reflect just one prior felony conviction. The agreement also stated that the prosecutor's "sentencing recommendation does not bind the court."

At sentencing a few months later, the pre-sentence report indicated that the defendant had two prior felony convictions. This revelation raised Lace's criminal history to II. This change increased the advisory sentencing range from 33-41 months to 37-46 months. The judge asked the prosecutor whether she objected to using a criminal history of II to calculate the advisory sentencing range. The prosecutor answered: "No, your honor. We were not aware of the defendant's first conviction at the time of the plea agreement because it was out of state. But I have reviewed the presentence investigative report now and checked his record, and it appears that first conviction certainly should have been included, and I think the new calculation is correct."

Lace objected to the new calculation, but the court used it anyway and sentenced the Lace to 46 months. Were the Lace's Rule 11 rights violated?

2. Partners in Crime. Two brothers, Owen and Aiden Stewart, were co-owners of an electronics store. They were charged with violating federal trademark law by selling electronic equipment from their store which carried the "Samsung" and "Apple" trademarks but were actually non-trademarked inferior quality items. Owen was charged with six counts of selling falsely trademarked goods; Aiden was charged with two counts.

In separate plea negotiations, both Owen and Aiden reached plea deals with the government. Owen agreed to plead guilty to one count of trademark violation and to cooperate with the government in other investigations of trademark infringement in the city. In exchange, the government agreed to stipulate to a sentence of 18 months. Aiden also agreed to plead guilty to one count, and the government agreed to stipulate to a sentence of 6 months.

At the change of plea hearing, the judge conditionally accepted both pleas, deferring to the pre-sentence report before making a final decision. During the next two months, Owen cooperated with the government on a number of sting operations for trademark violations throughout the city, resulting in multiple arrests.

At sentencing, the pre-trial report came back, showing that Owen had in fact been operating his store for six years and that for nearly that entire time, he had been violating trademark law with nearly every sale. The judge stated: "With this history, there is no way I can agree to an eighteen month sentence. He deserves a lot more than eighteen months. So I am rejecting this plea bargain." The court then decided to sentence Owen to 48 months in prison. Owen objected, arguing that because he had already performed part of the bargain by cooperating with the government for two months, he deserved specific performance for the sentence. The prosecutor realized that if the entire scope of Owen's conduct was proven at trial, Owen would probably get a sentence of over 72 months after conviction, so the prosecutor also objected, arguing that the defendant should now be allowed to withdraw his plea and proceed to trial. What is the correct procedure?

The judge was willing to accept Aiden's plea, but Aiden moved to withdraw his plea. His attorney argued that Aiden had been confused on the day of the plea and had not understood fully all of the collateral consequences of his conviction. Specifically, because he was pleading to a felony, the state would revoke his license to own a business, thus forcing him and his brother to close the store. Should Aiden be allowed to withdraw his plea?

3. First Fire All the Lawyers. A grand jury charged Marco Rodriguez with three counts of distributing methamphetamine. The trial judge determined that Rodriguez was indigent and appointed counsel to represent him. The judge also set bail at $5,000, which Rodriguez was unable to post.

Four months after the arraignment, Rodriguez sent a letter to the trial judge complaining about his attorney. He claimed that his attorney had only met with him once and since then had simply sent him documents to sign without explaining what they were. He also complained that the attorney had sent him copies of the discovery in the case, but that all the documents were in English, a language which he could not read.

The trial judge showed the letter to the defense attorney, who went and met with Rodriguez in person. At the meeting, the defense attorney described a plea offer the prosecutor had made, which would involve Rodriguez pleading guilty to one count and receiving a five year sentence. Rodriquez agreed to the deal.

Two weeks later, only a few days before the change of plea hearing, Rodriguez sent another letter to the trial judge, saying that his lawyer had pressured him into taking the deal and that friends of his at the jail were advising him not to take the plea because he was likely to win at trial. Rodriguez said he wanted to fire his attorney, get a new attorney, and go to trial.

At the change of plea hearing, the trial judge called the prosecutor, the defense attorney, the defendant, and an interpreter into his chambers. He had the prosecutor repeat the terms of the plea deal and then asked the defense attorney for his recommendation. The defense attorney stated that he believed Rodriguez should take the deal. The defendant then reiterated that he did not want to take the deal and that he wanted a new attorney. The judge then said the following:

> Mr. Rodriguez, you have the right to get a new attorney and to go to trial if you want to, but I don't want to see you pass up a good thing. I worry you are getting advice from some of the people in jail with you, and those people aren't lawyers, they aren't trained in the law. They don't really know whether this is a good deal or not; they don't know the law and they don't know anything, really, about your case. Mr. Ferguson here, he is a lawyer and he knows this case and he thinks that you should take this deal. This deal allows you to get a much shorter sentence than you would get if you went to trial and were found guilty. If you are found guilty, the sentencing guidelines say you will get a minimum of ten years in prison. If you take this deal, the prosecutor drops most of the charges and you get a discount for cooperating. But if the jury finds you guilty, you don't get the discount; you get a very severe sentence. So whether you like this lawyer or not, you need to think very seriously about whether this is a good deal for you.

The defense attorney and the defendant then had a conversation for about fifteen minutes, after which all the parties went into open court and the defendant pled guilty pursuant to the plea agreement.

The defendant is now challenging his plea on appeal, arguing that the judge improperly involved himself in the plea bargaining process. Should the appellate court allow Rodriguez to withdraw his plea?

FROM THE COURTROOM

BORDENKIRCHER v. HAYES

United States Supreme Court, 1978
434 U.S. 357

[Justice STEWART delivered the opinion of the Court.]

[Justice BLACKMUN filed dissenting opinion, which was joined by Justice BRENNAN and Justice MARSHALL.]

[Justice POWELL filed a dissenting opinion.]

. . .

I

The respondent, Paul Lewis Hayes, was indicted by a Fayette County, Ky., grand jury on a charge of uttering a forged instrument in the amount of $88.30, an offense then punishable by a term of 2 to 10 years in prison. After arraignment, Hayes, his retained counsel, and the Commonwealth's Attorney met in the presence of the Clerk of the Court to discuss a possible plea agreement. During these conferences the prosecutor offered to recommend a sentence of five years in prison if Hayes would plead guilty to the indictment. He also said that if Hayes did not plead guilty and "save[d] the court the inconvenience and necessity of a trial," he would return to the grand jury to seek an indictment under the Kentucky Habitual Criminal Act, which would subject Hayes to a mandatory sentence of life imprisonment by reason of his two prior felony convictions. Hayes chose not to plead guilty, and the prosecutor did obtain an indictment charging him under the Habitual Criminal Act. It is not disputed that the recidivist charge was fully justified by the evidence, that the prosecutor was in possession of this evidence at the time of the original indictment, and that Hayes' refusal to plead guilty to the original charge was what led to his indictment under the habitual criminal statute.

A jury found Hayes guilty on the principal charge of uttering a forged instrument and, in a separate proceeding, further found that he had twice before been convicted of felonies. As required by the habitual offender statute, he was sentenced to a life term in the penitentiary. The Kentucky Court of Appeals rejected Hayes' constitutional objections to the enhanced sentence, holding in an unpublished opinion that imprisonment for life with the possibility of parole was constitutionally permissible in light of the previous felonies of which Hayes had been convicted, and that the prosecutor's decision to indict him as a habitual offender was a legitimate use of available leverage in the plea-bargaining process.

. . . We granted certiorari to consider a constitutional question of importance in the administration of criminal justice.

II

It may be helpful to clarify at the outset the nature of the issue in this case. While the prosecutor did not actually obtain the recidivist indictment until after the plea conferences had ended, his intention to do so was clearly expressed at the outset of the plea negotiations. Hayes was thus fully informed of the true terms of the offer when he made his decision to plead not guilty. This is not a situation, therefore, where the prosecutor without notice brought an additional and more serious charge after plea negotiations relating only to the original indictment had ended with the defendant's insistence on pleading not guilty. As a practical matter, in short, this case would be no different if the grand jury had indicted Hayes as a recidivist from the outset, and the prosecutor had offered to drop that charge as part of the plea bargain.

The Court of Appeals nonetheless drew a distinction between "concessions relating to prosecution under an existing indictment," and threats to bring more severe charges not contained in the original indictment—a line it thought necessary in order to establish a prophylactic rule to guard against the evil of prosecutorial vindictiveness. Quite apart from this chronological distinction, however, the Court of Appeals found that the prosecutor had acted vindictively in the present case since he had conceded that the indictment was influenced by his desire to induce a guilty plea. The ultimate conclusion of the Court of Appeals thus seems to have been that a prosecutor acts vindictively and in violation of due process of law whenever his charging decision is influenced by what he hopes to gain in the course of plea bargaining negotiations.

III

We have recently had occasion to observe: "[W]hatever might be the situation in an ideal world, the fact is that the guilty plea and the often concomitant plea bargain are important components of this country's criminal justice system. Properly administered, they can benefit all concerned." The open acknowledgment of this previously clandestine practice has led this Court to recognize the importance of counsel during plea negotiations, the need for a public record indicating that a plea was knowingly and voluntarily made, and the requirement that a prosecutor's plea-bargaining promise must be kept. The decision of the Court of Appeals in the present case, however, did not deal with considerations such as these, but held that the substance of the plea offer itself violated the limitations imposed by the Due Process Clause of the Fourteenth Amendment. For the reasons that follow, we have concluded that the Court of Appeals was mistaken in so ruling.

IV

This Court held in *North Carolina v. Pearce*, 395 U.S. 711, that the Due Process Clause of the Fourteenth Amendment "requires that vindictiveness against a defendant for having successfully attacked his first conviction must play no part in the sentence he receives after a new trial." The same principle was later applied to prohibit a prosecutor from reindicting a convicted misdemeanant on a felony charge after the defendant had invoked an appellate remedy, since in this situation there was also a "realistic likelihood of 'vindictiveness.'"

In those cases the Court was dealing with the State's unilateral imposition of a penalty upon a defendant who had chosen to exercise a legal right to attack his original conviction—a situation "very different from the give-and-take negotiation common in plea bargaining between the prosecution and defense, which arguably possess relatively equal bargaining power." The Court has emphasized that the due process violation in cases such as *Pearce* and [*Blachledge v. Perry*, 417 U.S. 21 (1974)] lay not in the possibility that a defendant might be deterred from the exercise of a legal right, but rather in the danger that the State might be retaliating against the accused for lawfully attacking his conviction.

To punish a person because he has done what the law plainly allows him to do is a due process violation of the most basic sort, and for an agent of the State to pursue a course of action whose objective is to penalize a person's reliance on his legal rights is "patently unconstitutional." But in the "give-and-take" of plea bargaining, there is no such element of punishment or retaliation so long as the accused is free to accept or reject the prosecution's offer.

Plea bargaining flows from "the mutuality of advantage" to defendants and prosecutors, each with his own reasons for wanting to avoid trial. Defendants advised by competent counsel and protected by other procedural safeguards are presumptively capable of intelligent choice in response to prosecutorial persuasion, and unlikely to be driven to false self-condemnation. Indeed, acceptance of the basic legitimacy of plea bargaining necessarily implies rejection of any notion that a guilty plea is involuntary in a constitutional sense simply because it is the end result of the bargaining process. By hypothesis, the plea may have been induced by promises of a recommendation of a lenient sentence or a reduction of charges, and thus by fear of the possibility of a greater penalty upon conviction after a trial.

While confronting a defendant with the risk of more severe punishment clearly may have a "discouraging effect on the defendant's assertion of his trial rights, the imposition of these difficult choices [is] an inevitable"—and permissible—"attribute of any legitimate system which tolerates and encourages the negotiation of pleas." It follows that, by tolerating and encouraging the negotiation of pleas, this Court has necessarily accepted as constitutionally legitimate the simple reality that the prosecutor's interest at the bargaining table is to persuade the defendant to forgo his right to plead not guilty.

It is not disputed here that Hayes was properly chargeable under the recidivist statute, since he had in fact been convicted of two previous felonies. In our system, so long as the prosecutor has probable cause to believe that the accused committed an offense defined by statute, the decision whether or not to prosecute, and what charge to file or bring before a grand jury, generally rests entirely in his discretion. Within the limits set by the legislature's constitutionally valid definition of chargeable offenses, "the conscious exercise of some selectivity in enforcement is not in itself a federal constitutional violation" so long as "the selection was [not] deliberately based upon an unjustifiable standard such as race, religion, or other arbitrary classification." To hold that the prosecutor's desire to induce a guilty plea is an "unjustifiable standard," which, like race or religion, may play no part in his charging decision, would contradict the very premises that underlie the concept of plea bargaining itself. Moreover, a rigid constitutional rule that would prohibit a prosecutor from acting forthrightly in his dealings with the defense could only invite unhealthy subterfuge that would drive the practice of plea bargaining back into the shadows from which it has so recently emerged.

There is no doubt that the breadth of discretion that our country's legal system vests in prosecuting attorneys carries with it the potential for both individual and institutional abuse. And broad though that discretion may be, there are undoubtedly constitutional limits upon its exercise. We hold only that the course of conduct engaged in by the prosecutor in this case, which no more than openly presented the defendant with the unpleasant alternatives of forgoing trial or facing charges on which he was plainly subject to prosecution, did not violate the Due Process Clause of the Fourteenth Amendment.

Accordingly, the judgment of the Court of Appeals is [r]eversed.

Mr. Justice BLACKMUN, with whom Mr. Justice BRENNAN and Mr. Justice MARSHALL join, dissenting.

I feel that the Court, although purporting to rule narrowly (that is, on "the course of conduct engaged in by the prosecutor in this case,") is departing from, or at least restricting, the principles established in *North Carolina v. Pearce*, and in *Blackledge v. Perry*. If those decisions are sound and if those principles are salutary, as I must assume they are, they require, in my view, an affirmance, not a reversal, of the judgment of the Court of Appeals in the present case.

In *Pearce*, as indeed the Court notes, it was held that "vindictiveness against a defendant for having successfully attacked his first conviction must play no part in the sentence he receives after a new trial." Accordingly, if on the new trial, the sentence the defendant receives from the court is greater than that imposed after the first trial, it must be explained by reasons "based upon objective information concerning identifiable conduct on the part of the defendant occurring after the time of the original sentencing proceeding," other than his having pursued the appeal or collateral remedy. On the other hand, if the sentence is imposed by the jury and not by the court, if the jury is not aware of the original sentence, and if the second sentence is not otherwise shown to be a product of vindictiveness, *Pearce* has no application.

Then later, in *Perry*, the Court applied the same principle to prosecutorial conduct where there was a "realistic likelihood of 'vindictiveness.'" It held that the requirement of Fourteenth Amendment due process prevented a prosecutor's reindictment of a convicted misdemeanant on a felony charge after the defendant had exercised his right to appeal the misdemeanor conviction and thus to obtain a trial de novo. It noted the prosecution's "considerable stake" in discouraging the appeal.

The Court now says, however, that this concern with vindictiveness is of no import in the present case, despite the difference between five years in prison and a life sentence, because we are here concerned with plea bargaining where there is give-and-take negotiation, and where, it is said, "there is no such element of punishment or retaliation so long as the accused is free to accept or reject the prosecution's offer." Yet in this case vindictiveness is present to the same extent as it was thought to be in *Pearce* and in *Perry*; the prosecutor here admitted that the sole reason for the new indictment was to discourage the respondent from exercising his right to a trial. Even had such an admission not been made, when plea negotiations, conducted in the face of the less serious charge under the first indictment, fail, charging by a second indictment a more serious crime for the same conduct creates "a strong inference" of vindictiveness. As then Judge McCree aptly observed, in writing for a unanimous panel of the Sixth Circuit, the prosecutor initially "makes a discretionary determination that the interests of the state are served by not seeking more serious charges." I therefore do not understand why, as in *Pearce*, due process does not require that the prosecution justify its action on some basis other than discouraging respondent from the exercise of his right to a trial.

Prosecutorial vindictiveness, it seems to me, in the present narrow context, is the fact against which the Due Process Clause ought to protect. I perceive little difference between vindictiveness after what the Court describes as the exercise of a "legal right to attack his original conviction," and vindictiveness in the "'give-and-take negotiation common in plea bargaining.'" Prosecutorial vindictiveness in any context is still prosecutorial vindictiveness. The Due Process Clause should protect an accused against it, however it asserts itself. The Court of Appeals rightly so held, and I would affirm the judgment.

It might be argued that it really makes little difference how this case, now that it is here, is decided. The Court's holding gives plea bargaining full sway despite vindictiveness. A contrary result, however, merely would prompt the aggressive prosecutor to bring the greater charge initially in every case, and only thereafter to bargain. The consequences to the accused would still be adverse, for then he would bargain against a greater charge, face the likelihood of increased bail, and run the risk that the court would be less inclined to accept a bargained plea. Nonetheless, it is far preferable to hold the prosecution to the charge it was originally content to bring and to justify in the eyes of its public.[72]

---

[72] That prosecutors, without saying so, may sometimes bring charges more serious than they think appropriate for the ultimate disposition of a case, in order to gain bargaining leverage with a defendant, does not add support to today's decision, for this Court, in its approval of the advantages to be gained from plea negotiations, has never openly sanctioned such deliberate overcharging or taken such a cynical view of the bargaining process. Normally, of course, it is impossible to show that this is what the prosecutor is doing, and the courts necessarily have deferred to the prosecutor's exercise of discretion in initial charging decisions.

Even if overcharging is to be sanctioned, there are strong reasons of fairness why the charges should be presented at the beginning of the bargaining process, rather than as a filliped threat at the end. First, it means that a prosecutor is required to reach a charging decision without any knowledge of the particular defendant's willingness to plead guilty; hence the defendant who truly believes himself to be innocent, and wishes for that reason to go to trial, is not likely to be subject to quite such a devastating gamble since the prosecutor has fixed the incentives for the

Mr. Justice POWELL, dissenting.

Although I agree with much of the Court's opinion, I am not satisfied that the result in this case is just or that the conduct of the plea bargaining met the requirements of due process.

Respondent was charged with the uttering of a single forged check in the amount of $88.30. Under Kentucky law, this offense was punishable by a prison term of from 2 to 10 years, apparently without regard to the amount of the forgery. During the course of plea bargaining, the prosecutor offered respondent a sentence of five years in consideration of a guilty plea. I observe, at this point, that five years in prison for the offense charged hardly could be characterized as a generous offer. Apparently respondent viewed the offer in this light and declined to accept it; he protested that he was innocent and insisted on going to trial. Respondent adhered to this position even when the prosecutor advised that he would seek a new indictment under the State's Habitual Criminal Act which would subject respondent, if convicted, to a mandatory life sentence because of two prior felony convictions.

The prosecutor's initial assessment of respondent's case led him to forgo an indictment under the habitual criminal statute. The circumstances of respondent's prior convictions are relevant to this assessment and to my view of the case. Respondent was 17 years old when he committed his first offense. He was charged with rape but pleaded guilty to the lesser included offense of "detaining a female." One of the other participants in the incident was sentenced to life imprisonment. Respondent was sent not to prison but to a reformatory where he served five years. Respondent's second offense was robbery. This time he was found guilty by a jury and was sentenced to five years in prison, but he was placed on probation and served no time. Although respondent's prior convictions brought him within the terms of the Habitual Criminal Act, the offenses themselves did not result in imprisonment; yet the addition of a conviction on a charge involving $88.30 subjected respondent to a mandatory sentence of imprisonment for life. Persons convicted of rape and murder often are not punished so severely.

---

average case.

Second, it is healthful to keep charging practices visible to the general public, so that political bodies can judge whether the policy being followed is a fair one. Visibility is enhanced if the prosecutor is required to lay his cards on the table with an indictment of public record at the beginning of the bargaining process, rather than making use of unrecorded verbal warnings of more serious indictments yet to come.

Finally, I would question whether it is fair to pressure defendants to plead guilty by threat of reindictment on an enhanced charge for the same conduct when the defendant has no way of knowing whether the prosecutor would indeed be entitled to bring him to trial on the enhanced charge. Here, though there is no dispute that respondent met the then-current definition of a habitual offender under Kentucky law, it is conceivable that a properly instructed Kentucky grand jury, in response to the same considerations that ultimately moved the Kentucky Legislature to amend the habitual offender statute, would have refused to subject respondent to such an onerous penalty for his forgery charge. There is no indication in the record that, once the new indictment was obtained, respondent was given another chance to plead guilty to the forged check charge in exchange for a five-year sentence.

No explanation appears in the record for the prosecutor's decision to escalate the charge against respondent other than respondent's refusal to plead guilty. The prosecutor has conceded that his purpose was to discourage respondent's assertion of constitutional rights, and the majority accepts this characterization of events.

It seems to me that the question to be asked under the circumstances is whether the prosecutor reasonably might have charged respondent under the Habitual Criminal Act in the first place. The deference that courts properly accord the exercise of a prosecutor's discretion perhaps would foreclose judicial criticism if the prosecutor originally had sought an indictment under that Act, as unreasonable as it would have seemed.[73] But here the prosecutor evidently made a reasonable, responsible judgment not to subject an individual to a mandatory life sentence when his only new offense had societal implications as limited as those accompanying the uttering of a single $88 forged check and when the circumstances of his prior convictions confirmed the inappropriateness of applying the habitual criminal statute. I think it may be inferred that the prosecutor himself deemed it unreasonable and not in the public interest to put this defendant in jeopardy of a sentence of life imprisonment.

There may be situations in which a prosecutor would be fully justified in seeking a fresh indictment for a more serious offense. The most plausible justification might be that it would have been reasonable and in the public interest initially to have charged the defendant with the greater offense. In most cases a court could not know why the harsher indictment was sought, and an inquiry into the prosecutor's motive would neither be indicated nor likely to be fruitful. In those cases, I would agree with the majority that the situation would not differ materially from one in which the higher charge was brought at the outset.

But this is not such a case. Here, any inquiry into the prosecutor's purpose is made unnecessary by his candid acknowledgment that he threatened to procure and in fact procured the habitual criminal indictment because of respondent's insistence on exercising his constitutional rights. We have stated in unequivocal terms . . . that . . . if the only objective of a state practice is to discourage the assertion of constitutional rights it is 'patently unconstitutional.' And in *Brady v. United States*, 397 U.S. 742, we drew a distinction between the situation there approved and the "situation where the prosecutor or judge, or both, deliberately employ their charging and sentencing powers to induce a particular defendant to tender a plea of guilty."

---

[73] The majority suggests that this case cannot be distinguished from the case where the prosecutor initially obtains an indictment under an enhancement statute and later agrees to drop the enhancement charge in exchange for a guilty plea. I would agree that these two situations would be alike only if it were assumed that the hypothetical prosecutor's decision to charge under the enhancement statute was occasioned not by consideration of the public interest but by a strategy to discourage the defendant from exercising his constitutional rights. In theory, I would condemn both practices. In practice, the hypothetical situation is largely unreviewable. The majority's view confuses the propriety of a particular exercise of prosecutorial discretion with its unreviewability. In the instant case, however, we have no problem of proof.

The plea-bargaining process, as recognized by this Court, is essential to the functioning of the criminal-justice system. It normally affords genuine benefits to defendants as well as to society. And if the system is to work effectively, prosecutors must be accorded the widest discretion, within constitutional limits, in conducting bargaining. This is especially true when a defendant is represented by counsel and presumably is fully advised of his rights. Only in the most exceptional case should a court conclude that the scales of the bargaining are so unevenly balanced as to arouse suspicion. In this case, the prosecutor's actions denied respondent due process because their admitted purpose was to discourage and then to penalize with unique severity his exercise of constitutional rights. Implementation of a strategy calculated solely to deter the exercise of constitutional rights is not a constitutionally permissible exercise of discretion. I would affirm the opinion of the Court of Appeals on the facts of this case.

43

Trial by Jury

Key Concepts

- Right to Jury: Only in "Non-Petty" Cases
- Size of Jury: Must be at Least Six Jurors
- Unanimity Not Required
- Selection of Jurors: For Cause Strikes, Peremptory Strikes, and *Batson* Challenges

A. Introduction and Policy. As discussed in **Chapter 42**, the overwhelming majority of criminal cases in this country are resolved not at trial, but by plea bargain. Nonetheless, the jury trial remains an important feature in the criminal justice system. The jury trial interposes a representative group of fellow citizens between the government and the accused. Describing the right to a jury trial, the Court has written, "That right is no mere procedural formality, but a fundamental reservation of power in our constitutional structure. Just as suffrage ensures the people's ultimate control in the legislative and executive branches, jury trial is meant to ensure their control in the judiciary."[1]

Jury trials are also significant in practical terms. Although jury trials are a relatively rare method of resolving a criminal case, they provide the benchmark for every plea bargaining session that occurs in the system. Prosecutors and defense attorneys who engage in plea bargaining evaluate the strength of the case based on their likely success at trial. How will the witnesses come across to a jury? What credibility issues might arise on cross-examination? And, most importantly, what are the chances the prosecutor can convince a jury the defendant is guilty beyond a reasonable doubt? In other words, plea bargaining is a negotiation that takes place in the shadow of the law; and the "law" in this case is what each side believes a jury is likely to do if the case goes to trial.

Most states provide constitutional or statutory protection of the right to a jury trial that exceeds the minimum safeguards recognized by the federal Constitution. For example, though the Constitution does not demand unanimity in jury verdicts, the state constitutions of all but two states require that a jury verdict in a criminal case be unanimous. Also, although many states provide for a jury trial in any criminal case that could result in incarceration, the Constitution only

[1] Blakely v. Washington, 542 U.S. 296, 306 (2004).

mandates a jury trial for cases in which there is the possibility of a punishment over six months.

B. The Law.

1. Constitutional Rules: Right to a Jury, Size of Jury, Unanimity, and Impartiality. The right to trial by jury is twice guaranteed in the Constitution. First, Article 3, Section 2, Clause 3 of the Constitution instructs that the "trial of all crimes, except in cases of impeachment, shall be by jury."[2] Next, the Sixth Amendment provides in relevant part:

> In all criminal prosecutions, the accused shall enjoy the right to a speedy and public trial, by an impartial jury of the state and district wherein the crime shall have been committed.[3]

Despite the right's twin mention, and the broad language used to describe it—"of all crimes," "in all criminal prosecutions"—it has long been settled that the constitutional right to a jury trial does not apply to the prosecution of every crime. Only those being prosecuted for non-petty crimes have a right to trial by jury. Petty crimes, on the other hand, may be prosecuted before just a judicial officer.

The particular label—felony v. misdemeanor—that a state has applied to an offense is not determinative of whether a right to jury trial exists. While there is no question felonies are "serious" offenses, there are many misdemeanors that may also justify that same categorization. It is also irrelevant to the question of seriousness within a particular jurisdiction how that offense is treated in other jurisdictions.[4] Instead, in deciding whether an offense is **petty or serious**, courts should look for objective indicators of seriousness.

Of the factors relevant to the assessment, the most critical one is the length of potential or **authorized punishment** upon conviction. If an offense is punishable by more than six months in jail it is presumptively a serious offense for which the accused enjoys the right to a jury trial. In contrast, offenses punishable by six months or less are presumptively petty, and not deserving of jury trial protection.[5] Sentencing **exposure** not the sentence **imposed** is thus a key determinant in assessing whether a defendant had a right to a jury trial. The one exception to this general rule is contempt charges.

---

[2] U.S. Const., art. III, § 2, cl. 3.

[3] U.S. Const. amend. VI.

[4] United States v. Nachtigal, 507 U.S. 1 (1993).

[5] Baldwin v. New York, 399 U.S. 66 (1970).

Judges typically enjoy broad discretion with regard to the sentence imposed for a criminal contempt conviction. In many states, the only limit on a contempt sentence is the constitutional bar on cruel and unusual punishment. For offenses like contempt, where no maximum penalty is authorized, it is impossible to make a prior assessment of seriousness. Accordingly, in contempt cases it is the "severity of the penalty actually imposed [that] is the best indication of the seriousness of the particular offense."[6]

In addition, even crimes that have a maximum punishment of less than six months imprisonment may be deemed "serious" if additional, non-incarcerative penalties can be imposed. However, to shift categorization of an offense from "petty" to "serious" those additional penalties "viewed together with the maximum prison term, [must be] so severe that the legislature clearly determined that the offense is a serious one."[7] The Court has recognized this possible category shifting only in theory, however. In each of the cases where the Court considered additional punishments it found them to fall well below the threshold needed to move a petty offense into the serious zone.

For example, the Court rejected the argument that additional punishment in the form of a three-month driver's license suspension was sufficient to render an offense "serious." The Court has also found that imposition of mandatory offender-paid counseling is not sufficient. Terms of community service wearing scarlet-letter-type clothing have also been found not to be enough. Similarly, the Court has rejected the contention that a $5,000 fine converted an offense to a serious crime justifying the right to a jury trial.[8] Along these same lines, the possibility of even significant terms of probation following completion of a period of incarceration generally will not alter the character of an offense from petty to serious.

However, lower courts have provided some examples of a shift from a petty offense to a serious one. For example, a trial judge determined that the defendant deserved a jury trial when he faced a potential fine of $100,000 in addition to the possible six-month sentence.[9]

The constitutional right to a jury trial also has implications for sentencing decisions. As you will read in greater detail in Section C.6, a judge may sentence a convicted person based only upon those essential facts that have either been admitted by the accused or that have been found by a jury.

---

[6] Frank v. United States, 395 U.S. 147, 149 (1969).

[7] Nachtigal, 507 U.S. at 4.

[8] Id.

[9] United States v. Donovo, No. A02-18 CR (JWS), 2002 WL 1874838 (D. Alaska Aug. 7, 2002).

The size of a jury is not expressed in the Constitution. At English common law and in America's early days, juries often consisted of twelve members. But, the Court has concluded that this number was more historical accident than utter necessity. In the Court's view, "the 12-man requirement cannot be regarded as an indispensable component of the Sixth Amendment."[10] States are thus free to select an appropriate size below twelve for criminal juries. Typically states allow smaller juries to recognize savings in the way of money or court time. But, in selecting the number of jurors required in state cases, states are not free to reduce the number below six. The Court has determined that six is the smallest number of jurors that may be empanelled consistent with the Constitution's jury trial guarantee.

Juries in federal courts are required to be unanimous. However, at least two states do not require unanimity.[11] Though this question has been the subject of repeated challenge, the Supreme Court has held that unanimity is not a requirement imposed on states by the Fourteenth Amendment. The Court determined that non-unanimous jury verdicts are neither the product of an inferior deliberative process, nor are they inconsistent with the central purpose of the jury—to interpose the community between the government and the accused. The one exception to this rule is six-person juries. If a state chooses to allow non-petty offenses to be tried by six-person juries, the verdicts of those juries must be unanimous to comport with the constitutional right to a jury trial.

Just as the constitutional right to counsel envisions a right to **effective** counsel (**Chapter 31**), the constitutional right to a jury trial envisions a trial by an **impartial** jury drawn from a fair cross section of the community.[12] "A fair trial in a fair tribunal is a basic requirement of due process."[13]

As you will read in **Chapter 44**, the fairness of a trial is often a question of matters internal to the trial process itself. However, on occasion, external matters—like pre-trial publicity—may impact the fairness of the proceeding. In such cases, the right of the accused to a fair trial may come into conflict with the First Amendment rights of others, like news agencies or the public. In striking a balance between these potentially competing concerns, "trial courts must take strong measures to ensure that the balance is never weighed against the accused."[14] The Court has consequently recognized any number of prophylactic measures including: continuances (to allow public outrage over a crime to abate); case transfers (to a venue where public sentiment is more tempered); jury sequestration; and gag orders on court staff, the parties and their lawyers.[15] The Court has been less tol-

[10] Williams v. Florida, 399 U.S. 78, 100 (1970).

[11] Johnson v. Louisiana, 406 U.S. 356 (1972).

[12] Berghuis v. Smith, 559 U.S. 314 (2010); Nebraska Press Ass'n v. Stuart, 427 U.S. 539 (1976).

[13] Irvin v. Dowd, 366 U.S. 717, 722 (1951) (quoting In re Murchison, 349 U.S. 133, 136 (1955)).

[14] Nebraska Press Ass'n, 427 U.S. at 553.

[15] Sheppard v. Maxwell, 384 U.S. 333 (1966).

erant, however, of prior restraints that ban press coverage of a case.[16] Indeed, the Court has found that television and other electronic media coverage of a trial are constitutionally permissible, even over defense objection, so long as "the presence of cameras [does not] impair[] the ability of the jurors to decide the case on only the evidence before them" and does not adversely affect "any of the participants [because] of the presence of the cameras and the prospect of broadcast."[17]

2. Statutory Rules: Waiver of Right, Size of Jury. In addition to the constitutional restrictions that govern the right to a jury trial, the Federal Rules of Criminal Procedure ("FRCP") also provide guidance. For example, FRCP 23 instructs:

Federal Rules of Criminal Procedure

Rule 23. Jury or Nonjury Trial

(a) Jury Trial. If the defendant is entitled to a jury trial, the trial must be by jury unless:

- **(1)** the defendant waives a jury trial in writing;
- **(2)** the government consents; and
- **(3)** the court approves.

(b) Jury Size.

- **(1) In General.** A jury consists of 12 persons unless this rule provides otherwise.
- **(2) Stipulation for a Smaller Jury.** At any time before the verdict, the parties may, with the court's approval, stipulate in writing that:
  - **(A)** the jury may consist of fewer than 12 persons; or
  - **(B)** a jury of fewer than 12 persons may return a verdict if the court finds it necessary to excuse a juror for good cause after the trial begins.
- **(3) Court Order for a Jury of 11.** After the jury has retired to deliberate, the court may permit a jury of 11 persons to return a verdict, even without a stipulation by the parties, if the court finds good cause to excuse a juror.

(c) Nonjury Trial. In a case tried without a jury, the court must find the defendant guilty or not guilty. If a party requests before the finding of guilty or not guilty, the court must state its specific findings of fact in open court or in a written decision or opinion.

[16] Nebraska Press Ass'n, 427 U.S. at 570.

[17] Chandler v. Florida, 449 U.S. 560, 581 (1981).

The first thing that is apparent from a plain reading of Rule 23 is that it does not purport to independently impose any requirements for when a jury trial should be held. Rather, the language of the rule defers to external metrics—"**if** the defendant is entitled to a jury trial." In the federal system, these external metrics are provided by Supreme Court decisions interpreting the right to jury trial provided in the Constitution.

To be valid, a defendant's waiver of his right to a jury trial must be knowing, voluntary, and intelligent.[18] In addition, notice that Rule 23 provides that a defendant's purported waiver of the right to a jury trial requires the government's consent and the trial court's approval. This consent requirement has been challenged and found to be constitutional.

In **Chapter 30** you read that the Sixth Amendment right to counsel carries with it a correlative right to self-representation—*i.e.*, the right to proceed **without** counsel. In 1965, a defendant charged with mail fraud sought to assert a similar correlative right with regard to jury trials. If an accused has a right to a jury trial, this defendant posited, there must be a correlative constitutional power to waive that right and demand trial before a judge. The Supreme Court however, rejected this argument: "The ability to waive a constitutional right does not ordinarily carry with it the right to insist upon the opposite of that right."[19] The only constitutional right a defendant enjoys regarding the specific mode of prosecution—*i.e.*, bench trial or jury trial—is the right to demand an impartial trial by jury.

In the state systems, the right to waive a jury trial is often governed by constitutional provision or by statute. Varying rules for acceptance of a defendant's decision to waive a jury trial apply depending upon the jurisdiction. In some, consent of the prosecutor is required. In others, the approval of the court is all that is needed. And, in still others, the choice is entirely up to the defendant.

Next, as Rule 23 makes clear, in the federal system, the number of jurors in criminal cases is set at twelve. There are just three exceptions to this rule. First, both parties may consent to a smaller number of jurors with the approval of the judge. Second, a smaller number of jurors may return a verdict, with the consent of the parties, if the judge finds it necessary to excuse one or more jurors after the trial has begun. Third and finally, eleven jurors may return a verdict, without the consent of the parties, if the judge finds it necessary to excuse a juror for good cause after deliberations have begun. As you will read, within constitutional constraints, the states are free to establish their own rules for the minimum number of jurors required in particular criminal cases.

---

[18] Johnson v. Zerbst, 304 U.S. 458 (1938).

[19] Singer v. United States, 380 U.S. 24, 34–35 (1965).

While Rule 23 governs the size of a jury, Rule 24 governs the selection of a jury:

Federal Rules of Criminal Procedure

Rule 24. Trial Jurors.

(a) **Examination.**

(1) **In General.** The court may examine prospective jurors or may permit the attorneys for the parties to do so.

(2) **Court Examination.** If the court examines the jurors, it must permit the attorneys for the parties to:

(A) ask further questions that the court considers proper; or

(B) submit further questions that the court may ask if it considers them proper.

(b) **Peremptory Challenges.** Each side is entitled to the number of peremptory challenges to prospective jurors specified below. The court may allow additional peremptory challenges to multiple defendants, and may allow the defendants to exercise those challenges separately or jointly.

(1) **Capital Case.** Each side has 20 peremptory challenges when the government seeks the death penalty.

(2) **Other Felony Case.** The government has 6 peremptory challenges and the defendant or defendants jointly have 10 peremptory challenges when the defendant is charged with a crime punishable by imprisonment of more than one year.

(3) **Misdemeanor Case.** Each side has 3 peremptory challenges when the defendant is charged with a crime punishable by fine, imprisonment of one year or less, or both.

(c) **Alternate Jurors.**

(1) **In General.** The court may impanel up to 6 alternate jurors to replace any jurors who are unable to perform or who are disqualified from performing their duties.

. . .

The purpose of jury selection is to ensure that all of the jurors are impartial. In addition, attorneys can use their limited number of peremptory challenges to strike jurors that they believe will be unsympathetic to their case. Attorneys need not give any reason for a peremptory challenge, but if the court determines an attorney is using peremptory challenges in a way that discriminates based on race or gender, the peremptory challenge will not be allowed. We will discuss peremptory challenges in greater depth in Section C.2 and C.3, below.

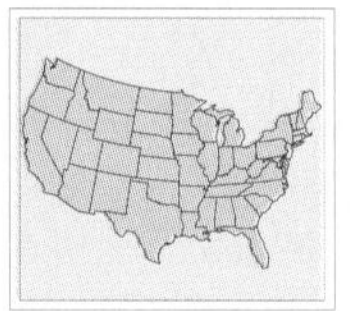

Most states also have constitutional, statutory, and rule-based schemes that govern the right to a jury trial. Many of these provisions are consistent with the protections and limitations offered by the Constitution. However, some states provide jury trial protections that exceed those that are constitutionally required. With just a handful of noted exceptions, the discussion that follows tracks the constitutional requirements for jury trials. Thus, in addition to familiarizing yourself with the law discussed in this chapter, you should also become conversant in any applicable local rules in your jurisdiction or practice area.

C. Applying the Law.

1. Petty v. Non-Petty Offenses. As you read above, if an offense is punishable by more than six months in prison, it is presumptively a serious offense and thus one for which the defendant is entitled to a jury trial. But, what if a defendant following conviction is sentenced to a period of actual incarceration that falls well below the six month cut-off for "petty" offenses? In a case involving a defendant convicted of simple battery, the Supreme Court held that the critical factor in assessing the right to a jury trial is the potential sentence, not the sentence that is actually imposed:

> **Example—*Duncan v. Louisiana*, 391 U.S. 145 (1968):** Gary Duncan was a nineteen year old living in Plaquemines Parish, Louisiana. Following racial integration of the local high schools, several of Duncan's younger cousins were transferred into a formerly all-white high school in the area. Duncan and his cousins were black. The cousins thereafter reported being victimized by various instances of racial violence at the school.
>
> One day Duncan was driving on a local highway and saw two of his cousins on the side of the road talking with four white teens. Duncan pulled over to find out if his cousins needed help. He got out of his car and after speaking to the group told his cousins to get into his car so that he could drive them home. As he was returning to the car himself, Duncan either touched or slapped one of the white teens on the elbow. Duncan was charged with misdemeanor simple battery.
>
> Duncan requested a jury trial, but this request was denied. Though simple battery is punishable by up to two years in prison,

Duncan was sentenced to sixty days in jail following a bench trial. A $150 fine was also imposed. Duncan appealed. He argued that his Sixth and Fourteenth Amendment rights had been violated. Louisiana responded that its limitation on jury trials to those cases involving sentences of capital punishment or hard labor was entirely consistent with the Sixth Amendment guarantee. The Supreme Court ultimately took the case to resolve the dispute.

Analysis: Duncan's right to a jury trial was violated. The Sixth Amendment, as imposed upon the states through the Fourteenth Amendment, guarantees an accused the right to a jury trial for all serious offenses.

The same wariness of absolute and unchecked power that is found elsewhere in our system of limited and balanced government is seen in the criminal justice system in the form of jury trials. The right to a jury trial interposes the people between the accused and the government. In this manner, jury trials offer a buffer against governmental oppression. "Providing an accused with the right to be tried by a jury of his peers gave him an inestimable safeguard against the corrupt or overzealous prosecutor and against the compliant, biased, or eccentric judge."[20]

There certainly is no right to a jury trial in **every** case. As the Court has long held, petty crimes can be (and routinely are) prosecuted without juries. In the federal system, petty crimes typically are those offenses that carry a possible penalty of no more than six months incarceration. The same constraint was true historically. And in most states surveyed at the time, petty offenses were those punishable by less than a year in jail.

In deciding whether an offense is a serious offense or a petty one, it is critical to consider the penalty that has been authorized by the legislature. The authorized penalty is an indication of the seriousness of the offense in the estimation of those elected to represent the will of the people. It is thus not the sentence actually imposed that reflects the seriousness of the offense, but the potential sentence that could be imposed.

Without deciding where the absolute upper limit of authorized sentences for petty offenses lies, it is safe to say that in this case, Duncan was not charged with a petty offense. His charge of simple battery was subject to punishment of up to two years incarceration. He was therefore entitled to a jury trial.

In *Duncan*, the Court determined that an offense punishable by a two-year period of incarceration was a serious offense warranting trial by jury. But, the *Duncan* Court did not say where exactly the dividing line was between "serious" and "petty" offenses. Two years later, the Court set a precise line and held that any

[20] Duncan v. Louisiana, 391 U.S. 145, 156 (1968).

accused facing a potential sentence of more than six months was charged with a serious offense and thus entitled to a jury trial.[21]

You may recall reading in **Chapter 30** that lawyers are not a constitutional necessity for defendants facing misdemeanor prosecution where a sentence of imprisonment is not imposed. In other words, the Sixth Amendment **right to counsel** is **not** delimited by the authorized punishment to which a convicted person is exposed. Instead, for misdemeanor offenders, the right to counsel turns upon the actual sentence handed down. As you read above though, a different rule applies to the question of the constitutional limits on the **right to a jury trial**. Where the legislature has identified an authorized punishment range, it is the authorized punishment not the actual punishment that answers the question of whether a right to a jury trial existed.

But what of cases where the legislature has not authorized any particular punishment range, such as contempt of court? In these cases, the Court determined that the appropriate rule is the same as the one used in misdemeanor right to counsel cases—actual punishment imposed:

> **Example—*Codispoti v. Pennsylvania*, 418 U.S. 506 (1974):** Dominick Codispoti, Herbert Langnes, and a co-defendant were prosecuted together. At their joint trial they each waived the right to counsel and proceeded *pro se*. Following the initial trial, the trial judge charged each man with several counts of contempt for their conduct during the proceedings. The men sought a jury trial for consideration of the contempt charges, but this request was denied.
>
> Following a separate trial before a new judge, Codispoti was convicted of seven contempt counts and Langnes was convicted of six contempt counts. The judge then sentenced each of the men to no more than six months on each of the contempt convictions but ran the sentences consecutively. As a result, Codispoti faced a cumulative term of incarceration of three and a half years. Langnes faced a cumulative term of incarceration of two years and eight months.
>
> Codispoti and Langnes then appealed, arguing that their right to trial by jury was violated. After this claim was rejected by the Pennsylvania Supreme Court, the United States Supreme Court accepted the case for review.

[21] Baldwin v. New York, 399 U.S. 66 (1970).

Analysis: The right to a jury trial was violated because the contempt charges were adjudicated in a single post-trial proceeding where a cumulative prison term was imposed.

As is true with other criminal offenses, "petty" criminal contempt charges can be tried without a jury, but "serious" criminal contempt charges must be tried to a jury unless the defendant has waived his rights. Although the seriousness of most offenses is evaluated by looking to the authorized sentence, in the case of contempt there typically is no authorized sentence. Legislatures often leave to the broad discretion of the trial judge the appropriate sentence to be imposed in any contempt case. Accordingly, rather than looking to the sentence authorized a court reviewing a contempt conviction must consider the sentence imposed to assess whether the right to a jury trial was triggered.

If a trial judge finds a defendant guilty of contempt **during** trial, a jury will not be required so long as a sentence of less than six months is imposed on the contempt conviction. Moreover, there is no limit on the number of such in-trial contempt charges that may be adjudicated. So long as each is "dealt with as a discrete and separate matter at a different point during the trial" and a sentence of not more than six months on any one contempt charge is imposed, no separate "contempt jury" will be required.[22] However, a different rule applies if a series of contempt citations are handled in a single post-trial proceeding.

In this case, it is true that individual sentences of no more than six months were handed down on each contempt conviction. But these sentences were then aggregated to years-long terms of imprisonment. In assessing whether a jury was required for those prosecutions "the salient fact remains that the contempts arose from a single trial, were charged by a single judge, and were tried in a single proceeding. The individual sentences imposed were then aggregated, one sentence taking account of the others and not beginning until the immediately preceding sentence had expired."[23]

One concurring justice in *Codispoti* advocated a different way of assessing Codispoti and Langnes's right to a jury trial. In Justice Marshall's view "[w]here the contemptuous acts arose out of a single course of conduct by the defendant . . . they should be treated as a single serious offense for which the Sixth Amendment requires a jury trial, whether the judge seeks to use his summary contempt power in individual instances during trial or tries the contempts together at the end of trial."[24] In other words, one way to evaluate the right to jury trial claim was as Justice Marshall did—evaluating the right by considering whether the contempt charges all arose out of a single source of conduct. The second way to evaluate the claim was as the majority did—evaluating the right by considering whether

[22] Id. at 515.

[23] Codispoti v. Pennsylvania, 418 U.S. 506, 517 (1974).

[24] Id. at 520 (Marshall, J., concurring in part).

the various contempt charges were adjudicated in a consolidated proceeding. The Court clearly rejected the single-source-of-conduct approach in favor of its consolidated-adjudication approach. Moreover, since *Codispoti*, the Court has narrowly limited the application of its consolidated-adjudication approach.

In theory, *Codispoti's* consolidated-adjudication approach could also be applied outside the context of contempt cases to trigger jury trial rights if a defendant was charged with a series of relatively minor offenses that were prosecuted in a single proceeding. Many years after *Codispoti*, the Court made clear that the approach applied only to contempt cases:

> **Example—*Lewis v. United States*, 518 U.S. 322 (1996):** Ray Lewis's supervisors at the Post Office suspected he was stealing cash from the mail he was processing. Accordingly, they set up a "sting" operation to route two marked envelopes through his station. The supervisors watched as Lewis opened the two pieces of test mail and removed the cash that had been planted inside.
>
> Thereafter, Lewis was charged in a two-count indictment with obstructing the mail. Obstructing the mail is a crime that carries a maximum penalty of six months. However, upon conviction Lewis theoretically faced a potential maximum penalty of one year in prison because both counts were tried in a single consolidated proceeding. Denying Lewis's request for a jury trial, the trial judge announced that she had no intention of sentencing him to anything more than six months in prison should he be convicted.
>
> The reviewing court agreed that the trial judge acted appropriately. The Supreme Court then accepted the case for review.

Analysis: Notwithstanding the fact that Lewis's two charges were adjudicated in a single proceeding, he did not enjoy a right to a jury trial where each count was properly classified as a petty offense.

The Sixth Amendment right to a jury trial does not extend to petty offenses. In assessing whether an offense is petty, courts should consider the authorized punishment. If that authorized punishment is six months or less, the offense is presumptively petty. At times, additional authorized penalties may be sufficiently severe to shift the presumption of pettiness. However, no such penalties existed in this case.

Obstructing the mails is an offense punishable by a maximum sentence of six months in jail. Accordingly, it is a petty offense. The aggregation of two such offenses for prosecution in a single trial does not change the nature of each individual offense. The decision in *Codispoti* does not require a different conclusion.

In the case of criminal contempt that was confronted by the Court in *Codispoti* there had been no legislative determination of the seriousness of the offense. This is because the criminal contempt at issue in that case did not have a statutorily defined maximum punishment. In assessing the seriousness of the offense there, the Court necessarily looked to the actual aggregate sentence that was imposed. But in this case there has been a legislative determination of seriousness.

"Where the offenses charged are petty, and the deprivation of liberty exceeds six months only as a result of the aggregation of charges, the jury trial right does not apply."[25]

As the Court noted in *Lewis*, in addition to the length of the authorized sentence, the seriousness of an offense for purposes of triggering jury trial rights is also informed by additional punishments that might be imposed. These additional punishments must be fairly serious, however, to shift an offense into the serious category. Consequently, in the cases the Court has considered, it has found that the additional punishments identified—*e.g.*, fines, probationary terms, counsel and community service projects—are **not** sufficiently draconian to warrant a finding of a right to a jury trial.

2. Jury Selection. Jury selection is the process by which the judge and the attorneys question the prospective jurors in order to assess whether each of them can impartially assess the evidence. If the trial judge determines that a prospective juror cannot be impartial, she is struck "for cause" from the jury pool (also known as the "venire"). Each attorney also has the right to strike a limited number of prospective jurors simply because the attorney believes the jurors would be unsympathetic to their case. These strikes are known as peremptories.

The process of jury selection is also known as *voir dire* (typically pronounced "vwah deer," though in some jurisdictions it may be pronounced "vwah die-ur"). The term, which derives from Old French, is translated alternately as "to speak the truth," or "to say what is true." The selection of jurors is governed by the Constitution. In the federal system, Rule 24 of the Federal Rule of Criminal Procedure also regulates the process. The states have comparable procedural rules governing their jury selection processes.

In all jurisdictions, the Office of the Jury Commissioner, the Office of the Clerk or some other administrative arm of the courts will sends out batches of summonses calling potential jurors in for service. Jurisdictions typically impose a variety of minimum qualifications on potential jurors including citizenship, residency and minimum age requirements. Many jurisdictions also exclude from service those

[25] Lewis v. United States, 518 U.S. 322, 330 (1996).

with recent felony records. The jury rolls in most jurisdictions are compiled from driver's license and voter registration records.

As a trial judge moves through her docket on any given day, she may determine that she has a case that is going to trial and will need a jury. When this occurs, the judge will call the jury office to have a group of potential jurors sent down to the courtroom for questioning. Many more potential jurors than are actually needed will be sent. This group—known as the "jury pool"—is then winnowed in the voir dire process.

The voir dire process in most places is conducted entirely by the trial judge; but in some jurisdictions lawyers are given substantial latitude to question the jurors directly. The process typically begins with a member of the court staff taking attendance to ensure that everyone has arrived. Once the court confirms that all the potential jurors are present, the jurors are sworn, and a brief introduction is usually provided. For example, the judge might introduce herself, the lawyers, and the parties. After giving the jurors a very brief description of the case, the court will then often ask the jurors questions to determine whether any jurors have biases that make them ill-suited for service in the particular case. For example, a potential juror may have a strong belief that the drug laws are unreasonable and should never be enforced, while another potential juror may have a close relationship with a police officer and consequently believe that law enforcement officers are more trustworthy than other witnesses. The exact range of questions asked varies from courtroom to courtroom.

Trial judges are afforded broad discretion in the conduct of voir dire, and there are just a handful of constitutional constraints to which the voir dire process is subject. Thus, the exact form and number of questions asked during the process are largely matters left to the trial judge's best judgment.[26] So too, the Constitution does not require that a question be asked during voir dire simply because it might help the lawyers for each side ferret out which jurors are most impartial.[27] "To be constitutionally compelled . . . the trial court's failure to ask [particular] questions must render the defendant's trial fundamentally unfair."[28]

Judges must inquire about juror biases, opinions and prejudices that may affect the consideration of the evidence.[29] As the Court has said, "[w]ithout an adequate voir dire the trial judge's responsibility to remove prospective jurors who will not be able impartially to follow the court's instructions and evaluate the evidence cannot be fulfilled."[30] Accordingly, though a judge need not ask prospective ju-

26 Rosales-Lopez v. United States, 451 U.S. 182 (1981).

27 Ristaino v. Ross, 424 U.S. 589 (1976).

28 Mu'Min v. Virginia, 500 U.S. 415, 425–26 (1991).

29 Aldridge v. United States, 283 U.S. 308 (1931).

30 Rosales-Lopez, 451 U.S. at 188.

rors about racial prejudice in every case,[31] if a case involves special circumstances that create a substantial reason to believe racial or ethnic prejudice might affect the impartial assessment of a case, the Constitution demands an inquiry into the issue:

> **Example—*Ham v. South Carolina*, 409 U.S. 524 (1973):** Gene Ham was a well-known civil rights organizer in his local community of Florence County, South Carolina. In 1971, Ham was charged with possessing marijuana. Ham had no prior criminal record. At trial, Ham's defense was that local law enforcement officials, angered by Ham's civil rights activism, had framed him. Accordingly, during voir dire Ham asked the trial judge to ask jurors about any racial prejudices they may hold against black Americans. The trial judge agreed to ask general questions about bias, prejudice and partiality; but refused to ask the more targeted questions that Ham proposed. Following trial, Ham was convicted and sentenced to a year and a half in prison.
>
> Ham appealed, arguing that his constitutional right to be tried by an impartial jury was violated by the trial court's refusal to inquire into the racial prejudice of prospective jurors.

Analysis: Ham's argument was correct. His conviction must be overturned.

The Fourteenth Amendment was adopted principally to keep states from discriminating against individuals on the basis of race. South Carolina created a jury selection process that authorized the trial judge to question jurors prior to their selection. The statutory process also permitted the removal of jurors for cause. In light of the statutory scheme established by the state, the Due Process clause of the Fourteenth Amendment further required that the prospective jurors be questioned about their racial biases.

The trial judge was not required to ask the question in the precise form proposed by Ham. Nor was the trial judge required to ask any particular number of questions probing potential racial bias. However, some inquiry on the specific issue was necessary.

Since Ham made a timely request for a question regarding racial bias, and since the particular facts of his case suggested that such a question might be especially relevant to the assessment of the evidence, reversal was required.[32]

---

[31] Ristaino, 424 U.S. at 589.

[32] Ham v. South Carolina, 409 U.S. 524 (1973).

The Court's decision in *Ham* should not be read as establishing a broad constitutional demand for voir dire inquiry into racial animus in every case. Inquiry is required by the Constitution only in those cases where the particular circumstances offer significant reason to believe that racial and/or ethnic prejudice might influence the jury's evaluation of the government's evidence. For example, in a capital case involving an interracial killing, the possibility of bias is sufficiently real as to require inquiry upon request into issues of racial bias.[33] In contrast, in a standard armed robbery case where the defendants happen to be white and the victim happens to be black, specific questioning of the prospective jurors about racial prejudice is not constitutionally required.[34]

The Constitution also does not require that prospective jurors be questioned about the precise content of any pretrial publicity to which they have been exposed. Instead, it is sufficient for a trial judge to ask generally about exposure to pretrial publicity, and then to inquire whether such exposure, if any, will affect the prospective juror's ability to fairly evaluate the case.[35]

After the questioning phase is completed, the pool of potential jurors is winnowed through the exercise of strikes. "Strikes" are the method by which jurors are eliminated from the final jury and excused from service on the case.

a. **"For Cause" Strikes.** The first round of strikes are "for cause," meaning a juror's responses to voir dire questions have revealed biases that make him unsuitable for service. A potential juror who has formed an opinion about the guilt of the accused is not impartial and therefore cannot serve on the jury. A juror may be removed for cause on the judge's own initiative if the judge believes it is clear that the juror cannot be impartial. Also, each attorney is allowed to challenge any juror for cause and argue to the judge that the juror should be struck. There is no limit to the number of for-cause challenges that each attorney can issue, though of course the attorney must convince the judge that the juror cannot be impartial before the judge will agree with the challenge and strike the juror.

   The demand for impartiality does not require that potential jurors have absolutely no knowledge of a case.[36] In the modern era of the 24-hour news cycle, it is often true that potential jurors will come to court with some knowledge about the crime charged or the person accused. The Constitution only requires that a potential juror "can lay aside his impression or opinion and render a verdict based on the evidence presented in court."[37]

---

33 Turner v. Murray, 476 U.S. 28 (1986).

34 Ristaino, 424 U.S. at 589.

35 Mu'Min v. Virginia, 500 U.S. 415 (1991).

36 Murphy v. Florida, 421 U.S. 794 (1975).

37 Irvin v. Dowd, 366 U.S. 717, 723 (1961); Dobbert v. Florida, 432 U.S. 282, 303 (1977).

In a capital case, a prospective juror may not be removed for cause simply because he has general objections to the death penalty. Such a juror may, however, be struck for cause if his objections to or affinity for capital punishment would "prevent or substantially impair the performance of his duties as a juror in accordance with his instructions and his oath."[38]

Jurors may also be removed in the initial round of strikes for other reasons unrelated to bias. For example, a juror may be excused for health reasons, because of serious scheduling conflicts, because of personal obligations that make service an extreme hardship, or because of language barriers.

b. Peremptory Strikes. Once the first round of strikes is completed, the lawyers for each side then have an opportunity to remove jurors that they don't believe will favor their side. This process is known as the use of peremptory strikes. Unlike a for-cause challenge, which must be backed by argument that the juror cannot be impartial, an attorney usually does not need to give any reason for a peremptory strike. Thus, while attorneys can issue an unlimited number of for-cause challenges, they are limited to a handful of peremptory challenges.

Peremptory strikes support "a defendant's right to trial by an impartial jury," however, "unlike the right to an impartial jury guaranteed by the Sixth Amendment, peremptory challenges are not of federal constitutional dimension." [39] Accordingly, the number of peremptory strikes that will be given to each side is most often a common law or statutory matter.[40] The specific number of peremptory strikes allowed is set, in most jurisdictions, based upon the seriousness of the offense charged. Oftentimes the defense will be given more peremptory strikes than the prosecution, but this is not always true.

Usually no reason at all is given for the exercise of a peremptory strike. The lawyer will simply ask that the juror be excused. Indeed, the point of peremptory strikes is to give the parties an opportunity to shape the jury based on their particular case strategy and view of the evidence. For example, in a case involving the murder of young child, the prosecution may feel that parents and primary school educators will be more receptive to the prosecution's evidence than single, childless, twenty-somethings. The prosecutor on such a case might consequently use all of her peremptories to remove college students, and other young, single individuals from the jury. The defense attorney, for the same reason, will probably seek to strike any parents with young children from the jury.

[38] Wainwright v. Witt, 469 U.S. 412, 424 (1985); Morgan v. Illinois, 504 U.S. 719 (1992).

[39] United States v. Martinez-Salazar, 528 U.S. 304, 311 (2000).

[40] Stilson v. United States, 250 U.S. 583 (1919).

The use of peremptory challenges is hardly an exact science—lawyers exercise such strikes relying upon assumptions drawn from only a scant quantity of information about a potential juror. Some attorneys have their own eccentric theories of human psychology that influence their choices—for example, "jurors who wear hats are sympathetic to criminal defendants" or "jurors who work for large companies are more willing to convict." There is no question that many of the superficial calculations driving peremptory challenges are inaccurate. For this reason, many experienced attorneys advocate not using peremptories at all and simply "going with the first twelve in the box." For now, though, peremptory strikes remain, in most jurisdictions, a definite and time-honored part of the jury selection process.

In addition to seating the jurors who will be serving on the jury, the court will also seat a certain number of alternate jurors. In federal court, where twelve-person juries are the norm, up to six alternates are allowed, but usually the judge will only seat one or two. The number of alternates will depend on the projected length of the trial. Parties are given extra peremptory challenges to use on alternate jurors.

Alternates sit with the jury during the trial, but are not allowed to participate in deliberations unless one of the actual jurors must be excused from her duties due to illness or improper conduct. If a juror must be excused after deliberations have begun and an alternate is sent in to replace her, the jury is instructed to begin deliberations all over again. As we have seen, a judge in the federal system also has the option of simply excusing the original juror and ordering the jury to finish deliberations with only the remaining eleven jurors.

After all the for-cause and peremptory strikes are exercised, and all of the jurors and alternates are seated, each party will be asked if the jury is acceptable. Assuming no objections, the jury will be sworn and the trial will begin.

3. Discriminatory Use of Peremptories and *Batson* Challenges. As you read above, lawyers usually do not have to offer any explanation for their desire to remove a juror with a peremptory strike. However, a lawyer may not exercise her peremptory strikes in a racially discriminatory manner—for example, to remove all black jurors from the panel. The Court has held that using peremptory strikes in this manner violates the Equal Protection Clause:

Example—*Batson v. Kentucky*, 476 U.S. 79 (1986): James Batson, a black man, was on trial for burglary and receipt of stolen goods. During voir dire, the prosecutor used peremptory challenges to strike all four black people from the jury pool. The resulting jury was all white. The defense attorney objected to the jury, arguing that using peremptory challenges to remove all of the black prospective jurors violated Batson's constitutional rights. The judge overruled the objection, saying that attorneys were allowed to use their peremptory challenges to strike anybody they wanted. After Batson was convicted, he appealed, and the case made its way to the Supreme Court.

Analysis: The Court held that once a defendant makes a *prima facie* showing that the prosecutor's use of peremptory challenges is discriminatory the prosecutor has the burden of providing a race-neutral explanation for the peremptory challenges. Since the defendant made a *prima facie* showing in this case and the prosecutor was never asked to give a race-neutral reason, the conviction must be reversed.

In earlier cases, the Supreme Court had already held that the state violates the Equal Protection Clause of the Fourteenth Amendment if it denies black citizens the right to be jurors on account of their race. However, most of the earlier cases involved state laws or practices which prohibited or discouraged black Americans from being members of the jury pool. In contrast, the peremptory challenge system, with its ancient roots in the British and American common law system, had remained effectively beyond challenge.

The Court noted that its interpretation of the Equal Protection Clause had evolved to the point where a "single invidiously discriminatory act" by the prosecutor was sufficient to violate the defendant's rights. Against this new background, the Court set out guidelines limiting the use of peremptory challenges.

First, the defendant must show that he is a member of a specific racial group, and that the prosecutor has exercised her peremptory challenges to remove members of that racial group from the jury pool. Second, the defendant must demonstrate facts and circumstances which raise an inference that the prosecutor struck those potential jurors *because* of their race. These facts could include a pattern of striking multiple individuals of the specified race, or questions or statements made by the prosecutor that give rise to an inference of discriminatory intent. Once the defendant has fulfilled these two factors, he has made out a *prima facie* case of discrimination.

At that point, the burden shifts to the prosecutor, who must give a race-neutral explanation for challenging the members of the specified race. This explanation does not have to be a reason strong enough to justify a challenge for cause, but it cannot be in any way related to the race of the potential juror. The prosecutor also must do more than simply deny that his challenge was racially motivated; he must articulate a specific, race-neutral reason for the strike. The trial court will then determine whether the prosecutor purposefully discriminated against the potential jury member on account of his race.

Batson was an attempt by the Supreme Court to strike a balance between a juror's right under the Equal Protection Clause not to be barred from the jury because of race, and the time-honored and strongly valued right of attorneys to exercise peremptory challenges on anyone for any reason—or no reason at all. Unsurprisingly, the *Batson* decision has been criticized by both sides of the debate. Some argue that any limitation on the peremptory challenge defeats the entire purpose of having these challenges, which is to allow an attorney to strike potential jurors without having to defend or explain the decision. On the other side of the debate, some claim that the *Batson* test is relatively toothless—although it is relatively easy for defendants to make a *prima facie* case of discrimination (a prosecutor striking more than one black member of the venire is sometimes sufficient), it is just as easy for the prosecutor to come up with some race-neutral reason for the challenge. Nonetheless, *Batson* has probably succeeded in preventing the most egregious and blatant of discriminatory practices, such as what occurred in *Batson* itself, where the prosecutor struck every black member of the venire in order to get an all-white jury.

Later the Supreme Court expanded *Batson* to cover peremptory challenges by defendants as well as prosecutors.[41] The Court held that the jurors themselves were denied equal protection when they were struck from the jury based on their race, regardless of which side struck them. The Court also held that a defendant exercising peremptory challenges constitutes "state action" and therefore implicates the Equal Protection Clause, because the peremptory challenge system involves government participation; selecting jury members in a criminal case is a "unique and constitutionally compelled government function" and regardless of which side issues the peremptory challenge, it is the judge—a government official—who strikes the jurors.[42]

Two years later, the Court expanded *Batson* again to cover peremptory challenges that exclude jurors based on gender. In *J.E.B. v. Alabama ex rel. T.B.*,[43] the state brought a paternity suit against the defendant. The state used nine of its ten peremptory challenges to exclude men from the jury, resulting in an all-female jury. The Supreme Court stated that:

> Discrimination in jury selection, whether based on race or on gender, causes harm to the litigants, the community, and the individual jurors who are wrongfully excluded from participation in the judicial process. The litigants are harmed by the risk that the prejudice that motivated the discriminatory selection of the jury will infect the entire proceedings. The community is harmed by the State's participation in the perpetuation of

[41] Georgia v. McCollum, 505 U.S. 42 (1992).

[42] Batson v. Kentucky, 476 U.S. 79 (1986); Hernandez v. New York, 500 U.S. 352 (1991); J.E.B. v. Alabama ex rel. T.B., 511 U.S. 127 (1994).

[43] J.E.B., 511 U.S. at 127.

> invidious group stereotypes and the inevitable loss of confidence in our judicial system that state-sanctioned discrimination in the courtroom engenders.
>
> When state actors exercise peremptory challenges in reliance on gender stereotypes, they ratify and reinforce prejudicial views of the relative abilities of men and women. Because these stereotypes have wreaked injustice in so many other spheres of our country's public life, active discrimination by litigants on the basis of gender during jury selection invites cynicism respecting the jury's neutrality and its obligation to adhere to the law. The potential for cynicism is particularly acute in cases where gender-related issues are prominent, such as cases involving rape, sexual harassment, or paternity. Discriminatory use of peremptory challenges may create the impression that the judicial system has acquiesced in suppressing full participation by one gender or that the "deck has been stacked" in favor of one side.[44]

Although the principle of *Batson* and its progeny is straightforward—race and gender cannot be a motivating factor in exercising peremptory challenges—the application of *Batson* can be tricky. What if the prosecutor's reason for excluding the potential jurors is indirectly related to race, but not specifically tied to race? Consider the following case:

> **Example—*Hernandez v. New York*, 500 U.S. 352 (1991):** Dionisio Hernandez was on trial for attempted murder. Many of the witnesses in the case were Latino, and some were going to testify in Spanish. Under the Rules of Evidence, whenever a witness testifies in a language other than English, the court employs an interpreter to translate the answers for the jury and for the official record. The jurors are instructed to only listen to the English translation, even if they can understand the foreign language used by the witness, so that all the jurors deliberate using exactly the same information.
>
> During voir dire, there were 63 members of the venire. After nine jurors had been empaneled, the defendant raised a *Batson* challenge, noting that the prosecutor had exercised four of his peremptory challenges on Latinos. Two of those four excluded jurors had been convicted of crimes, so the prosecutor had an alternate race-neutral reason for excluding them. With regard to the other two, the prosecutor explained that he had a concern

---

[44] Id. at 140.

that those two witnesses would listen to the original testimony of the Spanish-speaking witnesses rather than the interpreter.[45]

The prosecutor also pointed out that apart from the translation issue, he had no motivation to keep Latinos off the jury because all of the victims and all of the civilian witnesses in the case were Latino.[46]

The defendant responded by pointing out the high correlation between Spanish-speaking individuals and Latinos, particularly in New York City, where the case was being tried.

The trial court found that the prosecutor had a race-neutral reason for striking the Latino jurors, and denied the defendant's *Batson* motion. After the defendant was convicted, he appealed the case all the way to the Supreme Court.

Analysis: In a divided plurality opinion, the Court affirmed the conviction, finding there had been no *Batson* violation. The four-justice plurality agreed that striking jurors merely because Spanish was their native language might be a *Batson* violation because of the strong correlation between native Spanish speakers and Latino ethnicity. However, that was not the reason stated by the prosecutor in this case.

As the prosecutor explained, he saw the pool of potential jurors in two groups—those who would accept the translator's interpretation of the testimony and those who might not. Both groups could have included some Latinos, both groups also could have included non-Latinos. "As explained by the prosecutor, the challenges rested neither on the intention to exclude Latino or bilingual jurors, nor on stereotypical assumptions about Latinos or bilinguals. . . . While the prosecutor's criterion might well result in the disproportionate removal of prospective Latino jurors, that disproportionate impact does not turn the prosecutor's actions into a per se violation of the Equal Protection Clause."[47]

The Court noted that the prosecutor's claim about the potential jurors' seeming unwillingness to follow the court's instructions could be a pretext, but held that determining whether the prosecutor was in effect lying about his reason was a question for the trial judge. Since the trial judge was present to see the potential jurors' responses to the instructions and voir dire questions, he or she is given significant discretion in making this determination.

Two justices concurred in the result, but found that the plurality went to too much

---

45 Id. at 356–57 (internal citations omitted).

46 Id. at 357.

47 Hernandez v. New York, 500 U.S. 352, 361 (1991).

trouble in denying the defendant's claim. These two justices held that *Batson* only prohibits intentional discrimination based on race (and gender), and thus does not preclude a peremptory challenge based on any other reason, even those that might happen to correlate with race. The concurrence thus implied that even if the prosecutor's challenge was based solely on the fact that the potential jurors were native Spanish speakers that motivation would not violate *Batson*.

The three dissenting justices did not believe the prosecutor carried his burden of proving that the strikes were race-neutral, for three reasons:

> First, the justification would inevitably result in a disproportionate disqualification of Spanish-speaking venirepersons. An explanation that is "race neutral" on its face is nonetheless unacceptable if it is merely a proxy for a discriminatory practice.
>
> Second, the prosecutor's concern could easily have been accommodated by less drastic means. As is the practice in many jurisdictions, the jury could have been instructed that the official translation alone is evidence; bilingual jurors could have been instructed to bring to the attention of the judge any disagreements they might have with the translation so that any disputes could be resolved by the court.
>
> Third, if the prosecutor's concern was valid and substantiated by the record, it would have supported a challenge for cause. The fact that the prosecutor did not make any such challenge should disqualify him from advancing the concern as a justification for a peremptory challenge.[48]

4. The Size of the Jury. Movies like *Twelve Angry Men* popularized the notion that a jury in a criminal case must always consist of twelve members. Contrary to popular belief, the twelve-member jury is not a constitutional mandate. The Supreme Court has held that the Constitution merely requires a jury that is large enough to allow for collaborative deliberation—and, according to the Court, the minimum number of jurors required for this collaborative deliberation is six:

> **Example—*Ballew v. Georgia*, 435 U.S. 223 (1978):** Claude Ballew managed a movie theater in Atlanta, Georgia that showed pornographic movies. In the fall of 1973, Ballew screened the film *Behind the Green Door*. After viewing the film several times, law enforcement officers seized copies of the movie, and arrested Ballew. Ballew was charged with the misdemeanor offense of distributing obscene materials. At the time, misdemeanor offenses in Georgia were prosecuted using five-person juries. Ballew's request for a twelve-person jury was therefore denied.

[48] Id. at 379 (Stevens, J., dissenting).

At the close of the evidence, the five members of the jury deliberated for under an hour before returning a guilty verdict. The judge then sentenced Ballew to one year in prison, a sentence that was suspended once Ballew paid a $2,000 fine.

Ballew's appeal eventually reached the Supreme Court.

Analysis: The five-member jury violated Ballew's Sixth Amendment right to a jury trial.

The purpose of that right is to interpose the community between the government and the accused. In thinking about the minimum number of jurors necessary to realize this purpose the starting place has historically been the twelve-member jury. At the nation's founding, juries generally included twelve members. However, that number seems to have been a matter of happenstance. The Sixth Amendment right to a jury trial does not necessarily envision a twelve member jury as the constitutional minimum. The question is how far below twelve the number may fall.

From the State's perspective, smaller juries are more economical and save the courts time. But these savings must be measured against the threat to the constitutional guarantee that smaller juries pose.

The size of the jury must be sufficiently large to "promote group deliberation, to insulate members from outside intimidation, and to provide a representative cross-section of the community."[49] A jury comprised of six jurors is certainly enough to accomplish these goals. A jury of smaller than six, on the other hand, begins to threaten the jury's purpose.

Studies show that smaller groups are likely not to engage in successful group decision-making. Smaller groups also may overlook or fail to remember critical bits of evidence. In addition, smaller groups can be more susceptible to the biases of individual members; and minority viewpoints in a smaller group tend to receive less meaningful consideration. In contrast, larger groups generally demonstrate a greater ability at self-critique than smaller groups. And studies have shown that the "risk of convicting an innocent person rises as the size of the jury diminishes."[50]

This evidence all points to the conclusion that a jury of fewer than six members cannot dependably serve the function intended by the Constitution. The five-person jury used in Ballew's case also cannot be justified by the State's interests in saving time and money. While a decrease in size from twelve to six may realize considerable savings in these areas, a move from six to five accomplishes virtually nothing.

[49] Ballew v. Georgia, 435 U.S. 223, 230 (1978).

[50] Id. at 234.

Ballew had a right to a jury of no fewer than six members. Accordingly, his conviction must be reversed.

5. The Need for Unanimity? In addition to the size of the jury, the Constitution also has something to say about the need for unanimous verdicts. The constitutional rule regarding unanimity is different for state and federal cases. In federal court, a jury may not convict unless it unanimously agrees that each element of the government's case was proven.[51] The Court has indicated that the unanimity requirement in federal cases is a direct consequence of the Sixth Amendment. "Unanimity in jury verdicts is required where the Sixth and Seventh Amendments apply."[52]

There is a significant limitation on this unanimity requirement. Although jurors in federal cases are required to unanimously agree that each element of the government's case has been satisfied, they are not obliged to unanimously agree on the particular **way** in which an element of the government's case was accomplished by the accused. For example, if "an element of robbery is force or the threat of force, some jurors might conclude that the defendant used a knife to create the threat; others might conclude he used a gun. But that disagreement—a disagreement about means—would not matter as long as all twelve jurors unanimously concluded that the Government had proved the necessary related element, namely, that the defendant had threatened force."[53]

In contrast, in criminal cases in state courts, the Sixth Amendment, as applied to the States through the Fourteenth, does not require unanimity. In other words, this is one of the rare provisions from the Bill of Rights which has not been incorporated. In 1972, the Court decided a pair of cases that established this rule—one arising out of Louisiana, the other arising out of Oregon:

> **Example—*Johnson v. Louisiana*, 406 U.S. 356 (1972):** Following a string of armed robberies, Frank Johnson was identified by one of the robbery victims as the assailant. He was thereafter charged with robbery. He elected a jury trial.
>
> Louisiana law permits criminal convictions by non-unanimous jury votes. In Johnson's case, nine jurors voted to convict and three voted to acquit. Johnson was thereafter found guilty of armed robbery. On appeal, he challenged the non-unanimous verdict in his case.

[51] Richardson v. United States, 526 U.S. 813, 817 (1999).

[52] Andres v. United States, 333 U.S. 740, 748 (1948).

[53] Id. at 817.

Analysis: The non-unanimous verdict in Johnson's case did not offend the Constitution.

The Sixth Amendment is made applicable to the States through the Fourteenth Amendment. However, the Due Process Clause of the Fourteenth Amendment does not insist upon a unanimous verdict in every criminal case. It is true that the prosecution must establish the defendant's guilty by proof beyond a reasonable doubt. But the existence of dissenting jurors does not indicate that the government's proof fell below the necessary threshold with regard to those jurors who were sufficiently convinced to convict. The "want of jury unanimity is not to be equated with the existence of a reasonable doubt."[54]

The Court found that there was no reason to believe that a jury that votes unanimously to convict has engaged in any more thorough a deliberative process than a jury that votes non-unanimously to convict. In support of this conclusion, the Court pointed to the absence of any studies suggesting that non-unanimous verdicts were the product of an inferior process: "Appellant offers no evidence that majority jurors simply ignore the reasonable doubts of their colleagues or otherwise act irresponsibly in casting their votes in favor of conviction, and before we alter our own longstanding perceptions about jury behavior and overturn a considered legislative judgment that unanimity is not essential to reasoned jury verdicts, we must have some basis for doing so other than unsupported assumptions."[55]

The *Johnson* decision focused heavily on the absence of empirical data to sustain a conclusion that non-unanimous verdicts were the result of an inferior deliberative process. The plurality opinion in the Oregon case, *Apodaca v. Oregon*,[56] took a slightly different approach. There, the Court concluded that the core function of the jury trial—to prevent government oppression—was no better served by a unanimous jury than a non-unanimous one: "In terms of this function we perceive no difference between juries required to act unanimously and those permitted to convict or acquit by votes of 10 to two or 11 to one . . . in either case, the interest of the defendant in having the judgment of his peers interposed between himself and the officers of the State who prosecute and judge him is equally well served."[57]

Since *Johnson* and *Apodaca*, several empirical studies have concluded that non-unanimous verdicts may in fact be the product of an inferior process in which the voices of minority jurors are not fully weighed. Nonetheless, the Court has repeatedly declined to reconsider its decision that the Constitution does not require unanimity in state jury verdicts.

[54] Johnson v. Louisiana, 406 U.S. 356, 363 (1972).

[55] Id. at 362.

[56] 406 U.S. 404 (1972).

[57] Id. at 411.

But what if in addition to abandoning a unanimity requirement, a state also decides to reduce its jury size to less than twelve? Recall, in establishing a constitutional minimum for jury size, the Court identified a number of concerns that are created by juries with fewer than six members. Does agreement by fewer than six people suffer from the same deficiencies? The Court took on this question in yet another case out of Louisiana, this one involving obscenity charges:

> **Example—*Burch v. Louisiana*, 441 U.S. 130 (1979):** Daniel Burch was charged with showing obscene movies. Under Louisiana law, his jury consisted of just six people. At the close of the evidence, Burch's six-person jury voted by a margin of 5-1 for conviction. This margin was all that was required by Louisiana law for a guilty verdict. The court sentenced Burch to a suspended seven-month sentence and a $1,000 fine. Burch then appealed. He contended that, on the facts of his case, the non-unanimous jury verdict violated his Sixth Amendment right to a jury trial. The Court granted cert to consider the question.

Analysis: Burch's right to a jury trial was violated by the 5-1 vote of his jury.

The Fourteenth Amendment secures for an accused a right to a jury trial to the same extent such right would be guaranteed under the Sixth Amendment if the case were tried in federal court. It is true that this right demands neither a twelve-member jury nor a unanimous verdict in every case. But, acknowledging the lack of these restraints does not completely resolve the question presented in this case, because constitutional concerns exist at the intersection of jury size and unanimity.

As the Court has previously found when a jury gets too small there is doubt it can satisfy its constitutional purpose. The process and substance of decision-making falter when groups become too small. In the case of the Sixth Amendment, a line has been drawn at the six-person jury. Juries that are smaller than this entail too great a likelihood of not functioning as intended.

Where a six-person jury returns a unanimous verdict, there is generally little reason to question the sufficiency of the deliberative process or the accuracy of the body's fact-finding. The non-unanimous verdict of a six-person jury, however, presents many of the same concerns as the forbidden five-person jury. "[W]hen a State has reduced the size of its juries to the minimum number of jurors permitted by the Constitution, the additional authorization of nonunanimous verdicts by such juries sufficiently threatens the constitutional principles that led to the establishment of the size threshold that any countervailing interest of the State should yield."[58]

---

[58] Burch v. Louisiana, 441 U.S. 130, 139 (1979).

Daniel Burch's conviction, which was returned by a vote of 5-1, violated his constitutional rights, and therefore must be overturned.

In the end, it may be that the Court's unanimity cases are less important than they at first may seem. Presently, Louisiana and Oregon are the only two states in the nation that do not require unanimous verdicts in criminal cases. Every other state and the federal government demand that criminal convictions be obtained by undivided jury agreement. Thus, while the right to a unanimous verdict is not protected by the Fourteenth Amendment, it is currently protected by state constitutional provision or statute in all states but two.

6. The Right to Jury Trial and Sentencing. Traditionally sentencing is understood not as a jury matter, but as a matter almost entirely within the discretion of a sentencing judge. However, a defendant has the right to have a jury decide all of the essential facts in her case, and this right occasionally raises concerns in the sentencing context.

The Court addressed this right in the case of *Apprendi v. New Jersey*, which held that "any fact that increases the penalty for a crime beyond the prescribed statutory maximum must be submitted to a jury, and proved beyond a reasonable doubt."[59] In the wake of *Apprendi*, an open question remained as to what the Court meant by the "prescribed statutory maximum." The government claimed that the "statutory maximum" was the highest possible sentence that might be imposed under the law that the defendant was accused of violating. Defense attorneys argued that the "statutory maximum" was the highest sentence that could be justified by the jury's findings or the defendant's admissions in the specific case.

This ambiguity was particularly significant given the prevalence of sentencing guidelines in the federal system and many state courts. A given crime might have a wide range of possible sentences and a high maximum sentence, but the sentencing guidelines would set out a narrow sentencing range for a specific defendant given his prior record and his conduct during the crime. Under the sentencing guidelines, the sentencing judge would determine whether the defendant's conduct during the crime made him eligible for any "enhancements" that would increase his sentencing range. If the government's interpretation of *Apprendi* was correct, this determination by the sentencing judge was constitutional as long as the sentencing judge did not increase the sentencing range beyond the statutory maximum of the crime. If the defense bar's interpretation of *Apprendi* was correct, the judge was not allowed to increase the defendant's sentencing range by making any additional findings of fact; she was bound by the specific facts found by the jury or admitted to by the defendant.

---

[59] 539 U.S. 466, 490 (2000).

In 2004, the Court decided a landmark case that settled the question on the side of the defendant:

> **Example—*Blakely v. Washington*, 542 U.S. 296 (2004):** Ralph Blakely "was evidently a difficult man to live with." After twenty-five years of marriage, his wife, Yolanda, began divorce proceedings. Shortly thereafter, Blakely forced his wife at knife-point into a box secured in the back of his truck. After begging her to stay with him, Blakely then waited at the house for the couple's 13-year old son, Ralphy, to arrive from school. When Ralphy got home, Blakely told Ralphy his mother was locked up in the back of the truck. Blakely also told Ralphy to follow him in a second car or Blakely would shoot Yolanda with a shotgun. Ralphy did as he was told. When they stopped at a gas station, Ralphy managed to get away for help. Blakely was later arrested at a friend's house after the friend turned him in.
>
> Blakely negotiated his original charge of first degree kidnapping down to a guilty plea on the lesser included offense of second degree kidnapping involving domestic violence and a firearm. Under Washington law, second degree kidnapping was punishable by a maximum sentence of 120 months. However, Washington also had a set of mandatory sentencing guidelines in place intended to limit the discretion of the sentencing judge. Under the sentencing guidelines, the judge could only sentence Blakely to 49-53 months in prison unless he had "substantial and compelling reasons" to deviate from the guidelines.
>
> At the sentencing hearing, Yolanda testified to her experience during the kidnapping. In addition, the judge heard the testimony of Ralphy, a police officer, and a medical expert. The trial judge sentenced Blakely to 90 months in prison. Specifically, the sentencing judge found that Blakely's conduct was deliberately cruel and issued 32 separate findings of fact based on the testimony presented at the hearing to back up this conclusion.
>
> Blakely appealed. He argued that the sentence enhancement deprived him of his right to have a jury find any facts relevant to his sentence beyond a reasonable doubt. After several reviewing courts affirmed, the Supreme Court took the case for review.

Analysis: Blakely's right to a jury's determination of essential sentencing facts was violated.

In this case, Blakely's admissions at the time he pled guilty subjected him to a maximum sentencing range of 49-53 months. In sentencing Blakely to some 90 months in prison, the sentencing court relied upon facts which were never submitted to a jury and had not been admitted by Blakely in the plea colloquy.

Blakely's right to have a jury determine the facts essential to his sentence was grounded in his right to a jury trial. "In a system that says a judge may punish burglary with 10 to 40 years, every burglar knows he is risking 40 years in jail. In a system that punishes burglary with a 10-year sentence, with another 30 added for use of a gun, the burglar who enters a home unarmed is **entitled** to no more than a 10-year sentence—and by reason of the Sixth Amendment the facts bearing upon that entitlement must be found by a jury."[60]

In the context of guilty pleas, a state could of course secure a valid waiver from the defendant to permit judicial fact-finding at sentencing. But no such waiver was obtained in this case.

Ralph Blakely received a sentence that was more than three years longer than it would have been had the sentencing judge relied entirely upon the facts admitted in connection with the plea. "The Framers would not have thought it too much to demand that, before depriving a man of three more years of his liberty, the State should suffer the modest inconvenience of submitting its accusation to 'the unanimous suffrage of twelve of his equals and neighbours,' rather than a lone employee of the State."[61]

The *Blakely* decision fundamentally changed the sentencing process in this country, since it held that any factor which increased the defendant's maximum sentence had to be determined by a jury. Soon after *Blakely* was decided, the Supreme Court applied the same principles to the federal sentencing guidelines, striking their mandatory application.[62] We will discuss sentencing in more detail in **Chapter 45.**

---

[60] Blakely v. Washington, 542 U.S. 296, 309 (2004).

[61] Id. at 313–14.

[62] United States v. Booker, 543 U.S. 220 (2005).

Quick Summary

The right to a jury trial is guaranteed in Article 3, Section 2, Clause 3 of the U.S. Constitution, as well as in the Sixth Amendment. However, the constitutional right to a jury trial does not apply in every criminal case. Serious crimes trigger the right to a jury trial, but petty crimes may be prosecuted before just a judicial officer.

In deciding whether a crime is petty or serious, the label a state has applied to an offense is not determinative. Instead, courts should look for objective indicators of seriousness. The most critical objective indicator of seriousness is the length of the authorized sentence upon conviction. Offenses that are punishable by more than six months in jail are presumptively serious offenses for which the accused enjoys the right to a jury trial. Offenses punishable by six months or less are presumptively petty, and not deserving of jury trial protection.

Though the length of authorized (not imposed) punishment is the measure in most cases, contempt cases operate under a different rule. For offenses like contempt, where no maximum penalty is authorized, the best indication of the seriousness of the offense is the sentence imposed.

Additional punishments, beyond authorized periods of incarceration, may also inform a reviewing court's understanding of the seriousness of the offense for purposes of defining jury trial rights. However, to shift an offense from the petty category to the serious category, any additional penalties must be fairly severe.

Under federal statutory law, a jury has twelve members. However, the size of a jury is not expressed in the Constitution, and so the twelve person jury is not a constitutional mandate. The smallest number of jurors that may be empanelled consistent with the Constitution's jury trial guarantee is six.

Unanimity is also not a constitutional guarantee in all cases. Juries in federal courts are required to be unanimous, but the only time a state criminal jury must be unanimous is if that jury consists of only six persons.

Just as the constitutional right to counsel envisions a right to **effective** counsel, the constitutional right to a jury trial envisions a trial by an **impartial** jury drawn from a fair cross section of the community.

Jury selection involves the attorneys making unlimited challenges for cause if they believe that certain potential jurors cannot be impartial. Attorneys are also given a small number of peremptory challenges to strike any potential jurors for any reason. However, attorneys are prohibited under the *Batson* rule from exercising these peremptory challenges with a discriminatory intent.

In addition to the Constitution, the Federal Rules of Criminal Procedure and state constitutional, statutory, and rule-based schemes govern the right to a jury trial. Many of these provisions are consistent with the protections and limitations offered by the Constitution. However, some states provide jury trial protections that exceed those that are constitutionally required.

Review Questions

1. The Old Switcheroo. In 1991, Leroy Huckleberry was walking down the street in Detroit when he was grabbed by two masked men, thrown in the back of a van, bound at his hands and feet and blindfolded. Eighteen hours later, Huckleberry was released after it became clear his family would not pay any ransom. DeShannon Fitzgerald and Romallis Colvin were later charged with the crime. Huckleberry could not identify either man's face, but did identify both men by their voices. Fitzgerald and Colvin were charged jointly and the trial was scheduled to proceed in front of Judge Wendy Baxter. Shortly before trial, Fitzgerald waived his right to a jury trial and agreed to proceed on the question of guilt before Judge Baxter. Judge Baxter engaged in an extended colloquy with Fitzgerald to ascertain that he understood his rights and was knowingly and intelligently waiving them. After being convinced that Fitzgerald was validly waiving his rights, Judge Baxter entered a notation on Fitzgerald's docket sheet that read "Waiver Colloquy; Bench Trial (Baxter, J.)." Co-defendant Colvin did not waive his jury trial right, and so jury selection in the case began.

The next day a new judge, Judge Leonard Townsend, took the bench. He explained that Judge Baxter had become seriously ill and would not be available to try the case. Judge Townsend therefore announced he would conduct Fitzgerald's bench trial and Colvin's jury trial. Concerned about Judge Townsend's reputation as a "law and order" judge, Fitzgerald immediately requested a jury trial. Judge Townsend denied the request, finding that Fitzgerald had validly waived his rights. At the close of the evidence, Judge Townsend found Fitzgerald guilty and sentenced him to life in prison. Fitzgerald appealed. He argued that his consent to a bench trial was only his consent to have Judge Baxter try him. His right to a jury trial, he argued, was therefore denied when he was forced to proceed before Judge Townsend. Is Fitzgerald correct?

2. Counsel's Waiver of the Right to a Jury? Sergio Duarte-Higareda was indicted along with three co-conspirators of possessing methamphetamine with the intent to distribute. Prior to trial, defense counsel announced that Duarte-Higareda was waiving his right to a jury trial. Counsel advised the court that he had spoken with Duarte-Higareda about the issue on two separate occasions. Counsel further informed the court that he thought the jury trial waiver would be beneficial to Duarte-Higareda. By way of explanation, counsel noted that waiving a jury trial would enable counsel to "devote his time to an upcoming rape trial for another client." Counsel was not specifically asked, and never explicitly described how the jury trial waiver would help Duarte-Higareda.

Duarte-Higareda, who did not speak English but who had the assistance of an interpreter, was present in the court room during counsel's conversation with the court and did not offer any correction or clarification. The trial court also did not seek to clarify directly with Duarte-Higareda whether he understood the waiver. The next day, Duarte-Higareda signed a detailed jury waiver form that was printed in English. There was no indication in the record whether the form was ever translated for him. At the subsequent bench trial, Duarte-Higareda was found guilty and sentenced to ten years in prison.

On appeal, Duarte-Higareda challenged the validity of his jury trial waiver. If you were a member of the appellate panel, how would you rule?

3. **The Excess (?) Burden of Drunk Driving.** Phillip Landry was arrested for driving while intoxicated. The maximum punishment for this offense was six months imprisonment or a $500 fine or both. Landry waived his right to counsel, but requested a jury trial. His request was denied. Landry was later convicted. He received a $300 fine and a six month sentence. In addition, the court suspended execution of Landry's sentence for two years and placed Landry on probation. The terms of Landry's probation required him to perform community service four days a week, attend daily driver's education classes, and attend a weekly substance abuse program. On appeal, Landry complained that his right to a jury trial had been violated. In particular, Landry pointed to the additional conditions that had been imposed and contended that they demonstrated that his crime was a "serious offense" for jury trial purposes. Will Landry's appellate challenge be successful?

4. **And Then There Were Eleven. . . .** Daphne Essex was accused of possessing heroin with the intent to distribute it. A jury of twelve, plus one alternate, was selected to hear the case. However, just after the jury was seated, defense counsel noticed that one of the jurors who had been peremptorily struck was accidentally seated among the twelve jurors. Both the prosecutor and the defense agreed that the alternate juror should be seated as the twelfth juror. The following exchange then took place between both lawyers, the defendant, and the court:

> THE COURT: That means we proceed without an alternate and it is understood that in the event we should have anything happen to one of them, they are unable to come, if it is not less than one juror you are willing to proceed with 11?
>
> DEFENSE COUNSEL: That's correct, your Honor.
>
> THE COURT: That's agreeable to your client?
>
> THE DEFENDANT: Yes.
>
> THE COURT: Very well. Is it agreeable to the Government?

GOVERNMENT COUNSEL: It is agreeable to the Government, your Honor, but this is an issue which, as the court well knows, has been litigated many times. If we could have a formal waiver from Miss Essex, that is, to indicate that she has been advised that she has an absolute right to have 12 jurors and that if she waives it she waives any right to appeal that issue, and she must be satisfied with a verdict of 11.

THE COURT: Do you understand, Miss Essex, that you are entitled to a jury of 12 and you would certainly have it if we had it. At the moment you are going to have 12. I am just saying that in the event something should happen to one of them, we don't have any alternates.

THE DEFENDANT: Yes, Ma'am.

THE COURT: So if something should happen to one, we would proceed with 11. Is that your understanding and you agree to that?

THE DEFENDANT: Yes, Ma'am, I do.

THE COURT: Very well.

The accidentally seated juror was then dismissed and the alternate was seated. At the close of the evidence, the jurors were sent out to deliberate. At approximately 6:00 that evening the jurors had not yet reached agreement and voted to return the following Monday to continue deliberations.

The following Monday, only eleven of the twelve jurors arrived. Defense counsel objected to the jury being allowed to deliberate and instead asked that steps be taken to locate the missing juror. The trial judge, however, found that the defense's earlier stipulation was sufficient to waive the right to a twelve person jury, and instructed the jurors to continue deliberating immediately. The trial judge took no steps to find the missing juror or to determine why he had not appeared. The eleven-member jury convicted Essex. On appeal, she maintained that her rights (under the Constitution and the Federal Rules of Criminal Procedure) had been violated. Will she be successful on appeal?

FROM THE COURTROOM

BALLEW v. GEORGIA

Supreme Court of the United States, 1978
435 U.S. 223

[Justice BLACKMUN announce judgment of the Court; filed opinion joined by Justice STEVENS].

[Justice STEVENS filed concurring statement].

[Justice WHITE filed statement concurring in judgment].

[Justice POWELL filed concurring opinion joined by Chief Justice BURGER and Justice REHNQUIST].

[Justice BRENNAN filed separate opinion joined by Justice STEWART and Justice MARSHALL].

This case presents the issue whether a state criminal trial to a jury of only five persons deprives the accused of the right to trial by jury guaranteed by him by the Sixth and Fourteenth Amendments. Our resolution of the issue requires an application of principles enunciated in Williams v. Florida, 399 U.S. 78 (1970), where the use of a six-person jury in a state criminal trial was upheld against similar constitutional attack.

I

In November 1973 petitioner Claude Davis Ballew was the manager of the Paris Adult Theatre at 320 Peachtree Street, Atlanta, Ga. On November 9 two investigators from the Fulton County Solicitor General's office viewed at the theater a motion picture film entitled "Behind the Green Door." After they had seen the film, they obtained a warrant for its seizure, returned to the theater, viewed the film once again, and seized it. Petitioner and a cashier were arrested. Investigators returned to the theater on November 26, viewed the film in its entirety, secured still another warrant, and on November 27 once again viewed the motion picture and seized a second copy of the film.

On September 14, 1974, petitioner was charged in a two-count misdemeanor accusation with

"distributing obscene materials in violation of Georgia Code Section 26-2101 in that the said accused did, knowing the obscene nature thereof, exhibit a motion picture film entitled 'Behind the Green Door' that contained obscene and indecent scenes . . ."

Petitioner was brought to trial in the Criminal Court of Fulton County. After a jury of 5 persons had been selected and sworn, petitioner moved that the court impanel a jury of 12 persons. That court, however, tried its misdemeanor cases before juries of five persons pursuant to [the Georgia Constitution and Georgia statutory law]. Petitioner contended that for an obscenity trial, a jury of only five was constitutionally inadequate to assess the contemporary standards of the community. He also argued that the Sixth and Fourteenth Amendments required a jury of at least six members in criminal cases.

The motion for a 12-person jury was overruled, and the trial went on to its conclusion before the 5-person jury that had been impaneled. At the conclusion of the trial, the jury deliberated for 38 minutes and returned a verdict of guilty on both counts of the accusation. The court imposed a sentence of one year and a $1,000 fine on each count, the periods of incarceration to run concurrently and to be suspended upon payment of the fines. After a subsequent hearing, the court denied an amended motion for a new trial.

. . .

In his petition for certiorari here, petitioner raised three issues: the unconstitutionality of the five-person jury; the constitutional sufficiency of the jury instructions on scienter and constructive, rather than actual, knowledge of the contents of the film; and obscenity vel non. We granted certiorari. Because we now hold that the five-member jury does not satisfy the jury trial guarantee of the Sixth Amendment, as applied to the States through the Fourteenth, we do not reach the other issues.

II

The Fourteenth Amendment guarantees the right of trial by jury in all state nonpetty criminal cases. The Court in Duncan applied this Sixth Amendment right to the States because "trial by jury in criminal cases is fundamental to the American scheme of justice." The right attaches in the present case because the maximum penalty for violating [the statute under which Ballew was charged] as it existed at the time of the alleged offenses, exceeded six months' imprisonment.

In *Williams v. Florida*, the Court reaffirmed that the "purpose of the jury trial, as we noted in Duncan, is to prevent oppression by the Government. 'Providing an accused with the right to be tried by a jury of his peers gave him an inestimable safeguard against the corrupt or overzealous prosecutor and against the compliant, biased, or eccentric judge.'" This purpose is attained by the participation of the community in determinations of guilt and by the application of the common sense of laymen who, as jurors, consider the case.

Williams held that these functions and this purpose could be fulfilled by a jury of six members. As the Court's opinion in that case explained at some length, common-law juries included 12 members by historical accident, "unrelated to the great purposes which gave rise to the jury in the first place." The Court's earlier cases that had assumed the number 12 to be constitutionally compelled were set to one side because they had not considered history and the function of the jury. Rather than requiring 12 members, then, the Sixth Amendment mandated a jury only of sufficient size to promote group deliberation, to insulate members from outside intimidation, and to provide a representative cross-section of the community. Although recognizing that by 1970 little empirical research had evaluated jury performance, the Court found no evidence that the reliability of jury verdicts diminished with six-member panels. Nor did the Court anticipate significant differences in result, including the frequency of "hung" juries. Because the reduction in size did not threaten exclusion of any particular class from jury roles, concern that the representative or cross-section character of the jury would suffer with a decrease to six members seemed "an unrealistic one." As a consequence, the six-person jury was held not to violate the Sixth and Fourteenth Amendments.

III

When the Court in *Williams* permitted the reduction in jury size—or, to put it another way, when it held that a jury of six was not unconstitutional—it expressly reserved ruling on the issue whether a number smaller than six passed constitutional scrutiny. The Court refused to speculate when this so-called "slippery slope" would become too steep. We face now, however, the two-fold question whether a further reduction in the size of the state criminal trial jury does make the grade too dangerous, that is, whether it inhibits the functioning of the jury as an institution to a significant degree, and, if so, whether any state interest counterbalances and justifies the disruption so as to preserve its constitutionality.

Williams v. Florida and *Colgrove v. Battin*, (where the Court held that a jury of six members did not violate the Seventh Amendment right to a jury trial in a civil case), generated a quantity of scholarly work on jury size. These writings do not draw or identify a bright line below which the number of jurors would not be able to function as required by the standards enunciated in *Williams*. On the other hand, they raise significant questions about the wisdom and constitutionality of a reduction below six. We examine these concerns:

First, recent empirical data suggest that progressively smaller juries are less likely to foster effective group deliberation. At some point, this decline leads to inaccurate fact-finding and incorrect application of the common sense of the community to the facts. Generally, a positive correlation exists between group size and the quality of both group performance and group productivity. A variety of explanations have been offered for this conclusion. Several are particularly applicable in the jury setting. The smaller the group, the less likely are members to make critical contributions necessary for the solution of a given problem. Because most juries are not permitted to take notes, memory is important for accurate jury deliberations. As juries decrease in size, then, they are less likely to have members who remember each of the important pieces of evidence or argument. Furthermore, the smaller the group, the less likely it is to overcome the biases of its members to obtain an accurate result. When individual and group decisionmaking were compared, it was seen that groups performed better because prejudices of individuals were frequently counterbalanced, and objectivity resulted. Groups also exhibited increased motivation and self-criticism. All these advantages, except, perhaps, self-motivation, tend to diminish as the size of the group diminishes. Because juries frequently face complex problems laden with value choices, the benefits are important and should be retained. In particular, the counterbalancing of various biases is critical to the accurate application of the common sense of the community to the facts of any given case.

Second, the data now raise doubts about the accuracy of the results achieved by smaller and smaller panels. Statistical studies suggest that the risk of convicting an innocent person (Type I error) rises as the size of the jury diminishes. Because the risk of not convicting a guilty person (Type II error) increases with the size of the panel, an optimal jury size can be selected as a function of the interaction between the two risks. Nagel and Neef concluded that the optimal size, for the purpose of minimizing errors, should vary with the importance attached to the two types of mistakes. After weighing Type I error as 10 times more significant than Type II, perhaps not an unreasonable assumption, they concluded that the optimal jury size was between six and eight. As the size diminished to five and below, the weighted sum of errors increased because of the enlarging risk of the conviction of innocent defendants.

Another doubt about progressively smaller juries arises from the increasing inconsistency that results from the decreases. Saks argued that the "more a jury type fosters consistency, the greater will be the proportion of juries which select the correct (i. e., the same) verdict and the fewer 'errors' will be made." From his mock trials held before undergraduates and former jurors, he computed the percentage of "correct" decisions rendered by 12-person and 6-person panels. In the student experiment, 12-person groups reached correct verdicts 83% of the time; 6-person panels reached correct verdicts 69% of the time. The results for the former-juror study were 71% for the 12-person groups and 57% for the 6-person groups. Working with statistics described in H. Kalven & H. Zeisel, *The American Jury* (1966), Nagel and Neef tested the average conviction propensity of juries, that is, the likelihood that any given jury of a set would convict the defendant. They found that half of all 12-person juries would have average conviction propensities that varied by no more than 20 points. Half of all six-person juries, on the other hand, had average conviction propensities varying by 30 points, a difference they found significant in both real and percentage terms. Lempert reached similar results when he considered the likelihood of juries to compromise over the various views of their members, an important phenomenon for the fulfillment of the common sense function. In civil trials averaging occurs with respect to damages amounts. In criminal trials it relates to numbers of counts and lesser included offenses. And he predicted that compromises would be more consistent when larger juries were employed. For example, 12-person juries could be expected to reach extreme compromises in 4% of the cases, while 6-person panels would reach extreme results in 16%. All three of these post-*Williams* studies, therefore, raise significant doubts about the consistency and reliability of the decisions of smaller juries.

Third, the data suggest that the verdicts of jury deliberation in criminal cases will vary as juries become smaller, and that the variance amounts to an imbalance to the detriment of one side, the defense. Both Lempert and Zeisel found that the number of hung juries would diminish as the panels decreased in size. Zeisel said that the number would be cut in half-from 5% to 2.4% with a decrease from 12 to 6 members. Both studies emphasized that juries in criminal cases generally hang with only one, or more likely two jurors remaining unconvinced of guilt. Also, group theory suggests that a person in the minority will adhere to his position more frequently when he has at least one other person supporting his argument. In the jury setting the significance of this tendency is demonstrated by the following figures: If a minority viewpoint is shared by 10% of the community, 28.2% of 12-member juries may be expected to have no minority representation, but 53.1% of 6-member juries would have none. Thirty-four percent of 12-member panels could be expected to have two minority members, while only 11% of 6-member panels would have two. As the numbers diminish below six, even fewer panels would have one member with the minority viewpoint and still fewer would have two. The chance for hung juries would decline accordingly.

Fourth, what has just been said about the presence of minority viewpoint as juries decrease in size foretells problems not only for jury decisionmaking, but also for the representation of minority groups in the community. The Court repeatedly has held that meaningful community participation cannot be attained with the exclusion of minorities or other identifiable groups from jury service. "It is part of the established tradition in the use of juries as instruments of public justice that the jury be a body truly representative of the community." The exclusion of elements of the community from participation "contravenes the very idea of a jury . . . composed of 'the peers or equals of the person whose rights it is selected or summoned to determine.'" Although the Court in *Williams* concluded that the six-person jury did not fail to represent adequately a cross-section of the community, the opportunity for meaningful and appropriate representation does decrease with the size of the panels. Thus, if a minority group constitutes 10% of the community, 53.1% of randomly selected six-member juries could be expected to have no minority representative among their members, and 89% not to have two. Further reduction in size will erect additional barriers to representation.

Fifth, several authors have identified in jury research methodological problems tending to mask differences in the operation of smaller and larger juries. For example, because the judicial system handles so many clear cases, decisionmakers will reach similar results through similar analyses most of the time. One study concluded that smaller and larger juries could disagree in their verdicts in no more than 14% of the cases. Disparities, therefore, appear in only small percentages. Nationwide, however, these small percentages will represent a large number of cases. And it is with respect to those cases that the jury trial right has its greatest value. When the case is close, and the guilt or innocence of the defendant is not readily apparent, a properly functioning jury system will insure evaluation by the sense of the community and will also tend to insure accurate factfinding.

. . .

IV

While we adhere to, and reaffirm our holding in *Williams v. Florida*, these studies, most of which have been made since *Williams* was decided in 1970, lead us to conclude that the purpose and functioning of the jury in a criminal trial is seriously impaired, and to a constitutional degree, by a reduction in size to below six members. We readily admit that we do not pretend to discern a clear line between six members and five. But the assembled data raise substantial doubt about the reliability and appropriate representation of panels smaller than six. Because of the fundamental importance of the jury trial to the American system of criminal justice, any further reduction that promotes inaccurate and possibly biased decisionmaking, that causes untoward differences in verdicts, and that prevents juries from truly representing their communities, attains constitutional significance.

Georgia here presents no persuasive argument that a reduction to five does not offend important Sixth Amendment interests. . . .

Georgia argues that its use of five-member juries does not violate the Sixth and Fourteenth Amendments because they are used only in misdemeanor cases. If six persons may constitutionally assess the felony charge in *Williams*, the State reasons, five persons should be a constitutionally adequate number for a misdemeanor trial. The problem with this argument is that the purpose and functions of the jury do not vary significantly with the importance of the crime. In *Baldwin v. New York*, 399 U.S. 66 (1970), the Court held that the right to a jury trial attached in both felony and misdemeanor cases. Only in cases concerning truly petty crimes, where the deprivation of liberty was minimal, did the defendant have no constitutional right to trial by jury. In the present case the possible deprivation of liberty is substantial. The State charged petitioner with misdemeanors . . . and he has been given concurrent sentences of imprisonment, each for one year, and fines totaling $2,000 have been imposed. We cannot conclude that there is less need for the imposition and the direction of the sense of the community in this case than when the State has chosen to label an offense a felony. The need for an effective jury here must be judged by the same standards announced and applied in *Williams v. Florida*.

[Next], the retention by Georgia of the unanimity requirement does not solve the Sixth and Fourteenth Amendment problem. Our concern has to do with the ability of the smaller group to perform the functions mandated by the Amendments. That a five-person jury may return a unanimous decision does not speak to the questions whether the group engaged in meaningful deliberation, could remember all the important facts and arguments, and truly represented the sense of the entire community. Despite the presence of the unanimity requirement, then, we cannot conclude that "the interest of the defendant in having the judgment of his peers interposed between himself and the officers of the State who prosecute and judge him is equally well served" by the five-person panel.

[In addition], Georgia submits that the five-person jury adequately represents the community because there is no arbitrary exclusion of any particular class. We agree that it has not been demonstrated that the Georgia system violates the Equal Protection Clause by discriminating on the basis of race or some other improper classification. But the data outlined above raise substantial doubt about the ability of juries truly to represent the community as membership decreases below six. If the smaller and smaller juries will lack consistency, as the cited studies suggest, then the sense of the community will not be applied equally in like cases. Not only is the representation of racial minorities threatened in such circumstances, but also majority attitude or various minority positions may be misconstrued or misapplied by the smaller groups. Even though the facts of this case would not establish a jury discrimination claim under the Equal Protection Clause, the question of representation does constitute one factor of several that, when combined, create a problem of constitutional significance under the Sixth and Fourteenth Amendments. . . .

V

With the reduction in the number of jurors below six creating a substantial threat to Sixth and Fourteenth Amendment guarantees, we must consider whether any interest of the State justifies the reduction. We find no significant state advantage in reducing the number of jurors from six to five.

The States utilize juries of less than 12 primarily for administrative reasons. Savings in court time and in financial costs are claimed to justify the reductions. The financial benefits of the reduction from 12 to 6 are substantial; this is mainly because fewer jurors draw daily allowances as they hear cases. On the other hand, the asserted saving in judicial time is not so clear. Pabst in his study found little reduction in the time for voir dire with the six-person jury because many questions were directed at the veniremen as a group. Total trial time did not diminish, and court delays and backlogs improved very little. The point that is to be made, of course, is that a reduction in size from six to five or four or even three would save the States little. They could reduce slightly the daily allowances, but with a reduction from six to five the saving would be minimal. If little time is gained by the reduction from 12 to 6, less will be gained with a reduction from 6 to 5. Perhaps this explains why only two States, Georgia and Virginia, have reduced the size of juries in certain nonpetty criminal cases to five. Other States appear content with six members or more. In short the State has offered little or no justification for its reduction to five members.

Petitioner, therefore, has established that his trial on criminal charges before a five-member jury deprived him of the right to trial by jury guaranteed by the Sixth and Fourteenth Amendments.

VI

The judgment of the Court of Appeals is reversed, and the case is remanded for further proceedings not inconsistent with this opinion.

It is so ordered.

[Justice STEVENS's concurring opinion has been omitted].

[Justice WHITE's concurring opinion has been omitted].

Mr. Justice POWELL, with whom THE CHIEF JUSTICE and Mr. Justice REHNQUIST join, concurring in the judgment.

I concur in the judgment, as I agree that use of a jury as small as five members, with authority to convict for serious offenses, involves grave questions of fairness. As the opinion of Mr. Justice Blackmun indicates, the line between five- and six-member juries is difficult to justify, but a line has to be drawn somewhere if the substance of jury trial is to be preserved.

I do not agree, however, that every feature of jury trial practice must be the same in both federal and state courts. Because the opinion of Mr. Justice Blackmun today assumes full incorporation of the Sixth Amendment by the Fourteenth Amendment contrary to my view in Apodaca, I do not join it. Also, I have reservations as to the wisdom-as well as the necessity-of Mr. Justice Blackmun's heavy reliance on numerology derived from statistical studies. Moreover, neither the validity nor the methodology employed by the studies cited was subjected to the traditional testing mechanisms of the adversary process. The studies relied on merely represent unexamined findings of persons interested in the jury system.

For these reasons I concur only in the judgment.

FROM THE COURTROOM

BLAKELY v. WASHINGTON

Supreme Court of the United States, 2004
542 U.S. 296

[Justice SCALIA delivered the opinion of the Court].

[Justice O'CONNOR filed a dissenting opinion in which Justice BREYER joined, and in which Chief Justice REHNQUIST and Justice KENNEDY joined in part].

[Justice KENNEDY filed dissenting opinion in which Justice BREYER joined].

[Justice BREYER filed dissenting opinion in which Justice O'CONNOR joined].

Petitioner Ralph Howard Blakely, Jr., pleaded guilty to the kidnaping of his estranged wife. The facts admitted in his plea, standing alone, supported a maximum sentence of 53 months. Pursuant to state law, the court imposed an "exceptional" sentence of 90 months after making a judicial determination that he had acted with "deliberate cruelty." We consider whether this violated petitioner's Sixth Amendment right to trial by jury.

I

Petitioner married his wife Yolanda in 1973. He was evidently a difficult man to live with, having been diagnosed at various times with psychological and personality disorders including paranoid schizophrenia. His wife ultimately filed for divorce. In 1998, he abducted her from their orchard home in Grant County, Washington, binding her with duct tape and forcing her at knifepoint into a wooden box in the bed of his pickup truck. In the process, he implored her to dismiss the divorce suit and related trust proceedings.

When the couple's 13–year–old son Ralphy returned home from school, petitioner ordered him to follow in another car, threatening to harm Yolanda with a shotgun if he did not do so. Ralphy escaped and sought help when they stopped at a gas station, but petitioner continued on with Yolanda to a friend's house in Montana. He was finally arrested after the friend called the police.

The State charged petitioner with first-degree kidnaping. Upon reaching a plea agreement, however, it reduced the charge to second-degree kidnaping involving domestic violence and use of a firearm. Petitioner entered a guilty plea admitting the elements of second-degree kidnaping and the domestic-violence and firearm allegations, but no other relevant facts.

The case then proceeded to sentencing. In Washington, second-degree kidnaping is a class B felony. State law provides that "[n]o person convicted of a [class B] felony shall be punished by confinement . . . exceeding . . . a term of ten years." Other provisions of state law, however, further limit the range of sentences a judge may impose. Washington's Sentencing Reform Act specifies, for petitioner's offense of second-degree kidnaping with a firearm, a "standard range" of 49 to 53 months. A judge may impose a sentence above the standard range if he finds "substantial and compelling reasons justifying an exceptional sentence." The Act lists aggravating factors that justify such a departure, which it recites to be illustrative rather than exhaustive. Nevertheless, "[a] reason offered to justify an exceptional sentence can be considered only if it takes into account factors other than those which are used in computing the standard range sentence for the offense." When a judge imposes an exceptional sentence, he must set forth findings of fact and conclusions of law supporting it. . . .

Pursuant to the plea agreement, the State recommended a sentence within the standard range of 49 to 53 months. After hearing Yolanda's description of the kidnaping, however, the judge rejected the State's recommendation and imposed an exceptional sentence of 90 months—37 months beyond the standard maximum. He justified the sentence on the ground that petitioner had acted with "deliberate cruelty," a statutorily enumerated ground for departure in domestic-violence cases.

Faced with an unexpected increase of more than three years in his sentence, petitioner objected. The judge accordingly conducted a 3–day bench hearing featuring testimony from petitioner, Yolanda, Ralphy, a police officer, and medical experts. After the hearing, he issued 32 findings of fact, concluding:

"The defendant's motivation to commit kidnapping was complex, contributed to by his mental condition and personality disorders, the pressures of the divorce litigation, the impending trust litigation trial and anger over his troubled interpersonal relationships with his spouse and children. While he misguidedly intended to forcefully reunite his family, his attempt to do so was subservient to his desire to terminate lawsuits and modify title ownerships to his benefit.

"The defendant's methods were more homogeneous than his motive. He used stealth and surprise, and took advantage of the victim's isolation. He immediately employed physical violence, restrained the victim with tape, and threatened her with injury and death to herself and others. He immediately coerced the victim into providing information by the threatening application of a knife. He violated a subsisting restraining order."

The judge adhered to his initial determination of deliberate cruelty.

Petitioner appealed, arguing that this sentencing procedure deprived him of his federal constitutional right to have a jury determine beyond a reasonable doubt all facts legally essential to his sentence. . . . We granted certiorari.

II

This case requires us to apply the rule we expressed in *Apprendi v. New Jersey*, 530 U.S. 466, 490 (2000): "Other than the fact of a prior conviction, any fact that increases the penalty for a crime beyond the prescribed statutory maximum must be submitted to a jury, and proved beyond a reasonable doubt." This rule reflects two longstanding tenets of common-law criminal jurisprudence: that the "truth of every accusation" against a defendant "should afterwards be confirmed by the unanimous suffrage of twelve of his equals and neighbours," and that "an accusation which lacks any particular fact which the law makes essential to the punishment is. . .no accusation within the requirements of the common law, and it is no accusation in reason." These principles have been acknowledged by courts and treatises since the earliest days of graduated sentencing; we compiled the relevant authorities in *Apprendi*, and need not repeat them here.

[In *Apprendi* and later in *Ring v. Arizona*, 536 U.S. 584 (2002)], . . . we concluded that the defendant's constitutional rights had been violated because the judge had imposed a sentence greater than the maximum he could have imposed under state law without the challenged factual finding.

In this case, petitioner was sentenced to more than three years above the 53–month statutory maximum of the standard range because he had acted with "deliberate cruelty." The facts supporting that finding were neither admitted by petitioner nor found by a jury. The State nevertheless contends that there was no *Apprendi* violation because the relevant "statutory maximum" is not 53 months, but the 10–year maximum for class B felonies . . . . It observes that no exceptional sentence may exceed that limit. Our precedents make clear, however, that the "statutory maximum" for *Apprendi* purposes is the maximum sentence a judge may impose solely on the basis of the facts reflected in the jury verdict or admitted by the defendant. In other words, the relevant "statutory maximum" is not the maximum sentence a judge may impose after finding additional facts, but the maximum he may impose without any additional findings. When a judge inflicts punishment that the jury's verdict alone does not allow, the jury has not found all the facts "which the law makes essential to the punishment," and the judge exceeds his proper authority.

The judge in this case could not have imposed the exceptional 90–month sentence solely on the basis of the facts admitted in the guilty plea. Those facts alone were insufficient because, as the Washington Supreme Court has explained, "[a] reason offered to justify an exceptional sentence can be considered only if it takes into account factors other than those which are used in computing the standard range sentence for the offense," which in this case included the elements of second-degree kidnaping and the use of a firearm. Had the judge imposed the 90–month sentence solely on the basis of the plea, he would have been reversed. The "maximum sentence" is no more 10 years here than it was 20 years in *Apprendi* (because that is what the judge could have imposed upon finding a hate crime) or death in Ring (because that is what the judge could have imposed upon finding an aggravator).

The State defends the sentence by drawing an analogy to those we upheld in *McMillan v. Pennsylvania*, 477 U.S. 79 (1986), and *Williams v. New York*, 337 U.S. 241 (1949).

Neither case is on point. *McMillan* involved a sentencing scheme that imposed a statutory minimum if a judge found a particular fact. We specifically noted that the statute "does not authorize a sentence in excess of that otherwise allowed for [the underlying] offense." *Williams* involved an indeterminate-sentencing regime that allowed a judge (but did not compel him) to rely on facts outside the trial record in determining whether to sentence a defendant to death. The judge could have "sentenced [the defendant] to death giving no reason at all." Thus, neither case involved a sentence greater than what state law authorized on the basis of the verdict alone.

Finally, the State tries to distinguish *Apprendi* and *Ring* by pointing out that the enumerated grounds for departure in its regime are illustrative rather than exhaustive. This distinction is immaterial. Whether the judge's authority to impose an enhanced sentence depends on finding a specified fact (as in *Apprendi*), one of several specified facts (as in *Ring*), or any aggravating fact (as here), it remains the case that the jury's verdict alone does not authorize the sentence. The judge acquires that authority only upon finding some additional fact.

Because the State's sentencing procedure did not comply with the Sixth Amendment, petitioner's sentence is invalid.

III

Our commitment to *Apprendi* in this context reflects not just respect for longstanding precedent, but the need to give intelligible content to the right of jury trial. That right is no mere procedural formality, but a fundamental reservation of power in our constitutional structure. Just as suffrage ensures the people's ultimate control in the legislative and executive branches, jury trial is meant to ensure their control in the judiciary. *Apprendi* carries out this design by ensuring that the judge's authority to sentence derives wholly from the jury's verdict. Without that restriction, the jury would not exercise the control that the Framers intended.

Those who would reject *Apprendi* are resigned to one of two alternatives. The first is that the jury need only find whatever facts the legislature chooses to label elements of the crime, and that those it labels sentencing factors—no matter how much they may increase the punishment—may be found by the judge. This would mean, for example, that a judge could sentence a man for committing murder even if the jury convicted him only of illegally possessing the firearm used to commit it—or of making an illegal lane change while fleeing the death scene. Not even *Apprendi*'s critics would advocate this absurd result. The jury could not function as circuitbreaker in the State's machinery of justice if it were relegated to making a determination that the defendant at some point did something wrong, a mere preliminary to a judicial inquisition into the facts of the crime the State actually seeks to punish.

The second alternative is that legislatures may establish legally essential sentencing factors within limits—limits crossed when, perhaps, the sentencing factor is a "tail which wags the dog of the substantive offense." What this means in operation is that the law must not go too far—it must not exceed the judicial estimation of the proper role of the judge.

The subjectivity of this standard is obvious. Petitioner argued below that second-degree kidnaping with deliberate cruelty was essentially the same as first-degree kidnaping, the very charge he had avoided by pleading to a lesser offense. The court conceded this might be so but held it irrelevant. Petitioner's 90–month sentence exceeded the 53–month standard maximum by almost 70%; the Washington Supreme Court in other cases has upheld exceptional sentences 15 times the standard maximum. Did the court go too far in any of these cases? There is no answer that legal analysis can provide. With too far as the yardstick, it is always possible to disagree with such judgments and never to refute them.

Whether the Sixth Amendment incorporates this manipulable standard rather than *Apprendi*'s bright-line rule depends on the plausibility of the claim that the Framers would have left definition of the scope of jury power up to judges' intuitive sense of how far is too far. We think that claim not plausible at all, because the very reason the Framers put a jury-trial guarantee in the Constitution is that they were unwilling to trust government to mark out the role of the jury.

IV

By reversing the judgment below, we are not, as the State would have it, "find [ing] determinate sentencing schemes unconstitutional." This case is not about whether determinate sentencing is constitutional, only about how it can be implemented in a way that respects the Sixth Amendment. Several policies prompted Washington's adoption of determinate sentencing, including proportionality to the gravity of the offense and parity among defendants. Nothing we have said impugns those salutary objectives.

Justice O'Connor argues that, because determinate-sentencing schemes involving judicial factfinding entail less judicial discretion than indeterminate schemes, the constitutionality of the latter implies the constitutionality of the former. This argument is flawed on a number of levels. First, the Sixth Amendment by its terms is not a limitation on judicial power, but a reservation of jury power. It limits judicial power only to the extent that the claimed judicial power infringes on the province of the jury. Indeterminate sentencing does not do so. It increases judicial discretion, to be sure, but not at the expense of the jury's traditional function of finding the facts essential to lawful imposition of the penalty. Of course indeterminate schemes involve judicial factfinding, in that a judge (like a parole board) may implicitly rule on those facts he deems important to the exercise of his sentencing discretion. But the facts do not pertain to whether the defendant has a legal right to a lesser sentence—and that makes all the difference insofar as judicial impingement upon the traditional role of the jury is concerned. In a system that says the judge may punish burglary with 10 to 40 years, every burglar knows he is risking 40 years in jail. In a system that punishes burglary with a 10–year sentence, with another 30 added for use of a gun, the burglar who enters a home unarmed is entitled to no more than a 10–year sentence—and by reason of the Sixth Amendment the facts bearing upon that entitlement must be found by a jury.

. . .

Justice Breyer argues that *Apprendi* works to the detriment of criminal defendants who plead guilty by depriving them of the opportunity to argue sentencing factors to a judge. But nothing prevents a defendant from waiving his *Apprendi* rights. When a defendant pleads guilty, the State is free to seek judicial sentence enhancements so long as the defendant either stipulates to the relevant facts or consents to judicial factfinding. If appropriate waivers are procured, States may continue to offer judicial factfinding as a matter of course to all defendants who plead guilty. Even a defendant who stands trial may consent to judicial factfinding as to sentence enhancements, which may well be in his interest if relevant evidence would prejudice him at trial. We do not understand how *Apprendi* can possibly work to the detriment of those who are free, if they think its costs outweigh its benefits, to render it inapplicable.

Nor do we see any merit to Justice Breyer's contention that *Apprendi* is unfair to criminal defendants because, if States respond by enacting "17–element robbery crime[s]," prosecutors will have more elements with which to bargain. Bargaining already exists with regard to sentencing factors because defendants can either stipulate or contest the facts that make them applicable. If there is any difference between bargaining over sentencing factors and bargaining over elements, the latter probably favors the defendant. Every new element that a prosecutor can threaten to charge is also an element that a defendant can threaten to contest at trial and make the prosecutor prove beyond a reasonable doubt. Moreover, given the sprawling scope of most criminal codes, and the power to affect sentences by making (even nonbinding) sentencing recommendations, there is already no shortage of in terrorem tools at prosecutors' disposal.

Any evaluation of *Apprendi's* "fairness" to criminal defendants must compare it with the regime it replaced, in which a defendant, with no warning in either his indictment or plea, would routinely see his maximum potential sentence balloon from as little as five years to as much as life imprisonment, based not on facts proved to his peers beyond a reasonable doubt, but on facts extracted after trial from a report compiled by a probation officer who the judge thinks more likely got it right than got it wrong. We can conceive of no measure of fairness that would find more fault in the utterly speculative bargaining effects Justice Breyer identifies than in the regime he champions. Suffice it to say that, if such a measure exists, it is not the one the Framers left us with.

The implausibility of Justice Breyer's contention that *Apprendi* is unfair to criminal defendants is exposed by the lineup of amici in this case. It is hard to believe that the National Association of Criminal Defense Lawyers was somehow duped into arguing for the wrong side. Justice Breyer's only authority asking that defendants be protected from *Apprendi* is an article written not by a criminal defense lawyer but by a law professor and former prosecutor.

Justice Breyer also claims that *Apprendi* will attenuate the connection between "real criminal conduct and real punishment" by encouraging plea bargaining and by restricting alternatives to adversarial factfinding. The short answer to the former point (even assuming the questionable premise that *Apprendi* does encourage plea bargaining) is that the Sixth Amendment was not written for the benefit of those who choose to forgo its protection. It guarantees the right to jury trial. It does not guarantee that a particular number of jury trials will actually take place. That more defendants elect to waive that right (because, for example, government at the moment is not particularly oppressive) does not prove that a constitutional provision guaranteeing availability of that option is disserved.

Justice Breyer's more general argument—that *Apprendi* undermines alternatives to adversarial factfinding—is not so much a criticism of *Apprendi* as an assault on jury trial generally. His esteem for "nonadversarial" truth-seeking processes, supports just as well an argument against either. Our Constitution and the common-law traditions it entrenches, however, do not admit the contention that facts are better discovered by judicial inquisition than by adversarial testing before a jury. Justice Breyer may be convinced of the equity of the regime he favors, but his views are not the ones we are bound to uphold.

Ultimately, our decision cannot turn on whether or to what degree trial by jury impairs the efficiency or fairness of criminal justice. One can certainly argue that both these values would be better served by leaving justice entirely in the hands of professionals; many nations of the world, particularly those following civil-law traditions, take just that course. There is not one shred of doubt, however, about the Framers' paradigm for criminal justice: not the civil-law ideal of administrative perfection, but the common-law ideal of limited state power accomplished by strict division of authority between judge and jury. As *Apprendi* held, every defendant has the right to insist that the prosecutor prove to a jury all facts legally essential to the punishment. Under the dissenters' alternative, he has no such right. That should be the end of the matter.

* * *

Petitioner was sentenced to prison for more than three years beyond what the law allowed for the crime to which he confessed, on the basis of a disputed finding that he had acted with "deliberate cruelty." The Framers would not have thought it too much to demand that, before depriving a man of three more years of his liberty, the State should suffer the modest inconvenience of submitting its accusation to "the unanimous suffrage of twelve of his equals and neighbours," rather than a lone employee of the State.

The judgment of the Washington Court of Appeals is reversed, and the case is remanded for further proceedings not inconsistent with this opinion.

It is so ordered.

[Justice O'CONNOR's dissent, which was joined by Justice BREYER, and by THE CHIEF JUSTICE and Justice KENNEDY as to all but Part IV–B is omitted].

[Justice KENNEDY's dissent, which was joined by Justice BREYER is omitted].

[Justice BREYER's dissent, which was joined by Justice O'CONNOR is omitted].

44

Trial Procedures

Key Concepts

- Stages of a Trial
- Sixth Amendment's Guarantees and Due Process Clause—Right to a Public Trial, Confrontation, and Compulsory Process
- Rules of Criminal Procedure Impose Additional Limits on Trial Procedures

A. Introduction and Policy. The Supreme Court has said that "a criminal trial does not unfold like a play with actors following a script."[1] No doubt every trial attorney would agree with that sentiment; unpredictability is an inevitable aspect of litigation. Even so, most trials follow a certain pattern: in most cases the introduction of evidence proceeds through the same predictable stages and usually in the same order.

Depending upon the nature of the charges being brought, before evidence can be presented, the decision must first be made as to whether a jury or a judge will be the fact-finder. If the latter is selected, the trial is referred to as a bench trial. In the vast majority of criminal trials, the fact-finder is a jury; the defendant has a right to a jury trial and will rarely waive that right. You read about the *voir dire* process and other rules governing juries in **Chapter 43**. This chapter will focus more broadly on the procedures that apply to all trials.

The first step in the trial is the giving of instructions. In a bench trial, instructions are not given because it would be nonsensical for a judge to instruct herself. In a jury trial, the judge will give the jury a set of very **preliminary instructions**. These preliminary instructions are usually not instructions on the law. Instead, the preliminary instructions include things like: comments on opening statements and the fact that they are not evidence; some statement about the likelihood of objections and the meaning of the court's ruling on them; an admonition to the jurors not to conduct outside research or visit any locations associated with the offense; instructions about note-taking; and the obligation of the jurors not to discuss the case with anyone or to begin deliberations until the trial is over. In recent years, the preliminary remarks to the jury increasingly include directives

[1] United States v. Young, 470 U.S. 1, 10 (1985).

not to post information about the case on social media outlets like Facebook and Twitter.

The burden in a criminal case is on the prosecution, so the prosecution has the first and last word in every criminal case. The prosecution's "first" word to the fact-finder about the evidence in the case usually comes in the form of an **opening statement**, which immediately follows the preliminary instructions. After the prosecution gives its opening, the defense may, but is not required to, give an opening statement as well. An opening statement is each side's best estimate of what they expect the evidence will (or will not) show. In jury trials, openings tend to be somewhat lengthier than openings at bench trials.

After openings, the next stage is the **presentation of evidence**. Evidence is introduced and admitted through the testimony of witnesses. Each witness's testimony has three primary phases. First, the party presenting the witness will conduct a **direct examination**. The opposing party will then have a chance to **cross-examine** the witness. And, finally, the initial party will have a chance for **re-direct examination**. In some cases, there may be additional phases of the examination—**re-cross** or further re-direct or further re-cross. In the phases of questioning that follow cross examination, however, parties may not simply go over the same material again and again with the witness. Instead, each party must confine its questions to new material that has come out during the last round of questioning.

In addition to witness testimony, evidence is also submitted to the trier of fact in the form of physical and documentary evidence. Usually such exhibits are introduced during a witness' testimony, but they may also come in by the agreement of the parties.

Once all of the prosecution's witnesses have been presented, the defense routinely asks the court to dismiss the case on the ground that the prosecution's evidence is insufficient to establish guilt beyond a reasonable doubt. The formal motion filed by the defense is called a **motion for judgment of acquittal**. If the motion is denied, the defense then has an opportunity to present its own evidence. Because the burden is on the prosecution, the defense has no obligation to present any evidence and guilt may not be inferred from the defendant's failure to present a case. If there is a **defense case**, however, the same pattern of direct-cross-redirect examination will repeat itself for each witness that the defense calls.

Following the defense case, the prosecution has an opportunity to present **rebuttal evidence**. This phase of the trial is not simply an additional opportunity for the prosecution to present witnesses. Instead, the prosecution's rebuttal case should focus on responding to evidence presented by the defense.

At the close of all the evidence, the defense will renew its motion for judgment. If that motion is denied, the case will then move to **jury instructions** (unless it is a bench trial) and **closing arguments**. In some jurisdictions closing arguments precede jury instructions. In others the reverse is true. Jury instructions are the court's opportunity to instruct the jury on the law. These instructions include both general instructions on the law and instructions on the law specifically relevant to the case. Typical instructions include:

- General matters like the presumption of innocence, the prosecution's burden, and the beyond a reasonable doubt standard.
- Elements of the offense(s) charged.
- If the defense has raised an affirmative defense like insanity or self-defense, the elements of that defense.
- If unanimity is required in the jurisdiction, an instruction on unanimity.
- A reminder that their deliberations should be based exclusively upon the evidence admitted at trial.
- An admonition to ignore evidence that has been stricken, and any comments the judge may have made during trial.
- An explanation of the verdict sheet, and instructions as to the particular order in which charges should be considered. (For example, if a defendant is charged with a greater offense as well as one or more lesser-included offenses, the trial judge may instruct the jury to consider the greater offense first and move on to consider the lesser-included offenses if and only if, the jury cannot come to agreement on the top charge).

In every jurisdiction, there are pattern jury instructions that judges use to craft jury instructions in each case. The law of the jurisdiction may require that some of these instructions be read verbatim. Other instructions can be tailored to the judge's voice.

Closing arguments are the parties' final opportunity to persuade the jury of their position. Unlike opening statements (which restrict a lawyer to describing what she expects the evidence to show), closing arguments allow the attorney for each side to explain to the jury what they believe the evidence has established. For both the prosecution and the defense, closing arguments are often tightly linked to the elements of the offense and attempt to explain how the evidence does (or does not) establish beyond a reasonable doubt that the defendant is guilty.

The fact-finder is then released for **deliberation**. If the jury is the fact-finder, once it reaches a decision, it sends a note to the judge indicating that a verdict has been reached. The jury is then called back into the courtroom to deliver the verdict before being thanked and discharged. If the trial is a bench trial, the judge will usually simply retire briefly to deliberate before returning to deliver the verdict from the bench.

Following entry of the verdict, the trial judge turns to the question of sentencing. In all but the most straightforward of cases, a sentencing date is set several weeks or months in the future. Sentencing is discussed in detail in **Chapter 45**. The defendant will also be advised of the opportunity for post-verdict motions, like motions for judgment notwithstanding the verdict or a motion for a new trial.

B. The Law. As in other areas of criminal procedure, the law governing trials in a particular jurisdiction can be found both in the United States Constitution and in the rules of criminal procedure that are applicable to that particular jurisdiction.

1. Constitutional Limitations. The two provisions of the Constitution that govern trial procedures are the Sixth Amendment and the Due Process Clause of the Fifth and Fourteenth Amendments.

The Sixth Amendment provides:

> In all criminal prosecutions, the accused shall enjoy the right to a speedy and public trial, by an impartial jury of the State and district wherein the crime shall have been committed, which district shall have been previously ascertained by law, and to be informed of the nature and cause of the accusation; to be confronted with the witnesses against him; to have compulsory process for obtaining witnesses in his favor, and to have the Assistance of Counsel for his defence.

Many of these constitutional guarantees regarding trial procedures have been covered in earlier chapters:

The constitutional guarantee of a speedy trial was analyzed in **Chapter 41**.

The right to an impartial jury was discussed in **Chapter 43.**

The right to a trial within the district where the crime was committed was part of the explanation of jurisdiction and venue in **Chapter 38**.

The right to notice of the charges was discussed in **Chapter 36**.

Finally, the right to the assistance of counsel was discussed in **Chapters 30, 31,** and **32**.

Thus, this chapter focuses on the three remaining constitutional rights: the right to a public trial, the right to confrontation, and the right to compulsory process.

First, the Sixth Amendment right to a public trial guarantees the accused a proceeding that is open to the community. This right flows directly to the criminal defendant and cannot be vicariously asserted by others who want to view the trial. News media outlets and the general public also have a right to be present at various stages of a criminal proceeding, but it is based on the First Amendment, not the Sixth Amendment.[2] We will discuss the right to a public trial in greater detail in Section C.1, below.

The Sixth Amendment also guarantees the right to confrontation. This right includes both a right to physically face the witnesses, and a right to cross-examine the government's witnesses. As you read in **Chapter 40**, the right to confrontation places limits on the admission of certain statements by non-testifying co-defendants. Another critical component of the confrontation right is the right of the accused to be present in the courtroom during all critical stages of trial. The Court has found, however, that certain unique forms of testimony (like a child witness' testimony via one-way closed circuit television) may be permitted in some cases without violating the defendant's confrontation rights.[3]

The Sixth Amendment also includes a right to compulsory process. This is one of several constitutional protections that assists the accused in meeting the government's evidence. This right has not been considered as frequently by the Court as the right to a public trial, but the Court's more recent cases have interpreted the right relatively narrowly. The right to compulsory process, the Court has said, does not promise the attendance and testimony of witnesses. Instead, the Constitution promises only that the defense will have the government's assistance (in the form of the subpoena power) in, "compelling the attendance of favorable witnesses at trial and the right to put before a jury evidence that might influence the determination of guilt."[4]

As you read in **Chapter 39**, the right does not include a right to discover the identity of witnesses known to the prosecutor. It also does not place an affirmative obligation on the government to produce exculpatory evidence. Instead, these claims are usually evaluated under the Due Process Clause. Furthermore, even though the accused has a right to compulsory process, the defense must still comply with otherwise applicable discovery obligations when his witness testifies. For example, the accused cannot call a witness but then refuse to provide the prosecutor with a copy of the witness' prior recorded statements.[5]

---

[2] Press-Enterprise Co. v. Superior Court of Cal., Riverside Cty., 464 U.S. 501 (1984).

[3] Maryland v. Craig, 497 U.S. 836 (1990).

[4] Pennsylvania v. Ritchie, 480 U.S. 39, 56 (1987).

[5] United States v. Nobles, 422 U.S. 225 (1975).

The Due Process Clause also guarantees a number of trial rights. Like the Sixth Amendment's Confrontation Clause, the Due Process Clause protects the defendant's right to be present during trial. Its guarantee is somewhat broader in scope than the Confrontation Clause right, since it applies even if the accused is not confronting the prosecution's witnesses or evidence. However, the accused's due process right to presence is triggered "to the extent that a fair and just hearing would be thwarted by his absence, and to that extent only."[6]

Because one of the primary interests of the constitutional right to be present is the right to cross-examine witnesses, the right obviously includes trial events like the taking of witness testimony.[7] In addition, the right includes other critical stages such as any significant communication between the judge and the jury.[8] The right is also understood to be the source of the ban against trials of the mentally incompetent—"the mentally incompetent defendant, though physically present in the courtroom, is in reality afforded no opportunity to defend himself."[9]

However, where an accused could have done nothing or would have gained nothing by being present, the Due Process Clause does not require the accused's attendance.[10] For example, an accused need not be present at a preliminary hearing to assess a witness' competence to testify if counsel for the accused was present at the hearing; no questions about the witness' substantive testimony are asked, and "the type of questions that were asked at the competency hearing . . . were easy to repeat on cross-examination at trial."[11]

The accused can waive his right to be present, either expressly or implicitly. For example, if an accused voluntarily absconds during trial, the trial may be continued in her absence.[12] An accused may also waive the right to presence by behaving in a seriously disruptive fashion. Federal Rule of Criminal Procedure 43 provides more detail regarding the right of the accused to be present. We will explore both the constitutional right and the statutory right in more detail in Section C.2.

The Due Process Clause also creates two other significant restraints on criminal trials: the presumption of innocence and the "beyond a reasonable doubt" standard. Presumption of innocence, means that an accused is presumed innocent at the beginning of the trial and guilt cannot be inferred from the fact that charges have been filed. The "beyond a reasonable doubt" standard has also been said to encourage respect for the criminal justice system by allowing "every individual going about his ordinary affairs [to] have confidence that his government cannot

6 United States v. Gagnon, 470 U.S. 522, 526 (1985).

7 Kentucky v. Stincer, 482 U.S. 730 (1987).

8 Rogers v. United States, 422 U.S. 35 (1975).

9 Drope v. Missouri, 420 U.S. 162, 171 (1975).

10 Gagnon, 470 U.S. at 527.

11 Stincer, 482 U.S. at 741.

12 Crosby v. United States, 506 U.S. 255 (1993).

adjudge him guilty of a criminal offense without convincing a proper factfinder of his guilt with utmost certainty."[13] Justice Harlan once wrote that the reasonable doubt standard reflects the fact that "we do not view the social disutility of convicting an innocent man as equivalent to the disutility of acquitting someone who is guilty."[14] Together, the presumption of innocence and the "beyond a reasonable doubt" reduce the risk of false convictions.

They also mean that the court must direct a verdict for the defendant if the evidence is legally insufficient to prove the prosecutor's case beyond a reasonable doubt. The court may never direct a verdict for the government, because that would violate the defendant's right to a jury trial.[15]

The fact that the prosecution shoulders the burden of proof in criminal cases as a constitutional matter does not, however, preclude imposing some burden on the defense. Though the government must prove "every fact necessary to constitute the crime,"[16] a state may lawfully require an accused to prove the elements of any asserted affirmative defense, such as insanity.

2. Rules of Criminal Procedure. In federal court, the Federal Rules of Criminal Procedure impose the next set of constraints upon trial procedures. Section VI of the Federal Rules, encompassing Rules 23 through 31, is devoted to the trial process:

> Rules 23 and 24 of the Rules of Criminal Procedure govern jury trials and the selection of the jury; and were discussed in **Chapter 43**.
>
> Rule 25 provides for the replacement of the trial judge if the original judge becomes incapacitated for some reason. If the new judge is taking over in the middle of a trial, she must certify that she is "familiar" with the trial record.
>
> Rule 26 of the Rules of Criminal Procedure codifies the constitutional command that the defendant's trial be a "public" one by instructing that, as a general matter, witness testimony "must be taken in open court."[17]
>
> Rule 26.3 provides for the granting of a mistrial, and instructs that the trial court give counsel for both sides an opportunity to be heard before a mistrial is granted.

[13] In re Winship, 397 U.S. 358, 364 (1970).
[14] Id. at 372 (Harlan, J., concurring).
[15] Sullivan v. Louisiana, 508 U.S. 275, 277 (1993).
[16] Patterson v. New York, 432 U.S. 197, 225 (1977).
[17] Fed. R. of Crim. P. 26.

Rule 29 is an extensive and detailed rule that governs the filing of a motion for judgment of acquittal.

Rule 29.1 provides the order for closing arguments—government, defense, and then government again.

Rule 30 provides for jury instructions and for the timing of any objection to those instructions.

Finally, Rule 31 requires a unanimous verdict that must be returned in open court:

Rule 31. Jury Verdict

(a) Return. The jury must return its verdict to a judge in open court. The verdict must be unanimous.

(b) Partial Verdicts, Mistrial, and Retrial.

(1) Multiple Defendants. If there are multiple defendants, the jury may return a verdict at any time during its deliberations as to any defendant about whom it has agreed.

(2) Multiple Counts. If the jury cannot agree on all counts as to any defendant, the jury may return a verdict on those counts on which it has agreed.

(3) Mistrial and Retrial. If the jury cannot agree on a verdict on one or more counts, the court may declare a mistrial on those counts. The government may retry any defendant on any count on which the jury could not agree.

(c) Lesser Offense or Attempt. A defendant may be found guilty of any of the following:

(1) An offense necessarily included in the offense charged;

(2) An attempt to commit the offense charged; or

(3) An attempt to commit an offense necessarily included in the offense charged, if the attempt is an offense in its own right.

(d) Jury Poll. After a verdict is returned but before the jury is discharged, the court must on a party's request, or may on its own, poll the jurors individually. If the poll reveals a lack of unanimity, the court may direct the jury to deliberate further or may declare a mistrial and discharge the jury.

In addition to Section VI, Section IX of the Federal Rules provides a number of rules which are directly relevant to the trial process. Rule 43 echoes the Sixth Amendment's guarantee that the accused be present at every stage of the trial. The rule also governs when presence is not required, including the waiver of the right to presence:

Rule 43. Defendant's Presence

(a) **When Required.** Unless this rule, Rule 5 [regarding video conferencing at the initial appearance], or Rule 10 [regarding video conferencing and waiver at the initial appearance and arraignment] provides otherwise, the defendant must be present at:

(1) the initial appearance, the initial arraignment, and the plea;

(2) every trial stage, including jury impanelment and the return of the verdict; and

(3) sentencing.

(b) **When Not Required.** A defendant need not be present under any of the following circumstances:

(1) Organizational Defendant. The defendant is an organization represented by counsel who is present.

(2) Misdemeanor Offense. The offense is punishable by fine or by imprisonment for not more than one year, or both, and with the defendant's written consent, the court permits arraignment, plea, trial, and sentencing to occur by video teleconferencing or in the defendant's absence.

(3) Conference or Hearing on a Legal Question. The proceeding involves only a conference or hearing on a question of law.

(4) Sentence Correction. The proceeding involves the correction or reduction of sentence under Rule 35 or 18 U.S.C. §3582 (c).

(c) **Waiving Continued Presence.**

(1) In General. A defendant who was initially present at trial, or who had pleaded guilty or nolo contendere, waives the right to be present under the following circumstances:

(A) when the defendant is voluntarily absent after the trial has begun, regardless of whether the court informed the defendant of an obligation to remain during trial;

(B) in a noncapital case, when the defendant is voluntarily absent during sentencing; or

(C) when the court warns the defendant that it will remove the defendant from the courtroom for disruptive behavior, but the defendant persists in conduct that justifies removal from the courtroom.

(2) **Waiver's Effect.** If the defendant waives the right to be present, the trial may proceed to completion, including the verdict's return and sentencing, during the defendant's absence, or may declare a mistrial and discharge the jury.

Other rules in Section IX include:

Rule 44, which describes the right to appointed counsel.

Rule 50, which instructs that for scheduling purposes, criminal trials should take precedent on the court's docket.

Rule 53, which prohibits a court from allowing the photographing or broadcasting of judicial proceedings unless the same is separately authorized by statute.

Rule 60, which provides certain rights for the victims of crimes, including: a right to notice, a right to attend the proceedings, and a right to be heard before the judge makes a decision about release of the accused, a plea or sentencing.

Because a trial is the method by which evidence is presented to the fact-finder, the process of a trial is also subject to substantial regulation by the rules of evidence. That subject is covered fully in a standard Evidence class in most law school curriculums, so we will not discuss it here. But close familiarity with the rules of evidence is a necessary prerequisite to a true understanding of trial procedures.

Finally, remember that every state will have its own set of criminal procedure rules, which will differ slightly from the Federal Rules of Criminal Procedure. Also, every jurisdiction will have local rules and case law, which will impose another layer of legal structure upon the trial process.

C. Applying the Law.

1. Courtroom Closure. The Sixth Amendment guarantees the accused a public trial. This right has been interpreted in a fairly direct manner by the United States Court. Thus, without a significant reason for excluding members of the public from the courtroom, a trial judge's decision to close the courtroom will likely result in reversal of any conviction:

Example—*Presley v. Georgia*, 558 U.S. 209 (2010): Eric Presley was charged with cocaine trafficking. Prior to jury selection, the trial judge saw a man sitting in the courtroom. He told the man to leave the courtroom (and leave the entire floor of the courthouse) because jury selection was about to begin and the court wished to use all of the seats in the courtroom for prospective jurors. The trial judge said that leaving the floor was required because the jurors would be out in the hallway too and he did not want the man communicating with the panel. The man explained that he was Presley's uncle, and the defense counsel objected to the closure of the courtroom as a violation of Presley's right to a public trial. The judge refused to change his order, but did invite Presley's uncle back later in the afternoon after the jury had been selected. After he was convicted, Presley sought a new trial on the ground that the exclusion of his uncle violated the Constitution.

Analysis: The Supreme Court reversed Presley's conviction, because the closure of the courtroom was impermissible.

The accused has a Sixth Amendment right to a public trial. This right extends well beyond the evidence-gathering phases of the trial. For example, the right has been found to extend to stages such as a pre-trial suppression hearing.[18] The defendant's right to a fair trial or the government's interest in keeping sensitive information secure may at times trump the right to a public trial. However, such circumstances are rare:

> "[T]he party seeking to close the hearing must advance an overriding interest that is likely to be prejudiced, the closure must be no broader than necessary to protect that interest, the trial court must consider reasonable alternatives to closing the proceeding, and it must make findings adequate to support the closure."[19]

There were a number of steps the trial judge could have taken instead of closing the courtroom. The court's failure to consider any such alternatives, as well as its failure to advance any real interest that would have been prejudiced by the uncle's presence in the room, required reversal of Presley's conviction.

2. The Right to Confrontation. The Sixth Amendment's right to confront witnesses includes both a right to be present at trial and a right to cross-examine witnesses. However, like the right to a public trial, this right may at times be

[18] Waller v. Georgia, 467 U.S. 39 (1984).

[19] Presley v. Georgia, 558 U.S. 209, 214 (2010) (quoting Waller v. Georgia at 48).

overcome by countervailing concerns. For example, an accused may waive his rights through conduct:

> **Example—*Illinois v. Allen*, 397 U.S. 337 (1970):** William Allen was indicted for armed robbery. Prior to the start of his trial, Allen told the trial judge that he wanted to proceed *pro se*. The trial judge agreed, but appointed stand-by counsel to "protect the record" for Allen. Jury selection then began. After a particularly long exchange with one prospective juror, the trial judge asked Allen to limit his questions to matters that were related to qualification to serve. After a heated exchange with Allen, the trial judge told stand-by counsel to complete voir dire. Allen, however, continued to talk and told the judge that stand-by counsel was not his lawyer. Allen also told the judge "When I go out for lunchtime, you're . . . going to be a corpse here."[20] Allen then snatched a file from stand-by counsel, ripped it in half and scattered the papers on the floor. The trial judge warned Allen that if he could not behave he would be excluded from the courtroom. To this, Allen responded, "There's not going to be no trial either. I'm going to sit here and you're going to talk and you can bring your shackles out and straight jacket and put them on me and tape my mouth, but it will do no good because there's not going to be no trial."[21] After more back and forth with the trial judge, Allen was excluded from the courtroom and jury selection proceeded in his absence.
>
> After a recess, Allen was brought back into the courtroom on his promise that he would behave. However, moments later Allen erupted again saying, "There is going to be no proceeding. I'm going to start talking and I'm going to keep on talking through the trial. There's not going to be no trial like this. I want my sister and my friends here in court to testify for me." Allen was again ordered out. Allen remained out of the courtroom for the duration of the government's case. He was brought back in for the defense case, which was conducted by stand-by counsel. Following his conviction, Allen challenged his exclusion from the courtroom as violating his Sixth and Fourteenth Amendment rights.

Analysis: Allen was properly excluded. The Constitution guarantees an accused the right to confront the witnesses against him, and a court should not lightly

---

[20] Illinois v. Allen, 397 U.S. 337, 340 (1970).

[21] Id.

discard constitutional rights. But, the Sixth and Fourteenth Amendments do not give the accused an excuse to behave any way he wants during trial. "[A] defendant can lose his right to be present at trial if, after he has been warned by the judge that he will be removed if he continues his disruptive behavior, he nevertheless insists on conducting himself in a manner so disorderly, disruptive, and disrespectful of the court that his trial cannot be carried on with him in the courtroom."[22]

The right to be present, once lost, is not lost permanently. As soon as the accused can comport himself appropriately, he should be afforded the right to re-enter.

In addition to excluding the accused from the courtroom, a trial judge may also bind and gag a disruptive defendant, or may cite the accused for contempt. However, there are problems that attach to each of the alternatives. A bound and gagged defendant is at least present in the courtroom and thus, in some sense, enjoying the Sixth Amendment right to confront witnesses. "But even to contemplate such a technique, much less see it, arouses a feeling that no person should be tried while shackled and gagged except as a last resort."[23] So too, the threat of a contempt citation may not impede the most dogged disorderly defendant. Exclusion of an unruly defendant therefore must remain an option.

Through bad behavior, Allen forfeited his Sixth and Fourteenth Amendment rights to be present at trial. "It would degrade our country and our judicial system to permit our courts to be bullied, insulted, and humiliated and their orderly progress thwarted and obstructed by defendants brought before them charged with crimes."[24]

Bad behavior is not the only way an accused may forfeit the right to confront witnesses. In addition, an accused may forfeit that right by not showing up:

> **Example—*Taylor v. United States*, 414 U.S. 17 (1973):** Richard Taylor was accused of selling cocaine. On the first day of his trial, Taylor appeared in court with his attorney for the morning session. When Taylor did not return for the afternoon session, the court recessed for the day. The next morning, Taylor's wife told the court she had taken a cab to the nearby town of Roxbury with Taylor the day before, but had not seen him since. She also said Taylor had not seemed sick the last time she saw him. Defense counsel moved for a mistrial on the ground that continuing the trial in Taylor's absence would violate his right to confront witnesses. The motion was denied based on the trial court's conclusion that Taylor was voluntarily absent. The court then invoked Rule 43 of the Federal Rules of Criminal Procedure to

[22] Id. at 343.

[23] Id. at 344.

[24] Id. at 346.

continue the trial. Taylor was convicted and sentenced to five years in prison. He then challenged the decision to continue the trial in his absence.

Analysis: The decision to continue the trial was entirely appropriate. Taylor did not suggest that his absence from trial was involuntary. There is also no question that Rule 43 allows a trial to be continued in the defendant's voluntary absence. Taylor understood he had a right to be present at every stage of his trial. "It seems equally incredible to us . . . that a defendant who flees from a courtroom in the midst of a trial—where judge, jury, witnesses and lawyers are present and ready to continue—would not know that as a consequence the trial could continue in his absence."[25] Under these circumstances, Rule 43 was appropriately invoked to continue the trial after Taylor decided not to return.

Rule 43 only allows the trial to continue without the defendant if the defendant's absence is **voluntary**. In Taylor's case, the defense attorney conceded that his client's absence was voluntary, and the wife's testimony seemed to corroborate that fact. But sometimes the defense contests this fact, and the prosecutor must convince the judge that the defendant's absence is in fact voluntary—that he is not ill or in the hospital or in custody after a new arrest.

The Court has been careful to note that while Rule 43 does allow a trial to be continued in a defendant's absence, the rule does not allow a trial to be **commenced** if the defendant is not present. In other words, if the defendant is present for the start of trial and then absconds, Rule 43 clearly authorizes the continuation of the trial. However, if trial has not yet begun and the defendant cannot be found, Rule 43 does not allow a trial *in absentia* from the outset. The Court has not yet determined whether the Constitution similarly forbids a full trial *in absentia*.[26]

Most recently, the Court has found that the accused's right to be present is not violated by a prosecutor's observation that the defendant was able to sit through the testimony of all the witnesses before providing the jury with his own version of events:

Example—*Portuondo v. Agard*, 529 U.S. 61 (2000): At Ray Agard's trial, Nessa Winder and her friend, Breda Keegan, testified that Ray Agard sexually assaulted Winder and threatened both women with a gun. Agard testified in his own defense. He admitted that he had sex with Winder, but asserted that it was consensual. During closing argument, defense counsel attacked

[25] Taylor v. United States, 414 U.S. 17, 20 (1973).

[26] Crosby v. United States, 506 U.S. 255 (1993).

the credibility of both women. The prosecutor responded over objection that "unlike all the other witnesses in this case the defendant has a benefit and the benefit that he has, unlike all the other witnesses, is he gets to sit here and listen to the testimony of all the other witnesses before he testifies. . . . That gives you a big advantage, doesn't it. You get to sit here and think what am I going to say and how am I going to say it? How am I going to fit it into the evidence?" Agard was convicted and later challenged the propriety of the prosecutor's closing argument.

Analysis: The prosecutor did not impermissibly burden Ray Agard's constitutional rights to be present and to confront witnesses against him when she suggested that Ray Agard's credibility was impacted by the fact that he was present during the testimony of other witnesses.

The prosecution may not suggest that an accused's failure to present a defense or otherwise to deny the prosecution's charges is evidence of guilt.[27] But this is because the burden of proof in criminal cases rests entirely with the prosecution. When a defendant chooses to take the stand, there is nothing wrong with the jury considering the fact that he has done so only after hearing what all the other witnesses have said. "When a defendant assumes the role of a witness, the rules that generally apply to other witnesses—rules that serve the truth-seeking function of the trial—are generally applicable to him as well."[28] Some rules, like sequestration, that apply to other witnesses do not apply to the defendant. But, other rules, like challenges to credibility, do. A witness who is able to listen to the testimony of other witnesses before testifying has an advantage, and the jury can be reminded of this fact before being asked to assess credibility.

Advances in technology have also forced the Court to confront novel questions about the scope of the defendant's right to confront witnesses. In a case involving a young victim of child sexual assault, the Court found that the defendant's confrontation rights did not require the victim's physical presence in the courtroom during her testimony:

Example—*Maryland v. Craig*, 497 U.S. 836 (1990): Sandra Craig ran a daycare center for young children. A six-year-old girl who attended pre-K and kindergarten at Craig's center accused Craig of sexual abuse. At trial on the charges, the child was allowed to testify via closed-circuit television. Pursuant to the state's procedures, the witness, the prosecutor, and defense counsel all went to a separate room for the witness to testify. This testimony was then projected into the courtroom for the judge,

[27] Griffin v. California, 380 U.S. 609 (1965).

[28] Portuondo v. Agard, 529 U.S. 61, 69 (2000).

jury, and defendant to watch. Though the witness could not see Craig, Craig was able to communicate electronically with her attorney. In addition, electronic communication with the court allowed objections to be made and ruled on instantly. Craig objected that the use of the closed-circuit procedure violated the Confrontation Clause.

Analysis: Craig's right to confront the witnesses against her was not violated by the use of the closed-circuit television procedure.

The Court said in *Coy v. Iowa* that "the Confrontation Clause guarantees the defendant a face-to-face meeting with witnesses appearing before the trier of fact."[29] The guarantees of the Confrontation Clause are primarily concerned with the reliability of evidence and its adequate testing through rigorous cross-examination. The core elements of the clause are therefore physical presence, the witness' swearing of an oath, cross-examination, and the trier of fact's ability to observe the demeanor of the witness when making the statement. The guarantee of face-to-face confrontation is rooted in part in reducing erroneous convictions and in part in "the strong symbolic purpose served by requiring adverse witnesses at trial to testify in the accused's presence."[30]

But despite the important ways in which face-to-face confrontation advances the goals of the Confrontation Clause, it is not an absolute guarantee. For example, certain hearsay statements are admissible at trial even though the defendant is not able to confront the declarant. While there is a constitutional preference for face-to-face confrontations, the guarantees of the Confrontation Clause encompass more than this singular form of interaction.

If it is necessary to advance an "important public policy" and "the reliability of the testimony is otherwise assured," face-to-face confrontation may be avoided.[31] The procedure used by the state retained three of the four core elements of the clause's guarantees—the oath, cross-examination, and the fact-finder's ability to observe the demeanor of the witness. The state had a compelling and well-documented interest in protecting young victims of sexual assault from further distress and suffering. That interest was adequate to justify impinging upon Craig's right to the face-to-face confrontation of her accuser. Moreover, while a state may not allow a child witness to testify outside of the courtroom simply because the child is uncomfortable in that setting and may not allow testimony outside of the defendant's presence based upon *de minimis* harm, an adequate showing was made as to the witness in this case that the child would be seriously traumatized not by the courtroom setting, but by the presence of the accused.

---

[29] Maryland v. Craig, 497 U.S. 836, 844 (1990).

[30] Id. at 847.

[31] Id. at 850.

3. Compulsory Process. The constitutional guarantee of compulsory process has been interpreted in a manner that is consistent with the Court's other cases on the constitutional right regarding access to evidence. Accordingly, an accused must establish more than that evidence might have been useful. To prove a violation of the constitutional right, the accused must be able to offer some proof of the materiality of the missing evidence:

> **Example—*United States v. Valenzuela-Bernal*, 458 U.S. 858 (1982):** Ricardo Valenzuela-Bernal illegally entered the United States with the help of smugglers. In return, Valenzuela-Bernal agreed to assist the smugglers by driving himself and five others from Escondido, California, to Los Angeles. During the drive, Valenzuela-Bernal passed through a U.S. Border Patrol checkpoint. Following a brief chase, first in the car and then on foot, Valenzuela-Bernal and three of the passengers were arrested by border patrol agents, and Valenzuela-Bernal was charged with transporting illegal aliens. After speaking with two of the passengers in the car, a prosecutor determined that they had no evidence relevant to the charged offense. Accordingly, these two were deported. The third passenger, Enrique Romero-Morales, was detained to provide evidence in the government's case against Valenzuela-Bernal.
>
> Valenzuela-Bernal argued that the deportation of the two passengers prevented him from interviewing the men and thus violated his constitutional right to compulsory process.

Analysis: Valenzuela-Bernal did not make a sufficient showing to establish that the deportation of the two passengers violated his constitutional rights.

The federal government has a dual obligation to prosecute those who violate the law and to deport those who are illegally in the country and subject to removal. The prompt apprehension and deportation of illegal immigrants at the nation's borders is, in Congress' view "the most effective method for curbing the enormous flow of illegal aliens across our southern border."[32] The removal of the passengers in this case was based on this immigration policy and on the realization that overcrowding in federal detention centers in southern California has created significant financial and security concerns for the officials that run them.

The Constitution guaranteed Valenzuela-Bernal the right to compulsory process to obtain witnesses that were favorable to the defense. To establish a violation of this right, Valenzuela-Bernal therefore had to do more than show that deportation of the passengers prevented him from securing their testimony. He also had

---

[32] United States v. Valenzuela-Bernal, 458 U.S. 858, 864 (1982).

to offer some proof that the witness' testimony would have been material and favorable. In the context of constitutionally guaranteed access to evidence, the Court has always required the defense to make such a showing of materiality. For example, in the case of the government's suppression of favorable evidence (*Brady*), or government delay that causes the loss of evidence prior to indictment, (or following indictment, a showing of materiality has always been required).

The demand for some showing of materiality does not shift in this case simply because the defense never had access to the witnesses to assess what the value of their testimony might have been. "[W]hile a defendant who has not had an opportunity to interview a witness may face a difficult task in making a showing of materiality, the task is not an impossible one. . . . [T]he events to which a witness might testify, and the relevance of those events to the crime charged [] may well demonstrate either the presence or absence of the required materiality."[33] Valenzuela-Bernal was not expected to offer a detailed explanation of what the witnesses' testimony would likely have been, but he did need to offer some proof. "Sanctions may be imposed on the Government for deporting witnesses only if the criminal defendant makes a plausible showing that the testimony of the deported witnesses would have been material and favorable to his defense, in ways not merely cumulative to the testimony of available witnesses."[34]

Trials are complicated undertakings that are governed by a host of rules, the bulk of which are provided by individual jurisdictions. Moreover, from a constitutional standpoint, the right to a public trial, the right to confrontation, and the right to compulsory process discussed in this chapter are only a fraction of the important constitutional protections that regulate the adjudication of a criminal case. Other trial rights, discussed in other chapters of this book, are equally central to the adversarial system and are equally relevant to trial procedures.

[33] Id. at 871.

[34] Id. at 873.

Quick Summary

Most criminal cases include the same stages of trial: preliminary instructions, opening statements, the presentation of evidence, jury instructions, closing statements,deliberation and the return of a verdict.

The trial process is primarily regulated by the rules of the individual jurisdiction in which the trial is held. However, the Sixth Amendment and the Due Process Clause also impose restraints on the progression of a trial. Those rights include the right to a public trial, the right to confront witnesses, and the right to compulsory process. The right to a public trial is construed very strictly by the Supreme Court; any closure must be justified by an "overriding interest" and must be narrowly tailored to serve that interest. The right to confront witnesses includes the right to be present at trial, but the defendant can waive that right if he is disruptive or he voluntarily absents himself once the trial begins. And the right to compulsory process only applies to witnesses who can provide material evidence to the case.

The burden of proof in any criminal case is on the prosecution, which must satisfy the fact-finder beyond a reasonable doubt of the accused's guilt before a conviction can be returned.

In addition to the limitations imposed by the Constitution, the relevant rules of criminal procedure also impose constraints upon trial procedures. And because a trial is the method by which evidence is presented to the fact-finder, the process of a trial is also subject to substantial regulation by the rules of evidence.

Review Questions

1. The Downside of Discovery. Christopher Young was tried on multiple counts of sexually abusing a child. Prior to trial, the government asked the court to exclude the testimony of several of Young's witnesses because the defense had not turned over certain discovery documents, and because the defense had not offered any indication of the nature of the witnesses' testimony. Defense counsel said only that he planned to introduce testimony "regarding inconsistencies in the alleged victim's version of events" and "documents indicating that the child's caregivers noticed nothing unusual about the child's demeanor or behavior while she was at day care during the relevant period of time." Ruling on the prosecution's motion, the court acknowledged that it had ordered the defense earlier to provide the prosecution with the requested discovery material, including additional information about the likely testimony of the proposed witnesses. The court also noted that it had granted at least one continuance to allow the defense an opportunity to provide this discovery. The trial court waited to rule on the motion until trial had commenced. When the defense still had not turned over the necessary discovery, the trial court precluded the defense witnesses from testifying, stating:

> There has been no further discovery by you, [defense counsel], to the state. So you did not comply with my order back in April of 1999. As you did not comply with my order . . . and did not give the state the discovery that I ordered you to give under the local discovery rules which allow the Court to order certain sanctions, and the sanction that I imposed in this case was that those witnesses would not be called as the state still had not—did not have sufficient information to adequately proceed to trial. I did not want to continue the trial because it was time to take this case to trial. And that's a remedy that I chose.

Young was convicted, and appealed on the ground that the exclusion of the defense evidence violated his constitutional rights. How should the appellate court rule?

2. Staying Under Cover. Vernon Bowden was accused of selling crack cocaine to an undercover police officer, Detective Billingy. Billingy testified to the transaction, in which Bowden sold Billingy twelve dollars worth of crack in a building on 126th Street in Manhattan. A second undercover officer, Detective Weathers, testified that he was following Billingy. He confirmed that he saw Billingy walk into the building with Bowden, after which he (Weathers) alerted the backup team to make an arrest. Unlike Billingy, Weathers did not testify in open court. Instead, prior to his testimony, the prosecution moved to close the courtroom. In support of its request, the prosecution presented Weathers's testimony that he was a current undercover officer who was working in the North Manhattan Narcotics District. Weathers maintained that he had "already been threatened by alleged drug dealers for being a cop. I'm supposed to be killed or whatnot [sic], mutilated, strangulated [sic]." Weathers told the court that he had bought drugs from some twenty-five people who were to his knowledge still on the street. The defense objected to the courtroom closure. But the trial court granted the request saying, "I believe the record now does substantiate closure of the courtroom, and I am not going to summarize it. I think it speaks for itself, not the least factor of which is the way information circulates throughout this system[.] [It] is perfectly conceivable to me that word will get out if I did not close the courtroom that an undercover officer would be testifying and that he will be identified, and it isn't necessary for people to be sitting in the courtroom." Weathers was allowed to present his testimony to the jury in the closed courtroom from which all members of the public were excluded, although the defendant Bowden was present the entire time. After he was convicted, Bowden challenged the courtroom closure. Was the trial judge correct to grant the prosecution's request?

3. The Taped Case for Guilt. Margo McKee was stabbed and beaten to death. After her body was discovered, the police investigation quickly came to focus on McKee's husband and four of his friends: Stephen Whelchel, Jeffrey Flota, Beth Massey and Nancy Hughes. During police questioning, everyone except Whelchel confessed to participating in McKee's murder. Two of the witnesses, Massey and Hughes, agreed to testify against the others in exchange for being charged as juveniles. McKee and Flota were thereafter convicted in a joint trial of murder. Whelchel was tried next. The state's evidence at Whelchel's trial consisted primarily of three taped statements. The first two were statements that McKee made during police questioning. The third was the taped statement of Flota taken under similar circumstances. The state also introduced the videotaped deposition of Flota's father. Whelchel's counsel was present for this deposition, which was conducted before the trial judge, and was given an opportunity to cross-examine the witness. Neither McKee, Flota, nor Flota's father testified at trial. Whelchel was eventually convicted. Whelchel challenged the admission of the three recorded statements and the videotaped deposition. In deciding whether the admission of this evidence violated Whelchel's rights under the Confrontation Clause, what factors would be relevant to your assessment?

FROM THE COURTROOM

PORTUONDO v. AGARD

Supreme Court of the United States
529 U.S. 61 (2000)

[SCALIA, J., delivered the opinion of the Court, in which REHNQUIST, C. J., and O'CONNOR, KENNEDY, and THOMAS, JJ., joined].

[STEVENS, J., filed an opinion concurring in the judgment, in which BREYER, J., joined].

[GINSBURG, J., filed a dissenting opinion, in which SOUTER, J., joined].

Justice SCALIA delivered the opinion of the Court.

In this case we consider whether it was constitutional for a prosecutor, in her summation, to call the jury's attention to the fact that the defendant had the opportunity to hear all other witnesses testify and to tailor his testimony accordingly.

I

Respondent's trial on 19 sodomy and assault counts and 3 weapons counts ultimately came down to a credibility determination. The alleged victim, Nessa Winder, and her friend, Breda Keegan, testified that respondent physically assaulted, raped, and orally and anally sodomized Winder, and that he threatened both women with a handgun. Respondent testified that he and Winder had engaged in consensual vaginal intercourse. He further testified that during an argument he had with Winder, he struck her once in the face. He denied raping her or threatening either woman with a handgun.

During summation, defense counsel charged Winder and Keegan with lying. The prosecutor similarly focused on the credibility of the witnesses. She stressed respondent's interest in the outcome of the trial, his prior felony conviction, and his prior bad acts. She argued that respondent was a "smooth slick character . . . who had an answer for everything," and that part of his testimony "sound[ed] rehearsed." Finally, over defense objection, the prosecutor remarked:

"You know, ladies and gentlemen, unlike all the other witnesses in this case the defendant has a benefit and the benefit that he has, unlike all the other witnesses, is he gets to sit here and listen to the testimony of all the other witnesses before he testifies.

. . . . .

"That gives you a big advantage, doesn't it. You get to sit here and think what am I going to say and how am I going to say it? How am I going to fit it into the evidence?

. . . . .

"He's a smart man. I never said he was stupid. . . . He used everything to his advantage."

The trial court rejected defense counsel's claim that these last comments violated respondent's right to be present at trial. The court stated that respondent's status as the last witness in the case was simply a matter of fact, and held that his presence during the entire trial, and the advantage that this afforded him, "may fairly be commented on."

. . . . .

II

Respondent contends that the prosecutor's comments on his presence and on the ability to fabricate that it afforded him unlawfully burdened his Sixth Amendment right to be present at trial and to be confronted with the witnesses against him, and his Fifth and Sixth Amendment rights to testify on his own behalf. Attaching the cost of impeachment to the exercise of these rights was, he asserts, unconstitutional.

Respondent's argument boils down to a request that we extend to comments of the type the prosecutor made here the rationale of *Griffin v. California*, 380 U.S. 609 (1965), which involved comments upon a defendant's refusal to testify. In that case, the trial court instructed the jury that it was free to take the defendant's failure to deny or explain facts within his knowledge as tending to indicate the truth of the prosecution's case. This Court held that such a comment, by "solemniz[ing] the silence of the accused into evidence against him," unconstitutionally "cuts down on the privilege [against self-incrimination] by making its assertion costly."

We decline to extend *Griffin* to the present context. As an initial matter, respondent's claims have no historical foundation, neither in 1791, when the Bill of Rights was adopted, nor in 1868 when, according to our jurisprudence, the Fourteenth Amendment extended the strictures of the Fifth and Sixth Amendments to the States. The process by which criminal defendants were brought to justice in 1791 largely obviated the need for comments of the type the prosecutor made here. Defendants routinely were asked (and agreed) to provide a pretrial statement to a justice of the peace detailing the events in dispute. If their story at trial-where they typically spoke and conducted their defense personally, without counsel-differed from their pretrial statement, the contradiction could be noted. Moreover, what they said at trial was not considered to be evidence, since they were disqualified from testifying under oath.

The pretrial statement did not begin to fall into disuse until the 1830's, and the first State to make defendants competent witnesses was Maine, in 1864. In response to these developments, some States attempted to limit a defendant's opportunity to tailor his sworn testimony by requiring him to testify prior to his own witnesses. Although the majority of States did not impose such a restriction, there is no evidence to suggest they also took the affirmative step of forbidding comment upon the defendant's opportunity to tailor his testimony. The dissent faults us for "call[ing] up no instance of an 18th- or 19th-century prosecutor's urging that a defendant's presence at trial facilitated tailored testimony." We think the burden is rather upon respondent and the dissent, who assert the unconstitutionality of the practice, to come up with a case in which such urging was held improper. They cannot even produce one in which the practice was so much as challenged until after our decision in *Griffin*. This absence cuts in favor of respondent (as the dissent asserts) only if it is possible to believe that after reading *Griffin* prosecutors suddenly realized that commenting on a testifying defendant's unique ability to hear prior testimony was a good idea. Evidently, prosecutors were making these comments all along without objection; *Griffin* simply sparked the notion that such commentary might be problematic.

Lacking any historical support for the constitutional rights that he asserts, respondent must rely entirely upon our opinion in *Griffin*. That case is a poor analogue, however, for several reasons. What we prohibited the prosecutor from urging the jury to do in *Griffin* was something the jury is not permitted to do. The defendant's right to hold the prosecution to proving its case without his assistance is not to be impaired by the jury's counting the defendant's silence at trial against him-and upon request the court must instruct the jury to that effect. It is reasonable enough to expect a jury to comply with that instruction since, as we observed in *Griffin*, the inference of guilt from silence is not always "natural or irresistible." A defendant might refuse to testify simply out of fear that he will be made to look bad by clever counsel, or fear "'that his prior convictions will prejudice the jury.'" By contrast, it is natural and irresistible for a jury, in evaluating the relative credibility of a defendant who testifies last, to have in mind and weigh in the balance the fact that he heard the testimony of all those who preceded him. It is one thing (as *Griffin* requires) for the jury to evaluate all the other evidence in the case without giving any effect to the defendant's refusal to testify; it is something else (and quite impossible) for the jury to evaluate the credibility of the defendant's testimony while blotting out from its mind the fact that before giving the testimony the defendant had been sitting there listening to the other witnesses. Thus, the principle respondent asks us to adopt here differs from what we adopted in *Griffin* in one or the other of the following respects: It either prohibits inviting the jury to do what the jury is perfectly entitled to do; or it requires the jury to do what is practically impossible.

Second, *Griffin* prohibited comments that suggest a defendant's silence is "evidence of guilt." The prosecutor's comments in this case, by contrast, concerned respondent's credibility as a witness, and were therefore in accord with our longstanding rule that when a defendant takes the stand, "his credibility may be impeached and his testimony assailed like that of any other witness." "[W]hen [a defendant] assumes the role of a witness, the rules that generally apply to other witnesses-rules that serve the truth-seeking function of the trial-are generally applicable to him as well."

Respondent points to our opinion in *Geders v. United States*, 425 U.S. 80, 87-91 (1976), which held that the defendant must be treated differently from other witnesses insofar as sequestration orders are concerned, since sequestration for an extended period of time denies the Sixth Amendment right to counsel. With respect to issues of credibility, however, no such special treatment has been accorded. *Jenkins v. Anderson*, 447 U.S. 231, (1980), illustrates the point. There the prosecutor in a first-degree murder trial, during cross-examination and again in closing argument, attempted to impeach the defendant's claim of self-defense by suggesting that he would not have waited two weeks to report the killing if that was what had occurred. In an argument strikingly similar to the one presented here, the defendant in Jenkins claimed that commenting on his prearrest silence violated his Fifth Amendment privilege against self-incrimination because "a person facing arrest will not remain silent if his failure to speak later can be used to impeach him." The Court noted that it was not clear whether the Fifth Amendment protects prearrest silence but held that, assuming it does, the prosecutor's comments were constitutionally permissible. "[T]he Constitution does not forbid 'every government-imposed choice in the criminal process that has the effect of discouraging the exercise of constitutional rights.'" Once a defendant takes the stand, he is "'subject to cross-examination impeaching his credibility just like any other witness.'"

Indeed, in *Brooks v. Tennessee*, 406 U.S. 605 (1972), the Court suggested that arguing credibility to the jury-which would include the prosecutor's comments here-is the preferred means of counteracting tailoring of the defendant's testimony. In that case, the Court found unconstitutional Tennessee's attempt to defeat tailoring by requiring defendants to testify at the outset of the defense or not at all. This requirement, it said, impermissibly burdened the defendant's right to testify because it forced him to decide whether to do so before he could determine that it was in his best interest. The Court expressed its awareness, however, of the danger that tailoring presented. The antidote, it said, was not Tennessee's heavy-handed rule, but the more nuanced "adversary system[, which] reposes judgment of the credibility of all witnesses in the jury." The adversary system surely envisions-indeed, it requires-that the prosecutor be allowed to bring to the jury's attention the danger that the Court was aware of.

Respondent and the dissent also contend that the prosecutor's comments were impermissible because they were "generic" rather than based upon any specific indication of tailoring. Such comment, the dissent claims, is unconstitutional because it "does not serve to distinguish guilty defendants from innocent ones." But this Court has approved of such "generic" comment before. . . . Thus, that the comments before us here did not, of their own force, demonstrate the guilt of the defendant, or even distinguish among defendants, does not render them infirm.

Finally, the Second Circuit held, and the dissent contends, that the comments were impermissible here because they were made, not during cross-examination, but at summation, leaving the defense no opportunity to reply. That this is not a constitutionally significant distinction is demonstrated by our decision in Reagan. There the challenged instruction came at the end of the case, after the defense had rested, just as the prosecutor's comments did here.

Our trial structure, which requires the defense to close before the prosecution, regularly forces the defense to predict what the prosecution will say. Indeed, defense counsel in this case explained to the jury that it was his job in "closing argument here to try and anticipate as best [he could] some of the arguments that the prosecution [would] be making." . . . . There is absolutely nothing to support the dissent's contention that for purposes of determining the validity of generic attacks upon credibility "the distinction between cross-examination and summation is critical."

In sum, we see no reason to depart from the practice of treating testifying defendants the same as other witnesses. A witness's ability to hear prior testimony and to tailor his account accordingly, and the threat that ability presents to the integrity of the trial, are no different when it is the defendant doing the listening. Allowing comment upon the fact that a defendant's presence in the courtroom provides him a unique opportunity to tailor his testimony is appropriate-and indeed, given the inability to sequester the defendant, sometimes essential-to the central function of the trial, which is to discover the truth.

. . . . .

Many long established elements of criminal procedure deprive a defendant of advantages he would otherwise possess-for example, the requirement that he plead to the charge before, rather than after, all the evidence is in. The consequences of the requirement that he be present at trial seem to us no worse.

. . . . .

For the foregoing reasons, the judgment of the Court of Appeals for the Second Circuit is reversed, and the case is remanded for further proceedings consistent with this opinion.

It is so ordered.

[The concurring opinion of Justice STEVENS, with whom Justice BREYER joined, is omitted].

[The dissenting opinion of Justice GINSBURG, with whom Justice SOUTER joined is omitted].

FROM THE COURTROOM

PRESLEY V. GEORGIA

Supreme Court of the United States, 2010
558 U.S. 209

PER CURIAM.

After a jury trial in the Superior Court of DeKalb County, Georgia, petitioner Eric Presley was convicted of a cocaine trafficking offense. The conviction was affirmed by the Supreme Court of Georgia. Presley seeks certiorari, claiming his Sixth and Fourteenth Amendment right to a public trial was violated when the trial court excluded the public from the voir dire of prospective jurors. The Supreme Court of Georgia's affirmance contravened this Court's clear precedents. Certiorari and petitioner's motion for leave to proceed in forma pauperis are now granted, and the judgment is reversed.

Before selecting a jury in Presley's trial, the trial court noticed a lone courtroom observer. The court explained that prospective jurors were about to enter and instructed the man that he was not allowed in the courtroom and had to leave that floor of the courthouse entirely. The court then questioned the man and learned he was Presley's uncle. The court reiterated its instruction:

"'Well, you still can't sit out in the audience with the jurors. You know, most of the afternoon actually we're going to be picking a jury. And we may have a couple of pre-trial matters, so you're welcome to come in after we . . . complete selecting the jury this afternoon. But, otherwise, you would have to leave the sixth floor, because jurors will be all out in the hallway in a few moments. That applies to everybody who's got a case.'"

Presley's counsel objected to "'the exclusion of the public from the courtroom,'" but the court explained, "'[t]here just isn't space for them to sit in the audience.'" When Presley's counsel requested "'some accommodation,'" the court explained its ruling further:

"'Well, the uncle can certainly come back in once the trial starts. There's no, really no need for the uncle to be present during jury selection. . . . [W]e have 42 jurors coming up. Each of those rows will be occupied by jurors. And his uncle cannot sit and intermingle with members of the jury panel. But, when the trial starts, the opening statements and other matters, he can certainly come back into the courtroom.'"

After Presley was convicted, he moved for a new trial based on the exclusion of the public from the juror voir dire. At a hearing on the motion, Presley presented evidence showing that 14 prospective jurors could have fit in the jury box and the remaining

28 could have fit entirely on one side of the courtroom, leaving adequate room for the public. The trial court denied the motion, commenting that it preferred to seat jurors throughout the entirety of the courtroom, and "it's up to the individual judge to decide . . . what's comfortable." The court continued: "It's totally up to my discretion whether or not I want family members in the courtroom to intermingle with the jurors and sit directly behind the jurors where they might overhear some inadvertent comment or conversation." On appeal, the Court of Appeals of Georgia agreed, finding "[t]here was no abuse of discretion here, when the trial court explained the need to exclude spectators at the voir dire stage of the proceedings and when members of the public were invited to return afterward."

The Supreme Court of Georgia granted certiorari and affirmed, with two justices dissenting. After finding "the trial court certainly had an overriding interest in ensuring that potential jurors heard no inherently prejudicial remarks from observers during voir dire," the Supreme Court of Georgia rejected Presley's argument that the trial court was required to consider alternatives to closing the courtroom. It noted that "the United States Supreme Court [has] not provide[d] clear guidance regarding whether a court must, *sua sponte*, advance its own alternatives to [closure]," and the court ruled that "Presley was obliged to present the court with any alternatives that he wished the court to consider." When no alternatives are offered, it concluded, "there is no abuse of discretion in the court's failure to *sua sponte* advance its own alternatives."

This Court's rulings with respect to the public trial right rest upon two different provisions of the Bill of Rights, both applicable to the States via the Due Process Clause of the Fourteenth Amendment. The Sixth Amendment directs, in relevant part, that "[i] n all criminal prosecutions, the accused shall enjoy the right to a speedy and public trial . . . ." The Court in *In re Oliver*, 333 U.S. 257, 273 (1948), made it clear that this right extends to the States. The Sixth Amendment right, as the quoted language makes explicit, is the right of the accused.

The Court has further held that the public trial right extends beyond the accused and can be invoked under the First Amendment. *Press–Enterprise Co. v. Superior Court of Cal., Riverside Cty.*, 464 U.S. 501 (1984) *(Press–Enterprise I)*. This requirement, too, is binding on the States.

The case now before the Court is brought under the Sixth Amendment, for it is the accused who invoked his right to a public trial. An initial question is whether the right to a public trial in criminal cases extends to the jury selection phase of trial, and in particular the voir dire of prospective jurors. In the First Amendment context that question was answered in *Press–Enterprise I*. The Court there held that the voir dire of prospective jurors must be open to the public under the First Amendment. Later in the same Term as *Press–Enterprise I*, the Court considered a Sixth Amendment case concerning whether the public trial right extends to a pretrial hearing on a motion to suppress certain evidence. *Waller v. Georgia*, 467 U.S. 39 (1984). The *Waller* Court relied heavily upon *Press–Enterprise I* in finding that the Sixth Amendment right to a public trial extends beyond the actual proof at trial. It ruled that the pretrial suppression hearing must be open to the public because "there can be little doubt that the explicit Sixth Amendment right of the accused is no less protective of a public trial than the implicit First Amendment right of the press and public."

While *Press–Enterprise I* was heavily relied upon in *Waller*, the jury selection issue in the former case was resolved under the First, not the Sixth, Amendment. In the instant case, the question then arises whether it is so well settled that the Sixth Amendment right extends to jury voir dire that this Court may proceed by summary disposition.

The point is well settled under *Press–Enterprise I* and *Waller*. The extent to which the First and Sixth Amendment public trial rights are coextensive is an open question, and it is not necessary here to speculate whether or in what circumstances the reach or protections of one might be greater than the other. Still, there is no legitimate reason, at least in the context of juror selection proceedings, to give one who asserts a First Amendment privilege greater rights to insist on public proceedings than the accused has. "Our cases have uniformly recognized the public-trial guarantee as one created for the benefit of the defendant." There could be no explanation for barring the accused from raising a constitutional right that is unmistakably for his or her benefit. That rationale suffices to resolve the instant matter. The Supreme Court of Georgia was correct in assuming that the Sixth Amendment right to a public trial extends to the voir dire of prospective jurors.

While the accused does have a right to insist that the voir dire of the jurors be public, there are exceptions to this general rule. "[T]he right to an open trial may give way in certain cases to other rights or interests, such as the defendant's right to a fair trial or the government's interest in inhibiting disclosure of sensitive information." "Such circumstances will be rare, however, and the balance of interests must be struck with special care." *Waller* provided standards for courts to apply before excluding the public from any stage of a criminal trial:

"[T]he party seeking to close the hearing must advance an overriding interest that is likely to be prejudiced, the closure must be no broader than necessary to protect that interest, the trial court must consider reasonable alternatives to closing the proceeding, and it must make findings adequate to support the closure."

In upholding exclusion of the public at juror voir dire in the instant case, the Supreme Court of Georgia concluded, despite our explicit statements to the contrary, that trial courts need not consider alternatives to closure absent an opposing party's proffer of some alternatives. While the Supreme Court of Georgia concluded this was an open question under this Court's precedents, the statement in Waller that "the trial court must consider reasonable alternatives to closing the proceeding" settles the point. If that statement leaves any room for doubt, the Court was more explicit in *Press–Enterprise I*:

"Even with findings adequate to support closure, the trial court's orders denying access to voir dire testimony failed to consider whether alternatives were available to protect the interests of the prospective jurors that the trial court's orders sought to guard. Absent consideration of alternatives to closure, the trial court could not constitutionally close the voir dire."

The conclusion that trial courts are required to consider alternatives to closure even when they are not offered by the parties is clear not only from this Court's precedents but also from the premise that "[t]he process of juror selection is itself a matter of importance, not simply to the adversaries but to the criminal justice system." The public has a right to be present whether or not any party has asserted the right. In *Press–Enterprise I*, for instance, neither the defendant nor the prosecution requested an open courtroom during juror voir dire proceedings; in fact, both specifically argued in favor of keeping the transcript of the proceedings confidential. The Court, nonetheless, found it was error to close the courtroom.

Trial courts are obligated to take every reasonable measure to accommodate public attendance at criminal trials. Nothing in the record shows that the trial court could not have accommodated the public at Presley's trial. Without knowing the precise circumstances, some possibilities include reserving one or more rows for the public; dividing the jury venire panel to reduce courtroom congestion; or instructing prospective jurors not to engage or interact with audience members.

Petitioner also argues that, apart from failing to consider alternatives to closure, the trial court erred because it did not even identify any overriding interest likely to be prejudiced absent the closure of voir dire. There is some merit to this complaint. The generic risk of jurors overhearing prejudicial remarks, unsubstantiated by any specific threat or incident, is inherent whenever members of the public are present during the selection of jurors. If broad concerns of this sort were sufficient to override a defendant's constitutional right to a public trial, a court could exclude the public from jury selection almost as a matter of course. As noted in the dissent below, "the majority's reasoning permits the closure of voir dire in every criminal case conducted in this courtroom whenever the trial judge decides, for whatever reason, that he or she would prefer to fill the courtroom with potential jurors rather than spectators."

There are no doubt circumstances where a judge could conclude that threats of improper communications with jurors or safety concerns are concrete enough to warrant closing voir dire. But in those cases, the particular interest, and threat to that interest, must "be articulated along with findings specific enough that a reviewing court can determine whether the closure order was properly entered."

We need not rule on this second claim of error, because even assuming, arguendo, that the trial court had an overriding interest in closing voir dire, it was still incumbent upon it to consider all reasonable alternatives to closure. It did not, and that is all this Court needs to decide.

The Supreme Court of Georgia's judgment is reversed, and the case is remanded for further proceedings not inconsistent with this opinion.

It is so ordered.

[The dissenting opinion of Justice THOMAS, with whom Justice SCALIA joined, is omitted].

45

Sentencing

Key Concepts

- Significant Discretion Is Vested in Sentencing Judges
- Constitutional and Statutory Constraints
- Once Mandatory Sentencing Guidelines Now Advisory Only

A. Introduction and Policy. Once the guilty verdict is returned or the guilty plea entered, the question shifts to what sentence should be imposed. As you may have learned in your first-year Criminal Law class, there are five primary theories of sentencing. For most of the twentieth century, American sentencing policy was focused on **rehabilitative** aims. However, as the crime rate began to rise in the late 1960s and early 1970s, rehabilitation gave way to **deterrence**, **incapacitation**, and **retribution** as the central goals of sentencing. More recently, **restoration** has been growing in popularity as a sentencing goal.

The aim of a criminal sentence that focuses on **rehabilitation** is to change the criminal offender—to fix or correct whatever traits caused her to offend in the first place. Although rehabilitative sentences are not as widespread in the modern criminal justice system, they are still handed down, especially for misdemeanor convictions. Drug treatment programs, mental health counseling, or anger management programs are all examples of rehabilitative sentences. The antithesis of a rehabilitative sentence is the death penalty, since it assumes the incorrigibility of the offender.

Although rehabilitation—if successful—offers the benefit of returning the offender to society as a law-abiding and productive citizen, it is not always appropriate for every crime. Many serious crimes—robbery, embezzlement, and murder, for example—frequently have deeper and more complex causes than can be cured by a court-ordered treatment program. Rehabilitation also has become less politically popular in recent decades; advocates of rehabilitative programs are frequently (and successfully) caricatured as being "soft on crime."

A second theory of punishment, **deterrence**, is premised on the theory that fear of future punishment will discourage criminal conduct. **Specific deterrence** is meant to discourage the particular offender from engaging in criminal behavior again. The goal is to make the first punishment sufficiently unpleasant that the offender remains law-abiding in order to avoid similar punishment in the future.

General deterrence, on the other hand, punishes a particular offender in order to convince all other potential offenders that the risk of criminal conduct is simply not worth it.

There is substantial debate about the effectiveness of deterrence. Many crimes are committed in the heat of the moment and thus cannot be deterred by a rational appeal to the offender's better judgment. For example, an individual who commits a crime while under the influence of drugs or while caught up in a fit of extreme emotion is unlikely to be considering the long-term consequences of his actions.

Incapacitation is a third punishment theory. Under this theory, the goal is quite simple: remove the offender from the streets so that he cannot offend again. Incapacitation works with regard to the specific offender because he is literally kept away from potential victims in society as long as he is behind bars. Some social scientists have traced the dramatic drop in crime in the 1990s at least partially to the fact that hundreds of thousands of criminals had been imprisoned for extraordinarily long sentences. However, this conclusion is the subject of vigorous debate.

Whether mass incarceration has actually substantially succeeded in decreasing the crime rate, it has certainly come at a high cost. Incarceration is a very expensive sentencing option. It was recently estimated that it costs approximately $29,000 a year to house an inmate in the federal system.[1] In some locations, the cost is much higher: in New York City, for example, the cost of incarceration jumps to an average of $168,000 a year per inmate for its local jail population.[2] By way of comparison, the average national cost of sending a child to public school is $11,000.[3]

Even the basic effectiveness of incarceration has been called into question. In recent years, a number of studies examining the destabilizing effects of mass incarceration on communities have suggested that widespread incapacitation may actually cause crime rates to rise rather than fall. This is because at some tipping point, locking up too many people from a single community disrupts family structures and other informal social networks and creates an environment that actually fosters crime. A final problem with regard to incapacitation is that an incarcerated offender is not completely prevented from committing a crime while

---

[1] Federal Register (March 18, 2013), available online at https://www.federalregister.gov/articles/2013/03/18/2013-06139/annual-determination-of-average-cost-of-incarceration.

[2] Marc Santora, "City's Annual Cost Per Inmate Is $168,000, Study Finds," New York Times (August 23, 2013), available online at http://www.nytimes.com/2013/08/24/nyregion/citys-annual-cost-per-inmate-is-nearly-168000-study-says.html.

[3] Lam Thuy Vo, "How Much Does the Government Spend to Send a Kid to Public School?" National Public Radio (June 21, 2012), available online at http://www.npr.org/blogs/money/2012/06/21/155515613/how-much-does-the-government-spend-to-send-a-kid-to-school.

behind bars; it is still possible to commit crimes against other inmates or against correctional officers.

In some sense, rehabilitation, deterrence and incapacitation are all similar in that they are forward-looking justifications for criminal punishment. They examine the consequences of criminal behavior and seek to avoid them by imposing a punishment that will fix, scare, or immobilize the offender. Thus, punishment is seen as a means to some end. **Retribution**, however, is backward-looking. Under a retributivist theory, the punishment is an end in itself; the offender is punished not to serve some greater purpose, but because he deserves to be punished for the immoral act that he has committed. Thus, under retributive theory, the punishment should fit the crime by matching in severity the offender's criminal conduct and the moral blameworthiness of the offender himself.[4] Retribution as a theory is focused on the proportionality and fairness of punishment. The offender should be penalized only as much (but no more) than is merited by his criminal behavior. Despite its relatively unobjectionable theoretical underpinnings, in the modern political era retribution has been used as justification for extremely harsh penal sanctions.

In contrast with the offender-centered retributive model, the fifth and final theory of criminal sentencing—**restoration**—seeks to restore the balance by restoring the victim to the condition she was in before the crime occurred. When a criminal act is committed, the offender often gains something at the expense of the victim. Restorative punishment attempts to rebalance this scale. For example, if the offender stole the victim's cell phone, a restorative model might impose restitution (in the amount of the stolen phone) upon the convicted defendant. Alternately, if the defendant sold drugs in a particular neighborhood, the judge would require the offender to undertake community service at the neighborhood's drug treatment center. Although restoration can be successful in healing the damage caused by the defendant and re-integrating the defendant into his community, restoration is rarely an articulated goal of criminal punishment for extremely serious offenses.

In order to accomplish one of these five goals of sentencing, the criminal justice system uses a number of different forms of sentences, such as death, incarceration, fines, forfeiture, restitution, and community service. But of all these options, incarceration is by far the most common punishment that is imposed. As a result, the United States currently has the largest prison population in the world, with over 2.2 million people incarcerated. In raw numbers, the next closest country is China, which incarcerates approximately 1.6 million of its citizens. On a per capita basis, our closest rival is Russia, which incarcerates 615 of every 100,000 people to America's 737 of every 100,000.

---

[4] Williams v. New York, 337 U.S. 241, 247 (1949).

As you read above, incarceration is an expensive form of punishment. In an era of budget shortfalls and severe prison overcrowding many states and the federal government are, therefore, looking for cheaper alternatives. These alternatives include short-term boot camps and the decriminalization of (or reduced punishment for) some minor possessory drug offenses.

One of the most controversial alternatives currently being used in lieu of prison time is public shaming. For example, a Cleveland resident was convicted after she drove down the sidewalk to avoid stopping for a school bus. She was sentenced to stand on the street corner for two days holding a sign that read, "Only an idiot would drive on the sidewalk to avoid a school bus." Similarly, a mail thief was sentenced to wear a sandwich board that read, "I am a thief. This is my punishment," as he stood in front of a post office for eight hours. Public shaming, which was a common form of punishment in colonial America, fell out of favor as urbanization set in and people lost strong connection with the communities in which they lived. However, it has seen a resurgence as governments look for a less expensive way to punish criminal offenders. The current use of public shaming as criminal punishment has withstood statutory and constitutional scrutiny.

There are also a host of indirect "punishments" that may flow from a criminal conviction. We discussed these penalties, known as "collateral consequences," when we discussed plea bargaining in **Chapter 42**. These collateral consequences include loss of the right to vote, exclusion from public benefits, loss of the right to own a firearm, or deportation. Many of these collateral consequences make reentry into society more difficult for ex-offenders. Recognizing that successful reentry makes communities safer, some state legislatures are working to limit collateral consequences in order to reduce the barriers to reentry.

B. The Law. Though sentencing judges enjoy extremely broad discretion in fashioning an appropriate punishment for one convicted of an offense, there are several legal limitations that constrain criminal sentences. These limitations come either from the Constitution or from statutes and other rules.

1. Constitutional Limits on Screening.

The Constitution has many different provisions that limit a sentencing judge's discretion: the Eighth Amendment prohibition against cruel and unusual punishment, the ban on ex post facto laws, the Sixth Amendment right to a jury trial, the Due Process Clause, the Equal Protection Clause, and the First Amendment right to free expression.

a. Perhaps the most well-known constitutional limit on sentencing is the **Eighth Amendment ban on cruel and unusual punishment.** The Amendment provides:

U.S. Constitution, Amendment VIII

Excessive bail shall not be required, nor excessive fines imposed, nor cruel and unusual punishments inflicted.

Whether a punishment is "cruel and unusual" is defined in large part by the current consensus in the United States: "[a] claim that punishment is excessive is judged not by the standards that prevailed in 1685 when Lord Jeffreys presided over the 'Bloody Assizes' or when the Bill of Rights was adopted, but rather by those that currently prevail."[5] Thus, in assessing an Eighth Amendment claim, a reviewing court should look to "evolving standards of decency that mark the progress of a maturing society."[6] In order to determine how the country's standard of decency has evolved, the Court looks to objective factors to the maximum possible extent, and the "clearest and most reliable objective evidence of contemporary values is the legislation enacted by the country's legislatures."[7] Therefore, the Supreme Court will frequently examine the laws of all fifty states to determine which of them agree or disagree with the particular sentencing regime at issue. This does not mean that Eighth Amendment cases are nothing more than an exercise in counting up how many states oppose certain policies; even when there does appear to be a consensus among the state laws, the Supreme Court Justices still apply their own judgment to decide whether they agree with the consensus.[8]

Thus, although the Clause unquestionably prohibits barbaric forms of traditional punishments like torture; it also prevents some more modern types of punishments—and even some punishments which might not have been deemed "cruel and unusual" at the time of the nation's founding—for example, imposing the death penalty on a defendant who committed a crime other than murder.[9]

In fact, one of the primary areas where the terms of the Eighth Amendment have come into play is in the context of capital punishment. In the early 1970s, the Supreme Court held that capital punishment violated the Eighth Amendment's ban on cruel and unusual punishment.[10] But, the Supreme Court quickly reversed course and just four years later it held that if properly administered, the death penalty can survive constitutional attack.[11]

---

[5] Atkins v. Virginia, 536 U.S. 304, 311 (2002).

[6] Graham v. Florida, 560 U.S. 48, 58 (2010).

[7] Atkins, 536 U.S. at 312.

[8] Id. at 312-3.

[9] Coker v. Georgia, 433 U.S. 584 (1977).

[10] Furman v. Georgia, 408 U.S. 238 (1972).

[11] Gregg v. Georgia, 428 U.S. 153 (1976).

According to the most recent Supreme Court cases, the Eighth Amendment places three limitations on the imposition of death sentences.

1. Capital sentencing schemes may not give the sentencers "unbridled discretion in determining the fates of those charged with capital offenses."[12] That is, the legislature must provide guidance to the judge or jury who is imposing sentence as to what factors to consider when making the decision.

2. At the sentencing hearing, the capital defendant must be allowed "to introduce any relevant mitigating evidence regarding his character or record and any of the circumstances of the offense."[13] The prosecutor will also present aggravating circumstances at the sentencing hearing, and the death sentencing schemes in most states require the sentencer to find at least one aggravating factor before imposing the death penalty.

3. The death penalty may not be imposed for a) a non-homicide crime;[14] b) a crime committed by someone under the age of 18;[15] or c) a crime committed by someone who is mentally retarded.[16]

Obviously, just because the Eighth Amendment allows capital punishment does not mean that states are required to impose it. Many states have abolished the death penalty for policy reasons or have imposed a moratorium on executions pending review of how it is applied in practice. Nonetheless, capital punishment remains a possible sanction in the majority of states and in the federal system.

In addition to sentences of death, the Eighth Amendment has also been used to challenge the length of incarceration. For more than a century, the Court has recognized that proportionality has constitutional dimensions.[17] Thus, a sentence that is grossly disproportionate to the offense (or the offender) may be unconstitutional.

This does not mean, however, that extremely harsh sentences are always unconstitutional. The Court has determined that "three-strikes" laws, which often impose severe mandatory punishment upon offenders who accumulate more than a specified number of convictions, are not constitutionally disproportionate.[18] By way of illustration, under such laws, a repeat offender was lawfully sentenced to twenty-five years to life in prison for two counts of soliciting prostitution

---

[12] California v. Brown, 479 U.S. 538, 541 (1987).

[13] Id.

[14] Enmund v. Florida, 458 U.S. 782 (1982), as limited by Tison v. Arizona, 481 U.S. 137 (1987).

[15] Roper v. Simmons, 543 U.S. 551 (2005).

[16] Atkins v. Virginia, 536 U.S. 304 (2002).

[17] Weems v. United States, 217 U.S. 349 (1910).

[18] Lockyer v. Andrade, 538 U.S. 63 (2003).

customers.[19] In another example, first-time felony offender Ronald Harmelin was sentences to life in prison after he was convicted of possessing approximately 650 grams (or just under three cups) of cocaine. The Supreme Court rejected Harmelin's constitutional challenge to his life sentence, explaining that "severe, mandatory penalties may be cruel, but they are not unusual in the constitutional sense, having been employed in various forms throughout our Nation's history."[20] We will discuss the disproportionality question in more detail in Section C.1, below.

In recent years, the Court has been particularly less tolerant of severe sentences that are imposed on children who commit criminal offenses. There are mechanisms in every state by which children who are charged with serious offenses can be moved out of the juvenile justice system and charged as adults. In two states, children as young as ten-years old may be transferred to adult court for prosecution. Once convicted in adult court, the child offender is then subject to the same sentencing range as an adult offender. However, in a trio of cases, the Court determined that the Eighth Amendment mandates a) that youthful offenders cannot be sentenced to death, b) that juveniles cannot receive mandatory life sentences, and c) that in non-homicide cases juveniles may not be sentenced to life without the possibility of parole ("LWOP").[21] We will discuss the special case of juvenile sentencing in Section C.3, below.

It bears mention that the cruel and unusual punishment provisions of the amendment do not apply to pre-trial detainees. A conviction is required before that portion of the amendment is triggered.[22]

b. The bar on **Ex Post Facto** laws, contained in Sections 9 and 10 of Article I of the Constitution, is another restraint on sentencing. As it pertains to sentencing, an ex post facto law is one that retroactively increases the punishment for a criminal act.[23] For example, the Ex Post Facto clause does not allow a convicted person to be sentenced under a new version of the Sentencing Guidelines if the newer Guidelines impose higher advisory sentencing ranges than were in place at the time the offense of conviction was committed.[24] Similarly, the Court has applied the Ex Post Facto Clause to invalidate a state's reduction of an inmate's "good time" credits.[25]

c. A third constraint on sentencing is provided by the **Sixth Amendment** (and in the case of a state sentence, by that amendment as applied to the states

[19] Nutt v. Knowles, 145 Fed. Appx. 221 (2005).

[20] Harmelin v. Michigan, 501 U.S. 957, 994–95 (1991).

[21] Miller v. Alabama, 132 S.Ct. 2455 (2012).

[22] Bell v. Wolfish, 441 U.S. 520, 535 n.16 (1979).

[23] California Dept. of Corrections v. Morales, 514 U.S. 491 (1995).

[24] Peugh v. United States, 133 S.Ct. 2072 (2013).

[25] Weaver v. Graham, 450 U.S. 24 (1981).

through the Fourteenth Amendment). As you read in **Chapter 43**, the right to a jury trial requires that an offender not be subjected to enhanced punishment for any fact (other than the fact of a prior conviction) that has not been determined by a jury.[26] A judge certainly may consider a wide range of information when selecting a sentence within a statutorily prescribed sentencing range. But, the court may not exceed that authorized range if the facts relied on to exceed the range were not found by the jury.[27] The prohibition against enhanced punishment based on non-jury-assessed facts also applies to the imposition of enhanced fines.[28] This doctrine has been the source of a number of significant Supreme Court cases recently with regard to the federal Sentencing Guidelines. We will discuss these cases in Section C.2, below.

d. A fourth set of constitutional constraint on sentencing are provided by the Fourteenth Amendment's **due process guarantee.** These include:

1. **Restrictions on the treatment of indigents.** For example, a court may not automatically revoke probation merely because an indigent offender is unable to pay a fine.

2. **Procedural limits upon the process of revoking parole or probation.** Before parole or a probationary sentence may be revoked, the fact-finding body must engage in an assessment of whether a condition of probation was actually violated; and must then determine whether the violation warrants revocation.[29] The probationer or parolee is entitled to notice of this assessment and a hearing at which he is afforded both an opportunity to present evidence and (usually) the opportunity to challenge the government's evidence. Although a certain level of procedural safeguards must be in place at this hearing, they need not be as extensive as those afforded at trial.[30]

3. **Limits on re-sentencing.** If a defendant's sentence is reversed on appeal, any new sentence may not be increased in retaliation for the successful appellate challenge.[31] To ensure the length of the new sentence is not the product of vindictiveness, the Court has said, "whenever a judge imposes a more severe sentence upon a defendant after a new trial, the reasons for his doing so must affirmatively appear."[32] Thus, a presumption of vindictiveness applies to harsher sentences following appeal. This presumption can be overcome only by positive evidence from the resentencing court

[26] Blakely v. Washington, 542 U.S. 296 (2004).

[27] Apprendi v. New Jersey, 530 U.S. 466 (2000).

[28] Southern Union Co. v. United States, 132 S.Ct. 2344 (2012).

[29] Black v. Romano, 471 U.S. 606 (1985).

[30] Morrissey v. Brewer, 408 U.S. 471 (1972); Gagnon v. Scarpelli, 411 U.S. 778 (1973).

[31] North Carolina v. Pearce, 395 U.S. 711 (1969).

[32] Wasman v. United States, 468 U.S. 559, 564-65 (1984).

justifying the enhancement. For example, the court could overcome the presumption by referring to intervening convictions the defendant amassed prior to the re-sentencing.[33]

4. **Restraints on capital sentencing.** For example, a person may not be executed based upon information that he did not have an opportunity to rebut. Consistent with this mandate, whenever future dangerousness is an issue, a capital sentencing jury must be informed that a defendant will not be parole-eligible if sentenced to life in prison.[34]

As the above list indicates, included within the due process constraints upon sentencing are limitations upon a court's ability to revoke parole or a probationary term; limitations upon the court's authority at the time of re-sentencing; and limitations upon the information that must be conveyed to capital sentencing juries.

e. **The Equal Protection Clause** imposes a fifth constitutional limit upon sentencing. The Equal Protection Clause does not require that all persons convicted of the same offense be sentenced to an identical form of punishment[35]—as with any equal protection claim, the defendant must prove the existence of purposeful discrimination which had an effect on his specific case.

But, a state may not convert an original non-incarcerative sentence into a term of imprisonment simply because an impoverished defendant is unable to pay associated fines and costs.[36] If "the probationer has made all reasonable bona fide efforts to pay the fine and yet cannot do so through no fault of his own, it is fundamentally unfair to revoke probation automatically without considering whether adequate alternative methods of punishing the probationer are available to meet the State's interest in punishment and deterrence."[37]

Imprisonment for nonpayment is not constitutionally barred in all circumstances, however. If the trial court finds that imprisonment is the only way for the government to accomplish its punishment objectives, jailing a probationer is appropriate even if he has made significant and legitimate efforts to repay his debt.[38] Imprisonment for nonpayment of a fine is also a viable option if a convicted person intentionally refuses to pay a fine that he has the resources to pay or if he refuses to take legitimate steps to secure the funds by, for example, finding a job.

[33] Id. at 569.

[34] Simmons v. South Carolina, 512 U.S. 154 (1994).

[35] Williams v. Illinois, 399 U.S. 235 (1970).

[36] Tate v. Short, 401 U.S. 395 (1971).

[37] Bearden v. Georgia, 461 U.S. 660 (1983).

[38] Id. at 672.

f. Finally, the **First Amendment** prohibits a sentencing court from punishing a defendant more harshly for his thoughts or beliefs.[39] The Court has noted that "a defendant's abstract beliefs, however obnoxious to most people, may not be taken into consideration by a sentencing judge."[40] Of course, if a defendant's articulated thoughts provide evidence of an element of the crime or are useful to the question of motive or intent, they are appropriate fodder at sentencing.

2. Non-Constitutional Limits on Sentencing and Sentencing Practices.

A sentencing judge only has the authority to sentence an offender within the range of punishments set out in the applicable statute. Thus, the primary limitation on a judge's sentencing discretion is the law that the federal or state legislature passed.

Many sentencing statutes provide a maximum amount of authorized punishment which any imposed sentence may not exceed. Such statutes are often worded using permissive language, indicating that a particular offense is punishable by "up to X years in prison." Legislatures also may establish mandatory (or mandatory minimum) sentences. These sentences constrain the discretion of the sentencing body by requiring that a specified minimal amount of punishment be imposed.

Within the authorized range, the judge or (as is often the case in capital offenses) the sentencing jury will select the sentence that is appropriate for the particular offender. **Rule 32** of the Federal Rules of Criminal Procedure is a long and detailed rule that governs sentencing in federal cases. It sets out the following procedures:

1. Sentencing hearings must be held "without unnecessary delay."[41] In practice, a sentencing hearing is held within a few months of the verdict. Apart from questions of scheduling, the primary cause for delay in sentencing is the time needed to prepare the presentence report, as described below.

2. Prior to the sentencing hearing, the probation department must conduct a presentence investigation[42] and prepare the presentence report.[43] The presentence report, provides the sentencing court with a host of useful information like the history and characteristics of the defendant; victim impact information; the availability of non-incarceration alternatives that might be of benefit to the defendant; and information relevant to questions of restitution and forfeiture.[44] Without written defense consent, the report may not be disclosed to anyone until after a guilty plea (or verdict) is entered.[45]

[39] Dawson v. Delaware, 503 U.S. 159 (1992).

[40] Wisconsin v. Mitchell, 508 U.S. 476, 487 (1993).

[41] Fed. R. Crim. Proc. 32(b)(1).

[42] Fed. R. Crim. Proc. 32(c).

[43] Fed. R. Crim. Proc. 32(d).

[44] Id.

[45] Fed. R. Crim. Proc. 32(e).

Once guilt has been assessed, the report must be disclosed to the parties and the court at least thirty-five days prior to sentencing, unless the defendant waives this timing requirement.[46] If the government or the defense have objections to the report, they may raise them. While the sentencing judge is free to rely upon information outside of the presentence report, she must notify the defense and the government if she is doing so in order to allow the parties time to respond.[47]

5. At the sentencing hearing, the prosecutor, the defense attorney, and the defendant all have a right to speak and argue for a specific sentence.[48] In addition, the prosecution and the defense may call witnesses at the sentencing hearing, and the victim also has a reasonable right to be heard.[49]

On the federal level, the judge's sentencing decision will be informed by the sentencing range suggested by the Sentencing Guidelines. These Guidelines, which are discussed in detail in Section C.2, below, were designed to produce greater nationwide consistency in sentencing by setting out identical sentencing ranges for all defendants with the same criminal history and the same severity of crime. The Guidelines used to be mandatory, but recent Supreme Court cases have held that they can only be used as advisory authority.

In gathering information for the sentencing hearing, the judge is not bound by constraints like the rules of evidence. Indeed, 18 U.S.C. § 3661 instructs that "no limitation shall be placed on the information a sentencing court may consider concerning the defendant's background, character, and conduct."[50] By gathering information widely, the sentencing court will ensure that any punishment imposed suits both the offense and the offender.[51] For example, if a sentence is overturned on appeal, upon resentencing the judge may consider the offender's post-sentencing rehabilitation (or re-offending) in deciding upon the new sentence. However, as you read above, any information considered by the judge which increases the authorized sentencing range must have been determined by the jury to comport with Sixth Amendment guarantees.

An imposed sentence may be **determinate** or **indeterminate**. Determinate sentencing imposes punishment for a fixed period—for example, when an offender is convicted of armed robbery and the judge imposes a flat 10-year sentence. The offender knows upon receiving the sentence that she will serve no more than 10 years in prison (and may serve less if the jurisdiction where she is sentenced allows

[46] Fed. R. Crim. Proc. 32(e)(2).

[47] Fed. R. Crim. Proc. 32(i).

[48] Fed. R. Crim. Proc. 32(i)(4).

[49] Fed. R. Crim. Proc. 32(i)(4)(B).

[50] Pepper v. United States, 131 S.Ct. 1229, 1235 (2011).

[51] Wasman v. United States, 468 U.S. 559 (1984).

"good time" credits, which reduce the period of incarceration for good behavior). In contrast, an indeterminate sentence imposes a range of appropriate punishment—for example, if the sentencing judge chose instead to sentence the armed robber to a term of 10-to-40 years in prison. In the case of an indeterminate sentence, the actual release date for the offender would be determined not by the sentencing judge but by the local parole board.

As noted in **Chapter 42**, the overwhelming majority of sentences imposed at both the state and federal level are the result of guilty pleas. We saw in that chapter that the extent to which a plea of guilty can guarantee imposition of particular punishment depends upon the terms of the agreement. The prosecutor might make no commitment about sentencing; she might agree to simply stay silent; or she might agree to join in the defendant's request for a specific sentence. Whether the judge is bound by the plea bargain will depend on the terms of the agreement. As you may recall, a "Type B" agreement only binds the prosecutor, who agrees to either stay silent or join in the defendant's request. The judge is then free to ignore the defendant's request and impose any sentence within the range. A "Type C" agreement locks in a specific sentence. At the time the defendant pleads guilty, the judge must either accept the agreement and be bound by the sentence it sets out, or reject the plea agreement in its entirety—meaning the defendant does not plead guilty. Although the sentencing judge will usually defer to the deal the parties have worked out, she should not accept a plea if she is not convinced that the agreed upon sentence "is an appropriate sentence within the applicable guideline range or, if not, that the sentence departs from the applicable guideline range for justifiable reasons."[52]

Finally, a comment about finality. As you know, the rules of criminal procedure are a careful balance between notions of finality and notions of fairness. As you will read in **Chapters 47** (Appeals) and **48** (Post-Conviction), once a conviction is handed down, the procedural balance tips decidedly in favor of finality. The same is true in the case of sentences. Once a sentence is handed down, it is for the most part final. The trial judge's ability to amend or modify the sentence is, in most states, strictly limited by rules and statutes that set firm limits on the time period during which a court retains jurisdiction over a sentence it has imposed. The same is true in the federal system. "Federal courts are forbidden, as a general matter, to modify a term of imprisonment once it has been imposed . . . subject to a few narrow exceptions."[53]

The finality of sentences also comes into play at the appellate level. On direct appeal, a federal appellate court reviews a sentence only for reasonableness. If the sentence is within the advisory Guidelines range, the appellate court may

[52] Freeman v. United States, 131 S.Ct. 2685, 2692 (2011).

[53] Id.

presume it to be reasonable. This "presumption reflects the fact that, by the time an appeals court is considering a within-Guidelines sentence on review, both the sentencing judge and the Sentencing Commission will have reached the same conclusion as to the proper sentence in the particular case."[54]

The presumption of reasonableness applies only to appellate courts, however. The Supreme Court has expressly instructed that a sentencing judge may not impose a Guidelines sentence based simply on a presumption that it is the appropriate one. Instead, the sentencing judge must consider the full array of information before her in deciding the appropriate sentence in a case.[55]

C. Applying the Law.

1. Proportionality Review. The Eighth Amendment's protection against cruel and unusual punishment prohibits not just barbaric punishment but also disproportionately lengthy punishment. However, outside of the context of capital cases, the Court has made clear that successful proportionality challenges are (and should be) "exceedingly rare." To succeed on such a challenge, the offender must do more than demonstrate that his sentence was very severe; the Eighth Amendment "forbids only extreme sentences that are **grossly disproportionate** to the crime."[56] Most recently, the Court found that a sentence of twenty-five years to life for stealing three golf clubs did not overcome this high hurdle:

> **Example—*Ewing v. California*, 538 U.S. 11 (2003):** California has a "three strikes" law that punishes repeat offenders more severely. If a defendant is convicted of a felony after having been once convicted of a serious or violent offense, his sentence in the new case is double that normally imposed. If the defendant has two or more prior serious or violent felonies, the court must impose a mandatory indeterminate sentence of at least twenty-five years to life.
>
> Gary Ewing was arrested after he slipped three golf clubs into his pants leg and walked out of a pro shop at a golf course in Los Angeles. The clubs were valued at $399 each. Ewing was convicted of felony grand theft of personal property in excess of $400. The prosecution gave notice of its intention to pursue a sentence under the three-strikes law. The prosecution pointed to Ewing's three prior convictions for burglary and one for robbery, for which he received a combined sentence of nine

[54] Rita v. United States, 551 U.S. 338, 347 (2007).

[55] Nelson v. United States, 555 U.S. 350 (2009).

[56] Ewing v. California, 538 U.S. 11, 23 (2003).

years in prison. Ewing was on parole from that nine-year sentence when he stole the golf clubs. The court sentenced Ewing to twenty-five years to life for stealing the golf clubs. Ewing then challenged his sentence under the Eighth Amendment, arguing that it was grossly disproportionate.

Analysis: The sentence of twenty-five years to life that Ewing received was constitutional.

When assessing a claim of constitutional disproportionality, three factors are relevant to the reviewing court's analysis: 1) the gravity of the offense and the harshness of the penalty; 2) the sentences imposed on other criminals in the same jurisdiction; and 3) the sentences imposed for commission of the same crime in other jurisdictions. In this case, consideration of the first factor alone makes clear that Ewing's sentence did not violate the Eighth Amendment.

Ewing characterized his offense as simply stealing three golf clubs. But, his offense is more accurately characterized as stealing nearly $1200 worth of merchandise after already having been convicted of at least two prior violent or serious felonies. In assessing the seriousness of his offense, the golf club theft cannot be viewed in a vacuum, but instead must be considered against the backdrop of his lengthy criminal history.

Three-strikes laws are a response by the states to the perceived threat of career criminals. In passing such laws, states have determined that the best way to protect the public from repeat offenders is to lock them away for extended periods. The legislative policy choice to manage repeat offenders in this way was well within the State's discretion, and nothing in the Eighth Amendment prohibited the choice that California made. The Court does "not sit as a 'superlegislature' to second-guess these policy choices. It is enough that the State of California has a reasonable basis for believing that dramatically enhanced sentences for habitual felons 'advances the goals of its criminal justice system in any substantial way.'"

The Court did not dispute that Ewing's sentence was extremely long. However the Court concluded that "it reflects a rational legislative judgment, entitled to deference, that offenders who have committed serious or violent felonies and who continue to commit felonies must be incapacitated."[57]

Since *Ewing*, the Court has clarified that the three *Ewing* factors are considered consecutively. First, the reviewing court considers the seriousness of the offense and the severity of the punishment. The court moves on to consider the sentences imposed on similar offenders in the same and other jurisdictions only if the initially assessment leads to a conclusion that the sentence was grossly disproportionate.

[57] Id. at 30.

Although it is difficult to prevail on a proportionality case, it is not impossible. Many years before its decision in *Ewing*, the Court found that a sentence of life without the possibility of parole for a seventh non-violent felony violated the Eighth Amendment:

> **Example—*Solem v. Helm*, 463 U.S. 277 (1983):** Jerry Helm had a drinking problem: when he drank, he committed crimes. In eleven years, Helm's criminal conduct resulted in six separate convictions for non-violent felonies. Helm was then charged with cashing a "no account" check for $100. The maximum penalty for this offense was normally five years in prison and a $5,000 fine. However, as a result of Helm's criminal history, he was sentenced under the state's recidivist statute to life in prison without the possibility of parole. The Supreme Court accepted the case for review.

Analysis: Helm's life sentence was grossly disproportionate to his offense of conviction and therefore violated the Eighth Amendment's ban on cruel and unusual punishment.

In determining whether a sentence is grossly disproportionate, a great deal of deference should be afforded the legislative determination to set the penalty at a particular point. But, even this healthy dose of deference will not insulate every sentence. "[A] single day in prison may be unconstitutional in some circumstances."[58]

In determining the proportionality of a sentence the court must be guided by objective criteria. In this case, those objective criteria reveal that Helm's sentence was too harsh.

Helm's crime was not particularly serious. It involved no violence or threat of violence, and the amount of the "no account" check he cashed was not particularly large. It is true that Helm was sentenced not just for cashing the check, but also for being a repeat offender. But, in assessing that status, the nature of his past crimes is relevant. All of Helm's prior crimes were non-violent and all were relatively minor. In comparison, the sentence that Helm received is the most severe a state might impose short of death.

The other crimes in the state that might have been punished with the sentence that Helm received were murder, treason, arson and kidnapping. The fact that Helm is being sentenced in the same fashion as those who have committed far more serious crimes is significant. Moreover, Helm could have received the sentence that he did in only one other state.

---

[58] Solem v. Helm, 463 U.S. 277, 290 (1983).

> In light of the relevant objective criteria in the instant case, the only rational conclusion is that Helm's "sentence is significantly disproportionate to his crime, and is therefore prohibited by the Eighth Amendment."[59]

Helm is one of just two cases to date where the Court has found that a sentence of a term of years was grossly disproportionate and thus a violation of the Constitution. The second case, *Graham v. Florida*, was decided more than a quarter-century after the *Helm* case and is discussed in Section 3, below.

2. Sentencing Guidelines. In the late 1970s and early 1980s, there was mounting concern at the federal level that the length of sentence an offender received had less to do with the offender's conduct and more to do with the particular proclivities of the sentencing judge. The politics of criminal justice were also shifting to a more tough-on-crime stance. In response, the Sentencing Reform Act of 1984 was passed with the goal of eliminating wide disparities in federal sentences. As the Court has said, the "Act aims to create a comprehensive sentencing scheme in which those who commit crimes of similar severity under similar conditions receive similar sentences."[60] The Act required judges to state reasons for their sentencing decisions on the record; it facilitated appellate review of federal sentences; it required determinate sentencing; and it abolished parole in the federal system.

Most importantly, the act created the U.S. Sentencing Commission, an independent arm of the federal judiciary that was tasked with drafting the Sentencing Guidelines. The Sentencing Guidelines were meant to reduce sentencing disparity across the country and to increase punishment for certain categories of offenders. The Guidelines became effective in 1987 and were mandatory. They severely restricted the discretion of federal sentencing judges and withstood repeated constitutional challenge up until 2005.[61]

The Guidelines required judges to engage in detailed calculations related to an offender's criminal history and the severity of the current offense to arrive at a "Guidelines range" for the appropriate sentence. The offender's criminal record ("criminal history category") is rated on a scale of one to six. The severity of the offense ("offense level") is rated on a scale of one to forty-three. The criminal history category and offense level for the particular offender are then plotted on a chart to arrive at the appropriate Guidelines sentencing range. A copy of the Guidelines' Sentencing Table is included at the end of this chapter. The mandatory nature of the Guidelines meant that deviation from the prescribed range was carefully circumscribed, and judges had little to no discretion to impose sentences other than what the calculations dictated.

---

[59] Helm, 463 U.S. at 303.

[60] Freeman v. United States, 131 S.Ct. 2685, 2694 (2011).

[61] Mistretta v. United States, 488 U.S. 361 (1989).

All this began to change in 2004, when the Supreme Court decided the case of *Blakely v. Washington.*[62] As described in **Chapter 43,** Blakely was convicted of kidnapping in state court, which subjected him to a sentencing range of 49-53 months under Washington state's sentencing regime. However, the trial judge heard extra testimony at the sentencing hearing which led him to conclude that Blakely's conduct was "deliberately cruel," which allowed the judge to increase the sentence to ninety months. The United States Supreme Court held that it was unconstitutional for a sentencing judge to increase the sentencing range based on facts from the sentencing hearing, because those facts had not been determined by a jury beyond a reasonable doubt.

Like the Washington state sentencing regime, the federal guidelines allow a judge to make factual determinations at the sentencing hearing in order to determine what sentencing range was appropriate for the defendant. Thus, it was only a matter of time before the Supreme Court applied the *Blakely* rule to the federal sentencing guidelines. And sure enough, in 2005 the Court determined that while federal sentencing courts should consult with and be guided by the Sentencing Guidelines, they are no longer mandatory:

> **Example—*United States v. Booker/United States v. Fanfan,* 543 U.S. 220 (2005):** Freddie Booker was charged with drug offenses. The jury heard evidence that Booker had ninety-two and a half grams of crack cocaine stashed in a duffel bag. Upon conviction, Booker was eligible for a statutory minimum sentence of ten years in prison and a statutory maximum sentence of life. However the relevant Guidelines assigned a sentence of 210 to 262 months in prison based on Booker's criminal history and the ninety-two and a half grams of cocaine base that the jury found he possessed. The sentencing judge found by a preponderance of the evidence that Booker actually possessed 566 grams of crack cocaine. This additional quantity of drugs raised Booker's calculated sentencing range under the Guidelines to a term of imprisonment of 360 months to life. The trial court imposed the higher sentence, which was rejected on appeal by the intermediate appellate court.
>
> Duncan Fanfan was convicted of conspiring to distribute more than 500 grams of cocaine. This quantity of drugs exposed Fanfan to a sentence of seventy-eight months in prison under the Sentencing Guidelines. As was true in Booker's case, the trial judge in Fanfan's case also found by a preponderance of the evidence that Fanfan was responsible for two and a half kilos of

[62] 542 U.S. 296 (2004).

cocaine and an additional 261.6 grams of crack cocaine. These additional facts increased Fanfan's sentencing exposure under the Guidelines to 188 to 235 months in prison. However, the sentencing court in Fanfan's case rejected the higher sentence based upon the conclusion that it was inconsistent with the Supreme Court's holdings in *Blakely*—that any fact that enhances the sentence imposed must be found by a jury.

The government in both cases appealed, arguing that the *Blakely* line of cases did not apply to the mandatory Sentencing Guidelines. The Supreme Court eventually accepted and consolidated the cases for review.

Analysis: The *Blakely* decision applies to sentences imposed under the Sentencing Guidelines. To remain consistent with the Constitution, the Guidelines must therefore be considered advisory only.

Any fact that increases a sentence beyond the relevant statutory maximum has to be determined by a jury. Under *Blakely*, the relevant "maximum" is the term of punishment that can be imposed based only on the facts found by the jury. While there can be no doubt that Congress hoped to create a mandatory sentencing scheme when it wrote the Sentencing Act, "that is not a choice that remains open."[63]

The question thus became one of remedy. The problem could have been remedied by striking the Guidelines in their entirety. Or, the problem could have been remedied by striking only those portions of the Guidelines that render them mandatory. The Court chose the latter course; and decided to "sever and excise two specific statutory provisions: the provision that requires sentencing courts to impose a sentence within the applicable Guidelines range . . . and the provision that sets forth [de novo] standards of review on appeal [for sentences outside of the Guidelines range]."[64]

Without the two mandatory provisions, a sentencing judge should take account of the Guidelines, but should also be guided by other considerations. Thus, the Guidelines even as revised will continue to advance Congress' original goal in promoting sentencing consistency.

The instant holding did not alter the Court's previous declaration that certain conduct not considered by the jury may be considered in calculating the appropriate sentencing. However, such non-jury-assessed conduct may be used only to determine the most appropriate sentence within the range authorized by the jury's conclusions.

---

[63] United States v. Booker, 543 U.S. 220, 265 (2005).

[64] Booker, 543 U.S. at 259.

The sentence imposed on Booker was improperly enhanced based upon facts not found by his jury. And the sentencing judge in *Fanfan* appropriately refused to enhance his sentence based upon facts that had not been considered by the jury.

The now "optional" nature of the Guidelines has been of uncertain practical impact. In the years since announcing the discretionary nature of the Guidelines, the Court has repeatedly noted that to encourage nationwide consistency, the Guidelines should nonetheless form the "initial benchmark" and "starting point" for any federal sentence.[65] For this reason, many federal judges continue to sentence within Guidelines' ranges.

But the Guidelines are no longer the only relevant consideration. Thus, since *Booker*, the Court has also powerfully affirmed the autonomy of judges to sentence below or beyond the Guidelines. Moreover, a trial judge's sentencing decision—no matter where it lies in relationship to the Guidelines—is reviewed only for reasonableness. In 2011, affirming a district court's decision to impose a sentence that was only the tiniest fraction of the suggested Guidelines range, the Court wrote, "although a sentencing court must give respectful consideration to the Guidelines, *Booker* permits the court to tailor the sentence in light of other statutory concerns as well."[66] Indeed, even if the district court's decision to sentence outside the Guidelines range is based upon candid disagreement with the Sentencing Commission's policy choices, the Court has said departure might be reasonable:

> **Example—*Kimbrough v. United States*, 552 U.S. 85 (2007):** Derrick Kimbrough pled guilty to four drug charges. The charges involved crack cocaine. Kimbrough's advisory Guidelines sentencing range was 228 to 270 months in prison. The sentencing court, however, found that the Guidelines range was too high, and thus sentenced Kimbrough to 180 months in prison. In sentencing Kimbrough, the judge commented that Kimbrough would have been subject to a range of just 97 to 106 months in prison if the drug involved had been powder cocaine only. (At the time, the Sentencing Guidelines created a wide discrepancy between sentences for possessing crack cocaine and sentences for possessing powder cocaine, such that a defendant possessing five grams of crack cocaine received the same sentencing range as a defendant who possessed 500 grams of powder cocaine). The appellate court reversed the sentence based on its conclusion that the sentencing judge's mere disagreement with the 100-to-1 ratio was insufficient justification for sentencing Kimbrough well below the relevant Guidelines range. The Supreme Court then accepted the case for review.

---

[65] Gall v. United States, 552 U.S. 38 (2007); Kimbrough v. United States, 552 U.S. 85 (2007).

[66] Pepper, 131 S.Ct. at 1241.

Analysis: The sentence imposed was entirely appropriate and should not have been reversed.

Powder cocaine and crack cocaine contain the very same active ingredient. When the Sentencing Guidelines were first enacted, crack was a relatively new drug about which little was known. The 100-to-1 ratio was established based on assumptions about crack cocaine that have since proven to be false. In the years since the Guidelines were enacted, the Sentencing Commission (and others) have called for a significant decrease in the existing crack/cocaine disparity based upon the new data.

There is no question that a reduction in sentencing disparities across the nation was, and remains, a serious consideration in deciding whether variance from the relevant Guidelines range is reasonable. But, a sentencing judge does not abuse her discretion when she concludes that "the crack/powder disparity yields a sentence greater than necessary" to accomplish legitimate sentencing goals. Kimbrough's sentencing judge properly calculated the applicable advisory range, and addressed all of the relevant sentencing considerations. The sentence that the judge imposed was four and a half years lower than the bottom of the advisory range. However, in imposing that sentence it was appropriate for the court to observe "that the 100-to-1 ratio itself created an unwarranted disparity." [67]

The Court has found that the now-advisory nature of the Sentencing Guidelines also impacts the way that appellate courts must review sentences. When evaluating a sentence, the appellate court first should consider whether the sentencing court committed procedural error. Such errors might include miscalculating the relevant Guidelines range; treating the Guidelines as mandatory; or imposing a sentence based on clearly erroneous facts. In the face of such error, remand for resentencing is appropriate. If such procedural errors were not committed, the reviewing court next must consider whether the sentence is substantively reasonable. In assessing the reasonableness of a sentence, the appellate court may presume that a sentence within the Guidelines range was reasonable. However, there is no countervailing presumption of unreasonableness for sentences outside of the range. Consequently, in all cases—whether a sentence falls above, below or within the Guidelines—the reviewing court must use "a deferential abuse-of-discretion standard."[68]

3. Sentencing and Juveniles. Young people can behave in impetuous and self-destructive ways. They do not perceive risk well and are much more subject to the influence of friends than are adults. Most young people eventually outgrow all of these traits. But, even though the bad behavior of most young people is usually

[67] Kimbrough v. United States, 552 U.S. 85 (2007).

[68] Gall v. United States, 552 U.S. 38 (2007).

transitory, until recently youths who engaged in criminal conduct could receive the same criminal sentence that would be imposed upon an adult.

Beginning in 2005, however, the Court issued a series of decisions that completely reshaped the sentencing landscape for juveniles. The Court first struck down death sentences for youthful offenders; then sentences of life without parole for non-homicide offenses; and finally mandatory life sentences for juveniles in any case:

> **Example—*Roper v. Simmons*, 543 U.S. 551 (2005):** When Christopher Simmons was a junior in high school he decided to murder someone. Simmons convinced two friends to join him. The three killed their victim after binding her hands, feet, and face, and throwing her off of a railroad trestle into the Meramec River where she drowned. Simmons was arrested after boasting about the crime.
>
> On appeal and in post-conviction, Simmons challenged the constitutionality of his death sentence. After the Missouri Supreme Court affirmed the sentence, the Supreme Court accepted the case.

Analysis: Sentencing a juvenile to death violates the Eighth Amendment's prohibition against cruel and unusual punishment.

The Eighth Amendment guarantees that convicted persons will not be subjected to excessive punishments. The government's obligation to respect the dignity interests of even the most heinous offenders lies behind the Amendment's proscriptions.

The same reason that young people "are not trusted with the privileges and responsibilities of an adult also explain why their irresponsible conduct is not as morally reprehensible."[69] Thus, as early as 1988, the Court recognized that the execution of offenders under the age of sixteen violates the Eighth Amendment.

A majority of the states have rejected the death penalty for those under the age of 18, as has every nation in the world other than the United States. The Eighth Amendment now requires the rejection of that penalty nationwide. The Eighth Amendment applies with "special force" to the death penalty, which is the harshest punishment that may be imposed. The characteristics of youth are inconsistent with the view that they are deserving of the worst punishment.

Saying that youth are not deserving of the death penalty in no way minimizes the horror of some of their crimes. But, an "unacceptable likelihood exists that the brutality or cold-blooded nature of any particular crime would overpower mitigating arguments based on youth as a matter of course, even where the juvenile

[69] Roper, 543 U.S. at 561.

offender's objective immaturity, vulnerability, and lack of true depravity should require a sentence less severe than death."[70]

When bright line rules are drawn, there is no question that there will be stark similarities to cases close to either side of the line. But eighteen is the age at which society has chosen to mark the difference between children and adults. It is therefore also "the age at which the line for death eligibility ought to rest."

Five years after the Court found that individuals could not be executed for crimes they committed as juveniles, the Court took the next step and determined that individuals also cannot be sentenced to life in prison without the possibility of parole for non-homicide crimes they committed as juveniles:

> **Example— *Graham v. Florida*, 560 U.S. 48 (2010):** When Terrance Graham was sixteen years old, he and three friends tried to rob a local restaurant. When the manager of the store yelled at them, they ran out of the back door. Graham was ultimately apprehended, charged as an adult, and pled guilty. Prior to sentencing, Graham wrote an apology note to the court explaining that the attempted robbery was his "first and last time getting in trouble." Graham assured the court he was going to turn his life around. The judge sentenced Graham to a three-year term of probation.
>
> Despite his pre-sentencing promise, Graham was arrested six months later. He and two older men broke into a home, held the occupants at gunpoint, and ransacked the house looking for valuables. Graham was arrested later that evening after a high speed chase with the police. At the time of the home invasion, Graham was one month shy of his eighteenth birthday.
>
> A probation revocation hearing was held, at which the court found Graham violated his earlier term of probation both by engaging in the high speed chase with police and by participating in the home invasion. The minimum sentence that Graham could receive for the violation was a five-year term of imprisonment. The maximum he could receive was life. Finding that "there is nothing that we can do for you," the judge sentenced Graham to life imprisonment. The parole system had been abolished in Florida, and so Graham's only hope of not dying in prison was a grant of executive clemency.

[70] Id. at 573.

Graham appealed the sentence, arguing that it violated the Eighth Amendment's proscription against cruel and unusual punishment. The Supreme Court ultimately accepted the case for review.

Analysis: Imposing a sentence of life without the possibility of parole ("LWOP") on an individual for a non-homicide offense they committed as a juvenile constitutes cruel and unusual punishment.

The Eighth Amendment's ban on cruel punishment "necessarily embodies a moral judgment. The standard itself remains the same, but its applicability must change as the basic mores of society change."[71] The Eighth Amendment's proportionality principle prohibits those punishments that are grossly disproportionate to the crime. As the prosecutor noted, the Court had concluded that a particular sentence was grossly disproportionate on only three prior occasions. On each of those occasions, the Court was evaluating the constitutionality of a death sentence—concluding that a death sentence was cruel and unusual for any non-homicide case, for youthful offenders, and for offenders with limited intellectual functioning.

Graham was not sentenced to death, but to an unspecified term of years. However, given the severity of this punishment and what is now known about juvenile brain development, the Court concluded that the "grossly disproportionate" doctrine should be applied beyond the capital sentencing context.

Though an overwhelming majority of states technically allow the imposition of juvenile LWOP sentences ("JLWOP"), just eleven jurisdictions have actually imposed such sentences. Moreover, of the hundreds of thousands of juveniles who are arrested and charged with felony offenses each year, only the tiniest fraction are sentenced to JLWOP. In the international arena, the United States stood alone in allowing JLWOP sentences for non-homicide offenses.

Juveniles are not as fully formed as adults. Their "lessened culpability [means they] are less deserving of the most severe punishments." Life without parole is the second most severe sentence that can be imposed in this country. For a sixteen-year old it is a particularly harsh sentence. "A 16-year-old and a 75-year-old each sentenced to life without parole receive the same punishment in name only."[72]

Sentencing youthful offenders to LWOP also cannot be justified as specifically advancing any penological goals. Retribution is a valid reason to impose punishment. But critical to retribution is the notion that the punishment should be calibrated to the moral culpability of the offender. Deterrence also cannot sufficiently justify such sentences because juveniles do not generally engage in any meaningful cost-benefit analysis prior to committing crimes. Incapacitation

---

[71] Graham v. Florida, 560 U.S. 48, 58 (2010).

[72] Graham, 560 U.S. at 71.

also cannot justify JLWOP sentences because "incorrigibility is inconsistent with youth." There is no question that some juveniles pose an immediate risk. And there is no question that some of these same juveniles will continue to present a danger to the community well into the future. But identifying at the outset which are in the latter group is impossible. Finally, rehabilitation cannot justify JLWOP sentences because "the penalty foreswears altogether the rehabilitative goal."[73]

"A State is not required to guarantee eventual freedom to a juvenile offender convicted of a nonhomicide crime. What the State must do, however, is give defendants like Graham some meaningful opportunity to obtain release based on demonstrated maturity and rehabilitation."[74]

In the review of *Graham*, readers should recognize that a different form of proportionality review is at issue in that case than what we considered in Section C.1, above. In Section C.1, we considered proportionality analysis examining a particular sentence imposed on a particular offender. That form of proportionality review, as explained, is conducted in two steps—first considering the seriousness of the offense and the severity of the punishment, and then turning to consider other sentences that have been imposed.

Unlike those earlier cases, the challenge in *Graham* was a categorical one. The litigants in *Graham* did not complain that Graham's specific sentence was too harsh for the precise crime he committed. Rather in *Graham*, the contention was that a sentence of life without the possibility of parole was unconstitutional if imposed on any juvenile in a non-homicide case. The form of proportionality review conducted in such categorical cases does not employ the two-step approach described in Section C.1, but instead considers "objective indicia of national consensus." These objective indicia include the number of jurisdictions that currently allow the challenged practice and the actual sentencing practices in those jurisdictions that allow the challenged practice. In addition, courts must make an assessment more like the traditional proportionality review, balancing the seriousness of the offense with the severity of punishment. However, this assessment is made across an entire class of offenders. Furthermore, with a categorical challenge, the reviewing court must consider whether the challenged sentencing practice is justified by the traditional theories of punishment discussed in the opening of this chapter. Finally, while international practices are not dispositive, the Court has also said they are "not irrelevant."[75]

In other words, *Roper* and *Graham* required categorical bans on two particular types of sentences—death sentences for all juvenile offenders, and life without parole sentences for non-homicide juvenile offenders—because of a mismatch be-

---

73 Id. at 73.

74 Id.

75 Graham, 560 U.S. at 80.

tween the characteristics of certain classes of offenders and the particular forms of severe punishments at issue. Meanwhile, in a separate strand of analysis decided decades before the *Roper* and *Graham* decisions, the Court had held that mandatory death sentences violate the Eighth Amendment.[76] In its most recent case involving juveniles, the Supreme Court knit these two lines of cases together to hold that, even in homicide cases, juveniles may not be sentenced to a mandatory term of life in prison without the possibility of parole:

> **Example—*Miller v. Alabama*, 132 S.Ct. 2455 (2012):** Evan Miller and Kuntrell Jackson were each 14-years old at the time they participated separately in the murder of two different victims. Miller's victim was knocked unconscious during a botched robbery attempt, and then died of asphyxiation after Miller and his co-defendant burned the victim's trailer in an effort to hide evidence of the crime. Jackson's victim was killed after he and two friends decided to rob a video store. When the owner of the store resisted Jackson's friend's demands for money, the friend shot and killed him. Both Miller and Jackson were sentenced to life without the possibility of parole pursuant to mandatory sentencing schemes in Alabama and Arkansas, respectively.
>
> The two cases worked their way separate to the Supreme Court for review, and were eventually consolidated for argument. On appeal, both boys challenged the constitutionality of their life sentences under the Eighth Amendment.

Analysis: The imposition of a mandatory life sentence without the possibility of parole upon a juvenile offender violates the Eighth Amendment's prohibition against cruel and unusual punishment.

As the Court found in *Roper* and *Graham*, children are materially different from adults for sentencing purposes. They are more impulsive, they are more susceptible to peer and family pressures; and they are less likely to be irredeemable. These characteristics make children less deserving of the harshest punishments. Even though *Roper* measured these characteristic against the severity of the death penalty and *Graham* compared them against the reduced seriousness of nonhomicide offenses, the observations about the characteristics standing alone must inform the assessment of Miller and Jackson's sentences.

The mandatory sentences at issue in this case prevented the sentencing judges from considering any of the mitigating characteristics of Miller and Jackson's youth. "Under these schemes, every juvenile will receive the same sentence as every other . . . And still worse, each juvenile (including these two fourteen-year-

[76] Woodson v. North Carolina, 428 U.S. 280 (1976).

olds) will receive the same sentence as the vast majority of adults committing similar homicide offenses—but really, as *Graham* noted, a greater sentence than those adults will serve."[77]

It may be the case that both boys deserve the severest punishment possible for their crimes. But in assessing what that punishment should be, the sentencing court should be able to evaluate all of the relevant circumstances—including the mitigating evidence of youth—before deciding that life without the possibility of parole is the most fitting sentence. For this reason, mandatory sentences of life without the possibility of parole violate the Eighth Amendment when imposed for conduct committed by a juvenile offender.

As the above discussion of *Roper*, *Graham*, and *Miller* makes clear the Court has gradually developed the law in the area of juvenile sentencing. *Roper* abolished the death penalty for juvenile murders. *Graham* prohibited non-paroleable life sentences for juveniles convicted of non-homicide crimes. And, *Miller* struck down mandatory life sentences for all juvenile offenders. The *Miller* Court left open a question that is likely to be the next step in the Court's *Roper*/*Graham*/*Miller* line of cases. Specifically, the Court declined to decide whether the Eighth Amendment prohibits a non-mandatory sentence of life without the possibility of parole if a juvenile has participated in a homicide offense. Some jurisdictions have already taken the plunge and prohibited such sentences.[78] Whether the Supreme Court will follow suit remains to be seen.

---

[77] Miller v. Alabama, 132 S.Ct. 2455, 2467-68 (2012).

[78] See, e.g., Diatchenko v. Dist. Atty., 466 Mass. 655 (2013).

Quick Summary

Sentencing judges enjoy extremely broad discretion in fashioning an appropriate punishment for one convicted of an offense. But this discretion is subject to a number of limitations.

The Constitution imposes limits on sentencing through the First, Sixth, and Eighth Amendments, as well as through the Ex Post Facto Clause, the Due Process Clause, and the Equal Protection Clause.

In addition to constitutional limits, a sentencing court's discretion is also limited by statute and by rule. The amount of authorized punishment is decided in the first instance by the legislature. Within the authorized range, the judge or (as is often the case in capital offenses) the sentencing jury will then select the sentence that is appropriate for the particular offender. The Federal Rules of Criminal Procedure provide guides for sentencing procedures, including things like presentence reports.

Another significant source of constraint upon the sentencing judge's discretion in federal courts and many state courts is provided by sentencing guidelines. Though once mandatory, these guidelines are now advisory only. Nonetheless, they continue to form the basis for the vast majority of sentences imposed in the federal system and in many state systems.

A sentence can either be determinate or indeterminate. Determinate sentences impose punishment for a fixed period, while indeterminate sentences impose a range of appropriate punishment.

The overwhelming majority of sentences imposed at both the state and federal level are the result of guilty pleas. The extent to which a plea of guilty can guarantee imposition of particular punishment is entirely dependent upon the terms of the agreement.

The United States has the largest prison population in the world. In an era of budget shortfalls and severe prison overcrowding, many states and the federal government are looking for cheaper alternatives to incarceration. It will take some time to see if these measures are effective in reducing mass incarceration.

On direct appeal, a federal appellate court reviews a sentence only for reasonableness. If the sentence imposed is within the advisory Guidelines range, the appellate court may (but is not required) to presume it to be reasonable. But, the presumption of reasonableness applies only to appellate courts. A sentencing judge may not impose a Guidelines sentence based on nothing more than a presumption that it is the appropriate one. Instead, the judge must consider all relevant information before deciding the appropriate sentence in a case.[79]

In recent years, the Supreme Court has been developing the sentencing law regarding juveniles. The Court has held that juvenile offenders cannot be sentenced to death nor to life in prison without parole (for non-homicide offenses), and they cannot receive a mandatory life sentence without the possibility of parole for any crime. These decisions have been based on the science of brain development in juveniles and an examination of evolving standards of decency, as exemplified by laws at the state level.

On the following page is a reproduction of the Sentencing Table for the United States Sentencing Guidelines. The Guidelines Manual sets out a complicated series of calculations for any individual crime: a given crime is assigned a "Base Offense Level" and then that level can be increased if certain factors are present in the defendant's case, such as if the defendant used a firearm or the victim was a child. The offense level can also be decreased if there were mitigating circumstances or if the defendant cooperates with the prosecutor. However, to give you some general idea of how crimes are graded, here are some sample base offense levels: theft of less than $5,000 of property has a base offense level of six; aggravated assault that causes serious bodily injury has a base offense level of nineteen; and possession of a kilogram of cocaine with intent to sell would have a base offense level of twenty-six.

The "Criminal History Category" places defendants in categories based on their prior convictions: for example, a defendant with one prior felony would usually be in Criminal History Category II, while a defendant with three prior felonies would usually be in Criminal History Category IV. Again, these numbers may need to be adjusted for specific types of prior convictions, such as if the prior crime involved violence or was committed while the defendant was on probation.

[79] Nelson v. United States, 555 U.S. 350 (2009).

U.S. SENTENCING GUIDELINES SENTENCING TABLE
(in months of imprisonment)

Criminal History Category (Criminal History Points)

	Offense Level	I (0 or 1)	II (2 or 3)	III (4, 5, 6)	IV (7, 8, 9)	V (10, 11, 12)	VI (13 or more)
Zone A	1	0-6	0-6	0-6	0-6	0-6	0-6
	2	0-6	0-6	0-6	0-6	0-6	1-7
	3	0-6	0-6	0-6	0-6	2-8	3-9
	4	0-6	0-6	0-6	2-8	4-10	6-12
	5	0-6	0-6	1-7	4-10	6-12	9-15
	6	0-6	1-7	2-8	6-12	9-15	12-18
	7	0-6	2-8	4-10	8-14	12-18	15-21
	8	0-6	4-10	6-12	10-16	15-21	18-24
Zone B	9	4-10	6-12	8-14	12-18	18-24	21-27
	10	6-12	8-14	10-16	15-21	21-27	24-30
Zone C	11	8-14	10-16	12-18	18-24	24-30	27-33
	12	10-16	12-18	15-21	21-27	27-33	30-37
Zone D	13	12-18	15-21	18-24	24-30	30-37	33-41
	14	15-21	18-24	21-27	27-33	33-41	37-46
	15	18-24	21-27	24-30	30-37	37-46	41-51
	16	21-27	24-30	27-33	33-41	41-51	46-57
	17	24-30	27-33	30-37	37-46	46-57	51-63
	18	27-33	30-37	33-41	41-51	51-63	57-71
	19	30-37	33-41	37-46	46-57	57-71	63-78
	20	33-41	37-46	41-51	51-63	63-78	70-87
	21	37-46	41-51	46-57	57-71	70-87	77-96
	22	41-51	46-57	51-63	63-78	77-96	84-105
	23	46-57	51-63	57-71	70-87	84-105	92-115
	24	51-63	57-71	63-78	77-96	92-115	100-125
	25	57-71	63-78	70-87	84-105	100-125	110-137
	26	63-78	70-87	78-97	92-115	110-137	120-150
Zone D	27	70-87	78-97	87-108	100-125	120-150	130-162
	28	78-97	87-108	97-121	110-137	130-162	140-175
	29	87-108	97-121	108-135	121-151	140-175	151-188
	30	97-121	108-135	121-151	135-168	151-188	168-210
	31	108-135	121-151	135-168	151-188	168-210	188-235
	32	121-151	135-168	151-188	168-210	188-235	210-262
	33	135-168	151-188	168-210	188-235	210-262	235-293
	34	151-188	168-210	188-235	210-262	235-293	262-327
	35	168-210	188-235	210-262	235-293	262-327	292-365
	36	188-235	210-262	235-293	262-327	292-365	324-405
	37	210-262	235-293	262-327	292-365	324-405	360-life
	38	235-293	262-327	292-365	324-405	360-life	360-life
	39	262-327	292-365	324-405	360-life	360-life	360-life
	40	292-365	324-405	360-life	360-life	360-life	360-life
	41	324-405	360-life	360-life	360-life	360-life	360-life
	42	360-life	360-life	360-life	360-life	360-life	360-life
	43	life	life	life	life	life	life

Commentary to Sentencing Table

Application Notes: 1. The Offense Level (1-43) forms the vertical axis of the Sentencing Table. The Criminal History Category (I-VI) forms the horizontal axis.

Review Questions

1. Race and the Death Penalty. Greg Mason and three other men set out to rob a store at gunpoint. They forced all the customers to lie on the ground, bound all of the employees, and stole all the money from the cash register. During the robbery, a police officer responded to a silent alarm that had been triggered. The officer entered the front of the store and was shot dead. Evidence indicated that the bullets came from Mason's gun, and that Mason later admitted the shooting to others. Mason was arrested and ultimately convicted of two counts of robbery and one count of murder in Georgia. Mason was black and the police officer that he killed was white.

At the sentencing hearing, the jury found two aggravated circumstances: the murder was committed during the course of an armed robbery, and the victim was a police officer engaged in the performance of his duties. Mason offered no mitigating circumstances and Mason was sentenced to death.

After his appeals were exhausted in state court, Mason filed a habeas petition in federal court, arguing that the Georgia capital sentencing process was administered in a racially discriminatory manner. As evidence, Mason cited a report that studied 2,000 murder cases in Georgia over the past ten years. The study showed that the death penalty was imposed in 22% of the cases in which the defendant was black and the victim white, but only 3% of the cases in which the defendant was white and the victim was black. Mason argued that this study proved that his sentence violated the Eighth Amendment's ban on cruel and unusual punishment. What factors should the reviewing court consider in evaluating Mason's claim?

2. In Prison Forever. Derek Surrey was convicted in Wyoming state court of felony grand larceny after he stole $600 of merchandise from his employer. He had two prior convictions, both for armed robbery, although the most recent was fifteen years earlier. Surrey's pre-sentence report noted that he had stayed out of trouble for fifteen years before his most recent crime, and that for that time he had been an upstanding member of his community, having bought a house, started a family, and attended community college. After his crime, Surrey felt immediate remorse, and the day after his theft, he returned the merchandise and confessed to his employer. The pre-sentence report also noted that his employer was willing to re-hire him and regretted the fact that she brought charges against him. He told the judge that he was willing to pay a large fine or undertake any amount of community service.

Under Wyoming law, a third felony conviction carries a mandatory sentence of life in prison without parole. At the sentencing hearing, the trial judge said on the record that "I wish I could do more for you—in my opinion you don't deserve a day in jail for this and you could give so much more back to your community with a non-incarcerative sentence. But my hands are tied." The judge then sentenced Surrey to life in prison without the possibility of parole. The case was appealed all the way to the Wyoming Supreme Court, which upheld the sentence.

You are Surrey's defense attorney bringing a habeas claim in federal court to attack Surrey's sentence as unconstitutional. What facts would you want to know before making your claim? What arguments would you make in your brief? What chance do you have of prevailing?

3. Four Defendants, Four Sentences. On one fateful day, four different defendants were sentenced in the federal district courthouse:

A. Defendant Adam had been convicted of kidnapping. Given Adam's prior criminal history, his sentencing range should have been 151-188 months. However, there was a clerical error in the pre-sentence report, and the report stated that his sentencing range was between 188-235 months. After reading the report, the judge sentenced Adam to 188 months in prison.

B. Defendant Brenda had been convicted of fraud after operating a pyramid scheme disguised as an investment opportunity. This crime has a base offense level of six, which gave Brenda (a first-time offender) a base sentencing range of 0-6 months. However, the offense level (and thus the range of sentences) increases depending on the amount of loss suffered by the victims. The charge that Brenda pled guilty to did not specify the amount of loss to her victims.

The probation officer investigated the case for the pre-sentence report and calculated that the losses to the victims were over $120,000. This fact added ten points to her base offense level to make it sixteen, which gave her a sentencing range of 21-27 months. The sentencing judge read the pre-sentence report, heard arguments from the prosecutor and defense attorney, and then sentenced Brenda to 24 months in prison.

C. Defendant Carl had been convicted of selling heroin. The pre-sentence report accurately stated that Carl's sentencing range was 121-151 months. There was no new information in the pre-sentence report, nor was there any new information provided at the sentencing hearing. However, the judge said on the record: "Carl, this is not your lucky day. I have heard some people say that selling drugs is a victimless crime. Well, I have never understood that argument. Drugs—and especially heroin—ruin people's lives. I think the only way to win the drug war is to get tough on people like you." The judge then sentenced Carl to 180 months in prison.

D. Defendant Dino had been convicted of unlawfully entering the United States. The probation officer investigated the case and found a number of specific offense characteristics that increased Dino's offense level. Based on this increased offense level, Dino's sentencing range was

24-30 months. At the sentencing hearing, the judge said: "My understanding is that for immigration crimes, the Sentencing Guidelines are mandatory. So I have no choice but to sentence you within this range." The judge gave Dino a 24-month sentence.

Each of these defendants is now challenging the sentence imposed on appeal. Assume each of the sentences that was imposed was below the statutory maximum for that crime. What should the appellate court do in each case?

FROM THE COURTROOM

UNITED STATES v. BOOKER

UNITED STATES v. FANFAN

Supreme Court of the United States, 2005
543 U.S. 220

[Justice Stevens delivered the opinion of the Court in part].

[Justice Breyer delivered the opinion of the Court in part]

[The separate dissenting opinions of Justices BREYER, STEVENS, SCALIA, and THOMAS have been omitted].

Justice STEVENS delivered the opinion of the Court in part.

The question presented in each of these cases is whether an application of the Federal Sentencing Guidelines violated the Sixth Amendment. In each case, the courts below held that binding rules set forth in the Guidelines limited the severity of the sentence that the judge could lawfully impose on the defendant based on the facts found by the jury at his trial. In both cases the courts rejected, on the basis of our decision in *Blakely v. Washington*, 542 U.S. 296 (2004), the Government's recommended application of the Sentencing Guidelines because the proposed sentences were based on additional facts that the sentencing judge found by a preponderance of the evidence. We hold that both courts correctly concluded that the Sixth Amendment as construed in *Blakely* does apply to the Sentencing Guidelines. In a separate opinion authored by Justice Breyer, the Court concludes that in light of this holding, two provisions of the Sentencing Reform Act of 1984(SRA) that have the effect of making the Guidelines mandatory must be invalidated in order to allow the statute to operate in a manner consistent with congressional intent.

I

Respondent Booker was charged with possession with intent to distribute at least 50 grams of cocaine base (crack). Having heard evidence that he had 92.5 grams in his duffel bag, the jury found him guilty of violating 21 U.S.C. § 841(a)(1). That statute prescribes a minimum sentence of 10 years in prison and a maximum sentence of life for that offense.

Based upon Booker's criminal history and the quantity of drugs found by the jury, the Sentencing Guidelines required the District Court Judge to select a "base" sentence of not less than 210 nor more than 262 months in prison. The judge, however, held a post-trial sentencing proceeding and concluded by a preponderance of the evidence that Booker had possessed an additional 566 grams of crack and that he was guilty of obstructing justice. Those findings mandated that the judge select a sentence between 360 months and life imprisonment; the judge imposed a sentence at the low end of the range. Thus, instead of the sentence of 21 years and 10 months that the judge could have imposed on the basis of the facts proved to the jury beyond a reasonable doubt, Booker received a 30–year sentence.

Over the dissent of Judge Easterbrook, the Court of Appeals for the Seventh Circuit held that this application of the Sentencing Guidelines conflicted with our holding in *Apprendi v. New Jersey*, 530 U.S. 466 (2000), that "[o]ther than the fact of a prior conviction, any fact that increases the penalty for a crime beyond the prescribed statutory maximum must be submitted to a jury, and proved beyond a reasonable doubt." The majority relied on our holding in *Blakely*, that "the 'statutory maximum' for *Apprendi* purposes is the maximum sentence a judge may impose solely on the basis of the facts reflected in the jury verdict or admitted by the defendant." The court held that the sentence violated the Sixth Amendment, and remanded with instructions to the District Court either to sentence respondent within the sentencing range supported by the jury's findings or to hold a separate sentencing hearing before a jury.

Respondent Fanfan was charged with conspiracy to distribute and to possess with intent to distribute at least 500 grams of cocaine in violation of 21 U.S.C. §§ 846, 841(a)(1), and 841(b)(1)(B)(ii). He was convicted by the jury after it answered "Yes" to the question "Was the amount of cocaine 500 or more grams?" Under the Guidelines, without additional findings of fact, the maximum sentence authorized by the jury verdict was imprisonment for 78 months.

A few days after our decision in *Blakely*, the trial judge conducted a sentencing hearing at which he found additional facts that, under the Guidelines, would have authorized a sentence in the 188–to–235–month range. Specifically, he found that respondent Fanfan was responsible for 2.5 kilograms of cocaine powder, and 261.6 grams of crack. He also concluded that respondent had been an organizer, leader, manager, or supervisor in the criminal activity. Both findings were made by a preponderance of the evidence. Under the Guidelines, these additional findings would have required an enhanced sentence of 15 or 16 years instead of the 5 or 6 years authorized by the jury verdict alone. Relying not only on the majority opinion in *Blakely*, but also on the categorical statements in the dissenting opinions and in the Solicitor General's brief in *Blakely*, the judge concluded that he could not follow the particular provisions of the Sentencing Guidelines "which involve drug quantity and role enhancement." Expressly refusing to make "any blanket decision about the federal guidelines," he followed the provisions of the Guidelines that did not implicate the Sixth Amendment by imposing a sentence on respondent "based solely upon the jury verdict in this case."

Following the denial of its motion to correct the sentence in Fanfan's case, the Government filed a notice of appeal in the Court of Appeals for the First Circuit, and a petition in this Court for a writ of certiorari before judgment. Because of the importance of the questions presented, we granted that petition, as well as a similar petition filed by the Government in Booker's case. In both petitions, the Government asks us to determine whether our *Apprendi* line of cases applies to the Sentencing Guidelines, and if so, what portions of the Guidelines remain in effect.

In this opinion, we explain why we agree with the lower courts' answer to the first question. In a separate opinion for the Court, Justice Breyer explains the Court's answer to the second question.

II

It has been settled throughout our history that the Constitution protects every criminal defendant "against conviction except upon proof beyond a reasonable doubt of every fact necessary to constitute the crime with which he is charged." It is equally clear that the "Constitution gives a criminal defendant the right to demand that a jury find him guilty of all the elements of the crime with which he is charged." These basic precepts, firmly rooted in the common law, have provided the basis for recent decisions interpreting modern criminal statutes and sentencing procedures.

. . .

In *Apprendi v. New Jersey*, the defendant pleaded guilty to second-degree possession of a firearm for an unlawful purpose, which carried a prison term of 5–to–10 years. Thereafter, the trial court found that his conduct had violated New Jersey's "hate crime" law because it was racially motivated, and imposed a 12–year sentence. This Court set aside the enhanced sentence. We held: "Other than the fact of a prior conviction, any fact that increases the penalty for a crime beyond the prescribed statutory maximum must be submitted to a jury, and proved beyond a reasonable doubt."

The fact that New Jersey labeled the hate crime a "sentence enhancement" rather than a separate criminal act was irrelevant for constitutional purposes. As a matter of simple justice, it seemed obvious that the procedural safeguards designed to protect Apprendi from punishment for the possession of a firearm should apply equally to his violation of the hate crime statute. Merely using the label "sentence enhancement" to describe the latter did not provide a principled basis for treating the two crimes differently.

In *Ring v. Arizona*, we reaffirmed our conclusion that the characterization of critical facts is constitutionally irrelevant. There, we held that it was impermissible for "the trial judge, sitting alone" to determine the presence or absence of the aggravating factors required by Arizona law for imposition of the death penalty. "If a State makes an increase in a defendant's authorized punishment contingent on the finding of a fact, that fact—no matter how the State labels it—must be found by a jury beyond a reasonable doubt." Our opinion made it clear that ultimately, while the procedural error in Ring's case might have been harmless because the necessary finding was implicit in the jury's guilty verdict, "the characterization of a fact or circumstance as an 'element' or a 'sentencing factor' is not determinative of the question 'who decides,' judge or jury."

In *Blakely v. Washington*, we dealt with a determinate sentencing scheme similar to the Federal Sentencing Guidelines. There the defendant pleaded guilty to kidnaping, a class B felony punishable by a term of not more than 10 years. Other provisions of Washington law, comparable to the Federal Sentencing Guidelines, mandated a "standard" sentence of 49–to–53 months, unless the judge found aggravating facts justifying an exceptional sentence. Although the prosecutor recommended a sentence in the standard range, the judge found that the defendant had acted with " 'deliberate cruelty' " and sentenced him to 90 months.

For reasons explained in . . . *Apprendi*, and *Ring*, the requirements of the Sixth Amendment were clear. The application of Washington's sentencing scheme violated the defendant's right to have the jury find the existence of " 'any particular fact' " that the law makes essential to his punishment. That right is implicated whenever a judge seeks to impose a sentence that is not solely based on "facts reflected in the jury verdict or admitted by the defendant." We rejected the State's argument that the jury verdict was sufficient to authorize a sentence within the general 10–year sentence for class B felonies, noting that under Washington law, the judge was required to find additional facts in order to impose the greater 90–month sentence. Our precedents, we explained, make clear "that the 'statutory maximum' for *Apprendi* purposes is the maximum sentence a judge may impose solely on the basis of the facts reflected in the jury verdict or admitted by the defendant." The determination that the defendant acted with deliberate cruelty, like the determination in *Apprendi* that the defendant acted with racial malice, increased the sentence that the defendant could have otherwise received. Since this fact was found by a judge using a preponderance of the evidence standard, the sentence violated *Blakely's* Sixth Amendment rights.

As the dissenting opinions in *Blakely* recognized, there is no distinction of constitutional significance between the Federal Sentencing Guidelines and the Washington procedures at issue in that case. This conclusion rests on the premise, common to both systems, that the relevant sentencing rules are mandatory and impose binding requirements on all sentencing judges.

If the Guidelines as currently written could be read as merely advisory provisions that recommended, rather than required, the selection of particular sentences in response to differing sets of facts, their use would not implicate the Sixth Amendment. We have never doubted the authority of a judge to exercise broad discretion in imposing a sentence within a statutory range. Indeed, everyone agrees that the constitutional issues presented by these cases would have been avoided entirely if Congress had omitted from the SRA the provisions that make the Guidelines binding on district judges; it is that circumstance that makes the Court's answer to the second question presented possible. For when a trial judge exercises his discretion to select a specific sentence within a defined range, the defendant has no right to a jury determination of the facts that the judge deems relevant.

The Guidelines as written, however, are not advisory; they are mandatory and binding on all judges. While subsection a) of § 3553 of the sentencing statute lists the Sentencing Guidelines as one factor to be considered in imposing a sentence, subsection (b) directs that the court "shall impose a sentence of the kind, and within the range" established by the Guidelines, subject to departures in specific, limited cases. Because they are binding on judges, we have consistently held that the Guidelines have the force and effect of laws.

The availability of a departure in specified circumstances does not avoid the constitutional issue, just as it did not in *Blakely* itself. The Guidelines permit departures from the prescribed sentencing range in cases in which the judge "finds that there exists an aggravating or mitigating circumstance of a kind, or to a degree, not adequately taken into consideration by the Sentencing Commission in formulating the guidelines that should result in a sentence different from that described." At first glance, one might believe that the ability of a district judge to depart from the Guidelines means that she is bound only by the statutory maximum. Were this the case, there would be no *Apprendi* problem. Importantly, however, departures are not available in every case, and in fact are unavailable in most. In most cases, as a matter of law, the Commission will have adequately taken all relevant factors into account, and no departure will be legally permissible. In those instances, the judge is bound to impose a sentence within the Guidelines range. It was for this reason that we rejected a similar argument in *Blakely*, holding that although the Washington statute allowed the judge to impose a sentence outside the sentencing range for " 'substantial and compelling reasons,' " that exception was not available for Blakely himself. The sentencing judge would have been reversed had he invoked the departure section to justify the sentence.

Booker's case illustrates the mandatory nature of the Guidelines. The jury convicted him of possessing at least 50 grams of crack in violation of 21 U.S.C. § 841(b)(1)(A)(iii) based on evidence that he had 92.5 grams of crack in his duffel bag. Under these facts, the Guidelines specified an offense level of 32, which, given the defendant's criminal history category, authorized a sentence of 210–to–262 months. Booker's is a run-of-the-mill drug case, and does not present any factors that were inadequately considered by the Commission. The sentencing judge would therefore have been reversed had he not imposed a sentence within the level 32 Guidelines range.

Booker's actual sentence, however, was 360 months, almost 10 years longer than the Guidelines range supported by the jury verdict alone. To reach this sentence, the judge found facts beyond those found by the jury: namely, that Booker possessed 566 grams of crack in addition to the 92.5 grams in his duffel bag. The jury never heard any evidence of the additional drug quantity, and the judge found it true by a preponderance of the evidence. Thus, just as in *Blakely*, "the jury's verdict alone does not authorize the sentence. The judge acquires that authority only upon finding some additional fact." There is no relevant distinction between the sentence imposed pursuant to the Washington statutes in *Blakely* and the sentences imposed pursuant to the Federal Sentencing Guidelines in these cases.

In his dissent, Justice Breyer argues on historical grounds that the Guidelines scheme is constitutional across the board. He points to traditional judicial authority to increase sentences to take account of any unusual blameworthiness in the manner employed in committing a crime, an authority that the Guidelines require to be exercised consistently throughout the system. This tradition, however, does not provide a sound guide to enforcement of the Sixth Amendment's guarantee of a jury trial in today's world.

It is quite true that once determinate sentencing had fallen from favor, American judges commonly determined facts justifying a choice of a heavier sentence on account of the manner in which particular defendants acted. In 1986, however, our own cases first recognized a new trend in the legislative regulation of sentencing when we considered the significance of facts selected by legislatures that not only authorized, or even mandated, heavier sentences than would otherwise have been imposed, but increased the range of sentences possible for the underlying crime. Provisions for such enhancements of the permissible sentencing range reflected growing and wholly justified legislative concern about the proliferation and variety of drug crimes and their frequent identification with firearms offenses.

The effect of the increasing emphasis on facts that enhanced sentencing ranges, however, was to increase the judge's power and diminish that of the jury. It became the judge, not the jury, who determined the upper limits of sentencing, and the facts determined were not required to be raised before trial or proved by more than a preponderance.

As the enhancements became greater, the jury's finding of the underlying crime became less significant. And the enhancements became very serious indeed.

As it thus became clear that sentencing was no longer taking place in the tradition that Justice Breyer invokes, the Court was faced with the issue of preserving an ancient guarantee under a new set of circumstances. The new sentencing practice forced the Court to address the question how the right of jury trial could be preserved, in a meaningful way guaranteeing that the jury would still stand between the individual and the power of the government under the new sentencing regime. And it is the new circumstances, not a tradition or practice that the new circumstances have superseded, that have led us to the answer first considered in *Jones* and developed in *Apprendi* and subsequent cases culminating with this one. It is an answer not motivated by Sixth Amendment formalism, but by the need to preserve Sixth Amendment substance.

. . .

IV

All of the foregoing supports our conclusion that our holding in *Blakely* applies to the Sentencing Guidelines. We recognize, as we did in *Jones*, *Apprendi*, and *Blakely*, that in some cases jury factfinding may impair the most expedient and efficient sentencing of defendants. But the interest in fairness and reliability protected by the right to a jury trial—a common-law right that defendants enjoyed for centuries and that is now enshrined in the Sixth Amendment—has always outweighed the interest in concluding trials swiftly. As Blackstone put it:

"[H]owever convenient these [new methods of trial] may appear at first, (as doubtless all arbitrary powers, well executed, are the most convenient) yet let it be again remembered, that delays, and little inconveniences in the forms of justice, are the price that all free nations must pay for their liberty in more substantial matters; that these inroads upon this sacred bulwark of the nation are fundamentally opposite to the spirit of our constitution; and that, though begun in trifles, the precedent may gradually increase and spread, to the utter disuse of juries in questions of the most momentous concerns."

Accordingly, we reaffirm our holding in *Apprendi*: Any fact (other than a prior conviction) which is necessary to support a sentence exceeding the maximum authorized by the facts established by a plea of guilty or a jury verdict must be admitted by the defendant or proved to a jury beyond a reasonable doubt.

Justice Breyer delivered the opinion of the Court in part.

The first question that the Government has presented in these cases is the following:

"Whether the Sixth Amendment is violated by the imposition of an enhanced sentence under the United States Sentencing Guidelines based on the sentencing judge's determination of a fact (other than a prior conviction) that was not found by the jury or admitted by the defendant."

The Court, in an opinion by Justice Stevens, answers this question in the affirmative. Applying its decisions in *Apprendi v. New Jersey*, and *Blakely v. Washington*, to the Federal Sentencing Guidelines, the Court holds that, in the circumstances mentioned, the Sixth Amendment requires juries, not judges, to find facts relevant to sentencing.

We here turn to the second question presented, a question that concerns the remedy. We must decide whether or to what extent, "as a matter of severability analysis," the Guidelines "as a whole" are "inapplicable ... such that the sentencing court must exercise its discretion to sentence the defendant within the maximum and minimum set by statute for the offense of conviction."

We answer the question of remedy by finding the provision of the federal sentencing statute that makes the Guidelines mandatory, 18 U.S.C. § 3553(b)(1) (Supp. IV), incompatible with today's constitutional holding. We conclude that this provision must be severed and excised, as must one other statutory section, § 3742(e) (2000 ed. and Supp. IV), which depends upon the Guidelines' mandatory nature. So modified, the federal sentencing statute, makes the Guidelines effectively advisory. It requires a sentencing court to consider Guidelines ranges, but it permits the court to tailor the sentence in light of other statutory concerns as well.

I

We answer the remedial question by looking to legislative intent. We seek to determine what "Congress would have intended" in light of the Court's constitutional holding. In this instance, we must determine which of the two following remedial approaches is the more compatible with the Legislature's intent as embodied in the 1984 Sentencing Act.

One approach, that of Justice Stevens's dissent, would retain the Sentencing Act (and the Guidelines) as written, but would engraft onto the existing system today's Sixth Amendment "jury trial" requirement. The addition would change the Guidelines by preventing the sentencing court from increasing a sentence on the basis of a fact that the jury did not find (or that the offender did not admit).

The other approach, which we now adopt, would (through severance and excision of two provisions) make the Guidelines system advisory while maintaining a strong connection between the sentence imposed and the offender's real conduct—a connection important to the increased uniformity of sentencing that Congress intended its Guidelines system to achieve.

Both approaches would significantly alter the system that Congress designed. But today's constitutional holding means that it is no longer possible to maintain the judicial factfinding that Congress thought would underpin the mandatory Guidelines system that it sought to create and that Congress wrote into the Act in 18 U.S.C. §§ 3553(a) and 3661 (2000 ed. and Supp. IV). Hence we must decide whether we would deviate less radically from Congress' intended system (1) by superimposing the constitutional requirement announced today or (2) through elimination of some provisions of the statute.

To say this is not to create a new kind of severability analysis. Rather, it is to recognize that sometimes severability questions (questions as to how, or whether, Congress would intend a statute to apply) can arise when a legislatively unforeseen constitutional problem requires modification of a statutory provision as applied in a significant number of instances.

In today's context—a highly complex statute, interrelated provisions, and a constitutional requirement that creates fundamental change—we cannot assume that Congress, if faced with the statute's invalidity in key applications, would have preferred to apply the statute in as many other instances as possible. Neither can we determine likely congressional intent mechanically. We cannot simply approach the problem grammatically, say, by looking to see whether the constitutional requirement and the words of the Act are linguistically compatible.

Nor do simple numbers provide an answer. It is, of course, true that the numbers show that the constitutional jury trial requirement would lead to additional decisionmaking by juries in only a minority of cases. Prosecutors and defense attorneys would still resolve the lion's share of criminal matters through plea bargaining, and plea bargaining takes place without a jury. Many of the rest involve only simple issues calling for no upward Guidelines adjustment. And in at least some of the remainder, a judge may find adequate room to adjust a sentence within the single Guidelines range to which the jury verdict points, or within the overlap between that range and the next highest.

But the constitutional jury trial requirement would nonetheless affect every case. It would affect decisions about whether to go to trial. It would affect the content of plea negotiations. It would alter the judge's role in sentencing. Thus we must determine likely intent not by counting proceedings, but by evaluating the consequences of the Court's constitutional requirement in light of the Act's language, its history, and its basic purposes.

While reasonable minds can, and do, differ about the outcome, we conclude that the constitutional jury trial requirement is not compatible with the Act as written and that some severance and excision are necessary. In Part II, infra, we explain the incompatibility. In Part III, infra, we describe the necessary excision. In Part IV, infra, we explain why we have rejected other possibilities. In essence, in what follows, we explain both (1) why Congress would likely have preferred the total invalidation of the Act to an Act with the Court's Sixth Amendment requirement engrafted onto it, and (2) why Congress would likely have preferred the excision of some of the Act, namely the Act's mandatory language, to the invalidation of the entire Act. That is to say, in light of today's holding, we compare maintaining the Act as written with jury factfinding added (the dissenters' proposed remedy) to the total invalidation of the statute, and conclude that Congress would have preferred the latter. We then compare our own remedy to the total invalidation of the statute, and conclude that Congress would have preferred our remedy.

II

Several considerations convince us that, were the Court's constitutional requirement added onto the Sentencing Act as currently written, the requirement would so transform the scheme that Congress created that Congress likely would not have intended the Act as so modified to stand. First, the statute's text states that "[t]he court" when sentencing will consider "the nature and circumstances of the offense and the history and characteristics of the defendant." In context, the words "the court" mean "the judge without the jury," not "the judge working together with the jury." A further statutory provision, by removing typical "jury trial" evidentiary limitations, makes this clear. The Act's history confirms it.

This provision is tied to the provision of the Act that makes the Guidelines mandatory. They are part and parcel of a single, unified whole—a whole that Congress intended to apply to all federal sentencing.

This provision makes it difficult to justify Justice Stevens' approach, for that approach requires reading the words "the court" as if they meant "the judge working together with the jury." Unlike Justice Stevens, we do not believe we can interpret the statute's language to save its constitutionality because we believe that any such reinterpretation, even if limited to instances in which a Sixth Amendment problem arises, would be "plainly contrary to the intent of Congress." Without some such reinterpretation, however, this provision of the statute, along with those inextricably connected to it, are constitutionally invalid, and fall outside of Congress' power to enact. Nor can we agree with Justice Stevens that a newly passed "identical statute" would be valid. Such a new, identically worded statute would be valid only if (unlike the present statute) we could interpret that new statute (without disregarding Congress' basic intent) as being consistent with the Court's jury factfinding requirement. If so, the statute would stand.

Second, Congress' basic statutory goal—a system that diminishes sentencing disparity—depends for its success upon judicial efforts to determine, and to base punishment upon, the real conduct that underlies the crime of conviction. That determination is particularly important in the federal system where crimes defined as, for example, "obstruct[ing], delay[ing], or affect [ing] commerce or the movement of any article or commodity in commerce, by ... extortion," or, say, using the mail "for the purpose of executing" a "scheme or artifice to defraud," can encompass a vast range of very different kinds of underlying conduct. But it is also important even in respect to ordinary crimes, such as robbery, where an act that meets the statutory definition can be committed in a host of different ways. Judges have long looked to real conduct when sentencing. Federal judges have long relied upon a presentence report, prepared by a probation officer, for information (often unavailable until after the trial) relevant to the manner in which the convicted offender committed the crime of conviction.

Congress expected this system to continue. That is why it specifically inserted into the Act the provision cited above, which (recodifying prior law) says that

"[n]o limitation shall be placed on the information concerning the background, character, and conduct of a person convicted of an offense which a court of the United States may receive and consider for the purpose of imposing an appropriate sentence."

This Court's earlier opinions assumed that this system would continue. That is why the Court, for example, held in *United States v. Watts* that a sentencing judge could rely for sentencing purposes upon a fact that a jury had found unproved (beyond a reasonable doubt).

The Sentencing Guidelines also assume that Congress intended this system to continue. That is why, among other things, they permit a judge to reject a plea-bargained sentence if he determines, after reviewing the presentence report, that the sentence does not adequately reflect the seriousness of the defendant's actual conduct.

To engraft the Court's constitutional requirement onto the sentencing statutes, however, would destroy the system. It would prevent a judge from relying upon a presentence report for factual information, relevant to sentencing, uncovered after the trial. In doing so, it would, even compared to pre-Guidelines sentencing, weaken the tie between a sentence and an offender's real conduct. It would thereby undermine the sentencing statute's basic aim of ensuring similar sentences for those who have committed similar crimes in similar ways.

. . .

This point is critically important. Congress' basic goal in passing the Sentencing Act was to move the sentencing system in the direction of increased uniformity. That uniformity does not consist simply of similar sentences for those convicted of violations of the same statute—a uniformity consistent with the dissenters' remedial approach. It consists, more importantly, of similar relationships between sentences and real conduct, relationships that Congress' sentencing statutes helped to advance and that Justice Stevens' approach would undermine. In significant part, it is the weakening of this real-conduct/uniformity-in-sentencing relationship, and not any "[i]nexplicabl[e]" concerns for the "manner of achieving uniform sentences," that leads us to conclude that Congress would have preferred no mandatory system to the system the dissenters envisage.

Third, the sentencing statutes, read to include the Court's Sixth Amendment requirement, would create a system far more complex than Congress could have intended.

How would courts and counsel work with an indictment and a jury trial that involved not just whether a defendant robbed a bank but also how? Would the indictment have to allege, in addition to the elements of robbery, whether the defendant possessed a firearm, whether he brandished or discharged it, whether he threatened death, whether he caused bodily injury, whether any such injury was ordinary, serious, permanent or life threatening, whether he abducted or physically restrained anyone, whether any victim was unusually vulnerable, how much money was taken, and whether he was an organizer, leader, manager, or supervisor in a robbery gang? If so, how could a defendant mount a defense against some or all such specific claims should he also try simultaneously to maintain that the Government's evidence failed to place him at the scene of the crime? Would the indictment in a mail fraud case have to allege the number of victims, their vulnerability, and the amount taken from each? How could a judge expect a jury to work with the Guidelines' definitions of, say, "relevant conduct," which includes "all acts and omissions committed, aided, abetted, counseled, commanded, induced, procured, or willfully caused by the defendant; and [in the case of a conspiracy] all reasonably foreseeable acts and omissions of others in furtherance of the jointly undertaken criminal activity"? How would a jury measure "loss" in a securities fraud case—a matter so complex as to lead the Commission to instruct judges to make "only ... a reasonable estimate"? How would the court take account, for punishment purposes, of a defendant's contemptuous behavior at trial—a matter that the Government could not have charged in the indictment?

Fourth, plea bargaining would not significantly diminish the consequences of the Court's constitutional holding for the operation of the Guidelines. Rather, plea bargaining would make matters worse. Congress enacted the sentencing statutes in major part to achieve greater uniformity in sentencing, i.e., to increase the likelihood that offenders who engage in similar real conduct would receive similar sentences. The statutes reasonably assume that their efforts to move the trial-based sentencing process in the direction of greater sentencing uniformity would have a similar positive impact upon plea-bargained sentences, for plea bargaining takes place in the shadow of (i.e., with an eye toward the hypothetical result of) a potential trial.

That, too, is why Congress, understanding the realities of plea bargaining, authorized the Commission to promulgate policy statements that would assist sentencing judges in determining whether to reject a plea agreement after reading about the defendant's real conduct in a presentence report (and giving the offender an opportunity to challenge the report). This system has not worked perfectly; judges have often simply accepted an agreed-upon account of the conduct at issue. But compared to pre-existing law, the statutes try to move the system in the right direction, i.e., toward greater sentencing uniformity.

The Court's constitutional jury trial requirement, however, if patched onto the present Sentencing Act, would move the system backwards in respect both to tried and to plea-bargained cases. In respect to tried cases, it would effectively deprive the judge of the ability to use post-verdict-acquired real-conduct information; it would prohibit the judge from basing a sentence upon any conduct other than the conduct the prosecutor chose to charge; and it would put a defendant to a set of difficult strategic choices as to which prosecutorial claims he would contest. The sentence that would emerge in a case tried under such a system would likely reflect real conduct less completely, less accurately, and less often than did a pre-Guidelines, as well as a Guidelines, trial.

Because plea bargaining inevitably reflects estimates of what would happen at trial, plea bargaining too under such a system would move in the wrong direction. That is to say, in a sentencing system modified by the Court's constitutional requirement, plea bargaining would likely lead to sentences that gave greater weight not to real conduct, but rather to the skill of counsel, the policies of the prosecutor, the caseload, and other factors that vary from place to place, defendant to defendant, and crime to crime. Compared to pre-Guidelines plea bargaining, plea bargaining of this kind would necessarily move federal sentencing in the direction of diminished, not increased, uniformity in sentencing. It would tend to defeat, not to further, Congress' basic statutory goal.

Such a system would have particularly troubling consequences with respect to prosecutorial power. Until now, sentencing factors have come before the judge in the presentence report. But in a sentencing system with the Court's constitutional requirement engrafted onto it, any factor that a prosecutor chose not to charge at the plea negotiation would be placed beyond the reach of the judge entirely. Prosecutors would thus exercise a power the Sentencing Act vested in judges: the power to decide, based on relevant information about the offense and the offender, which defendants merit heavier punishment.

In respondent Booker's case, for example, the jury heard evidence that the crime had involved 92.5 grams of crack cocaine, and convicted Booker of possessing more than 50 grams. But the judge, at sentencing, found that the crime had involved an additional 566 grams, for a total of 658.5 grams. A system that would require the jury, not the judge, to make the additional "566 grams" finding is a system in which the prosecutor, not the judge, would control the sentence. That is because it is the prosecutor who would have to decide what drug amount to charge. He could choose to charge 658.5 grams, or 92.5, or less. It is the prosecutor who, through such a charging decision, would control the sentencing range. And it is different prosecutors who, in different cases—say, in two cases involving 566 grams—would potentially insist upon different punishments for similar defendants who engaged in similar criminal conduct involving similar amounts of unlawful drugs—say, by charging one of them with the full 566 grams, and the other with 10. As long as different prosecutors react differently, a system with a patched-on jury factfinding requirement would mean different sentences for otherwise similar conduct, whether in the context of trials or that of plea bargaining.

Fifth, Congress would not have enacted sentencing statutes that make it more difficult to adjust sentences upward than to adjust them downward. As several United States Senators have written in an amicus brief, "the Congress that enacted the 1984 Act did not conceive of—much less establish—a sentencing guidelines system in which sentencing judges were free to consider facts or circumstances not found by a jury or admitted in a plea agreement for the purpose of adjusting a base-offense level down, but not up, within the applicable guidelines range. Such a one-way lever would be grossly at odds with Congress's intent." Yet that is the system that the dissenters' remedy would create.

For all these reasons, Congress, had it been faced with the constitutional jury trial requirement, likely would not have passed the same Sentencing Act. It likely would have found the requirement incompatible with the Act as written. Hence the Act cannot remain valid in its entirety. Severance and excision are necessary.

. . . .

V

In respondent Booker's case, the District Court applied the Guidelines as written and imposed a sentence higher than the maximum authorized solely by the jury's verdict. The Court of Appeals held *Blakely* applicable to the Guidelines, concluded that Booker's sentence violated the Sixth Amendment, vacated the judgment of the District Court, and remanded for resentencing. We affirm the judgment of the Court of Appeals and remand the case. On remand, the District Court should impose a sentence in accordance with today's opinions, and, if the sentence comes before the Court of Appeals for review, the Court of Appeals should apply the review standards set forth in this opinion.

In respondent Fanfan's case, the District Court held *Blakely* applicable to the Guidelines. It then imposed a sentence that was authorized by the jury's verdict—a sentence lower than the sentence authorized by the Guidelines as written. Thus, Fanfan's sentence does not violate the Sixth Amendment. Nonetheless, the Government (and the defendant should he so choose) may seek resentencing under the system set forth in today's opinions. Hence we vacate the judgment of the District Court and remand the case for further proceedings consistent with this opinion.

As these dispositions indicate, we must apply today's holdings—both the Sixth Amendment holding and our remedial interpretation of the Sentencing Act—to all cases on direct review. That fact does not mean that we believe that every sentence gives rise to a Sixth Amendment violation. Nor do we believe that every appeal will lead to a new sentencing hearing. That is because we expect reviewing courts to apply ordinary prudential doctrines, determining, for example, whether the issue was raised below and whether it fails the "plain-error" test. It is also because, in cases not involving a Sixth Amendment violation, whether resentencing is warranted or whether it will instead be sufficient to review a sentence for reasonableness may depend upon application of the harmless-error doctrine.

It is so ordered.

FROM THE COURTROOM

MILLER v. ALABAMA

JACKSON v. HOBBS

Supreme Court of the United States, 2012
132 S.Ct. 2455

[Justice KAGAN delivered the opinion of the Court].

[Justice BREYER filed a concurring opinion, in which Justice SOTOMAYOR joined].

[CHIEF JUSTICE ROBERTS filed a dissenting opinion, in which Justices SCALIA, THOMAS, and ALITO joined].

[Justice THOMAS filed a dissenting opinion, in which Justice SCALIA joined].

[Justice ALITO filed a dissenting opinion, in which Justice SCALIA joined].

Justice KAGAN delivered the opinion of the Court.

The two 14–year–old offenders in these cases were convicted of murder and sentenced to life imprisonment without the possibility of parole. In neither case did the sentencing authority have any discretion to impose a different punishment. State law mandated that each juvenile die in prison even if a judge or jury would have thought that his youth and its attendant characteristics, along with the nature of his crime, made a lesser sentence (for example, life with the possibility of parole) more appropriate. Such a scheme prevents those meting out punishment from considering a juvenile's "lessened culpability" and greater "capacity for change," and runs afoul of our cases' requirement of individualized sentencing for defendants facing the most serious penalties. We therefore hold that mandatory life without parole for those under the age of 18 at the time of their crimes violates the Eighth Amendment's prohibition on "cruel and unusual punishments."

I

A

In November 1999, petitioner Kuntrell Jackson, then 14 years old, and two other boys decided to rob a video store. En route to the store, Jackson learned that one of the boys, Derrick Shields, was carrying a sawed-off shotgun in his coat sleeve. Jackson decided to stay outside when the two other boys entered the store. Inside, Shields pointed the gun at the store clerk, Laurie Troup, and demanded that she "give up the money." Troup refused. A few moments later, Jackson went into the store to find Shields continuing to demand money. At trial, the parties disputed whether Jackson warned Troup that "[w]e ain't playin'," or instead told his friends, "I thought you all was playin'." When Troup threatened to call the police, Shields shot and killed her. The three boys fled empty-handed.

Arkansas law gives prosecutors discretion to charge 14–year–olds as adults when they are alleged to have committed certain serious offenses. The prosecutor here exercised that authority by charging Jackson with capital felony murder and aggravated robbery. Jackson moved to transfer the case to juvenile court, but after considering the alleged facts of the crime, a psychiatrist's examination, and Jackson's juvenile arrest history (shoplifting and several incidents of car theft), the trial court denied the motion, and an appellate court affirmed. A jury later convicted Jackson of both crimes. Noting that "in view of [the] verdict, there's only one possible punishment," the judge sentenced Jackson to life without parole. Jackson did not challenge the sentence on appeal, and the Arkansas Supreme Court affirmed the convictions.

Following *Roper v. Simmons,* in which this Court invalidated the death penalty for all juvenile offenders under the age of 18, Jackson filed a state petition for habeas corpus. He argued, based on *Roper's* reasoning, that a mandatory sentence of life without parole for a 14–year–old also violates the Eighth Amendment. The circuit court rejected that argument and granted the State's motion to dismiss. While that ruling was on appeal, this Court held in *Graham v. Florida* that life without parole violates the Eighth Amendment when imposed on juvenile nonhomicide offenders. After the parties filed briefs addressing that decision, the Arkansas Supreme Court affirmed the dismissal of Jackson's petition. The majority found that *Roper* and *Graham* were "narrowly tailored" to their contexts: "death-penalty cases involving a juvenile and life-imprisonment-without-parole cases for nonhomicide offenses involving a juvenile." Two justices dissented. They noted that Jackson was not the shooter and that "any evidence of intent to kill was severely lacking." And they argued that Jackson's mandatory sentence ran afoul of *Graham* 's admonition that " '[a]n offender's age is relevant to the Eighth Amendment, and criminal procedure laws that fail to take defendants' youthfulness into account at all would be flawed.'"

B

Like Jackson, petitioner Evan Miller was 14 years old at the time of his crime. Miller had by then been in and out of foster care because his mother suffered from alcoholism and drug addiction and his stepfather abused him. Miller, too, regularly used drugs and alcohol; and he had attempted suicide four times, the first when he was six years old.

One night in 2003, Miller was at home with a friend, Colby Smith, when a neighbor, Cole Cannon, came to make a drug deal with Miller's mother. The two boys followed Cannon back to his trailer, where all three smoked marijuana and played drinking games. When Cannon passed out, Miller stole his wallet, splitting about $300 with Smith. Miller then tried to put the wallet back in Cannon's pocket, but Cannon awoke and grabbed Miller by the throat. Smith hit Cannon with a nearby baseball bat, and once released, Miller grabbed the bat and repeatedly struck Cannon with it. Miller placed a sheet over Cannon's head, told him "'I am God, I've come to take your life,'" and delivered one more blow. The boys then retreated to Miller's trailer, but soon decided to return to Cannon's to cover up evidence of their crime. Once there, they lit two fires. Cannon eventually died from his injuries and smoke inhalation.

Alabama law required that Miller initially be charged as a juvenile, but allowed the District Attorney to seek removal of the case to adult court. The D.A. did so, and the juvenile court agreed to the transfer after a hearing. Citing the nature of the crime, Miller's "mental maturity," and his prior juvenile offenses (truancy and "criminal mischief"), the Alabama Court of Criminal Appeals affirmed. The State accordingly charged Miller as an adult with murder in the course of arson. That crime (like capital murder in Arkansas) carries a mandatory minimum punishment of life without parole.

Relying in significant part on testimony from Smith, who had pleaded to a lesser offense, a jury found Miller guilty. He was therefore sentenced to life without the possibility of parole. The Alabama Court of Criminal Appeals affirmed, ruling that life without parole was "not overly harsh when compared to the crime" and that the mandatory nature of the sentencing scheme was permissible under the Eighth Amendment. The Alabama Supreme Court denied review.

We granted certiorari in both cases, and now reverse.

II

The Eighth Amendment's prohibition of cruel and unusual punishment "guarantees individuals the right not to be subjected to excessive sanctions." That right, we have explained, "flows from the basic 'precept of justice that punishment for crime should be graduated and proportioned'" to both the offender and the offense. As we noted the last time we considered life-without-parole sentences imposed on juveniles, "[t]he concept of proportionality is central to the Eighth Amendment." And we view that concept less through a historical prism than according to "'the evolving standards of decency that mark the progress of a maturing society.'"

The cases before us implicate two strands of precedent reflecting our concern with proportionate punishment. The first has adopted categorical bans on sentencing practices based on mismatches between the culpability of a class of offenders and the severity of a penalty. So, for example, we have held that imposing the death penalty for nonhomicide crimes against individuals, or imposing it on mentally retarded defendants, violates the Eighth Amendment. Several of the cases in this group have specially focused on juvenile offenders, because of their lesser culpability. Thus, *Roper* held that the Eighth Amendment bars capital punishment for children, and *Graham* concluded that the Amendment also prohibits a sentence of life without the possibility of parole for a child who committed a nonhomicide offense. *Graham* further likened life without parole for juveniles to the death penalty itself, thereby evoking a second line of our precedents. In those cases, we have prohibited mandatory imposition of capital punishment, requiring that sentencing authorities consider the characteristics of a defendant and the details of his offense before sentencing him to death. Here, the confluence of these two lines of precedent leads to the conclusion that mandatory life-without-parole sentences for juveniles violate the Eighth Amendment.

To start with the first set of cases: *Roper* and *Graham* establish that children are constitutionally different from adults for purposes of sentencing. Because juveniles have diminished culpability and greater prospects for reform, we explained, "they are less deserving of the most severe punishments." Those cases relied on three significant gaps between juveniles and adults. First, children have a "'lack of maturity and an underdeveloped sense of responsibility,'" leading to recklessness, impulsivity, and heedless risk-taking. Second, children "are more vulnerable ... to negative influences and outside pressures," including from their family and peers; they have limited "contro[l] over their own environment" and lack the ability to extricate themselves from horrific, crime-producing settings. And third, a child's character is not as "well formed" as an adult's; his traits are "less fixed" and his actions less likely to be "evidence of irretrievabl[e] deprav[ity]."

Our decisions rested not only on common sense—on what "any parent knows"—but on science and social science as well. In *Roper*, we cited studies showing that "'[o]nly a relatively small proportion of adolescents'" who engage in illegal activity "'develop entrenched patterns of problem behavior.'" And in *Graham*, we noted that "developments in psychology and brain science continue to show fundamental differences between juvenile and adult minds"—for example, in "parts of the brain involved in behavior control." We reasoned that those findings—of transient rashness, proclivity for risk, and inability to assess consequences—both lessened a child's "moral culpability" and enhanced the prospect that, as the years go by and neurological development occurs, his "'deficiencies will be reformed.'"

Roper and *Graham* emphasized that the distinctive attributes of youth diminish the penological justifications for imposing the harshest sentences on juvenile offenders, even when they commit terrible crimes. Because "'[t]he heart of the retribution rationale'" relates to an offender's blameworthiness, "'the case for retribution is not as strong with a minor as with an adult.'" Nor can deterrence do the work in this context, because "'the same characteristics that render juveniles less culpable than adults'"—their immaturity, recklessness, and impetuosity—make them less likely to consider potential punishment. Similarly, incapacitation could not support the life-without-parole sentence in *Graham*: Deciding that a "juvenile offender forever will be a danger to society" would require "mak[ing] a judgment that [he] is incorrigible"—but "'incorrigibility is inconsistent with youth.'" And for the same reason, rehabilitation could not justify that sentence. Life without parole "forswears altogether the rehabilitative ideal." It reflects "an irrevocable judgment about [an offender's] value and place in society," at odds with a child's capacity for change.

Graham concluded from this analysis that life-without-parole sentences, like capital punishment, may violate the Eighth Amendment when imposed on children. To be sure, *Graham's* flat ban on life without parole applied only to nonhomicide crimes, and the Court took care to distinguish those offenses from murder, based on both moral culpability and consequential harm. But none of what it said about children—about their distinctive (and transitory) mental traits and environmental vulnerabilities—is crime-specific. Those features are evident in the same way, and to the same degree, when (as in both cases here) a botched robbery turns into a killing. So *Graham's* reasoning implicates any life-without-parole sentence imposed on a juvenile, even as its categorical bar relates only to nonhomicide offenses.

Most fundamentally, *Graham* insists that youth matters in determining the appropriateness of a lifetime of incarceration without the possibility of parole. In the circumstances there, juvenile status precluded a life-without-parole sentence, even though an adult could receive it for a similar crime. And in other contexts as well, the characteristics of youth, and the way they weaken rationales for punishment, can render a life-without-parole sentence disproportionate. "An offender's age," we made clear in Graham, "is relevant to the Eighth Amendment," and so "criminal procedure laws that fail to take defendants' youthfulness into account at all would be flawed." The Chief Justice, concurring in the judgment, made a similar point. Although rejecting a categorical bar on life-without-parole sentences for juveniles, he acknowledged "*Roper's* conclusion that juveniles are typically less culpable than adults," and accordingly wrote that "an offender's juvenile status can play a central role" in considering a sentence's proportionality.

But the mandatory penalty schemes at issue here prevent the sentencer from taking account of these central considerations. By removing youth from the balance—by subjecting a juvenile to the same life-without-parole sentence applicable to an adult—these laws prohibit a sentencing authority from assessing whether the law's harshest term of imprisonment proportionately punishes a juvenile offender. That contravenes *Graham's* (and also *Roper's*) foundational principle: that imposition of a State's most severe penalties on juvenile offenders cannot proceed as though they were not children.

And *Graham* makes plain these mandatory schemes' defects in another way: by likening life-without-parole sentences imposed on juveniles to the death penalty itself. Life-without-parole terms, the Court wrote, "share some characteristics with death sentences that are shared by no other sentences." Imprisoning an offender until he dies alters the remainder of his life "by a forfeiture that is irrevocable." And this lengthiest possible incarceration is an "especially harsh punishment for a juvenile," because he will almost inevitably serve "more years and a greater percentage of his life in prison than an adult offender." The penalty when imposed on a teenager, as compared with an older person, is therefore "the same ... in name only." All of that suggested a distinctive set of legal rules: In part because we viewed this ultimate penalty for juveniles as akin to the death penalty, we treated it similarly to that most severe punishment. We imposed a categorical ban on the sentence's use, in a way unprecedented for a term of imprisonment. And the bar we adopted mirrored a proscription first established in the death penalty context—that the punishment cannot be imposed for any nonhomicide crimes against individuals.

That correspondence—*Graham's* "[t]reat[ment] [of] juvenile life sentences as analogous to capital punishment,"—makes relevant here a second line of our precedents, demanding individualized sentencing when imposing the death penalty. In Woodson, we held that a statute mandating a death sentence for first-degree murder violated the

Eighth Amendment. We thought the mandatory scheme flawed because it gave no significance to "the character and record of the individual offender or the circumstances" of the offense, and "exclud[ed] from consideration ... the possibility of compassionate or mitigating factors." Subsequent decisions have elaborated on the requirement that capital defendants have an opportunity to advance, and the judge or jury a chance to assess, any mitigating factors, so that the death penalty is reserved only for the most culpable defendants committing the most serious offenses.

Of special pertinence here, we insisted in these rulings that a sentencer have the ability to consider the "mitigating qualities of youth." Everything we said in *Roper* and *Graham* about that stage of life also appears in these decisions. As we observed, "youth is more than a chronological fact." It is a time of immaturity, irresponsibility, "impetuousness[,] and recklessness." It is a moment and "condition of life when a person may be most susceptible to influence and to psychological damage." And its "signature qualities" are all "transient." *Eddings* is especially on point. There, a 16–year–old shot a police officer point-blank and killed him. We invalidated his death sentence because the judge did not consider evidence of his neglectful and violent family background (including his mother's drug abuse and his father's physical abuse) and his emotional disturbance. We found that evidence "particularly relevant"—more so than it would have been in the case of an adult offender. We held: "[J]ust as the chronological age of a minor is itself a relevant mitigating factor of great weight, so must the background and mental and emotional development of a youthful defendant be duly considered" in assessing his culpability.

In light of *Graham's* reasoning, these decisions too show the flaws of imposing mandatory life-without-parole sentences on juvenile homicide offenders. Such mandatory penalties, by their nature, preclude a sentencer from taking account of an offender's age and the wealth of characteristics and circumstances attendant to it. Under these schemes, every juvenile will receive the same sentence as every other—the 17–year–old and the 14–year–old, the shooter and the accomplice, the child from a stable household and the child from a chaotic and abusive one. And still worse, each juvenile (including these two 14–year–olds) will receive the same sentence as the vast majority of adults committing similar homicide offenses—but really, as *Graham* noted, a greater sentence than those adults will serve. In meting out the death penalty, the elision of all these differences would be strictly forbidden. And once again, *Graham* indicates that a similar rule should apply when a juvenile confronts a sentence of life (and death) in prison.

So *Graham* and *Roper* and our individualized sentencing cases alike teach that in imposing a State's harshest penalties, a sentencer misses too much if he treats every child as an adult. To recap: Mandatory life without parole for a juvenile precludes consideration of his chronological age and its hallmark features—among them, immaturity, impetuosity, and failure to appreciate risks and consequences. It prevents taking into account the family and home environment that surrounds him—and from which he cannot usually extricate himself—no matter how brutal or dysfunctional. It neglects the circumstances of the homicide offense, including the extent of his participation in the conduct and the way familial and peer pressures may have affected him. Indeed, it ignores that he might have been charged and convicted of a lesser offense if not for incompetencies associated with youth—for example, his inability to deal with police officers or prosecutors (including on a plea agreement) or his incapacity to assist his own attorneys. And finally, this mandatory punishment disregards the possibility of rehabilitation even when the circumstances most suggest it.

Both cases before us illustrate the problem. Take Jackson's first. As noted earlier, Jackson did not fire the bullet that killed Laurie Troup; nor did the State argue that he intended her death. Jackson's conviction was instead based on an aiding-and-abetting theory; and the appellate court affirmed the verdict only because the jury could have believed that when Jackson entered the store, he warned Troup that "[w]e ain't playin'," rather than told his friends that "I thought you all was playin'." To be sure, Jackson learned on the way to the video store that his friend Shields was carrying a gun, but his age could well have affected his calculation of the risk that posed, as well as his willingness to walk away at that point. All these circumstances go to Jackson's culpability for the offense. And so too does Jackson's family background and immersion in violence: Both his mother and his grandmother had previously shot other individuals. At the least, a sentencer should look at such facts before depriving a 14–year–old of any prospect of release from prison.

That is true also in Miller's case. No one can doubt that he and Smith committed a vicious murder. But they did it when high on drugs and alcohol consumed with the adult victim. And if ever a pathological background might have contributed to a 14–year–old's commission of a crime, it is here. Miller's stepfather physically abused him; his alcoholic and drug-addicted mother neglected him; he had been in and out of foster care as a result; and he had tried to kill himself four times, the first when he should have been in kindergarten. Nonetheless, Miller's past criminal history was limited—two instances of truancy and one of "second-degree criminal mischief." That Miller deserved severe punishment for killing Cole Cannon is beyond question. But once again, a sentencer needed to examine all these circumstances before concluding that life without any possibility of parole was the appropriate penalty.

We therefore hold that the Eighth Amendment forbids a sentencing scheme that mandates life in prison without possibility of parole for juvenile offenders. By making youth (and all that accompanies it) irrelevant to imposition of that harshest prison sentence, such a scheme poses too great a risk of disproportionate punishment. Because that holding is sufficient to decide these cases, we do not consider Jackson's and Miller's alternative argument that the Eighth Amendment requires a categorical bar on life without parole for juveniles, or at least for those 14 and younger. But given all we have said in *Roper*, *Graham*, and this decision about children's diminished culpability and heightened capacity for change, we think appropriate occasions for sentencing juveniles to this harshest possible penalty will be uncommon. That is especially so because of the great difficulty we noted in *Roper* and *Graham* of distinguishing at this early age between "the juvenile offender whose crime reflects unfortunate yet transient immaturity, and the rare juvenile offender whose crime reflects irreparable corruption." Although we do not foreclose a sentencer's ability to make that judgment in homicide cases, we require it to take into account how children are different, and how those differences counsel against irrevocably sentencing them to a lifetime in prison.

. . .

Alabama and Arkansas (along with the Chief Justice and Justice Alito) next contend that because many States impose mandatory life-without-parole sentences on juveniles, we may not hold the practice unconstitutional. In considering categorical bars to the death penalty and life without parole, we ask as part of the analysis whether " 'objective indicia of society's standards, as expressed in legislative enactments and state practice,' " show a "national consensus" against a sentence for a particular class of offenders. By our count, 29 jurisdictions (28 States and the Federal Government) make a life-without-parole term mandatory for some juveniles convicted of murder in adult court. The States argue that this number precludes our holding.

We do not agree; indeed, we think the States' argument on this score weaker than the one we rejected in *Graham*. For starters, the cases here are different from the typical one in which we have tallied legislative enactments. Our decision does not categorically bar a penalty for a class of offenders or type of crime—as, for example, we did in *Roper* or *Graham*. Instead, it mandates only that a sentencer follow a certain process—considering an offender's youth and attendant characteristics—before imposing a particular penalty. And in so requiring, our decision flows straightforwardly from our precedents: specifically, the principle of *Roper*, *Graham*, and our individualized sentencing cases that youth matters for purposes of meting out the law's most serious punishments. When both of those circumstances have obtained in the past, we have not scrutinized or relied in the same way on legislative enactments. We see no difference here.

In any event, the "objective indicia" that the States offer do not distinguish these cases from others holding that a sentencing practice violates the Eighth Amendment. In Graham, we prohibited life-without-parole terms for juveniles committing nonhomicide offenses even though 39 jurisdictions permitted that sentence. That is 10 more than impose life without parole on juveniles on a mandatory basis. And in *Atkins*, *Roper*, and *Thompson*, we similarly banned the death penalty in circumstances in which "less than half" of the "States that permit [ted] capital punishment (for whom the issue exist[ed])" had previously chosen to do so. So we are breaking no new ground in these cases.

Graham and *Thompson* provide special guidance, because they considered the same kind of statutes we do and explained why simply counting them would present a distorted view. Most jurisdictions authorized the death penalty or life without parole for juveniles only through the combination of two independent statutory provisions. One allowed the transfer of certain juvenile offenders to adult court, while another (often in a far-removed part of the code) set out the penalties for any and all individuals tried there. We reasoned that in those circumstances, it was impossible to say whether a legislature had endorsed a given penalty for children (or would do so if presented with the choice). In Thompson, we found that the statutes "t[old] us that the States consider 15–year–olds to be old enough to be tried in criminal court for serious crimes (or too old to be dealt with effectively in juvenile court), but t[old] us nothing about the judgment these States have made regarding the appropriate punishment for such youthful offenders." And *Graham* echoed that reasoning: Although the confluence of state laws "ma[de] life without parole possible for some juvenile nonhomicide offenders," it did not "justify a judgment" that many States actually "intended to subject such offenders" to those sentences.

All that is just as true here. Almost all jurisdictions allow some juveniles to be tried in adult court for some kinds of homicide. But most States do not have separate penalty provisions for those juvenile offenders. Of the 29 jurisdictions mandating life without parole for children, more than half do so by virtue of generally applicable penalty provisions, imposing the sentence without regard to age. And indeed, some of those States set no minimum age for who may be transferred to adult court in the first instance, thus applying life-without-parole mandates to children of any age—be it 17 or 14 or 10 or 6. As in *Graham*, we think that "underscores that the statutory eligibility of a juvenile offender for life without parole does not indicate that the penalty has been endorsed through deliberate, express, and full legislative consideration." That Alabama and Arkansas can count to 29 by including these possibly (or probably) inadvertent legislative outcomes does not preclude our determination that mandatory life without parole for juveniles violates the Eighth Amendment.

B

Nor does the presence of discretion in some jurisdictions' transfer statutes aid the States here. Alabama and Arkansas initially ignore that many States use mandatory transfer systems: A juvenile of a certain age who has committed a specified offense will be tried in adult court, regardless of any individualized circumstances. Of the 29 relevant jurisdictions, about half place at least some juvenile homicide offenders in adult court automatically, with no apparent opportunity to seek transfer to juvenile court. Moreover, several States at times lodge this decision exclusively in the hands of prosecutors, again with no statutory mechanism for judicial reevaluation. And those "prosecutorial discretion laws are usually silent regarding standards, protocols, or appropriate considerations for decisionmaking."

Even when States give transfer-stage discretion to judges, it has limited utility. First, the decisionmaker typically will have only partial information at this early, pretrial stage about either the child or the circumstances of his offense. Miller's case provides an example. As noted earlier, the juvenile court denied Miller's request for his own mental-health expert at the transfer hearing, and the appeals court affirmed on the ground that Miller was not then entitled to the protections and services he would receive at trial. But by then, of course, the expert's testimony could not change the sentence; whatever she said in mitigation, the mandatory life-without-parole prison term would kick in. The key moment for the exercise of discretion is the transfer—and as Miller's case shows, the judge often does not know then what she will learn, about the offender or the offense, over the course of the proceedings.

Second and still more important, the question at transfer hearings may differ dramatically from the issue at a post-trial sentencing. Because many juvenile systems require that the offender be released at a particular age or after a certain number of years, transfer decisions often present a choice between extremes: light punishment as a child or standard sentencing as an adult (here, life without parole). In many States, for example, a child convicted in juvenile court must be released from custody by the age of 21. Discretionary sentencing in adult court would provide different options: There, a judge or jury could choose, rather than a life-without-parole sentence, a lifetime prison term with the possibility of parole or a lengthy term of years. It is easy to imagine a judge deciding that a minor deserves a (much) harsher sentence than he would receive in juvenile court, while still not thinking life-without-parole appropriate. For that reason, the discretion available to a judge at the transfer stage cannot substitute for discretion at post-trial sentencing in adult court—and so cannot satisfy the Eighth Amendment.

IV

Graham, *Roper*, and our individualized sentencing decisions make clear that a judge or jury must have the opportunity to consider mitigating circumstances before imposing the harshest possible penalty for juveniles. By requiring that all children convicted of homicide receive lifetime incarceration without possibility of parole, regardless of their age and age-related characteristics and the nature of their crimes, the mandatory sentencing schemes before us violate this principle of proportionality, and so the Eighth Amendment's ban on cruel and unusual punishment. We accordingly reverse the judgments of the Arkansas Supreme Court and Alabama Court of Criminal Appeals and remand the cases for further proceedings not inconsistent with this opinion.

It is so ordered.

[The concurring opinion of Justice BREYER, with whom Justice SOTOMAYOR joined, has been omitted].

Chief Justice ROBERTS, with whom Justice SCALIA, Justice THOMAS, and Justice ALITO join, dissenting.

Determining the appropriate sentence for a teenager convicted of murder presents grave and challenging questions of morality and social policy. Our role, however, is to apply the law, not to answer such questions. The pertinent law here is the Eighth Amendment to the Constitution, which prohibits "cruel and unusual punishments." Today, the Court invokes that Amendment to ban a punishment that the Court does not itself characterize as unusual, and that could not plausibly be described as such. I therefore dissent.

The parties agree that nearly 2,500 prisoners are presently serving life sentences without the possibility of parole for murders they committed before the age of 18. The Court accepts that over 2,000 of those prisoners received that sentence because it was mandated by a legislature. And it recognizes that the Federal Government and most States impose such mandatory sentences. Put simply, if a 17–year–old is convicted of deliberately murdering an innocent victim, it is not "unusual" for the murderer to receive a mandatory sentence of life without parole. That reality should preclude finding that mandatory life imprisonment for juvenile killers violates the Eighth Amendment.

. . . .

Mercy toward the guilty can be a form of decency, and a maturing society may abandon harsh punishments that it comes to view as unnecessary or unjust. But decency is not the same as leniency. A decent society protects the innocent from violence. A mature society may determine that this requires removing those guilty of the most heinous murders from its midst, both as protection for its other members and as a concrete expression of its standards of decency. As judges we have no basis for deciding that progress toward greater decency can move only in the direction of easing sanctions on the guilty.

. . . . [B]y the 1980's, outcry against repeat offenders, broad disaffection with the rehabilitative model, and other factors led many legislatures to reduce or eliminate the possibility of parole, imposing longer sentences in order to punish criminals and prevent them from committing more crimes. Statutes establishing life without parole sentences in particular became more common in the past quarter century. And the parties agree that most States have changed their laws relatively recently to expose teenage murderers to mandatory life without parole.

. . . .

Here the number of mandatory life without parole sentences for juvenile murderers, relative to the number of juveniles arrested for murder, is over 5,000 times higher than the corresponding number in *Graham*. There is thus nothing in this case like the evidence of national consensus in *Graham*.

. . . .

To say that a sentence may be considered unusual because so many legislatures approve it stands precedent on its head.

. . . .

In the end, the Court does not actually conclude that mandatory life sentences for juvenile murderers are unusual. It instead claims that precedent "leads to" today's decision, primarily relying on *Graham* and *Roper*. . . . If the Court is unwilling to say that precedent compels today's decision, perhaps it should reconsider that decision.

In any event, the Court's holding does not follow from *Roper* and *Graham*. Those cases undoubtedly stand for the proposition that teenagers are less mature, less responsible, and less fixed in their ways than adults—not that a Supreme Court case was needed to establish that. What they do not stand for, and do not even suggest, is that legislators—who also know that teenagers are different from adults—may not require life without parole for juveniles who commit the worst types of murder.

. . . .

Today's decision does not offer *Roper* and *Graham*'s false promises of restraint. Indeed, the Court's opinion suggests that it is merely a way station on the path to further judicial displacement of the legislative role in prescribing appropriate punishment for crime. The Court's analysis focuses on the mandatory nature of the sentences in this case. But then—although doing so is entirely unnecessary to the rule it announces—the Court states that even when a life without parole sentence is not mandatory, "we think appropriate occasions for sentencing juveniles to this harshest possible penalty will be uncommon." Today' holding may be limited to mandatory sentences, but the Court has already announced that discretionary life without parole for juveniles should be "uncommon"—or, to use a common synonym, "unusual."

Indeed, the Court's gratuitous prediction appears to be nothing other than an invitation to overturn life without parole sentences imposed by juries and trial judges. If that invitation is widely accepted and such sentences for juvenile offenders do in fact become "uncommon," the Court will have bootstrapped its way to declaring that the Eighth Amendment absolutely prohibits them.

. . . . The principle behind today's decision seems to be only that because juveniles are different from adults, they must be sentenced differently. There is no clear reason that principle would not bar all mandatory sentences for juveniles, or any juvenile sentence as harsh as what a similarly situated adult would receive. Unless confined, the only stopping point for the Court's analysis would be never permitting juvenile offenders to be tried as adults. Learning that an Amendment that bars only "unusual" punishments requires the abolition of this uniformly established practice would be startling indeed.

* * *

It is a great tragedy when a juvenile commits murder—most of all for the innocent victims. But also for the murderer, whose life has gone so wrong so early. And for society as well, which has lost one or more of its members to deliberate violence, and must harshly punish another. In recent years, our society has moved toward requiring that the murderer, his age notwithstanding, be imprisoned for the remainder of his life. Members of this Court may disagree with that choice. Perhaps science and policy suggest society should show greater mercy to young killers, giving them a greater chance to reform themselves at the risk that they will kill again. But that is not our decision to make. Neither the text of the Constitution nor our precedent prohibits legislatures from requiring that juvenile murderers be sentenced to life without parole. I respectfully dissent.

[The dissenting opinion of Justice THOMAS, with whom Justice SCALIA joins, is omitted].

[The dissenting opinion of Justice ALITO, with whom Justice SCALIA joins, is omitted].

46

Double Jeopardy

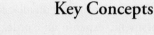

Key Concepts

- Prohibits Multiple Prosecutions and Multiple Punishments
- Does Not Encumber Legislature; Restrains Courts and Prosecutors
- *Blockburger* "Same Offense" Test: Does Each Offense Require Proof of an Additional Fact that the Other Does Not?
- Dual Sovereigns Are Unimpeded by the Terms of the Double Jeopardy Clause

A. Introduction and Policy. The Fifth Amendment to the United States Constitution guarantees that no person shall be "subject for the same offence to be twice put in jeopardy of life or limb."[1] In it simplest construction, this language means the government may not repeatedly prosecute an individual for the same crime. The protection offered by the Double Jeopardy Clause protects a defendant in three ways:

1. A defendant may not be prosecuted for the same offense following an acquittal;
2. A defendant may not be prosecuted for the same offense following a conviction; and
3. A defendant may not receive multiple punishments for the same offense.[2]

The prohibition against multiple trials (primarily the concern of items (1) and (2), above) is driven by twin policy objectives. The first is an interest in the finality of judgments, which "protects the accused from attempts to relitigate the facts underlying a prior acquittal, and from attempts to secure additional punishment after a prior conviction and sentence."[3]

---

1 U.S. Const. amend. V.

2 Ohio v. Johnson, 467 U.S. 493 (1984).

3 Brown v. Ohio, 432 U.S. 161, 165-66 (1977).

The prohibition against multiple trials is also driven by the need to prevent abuse of the prosecutor's relatively unregulated power to bring charges. As the Court has said:

> the State with all its resources and power should not be allowed to make repeated attempts to convict an individual for an alleged offense, thereby subjecting him to embarrassment, expense and ordeal and compelling him to live in a continuing state of anxiety and insecurity, as well as enhancing the possibility that even though innocent he may be found guilty.

In contrast, the prohibition against multiple punishments finds its source elsewhere. That prohibition is "designed to ensure that the sentencing discretion of courts is confined to the limits established by the legislature."[4] If the legislature intended cumulative punishments, then cumulative punishments may be imposed in a single trial.[5] Accordingly, courts will defer to the intentions of the legislature when analyzing a multiple punishment claim. The prohibition against multiple punishments only restrains prosecutors and judges, not the legislature.[6] In this way, the multiple punishment bar reflects an appreciation for the separation of powers. As the Court noted, "within our federal constitutional framework the legislative power, including the power to define criminal offenses and to prescribe the punishments to be imposed upon those found guilty of them, resides wholly with the Congress."[7]

Finally, keep in mind that all of the double jeopardy limitations discussed apply only if a single sovereign is seeking multiple prosecutions or punishments. Dual sovereigns—like a state and the federal government, or two different states—may prosecute the same offender for the same conduct.[8] For double jeopardy purposes, a state and all of its political subdivisions (counties, cities, towns, etc.) constitute a single sovereign.[9] So too, federal courts are treated as the same sovereign as territorial courts.[10] Native American tribal courts, however, are **not** the same sovereign as federal courts for double jeopardy purposes.[11]

B. The Law. In evaluating a double jeopardy claim, the first question to decide is whether the defendant was ever "in jeopardy" for the initial charge. The double jeopardy rule does not prohibit a prosecutor from charging a defendant twice for

---

4 Ohio v. Johnson, 467 U.S. 493, 497 (1984).

5 Missouri v. Hunter, 459 U.S. 359 (1983).

6 Garrett v. United States, 471 U.S. 773 (1985).

7 Whalen v. United States, 445 U.S. 684, 689 (1980).

8 Heath v. Alabama, 474 U.S. 82 (1985).

9 Waller v. Florida, 397 U.S. 387 (1970).

10 United States v. Wheeler, 435 U.S. 313 (1978).

11 United States v. Lara, 541 U.S. 193 (2004).

the same crime; it only prevents a defendant from being placed in jeopardy twice for the same crime. Often a prosecutor will bring charges against a defendant, then dismiss the charges (perhaps because of a problem with the pleadings), and then bring the same charges again a few days later. This does not violate the double jeopardy rule because technically the defendant was never "in jeopardy" for the initial charge. As noted in **Chapter 41**, the prosecutor may eventually run into problems with the speedy trial clock if she continues to dismiss the charges and re-file them, but this is a separate consideration from the double jeopardy bar.

In the parlance of courts, a defendant is not in jeopardy until jeopardy has "attached." "Attachment" defines the particular point in a criminal proceeding when the Double Jeopardy Clause is triggered.[12] The Supreme Court has determined that jeopardy does not attach until the commencement of proceedings before a trier of fact with the authority to decide questions of guilt or innocence. Thus, the first part of the double jeopardy rule is:

> In jury trials, jeopardy does not attach until the jury is empaneled and sworn.[13] In bench trials, jeopardy does not attach until the court begins to hear evidence—usually when the first witness is sworn in to testify.[14]

Once you have determined that jeopardy once attached, the next question is whether the facts present a threat of double jeopardy. The Double Jeopardy Clause protects against multiple prosecutions or multiple punishments for "the same" offense. In deciding whether two offenses are "the same" for double jeopardy purposes, courts use the ***Blockburger* test**:

> Two offenses are distinct as long as each offense "requires proof of an additional fact which the other does not."[15] As long as each charged offense requires proof of at least one unique fact from the other charged offense, the test is satisfied and the two offenses are not "the same." However, if each offense does not have an independent element, they are "the same" offense for double jeopardy purposes, and multiple trials and multiple prosecutions will be prohibited.

As discussed in **Chapter 36** on pleadings, the classic example of offenses that are considered "the same" for double jeopardy purposes are greater and lesser-included offenses. If Crime A contains all the elements of Crime B, but also includes one or more additional elements, Crime A is a greater offense of Crime

---

12 Serfass v. United States, 420 U.S. 377, 388 (1975).

13 Id. at 388.

14 Id.

15 Blockburger v. United States, 284 U.S. 299, 304 (1932).

B (and Crime B is a lesser-included offense of Crime A). For double jeopardy purposes, Crime A and Crime B are the "same" crime. For example, possession of heroin is a lesser-included offense of possession of heroin with the intent to sell. If the defendant has already been tried for possession of heroin and the case has reached a final disposition, he cannot be charged with possession of that same heroin with the intent to sell. Moreover, it does not matter which offense is prosecuted first. Double jeopardy protections preclude subsequent prosecution of either the greater offense or the lesser-included offense.

Once a court determines that the two offenses are "the same" offense, the next step is to determine how—and whether—the first offense was resolved:

> The Double Jeopardy Clause does not apply until the first prosecution has been resolved.
>
> If the first prosecution was resolved by a conviction, the prosecutor is barred from charging the defendant again for the same offense.
>
> If the first prosecution was resolved by an acquittal, not only is the prosecutor barred from charging the defendant again for the same offense, but the doctrine of collateral estoppel may apply to prevent the prosecutor from filing any charge which depends on an issue of fact that was already definitively determined by the acquittal.
>
> For the purposes of double jeopardy analysis, an "acquittal" includes:
>
> A ruling by the court that the evidence is insufficient to convict;
>
> A factual finding that necessarily establishes the criminal defendant's lack of criminal culpability; or
>
> Any other ruling which relates to the ultimate question of guilt or innocence.[16]

Thus, in analyzing a double jeopardy claim, the court must first determine whether jeopardy "ended" for the first offense—that is, whether the first case reached a final resolution. Generally, a case is only resolved by a conviction or by an acquittal—although as noted above, courts have defined "acquittal" relatively broadly in this context.

There a number of ways a criminal case can appear to come to an end without actually reaching a final resolution:

[16] Evans v. Michigan, 133 S.Ct. 1069, 1075 (2013).

1. If a trial judge enters a judgment of acquittal notwithstanding the jury's guilty verdict, the government may appeal that judgment and, if successful, have the jury's guilty verdict reinstated.[17]

2. If a defendant moves to dismiss the indictment after a guilty verdict, the government can appeal the dismissal.[18]

3. If the case ends with a conviction that is overturned by an appellate court (for reasons unrelated to the sufficiency of the evidence), the prosecution may usually re-file the charges.[19] (As we will see below, if the appellate court overturns the conviction based on insufficiency of the evidence, the case is deemed to be resolved, and the double jeopardy bar applies).[20]

Likewise, most procedural rulings that result in the early termination of a trial, such as dismissals and mistrials, do not trigger the double jeopardy doctrine. A dismissal of a case only triggers the double jeopardy bar if the dismissal was based on the judge's determination that the defendant was not in fact guilty (for example, a ruling that the evidence was insufficient to convict). If the case is dismissed purely on procedural grounds, the prosecution may appeal the dismissal and may retry the defendant if successful on appeal.[21]

Finally, most mistrials do not trigger the double jeopardy doctrine. If a mistrial is granted because of "manifest necessity" (for example, a hung jury is unable to reach a verdict[22]), the case has not been resolved and the prosecutor can re-file the charges.[23] Also, double jeopardy does not apply if the defendant moves for a mistrial or otherwise acquiesces in the early termination of proceedings.[24] The only exception to this rule is if the judge determines that the prosecutor intentionally provoked the defense request.[25]

If the initial offense reached a final resolution, a court will look to whether the prior charge ended in a conviction or an acquittal. If the case is resolved with a conviction, the double jeopardy doctrine merely prohibits a second prosecution for the same offense.

However, a prior acquittal provides a more robust double jeopardy protection. The Court has repeatedly said that acquittals are afforded "special weight" for double jeopardy purposes.

17 United States v. Wilson, 420 U.S. 332 (1975).
18 Sanabria v. United States, 437 U.S. 54 (1978).
19 Smith v. Massachusetts, 543 U.S. 462 (2005).
20 Burks v. United States, 437 U.S. 1 (1978).
21 United States v. Scott, 437 U.S. 82 (1978).
22 Arizona v. Washington, 434 U.S. 497 (1978).
23 Renico v. Lett, 559 U.S. 766 (2010).
24 United States v. Dinitz, 424 U.S. 600 (1976).
25 United States v. DiFrancesco, 449 U.S. 117 (1980); Oregon v. Kennedy, 456 U.S. 667 (1982).

The bar against re-prosecution following acquittal has been described as "the most fundamental rule in the history of double jeopardy jurisprudence,"[26] and applies with equal strength whether the acquittal was made by a judge or a jury.[27] Like convictions, acquittals create an absolute prohibition against retrial—and this prohibition applies even if the acquittal is grounded in a mistake—for example, the erroneous exclusion of evidence;[28] a mistaken view of the prosecution's evidentiary hurdle; or a misunderstanding of the applicable law.[29]

In addition, an acquittal may also give rise to the doctrine of collateral estoppel, otherwise known as issue preclusion. The collateral estoppel rule will preclude future litigation of any issue that "was necessarily decided by a jury's acquittal in a prior trial."[30]

As noted in **Chapter 36,** determining whether a particular issue has been resolved by a prior case can be a difficult task. The defendant has the burden of establishing that the acquittal in the prior case necessarily means that the finder of fact has resolved the specific issue in question.[31] Jury verdicts tend to be very general (e.g., by simply stating that the defendant is "not guilty"), so it may be ambiguous what specific issues the jury resolved in reaching their decision to acquit.

However, occasionally the facts and circumstances of the case will make the jury's decision more transparent. For example, assume a victim is robbed and murdered during a single criminal episode by one assailant. The facts are such that whoever was responsible for one crime was necessarily responsible for the other. The accused is charged first with the murder, but is acquitted. Under these circumstances, even though murder and robbery are not "the same" offense, the government would nonetheless be prevented on double jeopardy grounds from subsequently prosecuting the robbery because the issue of the defendant's identity as the assailant has already been resolved by the acquittal in the murder case. To decide which issues of fact have been resolved by an earlier acquittal, the reviewing court should be guided by "the record of a prior proceeding, taking into account the pleadings, evidence, charge, and other relevant matter."[32]

Neither the double jeopardy doctrine nor the collateral estoppel rule applies to subsequent proceedings with a lower standard of proof. [33] For example, when a gun owner is acquitted of illegal gun running charges, the prosecutor would be precluded from bringing any further criminal charges which relied on the fact that

[26] United States v. Martin Linen Supply Co., 430 U.S. 564 (1977).

[27] Fong Foo v. United States, 369 U.S. 141 (1962); Smith v. Massachusetts, 543 U.S. 462 (2005).

[28] Sanabria v. United States, 437 U.S. 54 (1978).

[29] Evans v. Michigan, 133 S.Ct. 1069 (2013).

[30] Yeager v. United States, 557 U.S. 110 (2009).

[31] Dowling v. United States, 493 U.S. 342 (1990).

[32] Ashe v. Swenson, 397 U.S. 436, 444 (1970).

[33] Dowling v. United States, 493 U.S. 342 (1990).

the defendant knowingly possessed illegal guns. However, the prosecutor would not be precluded from seizing the weapons in an *in rem* forfeiture action, even though such a seizure would depend on proof that the defendant knowingly possessed illegal guns. This is because the forfeiture is governed by a preponderance of the evidence standard, not a reasonable doubt standard.[34] Similarly, acquitted conduct may be admitted as "other bad acts" evidence under Rule 404(b) of the Federal Rules of Evidence (or its state counterpart).

Though the Court has been capacious in defining an "acquittal" for double jeopardy purposes, there are two "not guilty" findings that the Court has refused to include in its definition of "acquittals." The first, noted above, occurs when a trial judge decides to set aside a jury's guilty verdict and enter a judgment of acquittal. Such a judgment does not have the same preclusive effect as a judgment of acquittal entered by the jury. Also, it is not considered an "acquittal" when an appellate court holds that the jury's guilty verdict was against the "weight of the evidence."[35]

Although the double jeopardy rule prohibits multiple punishments for the same criminal conduct, it generally does not prohibit the imposition of a harsher sentence if a case is re-tried after an appeal. For example, assume that Debbie Defendant was convicted at her first trial and then sentenced to life imprisonment by a sentencing court. Debbie then successfully appealed her conviction and her case was remanded for retrial. Following retrial, the sentencing court sentenced Debbie to death. The Supreme Court has found that under these circumstances, the death sentence imposed following the second trial is not prohibited by double jeopardy. In the Court's view, "the imposition of a particular sentence usually is not regarded as an 'acquittal' of any more severe sentence that could have been imposed."[36]

There is, however, one narrow set of circumstances in which double jeopardy prohibitions will prevent the imposition of a harsher sentence: when the initial sentencing decision was made by a jury at a bifurcated capital sentencing hearing at which the prosecution's burden was proof beyond a reasonable doubt. According to the Supreme Court, if the initial capital sentencing decision was to impose some punishment other than death, the hearing operates much like a criminal trial with the defendant essentially being "acquitted" of the death penalty.[37] In addition, as you read in **Chapter 45**, there are due process limits on the imposition of harsher sentences upon retrial.

Finally, remember that the Double Jeopardy Clause only prohibits a second criminal prosecution or punishment. Civil actions do not trigger double jeopardy

---

[34] United States v. One Assortment of 89 Firearms, 465 U.S. 354 (1984).

[35] Tibbs v. Florida, 457 U.S. 31 (1982).

[36] Bullington v. Missouri, 451 U.S. 430 (1981).

[37] Id.

concerns.[38] However, in some cases it may be difficult to determine whether the second proceeding is civil or criminal—for example, in civil forfeiture cases or proceedings in juvenile court.

To decide whether an action is civil or criminal, the reviewing court should look first to the authorizing statute. But, this is just the first step in the analysis. There are times when a penalty even though categorized as "civil" will be "so punitive either in purpose or effect as to transform what was clearly intended as a civil remedy into a criminal penalty."[39] There are seven factors a court should consider in deciding how to categorize an action for double jeopardy purposes:

1. Whether the sanction involves an affirmative disability or restraint;
2. Whether it has historically been regarded as a punishment;
3. Whether it comes into play only on a finding of scienter;
4. Whether its operation will promote the traditional aims of punishment—retribution and deterrence;
5. Whether the behavior to which it applies is already a crime;
6. Whether an alternative purpose to which it may rationally be connected is assignable for it; and
7. Whether it appears excessive in relation to the alternative purpose assigned.[40]

If a penalty has been designated by the legislature as civil, a defendant will need to offer "clear proof" that it is in reality criminal in order to convert it for double jeopardy purposes.[41] In keeping with these rules, the Court has found the Double Jeopardy Clause does not prohibit the indefinite civil commitment of dangerous sexual predators even after they have served a criminal sentence for such conduct.[42] The Clause also "does not bar the institution of a civil, *in rem* forfeiture action after the criminal conviction [or acquittal] of the defendant."[43] It should be noted, however, that the Court has suggested a constitutional difference between "*in rem* civil forfeitures [which are actions against the guilty property] and *in*

---

[38] United States v. Ursery, 518 U.S. 267 (1996).
[39] Hudson, 522 U.S. at 99.
[40] Id. at 99–100.
[41] United States v. Ward, 448 U.S. 242 (1980).
[42] Kansas v. Hendricks, 521 U.S. 346 (1997).
[43] United States v. Bajakajian, 524 U.S. 321, 332 (1998); One Lot Emerald Cut Stones and One Ring v. United States, 409 U.S. 232 (1972).

personam civil penalties such as fines [which are actions against the individual.]"[44] The former generally have no double jeopardy implications while the latter may.[45]

Finally, while the juvenile justice system was for many years characterized as "civil" in nature, the Court has recognized that a candid appraisal of the juvenile justice process leads to a conclusion that such proceedings are actually "criminal" in nature in the context of the Double Jeopardy Clause.[46]

C. Applying the Law.

1. Retrial Following a Prior Acquittal. The first and most basic rule encompassed by the double jeopardy protection is that an acquittal bars any future prosecution for the same offense. In one of the early cases discussing this principle, the Court clarified that the preclusive effect of an acquittal differs drastically from the impact (for double jeopardy purposes) of a conviction:

> **Example—*Ball v. United States*, 163 U.S. 662 (1896):** Millard Fillmore Ball was tried along with two co-defendants (John C. Ball and Robert Boutwell) for the shooting death of William T. Box. The jury convicted John Ball and Robert Boutwell, but acquitted Millard Ball of the murder.
>
> John Ball and Robert Boutwell were sentenced to death. However, on appeal the Supreme Court held that their convictions should be overturned because the indictment's failure to identify the time and place of Box's death rendered it fatally defective.
>
> The government re-indicted the case, again charging all three men with murder. Each of the men maintained that the double jeopardy clause prevented further prosecution. John Ball and Robert Boutwell argued that their prior conviction precluded their re-indictment on murder charges; while Millard Ball maintained that his prior acquittal prevented further prosecution. All three double jeopardy claims were rejected, and the men were convicted and sentenced to death. The defendants appealed to the Supreme Court.

Analysis: The second prosecution of Millard Ball following his acquittal was prevented by the prohibition against double jeopardy. However, the further prosecution of John Ball and Robert Boutwell was not similarly precluded.

[44] Ursery, 518 U.S. at 275.

[45] Bajakajian, 524 U.S. 321.

[46] Breed v. Jones, 421 U.S. 519 (1975).

There were two judgments below. The first was a conviction as to John Ball and Robert Boutwell. The second was the acquittal of Millard Ball. Millard Ball did not seek a writ of error with regard to his acquittal and the government could not have. The trial court's discharge of Ball's case in light of the acquittal thus stands unimpeached.

Moreover, the decision by John Ball and Robert Boutwell to challenge the sufficiency of the indictment in their cases had no impact on the judgment in Millard Ball's case. Millard Ball's acquittal stood as an absolute bar to his second prosecution for Box's murder.

A similar result does not obtain, however, with regard to John Ball and Robert Boutwell. The judgment against both men was reversed at their own insistence. "[A] defendant who procures a judgment against him upon an indictment to be set aside may be tried anew upon the same indictment, or upon another indictment, for the same offense of which he had been convicted."[47]

In addition to the principle set out in *Ball*, an acquittal can also give rise to the principle of collateral estoppel. This principle states that "when an issue of ultimate fact has once been determined by a valid and final judgment, that issue cannot again be litigated between the same parties in any future lawsuit."[48]

Of course, when a jury decides to acquit a defendant it almost never offers the reasons for the acquittal. Thus, the court analyzing the double jeopardy claim must decide whether an issue of ultimate fact has been determined by the acquitting jury. This was precisely the situation confronted by the Court in *Ashe v. Swenson*.[49]

Example—*Ashe v. Swenson*, 397 U.S. 436 (1970): Six men were playing poker late into the night in the basement of a house when masked men broke into the house and stole their money and other property. It was never clear whether there were three or four masked men. The robbers stole a car from one of the victims and left the scene of the crime. A few hours later, the car was recovered in an empty field, and three men were arrested walking together on a highway nearby. A fourth man, Bob Ashe, was arrested a few minutes later some distance away.

Ashe was eventually charged with robbing Donald Knight, one of the poker players. Knight and three other poker players testified at the trial, describing the robbery and the items that were stolen. The government had very strong proof that Knight and the other

---

[47] Ball v. United States, 163 U.S. 662, 672 (1896).

[48] Ashe v. Swenson, 397 U.S. 436, 443 (1970).

[49] 397 U.S. 436 (1970).

players had been robbed, and on cross-examination Ashe's attorney did not challenge the fact that a robbery occurred. However, the evidence that Ashe was one of the robbers was particularly weak. Two of the witnesses testified that there were only three robbers, and did not identify Ashe as one of the robbers; another could only identify Ashe by voice; and the fourth only identified Ashe by his size and height. Ashe's attorney attacked the accuracy of these identifications on cross-examination. The jury found Ashe not guilty.

Six weeks later the prosecutor charged Ashe again, this time with robbing a different participant in the poker game. Ashe moved to dismiss the indictment, but his motion was denied. In the second trial, the same witnesses testified, but the identification evidence against Ashe was much stronger: the two witnesses who could not identify him at all now identified him by his features, size, and mannerisms; another witness who before only identified him by his size and height now also identified him by his voice. Ashe was found guilty and sentenced to thirty-five years. Ashe appealed the case to the state supreme court and lost. Years later, he brought a habeas corpus proceeding in federal court, which reached the Supreme Court.

Analysis: The Court reversed the conviction, holding that the doctrine of double jeopardy barred Ashe's second prosecution for the robbery. After examining the record from the first trial, the only logical conclusion was that the first jury concluded that there was insufficient evidence to prove that Ashe was one of the robbers:

After the first jury had acquitted the petitioner of robbing Knight, Missouri could certainly not have brought him to trial again upon that charge. Once a jury had determined upon conflicting testimony that there was at least a reasonable doubt that the petitioner was one of the robbers, the State could not present the same or different identification evidence in a second prosecution for the robbery of Knight in the hope that a different jury might find that evidence more convincing. The situation is constitutionally no different here, even though the second trial related to another victim of the same robbery. For the name of the victim, in the circumstances of this case, had no bearing whatever upon the issue of whether the petitioner was one of the robbers.[50]

In the Court's view, the only issue that was rationally in dispute at the first trial "was whether [Ashe] had been one of the robbers. And the [first] jury by its verdict found that he had not."[51]

---

[50] Id. at 446.

[51] Id. at 445; see also Green v. United States, 355 U.S. 184 (1957).

Not every case presents as clearly as *Ashe* an obvious delineation of the issues that were decided. In deciding whether a particular issue was resolved by the first jury, the reviewing court must avoid speculation:

> **Example—*Yeager v. United States*, 557 U.S. 110 (2009):** F. Scott Yeager was a senior vice president at Enron Broadband Services ("EBS"), a company owned by Enron. Enron aggressively marketed EBS's efforts to develop a new national telecommunications system. At one marketing conference, Yeager and others made false or misleading statements about the viability of the telecommunications project. In the days and months after these statements were made, Enron's stock price soared. During this period, Yeager sold shares of his Enron stock, reaping more than $19 million in profit. Ultimately, the telecommunications project never launched due to technological problems.
>
> Yeager was charged with 126 counts that could roughly be grouped into "fraud counts" and "insider trading counts." Specifically, it was the government's contention that Yeager and others lied about the viability of the telecommunications project to artificially inflate the price of Enron stock.
>
> The jury deliberated for four days before advising the trial judge that it could only reach a verdict on some of the counts. With the agreement of the parties, the trial judge accepted the partial verdict. The jury acquitted Yeager on the fraud counts but announced that it remained hung on the insider trading counts, a mistrial was therefore declared as to these counts.
>
> Several months later, the prosecution re-indicted Yeager on some of the insider trading counts. Yeager moved to dismiss, arguing that his acquittal on the fraud counts served as an absolute bar to further prosecution on the insider trading counts. In particular, Yeager maintained that the acquittals meant the jury necessarily concluded he did not "possess material, nonpublic information about the performance of the [telecommunications] project or its value to Enron."[52] Where this fact was required for conviction on the insider trading counts, Yeager argued that further prosecution was prevented by the Double Jeopardy Clause.

[52] Yeager v. United States, 557 U.S. 110, 115 (2009).

After the trial court denied his motion to dismiss, Yeager appealed. Because of the inconsistency between the jury's treatment of the two sets of counts (hung/acquittal), the intermediate appellate court found that issue preclusion would not bar a new trial. Yeager then appealed to the Supreme Court.

Analysis: The acquittal on the fraud counts absolutely barred further prosecution of any issue already decided by the acquittals.

The Double Jeopardy Clause exists to prevent harassment of defendants and to preserve the finality of judgments. When a prosecutor seeks to retry a defendant after a jury has failed to reach a verdict, there is a danger of harassment. However, courts have determined that jury deadlock creates a "manifest necessity" for a mistrial, and therefore it does not bar a permitted second prosecution.

However, this case raised a second problem beyond the manifest necessity of the mistrial. The Supreme Court also had to deal with the preclusive effect of the fraud count acquittals. This factor implicates the second rationale behind the Double Jeopardy Clause: appreciation for the finality of judgments.

An acquittal precludes retrial because the prosecution should not be allowed to re-litigate issues that have already been decided in the defendant's favor. The question therefore is which issues can be said to have been decided by an acquittal. To answer this question, the reviewing court should look to the trial record, including the pleadings, the evidence, the charging document, and other similarly relevant materials.

In the instant case, the lower appellate court looked beyond these materials to the counts in which the prior jury could not reach a verdict. But these counts should not be part of the analysis. "Because a jury speaks only through its verdict, its failure to reach a verdict cannot—by negative implication—yield a piece of information that helps put together the trial puzzle."[53]

Any number of reasons might have caused the jury not to reach a verdict on the insider trading counts. Suggesting, as the lower appellate court did, that this inability necessarily meant the jury had not resolved whether Yeager possessed insider information "is not reasoned analysis; it is guess work."[54] When deciding which issues are precluded by a prior acquittal, the jury's inability to reach a verdict on any counts is irrelevant to the analysis. The meaning of a jury's decision is found in what the jury decided, not in what it failed to resolve.

In this case, it seems likely that the possession of insider information in connection with Yeager's stock sales was an ultimate fact that was necessarily resolved by the jury when it acquitted him on the fraud counts. On remand, the lower court should determine (based exclusively on the record and not on the hung counts) whether this was the case.

[53] Id. at 121.

[54] Id. at 122.

In some cases, the meaning of an acquittal is far clearer than it was in the *Yeager* case. For example, when a trial judge enters a judgment of acquittal, she frequently provides reasons for her decision. The rule against re-prosecution after an acquittal is absolute. It even applies if the acquittal was clearly in error:

> **Example—*Evans v. Michigan*, 133 S.Ct. 1069 (2013):** Officers with the Detroit Police Department saw Lamar Evans running away from the scene of a house fire with a gas can in his hand. The police caught Evans and he confessed to having set the fire. The house did not have tenants at the time of the arson.
>
> Two provisions of the Michigan Code related to deliberately setting fires. The first criminalized the burning of a "dwelling house." The second criminalized the burning of "other real property." The elements of the two are identical, with the only exception being that the first (the greater offense) requires the prosecution to prove the extra element that the burned property was a "dwelling." The government charged Evans under the lesser-included "other real property" provision.
>
> The government established at trial that Evans was responsible for burning down the house, and then closed its case. Evans moved for judgment of acquittal, arguing that the government had not proven the property he burned was not a dwelling house. In support of his argument, Evans directed the trial court to the pattern jury instructions, which noted, "an essential element is that the structure burned is not a dwelling house." The trial court found that while the property clearly was not occupied at the time of the fire, the owner of the property had testified that it "was a dwelling house." Consequently, the court granted Evans's motion and entered a directed verdict of acquittal.
>
> The prosecution appealed, and the appellate court reversed. The appellate court found the prosecution had no burden to disprove the nature of the structure. The court also rejected Evans's claim that he could not be re-prosecuted because of his prior acquittal. After the Michigan Supreme Court affirmed, the U.S. Supreme Court accepted the case for review.

Analysis: The Double Jeopardy Clause of the Fifth Amendment prevented Evans's retrial on the arson charge.

Retrial following acquittal is prohibited by the Double Jeopardy Clause even if a court-ordered acquittal is "based upon an egregiously erroneous foundation."[55] The accuracy of an acquittal is simply not a matter of concern to the protections provided by the bar on double jeopardy.

An "acquittal" for double jeopardy purposes is "any ruling that the prosecution's proof is insufficient to establish criminal liability for an offense."[56] In this sense, acquittals differ from procedural rulings that may result in the termination of the prosecution's case, but do not speak to the question of guilt or innocence.

In Evans's case, the ruling by the trial court undoubtedly spoke to the question of guilt or innocence. The trial court found that the evidence produced by the prosecutor was insufficient to meet its burden. It is equally true that the trial court reached this conclusion based upon an incorrect understanding of the prosecution's evidentiary burden. But that makes absolutely no difference to the double jeopardy analysis. The trial court's "judgment, however erroneous it was, precludes re-prosecution on this charge."[57]

As was true in *Evans*, acquittals most typically occur at the close of evidence. However, there are times when a judge may decide to dismiss certain charges mid-trial. If such a dismissal is based upon the trial court's determination that the prosecution has not met its burden as to those counts, the dismissal functions as an acquittal.[58]

If a trial judge has second thoughts after granting such a dismissal, the judge's ability to revisit the mid-trial acquittal will depend upon how far along the trial has progressed prior to the reconsideration. If the dismissal was entered without qualification and "the trial has proceeded to the defendant's introduction of evidence, the acquittal must be treated as final, unless the availability of reconsideration has been plainly established by pre-existing rule or case authority expressly applicable to midtrial rulings on the sufficiency of the evidence."[59]

2. Retrial Following a Prior Conviction. In addition to precluding re-prosecution following an acquittal, the double jeopardy ban on multiple prosecutions also precludes re-prosecution for the same offense following a conviction. For double jeopardy purposes the "same" offense includes conviction on a lesser-included offense:

---

55 Evans v. Michigan, 133 S.Ct. 1069, 1074 (2013).

56 Id.

57 Id. at 1078.

58 Smalis v. Pennsylvania, 476 U.S. 140 (1986).

59 Smith, 543 U.S. 462.

Example—*Brown v. Ohio*, 432 U.S. 161 (1977): Nathaniel Brown stole a car in East Cleveland in late November. Nine days later, in early December, Brown was arrested when he was found in a neighboring town driving the car. The police in the neighboring town charged Brown with the offense of "joyriding." Joyriding was defined as "taking or operating a car without the owner's consent." The date listed for the offense was the December date of Brown's arrest. After Brown pled guilty, he was sentenced to thirty days in jail and was fined $100.

Shortly after his release from jail, Brown was charged in a two-count indictment in East Cleveland. The indictment charged Brown with auto theft and joyriding. The date of these offenses was listed as the November date when Brown initially took the car. Brown challenged the second prosecution on double jeopardy grounds, but his motion was denied by the trial court. Brown pled guilty to the theft count. He received a six month suspended sentence and one year of probation.

The reviewing court found that the two prosecutions were "based on two separate acts of the appellant, one which occurred on November 29th and one which occurred on December 8th."[60] The Supreme Court then accepted the case for review.

Analysis: Brown could not be prosecuted in East Cleveland for theft of the car because he had already been convicted of the lesser-included offense of joyriding in Wickliffe.

The Double Jeopardy Clause protects individuals from being prosecuted twice for the same offense. The Constitution does not require complete equivalence between two offenses for them to be considered the "same" for double jeopardy purposes. There is no question that joyriding is a lesser-included offense of automobile theft under Ohio law. The question is whether that fact makes the two offenses "the same" for double jeopardy purposes.

The test for determining whether two offenses are "the same" is the *Blockburger* test. Under this test, the elements of the two offenses must be examined. If each offense requires proof of an element that the other offense does not, the two offenses are not "the same" for double jeopardy purposes. This is true even if there is otherwise significant overlap in the other elements or even in the evidence needed to prove guilt of either crime.

---

60 Brown v. Ohio, 432 U.S. 161, 164 (1977).

If a judge could not impose separate punishments for two offenses at the close of a single trial, the prosecution cannot attempt to accomplish an identical result simply by prosecuting the accused in two separate trials. The protections of double jeopardy impede either result.

Joyriding is defined as the "taking or operating of a vehicle without the owner's consent." Auto theft is "joyriding with the intent permanently to deprive the owner of possession."[61] Thus, to establish the offense of joyriding there is no unique element that the prosecution must establish that is not also required to establish the offense of auto theft. This is indeed the nature of a lesser-included offense. "The greater offense is therefore by definition the 'same' for purposes of double jeopardy of any lesser offense included in it."[62]

It makes no difference to the double jeopardy question which offense was tried first. "Whatever the sequence may be, the Fifth Amendment forbids successive prosecution and cumulative punishment for a greater and lesser included offense."[63]

Finally, it is immaterial that the two prosecutions Brown faced identified different dates in the charging documents. The Ohio legislature defined as a single offense the taking and use of a single car. Regardless of how many days the car was actually in the thief's possession, the action is still just one offense. Accordingly, because Brown had been convicted of the lesser-included offense of joyriding, the Double Jeopardy Clause prohibited his subsequent prosecution for the greater offense of auto theft.

Interestingly, the Court has suggested that the preclusive effect of a prior conviction for a lesser-included offense depends in part on whether the prosecution planned to resolve the greater and lesser-included offenses in a single proceeding or in successive ones. In *Brown*, the prosecution first convicted the defendant of the offense of "joyriding." It was only after this initial proceeding was resolved that the State charged Brown with the greater offense of auto theft—charges which were barred by double jeopardy protections.

But would the double jeopardy bar have operated in the same manner if the State had charged Brown simultaneously with both offenses (as it did in the East Cleveland indictment) and he simply chose to plead guilty only to joyriding? In other words, is protection against double jeopardy required if the State intends only a single proceeding, but the accused triggers the successive handling of charges? The Court considered this question seven years after *Brown* and found that the double jeopardy bar operates differently where an action by the accused sets in motion the complained of subsequent prosecution for "the same" offense:

---

[61] Id. at 167.

[62] Id. at 168.

[63] Id.

Example—*Ohio v. Johnson*, 467 U.S. 493 (1984): Thomas Hill was shot and killed in his apartment and a number of items were taken. Kenneth Johnson was quickly charged in a single indictment with four counts in connection with the murder. These charges were murder, manslaughter (a lesser-included offense), grand theft, and aggravated robbery (a lesser-included offense).

Johnson agreed to plead guilty to the two lesser-included offenses—involuntary manslaughter and aggravated robbery. The trial judge accepted the pleas. Then on a defense motion, and, over the State's objection, the trial judge dismissed the murder and grand theft counts. The trial judge accepted Johnson's argument that the prohibition against double jeopardy prevented Johnson's further prosecution on the more serious counts in light of Johnson's conviction on the lesser-included offenses. The State appealed.

Analysis: Under the circumstances presented, Johnson's convictions for involuntary manslaughter and aggravated robbery did not bar his further prosecution for murder and grand theft.

The Double Jeopardy Clause offers three protections. "It protects against a second prosecution for the same offense after an acquittal. It protects against a second prosecution for the same offense after conviction. And it protects against multiple punishments for the same offense."[64]

The justifications for the first two forms of protection are identical—a concern for the negative impacts of repetitive prosecutions and a respect for the finality of judgments. Where (as in *Brown*) such concerns are implicated, double jeopardy will prevent "prosecution of a defendant for a greater offense when he has already been tried and acquitted or convicted on the lesser included offense."[65]

Here, however, the prosecution anticipated only a single trial. It was Johnson's choice to resolve only some of the charges he faced in the indictment. There was no final judgment on the counts to which Johnson did not plead. Moreover, on these facts, there is no cause for concern about repetitive prosecutions. The government never "had the opportunity to marshal its evidence and resources more than once or to hone its presentation of its case through a trial."[66]

When a jury convicts an accused of a lesser-included offense but not of the greater, there is a sense that the jury has implicitly acquitted the accused of the greater

---

[64] Ohio v. Johnson, 467 U.S. 493, 498 (1984).

[65] Id. at 501.

[66] Id.

offense. The acceptance of a guilty plea on a lesser-included offense, however, does not create a similar inference.

Finally, the double jeopardy protection against multiple punishments does not stand in the way of Johnson's further prosecution, it only affects his potential punishment after conviction. If Johnson is convicted of either of the greater offenses at trial, the trial court would then have to resolve the question of multiple punishments.

The Court did note that the rule against multiple punishment considers whether the legislature intended to create separate offenses or cumulative punishments. Here, the Ohio Legislature seemingly did not intend that cumulative punishment could be imposed for the greater and lesser-included offenses at issue in this case; however, this would be a matter to determine if (and when) Johnson is convicted of either.[67]

Tracking the logic of *Johnson*, the Court has also found that double jeopardy does not bar successive prosecutions where it is the accused who insists upon separate trials, despite the State's request to consolidate.[68]

3. "Same Offense" Preclusion v. "Collateral Estoppel" Preclusion. Double jeopardy protections differ depending upon whether a defendant alleges a) she is being prosecuted for an offense for which she has already been acquitted/convicted, or b) further litigation is collaterally estopped because an issue has been resolved by a prior acquittal. Collateral estoppel provides a narrower basis for relief than "the same offense" doctrine.

By way of example, assume you have been charged with first and second degree murder in connection with a single killing. The jury convicts you only of the lesser-included offense (second degree murder). As you read in *Brown*, that conviction would prevent the prosecution from ever re-prosecuting you for the greater offense (first degree murder). In addition, as you read in *Johnson*, the conviction on the lesser offense but not on the greater allows a presumption that you have been "acquitted" of first degree murder. Thus, for issue preclusion purposes, any issue that was necessarily resolved in connection with the first degree murder charge can never be re-litigated by the prosecution.

However, the collateral estoppel rule has a significant limitation: The jury's silence on the greater offense only collaterally estops further litigation of an issue presented in the case if "the record establishes that the issue was actually and necessarily decided in the defendant's favor."[69] If there is doubt, re-litigation of

---

[67] Id. at 502.

[68] Jeffers v. United States, 432 U.S. 137 (1977).

[69] Schiro v. Farley, 510 U.S. 222 (1994).

the single issue may be allowed if it is part of a different offense, even though a future prosecution for the greater offense would not be.

Let's look briefly at an example of how this plays out in the real world:

> **Example—*Schiro v. Farley*, 510 U.S. 222 (1994):** Thomas Schiro was accused of the brutal rape and murder of Laura Luebbehusen. At trial, the defense did not dispute that Schiro had killed Luebbehusen. Rather, the defense theory was Schiro was insane or mentally ill. The jury was asked to consider Schiro's guilt under three different counts—intentional murder, felony murder based on the rape, and felony murder based on other criminal conduct. The jury convicted Schiro of the second count (felony murder based on the rape) but left the rest of the verdict sheet blank.
>
> The State sought the death penalty. As an aggravating factor, the state argued that Schiro had intentionally killed Luebbehusen while raping or attempting to rape her. The trial judge sentenced Schiro to death finding that the State had established the aggravating factor beyond a reasonable doubt. Schiro appealed. He argued that the jury's conviction on the second count and silence on the first functioned as an "acquittal" of intentional murder. Accordingly, Schiro maintained, he should not have to re-litigate that issue. After the state and federal habeas courts rejected Schiro's claim, the Supreme Court accepted the case for review.

Analysis: The Double Jeopardy Clause did not preclude the State's efforts to seek the death penalty on the ground that Schiro had intentionally killed Luebbenhusen.

The Double Jeopardy Clause does protect against multiple prosecutions. But, the sentencing proceeding at issue here was not a successive prosecution for intentional murder for double jeopardy purposes. A defendant's first sentencing proceeding is simply a portion of the initial prosecution. Schiro was not forced to face a second trial on the question of his guilt. He also was not asked to endure successive death penalty proceedings. "[A]s applied to successive prosecutions, the Clause is written in terms of potential risk of trial and conviction, not punishment."[70]

Moreover, Schiro's death sentence is not precluded by collateral estoppel notions. Collateral estoppel or issue preclusion requires only that an accused not be forced

[70] Schiro, 510 U.S. at 231.

to re-litigate against the state an issue of ultimate fact that has already been decided in his favor. The burden is on Schiro to establish that the jury "acquitted" him on the issue of intentional murder. This he cannot do.

The felony murder charge on which Schiro was convicted was not a lesser-included offense of the intentional murder count. Thus, it cannot be said that the conviction on felony murder but not on intentional murder resolved the question of intent. Moreover, the trial record does not support a claim that the intent question was necessarily resolved by the jury's verdict. The jury received instructions suggesting that intent was an element of each of the murder counts; Schiro confessed to the killing; and the jury may have believed it could return only one verdict. Under these circumstances, "Schiro has not met his burden to demonstrate that the issue whose relitigation he seeks to foreclose was actually decided in his favor."[71]

4. Double Jeopardy Issues at the End of a Trial. Prosecutors must be especially aware of potential double jeopardy issues at the end of a trial for any crime that contains a lesser included offense. If the prosecutor has proven the lesser included offense, but has not proven the extra element for the greater offense, she may want to ask the trial judge to instruct the jury that they have the ability to convict the defendant of the lesser included offense. If the prosecutor does not ask for such an instruction, the jury may believe it has no choice but to acquit the defendant of the greater offense. Once that acquittal takes place, the prosecutor is prohibited from bringing new charges on the lesser included offense.

For example, assume the defendant is on trial for hitting the victim in the ribs with a baseball bat. He is charged with felony assault, the elements of which are:

1. Intent to cause physical injury;
2. Causing physical injury; and
3. Using a weapon.

At trial, the prosecutor proves the first two elements beyond a reasonable doubt, but the evidence that the defendant used a baseball bat is weak. The jury acquits the defendant. The prosecutor, realizing his mistake, brings a new charge against the defendant: misdemeanor assault. The elements of this crime are:

1. Intent to cause physical injury; and
2. Causing physical injury

[71] Id. at 236.

The defendant moves to dismiss this new charge on double jeopardy grounds and wins. The new charge does not contain any elements that are different from the original charge; therefore, it is not a separate offense—it is a lesser included offense. The defendant's acquittal of the greater offense will prevent his subsequent prosecution on the lesser included.

What could the prosecutor have done to avoid this result? After the evidence was submitted for the first trial, he should have asked the judge to charge the jury that if they found elements 1 and 2 but not 3, they could convict the defendant of misdemeanor assault. This is in effect adding a new charge to the charging instrument just before the jury begins to deliberate. The jury cannot convict the defendant of both misdemeanor assault and felony assault, but since both charges are included on the same charging instrument, the jury is able to decide whether the more serious crime has been proven. If the prosecutor does not request the charge on a lesser included offense and the jury acquits of felony assault, the defendant's double jeopardy rights preclude any future prosecution for the same offense.

On the other hand, sometimes a prosecutor will not want to agree to a lesser-included-offense instruction because she believes she has proven the extra element and does not want the jury to compromise on a less serious count. In the example above, assume the prosecutor believes she has proven all three elements of aggravated assault, but worries that the defendant appears sympathetic to the jury. In that case, the defense attorney might ask for a lesser-included-offense charge, hoping that although the jury will feel compelled to convict the defendant, it will be more comfortable convicting him of a lesser crime. The prosecutor may then refuse the lesser-included-offense charge and insist on an "all-or-nothing" verdict from the jury.

Of course, the actual decision about whether to give a lesser-included-offense instruction rests with the judge, and she should only give such an instruction if a reasonable juror could potentially determine that the elements of the lesser included crime are met but the extra element is not. In the above example, if there is no question that the defendant struck the victim with a baseball bat, and the defense is based on self-defense or lack of criminal intent, then the judge should refuse to give a lesser-included-offense instruction.

5. Retrial After a Mistrial. One common instance of retrial occurs when the initial trial ends prematurely because a mistrial is granted by the trial judge. Mistrials can be granted for a number of different reasons: if the jury hears prejudicial evidence, or if a lawyer says something in front of the jury that should not have been said, or if the jury is unable to reach a verdict.

A retrial is permitted after a mistrial if the defense requests or otherwise consents to the mistrial,[72] or if there is a "manifest necessity for the act [of declaring the mistrial] or the ends of public justice would otherwise be defeated."[73] The only exception to this rule arises when the prosecution has deliberately provoked the mistrial.

The decision of whether the mistrial was due to a manifest necessity is left to the broad discretion of the trial court. The Court has made clear that this discretion should be exercised only "in very extraordinary and striking circumstances,"[74] but the Court has provided some guidelines for making the assessment:

> **Example—*Arizona v. Washington*, 434 U.S. 497 (1978):** George Washington was accused of killing the night clerk in an Arizona hotel. He was convicted, but that conviction was overturned after it was discovered the prosecution withheld exculpatory evidence. During opening statements of the second trial, defense counsel told the jurors that at the first trial, the prosecution had "suppressed and hidden" and "purposely withheld" evidence from Washington. At the end of opening statements, the prosecution moved for a mistrial. After considering the arguments of both sides, the mistrial was granted.
>
> The reviewing courts agreed that defense counsel's statement were improper, but found that the trial court had not considered other alternatives and had not made an explicit finding that the mistrial was manifestly necessary. Therefore, the Double Jeopardy Clause barred another prosecution. The Supreme Court then accepted the case for review.

Analysis: The Court held that the re-prosecution of Washington will not violate the Double Jeopardy Clause.

The prohibition against double jeopardy recognizes an accused's "valued right to have his trial completed by a particular tribunal."[75] There are times, however, when this right of the accused is outweighed by the interest in allowing the prosecution "one full and fair opportunity to present his evidence to an impartial jury."[76] Where such circumstances exist, it may be necessary to declare a mistrial, even over defense objection. The burden is on the prosecutor to demonstrate that manifest necessity for such a mistrial existed.

---

72 Dinitz, 424 U.S. 600.

73 Wilson, 420 U.S. at 344.

74 Downum v. United States, 372 U.S. 734, 736 (1963).

75 Washington, 434 U.S. at 504.

76 Id. at 505.

The term "necessity" as used in the "manifest necessity" standard should not be read literally—that is, the prosecutor need not prove that there was no option other than a mistrial. On the other hand, "there are degrees of necessity and we require a 'high degree' before concluding that a mistrial is appropriate."[77] Some explanations will be viewed skeptically if offered as justification for a mistrial. For example, suspicion is warranted if an essential prosecution witness is unavailable or if there is some suggestion that the prosecution sought the mistrial to harass the accused or to gain a tactical advantage.

In this case, a mistrial was not literally "necessary"—some judges might have simply chosen to instruct the jury and proceed with trial. However, "the overriding interest in the evenhanded administration of justice requires that we accord the highest degree of respect to the trial judge's evaluation of the likelihood that the impartiality of one or more jurors may have been affected by the improper comment."[78]

In deciding whether to grant a mistrial, the trial judge must, of course, be guided by the defendant's right to have his case heard by the jury selected. But the defendant's right is not the only consideration. The trial judge is in the best position to see and hear the jurors. The trial judge is familiar with the evidence and is able to listen to the tone of the opening argument as it was delivered. If the trial judge acts "irrationally or irresponsibly" in granting a mistrial, reversal is warranted. But otherwise the trial judge's mistrial decision should be affirmed.

In this case, there is no suggestion that the trial judge acted rashly. After hearing the prosecution's motion, the trial judge expressed concerns about the double jeopardy implications of a mistrial. The trial court also deferred ruling to allow both sides time to argue their positions. "Since he exercised 'sound discretion' in handling the sensitive problem of possible juror bias created by the improper comment of defense counsel, the mistrial order is supported by the 'high degree' of necessity which is required in a case of this kind."[79]

Moreover, the trial judge was not required to place explicit findings regarding the "manifest necessity" on the record for the grant of the mistrial to be affirmed. As long as the record provides adequate explanation of the ruling, "the failure to explain that ruling more completely does not render it constitutionally defective."[80]

In addition to the sort of highly prejudicial comments seen in *Washington*, manifest necessity for a mistrial has also been found in cases where the jury cannot reach a verdict and where the trial judge's discovers juror bias.[81]

---

77 Id. at 506.

78 Id. at 511.

79 Id. at 516.

80 Id. at 517.

81 Downum, 372 U.S. 734.

6. Retrial After a Conviction Is Reversed on Appeal. The vast majority of appellate reversals are prompted by procedural irregularities during trial that do not directly implicate the question of guilt. For example, a conviction might be reversed because evidence was improperly admitted or because the prosecutor made improper and prejudicial closing arguments. Following such procedural reversals, double jeopardy presents no impediment to the prosecution's ability to retry the case. Indeed, the form of relief most often granted by the appellate court is a "remand for new trial."

However, sometimes a reviewing court is asked to consider directly the strength of the government's evidence. This sort of substantive evidentiary review can take two forms. First, it might be a review for the legal sufficiency of the government's evidence (as discussed in **Chapter 47**). Alternately, the review might consider the "weight of the evidence." Weight of the evidence review is not allowed in every jurisdiction. Where it is allowed, however, it requires the appellate court to sit as a so-called "thirteenth juror" to determine whether the conviction was appropriate. If an appellate court reverses because the conviction is against the weight of the evidence, it does not mean the government's evidence was legally insufficient. It simply means the appellate court found on balance the evidentiary proof tipped in favor of an acquittal.

For double jeopardy purposes, a reversal for insufficient evidence precludes further prosecution for the same offense.[82] In 1982, an accused who had his conviction reversed under a weight of the evidence review asked that a similar rule be applied in his case:

> **Example—*Tibbs v. Florida*, 457 U.S. 31 (1982):** Cynthia Nadeau and her friend Terry Milroy were hitchhiking their way from the Gulf Coast of Florida to a city in the Florida Keys. On February 3, just outside of Fort Meyers, a man in a green truck offered to give the two a ride. Shortly after Nadeau and Milroy got into the truck the man turned into a field. The man drew a gun on Milroy and told Nadeau to strip so that he could have sex with her. After sexually assaulting Nadeau, the man agreed that Milroy could leave. But, as Milroy was walking away the man shot him twice, killing him. A short time later, Nadeau made a run for a nearby house where she was able to use the telephone to contact police.
>
> Several days later, the police picked up Delbert Tibbs, who was hitchhiking in northern central Florida more than two hundred miles from the crime scene. According to the arresting officer,

[82] Burks, 437 U.S. 1.

Tibbs matched the description provided by Nadeau. Thereafter, Nadeau identified Tibbs as her assailant in a photo array, in a pre-trial lineup, and at trial.

Tibbs testified in his own defense asserting a case of mistaken identity. He maintained that he had been many hundreds of miles away in Daytona Beach at the time the crime was committed. Tibbs was able to partially corroborate this claim with the testimony of two Salvation Army Transit Lodge workers who confirmed Tibbs stayed at their motel for at least part of the time he claimed to be in Daytona Beach. On rebuttal, the prosecutor impeached Tibbs by introducing evidence (a registration card from a Salvation Army Transit Lodge in Orlando) that Tibbs was not in Daytona Beach the entire time he said he was. The jury convicted Tibbs and the court sentenced him to death.

The Florida Supreme Court reversed the conviction. The court found the only direct evidence of guilt was provided by Nadeau, who admitted to smoking marijuana before the crimes and who initially identified Tibbs during a suggestive photo array procedure. The reviewing court was also troubled by the fact that the truck, keys, and gun were never found. Furthermore, the court found that the rebuttal evidence offered by the prosecution had been manufactured. Based upon these and other findings, the court found that a new trial was required "in the interests of justice."

On remand, the trial court dismissed the indictment. It concluded that retrial was precluded by the double jeopardy clause because the reviewing court's reversal was akin to an acquittal. The case was eventually appealed to the Supreme Court.

Analysis: Tibbs's retrial was not prevented by double jeopardy concerns.

As a general rule, a defendant who is successful in having his conviction overturned on appeal may not use double jeopardy concerns as a sword to defeat further prosecution. There is just one narrow exception to this general rule: retrial is barred if a conviction is reversed because the evidence is legally insufficient. This narrow exception is justified by the special relationship that acquittals bear to the question of double jeopardy. "A reversal based on the insufficiency of the evidence has the same effect [as an acquittal] because it means that no rational factfinder could have voted to convict the defendant."

There is no question that repeated trials typically enhance the prosecutor's ability to secure a conviction. But there is less concern for prosecutorial gamesmanship when a conviction is reversed because a reviewing court simply disagrees with the jury's guilty verdict. "A reversal on this ground, unlike a reversal based on insufficient evidence, does not mean that acquittal was the only proper verdict."[83] Instead, the disagreement between the reviewing court and the jury on the appropriate verdict should be treated in much the same way that disagreement between deadlocked jurors is treated for double jeopardy purposes—by allowing retrial.

The only remaining question is whether the reversal here was on sufficiency or weight grounds. The reversal in this case, though not plainly labeled a "weight of the evidence" reversal, was clearly just that. The reviewing court essentially concluded that Tibbs's testimony and the defense case were more believable than Nadeau's testimony and the prosecution case. "This resolution of conflicting testimony in a manner contrary to the jury's verdict is a hallmark of review based on evidentiary weight, not evidentiary sufficiency."[84] Accordingly, the Double Jeopardy Clause presented no impediment to Tibbs's retrial.

7. The Question of Sentencing. Defendants can also raise double jeopardy challenges at the sentencing phase. These challenges arise in two different situations. The first situation involves a defendant whose initial conviction is overturned on appeal, and who is tried and convicted again. The defendant then argues that the judge will violate his double jeopardy rights if she sentences him to a harsher punishment after his retrial than he received after the initial trial.

The second situation occurs when a prosecutor appeals the sentence handed down by a judge because she believes the judge was too lenient at sentencing. The defendant then argues that this appeal by the prosecutor violates his double jeopardy rights.

We will first consider the issue of re-sentencing after a defendant has successfully appealed and then been convicted a second time. The Clause's protection against multiple punishments provides a basis for banning a harsher sentence on retrial. However, with just one narrow exception, the Court has largely rejected such claims, concluding that imposition of a particular sentence is not the functional equivalent of an "acquittal" of harsher punishments.[85] Accordingly, imposition of a lengthier sentence following a retrial is not prohibited by the Double Jeopardy Clause.

For example, imagine that a defendant, Jenny Jones, was convicted and sentenced to one year in prison for violently assaulting her boyfriend. On appeal, Jones ar-

[83] Tibbs, 457 U.S. at 42.

[84] Id. at 46.

[85] DiFrancesco, 449 U.S. at 134.

gued that reversal was required because the prosecutor told the jurors they would be "laughed at" if they didn't convict. The appellate court agreed, and found that a new trial was warranted. On retrial, the government was again able to secure a conviction. But after the second conviction, the sentencing court imposed a two-year period of incarceration. Arguing that the harsher sentence violated double jeopardy protections, Jones posited that the initial one-year sentence should be understood as an implicit "acquittal" of any harsher sentences that might have been imposed. The Supreme Court has rejected this argument. Accordingly, the court's sentencing discretion on retrial would not be circumscribed under the Double Jeopardy Clause by the one-year prison term that Jones initially received.

The Supreme Court has found one exception to this rule: if the sentencing scheme requires the sentencing judge or jury to make sentencing decisions in a manner that is comparable to methods used to assess guilt, the initial sentencing decision will be treated as an "acquittal" of harsher punishments that might have been imposed. Thus, under these conditions, if the case is re-tried and the defendant is convicted a second time, double jeopardy concerns dictate that he cannot be sentenced to a harsher punishment than he received after the first conviction.

So far, the Court has limited the application of this rule to capital cases:[86]

> **Example—*Bullington v. Missouri*, 451 U.S. 430 (1981):** Robert Bullington was accused of kidnapping and drowning a young woman. A jury convicted him of the murder. According to the standard sentencing procedures for capital cases, the jury was next asked to consider the evidence of aggravation or mitigation in deciding whether to impose a death sentence. After considering this evidence, the jury voted unanimously to sentence Bullington to life without the possibility of parole for fifty years.
>
> Bullington appealed his conviction, and it was overturned on procedural grounds. His case was remanded for retrial. Prior to the second trial, the government again announced its intention to seek a death sentence. Bullington took an immediate appeal. It was his contention that the jury's decision not to sentence him to death at the first trial functioned as an "acquittal" of capital punishment and thereby precluded the prosecution's ability to seek death again.

Analysis: Bullington could not be sentenced to death should he be convicted at the end of his second trial.

[86] Monge v. California, 524 U.S. 721 (1998).

There is no question that the Double Jeopardy Clause prevents the retrial of a person who has been acquitted of certain conduct. But there has been little expansion of this reasoning into the sentencing realm because the imposition of a specific sentence is not viewed as an "acquittal" of any other punishments that might have been imposed.

The type of evidence that usually informs the sentencing decision is very different from the type of evidence that informs questions of guilt. Sentencing evidence is largely developed outside of the courtroom, and the standards that govern the decision-making process do not require proof beyond a reasonable doubt. Indeed, in most cases, "there are virtually no rules or tests or standards," and the sentencing decision is entirely a discretionary one.[87] In the run-of-the-mill sentencing case previously decided by the Court, therefore, there was little reason to conclude that standard double jeopardy notions should be imported into the sentencing context. However, the same cannot be said of the capital sentencing scheme that Bullington faced.

Once a jury convicts an accused of capital murder in Missouri, it must choose between two possible sentences—death or life imprisonment without the possibility of parole for fifty years. A separate sentencing hearing is held to present the jury with evidence in mitigation and aggravation. If the jury unanimously agrees that one of the ten aggravating circumstances has been established by proof beyond a reasonable doubt, it may (but is not required to) sentence the convicted person to death. The jury is always free to choose life, even it if finds the aggravating evidence outweighs the mitigation. The capital sentencing scheme that Bullington faced at his first trial was thus roughly akin to the guilt phase of a trial.

Under these circumstances, when the jury at Bullington's first trial sentenced him to life that necessarily meant it acquitted him of whatever aggravating factors were necessary to sentence him to death. In the double jeopardy context, an "acquittal" such as this is an absolute bar to retrial. "Having received 'one fair opportunity to offer whatever proof it could assemble' the State is not entitled to another."[88]

The second question with regard to the impact of double jeopardy on sentencing occurs when a prosecutor appeals a sentencing decision that she feels was too lenient. This arises most often in the context of career offender sentencing statutes, which typically allow the sentencing judge to impose a harsher sentence on a convicted person if certain factual predicates are found. These factual predicates are often prior convictions for certain specified crimes. If the prosecutor appeals one of these sentences, the defendant can argue that this appeal violates his double jeopardy rights. However, the Court has consistently rejected these claims:

[87] Bullington, 451 U.S. at 444.

[88] Id. at 446.

Example—*United States v. DiFrancesco*, 449 U.S. 117 (1980): Eugene DiFrancesco and his partners were hired by property owners to burn down their buildings in exchange for a share of the insurance proceeds. The scheme resulted in a total fraud against the insurers in the amount of $480,000. DiFrancesco was convicted of racketeering and conspiracy charges in connection with his role in the scheme. He was not immediately sentenced because of a second prosecution that was pending. In the second (unrelated) case, DiFrancesco was convicted of bombing a federal building and of related offenses. For the second case, DiFrancesco received a nine-year sentence. The sentencing for the first conviction was then scheduled.

The government announced that it intended to sentence DiFrancesco under the Organized Crime Control Act, which allowed convicted persons to be sentenced to enhanced punishment if they were "dangerous special offenders." The Act also allowed the government to appeal any sentence imposed under it. The sentencing judge found DiFrancesco was a "dangerous special offender," and sentenced him to two concurrent ten-year terms for his racketeering and conspiracy convictions. These sentences was to run concurrent with the earlier arson sentence. Thus, DiFrancesco was required to serve only one additional year in prison beyond his earlier sentence. The government appealed.

The reviewing court dismissed the government's appeal as prohibited by double jeopardy concerns. The Supreme Court then took the case for review.

Analysis: The statutory sentencing scheme allowing the government to appeal a sentence that it viewed as too light did not infringe upon double jeopardy protections.

The Double Jeopardy Clause does not function as an absolute bar to a government appeal in every criminal case. An appeal in DiFrancesco's case would be prohibited only if his sentence enjoys the same finality and conclusiveness that is properly afforded an acquittal.

However, sentences have never enjoyed the same finality as acquittals. It has long been true that there is no double jeopardy bar to the imposition of a harsher sentence on retrial. There is also little reason to believe that the same concerns for "embarrassment, expense, anxiety, and insecurity," that justify giving preclusive effect to acquittals are relevant to sentencing decisions.

The government appeal is also not barred by the double jeopardy ban on multiple punishments. The multiple punishment provisions prevent only the imposition of "a greater sentence than the legislature has authorized."[89] Here the career offender provision under which DiFrancesco was sentenced, and under which the government appealed, was specifically authorized by Congress.

Sentencing judges have traditionally enjoyed extremely broad discretion to sentence convicted offenders as they see fit. The statutory provision authorizing a government appeal of the sentence was a direct attempt by Congress to check that discretion and address what it saw as the problem of judges sentencing organized crime figures too leniently. Thus, the statute "[i]s not an example of 'Government oppression' against which the Double Jeopardy Clause stands guard."[90]

Finally, remember that the Double Jeopardy Clause does not restrict a legislature's ability to impose cumulative punishment for the same offense.[91] While it is true that legislatures "ordinarily do[] not intend to punish the same offense under two different statutes,"[92] there is no constitutional rule forbidding legislatures from doing so. Thus, a legislature may create two different statutes which cover the same criminal conduct, which could legally result in cumulative sentences.[93] Consequently, where "a legislature specifically authorizes cumulative punishment under two statutes, regardless of whether those two statutes proscribe the same conduct under *Blockburger*, a court's task of statutory construction is at an end and the prosecutor may seek and the trial court or jury may impose cumulative punishment under such statutes in a single trial."[94]

[89] DiFrancesco, 449 U.S. at 139.

[90] Id. at 143.

[91] Albernaz v. United States, 450 U.S. 333 (1981).

[92] Whalen, 445 U.S. 684.

[93] Hunter, 459 U.S. 359.

[94] Id. at 368-69.

Quick Summary

The double jeopardy guarantees of the Fifth Amendment (applied to the States through the Fourteenth) prevent the government from repeatedly prosecuting an individual for the same criminal offense and from imposing multiple punishments for the same offense.

In jury trials, jeopardy attaches once the jury "is empaneled and sworn."[1] In bench trials, jeopardy attaches "when the court begins to hear evidence." The *Blockburger* test is used to decide whether two offenses are "the same" for double jeopardy purposes. Under this test, if each offense does require proof of at least one unique fact, the two offenses are not "the same."

The most robust double jeopardy protection is provided by a prior acquittal. The double jeopardy protection afforded by a prior acquittal applies equally to verdicts of acquittal that have been entered by a judge and by a jury. Acquittals also bar retrial even if the acquittal is grounded in a mistake. In addition, acquittals preclude both retrial for the same offense, and future litigation of any issue that "was necessarily decided by a jury's acquittal in a prior trial." Thus, the notion of issue preclusion (or collateral estoppel) is embedded in the double jeopardy protection. But, the government may re-litigate an issue that has been resolved in a prior proceeding if the subsequent proceeding is governed by a lower standard of proof.

If a defendant has been convicted of an offense, she may not again be forced to endure a repeated prosecution for the same offense. But further proceedings are permissible if: a trial judge enters a judgment of acquittal notwithstanding the jury's guilty verdict; if a defendant moves to dismiss the indictment after a guilty verdict; or if a conviction is overturned by an appellate court for reasons unrelated to the sufficiency of the evidence.

Mistrials are another form of early trial termination that may implicate double jeopardy concerns. Where there is "manifest necessity" for a mistrial, the prosecution is not limited by double jeopardy in its ability to re-file charges. But, if manifest necessity did not exist, and a mistrial is granted over defense objection, retrial is not permitted. The most common example of manifest necessity is a jury's inability to agree upon a verdict.

---

[1] Martinez v. Illinois, 134 S. Ct. 2070 (2014).

Double jeopardy concerns are not as acute in the sentencing context. First, double jeopardy protections are aimed primarily at ensuring that a court does not impose greater punishment than the legislature has authorized. Beyond this, the Court has found that double jeopardy concerns do not preclude harsher sentences on retrial. The one circumstance in which double jeopardy prohibitions will apply to a harsher sentence on retrial is in the death penalty context.

The Double Jeopardy Clause generally does not preclude civil actions. However, there are times when a penalty even though categorized as "civil" will be sufficiently punitive to transform it into a criminal penalty.

Finally, while the juvenile justice system was for many years characterized as "civil" in nature, the Court has recognized that a candid appraisal of the juvenile justice process requires a conclusion that double jeopardy applies with equal force in that context.

Review Questions

1. The Case of the Bank Executive and His Real Estate Fraud. Michael Morgan was the founder, CEO and member of the Board of Directors at Charter Federal Saving and Loan Association. The bank used a wholly owned subsidiary, Bedford Equities, that it used to buy real estate. In 1990 the federal government began investigating Morgan. In 1993, he was charged with certain civil offenses. He settled these civil charges with a consent order and consent judgment. The civil charges related to four real estate transactions and alleged that Morgan had concealed payments received in connection with the four transactions or otherwise falsified transaction documents. Though Morgan did not admit liability, he was banned from future participation in FDIC insured businesses, and agreed to pay $1.8 million in restitution and penalties to resolve the civil offenses.

Eight months later, a federal grand jury charged Morgan in a six-count indictment with bank fraud and other charges related to the four real estate transactions. The criminal charges arose from the exact conduct that was the subject of the civil settlement. Morgan moved to dismiss the indictment, alleging that it was in violation of his Fifth Amendment right against double jeopardy. If you are the trial judge deciding the motion, how will you rule?

2. The Case of the Prosecutor's Improper Cross. James Gilmore was prosecuted for his role in a fraudulent investment scheme. During trial, the prosecutor repeatedly and improperly asked one of Gilmore's confederates about her assertion of her Fifth Amendment privilege against self-incrimination during an earlier SEC investigation. More than 25 times during the cross-examination, the prosecutor incorrectly referenced the confederate's assertion of the privilege. Following conviction, the trial court granted a defense motion for new trial. The court found that the prosecutor's repeated and highly prejudicial misconduct necessitated reversal of the conviction. The trial court, however, denied the defense motions for judgment of acquittal notwithstanding the jury's verdict. In the trial court's estimation, the evidence had been sufficient. Gilmore then filed a motion to dismiss the indictment. Gilmore maintained that the prosecutor's deliberate and egregious misconduct rendered any retrial a violation of his double jeopardy rights. Should the motion to dismiss be granted?

3. The Case of Copying Child Pornography. Police began investigating Christopher Emly after they traced several child pornography files to a computer at his mother's house. During a search of the residence conducted pursuant to a warrant, the police seized a laptop. On the laptop, the police found some 629 images of child pornography. In addition, the police seized an SD card from Emly's bedroom. On this card, the police found copies of 481 of the images found on the laptop. The police also found 6 to 8 of the same images of child pornography on both a CD and a computer hard drive found in the bedroom. These 6 to 8 images were among those found on the SD card, and had originally been on the laptop but were automatically deleted.

Emly was indicted by a federal grand jury. He was charged in one count with "using his laptop to receive child pornography files." He was also charged in three separate possession counts with the images found on the SD card, the CD, and the computer hard drive. The possession charges all alleged possession on the same day—the day the materials were seized from Emly's bedroom. Prior to trial, Emly moved to merge the three possession counts into one, but the court denied his motion.

Emly was convicted of the receipt count and all three possession counts. The court sentenced him to 228 months in prison on the receipt count and 120 months on each possession count. The sentences were set to run concurrently. Emly appealed arguing that his convictions and sentences violated the Double Jeopardy Clause. Will he be successful? If he is, what will the practical effect of his victory be?

4. The Case of the Sentencing Error. Kennon D. Thomas pled guilty to one count of being a felon in possession of a firearm. Prior to his sentencing, the court ordered a pre-sentence report ("PSR"). The PSR recommended a sentence based on its conclusion that Thomas had two prior convictions for crimes of violence. At the sentencing hearing, however, the court accepted Thomas's assertion that his prior convictions were not crimes of violence. The court sentenced Thomas to 33 months in prison. The government properly appealed, challenging the lower court's conclusion that Thomas's priors were not crimes of violence. The appellate court reversed, agreeing with the government (and the PSR) that the prior convictions were in fact for crimes of violence. The case was remanded for resentencing. Upon resentencing, the court sentenced Thomas with the understanding that his priors were crimes of violence. Based on Thomas's failure to appear at an earlier scheduled resentencing hearing, the court also imposed sentencing penalties for obstruction of justice and the failure to accept responsibility. Thomas was ultimately resentenced to 110 months in prison. He appealed, arguing that his new sentence was precluded by Double Jeopardy concerns. How should the appellate court now rule?

FROM THE COURTROOM

BLOCKBURGER v. UNITED STATES

Supreme Court of the United States, 1932
284 U.S. 299

Mr. Justice SUTHERLAND delivered the opinion of the Court.

The petitioner was charged with violating provisions of the Harrison Narcotic Act. The indictment contained five counts. The jury returned a verdict against petitioner upon the second, third, and fifth counts only. Each of these counts charged a sale of morphine hydrochloride to the same purchaser. The second count charged a sale on a specified day of ten grains of the drug not in or from the original stamped package; the third count charged a sale on the following day of eight grains of the drug not in or from the original stamped package; the fifth count charged the latter sale also as having been made not in pursuance of a written order of the purchaser as required by the statute. The court sentenced petitioner to five years' imprisonment and a fine of $2,000 upon each count, the terms of imprisonment to run consecutively; and this judgment was affirmed on appeal.

The principal contentions here made by petitioner are as follows: (1) That, upon the facts, the two sales charged in the second and third counts as having been made to the same person constitute a single offense; and (2) that the sale charged in the third count as having been made not from the original stamped package, and the same sale charged in the fifth count as having been made not in pursuance of a written order of the purchaser, constitute but one offense, for which only a single penalty lawfully may be imposed.

One. The sales charged in the second and third counts, although made to the same person, were distinct and separate sales made at different times. It appears from the evidence that, shortly after delivery of the drug which was the subject of the first sale, the purchaser paid for an additional quantity, which was delivered the next day. But the first sale had been consummated, and the payment for the additional drug, however closely following, was the initiation of a separate and distinct sale completed by its delivery.

The contention on behalf of petitioner is that these two sales, having been made to the same purchaser and following each other, with no substantial interval of time between the delivery of the drug in the first transaction and the payment for the second quantity sold, constitute a single continuing offense. The contention is unsound. The distinction between the transactions here involved and an offense continuous in its character is well settled, as was pointed out by this court in the case of *In re Snow*, 120 U. S. 274. There it was held that the offense of cohabiting with more than one woman was a continuous offense, and was committed, in the sense of the statute, where there was a living or dwelling together as husband and wife. The court said:

'It is, inherently, a continuous offense, having duration; and not an offense consisting of an isolated act. * * *

'A distinction is laid down in adjudged cases and in text-writers between an offense continuous in its character, like the one at bar, and a case where the statute is aimed at an offense that can be committed uno ictu.'

The Narcotic Act does not create the offense of engaging in the business of selling the forbidden drugs, but penalizes any sale made in the absence of either of the qualifying requirements set forth. Each of several successive sales constitutes a distinct offense, however closely they may follow each other. The distinction stated by Mr. Wharton is that, 'when the impulse is single, but one indictment lies, no matter how long the action may continue. If successive impulses are separately given, even though all unite in swelling a common stream of action, separate indictments lie.' Wharton's Criminal Law (11th Ed.) § 34. Or, as stated in note 3 to that section, 'The test is whether the individual acts are prohibited, or the course of action which they constitute. If the former, then each act is punishable separately. * * * If the latter, there can be but one penalty.'

In the present case, the first transaction, resulting in a sale, had come to an end. The next sale was not the result of the original impulse, but of a fresh one-that is to say, of a new bargain. The question is controlled, not by the *Snow* Case, but by such cases as that of *Ebeling v. Morgan*. There the accused was convicted under several counts of a willful tearing, etc., of mail bags with intent to rob. The court stated the question to be 'whether one who, in the same transaction, tears or cuts successively mail bags of the United States used in conveyance of the mails, with intent to rob or steal any such mail, is guilty of a single offense, or of additional offenses because of each successive cutting with the criminal intent charged.' Answering this question, the court, after quoting the statute said:

'These words plainly indicate that it was the intention of the lawmakers to protect each and every mail bag from felonious injury and mutilation. Whenever any one mail bag is thus torn, cut, or injured, the offense is complete. Although the transaction of cutting the mail bags was in a sense continuous, the complete statutory offense was committed every time a mail bag was cut in the manner described, with the intent charged. The offense as to each separate bag was complete when that bag was cut, irrespective of any attack upon, or mutilation of, any other bag.'

Two. Section 1 of the Narcotic Act creates the offense of selling any of the forbidden drugs except in or from the original stamped package; and section 2 creates the offense of selling any of such drugs not in pursuance of a written order of the person to whom the drug is sold. Thus, upon the face of the statute, two distinct offenses are created. Here there was but one sale, and the question is whether, both sections being violated by the same act, the accused committed two offenses or only one.

The statute is not aimed at sales of the forbidden drugs qua sales, a matter entirely beyond the authority of Congress, but at sales of such drugs in violation of the requirements set forth in sections 1 and 2, enacted as aids to the enforcement of the stamp tax imposed by the act.

Each of the offenses created requires proof of a different element. The applicable rule is that, where the same act or transaction constitutes a violation of two distinct statutory provisions, the test to be applied to determine whether there are two offenses or only one, is whether each provision requires proof of a fact which the other does not. In [*Gavieres v. United States*] this court quoted from and adopted the language of the Supreme Court of Massachusetts in *Morey v. Commonwealth*: 'A single act may be an offense against two statutes; and if each statute requires proof of an additional fact which the other does not, an acquittal or conviction under either statute does not exempt the defendant from prosecution and punishment under the other.' Applying the test, we must conclude that here, although both sections were violated by the one sale, two offenses were committed.

. . .

Three. . . . Nor is there merit in the contention that the language of the penal section of the Narcotic Act, 'any person who violates or fails to comply with any of the requirements of this act,' shall be punished, etc., is to be construed as imposing a single punishment for a violation of the distinct requirements of sections 1 and 2 when accomplished by one and the same sale. The plain meaning of the provision is that each offense is subject to the penalty prescribed; and, if that be too harsh, the remedy must be afforded by act of Congress, not by judicial legislation under the guise of construction. Under the circumstances, so far as disclosed, it is true that the imposition of the full penalty of fine and imprisonment upon each count seems unduly severe; but there may have been other facts and circumstances before the trial court properly influencing the extent of the punishment. In any event, the matter was one for that court, with whose judgment there is no warrant for interference on our part.

Judgment affirmed.

47

Appeals

Key Concepts

- Discretionary Review v. Review as a Matter of Right
- Final Judgment Rule and Interlocutory Appeals
- Preservation of Appellate Claims
- Harmless Error
- Standards of Review: *De Novo*, Clear Error, Abuse of Discretion

A. Introduction and Policy. After the jury has returned a guilty verdict and the defendant has been sentenced, the defendant can appeal the case to another court to review the judgment and sentence. And, although a prosecutor cannot challenge an acquittal by a jury, she can appeal certain adverse decisions by a trial judge. In this chapter we will consider some of the primary standards that govern that review process. But first let's discuss some of the nuts and bolts of appellate litigation:

1. Two-Tiered Appellate Systems. There are two layers of appellate courts in most states and in the federal system. The first layer of courts sits immediately above the trial courts. This layer is known as the **intermediate appellate court**. Intermediate appellate courts have the authority to review the decisions of the trial courts, though that review is cabined, to a greater or lesser extent, by the various standards of review you will read about below—*de novo*, abuse of discretion, clear error, etc.

In the federal system, this intermediate layer of courts is called the United States Courts of Appeal. While the federal trial courts cover a geographic territory that is contained within a single state (e.g., the United States District Court for the District of Maryland), the federal appellate courts cover larger geographic regions known as "circuits." For example, the United States Court of Appeals for the Second Circuit reviews the decisions of the federal trial courts in New York, Vermont and Connecticut.

In addition to the eleven numbered circuits, there are also the Court of Appeals for the D.C. Circuit and the Court of Appeals for the Federal Circuit. The D.C. Circuit's jurisdiction extends only to Washington, D.C., but it plays a significant role in shaping national law because it is the site of numerous appeals involving federal agencies. The Federal Circuit is unlike any of the other circuits—it has nationwide jurisdiction over specific subject areas, such as patent suits or suits for money damages against the United States.

In the state court systems, not every state has an intermediate appellate court. But, in those states with such courts, they are not as predictably structured as those in the federal system. In some states, like Maryland or Mississippi, there is just a single intermediate appellate court with statewide jurisdiction over all the trial courts. In other states, like New York and California, the intermediate appellate court is divided into districts or departments that only hear appeals from a pre-defined portion of the state.

Above the intermediate appellate courts sits the high court in the particular jurisdiction, also known as the "**court of last resort**." In the federal system, this court is the United States Supreme Court. In the state systems, the name of the high court will vary. For example, in New York (as is true in many states), the Supreme Court is the trial court, while the court of last resort is called the Court of Appeals. Unlike the intermediate appellate courts, which generally tend to be courts of error correction, the high court in most jurisdictions will hear only those cases with a significant legal impact. The one significant exception to this general rule arises in states where there is not an intermediate appellate court. In such states, the court of last resort is also a court of error correction.

2. Getting Into the Appellate Court. Appeals may be either "**discretionary**" or "**as a matter of right**." The ease with which you can get into the appellate court will first be determined by which type of appeal you are bringing. It is harder to get into court with a discretionary appeal because they don't have to be accepted by the court. In contrast, it couldn't be easier to get into court with an appeal that you are taking as a matter of right. This is because as the name suggests in such cases the litigant has an unambiguous right to seek review. In most criminal cases the first round of review is an appeal as a matter of right.

Getting into court when you have a right to appeal is a simple matter of filing what is known as a **notice of appeal**. The notice of appeal is a straightforward form that notifies the court an appeal is being taken. A sample notice of appeal is attached at the end of this chapter. Though it is rare, some jurisdictions do require a particular format for the notice of appeal. You should therefore check the local rules to ensure that any format you are using is appropriate. Sample notices are also oftentimes available on court websites or are attached as appendices to the court rules or the relevant rules of appellate procedure.

Though the notice of appeal is a fairly simple form to draft, there are deadlines that must be strictly adhered to in order to secure the right to appeal. In the federal system, Rule 4 of the Federal Rules of Appellate Procedure gives a convicted person just fourteen days from the entry of judgment to file the notice of appeal. In many states, that deadline is longer. Though it varies from state to state, within thirty days of sentencing is a fairly common cutoff.

Once the notice of appeal is timely filed and the case is docketed in the appellate court, the labels of the parties changes. The party who appeals (usually the defendant) becomes the "appellant," and the opposing party becomes the "appellee."

The process for getting into an appellate court for a discretionary appeal is a bit more complicated. As noted above, the courts of last resort in the federal and state systems are (for most matters) not courts of error. Instead, these courts tend to consider open questions of law, questions that are in need of further clarification, or questions that will likely have an impact beyond the four corners of the case being considered. Accordingly, to secure review in these courts, you must convince the court that your legal claims are of the sort the court generally finds will merit its consideration.

The preliminary application for discretionary review, called a **petition for writ of certiorari** (or "cert petition" for short) usually includes a discussion of the ambiguity of the existing law and a request for further guidance or clarification. In this sense, writing a cert petition is a much different task than drafting an appellate brief (where you are presumably telling the reviewing court that the decided law clearly favors your client's position). Moreover, unlike the notice of appeal, which is a single-page document, the cert petition can be detailed and complex, including a complete discussion of the material facts and the relevant law.

Once a discretionary appeal is accepted, the labels of the parties again change. The losing party in the intermediate appellate court (who sought review in the high court) becomes the "petitioner," and the victor in the intermediate appellate court becomes the "respondent" as the case moves up.

Below is a simplified chart reflecting the flow of cases from the trial court to the highest appellate court. The dashed line between the intermediate appellate court and the court of last resort reflects the discretionary nature of that review:

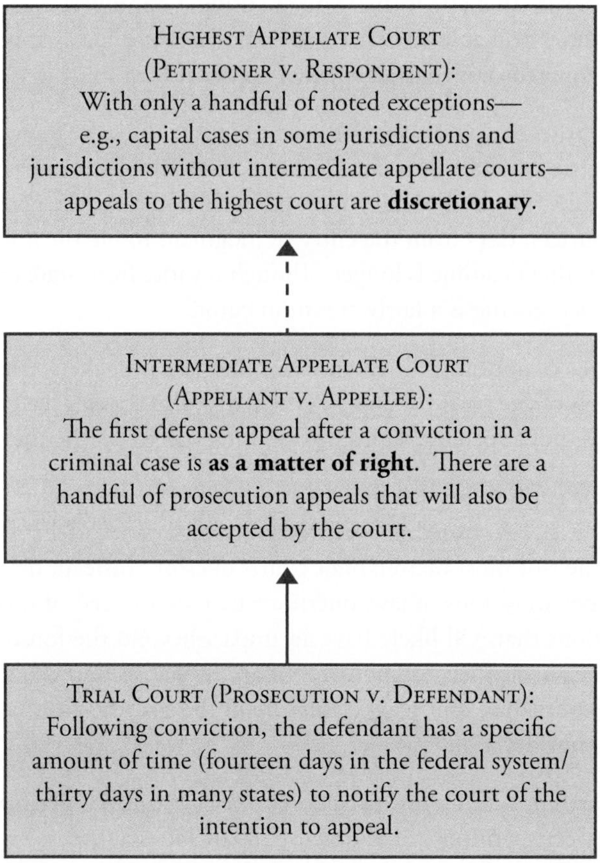

Highest Appellate Court
(Petitioner v. Respondent):
With only a handful of noted exceptions—
e.g., capital cases in some jurisdictions and
jurisdictions without intermediate appellate courts—
appeals to the highest court are **discretionary**.

↑ (dashed)

Intermediate Appellate Court
(Appellant v. Appellee):
The first defense appeal after a conviction in a
criminal case is **as a matter of right**. There are a
handful of prosecution appeals that will also be
accepted by the court.

↑

Trial Court (Prosecution v. Defendant):
Following conviction, the defendant has a specific
amount of time (fourteen days in the federal system/
thirty days in many states) to notify the court of the
intention to appeal.

3. Making A Case. In the appellate court, the presentation of your case is done first through written briefs and then (where allowed) through oral argument. After a careful review of the trial transcript and other relevant portions of the trial record, the appellant will draft a brief that sets forth the legal errors she is raising in the case. The brief should provide a legal analysis that contains ample citation to relevant case law and should articulate the relief that is sought. In a criminal case (assuming a defense appeal), the relief sought by the appellant may include a request for reversal of the conviction, a request for a new trial, or a request for sentencing relief. As you read in **Chapter 46**, there are also times when a government appeal is permitted. In such cases, the relief sought is often reinstatement of a guilty verdict, reversal of a suppression decision (where the suppression precludes prosecution), or a sentencing challenge.

After the appellant files her principal brief, the appellee (usually the government) will have an opportunity to file a response brief to answer the appellant's arguments. As you will read, in addition to making substantive legal arguments, the government also commonly argues preservation and harmless error as reasons why reversal of a conviction is not warranted. After the response brief is filed, the appellant has the final written word in the reply brief.

Every appellate court has specific rules that must be followed with regard to the formatting of briefs. For example, Rule 28 of the Federal Rules of Appellate Procedure

1. Identifies the specific sections that each appellate brief must include;

2. Describes the ordering of certain tables; and

3. Explains the correct format for citing references.

There are also rules for the maximum number of words that may be included, for the maximum page length, and other such specifics.[1] State systems all have similar guidelines. Before filing an appellate brief for the first time in a particular jurisdiction, careful review of the requirements provided in the relevant rules is advised. Something as simple as filing a brief with too many pages or the wrong-sized font may be cause for the court to reject an argument.

After the briefs have been filed, most jurisdictions grant the parties an **oral argument**. Oral arguments usually run about thirty minutes per side. The parties use oral arguments to help the judges better understand the legal arguments and to answer questions that the court may have or to clarify issues in the record. Some jurisdictions do not automatically allow an oral argument. In the federal courts, for example, Rule 34 of the Federal Rules of Appellate Procedure provides for an oral argument unless all three judges on the panel agree that it is unnecessary.

Intermediate appellate courts decide cases in panels, usually composed of three judges. In theory, sitting in panels allows intermediate appellate judges to engage in more collaborative decision-making than is possible at the trial level. After considering the briefs and hearing oral arguments, the judges on the panel can fully discuss the issues presented to arrive at the most appropriate resolution of the claims.

In reality, however, the collaborative nature of decision-making in the intermediate appellate courts does not always live up to the ideal. Because of significant caseload pressures, many appellate panels divide up the opinion writing responsibilities for the cases under consideration before oral argument. Thus, in some courts there will be times when only the judge assigned to write the opinion will have fully reviewed the briefs and the appellate record.

Though intermediate appellate courts generally sit in panels of three, there will be times when the court sits *en banc*, so that all of the judges on the intermediate

[1] See, e.g., F.R.A.P. 32.

appellate court (not just some portion of them) will sit to hear a case. The federal rules and about half of the states allow for *en banc* rehearing of a case. In some jurisdictions, this may mean as many as fourteen or fifteen judges are considering the appeal.

The highest court does not sit in panels, but rather sits as a whole court. Thus, when the United States Supreme Court considers cases, all nine justices will be present for argument and will have reviewed the briefs in the cases. With only a small number of exceptions, the same is true for the high courts in the states. Because of the discretionary nature of many high court dockets, the workload is generally lower, affording each of the judges more time to review all of the materials relevant to each case being considered.

Every state in the nation affords some right to appeal in criminal cases. However, unlike the constitutional right to a jury trial, there is no federal constitutional right to an appeal.[2] Nonetheless, if a state has created a statutory (or state constitutional) right to appeal, the United States Constitution requires that the right be administered in an evenhanded manner. States therefore may not allow access to appeals for the rich but not the poor without raising equal protection and due process concerns. As the Court has said, in "criminal trials a State can no more discriminate on account of poverty than on account of religion, race, or color."[3]

In the federal system, the entire direct review process consists of just two phases—the first in the Court of Appeals and the second (possibly) in the United States Supreme Court. In the state systems, the first two phases of the direct review process similarly entail review in the relevant intermediate and high appellate courts. But, if there is a federal issue involved in the appeal, an appellate litigant who has lost in the state's highest court may seek further review in the United States Supreme Court. If the Supreme Court agrees to take the case, it will consider only the questions of federal law in the case. For example, if a defendant argues in state court that the admission of certain testimony in her case violated both a state evidentiary rule and her constitutional right to confront witnesses, the United States Supreme Court would consider only the latter claim.

Once the process of appellate review is completed, a case moves into the collateral review phase (also known as the post-conviction process). Collateral review, which is no longer considered a direct attack on the conviction and/or sentence, is discussed in **Chapter 48**.

---

[2] McKane v. Durston, 153 U.S. 684 (1894).

[3] Griffin v. Illinois, 351 U.S. 12, 17 (1956).

B. The Law. Once a party reaches the appellate court, she still must navigate a series of hurdles before obtaining relief. Here is an overview of the rules governing the appellate process:

1. A party may generally appeal only the final judgment of the trial court. There are two exceptions to this rule:
   a. Either party may appeal a final collateral order of the trial court; and
   b. The government may appeal significant pre-trial evidentiary rulings.
2. The issue being appealed must be within the scope of review of the appellate court.
3. The issue being appealed must have been preserved in the lower court by a timely objection. However, if the error in the lower court was plain error the appellate court may consider the issue even if it was not preserved at the lower court level.
4. The standard of review will dictate how much deference the appellate court should afford the trial court's original decision. There are three standards of review. Identifying which standard applies will depend on the type of appellate claim being raised:
   a. *De novo*;
   b. Plain error;
   c. Abuse of discretion.
5. For the overwhelming majority of appellate claims, even if the appellate court finds that the trial court made an error, the appellate court will not overturn the trial court's decision if it was a harmless error; that is, if the mistake likely did not affect the result of the trial.

The most basic hurdle is to ensure the problem the party is complaining about is actually appealable. The **final judgment rule** states that an appellate court can only review final judgments of the lower court. This rule is based on the statutory language of the provision which gives the appellate court its jurisdiction. In the federal courts, this statute is found at 28 U.S.C. § 1291, which states that, "[t]he courts of appeals . . . shall have jurisdiction of appeals from all **final decisions** of the district courts of the United States."[4]

A final judgment is one that terminates the dispute between the parties. In a criminal case that termination occurs, typically, with a conviction or an acquittal. The purpose of the final judgment rule is to avoid piecemeal litigation. Without

[4] 28 U.S.C. § 1291 (emphasis added).

such a rule, either party could halt the trial proceedings after any adverse decision and move the case into appellate court for months at a time. This would make it nearly impossible to move a case through the trial process in an efficient and orderly manner.

For example, assume the defendant was arrested in her car and drugs and drug paraphernalia were seized at the time of the arrest. The defense attorney files a motion to suppress this evidence on the ground that reasonable articulable suspicion did not exist for the stop. If the defendant loses the suppression motion, the evidence will be admitted at trial. The defense attorney cannot immediately challenge the admission of the evidence because that decision is not a "final judgment." Rather, the defense attorney must wait until after the defendant is convicted to challenge the suppression ruling, along with any other appellate claims that may develop during the course of the trial.

An appeal that is taken from a trial court decision which is not a final judgment is called an **interlocutory appeal**. Interlocutory appeals are generally barred,[5] but there are two exceptions to this rule.

The first is known as the "**collateral order doctrine**."[6] Because the doctrine was first articulated in *Cohen v. Beneficial Industrial Loan Corp.*, you may at times hear the doctrine referred to as the "*Cohen* doctrine." The collateral order doctrine allows either party to appeal a final decision that does not resolve the ultimate dispute between the parties, but that does finally resolve a collateral issue in the case. A decision will be deemed "final" (and thus reviewable under the collateral order doctrine) if three conditions are met:

1. The decision conclusively disposes of the question;
2. The decision resolves "an issue completely collateral to the cause of action asserted;" and
3. The decision "involved an important right which would be lost probably irreparably, if review had to await final judgment."[7]

The next exception to the final judgment rule applies only to interlocutory appeals brought by the prosecutor. As you read in **Chapter 46**, many government appeals are constrained by double jeopardy concerns. However, where double jeopardy concerns are not implicated, 18 U.S.C. § 3731 expressly authorizes government appeals in enumerated circumstances. Specifically, § 3731 allows the government to appeal "from a decision or order . . . suppressing or excluding evidence . . . not made after the defendant has been put in jeopardy . . . if the United States at-

[5] Ortiz v. Jordan, 131 S.Ct. 884, 889 (2011).

[6] Cohen v. Beneficial Industrial Loan Corp., 337 U.S. 541 (1949).

[7] Abney v. United States, 431 U.S. 651, 658 (1977).

torney certifies . . . that the evidence is a substantial proof of a fact material in the proceeding."[8] Thus, the government can appeal a pre-jeopardy ruling excluding evidence if it certifies that the evidence was especially significant. The suppression of evidence like an identification of the accused, a confession by the accused, or a piece of significant physical evidence found on the defendant will often satisfy this standard. In contrast, the preclusion of a third-party statement as hearsay likely will have more difficulty overcoming the hurdle.

Allowing the government to appeal the exclusion of evidence creates an asymmetry, since an aggrieved defendant may not immediately appeal the denial of a suppression motion. However, this asymmetry makes sense. If the suppression of evidence substantially inhibits the government's ability to move forward with a prosecution, allowing an instant appeal is appropriate because the government will otherwise not have a meaningful opportunity to challenge such a ruling. In contrast, if a suppression motion is denied, the aggrieved defendant has an adequate opportunity to challenge the correctness of that order upon conviction. And, if he is not convicted, the ruling, even if erroneous, caused no lasting harm.

Note that § 3731 also gives the government the right to appeal in two other situations. The government can appeal from the dismissal of an indictment and from a judgment by the court to acquit notwithstanding a guilty verdict; and it can appeal a decision "granting the release of a person charged with or convicted of an offense," or otherwise modifying the conditions or fact of release.

After ensuring that the matter is appealable, the attorney who wishes to appeal the case must identify an issue that is within the appellate court's **scope of review**. Appellate courts are given statutory authority to review the lower courts' decisions, but some issues are beyond the authority of the appellate court. Scope of review refers to that constellation of issues that are properly heard by the court. The most common example of this is that federal appellate courts cannot review questions of purely state law. For example, if you are in federal court on direct appeal, you will not be able to argue that your conviction must be overturned because a municipal ordinance was violated by the police when they filed your arrest paperwork.

The issue being appealed must also have been **preserved** for appeal at the trial level. This generally means that the attorney who is now appealing the case must have brought the issue to the trial court's attention at the time the decision was made in order to give the trial court a chance to rectify its own mistake. Federal Rule of Criminal Procedure 51 provides that a "party may preserve a claim of error by informing the court—when the court ruling or order is made or sought—of the action the party wishes the court to take or the party's objection to the court's action and the grounds for that objection."[9]

[8] 18 U.S.C. § 3731.

[9] F.R.C.P. 51(b).

Every jurisdiction has its own specific rules describing what must be done to adequately preserve an error for appellate review. The rules sometimes define the requisite level of specificity or the need to renew a particular trial objection to preserve the issue.[10] However, these details are also often provided in the common law.[11] For example, in some jurisdictions, though not expressly stated in the rules, certain objections to the voir dire process will not be preserved unless the objection is also renewed at the time the final jury is sworn. You should therefore be careful to review local practice and precedent to ensure that your objection will be both appropriately-timed and sufficient to preserve any claimed error.

If a party fails to object to an error at trial, he will typically be precluded from bringing it up on appeal. Courts will consider the unobjected-to error as "forfeited," and forfeited claims do not usually offer a basis for appellate relief. As the Court has said, "No procedural principle is more familiar to this Court than that a right may be forfeited in criminal as well as civil cases by the failure to make timely assertion of the right before a tribunal having jurisdiction to determine it."[12] For example, assume the prosecutor calls a police detective to the stand who testifies about a statement the defendant made as he was being arrested and the defense attorney does not object to the testimony. On appeal, the defense attorney wants to argue that the defendant's statement was not spontaneous but was a response to custodial interrogation. Absent an objection by the defense lawyer at the time the testimony is given, the appellate court will not be permitted to review that claim.

However, some mistakes are so obvious and so damaging that it is unduly harsh to preclude appellate correction simply because trial counsel did not object. Thus, the preservation rule is subject to the **plain error** doctrine. Plain error, which is described in Rule 52(b) of the Federal Rules of Criminal Procedure, provides in relevant part:

> If the trial court makes an error which:
>
> 1. Has not been intentionally abandoned;
> 2. Is obvious;
> 3. Affects substantial rights; and
> 4. Seriously affects the fairness, integrity, or public reputation of juridical proceedings
>
> Then the appellate court may, but is not required to, consider the error even if the trial counsel did not object at the time the decision was made.[13]

[10] See, e.g., F.R.C.P. 30.

[11] Jones v. United States, 527 U.S. 373, 387-88 (1999).

[12] Puckett v. United States, 556 U.S. 129 (2009).

[13] F.R.C.P. 52(b); Johnson v. United States, 520 U.S. 461, 466 (1997).

It is very difficult to satisfy all of the steps in the plain error analysis. In the Court's view, an exercise of discretion under the plain error doctrine is appropriate only if the reviewing court can say that a "miscarriage of justice would otherwise result."[14]

Some states have deployed the plain error analysis differently in the context of so-called "structural errors." These states have found that structural errors (those more serious errors that affect the fundamental soundness of the trial's framework) necessarily affect substantial rights (thus satisfying the third prong of a plain error analysis) even without a showing of individual prejudice. The federal system, however, has not embraced this approach. Indeed, as recently as 2009, the Court "declined to resolve whether 'structural' errors—those that affect 'the framework within which the trial proceeds'—automatically satisfy the third prong of the plain error test."[15] And the following year, the Court was only willing to suggest the "possibility that certain errors, termed 'structural errors,' might 'affect substantial rights' regardless of their actual impact on an appellant's trial."[16] As you will read shortly, however, the structural error distinction has been explicitly embraced by the Supreme Court with regard to the question of harmless error.

It is important to note the difference between a claim that is **forfeited** through lack of preservation (which may still be reviewed through the plain error doctrine) and a right which is intentionally **waived** by a party (which cannot be). Forfeiture is the untimely assertion of a right. Waiver, on the other hand, involves the intentional and deliberate relinquishment of a known right.[17] As the Court has found, where there is a valid waiver, "there would be no error at all and plain-error analysis would add nothing."[18]

Establishing that there was a final judgment, that the claims lie within the court's scope of review, and that the claims have been properly preserved only gets the litigant into the appellate court. The next step is to convince the appellate court that a mistake was actually made. When the appellate court reviews the claim for error, it will apply a specific **standard of review** to the trial court's decision. The standard of review refers to the amount of deference an appellate court will give to the lower court's ruling. There are three primary standards of appellate review in all criminal appeals:

1. ***De Novo.*** Questions of law are reviewed *de novo*. This means the appellate court will afford no deference to the lower court's decision. Instead the question is reviewed as if for the first time by the appellate court.

---

[14] United States v. Frady, 456 U.S. 152 (1982).

[15] Puckett v. United States, 556 U.S. 129, 140 (2009).

[16] United States v. Marcus, 560 U.S. 258, 263 (2010).

[17] United States v. Olano, 507 U.S. 725, 733 (1993).

[18] Puckett, 556 U.S. at 138.

Mixed questions of law and fact are also usually reviewed *de novo*. A mixed question of law and fact will arise when the facts and applicable legal rules are not in dispute but the question is whether the facts at issue satisfy the applicable legal standard. For example, whether a suspect was handcuffed by the police is a question of fact. Whether the official restraint of movement constitutes an arrest is a question of law. But, whether the handcuffing of the suspect in your case was sufficient to convert a temporary stop into an arrest will be a mixed question of law and fact.

Another application of this standard that bears particular mention is a **sufficiency of the evidence** review. Sufficiency is a question of law and thus is considered *de novo*. In assessing sufficiency, however, the appellate court must view the evidence in the light most favorable to the party that prevailed below—in criminal cases, this would always be the prosecution.

2. **Clear Error.** All questions of fact are reviewed for clear error. This is a very deferential standard that allows the appellate court to reverse the lower court's factual findings only if they are clearly erroneous. A finding of clear error requires a "definite and firm conviction that a mistake has been committed."[19]

3. **Abuse of Discretion.** For matters that are committed to the trial court's discretion, the reviewing court will not reverse unless it finds the lower court abused its discretion. An appellate court will reverse the lower court's decision under this standard only if the lower court acted outside of the wide range of permissible options available to it. However, this is not to say that the lower court has free rein. "[D]iscretionary choices are not left to the court's inclination, but to its judgment; and its judgment is to be guided by sound legal principles."[20] The particular form of *voir dire* questions or the admission of certain pieces of evidence (like autopsy photos) are the sorts of routine trial matters that are usually committed to the trial court's sound judgment and thus only reviewed for an abuse of discretion.

As the above reflects, some standards of review do not impose any significant burden on the litigants. Others give a large amount of deference to the trial court and so may be a severe impediment to relief in the appellate court.

Assume that an appellant has identified a final judgment (or collateral order) that presents an issue within the appellate court's scope of review that was preserved by trial counsel and that can withstand scrutiny under the relevant standard of review. This does still not guarantee success. The final hurdle any appellate litigant must overcome is the question of **harmless error**.

---

[19] Easley v. Cromartie, 532 U.S. 234, 242 (2001).

[20] United States v. Taylor, 487 U.S. 326, 336 (1988).

Harmless error is described in Rule 52(a) of the Federal Rules of Criminal Procedure:

> Any error, defect, irregularity, or variance that does not affect substantial rights must be disregarded.[21]

Thus, while the plain error doctrine that you read about above works to save claims for appellate review that are otherwise unpreserved, the harmless error doctrine operates in the other direction. The harmless error doctrine instructs appellate courts to essentially ignore mistakes in the trial process that do not meaningfully impact the trial's outcome. There is a sense that "errors are a constant in the trial process,"[22] and awarding relief every time an error is made would cause the system to grind to a halt. Accordingly, an error will not survive harmless error analysis in the federal system and in many states unless the reviewing court can "declare a belief that it was harmless beyond a reasonable doubt."[23]

When assessing the harm of a particular error, the significance of the error is one part of the equation, the strength of the government's case is another.[24] The more overwhelming the evidence of guilt, the more likely any complained of errors will be deemed harmless.

There are a small number of issues which are immune from the harmless error analysis—that is, which will allow for reversal without the appellant having to prove that the error likely changed the outcome of the trial. These errors, deemed "structural errors," defy analysis under the harmless error standard because they "affect the [very] framework within which the trial proceeds, such that it is often difficult to assess the effect of the error."[25] Errors that the Supreme Court has found are not subject to harmless error analysis include:

1. The total deprivation of the right to counsel;
2. The presence of a biased judge;
3. Racial bias in the composition of the grand jury;
4. The deprivation of the right to self-representation; and
5. Deprivation of the right to a public trial.

---

21 F.R.C.P. 52(a).

22 United States v. Padilla, 415 F.3d 211, 224 (C.A.1 2005) (en banc) (Boudin, C.J., concurring).

23 Chapman v. California, 386 U.S. 18 (1967).

24 United States v. Young, 470 U.S. 1 (1985).

25 United States v. Marcus, 560 U.S. 258, 263 (2010).

All other errors, including most constitutional errors, are subject to harmless error analysis.

Under a plain error analysis, the burden of persuasion rests with the convicted defendant to establish prejudice. In contrast, for harmless error it is the government that bears the burden of persuasion with regard to prejudice.[26]

C. Applying the Law.

1. Final Judgments and Collateral Orders. In most criminal cases, the appealable final order is the judgment of conviction. However, before judgment is entered, there may be other issues that a party would like to have immediately reviewed. In many cases, it will be easy to identify an issue as falling within the collateral order doctrine. At other times, however, the task is a greater challenge. One of the easier issues is a double jeopardy challenge. As you read in **Chapter 46**, the protection against double jeopardy protects the accused against twice being put at **risk** of conviction. It thus makes sense that an accused need not sit through the trial she seeks to avoid before appealing because by that point the harm complained of—the risk of the second prosecution—would already have occurred:

> **Example—*Abney v. United States*, 431 U.S. 651 (1977):** Donald Abney and two others threatened the owner of liquor store and made demands for $200 in "weekly taxes." Thereafter, Abney and his friends were charged in a one count indictment with both the substantive crime of attempting to extort the liquor store owner, and with the inchoate crime of conspiring to commit the extortion. The trial court instructed the jury that to return a conviction it had to find the defendants guilty of both the conspiracy and the extortion. Thereafter, all three men were convicted.
>
> On appeal, the convictions were overturned because certain evidence was improperly admitted. The appellate court also found that the one count indictment was duplicitous in that it charged more than one offense in a single count. The court therefore instructed the prosecution on remand to choose either the conspiracy or the attempted extortion theory. The prosecution determined that it would proceed on the conspiracy theory.

[26] United States v. Olano, 507 U.S. 725, 734 (1993).

Once the prosecution announced its intention to re-prosecute, Abney and the others filed a motion to dismiss the indictment. They raised two claims. First, they contended that retrial violated the Double Jeopardy Clause. Next, they maintained the indictment was still duplicitous. The motion to dismiss was denied by the trial court and Abney immediately appealed. On appeal, in addition to arguing that Abney's claims were substantively without merit, the government also claimed as a threshold matter that the appeal should not be heard because it was not a final judgment. The intermediate appellate court heard the appeal, but rejected both claims. Abney and his co-defendants then sought discretionary review in the Supreme Court.

Analysis: The Supreme Court also rejected Abney's claims. The double jeopardy challenge was immediately appealable under the collateral order doctrine, but the retrial of Abney and his co-defendants did not violate their double jeopardy protections. Meanwhile, the substantive challenge to the indictment did not fall within the collateral order doctrine, and therefore was an impermissible interlocutory appeal that would not be considered on the merits.

Because there is no constitutional right to an appeal, Congress may establish the parameters for appeals. One such parameter that Congress has clearly articulated is strong disapproval for the piecemeal litigation that results when interlocutory appeals are permitted. Accordingly, "[f]inality of judgment has been required [by 28 U.S.C. § 1291] as a predicate for federal appellate jurisdiction."[27]

The pretrial denial of a motion to dismiss does not typically resolve the underlying issues that are presented in the criminal prosecution. For this reason, the denial of the motion was not a "final judgment" within the meaning of § 1291. However, such a motion does fall within the exception to the final judgment rule to the extent it is based upon an assertion of double jeopardy protections. This is true because the double jeopardy claim satisfies the three conditions needed to qualify as a collateral order.

First, the lower court's order was a decisive rejection of Abney's double jeopardy claim. "There are simply no further steps that can be taken in the District Court to avoid the trial the defendant maintains is barred by the Fifth Amendment's guarantee."[28] Second, the double jeopardy claim is completely independent of the question of Abney's guilt. Third and finally, the Double Jeopardy Clause protects against the risk of a second trial and against the strain, embarrassment and expense associated with the same. Consequently, if immediate appellate review of the double jeopardy claims is not allowed, the protection that is afforded by the

[27] Abney v. United States, 431 U.S. 651, 656 (1977).

[28] Id. at 659.

Clause will be substantially eroded. For these reasons, the denial of the motion to dismiss on double jeopardy grounds is immediately appealable.

Turning to the merits of Abney's claim, the Court disagreed with Abney's contention that his retrial was prohibited by double jeopardy concerns. At the original trial, the prosecutor proceeded on both theories charged in the single count—conspiracy and attempted extortion. The trial court accordingly instructed the jury that it had to find proof beyond a reasonable doubt of both crimes to convict. The verdict of guilt therefore cannot, on these facts, be understood as the jury making a choice between two competing theories of guilt. Rather, the verdict represents a conclusion that the government established the existence of both offenses. Because Abney was not implicitly acquitted of either offense, his retrial following reversal on appeal does not raise double jeopardy concerns.

Finally, though the double jeopardy challenge was an immediately appealable collateral order, the same cannot be said for Abney's other substantive challenge—his claim that the indictment is duplicitous. "[A]n order denying a motion to dismiss an indictment for failure to state an offense is plainly not 'collateral' in any sense of that term; rather it goes to the very heart of the issues to be resolved at the upcoming trial."[29] It is also true that Abney's challenge to the infirmity of the indictment can be adequately reviewed (if necessary) on appeal following a final judgment. The case should be remanded for retrial.

2. Preservation and Plain Error. Preservation requirements are beneficial in that they make the trial the "main event." Recognizing that errors will not be corrected on appeal absent an objection, the parties and their lawyers focus time and attention at a point when the trial judge is best able to address errors in a fair and efficient manner. Such rules also respect the role of the trial judge by giving her the first opportunity to address problems that arise during trial. It is also unquestionably more efficient to have an error corrected promptly by the trial court rather than, as may be the case on appeal, many years after the conviction has been entered.

Another commonly advanced but more controversial rationale that has been suggested for the preservation requirement is to prevent sandbagging. The Supreme Court has often commented that "the contemporaneous-objection rule prevents a litigant from 'sandbagging' the court—remaining silent about his objection and belatedly raising the error only if the case does not conclude in his favor."[30]

Many in the defense community question the legitimacy of the notion that preservation is required to avoid deliberate gamesmanship by the defense bar. As they note, if correction of an error will prevent conviction in the first instance, it would

[29] Id. at 662.

[30] Puckett v. United States, 556 U.S. 129, 134 (2009).

be the rarest (or most incompetent) of defense attorneys who would actual forgo prompt correction and risk a guilty verdict simply to retain an issue for presentation on appeal. Expressing a similar sentiment in the context of post-conviction remedies, a Florida inmate once wrote, "I have never witnessed a situation in which a *pro se* prisoner wished to delay his . . . remedies. . . . Intentionally or needlessly delaying the pursuit of these remedies would be illogical and contrary to the reason we file the petitions in the first place."[31]

Whatever the underlying rationale for the preservation requirement, there are times when rigid adherence to its demands will work injustice to the party bringing the appeal. As you read above, the plain error doctrine therefore acts as a safety valve which allows litigants to present claims on appeal that otherwise would be considered forfeited by counsel's failure to object below. However, the standard for applying the plain error doctrine is difficult to reach, and the Court has said this is "as it should be:"[32]

> **Example—*Johnson v. United States*, 520 U.S. 461 (1997):** Law enforcement was investigating Earl James Fields's involvement in a large drug trafficking operation. According to information obtained by investigators, Fields had accumulated more than $10 million from the business. During the investigation, Fields's girlfriend, Joyce Johnson, was questioned under oath in a federal grand jury. When asked about the source of funds she used to purchase various properties held in her name, Johnson answered that her deceased mother gave her a box of cash originally given to the mother in 1985 or 1986 by a man named Gerald Talcott.
>
> Soon thereafter, Johnson was indicted for perjury. The government's evidence established that one of the properties Johnson owned was purchased with eight cashier's checks, two of which were from a corporation that Fields owned. It was also revealed that Gerald Talcott died in 1982, several years before Johnson claimed he had given her mother the box of money. After the evidence was submitted, the trial court gave the jury its final instructions, including an instruction that the jury should find Johnson's statements were material. Johnson was convicted and sentenced to 30 months in prison.
>
> Before Johnson could file an appeal, the Supreme Court determined that materiality is an element of perjury that should be

[31] Thomas O'Bryant, The Great Unobtainable Writ, 41 Harv. C.R.-C.L. L. Rev. 299, 306 (2006).

[32] United States v. Dominguez Benitez, 542 U.S. 74, 83 n.9 (2004).

submitted to the jury. Thus, Johnson argued on appeal that reversal was required because her jury had been instructed to find materiality. Though counsel had not objected to the instruction at trial, Johnson contended that the error should be reviewed as plain error. The intermediate appellate court denied relief, finding that Johnson had not satisfied the third prong of plain error review—an error affecting substantial rights. The Supreme Court then took the case for review.

Analysis: The trial court's materiality instruction was not plain error. Therefore, reversal of Johnson conviction was unwarranted.

There is no question that materiality is a question that must be decided by the jury. But the clarity or seriousness of a claimed error does not exempt it from application of the Rules of Criminal Procedure. Those rules require either a timely objection to a claimed error or satisfaction of the plain error test.

Here, there was no objection by trial counsel. To satisfy the plain error test, Johnson must show there was an error that was plain and that affected her substantial rights. There certainly was an error. Error is present if there is deviation from a legal rule,[33] and the Supreme Court had just held that materiality is a jury question and the court's instruction to Johnson's jury to the contrary was incorrect.

The next prong requires consideration of whether the error was plain. Here, the case that established the error in Johnson's case was not decided until after her conviction. "Plain" as used in this context means "clear or equivalently, obvious."[34] It is also the case that an error must be plain under "current law" to satisfy the second prong of plain error. Certainly an argument could be made that the error in Johnson's case was not "plain" under "current" law, if "current" is understood to mean at the time of her conviction. However, "in a case such as this—where the law at the time of trial was settled and clearly contrary to the law at the time of appeal—it is enough that an error be 'plain' at the time of appellate consideration."[35]

Finally, Johnson had to demonstrate that the plain error in her case affected substantial rights. The Court assumed for the sake of argument that Johnson established this prong as well. But, she nonetheless was not entitled to relief. Even after all three prongs of the plain error test are established, a court should only exercise its discretion to grant relief if the claim "seriously affects the fairness, integrity or public reputation of judicial proceedings."[36] That showing could not be made in Johnson's case.

There was overwhelming evidence of the materiality of Johnson's statements. Indeed, Johnson did not, and could not, seriously argue that her statements

---

[33] United States v. Olano, 507 U.S. 725, 732–33 (1993).

[34] 520 U.S. at 467.

[35] Johnson v. United States, 520 U.S. 461, 468 (1997).

[36] Id. at 469.

about the source of funds she used to purchase and improve properties were not material to the grand jury's investigation into her boyfriend's illegal drug empire. Under these circumstances, it would be inappropriate to redress the improper jury instruction as plain error.

As the discussion of *Johnson* reflects, the Court at one time described the plain error doctrine as a three-pronged standard that should be applied only if there was a serious effect upon the fairness, integrity or public reputation of the trial. In its more recent articulations of the plain error doctrine, the Court has described the final consideration of the appellate court—that "the error seriously affects the fairness, integrity or public reputation of judicial proceedings—as the fourth and last prong of the plain error analysis."[37] In other words, the Court has moved from describing the analysis as "a three prong test to be exercised when a final condition is met" to "a four prong test."

3. Harmless Error. As you read above, harmless error is the final hurdle any appellate litigant must overcome before relief will be granted. The harmless error doctrine advances the "principle that the central purpose of a criminal trial is to decide the factual question of the defendant's guilt or innocence and promotes public respect for the criminal process by focusing on the underlying fairness of the trial rather than on the virtually inevitable presence of immaterial error."[38] In other words, every trial is bound to have some errors, but reversal of a conviction is not appropriate if those errors do not infect the basic fairness of the trial proceeding. On its face, this sounds like a straightforward rule. However, things get a little more complicated in the implementation of the doctrine.

The first complication is that certain errors are so fundamental they are categorized as "structural" errors and as such are never deemed "harmless." As noted above, there are only five types of errors that fall into this category, such as a judge who is biased against the defendant or the deprivation of the right to a public trial. Some commentators have argued that this category should be expanded to include all constitutional violations, under the theory that constitutional protections are so fundamental that a violation of one is itself the harm. However, the Court has consistently rejected any such expansion. Along with the countless minor errors that occur during criminal trials, the Court has also concluded that constitutional errors may at times be "harmless." Indeed, even significant constitutional protections, like the ban on coerced confessions, have been subjected to harmless error reviewas demonstrated in *Arizona v. Fulminante*, a case we have already seen in Chapter 25:

---

[37] United States v. Marcus, 560 U.S. 258 (2010).

[38] Delaware v. Van Arsdall, 475 U.S. 673, 681 (1986).

Example—Arizona v. Fulminante, 499 U.S. 279 (1991): Oreste Fulminante called the police in Mesa, Arizona one morning to report that his stepdaughter Jeneane was missing. Fulminante had been watching the child while her mother, Fulminante's wife, was in the hospital. Two days later, Jeneane's body was found in the desert. She had been strangled and shot twice in the head. Fulminante was suspected in Jeneane's killing, but the police lacked adequate evidence to connect him to the crime.

A year later, Fulminante was incarcerated in New York on federal weapons charges. While Fulminante was in prison, he befriended another inmate, Anthony Sarivola. Sarivola was known around the prison as a mafia figure. Unbeknownst to Fulminante, Sarivola was actually a convicted former police officer who was working as a paid informant for the FBI.

When rumors began to swirl that Fulminante was responsible for the murder of a little girl back in Arizona, he received threats from other inmates. Sarivola offered to protect Fulminante (a seemingly credible offer in light of his presumed mob connections) but said he would only offer such protection if Fulminante "came clean." Fulminante then confessed that he choked and sexually assaulted Jeaneane. Fulminante told Sarivola that he made Jeneane beg for her life, before shooting her twice in the head. About a year later, Fulminante was charged in Arizona with Jeneane's murder.

At trial, Fulminante moved to suppress his confession to Sarivola (and a subsequent confession to Sarivola's wife, Donna) on the ground that they were coerced. His motion was denied and the two confessions were introduced. Fulminante was convicted and sentenced to death. He then appealed. The state supreme court reversed, finding that Fulminante's confession was coerced and that such error was not subject to harmless error review. The case was then appealed to the Supreme Court to determine whether Fulminante's confession was coerced, whether the admission of a coerced confession is properly subjected to harmless error analysis, and finally whether the admission was harmless in this case.

Analysis: The admission of Fulminante's coerced confession was an error properly reviewed under the harmless error analysis. However, where the admission of that confession likely influenced the verdict, reversal was required.

Fulminante's confession was coerced. Sarivola did not have to engage in his own acts of physical brutality to make the confession he eked out of Fulminante the product of coercion. A credible threat of violence is sufficient to establish coercion. Here, Sarivola took advantage of the credible threats from other inmates to convince Fulminante to confess.[39]

However, the finding of a coerced confession does not end the analysis. If an appellate error is harmless it will not generally warrant relief. While it is true that Fulminante alleges a constitutional violation, the vast majority of constitutional claims are subject to harmless error review. In determining which constitutional errors are subject to harmless error analysis and which are not, it is important to consider the nature of the error. Many constitutional errors are simply "trial errors." Such errors are not exempt from a harm analysis because they do not infect the structural integrity of the trial process.

In contrast, there are other constitutional errors that are not well-suited to an analysis of harm. These errors affect the integrity of the trial apparatus and render it structurally unsound. Excluding such structural defects from a harm analysis is appropriate because they are so fundamental that "a criminal trial [conducted in their presence] cannot reliably serve its function as a vehicle for determination of guilt or innocence, and no criminal punishment may be regarded as fundamentally fair."[40] Accordingly, in the case of structural error, relief is appropriate even if the appellant cannot make an individualized showing of harm.

Errors that have been deemed structural are errors like the absence of trial counsel or racial discrimination in the selection of the grand jury. The admission of an involuntary confession is not of the same fundamental quality as these errors. Instead it is more like other trial errors that are routinely seen in many cases. "Of course an involuntary confession may have a more dramatic effect on the course of a trial than do other trial errors . . . but this simply means that a reviewing court will conclude in such a case that its admission was not harmless error; it is not a reason for eschewing the harmless-error test entirely."[41]

On this record it cannot be said that the admission of Fulminante's coerced confession to Anthony Sarivola was harmless beyond a reasonable doubt. Absent the confessions to Sarivola and his wife, the evidence was insufficient to establish Fulminante's responsibility for Jeneane's murder. In addition, absent the confession to Sarivola it is likely the jury would have rejected Donna's somewhat unbelievable claim that Fulminante confessed the details of Jeneane's murder to her upon their first meeting. Fulminante is entitled to a new trial because the admission of his coerced confession was not harmless.

---

[39] Arizona v. Fulminante, 499 U.S. 279, 288 (1991).

[40] Id. at 310.

[41] Id. at 312.

The *Fulminante* Court applied a test for harmless error that was originally set out in *Chapman v. California*. There the Court wrote: "[t]he question is whether there is a reasonable possibility that the evidence complained of might have contributed to the conviction."[42] Phrased in the contrary, the question is whether the reviewing court can "declare a belief that [the error] was harmless beyond a reasonable doubt."[43] This construction of the standard has been embraced in a number of state courts as well.

4. Sufficiency of the Evidence. One final rule that you may see on appeal applies during challenges to the sufficiency of the evidence. As you read above, such a claim is evaluated *de novo* because whether evidence is sufficient to sustain a conviction is a question of law. But, how should the evidence be evaluated? Should the appellate court assess the credibility of the witnesses in the case to reweigh the evidence that was presented to the jury? The Court has said no.

When assessing a defendant's sufficiency claim on direct review, the appellate court must view the evidence in the light most favorable to the prosecution:

> **Example—*Jackson v. Virginia*, 443 U.S. 307 (1979):** James Jackson befriended Mary Cole, a corrections employee, during the time he was an inmate at the local county jail. After Jackson's release, Cole arranged for Jackson to live with her son and daughter-in-law. On the day of Cole's murder, she was seen with Jackson in a local diner. Both Cole and Jackson were intoxicated. A sheriff's deputy who saw the two in the diner asked Jackson if he wanted the sheriff to hold onto his gun until he and Cole sobered up. Jackson said that would not be necessary because he and Cole were going to have sex. The deputy also saw a knife in Jackson's car.
>
> A day and a half later, Cole's body was found in a parking lot. She had been shot twice in the chest. Jackson did not dispute that he was the one who shot Cole. But, he maintained alternately that the shooting was an accident, had been done in self-defense, or had been done without the requisite intent due to his intoxication. Jackson asserted that Cole attacked him with the knife after he rebuffed her sexual advances. He then grabbed the gun to protect himself and when Cole grabbed for it, it went off accidentally. The trial judge found Jackson guilty of first degree murder and sentenced him to 30 years in prison.

---

[42] Chapman v. California, 386 U.S. 18, 23 (1967).

[43] Id. at 24.

Jackson then filed a series of challenges to his conviction, asserting among other things that the evidence was insufficient to sustain a conviction. A federal habeas court agreed, finding the evidence was not sufficient to establish premeditation. The intermediate appellate court, however, found that where there was "some evidence" of premeditation, the conviction should have been affirmed. The case then was accepted by the Supreme Court for consideration of Jackson's sufficiency claim.

Analysis: Though the intermediate appellate court applied the wrong test for sufficiency, Jackson's conviction was properly affirmed because the evidence of his guilt was more than legally sufficient.

The Constitution allows a criminal conviction only after guilt has been established beyond a reasonable doubt for every element of the charged offense. Therefore, when the sufficiency of the evidence is challenged, an appellate court must review that evidence to ensure it surpasses the constitutional threshold. The reviewing court's task is not to determine whether it agrees with the guilty verdict.

Rather, "the relevant question is whether, after viewing the evidence in the light most favorable to the prosecution, any rational trier of fact could have found the essential elements of the crime beyond a reasonable doubt."[44] By viewing the evidence in the light most favorable to the prosecution, the reviewing court ensures the jury retains its primary role as the evaluator of credibility.

When viewed in this fashion, the prosecution's evidence was clearly sufficient to support Jackson's conviction for first-degree murder. That Jackson shot Cole was not a matter in dispute. Instead the only question was whether he shot her with the requisite intent. As the trial judge well knew, premeditation may be formed in an instant and does not require an extended period of development. The circumstantial evidence supported a conclusion beyond a reasonable doubt that Jackson acted intentionally.

Cole was shot twice at close range. After the shooting, rather than getting help for Cole, Jackson fled to North Carolina. Moreover, he was able to drive the entire distance from Virginia to North Carolina immediately after the shooting without getting into an accident, undercutting his claim that he was excessively intoxicated. In addition, prior to the shooting, Jackson declared his intention to have sex with the victim making it somewhat implausible that Cole attacked him when he rejected her advances. "His claim of self-defense would have required the trial judge to draw a series of improbable inferences from the basic facts, prime among them the inference that [Jackson] was wholly uninterested in sexual activity with the victim but that she was so interested as to have willingly removed part of her clothing and then attacked him with a knife when he resisted her advances,

44 Jackson v. Virginia, 443 U.S. 307, 319 (1979).

even though he was armed with a loaded revolver that he had just demonstrated he knew how to use."[45]

The prosecution was not required to negate every hypothetical theory of innocence. Instead, its burden was only to establish Jackson's guilt beyond a reasonable doubt. On this record, the prosecution met its burden.

In other words, when assessing the sufficiency of the evidence the question that must be answered is whether "any rational juror could have convicted."[46] In describing this standard, the Court has said the use of the word "could" focuses the reviewing court's analysis on "the power of the trier of fact to reach its conclusion," not on the trier of fact's "likely behavior."[47] The test is, therefore, descriptive not prescriptive—what the jury could have done, not what it should have done on the evidence presented. As you read in **Chapter 43**, the prescriptive test for analyzing evidence is the weight of the evidence review that is conducted in some appellate jurisdictions.

Note that the rule that prohibits the appellate court from reassessing witness credibility only apples to direct appeals. As you will see in **Chapter 48,** a court conducting a post-conviction review is sometimes allowed to engage in reassessment of witness credibility.

---

45 Jackson, 443 U.S. at 325.

46 Schlup v. Delo, 513 U.S. 298, 330 (1995).

47 Id.

Quick Summary

A direct appeal is the first round of review that a criminal conviction receives.

Appellate practitioners must navigate a series of hurdles before they can obtain relief. First, the appellant must ensure her claim satisfies the final judgment rule, which provides that appellate courts only have jurisdiction over final decisions. The purpose of the final judgment rule is to avoid piecemeal litigation.

Appeals that are not taken from a final judgment are called "interlocutory," and are generally prohibited. The only exception to this rule is provided by the "collateral order doctrine." The collateral order doctrine allows an appeal to be taken from a final decision that does not resolve the ultimate dispute between the parties, but that does finally resolve a collateral issue in the case. To constitute an appealable collateral order the decision must:

1. conclusively dispose of the question;
2. resolve "an issue completely collateral to the cause of action asserted; and
3. "involve an important right which would be lost probably irreparably, if review had to await final judgment."

Scope of review is the next hurdle for an appellate litigant. It refers to the array of issues that are properly heard by the court. The appellate litigant must also ensure the claim was preserved at trial. Generally preservation demands a timely and sufficient objection in the trial court to any claimed error. The failure to object will typically preclude consideration on appeal.

Errors that are plain and that affect substantial rights may be reviewed by the appellate court even in the absence of an objection. However, the court's discretion to review a plain error should be exercised sparingly. An appellate court will apply the plain error doctrine only if "the error 'seriously affects the fairness, integrity, or public reputation of judicial proceedings.'"

The standard of review that applies to an appellate claim may or may not present a further challenge to the appellate litigant depending upon the amount of deference the standard requires. The primary standards of appellate review in criminal appeals are *de novo* (questions of law/mixed questions of law and fact/legal sufficiency of the evidence); clear error (questions of fact); and abuse of discretion.

The final hurdle any litigant must overcome is the question of harmless error. Even if the appellate court agrees that an error was committed by the trial court, the judgment will stand if the appellate court can "declare a belief that [the error] was harmless beyond a reasonable doubt." The more overwhelming the evidence of guilt, the more likely any complained of errors will be deemed harmless. For only a handful of structural errors, harmless error analysis will not apply and the appellant will not be required to show individual prejudice.

Review Questions

1. Daddy Dearest. Dr. Rakesh Punn, a pediatrician, was being investigated by both state and federal law enforcement for a variety of crimes including unlawful surveillance of his patients, child pornography, and health care fraud. During the state investigation two of Punn's adult children made statements to the local police that implicated Punn. Eventually, a federal grand jury indicted Punn on 7 counts of sexually exploiting children, and 29 counts of health care fraud. Prior to trial, Punn moved to suppress evidence that had been seized from his home. Two days before the government's deadline for responding to the suppression motion, the government subpoenaed Punn's two adult children to appear before a federal grand jury. Punn moved to quash the subpoenas, arguing that they had been improperly issued to aid the government in preparing for the upcoming trial. The trial court denied the motion, and Punn took an immediate appeal of the denial to the intermediate appellate court. The government moved to dismiss the appeal, arguing that the denial of the motion to quash was not a final order. How should the appellate court rule?

2. 1 + 1 + 1 +1 + 1 + 1 + 1 + 1 + 1 is 10. Jamonn Lamont Lindsey was tried for conspiracy, armed bank robbery and brandishing a firearm during a crime of violence. The prosecution's evidence suggested that Lindsey, Jeffrey Gibson and a third man known only as "Lil Ball" stole $132,464 from a Banco Popular in Wilmington, California.

By statute, Lindsey was afforded ten peremptory challenges during *voir dire.* However, due to the district court's counting error, Lindsey was allowed to exercise only nine of his ten peremptory challenges. After the government exercised its tenth and last challenge, the trial judge stated, "All right. And the defense has no further peremptories." The trial judge instructed the clerk to swear in the jury panel. Contrary to the trial judge's assertion, Lindsey in fact had one final peremptory challenge to exercise. However, defense counsel did not bring the error to the court's attention and did not otherwise object. At the close of the evidence, Lindsey was convicted of all counts. Lindsey argued on appeal that the peremptory challenge error required automatic reversal of his conviction. In particular, he asserted that denial of an adequate number of peremptory challenges was an error for which there can be no harmless-error review. Will Lindsey be successful on appeal?

3. The Taxman Cometh. Fabian Muyaba was charged with conspiracy to commit tax fraud. The government produced the following evidence at trial:

Muyaba worked at a company called Reliable Tax Services.

> While at this company, Muyaba improperly changed the filing status on clients' returns (from "single" to "head of household"); claimed losses on returns for non-existent businesses; charged clients substantial fees; used different Electronic Filer Identification Numbers each year; and refused to give copies of the filed returns to clients.
>
> Muyaba had a cubicle at Reliable and several Reliable clients remembered him as their return preparer.

Muyaba took the stand in his own defense. He testified at length about his education and tax training. He told the jury he had been improperly implicated in the Reliable scheme by an employee at that company who was looking for lenient treatment from the government on her own criminal charges. Muyaba further testified that though he had never worked for Reliable, he did run a return preparer business by the name of Efficient Tax Services. Muyaba produced documents that confirmed his ownership of Efficient.

At the close of the evidence, the jury convicted Muyaba. On appeal, he sought reversal by challenging the sufficiency of the government's evidence. Will he succeed?

STATE OF MARYLAND	*	**IN THE**
	*	**CIRCUIT COURT**
v.	*	**FOR**
	*	**BALTIMORE CITY**
JOSEPH CARTER	*	**Case No. 18727238, 39**

NOTICE OF APPEAL

Notice is hereby given that Joseph Carter appeals to the Court of Special Appeals of Maryland from the judgment in the above-captioned case.

Respectfully submitted,

___________/s/_________________

Renée M. Hutchins
Counsel for Joseph Carter
University of Maryland School of Law
500 W. Baltimore Street, Suite 360
Baltimore, MD 21201-1786
(410) 706-3295
rhutchins@law.umaryland.edu

CERTIFICATE OF SERVICE

I HEREBY CERTIFY that on this 21st day of April, 2012, a copy of the foregoing was mailed to the Office of the State's Attorney, Baltimore City, 208 Mitchell Courthouse, 110 North Calvert Street, Baltimore, MD 21202.

___________/s/_________________

Renée M. Hutchins

FROM THE COURTROOM

JACKSON v. VIRGINIA

Supreme Court of the United States, 1979
443 U.S. 307

Mr. Justice STEWART delivered the opinion of the Court.

The Constitution prohibits the criminal conviction of any person except upon proof of guilt beyond a reasonable doubt. The question in this case is what standard is to be applied in a federal habeas corpus proceeding when the claim is made that a person has been convicted in a state court upon insufficient evidence.

I

The petitioner was convicted after a bench trial in the Circuit Court of Chesterfield County, Va., of the first-degree murder of a woman named Mary Houston Cole. Under Virginia law, murder is defined as "the unlawful killing of another with malice aforethought." Premeditation, or specific intent to kill, distinguishes murder in the first from murder in the second degree; proof of this element is essential to conviction of the former offense, and the burden of proving it clearly rests with the prosecution.

That the petitioner had shot and killed Mrs. Cole was not in dispute at the trial. The State's evidence established that she had been a member of the staff at the local county jail, that she had befriended him while he was imprisoned there on a disorderly conduct charge, and that when he was released she had arranged for him to live in the home of her son and daughter-in-law. Testimony by her relatives indicated that on the day of the killing the petitioner had been drinking and had spent a great deal of time shooting at targets with his revolver. Late in the afternoon, according to their testimony, he had unsuccessfully attempted to talk the victim into driving him to North Carolina. She did drive the petitioner to a local diner. There the two were observed by several police officers, who testified that both the petitioner and the victim had been drinking. The two were observed by a deputy sheriff as they were preparing to leave the diner in her car. The petitioner was then in possession of his revolver, and the sheriff also observed a kitchen knife in the automobile. The sheriff testified that he had offered to keep the revolver until the petitioner sobered up, but that the latter had indicated that this would be unnecessary since he and the victim were about to engage in sexual activity.

Her body was found in a secluded church parking lot a day and a half later, naked from the waist down, her slacks beneath her body. Uncontradicted medical and expert evidence established that she had been shot twice at close range with the petitioner's gun. She appeared not to have been sexually molested. Six cartridge cases identified as having been fired from the petitioner's gun were found near the body.

After shooting Mrs. Cole, the petitioner drove her car to North Carolina, where, after a short trip to Florida, he was arrested several days later. In a post-arrest statement, introduced in evidence by the prosecution, the petitioner admitted that he had shot the victim. He contended, however, that the shooting had been accidental. When asked to describe his condition at the time of the shooting, he indicated that he had not been drunk, but had been "pretty high." His story was that the victim had attacked him with a knife when he resisted her sexual advances. He said that he had defended himself by firing a number of warning shots into the ground, and had then reloaded his revolver. The victim, he said, then attempted to take the gun from him, and the gun "went off" in the ensuing struggle. He said that he fled without seeking help for the victim because he was afraid. At the trial, his position was that he had acted in self-defense. Alternatively, he claimed that in any event the State's own evidence showed that he had been too intoxicated to form the specific intent necessary under Virginia law to sustain a conviction of murder in the first degree.

The trial judge, declaring himself convinced beyond a reasonable doubt that the petitioner had committed first-degree murder, found him guilty of that offense. The petitioner's motion to set aside the judgment as contrary to the evidence was denied, and he was sentenced to serve a term of 30 years in the Virginia state penitentiary. A petition for writ of error to the Virginia Supreme Court on the ground that the evidence was insufficient to support the conviction was denied.

. . .

We granted certiorari to consider the petitioner's claim that under *In re Winship*, a federal habeas corpus court must consider not whether there was any evidence to support a state-court conviction, but whether there was sufficient evidence to justify a rational trier of the facts to find guilt beyond a reasonable doubt.

II

Our inquiry in this case is narrow. The petitioner has not seriously questioned any aspect of Virginia law governing the allocation of the burden of production or persuasion in a murder trial. As the record demonstrates, the judge sitting as factfinder in the petitioner's trial was aware that the State bore the burden of establishing the element of premeditation, and stated that he was applying the reasonable-doubt standard in his appraisal of the State's evidence. The petitioner, moreover, does not contest the conclusion of the Court of Appeals that under the "no evidence" rule of *Thompson v. Louisville*, his conviction of first-degree murder is sustainable. And he has not attacked the sufficiency of the evidence to support a conviction of second-degree murder. His sole constitutional claim, based squarely upon *Winship*, is that the District Court and the Court of Appeals were in error in not recognizing that the question to be decided in this case is whether any rational factfinder could have concluded beyond a reasonable doubt that the killing for which the petitioner was convicted was premeditated.

The question thus raised goes to the basic nature of the constitutional right recognized in the *Winship* opinion.

III

A

This is the first of our cases to expressly consider the question whether the due process standard recognized in *Winship* constitutionally protects an accused against conviction except upon evidence that is sufficient fairly to support a conclusion that every element of the crime has been established beyond a reasonable doubt. . . . [T]he answer to that question, we think, is clear.

It is axiomatic that a conviction upon a charge not made or upon a charge not tried constitutes a denial of due process. These standards no more than reflect a broader premise that has never been doubted in our constitutional system: that a person cannot incur the loss of liberty for an offense without notice and a meaningful opportunity to defend. A meaningful opportunity to defend, if not the right to a trial itself, presumes as well that a total want of evidence to support a charge will conclude the case in favor of the accused. Accordingly, we held in the *Thompson* case that a conviction based upon a record wholly devoid of any relevant evidence of a crucial element of the offense charged is constitutionally infirm. The "no evidence" doctrine of *Thompson v. Louisville* thus secures to an accused the most elemental of due process rights: freedom from a wholly arbitrary deprivation of liberty.

The Court in *Thompson* explicitly stated that the due process right at issue did not concern a question of evidentiary "sufficiency." The right established in *In re Winship*, however, clearly stands on a different footing. *Winship* involved an adjudication of juvenile delinquency made by a judge under a state statute providing that the prosecution must prove the conduct charged as delinquent-which in *Winship* would have been a criminal offense if engaged in by an adult-by a preponderance of the evidence. Applying that standard, the judge was satisfied that the juvenile was "guilty," but he noted that the result might well have been different under a standard of proof beyond a reasonable doubt. In short, the record in *Winship* was not totally devoid of evidence of guilt.

The constitutional problem addressed in *Winship* was thus distinct from the stark problem of arbitrariness presented in *Thompson v. Louisville*. In *Winship*, the Court held for the first time that the Due Process Clause of the Fourteenth Amendment protects a defendant in a criminal case against conviction "except upon proof beyond a reasonable doubt of every fact necessary to constitute the crime with which he is charged." In so holding, the Court emphasized that proof beyond a reasonable doubt has traditionally been regarded as the decisive difference between criminal culpability and civil liability. The standard of proof beyond a reasonable doubt, said the Court, "plays a vital role in the American scheme of criminal procedure," because it operates to give "concrete substance" to the presumption of innocence to ensure against unjust convictions, and to reduce the risk of factual error in a criminal proceeding. At the same time by impressing upon the factfinder the need to reach a subjective state of near certitude of the guilt of the accused, the standard symbolizes the significance that our society attaches to the criminal sanction and thus to liberty itself.

The constitutional standard recognized in the *Winship* case was expressly phrased as one that protects an accused against a conviction except on "proof beyond a reasonable doubt . . . ." In subsequent cases discussing the reasonable-doubt standard, we have never departed from this definition of the rule or from the *Winship* understanding of the central purposes it serves. In short, *Winship* presupposes as an essential of the due process guaranteed by the Fourteenth Amendment that no person shall be made to suffer the onus of a criminal conviction except upon sufficient proof-defined as evidence necessary to convince a trier of fact beyond a reasonable doubt of the existence of every element of the offense.

B

Although several of our cases have intimated that the factfinder's application of the reasonable-doubt standard to the evidence may present a federal question when a state conviction is challenged, the Federal Courts of Appeals have generally assumed that so long as the reasonable-doubt instruction has been given at trial, the no-evidence doctrine of *Thompson v. Louisville* remains the appropriate guide for a federal habeas corpus court to apply in assessing a state prisoner's challenge to his conviction as founded upon insufficient evidence. We cannot agree.

The *Winship* doctrine requires more than simply a trial ritual. A doctrine establishing so fundamental a substantive constitutional standard must also require that the factfinder will rationally apply that standard to the facts in evidence. A "reasonable doubt," at a minimum, is one based upon "reason." Yet a properly instructed jury may occasionally convict even when it can be said that no rational trier of fact could find guilt beyond a reasonable doubt, and the same may be said of a trial judge sitting as a jury. In a federal trial, such an occurrence has traditionally been deemed to require reversal of the conviction. Under *Winship*, which established proof beyond a reasonable doubt as an essential of Fourteenth Amendment due process, it follows that when such a conviction occurs in a state trial, it cannot constitutionally stand.

A federal court has a duty to assess the historic facts when it is called upon to apply a constitutional standard to a conviction obtained in a state court. For example, on direct review of a state-court conviction, where the claim is made that an involuntary confession was used against the defendant, this Court reviews the facts to determine whether the confession was wrongly admitted in evidence. The same duty obtains in federal habeas corpus proceedings.

After *Winship* the critical inquiry on review of the sufficiency of the evidence to support a criminal conviction must be not simply to determine whether the jury was properly instructed, but to determine whether the record evidence could reasonably support a finding of guilt beyond a reasonable doubt. But this inquiry does not require a court to "ask itself whether it believes that the evidence at the trial established guilt beyond a reasonable doubt." Instead, the relevant question is whether, after viewing the evidence in the light most favorable to the prosecution, any rational trier of fact could have found the essential elements of the crime beyond a reasonable doubt. This familiar standard gives full play to the responsibility of the trier of fact fairly to resolve conflicts in the testimony, to weigh the evidence, and to draw reasonable inferences from basic facts to ultimate facts. Once a defendant has been found guilty of the crime charged, the factfinder's role as weigher of the evidence is preserved through a legal conclusion that upon judicial review all of the evidence is to be considered in the light most favorable to the prosecution. The criterion thus impinges upon "jury" discretion only to the extent necessary to guarantee the fundamental protection of due process of law.

That the *Thompson* "no evidence" rule is simply inadequate to protect against misapplications of the constitutional standard of reasonable doubt is readily apparent. "[A] mere modicum of evidence may satisfy a 'no evidence' standard . . . ." Any evidence that is relevant-that has any tendency to make the existence of an element of a crime slightly more probable than it would be without the evidence could be deemed a "mere modicum." But it could not seriously be argued that such a "modicum" of evidence could by itself rationally support a conviction beyond a reasonable doubt. The *Thompson* doctrine simply fails to supply a workable or even a predictable standard for determining whether the due process command of *Winship* has been honored.

. . .

IV

Turning finally to the specific facts of this case, we reject the petitioner's claim that under the constitutional standard dictated by *Winship* his conviction of first-degree murder cannot stand. A review of the record in the light most favorable to the prosecution convinces us that a rational factfinder could readily have found the petitioner guilty beyond a reasonable doubt of first-degree murder under Virginia law.

There was no question at the trial that the petitioner had fatally shot Mary Cole. The crucial factual dispute went to the sufficiency of the evidence to support a finding that he had specifically intended to kill her. This question, as the Court of Appeals recognized, must be gauged in the light of applicable Virginia law defining the element of premeditation. Under that law it is well settled that premeditation need not exist for any particular length of time, and that an intent to kill may be formed at the moment of the commission of the unlawful act. From the circumstantial evidence in the record, it is clear that the trial judge could reasonably have found beyond a reasonable doubt that the petitioner did possess the necessary intent at or before the time of the killing.

The prosecution's uncontradicted evidence established that the petitioner shot the victim not once but twice. The petitioner himself admitted that the fatal shooting had occurred only after he had first fired several shots into the ground and then reloaded his gun. The evidence was clear that the two shots that killed the victim were fired at close, and thus predictably fatal, range by a person who was experienced in the use of the murder weapon. Immediately after the shooting, the petitioner drove without mishap from Virginia to North Carolina, a fact quite at odds with his story of extreme intoxication. Shortly before the fatal episode, he had publicly expressed an intention to have sexual relations with the victim. Her body was found partially unclothed. From these uncontradicted circumstances, a rational factfinder readily could have inferred beyond a reasonable doubt that the petitioner, notwithstanding evidence that he had been drinking on the day of the killing, did have the capacity to form and had in fact formed an intent to kill the victim.

The petitioner's calculated behavior both before and after the killing demonstrated that he was fully capable of committing premeditated murder. His claim of self-defense would have required the trial judge to draw a series of improbable inferences from the basic facts, prime among them the inference that he was wholly uninterested in sexual activity with the victim but that she was so interested as to have willingly removed part of her clothing and then attacked him with a knife when he resisted her advances, even though he was armed with a loaded revolver that he had just demonstrated he knew how to use. It is evident from the record that the trial judge found this story, including the petitioner's belated contention that he had been so intoxicated as to be incapable of premeditation, incredible.

Only under a theory that the prosecution was under an affirmative duty to rule out every hypothesis except that of guilt beyond a reasonable doubt could this petitioner's challenge be sustained. That theory the Court has rejected in the past. We decline to adopt it today. Under the standard established in this opinion as necessary to preserve the due process protection recognized in *Winship*, a federal habeas corpus court faced with a record of historical facts that supports conflicting inferences must presume-even if it does not affirmatively appear in the record-that the trier of fact resolved any such conflicts in favor of the prosecution, and must defer to that resolution. Applying these criteria, we hold that a rational trier of fact could reasonably have found that the petitioner committed murder in the first degree under Virginia law.

For these reasons, the judgment of the Court of Appeals is affirmed.

It is so ordered.

[The concurring opinion of Mr. Justice STEVENS, with whom THE CHIEF JUSTICE and Mr. Justice REHNQUIST joined has been omitted].

FROM THE COURTROOM

ARIZONA v. FULMINANTE

Supreme Court of the United States, 1991
499 U.S. 279

Justice WHITE delivered an opinion, Parts I, II, and IV of which are the opinion of the Court.

The Arizona Supreme Court ruled in this case that respondent Oreste Fulminante's confession, received in evidence at his trial for murder, had been coerced and that its use against him was barred by the Fifth and Fourteenth Amendments to the United States Constitution. The court also held that the harmless-error rule could not be used to save the conviction. We affirm the judgment of the Arizona court, although for different reasons than those upon which that court relied.

I

Early in the morning of September 14, 1982, Fulminante called the Mesa, Arizona, Police Department to report that his 11–year–old stepdaughter, Jeneane Michelle Hunt, was missing. He had been caring for Jeneane while his wife, Jeneane's mother, was in the hospital. Two days later, Jeneane's body was found in the desert east of Mesa. She had been shot twice in the head at close range with a large caliber weapon, and a ligature was around her neck. Because of the decomposed condition of the body, it was impossible to tell whether she had been sexually assaulted.

Fulminante's statements to police concerning Jeneane's disappearance and his relationship with her contained a number of inconsistencies, and he became a suspect in her killing. When no charges were filed against him, Fulminante left Arizona for New Jersey. Fulminante was later convicted in New Jersey on federal charges of possession of a firearm by a felon.

Fulminante was incarcerated in the Ray Brook Federal Correctional Institution in New York. There he became friends with another inmate, Anthony Sarivola, then serving a 60–day sentence for extortion. The two men came to spend several hours a day together. Sarivola, a former police officer, had been involved in loansharking for organized crime but then became a paid informant for the Federal Bureau of Investigation. While at Ray Brook, he masqueraded as an organized crime figure. After becoming friends with Fulminante, Sarivola heard a rumor that Fulminante was suspected of killing a child in Arizona. Sarivola then raised the subject with Fulminante in several conversations, but Fulminante repeatedly denied any involvement in Jeneane's death. During one conversation, he told Sarivola that Jeneane had been killed by bikers looking for drugs; on another occasion, he said he did not know what had happened. Sarivola passed this information on to an agent of the Federal Bureau of Investigation, who instructed Sarivola to find out more.

Sarivola learned more one evening in October 1983, as he and Fulminante walked together around the prison track. Sarivola said that he knew Fulminante was "starting to get some tough treatment and whatnot" from other inmates because of the rumor. Sarivola offered to protect Fulminante from his fellow inmates, but told him, "'You have to tell me about it,' you know. I mean, in other words, 'For me to give you any help.'" Fulminante then admitted to Sarivola that he had driven Jeneane to the desert on his motorcycle, where he choked her, sexually assaulted her, and made her beg for her life, before shooting her twice in the head.

Sarivola was released from prison in November 1983. Fulminante was released the following May, only to be arrested the next month for another weapons violation. On September 4, 1984, Fulminante was indicted in Arizona for the first-degree murder of Jeneane.

Prior to trial, Fulminante moved to suppress the statement he had given Sarivola in prison, as well as a second confession he had given to Donna Sarivola, then Anthony Sarivola's fiancée and later his wife, following his May 1984 release from prison. He asserted that the confession to Sarivola was coerced, and that the second confession was the "fruit" of the first. Following the hearing, the trial court denied the motion to suppress, specifically finding that, based on the stipulated facts, the confessions were voluntary. The State introduced both confessions as evidence at trial, and on December 19, 1985, Fulminante was convicted of Jeneane's murder. He was subsequently sentenced to death.

Fulminante appealed, arguing, among other things, that his confession to Sarivola was the product of coercion and that its admission at trial violated his rights to due process under the Fifth and Fourteenth Amendments to the United States Constitution. After considering the evidence at trial as well as the stipulated facts before the trial court on the motion to suppress, the Arizona Supreme Court held that the confession was coerced, but initially determined that the admission of the confession at trial was harmless error, because of the overwhelming nature of the evidence against Upon Fulminante's motion for reconsideration, however, the court ruled that this Court's precedent precluded the use of the harmless-error analysis in the case of a coerced confession. The court therefore reversed the conviction and ordered that Fulminante be retried without the use of the confession to Sarivola. Because of differing views in the state and federal courts over whether the admission at trial of a coerced confession is subject to a harmless-error analysis, we granted the State's petition for certiorari. Although a majority of this Court finds that such a confession is subject to a harmless-error analysis, for the reasons set forth below, we affirm the judgment of the Arizona court.

II

We deal first with the State's contention that the court below erred in holding Fulminante's confession to have been coerced. The State argues that it is the totality of the circumstances that determines whether Fulminante's confession was coerced, but contends that rather than apply this standard, the Arizona court applied a "but for" test, under which the court found that but for the promise given by Sarivola, Fulminante would not have confessed. In support of this argument, the State points to the Arizona court's reference to *Bram v. United States*. Although the Court noted in *Bram* that a confession cannot be obtained by "'any direct or implied promises, however slight, nor by the exertion of any improper influence,'" it is clear that this passage from Bram, which under current precedent does not state the standard for determining the voluntariness of a confession, was not relied on by the Arizona court in reaching its conclusion. Rather, the court cited this language as part of a longer quotation from an Arizona case which accurately described the State's burden of proof for establishing voluntariness. Indeed, the Arizona Supreme Court stated that a "determination regarding the voluntariness of a confession . . . must be viewed in a totality of the circumstances," and under that standard plainly found that Fulminante's statement to Sarivola had been coerced.

In applying the totality of the circumstances test to determine that the confession to Sarivola was coerced, the Arizona Supreme Court focused on a number of relevant facts. First, the court noted that "because [Fulminante] was an alleged child murderer, he was in danger of physical harm at the hands of other inmates." In addition, Sarivola was aware that Fulminante had been receiving "'rough treatment from the guys.'" Using his knowledge of these threats, Sarivola offered to protect Fulminante in exchange for a confession to Jeneane's murder, and "[i]n response to Sarivola's offer of protection, [Fulminante] confessed." Agreeing with Fulminante that "Sarivola's promise was 'extremely coercive,'" the Arizona court declared: "[T]he confession was obtained as a direct result of extreme coercion and was tendered in the belief that the defendant's life was in jeopardy if he did not confess. This is a true coerced confession in every sense of the word."

We normally give great deference to the factual findings of the state court. Nevertheless, "the ultimate issue of 'voluntariness' is a legal question requiring independent federal determination."

Although the question is a close one, we agree with the Arizona Supreme Court's conclusion that Fulminante's confession was coerced. The Arizona Supreme Court found a credible threat of physical violence unless Fulminante confessed. Our cases have made clear that a finding of coercion need not depend upon actual violence by a government agent; a credible threat is sufficient. As we have said, "coercion can be mental as well as physical, and . . . the blood of the accused is not the only hallmark of an unconstitutional inquisition." As in *Payne*, where the Court found that a confession was coerced because the interrogating police officer had promised that if the accused confessed, the officer would protect the accused from an angry mob outside the jailhouse door, so too here, the Arizona Supreme Court found that it was fear of physical violence, absent protection from his friend (and Government agent) Sarivola, which motivated Fulminante to confess. Accepting the Arizona court's finding, permissible on this record, that there was a credible threat of physical violence, we agree with its conclusion that Fulminante's will was overborne in such a way as to render his confession the product of coercion.

III

[Part III of Justice White's opinion has been replaced with Part II of Justice Rehnquist's opinion, which was the opinion of the Court.

Since this Court's landmark decision in *Chapman v. California*, in which we adopted the general rule that a constitutional error does not automatically require reversal of a conviction, the Court has applied harmless-error analysis to a wide range of errors and has recognized that most constitutional errors can be harmless.

The common thread connecting these cases is that each involved "trial error"—error which occurred during the presentation of the case to the jury, and which may therefore be quantitatively assessed in the context of other evidence presented in order to determine whether its admission was harmless beyond a reasonable doubt. In applying harmless-error analysis to these many different constitutional violations, the Court has been faithful to the belief that the harmless-error doctrine is essential to preserve the "principle that the central purpose of a criminal trial is to decide the factual question of the defendant's guilt or innocence, and promotes public respect for the criminal process by focusing on the underlying fairness of the trial rather than on the virtually inevitable presence of immaterial error."

. . .

The admission of an involuntary confession—a classic "trial error"—is markedly different from the other two constitutional violations referred to in the *Chapman* footnote as not being subject to harmless-error analysis. One of those violations, involved in *Gideon v. Wainwright*, was the total deprivation of the right to counsel at trial. The other violation, involved in *Tumey v. Ohio*, was a judge who was not impartial. These are structural defects in the constitution of the trial mechanism, which defy analysis by "harmless-error" standards. The entire conduct of the trial from beginning to end is obviously affected by the absence of counsel for a criminal defendant, just as it is by the presence on the bench of a judge who is not impartial. Since our decision in *Chapman*, other cases have added to the category of constitutional errors which are not subject to harmless error the following: unlawful exclusion of members of the defendant's race from a grand jury; the right to self-representation at trial; and the right to public trial. Each of these constitutional deprivations is a similar structural defect affecting the framework within which the trial proceeds, rather than simply an error in the trial process itself. "Without these basic protections, a criminal trial cannot reliably serve its function as a vehicle for determination of guilt or innocence, and no criminal punishment may be regarded as fundamentally fair."

It is evident from a comparison of the constitutional violations which we have held subject to harmless error, and those which we have held not, that involuntary statements or confessions belong in the former category. The admission of an involuntary confession is a "trial error," similar in both degree and kind to the erroneous admission of other types of evidence. The evidentiary impact of an involuntary confession, and its effect upon the composition of the record, is indistinguishable from that of a confession obtained in violation of the Sixth Amendment—of evidence seized in violation of the Fourth Amendment—or of a prosecutor's improper comment on a defendant's silence at trial in violation of the Fifth Amendment. When reviewing the erroneous admission of an involuntary confession, the appellate court, as it does with the admission of other forms of improperly admitted evidence, simply reviews the remainder of the evidence against the defendant to determine whether the admission of the confession was harmless beyond a reasonable doubt.

Nor can it be said that the admission of an involuntary confession is the type of error which "transcends the criminal process." This Court has applied harmless-error analysis to the violation of other constitutional rights similar in magnitude and importance and involving the same level of police misconduct. For instance, we have previously held that the admission of a defendant's statements obtained in violation of the Sixth Amendment is subject to harmless-error analysis. In *Milton v. Wainwright*, the Court held the admission of a confession obtained in violation of *Massiah v. United States* to be harmless beyond a reasonable doubt. We have also held that the admission of an out-of-court statement by a nontestifying codefendant is subject to harmless-error analysis. The inconsistent treatment of statements elicited in violation of the Sixth and Fourteenth Amendments, respectively, can be supported neither by evidentiary or deterrence concerns nor by a belief that there is something more "fundamental" about involuntary confessions. This is especially true in a case such as this one where there are no allegations of physical violence on behalf of the police. A confession obtained in violation of the Sixth Amendment has the same evidentiary impact as does a confession obtained in violation of a defendant's due process rights. Government misconduct that results in violations of the Fourth and Sixth Amendments may be at least as reprehensible as conduct that results in an involuntary confession. For instance, the prisoner's confession to an inmate-informer at issue in *Milton*, which the Court characterized as implicating the Sixth Amendment right to counsel, is similar on its facts to the one we face today. Indeed, experience shows that law enforcement violations of these constitutional guarantees can involve conduct as egregious as police conduct used to elicit statements in violation of the Fourteenth Amendment. It is thus impossible to create a meaningful distinction between confessions elicited in violation of the Sixth Amendment and those in violation of the Fourteenth Amendment.

Of course an involuntary confession may have a more dramatic effect on the course of a trial than do other trial errors—in particular cases it may be devastating to a defendant—but this simply means that a reviewing court will conclude in such a case that its admission was not harmless error; it is not a reason for eschewing the harmless-error test entirely. The Supreme Court of Arizona, in its first opinion in the present case, concluded that the admission of Fulminante's confession was harmless error. That court concluded that a second and more explicit confession of the crime made by Fulminante after he was released from prison was not tainted by the first confession, and that the second confession, together with physical evidence from the wounds (the victim had been shot twice in the head with a large calibre weapon at close range and a ligature was found around her neck) and other evidence introduced at trial rendered the admission of the first confession harmless beyond a reasonable doubt.]

IV

Since five Justices have determined that harmless-error analysis applies to coerced confessions, it becomes necessary to evaluate under that ruling the admissibility of Fulminante's confession to Sarivola. *Chapman v. California* made clear that "before a federal constitutional error can be held harmless, the court must be able to declare a belief that it was harmless beyond a reasonable doubt." The Court has the power to review the record de novo in order to determine an error's harmlessness. In so doing, it must be determined whether the State has met its burden of demonstrating that the admission of the confession to Sarivola did not contribute to Fulminante's conviction. Five of us are of the view that the State has not carried its burden and accordingly affirm the judgment of the court below reversing respondent's conviction.

A confession is like no other evidence. Indeed, "the defendant's own confession is probably the most probative and damaging evidence that can be admitted against him . . . . [T]he admissions of a defendant come from the actor himself, the most knowledgeable and unimpeachable source of information about his past conduct. Certainly, confessions have profound impact on the jury, so much so that we may justifiably doubt its ability to put them out of mind even if told to do so." While some statements by a defendant may concern isolated aspects of the crime or may be incriminating only when linked to other evidence, a full confession in which the defendant discloses the motive for and means of the crime may tempt the jury to rely upon that evidence alone in reaching its decision. In the case of a coerced confession such as that given by Fulminante to Sarivola, the risk that the confession is unreliable, coupled with the profound impact that the confession has upon the jury, requires a reviewing court to exercise extreme caution before determining that the admission of the confession at trial was harmless.

In the Arizona Supreme Court's initial opinion, in which it determined that harmless-error analysis could be applied to the confession, the court found that the admissible second confession to Donna Sarivola rendered the first confession to Anthony Sarivola cumulative. The court also noted that circumstantial physical evidence concerning the wounds, the ligature around Jeneane's neck, the location of the body, and the presence of motorcycle tracks at the scene corroborated the second confession. The court concluded that "due to the overwhelming evidence adduced from the second confession, if there had not been a first confession, the jury would still have had the same basic evidence to convict" Fulminante.

We have a quite different evaluation of the evidence. Our review of the record leads us to conclude that the State has failed to meet its burden of establishing, beyond a reasonable doubt, that the admission of Fulminante's confession to Anthony Sarivola was harmless error. Three considerations compel this result.

First, the transcript discloses that both the trial court and the State recognized that a successful prosecution depended on the jury believing the two confessions. Absent the confessions, it is unlikely that Fulminante would have been prosecuted at all, because the physical evidence from the scene and other circumstantial evidence would have been insufficient to convict. Indeed, no indictment was filed until nearly two years after the murder. Although the police had suspected Fulminante from the beginning, as the prosecutor acknowledged in his opening statement to the jury, "[W]hat brings us to Court, what makes this case fileable, and prosecutable and triable is that later, Mr. Fulminante confesses this crime to Anthony Sarivola and later, to Donna Sarivola, his wife." After trial began, during a renewed hearing on Fulminante's motion to suppress, the trial court opined, "You know, I think from what little I know about this trial, the character of this man [Sarivola] for truthfulness or untruthfulness and his credibility is the centerpiece of this case, is it not?" The prosecutor responded, "It's very important, there's no doubt." Finally, in his closing argument, the prosecutor prefaced his discussion of the two confessions by conceding: "[W]e have a lot of [circumstantial] evidence that indicates that this is our suspect, this is the fellow that did it, but it's a little short as far as saying that it's proof that he actually put the gun to the girl's head and killed her. So it's a little short of that. We recognize that."

Second, the jury's assessment of the confession to Donna Sarivola could easily have depended in large part on the presence of the confession to Anthony Sarivola. Absent the admission at trial of the first confession, the jurors might have found Donna Sarivola's story unbelievable. Fulminante's confession to Donna Sarivola allegedly occurred in May 1984, on the day he was released from Ray Brook, as she and Anthony Sarivola drove Fulminante from New York to Pennsylvania. Donna Sarivola testified that Fulminante, whom she had never before met, confessed in detail about Jeneane's brutal murder in response to her casual question concerning why he was going to visit friends in Pennsylvania instead of returning to his family in Arizona. Although she testified that she was "disgusted" by Fulminante's disclosures, she stated that she took no steps to notify authorities of what she had learned. In fact, she claimed that she barely discussed the matter with Anthony Sarivola, who was in the car and overheard Fulminante's entire conversation with Donna. Despite her disgust for Fulminante, Donna Sarivola later went on a second trip with him. Although Sarivola informed authorities that he had driven Fulminante to Pennsylvania, he did not mention Donna's presence in the car or her conversation with Fulminante. Only when questioned by authorities in June 1985 did Anthony Sarivola belatedly recall the confession to Donna more than a year before, and only then did he ask if she would be willing to discuss the matter with authorities.

Although some of the details in the confession to Donna Sarivola were corroborated by circumstantial evidence, many, including details that Jeneane was choked and sexually assaulted, were not. As to other aspects of the second confession, including Fulminante's motive and state of mind, the only corroborating evidence was the first confession to Anthony Sarivola. Thus, contrary to what the Arizona Supreme Court found, it is clear that the jury might have believed that the two confessions reinforced and corroborated each other. For this reason, one confession was not merely cumulative of the other. While in some cases two confessions, delivered on different occasions to different listeners, might be viewed as being independent of each other, it strains credulity to think that the jury so viewed the two confessions in this case, especially given the close relationship between Donna and Anthony Sarivola.

The jurors could also have believed that Donna Sarivola had a motive to lie about the confession in order to assist her husband. Anthony Sarivola received significant benefits from federal authorities, including payment for information, immunity from prosecution, and eventual placement in the federal Witness Protection Program. In addition, the jury might have found Donna motivated by her own desire for favorable treatment, for she, too, was ultimately placed in the Witness Protection Program.

Third, the admission of the first confession led to the admission of other evidence prejudicial to Fulminante. For example, the State introduced evidence that Fulminante knew of Sarivola's connections with organized crime in an attempt to explain why Fulminante would have been motivated to confess to Sarivola in seeking protection. Absent the confession, this evidence would have had no relevance and would have been inadmissible at trial. The Arizona Supreme Court found that the evidence of Sarivola's connections with organized crime reflected on Sarivola's character, not Fulminante's, and noted that the evidence could have been used to impeach Sarivola. This analysis overlooks the fact that had the confession not been admitted, there would have been no reason for Sarivola to testify and thus no need to impeach his testimony. Moreover, we cannot agree that the evidence did not reflect on Fulminante's character as well, for it depicted him as someone who willingly sought out the company of criminals. It is quite possible that this evidence led the jury to view Fulminante as capable of murder.

Finally, although our concern here is with the effect of the erroneous admission of the confession on Fulminante's conviction, it is clear that the presence of the confession also influenced the sentencing phase of the trial. Under Arizona law, the trial judge is the sentencer. At the sentencing hearing, the admissibility of information regarding aggravating circumstances is governed by the rules of evidence applicable to criminal trials. In this case, "based upon admissible evidence produced at the trial," the judge found that only one aggravating circumstance existed beyond a reasonable doubt, i.e., that the murder was committed in "an especially heinous, cruel, and depraved manner." In reaching this conclusion, the judge relied heavily on evidence concerning the manner of the killing and Fulminante's motives and state of mind which could only be found in the two confessions. For example, in labeling the murder "cruel," the judge focused in part on Fulminante's alleged statements that he choked Jeneane and made her get on her knees and beg before killing her. Although the circumstantial evidence was not inconsistent with this determination, neither was it sufficient to make such a finding beyond a reasonable doubt. Indeed, the sentencing judge acknowledged that the confessions were only partly corroborated by other evidence.

In declaring that Fulminante "acted with an especially heinous and depraved state of mind," the sentencing judge relied solely on the two confessions. While the judge found that the statements in the confessions regarding the alleged sexual assault on Jeneane should not be considered on the issue of cruelty because they were not corroborated by other evidence, the judge determined that they were worthy of belief on the issue of Fulminante's state of mind. The judge then focused on Anthony Sarivola's statement that Fulminante had made vulgar references to Jeneane during the first confession, and on Donna Sarivola's statement that Fulminante had made similar comments to her. Finally, the judge stressed that Fulminante's alleged comments to the

Sarivolas concerning torture, choking, and sexual assault, "whether they all occurred or not," depicted "a man who was bragging and relishing the crime he committed."

Although the sentencing judge might have reached the same conclusions even without the confession to Anthony Sarivola, it is impossible to say so beyond a reasonable doubt. Furthermore, the judge's assessment of Donna Sarivola's credibility, and hence the reliability of the second confession, might well have been influenced by the corroborative effect of the erroneously admitted first confession. Indeed, the fact that the sentencing judge focused on the similarities between the two confessions in determining that they were reliable suggests that either of the confessions alone, even when considered with all the other evidence, would have been insufficient to permit the judge to find an aggravating circumstance beyond a reasonable doubt as a requisite prelude to imposing the death penalty.

Because a majority of the Court has determined that Fulminante's confession to Anthony Sarivola was coerced and because a majority has determined that admitting this confession was not harmless beyond a reasonable doubt, we agree with the Arizona Supreme Court's conclusion that Fulminante is entitled to a new trial at which the confession is not admitted. Accordingly the judgment of the Arizona Supreme Court is

Affirmed.

[Part II of Chief Justice REHNQUIST's opinion, which was the opinion of the Court, has been inserted as Part III in the opinion above; the balance of his opinion has been omitted].

[The opinion of Justice KENNEDY, concurring in the judgment has been omitted].

48

Post-Conviction

Key Concepts

- Exhaustion of State Court Remedies Is Required
- State Court Decision Must Be Contrary to or an Unreasonable Application of Federal Law to Warrant Habeas Relief
- A Showing of Cause and Prejudice May Excuse Procedural Defaults
- Gateway Innocence v. Stand-Alone Innocence

A. Introduction and Policy.

1. A Word About Terminology. In **Chapter 47** we discussed the various policies, rules, and considerations that impact the direct review of a case on appeal. In this chapter, we will consider what happens after the appellate process is over. Technically, anything that occurs after the jury (or judge) returns a guilty verdict could be described as the "post-conviction" phase of a criminal case. Indeed, the Federal Rules of Criminal Procedure include under the subheading "Post-Conviction Procedures" items like "Sentencing," "Revoking or Modifying Probation," and "New Trial" motions. Among practicing attorneys, however, the term "post-conviction" is a term of art which refers to the collateral attacks on a conviction that are launched **after** the conviction is affirmed on direct appeal.

The challenge of labeling is not without cause. For many years, in both the states and the federal system, a "writ of habeas corpus" (either statutory or common law) was the dominant avenue for relief following a conviction. However, that phraseology began to shift as many states consolidated and codified their collateral options into systems loosely referred to as the "post-conviction process." Attorneys who had come up in the former systems continued to refer to all collateral challenges as "habeas," while newer attorneys more often called such challenges "post-conviction" attacks. Furthermore, any change in phraseology oftentimes depended upon whether the state in which an attorney practiced had a) codified its collateral review process by adopting the Uniform Post-Conviction Procedure Act; b) maintained common law remedies; or c) pursued some other avenue entirely. At the same time, in the federal system, traditional "habeas" relief was being overhauled into a new statutory scheme that was not actually called "habeas." And, to complicate matters further, the traditional "habeas" remedy was kept on the books, though largely relegated to only a minor role.

For purposes of this chapter, unless specific limitation is indicated, the term "post-conviction" will be used throughout to refer collectively to both state post-conviction proceedings and federal habeas proceedings. The term "state post-conviction" will be used to refer only those collateral proceedings in state court. And, the term "habeas proceedings" will be used to refer only to collateral attacks in federal court, whether they are brought by state or federal prisoners.

2. Post-Conviction Review. "Post-conviction" is an umbrella-like label that includes many different forms of collateral attack upon a conviction after the appellate process has been exhausted. In a direct appeal, the defendant is usually arguing that the trial court made a mistake about the law, or that no reasonable jury could have convicted him based on the evidence that was presented. In a post-conviction challenge, the defendant is usually arguing that there was some fundamental unfairness in the trial process that is inconsistent with state or federal law, or that new evidence has arisen since his conviction that significantly undermines confidence in his guilt. Post-conviction challenges are less common than direct appeals and less likely to succeed.

One of the primary differences between the review available on direct appeal and the review available in post-conviction concerns the source of the error. As you read in **Chapter 47**, on direct appeal, the appellant is limited to matters that appear in the trial record. No similar limitation applies to an applicant's first round of post-conviction review. Thus, in thinking about one basic difference between the two stages of review, it might help you to conceptualize a direct appeal as pointing to those things that happened at trial that should not have. In contrast, you might conceptualize a post-conviction as introducing new evidence to show what should have happened at trial but didn't.

An appellate court does not, as a general matter, accept new evidence. If an issue does not appear in the appellate record, it will be nearly impossible for a successful appellate claim to be brought. But, with post-conviction claims, new evidence is the most frequent basis for claims raised. For example, to demonstrate that your attorney was ineffective, it may be necessary to introduce evidence of what she failed to do. To demonstrate that a prosecutor hid evidence, the exculpatory evidence that was not originally disclosed must be presented. To show that a witness lied, the witness' recantation must be offered to the post-conviction court. All of these matters require the introduction of new evidence—either documentary or through live witnesses. In this sense then, post-conviction proceedings (at least in state courts) are much more like trials than the direct appeals that precede them.

It would be impossible to consider exhaustively each of the collateral remedies that are available to state and federal prisons in a single chapter. Entire books and law review articles have been dedicated to detailed analysis of the array of federal and state post-conviction remedies. In this chapter, the goals are far more modest.

First, you will become generally acquainted with the statutory remedies that are available in the federal system for state and federal inmates. Next, we will turn to the most significant legal standards that govern post-conviction practice in the federal courts. Finally, we will close with a discussion of the role of actual innocence.

State post-conviction procedures are available in every state, but they vary widely depending on the jurisdiction. As usual, you must familiarize yourself with the rules governing post-conviction practice in your state. Because of the restrictions that have been imposed on federal habeas, it is the state post-conviction process that increasingly offers the greatest opportunity for relief from a wrongful conviction.

As you have read over the last forty-odd chapters, a criminal trial consists of a number of simultaneously moving parts. We trust the results of the system are accurate when these parts are all working properly. The adversarial system thus depends on the defense attorney, the prosecutor, the jury, the witnesses, the trial judge, and the appellate judges to do their jobs correctly. But the system does not always work correctly. Innocent people are sometimes convicted, and guilty people are sometimes acquitted. This second type of error (the wrongful acquittal of the guilty) is a cost we are willing to pay to ensure that our constitutional rights are protected and to guard against wrongful convictions. Thus, the system is theoretically weighted to err on the side of wrongful dismissal or acquittal. For example, the prosecutor has the burden of proof, and the burden is set very high. This weighting against the prosecutor extends to post-trial proceedings as well: if the prosecutor loses at trial, she is not able to appeal or collaterally attack an acquittal.

However, even with this built-in weighting, errors still occur in the other direction. The reasons for wrongful convictions are varied: Defense attorneys fail to prepare. Prosecutors hide exculpatory evidence or engage in other misconduct. Witnesses lie. Judges mismanage trials. The appellate process is designed to recognize and correct some errors, but it cannot correct them all. Thus, post-conviction remedies are a necessary backstop to address those situations when the adversarial system does not work properly and a person is wrongfully convicted.

Current post-conviction case law largely focuses on a respect for the finality of judgments. This has meant in many respects increased deference to trial courts, stricter enforcement of deadlines, and the imposition of heightened standards to warrant relief. The forces driving the tightening of these rules are multi-faceted. But, at least one concern is the problem of limited resources. In the criminal justice system, the vast majority of resources are dedicated to the initial adjudication phase—that is, to getting an accurate decision the first time around. Therefore, once an accused has been adjudged guilty and any direct appeals are finished, legislatures and courts are disinclined to spend more resources second-guessing the primary decision-making process.[1]

B. The Law. In the very early years, many of the remedies that were available to collaterally attack a conviction were a product of the common law. Increasingly, the remedies for post-conviction relief have been formalized in statutory provisions.

There are five major collateral remedies available in the federal system. The availability of any one of these remedies depends upon where the judgment of conviction being attacked was entered—state or federal court—and whether the claimant is incarcerated.

1. 28 U.S.C. § 2254: Petition for Writ of Habeas Corpus. This is the most common form of post-conviction remedy. It is used by individuals who have been convicted in state court and who have exhausted all of their state court remedies.

2. 28 U.S.C. § 2255: Motion to Vacate, Set Aside or Correct a Sentence. This is the primary post-conviction claim brought by federal prisoners. It is used to challenge federal convictions on the grounds that the trial court made jurisdictional or constitutional error or otherwise violated federal law.

3. 28 U.S.C. § 2241: Petition for Writ of Habeas Corpus. This claim is brought by federal prisoners who want to challenge the execution of their sentence. It is also available if the prisoner can demonstrate that § 2255 is inadequate or ineffective.

4. 28 U.S.C. § 1651: Motion for Writ of Error Coram Nobis. This is an old common law writ which can be used in many different situations, but it is an "extraordinary" remedy that can only be used if other remedies are not available.

5. Federal Rule Criminal Procedure 35(b): Motion to Correct or Reduce a Sentence. This is the only post-conviction claim which is brought by the prosecutor. It is used when the prosecutor seeks to lower the prisoner's sentence after the prisoner provides cooperation to the state.

---

[1] United States v. Frady, 456 U.S. 152 (1982).

Sections 1651, 2241 and 2255 and Federal Rule of Criminal Procedure 35(b) are each forms of relief that are available only to people who have been convicted of federal offenses. State prisoners are limited to relief under § 2254. Since § 2254 is far and away the most commonly used form of post-conviction relief in the federal system, we will discuss it first.

1. 28 U.S.C. § 2254 governs claims that ask the federal courts to review a state conviction.

28 U.S.C. § 2254

This form of relief is available to "a person in custody pursuant to the judgment of a State court only on the ground that he is in custody in violation of the Constitution or the laws or treaties of the United States."[2]

In order to get relief under this statute, the state prisoner must have either:

"Exhausted the remedies available in the court of the State;"[3] or

Show that a state process for addressing her claims was not available; or

Show that the circumstances of her case are such that the state process is ineffective.[4]

If the prisoner presented his claims to the state court but they were either filed too late or were filed improperly, the claims will be deemed procedurally defaulted and this statute will not provide relief unless the prisoner can demonstrate either:

"Cause and prejudice" for the default; or,

A sufficiently compelling showing of "gateway innocence."

If the prisoner's constitutional claims were resolved on the merits by the state courts, those judgments will not be disturbed in federal habeas unless the state court's decision was either "contrary to, or involved an unreasonable application of, clearly established Federal law, as determined by the Supreme Court of the United States."[5]

A prisoner must file his claim within:

One year from the time their convictions became final; or

---

[2] 28 U.S.C. § 2254(a).

[3] § 2254(b)(1)(A).

[4] § 2254(b)(1)(B).

[5] § 2254(d)(1).

> If the claim is based on a constitutional right that was newly recognized by the Supreme Court and has retroactive effect, one year from the date on which the constitutional right the claim invokes was initially recognized by the Supreme Court;[6] or If the claim is based on newly discovered facts, one year from the date that the facts could have been discovered through the exercise of due diligence.[7]

The **exhaustion requirement** means that an applicant must first present his federal claims to the state courts using whatever avenues of relief are available. As the statute explains, "[a]n applicant shall not be deemed to have exhausted the remedies available in the courts of the State, within the meaning of this section if he has the right under the law of the State to raise, by any available procedure the question presented."[8] The exhaustion requirement is a one-way street: if the defendant has failed to exhaust his claims, the court will not grant his petition, but the court could still decide to deny the petition on the merits, thus precluding him from bringing it at a later time.[9]

If the applicant has not exhausted his claims, he must demonstrate that state relief was either unavailable or would be ineffective. We will discuss these exceptions further in Section C.1.

Another significant bar to federal habeas review is the notion of **procedural default**. Procedural default is a concept that is very closely related to the exhaustion requirement. One way to understand the relationship between the two is to think of an applicant's failure to exhaust his state court remedies as just one way in which he might procedurally default his claims. However, procedural default is a concept that extends well beyond an applicant's complete failure to present a claim to the state courts. In addition, procedurally defaulted claims are those claims that have been rejected by the state courts not on the merits but because they were not timely filed or were filed improperly.

The doctrine of procedural default is based on "the comity and respect that must be accorded to state-court judgments."[10] In order to succeed on a procedurally defaulted claim, the applicant must make one of two showings—"cause and prejudice" or "gateway innocence." **Cause and prejudice** requires an applicant to show that his failure to properly raise the claim in state court was caused by some external factor and that the failure to properly raise the claim has prejudiced his rights. **Gateway innocence** requires an applicant to present newly discovered

---

[6] § 2244(d)(1)(C).

[7] § 2244(d)(1)(D).

[8] § 2254(c).

[9] § 2254(b)(2).

[10] House v. Bell, 547 U.S. 518, 536 (2006).

evidence that makes it more likely than not no reasonable juror would have found the applicant guilty beyond a reasonable doubt. We will consider these terms further in Sections C.2 and C.3.

The final set of rules governing Section 2254 petitions were added by the Antiterrorism Effective Death Penalty Act ("AEDPA," pronounced "ED-pah"), which is codified at 28 U.S.C. § 2244. AEDPA was enacted in 1996 in response to perceived abuses of existing habeas remedies. The sense was the federal judiciary was spending an ever-increasing percentage of its time resolving state prisoner habeas claims.

To solve this perceived problem, AEDPA created standards-based and temporal limits, all of which substantially weakened the degree of scrutiny to which federal courts subjected state court rulings on constitutional claims. Under AEDPA's modifications, the standards in the federal courts are now highly deferential to state court judgments. Specifically, a federal court will not grant relief unless it determines that the state court's post-conviction decision is contrary to or an unreasonable application of federal law.

A state court's decision is "**contrary to**" clearly established federal law if the state court has arrived at an opposite conclusion of law to that reached by the Supreme Court; or on materially indistinguishable facts has reached a contrary result. A state court decision involves an "**unreasonable application**" of federal law if the court identifies the correct legal rule, but then a) applies that rule unreasonably to the facts of the case; or b) refuses to extend the rule to a context where it clearly applies; or c) extends the rule to a context where it clearly does not apply.

If the state court decision was based on a factual determination, the decision is presumed to be correct, and the applicant can only rebut the presumption if there is clear and convincing evidence of an error.[11] This means the federal court will not overturn a state court's factual judgment unless the decision "was based on an unreasonable determination of the facts in light of the evidence presented in the State court proceeding."[12]

In other words, it is not enough for a federal court to simply disagree with the state court's post-conviction determination of the facts or the law. Indeed, it is not even enough that the state court's decision was incorrect. Instead, to warrant federal habeas relief, the federal court must find the state court's judgment was patently unreasonable. We will explore this issue in more detail in Section C.4.

In addition to weakening the standards by requiring deference to state court findings, AEDPA also imposed time limits that required state applicants to move

11 § 2254(e)(1).

12 § 2254 (d)(2).

into federal court within one year of their convictions becoming final; or one year from when the right they are relying upon was recognized; or one year from the date on which they should have learned the new facts which they are citing. Under this rule, a conviction becomes "final" upon the conclusion of appellate review in the state courts or upon conclusion of the time available for seeking appellate review.[13]

Just like the speedy trial provisions you read about in **Chapter 41,** the one-year statute of limitations period can be suspended or "tolled." Section 2254's clock tolls during any periods that the applicant is actively pursuing state post-conviction remedies in the state courts. The minute the applicant's conviction becomes final, the 2254 "clock" begins running. As soon as the applicant files for post-conviction relief in state court, the clock stops. Once the denial of post-conviction relief in the state court is final, the clock starts again. The amount of real time that passes is immaterial. The question is whether, between all its starts and stops, the 2254 clock has accrued more than a year's worth of time. "Statutory tolling" is the term used to refer to all the points when the clock was stopped because this form of tolling is expressly recognized in the statutory language.[14]

In addition, the one-year limitations period is subject to what is known as "equitable tolling." Equitable tolling allows a federal court to overlook delay in filing if the applicant can show "(1) that he has been pursuing his rights diligently, and (2) that some extraordinary circumstance stood in his way and prevented timely filing."[15] "Garden variety" attorney error—like miscalculating a filing deadline—will not constitute an extraordinary circumstance justifying equitable tolling.[16] However, a court is likely to apply equitable tolling if there is a "serious instance of attorney misconduct."[17] An example of serious attorney misconduct would include a lawyer's failure to file a petition despite the client's "many letters that repeatedly emphasized the importance of his doing so," coupled with the lawyer's failure to "do the research necessary to find out the proper filing date," and the lawyer's failure to inform the client of facts necessary to allow the client to timely file on his own behalf despite the client's request for such information.[18]

Notwithstanding the various tolling provisions, the one-year limitations period imposed by AEDPA has foreclosed federal habeas review for a significant number of state applicants. As many practitioners will tell you, one year is a remarkably short period in which to completely reinvestigate a case, identify and research constitutional claims and prepare habeas pleadings. This challenge becomes

---

13 28 U.S.C. § 2244(d)(1).

14 § 2244(d)(2).

15 Holland v. Florida, 560 U.S. 631, 649 (2010).

16 Id. at 651

17 Id. at 652.

18 Id.

even greater when the one-year limitations period is overlaid with the exhaustion requirement. In many states, prisoners have no right to counsel to assist in the preparation of state post-conviction pleadings. In addition, in many states the limitations period for filing for state post-conviction relief is far longer than the one year allowed in federal court—yet under the federal rules, the state pleadings must be filed first to satisfy the exhaustion requirement.

As an example, take the State of Maryland. Maryland law allows state prisoners ten years after their sentence is imposed to file for state post-conviction relief. The state statute authorizing post-conviction procedures grants a right to counsel, but this right has been read to require counsel only after a request for post-conviction relief has been filed. Accordingly, if a state prisoner takes even a fraction of the ten years she has to file a timely state post-conviction petition, her federal petition will be untimely. This is because time spent investigating, drafting and researching a state post-conviction pleading does not toll the federal clock. It is only the time that the pleading is pending in state court that counts.

There are also restrictions regarding the **factual record** used for these claims. In general, federal courts must rely upon the factual record developed during the exhaustion process in the state courts.[19] The Court has explicitly noted that the only time federal fact-finding is appropriate is if a state court has not decided a claim on the merits.[20] This is true even if additional facts are discovered after the state review is complete that weigh upon the correctness of a conviction.

Where it is appropriate for a federal court to consider new facts, the facts must be introduced into the record. Introducing facts can be done by way of affidavit or through live witnesses. Live witnesses can only present their evidence at a hearing, but a federal judge considering a habeas petition is not required to grant a hearing. A hearing in federal court is only warranted if:

a. The applicant shows that the new factual assertions "establish by clear and convincing evidence that but for constitutional error, no reasonable fact-finder would have found the applicant guilty of the underlying offense."[21] (In layman's terms, this means that the applicant must establish that the new evidence presented completely undermines confidence in his guilt); and

b. The claim presents a question concerning a new, retroactively applied rule of constitutional law; or the claim depends upon facts that could not have been discovered earlier. In assessing whether a factual basis for a claim could have been discovered earlier, the standard is due diligence.[22]

---

[19] § 2254(g).

[20] Cullen v. Pinholster, 131 S.Ct. 1388 (2011).

[21] § 2254(e)(2)(B).

[22] § 2254(e)(2).

A few final notes about § 2254 claims:

a. With the exception of capital cases,[23] there is not a right to counsel in federal habeas proceedings. The federal habeas court does have the authority to appoint counsel to indigent petitioners if it deems representation necessary.[24]

b. Though the trial of a mentally incompetent person violates the Constitution no similar ban exists in the habeas context. If a habeas petitioner is mentally incompetent, the habeas proceeding need not be stayed. There is no right to competence during a habeas proceeding.[25]

c. Ineffectiveness of trial and appellate counsel are claims that are commonly seen in federal habeas petitions. However, ineffective assistance of counsel at the post-conviction stage **cannot** be the basis for relief under this section.[26] Thus, if the applicant is challenging a lawyer who represented him in a collateral attack on his conviction, even the lawyer's gross incompetence cannot form the basis for habeas relief. However, while the ineffectiveness of post-conviction counsel does not form an independent habeas claim, it may amount to "cause" that excuses a procedural default that would otherwise bar other substantive claims.[27]

   For example, imagine that Dianne Derek is convicted of murder. Trial counsel does no investigation of the case. On appeal, a new attorney raises several challenges which are rejected as unpreserved because of trial counsel's failure to object. The case then moves into state post-conviction. A new lawyer is assigned to represent Derek. This lawyer completely reinvestigates the case and finds a videotape of the murder that clearly shows someone other than Derek stabbing the victim. Counsel also locates six police officers who would have testified that they were in a bar with Derek celebrating Police Week across town at the time of the murder. After identifying this evidence and drafting the state post-conviction petition, however, the new counsel develops a serious drinking problem that causes him to file the petition three years late despite Derek's repeated and detailed written requests that counsel move forward with the case. When counsel eventually files, all claims are rejected by the state court as procedurally defaulted. The case then moves into federal habeas. Habeas counsel asserts that trial counsel was ineffective for failing to find the videotape and the police witnesses. Habeas counsel also maintains that state post-conviction counsel was ineffective for failing to raise the claims in a timely fashion. The ineffectiveness of trial counsel would be a

[23] 28 U.S.C. § 2261.

[24] § 2254(h).

[25] Ryan v. Gonzales, 133 S.Ct. 696 (2013).

[26] § 2254(i).

[27] Martinez v. Ryan, 566 U.S. 1 (2012).

viable claim in federal habeas (if not for the procedural default). And, while the ineffectiveness of state post-conviction counsel does not provide a direct basis for habeas relief, it would provide a basis for excusing the procedural default—thereby enabling trial counsel's ineffectiveness to be considered by the federal court.

d. Much in the same way that ineffective post-conviction counsel will not constitute an independent basis for habeas relief, a claimed violation of the Fourth Amendment also will not establish grounds for relief.[28] However, a habeas applicant may assert a Sixth Amendment claim that counsel was ineffective for failing to seek the suppression of evidence.[29]

e. Section 2254 claims are heard by a federal district court. If the district court denies relief, the circuit court has the discretion to hear the case on appeal. To obtain review, the applicant must apply for and receive a certificate of appealability from the United States Court of Appeals for the relevant circuit. To be entitled to a certificate of appealability, the applicant must make a "substantial showing" of the denial of constitutional rights.[30] On the other hand, if the applicant wins his case in the district court, the government can appeal directly, without first obtaining a certificate of appealability.[31]

f. An applicant is limited to just one habeas petition per case. A second or successive petition may only be filed with the permission of the court, and must rely either on a new retroactive rule of constitutional law, or a factual predicate that could not previously have been discovered.[32]

2. 28 U.S.C. § 2255 is the primary statute used by prisoners in federal custody to challenge the legality of their sentence. It allows applicants to seek release on the grounds that "the sentence was imposed in violation of the Constitution or laws of the United States, or that the court was without jurisdiction to impose such sentence, or that the sentence was in excess of the maximum authorized by law, or is otherwise subject to collateral attack."[33] If convinced on the merits, the federal habeas court may vacate, set aside or correct the applicant's sentence.

If the court is able to determine conclusively on the paper record that relief is not warranted, the court can deny the petition without a hearing. Otherwise, the court should hold a hearing to decide the issues and make findings of fact and law. The applicant does not have to be present for the hearing.[34]

28 Stone v. Powell, 428 U.S. 465 (1976).
29 Kimmelman v. Morrison, 477 U.S. 363 (1986).
30 28 U.S.C. § 2253(c)(2).
31 Fed. R. App. Proc. 22(b)(3).
32 28 U.S.C. § 2244(b)(2).
33 28 U.S.C. § 2255(a).
34 28 U.S.C. § 2255(c).

As is true under § 2254, there is no right to counsel. But, counsel may be appointed at the discretion of the federal court.[35]

3. 28 U.S.C. § 2241 is the codification of the original common law writ of habeas corpus. It is primarily used by inmates to challenge the execution of their sentence as opposed to the trial or sentencing itself. For example, an inmate would bring a § 2241 motion against the bureau of prisons to argue that his sentence has been completed and so he should be released, or that he did not receive credit he deserved for good time on his sentence. Thus, § 2241 is only available to individuals who are currently in federal custody.

Section 2241 also provides a backup to § 2255 in that a defendant can bring a § 2241 motion to challenge his conviction if a § 2255 motion would be inadequate or ineffective. In addition, § 2241 is also the mechanism by which prisoners can be transferred from prison to court to testify.[36] If a petition is being used for this purpose, it will be titled a "Petition for Writ of Habeas Corpus Ad Testificandum."

4. The Writ of Error Coram Nobis was historically a common law writ that allowed for the correction of factual errors to the extent those errors affected the validity of a conviction. Early on, the writ was seen as a mechanism for the correction of technical errors in a judgment, like errors by a court clerk. However, the writ has long since expanded beyond its humble beginnings.[37] Currently, the writ is available to correct fundamental legal or factual errors.[38] However, coram nobis is available only if alternative remedies are not.

There is no statutory provision that specifically allows a writ of error coram nobis to be sought. However, **28 U.S.C. § 1651**, sometimes referred to as the "All Writs Section," has been interpreted by the Supreme Court as allowing the filing of such a writ in federal court.[39] This statutory provision provides in relevant part, "The Supreme Court and all courts established by Act of Congress may issue all writs necessary or appropriate in aid of their respective jurisdictions and agreeable to the usages and principles of law."

The Court has found that the All Writs Act is not a separate source of subject-matter jurisdiction for the reviewing court. Rather, the jurisdiction to consider or grant the relief requested must already be possessed by the court. A coram nobis action is, thus, a continuation of the original criminal proceeding and is not a separate civil action in the same way that a habeas proceeding is.[40]

---

35 § 2255(g).

36 28 U.S.C. § 2241(c)(5).

37 United States v. Denedo, 556 U.S. 904, 911 (2009).

38 Id. at 912-13.

39 United States v. Morgan, 346 U.S. 502 (1954).

40 Denedo, 556 U.S. at 913-14.

Reflecting its ancient common law origins, the writ has been used to address problems as varied as inquiring as to the "imprisonment of a slave not subject to imprisonment, [the] insanity of a defendant, a conviction on a guilty plea through the coercion of fear of mob violence, [and the] failure to advise of right to counsel."[41] More recently, the writ has been used to challenge the legality of a state court conviction that was used to enhance subsequent sentencing in federal court.[42] The applicant had served his term of punishment on the state conviction, but asserted that his guilty plea in that case was secured without the assistance of counsel.

Relief by way of writ of error coram nobis can be difficult to obtain. The writ is an extraordinary remedy and "an extraordinary remedy . . . should not be granted in the ordinary case."[43] In deciding whether coram nobis relief is appropriate, the court should consider things like the relative strength of the claim, the delay in seeking relief, whether the applicant knew (or should have known) of the claims sooner, and the impact upon the finality of judgments.[44]

5. Rule 35(b) of the Federal Rules of Criminal Procedure is the final major avenue of relief in the federal courts. Unlike the other provisions that have been discussed to this point, a Rule 35(b) motion may only be filed by the prosecution. In addition, the sentence reduction offered is only available to federal prisoners.

In general, a Rule 35(b) motion can be filed by the prosecution within one year of sentencing if the inmate has "provided substantial assistance in investigating or prosecuting another person."[45] Beyond the one year mark, sentence reduction upon government motion will only be allowed in three circumstances: a) if the inmate only learned the information after the one year period expired; b) if the information was provided within the one year limit, but did not become useful to the government until later; or c) if the inmate did not realize the usefulness of the information until after the deadline expired.

A successful motion filed pursuant to the rule may afford a substantial benefit to the inmate. The court is even authorized to reduce the sentence below any applicable statutory minimums.[46]

---

41 Morgan, 346 U.S. at 508.

42 Id.

43 Nken v. Holder, 556 U.S. 418 (2009) (Kennedy, J., concurring).

44 Denedo, 556 U.S. at 917.

45 F.R.C.P. 35(b)(1).

46 F.R.C.P. 35(b)(4).

C. Applying the Law.

1. Overcoming Exhaustion: Unavailable or Ineffective State Remedies. Exhaustion of available state court remedies is the first requirement for an applicant seeking federal review of a state conviction. An applicant who cannot demonstrate exhaustion will generally be declined a merits-review of his claims in the federal courts. However, the language of the statute also indicates that exhaustion is not required if state remedies are "unavailable" or "ineffective." This situation most commonly arises when a state court takes an excessive amount of time to resolve an applicant's state post-conviction claims:

> **Example:** Martin Cristin was tried in absentia in Pennsylvania and convicted of theft by deception. He was sentenced to fifteen to thirty years in prison. The period in which to file an appeal came and went without Cristin filing a notice of appeal. Approximately two months later, Cristin surrendered himself to law enforcement officers. Cristin filed a timely petition for post-conviction relief in the state court alleging ineffective assistance of counsel, and other constitutional claims.
>
> Twenty-seven months passed without the state court resolving Cristin's petition. Cristin then filed a petition in federal court seeking habeas relief. One week after Cristin filed his federal petition, the state court rejected his claims in their entirety. Cristin did not appeal the state court's denial of relief. The district court initially found that federal review was barred by Cristin's failure to exhaust his state court remedies—specifically, the court pointed to Cristin's failure to appeal either his conviction or the denial of post-conviction relief. However, on reconsideration, the court found that while Cristin was not excused from the exhaustion requirement, he could demonstrate both cause and prejudice for his failures to appeal. On the merits, the court then found that habeas relief was appropriate in light of the numerous constitutional violations present in Cristin's case. The state appealed to the Third Circuit.

Analysis: The circuit court found that Cristin did not exhaust his state court remedies and there was no basis for finding that he did not have to overcome this basic hurdle.

Exhaustion is closely related to the doctrine of procedural default. "A prisoner has not exhausted his remedies in state court 'if he has the right under the law of the

State to raise, by any available procedure, the question presented.'"[47] Cristin no longer had an available state court remedy to pursue his claims. But, the simple absence of remaining state court remedies does not end the federal inquiry. In addition, the federal court has to consider whether that absence is the result of the applicant properly exhausting his remedies by fairly presenting any claims to the state court. Fair presentation requires a state prisoner to pursue his federal claims at "all levels of state court adjudication." In the absence of such fair presentation, a federal habeas court cannot hear the claims because they are procedurally defaulted.

Cristin's constitutional claims could have been presented to the state courts either on the direct appeal of his conviction, or on the appeal of the denial of post-conviction relief. He did neither.

Cristin maintained that his failure to exhaust his state court remedies was not a bar to federal review because the state court's delay in resolving his post-conviction claim made relief effectively unavailable. It is true that inexcusable or inordinate delay in the state court's resolution of a pleading may render the state court remedy "unavailable," thereby allowing federal habeas review without exhaustion. However, such delay must be fairly substantial to justify such relief. In the Third Circuit, a thirty-three month delay "remains the shortest delay held to render state collateral proceedings ineffective for purposes of the exhaustion requirement."[48] While the state court should have resolved Cristin's claims more expeditiously, the twenty-seven month delay in his case was not adequate to render state relief "effectively unavailable." This is particularly true where at least some activity on Cristin's claims was happening in the state court for at least a portion of the time.

Cristin was required to exhaust his claims but did not. Therefore, relief in the federal court would only be appropriate if Cristin could show either (1) cause and prejudice for the default or (2) that he is actually innocent, and thus a fundamental miscarriage of justice will occur if his claims are not reviewed. Cristin could show neither, so he was not entitled to federal habeas relief.

2. Overcoming Procedural Default: Cause and Prejudice. As you read above, under § 2254 the exhaustion requirement is a significant hurdle that state prisoners must overcome before their claims will be reviewed in federal habeas. If a state prisoner does not present a claim to the state court (or presents it improperly) that claim will be considered "procedurally defaulted." A procedurally defaulted claim cannot, as a general matter, form the basis for federal habeas relief.

If, however, a state prisoner can demonstrate cause for and actual prejudice as a result of the procedural default, the federal court considering the habeas

---

47 Cristin v. Brennan, 281 F.3d 404, 410 (3d Cir. 2002).

48 Id. at 411.

claim may overlook the default.[49] Cause comes in different forms, but generally, "cause" for the procedural default must be something objectively external to the defense.[50] For example, "a showing that the factual or legal basis for a claim was not reasonably available to counsel . . ., or that some interference by officials . . . made compliance impracticable, would constitute cause under this standard."[51] In contrast, where the reason for the default is attorney error, the simple negligence or inadvertence of state post-conviction counsel generally will not qualify as "cause."[52]

However, though the Court has demanded "something external to the defense" to establish cause, it has also recognized that attorney error may amount to cause under three circumstances:

First, the **constitutional ineffectiveness** of appellate counsel may establish cause for default.[53]

Second, if the procedural default was caused by the **unannounced abandonment** of the client by state post-conviction counsel, it may be excused.[54]

Finally, where the federal habeas action presents a procedurally defaulted claim of trial counsel's ineffectiveness, the ineffectiveness of state post-conviction counsel may establish cause in the narrow circumstance where the trial level IAC claim has substance and the state post-conviction proceeding was the **first real opportunity** to raise this claim of trial level IAC:

> **Example—*Trevino v. Thaler*, 133 S.Ct. 1911 (2013):** Carlos Trevino was convicted of murdering Linda Salinas. Following his conviction, the court held a capital sentencing hearing. After the state presented its aggravating evidence, defense counsel called Trevino's aunt. She testified to Trevino's "difficult upbringing." She also told the jury that Trevino's mother had a drinking problem, that Trevino had dropped out of high school and that his family received public assistance. The jury found that Trevino was a future danger, that he was actually responsible for Salinas's death, and that there was not sufficient mitigating evidence to warrant mercy. Accordingly, Trevino was sentenced to death. Trevino's appeal was rejected by the Texas high court. Trevino was then appointed a post-conviction attorney to handle his state post-conviction claims. These were denied as well.

---

49 McCleskey v. Zant, 499 U.S. 466 (1991).

50 Coleman v. Thompson, 501 U.S. 722 (1991).

51 Murray v. Carrier, 477 U.S. 478, 488 (1986).

52 Maples v. Thomas, 132 S.Ct. 912, 922 (2011).

53 Martinez v. Ryan, 132 S.Ct. 1309 (2012).

54 Maples v. Thomas, 132 S.Ct. 912 (2012).

Trevino then sought federal habeas relief. For the first time, counsel for Trevino alleged that his trial attorney was constitutionally ineffective because the trial attorney had not adequately investigated evidence of mitigation. In support of this claim, habeas counsel presented the significant mitigation that he had uncovered during his own investigation. This evidence included evidence that Trevino suffered from Fetal Alcohol Syndrome and repeated head trauma, that he had been both physically and emotionally abused as a child, that he had used drugs and alcohol since childhood, and that he had impaired cognitive abilities.

Rather than dismissing the claim because Trevino had failed to exhaust his state court remedies, the federal habeas court agreed to stay its proceedings to allow counsel to present the ineffective assistance claim to the state court. The state court refused to consider the claim, finding it had been procedurally defaulted by Trevino's failure to raise it during his state post-conviction. When the case returned to the federal habeas court, that court found the procedural default precluded habeas relief on the federal level. On appeal, the Fifth Circuit agreed. The Supreme Court then granted cert.

Analysis: The ineffectiveness of Trevino's state post-conviction attorney **may** amount to "cause" that excuses his procedural default.

Procedural default occurs when a habeas applicant has failed "to raise a claim of error at the time or in the place that state law requires."[55] In this case, Trevino's ineffective assistance of trial counsel claim was not presented to the appellate court or to the state post-conviction court that heard his case. It was not until Trevino got into federal court that he raised the ineffectiveness of trial counsel for the first time. This sort of procedural default of a claim in state court ordinarily creates a bar to federal habeas relief. The only way to get around this bar is to establish cause for the procedural default and prejudice as a result of the claimed violation.

Trevino maintained that he should not face the ramifications of his procedural default because his state post-conviction counsel's ineffectiveness amounted to "cause" for the default in his case. As a general rule, "an attorney's ignorance or inadvertence in a post-conviction proceeding does not qualify as cause to excuse a procedural default."[56] This general rule advances the notion that federal courts should not interfere "with a State's application of its own firmly established,

[55] Trevino v. Thaler, 133 S.Ct. 1911, 1917 (2013).

[56] Id. at 1917 (quoting Martinez v. Ryan, 566 U.S. 1 (2012); and citing Coleman v. Thompson, 501 U.S. 722 (1991)).

consistently followed, constitutionally proper procedural rules."[57] A state court's finding that a claim has been procedurally default is therefore treated as an "independent and adequate state ground" for the denial of relief that will not be disturbed by the federal court.

There are, however, exceptions to the general rule. The remedy of federal habeas relief is a critical mechanism for ensuring that people are not imprisoned in violation of federal law. Accordingly, there are times when a post-conviction attorney's error may amount to cause.

"A procedural default will not bar a federal habeas court from hearing a substantial claim of ineffective assistance at trial if, in the initial-review collateral proceeding, there was no counsel or counsel in that proceeding was ineffective."[58] Trevino has not had an opportunity to establish that his ineffective assistance of trial counsel claim likely has merit. He also has not had an opportunity to establish whether his state post-conviction attorney was ineffective. The lower court will need to resolve both of these issues on remand to determine whether cause for the procedural default in Trevino's case exists.

Securing application of the exception recognized in *Trevino* requires proof of three separate elements. First, the claim of trial counsel's ineffectiveness has to be substantial. In other words, it must have some substance and cannot be frivolous or likely without merit. Second, at the state post-conviction proceeding, counsel must have performed ineffectively in failing to raise the issue of trial counsel's ineffectiveness. And, third, the state post-conviction hearing has to have been the first meaningful opportunity the habeas applicant had to raise the ineffective assistance of trial counsel claim. Where these three elements are not met, state post-conviction counsel's ineffectiveness will not provide "cause" to excuse a procedural default and a federal habeas court will not consider the claim.

Establishing prejudice is a much more straightforward affair (though no less onerous a burden). The applicant must show some "actual prejudice" arising from the alleged constitutional violation.[59] For example, working from the *Trevino* facts, to establish prejudice in his case, Trevino would need to establish that his trial attorney's ineffectiveness actually prejudiced his chances of being found not guilty or of being sentenced to death.

3. Overcoming Procedural Default: Gateway Innocence. As you have read, procedural default is generally an absolute bar to habeas relief absent a showing of cause and prejudice. In addition to cause and prejudice, the Court has found that a sufficient showing of actual innocence will also serve as a "gateway" through which a procedurally defaulted claim may pass into federal habeas review. As you

[57] Id.

[58] Id. at 1921.

[59] Coleman v. Thompson, 501 U.S. 722, 750 (1991).

will read below, so-called "gateway innocence" is not an independent claim for habeas relief. Rather, it is a basis for having other claims that have been procedurally defaulted heard by the habeas court:

> **Example—*House v. Bell*, 547 U.S. 518 (2006):** Carolyn Muncey was home alone with her two children one evening. After the children had been sent to bed, they heard someone knock on the door. They then heard a deep voice asking where Mr. Muncey was. The children then heard Mrs. Muncey crying and saying, "Oh God, no, not me." The children fell back to sleep until their father came home some time later. When he asked the children where their mother was, they said she had not been home in some time. Mr. Muncey then took the kids to a neighbor's and went out looking for his wife in the woods behind his house to no avail.
>
> The next day neighbors and relatives were out still looking for Ms. Muncey. One cousin, Billy Ray Hensley, was driving toward the Muncey home when he saw Paul Gregory House, a friend of the Munceys, near an embankment wiping his hands on a black rag. House told Hensley he was looking for Mr. Muncey but suspected he was out drinking. Suspicious of House's presence, the relative later searched the embankment with a friend and found Mrs. Muncey's body dumped in the woods a little ways down the embankment about 100 yards from her house. She was dressed in her nightgown and it appeared she had been killed by a hard blow to the front of her head that cause both a laceration, brain trauma and severe internal bleeding into her skull. According to the medical examiner, Mrs. Muncey died the night before between 9:00 and 11:00 p.m.
>
> House was questioned by the police and provided an account of the previous evening that was later proven to be at least partially untrue. Police officer seized the pants House had on the night of the murder. These pants were packed with vials of blood from the autopsy and other evidence, and transported in the trunk of a police car to the FBI lab in Washington, DC.
>
> At trial, the State presented evidence that semen found on Mrs. Muncey's underpants and nightgown was consistent with House's blood type. The State also presented evidence that blood stains found on House's pants came from Mrs. Muncey. House's shoes were found several months after the murder in a field near his

girlfriend's home. The jury did not hear (and the defense was not told) that the State tested the shoes and did not find blood on them. After considering the evidence, the jury convicted House and recommended that he be sentenced to death.

House's conviction was affirmed on direct appeal. His initial state post-conviction was also denied. In a second state post-conviction, House argued that his trial attorney provided ineffective assistance by failing to adequately investigate the case or seek expert assistance. In support of this claim, House presented substantial evidence of actual innocence. However, the state court rejected the evidence, finding that House had procedurally defaulted the claim by failing to raise it in his initial state post-conviction proceeding. House then moved into federal court on a habeas petition. After his claims were rejected on procedural default grounds, the Supreme Court took the case for review.

Analysis: House presented a sufficiently convincing case of "gateway innocence" to justify consideration in federal habeas of his procedurally defaulted claim.

It is typically true that claims that have been procedurally defaulted in state court cannot be considered on federal habeas review. The primary exception to this rule is if the habeas applicant can demonstrate cause and prejudice for his default. However, the Court has also recognized a "miscarriage of justice" exception to "balance the society interests in finality, comity, and conservation of scarce judicial resources with the individual interest in justice that arises in the extraordinary case."[60]

To establish such an extraordinary case, a habeas applicant must show that newly discovered evidence makes it "more likely than not that no reasonable juror would have found petitioner guilty beyond a reasonable doubt."[61] In evaluating this evidence, the habeas court should consider the entire collection of evidence, even inadmissible new evidence, to assess whether any reasonable juror would have convicted. The habeas court need not be absolutely certain of innocence. But, the burden is nonetheless a significant one. Moreover, the court need not view the evidence in the light most favorable to the prosecution (as would be appropriate for a sufficiency review). Indeed, if necessary, the court may reevaluate issues like a trial witness' credibility.

House presented such evidence. New DNA evidence established that the source of the semen on Mrs. Muncey's clothing was her husband and not House. In addition, there was substantial new evidence that the bloodstains found on House's pants were a result of evidence contamination (the vials of blood that were packed

---

60 House v. Bell, 547 U.S. 518, 536 (2006).

61 Id. at 537.

with the pants leaked during transport) and not a result of his presence at the scene. There was also evidence that Mr. Muncey made a drunken confession to the crime to two neighbors during House's trial. Several witnesses testified to Mr. Muncey's physical abuse of his wife, including on the night of her murder. And, there was new evidence presented that after the murder, Mr. Muncey visited a neighbor in an effort to construct a false alibi.

The newly discovered evidence did not conclusively exonerate House. There was still circumstantial evidence that he was the killer—the daughter's testimony that a man with a deep voice was at the door the evening of Mrs. Muncey's death, his presence in the rough vicinity of the body on the morning it was found, the blood on his pants, and his bizarre (and ultimately false) story to the police. But, the new evidence did punch serious holes in the State's theory of guilt. "Accordingly, and although the issue is close, we conclude that this is the rare case where—had the jury heard all of the conflicting testimony—it is more likely than not that no reasonable juror viewing the record as a whole would lack reasonable doubt."[62]

The first thing that is readily apparent from even the most glancing review of *House* is the incredibly high burden a habeas applicant must overcome to establish a claim of gateway innocence. House a) presented the confession of an alternate (and far more likely) suspect, b) convincingly explained the presence of the victim's blood on his clothing, and c) conclusively established that the other biological evidence found on the victim belonged to the alternate suspect Mr. Muncey. However, even with all of this newly discovered evidence the *House* Court still concluded that the case was "close." Indeed, the Court plainly noted that the more traditional forms of evidence that are seen in most post-conviction cases, "incriminating testimony from inmates, suspects, or friends or relations of the accused" would not have been afforded the same weight as the evidence that House was able to produce.[63]

In addition, you should be very careful to distinguish the "gateway innocence" that was recognized in *House* from a substantive claim of actual innocence. Gateway innocence only allows a habeas applicant to present other claims of error. For example, as in *House*, the other claims might involve a question of trial counsel's effectiveness or the misconduct of the prosecutor. A claim of substantive innocence, in contrast, asks for relief not because there are other constitutional violations present, but because the actual innocence is itself a constitutional violation. Because such a claim does not rely upon other underlying claims of error it is sometimes referred to as "**freestanding innocence**."

To date, the Supreme Court has only acknowledged the possibility that a claim of freestanding innocence might exist. A hypothetical claim of freestanding in-

[62] Id. at 554.

[63] Id. at 552.

nocence was first recognized by the Court in *Herrera v. Collins*[64] and then again in *Schlup v. Delo*[65]. However, in neither case did the Court actually find that such a claim existed. The Court then took the question up a third time in *House* and again refused to definitively recognize the claim. Instead, the Court has "assumed without deciding that 'in a capital case a truly persuasive demonstration of "actual innocence" made after trial would render the execution of a defendant unconstitutional, and permit habeas relief if there were no state avenue open to process such a claim.'"[66]

It is entirely uncertain whether a claim of freestanding innocence will ever be recognized. What is certain is that the threshold for establishing any such claim is even higher than that for a claim of gateway innocence. Though finding that House's evidence satisfied the threshold for gateway innocence, the Court concluded that "House's showing [fell] short of the threshold implied in *Herrera*" for freestanding innocence.[67]

4. Contrary to/Unreasonable Application of Federal Law. If the state court's post-conviction determination was based on the merits of the case, the habeas applicant must demonstrate that the decision of the state court was contrary to or an unreasonable application of clearly established federal law. The Court has described this standard as a very high burden, and its application of the standard is consistent with that description:

> **Example—*Cullen v. Pinholster*, 131 S.Ct. 1388 (2011):** Scott Pinholster convinced two friends to help him burglarize a local drug dealer's home. As the burglary was underway, two men who knew the homeowner arrived and shouted that they were going to call the police. Pinholster stabbed both men repeatedly, killing them.
>
> Two weeks later, one of Pinholster's two friends turned himself in to the police. Pinholster was arrested and charged with capital murder. Prior to trial, Pinholster decided to proceed *pro se*. During this period, the state sent a notice of aggravating circumstances that it intended to introduce at the penalty phase of the trial. Subsequently, defense attorneys were appointed. At the guilt phase, Pinholster testified in his own defense. He told the jurors that he was a robber not a murderer. He also told the jurors that his weapon of choice was a gun not a knife. He

[64] 506 U.S. 390.

[65] 513 U.S. 298.

[66] Id. at 554 (citing Herrera v. Collins, 506 U.S. 390, 417 (1993).

[67] Id. at 555.

admitted that he had burglarized the home, but testified that he left before anyone arrived. He maintained that the friend who turned himself in was the one who returned to the home to see if he could find any other valuables, and that it was that friend who was the murderer.

Following conviction, the defense attorneys initially moved to exclude any aggravating evidence on the ground that the defense had not received notice of the state's intention to introduce such evidence. Counsel also maintained that they had not prepared much in the way of mitigation because they had not gotten the notice. When asked if a continuance would help, however, the defense maintained that Pinholster's mother was the only likely defense witness and that additional time would not make a difference. The trial court rejected the defense request to exclude, finding that notice had been sent to Pinholster while he was *pro se*. The prosecution presented a great deal of aggravating evidence. The defense presented only the testimony of Pinholster's mother. Pinholster was sentenced to death.

Following the denial of relief in the state courts, Pinholster moved into federal habeas. The district court granted habeas relief, finding that trial counsel was ineffective at the sentencing phase based in part on evidence introduced during an evidentiary hearing in federal court. The federal appellate court affirmed, and the Supreme Court then accepted the case for review.

Analysis: The state court's denial of relief was neither contrary to nor an unreasonable application of clearly established federal law.

Whenever a habeas petition contains a claim that has been adjudicated on the merits by the state court, that state court decision should not be overturned unless it is contrary to or an unreasonable application of federal law. This highly deferential standard is one that is deliberately difficult for habeas applicants to meet.

In reviewing the state court's decision, the federal habeas court should confine its review to the record that was before the state court. Material that was introduced during a federal evidentiary hearing is irrelevant to the question of whether the state court's decision fell within either of the two categories warranting reversal under § 2254(d)(1)—"contrary to" or "an unreasonable application of." "It would be strange to ask federal courts to analyze whether a state court's adjudication resulted in a decision that unreasonably applied federal law to facts not before the state court."[68]

Though the evidentiary hearing in federal court that § 2254 permits is not relevant to claims that have been decided on the merits by a state court; it is relevant to claims that have **not** been so decided, like procedurally defaulted claims.

Considering only the record before the state court, it cannot be said that that court's decision was contrary to or an unreasonable application of federal law. The relevant federal law here is *Strickland*, because Pinholster maintains that his trial attorney was ineffective during the sentencing phase of his trial.

The record reflects that the defense attorneys' performance at the sentencing hearing was a matter of trial strategy. Their protestation appears to have been an unsuccessful ploy by counsel to have the state's aggravating evidence excluded. "Other statements made during the argument regarding the motion to exclude suggest that defense counsel were trying to take advantage of a legal technicality and were not truly surprised."[69]

There is evidence in the record that counsel did in fact conduct some investigation of mitigating evidence. And, there is strong support in the record for the conclusion that only a handful of viable mitigation strategies were available to counsel where Pinholster was an unsympathetic client who had already negatively impressed the jury with his boasting claims during trial that suggested he was proud of his criminal history. Limiting the mitigation to generating sympathy for Pinholster's mother (a recognized mitigation strategy in California) did not amount to deficient performance under *Strickland*. Based on this conclusion, it cannot be said that the state supreme court unreasonably applied federal law to the facts of Pinholster's case.

The defendant also did not demonstrate that the state supreme court unreasonably applied the law to the question of prejudice in Pinholster's case. There was a substantial amount of aggravating evidence presented by the state. The newly discovered evidence that was before the state post-conviction court was substantially similar, though in some respects slightly more detailed, to the evidence of mitigation that the jury heard. "Given what little additional mitigating evidence Pinholster presented in state habeas, we cannot say that the California Supreme Court's determination was unreasonable."[70]

However, while it is difficult to establish that a state court decision was "contrary to" or "an unreasonable application of" federal law, it is not impossible to do so:

[68] Cullen v. Pinholster, 131 S.Ct. 1388, 1399 (2011).

[69] Id. at 1404.

[70] Id. at 1410.

Example—*Williams v. Taylor*, 529 U.S. 362 (2000): An elderly man named Harris Stone was found dead in his home. The police found evidence of alcohol poisoning and assumed that Stone simply drank himself to death. They closed the case. Six months later, Terry Williams, who was incarcerated at the local jail for another offense, wrote a letter to the police confessing to Stone's murder, and confessing to an unsolved assault on an elderly woman that left her in a persistent vegetative state. Williams said in his confession that he killed Stone because Stone refused to give him money. After hitting Stone once on the chest and once on the back with a small pickaxe, Williams took three dollars from Stone's wallet.

Williams was charged with capital murder for Stone's death. His attorney began preparing for the sentencing hearing a week before the trial began. At the hearing, counsel devoted much of his time to telling the jury that it was hard to find reasons not to execute Williams. Counsel also introduced the testimony of Williams's mother and of two neighbors, all of whom testified that Williams was a "nice boy," who was not violent. Counsel also introduced a taped portion of a psychiatrist's testimony. In the tape, the psychiatrist recounted that in an earlier robbery Williams had removed the bullets from his gun so no one would get hurt. After hearing the state's expert testimony regarding Williams's likelihood of future dangerousness, the jury recommended a death sentence.

Williams filed a state post-conviction petition. The judge found that Williams's trial counsel was ineffective. In particular, the court pointed to the substantial mitigating evidence that had not been uncovered by counsel because of an erroneous belief that state law did not permit access to the records in question. The newly discovered evidence reflected, among other things, that Williams suffered significant abuse as a child. His parents were convicted of criminal neglect of Williams and his siblings. While his parents were in prison, Williams was sent to at least one foster home where he was again abused. There was also newly discovered evidence that Williams was borderline mentally retarded, had suffered significant head trauma as a child, which may have caused brain impairment, and only had a sixth-grade education.

The state supreme court overturned the grant of post-conviction relief based upon its conclusion that Williams had not established sufficient prejudice to satisfy the *Strickland* standard.

Williams then moved into federal habeas. The federal habeas court concluded the state supreme court had decided Williams's case in a way that was contrary to clearly established federal law. The Fourth Circuit reversed, and the Supreme Court then accepted the case for review.

Analysis: The state supreme court's decision was contrary to and an unreasonable application of clearly decided federal law.

A state prisoner is entitled to federal habeas relief if he can show the state court has resolved his claim in a way "that was contrary to, or involved an unreasonable application of, clearly established Federal law, as determined by the Supreme Court of the United States."[71]

The first category of relief—contrary to—includes cases in which "the state court arrives at a conclusion opposite to that reached by [the Supreme Court] on a question of law."[72] A state court's decision will also be contrary to federal law if the state court reaches an opposite result on facts that are meaningfully identical to facts already considered by the Supreme Court. The fact that a federal court might disagree with the state court's conclusion is not enough. To warrant habeas relief, the state court decision must be mutually opposed to federal law.

The second category of relief—an unreasonable application—includes cases in which "the state court identifies the correct governing legal rule . . . but unreasonably applies it to the facts of the particular state prisoner's case."[73] A decision will also constitute an unreasonable application if the state court "unreasonably extends a legal principle from [Supreme Court] precedent to a new context where it should not apply or unreasonably refused to extend that principle to a new context where it should apply."[74] Unreasonableness amounts to something more than simple incorrectness.

Williams challenged the effectiveness of his trial counsel during the sentencing phase of his capital trial. There is no question that the standard for resolving this question was "clearly established" at the time of Williams's trial. The standard for resolving questions about counsel's effectiveness was settled long ago with the Court's decision in *Strickland v. Washington.*

---

71 § 2254(d)(1).

72 Williams v. Taylor, 529 U.S. 362, 405 (2000).

73 Id. at 407.

74 Id.

The state post-conviction court found that with regard to *Strickland*'s first prong trial counsel performed deficiently at Williams's sentencing hearing. The state supreme court assumed this to be the case.

With regard to the prejudice prong, the state supreme court found that Williams had not sufficiently established prejudice. In so holding, the state supreme court's decision was both contrary to and an unreasonable application of federal law. The state supreme court found that the prejudice inquiry under *Strickland* included an inquiry into fundamental fairness. The Court, however, has never suggested that fundamental fairness is a component of the *Strickland* prejudice inquiry for people like Williams who can "show that his lawyer was ineffective and that his ineffectiveness probably affected the outcome of the proceeding."[75] The state supreme court's ruling was therefore contrary to clearly established federal law.

It was also an unreasonable application of that law. The state supreme court applied the wrong standard for determining the effectiveness of trial counsel. The court also was unreasonable in its evaluation of the totality of the evidence relevant to the question of sentencing. By focusing narrowly on the question of whether Williams had rebutted the future dangerousness evidence, the court failed to appreciate that "evidence unrelated to dangerousness may alter the jury's selection of penalty, even if it does not undermine or rebut the prosecution's death-eligibility case."[76]

Where the state supreme court's decision was both contrary to and an unreasonable application of federal law, it must be reversed.

[75] Id. at 393.

[76] Id. at 398.

Quick Summary

There are five major collateral remedies available in the federal system. They are:

1. 28 U.S.C. § 2254: Petition for Writ of Habeas Corpus (state prisoner);
2. 28 U.S.C. §2255: Motion to Vacate, Set Aside or Correct a Sentence;
3. 28 U.S.C. § 2241: Petition for Writ of Habeas Corpus (federal prisoner);
4. U.S.C. § 1651: Motion for Writ of Error Coram Nobis; and
5. FRCP 35(b): Motion to Correct or Reduce a Sentence.

The most commonly used form of post-conviction relief in the federal system is the procedure used by state prisoners, 28 U.S.C. § 2254. This section is available to "a person in custody pursuant to the judgment of a State court only on the ground that he is in custody in violation of the Constitution or the laws or treaties of the United States." To access the federal habeas court, a state prisoner has to first present his claims to the state courts. This is known as "exhaustion." In the absence of exhaustion, with just two minor exceptions, the § 2254 petition will be barred. The failure to present claims to the state courts can lead to a conclusion in federal court that the claims are procedurally defaulted and therefore not a basis for federal relief.

An applicant's failure to exhaust state remedies is not the only way that federal relief will be barred. Sometimes a state prisoner does present claims to a state court but those claims are rejected because they were filed too late or were filed improperly. When this happens and the state court refuses to hear the claims on the merits, these claims too will be considered "procedurally defaulted." Much like an unexhausted claim, a claim that is procedurally defaulted because it was filed improperly generally cannot provide a basis for federal habeas relief. However, a procedurally defaulted claim can be considered in federal habeas if the habeas applicant can demonstrate "cause and prejudice" for the default. A sufficient showing of "gateway innocence" or a fundamental miscarriage of justice also will permit a procedurally defaulted claim in a habeas petition to be considered.

If a prisoner's constitutional claims were resolved on the merits by the state courts, those judgments will not be disturbed in federal habeas unless the state court's decision was "contrary to, or involved an unreasonable application of, clearly established Federal law, as determined by the Supreme Court of the United States." If the state court decision was based on a factual determination the decision is presumed to be correct, and the presumption is undermined only by clear and convincing evidence of an error.

State prisoners must move into federal court within one year of their convictions becoming final (i.e., upon the conclusion of appellate review in the state courts or upon conclusion of the time available for seeking appellate review). The one-year statute of limitations period will be suspended (or "tolled") during any periods that the state prisoner is actively pursuing state post-conviction remedies in the state courts. In addition, the one-year limitations period is subject to what is known as "equitable tolling."

A habeas petitioner is entitle to file just one habeas petition, and the right to counsel in federal habeas proceedings is only extended to capital cases. Appellate review for an unsuccessful habeas applicant is discretionary, and is accomplished by obtaining a certificate of appealability.

Federal prisoners seeking habeas relief must file under 28 U.S.C. § 2255. Federal prisoners also may seek review of their convictions or sentences under 28 U.S.C. § 2241. The government may bring a post-conviction claim under Federal Rule of Criminal Procedure 35(b) in order to reduce the sentence of a prisoner who has provided cooperation.

Finally, the Writ of Error Coram Nobis is available to correct fundamental legal or factual errors. However, coram nobis is available only if alternative remedies are not.

Review Questions

1. The Belated Claim of the Inadequate Indictment. Cyrus Braswell was indicted by a federal grand jury. The indictment included multiple counts that accused Braswell of, among other things, "distributing a Schedule II controlled substance;" "possessing a Schedule II controlled substance with the intent to distribute it;" and "maintaining a place for drug trafficking." Braswell was convicted of all counts and sentenced to some 400 months in prison. Braswell's conviction was affirmed on direct appeal.

Braswell then filed several post-trial motions, including a motion for new trial, a motion for acquittal notwithstanding the verdict, and a motion for change of venue. All motions were denied. Braswell filed a habeas petition under 28 U.S.C. § 2255. After the petition had been preliminarily considered by a habeas court, Braswell filed an additional claim that his indictment had not identified the drugs (cocaine and marijuana) that were identified in the jury instructions. The court, over government objection, agreed to hear the claim. The court construed the claim as a claim that trial counsel had provided constitutionally ineffective assistance by failing to object to the sufficiency of the indictment. The court then rejected the claim on its merits, finding that counsel was not constitutionally ineffective.

Braswell sought and received a certificate of appealability on the single question of whether his constitutional rights were violated by the lack of specificity in the indictment. The government contended on appeal that any consideration of the claim was precluded because the claim was procedurally barred. If you were a member of the appellate panel, would you urge your fellow panelist to consider the merits of the claim? If so, why? If not, why not?

2. Straight No Chaser. Albert Roy was convicted on two counts of first-degree sodomy. His conviction was affirmed on direct appeal by the Oregon Court of Appeals on August 23, 1995. Discretionary review to the Oregon Court of Appeals was available, but Roy did not file a request for such consideration. Roy also did not seek review in the United States Supreme Court. As a result, his conviction became final pursuant to state law on November 1, 1995.

On February 7, 1996, Roy was transferred from the prison in Oregon to a prison in Arizona. He stayed at this prison until April 25, 1997, at which point he was returned to the prison in Oregon. However, on February 28, 1997, while he was still in Arizona, Roy filed a petition for habeas relief in federal court in Arizona. The petition was transferred to the federal trial court in Oregon on August 28, 1998. It was ultimately denied.

However, while the federal petition was still pending, Roy filed a petition for post-conviction relief in state court in Oregon. Though timely, this petition was denied on the merits. After review in the state appellate courts, the denial of state post-conviction relief became final on December 5, 2000. On May 23, 2001, Roy then filed a second petition for habeas relief in the federal court.

You are a young line attorney in the local federal public defender's office. You have been assigned to advise Roy in connection with his 2001 habeas petition. Upon a quick review of the substance of his claims, you think he has some pretty strong claims of trial counsel's ineffectiveness. But, he does not assert actual innocence. At your first meeting, Roy asks you to "Give it to me straight counselor. Am I going to win this case?" What will you tell him? If you don't think you have enough information to make an honest assessment, what more would you like to know?

FROM THE COURTROOM

HOUSE V. BELL

Supreme Court of the United States, 2006
547 U.S. 518

[KENNEDY, J., delivered the opinion of the Court, in which STEVENS, SOUTER, GINSBURG, and BREYER, JJ., joined].

[ROBERTS, C. J., filed an opinion concurring in the judgment in part and dissenting in part, in which SCALIA and THOMAS, JJ., joined].

[ALITO, J., took no part in the consideration or decision of the case].

Some 20 years ago in rural Tennessee, Carolyn Muncey was murdered. A jury convicted petitioner Paul Gregory House of the crime and sentenced him to death, but new revelations cast doubt on the jury's verdict. House, protesting his innocence, seeks access to federal court to pursue habeas corpus relief based on constitutional claims that are procedurally barred under state law. Out of respect for the finality of state-court judgments federal habeas courts, as a general rule, are closed to claims that state courts would consider defaulted. In certain exceptional cases involving a compelling claim of actual innocence, however, the state procedural default rule is not a bar to a federal habeas corpus petition. After careful review of the full record, we conclude that House has made the stringent showing required by this exception; and we hold that his federal habeas action may proceed.

I

We begin with the facts surrounding Mrs. Muncey's disappearance, the discovery of her body, and House's arrest. Around 3 p.m. on Sunday, July 14, 1985, two local residents found her body concealed amid brush and tree branches on an embankment roughly 100 yards up the road from her driveway. Mrs. Muncey had been seen last on the evening before, when, around 8 p.m., she and her two children—Lora Muncey, aged 10, and Matthew Muncey, aged 8—visited their neighbor, Pam Luttrell. According to Luttrell, Mrs. Muncey mentioned her husband, William Hubert Muncey, Jr., known in the community as "Little Hube" and to his family as "Bubbie." As Luttrell recounted Mrs. Muncey's comment, Mr. Muncey "had gone to dig a grave, and he hadn't come back, but that was all right, because [Mrs. Muncey] was going to make him take her fishing the next day." Mrs. Muncey returned home, and some time later, before 11 p.m. at the latest, Luttrell "heard a car rev its motor as it went down the road," something Mr. Muncey customarily did when he drove by on his way home. Luttrell then went to bed.

Around 1 a.m., Lora and Matthew returned to Luttrell's home, this time with their father, Mr. Muncey, who said his wife was missing. Muncey asked Luttrell to watch the children while he searched for his wife. After he left, Luttrell talked with Lora. According to Luttrell:

"[Lora] said she heard a horn blow, she thought she heard a horn blow, and somebody asked if Bubbie was home, and her mama, you know, told them—no. And then she said she didn't know if she went back to sleep or not, but then she heard her mama going down the steps crying and I am not sure if that is when that she told me that she heard her mama say—oh God, no, not me, or if she told me that the next day, but I do know that she said she heard her mother going down the steps crying."

While Lora was talking, Luttrell recalled, "Matt kept butting in, you know, on us talking, and he said—sister they said daddy had a wreck, they said daddy had a wreck."

At House's trial, Lora repeated her account of the night's events, this time referring to the "wreck" her brother had mentioned. To assist in understanding Lora's account, it should be noted that Mrs. Muncey's father-in-law—Little Hube's father—was sometimes called "Big Hube." Lora and her brother called him "Paw Paw." We refer to him as Mr. Muncey, Sr. According to Lora, Mr. Muncey, Sr., had a deep voice, as does petitioner House.

Lora testified that after leaving Luttrell's house with her mother, she and her brother "went to bed." Later, she heard someone, or perhaps two different people, ask for her mother. . . .

Lora did not describe hearing any struggle. Some time later, Lora and her brother left the house to look for their mother, but no one answered when they knocked at the Luttrells' home, and another neighbor, Mike Clinton, said he had not seen her. After the children returned home, according to Lora, her father came home and "fixed him a bologna sandwich and he took a bit of it and he says—sissy, where is mommy at, and I said—she ain't been here for a little while." Lora recalled that Mr. Muncey went outside and, not seeing his wife, returned to take Lora and Matthew to the Luttrells' so that he could look further.

The next afternoon Billy Ray Hensley, the victim's first cousin, heard of Mrs. Muncey's disappearance and went to look for Mr. Muncey. As he approached the Munceys' street, Hensley allegedly "saw Mr. House come out from under a bank, wiping his hands on a black rag." Just when and where Hensley saw House, and how well he could have observed him, were disputed at House's trial. Hensley admitted on cross-examination that he could not have seen House "walking up or climbing up" the embankment, rather, he saw House, in "[j]ust a glance," "appear out of nowhere," "next to the embankment." On the Munceys' street, opposite the area where Hensley said he saw House, a white Plymouth was parked near a sawmill. Another witness, Billy Hankins, whom the defense called, claimed that around the same time he saw a "boy" walking down the street away from the parked Plymouth and toward the Munceys' home. This witness, however, put the "boy" on the side of the street with the parked car and the Munceys' driveway, not the side with the embankment.

Hensley, after turning onto the Munceys' street, continued down the road and turned into their driveway. "I pulled up in the driveway where I could see up toward Little Hube's house," Hensley testified, "and I seen Little Hube's car wasn't there, and I backed out in the road, and come back [the other way]." As he traveled up the road, Hensley saw House traveling in the opposite direction in the white Plymouth. House "flagged [Hensley] down" through his windshield, and the two cars met about 300 feet up the road from the Munceys' driveway. According to Hensley, House said he had heard Mrs. Muncey was missing and was looking for her husband. Though House had only recently moved to the area, he was acquainted with the Munceys, had attended a dance with them, and had visited their home. He later told law enforcement officials he considered both of the Munceys his friends. According to Hensley, House said he had heard that Mrs. Muncey's husband, who was an alcoholic, was elsewhere "getting drunk."

As Hensley drove off, he "got to thinking to [him]self—he's hunting Little Hube, and Little Hube drunk—what would he be doing off that bank . . . ." His suspicion aroused, Hensley later returned to the Munceys' street with a friend named Jack Adkins. The two checked different spots on the embankment, and though Hensley saw nothing where he looked, Adkins found Mrs. Muncey. Her body lay across from the sawmill near the corner where House's car had been parked, dumped in the woods a short way down the bank leading toward a creek.

Around midnight, Dr. Alex Carabia, a practicing pathologist and county medical examiner, performed an autopsy. Dr. Carabia put the time of death between 9 and 11 p.m. Mrs. Muncey had a black eye, both her hands were bloodstained up to the wrists, and she had bruises on her legs and neck. Dr. Carabia described the bruises as consistent with a "traumatic origin," i.e., a fight or a fall on hard objects. Based on the neck bruises and other injuries, he concluded Mrs. Muncey had been choked, but he ruled this out as the cause of death. The cause of death, in Dr. Carabia's view, was a severe blow to the left forehead that inflicted both a laceration penetrating to the bone and, inside the skull, a severe right-side hemorrhage, likely caused by Mrs. Muncey's brain slamming into the skull opposite the impact. Dr. Carabia described this head injury as consistent either with receiving a blow from a fist or other instrument or with striking some object.

The county sheriff, informed about Hensley's earlier encounter with House, questioned House shortly after the body was found. That evening, House answered further questions during a voluntary interview at the local jail. Special Agent Ray Presnell of the Tennessee Bureau of Investigation (TBI) prepared a statement of House's answers, which House signed. Asked to describe his whereabouts on the previous evening, House claimed—falsely, as it turned out—that he spent the entire evening with his girlfriend, Donna Turner, at her trailer. Asked whether he was wearing the same pants he had worn the night before, House replied—again, falsely—that he was. House was on probation at the time, having recently been released on parole following a sentence of five years to life for aggravated sexual assault in Utah. House had scratches on his arms and hands, and a knuckle on his right ring finger was bruised. He attributed the scratches to Turner's cats and the finger injury to recent construction work tearing down a shed. The next day House gave a similar statement to a different TBI agent, Charles Scott.

In fact House had not been at Turner's home. After initially supporting House's alibi, Turner informed authorities that House left her trailer around 10:30 or 10:45 p.m. to go for a walk. According to Turner's trial testimony, House returned later—she was not sure when—hot and panting, missing his shirt and his shoes. House, Turner testified, told her that while he was walking on the road near her home, a vehicle pulled up beside him, and somebody inside "called him some names and then they told him he didn't belong here anymore." House said he tried to ignore the taunts and keep walking, but the vehicle pulled in behind him, and "one of them got out and grabbed him by the shoulder . . . and [House] swung around with his right hand" and "hit something." According to Turner, House said "he took off down the bank and started running and he said that he—he said it seemed forever where he was running. And he said they fired two shots at him while he took off down the bank . . . ." House claimed the assailants "grabbed ahold of his shirt," which Turner remembered as "a blue tank top, trimmed in yellow," and "they tore it to where it wouldn't stay on him and he said—I just throwed it off when I was running." Turner, noticing House's bruised knuckle, asked how he hurt it, and House told her "that's where he hit." Turner testified that she "thought maybe my ex-husband had something to do with it."

Although the white Plymouth House drove the next day belonged to Turner, Turner insisted House had not used the car that night. No forensic evidence connected the car to the crime; law enforcement officials inspected a white towel covering the driver seat and concluded it was clean. Turner's trailer was located just under two miles by road, through hilly terrain, from the Muncey residence.

Law enforcement officers also questioned the victim's husband. Though Mrs. Muncey's comments to Luttrell gave no indication she knew this, Mr. Muncey had spent the evening at a weekly dance at a recreation center roughly a mile and a half from his home. In his statement to law enforcement—a statement House's trial counsel claims he never saw—Mr. Muncey admitted leaving the dance early, but said it was only for a brief trip to the package store to buy beer. He also stated that he and his wife had had sexual relations Saturday morning.

Late in the evening on Monday, July 15—two days after the murder—law enforcement officers visited Turner's trailer. With Turner's consent, Agent Scott seized the pants House was wearing the night Mrs. Muncey disappeared. The heavily soiled pants were sitting in a laundry hamper; years later, Agent Scott recalled noticing "reddish brown stains" he "suspected" were blood. Around 4 p.m. the next day, two local law enforcement officers set out for the Federal Bureau of Investigation in Washington, D.C., with House's pants, blood samples from the autopsy, and other evidence packed together in a box. They arrived at 2 a.m. the next morning. On July 17, after initial FBI testing revealed human blood on the pants, House was arrested.

II

The State of Tennessee charged House with capital murder. At House's trial, the State presented testimony by Luttrell, Hensley, Adkins, Lora Muncey, Dr. Carabia, the sheriff, and other law enforcement officials. Through TBI Agents Presnell and Scott, the jury learned of House's false statements. Central to the State's case, however, was what the FBI testing showed—that semen consistent (or so it seemed) with House's was present on Mrs. Muncey's nightgown and panties, and that small bloodstains consistent with Mrs. Muncey's blood but not House's appeared on the jeans belonging to House.

Regarding the semen, FBI Special Agent Paul Bigbee, a serologist, testified that the source was a "secretor," meaning someone who "secrete[s] the ABO blood group substances in other body fluids, such as semen and saliva"—a characteristic shared by 80 percent of the population, including House. Agent Bigbee further testified that the source of semen on the gown was blood-type A, House's own blood type. As to the semen on the panties, Agent Bigbee found only the H blood-group substance, which A and B blood-type secretors secrete along with substances A and B, and which O-type secretors secrete exclusively. Agent Bigbee explained, however—using science an amicus here sharply disputes, that House's A antigens could have "degraded" into H. Agent Bigbee thus concluded that both semen deposits could have come from House, though he acknowledged that the H antigen could have come from Mrs. Muncey herself if she was a secretor—something he "was not able to determine,"—and that, while Mr. Muncey was himself blood-type A (as was his wife), Agent Bigbee was again "not able to determine his secretor status." Agent Bigbee acknowledged on cross-examination that "a saliva sample" would have sufficed to determine whether Mr. Muncey was a secretor; the State did not provide such a sample, though it did provide samples of Mr. Muncey's blood.

As for the blood, Agent Bigbee explained that "spots of blood" appeared "on the left outside leg, the right bottom cuff, on the left thigh and in the right inside pocket and on the lower pocket on the outside." Agent Bigbee determined that the blood's source was type A (the type shared by House, the victim, and Mr. Muncey). He also successfully tested for the enzyme phosphoglucomutase and the blood serum haptoglobin, both of which "are found in all humans" and carry "slight chemical differences" that vary genetically and "can be grouped to differentiate between two individuals if those types are different." Based on these chemical traces and on the A blood type, Agent Bigbee determined that only some 6.75 percent of the population carry similar blood, that the blood was "consistent" with Mrs. Muncey's (as determined by testing autopsy samples), and that it was "impossible" that the blood came from House.

A different FBI expert, Special Agent Chester Blythe, testified about fiber analysis performed on Mrs. Muncey's clothes and on House's pants. . . . he acknowledged that . . . "blue jean material is common material," so "this doesn't mean that the fibers that were all over the victim's clothing were necessarily from [House's] pair of blue jeans." On House's pants, though cotton garments both transfer and retain fibers readily, Agent Blythe found neither hair nor fiber consistent with the victim's hair or clothing.

In the defense case House called Hankins, Clinton, and Turner, as well as House's mother, who testified that House had talked to her by telephone around 9:30 p.m. on the night of the murder and that he had not used her car that evening. House also called the victim's brother, Ricky Green, as a witness. Green testified that on July 2, roughly two weeks before the murder, Mrs. Muncey called him and "said her and Little Hube had been into it and she said she was wanting to leave Little Hube, she said she was wanting to get out—out of it, and she was scared." Green recalled that at Christmastime in 1982 he had seen Mr. Muncey strike Mrs. Muncey after returning home drunk.

As Turner informed the jury, House's shoes were found several months after the crime in a field near her home. Turner delivered them to authorities. Though the jury did not learn of this fact (and House's counsel claims he did not either), the State tested the shoes for blood and found none. House's shirt was not found.

The State's closing argument suggested that on the night of her murder, Mrs. Muncey "was deceived . . . . She had been told [her husband] had had an accident." The prosecutor emphasized the FBI's blood analysis, noting that "after running many, many, many tests," Agent Bigbee "was able to tell you that the blood on the defendant's blue jeans was not his own blood, could not be his own blood. He told you that the blood on the blue jeans was consistent with every characteristic in every respect of the deceased's, Carolyn Muncey's, and that ninety-three (93%) percent of the white population would not have that blood type . . . . He can't tell you one hundred (100%) percent for certain that it was her blood. But folks, he can sure give you a pretty good—a pretty good indication."

In the State's rebuttal, after defense counsel questioned House's motive "to go over and kill a woman that he barely knew[,] [w]ho was still dressed, still clad in her clothes," the prosecutor referred obliquely to the semen stains. While explaining that legally "it does not make any difference under God's heaven, what the motive was," the prosecutor told the jury, "you may have an idea why he did it,":

"The evidence at the scene which seemed to suggest that he was subjecting this lady to some kind of indignity, why would you get a lady out of her house, late at night, in her night clothes, under the trick that her husband has had a wreck down by the creek? . . . Well, it is because either you don't want her to tell what indignities you have subjected her to, or she is unwilling and fights against you, against being subjected to those indignities. . . . That is what the evidence at the scene suggests about motive."

In addition the government suggested the black rag Hensley said he saw in House's hands was in fact the missing blue tank top, retrieved by House from the crime scene. And the prosecution reiterated the importance of the blood. "[D]efense counsel," he said, "does not start out discussing the fact that his client had blood on his jeans on the night that Carolyn Muncey was killed . . . . He doesn't start with the fact that nothing that the defense has introduced in this case explains what blood is doing on his jeans, all over his jeans, that is scientifically, completely different from his blood." The jury found House guilty of murder in the first degree.

The trial advanced to the sentencing phase. . . . The jury recommended a death sentence, which the trial judge imposed.

III

The Tennessee Supreme Court affirmed House's conviction and sentence, describing the evidence against House as "circumstantial" but "quite strong." Two months later, in a state trial court, House filed a . . . petition for postconviction relief . . . . House's counsel offered no proof beyond the trial transcript. The trial court dismissed the petition . . . . In an unpublished opinion the Tennessee Court of Criminal Appeals affirmed, and both the Tennessee Supreme Court and this Court denied review.

House filed a second postconviction petition in state court reasserting his ineffective-assistance claim and seeking investigative and/or expert assistance. After extensive litigation regarding whether House's claims were procedurally defaulted the Tennessee Supreme Court held that House's claims were barred under a state statute providing that claims not raised in prior postconviction proceedings are presumptively waived, and that courts may not consider grounds for relief "which the court finds should be excluded because they have been waived or previously determined." This Court denied certiorari.

House next sought federal habeas relief, asserting numerous claims of ineffective assistance of counsel and prosecutorial misconduct. . . . . Presenting evidence we describe in greater detail below, House attacked the semen and blood evidence used at his trial and presented other evidence, including a putative confession, suggesting that Mr. Muncey, not House, committed the murder. The District Court nevertheless denied relief, holding that House had neither demonstrated actual innocence of the murder under *Schlup* nor established that he was ineligible for the death penalty under *Sawyer*.

The Court of Appeals for the Sixth Circuit granted a certificate of appealability . . . .

[A]n eight-judge majority affirmed the District Court's denial of habeas relief. . . .

We granted certiorari, and now reverse.

IV

As a general rule, claims forfeited under state law may support federal habeas relief only if the prisoner demonstrates cause for the default and prejudice from the asserted error. The rule is based on the comity and respect that must be accorded to state-court judgments. The bar is not, however, unqualified. In an effort to "balance the societal interests in finality, comity, and conservation of scarce judicial resources with the individual interest in justice that arises in the extraordinary case," the Court has recognized a miscarriage-of-justice exception. "'[I]n appropriate cases,'" the Court has said, "the principles of comity and finality that inform the concepts of cause and prejudice 'must yield to the imperative of correcting a fundamentally unjust incarceration.'"

In *Schlup*, the Court adopted a specific rule to implement this general principle. It held that prisoners asserting innocence as a gateway to defaulted claims must establish that, in light of new evidence, "it is more likely than not that no reasonable juror would have found petitioner guilty beyond a reasonable doubt." This formulation, *Schlup* explains, "ensures that petitioner's case is truly 'extraordinary,' while still providing petitioner a meaningful avenue by which to avoid a manifest injustice." In the usual case the presumed guilt of a prisoner convicted in state court counsels against federal review of defaulted claims. Yet a petition supported by a convincing *Schlup* gateway showing "raise[s] sufficient doubt about [the petitioner's] guilt to undermine confidence in the result of the trial without the assurance that that trial was untainted by constitutional error"; hence, "a review of the merits of the constitutional claims" is justified.

. . . . Our review in this case addresses the merits of the *Schlup* inquiry, based on a fully developed record, and with respect to that inquiry *Schlup* makes plain that the habeas court must consider "'all the evidence,'" old and new, incriminating and exculpatory, without regard to whether it would necessarily be admitted under "rules of admissibility that would govern at trial." Based on this total record, the court must make "a probabilistic determination about what reasonable, properly instructed jurors would do." The court's function is not to make an independent factual determination about what likely occurred, but rather to assess the likely impact of the evidence on reasonable jurors.

Second, it bears repeating that the *Schlup* standard is demanding and permits review only in the "'extraordinary'" case. At the same time, though, the *Schlup* standard does not require absolute certainty about the petitioner's guilt or innocence. A petitioner's burden at the gateway stage is to demonstrate that more likely than not, in light of the new evidence, no reasonable juror would find him guilty beyond a reasonable doubt—or, to remove the double negative, that more likely than not any reasonable juror would have reasonable doubt.

Finally, as the *Schlup* decision explains, the gateway actual-innocence standard is "by no means equivalent to the standard of *Jackson v. Virginia*, 443 U.S. 307 (1979)," which governs claims of insufficient evidence. When confronted with a challenge based on trial evidence, courts presume the jury resolved evidentiary disputes reasonably so long as sufficient evidence supports the verdict. Because a *Schlup* claim involves evidence the trial jury did not have before it, the inquiry requires the federal court to assess how reasonable jurors would react to the overall, newly supplemented record. If new evidence so requires, this may include consideration of "the credibility of the witnesses presented at trial."

. . . .

With this background in mind we turn to the evidence developed in House's federal habeas proceedings.

DNA Evidence

First, in direct contradiction of evidence presented at trial, DNA testing has established that the semen on Mrs. Muncey's nightgown and panties came from her husband, Mr. Muncey, not from House. The State, though conceding this point, insists this new evidence is immaterial. At the guilt phase at least, neither sexual contact nor motive were elements of the offense, so in the State's view the evidence, or lack of evidence, of sexual assault or sexual advance is of no consequence. We disagree. In fact we consider the new disclosure of central importance.

From beginning to end the case is about who committed the crime. When identity is in question, motive is key. The point, indeed, was not lost on the prosecution, for it introduced the evidence and relied on it in the final guilt-phase closing argument. Referring to "evidence at the scene," the prosecutor suggested that House committed, or attempted to commit, some "indignity" on Mrs. Muncey that neither she "nor any mother on that road would want to do with Mr. House." Particularly in a case like this where the proof was, as the State Supreme Court observed, circumstantial, we think a jury would have given this evidence great weight. Quite apart from providing proof of motive, it was the only forensic evidence at the scene that would link House to the murder.

. . . . A jury informed that fluids on Mrs. Muncey's garments could have come from House might have found that House trekked the nearly two miles to the victim's home and lured her away in order to commit a sexual offense. By contrast a jury acting without the assumption that the semen could have come from House would have found it necessary to establish some different motive, or, if the same motive, an intent far more speculative. When the only direct evidence of sexual assault drops out of the case, so, too, does a central theme in the State's narrative linking House to the crime. In that light, furthermore, House's odd evening walk and his false statements to authorities, while still potentially incriminating, might appear less suspicious.

Bloodstains

The other relevant forensic evidence is the blood on House's pants, which appears in small, even minute, stains in scattered places. As the prosecutor told the jury, they were stains that, due to their small size, "you or I might not detect[,] [m]ight not see, but which the FBI lab was able to find on [House's] jeans." The stains appear inside the right pocket, outside that pocket, near the inside button, on the left thigh and outside leg, on the seat of the pants, and on the right bottom cuff, including inside the pants. Due to testing by the FBI, cuttings now appear on the pants in several places where stains evidently were found. (The cuttings were destroyed in the testing process, and defense experts were unable to replicate the tests.) At trial, the government argued "nothing that the defense has introduced in this case explains what blood is doing on his jeans, all over [House's] jeans, that is scientifically, completely different from his blood." House, though not disputing at this point that the blood is Mrs. Muncey's, now presents an alternative explanation that, if credited, would undermine the probative value of the blood evidence.

. . . .

In sum, considering "'all the evidence,'" on this issue, we think the evidentiary disarray surrounding the blood, taken together with Dr. Blake's testimony and the limited rebuttal of it in the present record, would prevent reasonable jurors from placing significant reliance on the blood evidence. We now know, though the trial jury did not, that an Assistant Chief Medical Examiner believes the blood on House's jeans must have come from autopsy samples; that a vial and a quarter of autopsy blood is unaccounted for; that the blood was transported to the FBI together with the pants in conditions that could have caused vials to spill; that the blood did indeed spill at least once during its journey from Tennessee authorities through FBI hands to a defense expert; that the pants were stored in a plastic bag bearing both a large blood stain and a label with TBI Agent Scott's name; and that the styrofoam box containing the blood samples may well have been opened before it arrived at the FBI lab. Thus, whereas the bloodstains, emphasized by the prosecution, seemed strong evidence of House's guilt at trial, the record now raises substantial questions about the blood's origin.

A Different Suspect

Were House's challenge to the State's case limited to the questions he has raised about the blood and semen, the other evidence favoring the prosecution might well suffice to bar relief. There is, however, more; for in the post-trial proceedings House presented troubling evidence that Mr. Muncey, the victim's husband, himself could have been the murderer.

. . .

In the habeas proceedings, . . . two different witnesses (Parker and Letner) described a confession by Mr. Muncey; two more (Atkins and Lawson) described suspicious behavior (a fight and an attempt to construct a false alibi) around the time of the crime; and still other witnesses described a history of abuse.

. . . .

Mr. Muncey testified at the habeas hearing, and the District Court did not question his credibility. Though Mr. Muncey said he seemed to remember visiting Lawson the day after the murder, he denied either killing his wife or confessing to doing so. Yet Mr. Muncey also claimed, contrary to Constable Wallace's testimony and to his own prior statement, that he left the dance on the night of the crime only when it ended at midnight. Mr. Muncey, moreover, denied ever hitting Mrs. Muncey; the State itself had to impeach him with a prior statement on this point.

It bears emphasis, finally, that Parker's and Letner's testimony is not comparable to the sort of eleventh-hour affidavit vouching for a defendant and incriminating a conveniently absent suspect that Justice O'Connor described in her concurring opinion in Herrera as "unfortunate" and "not uncommon" in capital cases, nor was the confession Parker and Letner described induced under pressure of interrogation. The confession evidence here involves an alleged spontaneous statement recounted by two eyewitnesses with no evident motive to lie. For this reason it has more probative value than, for example, incriminating testimony from inmates, suspects, or friends or relations of the accused.

The evidence pointing to Mr. Muncey is by no means conclusive. If considered in isolation, a reasonable jury might well disregard it. In combination, however, with the challenges to the blood evidence and the lack of motive with respect to House, the evidence pointing to Mr. Muncey likely would reinforce other doubts as to House's guilt.

. . . .

This is not a case of conclusive exoneration. Some aspects of the State's evidence—Lora Muncey's memory of a deep voice, House's bizarre evening walk, his lie to law enforcement, his appearance near the body, and the blood on his pants—still support an inference of guilt. Yet the central forensic proof connecting House to the crime—the blood and the semen—has been called into question, and House has put forward substantial evidence pointing to a different suspect. Accordingly, and although the issue is close, we conclude that this is the rare case where—had the jury heard all the conflicting testimony—it is more likely than not that no reasonable juror viewing the record as a whole would lack reasonable doubt.

V

In addition to his gateway claim under *Schlup*, House argues that he has shown freestanding innocence and that as a result his imprisonment and planned execution are unconstitutional. In *Herrera*, decided three years before *Schlup*, the Court assumed without deciding that "in a capital case a truly persuasive demonstration of 'actual innocence' made after trial would render the execution of a defendant unconstitutional, and warrant federal habeas relief if there were no state avenue open to process such a claim." . . . House urges the Court to answer the question left open in *Herrera* and hold not only that freestanding claims are possible but also that he has established one.

We decline to resolve this issue. We conclude here, much as in *Herrera*, that whatever burden a hypothetical freestanding innocence claim would require, this petitioner has not satisfied it. To be sure, House has cast considerable doubt on his guilt—doubt sufficient to satisfy *Schlup*'s gateway standard for obtaining federal review despite a state procedural default. In *Herrera*, however, the Court described the threshold for any hypothetical freestanding innocence claim as "extraordinarily high." The sequence of the Court's decisions in *Herrera* and *Schlup*—first leaving unresolved the status of freestanding claims and then establishing the gateway standard—implies at the least that *Herrera* requires more convincing proof of innocence than *Schlup*. It follows, given the closeness of the Schlup question here, that House's showing falls short of the threshold implied in *Herrera*.

* * *

House has satisfied the gateway standard set forth in *Schlup* and may proceed on remand with procedurally defaulted constitutional claims. The judgment of the Court of Appeals is reversed, and the case is remanded for further proceedings consistent with this opinion.

It is so ordered.

[The opinion of Chief Justice ROBERTS, with whom Justice SCALIA and Justice THOMAS join, concurring in the judgment in part and dissenting in part, has been omitted].

TABLE OF CASES

The principal cases are in bold type.

SUBJECT MATTER INDEX

Page numbers in **bold** refer to the first or primary discussion of a topic